The Complete Tightwad Gazette

The Complete Tightwad Gazette

Promoting Thrift as a Viable Alternative Lifestyle

Amy Dacyczyn

a.k.a. The Frugal Zealot

Villard • New York

A few years have passed since the *Tightwad* books were first published. We were unable, for this edition, to double-check the contact information for each and every resource mentioned in the book. Some telephone numbers and addresses may have changed; before you write to a company or organization, we recommend trying to call to confirm the address and that they still offer the service(s) we mention. Please understand our spirit of economy if some of the information is no longer current.

 Published in the United States by Villard Books, a division of Random House, Inc., New York, and simultaneously in Canada by Random House of Canada Limited, Toronto.

ISBN 0-7394-0439-3

Random House website address: www.atrandom.com

Printed in the United States of America

A Word of Caution

Tightwads are by nature unconventional. We push the normal limits to make things last longer. We reuse things in unusual ways. We experiment constantly to find new, cheaper ways to do almost everything. Because this book draws upon the experiences of tightwads throughout the country, there is a chance we will inadvertently publish information that is technically illegal or not safe. On the other hand, all of the information in this book was previously published in a newsletter that was read by tens of thousands of people. Whenever any reader pointed out a concern, I thoroughly researched the question and then made a judgment as to the validity of the concern. These judgments are all incorporated in this book.

Based on this, to the best of my knowledge all of the ideas in this book are legal. Likewise I believe that all of the ideas meet a reasonable level of safety. I pointed out any significant hazard I was aware of, but I did not point out safety concerns if the hazard was extremely remote. For example, when I suggested turning out the lights to save electricity, I did not warn you about the hazard of stumbling over your toddler's pull toy in the darkness.

When using ideas in this book you must exercise your personal judgment and take reasonable precautions.

Contents

Introduction

Two years have breezed by since I sent the last issue of my newsletter, *The Tightwad Gazette,* to press. While my family and I continue to live frugally, I've retired from writing about that subject and have since become absorbed in a series of other projects. Then last summer, when *The Tightwad Gazette* seemed like the distant past, my paint-scraping project was interrupted by a call from my agent. It was a surreal moment: Covered with paint chips and perspiration, and still breathless from scurrying down a ladder and jogging to the house to take the phone, I learned Villard had proposed combining my three books into one. I said, "Well, whatever," and returned to my task. Upon more reflection, the idea grew on me. I'm particularly happy that this book contains information not included in the previous three books. This single reference work embodies more than six years of hard work and the best tightwad ideas gleaned from thousands of readers. It's the book I wish I'd had when I began my adult life.

I realize that, with this book, some readers are encountering *The Tightwad Gazette* for the first time, so I'll provide some background. As for those who are returning as old friends, later in this introduction they will find an update on my family's happy, frugal life.

Way back in 1990, when I decided I wanted to write about frugality, I knew I didn't want to write a book. During the previous years, when I was fine-tuning my own frugality, I had read just about every book I could find on the topic. I saw that because each author solely wrote from his or her own experience, each book had strengths and gaps.

To me, a newsletter seemed better suited to the subject. It allowed me to make frugality more interesting and fun by balancing types of information and diversifying the ways in which I demonstrated ideas. I solicited participation from my tens of thousands of readers, so that even if my knowledge wasn't well rounded, my newsletter could be. I constantly learned new ideas from my readers. Both the newsletter and I benefited from the unparalleled resources of these fellow tightwads.

After my newsletter became successful, I began to receive offers from publishers who wanted me to write a book. I rejected such offers for over a year—my children were

quite young, and I didn't have the time or ambition to generate that much additional material.

Then Villard approached me with the idea of synthesizing issues of the newsletter published during the first two years into a book. My first reaction was that this would make an awkward book. The articles wouldn't fit into neat, obvious chapters. Some articles could be categorized into several chapters, while others would fit into none. And if similar articles were lumped together, the book would lose much of the surprise and spirit that made the newsletter fun to read. So after much pondering, we decided to structure the book in a fairly loose format. In retrospect, it proved to be the right choice. Many readers shared how enjoyable the book was for them. One noted that because she couldn't simply flip to the few chapters that interested her, she was forced to read everything and thus found she learned much more.

At the time I agreed to publish the first book, I understood that in doing so my newsletter would have a limited run. Many publications repeat articles every year or so, but because books are permanently out there, I couldn't repeat myself. But books were better for the audience. By the time I had been publishing for two years, I had frequently communicated with people who were so financially desperate they were genuinely unable to afford buying my back issues. Once the issues were compiled in books, and those books were in libraries, the information could be freely accessed by anyone. (I always felt the most honored by those who bought the books after they read their library's copies.)

The first book, *The Tightwad Gazette,* became a national bestseller in 1993. It was followed by *The Tightwad Gazette II* in 1995 and *The Tightwad Gazette III* in 1997. Each book represents two years, or twenty-four issues of the newsletter.

Although we strove for continuity in the newsletter and the three books, there are differences. Some differences reflect the styles of various book editors, but most reflect changes in my own life as well as the natural progression of writing on one topic.

First and most obvious, over the course of the six-year period, my children and my family grew. After I had been publishing for a year I gave birth to a set of twins, my fifth and sixth children. Quite naturally, certain parts of the family budget changed—for example, our family's food expenses grew from $150 per month in 1990 to about $200 in 1996.

Then there were remarkable changes in our business. During the first year I published, my husband, Jim, still went to a job every day, so I wore all the hats in the business while caring for my four small children. I had fewer than 1,700 readers and I found it surprisingly difficult to fill the reader-letter page. As a result, the amount of space devoted to reader participation was small. And I had no formal training as a journalist, so I didn't know how to thoroughly research topics. Due to my limited time, reader letters, and skills, I found it easiest to write from my well of personal experience.

In March 1991, our newsletter gained national press attention and our subscriber base mushroomed to over 40,000. In June, the twins

were born. Jim retired from the Navy to manage our business. But even this was not enough. Our lives were chaotic, and I was not doing my best work. Not only wasn't I having fun, I was rapidly approaching burnout. After struggling for a year, we decided we had to hire more qualified staff. Aside from employing a half-dozen office workers, I hired a "real" writer, a journalist named Brad Lemley. Brad taught me how to craft better articles, as well as how to do research and interview experts. He shared in much of the research and writing during the last four and a half years. Were it not for his help, his ideas, and especially his good humor, the newsletter would have had a much shorter run.

So just as I was running out of ideas from my personal experience, I was able to shift into writing articles outside of my experience. And because my subscriber base was much larger, the quality of the readers' letters improved and the newsletter reflected more of my readers' experiences.

Back when I signed my first book contract, I envisioned three books that would, together, represent a complete body of work. My plan was to retire the newsletter after six years, which meant I would have to give my subscribers a year's notice after I had published for five years. As we approached that time, we were undecided about how much more good information we still had to write. Brad kept saying, "There's lot's more—we still haven't written about going to college cheaply." Then one month we published *that* article, and suddenly we understood there *was* a limit.

It took us several extra months to decide to retire, bringing the newsletter's run to six years and seven months. At the time the manuscript for the third book went to press, we were still writing some good stuff. I have always regretted the "untidiness" of those last issues, and the fact that book readers never enjoyed that valuable information. In the last issue, we published eight pages of reader success stories culled from a three-pound file of letters we had saved. I especially wanted to share these testimonials. So when Villard proposed combining the three books into one big one, my immediate reaction was that the inclusion of the last seven issues, especially the success stories, would make the title *The Complete Tightwad Gazette* very fitting.

For those who might scoff that many of the ideas in *The Tightwad Gazette* are too extreme and offbeat, or might doubt that such ideas would really make a difference, I would suggest reading the success stories *first*. They begin on page 909. These success stories prove that this information works for real people in the real world. And they prove what I have always believed: If you want more money, you can either find a higher paying job or you can save more money. My readers have had their dreams come true because they chose the latter of these two options.

While I have managed to cover most of what readers might need to know about being frugal, no reader can expect to find answers to every question in his or her own life. An article called "A Reader's Guide to *The Tightwad Gazette*," which begins on page 305,

addresses this in depth. Throughout this book you'll find numerous articles in which I go into laborious detail explaining how I arrived at my conclusions. Such articles should be viewed as models for readers to use in solving their own problems. Once a newsletter subscriber wrote to ask me if homemade bread dough could be frozen and then thawed for later use. I wrote her back saying that I didn't know the answer to her question, but I did know she spent more on a postage stamp to ask me than she would have if she had conducted her own frozen-dough experiment.

My final decision to retire occurred when I knew I had written most of what I had within me to share on the topic. Certainly I could have kept churning out repetitive articles for many years, but that wouldn't have been satisfying to me, or a good value for the audience. There was a point when I knew the scales had shifted—when I felt the audience and I had little more to gain by my continuing to publish the newsletter, and when I saw that continuing meant I would be giving up much more. The newsletter was always demanding of my time and creative energy. I wanted to have more time to spend with my growing children, and I also wanted to pursue other interests. I have never regretted this decision.

This seems to be as good a place as any to respond to the common criticism that my ideas are too extreme. The very purpose of a newsletter is to meet a need that is not met by the mainstream media. Traditional financial and consumer writers offer safe, halfway advice: They'll tell you how to feed a family of four for $84 per week (when it can be done for half that amount). The same writers will tell you it's becoming increasingly difficult, if not impossible, for families to make ends meet. In fact, by adhering to the "safe" advice, many families would *not* make ends meet. *The Tightwad Gazette* came about as a reaction to this traditional viewpoint, because I knew that people could achieve the "impossible" with a little discipline, a little creativity, and a willingness to do things that mainstream thinkers deem extreme.

The purpose of this book is to suggest options and explore the boundaries. Not every idea is appropriate for every reader. Even I do not use every idea suggested by newsletter readers. The readers of this book can pick and choose. Those readers who are financially comfortable will likely choose to implement fewer ideas than the financially desperate. In addition, this book is not a textbook about frugality. Much of what readers will find is included solely to express the sport and fun of frugality. It's a celebration of a way of life.

Finally, I wanted to share some of our lives during the last two years. Those readers who want to learn how Jim and I are able to retire early should refer to the article called "An Unemployment Opportunity," which appears on page 831. While our net worth is more significant than most families, technically our "income" is comprised of Jim's military retirement, money from rental houses, and what little money we draw from our investments.

Some people may suspect, now that we're out of the limelight, that we've stopped being frugal or that

we've conveniently retired just as our oldest kids reached the "financially impossible" teenage years. Neither is true. Our tightwad life goes on, much as it did before. Neal is eleven, Rebecca is nine, and the twins, Brad and Laura, are now seven. Our oldest, Alec, is now fifteen, and the cynical predictions we heard haven't occurred. A year ago we had to buy him his first new jeans, as he is now adult-sized and harder to fit with secondhand finds. But nearly all our family wardrobe continues to come from yard sales and thrift shops. Jamie, now thirteen, was the only child who showed resistance to frugality, and even that was limited to half a dozen occasions. The article "Retail Revelation," which appears on page 760, is an example of one way I dealt with this. In retrospect I see that this tense period was more about her going through a stage, and she has since become quite frugal and accepting of the lifestyle. The article "My Teenage Plan," which appears on page 185, was written back when Alec was seven. At the time it was written, the article was pooh-poohed as naïve. Nevertheless, it has worked as I predicted. Jim and I buy the kids new stuff when we have been unable to fill their needs from the used market. If the kids want a new lunch box when we have an adequate supply of good used ones, they know they have to pay for it themselves. They have accepted this policy without question. Jamie, who once (inaccurately) complained she had never owned a new pair of shoes, finally bought herself a new pair of sneakers—which she outgrew within a few months. She has since been very content with the twenty-five-cent shoes, sneakers, boots, and sandals from our church thrift shop. By doing extra chores around the house, the children have all earned sufficient amounts of money to buy most of their wants, but they generally choose to hang on to it, spending small amounts on yard sale treasures.

During the last two years, since Jim and I "retired," we've worked very hard at various projects. Jim enjoys balancing the many activities required to keep up with our large home and family. He is a putterer at heart. His garden has become much larger. During one good wild-grape year, he successfully experimented with wine making (in contrast, most of his rhubarb-wine experiment blew up in the cellar).

Unlike Jim, I tend to become absorbed in big projects that keep me busy for weeks or months at a time. These projects range from painting the back side of our huge barn (forty feet wide and forty-nine feet to the peak) to researching my great-grandfather's trip to Russia during the Bolshevik Revolution. I've thought about beginning another career, but while various ideas were interesting, they felt hollow after years of publishing a newsletter that had helped so many.

But then I stumbled into a part-time volunteer opportunity. About a year ago I was elected church deacon (an honor that seems to be bestowed on most church members sooner or later). I chose the responsibility of overseeing the church thrift shop, which is run out of our town's old Grange building, now owned by the church. It's a huge task, previously run with a half day of deacon and volunteer

effort each week. The shop is open two hours on Saturday morning, and all clothing items are priced from a dime to a dollar. At those prices, the Grange typically sells hundreds of items each week. For most of the past year I've put in at least two days a week, with the result that sales have increased enough that the deacons will be able to pay for an expensive foundation repair within a year or so. This volunteer project interests me on many levels. I like business. I'm interested in the maintenance of this historically important building. I really like the whole idea of this community service project, which enables a large number of people to save a huge amount of money. But one of the best parts of this for me is that Jamie worked with me about two days a week last summer and now she happily wears clothing she found while volunteering. For me, the Grange feels like the final piece of a puzzle as it has allowed me the means to interact with and serve my community in a way I couldn't when I was still publishing.

In the last issue, published in December 1996, I wrote an article called "A Look Back," which offers an inside view of the history of the newsletter (see page 906). Now, two years later, I view the newsletter as if I were watching a distant roller-coaster ride. *The Tightwad Gazette* was a ride with many ups and downs. It was often surprising, exhilarating, intense, and stressful—my constant interaction with the media having much to do with those extremes. We once estimated that I have given over 750 interviews in six years. Now, with my new perspective, I am amazed that I climbed on that ride. I'm glad I did, but it feels more natural to be on solid ground again.

Frugality enabled me to achieve the life I wanted. I felt so grateful for that lifestyle, I wanted to share it in a newsletter. What we didn't expect was that the newsletter would enable us to enjoy an early, albeit frugal, retirement. I'm glad that happened too.

I started the newsletter because I recognized that I had a lot of stories in me and in my family. Now that I'm no longer writing, every once in a while something happens and I feel a twinge of regret for having no outlet for sharing it. For instance, I recently brought home a winter jacket from our local church thrift shop. I showed it to Neal, now eleven years old, and asked if he would like it. Neal was initially reluctant, but when he suddenly spied the fancy Northwest Territory label sewn inside the jacket, his eyes about popped out and he nodded eagerly. I made some comment about this being the first time he had ever seemed to care about a designer label. He responded, "No, you don't understand," and then pointed to the handwritten name of the former owner, which was scrawled with ballpoint pen on the label. It was the name of Neal's longtime best friend. I had to laugh about this, because many years ago I ran up against the immovable skepticism of the editor of a major women's magazine. Dissatisfied with the answers I had given, the editor demanded, "Have your children ever gone to school and found they were wearing the clothes that used to belong to one of their classmates?" She imagined such an occurrence would be a trauma. I responded that it hadn't ever happened, but even if it did, would it

be a terrible shame? Turns out Neal's knowledge of the previous ownership made this jacket much more desirable.

We have appreciated the support and good ideas of our readers, and in return, I hope we have contributed a little to helping others move closer to, or even achieve, their own version of "the amazing life."

The Tightwad Gazette

Preface

I never wanted to write a book. Every book I have ever read on the subject of thrift or money management was as dry as . . . well . . . vacuum cleaner bag dust. As each author wrote about his or her areas of expertise, large areas were left unaddressed. And because learning is an ongoing process, any book would have to be too final and incomplete.

Within the format of a newsletter I have found that I could make my subject matter interesting and fun by balancing types of information and diversifying the manner by which I demonstrated ideas. I solicit reader participation, which provides an enormous pool of expertise to draw upon. So even if my knowledge isn't well rounded, the newsletter can be, and because I constantly learn from my readers the newsletter is a growth process for me as well.

Before accepting this offer from Villard I turned down publishers for more than a year. My primary reason for beginning a newsletter was my belief that a home business would give me more time with my children. My husband and I have six, nine years old and under. I simply did not have the time or ambition to generate new material for a book. Doing so would shortchange my family and undermine my newsletter. However, what I had written to that point was very incomplete.

A *Tightwad Gazette* book became a possibility when Villard proposed that a compilation of articles could work. This book is a collection of the majority of the material covered in the first two years of my newsletter.

Organizing it presented problems. From the onset we saw that no one method would encompass all the material. Articles did not fit into neat obvious chapters. Some articles could fit into several categories, while others fit into none. Lumping similar material together would make the entire book dry as . . . well . . . you know. On the other hand, I knew that people who had bought all the back issues of the newsletter often read through the entire stack in a single sitting.

With this understanding we decided to assemble the book with the loosest possible structure. Because *The Tightwad Gazette* is written month to month, we or-

ganized material based on times of the year, even though only about 40% of the material is seasonal. You can therefore assume that 60% of the material included under each season may be relevant to any time of year.

This *Tightwad Gazette* compilation is not, and was never intended to be, a complete handbook on thrift. After two years of writing the newsletter I have barely scratched the surface, and I have more ideas for things to write about today than when I began. As it is only a beginning for me, likewise it is a beginning for you to rethink your lifestyle.

I have written from the viewpoint of "Give a man a fish and he'll eat for a day. Teach him to fish and he'll eat for life." This book does not contain all the answers. Hopefully, it does contain the necessary tools for you to discover answers for yourself.

THEY CALL ME "THE FRUGAL ZEALOT"

I am a compulsive tightwad. People who know me believe that I worry too much about money, that I don't spend enough on myself, and that I don't know how to have any fun. Even depression-era relatives think that I am too thrifty. One Christmas an aunt gave me two boxes of aluminum foil after learning that I recycled the stuff. (I made it last for years.) And when I was first labeled "The Frugal Zealot" even *I* had to smile.

It was not always this way. Before the fever gripped me I had a very normal and healthy love for spending.

The change occurred when I got married and began to pursue my dream. I had always wanted a large family and a rural pre-1900 New England farmhouse (with attached barn). I had a crazy notion that I could have both without the two-income/daycare frenzy that has become the norm for the modern American family.

Our first child was born nine months (and 15 minutes) after the ceremony. I set aside my career in graphic design to be a mom. It was during this time that I discovered daytime talk shows and first heard the commonly held myths expounded by intelligent audience members.

"Nowadays, a family has to have two incomes to make ends meet."

"Nowadays, it is impossible for a young couple to get into the housing market."

"Nowadays, families cannot afford to raise more than two children."

As if the message could magically be shot back through the television tube, I raised my fist and shouted, "It is not true, it can be done." And so began my quest ... to prove that it could be done ... that it was still possible to raise a large family and buy a house without two full-time incomes.

Saving money, rather than earning money, became the means to my goal. I became a recycler first of aluminum foil, then of Ziploc bags, and now, I publicly confess, I have become a recycler of vacuum cleaner bags. (No Christmas presents please.)

My challenge in life became how low could I get our food budget and still have a varied, healthful diet, or how wonderful I could make a child's birthday with a $25 budget, or how many years I could go without buying wrapping paper.

I made it my personal mission to create ways to recycle plastic milk jugs, bread tabs, brown

paper bags, egg cartons, and those frozen juice lid things.

To fine-tune our spending I became a student of thrift. I routinely calculated such things as the cost of drying a load of laundry, or the cost savings in cloth diapers, or the cost difference of making food from scratch versus buying convenience foods.

When Oprah had a show featuring cheapskates I didn't laugh. I took notes.

Although I was the chief architect of our family economic plan, my husband became a willing convert. In addition he taught me the ways of scrounging and organized packratting. (A level beyond cheap is to get it for free.)

It worked.

In 1989 we realized our dream. Our family (then it was four children; now, with the advent of twins two years later, it's six) moved into our rural pre-1900 New England farmhouse (with attached barn).

Were we too thrifty?

When we got married, our joint financial assets barely paid for the budget wedding. We owned almost nothing. In other words we started from *zero.*

Over the years our average income has been less than $30,000 (including my husband's Navy salary and all allowances, plus my spotty free-lance income). In less than seven years we saved $49,000, made significant purchases (vehicles, appliances, furniture) of $38,000, and were completely debt-free! That is an annual savings/investment rate of over $12,500 per year, or 43% of our gross income.

It is difficult to compare finances of different families except in the military, where all things are roughly equal. Of the scores of families we have known, most lived paycheck to paycheck, moonlighted, or relied on a second income. I know of only one other family that were accomplished savers. Their annual savings/investment rate was about half of ours.

Without a down payment we would have been able to buy only a small starter home. Instead we purchased a wonderful house that exceeded our expectations, a house vastly superior to the 176 other houses we saw during a 15-month period. If we had saved a few thousand less we would not own it today.

No, we weren't too thrifty.

Certainly the recycling of aluminum foil did not greatly contribute to our dream. Rather it was the attention to all the thousands of ways we spent our money that made a tremendous difference.

Our success was very much a gradual learning process. We made many big mistakes. Had we known in the beginning what we know now I am sure we could have saved several thousand more.

Thus having proven that it could be done—that financial goals could be achieved through saving more rather than earning more—I have become a crusader for the causes of thrift and frugality. I have been guilty of preaching its virtues beyond the point when eyes glazed over. My ideas seemed to fall on the deaf ears of the financially strapped.

For years now my husband and I have felt we were loners . . . mavericks in the realm of personal economics.

But then one day it hit me. Maybe we *aren't* alone. Maybe there are others—penny-pinchers horrified at the holes in the pockets of those they know and love.

Maybe they feel alone, too. We need a forum for mutual support and the exchange of frugal ideas. Tightwads need to join forces!

So with my background in graphics, a joy of writing, and a conviction that the world can be saved through thrift I have decided to go where no tightwad has gone before—I have decided to write a book.

Hence, the birth of *The Tightwad Gazette.*

Amy Dacyczyn
a.k.a. The Frugal Zealot

MRS. DA...DA...?

Dear Amy,
How do you pronounce your name?

Name withheld by request
Salina, Utah

It's pronounced "decision," as in, "I made a decision to marry a guy of Ukrainian ancestry."

The week before I got married I called utility companies to notify them of my upcoming name change. The woman from the electric company asked, "What's your last name now?" I said, "Davis." She then asked, "What will your name change to?" I replied, "Dacyczyn . . . D-A-C-Y-C-Z-Y-N." After a lengthy pause the electric company lady asked, "Don't you want to think about this a little longer?"

Tightwaddery is not for everyone. I am keenly aware that most people really don't care a hoot about any of this stuff. Some are doing just fine, thank you. They have enough money to do everything they want. A larger segment does need to manage their finances better but are unwilling to make the needed changes. Past experience taught me quickly that I couldn't win them over. No amount of information will cause them to rethink their lifestyle.

This information is geared for the rest of the people who do not find thrift a radical concept.

Tightwads are a small elite group. But while few in number they come in endless varieties. There are borderline tightwads and spartan tightwads and all shades in between.

There are budding tightwads who feel overwhelmed and think "How does she expect me to bake bread, make wrapping paper, braid rugs and shop at fourteen different grocery stores?" Relax. It took me years to reach my level of skill and I am still learning. Choose one new idea a week. One new skill per month. When you have mastered it you'll be ready to take on a new challenge.

There are old-hand tightwads who may learn only one or two new ideas per chapter. Their primary reason for reading this will be to have *The Tightwad Gazette* to wave in the faces of spendthrift family and friends and say, "See! Look here! I'm not crazy. Someone else thinks the same way I do."

Not every tightwad is saving for a pre-1900 New England farmhouse (with attached barn).

Some live in a shack so they can afford a fleet of snowmobiles and all-terrain vehicles. As long as they are financially responsible—their kids have enough to eat, the bills are paid, and they have adequate insurance and savings for emergencies—that is absolutely acceptable.

There are working moms who want to find a way to be home with their children and there are stay-at-home moms who want to get out of the house . . . return to college or start a business. Thrift can address both these goals.

The Tightwad Gazette is for both men and women. Especially if there is a lack of spouse cooperation, tightwads need to cross over into "other-sex-dominated territories." Men can learn to bake bread, do the grocery shopping, and scrounge yard sales. Women can learn to swing a hammer and do a tune-up. Don't point a finger. Instead, do whatever it takes to reach your goal.

The size of the dream, the size of the income, and the length of time allowed to meet the goal determine the degree of thrift tightwads will resort to.

I do not expect that every reader will recycle aluminum foil, Ziploc bags, and yes, vacuum cleaner bags. *The Tightwad Gazette* will present a cornucopia of ideas, approaches, and knowledge that has worked for us, as well as for the readership. Each tightwad must weigh and decide what is compatible to his or her lifestyle.

Yeah, I've been called The Frugal Zealot, and we have had above average success with an average income. But I do not claim expert status. I still have a lot to learn but am excited about a book that serves as a clearinghouse of ideas . . . that draws upon the collective wisdom of the finest frugal minds in the country.

GOALS OF THE TIGHTWAD GAZETTE

- To give tightwaddery a good name
- To provide the widest possible sharing of the tightwad philosophy
- To be a clearinghouse of frugal ideas through active participation of tightwads everywhere
- To explode all myths wrongly associated with tightwads
- To promote tightwaddery as a viable alternative lifestyle
- To provide support to tightwads who feel they're all alone out there
- To gain recognition for tightwads as a minority
- To provide an income for the author, who doesn't want to go out and get a real job
- To demonstrate, in all sincerity, that thrift can help families of all economic levels achieve their financial goals and to have greater economic freedom

REASONS WHY PEOPLE CAN'T SAVE MONEY

I'M JUST NO GOOD AT COOKING.
MY WIFE SPENDS EVERYTHING I SAVE.
I'M JUST NOT CREATIVE LIKE YOU.
TEENAGERS ARE SO EXPENSIVE.
IT'S HARD TO MAKE ENDS MEET NOWADAYS.
I'M TOO BUSY TO CHASE AFTER SALES.
I CAN NEVER FIND WHAT I WANT AT THRIFT SHOPS.
I DON'T HAVE TIME TO...
MY FAMILY WON'T EAT CASSEROLES

WE WILL DEAL WITH THESE REASONS IN THE PAGES AHEAD.

WHAT CAN YOU DO TO GET STARTED?

The most elementary exercise for any aspiring tightwad is to record spending habits for a period of three months. Write down *everything* from the mortgage payment to the candy bar at the checkout counter.

All your expenses will be one of two types. Essential and optional. Essential expenses are things that you absolutely cannot cut. Optional expenses are nonessential. For example, your phone bill has a minimum service charge that you must pay to have telephone service and a breakdown for long-distance calls. The $10 call to your mother was optional. Your food bill contains items necessary for basic nutrition and nonnutritious items like coffee, candy, and soda, which are optional.

No one but you can say exactly where the line between essential and optional expenses falls. That depends on *your* value system. The point is to understand how much you *really* have left over to play with.

If you take home $20,000 and of that $15,000 is already allocated for essential expenses, the $5,000 remaining is what you have left for optional expenses. In that light, making a small adjustment to save $1,000 a year makes more sense. As you further fine-tune your spending, you may real-

ize that only $12,000 of your take home is actually essential and you have even more room for savings.

By tracking your spending in this way, for the first time, you will have a truly clear picture of where your money is going and where your best options for cutbacks are. It also will give you a valuable gauge for comparison as you gain success at managing your money.

EYE OPENER

Dear Amy,

Thank you for sending the premiere issue of your *Tightwad Gazette.* As you suggested I did the necessary vs. optional lists. Wow! Just going over my checkbook, as of 1/14/91 we spent over $300 on optional items (to 3/19/91). That's not including items purchased with cash!

Pearl Nagoshi
Budd Lake, New Jersey

WE REGRETFULLY INFORM YOU . . .

. . . that in an effort to bring you real usable information on a limited number of pages we will *not* be able to feature the following types of articles:

Beauty makeovers
Hollywood gossip
Romance novels
$40,000 only-dreamin' kitchens
Fashions as dictated by designers that do not reside on planet Earth
Nouvelle cuisine recipes
Royal family updates

10 PAINLESS WAYS TO SAVE $100 THIS YEAR

1 Purchase 10 articles of clothing at thrift shops and yard sales this year instead of paying department store prices.

2 Hang four loads of laundry per week instead of using your dryer.

3 Once a month make a pizza from scratch instead of having one delivered.

4 Write a good letter instead of making a monthly long-distance phone call.

5 Reduce your soda consumption by four cans per week.

6 Bake one batch of bread (two loaves) per week.

7 Save $50 each on two children's birthday parties by making homemade decorations, cake, wrapping paper, and one present.

8 Reduce your smoking by three cigarettes per day (or give up smoking altogether and save even more).

9 Reduce your whole milk consumption by two gallons per week, substituting dry milk in cooking, homemade cocoa mix, and in half-and-half for drinking.

10 Pack four inexpensive school lunches per week.

Fall

EVERYTHING YOU ALREADY KNOW

Telling you how to save money is like telling you how to lose weight. Everybody knows how to lose weight. You need to eat fewer calories than your body uses. To save money you need to spend fewer dollars than you earn. In both cases you need to adjust your rate of consumption to your rate of work.

The "Don't save more, earn more" philosophy is a very one-sided approach. And it has one big flaw. Nearly everyone that earns more automatically spends more. For this reason, regardless of their incomes, many families seem to have exactly enough to get by.

Telling you to earn more instead of saving more is like saying "Don't eat less, exercise more."

When I learned that walking a mile burned up the same amount of calories as in an apple I wondered how many miles I would have to run to burn the calories in a candy bar. It made more sense to give up the candy bar.

Most Americans are running to burn up candy bars. They are running out of the house, running to the daycare center, running on the job . . . so they can *afford* candy bars and Nintendo games, meals at McDonald's, and designer sneakers.

There is no doubt that the minimum wage earner does need to earn more to afford apples—the basics of life.

But for most of us whether we choose to earn more or to save more depends on how easy, accessible, and enjoyable *more* work is.

For me, working more, especially when I had to leave home, creates a high level of stress. Juggling business and babies is a job in itself. The client's needs must come first if I am to maintain a professional image.

Likewise few dedicated fathers like to moonlight for minimum wage. In some cases more work is not available.

Earning more in the same eight-hour day often requires capital and years to make the transition to start a new business or to obtain additional education.

In the meantime, earning more boils down to working more and being away from home more hours. It means less time to call your own.

There is a point at which the quality of life and the standard of living depart . . . where earning more results in a personal cost and erodes the quality of life.

The solution is to find the right balance of earning more and sav-

ing more. You need to couple your earning effort and your saving effort to achieve the highest quality of life.

When you do earn more, resist the temptation to spend more. Discipline yourself to saving whatever possible of what you do earn and reinvest in ways to either earn more or save more.

Sometimes I feel like I am telling you everything you already know. It is much like when I joined Weight Watchers years ago. At the time I joined I already knew how to lose weight, yet I continued to attend long after I had reached my goal. Weight Watchers' success is in their structure as a support network.

The purpose of *The Tightwad Gazette* is much the same. You will learn some new nitty-gritty strategies and it will bring into focus what you already know. But I hope you will also come to regard it as a national tightwad network, providing support as you work toward reaching your goal.

A SPENDTHRIFT HORROR STORY

Dear Amy,

One and a half years ago we felt a calling to move to Austin, Texas, where my family resides. We had no job lined up in Texas and did not know how long we would be there. We had a $9,000 check coming to us. When we received it we spent like crazy, buying furniture and appliances we didn't really need.

Two months later we made the final decision, by force, to move to Texas. My husband lost his job and the condo we rented for three and a half years sold under us. We proceeded to put all our "new stuff" in storage in New Jersey. We have not seen these things in the last year and a half, and we continue not only to pay storage, but also to kick ourselves for spending the $9,000 on it. It would have come in handy in Texas.

Save your money. You never know what could happen in two months. Arg!

Isabel Renbjor
Austin, Texas

LUNCH BOX BASICS

I'm not naive. I know that while my kids might be happy now to take box lunches to school, someday the honeymoon will be over. I envision one day Alec will get off the school bus, march into the house with a mission, plunk his red plastic lunch box on the counter, and announce he wants school lunches like the rest of the kids. After six months of intensive negotiations I will lose . . . maybe.

In our community a grammar school lunch costs 90¢. I can prepare a box lunch for 45¢. This means that every year a child takes a box lunch I can save $81. If all six kids take box lunches through grammar school I can save $2,916.

WHAT TO PUT IT IN

If you haven't purchased a new $5 lunch box for your grade schooler you might check out your thrift shop. I frequently see several at a time.

You can refurbish a lunch box by replacing the old peeling side panel art commonly found on plastic lunch boxes. I have done this either by having a child create his own artwork or by using a large interesting photograph such as might be found on an old calendar. On one occasion a free photography magazine arrived in the mail that had a large cover photo of a dinosaur mural. This refurbished Alec's lunch box, making it the envy of his friends.

I was able to accomplish this with minimal expense since I have the proper tools and materials on hand. If you need to buy materials, realize that tools and leftover materials can be used in future projects, and so the real expense is smaller than the initial investment.

You need clear contact paper and one-coat rubber cement. One-coat dries so that it is tacky and stickerlike.

Trim out your new art to the exact size of the old art, rounding the corners. If you can remove the old art in one piece use it for a pattern.

Coat the back of the art with the rubber cement and let it completely dry. Adhere the front of the art to a larger piece of clear contact paper. Trim the contact paper 1/8 to 1/4 inch larger than the art. Carefully adhere the art to the lunch box. Rub down well, paying special attention to the edges of the contact paper. Washed carefully, this waterproof sticker will last a year.

WHAT TO PUT IN IT

All of the following items are presumed to have been purchased as cheaply as possible or made from scratch.

Sandwiches like bologna, turkey, tuna, egg salad, and peanut butter and jelly cost between 10¢ to 20¢.

A cup of soup in a thermos costs between 5¢ and 10¢.

Rewarmed casserole or chili costs as little as 15¢.

Balance the "main course" with one or two of the following items, which can be put into a reused baggie or butter tub. All of these cost between 1¢ and 10¢.

Vegetable sticks
A muffin or biscuit with jam
Popcorn
Homemade cookies
Canned fruit or applesauce
Trail mix made with raisins, seeds, nuts, coconut, chocolate chips, cold cereal, Chinese noodles, etc.
Homemade yogurt, pudding, or Jell-O
Crackers
Bread sticks
Fresh fruit

A cup of juice or half-and-half milk (that is, half whole, half powdered) costs about 12¢. To ensure that it stays cold try this method:

Thoroughly wash the thermos. Pour one inch of beverage in it.

Place the cup loosely over the top (to keep out freezer odors) and put the thermos in the freezer overnight. In the morning, when you pack lunches, fill the remainder of the thermos with the same beverage. By lunch the ice should be completely melted and the beverage should still be cold. Ask your children about the lunchtime results and adjust the amount of frozen beverage if needed.

Under no circumstances use prepackaged individual-sized snack foods and juice packs. I would suggest that you fork out the money for school lunches first. Below is an example of an expensive box lunch.

GREAT QUOTES

"I would rather have my people laugh at my economies than weep for my extravagance."

—King Oscar of Sweden (1829–1907)

"To secure the greatest amount of pleasure with the least possible outlay should be the aim of all economic effort."

—Francois Quesnay (1694–1774), French economist

"The world has enough for everyone's need, but not enough for everyone's greed."

—Attributed to Mahatma Gandhi (1869–1948)

THE EXPENSIVE BOX LUNCH

(Do not try this in your own home.)

Tom's peanut butter cheese crackers (25¢)

Doritos snack size (29¢ for eight chips including broken pieces)

Del Monte fruit cup (43¢ for 4½ ounces)

Sunkist Fun Fruits Dinosaurs (33¢, or 4¢ per dinosaur)

Mott's apple-grape juice pack (33¢)

TOTAL: $1.63

"The safest way to double your money is to fold it over once and put it in your pocket."

—Frank McKinney Hubbard (1868–1930)

"Wealth consists not in having great possessions but in having few wants."

—Epicurus (341–270 B.C.)

Here's one for the Dacyczyns: "It is not economical to go to bed early to save candles if the results are twins."

—Chinese proverb

YOU AND THE FINANCIAL EDGE

You know someone who arrives 20 minutes late for everything. It could be late to work, to church, or for a date. He is always late because the 20 minutes falls within his margin of acceptability.

When they turn the clocks back from daylight savings to standard time, you'd figure he would now be 40 minutes early. However, he makes the mental adjustment and arrives the same 20 minutes late.

You also know people who arrive exactly on time, and people characterized by chronic earliness. Likewise these people set their mental clocks so that they arrive within a time frame that is acceptable to them. In the case of the extenuating circumstance the early bird may arrive on time, the on-time person may be 20 minutes late, and the straggler will arrive 40 minutes late.

Your personal inner clock functions in the same manner as your sense of where you are in relation to "the financial edge." You have an inner sense of how close you can come to meeting your financial obligations and still feel comfortable.

During my single working years I maintained a checking account balance of $1,000 to $1,500. When my balance exceeded $1,500 I would spend. When the balance dropped below $1,000 I would cease extravagant activity. I could have saved more, but I felt comfortable with the $1,000 to $1,500 range from the edge.

Those who feel comfortable closer to the edge frequently find themselves saying, "I have only $10 to get me to the next paycheck."

What of the individual who lives beyond his means? He builds a mental gangplank out beyond the edge where he teeters precariously.

The "$10-to-paycheck-guy" and the "gangplank-guy" will point to the extenuating circumstances

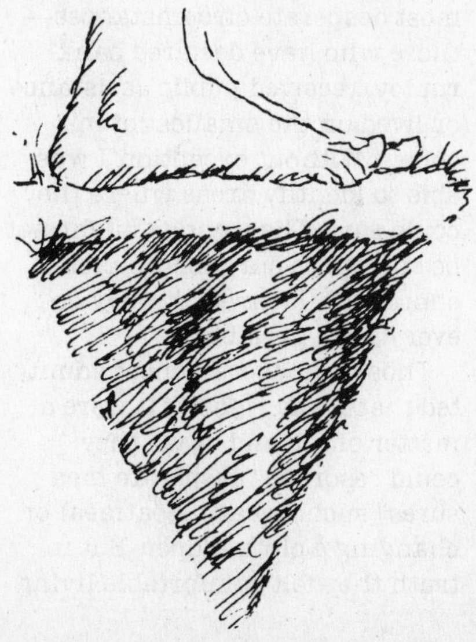

that lead to his position near or beyond the edge. When an unexpected expense comes along propelling them to financial depths, they do not accept responsibility. However, the person who maintains a cushion, given the same circumstance, will occasionally approach the edge but quickly work his way back to his comfort zone.

I have been a closet amateur budget analyst for many years. People have told me about the shortage of income that leads them to their troubles. Because my opinion was not asked for I didn't point out the Froot Loops in the cupboards, the Pampers in the bathroom, and the cable TV.

Even more responsible families on modest incomes nearly always have areas in which they could economize. They could give up red meat in favor of dried beans or whole milk in favor of mixed.

My standing as a "professional budget analyst" enjoys a briefer history. Recently I have talked or corresponded with people in the most desperate circumstances—those who have declared bankruptcy, received public assistance, or lived on the smallest of incomes. Without exception I was able to identify areas where they could save. The savings might not be enough to cure the financial shortfall, but rarely do they do everything possible.

Those who were honest admitted that I was right. If it were a matter of life and death they could resort to "desperate measures" such as eating oatmeal or changing a cloth diaper. But in truth they felt comfortable living on the financial edge.

I have not scrutinized every budget on the planet Earth, and I know rare individuals exist who live on the edge while making every frugal choice possible. However, I have not seen it.

The majority of the desperate hesitate to make the choices that our family has done routinely for years.

In the same way that the late guy still arrives late with the gift hour due to the return to standard time, many of those living on the edge or out on the gangplank fail to benefit by increased income. They might have more stuff or more fun, but they instinctively maintain the same distance to the edge regardless.

If they cannot pay a bill because "the transmission gave out," truthfully the problem is not mechanical at all. Rather the fault can be found with all the extras that they were not willing to give up in order to have the needed cushion.

For most of us our relationship to the financial edge comes down to a matter of choice. The choice may be the decisions we make today, or we may be living with choices we have made in the past. While the past choices cannot be changed, remarkably the ones we make today become tomorrow's past choices.

We can make choices that allow us to take a giant step back from the financial edge and set up a cushion. A sustained effort to scale back will result in savings for more than just a cushion. We can save for long-term goals and increased financial independence.

BUILDING MATERIALS

Dear Amy,

I am sick to death of our unfinished basement. Can you give us some suggestions as to where I can get super cheap drywall, lumber, etc.?

Lee Ann Welka
Brooklyn Park, Minnesota

Dear Lee Ann,

Jim and I usually find that shopping around for the best price is the only way we can consistently get building materials cheaply . . . if new materials are ever cheap. On occasion we scrounge small quantities of lumber, which will do for small projects and minor repairs, but for the major projects we cannot find enough.

The solution is to divert funds from other areas of finances. We routinely pinch on food, clothing, and entertainment, so that we always have money to buy the things that are hard to economize on.

I have seen advertisements for people willing to tear down buildings in exchange for lumber.

Along with that idea another reader recently wrote the following about her luck (and talent) for scrounging building materials:

Dear Amy,

Both my husband and I watch for places that are being remodeled or torn down for whatever reason, and those people generally want new stuff as replacement . . . well, there is a lot to salvage at times. Sometimes my husband is even able to help someone tear down, and he looks for useful items to salvage. We even found insulation without the backing from a fire sale that was quite useful. Also we have found windows better than ours. Most of these items were better than we had and even though secondhand we put them to good use. We even built a deck behind our house.

Time and effort have to be spent looking. With more people in the remodeling mode because of the economy you might be surprised at what you find, even in yard sales.

Ann Gardner
Conway, New Hampshire

DRYER SHEETS

Dear Amy,

Dryer sheets do not require a full sheet to reduce static. I've found I can tear one sheet into four strips and use one strip per load, thus making one box last four times as long.

Deb Knight
Westbrook, Maine

Dear Amy,

Make dryer sheets by using a big bottle of Downy and old face cloths. Pour 1 to 2 tablespoons on the face cloths and use the same as you would use a dryer sheet. You don't have to rewash the face cloths often.

Polly Dzurak
Quincy, Massachusetts

Dear Amy,

I don't buy dryer sheets anymore. I live in an apartment building. I just reuse the dryer sheets other tenants have discarded. They work great.

Kathy Ranta
Coon Rapids, Minnesota

(I asked Jim, "How come we don't use dryer sheets?" Jim replied, "We don't use our dryer!" Air-dried clothing is so stiff it couldn't possibly cling. FZ)

THE SCHOOL RECYCLER

Charlotte Johns of Bison, Oklahoma, sent in an idea for making a "new" carrier for "old" school supplies. I thought it could be used for other applications as well; a kit of small tools, a manicure set, crochet needles, etc.

Use heavyweight fabrics. Examples include denim (from last year's cutoffs) or quilted fabric. Charlotte has used seed sacks.

Fabric should be double layered. Sew two layers, right side together. Leave one end open and reverse. Press into a workable square or rectangle.

To finish, fold up bottom flap and stitch. Make spaces for pencils, pens, crayons, a paint box, scissors, etc.

Stitch on the pocket for the eraser and sharpener. The opening will be on the inside at the top when it folds down.

Finally, sew on a tie made of the same material, or a ribbon.

A possible modification to this design might be an additional flap sewn from the top to prevent any supplies from falling out once the recycler is tied.

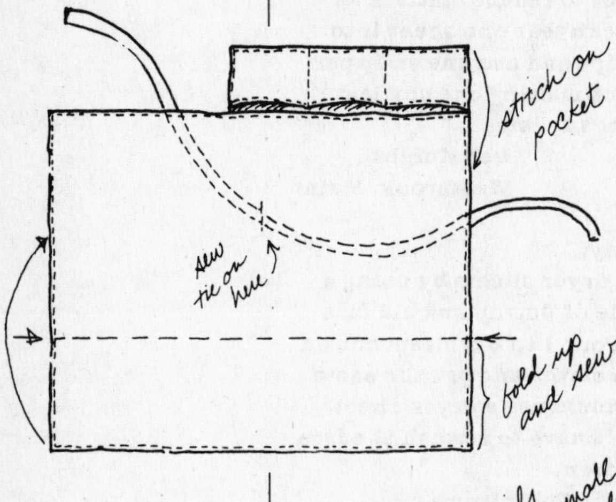

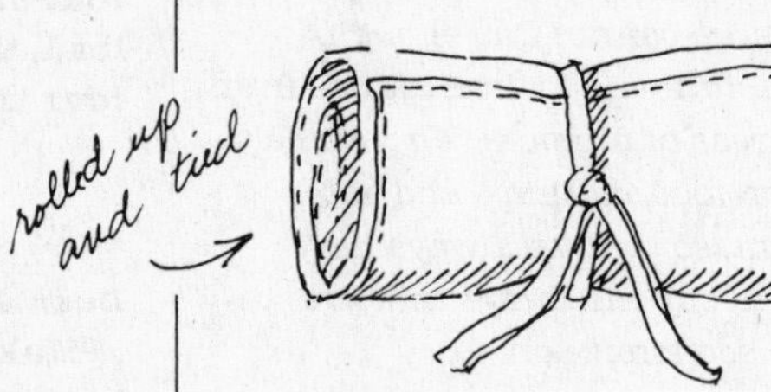

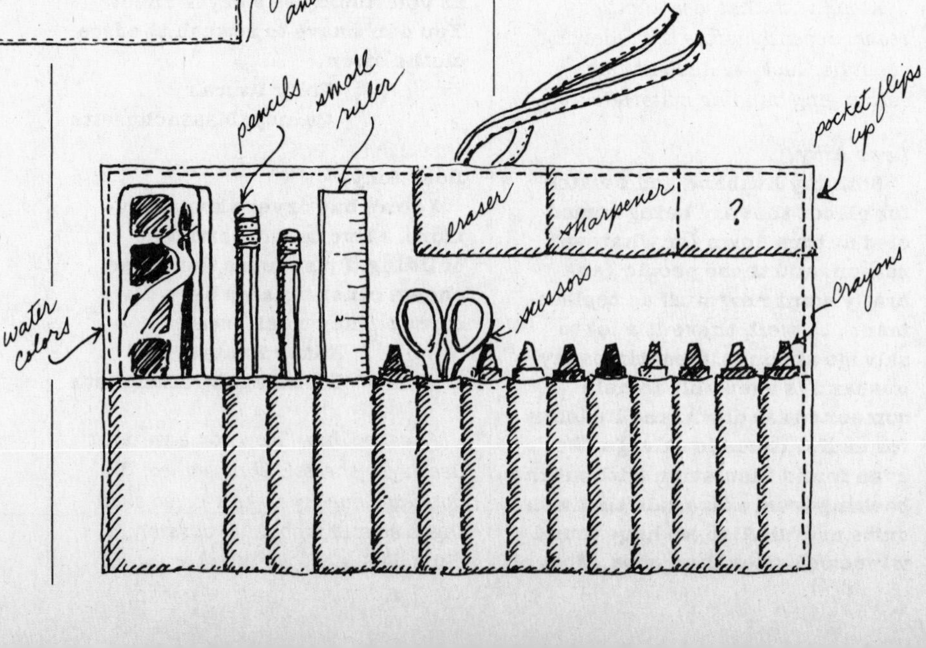

"HOW CAN I SAVE ON BABY FORMULA?"

Many readers have requested a homemade baby formula recipe. These queries coincided with the following baby formula recipe sent in:

2 12-oz cans of evaporated milk
32 oz water
2 Tbsp Karo syrup
3 ml Poly Vi Sol vitamins

Commercial formula costs roughly three times as much as this recipe, or between $816 and $967 per year.

In the interest of passing along good information, I began a phone call trek to verify the appropriateness of this recipe, or to find an approved recipe.

I called the American Academy of Pediatrics and spoke with two of their advisers. They gave me the name of a lab that develops baby formula. I also spoke with three other nutritionists, including one from Women and Infant Children.

None of the professionals I spoke with felt that homemade formulas were a very good option. Prepared correctly, they rank a distant third behind breast-feeding and commercial formula. They are probably adequate but not optimum.

However, under certain circumstances homemade formulas may be fine to use. Before considering its use you need to know more about infant nutrition, and formula in general.

A generation ago most of us were fed formula made with evaporated milk. It was the best formula available at the time. Parents in many other countries still make their own today. However, the new commercial formulas more closely resemble breast milk and are more complete.

Homemade formulas use evaporated milk because it has been sufficiently heated to denature or break down the protein of cow's milk, in the same way that commercial formulas are manufactured. No newborn should be fed regular cow's milk, which is too hard for the child to digest. Ten to 20% of the infants will suffer from minor stomach bleeding, which would be undetectable and could lead to an iron deficiency.

Evaporated milk is on the low end of the range for essential fatty acids. Concern was expressed over prolonged use of evaporated milk for that reason. A generation ago this issue was not as great because children started solid foods as early as four months. Essential fatty acids are found in a variety of foods. However, it is now believed that the introduction of solid foods too early can cause lifelong allergies. Today many doctors advise waiting until at least six months before introducing solid foods.

Essential fatty acids are important to brain development.

Homemade formula contains Karo syrup. There has been some concern raised over the possibility of infant botulism, such as is the case with honey. The AAP was not aware of any documented cases, and therefore did not feel that there was any need for concern. The lack of documented cases may be a result of the fact that very few babies are fed Karo syrup today. The WIC nutritionist thought that granulated sugar might be a better addition.

The formula lab felt that infant formula would need a vitamin supplement that contains vitamin C, iron, and folic acid. Poly Vi Sol vitamins have vitamin C and iron, but no folic acid. (Folic acid aids in the absorption of iron.) The vitamins should be given to an infant separately if the formula is heated up beyond room temperature, since heat destroys many vitamins.

The professionals I spoke with felt concern over the preparation of the homemade formulas. If a parent were highly conscientious this need not be a factor, but incorrect mixing could be a problem, especially if the milk were not sufficiently diluted. The same argument could be made about mixing powdered commercial formulas.

When asked about the cost difference, and whether the savings could justify use of homemade formulas, the reaction was mixed. They truthfully pointed out that most household budgets include many nonessentials. A potential annual savings in the hundreds of dollars could be important to "the working poor," but most families should look to other cuts first.

What of the argument "We were all raised on it and we turned out fine"? One expert described that as the Dr. Welby approach to medicine. The theory is cozy and warm but not very scientific. The same applies to the argument "My children look healthy, so I must be doing it right." The best information currently available points to specific nutritional guidelines. While experts frequently disagree, and new evidence always comes along, we should not discount the opinions of those who have studied the question for years.

Where does this leave us? Breast-feeding is still the best option for feeding infants, from a nutritional and economic standpoint. A breast-feeding mother needs an additional two cups of milk per day, which costs about a quarter. If you are having difficulty, call your local chapter of the La Leche League for help. Statistically only about 10% of mothers are physically unable to breast-feed infants. The remainder of mothers who use formula do so by choice or because of problems with work schedules.

Some of the nutritionists feel that babies who eat a well-balanced diet of solid food twice a day can be switched to a homemade formula, and some pediatricians may approve whole milk around eight months.

The interest in reviving the old recipes stems from a real concern over the dramatic rise in the cost of commercial formulas. The Federal Trade Commission is currently investigating three major formula manufacturers for price fixing. However, this does not invalidate the product.

If a mother cannot breast-feed, commercial formula remains a strong second. Before using any homemade formula recipe, consult your pediatrician.

BABY FORMULA UPDATE

Dear Amy,

I am writing concerning the article "How Can I Save on Baby Formula?" As you pointed out, only 5% to 10% of women are physically unable to breast-feed, meaning that the majority of women who do choose to bottle-feed do so for personal reasons. I would like it noted for your cost-conscious readers that the expense of feeding breast-milk substitute to a baby must also include added medical expenses. A recent study in *The American Physician* found that artificially fed infants are treated by their doctor three times as often as breast-fed infants. In their first year, only 25% of breast-fed infants were brought to their doctor for illness, while 97% of artificially fed infants needed medical treatment. With the cost of doctor visits ranging from $30 to $50 per visit, breast-feeding could save a family a lot of money and a baby from a lot of unnecessary pain.

Beverly Wilder
Lawrenceville, Georgia

(Without having read it, I don't know the criteria for this study. It occurs to me that formula-fed babies are more likely to be in daycare, and thus more likely to be exposed to germs. This may account for some of the higher incidence of illness of the formula-fed babies. FZ)

TACKY & CHEAP

Dear Amy,

Use duct tape, or masking tape, for taping jobs where the tape does not need to be clear. Duct tape is also excellent for package sealing. The P.O. frowns on it, for unknown reasons, but many people are using it. Masking tape does not have the strength needed for most packages.

John Etter
Hood River, Oregon

(OK, this tightwad sends me in this idea, and in the interest of passing along good information, I, the greatest mathematical midget of all time, have to work out how to compare:

Duct 2 in × 60 yds. for $6
Masking 1 in. × 60 yds. for $1
Clear ½ in. × 12.5 yds. for 69¢

I finally figured based on ½ in. × 1 yd. After at least 30 minutes of intense calculations I have determined that a hunk of duct tape would cost 2½¢ (2.5¢), masking tape would cost under a penny (.83¢), and clear tape would cost over 5¢ (5.7¢). Phew! FZ)

HOW BIG IS A CORD OF WOOD?

I have a friend, and subscriber, who sells wood part time. He tells me that from time to time he finds that people do not get their money's worth when they purchase firewood.

The problem arises over confusion between a "full cord" and a "face cord" of wood.

A full cord of firewood is a stack of wood that equals 128 cu. ft. Although usually defined as 4′ × 4′ × 8′, obviously it can be an equal dimension, such as 2′ × 4′ × 16′.

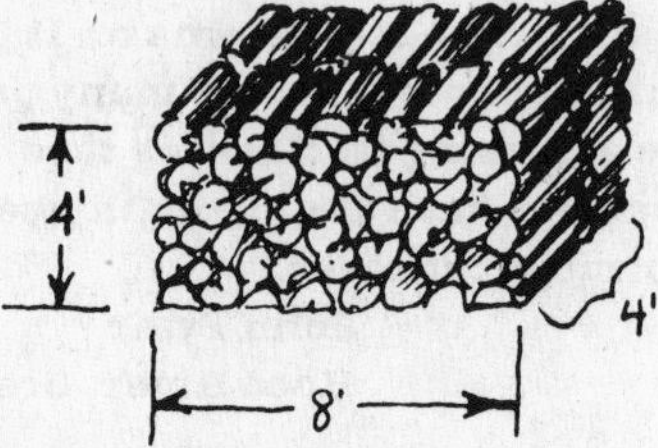

A face cord is a stack of firewood where the "face" is the traditional 4′ × 8′, but the depth is not the 4′ measurement. This can occur when the wood has been cut in an odd length so that it stacks up to an odd depth. Such as two rows deep of 18″ wood adds up to 3′ deep. If you have purchased a face cord, which equals 3′ × 4′ × 8′, you've only bought 75% of a full cord.

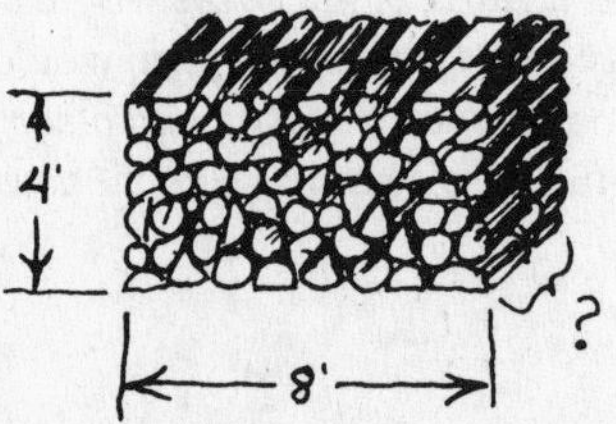

PRESCRIPTIONS

Dear Amy,

I am sensitive to certain medicines and sometimes get side effects. Many times after purchasing a full bottle of prescription pills that is outrageously expensive, after taking one or two, my doctor would switch me to another brand. I'd be stuck with the bottle of pills. When I complained to my pharmacist, I learned I could buy as few or as many pills as I want at a time. Since then, I have purchased as few as three at a time. This has saved me lots of money, plus I can stick to my budget and buy pills by the day or the week.

Doreen Gully
Silver Spring, Maryland

PILL POINTER

Dear Amy,

A reader wrote in about buying prescriptions in small amounts. That is fine for people who are worried about allergic reactions, etc. However, you do end up paying more per pill that way. The pharmacy not only charges for the pills but also a dispensing fee (of about $3) each time they fill a prescription. If you have insurance you pay the copayment each time you get it filled. I know this because I used to work in a pharmacy.

Chris Bean
Sevartz Creek, Michigan

CALCULATING THE NET VALUE OF THE SECOND INCOME

Some time ago I met a woman at a party who told me she worked

because she *had* to. I should have let this comment slide by, but I didn't. Instead I interrogated her mercilessly until I was able to get her to admit she worked because she *wanted* to. She did not appreciate my attempt to enlighten, and I did regret doing it.

If you have concluded that I think mothers who work outside the home are subhuman, you are wrong. I just get a little off kilter when middle-income families do not assume responsibility for their choices.

This woman, it turned out, was a teacher, and she was genuinely enriched by her job. She just had unresolved feelings about her role as a parent.

Families choose a two-income lifestyle for very good reasons. In the lowest-income groups it is usually an economic necessity. I know of many cases when the wife works because her husband's job lacks security or sufficient benefits. Usually the purpose of the second income is to elevate the standard of living.

All these reasons can be valid. It would be clearly stupid of me to nitpick the choices of working moms when I am indebted to many. Some wonderful schoolteachers and delivery room nurses come to mind.

This lengthy prelude is, admittedly, literary clutter because this article is not about values. My biggest concern about the traditional two-income structure is that it can be extremely inefficient.

To illustrate this I am using a scenario of a family of four with two incomes of $25,000 and $15,000. Neither spouse is self-employed (thereby paying less social security), and both have equal benefits.

The most complicated factor to figure is the bigger tax bite. I am presuming my couple does not

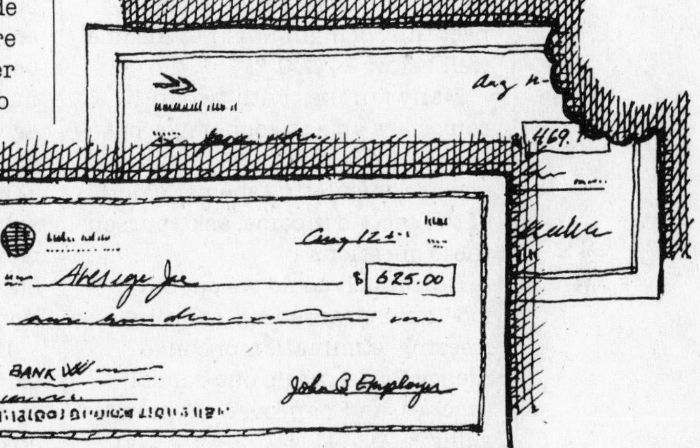

itemize. A $15,000 income loses about 12% to federal and state income tax, and social security. A $25,000 income has about 18% withheld. But as these two incomes combine, our couple moves into a higher tax bracket. A $40,000 income has about 22% withheld. In reality what this means is that the $15,000 loses 27% to the tax bite. To determine this I figured the couple's taxes with a $40,000 income and a $25,000 income. The difference is then subtracted from the $15,000 income.

$40,000 income pays $8,638
$25,000 income pays $4,516
additional taxes = $4,122

When the difference is subtracted from $15,000, the net is $10,878.

My couple has two children in daycare at a cost of $120 per week. (Daycare costs exceed $100 per child weekly in urban areas. Infants cost even more.) After factoring in the child care tax deduction, the income drops to $5,838 annually. Transportation, costlier hair care, and a professional wardrobe can further impact this, bringing the net income well below $4,000.

Many families with two incomes are able to economize, but the reality is that most do not. If you are calculating the net value of the second income, ask yourself these questions:

How much could we cut our food bill by gardening, canning, freezing, elimination of convenience foods, meals out, school lunches, and improved shopping skills?

How much could we save by spending more time shopping for better prices on the purchase of household goods?

Could we eliminate services we currently buy because of a lack of time, such as home maintenance and renovation, tax preparation, house cleaning, tutoring, etc.?

How much could be saved on birthdays and holidays by making gifts?

How much could be saved by writing letters instead of making long-distance phone calls?

How much could we save on clothing by yard saling, watching sales, sewing, and repairing clothing?

How much could we save by using cloth diapers and hanging laundry?

If wood heat is a factor, how much could we save by 100% wood use and providing some labor?

In addition to the endless ways to save money with more free time, families with lower incomes qualify for special benefits. In Maine families earning $30,000 or less qualify for subsidized loans if they are a first-time home buyer. (Our income was low enough, but we were disqualified because we had saved too much money!) As children reach college age they can obtain more loans and scholarships.

When you calculate the net value of your second income, work out your taxes both ways. State taxes and individual deductions will vary.

If you decide you want to scale back to one income, you must be sure you are willing to actually economize in the ways you factored in.

If you are single or newly married and wish to achieve a single income lifestyle, be aware that it requires aggressive planning. It is not a matter of luck. Many double-income families who believe they work because they have to are in reality paying for past choices.

If you both love your jobs . . . great. But if you would like to work less or leave your job altogether, an evening with a calculator may turn up a pleasant surprise.

TWO INCOMES

Dear Amy,

It seems that you have started your gazette at just the right time. People are beginning to

wake up and realize that they are not saving a lot by working two jobs. I know I wished I had stayed home with our son. We could have saved so much. Since I gave up a full-time job in favor of a part-time weekend job, my husband has admitted that the quality of our lives has improved and that we are doing better now.

Matilda Carreras
Malden Massachusetts

(She also included an article that appeared in the August 1990 issue of Parents *magazine called "Can You Afford to Quit?" It came to an identical conclusion as my article "Calculating the Net Value of the Second Income." Check your library for back issues of* Parents *magazine. FZ)*

PIGGYBACK POSTAGE

Dear Amy,

To save on postage, form a neighborhood group to use a common envelope and stamp to mail bills. In our neighborhood all the telephone bills are due on the 4th, water bills on the 10th, etc. When three neighbors combine their bills with a fourth neighbor, 87¢ is saved. This is not a big savings, especially when divided by several families, but can foster a spirit of "community tightwaddery."

Connie Tefteller
La Vernia,
Texas

HOMEMADE GRANOLA

The homemade granola contributions from several readers and the gift of a few pounds of Georgia pecans inspired me to dig out my granola recipe. Presuming that you buy the ingredients cheaply enough and you avoid the option of nuts, this recipe will make a 2-oz. serving for about 10¢ to 12¢, or half the price of name-brand cereals and less than a third of many commercial granolas.

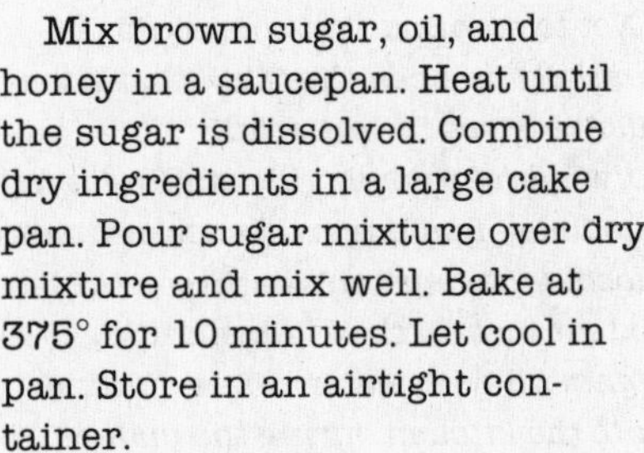

¾ cup brown sugar
⅓ cup vegetable oil
⅓ cup honey
5 cups oatmeal
½ cup raisins*
½ cup dry milk
¾ teaspoon cinnamon
pinch of salt

Mix brown sugar, oil, and honey in a saucepan. Heat until the sugar is dissolved. Combine dry ingredients in a large cake pan. Pour sugar mixture over dry mixture and mix well. Bake at 375° for 10 minutes. Let cool in pan. Store in an airtight container.
Optional: add nuts, wheat germ, coconut, dates, etc.
* add raisins after cooking

TOILET PAPER STRATEGY

Dear Amy,

This is what I discovered when my umpteen grandchildren came to visit: The bathroom was in constant use and I had to run to the store to renew my supply of toilet paper. That roll of paper was letting them grab miles of it at a time, and so before I replaced a roll, I stood on it with one foot. It was no longer round like a circle but was creased instead. When the roll was put back it would

turn around three times and tear off easy. It saves money, trees, and a stuffed-up sewer line.

Mrs. Mary Fedorka
Jamestown, New York

(Not to mention that this could potentially dampen the thrill that a toddler receives from gleefully unwinding a whole roll, stuffing it in the toilet, flushing half a dozen times, flooding the upstairs bathroom to the extent that all the kitchen ceiling lights fill with water before spilling into the kitchen during the major monthly mailing. FZ)

THE SCROUNGED HALLOWEEN COSTUME

Chances are that you will not be creating a Halloween costume for a six-year-old boy who wants to be a robot. In fact, it is possible to live one's entire life without being pressed into any costume designing.

This article is really about creating something from nothing. The process is the same as putting together a gourmet meal from leftovers or building a wheelbarrow from salvaged materials.

If it happens that there is a six-year-old in your house that does want to be a robot, do not read this as a "paint by numbers" how-to article.

The creative tightwad method requires that you draw from your own resources—your talents and materials you can obtain cheaply or are in surplus. You do not have the same materials on hand that I did. You may not have the same skills or husband waiting in the wings willing to lend technical support.

Before asking your child what he wants to be this year, access your resources. One year the only material I had to make costumes was from a pile of old black Navy uniforms. I told the children they could be anything they wanted to be as long as it was something black. When you are stuck for an idea, let your available materials be your springboard.

The following year Alec told me he wanted to be a transformer. I accessed my resources and decided even I wasn't that creative. We compromised with a robot design. The springboard was a milk jug mask design I had developed a few years before. Having just moved we had a surplus of cardboard boxes and a discarded dryer duct. I had a can of silver spray paint and I gambled that Jim would have some electronic or mechanical stuff kicking around.

The result was a successful collaboration of Jim's and my skills. We made our community debut at the church Halloween party. Alec won the "Most Creative Costume" award, but the real prize was seeing him surrounded by a crowd of older boys checking out the front door panel. One voice

a mask made from a milk jug painted silver

a spark plug

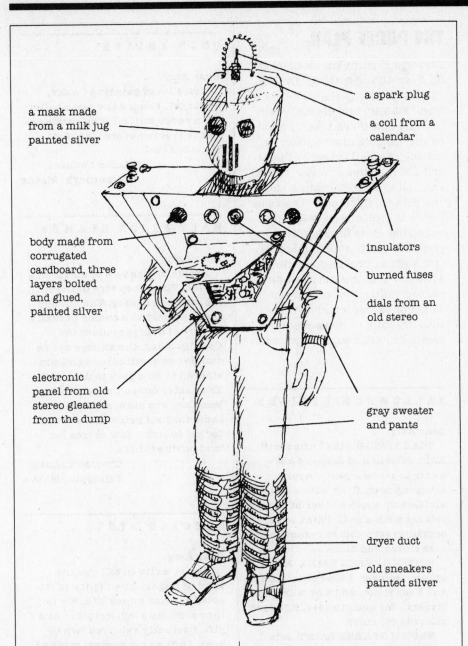

a coil from a calendar

body made from corrugated cardboard, three layers bolted and glued, painted silver

insulators

burned fuses

dials from an old stereo

electronic panel from old stereo gleaned from the dump

gray sweater and pants

dryer duct

old sneakers painted silver

announced, "This is the best costume any kid could ever have!"

My children are not always clad with award-winning efforts. The two-year-old was shortchanged with a fire hat and red raincoat.

This kind of quality-time project has value beyond the production of a good costume. The dime store ones are cheap enough. But by observing you, children learn how to create and they learn craft. These powerful memories imprint a more important message. They come to understand the superiority of the creative tightwad method.

THE PUREE PLAN

Carve your pumpkin on October 30. Save all the cuttings. On November 1 salvage the jack-o'-lantern. Cut it up and discard peels and any blackened areas. Prepare as you would winter squash by cutting in small cubes. Fill a pot and add 2 inches of water. Cover and boil until soft. Drain water and process in blender. Freeze in (reused) Ziploc bags in 2-cup quantities. Save for Thanksgiving pumpkin pie, pumpkin pudding (pie with no crust), or muffins. After puree is thawed it is often watery, unlike the canned version. Use excess water to mix with dry milk to make mock cream or milk needed in your recipe.

HALLOWEEN RECIPES

Dear Amy,

SCAR TISSUE. Mix unflavored Knox gelatin and drops of hot water to make a paste. Apply drooping open flesh with a spatula. Gently apply a layer of baby powder with a puff. Paint with acrylic craft paint to resemble scar tissue and blood.

WHITE GREASE PAINT. Mix 2 tsp shortening, 5 tsp cornstarch and 1 tsp flour. Add 2 or 3 drops of glycerin for smoothness. Add food coloring for color.

BROWN GREASE PAINT. Mix 1 tsp shortening and 2½ tsp cocoa. Add 2 or 3 drops of glycerin.

Both grease paints wash off with baby oil, cold cream, or Crisco.

Merrie Hallman
Liv Manor, New York

COLD ROLLER

Dear Amy,

I do a lot of painting (walls, ceilings). I reuse the same roller with cover still on it by putting it in the freezer overnight. Just thaw to reuse.

Elaine Levine
Scarborough, Maine

HALF-PRICE STAMPS

Dear Amy,

People buy sheets of all stamps issued. Then they tire of them, die, or need money. The stamps are then sold to a dealer (usually as part of a larger collection). Usually older, the stamps are in smaller denominations and considered to be a pain to deal with. The dealer doesn't want them unless they are rare, and will sell them for half price. It's worth it for me to lick a few extras for that basic savings.

Charles Tanner
Falmouth, Maine

SUCCESS STORY

Dear Amy,

I must write to tell you the kind of impact *The Tightwad Gazette* has had on my life. My father sent me a subscription as a gift. I actually received two issues. In the past several weeks I have read each at least six times and highlighted the main points.

Last Monday I went shopping, keeping in mind your suggestions for savings. My normal bill for 10 days' worth of food for 3 was about $110. This past Monday I purchased the same amount of food, just different types. To my

total glee the bill was $60.94! Almost half. And, yes, I did buy the dry milk and so far my family has not noticed the switch.

Morgan M. Franks
Hackettstown, New Jersey

(Learning how to feed a family for as little as we do can take a year or more to learn, especially if gardening is to be a part of the plan. Morgan's ability to nearly cut her food bill in half in a matter of weeks is terrific. FZ)

AIR FRESHENER

Dear Amy,

We find that instead of using the highly perfumed and expensive room refreshers, such as Airwick and Glade, we can easily get rid of unpleasant odors by simply lighting a match. We have not yet tried it as an underarm deodorant!

Jim Spaulding
Northfield, Massachusetts

STAIN REMEDY

Dear Amy,

My father-in-law had made me savvy to the dishwasher detergent/all-fabric bleach combo* years ago. But for even tougher stains, a paste of Barkeeper's Friend cleanser on the stain for about five minutes has had remarkable results for me.

Anne Fairfield
Wiscasset, Maine

(This reader refers to my stain recipe on page 272. FZ)*

.,.,.,

GETTING A BARGAIN EVERY TIME

We had a burst of company the first summer after we bought the house . . . relatives coming to see our new home for the first time. Part way through the umpteenth house tour I realized that every other sentence coming out of my mouth started to the effect of: "We bought this at a yard sale" or "Jim scrounged this. . . ." After taking a quick inventory of our household stuff, it became obvious of the high percentage of goods we have obtained as the result of expert bargain hunting. I could more easily single out the items purchased in department-store desperation.

Our style of acquisition is strikingly different from most families I know. Typically people tend to notice today that they will need a new something tomorrow, run to Kmart, and put it on a charge card. They purchase, paying full price with interest. If they change their mind about their rushed purchase, they yard sale it for a 90% loss of their investment. (And someone like me buys it.)

If you are an impulse buyer, the first strategy you need to employ is *foresight.* You need to anticipate needs as far in advance as possible. Time is the key to finding bargains. It is not unreasonable to spend years shopping for a house, a year shopping for a car, or six months shopping for a tool.

During this period you should do extensive research. You need to determine your exact needs. Decide if you can get by with the inexpensive simpler model or if you really need the more expen-

sive one with all the features. Will a used item serve your needs as well? If so spend time in thrift shops, flea markets, and at yard sales, etc. to determine the "going price." Also look into your local swap magazine.

Only after you have done extensive research will you be certain you have found a genuine bargain.

It goes without saying that during this time you should plan your finances so that you have the available cash at the time you need it. If you know you will purchase a house in three years, do the homework to determine the down payment you'll need. Sometimes people miss smaller bargains for lack of funds. As a woman once told me, "Yes, I saw that sale on chicken, but I didn't have $10 to spare at the time."

Patience is the second element. It takes time to find your bargain. You need to stretch out your "looking-around time" as much as possible. Do not even consider paying full price for anything, and persist with your hunt.

Third, *improvise.* Often you will not find your bargain before the need comes due—the camping trip is next weekend and you are short two sleeping bags. Can you temporarily borrow the item you need? Can you rent the tool for one or two occasions? Can you make a widget that will do for a short time? In other words, bedrolls work almost as well as sleeping bags.

It does happen that some items never go on sale or turn up at a yard sale. When you get to this point you will be confident that you have done your best in finding a bargain. Pay full price only when you are certain that you have exhausted all possibilities.

How long is too long to wait? A good rule of thumb is to buy when it costs you money *not* to own it. Examples include a car, a washer, or a new business suit.

Otherwise, be stubborn and persistant.

I ruined our $14 teakettle by allowing the water to boil out. (Murphy's Law dictates that you will destroy new expensive purchases first.) We improvised by using a coffee perker (minus the guts) until I ruined that one two weeks later. In the following months we limped along boiling water in a pot, waiting for a bargain.

Then Jim found another perker (minus the guts) for $1 in a thrift shop. Since the destruction of two hot water vessels (and a couple of pots over the years) constitutes a habit, we are employing foresight. We are continuing our search for other cheap teakettles.

THE PRICE BOOK

I was four years into my thrift quest before I realized I needed to develop some sort of book to keep track of prices. I often wonder if all the various sizes and brands is part of a huge conspiracy to confuse consumers. With this possibility in mind, I set out to beat them at their own game.

Although prices on many items can vary widely from store to store, they probably average out overall. But what if I could buy only the cheapest products at each store?

We shop at a supermarket, a natural foods store, a day-old-bread store, a warehouse store, a smaller overpriced store with terrific sales, and we buy a few items from local farmers. (We don't shop at the Navy commissary because it is located an hour away from us and the savings are marginal.)

My price book is a small loose-leaf binder. Each page contains prices for one item, and the pages are in alphabetical order for quick reference. I include my code for the store name, the brand, the size of the item, the price, and the unit price.

I began by writing down prices on sale flyers and from my grocery slips. I made a few trips to compare prices of specific items.

It quickly became evident that not every sale was really a sale. But when I did find a good buy, and I could verify it with months of records . . . what power! I could stock up with confidence.

At first you may think this is too much work and the idea of shopping at so many stores will be inconceivable. It will pay off. A good strategy is to shop at different stores each week of the month so that within a 30-day cycle you can hit them all. We have our shopping system down to once a month with only a few short trips to hit unbeatable sales.

The keeping of a price book revolutionized our shopping strategy more than anything else we did. For the first time we had a feeling of control over our food budget.

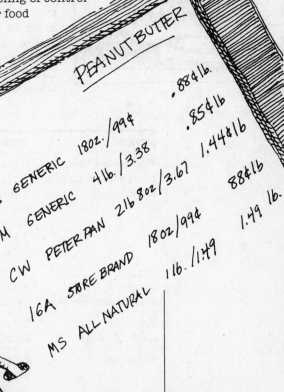

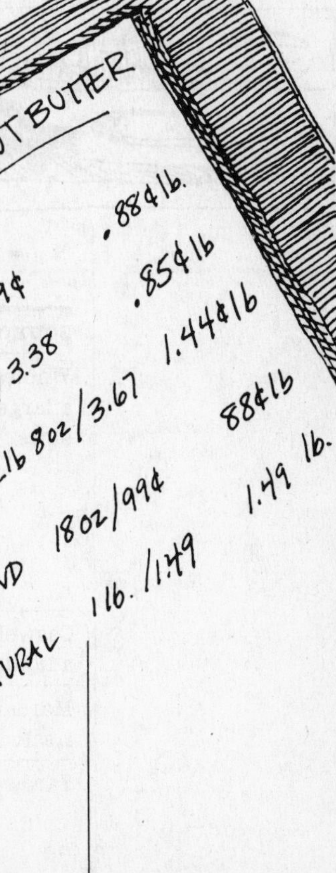

PEANUT BUTTER
SNS GENERIC 18oz./99¢ .88¢lb.
CM GENERIC 4lb./3.38 .85¢lb
CW PETER PAN 2lb 8oz/3.67 1.44¢lb
16A STORE BRAND 18oz/99¢ 88¢lb
MS ALL NATURAL 1lb./1.49 1.49 lb.

AN URBAN EXCURSION

Twice a month I venture into the "city" to pick up or drop off printing. Each 50-mile round trip saves money on the cost of printing my newsletter. To make this effort more profitable I hit thrift shops, day-old bread stores, yard sales, discount stores, etc. On page 33 is a table that depicts the results of a real outing. The entire trip, with all the stops, took three hours. We estimated our savings based on typical supermarket or department store prices.

If you travel to an area other than where you regularly shop, I recommend that you make a point of investigating any stores that might offer a discount, and record items into your price book. In the future when you make a trip, make it a point to pick up items with worthwhile prices. Always compare prices with your price book (see below) and never assume any discount store offers best prices on every item.

Not including the savings on printing and factoring in gas, this trip earned (saved) us a tax-free $32 per hour.

GROCERY PRICES

Dear Amy,

Thanks for the idea on pricing all area stores. I was so surprised when my impressions were completely wrong. Even the discount warehouse was higher than our local store on a few items. Also the food co-op we participate in had some great bargains and some items way overpriced!

Joyce Bussell
Jensen Beach, Florida

SOURCE	ITEM	COST	EST. SAV.
Wholesale Depot, a large warehouse store	2 gal. generic shampoo	$ 4.18 ea	$ 7.48
	1 gal. generic conditioner	4.18 ea	3.74
	1 ltr soda	free	1.00
	50 lbs Purina dog food	15.99	1.09
	12″ x 2,000′ plastic wrap	4.83	9.07
	40 lbs generic detergent	9.99	12.50
	1 gal. Murphy's Oil Soap	7.63	1.93
	1½ lbs dog chews	4.88	.49
Caswell's, a liquidation center	8 12-oz apple juice conc.	.57 ea	2.00
	24 20-oz cans of pineapple	.49 ea	6.00
Marden's, a salvage store	5 rolls of clear tape	.20 ea	2.50
	25 mailing envelopes	.11 ea	3.25
Yard sales	27 qt. canning jars	3.00	9.50
	soup thermos	.25	1.75
	snowsuit	.50	24.00
	boys' denim jacket	1.00	14.00
	Total	$76.12	$100.30

HOW TO BUY FOOD IN BULK

The typical American shops once a week. Each trip includes a walk down every aisle as he puts enough in his cart to last seven days. This shopping style is time consuming and expensive.

We have fallen into this pattern perhaps because we tend to be paid weekly, or because a small percentage of groceries (milk, produce) has a shelf life of about a week. Sales also run weekly.

Even if the shopper were to stop in weekly for produce, milk, and the unbeatable sale, touring each aisle need not be necessary.

Bulk buying, or stocking up, saves money, and although you may shop at more than one store it need not require more time, and will probably *save* time.

The first rule of bulk buying is to know your prices. Never assume that one source of food has the lowest price on every item, regardless of the type of store. To effectively determine the lowest price you must establish some method of tracking prices and frequency of sales. We use a price book system, as discussed in the preceding article. This information tells you which store to buy each item from and how much to buy. A few hours spent doing this research can save you hundreds of dollars over the year. Do not unforgo this step, thinking it is too much work. I have had many readers write saying they tried the price book and "It works!"

Secondly you must investigate all sources of food in your area. Aside from grocery stores, check out warehouse stores, salvage stores, food co-ops, and even local farmers. As a general rule the loss leader sale items, which appear on the cover and back of sale flyers, will beat the prices of any wholesale source of food. The grocer takes a loss on these items figuring you will buy other products at the regular price. However, many staples never go on sale, so you will look for other sources for these items.

Bulk buying isn't just for big families. Simply put, buy enough to get you to the next sale or enough until it's convenient for you to stop there again. For example, we go past a bakery thrift shop twice a month. Each time I buy two weeks' worth of bread. We never make a special trip. Obviously a large family buys more than a single person. Each buys in bulk according to his need.

Note the date of any rare, unbeatable sales. In some cases you might detect a pattern of frequency. If you determine that peanut butter goes on sale once every three months, you should buy a three-month supply.

Many bulk foods are packaged in large quantities. The 50-pound sack of oatmeal will not be practi-

cal for the small family. Co-ops came into existence to address this need. Generally in the form of a buying club, groups of families band together to buy large quantities and split them up into smaller ones. As formal organizations, members are usually asked to donate a few hours of labor per month.

Food co-ops vary greatly in character. Some deal only with organic foods while others carry a line of frozen and prepackaged foods. Finding one that suits your needs may prove difficult.

An alternative is the informal co-op. A small group of friends, who buy similar foods, agrees to split up large quantities or pick up large quantities of sale items for others in the group. This saves time, gasoline, and money. These options address the needs of the smaller family units and those people with storage and time limitations.

To find additional room for bulk foods, rethink the spaces in your home. If you were offered $50 per month to rent out the space under your bed would you do it? People tend to think that all food must be stored in kitchen cabinets. However, a closet can be converted to a pantry and unused spaces, such as under your bed, can store a case of bargain canned pineapple. Buying in bulk can save the average family at least $50 per month.

To buy in bulk most effectively you should have a freezer. Used for garden surplus as well, the savings far outweigh the cost of electricity. The largest Sears freezer costs under $6 per month to operate. If you do not have a garden, you should select a smaller model. While some families and singles genuinely may not have room for a freezer, I have known renters who worked out arrangements to leave their freezer in the apartment basement. Freezers come with a lock.

Many people do not buy in bulk because they live paycheck to paycheck. Available dollars must be used to buy food for this week, not next month. The inability to bulk buy is one of the many ways that being "poor" makes your lifestyle more expensive. Make a small beginning. Eat more meatless meals or eliminate some nonessential grocery items. Use the surplus to begin buying in bulk. The savings will provide more spare cash to reinvest. Within a few months you should not have to think twice about affording to buy in bulk.

To make the most of buying in bulk you will probably have to let go of budgetary guidelines (allowing yourself only a very strict amount to be spent per week). You should not miss a great sale because you've already spent your quota. Instead work toward an average. As you begin to buy in bulk your food bill will be high the first month, but eventually the average will drop to a new low as you gradually eat a larger percentage of foods purchased at the lowest possible price.

After three years of living in this area we still find new sources of inexpensive foods. Even within the past few weeks we have found less expensive sources of cheese, chicken, and powdered milk. Two of these sources were through word of mouth. Ask around, especially of those people you know to be

shrewd shoppers. Try to find wholesale distributors in your Yellow Pages. One in our area primarily sells to bakeries, and is listed under "Bakery Supplies." A wholesale distributor may or may not sell to individuals. Or they may have minimum order requirements. However, they can give you the names of a storefront co-op or buying club that they sell to.

If you are unable to locate sources of bulk foods send an SASE to:

Co-op Directory Services
919 21st Ave. South
Minneapolis, MN 55404

This service will provide you with the name of a regional wholesaler who can give you the names of local co-ops, buying clubs, or storefronts.

Learning to bulk buy, like the acquisition of any new skill, requires an initial investment of time. The long-range dividends are unquestionable.

RIBBON TRICK

Dear Amy,

One tightwad tip that you might not have heard of is to spray faded (but not torn) typewriter ribbons with WD-40, which renews some oil used in typewriter ribbon inks.

Joseph Hagedorn
Cincinnati, Ohio

FREE RIDE

Dear Amy,

In 25 years of driving over 30,000 miles a year, I haven't spent a cent to own the cars.

When I first started in business, I called the local commercial credit office to inquire about repossessed cars. They had dozens, and I bought two for a total of $500 . . . sold one for $600, and that began my odyssey of not spending money for cars.

When I tired of that car (remember I got that car and $100 to start) I ran an ad to sell my "Classic 1959 Plymouth" and sold it for $400. I used that $400 to buy a 1962 Volvo, drove it two years, ran another "classic" ad and sold it for $600. I bought another Volvo for $500 . . . and I've repeated the process about 15 times.

Part of the formula involves negotiating. I might look at 10 cars (all private sales, no dealers) before I find one I like that can be bought right. I pull out my money in $100 bills, explain that I'm on my way to look at another car, but if I could buy theirs for *X* (usually half of what they are asking) I can give them cash now.

Sometimes I have to drive away and look at more cars, but 15 times they accepted my offer.

I prefer Volvos, as they last, hold value, and give great service. I do my own maintenance, using a Chilton's guide or the manual for that model car. I change the oil every 3,000 miles, keep them clean, had several Maaco $100 paint jobs, and always have whitewall tires.

Bill Niland
Topsfield, Massachusetts

GOOD DEAL

Dear Amy,

I recently discovered "price adjustment policies." I first learned of them from a discount department store. If I make a purchase and that item goes on sale, within 30 days, I can take my receipt to Customer Service for a cash refund of the difference. I have already received $5 back on school supplies.

I called other larger department stores and specialty shops in my area and learned they also had the same unwritten policy. One store even has a policy that if I make a purchase of an item that I know had been on sale within the past 30 days, they will give me the former sale price. All the stores I researched also gave a price adjustment for items that are on layaway that go on sale.

Some stores make the offer for seven days after the purchase only. Only one store wanted to see a dated sales receipt and the merchandise. Some stores have exclusions, such as for clearance of special-event sales. One store would make a price adjustment if a competitor had the same item on sale.

D. T. Mercer
Loma, Colorado

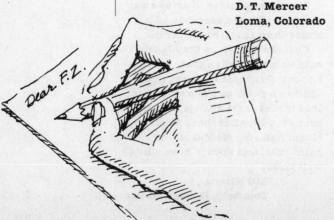

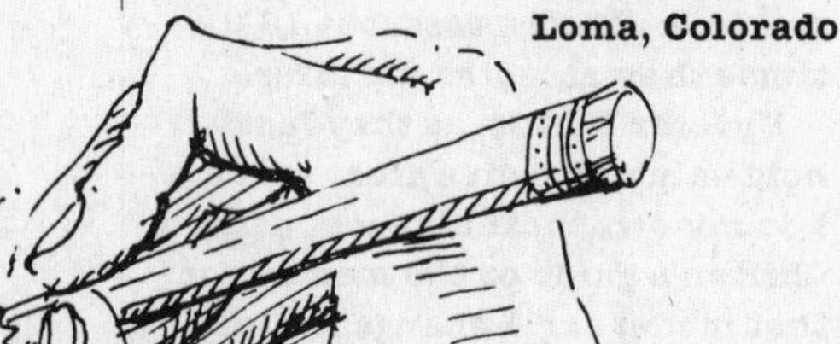

PAPER SAVER

Dear Amy,

I work in a busy office that utilizes personal computers and printers that use up a lot of paper. There is an extraordinary amount of paper wasted after printing. I save any blank or unused sheets. By the end of the day I might have 5 to 10 sheets. I use these to make envelopes.

Make a template from a piece of cardboard the same size as a business- or letter-size envelope. Then cut the paper 10″ × 10″ for legal size, or 7½″ × 7½″ for a letter-size envelope. Place the template in the middle of the paper on an angle. Using the template as a guide, first fold the sides, next the bottom, and finally the top. Use glue or glue stick to secure.

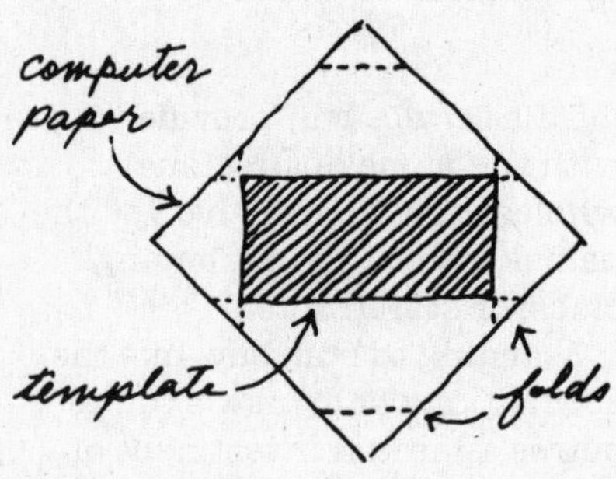

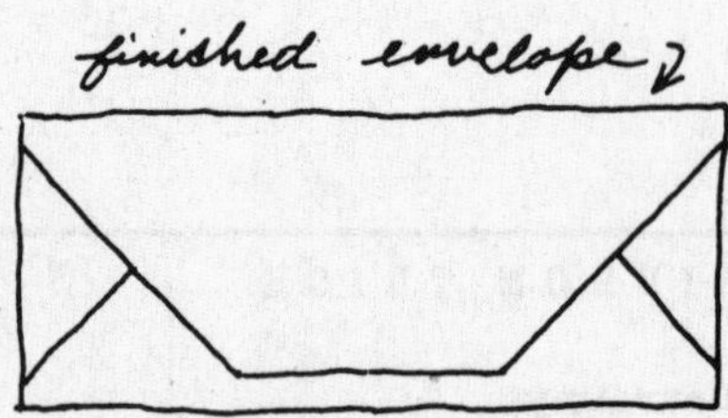

Margaret Williams
DeLand, Florida

A READER QUESTION

Dear Amy,
I am interested in finding out how your husband purchased a new car and saved so much money. I am desperate for some ammo when dealing with car dealers. It's a jungle out there!

Judith Perry
Lee, Massachusetts

Dear Judith,

Purchasing a new car can only be considered economical if you plan to own it for more than 10 years, you maintain it meticulously, and you buy it with cash. The exception would be if your cash is invested in a safe plan that has a higher interest rate than the interest rate you could get for a car loan. At least try to pay off the loan quickly.

Figuring that you expect to own this vehicle for 10 or more years, plan ahead. Don't buy a compact car if you are planning a family. Carefully consider the options you want. When purchasing our Horizon we decided to save $250 and not get the rear window wiper and defogger. However, there were many frigid mornings of frost scraping that we wished we had gotten it.

The ammo to which you refer can be found at bookstores . . . a new car buyer's guide. Find one that pertains to the type of vehicle you want, tells you the suggested list price and dealer's cost. The dealer's cost is broken down by models and options.

After you decide on the model you want, visit a dealer to learn the codes for options and which options go together.

Make up a list of options with the codes, dealer's cost, and the suggested list price. Total up the prices. From this determine what you feel is an allowable profit, bearing in mind that the dealer will get further discounts below the dealer cost.

A $200 to $500 profit will be adequate.

Start making the rounds of dealers and tell them what you would be willing to pay. If they do not want to meet your price, go elsewhere. To speed up the process you can mail copies of your specifications and price you are willing to pay to other area dealers.

Also check on buying clubs or organizations that can get you a group discount.

In general, remember that sometimes at the end of the month dealers become desperate to make a sales quota. Don't let dealers talk you into buying something other than what you have decided you want.

Avoid trading in. You'll get a better price for your old car through a private sale.

Ignore sales and rebates. These are designed to confuse you.

If you buy "off-the-lot" you will likely pay for options you didn't really

want, and not get ones you really wanted. The dealer has money tied up in a lot car and won't give you as good a deal.

In general, dealerships will not sell any car at a loss. They don't operate like grocery stores, which sell one item at a loss to get you to buy several more. You will buy only one car from them. However, they will cut their profits to the bone.

Your only consideration should be the bottom line. How much you "save" is not as important as how much you spend.

Using this method Jim has gotten roughly 20% off the sticker price of two vehicles.

MYSTERIES OF THE MODERN WORLD

Why is it that if I had placed my six children in daycare at a cost of about $250 per week, and I worked a job grossing $100 per week, our family would have qualified for a larger mortgage loan?

Why do people moonlight for a few more dollars to make ends meet and then buy convenience foods because of a lack of time?

Why is it that people won't donate to charities, but will buy overpriced merchandise they do not need because it's for a good cause?

THE SPIDER WEB GAME

The standard games for Halloween are always great . . . they're traditional. Here's one you might never have heard of. This is called the Spider Web Game.

You are having a small party with about 10 people. You need a few balls of white string and 10 prizes. You tie an end of string around a prize and hide it. Then you unroll the ball of string and wind it around the room, wrapping it taut around chair legs, door knobs, window hardware, etc. Make a complex design. The string should not be loose on the floor. Tie the other end around a stick or small piece of cardboard. Repeat until you have made 10 string trails that crisscross and tangle up together. Design your game so that all the trails begin near the door. When your guests arrive they get their own stick to wind their string on as they follow their own trail.

This game is appropriate for guests of all ages (as long as they are limber enough to crawl under and over the string maze). You can make shorter trails for younger kids and longer, more difficult ones for older kids and adults. You can also choose specific prizes for age and sex. Just

label the stick or cardboard with a name as you finish each trail.

I used this idea for a birthday party game one time. By the time I finished setting up the game I figure I burned up a few thousand calories. I finished at the front door. Then I realized I had forgotten something in one of the bedrooms . . . on the other side of the string web. It took a full 10 minutes to get across the room and back.

(Naturally, when you finish the Spider Web Game you must save the string.)

NEW/OLD QUILTS

Dear Amy,

Everyone loves handmade quilts; however, with the rising cost of material and batting, they become very expensive to make, and with the rising cost of heating they become very necessary to have.

To save money and recycle you can take an old quilt (factory made or handmade) that is stained or getting frayed and recover it. Yard sales often have stained quilts for very low prices.

You can use sheets for backing purchased at white sales and factory outlets. Use scraps of material collected over time (shirts ready for the rag bag usually have a nice square or two, as well as material left over when you cut off jeans).

After winter you can use this to display in your frugal country home.

Betty Candage
Auburn, Maine

CORN CASSEROLE

Dear Amy,

I had three ears of leftover corn, and ½ onion in the fridge. I cut the corn off the cob, chopped the onion, and threw them into a bowl together with a big handful of stale crackers, an egg, dry milk, a tablespoon of sugar, a little water, and blended it. Cooked it about ¾ hour in a 350° oven. My crew loved it!

Attalie Boynton
Readfield, Maine

SPENDTHRIFT HORROR STORY

Leeds, Maine, is a very rural farm community. Most of the families have practiced thrift for generations as a matter of survival. In this tightwad environment I am finding my fervor slipping and feel a need to go to a mall just to get my batteries recharged. Therefore I appreciate spendthrift horror stories like the following submission.

Dear Amy,

A friend and I were talking about sorting through fall and winter clothing for our sons. She thought she had done well in only paying $700 for school clothes and an additional $150 at department stores for her three-year-old. She also threw out all her son's size 5 clothes. My son has just outgrown his size 4 clothes. I would have happily traded my 4's for her 5 and 6 clothes. We would have both benefited. Of course she put her new purchases on credit cards. Ouch!

Matilda Carreras
Billerica, Massachusetts

THREE WAYS TO SAVE

There are three basic methods to save money.

1. Buy it cheaper
2. Make it last longer
3. Use it less

Using all three strategies may not work or be desirable in all situations. For instance, you shouldn't brush your teeth less. Or maybe you prefer the taste of the more expensive brands. But if you can combine strategies the results are dramatic.

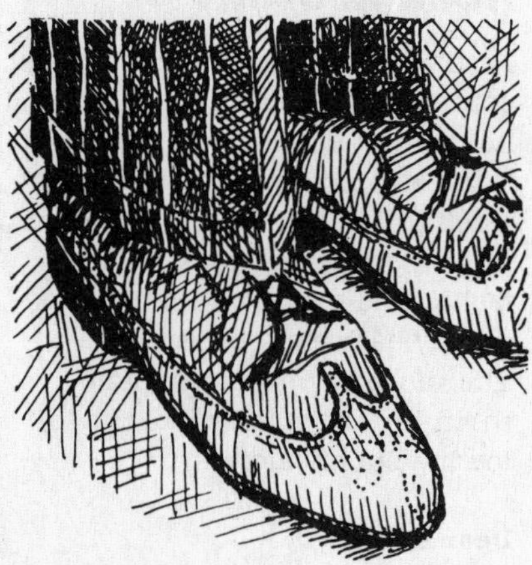

EXAMPLE:

You currently wear out one $75 pair of business shoes every six months, for an annual shoe cost of $150.

STRATEGY OPTIONS:

1. Before your shoes wear out you find a sale of your favorite brand for $60. You buy two pairs.

2. You double the life of the shoes by getting them reheeled for $10.

3. You double the life of your shoes by wearing last year's old shoes for street use.

RESULTING ANNUAL COST:

Strategy 1: $120
Strategy 2: $85
Strategy 3: $75

Strategies 1 and 2: $70
Strategies 1 and 3: $60
Strategies 2 and 3: $42.50

Strategies 1, 2, and 3: $35

EXAMPLE:

You are buying one can of coffee per month at $5.12 per can.

STRATEGY OPTIONS:

1. You switch brands and purchase coffee with a coupon.

2. You make your coffee go farther by reusing your grounds with half as much fresh grounds added to the old ones.

3. You decide to drink half as much coffee.

RESULTING MONTHLY COST:

Strategy 1: $1.18
Strategy 2: $3.84
Strategy 3: $2.56

Strategies 1 and 2: $.88
Strategies 1 and 3: $.59
Strategies 2 and 3: $1.92

Strategies 1, 2, and 3: $.44

EXAMPLE:

You currently spend $75 per month for gasoline.

STRATEGY OPTIONS:

1. You switch to pumping your own gas, and you learn where the cheapest stations are and fill up when in the area for a 10% cost savings.

2. You get a tune-up, change your oil, and make sure your tires are pumped to the right pressure. Even when the cost of the service is factored in, your improved mileage saves you 15% on gas for the year.

3. You reduce your transportation cost a third by car pooling, combining more errands, and walking more.

RESULTING MONTHLY COST:

Strategy 1: $67.50
Strategy 2: $63.75
Strategy 3: $50.00

Strategies 1 and 2: $57.37
Strategies 1 and 3: $45.00
Strategies 2 and 3: $42.33

Strategies 1, 2, and 3: $38.25

EXAMPLE:

You get your hair cut every six weeks for $25, including tip, for an annual cost of $216.67.

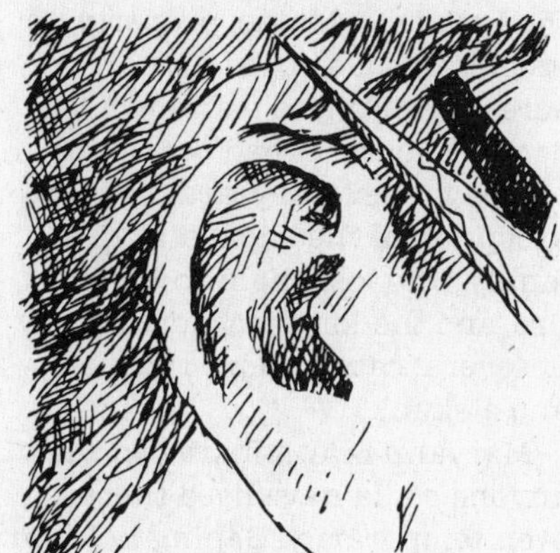

STRATEGY OPTIONS:

1. You shop around and find a less prestigious salon that does as good a job for $12.50.

2. No savings here. I haven't figured out how to make hair grow slower yet.

3. You trim your hair around the ears yourself so that you need to get a professional cut once every eight weeks.

RESULTING ANNUAL COST:

Strategy 1: $108.34
Strategy 3: $162.50

Strategies 1 and 3: $81.25

LIFESTYLES OF THE FRUGAL AND OBSCURE

Dave Smith told me he would have been better off burning the place and starting from scratch. I wondered at his sincerity, as the 43-year-old electrical contractor takes obvious pride in owning a home appraised at four times his investment.

The Smiths' home is a prime example of how ingenuity and a willingness to work can yield huge savings in home remodeling.

In 1988 the Smiths purchased the Readfield, Maine, property for its picturesque six and a half acres, planning to tear down the derelict house. It had been unoccupied for several years, with the exception of the short stay of a family who lost their home in a fire, and the long-term occupancy of several cats, sundry rodents, and a skunk.

Maryann Smith marveled that anyone could have lived there, even temporarily. Gaping holes in the walls allowed icy wind to blow through, the ceiling was falling down, and the critter invasion had left it less than sanitary. Judging from the pictures in their scrapbook, I, too, would have doubted the building's salvageability.

But something stirred Dave's Scotch instincts, and one day he lifted a crowbar. During the following three years he gutted the main house, and dismantled and rebuilt the addition. Today the home has a new roof, a shingled gray exterior, and a wrap-around deck. The interior features arched doorways, a new kitchen, two new baths, and a cathedral ceiling in the living room.

With a passion, Dave reused old materials. He pulled out the worn floor joists, turned them over, and reinstalled them for a fresh nailing edge. Maryann spent endless hours pulling nails out of old boards. Dave used scraps of old lumber to make new trim for windows and doors. He used wood in rougher condition for the internal structure of cabinets and other places where it would not be seen.

To purchase new materials cheaply, Dave learned which lumber yards would negotiate on materials they had been unable to sell. He bought five interior doors for the price of three because the packaging had been damaged. He bought odd lots of ceramic floor tile reduced in price because of barely visible color differences. The home has marble details purchased from an out-of-state factory outlet. Typically, a one-foot square that might cost $9 locally, cost 50¢.

Dave's job provides ample opportunity to scavenge discarded materials. The cellar lighting came from stores that were replacing and disposing of their old fixtures.

He constructed a water tank from a section of 18-inch-diameter stainless-steel pipe with a plate welded on the top and bottom. Most of the fittings were also scavenged. A new-looking sink for the laundry room came from another job site.

The house's unique feature, a two-floor spiral staircase, is a feat of engineering and welding. Dave scrounged scrap electrical conduit for years before he had enough to complete the framework.

Dave also keeps a lookout on trips to the dump. An old set of drawers provided porcelain knobs for the laundry room cabinet.

He scavenged some 15,000 old bricks from a burned mill and other sources to build walkways, steps, and garden walls.

Dave saves all leftover materials. He built an attractive kitchen countertop from scraps of hardwood flooring laid on a 45-degree angle. He used leftover ceramic floor tile from the kitchen for the countertop in the laundry room and leftover ceiling lumber for flooring in a bathroom. The lack of huge piles of surplus materials bears witness to his persistence in finding ways to use them.

Dave took advantage of inexpensive alternatives. He used dowels, which are low cost and versatile, to make spindles for his staircase and uprights for bookcases. By ripping them in half, Dave made counter trim for a fifth of the price of ready-made trim. Stucco, made from cement and sand, made a smooth covering on the interior of the cement-block foundation downstairs.

The Smiths' resourcefulness extends to some of the things within their home. Dave made a coat rack by soldering together leftover copper pipe. They were given a 28-year-old washer (fixed with $6 worth of parts) and a dryer (fixed with a few minutes of soldering). They bought televi-

sions for $10 and $45 from a local handyman. The workshop has a large rubber mat—formerly a conveyor belt—on the floor.

In the warmer months Maryann's green thumb provides the flowering plants for the deck while Dave provides the audio treat. He makes wind chimes from copper and aluminum pipe, and experiments with different designs for optimum resonance.

During my December house tour I couldn't help notice the lush 9-foot Christmas tree, and silently wagered it cost a bit more than the Charlie Brown special our family hauled from the woods. In Maine such a tree might go for $50, but few people have a ceiling high enough for one as big. I learned Dave waits until just before Christmas and dickers for a tree that didn't sell. This one cost $9.

The Smiths' home needs one more purchase to make it complete . . . they have not installed carpeting yet. When I asked when they would, Dave stroked his full auburn mustache and answered, "When we find a good deal."

EASY ZIPPER REPAIR

One of the best thrift shop/yard sale bargains can be an article of clothing with a broken zipper. They are frequently marked down because most people shy away from "the monumental task" of replacing a broken zipper. However zipper repair can involve only a few minutes to an hour of time.

I will purchase an item with a broken zipper if it's practically free (maybe 25¢) and it's a hard-to-come-by commodity, such as a child's jacket, a snowsuit, or a backpack. If I point out the damage to the yard sale or thrift shop proprietor I might get the garment free.

There are several cases in which zipper replacement isn't feasible. I wouldn't replace a zipper on an article of clothing that could be easily found again, such as pants. Some zippers were sewn into the garment from the inside before it was finished, such as zippers on pockets. In this case, a zipper replacement might be extremely complex and time consuming. Some coats have zippers in combination with large snaps. Zipper replacement may be impossible if the snaps would get in the way of machine sewing. I wouldn't bother replacing a zipper on a garment that has other undesirable qualities such as stains, excessive wear, or a dated look.

I also look closely to make sure the zipper really needs replacing. A close-ended (or dress) zipper with a break near the bottom may be repaired without replacement. My daughter broke the zipper on her backpack an inch from the

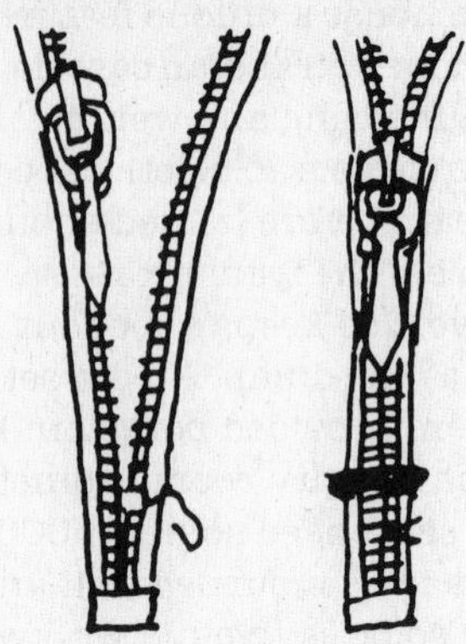

bottom (or beginning). By snipping off the damaged and stretched plastic zipper teeth I was able to restart the zipper. Then I hand sewed the zipper securely just above the break to prevent it from coming apart again.

A separating zipper, such as on a jacket, with a break at the top that allows the zipper pull to come off track, can also be repaired with thread. Simply make a new "zipper stopper" by sewing several layers of thread below the break.

If the zipper pull is missing you can replace it with a small metal ring, a tiny metal ring with some type of charm, or even with a paperclip.

Before replacing an unfixable zipper, consider other possible alternatives. My daughter's jacket had a broken zipper covered by a large flap with Velcro fasteners. If the coat had a zipper in combination with snaps I could have simply removed the zipper. I also considered adding buttons to the jacket by making

buttonholes on the flap. Ultimately I decided that replacing the zipper would be best.

If you determine that a zipper must be replaced completely, carefully look at the construction of the garment. Usually the broken zipper can be replaced by ripping out only two or three seams. If the procedure looks more complex, make notes as to the sequence that you follow to rip out the seams. You will want to put in the new zipper by reversing the sequence.

A new zipper, especially a heavy one for a jacket, can cost as much as $4. You can save money by scavenging a zipper from another garment. In the case of Jamie's jacket, I scavenged a zipper from a worn windbreaker, which I purchased at a $1-per-bag sale at a thrift shop. Because I purchased several other items, the zipper was essentially free. (You can save money on buttons this way as well.)

Used zippers offer two basic advantages. They are preshrunk, and because they've held up for a period of time already, they probably will continue to hold up. I would try to get a metal zipper over a plastic one, because of the durability factor.

When scavenging a zipper it might not be necessary to get a precise color match, especially if the zipper is hidden by a flap. In the case of Jamie's jacket, the black scavenged zipper looked fine with a multicolored design. The old zipper in her jacket extended to the tips of the collar. I stopped the new zipper at the throat, and stitched the collar closed.

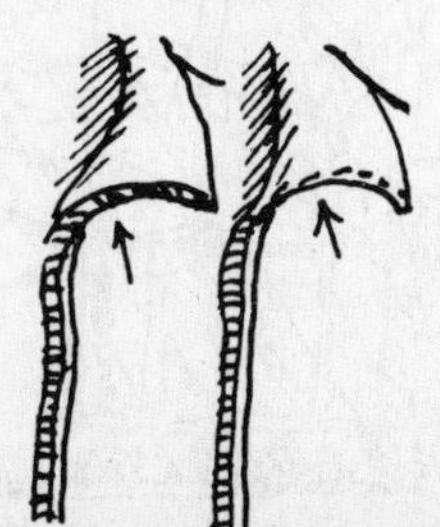

In addition, the zipper doesn't have to be the same length—it can be longer. You can use a longer zipper by cutting it at the precise length needed and sewing "zipper stoppers" or you can cut the zipper ⅜ inch longer than needed and fold the surplus under at a 45-degree angle. When you sew the zipper in place you will secure the end in the seam.

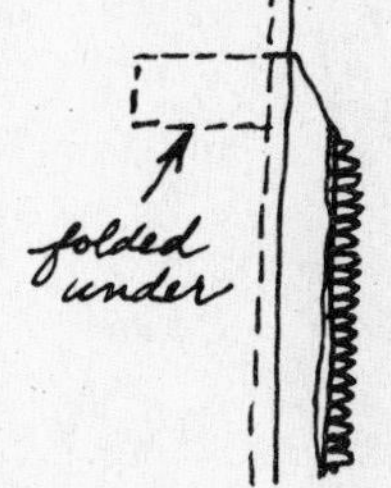

The trick to replacing a zipper is good preparation. First pin the zipper into position and then baste. (Basting is hand sewing with a large running stitch.) Remove the pins before machine stitching, and the basting afterwards. If the zipper lies flat, lines up well, and works well in the basting stage, you ensure the best result when you machine stitch. Basting is especially important if the garment has an inner and outer piece of fabric to line up when stitching the zipper in place.

Always machine stitch from the visible side. It can be hard to make both the inside and outside perfect, so remember that you want the outside to look best. Be sure to keep the material a uniform distance away from the zipper so it can't get caught when zipping.

A sewing machine is an important tool to save money in clothing repair. First attempts to learn new skills can be frustrating, but they're an important time investment that can lead to future savings.

BAGGIE BASICS

Letters from readers lead me to believe that there is some mystery about the proper method to wash out plastic bags. Here are a few pointers to illuminate this basic tightwad task:

I only wash out sturdy Ziploc (or other brand equivalent) bags. The flimsy sandwich bags do not seem to dry as well.

I never save any bag that was used to store meats. Greasy bags are hard to wash as well. I store meats in other bags or plastic wrap. Most important, I never, ever reuse any bag that stored raw poultry.

Due to these precautions, I can personally report that in nearly 10 years of Baggie washing I have yet to lose a family member to food poisoning.

Wash bags in the same dishwater in which you wash dishes (so that the cost of water does not become a factor). Wash bags while the water is still fairly clean.

To wash a bag that held something goopy, such as pumpkin puree, turn it inside out over your hand and wash with a dishrag. Ones that contained something relatively dry and solid, like carrot sticks, require only minimal swishing.

Entrepreneurs have devised several kinds of plastic-bag drying racks that you can buy. The problem is I don't want such an odd contraption taking up space in my kitchen.

I drape washed bags over kitchen utensils already drying in the dish rack. If I run out of utensils to hang them on, I whip out a skewer or chopstick and prop it in the drainer.

Most of my Baggies are used for school lunches. With two kids in school I wash as many as six per day. When I have six kids in school my dish drainer is an unsightly tower of as many as 18 Baggies, assorted utensils, skewers, and chopsticks.

(As I was writing this article an idea came across my desk. Janet Groleau of Menominee, Michigan, wrote that you can make a noodle dryer out of

Tinkertoys. A vision of a Tinkertoy bag dryer came to me. OK. Far-fetched, but funny.)

Dry bags inside out. That way, even if the bags don't completely dry, any remaining droplets will be on the outside.

There are several ways to squeeze more life from bags. During a radio interview, a caller told me that when the seams on the "zipper" start to split on the edges, he fuses them with the tip of an iron.

If the zipper begins to separate completely from the bag, cut it off altogether and use a bread tab to close it.

If a bag has a small hole, don't throw it away yet—use it for foods that don't need to be air-tight, like popcorn.

Here's my answer to the most critical Baggie-washing question: When do you throw it away? When washing the bag, fill it with water and hold it up. If the bag resembles a sprinkler you may throw it away. I've never tracked an average Baggie life span, but I have used them until the white block (where you write the bag's contents) has worn off.

One could argue that we should use plastic freezer containers and plastic food containers for lunch boxes. The argument has some merit, but I couldn't fit three plastic containers and a thermos in one lunch box.

Except for the Ziploc bags we buy for freezing garden produce and recycle for household use, we never buy any plastic bags. Think about the plastic bags you throw away daily. Panty hose comes in a bag with a sheet of cardboard. I reuse the bags that brown sugar comes in. One of my staff takes lightweight produce bags back to the grocery store and refills them (even though they're free . . . this is an environmental tip, not an economic one).

Any bag with paint, such as a bread bag, should not be used inside out.

For all of you longtime tightwads, who can't believe I have devoted space to such basic information . . . be patient with me. I'm educating novices as well. (You should read my mail.) For you folks, I'm including some information you probably don't know—how much money washing plastic bags saves.

One reader enlarged upon my Time and Money Chart on page 102, where I show that to determine the hourly worth of any money-saving activity, you calculate how many times you could do the task in an hour and multiply that figure by the savings per task.

In her study, which she did for a class she is taking, she calculated the savings from washing out plastic bags:

"I can wash out a plastic Baggie used to store broccoli in the freezer in 11 seconds, saving .05¢ per bag . . . or I can throw the bag away and reach under the counter to get a new Baggie in 5 seconds."

Figuring that she spends 6 seconds to save .05¢, she calculated the savings rate of washing Baggies is $30 per hour.

So if you get nothing else from this article, you can at least stop feeling crazy for washing plastic bags.

EPITAPHS

Dear Amy,

For me to consider becoming a tightwad is almost revolutionary. My husband used to say that he'd put two phrases on my tombstone: (1) Nothing feels like real gold. (2) My wife wasn't happy unless she paid full price.

Janet Stanhope
Auburn, Maine

AMAZING REFUND

Dear Amy,

My best bargains are usually at the reduced rack at the grocery store. I went in one day and they had 12 boxes of Tide (39 oz). They had been damaged by a blade used to open the cartons. The reduced price was $1. I had coupons for $1, so all I paid was 5¢ tax. My mother cut the net weight from the boxes and sent them in for a $2 refund each.

Patricia Williams
Rockland, Maine

HOMEMADE WEIGHTS

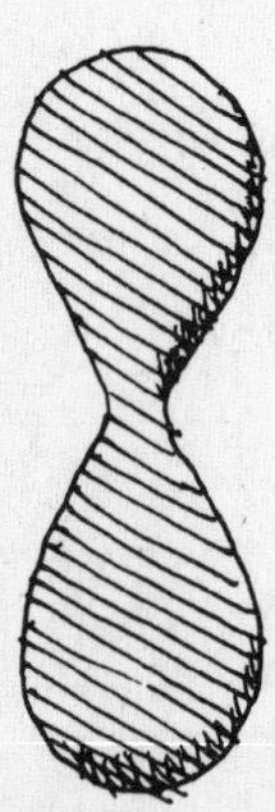

Dear Amy,

To make dumbbells of different weights take long, strong, plastic bags and fill with sand to the required weight. Put into cloth bag (you may have to sew these), or leg sections from pants, sleeves, long socks, or stockings. Distribute sand equally at each end leaving a narrow section in the center for a hand or foot.

Arnie Anfinson
Seattle, Washington

NOT JUST LENTILS AND OATMEAL

People frequently express astonishment at our family's food budget and have requested a menu. (We feed Jim, myself and our six children, ages 9 to 1-year-old twins, on $180 per month.)

You asked for it, you got it. I recorded the meals we ate during a 14-day period in March. Because I wanted to depict the way we really eat, I purposely did not plan special meals for the benefit of publication.

While the menu shown opposite is typical, it doesn't reflect our entire repertoire. We tend to eat according to what foods happen to be on sale. For example, during previous weeks we ate less cheese and more turkey.

The lunch menu shows what I put into school lunches. All sandwiches were made with whole-wheat bread. I didn't record the weekend's every-man-for-himself lunch menu.

I put an asterisk on foods that were homegrown.

Our diet does have its share of humble meals and repetition, due in part to a lack of time. We still manage to avoid all convenience foods, and counter with meals that require very little preparation time.

While our diet may not be glamorous, it's nourishing and offers a reasonable amount of variety. Jim and I also have excellent blood pressure and cholesterol numbers.

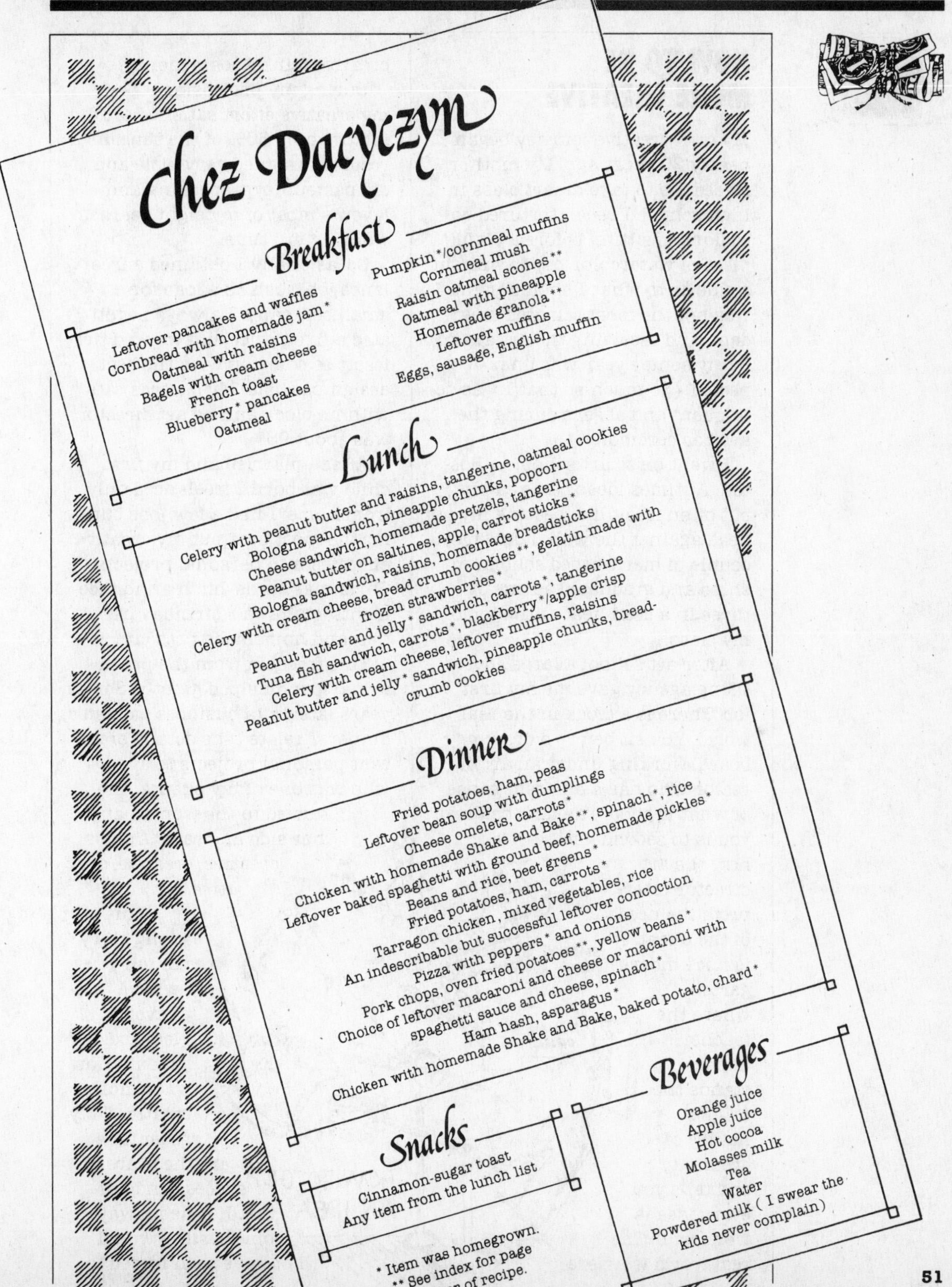

Chez Dacyczyn
Breakfast
Leftover pancakes and waffles
Cornbread with homemade jam*
Oatmeal with raisins
Bagels with cream cheese
French toast
Blueberry* pancakes
Oatmeal
Pumpkin*/cornmeal muffins
Cornmeal mush
Raisin oatmeal scones**
Oatmeal with pineapple
Homemade granola**
Leftover muffins
Eggs, sausage, English muffin
Lunch
Celery with peanut butter and raisins, tangerine, oatmeal cookies
Bologna sandwich, pineapple chunks, popcorn
Cheese sandwich, homemade pretzels, tangerine
Peanut butter on saltines, apple, carrot sticks*
Bologna sandwich, raisins, homemade breadsticks
Celery with cream cheese, bread crumb cookies**, gelatin made with frozen strawberries*
Peanut butter and jelly* sandwich, carrots*, tangerine
Tuna fish sandwich, carrots*, blackberry*/apple crisp
Celery with cream cheese, leftover muffins, raisins
Peanut butter and jelly* sandwich, pineapple chunks, bread-crumb cookies
Dinner
Fried potatoes, ham, peas
Leftover bean soup with dumplings
Cheese omelets, carrots*
Chicken with homemade Shake and Bake**, spinach*, rice
Leftover baked spaghetti with ground beef, homemade pickles*
Beans and rice, beet greens*
Fried potatoes, ham, carrots*
Tarragon chicken, mixed vegetables, rice
An indescribable but successful leftover concoction
Pizza with peppers* and onions
Pork chops, oven fried potatoes**, yellow beans*
Choice of leftover macaroni and cheese or macaroni with spaghetti sauce and cheese, spinach*
Ham hash, asparagus*
Chicken with homemade Shake and Bake, baked potato, chard*
Snacks
Cinnamon-sugar toast
Any item from the lunch list
Beverages
Orange juice
Apple juice
Hot cocoa
Molasses milk
Tea
Water
Powdered milk (I swear the kids never complain)
* Item was homegrown.
** See index for page number of recipe.

HOW TO BE MORE CREATIVE

My own creative journey began nearly 20 years ago. My mother forced me to take an art class in high school. I recall tortured occasions of sitting before a blank piece of watercolor paper without a clue as to what I should paint. I was not the most talented student, and receiving the art award in my senior year was unexpected. (So much so that I was delinquent and absent during the awards ceremony.)

I went on to art school in Boston. At times ideas came easily but often it felt like beating my head against the wall. I did snag a couple of merit-based scholarships and graduated as one of three in a dead heat at the top of my class.

After art school a large advertising agency gave me my first job. There is a clock in the real world. You sit before a drawing board, working under an art director who has a different sense of what is good. The task before you is to second guess how the art director interprets the needs of the client. It is not kindergarten, where the teacher understands the fragile nature of creativity and tells you every idea is wonderful. The real world is where creative failure costs money.

During my professional peak my creative effort satisfied art directors only 50% of the time. As a result I designed very little and did pasteup, typespecking and layouts most of my eight years working full time.

Occasionally I obtained a freelance job, such as a logo for a small company. I always negotiated a fixed price and worked tirelessly to come up with the best design possible. My success rate with no clock and no art director was about 95%.

After I married and my first child was born I freelanced only from home. I had a few jobs but for the most part put my creative energies into personal projects. Christmas cards, birth announcements, children's birthday parties, and homemade presents.

This freedom from the professional grind helped greatly. Some years later, at a business women's dinner, I related the details of recent personal projects to a lady who was one of my clients. She turned to the woman at her side and said "Amy is creative, creative, creative."

This is a long story to tell you what I have learned about "How to be more creative." My credentials are the years of success and failure. If it had always come easily I would not have been forced to

HOW TO GET AN IDEA

analyze. But through my roller coaster ride I have come to understand something of the nuts and bolts process of creativity.

People tend to believe that creativity is a mystical gift reserved for a few. They think this mistaking creativity for "craft." Creativity is the process. Craft is the product. When there is a lack of a recognized outlet, such as writing, art, or music, creativity goes unnoticed.

Creativity is nothing more and nothing less than solving a problem in an original way. As humans we all have this spark. We string together words to express our thoughts. We do not memorize and repeat the sentences that we speak. We put together new word combinations continually.

Creativity occurs in subtle ways. While preparing a familiar recipe and you realize that you lack an ingredient and make a substitution. Or while folding laundry the way your mother taught you 20 years ago, you discover that by rearranging piles in a different order you can save time. Or you have a problem with a co-worker and attempt a new strategy to make the relationship work better. Or you figure how to build a lathe out of salvaged materials and a washing machine motor. These are all forms of creativity.

TEN STEPS TO A MORE CREATIVE YOU

Step 1. Realize that you *are* creative. Look for it in your daily life and nurture that part of yourself.

Step 2. Give yourself mental space, a clear field. We tend to fill up our days with the TV, car radio, reading the paper, chats with friends on the phone. Instead do that "mindless task" in quiet. This type of activity dominates my life . . . housework, mowing lawn, scraping paint. Boredom never strikes, as the mental gears whirl continually. I write only after mentally rehearsing paragraphs a dozen times.

When someone says, "I'm just not creative like you," I reply "No, I just thought about it longer."

Step 3. Never *ever* compare yourself to others, but rather enjoy your own innovations. I stumbled over this block working in the shadow of many award-winning designers. No matter how good I could become there would still be someone better. Later I realized that no matter how bad I was there was always someone worse. Compare yourself only to yourself. "This is how good I am today. I am better than I was yesterday and I will be better tomorrow."

Step 4. I use a strategy I call "putting the problem into the mental computer." Your brain functions continually, even as you sleep. Study the parameters of your problem and then let it rest for a few days. Very often your mental computer will spit out the solution unexpectedly as you shower or drive to work. This works much better than trying to perform as the clock ticks away. If you are trying to come up with a great party idea, give yourself a couple months of mental back-burner time.

Step 5. Brainstorm. Toss the idea around with another person. Be flexible and say or write down every "stupid" thought that

comes. Very often another person can take your idea and add a twist that makes it great. Jim is my brainstorming partner. He is very good at telling me when my idea is good and I should run with it. Sometimes something isn't working just right and he can look at it and come up with a better sentence or illustration idea.

Step 6. Find a springboard, a starting place. For the tightwad this usually means determining which resources are cheap or in surplus. Build from that point.

Step 7. Do not share your creative ideas with anyone who continually tells you they are dumb. This is often a spouse or a parent. Professionally I should have switched jobs until I found an art director who shared a similar creative style. The art directors that didn't like my ideas were not more creative than me. Often they were *less* creative. Mostly it was a matter of seeing things differently. But, the constant message that I was doing it wrong took its toll. A mouse does not go down the same hole over and over if he fails to find cheese.

After I stopped working under art directors and created for myself, or for my clients in my own way, I began to realize that I was creative after all.

Step 8. Practice. As with any skill, accessing your creative ability improves the more you do it. You will develop your own methods and strategies to fall back on when tackling new problems.

Step 9. Avoid negative stress. This also tends to block creativity, as your mind focuses on that problem instead. Try to limit contact with individuals who bring on these problems. If it is someone within your household, try to limit your reaction to their actions.

Step 10. Start small. When you bite off more than you can chew you set yourself up for failure. Instead set small easily attainable goals to build a sense of success. In subsequent projects stretch yourself to slightly more ambitious undertakings.

Sometime as you were reading the beginning of this piece you thought, "What the heck does creativity have to do with thrift?"

Tightwaddery without creativity is deprivation. When there is a lack of resourcefulness, inventiveness, and innovation, thrift means doing without.

When creativity combines with thrift you may be doing it without money, but you are not doing without.

HEADBAND HOW-TO

My daughter Jamie, at the age of six, had a field day with a pair of shears and cut off a lock of her (already thin) hair at the earlobe. Rather then resorting to a drastic short haircut I thought I'd have her wear headbands until it grew out.

Remember those cloth headbands we wore in the 60s and 70s? You can't buy them anymore. The sweat bands now on the market work, but are limited. The plastic ones don't stay on well, and a younger sibling snaps them in half within a week.

As I pondered this dilemma I saw a classmate of my daughter's wearing a pretty cloth headband.

I asked, and her mother admitted that she made it.

She made a tube of fabric from a 2½" × 32" strip, sewing the right side together, about a half inch from the edge. She turned the tube inside out and inserted a 19" × ¾" piece of elastic. Then she machine sewed the elastic ends together, and then hand sewed the cloth tube ends together, neatly tucking under the cut edge.

The resulting headband has a ruffled or gathered look. Her headband was of a calico material. I have some pink satin I'd like to try first. The length of elastic and strip of cloth are based on a six-year-old head size.

REAL MAIL

When the price of the first-class stamp soared to 29¢, Ralph Nader complained on television talk shows, and perhaps a few subscribers wondered if *The Tightwad Gazette* would cost more. (It didn't.)

Despite concern over postal rates, the first-class letter remains one of our best bargains. By comparison the instant the telephone receiver clicks back into position a long-distance phone call becomes an expensive intangible memory.

For this reason nearly all my long-distance communication takes the form of *real mail.*

I regard the letters I receive to be a gift from the sender, and from the best writers, a treasure to be savored.

I spend more time writing letters than most people I know, and I am told (seldom by return mail) that they are wonderful. Friends have been known to read choice excerpts to their mothers, who have never met me, during long-distance phone conversations. (Yes, I have befriended a spendthrift or two.)

A business envelope with about five sheets of paper can be mailed with a first-class stamp. Using 15-pitch type, small margins, single spacing, and two sides of the paper your entire autobiography can be mailed first class as far as such remote areas as Alaska, Guam, or Leeds, Maine.

My mother saves my letters and returns them by the stack, which double as a journal for me. When rereading a letter written only a few years ago I am amazed at how many events I had forgotten.

Writing letters helps to develop writing skills. For any beginning writer the best material comes from personal experience, mak-

ing letters a perfect training ground. And any acquired skill is a potential money maker.

Any researcher of genealogy knows how important letters are in providing insight to an ancestor who might otherwise be known only through birth and death records. In terms of more recent family members, it is a real trip to read the "gee whiz" literary style of your then 20-year-old father.

If you are blank-page-phobic, a few suggestions to get you going are shown below:

WOOD AND OIL

We have an efficient wood/oil furnace and an ample supply of wood purchased at $60 per cord (go-get-it-yourself), but we need some oil for when we are not home.

It seems like a sure bet that wood burning will be cheaper

1 For a day or so before you plan to write, keep a pencil and paper handy to jot down ideas of items to include in your letter.

2 If you think there is little newsworthy in your life, remember that those who love you are interested in the "dull" goings on, too.

3 Try to include humorous stories. While I often have soapbox topics on my mind, I try to remember that grandmas are more interested in childhood comic action.

4 My mother and I write what we call "familygrams." These are a sort of general letter that go out to about 25 people. They can be photocopied or reproduced on a memory typewriter or computer. This enables us to communicate more in depth with a larger group of people. Though it sounds impersonal, considering the rarity of real mail, it is easy to see how people enjoy them.

5 Write as if you were speaking to the reader using common everyday language. Think of how your letter will sound to the recipient. Use descriptive and colorful images.

6 Former generations considered a typed letter inappropriate. Now home computers are commonplace. Use whatever technology you have available to make letter writing easier. Typing gives them a more polished look and improves readability. You will have a greater sense of accomplishment than if you pen several pages of chicken scratchings.

7 Include other items like a joke you heard recently, a new recipe, clippings, a child's drawing, and photographs.

8 When you reread your completed letter and think it too lackluster, mail it anyway. Any letter is better than no letter.

than oil. If you are thinking you might buy wood this fall and fire up the wood stove to avoid the rising oil prices you will also pay high prices for wood.

The question becomes, When is wood cheaper than oil?

Depending on the variety of hardwood, a cord of wood equals 130 to 200 gallons of oil.

Fall prices for dry wood are about $120 per cord, or even higher. Let's say that you buy wood of average quality and it produces the same heat as 165 gallons of oil.

To figure the break point you need to calculate when 165 gallons of oil equals $120 or . . .

$120 divided by 165 equals 75¢

. . . so when oil costs 75¢ per gallon and wood is $120 per cord they cost the same. As oil and wood prices stand, even a late purchase of wood will be cheaper than a late purchase of oil.

THE SCOOP ON COUPONS

It feels like tightwad sacrilege to suggest that there might be anything wrong with coupon use. But consider that manufacturers provide coupons to entice consumers to buy their products. Multiple coupons for a single product, which have decreasing values, such as 75¢ off, 50¢ off, and 25¢ off, are a dead giveaway that they hope to hook you by creating a habit.

There's a right way and a wrong way to use coupons. All coupon users believe they are using coupons the right way. "I never use a coupon to buy something I wouldn't buy anyway." However, if a majority of users did it the right way, manufacturers would be losing money and would stop offering coupons. So, consider the following questions:

HOW MUCH DO COUPONS REALLY SAVE?

Readers frequently send me sales slips to demonstrate how much they save using coupons. With bold sweeps of colored markers they circle the figure that shows how much the coupons used added up to. They're circling the wrong figure. The most important figure on your sales slip is how much you spend on groceries . . . not how much you save using coupons.

Sometimes, even with doubling your coupons you might be spending more money on items than if you had resorted to a different strategy. Always compare the price after coupons with alternative products, making the same item from scratch, or not buying the product at all (as in the case of things like soda, candy, etc.). Below is a table that demonstrates this. ("A.D.C." stands for the price "after double coupons.")

Even if the price after coupon is less than an alternative coupon, users frequently fail to calculate the true savings. Let's say you get $1.00 off brand A spaghetti sauce, which costs $1.89. Brand B, a sauce of equal quality, costs $1.29. Obviously you buy brand A, but your savings is not $1.00—it's really 40¢. This may seem like I'm quibbling. But it's important to understand your genuine savings because coupon use takes time. You need to know how much extra time you're spending compared to how much money you're saving. You also need to factor in the cost of obtaining the coupon, if there is any, such as the purchase of magazines and newspapers.

HOW MUCH TIME DO COUPONS REQUIRE?

Reports from readers vary. Some claim they only spend a few minutes extra per week. These individuals are moderate coupon users who tend to be very organized. An excellent way to do this is to keep your coupons in a small file box and organize them by type. On about the 20th of each month you should go through

PRODUCT	PRICE	A.D.C.	ALTERNATIVE STRATEGY
Lite & Lively Yogurt 6-pk.	$1.67	$1.16	store brand costs 80¢, homemade costs less
Aunt Jemima Syrup 24 oz.	3.19	2.44	store brand costs $1.99, homemade costs 66¢
Betty Crocker Scalloped Potatoes	1.09	.59	prepared from scratch costs less
Dixie 5 oz. Kitchen Cups 100 ct.	1.69	.69	use plastic, permanent cups instead
12 Country Kitchen Hamburger Rolls	1.39	.99	same brand costs 77¢ at bakery thrift store
Baby Fresh Wipes 84 ct.	2.99	2.39	make your own version . . . a washcloth works, too
Kraft Dressing 16 oz.	1.55	1.15	make your own version for 30% the cost
Kellogg's Variety Pack 9.58 oz.	3.19	2.19	at 22¢ per box almost any scratch breakfast is less
Huggies Disposable Diapers	9.99	8.99	home-laundered cloth costs a couple dollars per week
Philadelphia Cream Cheese 12 oz.	1.89	1.59	store brand costs $1.29
Special K Eggo Waffles 8 ct.	1.29	.69	prepared from scratch costs less, freeze surplus

your coupons looking for ones that might expire. Always take your file box with you when you shop. You might run across an unexpected sale or a good deal in the damages bin.

On the other end of the spectrum, very serious coupon users, those who also spend time refunding, can spend as much as 10 to 15 hours per week clipping coupons, studying sale flyers, soaking off and filing labels, and saving packaging and receipts. Serious refunders also subscribe to refund newsletters. Through these they swap "complete deals" or the refund with the required proof of purchase and receipt to get the refund. The most diligent can reap more than $100 per month in refunds and rebates. They also may get enough free gifts to make a significant dent in their Christmas budget. Sometimes refunders boost their coupon and refund results because family and friends save their proofs of purchase and coupons for them. In this case the coupon user/refunder benefits because an original purchaser paid an inflated price.

Another time element often not considered is how much additional time is spent in the supermarket. It takes more time making individual price comparisons and purchases. In contrast, other strategies, such as bulk buying of sale items, reduce shopping time.

WHAT DO PEOPLE BUY WITH COUPONS?

Our family generally uses coupons to buy nonfood items, and food items that cannot be prepared from scratch. But most food coupons are for convenience foods. Often the foods are more processed. Even when these items can be purchased cheaply, it should be considered that your family is acquiring a taste for these more expensive and less healthful items. This could potentially create bigger grocery bills in the future. Many of the products have more packaging as well. So even when Jell-O Pudding Snack Paks are near free, I seriously question these purchases because of the environmental issue of the excess trash created.

WHAT ABOUT THE "COUPON QUEENS" FEATURED BY THE MEDIA?

Most of us have seen newspaper articles or television shows featuring coupon experts who demonstrate their skills by taking reporters shopping and buying $134.86 of groceries, but after all the coupons are subtracted pay only $54.73. This type of shopping trip requires months of planning, and is not typical of these shoppers' usual trips to the store. On the average these shoppers claim their real savings is closer to 25 to 40%. Again, it's important to remember that these are savings on the prices of products that may be inflated in price.

Consider the real figures sent in by Mary Kenyan of Independence, Iowa. She saves 10% to 30% on a grocery bill of $385 per month. She feeds a family of six, with four children ages 2 to 11. Her grocery bill does not include her husband's work lunches, but they never eat out.

Figuring that she saves an average of 20% on her grocery bill using coupons, she actually spends about $308 per month. She receives $110 per month (after postage) from refunds. Of that figure roughly 65% comes from refunds from items she purchased at the grocery store, or $71.50. She has offsetting expenses of about $12.54 for additional postage and magazine and newspaper subscriptions. She gets her refund newsletters free in exchange for credits for submissions. This works out to a bottom line grocery bill of $249.04 per month. In addition she receives roughly 10 free gifts per month of varying values through refunding.

The average family of six spends $500 per month on groceries. In comparison, Mary's grocery budget compares well. However, with very little coupon use many families of equal size spend under $200 per month on groceries. A mixed approach, which includes some coupon use, will produce the lowest possible grocery bill. Readers have written that when they began to incorporate other strategies, they used fewer coupons and their grocery bills dropped.

If you genuinely dislike couponing and refunding, use other strategies (like gardening, bulk buying, and baking from scratch) that will save you as much if not more money on your grocery bill.

If, however, you find that refunding and couponing is an enjoyable hobby, and you genuinely are saving money, this is a valid way to spend your time. To read more about the coupon/refund strategy look for *Cashing In at the Cash Register* by Susan Samtur, commonly available at the library.

Refund newsletters include:

Money Talk
P.O. Box 1677
Kingston, PA 18704

Refunding Makes Cents
Box R
Farmington, UT 84025

Roadrunner Refunder
6535 West Ellis
Laveen, AZ 85339

WHAT TO DO WITH . . .

Pickle Juice.

A. Use in marinade or create your own salad dressings.

B. Sweet Pickled Chops. Arrange four chops in a shallow pan and sprinkle with salt. Place a slice of onion and a tablespoon of catsup on the top of each. Pour ½ cup of sweet pickle juice around chops. Cover and bake for 1 hour at 350°.

Bread Bags. Use as freezer bags for short-term storage, especially when re-packaging family packs of sale meats. Knot excess to close, and cut open when ready for use. Never reuse any plastic bag that has stored meats. Don't store food in inside-out bags.

Toilet Paper Tubes. Use to gather up unsightly loose excess electrical cord on kitchen appliances, lamps, entertainment center, etc.

A Half-Eaten Apple. Cut off remaining good parts and save to make an individual apple crisp. To make crumb mixture combine 1 tsp each of brown sugar, flour, oatmeal, and margarine. Add a dash of cinnamon. Top apples and microwave.

Milk Jug Rings. Use to keep socks together when laundering. Store in drawer with rings. When taking socks out, keep ring on bureau. Replace ring around soiled socks before tossing in hamper.

Dried-out Bread. Save slices in a freezer container or bread bag until you need to make bread crumbs. Grind up in your blender or food processor. When using as a topping toss in melted margarine, and season.

Dryer Lint. My neighbor and organic gardening expert was out for her evening stroll when I bounded down to the road with a breathless query, "Can you compost dryer lint?" Her official answer is yes, if the lint is from cotton material. Synthetic lint can be composted for flower garden use.

Yellow-flowered Broccoli.

A. Tell your family it is a rare gourmet variety.

B. If they're not quite that gullible use in quiche. The yellow egg and cheese mixture combine to create an effective camouflage.

Crayon Bits. Place a variety of colors in a muffin tin and melt in the oven. Cool. This makes a scribble cookie. Each one has its own unique color and pattern. Use for an inexpensive stocking stuffer.

Carrot Peels, Onion Skins, and Celery Leaves. Jeff Smith, the frugal gourmet, (no relation) uses these when cooking up turkey and chicken bones for soup stock.

Worn Towels and Washcloths. A worn towel can be cut lengthwise into strips to make a back washer. (Contributed by Alma Trider, Leeds, ME.) Washcloths can be cut in quarters to make reusable "handiwipes" or "baby wipes." Store damp in a plastic bag when traveling.

An Old Yellow Pages. Use for a gluing surface. Once the top page is used tear off for a fresh surface. The yellow color makes it easy to spot tiny pieces of white paper that would otherwise become lost on white pages or newspaper.

Mesh Onion Bags. Cut off metal clip and knot. Use to store

soap bits. The mesh and soap combine to form an effective cleaning agent when washing hands. (Contributed by Polly Davis, Shirley, MA.)

A Tuna Fish Can. Use to make cookie cutters. Cut off bottom of can and shape with two pliers, preferably needle nose. When making a symmetrical design begin working at opposite points of the can.

Leftover Rice. Make a rice crust for a quiche by combining 1½ cups of cooked rice, 1 ounce of shredded cheese, and an egg. Pat out in a pie plate. For a larger quiche dish increase rice and cheese portions slightly. Do not Pam or grease the dish. Bake at 425° for 20 minutes.

Old Cloth Diapers. Obviously these make excellent cleaning rags; however, I have found their best use is for washing windows. Because they are highly absorbent they beat paper towels and newspaper for a streak-free final wipe.

A Coat Hanger. Make a Baggie dryer by bending as shown. This idea is for the man in my church who said to me, "Have you any idea what you've started? Now when I wash dishes my wife has me hanging Baggies on a clothesline in the pantry!"

A STOLEN THANKSGIVING SOAP BOX SPEECH

Most of this article is a direct steal from a lay sermon preached by my neighbor.

Charlie Woodward works for the Rural Community Action Ministry, which provides a variety of services for low-income families. He serves as the chairman for the Maine Coalition for the Homeless, frequently meets with state officials, and is considered to be an expert on rural poverty.

I had heard bits and pieces of this sermon before. I have picked his brain on a number of occasions to understand why poor people are poor. Invariably the conversations have concluded as Charlie patiently reminded me that we have not all been born with the same gifts.

A gift is anything that we have that we did not work for. People born to wealth have more advantages than those born in poverty. People with a high intelligence will probably fare better than those born with low intelligence. It is known that people who are blond, tall, and good-looking will be more likely to succeed than those who are not.

Most of us feel that being born in the United States is a gift. While not all of us are rich, we are likely to have greater opportunities for education, health care, and employment than those living in Third World countries.

Health is a gift, at least the health with which we were born. Most of us are botching it to some degree or another. But our genetic package plays a large role in why some can abuse their health and never get sick while others work at being healthy and still get sick.

Those of us who were raised in good families have a gift. Not everyone was raised with love, security, positive feedback, and values. Charlie believes that the "work ethic" is also a gift. Some parents taught it to their kids and some parents did not.

Many examples come to mind of individuals who have overcome a lack of gifts. These people always have a variety of other gifts.

The bottom line is to understand that what we have and who we are has a lot to do with factors we received in a package deal when we came into the world. If that realization doesn't make you thankful, nothing will.

I believe we need to use all our gifts as well as we can to provide security and quality of life for our families. Most of us do this well enough to have a surplus of either time or money.

Clearly some people are short on gifts and some have gifts and do not use them well. For both groups their security and quality of life runs a deficit. All the grumbling about those who receive public assistance is really about deciding into which group people fall. The questions I have asked have only yielded the knowledge that experts do not agree and there are many murky gray areas.

But what of the rest of us whose gifts (and usually some effort) have yielded a surplus? It is easy to find people who have surpluses . . . most of us do. And most of us squander huge amounts of surplus money or time on personal gratification and give very little or nothing in return.

The attitude of "I worked hard and I deserve . . ." does not consider the very large degree that our gifts contributed to what we have.

The frugal lifestyle allows us to engineer the maximum surplus of time, energy, and/or money while using a minimum of resources. Since we are gifted differently, our surplus will also be different. We can, and should, use our surpluses to help smooth the peaks and valleys or unequal gift distribution.

Clearly I do not advocate squandering of resources, but neither do I advocate hoarding or stinginess.

By donating some of our surplus time, energy, and money we express thankfulness for the abundance of gifts with which we were born. (See, Charlie, I *was* paying attention.)

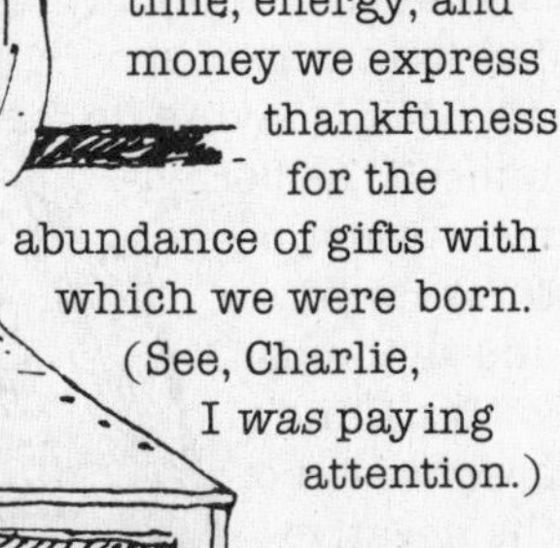

A VOICE FROM THE PAST

Had I known there were so many books written on the subject of thrift I probably would not have begun *The Tightwad Gazette.*

In the past several months readers have suggested or mailed some of these to me. One sent by a sister, probably in fun, is a reproduction of an 1833 work.

The American Frugal Housewife, written by a Mrs. Child bears a curious subtitle. She dedicated the book "To Those Who Are Not Ashamed of Economy."

Although frugality may have enjoyed a larger general acceptance during her time, clearly she felt it was falling out of fashion. She frequently quotes Benjamin Franklin's words on thrift. After pondering that I also wondered at the 18th-century attitude of thrift, since Franklin felt compelled to write his thoughts on the subject.

Mrs. Child wrote: "Economy is generally despised as low virtue, tending to make [characterize] people ungenerous and selfish. This is true of avarice; but not so of economy. The man who is economical, is laying up for himself the permanent power of being useful and generous."

Mrs. Child's observation of the negative attitude toward thrift might also be seen from earlier times. Since the development of the English language, we have no positive nouns for a frugal person. Instead we have "cheapskate," "skinflint," "penny-pincher," "miser," and "tightwad." Even the positive adjectives that the English language gives us, like "frugal" or "thrifty," have come to have a dull or boring connotation. We associate these words with Depression-era fuddy-duddy thinking.

(My choice of the word "tightwad" reflects my belief that thrift is not dull, but actually fun, and defies the attitude of our culture. If I had called my publication "The Frugal Person's Newsletter" the media wouldn't have paid attention.)

The American Frugal Housewife is not to be considered required reading. Much of it reads like a 19th-century Heloise, offering tips that have little relevance for our time. The essays sound like something one might have heard from an elderly schoolteacher. And as the title suggests, the book is by no means gender neutral.

Buy a barrel of really strong vinegar...

However, I was also struck by the similar overall strategies and philosophies that still apply (and parallel ideas that I have written).

"It is wise to keep an exact account of all you expend . . .

it makes you more careful in spending money, and it enables your husband to judge precisely whether his family live within his income." (Record spending.)

"If you have two dollars a day, let nothing but sickness induce you to spend more than nine shillings; if you have half a dollar a day, be satisfied to spend forty cents." (Regardless of your income level do not spend everything you earn.)

"Let [women] prove, by exertion of ingenuity and economy, that neatness, good taste, and gentility, are attainable without great expense." (Use creativity and thrift to improve the quality of life, rather than spending more money.)

"Make your own bread and cake. Some people think it is just as cheap to buy of the baker and confectioner; but it is not half as cheap." (Avoid convenience foods and instead prepare food from scratch.)

"It is poor economy to buy vinegar by the gallon. Buy a barrel, or half a barrel, of really strong vinegar when you begin housekeeping." (Buy in bulk.)

"It is a great deal better for boys and girls on a farm to be picking blackberries at six cents a quart, than to be wearing out clothes in useless play. They enjoy themselves just as well." (All family members should develop hobbies that save money rather than ones that are nonproductive . . . or ones that cost money.)

"Patchwork is good economy. It is indeed a foolish waste of time to tear cloth into bits for the sake of rearranging it anew in fantastic figures; but a family may be kept out of idleness, and a few shillings saved, by thus using scraps of gowns, curtains, etc." (Whenever possible reuse materials you already have rather than buying new materials at craft shops.)

"To associate with influential and genteel people with an appearance of equality unquestionably has its advantages, but like all other external advantages, these have their proper price, and may be bought too dearly. Self-denial, in proportion to the narrowness of your income, will eventually be the happiest and

FZ's World

DARN, A HOLE RIGHT IN THE FRONT OF A PERFECTLY GOOD JERSEY!

HMM... WHAT COULD I MAKE WITH ALL THAT JERSEY MATERIAL?
JAZZY UNDERWEAR?
OF COURSE I WOULD NEED ABOUT 50¢ WORTH OF ELASTIC... AND IT WOULD TAKE A COUPLE OF HOURS TO SEW...
AND YOU CAN BUY A PAIR OF NEW UNDERWEAR FOR $1.

SOMETIMES I THINK I'M TREADING DANGEROUSLY CLOSE TO THE EDGE OF THE GREAT ABYSS OF SKINFLINTIAN COMPULSION.
I'LL MAKE JAZZY RAGS INSTEAD!
Amy D

TAKE THE TIGHTWAD TEST

Are you a tightwad or a spendthrift? Read the questions and circle the most appropriate answer. After you have completed the test, compare your answers to those below.

1. A movie that you would *love* to see is playing. You . . .

A. Drop off the kids at the sitter, pay top dollar for tickets, and buy overpriced theater popcorn and soda.
B. Wait for the movie to come to cable TV or on video to rent.
C. Wait 10 years for the movie to come to primetime TV.

2. Your children are thirsty. You say . . .

A. "Help yourself. There's plenty of soda in the fridge."
B. "Help yourself. There are plenty of juice packs in the fridge."
C. "Help yourself. There's plenty of water."

3. Your family is midway through a four-hour car trip. You pull into McDonald's and . . .

A. Order a round of Happy Meals.
B. Order a round of burgers and shakes.
C. Use the restrooms only. Later you break out the peanut butter and jelly sandwiches in the car.

4. Your spouse says your family needs to increase its food budget. You say . . .

A. "No problem."
B. "What food budget?"
C. "Wouldn't this be a great time to start that diet, dear?"

5. You think the most perfect toy for your four-year-old is . . .

A. A battery-powered riding toy.
B. Nintendo games.
C. A cardboard box.

6. A thrilling family outing for you typically would be . . .

A. A day at the amusement park.
B. A day on the ski slopes.
C. A trip to the double-coupon store to combine coupons, sales, damaged goods, and store brands for the maximum possible volume of groceries.

7. Your teenager says he will die if he can't have a $75 pair of designer sneakers. You say . . .

A. "Anything for you, kid."
B. "If we have any money left over at the end of the month."
C. Nothing, being unable to speak through the peals of laughter.

8. If you and your spouse receive a gift coupon for a rare romantic dinner at a restaurant, your conversation would include . . .

A. Recollections of your courtship.
B. Compliments on your spouse's stunning appearance.
C. Calculations of how cheaply this meal could be prepared at home.

ANSWERS: If you had to turn this page upside down to learn the right answers you failed the test.

most respectable course for you and yours." (Don't try to keep up with the Joneses. Instead live within your means.)

CREDIT UNIONS VS. BANKS

A reader suggested that I write an article comparing credit unions to banks. I thought, "Great idea! This will give me another of those heavyweight financial-type articles."

In theory, no one should ever use a bank. Credit unions are nonprofit organizations, and they return surplus funds to their customers in the form of less expensive services.

I actually discovered that the rates between the two types of institutions often overlap to a large degree. Some credit unions are too small to offer better rates than banks, but if you have access to a large credit union the advantages are unquestionable.

The chart on page 66 indicates 1991 rates and fees based on three large credit unions and four major banks in our area. I have indicated the ranges where they existed.

Although interest rates on mortgages, checking, and savings accounts are similar, there is a significant difference in car loans and interest on credit cards. These credit unions offer free checking and a lesser annual fee (or none at all) for credit cards.

While most banks resell mortgage loans to loan institutions often credit unions do not. This can work to your advantage since loans that are resold must meet tighter requirements. We were able to get a mortgage based against 34% of our income rather than the standard 28%.

Loans through a credit union frequently are repaid with an allotment system. This can work to your disadvantage since a bank may not recognize the loan as part of your credit history. Because you didn't write a check each month, in theory, you have not demonstrated personal responsibility. As a result you might have trouble getting a loan through a bank in the future.

Credit unions often do not have automatic teller machines. Banks that have a national network offer the advantage of ready cash anywhere, at anytime. Credit unions have fewer branch offices, making them less convenient.

Comparing banks to credit unions is much like comparing supermarkets to warehouse stores. Generally one is better

than the other, but not always. In the same way that supermarkets run sales, banks can offer great deals to entice customers. At one time we had our sizable nest egg in a bank savings account with an interest rate of 8½%.

It is a fairly simple matter to join a credit union. One needs only to open a savings account with a minimum of $25 (or less in some cases). Therefore you can have a checking account in a bank and a credit union if both offer options that you need.

SERVICES COMPARED	BANKS	CREDIT UNIONS
30-year fixed mortgage	9.125% to 10%	9.5% to 9.9%
used car loan interest rate	12.75% to 16.75%	10.9% to 12.5%
new car loan interest rate	12.75% to 13.25%	10.9% to 11.5%
checking account fee	$6 per month under minimum balance	free
checking account interest rate	4.75% to 5.25%	5% to 6%
savings account interest rate	5.25%	5% to 6%
annual fee for credit cards	$12	$0 to $8
credit card interest rate	18% to 19.8%	12% to 14%

YOUR POULTRY PURCHASE

1. Buy your turkey several months in advance, when the price bottoms out at 39¢ lb.

2. If you didn't do that you will likely pay between 69¢ and 79¢ per pound. If you purchase a larger turkey (over 18 to 20 lbs) the price usually drops as much as 20¢ per pound. Many smaller households are reluctant to purchase the larger turkeys. But often a larger turkey will be cheaper than a smaller turkey.

Buy the larger one and freeze the leftovers in meal-size portions to eat during the next few months.

3. Beware of "the deal." A few years ago one store advertised a "free turkey" with the purchase of brand A ham. We discovered that brand B ham was far cheaper than brand A. After about 10 minutes of intense calculation we found that the cost difference was such that we could purchase brand B ham and a separate turkey (which was on sale at 29¢ per pound) and save money.

SQUEAKY WHEEL GREASED

Dear Amy,

Several times I have taken it upon myself to critique a product and send in my opinion to the address on the box. I usually tell them what I feel could be improved on or the benefits of using their products. I have always received something free back, whether it be more of the same product or coupons for free products, and all it cost me was a stamp.

Name withheld by request
Lincoln, Nebraska

DRYER POINTERS

Our family washes about 50 loads of laundry per month—100% dryer use would add at least $20 to our electric bill. Our attic clothesline allows us to air dry laundry year-round.

The only clothing still dried the conventional way (in the dryer) is the cloth diapers. Air-dried diapers resemble shingles, both in appearance and texture. I regard happy babies to be a bargain.

I heard, secondhand, from an energy expert, that smaller dryer

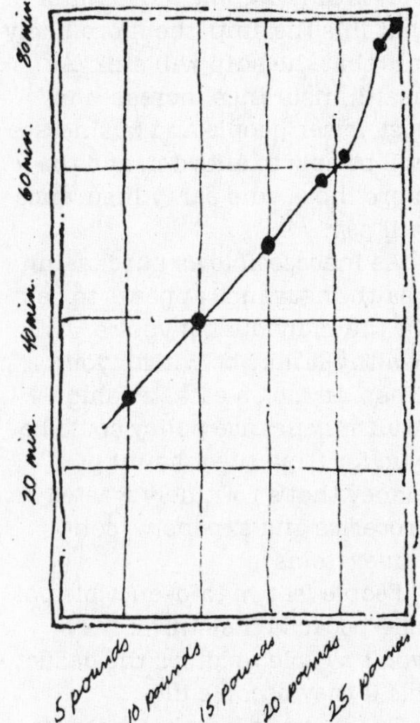

loads are more efficient. This was contrary to what I thought, so I devised an experiment to test this theory. Cloth diapers made an excellent control load, providing uniform consistency. Since they are also small items, I was able to precision-weigh loads in five-pound increments on my doctor's scale. I checked the drying loads frequently and removed the diapers at the brink of dryness. The chart above shows my results.

According to my findings 20 pounds of laundry appears to be the most energy-efficient load, with only a slight upturn (loss of efficiency) beyond that point. The important thing to note is that under 20 pounds the loads *are* inefficient. You can see that 10 pounds required 40 minutes of dryer time and 20 pounds required 60 minutes of dryer time. One large load versus two small saves 20 minutes of dryer time; 25 pounds of diapers equals a very full laundry basket and is all my 18-gallon washer will handle. It is also all the diapers, except two, that we own. (Actually I had to toss in a dampened washcloth to weigh in at exactly 25 pounds.) I did not test beyond that point, and perhaps a more dramatic loss of efficiency would be evident.

Your electric dryer costs about 44¢ per hour to operate based on 9¢ per KWH. Your iron, in comparison, costs about 9¢. Aren't we all guilty of using our dryer for an iron?

Air-dried clothing does come out wrinkled. I have found that about half a day of wear removes most wrinkles. If this method undermines your public image, try drying the clothing in the dryer for a few minutes before hanging. You'll find this works very well.

When I have to iron I save it for when I want to watch something really stupid on TV. This provides me justification for the mental mush.

Finally, these parting words of wisdom. *Clean your lint trap!*

THE EGG-CARTON PRINCESS CROWN

When my daughter, then going through her fairytale stage, asked me to make her a "princess crown," I went to my craft material bin (some folks call it a trash can) in search of some sort of discarded carton that would be suitable. An egg carton was on the top and the idea came to me.

I cut the egg carton through the cups lengthwise. I also cut the two rows of cups apart. This gave me four strips. By bending the strips in half circles, two could be stapled together to form a circle or crown. (Use insides with insides and outsides with outsides so the two sections will be the same.) I cut away a little on the end of each strip so they would overlap to make a better joint. The crown is exactly the right size for the head of a small child.

We spray painted ours silver with a can of paint that I found beside the road while collecting cans. We also used glitter left over from a Christmas project.

I have found that some egg cartons lack enough flexibility to bend properly. You'll have to experiment. Some carton designs have dips in the lid. These cut in the same way make a different sort of crown.

Decorate your crown with materials you have on hand—bits of colored paper, buttons, ribbon, stickers, etc. Be creative!

A REALLY DULL ARTICLE ABOUT HEALTH INSURANCE

> WARNING: The following article contains important but boring information. Reading it may be hazardous to your alertness. Reader discretion is advised.

Health insurance rates continue to climb dramatically, in part because the costs of the uninsured are passed on to those who have insurance. Like a ship that is sinking, the more water that fills the ship, the more likely it is that the ship will sink. As health insurance increases in cost, fewer people and businesses will be able to afford it, and the more those who carry insurance will pay.

As inaccessible as purchasing health insurance appears to be for the individual, if you're healthy it may be within your grasp. In fact, a catastrophic health insurance policy could be paid for from the amount of money that's routinely wasted on groceries and expensive consumer items.

People fear high-deductible policies because they think they won't be able to afford the deductible if they become ill.

To illustrate how high-deductible policies work I obtained rates for a woman my age in my part of the country. I compared rates of policies with a $500 deductible, a $1,000 deductible, and a $2,500 deductible. After the deductible is met the policy holder must pay 20% of the bills up to $5,000. This 20% is called the copayment.

DEDUCT-IBLE	MONTHLY RATE	ANNUAL RATE	WORST SCE-NARIO
$ 500	$158	$1,896	$3,396
$1000	$137	$1,644	$3,644
$2500	$105	$1,260	$4,760

The above table shows what it would cost with the three plans.

The annual rate is the "best scenario"—you have no medical bills and pay only the insurance premium.

I calculated the "worst scenarios" by using this equation:

The annual rate + the deductible + 20% of $5000 = your total cost

For example, to figure the worst scenario for the $500 deductible.

$1,896 + $500 + $1,000 = $3,396

If you choose the $2,500 deductible over the $500 deductible and have no medical expenses, you will save $636 over the year. If you have a medically expensive year the worst that could happen is that you would have to pay an additional $1,364. Although you have to pay the first $2,500, in reality you are not "out" the entire $2,500. In less than two healthy years your premium savings would pay for the additional $1,364.

The chart below shows that if you incur $1,500 of medical bills your annual cost will be about the same regardless of the deductible you choose.

Many people who are looking at insurance will not opt for the higher deductible because they don't have that much cash in the bank. However, most doctors and hospitals will work out a pay-

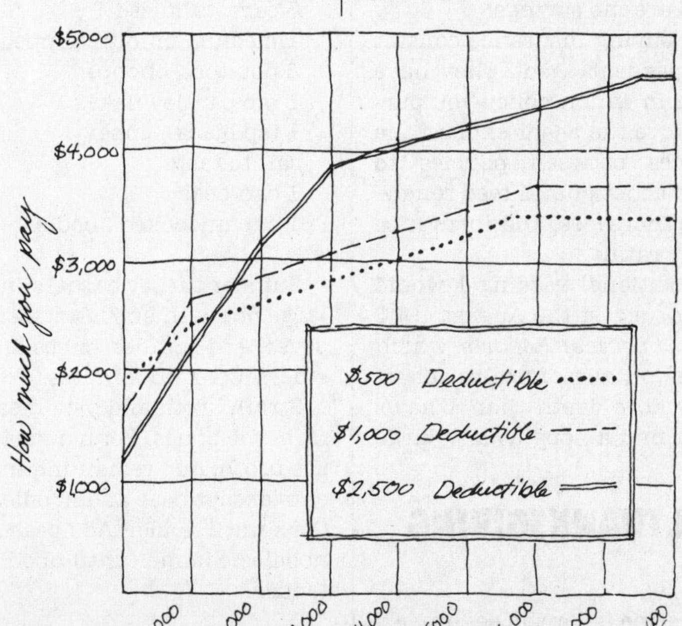

ment schedule if you are caught short. So get the higher deductible and discipline yourself to save the premium difference. Do not bank on the generosity of the medical establishment, for although they might be flexible, the cost of your unpaid bills gets passed on to other consumers.

If you're purchasing insurance for a family, the deductibles get scarier and it becomes more confusing to calculate the worst scenario. Companies vary in how they handle multiple deductibles. Many offer a cap . . . once three family members meet the deductible, the other family members don't have to. However, you must keep these huge numbers in perspective. In healthy families it's rare for one family member to have a high medical cost, let alone for one family to have three separate major illnesses or accidents. And while the worst scenario is huge, so are the savings.

When buying insurance consult an independent agent. They have no stake in which policy you purchase. Have the agent explain the differences between policies to you. Ask about guaranteed renewals, rate increases, and insurance company ratings.

For additional reading I would strongly suggest the August 1990 issue of *Consumer Reports,* which discusses pitfalls of health insurance in more depth than I have. You can find a copy at any large library.

AFTER THANKSGIVING SOUP

This recipe is for the beginner tightwad who has yet to learn that turkey carcasses and bones from other meats should be used for soup making. Leftovers from this soup should become the first ingredient in your grand adventure of refrigerator stew cookery.

Longtime practitioners of the Zen of Advanced Tightwaddery not only do this as second nature but also regard soup recipes to be an unnatural restraint, preferring instead to fly by the seat of their pants. Here's a tip for those folks:

Add vinegar to the water when you cook bones for soup. It will draw out calcium from the bones into your soup broth. Add 1 oz of vinegar to 1 quart. of water up to 4 oz of vinegar no matter how much water you use. You won't taste the vinegar in the final soup.

1 turkey carcass
4 chicken bouillon cubes
2 ribs celery, chopped
3 carrots, sliced
1 medium onion, chopped
2 potatoes, chopped
1 tsp parsley flakes
1 tsp black pepper
salt to taste
1 can peas
1 cup uncooked noodles

Simmer turkey carcass in a large pot with enough water to cover. Add bouillon cubes and spices. Cook 45 minutes.

Strain broth and pick meat from the bones. Return meat to the broth. Add remaining ingredients except peas and noodles. Cook until tender. Add peas and noodles. Simmer until noodles are tender.

(Contributed by Vicky Smith, North Little Rock, Arkansas)

KIDS' CLOTHES

Dear Amy,

I always buy my children's clothes at the end of the season for the next year. I buy one size larger than they are now. Around Labor Day there are still some summer items not sold. Last year I bought $10 pajamas for $1 and $2. And $5 and $6 tops for 75¢ to $1. Later in the fall there are still odds and ends left and I got several shirts for 50¢. I store clothes for next year in a closet in a trash bag.

Diana Meyer
St. Louis, Missouri

PLASTIC LIDS

Dear Amy,

In summer, we made our own Popsicles in plastic cups. We inserted recycled sticks (boiled to sanitation) in the little circles we cut out of large plastic lids to hold the stick upright in cup until frozen.

At Halloween we'd use the same plastic tops, especially the white ones, and cut vampire teeth, which one could put across one's gum and lip. These were also used as party favors.

Jean Grover
Oregon City, Oregon

TRANSCENDENTAL WOOD REFINISHING

I am a novice on the subject of refinishing wood in general, but when it comes to stripping old varnish, it seems I know of a method that few others do.

I learned about it when all other attempts to remove the old darkened varnish from our 100-year-old home's woodwork failed. Like most people would, I first tried all sorts of expensive chemicals. These made the finish gummy, and it still would not come off.

It turns out, as another owner of a Victorian home told me, old varnish can be removed with a simple paint scraper. I raced home to try it, and son-of-a-gun, it worked like a charm.

I had worried that it would scratch the surface, but several refinished doors, yard upon yard of trim, and a walnut bookcase later, I got compliments . . . and not a botched job yet.

If I were beginning a new project, I would first try denatured alcohol. Sometimes this will remove old varnish with no scraping. I had an antique bureau with stained, darkened varnish sitting around for a year before I tried denatured alcohol. Three hours later I had removed all the finish with ease. I just applied the denatured alcohol, let it sit for a

minute, and wiped off the dissolved finish with a rag.

If the varnish proves to be more stubborn, scraping is the next option. Old varnish scrapes off in a powdery form with relative ease. I scrape very lightly.

I use a standard paint scraper with disposable blades, which I sharpen on a bench grinder (bought at a yard sale for $10). If you don't have access to a grinder, you might try a whetstone. New blades, just out of the package, are not as sharp as ones sharpened on a grinder.

I discovered that if I grind the blades so that they have a slight convex curve, they work much better on flat surfaces.

I scrape concave curves with a sharpened spoon, and grooves can be scraped with the tip of a small screwdriver.

Once I have scraped an entire surface, which takes maybe three hours for a paneled door, I wipe the scraped area with a little denatured alcohol on a rag or a piece of steel wool. This dissolves and smooths out any varnish residue. After it dries I look for shiny spots, which indicate remaining varnish, and scrape those areas again. Then I hit rescraped areas with a little more denatured alcohol.

For the final finish I favor the low-luster look of linseed oil. It wipes on easily with a rag.

I like the scraper method because it's cheap, I can work small sections at a time, and I can clean up with a little quick sweeping and damp mopping. If I get the urge, I can pick up the project by getting the scraper out of the kitchen drawer. I don't need to get out chemicals, rubber gloves, newspapers, etc. Other methods produce more waste . . . more gunky steel wool, dirty rags, and sometimes wastewater (the toxic chemicals should not be dumped down the sink).

The denatured alcohol/scraper method does not work for all finishes, and predicting which method will work for a piece of furniture you're contemplating buying is difficult. But try the least expensive methods first.

Scraping might require a little more time, but I enjoy the peace of mindless work. After about three days of scraping I enter a (chemical-free) trancelike state. Lofty and profound thoughts flow into my consciousness. The scraper, the wood, and I become one.

THE POPCORN CHALLENGE

As the crack staff investigative reporter, I am planning a series of articles exposing the practice of the food industry to make healthful and cheap food more expensive, all in the name of—yes, you guessed it—*Convenience!*

The focus of this article is microwave popcorn.

To illustrate the factors of cost versus savings of time we devised a race—a pop-off—pitting a nationally recognized "gourmet" microwave popcorn against 15-year-old homegrown popcorn popped in a hot-air popcorn popper.

My husband, Jim, went undercover to a chain grocery store, where he would not be recognized, and made the actual purchase of the microwave popcorn.

Jim became the competitor designate of the Microwave Team, while I headed up the Homegrown Team.

He placed the microwave popcorn on a handy pantry shelf while I did a final check to be sure all was in place for traditional popping.

I wore track shoes and loosened up with stretching exercises while Jim relaxed, cocky and confident in hiking boots.

We assumed like starting positions on the sofa (couch potatoesque). Our oldest son fired the toy starting gun, and we were off.

The Microwave Team cheated shamelessly, holding, elbowing, and blocking my path. Forced to abandon my preplanned route, instead I sped down the hall, dodging four excited cheering children, and arrived in the pantry with a two-second advantage.

With fluid catlike movements I prepared my popcorn while Jim fumbled with unfamiliar packaging before getting his popcorn into the microwave.

The commotion settled into a tense stillness as we waited to the competitive hums of popper and microwave.

Being a knowledgeable tightwad, you have probably ascertained that the microwave popcorn is far more expensive. The packaging boasts 12 cups of popcorn per bag. This is a gross exaggeration. Fully popped the 75¢ bag yielded only 6 cups (12½¢ per cup). Traditional "gourmet" popcorn costs 30¢ per batch of 10 cups (3¢ per cup). Generic popcorn can be purchased for as little as 9¢ per batch of 9 cups (1¢ per cup).

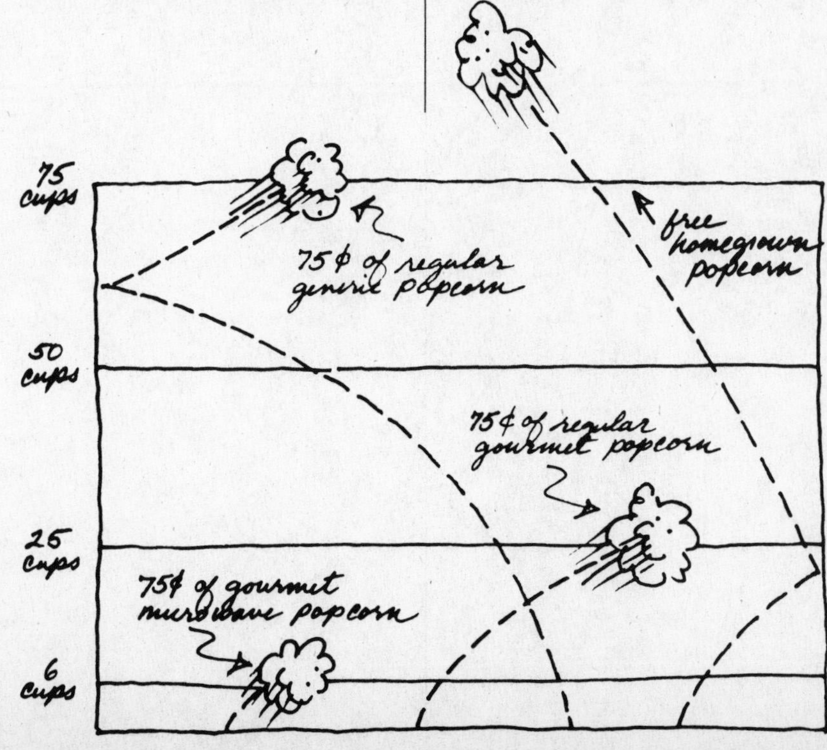

If your family pops two batches of traditional generic popcorn per week, instead of preparing an equivalent amount of microwave popcorn, you will save nearly $100 over the course of the year.

But how much *time* does microwave popcorn save?

Meanwhile, back in the pantry, the competitive humming gave way to the explosive fury of the Homegrown challenger: 3½ minutes into the race the traditionally popped popcorn was buttered and salted while the microwave popcorn emitted its first humble bursts. Jim had to wait an additional two minutes in the pantry for his to finish popping while the Homegrown Team relaxed victoriously on the sofa (couch potatoesque) in time for the start of the next program.

Note: some people spray a paper bag with cooking spray to make "homemade microwave popcorn." This is more flammable than the store bought type, and if attempted should be watched carefully.

Winter

THE CHRISTMAS FULFILLMENT DRAMA

In December most of us who share the holidays with children will observe a drama called the "fulfillment curve," played out within the space of two or three hours.

This drama, or idea, is one of many great insights in the book called *Transforming Your Relationship with Money and Achieving Financial Independence* by Joe Dominguez.

His theory is that when we spend money on the basics of survival—food, shelter, warmth, clothing—we receive maximum fulfillment for the dollars spent. To a slightly lesser degree we are fulfilled as we begin to spend on a few comforts and luxuries. Beyond this, however, the curve peaks and begins to drop so that we receive *less* fulfillment for the dollars spent (see chart below).

THE FULFILLMENT CURVE

It is not that spending money stops being fun altogether, but that the ratio of dollars spent to fulfillment received drops off. Ideally we should recognize where the peak is and consciously taper our spending beyond that point. If we do continue to spend we trade more hours of work to earn money to buy less and less fulfillment.

His book further outlines the way this works in relation to a scenario couple over a period of years.

Simpler examples come to mind, such as the fulfillment received from the first spoonful from a half gallon of ice cream versus the last one scraped from the bottom of the carton 20 minutes later. Or the fulfillment received from the first $200 car as a teenager versus the $20,000 car bought 10 years later. The new car was nice . . . but not 100 times as nice.

When I first read this book I instantly recognized the truth of the fulfillment curve as I thought about Christmas mornings (and birthdays) I have witnessed with children. Every parent who has overshot the peak knows exactly what I'm writing about.

The Christmas morning fulfillment drama opens with a scene of the Smuckster family gathered around an enormous stack of gifts. Clyde and Bunni anxiously anticipate the reaction of their son Hubert.

Act 1. Hubert opens up two presents—a Sno-Boggan and the King's Mountain Fortress Lego set. He is ecstatic and wants to play with the Legos, but Clyde insists he must open all his presents first.

Act 2. Hubert continues opening presents and receives a Creepy Cruiser Car, Beetle Juice Neighborhood Nasty figures, and a Mario Brothers pinball game. His eyes are big as saucers as he exclaims, "Cool! What else is for me?"

Act 3. More tearing and flinging of paper reveals a Hasbro WWF Wrestling Ring, the Jetsons videotape and a Nasta Air Guitar. Hubert's inner monster begins to show itself as he disdainfully points and says, "I didn't want that wrestling thing."

Act 4. Hubert opens Teenage Mutant Ninja Turtle figures, a Nintendo Game Boy, and a Nikko Big Bubba radio control truck. "Not this one. I told you I wanted the Black Thunder truck."

Bunni consoles him, "Don't worry, sweetie, we'll just take this one back and get the one you want." Hubert sulks, pokes through the empty wrappings and says, "Is that all I got?"

The peak of the fulfillment curve is different for every family. The drama may play out more subtly in your family. Sometimes the only indicator is a lessening of enthusiasm. But wherever it is for you, spending beyond the peak fails to add significantly to your holiday experience. The Smucksters' Christmas would have been perfect had it been a one-act play.

The peak seems to vary depending on the age of the child. (Your teenager may deny there is any such peak.) It is largely determined by our current culture, as any senior citizen will verify. When children have become accustomed to a large volume of material goods, more presents are required to satisfy them.

I am not suggesting that we revert to Dickensian holidays. We have found that Christmas and birthdays lack the "Wow!" when we have relied solely on scrounged and homemade presents. We seem to hit the peak when we focus on the purchase of one special new item of about $20, especially for the older children, and fill in around the edges with other things.

One Christmas our daughter, Jamie, desperately wanted P.J. Sparkles, a doll that lights up when hugged. We didn't locate the doll until her birthday in March. Jamie danced with joy when she opened the present, and I still put the pair to sleep together every night. It was unquestionably a "good spend."

THE HOT COCOA COMPARISON

This chart is based on price per serving, but that does not show the real story. Whenever we look at the cost of food we must consider how much nutrition our money is buying. The percentage

figure under each type of cocoa indicates the percent of the USRDA (U.S. Recommended Daily Allowance) of calcium each 6-ounce serving contains. Milk products do contain other nutrients, but we primarily look to them for calcium.

According to the information on a box of dry milk, 6 ounces of milk provides about 22½% of the RDA of calcium. The packaging information of the commercial mixes lists nutrition.

A reader sent in a homemade mix recipe, but when I made it up I found that, although it tasted very good, it was about the same price per serving as some commercially prepared brands. I calculated the volume of dry milk to nonnutritious ingredients to determine the percent of USRDA of calcium.

To determine how much nutrition your money is buying, divide the cost per serving by the percent of USRDA of calcium. I found that the tightwad mix provides about 3% per penny spent while the next most nutritious mixes, Hills Bros. and the reader's mix provide 1½%. Swiss Miss and Carnation are the bad guys coming in at under ¼% per penny spent.

Tightwad Hot Cocoa Mix

I mix ⅓ cup of dry milk with 1 teaspoon of cocoa and sugar each. Add 1 cup of hot water. Or mix with cold water and prepare in the microwave.

The Reader's Hot Cocoa Mix

10⅔ cups dry milk
6 oz of nondairy coffee creamer
1 pound of Nestlé's Quik
⅓ cup confectioner's sugar

Mix the ingredients in a large bowl and store in covered container. To prepare hot cocoa, mix ½ cup of the mix with 1 cup of hot water.

THE ENVELOPE RECYCLER

Dear Amy,

Want some cheap return-address labels? Here's how to get some. Cut out all of the mailing labels from your junk mail that have your address all nicely preprinted. Attach them to your envelopes with a glue stick, white glue, or tape.

Pat Flewelling
Leeds, Maine

(This is one of those things we tightwads do even though we know they don't contribute much to our financial dream. One of my other readers takes this a step further. Homemade labels can be made big enough to cover old return addresses. He reuses an envelope by patching it with one of these, and a blank label over the other address, and then adds a new stamp. The letters come with a double postmark. FZ)

CLEANING SOLUTION

Dear Amy,

This was given to me by a home economics teacher. It is just as effective as high-priced cleaning solutions.

½ cup ammonia
⅓ cup vinegar
2 Tbsp baking soda
1 gallon water

Alice Kinsman
Auburn, Maine

A TIGHTWAD QUERY

Dear Amy,

Still haven't figured out how to recycle toilet paper. I keep wondering about toilet paper that is advertised as recycled!

Arnie Anfinson
Seattle, Washington

SAVES ON SHAVES

Dear Amy,

My husband never believed me until he tried it, but drying your razor after you rinse it clean saves tons of shaves. My blades for my legs last for months.

Marina Andrew
Forest Lake, Minnesota

DO ONE BETTER

Dear Amy,

In reference to the "Saves on Shaves" contribution, I can do one better. After you clean and dry your razor blade, coat it with that ever-present-in-your-medicine-chest Vaseline or cold cream. This keeps the air from coming in contact with the cutting edge and causing rust. It also helps to lubricate the next shave.

Louis Pifer
Delano, California

THE INVESTMENT PURCHASE AND THE DISPOSABLE PURCHASE

During our honeymoon Jim and I went antiquing and stayed at country inns. Although we bought a few other items we primarily searched for an antique cannonball bed (a wooden bed frame with a ball on the top of the ornately turned corner posts).

We poked through scores of shops over a period of 10 days and turned up only a dozen in various conditions, costing between $300 and $800. After crisscrossing our way through the New England states we finally located one in perfect condition only a few miles from Jim's parents' house. Because we had shopped so thoroughly we knew the $425 price tag was perhaps not a steal, but certainly fair.

The bed, being a genuine antique, was too short and needed to have the rails lengthened by a woodworker. Then we had a custom box spring made to fit. Before we slept in it we had spent $700.

About this same time we also became very conscious of our food bill and refused to pay 59¢ for a can of tuna fish. We knew it would go on sale for 49¢ the next week.

Was this craziness or true tightwaddery?

The tuna fish is a disposable purchase. The bed is an investment purchase, not only because antiques appreciate in value but also because we will own it for 50 to 60 years. This bed annually costs us about the same as a pair of movie tickets.

Disposable purchases are those things that we buy for short-term use, such as food, clothing, and entertainment. Certainly food is an investment in nutrition, but tuna fish provides a similar food value to lobster. A business suit may be an investment but children's clothing can only be considered a disposable purchase. Entertainment is an investment in family time, but generally free entertainment can be as fulfilling.

Some purchases fall into a gray area. Automobiles, for example,

may be either depending on your car ownership philosophy.

Early on we recognized it was poor financial management to spend most of our money on disposable things. In the same way it did not seem wise to compromise on intermediate-priced items that we didn't like. As a result the cannonball bed remains our most extravagant household purchase. Other than half a dozen items that we have paid more than $100 for, the remainder of our house is furnished in an Early Marriage (thrift shop) style, liberally accessorized with wooden crates. We have temporarily shifted some of these purchases from the investment to the disposable category.

When I was single most of my discretionary income went for disposable things. Over an eight-year period I spent about $5,000 just on movies and meals out. Today I cannot name one tenth of the movies I saw and recall very few meals out.

During the same time I spent less than $400 on three chairs, a coffee table, and a cabinet. Now, 10 years later, these items still see daily use.

Without resorting to deprivation we try to spend a minimum on disposable purchases. In 1990 we spent less than $250 to clothe six people, less than $350 on birthdays and Christmas, and I am hard pressed to think of anything spent for entertainment. I know of only one family that spends less than we do for food.

By comparison we spent about $2,000 on a used garden tractor and several tools, which will save us many times their cost.

When we do spend on an investment purchase we shop for months, or even years. We look for the best value, not necessarily the cheapest solutions. If we plan to live with an item, perhaps forever, we do not compromise on what we like.

Although my $5,000 expenditure on movies and dinners

out is shocking it also typifies the down-the-drain spending habits of many people. They merely have not added it up yet. The lack of financial progress over a period of years dramatizes the long-term result of this type of spending. When gratification depends on the purchase of disposable things, spending must continue at the same level forever. Factoring in growing families and inflation more money needs to be spent to achieve the same level of gratification.

Although I have illustrated this concept with material goods, investment purchases can include less tangible things, such as education as well as the buying of financial freedom through a variety of strategies.

Jim and I are working toward a mix of acquiring material goods and buying financial freedom. We have done this to a degree when we bought a "two-income house" on one income. As inflation shrinks the value of the mortgage and as we pay it off early a smaller percentage of our income will go for housing.

The prudent (and restrained) expenditure on lesser investment purchases works toward this same goal. The first few years we were married we spent a great deal on investment purchases. The "extravagant" investment purchases, such as our cannonball bed, will never need to be replaced. Good appliances and tools save money. Today we need to spend far less on things of permanence.

As toddlers inevitably grow to be teenagers we expect our budget for disposable purchases will increase. (Although, amazingly, tuna fish still goes on sale for 49¢ a can.)

Some who are not lovers of antiques will argue the merits of our expenditure for a cannonball bed, pointing out that a mattress can be supported equally well by the floor. Nevertheless our financial plan continues to include the replacement of wooden crates with real furniture.

BOOK SMARTS

Dear Amy,

My main entertainment is reading. I use the library a lot, but I also like to own certain books. One bookstore in town offers 25% off all new books in July and December. I keep a list and buy during these two months.

I also frequent used-book stores. I trade in books I no longer want for "new" ones. When I run low on books to trade in, I go to a flea market or garage sale and offer to buy all their books for 10¢ each. I can get 100 books for $10. After reading the ones I am interested in I take the rest to the used bookstore to trade in.

I generally get $100 to $200 in credit this way, and can exchange it for other books, which I read and exchange again. For $10 and 100 books I can get 150 to 175 books to read. This is a lot of entertainment for $10. (Bookstores generally don't accept the small romance books because they have hundreds of them.)

Barbara Turner
Colorado Springs, Colorado

BARGAINS IN BACK

Dear Amy,

I work in a drugstore. We are always repricing items in our store, which means, in general, *raising them.* Yesterday I repriced Solarcaine at $5.49, and in the process noticed that there was some Solarcaine on the back of the shelf still at $3.95. It had missed being marked up for some time.

So, don't buy the product right in front. Look at all the packages, especially the ones in the back. This works best in older stores that don't use a laser reader.

Tightwad Jim
Phoenix, Arizona

LIGHT TRICK

Dear Amy,

My 74-year-old father lives in an 1867 home with only a very few conveniences. The elderly have always "made do" and so "does" my father. A ceiling kitchen light pull chain was pulled off one day when the light was "on," and so he couldn't turn it off (or off and on again). Rather than call in an electrician to fix the problem, my father found a green plastic garden pot, placed a styrofoam cup inside, which he then nailed to an old broom handle. As the old fixture is up on a 10-foot or so high ceiling, my parents have no problem turning the bulb to the right or left for "on" and "off." You see, the styrofoam cup gets a good grip on the bulb.

So goes life at my parents' house. There is a special place on the wall beside the kitchen table for this conversation piece, which they have used now for years!

I think an award should be given to this senior citizen tightwad.

Suzanne Foster
Winthrop, Maine

THE GIFT WHEEL

This inspiration comes from Duane and Muriel McIntire of Rolling Hills Estates, California, They have seven children. With all the grandchildren, gift giving had become too expensive. While many families draw names, this wheel method is superior because no family member will get the same person more than one time in eight years.

The McIntires' wheel (see opposite) is divided into eight sections—one section for each of their children and one section for them. You will divide yours by the number of people in your family.

Cut a large circle (about 5") and a small circle (about 4") from a piece of cardboard. Trace the correct size jar lids if you don't have a compass. Divide each circle into the appropriate number of sections. Poke a hole in the center of each of the circles and attach them with a brass fastener. Write names of family members around the outer edge of each circle. The sequence of names should be the same on each circle.

In the outer circle write this year's date in the first section, next year's date in the second section, and so on around the circle. With a different color mark an index line on any of the section lines on the inner circle.

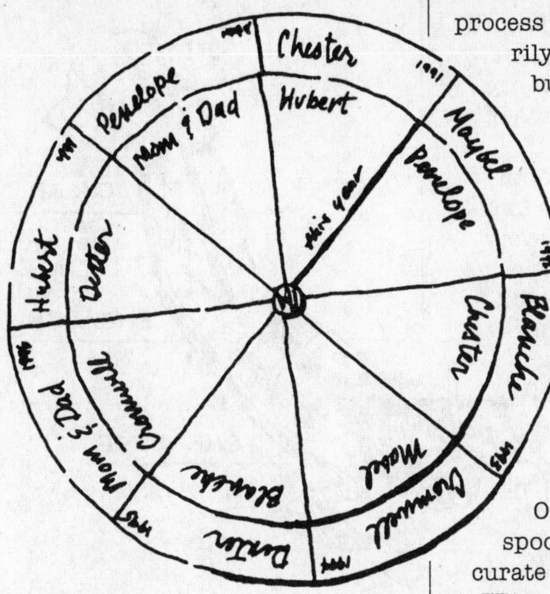

Each year you rotate the wheel by realigning the index line with the new date. The name on the inside wheel gives to the person on the outside wheel.

SEEKING THE MINIMUM LEVEL

People are creatures of habit. We do things because we have always done them that way, or because our parents always did them that way, or because a teacher taught us that way, or because an "expert" said to do it that way. We seldom challenge why we do things the way we do. As a result we persist in expensive behaviors, purely out of habit.

To form new, frugal habits, develop an awareness about all the small actions you do every day. Explore new ways to do things . . . seek the minimum level. Scale down step by step until the process does not work satisfactorily for your standards. Then bump it up one level.

When you wash dishes, do you always fill the sink to the top? If you're doing a small number of dishes a sink half full of water may suffice. Do you always put a two-second squirt of dishwashing liquid in the water? See if a one-second squirt will work. Or measure it in a teaspoon so that you have an accurate gauge.

When you wash laundry, do you always put the recommended amount of detergent in each load? Isn't it handy the way the manufacturers provide you with a plastic scoop in each box so you never think about using less? Think about how dirty each load is and add detergent accordingly. Often a half scoop will work as well.

Our grandmothers boiled cloth diapers. Our mothers bleached them. Experiment with your laundering procedure. Can you use less bleach? Do you need bleach? Will the ultraviolet rays from outdoor air drying be sufficient? Do you need to wash in hot water? Keep bumping down the procedure until it seems to bother your baby. Then move back up one level. It seems mean, but it may take three years before your child is potty trained, so you could save hundreds of dollars.

If your dryer doesn't have a moisture sensor, do you always set the dial at a certain point? Try setting it for less time, until you find how little time you really

need to dry your clothes. Record your findings for the different lengths of time required to dry different types and amounts of laundry.

Do you use an inch of toothpaste because a brush has inch-long rows of bristles and every toothpaste advertisement you've ever seen portrays a neat, full, bristle-length swath? Experiment to see if a ½ inch of toothpaste works as well.

When you pour bath water, do you habitually fill the tub to eight inches deep when four would do the same job? When you shampoo, do you experiment to find the least amount that will work? If you pour a quarter-sized dab in your palm, try using a nickel-sized one. When you shower, do you need to wash your hair each time? Do you need a shower every day or would a sponge bath suffice on days you're not going to work?

If you blow-dry your hair, are there days when air drying would be suitable? Do you need the full makeup regimen every day? Maybe some days you could scale it down—not use eye makeup or not use any at all.

To avoid the expense of canned shaving cream, a friend of mine put a chunk of soap in the bottom of a mug and used a shaving brush to whip it to a froth and apply it. He got good results, but one day, fresh from the shower, he tried shaving his still-wet face with no cream at all. Because his beard is relatively light, it worked. Now he only uses the mug and brush on days when he doesn't shower.

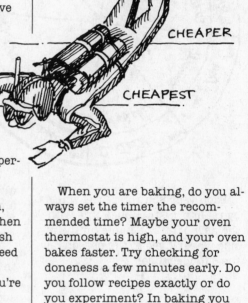

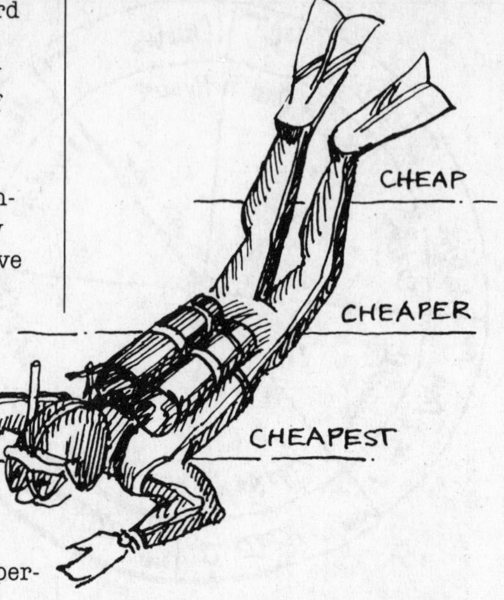

When you are baking, do you always set the timer the recommended time? Maybe your oven thermostat is high, and your oven bakes faster. Try checking for doneness a few minutes early. Do you follow recipes exactly or do you experiment? In baking you can try using less sugar, eggs, and oil. Find the point where you notice a significant taste difference, and then increase the sugar, eggs, or oil slightly.

When you eat and drink, do you always fill plates and cups full? Maybe a partial cup of coffee or a smaller portion would satisfy you as much. If you have a chocolate craving at the checkout line, do you really need the extra-large-size chocolate bar? Maybe a small Peppermint Patty would satisfy you.

Do you always buy brand-name foods because your one experiment with store brands was unsatisfactory? Keep experimenting to find lower-cost brands that

work for your needs. And bear in mind, just because a brand tastes different, it doesn't mean it tastes worse.

Could your heat thermostat be set lower? Move it down and put on a sweater. How high is your water heater set? Turn it down to 125°. (Do not experiment lower—it needs to be this hot to kill bacteria.) Could any of your lights be a lower wattage, especially in hallways? If you find the dimness of the lower-wattage bulbs bothersome, put the brighter ones back in.

How many gifts do you give for birthdays? Would fewer be as satisfying? We set a $50 limit on the total cost of gifts and the party, but found we were often able to do an entire birthday for about $25. If you find your reduced spending level is not quite satisfactory, increase the budget slightly.

Most important, when you establish your budget, do you always spend the allowed amount, or do you try to spend less on the areas of your budget that are flexible?

When you seek the minimum level you may be breaking old habits. Give yourself time to get used to the new lower level. It may take a few months to adjust so that the change feels comfortable. And at that point try the experiment again.

RAISIN OATMEAL SCONES

1 ½ cups flour
1 cup uncooked oatmeal
1 tsp baking soda
½ tsp salt
¼ cup softened margarine
½ cup raisins
¾ cup sour milk (milk with 2 tsp of vinegar added)
1 egg, beaten

Preheat oven to 400°. Mix dry ingredients; cut in margarine and raisins. Stir in enough sour milk just to moisten. Divide the dough in half. Flour hands and pat dough into two circles on a greased cookie sheet about ½ inch

thick. Cut into quarters. Bake for 10 minutes. Brush on egg and then bake until golden brown. Serve with honey, margarine, or jam.

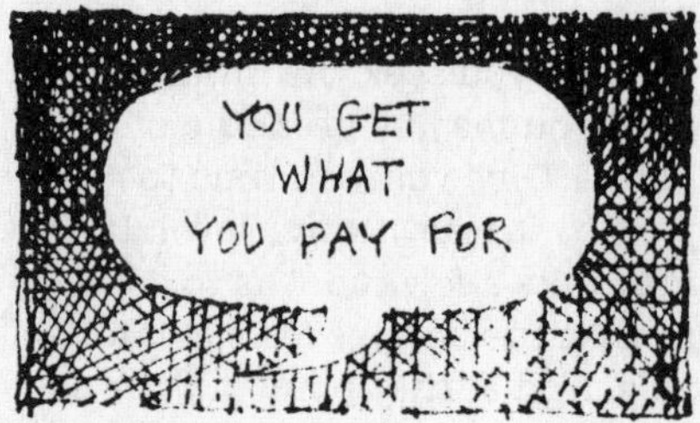

This hindsight wisdom translates into "expensive is good" and "inexpensive is bad." If it were true there would be no bargains.

Consumers are so deeply conditioned with this notion that they are suspicious when goods and services are "too low."

Did you ever wander down a store aisle of expensively priced shampoos and think, "Who buys this stuff?" In fact buyers of "quality" products are often purchasing advertising, glitzy packaging, and high corporate overhead.

Certainly there are times that my good deals turn out to be not so good and I hear that little voice whisper the familiar hindsight wisdom: "You get what you pay for." But those times are rare and the financial risks are small compared to all the savings that have come from the bargain hunting.

Every tightwad has a list of favorite steals. Here's a few of our recent good deals.

- A year-old probably-purebred German shepherd from the animal shelter for a $20 donation.
- Bulk purchased yeast at about 7% of the price of those little packages.
- A like-new Battleship game for 39¢ at the thrift shop.
- An antique wood cookstove found buried in a garage, rusted and in pieces. This, purchased for $100, is now worth about $500 after a few hours of elbow grease.
- An unopened half gallon of carpenter's glue for $3, originally priced at $17.95.

Finding bargains requires experimentation, research, and a little patience. Basing your purchases on the "you get what you pay for" presumption is easy, effortless . . . and expensive.

BEST BARGAINS

Toothpaste. Next time you sit in the dentist's chair, think about how much toothpaste could be purchased for the cost of that filling.

The Public Library. This remarkable institution makes information, knowledge, and self-education available to everyone at no cost.

Thinness. Despite the enormous weight loss industry, thinness is in fact very cheap. It does not require expensive diet foods, clubs, or counseling. One simply eats less. In many cultures only the wealthy can achieve the desired weight.

Paper. In an interview Bette Midler spoke of the extravagant presents fans send to her daughter. Sending these to children of low-income families seemed more logical to her. She added, "Besides, I kind of think the best present for a kid is a pencil and a piece of paper."

Public Places. Within any geographic area there are a number of places of interest that are free and open to all. Among my personal favorites are Trinity Chapel in Boston and Halibut Point in Gloucester, MA.

Television. Advertisers pick up the tab for this form of free entertainment. Note: this is only a bargain if you select worthwhile programming and if you have the presence of mind to ignore the commercials.

A 29¢ Postage Stamp. Consider the volume of information that can be included under an ounce and that the U.S. Postal Service will carry it thousands of miles for the same price.

A Single Zucchini Seed. As most of us wrap up the gardening season this is self-explanatory.

TWO CHRISTMAS PROJECTS

If you're like me, by this time you are frantically looking for one more good, last-minute idea that doesn't require learning a new skill. And you are vowing to start earlier next year. Here is a project for this year, and one to begin for next year.

Bread Bears

(This recipe comes from the Rodale Press Christmas magazine.)

1 package dry yeast
¼ cup warm water
½ cup softened butter
¼ to ½ cup honey
3 tsp freshly grated lemon peel

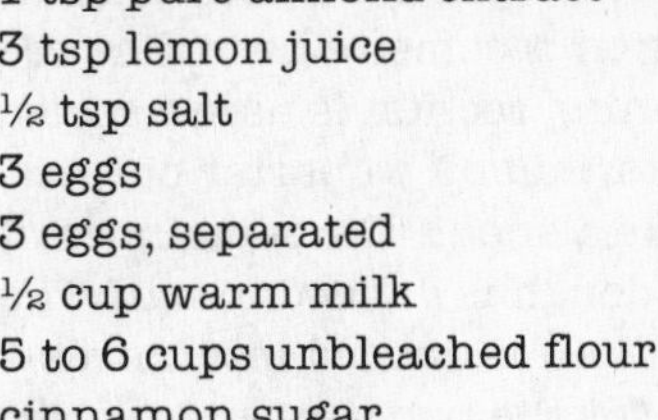

1 tsp pure almond extract
3 tsp lemon juice
½ tsp salt
3 eggs
3 eggs, separated
½ cup warm milk
5 to 6 cups unbleached flour
cinnamon sugar

Combine yeast with water; stir with fork until dissolved and set aside.

In a large bowl of an electric mixer, cream butter, honey, lemon peel, almond extract, lemon juice, and salt until mixture is fluffy. Beat in eggs and egg yolks one at a time. (Reserve three egg whites for glaze.)

With a spatula, blend in milk and yeast mixture.

Beat in two cups of flour to make a smooth batter. Add enough flour to make a stiff dough.

Turn dough onto a lightly floured surface. Knead it until the texture is smooth . . . about 10 minutes. Place in a buttered bowl,

cover lightly with a cloth, and allow it to rise in a warm place for an hour, or until doubled in bulk.

Turn the dough out onto a lightly floured surface; punch it down and let it rest for 10 minutes.

To assemble bears:

Each recipe makes two 12" bears, or four 8" bears. Or you can make a number of smaller ones. Divide your dough into circles, one for each bear. Each circle is divided according to the directions below to get the right proportions. (Or you can eyeball it.)

Divide each circle in half. One half makes up the body. Divide the second half into sections. One section becomes a head. The remaining section is useu for body parts. Pull off a quarter of it to make a snout. The remainder of the dough is divided in half. The first half is divided into thirds—one for the two ears and two for two arms. The last of the dough is divided in half to make two legs.

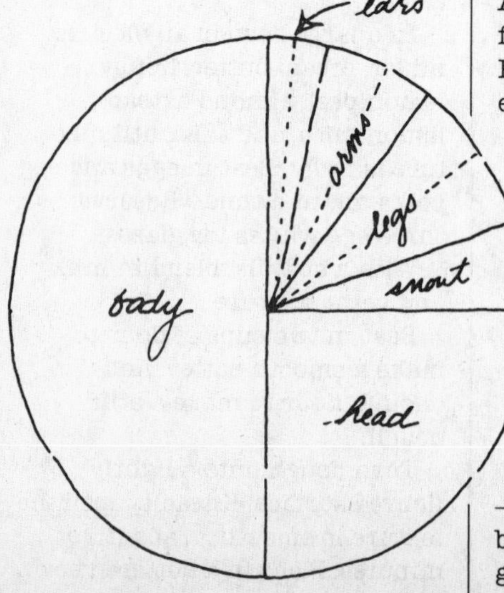

Roll the body section into a smooth ball and place in the center of a greased cookie sheet and flatten slightly. Roll the head section smooth and attach it to the body. Roll the snout and ear sections and attach them. The arms and legs sections are rolled into cylinders and attached. Use a small amount of water to stick together bear parts.

To finish the bear, press indentations with your index finger to make eyes and belly button. Put a blanched almond in each eye socket so that it will hold its shape while baking.

Cover the bear with a clean cloth and let it rise for one hour in a draft-free space.

Preheat the oven to 375°.

Beat one egg white with 1 tsp of water. Using a pastry brush paint the entire top surface of the bear with the egg glaze. Sprinkle with cinnamon sugar. (To make cinnamon sugar mix ½ cup granulated sugar to 1 tsp cinnamon.)

Bake the bears, 30 to 45 minutes, or until golden brown. (Smaller bears take less time.) After baking remove the nuts from the eyes. Let cool for 1 hour. Place raisins or candies in the eyes.

Tie brightly colored ribbon around the bear's neck. Place a large bear on a foil-covered cardboard and cover with plastic wrap. Or give several small bears in a basket. If you feel really inspired you could make an entire bear family to correspond with the sizes of family members you are giving to—a mommy and daddy and baby bears. Use red ribbon for girls and green for boys.

A Fruit Stone Wreath

Contributed by Nancy Wilson of Warren, Maine.

The stones or pits from peaches, prunes, and cherries have differing textures and natural colors. These can be saved to make a unique and attractive wreath.

After collecting a large number, wash the pits well. Soak briefly in bleach and rinse.

The pits are then glued to a sanded circle of ¼-inch plywood using Elmer's glue. Before beginning the gluing, plan a design using the different colors and textures of the pits.

To complete your wreath wire it over an evergreen wreath. It can be hung or laid flat as a centerpiece with a candle or made to fit around a punch bowl.

DEALING WITH DESIGNER CLOTHES

1. Give your child a clothing budget ample enough to cover his basic needs. Provide him with special jobs he can do to earn the difference between the $25 sneakers and the $75 sneakers. The pay scale should not rise above slave labor.

2. Form a parents' group specifically to strike against this unfair demand. If fewer parents caved in, fewer children would have designer clothes. Simple mathematics reveal that if fewer kids have designer clothes, more kids must wear generic clothes. Therefore, fewer designer-clad kids are around to pressure everyone else.

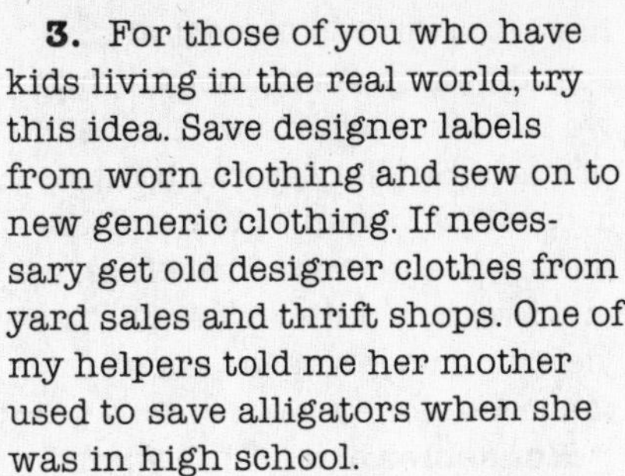

3. For those of you who have kids living in the real world, try this idea. Save designer labels from worn clothing and sew on to new generic clothing. If necessary get old designer clothes from yard sales and thrift shops. One of my helpers told me her mother used to save alligators when she was in high school.

INTERIOR DECORATING FOR TIGHTWADS

I have had this same experience on several occasions: I visit the home of someone on a small income, frequently a senior citizen. The home is tidy, orderly, and inviting. I like being there.

Maybe the hostess asks me to get the milk. Only then I notice that the refrigerator is of a vintage bordering on antique. The paint has worn through near the handle from decades of openings. But the refrigerator is also lacking in fingerprints and the litter of shopping lists and phone messages adhered with cute magnets and clear tape. An attractive arrangement of dried bittersweet in a stoneware jug replaces the usual crown of permanent clutter.

A further tour throughout the home would reveal a similar pattern. Furniture might be mismatched but good-looking. Woodwork might need to be repainted, but it is clean. Nothing is brand new, but somehow the entire home has an appeal.

Where we live has a marked effect on our sense of well-being. If we are happy in our home we

have less need to leave it and spend money. As tightwads, how we feel about where we live is important. But we approach interior decorating in a unique manner—money *is* an object. Therefore, we must resort to the strategies that yield the most improvement for the least money.

Housecleaning. This should be your first interior design consideration. Without investing any money you can achieve the most dramatic results.

Make a concentrated effort to eliminate the permanent pile of clutter, minimize eyesores, and put things away. If things are out of place because you don't have a place for them, then designate a place.

People who live in small places should eliminate unnecessary items such as the multicolored mushroom candle that has been sitting on your counter for years, that you never liked in the first place, and serves no useful purpose. Smaller places are harder to keep clean, so the less stuff you have the better.

When you eliminate stuff, hold a yard sale, donate, or ask around to find someone who wants it.

Rearranging. Redecorate by putting old things in new places. I saw a television program about an interior designer who could makeover a home without buying anything new. She worked on the assumption that whatever her clients already owned was there by their choosing, so they probably liked it. Instead she focused on using the things the clients already owned in more pleasing arrangements.

Recently I noticed that I had been storing a nice basket in the basement. I brought it upstairs where it could be seen in the kitchen. We repotted some of our plants and one found its way to a new spot in the living room. I had a frame with artwork that I didn't like. I replaced the art with a decorative card someone had sent me. That picture filled an empty spot on the kitchen wall. In each case the small change felt satisfying.

When you clean house and rearrange you can still keep the decorative items that please you, but try to group your treasures to create a focal point. Rooms also need areas that are clutter-free and restful to the eyes. You might put your collection of baseball memorabilia on one set of shelves. Your collection of baskets can hang in a grouping on one wall. Don't scatter them evenly around the room.

Eclecticism. This bona fide style of interior design allows you to mix furniture of all types. It lends itself perfectly to the tightwad approach. We tend to collect mismatched stuff from yard sales,

the curb, the secondhand shop, and Great-Aunt Ethel's attic.

Eclecticism defies the expensive approach of buying an entire room of furniture direct from the Ethan Allen showroom (and buying it on time). Some people feel compelled to buy things that match because they lack confidence in their own tastes. While being "safe," purchasing furniture in sets can result in a sterile and impersonal look. Your home should reflect you and not a designer.

Eclecticism is a great liberator. You can't make a mistake as long as you choose things that you like. It doesn't have to match or conform to someone else's standard of tastefulness. (This means if you really love it, you can keep the painting of bullfighters on black velvet.)

The Potpourri Approach. A potpourri is a grouping of items that are similar but not identical.

Rather than having one large picture, collect a variety of small frames and paint them the same color. Hang these in a grouping. You might like vintage silverware but find only a few pieces at a time. Collect a variety and set your table with a mix of pieces. If you can't afford a set of china pick up odd pieces of the same color (most likely white). Mismatched but similar dining chairs can be painted the same color.

You don't want to hide the mismatches, but rather take pleasure in the diversity.

Do-It-Yourself. When you refinish furniture, paint your own art, or grow your own houseplants from seedlings, you invest part of yourself in those items. They feel more personal to you because you have a history with them.

You can save a lot when you learn to see the potential of something that needs work. It might be priced low because other potential buyers lack vision.

The first time we laid eyes on our house, our enthusiasm wasn't dampened by the disastrous kitchen. So we bought the house and forged ahead. We removed all the peeling wallpaper, patched the old plaster, and painted over the dingy yellow with white paint. We repaired the holes in the ceiling with a large piece of Sheetrock we found in the barn. We removed the old cracked floor tiles and sanded and finished the wood floor underneath. We found a section of counter from an old country store in the shed, painted and refinished it, and use it as a work island. The total cost of our make-do-for-now redecoration was only $200.

Flexibility. Your interior design plan should be flexible. Carefully choose things over time and as bargains come your way. As you acquire better things you will want to be able to use your earlier acquisitions in other parts of your home. Our "entertainment

center" is made of boards, cement blocks, and bricks.

When we replace it, the materials can be reused for other projects. We bought four small reproduction oriental rugs at a yard sale. (They are worn enough to look almost authentic.) We have used these in a grouping on our living-room floor. If we buy a large rug the small ones can be used in other parts of the house.

If you move frequently you'll want to acquire smaller, more versatile things. I had a friend who secretly sawed and replaced the banister of her new apartment house so she could get the couch up the stairs. More responsible friends have sold their couches at a loss. Large pictures, rugs, and furniture lack flexibility and may not work well in a new home.

Breaking with Convention. In a letter that contained pictures and descriptions, one reader shared a number of unconventional ideas that work well. She and her husband bought a surplus library card catalog, refinished it, and use it for silverware, napkins, placemats, wrapping paper, dominoes, etc. They have an interesting old street light for a lamp. An old chifforobe became a cabinet for their television and stereo.

If you accept the unconventional, the range of inexpensive alternatives increases. Some types of outdoor furniture work well indoors. A glass brick can become a vase. Discarded lockers can be painted and used for storage in a child's room. A restaurant booth can become a breakfast nook.

Stick with Classics. Interior design, like clothing, undergoes style changes. With clothing, black is the classic color. In interior design the classic color is white. The harvest golds and avocados have long since enjoyed their heyday. But the white appliances from the '50s go with the ones from the '90s.

Likewise, white painted walls are not only the cheapest solution but also highly universal and timeless. Look through magazines that feature country and contemporary homes. Roughly 75% of the featured rooms have white painted walls.

The colors in design change every few years. The bright colored countertops of the '70s look dated today. The Williamsburg blue and salmons of the '80s will give way to something new.

Clear finished wood is also classic, as are most natural colors. Accessorize with colors in ways that you can change easily if you tire of them.

Avoid trendy design motifs. A few years ago mushrooms were popular. Today's cows and cats seem to be gaining ground on the "ducky decor" of more recent years. We have a nation of folks continually replacing matching canisters, potholders, and toaster covers.

Think. (It's cheap.) I have often suspected that people haven't really identified what it is about their home that bothers them. The general sense of confusion, frustration, or dissatisfaction they feel about their homes might be resolved by a good cleaning, a move of the furniture, or a fresh coat of paint.

Dear Amy,

My aloe vera plant supplies me with better burn ointment than I've ever bought. Its juices erase the minor burns my careless fingers get while cooking, and heal cuts and scrapes, too. This plant has also been reported to absorb household air pollutants. In a north window, with no direct sun, my aloe vera energetically produces offspring, which make lovely free gifts.

Westy Melby
Boone, Colorado

BABY FOOD

Dear Amy,

I work with mothers and infants a lot. Often they get excited over saving money by making their own baby food. Baby food, however, is what sociologists term "an acquired need." While it may be the social custom to use it, or expectation to use it, it is entirely the fabrication of baby food companies and only serves to fill their pockets. It can certainly be done away with. A breast-fed infant can go directly to table food when ready. I always figured if a baby *needed* strained peas at three months, I'd have a third one for strained peas.

Patti Clark
Camden, Maine

READER POTPOURRI

Dear Amy,

My aunt used an adding machine in her business. She never tears the tape off until it is used up, and then she rewinds it inside out and uses it the second time.

Jean Roberts
Alton, New Hampshire

Dear Amy,

When I make a pot of coffee, I put the rest in a thermos. It sits on the counter until I want coffee later.

Diane Bull
Rockford, Illinois

Dear Amy,

My mother used to cut a roll of paper towels in half up to the cardboard tube so that a half sheet was used most of the time.

Karen Pence
West Baldwin, Maine

Dear Amy,

Use the cuffs from old worn socks as cuff protectors on children's shirt cuffs when they are doing crafts etc.

Anne Cutter
Westbrook, Maine

FREE NEWSPAPERS

Dear Amy,

Usually small local stores have copies of the Sunday paper left over. They only have to send in a portion of the paper for credit and are often willing to part with the excess parts, such as coupons. This works with the dailies, too. When folks shop as we do, coupons really help.

Charles Tanner
Falmouth, Maine

THE GLASS-TOP CANNING JAR DILEMMA

We have about 400 surplus quart glass-top wire-bail canning jars—people keep giving them to us. These are becoming obsolete as the rubber rings get harder to find.

There must be millions of surplus jars throughout the country in need of a new use. Aside from potential food storage containers I have pondered about what could be put in them to make gifts, such as soup, coffee mixes, or Epsom salts. I requested ideas for the soon-to-be-obsolete and abundant glass-top canning jar. Teresa Totaro of Powhatan, Virginia, suggests we rub it, polish it, talk to it, adore it, and say the magic words: "We think we found different uses for them now, unless a genie finds a new source of rubber canning rings." It must have worked. A reader sent an address for rubber rings with tabs:

Hershberger Country Store
50940 T.R. 220 Rt.1
Baltic, OH 43804

The Hershbergers are Amish, and do not have a phone. Their catalog is free with an order or costs $2. Regular jar rubbers cost 98¢ per dozen, and wide-mouth ones cost $1.25 per dozen, plus a fee for shipping and handling.

An alternative source costs about 40% more:

Vermont Country Store
Mail Order Office
P.O. Box 3000
Manchester, Ctr., VT 05255-3000
(802) 362-2400

Glass-top canning jars may not be as plentiful in different parts of the country as they are in New England, as several readers indicated. They are often thrown away here. I found many boxes of them on the curb during spring cleaning (sanctioned trash-picking) season. Older people often have jars in their cellars with

40-year-old contents, and they are often pleased to have a younger person express interest. However, even here jars can sell for $1 to $6 per jar depending on the type. The blue-tinted ones are valuable.

You might be able to find a free source (if you *aren't* overloaded with them) if you think about possible likely sources such as your glass recycling center. Because these jars are collectible, old-fashioned, and attractive they make visually pleasing containers.

Containers for Office Use: rubber bands that come around flyers, paper clips, pens, and pencils

Decorative Storage: Indian corn, buttons, marbles, sea shells, small pine cones, beads, stones

Containers for Kitchen Use: miniature canisters, wooden spoon holder, match holder, silverware holder for entertaining

Containers for Bathroom Use: cotton balls, cotton swabs, colored soaps, bubble bath, Epsom salts

Containers for Food: dried beans, pasta, candy, popcorn, dried fruits, bouillon cubes, hot chocolate mix, bulk-purchased foods that come in plastic bags or large containers

Containers for Homemade Gifts: croutons, marigold and sunflower seeds, potpourri, "play dough," bean soup, or coffee mixes

Containers for Kids: barrettes, ponytail holders, crayons, change

Terrariums: Make a miniature garden inside and seal closed. It will not need watering. If vapors cloud the inside of the jar remove the glass top for a day.

Honey-Do Jar: Inside is a list of repairs or fix-it jobs that need attention. Next to the Honey-Do Jar is a Honey-Thank-You Jar. Each time your spouse completes a honey-do he gets a honey-thank-you coupon, which is good for things like a back rub or a special meal. (Kevin and Callie Smith, Albany, Oregon)

Candleholder: Fill partway with sand and place a small candle in sand. Replace top to put candle out. Good for outdoor use.

Gag Gift: If you return from a trip, label an empty jar "warm air from Florida," "cold air from Colorado," or "winnings from Las Vegas." (LaDonna Jewson, Wasaba, Minnesota)

Scene Jar: Alexia Cripps of Fort Ripley, Minnesota, has a jar with a nest and artificial bird in it. The jar lies on its side on a small *U*-shaped frame.

Keepsake Jar: Save your child's small treasures. Give the jar to your grandchildren some day. (Darlene Black, Alexandria, Virginia)

MAILING OUT YOUR CHRISTMAS PACKAGES

HOW TO PACK YOUR BOX

The United States Postal Service and United Parcel Service suggest similar guidelines for mailing packages, and may reject parcels if not packaged to their specifications.

Both do not like twine, string, and masking and cellophane tape.

The string and twine can get caught in machinery. Masking and cellophane tape lose their tackiness if frozen. In each case, even if your package is accepted for mailing, you run greater risk that it will not arrive intact. UPS discourages the use of brown wrapping paper. If used for mail through the post office, write your name on the inside box, as well as the outside paper. Do not use brown paper bags. Stamps do not adhere to it as well.

Both services recommend using a sturdy cardboard (preferably corrugated) box sealed with packing, duct, or other strong tape. The outside of the box can have other markings, but any words should be crossed off with a marker. The size of the address is not important, but should be written with a marker that won't bleed when wet. For added protection you can include a second address inside the box. Clearly mark "To" and "From" as well. A label should not be adhered over a taped seam.

When you pack your gifts inside the box use crumpled newspaper or bubble wrap. "Foam peanuts" must be packed tightly because they can shift around when loose. Six inches all around packed items is recommended, and 2 inches between items in a box. Very delicate items can be double-boxed for added protection.

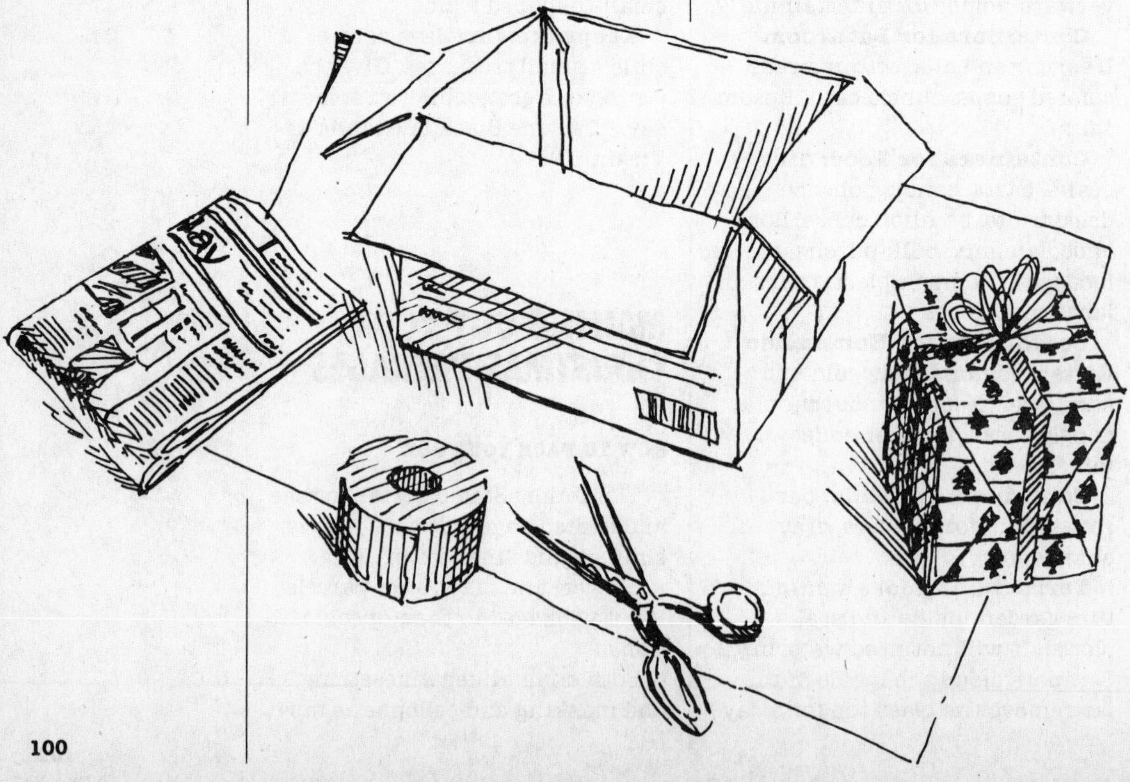

If you're mailing something small and unbreakable, consider a padded envelope . . . but not a new one from the post office. Any business receives a number of these, which can be reused by resealing

with duct tape or staples. Businesses, especially ones that order supplies through the mail, may have a selection of boxes in various sizes, complete with packing material. The best source I ever found for clean, sturdy boxes was the Dumpster behind an office supply/copy shop. (I asked first.) I have also cut large boxes down to make smaller ones, to save on weight.

WHICH SERVICE SHOULD YOU USE?

I've always wondered, but had never researched, the cheapest way to mail packages. I obtained rates from the post office and UPS. I spent many bleary-eyed hours poring over rate charts and making color-coded graphs for UPS ground delivery, and the postal service's 4th class and priority mail. It was my hope to nail down clear guidelines; however, my findings indicate that there are too many variables to provide simple answers.

In the case of both services it is cheaper to mail one large package than two or more smaller ones that equal the weight of the larger one. If you are mailing to several households in the same town you might consider putting all your gifts in one package, especially if the households share a common Christmas.

Although the two services have some basic similarities they have the following differences:

Speed. UPS takes 6 days to ship a package cross-country, and fewer days when shipping to closer locations; 4th-class mail through the post office generally takes 8 days to get cross-country. UPS claims a 1-day delay during the holiday peak, whereas the post office admits that 4th class can require 7 to 14 days to get anywhere during this time. Priority mail takes 2 to 3 days to ship a package cross-country. If you mail early, speed should not be a factor.

Safety. UPS insures packages for $100 at no charge. The post office charges $1.60 for $100 worth of insurance and 75¢ for $50 worth of insurance. UPS also has a tracking service so that you can find out where your package is if delayed. Most people do not inquire with their relatives to learn if their package arrived on time, and so the tracking may be of no use. I have had only one gift break in transit in 15 years of mailing. I had packaged it poorly. Like most people, I am not very concerned about insuring Christmas gifts.

Convenience. The post office offers the advantage of more locations. We are 30 minutes from a UPS facility and would have to plan to drop off a package when we are doing other errands. Even so, the facility has an out-of-the-way location.

You can also mail UPS from a "storefront shipper," which is either a mailing business or a service operated by a local hardware or other store. These vendors charge a handling fee per package above the UPS rate. It might cost a few dollars extra, and may be worth it if you live very far from a UPS facility.

UPS will pick up for a $5 fee, and you must pay cash for the shipping charge and pickup. They

charge $5 for the first time they pick up during a given week regardless of the number of packages, and the same $5 entitles you to an unlimited number of pickups during the same week.

If you know someone with an account, such as your employer or a friend with a business, you may be able to ship your personal package from their address without paying an additional pickup charge. The package must have the name and return address of the person the account belongs to. You can put your name inside the package so that the recipient knows it's from you. (I asked UPS point blank, and the service representative said that this was ethical.)

Economy. To compare rates let's set aside the issues of speed, safety, and convenience. And let's presume you don't have to pay a UPS pickup fee or storefront shipper fee.

In general, the heavier the package and the greater the distance, the more you will save by using UPS. The postal service is slightly cheaper when you mail under 2 lbs. UPS costs about the same or less than the post office on weights between 2 and 30 lbs.

Here's the tricky part. The cost savings can vary from only a few cents to many dollars per package. It's hard to make general rules because UPS's rates increase in a straight line, whereas 4th-class rates progress on a curve. Eventually the two rates cross over when you get to the heavier weights of 30 to 40 lbs. The further you mail a package the more exaggerated this curve is, and therefore the greater the cost

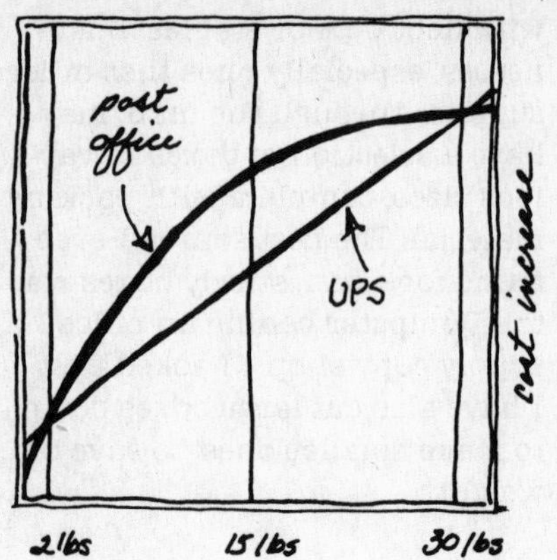

spread. Because of this curve, the UPS savings may be small on very light or very heavy packages, but significant on middle-range packages of 10 to 15 lbs.

But when mailing a package of any weight less than 1,500 miles the cost spread seldom exceeds $1, compared to an approximate $10 UPS savings for mailing a 10-lb package from Maine to California.

I also compared and charted the postal service's priority mail and 4th class. This chart was not without quirks. All the priority mail rates for mailing clear across country (or to what both services call "Zone 8") were only about 5¢ higher than 4th class until you get over 15 lbs. However, when mailing shorter distances the cost spread is far greater—$5 or more in some instances.

Have I lost you yet? The fact that this is so complex demonstrates why no one seems to have figured it out. And there are too many variables to give you cut-and-dried guidelines. Here's my conclusion:

Let your fingers do the walking. Consult the phone book for the UPS 800 number in your part of the country. Find the location of the nearest UPS facility or storefront shipper. Estimate the weight of your package, stand on a scale with and without it, and subtract the difference. Weigh it on a food scale or compare the weight to a 5-lb bag of flour. Call both the post office and UPS facility or storefront shipper for rates based on your weight estimate. Then figure out if the gasoline and hassle of using UPS is worth the savings in your situation.

If you are mailing several packages, a heavy package, or a package across country, it may be worthwhile to use UPS.

As a final note, choosing lightweight gifts is the best way to save on the cost of mailing. Don't do as I did one year . . . I mailed jars of homemade jam and pickles. The cost of the postage exceeded the value of the gifts.

THE TIME AND MONEY CHART

Many people think of their hourly worth in terms of their gross pay and presume that any effort that provides a smaller hourly yield isn't worth their time. On the other end of the spectrum, some people spend all their time doing things that provide very small economic yields (and that they dislike doing), while forgoing activities that save a greater amount of money.

The table on page 102 demonstrates the hourly worth of many tasks Jim and I have done. I often

time how many minutes a job requires to determine how many times I could, in theory, complete the job in an hour. I then calculate how much money a job saves. I multiply the times per hour by the savings per job to determine the hourly value. For example: A 10-minute task saves $2. The task could be done six times an hour. The hourly worth is $12 per hour.

Often the hourly savings appears to be deceptively small. You should also calculate your real hourly worth in the professional world. I could work as a graphic designer if I commuted an hour each way. Factoring in additional dressing and grooming time, dropping kids at a sitter's, the lost lunch hour, commuting and after-work-crash-from-exhaustion time, it really requires 60 hours for a 40-hour work week. I could earn $15 per hour. If I subtract taxes, the cost of child care, wardrobe, and transportation my $15 could become whittled down to $5 per hour. It would require 60 hours to earn $200 . . . or I would earn $3.33 per hour. (Hopefully your hourly rate is not so dismal.)

My chart includes two other columns that rate other reasons why I choose to do an activity.

MONEY-SAVING ACTIVITIES	HOURLY RATE	OTHER VALUES	ENJOY-MENT
Jim can make two cheese pizzas in 20 minutes including clean-up time (and not including rising and baking time). The cost of the homemade pizza is $2. It costs $18 to have two similar pizzas delivered.	$48	3	3
A couple of years ago my father-in-law gave me two bushels of small pears, which I canned with 40 hours of time. We estimate the savings was $40.	$1	4	2
If you change your oil and filter it might save you $7 for 15 minutes' effort including oil disposal at your convenience, as compared to having it done.	$28	1	1
I can hang a load of laundry and take it down in 15 minutes for a savings of 44¢ per load. (The savings increases when hanging heavy, large items.)	$1.76	5	3
It takes me 15 minutes to make two box lunches that cost about 45¢. A school lunch costs 95¢.	$2	3	2
Cloth diapers save about $7 per week when factoring in the cost of laundering. They require an hour of time per week.	$7	4	3
I spent 5 hours making a Halloween costume for my child. I could have purchased a similar one for $10.	$4	5	5
Jim made a 15-minute stop while on the way to do other errands, and bought three cases (72 jars) of sale peanut butter. He saved 60¢ per jar.	$86.40	1	2
I can cut a boy's head of hair in 30 minutes.	$12	3	3
Jim spent 20 hours shopping and negotiating for a new car, and saved $2,000 off the sticker price.	$100	1	4
We make jam from our own rhubarb. We can make 15 jars an hour at a cost of 40¢ per jar, or a savings of at least $1 per jar.	$15	4	4
It takes 5 seconds to save a clean but used piece of aluminum foil. (Yes, we actually timed this.) A 1′ square of the store brand costs 2½¢.	$18	3	3
I could go to work as a graphic designer.	$3.33	1	1

"Other Values" might show that I do something because it is environmentally sound or healthier. I also do some things because I can combine the savings effort with family time. Kids learn from watching parents do-it-themselves, even if they are only passively involved.

The "Enjoyment" column rates how much personal satisfaction I derive from an activity. I am constantly amazed to discover that some people despise the very things I enjoy doing.

In the case of both these columns the higher the number the more I enjoy or feel I get other values from the activity. I also rated the enjoyment and value that I personally get from doing graphic design. Others, especially those in service professions, would rate their jobs much higher.

The purpose of having such a chart, if only mentally, is to help you decide which tasks to drop when your schedule fills up. Consider the hourly rate, the enjoyment factor, and other values that the task brings.

Everyone needs a source of income, but we also need a way to gauge if we should work additional hours away from home. People who work outside the home frequently forgo ways to save, which have higher economic yields, because they lack time.

If you have some financial flexibility you can choose an enjoyable task with a small financial yield. If both time and money are in short supply you might have to stick with tasks with the highest hourly yields, even if they provide little enjoyment. But there are so many ways to save money you should not have to do tasks that provide a small hourly yield, offer little enjoyment, and satisfy no other values.

Because we all possess different abilities, resources, likes, and values, no two tightwads would fill out this chart the same way. There is no "right way" to be a tightwad.

TIME SAVERS

You know you're tired when you're washing the pizza pan, and the last slice of pizza floats to the top of the dishwater. Or when you're putting a sleeper on a baby and for some reason the sleeves don't have holes for the hands, but the sleeper legs have holes for the feet.

I have redefined the concept of "no time"... which has not gone unnoticed by the readers. My most commonly requested article is "How *do* You Do It All?" Well . . .

1. I don't do anything as well as we would like.

2. I don't do it all. Jim has retired from the Navy and now runs our household full time.

However, so's not to disappoint those who wanted some ideas . . . here are some ideas that I use during crisis times.

Housework Division. Some types of housework are a form of organization, whereas some things are cleaning only. During my busiest of times I keep up with organizational tasks, but let the cleaning slide.

The most important organizational tasks are washing dishes and washing laundry. I place a priority on keeping up with these two things because they create a loss of time if I get behind. Dirty dishes take up space on the counter and make food preparation more time consuming. If I don't keep up with laundry I lose time "hunting for matched socks." In addition, these types of tasks accumulate if I don't keep up with them.

Tasks that are cleaning only tend to not accumulate. Vacuuming takes the same amount of time regardless of whether I do it every day or once a week. The work in washing windows is about getting out ladders and buckets.

But if I postpone dishes it's just going to require more time when I finally wash them. So to save time I try to do the noncumulative cleaning less frequently.

I like things to be clean, but it's not important to survival when I'm busiest.

The Container Principle. Use the container method to quick clean your home. Items in a loose pile are mess. Items in a container are neat. Dirty dishes on the counter are messy. Dirty dishes stacked in the sink are neat (or neater). Laundry on the floor is a mess. Laundry in a basket is neat. Miscellaneous junk in view is a mess. Miscellaneous junk in a junk drawer is neat.

I use two variations of this basic idea:

Use "intermediate containers" for temporary storage. You can sort them later when you have more time. For example, we have three kitchen junk drawers: the paper drawer, the tool drawer, and the real junk drawer. I can put things in these drawers to clean the kitchen quickly. Once every several months I might

clean out the paper drawer, throwing away or filing as needed. I have a basket in the living room to store kids' toys, shoes, books, etc. The first kid who wants to watch TV has to put the stuff away.

Use a "roving container" when the entire house is a mess with all types of things out of place. You have a laundry basket and a preplanned route in which you hit every room in your house without doubling your tracks. As you follow the route pick up the things that are out of place and drop them off in the appropriate place. By the time you complete the route twice, everything will be back in place.

Equipment Investment. Most folks opt for time savers that provide a onetime benefit. TV dinners. Disposable diapers. Hiring a kid to mow the lawn. A long-distance call. The money is lost after a single use. To maintain the same level of free time they must continue to buy single-use time savers.

Equipment or tools represent money invested in permanent time savers. In a rural area there is a long list of necessary tools. We have had to acquire many (a computer, a garden tractor, a weed whacker, a utility trailer, a table saw), all of which were purchased used or at extremely good sale prices. We did not do this so we could watch TV, but rather so that we could sleep.

However, the wise purchase of tools does not include buying a Shopsmith, making one bookcase, and letting it gather dust in your garage.

The Federal Express System. The guy that conceived Federal Express got the idea while a student in business school. If I remember correctly his paper got a failing grade. He persisted, and now several companies have copied his idea. Basically he saw that the postal service was inefficient in its method of delivery. He thought it would be quicker to take all packages to a central location to sort and send on to their destinations. Even when a package has to go only a few miles from origination to destination, it still goes through the central sorting location thousands of miles away. In the scheme of the big picture this is more efficient.

I have applied this idea to picking up children's rooms. All the dumped toys are swept to a central pile. I surround the pile with the various containers, and sort. Toys with further destinations are all taken at once. I have tried in vain to teach this idea to my children but they persist with the postal service method.

Mass-Production. It is more efficient to repeat the same action several times rather than doing many individual tasks at random. In practical application I do things like make double and triple batches. I stand the kids in a line to comb hair and wash faces. When I read them a book everyone must be present. I mass-produce Christmas presents when I hit upon an idea that nearly everyone would like. I write a very good general family letter, reproduce it, and include a short personal note. Canning is a good example of this principle. In a day a year's supply of spaghetti

sauce can be canned. This is more efficient than making from scratch every Wednesday night, and cheaper than store bought.

Employee Training. The best companies distinguish themselves by teaching their workers new skills. Even though this takes away from short-term productivity, in the long run it is more profitable. In the same way, you need to take the time to learn new skills. I know many women, who have been married for years, that claim they can't bake anything. Silly. They could learn to whip up a batch of muffins faster then a drive to the convenience store. I learned computer basics so that I could produce my newsletter quicker. Learning new skills often seems overwhelming. It is important to shut down production for a period, study, regroup, and then start up again.

SWAP SHOP

Dear Amy,

We have a large extended family and a family newsletter that goes out quarterly. "The 1st Annual Shryock Swap Shop" is an itemized list of all treasures taking up space in attics, garages, barns, sheds, and cabinets published for giveaway, trade, nominal fee, or Christmas gifts. I have wanted to do this for a long time. It wasn't until I read *The Tightwad Gazette* that I finally motivated myself to do it.

Bernadette Barber
Lusby, Maryland

TIN PUNCH

Dear Amy,

It cost my husband and me a measly $6 to install our look-alike "tin" punch cabinets. Newspapers discard the large aluminum sheets (known as "plates") they use for printing purposes. They are printed on one side and blank on the other. We bought a nice stack for $6, enough for a very large kitchen.

After a quick cleanup in the tub to remove excess printer's ink, we cut the metal with tin snips down to a size that would fit our kitchen cabinets. A crayon rubbing of our sister-in-law's pie safe provided us with an authentic antique design. We traced this to a sheet of paper and taped the paper to the metal panels, blank side up.

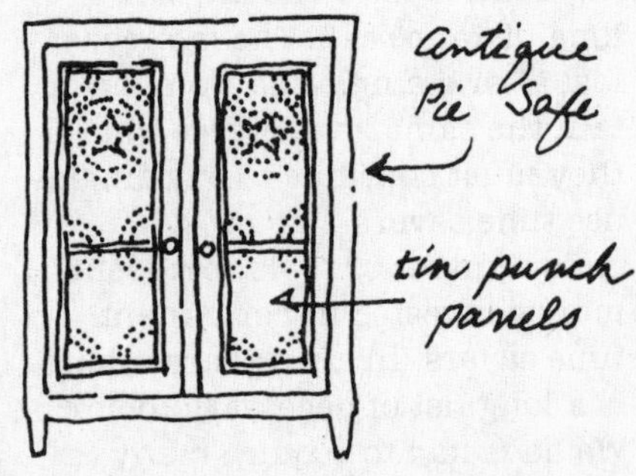

With a hammer and nail, and a piece of wood underneath for protection, we hammered the design, right through the paper, dot by dot.

Denise Lohr-Stuckey
Beech Grove, Indiana

TIPS FOR BETTER GIFT GIVING

The flip side of the gift-giving question is the stress surrounding gift receiving. At one time or another most of us have had that sickening feeling of receiving things we don't want.

Gift giving is fun, and I am not going to suggest that we do without it. But aside from spending beyond our means, the biggest financial mistake we make is spending badly. So I am going to say for you all what you want to say to others, but don't have the nerve to. The following are a number of random thoughts based on the feelings expressed by readers and friends. There are always exceptions to these suggestions.

Christmas gifts do not have to be a surprise. Most people would forgo the surprise element to assure that they will receive things they will genuinely appreciate. So if you are not sure your gift idea will be appreciated ask the recipient in advance. Give them that opportunity to decline. Or ask the recipient to make a list for you.

If you don't know what to give, select an expendable gift—things such as food items, postage stamps, stationery, film, and gift certificates are always winners. These are especially good for elderly people, or people with limited space.

Replace an item that is worn-out. If the recipient has a worn-out widget, chances are they want a widget in their home, but haven't gotten around to replacing their old one. Examples of things to replace include worn towels, an old wallet, holey socks, appliances that are acting up, etc.

Avoid gifts that decorate people's homes for them, especially gifts that demand to be located in a prominent part of the home. Exceptions may include family photos and holiday decorations. One reader tells me: "I look around my house and everything I see that I don't like was given to me." It is not a matter of the thing being in poor taste but that the recipient would not have chosen it for his own home. This category would also include large appliances. If uncertain, ask!

Consider giving modestly to the only child. These kids frequently become the entire holiday focus of a host of relatives, who swamp them with gifts. The parents have the chore of dealing with a temperamental overwhelmed child and a mountain of gifts they have no room to store. Consult the parents as to what and how much they feel might be appropriate for their child.

If you are purchasing for a young relative ask for suggestions so you can target a void. "He has 14 good shirts but really needs pajamas." Children often have toys that can be added on to

. . . a few more tracks for the train set, or a set of Barbie clothes.

New presents appropriate for almost any child include art or "office" supplies. I like multipiece toys such as Tinker Toys and Legos, which have provided more entertainment than any other present my children received. If the child already has these, then "more is better." Choose durable toys, as any mother can testify to throwing away bushels of broken ones. Do not buy battery-operated toys for younger children, as they tend to lose the batteries.

Give the recipient money to go toward a specific item that you do not feel knowledgeable enough to pick for them. One woman received a sewing machine. Although she wanted one, the model she received was too complex for her needs. Jim likes to fish, but I don't know enough about this hobby to buy for him. Instead I give him "permission" to buy. One year I taped a drafting compass to a toy boat, and wrapped it. After scratching his head a few minutes Jim deduced that I was granting him permission to purchase a boat compass.

Give people presents that complete part of a set of something people already have. The most obvious example includes buying pieces to go with the recipient's open-stock china.

Avoid the "domino principle" in gift giving. I look good in pink. Because I had a couple of pink shirts people kept giving me pink shirts, often exactly the same style as the pink shirts I already have. Now I receive pink shirts with a note of explanation: "I saw this and thought it looked just like you."

Often giving the same gift to someone year after year, regardless of the cost, will not be successful. Wouldn't it be dull if everyone gave everyone the same gift every year? Even a little variation from your theme will take the edge off predictability.

Under certain circumstances giving used gifts can be appropriate . . . usually when you are giving to another tightwad who knows and appreciates the value of used items. This sort of activity could include the swap of an interesting puzzle (which you would only use one time anyway), a great sweater the style and condition fitting a Cosby (or Huxtable), a book, or a tool your spouse has had his eye on. In all cases the gift should be very special, uniquely appropriate for the recipient, and given to someone who will admire your resourcefulness, rather than think you are merely cheap. You could make it a family sport to see who can find the best used stuff for Christmas.

Offer the recipient a service. You might offer a winter's worth of snow shoveling to an elderly person, or offer a night's babysitting to parents of young children. If you possess a specific skill offer that.

I love joke presents. They are cheap and entertaining.

I went to my uncle's first year wedding anniversary party. Being cheap as I am, and unsure if a gift was appropriate, I opted for a joke present. Previously I had found large rusty railroad square nuts while collecting aluminum cans. I bought two candles and matching paper napkins. Voila! I had a gift of matching candleholders and napkin rings. I wrapped the box in newspaper and spray painted it silver. I made a ribbon and bow of plastic wrap creating an iridescent elegant look.

When my uncle and his wife started to open the package they repeatedly gushed, "You really shouldn't have," and I repeatedly assured them, "It was really nothing." The wrapping and gift made us all laugh until we cried.

Make homemade gifts. Erma Bombeck tells of the Christmas when everyone decided to give only homemade presents. It was a disaster and they never tried it again. I think they started too big and gave up too soon.

A well-made and creative homemade gift has more value than a comparable store bought present. I try to settle on one idea that many people will like and then mass-produce.

Unfortunately some families do not appreciate these and regard them as cheap and inferior. If you are dealing with this, make their conversion your special mission and expect the process to take several years.

Gifts should be selected based on needs, internally generated desires and consistent with budgets. The fact that an advertiser has created a desire in your child by showing him a product scores of times does not mean you must succumb. During the holiday season, we are bombarded with ads for Isotoner gloves, Clappers, and Chia Pets. Consider avoiding these like the plague.

THE CASE OF THE LIGHTS LEFT ON

The computer hummed but the blank blue screen gave evidence of a silent keyboard. I stared through the window, focusing on the pale green lichen on a small sapling in the wooded area beyond. But my brain scanned the far corners of my consciousness for an idea to fill an empty page of *The Tightwad Gazette.*

The newsletter serves as a mere bread-and-butter sideline of a larger enterprise—FZ Private Investigation. Or F.Z.P.I. for short.

The phone rang, jolting me back into the present. I reached for the nearby almond-colored receiver, but paused before its smooth coolness filled my hand. With a stern drill sergeant tone I barked a command in the direction of nearby toddler mayhem. "OK, you guys, listen up, anyone makes a peep while I'm on the phone and you're in *big trouble.* Got it?" Instant silence.

I picked up the receiver on the third ring and answered in a calmer professional voice, "FZ Private Investigations."

"Frugal Zealot, Frugal Zealot!

I'm desperate; you gotta help me."

I recognized the frantic voice as belonging to a local subscriber. "Yes, Zelda, what can I do for you?"

"It's my husband . . . I . . . we've been arguing. It's driving us apart."

I broke in. "Hold on. This sounds like a job for a marriage counselor. I'm not qualified—"

"But," Zelda continued, "this *is* a job for FZ. It's about saving money. My husband, Zebulon, and I have been having this argument about the electric bill and we can't agree."

"What seems to be the problem?"

"Can you tell us if it's cheaper to turn out the lights if you leave the room, or to leave them on? Some people say that if you are

coming back in a few minutes it's cheaper just to leave them on."

"Wow, I never heard that one. I'll have to make an inquiry with my energy consultant and get back to you." I felt guilty. I knew she wanted some kind of answer now, so I offered what I could. "Zelda, I can tell you that the problem is not as big as it seems. Lighting makes up a small portion of our electric bill. Do you know that it costs less than a penny to operate a 100-watt bulb for an hour? Here in Maine we pay 9 cents per kilowatt-hour. A kilowatt-hour is 1,000 watts of electricity per hour."

"Is that all?" Zelda exclaimed incredulously.

"Of course most of us don't use 100-watt bulbs, we use 60 or 75 watts, which cost even less. All those bits of pennies do add up, but not compared to other appliances like the dryer and water heater. Your dryer, for instance, uses 4,500 watts, so it costs about 44¢ per hour to run. It makes more sense to hang laundry instead of flicking lights on and off."

"Huh! That's pretty interesting, but could you still find out about turning the lights off when you leave the room for less than half an hour?" Zelda asked.

"Right, FZ Private Investigations is on the case. I'll call as soon as I learn anything." The receiver clicked back into position, signaling the resumption of toddler mayhem.

Two hours later my energy consultant arrived home from work. As he crossed the threshold I summoned him into the corporate headquarters. "Hey, guess what? FZ Private Investigations has a case you can help with. It has to do with electricity." As an interior communication specialist with the Navy for more than 20 years, Jim's qualifications were beyond dispute. I related the conversation I had with Zelda.

I knew the answer was not simple when he pulled up a thrift shop office chair. "Actually, it can be true that it's cheaper to leave the lights on if you are coming back within a few minutes."

"That doesn't make sense."

Jim continued, "Turning bulbs on and off wears them out. Since compact fluorescents are the most expensive type to replace, when leaving the room for less than half an hour, you should leave them on. When leaving for less than 15 minutes, leave tube fluorescents on, and when leaving for less than 5 minutes, leave incandescents on."

I was amazed at having been a tightwad so long without knowing this. I asked him, "Would you mind starting supper? I've got a marriage to save."

In rapid fashion I punched Zelda's number on the Touch-tone dial of the nearby almond-colored receiver, its smooth coolness again filling my hand. Zebulon answered. When he informed me that Zelda was out I related what I learned to him instead. As I spoke he finished all my sentences. Using my keen detective acumen I deduced which side of the argument he had taken.

Epilogue: Thanks to FZ Private Investigations, six months later Zelda and Zebulon remain happily married, no longer arguing about lighting. Their two sons, Zeke and Zeus, thrive in the contented bicker-free home life.

This story is based on events that actually occurred. The names have been changed to protect those who had no intention of becoming subject matter for *The Tightwad Gazette*. Some events have been changed or amplified for the purposes of clarity and enhanced humor.

FAST-FOOD COMBAT

Dear Amy,

Do you, or any of your readers, have strategies to combat "after game" stops to McDonald's and other fast-food joints? My 14-year-old daughter is involved in band and chorus. Many times she has gone with these groups to play or sing in various performances. She also runs cross-country, which means she meets away from school. Inevitably there is always a stop for supper or lunch. At times I feel like everytime I'm turning around, I'm handing her money for a meal. It adds up after a while. Has anyone you know of come up with a workable solution?

Kathy Closson
Wiscasset, Maine

In response to this letter I asked for help from readers. Suggestions came from parents, the wife of a coach, a bus driver, a 13-year-old boy, and many people who used to be teenagers. They suggested:

1. "Have her earn all or part of the money." (5 votes)

2. "Talk with other parents and adults who coordinate activities for a cooperative solution." (4 votes)

3. "Give her an allowance to cover expenses and have her budget." (4 votes)

4. "Suggest she brown-bag it." (3 votes)

5. "Educate her about the costs and health issues." (2 votes)

6. "Cut back on school activities." (1 vote)

Parents want the best for their children . . . and sometimes they forget that adults have rights, too. After-school activities can require large amounts of chauffeur time, as well as expense. It may be worthwhile to figure out how much time the parents are giving, as well as money. Add up the monthly outlay of cash toward meals and calculate how many hours the parents are working to pay for the fast-food meals per month.

Second, it's hard to ask teens to earn some of the money to pay for the meals when they're busy with so many activities. I would suggest the daughter give up one activity and spend the free time doing extra chores, or an outside job. Fair is fair. If the teen wants Mom to give of her time and money there should be some equitable exchange. I do this all the time in the form of you-help-me-with-the-dishes-and-then-I'll-play-cards-with-you.

Some of the suggestions for parent cooperation were quite interesting. Peer pressure is fueled by the fact that parents tend to be too busy to get to know other parents. We don't want our kid to be the odd one out. But whenever I'm experiencing similar concerns I talk to other parents and learn my views are shared. It's just that there is no organized effort to bring about a change. And remember, there's no shame about admitting to your children or to other parents that you have budget constraints.

A school bus driver from Columbus, Ohio, wrote that they coordinate with a few other parents to make sandwiches, bring drinks, fruit, etc. Each child brings $1. If the groups are close to home Kate Lott of St. Louis, Missouri, suggests bringing them home.

Bonnie Click of Tucson, Arizona, suggests that you sit down with your kids and plan out all their financial needs for the year. Include clothing, shoes, entertainment, sports, and equipment fees, etc. Also include an untouchable 10% for savings, and another untouchable 10% for church giving, if that's part of your family values. Get their input and settle on something reasonable. The parent puts in 90% and the kids are expected to earn the other 10% (or whatever ratio you decide upon). Divide the money into 12 envelopes, one for each month. Teach them how to budget, and then stand firm and don't lend them a dime. "It's amazing, absolutely amazing, how unattractive their previously high-demand food can become when they have to pay for it."

As a final note about peer pressure, I must be out of touch. Seems to me that we ask our children to learn many hard lessons in life so that they will be fully equipped to deal with the adult world. For some reason we don't ask them to learn that it's OK to be different. Wouldn't it be a great victory if our children learned they could be different from their friends and still be liked?

THE CHEAPSKATE POSTAL SCALE

We've been hitting the used bookstores for books on saving money. I picked up a copy of *All-New*

Hints from Heloise. I cruised through it in rapid fashion and came upon one new idea that tickled me.

If you don't have a postal scale how do you make sure your letter is under one ounce? You need a 12" ruler, a pencil, and five quarters. Put the ruler on the pencil so that it is centered over the 6" mark, or in the center. Place the quarters (which weigh 1 oz) on the 3" mark. Center your sealed envelope on the 9" mark. (The 3" and 9" marks are the same distance from the ends of the ruler.) If the quarters don't move you know your letter is under 1 oz.

Aside from the fact that I think this is a very clever and astonishingly simple idea, it propelled me to further thought. The appeal of this postal scale idea is that it's made up of simple household items, that have another use. When you are finished, the pencil goes back in the cup, the ruler goes back in the drawer, and the quarters are returned to your pocket. You don't have an extra gadget on your desk taking up space.

I wondered what other gadgets do we think we need that could be conveniently replaced with simple household items? Since living in a small space is a great way to save on the cost of housing, learning to live with less stuff is crucial.

CHEAPSKATE WRAPPING

It's not that tightwads can't afford wrapping paper, but rather the thrill and the challenge to see how many years we can go without actually *buying* it. Five years have passed since our last purchase of a K mart special. Our success results from employing a variety of strategies.

Reusing Wrapping Paper. This idea must be as old as Christmas. We try to give smaller presents than our relatives give us, since clearly old paper must be cut down with every use. (If your relatives are also tightwads you'll be exchanging tie tacks and thimbles within five years.) Be creative and put a bow where old tape left a hole smack in the middle of an otherwise

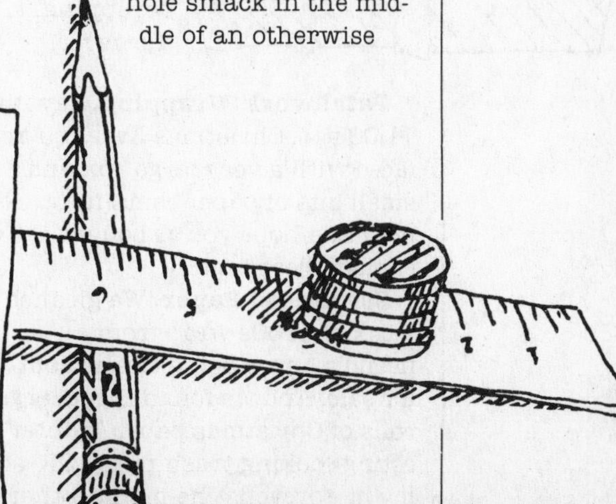

perfectly good chunk, or plan your ribbon placement to hide the old fold. Consider taping matching pieces together to make a larger sheet. Cover the seam with ribbon.

Alternative Wrapping. This includes comics from the Sunday paper, shelf paper, the paper from a bouquet of cut flowers, a piece of red-checkered paper tablecloth such as the type used for church dinners (we have a roll that came with the house), wallpaper, old maps, or the paper or plastic from a colored department store bag.

Tightwad Wrapping. This is when you capitalize on your reputation and use paper that is clearly old and very mangy. Or use common household materials like newspaper, duct tape, bailing twine, garbage bags, oatmeal cartons, etc. Plastic wrap pulled taut or twisted makes great ribbon. Do not use this for the actual wrapping, however.

Patchwork Wrapping. Say it's 11:00 P.M., Christmas Eve. You are faced with a very large box and small bits of paper remaining. Get busy and hope you've bought enough clear tape.

Scrounged Paper. We gleaned a box of 1960s wrap from a friend's house being cleaned out for sale. And we found three large rolls of Christmas paper in interesting-looking trash piles (OK, so my motorcyclist he-man brother-in-law wasn't thrilled about the Strawberry Shortcake paper.)

Angle Wrapping. As far as I know I invented this. It takes a bit of practice and doesn't look as good but uses far less paper. Instead of placing a box square on a sheet of paper place it on an angle. Fold sides of paper up one at a time. Practice with newspaper first.

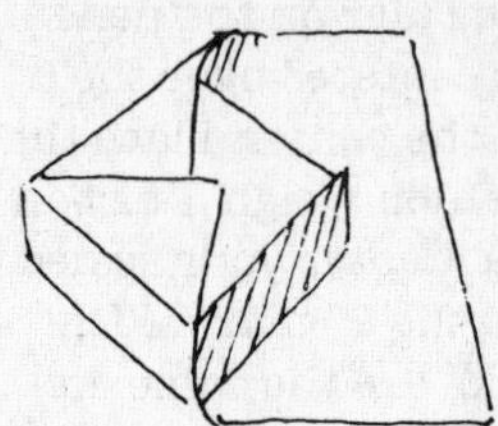

Permanent Wrapping. If you can imagine a Christmas tradition without frantic and wild tearing of paper, consider permanent wrapping solutions.

Make drawstring sacks that can be used from year to year. When wrapping a box use a larger square of fabric or a scarf from the thrift shop.

If you have the storage space you can also make present boxes —boxes with removable tops that are permanently decorated with paper or fabric.

Be resourceful in your acquisition of fabric. Use pinking shears to cut squares out of a dated garment. An old prom dress might be hopelessly out of fashion, but may yield several nice squares of fabric. The final hour of rummage sales often features one bag of clothes for $1. Try to pick articles that you can't imagine anyone would be caught dead wearing . . . but also have new-looking decorative or shiny material. Something that is too gaudy to wear might make great wrapping.

Use permanent methods for ribbon alternatives as well. This might include rickrack, gold

braid, strips of fabric cut with pinking shears, or elastic ties.

I read of one family that discovered other advantages to permanent wrapping solutions. The children enjoyed hauling their loot in the sacks and enjoyed replaying Christmas by reopening their sacks over and over. In addition, the living room did not have the usual litter of discarded wrapping paper.

As the tradition in this family continued from year to year, family members devised new usable gift containers. Some were appliquéd, embroidered, handwoven, or quilted. Someone even made a cedar box with the recipient's name woodburned on it. In their family the recipient's name and year are permanently marked on the wrapping, creating a family history after years of use.

Very large presents can be "wrapped in a closet" or other hiding place. Make a string trail or trail of paper clues.

Homemade Wrapping. I mention this last on purpose. Making wrapping paper is time consuming, and it also requires having a cheap source of large sheets of paper. Brown paper is commonly used. I have ironed out large sheets of packing paper left over from our move.

In addition, you need to have an easy way to make some type of repeat pattern. A shape cut into an art gum eraser makes a rubber stamp. You can make stencils from thin cardboard, like a margarine carton. Use crayon to feather in the design.

Or leave the paper plain and concentrate on decorating it with cut paper (such as snowflakes) or torn paper (to make a contemporary pattern). Adhere with white glue.

Marbled paper can be made by ironing crayon shavings between a piece of paper and a piece of wax paper. Instead of using tape seal the wrap with a warm iron.

Ribbons and Ties. Last year's ribbon can be gently ironed to look fresh again. If you have a variety of short pieces create a weave look as shown below, taping the underside.

One reader suggests one can macrame yarn and cheap ribbon into ribbon to wrap presents. Also cut fabric into strips to make ribbon.

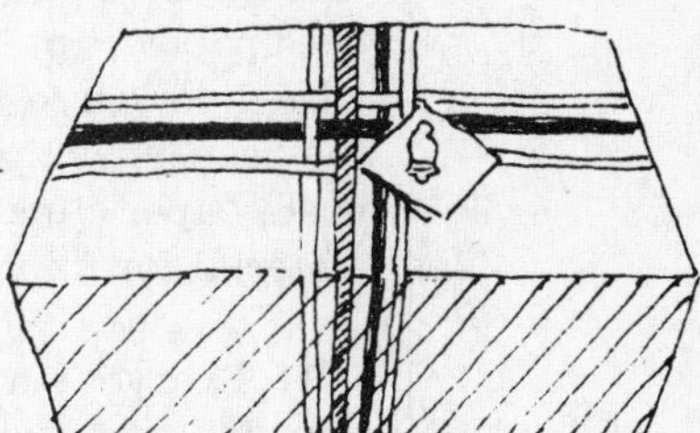

BEST ADDRESS

Jim and I are frequently amused by the variation of ways people address mail to us. Generally they either do not know how to spell "tightwad" or "gazette." Sometimes they write to the *Cheapskate Gazette* or *Penny Pincher Gazette.*

After a local television news spot, we received a postcard requesting information addressed in the following manner:

To That Woman Who Was on Channel 6 News, a "Gazette" About Cost-Cutting. Don't Know Her Name Nor the Gazette's Name . . . but Thank You. Leeds, Maine 04263

Bob White
Litchfield, Maine

PAPER CLIPPERY

Recently I repaired the rim of our laundry basket with paper-clip wire faster than I could have gone through a department store checkout line (which isn't saying a lot). As I "drilled" holes on either side of the break with the tip of an X-Acto blade and threaded through straightened paper-clip wire, I pondered the properties that make paper clips likely material for fix-it projects:

1. Everyone has more paper clips kicking around than things in need of clipping together.
2. They bend easily.
3. In a semi-unbent state the natural hook shape offers several possibilities.
4. Fully unbent, paper-clip wire has a handy length.

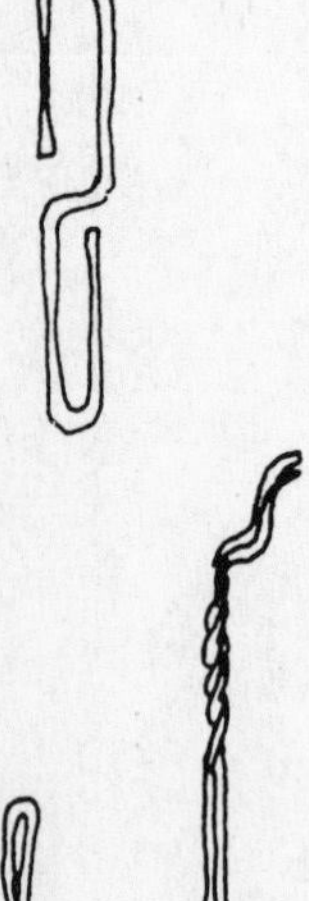

And I wondered how many repairable items had been thrown away for lack of a paper clip and a little resourcefulness.

For example, when I dropped my Dustbuster the plastic broke above the "catch" so that the cover and handle would no longer hold together, making the Dustbuster unusable. I repaired the Dustbuster in a manner similar to the way I repaired my laundry basket.

One of my staff has used a paper-clip hook in place of a drapery hook. I have used paper-clip hooks to hang Christmas stockings. A sturdier hook, such as one that might be used for a pegboard, can be fashioned by doubling and twisting the wire from a large paper clip.

Jim keeps our three electric staplers working with paper clips. The cotter pins break and he makes new ones from paper clips.

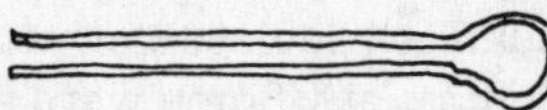

The chain in a friend's toilet tank broke. He replaced it with a paper-clip chain. He found they worked well because he could adjust the length of the chain as needed. Because paper clips rust he will have to replace his chain in time. (A new toilet chain costs about $12). Or a paper-clip chain could replace a missing chain on a tea ball.

Paper clips in combination with rubber bands can be handy. You can make a miniature bungee cord with a fat rubber band and two paper clips. (As with real bungee cords, any hook attached to a snapping piece of elastic presents obvious dangers. Use with caution.)

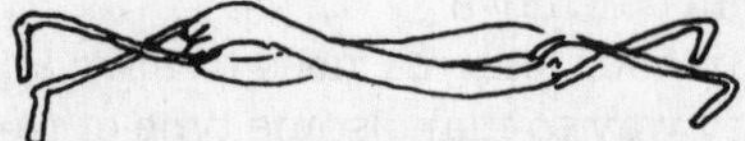

You can replace the broken elastic on a child's Halloween mask with looped-together rubberbands and two paper clips.

You can use a small piece of paper-clip wire to temporarily fix the broken hinge

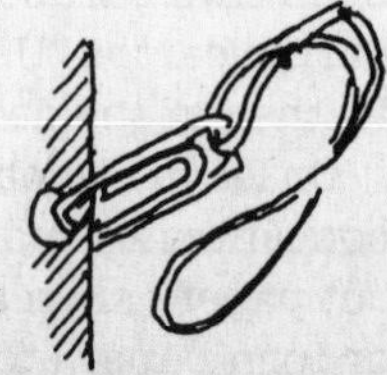

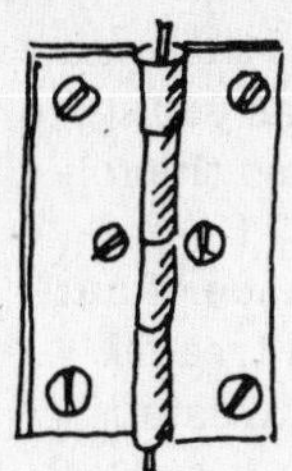

on a pair of glasses. Bend in such a way so there are no sharp ends sticking out.

If you have a small hinge with a pin, you can replace a broken or lost pin with a piece of paper-clip wire.

My grandmother gave me a fluted copper plate that I wanted to hang on the wall. I used two miniature bungee cords and a paper-clip hook. You might not

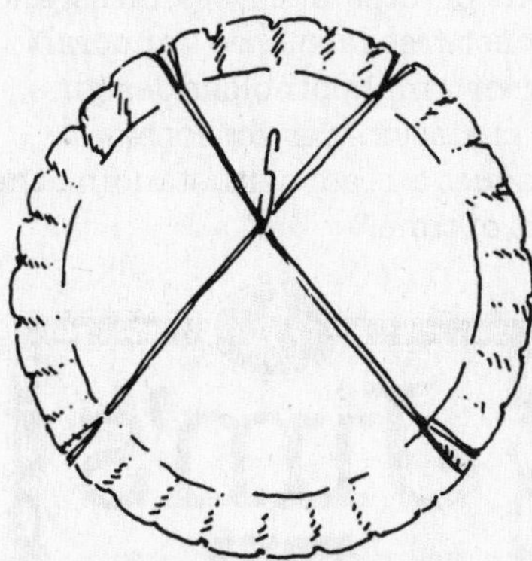

want to hang a $40 antique plate in this way, but the traction of the rubber band seems to make this more secure than the spring-type plate hangers.

Yes, the scope of possibilities of paper clippery is endless. I've always said you can fix just about anything with a paper clip, a hanger, twist tie, rubber bands and/or duct tape.

BEST FEEDBACK

Dear Amy,

You are doing a wonderful job. You have helped me decide that I can retire at the earliest opportunity and do what I think is necessary without regard to loss of marginal income.

Ron Fisher
Dixon, California

CHEAPER CHECKS

You can save money on the cost of printing checks if you order them by mail.

When you buy directly from a bank or savings institution, 200 plain ones can cost as much as $15.76—more for the fancy ones.

Checks printed by independent companies cost 40% to 65% less.

The article suggests two companies. Current Inc., a mail-order greeting card company in Colorado Springs, Colorado (800-426-0822), has a special introductory offer of 200 checks for $6.95 plus 70¢ shipping and handling.

The second company is Checks in the Mail, Irwin, California (800-733-4443). Its introductory offer is $4.95 for 200 checks.

Both companies offer wallet-type checks and a selection of a dozen or so designs. Current Inc. requests a check reorder form from your bank checks, a deposit slip, and a payment check. Each order takes about four weeks.

Advice for Seniors. Many banks offer free checking and checks with no minimum balance for seniors. Ask; they might not volunteer the information.

TAG IT

To enhance an otherwise ordinary homemade gift, I make an interesting or amusing tag to dress it up.

Since these tags are for mass produced presents, cheap reproduction is the first objective. Any black-and-white image can be produced well on a quality copy machine. You can paste up art and type, photocopy, white-out cut marks, and photocopy again for a clean copy. Combine hand lettering, typewriter type, any black-and-white printed drawing, original drawings, or left over press type.

If you have a computer with graphics capability, this will also produce a good tag. A few of my relatives without formal training are producing their own tags, labels, and cards with very respectable results.

Don't worry if your tags are not very professional looking. The most important element in any design is a good idea. I have a problem in that my tags can look so professional that recipients do not realize they are homemade. I have learned to customize (put their name or mine on it) or to not be too neat.

The Blue Jean
Potholder

One year I made very successful potholders out of scrap blue jean material topstitched with gold thread. I cut up an old torn quilted cowboy blanket that had been Jim's since he was young, to use as a filler. I included the following tag.

"Our products are made of naturally seasoned denim treated with an unpatented multistep process.

"First sewn into pants and worn by actual human beings, the material is exposed to sweat, grime, sunlight, and hundreds of washes to achieve an authentic fade and uniquely comfortable feel. Then using only select portions of unpatched, seamless, and pocket-free fabric we handcraft our original potholder design.

"THE BLUE JEAN POTHOLDER, a product already withstanding the test of time."

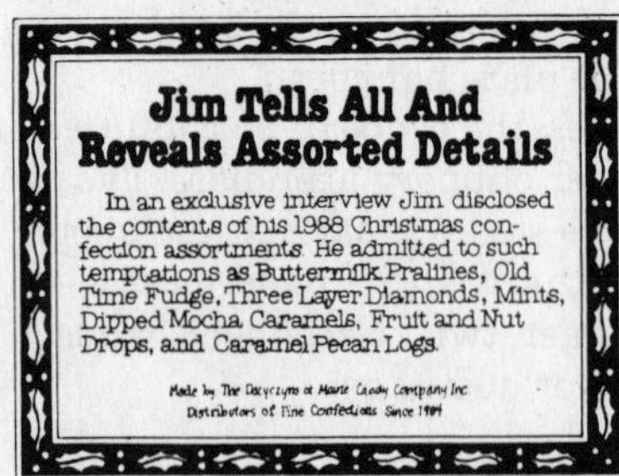

Jim has made candy for Christmas for the past few years. The acquisition of tins becomes the most expensive element of this gift. Three years ago we purchased plain red tins on sale in January and saved them for the

"HOW DO YOU MAKE BLUE JEAN POTHOLDERS?"

Following my mention of making potholders from blue jean material, readers asked for a set of instructions. They can be made in any shape, but mine were octagonal.

Choose clean unworn sections of old jeans. You will need four 8″ pieces to make two potholders. If cutting from more than one pair of jeans be sure they match in color and type of denim.

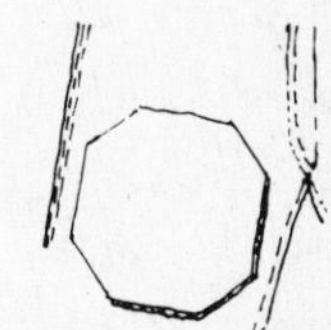

Make a cardboard stencil the shape and size you want your potholder to be. Using a ballpoint pen trace the stencil on the reverse side of two pieces of jean material. Cut ½″ outside the line.

Pin a marked piece to an unmarked piece, right sides together. Stitch pieces on the ink line, leaving an opening of about 2″. Trim excess close to the stitch line.

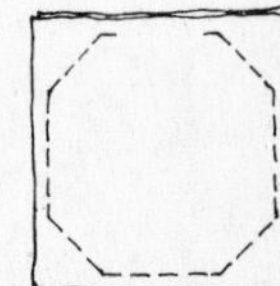

Turn inside out. Use a blunt but pointed object to make good corners. Iron flat.

Use your stencil and draw your shape on a piece of filler. Cut about ¼″ to the inside of the line. The filler can be of a variety of reused materials you have on hand, such as an old mattress pad, old flannel blankets, etc. Roll filler and insert into opening of potholder.

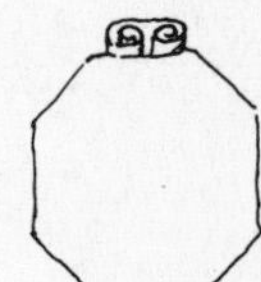

To make a loop cut a piece 5″ × 1½″. Fold in half the long way, wrong sides together, and iron flat.

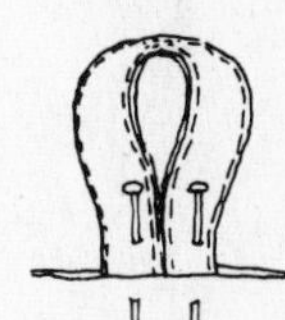

Top stitch 1/16″ away from the folded edge. Turn raw edge under to make a 7/16″-wide strip and topstitch 1/16″ away from the other edge. To save time make longer strips and cut down as needed.

Insert loop ends into potholder opening as shown so that the same side of each end faces forward. Pin securely into position.

Using gold-colored thread topstich the potholder about 1/16″ away from the edge. Topstitch a second time 5/16″ (a tad larger than ¼″) away from the first stitching. I used the edge of my presser foot as a guide.

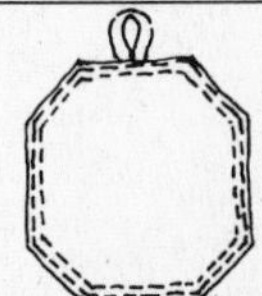

Using ballpoint pen, draw a light line from point to point of octagon as shown. Draw a second line 5/16″ to the inside of the first. Topstitch on top of drawn lines.

I finished my potholders with an amusing gold colored tag.

following year. I made these (front and back) labels to glue on to the tins.

He produces six to eight varieties and mixes them to make an assortment.

We keep a few extras on hand for a spur-of-the-moment gift, but most go to tough-to-buy-for relatives.

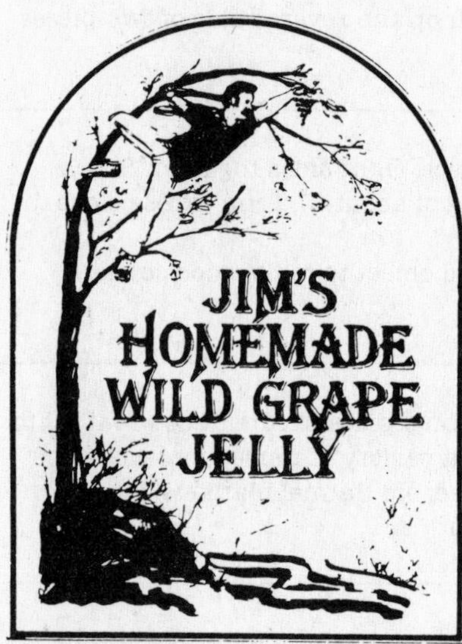

This tag was included on a jar of homemade jelly. The inside copy is a slightly overblown version of real events.

THE "JIM'S HOMEMADE WILD GRAPE JELLY" STORY

In September of 1986, while visiting the estate of his parents in Montague, Massachusetts, James Dacyczyn noted the pungent aroma of wild grapes in the wind. He remarked of it to his wife of nearly four years. Amy, a woman of enterprising character (and slightly pregnant condition) proposed a quest to harvest the fruit.

After careful preparation they entered the wood with bucket in hand. The terrain had grown fierce since his youth. Brambles, briars, swamps, and swarms of mosquitoes lay between the couple and their goal. Scratched, bitten, and muddied they finally came upon the grapes growing high atop slender saplings on an embankment that dropped sharply to the raging waters of the Sawmill River (1 foot deep and 10 feet wide).

Having come so far and braved such dangers James's determination was not lessened as he climbed the sapling to the upper branches to where the vines grew. Hanging far over the river he filled his bucket with the wild and elusive fruit. With each movement the sound of wild grapes could be heard plunking into the water 30 feet below.

To ensure maximum flavor the grapes were rushed to the kitchen of James's mother where they were transformed into the first jars of "Jim's Homemade Wild Grape Jelly."

HOMEMADE PANCAKE SYRUP

Three readers submitted recipes for homemade pancake syrup. We tested them all and priced them out. The most economical was one sent in by a nonsubscriber. It yielded 3¾ cups (30 oz) for 79¢. All recipes submitted tasted far better than the generic stuff we have been using. (Even the kids noticed.)

For the Maine readers . . . we purchased our maple extract at Meyer's Country Cupboard in Greene. It cost $2 for 8 oz, which is better than the supermarket price of $1.79 for 4 oz. However, if you have to pay supermarket prices it will increase the price of the recipe by about only 11¢.

Maple extract is not the same as maple flavoring. Truthfully, I was not able to find anyone who could tell me the precise difference; however, apparently the flavoring is not as concentrated. One of the recipes submitted, with a 16-oz yield, called for 1 Tbsp of flavoring . . . or half of a 1-oz $1.29 bottle. My teaspoon of maple extract cost just over 4¢.

Store bought syrup from generic to name brands cost between $1.59 to $3.19 for 24 oz. Since it takes only minutes to make a batch, the savings is worthwhile.

One of the differences between this recipe and the other that used extract is that the other did not call for butter flavoring. If you do not have it on hand try the recipe without.

Pancake Syrup

3 cups granulated sugar
1½ cups water
3 Tbsp molasses
1 tsp vanilla
2 tsp butter flavoring
1 tsp maple extract

Bring all to a boil, stirring until sugar dissolves (a good rolling boil). Turn off burner, but leave pot on burner until bubbling stops.

SLASHING YOUR GROCERY BILL

Our monthly food bill of $180 per month reflects the true cost of feeding our family. It includes all edible items, school lunches, the extremely rare meal out, canning supplies, and seeds. It does not include cleaning supplies, pet foods, toothpaste, etc. These items are often purchased in department or drug stores and may not be included in most people's grocery bills.

Although our oldest is only nine, most of my six children eat more than I do. But even compared to a family of four, we spend half of the national average for food.

There is no magic in our ability to do this but rather by using a variety of strategies. Not everyone wishes to do as we do. Some strategies only require better organization, but not a change in diet or more time. Obviously rural families have gardening options and suburban or urban families have greater shopping options.

1. Gardening (Families with limited space should look for books on urban gardening.)

2. Preservation of garden surplus (home canning, freezing, etc.)

3. A price book (or some system to keep track of prices between various stores)

4. Bulk buying (purchasing sale items, or good deals in stores you seldom shop, in quantities to get you through to the next sale)

5. Elimination of nonnutritious foods (soda, ice cream, candy . . . our remaining holdouts are coffee, tea, sugar, and cocoa)

6. Elimination of convenience foods (especially foods packaged in single-serving containers)

7. Choosing less expensive foods (the cheaper tuna, powdered milk, cheaper vegetables and fruits)

8. Buying store/generic brands

9. Buying marked-down damaged goods (also check deli for marked-down cheese and coldcut ends)

10. Coupons (we seldom use coupons as those products are generally more expensive than store brands or are for cold cereal. Also stores in our area do not offer double coupons. However, some people do very well with them.)

11. Vegetarianism (cut back on meat and substitute dried beans and whole grains.)

12. Portion comparison (Instead of comparing boxes of raisin bran, compare raisin bran to oatmeal or pancakes, or instead of buying steak when on sale compare portion price to that of chicken.)

13. Free food (garden surplus from neighbors, wild berries, food obtained through barter, groceries gotten free for buying $7.50 worth at some stores, etc.)

14. Preparing foods from scratch

15. Maintaining an optimum weight (Since your metabolism increases the more you eat, reducing your weight can make a significant difference on your food bill.)

16. Waste nothing (This includes making sure that children finish meals, cooking a turkey carcass for soup stock, and eating leftovers.)

17. Eat fewer meat and potato meals (Casseroles, soups, stews, stir-fry meals, etc. are generally less expensive.)

CHRISTMAS GIFT IDEAS FROM THE READERS

Make a "This Is Your Life" audio or videotape honoring a friend or relative. Include staged interviews with the honoree's family, friends, former teachers, and coworkers. Add narration as you tour places from their past—schools, former hangouts, etc. (Kim Frodelius, Solvay, New York)

Make a "beader" for a toddler using heavy-gauge wire, a block of hardwood, and nontoxic, brightly colored large beads. Drill a hole in the block the exact size of the wire, insert an end of wire and secure with epoxy. (Or secure from underneath with an electrical staple.) Bend the wire into curves and loops and secure at the opposite end. Tight loops can be made by wrapping around a clothes rod. Repeat with two more pieces of wire. Finish the wood with food-grade linseed oil. Make sure all edges are rounded and well sanded. (Susan Wiederhold, Austin, Texas)

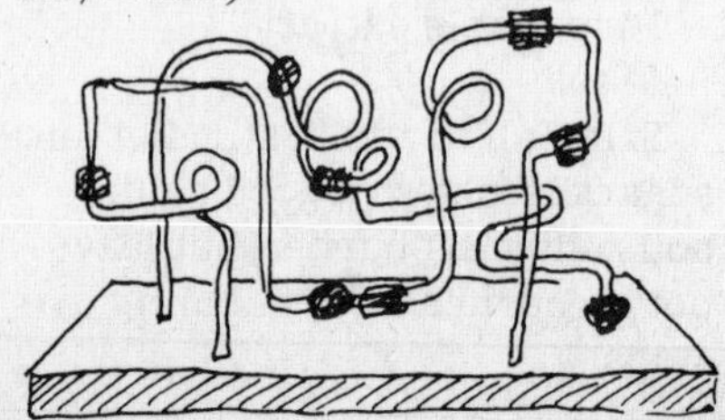

Buy magazines from antique stores dated the month and year of the birth date of the person you are buying for. Try to find magazines featuring their specific interests (such as an aviation magazine for a pilot). The average cost is about $3 per magazine. Recipients enjoy looking at ads of the new fangled gizmos of the year they were born. (Marsha Briggs, Placeville, California)

Make a "bandabout" (shown at right) for an older child from a sanded and finished 4½"-square block of wood about 1" thick. You also need 36 steel brads and a bag of colored rubber bands. With a light pencil divide the block horizontally, vertically, and diagonally. The brads are nailed into position as follows: begin nailing brads ½" away from the edge. Nail 4 brads on the diagonals allowing a ¾" space between. Nail 3 brads on each horizontal and vertical allowing a ½" space between. Nail another brad on each side of the outside brad of the horizontal and vertical line, allowing a ½" space between. The child can stretch the bands around to create designs. (Debra Posthumus Forbes, Portage, Michigan)

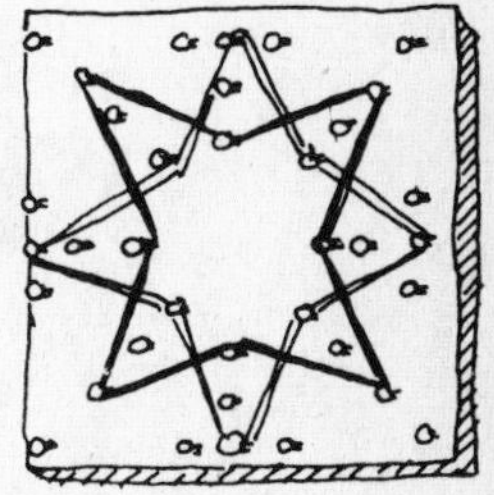

Make a clove-studded orange for an air freshener or moth deterrent. You need an orange and about 2 ounces of cloves. Use a small nail to make holes in the orange and push the cloves in, packing them tightly, using a thimble if needed. Allow the orange to dry for two weeks. The finished orange can be tied with a ribbon to hang in a closet, put in a drawstring bag for use in a drawer, or left plain for bathroom use. The total cost is about $6 with grocery store cloves or $1 with bulk-purchased cloves from a health food store. (Rebecca Hein, Casper, Wyoming)

Make cassette tapes of your child's favorite books. Record yourself reading the book and don't forget to say "Turn the page." (Elizabeth Gormley, Seguin, Texas)

Make up a price book for the "wannabe tightwad" in your life (see page 31). Credit for this idea goes to one of our staff workers who is making one for a relative.

Package your homemade jams and jellies in this unique manner: buy single wine goblets at the thrift store or yard sales. Put hot jam into goblets. Pour a thin coat of wax to seal. Take more melted wax and whip it with beaters until it reaches a foamlike consistency. Spoon the whipped wax on top of the sealed jam so that it looks like whipped cream. For easy wax removal don't use goblets that taper from a narrow top to a wider middle. Optional: decorate further with glitter, plastic flowers, and leaves.

If you are giving to a real tightwad they will appreciate a gift certificate to their favorite thrift or consignment shop for maximum value for dollars spent. Additionally, proceeds from thrift shops benefit needy individuals. (Elizabeth Roberts, Readfield, Maine)

Make designer placemats out of the fabric from sample books, which can be obtained by asking a home decor business for their old books. You would need twelve 3½" fabric squares to make one placemat

three squares deep and four squares long. Sew to plain-colored backing. (Doris Ray, Harrison, Maine)

Give a gift certificate for a year's subscription to *The Tightwad Gazette* newsletter. Make copies of your subscription and hand deliver. (Tina Hoag, Alfred, Maine.)

Make pumpkin bread in coffee cans. Each batch makes four or five nice-sized loaves. After baking, cans can be wrapped in plastic leaving a pompom on top. Decorate with ribbon, or ornament. The recipe appears on page 127. (Kathy Haubner, Cincinnati, Ohio)

Make brightly colored wire jewelry from the wires in telephone cable. Scout around at construction sites or ask the phone company for scraps. Cut 12″ pieces with scissors. Make a loop on one end. Start wrapping the wire to build up in the middle. Make a second loop with the last ¾″, burying the end. Take another wire, make a loop, and attach to the first wire. Repeat previous steps. If final necklace is large

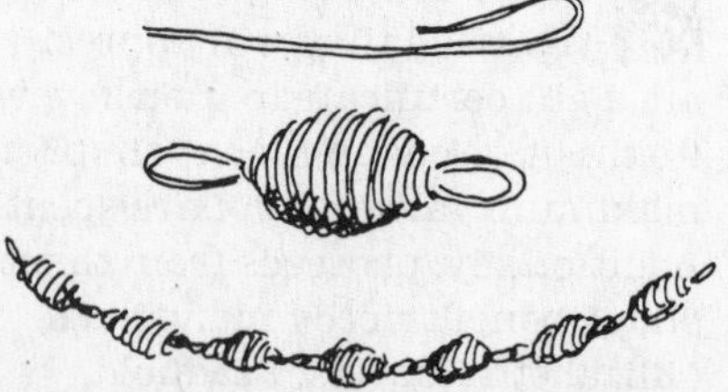

enough to fit over a head no clasp is needed. If you make a rainbow progression of colors the necklace can be shifted to complement different-colored outfits. Matching earrings can be made by attaching to earring findings.

Make up international coffee and tea mixes and give them in Mason jars. The recipes appear on page 126. Ask around . . . Mason jars can usually be had for free.

Give an elderly person a roll of 100 stamps to pay bills and write letters. It costs $29.00, but it's practical. (Judy Kilmer, Byron Center, Michigan)

Make up a bean soup mix with different beans and spices layered attractively in a glass jar with a pretty lid. Include a copy of the directions. See recipe on page 127.

Make firestarters by dipping pine cones in hot wax. These work better than crumpled newspapers for starting fires. Put them in a decorative basket. (Marion Kuklewicz, Turners Falls, Massachusetts)

Purchase Epsom salts in a milk carton. Put about ½ cup each of salts in several small bowls. Add food coloring to make a variety of soft colors. Using a paper funnel put layers of colored salts in bottles or jars. Tip the bottles or jars at different angles to make designs that look like mountains, sunsets, and oceans.

Buy sale-priced sweatsuits (about $4) and decorate the tops. You can cut flowers out of fabric and adhere with Stitch Witchery (an iron-on adhesive used to fuse two pieces of fabric together) and finish the edges with fabric paint. Or make a splatter design for your teenager. (Anna Weisend, Cleveland, Ohio)

If you have someone on your list who has just recently married into your family make them an important-date calendar. Purchase an inexpensive calendar and mark birth dates and anniversaries of family members.

Also list family addresses on the back of the calendar for easy access. (Debbie Owens, Albuquerque, New Mexico)

Make hair bows. Look closely at how store bows are made and duplicate. Or make a simple bow from a 5″ × 9″ fabric scrap. Fold the 5″ edges to the center so that they slightly overlap. Fold the 9″ edges to the center so they slightly overlap. Flip over and fanfold the center. Secure with small rubber band or thread. Cut a 3″ × ¼″ piece of ribbon to cover the rubber band or thread. Secure with hot glue. Glue finished bow to a barrette or French clip. Decorate the center with ribbon rosebuds, pearl strings, colorful buttons, etc.

Make up gift baskets with baskets purchased at yard sales or craft outlet stores. For a teacher you might fill with decorative soaps and bath items. For a young girl you might fill with sewing notions to make her first sewing basket. Use your surplus notions to keep this inexpensive. This might also include directions for a project and a coupon for free lessons from you. (Susan Pugh, Statesville, North Carolina)

If you can do calligraphy you can letter favorite Bible verses or sayings. Put in yard sale frames. Or purchase a kit and practice for next year. You can also press flowers for decoration. (Susie Finley, Albuquerque, New Mexico)

Make spice hot mats. You need cinnamon sticks, whole cloves, rice, and fabric scraps. Crush 4 cinnamon sticks and 2 Tbsp. whole cloves. Mix with one cup of rice. Cut a 7″ × 7″ square of denim and printed fabric. Hem all raw edges. Sew the two squares together on three sides (wrong sides together). Sew three even slots toward the open end. Fill with rice mix and sew the opening closed. A spicy aroma will fill the room when a hot dish or pot is placed on mat. Store in Ziploc bags to preserve the scent. (Penny McCauley, Hurley, New Mexico)

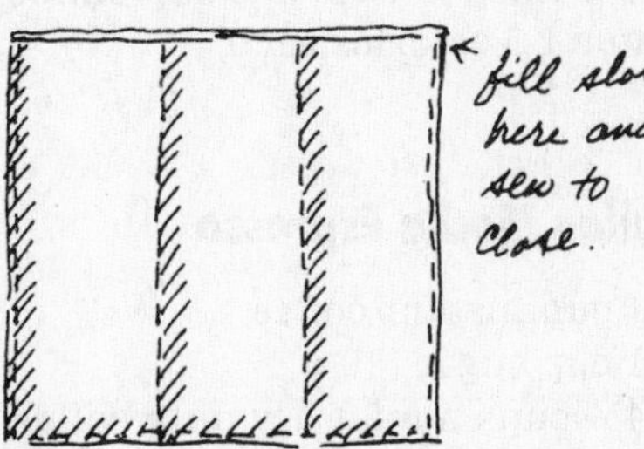

Make gag family portraits by cutting humorous or interesting photos of people out of magazines. Cut out the faces of family members from surplus snapshots. Glue snapshot faces over the faces in the photos. You and your husband can become Fred and Ethel. Uncle Hubert can have the physique of a body builder, etc. These can be given as cards or put into yard sale frames. (Doreen Gulley, Silver Spring, Maryland)

Make a tooth fairy pillowcase for a family with many small children. Buy or make a pillowcase and sew on a small pocket to hold the tooth. Decorate

creatively with rickrack, lace, or gold braid. Or paint a fairy design with tube paints. (Ruth Palmer, Glendale, Utah)

CHRISTMAS GIFT RECIPES

Cafe Vienna

½ cup instant coffee
⅔ cup sugar
⅔ cup nonfat dry milk solids
½ tsp cinnamon

Stir ingredients together. Process in a blender until powdered. Use 2 teaspoons to one cup of hot water. 35 calories each.

Italian Mocha Espresso

1 cup instant coffee
1 cup sugar
4½ cups nonfat dry milk solids
½ cup cocoa

Stir ingredients together, Process in a blender until powdered. Use 2 tablespoons to one small cup of hot water. Serve in demitasse cups. 60 calories each.

Swiss Mocha

½ cup instant coffee
½ cup sugar
1 cup nonfat dry milk solids
2 Tbsp cocoa

Stir ingredients together. Process in a blender until powdered. Use 2 tablespoons for each 4 oz cup of hot water. 40 calories each.

Cafe Cappuccino

½ cup instant coffee
¾ cup sugar
1 cup nonfat dry milk solids
½ tsp dried orange peel mashed in a mortar and pestle

Stir ingredients together. Process in a blender until powdered. Use 2 tablespoons for each cup of hot water. 40 calories each.

Spiced Tea

2 cups water
1 cup Tang or orange drink
1 cup instant tea
1 tsp each cloves and cinnamon

Combine and mix with hot water to taste.

The recipes below were sent in by a second reader. She suggests making up a basket with mugs (yard sale), cookies, and these two mixes.

Orange Cinnamon Coffee

⅓ cup ground coffee
1½ tsp grated orange peel
½ tsp vanilla extract
½ tsp cinnamon

Butter, Nut & Rum Coffee

⅓ cup ground coffee
½ tsp nutmeg
butter, nut, and rum flavoring

Blend coffee and dry ingredients in a blender. Blend in flavoring and extracts. Scrape sides and

blend 15 seconds more. Each recipe makes one 8-cup pot.

Place each coffee mix in a filter. Place filter on a square of plastic wrap. Draw together with a ribbon.

Bean Soup Mix

¼ cup white beans
¼ cup kidney beans
¼ cup split peas
¼ cup pinto beans
2 Tbsp pot barley

Layer these beans in a jar with a lid.

2 Tbsp parsley
2 Tbsp dried onions
1 bay leaf
2 Tbsp powdered beef broth

Wrap these spices in plastic wrap and place on top of bean layers.

Cooking directions: wash beans and soak overnight. Drain and top with 6 cups of water and simmer until done. Add one can of tomato soup. Also add one pound of fried and drained hamburger. Simmer a few more minutes.

Do not add salt of any kind until the last five minutes. It toughens the beans and the cooking time will be twice as long.

Pumpkin Bread

3 eggs
4 cups sugar
1 cup oil
1 16-oz can of pumpkin
5 cups flour
2 tsp soda
1 tsp salt
1½ Tbsp cinnamon
1 tsp allspice
½ Tbsp cloves or nutmeg
1 cup applesauce
½ to 1 cup chopped nuts
1 cup dates or raisins

Beat eggs. Mix in sugar. Mix in oil and pumpkin. Combine dry ingredients and add to moist batter. Mix in applesauce, nuts, and raisins.

Grease and flour five 1-lb coffee cans. Fill with batter over ½ full. Bake at 350° for 1 hour.

25 HOMEMADE PRESENTS FOR KIDS

Unless your children have been brainwashed extremely well they will not appreciate receiving *only* homemade presents for Christmas, but I like to give each child at least one.

Store bought toys must meet safety guidelines. Likewise when making homemade presents also consider age appropriateness and durability for safety reasons.

Most of the December women's magazines will offer homemade present ideas. These usually require that you buy kits, ready-made components, or materials from craft shops. Instead I suggest you first look to materials you already have—things that could be reused or recycled. Then, if necessary, purchase inexpensive new materials, and save any leftovers for future projects. Here are a few ideas:

1. Bean Bags (Use durable material scraps and dried beans left over from your unsuccessful ven-

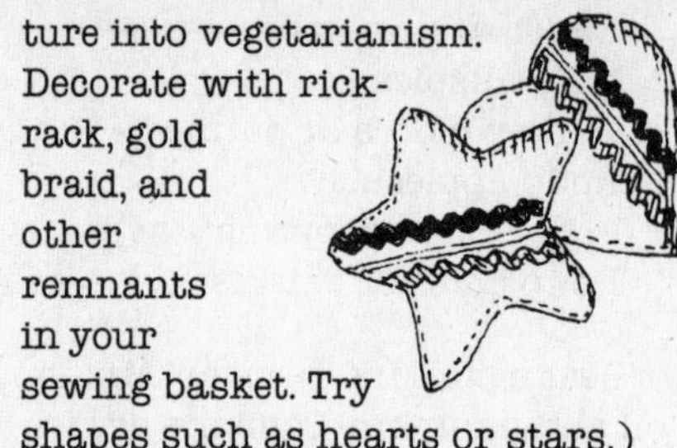

ture into vegetarianism. Decorate with rick-rack, gold braid, and other remnants in your sewing basket. Try shapes such as hearts or stars.)

2. A Scrap Book (Reuse an old check binder, notebook, or make traditional tie type. Construction paper can be bought all one color for $2.50 per 50 sheets. If you have the ability, custom design a cover or first page with the child's name.)

3. A Hobby or Rocking Horse

4. A Dress-Up Box (Fill with yard sale finds or items donated by Great-Aunt Ethel.)

5. A Treasure Box (Make from scrounged and durable wooden box with lid, add hinges and a padlock.)

6. Play Food (Fisher-Price is too expensive. Save all small food containers like spice cans and plastic containers. Also look for plastic fruit—not grapes—at yard sales. Cardboard containers, such as pudding boxes, can be filled with solid styrofoam and covered with clear contact paper. Look for possibilities in scraps of raw material you have. I made kid-size play bread cut out of 3/8″ foam rubber and colored the edges with brown marker.)

7. A Lady's Pocketbook (For the young child who likes to empty Mom's. Fill a thrift shop purse with a ring of old keys, wallet with play paper money, pictures, old credit cards, empty compact, etc.)

8. Play Dough (Recipe on page 194.)

9. Doll Blankets and Pillow (I have made them from dog-chewed pink satin-trimmed blanket.)

10. Denim Vest (Use scrap denim, especially stone-washed, and decorate with patches or embroidery.)

11. Gingerbread Cookies (Make large and decorative with frosting and silver balls. Customize with child's name.)

12. Drawstring Bag (Large or small depending on loot to be stored.)

13. A Work Bench (Build boy-size, utilizing scrap building materials.)

14. Child's Room Accessories (such as small and colorful braided rug, wall hanging, fanciful throw pillows, or sign with his name).

15. An Apron (with many pockets for tools or play kitchen utensils).

16. Wooden Blocks

17. A Stuffed Animal or Ball (Quilters frequently have a surplus of batting scraps. They may be willing to give this to you, or at least sell significantly cheaper than a craft store.)

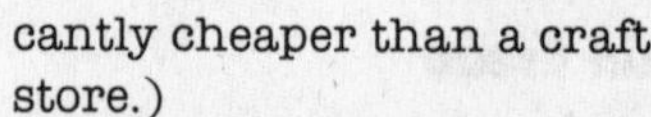

18. An Invention Box (A collection of gears, nuts and bolts, nails, wood, etc. that your inventor can create from. It might also include things she can take apart such as an old alarm clock.)

19. A Picture Album (Make using surplus pictures of the child's family with acetate pages. Tape completely on all edges.)

20. Sock Puppets (Use any odd sock you have saved for more than five years.)

21. Doll Clothing (This is another way to use up little scraps in your sewing basket. Make new outfits for the special doll.)

22. Coupons (Good for not picking up room on one occasion, a batch of favorite cookies, staying up late, an afternoon outing of their choice, getting Dad to make time to help with a special project, etc.)

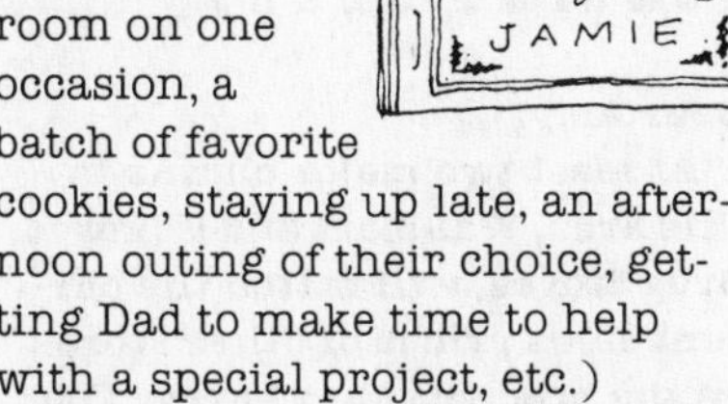

23. Bulletin Board (Adhesive cork tile on a scrap of plywood with thin wood frame, decorate with pictures of favorite things and child's name.)

24. Large Floor Pillow (for watching TV).

25. A New Paint Job (Instead of purchasing a new bike or wagon, surprise your child by giving the old bike a facelift. Aside from new paint, replace worn accessories, steel wool any rust, and clean off dirt and grease. Below is a way I devised to make streamers. They aren't as durable as the store kind but provide thrills for a month or so.)

To make bike streamers (shown at right) choose a durable plastic bag at least the weight of a bread bag. Cut many long strips 1/4″ wide. Twist paper clip as shown to secure strips. Add electrical or adhesive tape. Paper clip pops into the small hole of the handle grips.

HOMEMADE BRUSHES

Dear Amy,

I make disposable, foam paint brushes. Cut plastic from a milk jug, fold and staple to a popsicle stick as shown. If your staples won't penetrate, soak the wood in warm water until it softens. Cut carpet padding (if you don't have any, you may be able to get scraps from a local carpet installer) as shown: the beveled edge can be cut with scissors, the split down the center is cut with an X-Acto knife. Slip the padding over the plastic and add a few more staples to hold in place. Adjust the size according to the paint job.

Jay Patterson
New Albany, Indiana

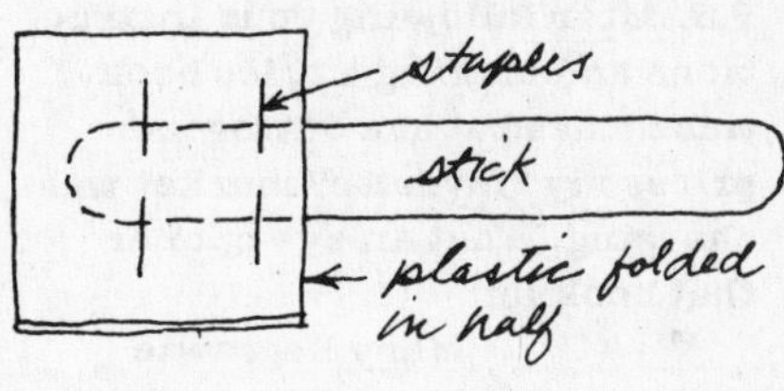

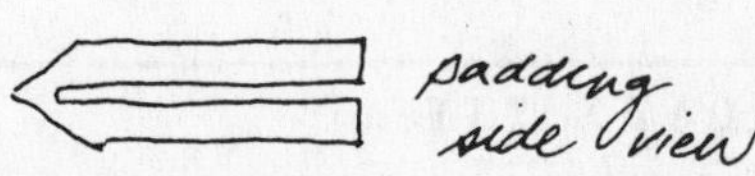

STOCK UP

Dear Amy,

Buying even a single share of stock in some companies can get you discounts. Tandy shareholders get discounts at Radio Shack. Marriott shareholders get discounts at the company's hotels. General Mills shareholders get a price break at Red Lobster restaurants. And stock in Disneyland/World makes you a member of the Magic Kingdom Club, which enti-

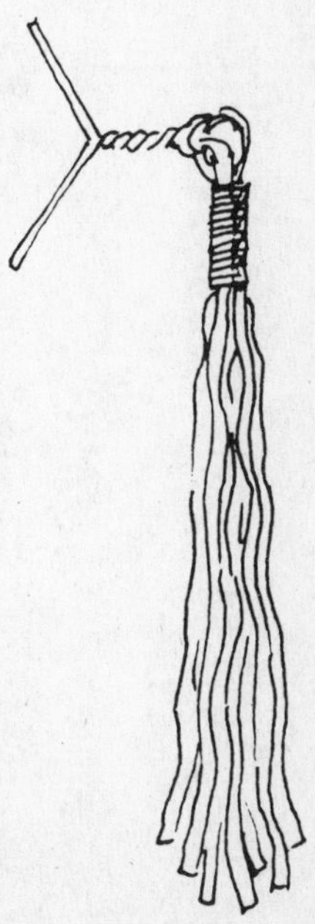

tles you to discounts in the parks, hotels, etc.

Linda G. Bukvic
Williamsburg, Ohio

USE YOUR NOODLE

Dear Amy,

Did you know that to cook pasta you don't need to boil the water for 10 minutes or whatever the directions state? My neighbor from India taught me that you bring the water to a boil (covered), add noodles, bring it back to a boil and then turn it off. Leave it covered for about 20 minutes, stirring once or twice to keep the noodles from sticking. It really works!

P.S. After following your instructions and making a price book, I was amazed at the outrageous prices my "favorite" market was charging. What an eye-opener that book is!

Mary Leggewie
Placentia, California

BLADE TIP

Dear Amy,

You can extend the life of the blade of a utility knife by carefully (using pliers) breaking the blade at the dotted line when it gets dull.

I. Appel
Ft. Lauderdale, Florida

(There is a special kind of utility knife available that makes this easy . . . its blade-inserts are scored, and one insert can be snapped off 12 times. These cost about the same as regular blades but may not be quite as rugged as regular utility blades.

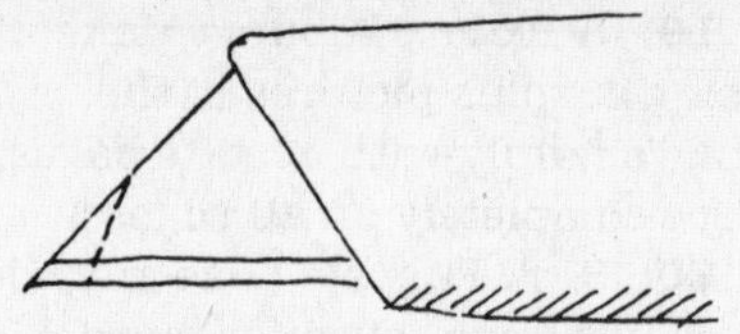

However, the same basic idea can be used for other types of blades. You can snap off or grind down the tip of an X-Acto blade from the back side to get a new tip. FZ)

DUELING DEALS

Dear Amy,

At least two major chains in this area, Wal-Mart and Eckerds Drug Stores, will match the current sales prices of other stores on the products they carry. You simply bring in the other store's advertisement and they will match the price. This is a real timesaver since I don't have to shop five stores for the best buys. I have found that other stores, such as Kmart, that don't advertise the policy, will match competitors' sale prices.

Teresa H. Morris
Garner, North Carolina

BREAD-CRUMB COOKIES

(a genuine tightwad recipe)

1¼ cups flour
1¼ cups sugar
½ tsp salt
½ tsp baking powder
⅓ cup cocoa
½ cup milk
1 egg
1½ tsp vanilla
⅔ cup melted shortening
2 cups bread crumbs

Sift together dry ingredients. Combine wet ingredients and add to dry mixture. Add melted shortening and bread crumbs. Drop by spoonfuls onto an ungreased cookie sheet. Bake at 350° for 15 minutes or until done.

This recipe works with the soy-flour-for-egg substitution (a heaping tablespoon of soy flour and one tablespoon of water substitutes for an egg). I have also had good success substituting ⅓ cup applesauce for ⅓ cup of the shortening.

Contributed by Ruth Palmer, Glendale, Utah

THE ART OF LEFTOVER WIZARDRY

We know it's time to use up leftovers when one of two things occurs: we run out of yard sale Tupperware and (donated) Cool Whip containers, or the freezer door no longer closes. More often than not Jim prepares meals, but he steps aside on leftover night to let me perform leftover wizardry.

Our house rule dictates that all leftovers go directly into the freezer, as any leftovers that go into the refrigerator may become forgotten and fertile territory for future growths.

I would prefer to report that we mark all our leftovers for date and content. In reality, the morning preceding leftover night I probe through the motley collection of containers, make educated guesses as to the probability of the frozen contents, and remove 20% more than I think I will need to implement my plan of action. (The extra 20% is in case I guess wrong.)

All tightwads have their preferred methods for dealing with leftovers, most of which fall into one of seven basic categories:

1. The Menu Management Method. There are no leftovers. This generally occurs when:

a. You have a family that devours everything regardless of how much you cook.

b. You're psychic and can accurately predict the appetite of all family members.

c. You live alone and possess a rare intuition that enables you to monitor internal signals indicating the size relationship between your eyes and your stomach.

If you fall into one of these three groups skip to the next article.

2. The Leftover Lunch. Always eat supper leftovers for lunch. Before Jim retired from the Navy he kept our leftovers in check by taking them for lunch to heat up in a microwave at work. Since his retirement, leftover management has become critical.

3. The Perpetual Soup Container. Leftover remnants, like sauces, bits of meat and vegetables, soups, etc., go into a large

container, such as a 5-lb peanut butter bucket, which occupies a permanent spot in the freezer. When the bucket is full, cross your fingers and thaw. The result can be surprisingly good, especially if you avoid combining conflicting spices.

A potpie variation of this theme was sent in by one reader. She saves leftovers in a plastic container, rinsing vegetables first, but not rinsing meats (to preserve the good flavor). When the container is full she heats up the leftovers, and then spoons them into a crust, vegetables first, then meat, and finally enough broth to cover vegetables and meat. If the leftovers don't yield enough broth, make more from bouillon and water. Cover with a second crust and bake at 350° until done.

4. Smorgasbord Night. Thaw a variety of leftovers, line up the family and let them choose what they want on their plate. Then warm in the microwave. Our kids love this, as it's the only time they can escape my "you-get-what-you-get-and-you're-lucky-to-get-it" philosophy passed on to me by a wiser soul (my mom).

A single woman told me she regularly holds get-togethers with others for a meal of exchanged leftovers. To her way of thinking, someone else's leftovers are new to her. To avoid "leftover glut" some families designate one night a week for a smorgasbord.

5. The TV Dinner Method. Obtain TV dinner trays or microwave dinner plates from spendthrifts. Fill these with leftovers and freeze. Use when the family cook has a night out and the other adult in the household

persists in a claim of kitchen incompetence.

6. Serial Leftovers. You deliberately make too much of something because you have a repertoire of recipes that use this item as an ingredient. For example, leftover ham gets packaged in portions specifically for future meals. Ham slices go in one package, smaller pieces are saved for a casserole, and the bone is saved for soup.

7. Leftover Wizardry. You perform a feat of magic, transforming leftovers into a completely new dish. The more skilled you become at this craft, the more types of leftovers you combine to make a single culinary sensation.

If you have a working knowledge of cooking you know there are few hard-and-fast rules. Look up any one recipe in as many cookbooks as you can lay your hands on—muffins, for example. You'll see that each recipe is different. Many ingredients are interchangeable. Leftover hot cereals and fruits, as well as some vegetables, can be used in making muffins, pancakes, waffles, and cakes.

Quiche makes a great leftover disguise, especially for mushy

vegetables. The following is my version of quiche, which may not be as tasty as richer counterparts, but healthier and economical. I make a rice crust from 1½ to 2 cups of leftover rice, 1 egg and 1 oz of grated cheese for an 8-inch pie plate. This mixture is patted into the plate and baked at 425° until firm. Put 1 cup of chopped leftover vegetables and 2 oz of grated cheese in the bottom of the crust. You can use any hard cheese for a quiche, although cheddar and Swiss are best. Use this opportunity to use up any dried-out pieces of cheese. Combine 2 beaten eggs, ⅔ cup dry milk powder, and 1 cup vegetable broth (saved water vegetables were cooked in) and a pinch of salt, pepper, and nutmeg. Cover the vegetables and cheese with egg mixture. Bake at 350° for 45 minutes or until solid.

To create casseroles you need only to combine meat and/or vegetables, a binder such as a white sauce, and a topping like bread crumbs or cheese.

Any basic cookbook tells you how to make a white (or béchamel) sauce and other variations. I save all bread crusts in a bag in my freezer to make crumbs for topping.

You can make a soup from casserole leftovers by adding liquid, and make a casserole from soup leftovers by removing liquid. For example, a soup that contains rice can be combined with more rice and baked with a cheese topping to make a casserole. Or a stew can be put in a shallow baking pan and topped with dumpling batter. The batter absorbs the excess liquid to make a casserole. Watery soup creations can be thickened either by topping with dumplings or by putting a portion of the soup in a blender, and mixing it back in.

When we make chicken cacciatore (chicken parts cooked in spaghetti sauce with onions and peppers) we always have leftover chicken-flavored sauce and vegetables. This can be combined with leftover rice and leftover baked chicken cut off the bone and chopped, and topped with cheese.

Be persistent in your use of leftovers. One summer we had an abundance of rhubarb and strawberries. Jim made strawberry shortcake, but he overbaked the biscuits. Then he made rhubarb jam, but misread the directions, resulting in a batch of runny rhubarb jam. He decided to make rhubarb betty (like apple betty) with ground, overbaked biscuits instead of bread cubes. The result was very dry. However, when we topped the betty with our rhubarb "syrup" it was . . . well . . . good enough to save it from the compost pile.

I would like to suggest a terrific book on leftover use. It is organized alphabetically by leftover—everything from apples to zucchini.

The Use-It-Up Cookbook
By Lois Carlson Willard
Practical Cookbooks
145 Malcolm Ave. SE
Minneapolis, MN 55414

It costs $9.95 per copy, including shipping.

MISSION (NOT QUITE) IMPOSSIBLE

(As you read imagine the *Mission Impossible* theme music played on Christmas bells.)

Objective: Your mission, should you choose to accept it, is to accomplish the scaling down of Christmas.

The Adversaries: This is a large and powerful syndicate made up of family members within your household including young children, teenagers, and yes, even your spouse. Other key players include relatives, friends, and friends of your children.

Your Partners: Anyone from the above group that you can possibly convert.

Prior History: Although the origins of the Christmas holiday date back to the birth of Christ, in recent generations it has become an event infiltrated by high levels of commercialism.

Tactic Suggestions: Depending on your adversaries and partners (and their respective ages) you may need to employ several of the following strategies.

1. Advertising Interception. Hide all incoming sale flyers and discourage Saturday morning cartoon watching. Avoid trips to the mall and toy store.

2. Create Diversions. Develop inexpensive family traditions such as attending the local church play, drives to see the gaudiest light display in town, stringing popcorn and cranberry garland, and involve even the youngest family members in gift giving.

3. Intelligence Gathering. Attempt to determine what other relatives intend to give to your children. Intercept incoming mailed gifts and determine contents by feel or carefully opening and resealing so that your activity is undetectable. This can prevent duplication. The exchanging of lists will discourage a shotgun approach to gift giving.

4. Alternative Excellence. In an effort to encourage adversary defection and win support, give superb scrounged and homemade gifts. Be creative in your acquisition of these items. Barter your gift-making skills with a parent who possesses another. Or barter with another family for used but very good outgrown toys.

5. The Family Council. Call a meeting of adversaries and partners. Provide facts and figures such as how long it took to pay off last year's Visa bill. Offer alternatives such as a present spending limit among adults. Couples can agree to purchase a single house present together or to simply spend the limited budget on the children. Try to help young children understand the importance of larger financial goals.

6. The Long-Range Plan. Accomplishing the scaling down from a Smuckster to a tightwad-style Christmas in one year may

be unrealistic and should not be attempted unless your circumstances are dire. Instead work toward a gentle transition over a period of a few years.

THE TIN ANGEL ORNAMENT

I couldn't resist including this idea, which has to be the ultimate tightwad tree ornament. You'll need a tin can lid, a paper clip, a birthday candle, an ornament hanger and a tiny glass ball ornament.

Cut the tin can lid as shown at the right. Then bend the lid to shape the angel. Make a halo out of the paper clip and attach glass ball, halo and candle.

THE SPENDTHRIFT CHRISTMAS DEBT CHART

Knowing that a few well-intentioned spendthrifts are reading I have included the handy-dandy credit card debt chart shown below. Simply choose the figure closest to the amount you estimate you will charge this Christmas and follow the column down to the number of months you think it will take to pay it off. If you plan to make the minimum payment, it will take 36 months to pay off. Using this chart you can roughly figure what this Christmas will *really* cost.

BREAD DOUGH RECIPES

The Flour and Salt Recipe

4 cups flour
1 cup salt
1½ cups water

Bake your completed designs in a 350° oven for at least 1 hour. Paint and when dry dip in polyurethane, shellac, or clear nail polish.

This recipe is used in many applications but most commonly for Christmas ornaments. One year I made one for everyone on my Christmas list. The most expensive aspect of this gift was the boxes to put them in. At that time Woolworth's was the only source of small boxes I could find.

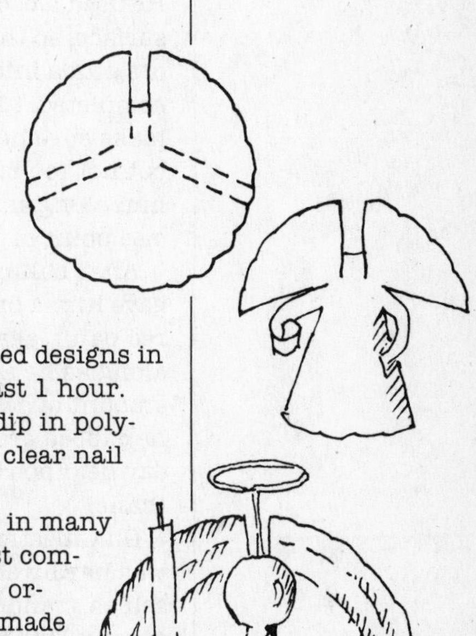

	$250	$500	$750	$1000	$1250	$1500
4 mos.	$259.44	$518.89	$778.33	$1,037.78	$1,297.22	$1,556.67
8 mos.	267.17	534.34	801.50	1,068.67	1,335.84	1,603.01
12 mos.	275.04	550.08	825.12	1,100.16	1,375.20	1,650.24
16 mos.	283.06	566.12	849.18	1,132.24	1,415.30	1,698.36
20 mos.	291.23	582.46	873.69	1,164.91	1,456.14	1,747.37
24 mos.	299.54	599.09	898.63	1,198.18	1,497.72	1,797.27
28 mos.	308.01	616.02	924.02	1,232.03	1,540.04	1,848.05
32 mos.	316.62	633.23	949.85	1,266.47	1,583.08	1,899.70
36 mos.	325.37	650.74	976.11	1,301.49	1,626.86	1,952.23

If you are not artistic, consider letting your kids make these for Christmas gifts. When my oldest was only three I helped him make abstract design ornaments. I provided Alec with 1-inch flattened balls that had an ornament hanger stuck in the back, and an assortment of household items with textures or designs, such as screws, bolts, a comb, spools, etc. He used a cookie sheet as a work surface, so that I could pop his creations into the oven when completed. I hovered about to make sure he designed enough, but not too much, and then moved him along as he reached the precise point of design perfection.

After baking the ornaments I gave him a brush and water-base red paint, again moving him along as he added the right amount of swishes. The next day he dabbed green paint. The last day he dipped them in polyurethane.

On Christmas morning Alec was hardly able to contain himself as grandmas opened the treasures. (This highlight by far superseded his interest in the presents given to him.)

The White Bread and Glue Recipe

(Possibly the only good use for white bread)

6 slices white bread
½ cup white glue

Remove the crusts from the bread and discard (i.e., save for bread crumbs). Tear bread into small pieces. Mix with glue and knead. This is quite messy. Persist and continue kneading until it makes a nice smooth consistency. You can mix food coloring into it. This dough does not need to be baked but dries hard as a rock in several days. (The color darkens and lightens to original color after dried for a week.)

This recipe will work for some projects where the flour and salt dough will not. It makes very nice jewelry for older children. When making beads, the holes should be at least 1/16″ as they become smaller when they dry. If you can find a source of pin backs you can epoxy them to dried dough.

JIM'S BEST CANDY RECIPE

Fruit and Nut Candy Bars

⅓ cup sugar
¼ cup light cream
¼ cup butter or margarine
1 3-ounce package cream cheese, softened
2 cups sifted powdered sugar
1 cup chopped mixed dried fruits
½ cup chopped nuts
½ tsp vanilla
1½ lbs white dipping chocolate

Line an 8″ × 8″ × 2″ baking pan with foil, extending foil over the edges of the pan. Butter the foil and set the pan aside.

In a heavy 2-quart saucepan combine the sugar, light cream, and the ¼ cup butter or margarine. Cook over medium heat to boiling, stirring constantly to dissolve the sugar. This should take about 8 minutes.

Cook over medium heat stirring

occasionally for 3 minutes. Mixture should boil at a moderate, steady rate over the entire surface. Remove pan from heat. Add cream cheese; stir until smooth. Add powdered sugar, dried fruits, nuts and vanilla; stir until well combined. Spread mixture into prepared pan. Chill about 1 hour, or until firm. When firm, lift foil to remove candy from pan; cut candy into 2″ × 1″ rectangles.

Melt the dipping chocolate. Carefully dip the rectangles, one at a time, into the melted chocolate. Let excess coating drip off rectangles. Place dipped rectangles on a baking sheet lined with waxed paper until dry. Store tightly covered in the refrigerator. Makes 32 candy bars.

DEBTS AND DOWN PAYMENTS

Since I wrote the premiere issue of *The Tightwad Gazette* newsletter I have come to understand the tremendous confusion about why "young people can't buy houses nowadays."

First-time home buyers see that they earn twice what their parents earn and assume they should be able to buy a house of the same value. But frequently a couple with a joint income of $50,000 fails to qualify for a $25,000 loan.

Couples that bought more than 10 years ago often do not understand the current value of their own homes or the income required to buy a similar home in today's market. If they were just starting out today many older couples would not be able to afford their own homes.

If you fall into one of these groups, an interesting exercise would be to take your income figures and debt figures (other than mortgage) to a bank and see how much you could borrow. Next go to a real estate office and get listings of houses you could afford based on the bank mortgage only. Actually drive to see what these homes look like. Pictures are deceiving.

For a young couple hoping to buy within a few years this exercise is imperative. For the older established couple it is merely entertainment.

Supposedly real estate has risen faster than the average wage. I don't know if this is true, as I look at the homes of our parents and their incomes at the time of purchase the figures are roughly proportional to today's market. Realtors I spoke with told me that houses appreciate about the same rate as inflation or 3% to 5% per year.

I can say that of the 177 houses we saw in our price range fewer than ten compare to a house my father bought without a down payment when he was in his early twenties. At the time we bought our house Jim was 40 and earning more proportionally, and we had more than $49,000 saved.

Double-digit interest rates stand out as the one glaring difference between today's economy and the old days. At the top of page 138 is a chart that shows roughly what a couple earning $30,000 could buy with different interest rates. Estimated taxes and insurance have been factored in.

Second, today's consumer debt

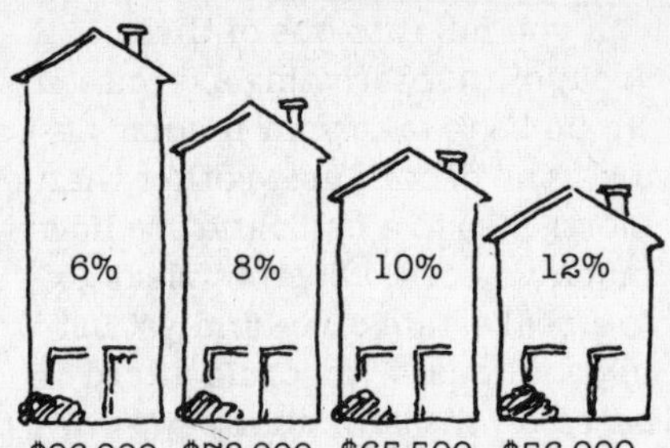

tends to be much higher. Some people blame TV for giving us an inaccurate picture of American life. Young couples tend to believe that they will live at the same standard of living that their parents gradually achieved over a period of years and the same standard of living as typical TV families.

In essence both sides are true. It is harder to buy a house today, but couples tend to wipe out their only real chance with high consumer debt. Banks still lend money the same way they always did. The mortgage, insurance, and property taxes cannot exceed 28% of the gross income, and that combined with other debts cannot exceed 36% of the gross income. Few banks will break away from these guidelines as they resell the loans to other institutions who insist on these figures. The chart below demonstrates buying power as impacted by consumer debt and down payments. (Based on 10% interest and a $30,000 income.)

$600 monthly debt	$20,000
$300 monthly debt	$54,000
$0 debt & $0 down	$65,500
$20,000 down	$85,500
$40,000 down	$105,500

There are several ways to buy more house than you can technically afford. (1) Trade up. Buy a starter home and resell it after five or so years. (2) Buy a duplex and rent half to help pay the mortgage. (3) Save up a large down payment. (4) Buy a fixer-upper if you have the skills, extra cash, and determination to actually do the work.

Many combinations of these methods work well. A question remains as how long to rent and save a down payment. There are several factors to determine which way—the trade-up method or the down payment method—is best. If you save up a big down payment you have to pay rent for those years. When you finally buy, your payments and total purchase price will be much less since you are financing less. But it will take several years to make up for the loss of the rent money. If you opt to trade up you must keep the home long enough to make a profit to make up for the realtor fees and the thousands in the process of purchasing a new home. (Points, lawyer fees, inspections, moving costs, etc.) And you have to buy in a buyer's market and sell in a seller's market. If you try to sell in a buyer's market you may not profit enough.

Clearly, it is very complex to weigh all the factors. We did one thing that gave us a tremendous economic boost. The first 18 months we were married, 8 of which I worked full time, we worked extremely hard to save. We lived in a dirt-cheap crummy third-floor three-and-a-half room apartment. During that period we saved half of all we were able to save in seven years.

Once children enter the picture, families need to rent larger

spaces with yards, as we did. Child-care costs severely compromise a couple's ability to earn. As a general rule parenthood slows (or stalls altogether) the climb up the economic mountain.

Whatever the market factors clearly the critical economic period in any marriage is the years before children. Typically couples tend to see this time as the final opportunity to have the fun "they deserve," squandering a valuable chance.

Instead they should live in the cheapest place possible for a short period of time—one to three years. Using this time to the maximum, earning and saving more, while not acquiring debt, couples can propel themselves into a higher standard of living they will enjoy the remainder of their lives.

GIFT GIVING THROUGH THE AGES

I am chatting with a friend in my kitchen, relating some of the Christmas ideas I am planning to include in the *Tightwad Gazette* newsletter. My friend sighs and says, "All this talk about Christmas is making me feel depressed."

In one sentence she expressed what a great many people feel about the holiday. Will I have enough money? Will I have enough time? How will I handle the conflicting family values about Christmas spending? What will I buy to thrill my husband, or wife, or child? Will people give me gifts I don't like?

My own personal Christmas stress tends to be about, Will I be able to pull another rabbit out of the hat this year? How will I solve the problem of finding wonderful *and* inexpensive gift ideas? Some years my gift giving has been brilliant, but other years I dug deep and found no rabbit.

So how is it that Christmas, a holiday about joy, peace, and festivity, has gotten to this point where we feel so overwhelmed and harried? Traditional gift giving, as we know it today, has only been a part of the holiday for less than 100 years.

Christmas was first celebrated in the fourth century. Prior to that time the early church frowned upon celebrating the birth of Christ. Roman pagans celebrated the winter solstice on December 17 and 25. St. Nicholas died on December 6 about A.D. 350. December 6 became the feast of St. Nicholas. January 6, the feast of the Epiphany, was celebrated as the date that the Magi

came. These four days eventually fused to become Christmas.

Each of these festivals brought its own tradition of gift giving. The participants in Roman festivals gave twigs from a sacred grove, and later gave candles, food, trinkets, and statues of gods. St. Nicholas was revered for his generosity, and it became the custom to give gifts on December 6 as well as on Christmas. The Magi brought gold, frankincense and myrrh to the Christ child.

In all cases gift giving was only a small part of the tradition. Participants decorated houses with evergreens, danced, sang, lit bonfires, ate, played games, made music, and told riddles.

Throughout history, with exception of the most wealthy families, people generally only gave gifts to young children and to the poor. Literature provides us with a few images from early Christmases in this country. The Laura Wilder *Little House* series depicts gifts for children of a tin cup and candy, or a hair comb. In the book she wrote of her husband's childhood, Almanzo Wilder received a jacknife and a hat in his stocking. Almanzo grew up in a relatively prosperous family. My own inlaws, who grew up in immigrant farm families during the Depression, tell of receiving nuts, an orange, and cookies in their stockings.

Jo Robinson and Jean Coppock Staeheli, authors of *Unplug the Christmas Machine* researched the commercialization of Christmas. They found that turn-of-the-century Christmas advertising featured toys for children and a few adult gifts called "notions." Adults might have exchanged a pouch of tobacco, a hat pin, or a handkerchief.

Robinson and Staeheli began to find ads that depicted more elaborate gifts in the early part of the century. The industrial revolution had made goods less expensive, and in the process, accelerated gift giving.

The fire was again fueled after World War I. It was feared that the prosperity brought about by the war would become a sluggish economy in peacetime. Advertisers fought back with a stepped-up campaign. In some cases, according to the authors, the ads were unconscionable, implying that more money spent on gifts showed how much you cared, and even assured domestic tranquillity. The ads played on people's insecurities about themselves as parents, spouses, and providers.

The ads worked, and people bought into the commercialism. Giving expensive gifts became a sign of their own prosperity.

The "Have a Natural Christmas 1987" publication by Rodale Press also outlines gift giving in the U.S. during this century. Although sales for toys were going full force, adult gift giving grew in fits and starts. Gifts remained practical, especially during the Depression. In the '40s small appliances made their entry as appropriate gifts, as well as the then-new board game Scrabble.

However, it wasn't until the prosperity of the '50s that more expensive gifts, such as we give today, became prevalent—jewelry, clothes, furniture, and liquor. This trend continues into the '90s, especially with the high percentage of double-income households. We don't have time to

be thoughtful . . . instead we throw money at the problem.

Today's holiday revolves around the gift giving. In most households, present opening is the climax of the day. Families may go on to visit extended family members, share a meal, or watch a ball game. After the paper and ribbon explosion subsides we are left with the Is-that-all-there-is? feeling. But from the years 400 until 1900, or the first 1,500 years of Christmas celebrations, gift giving played a minor role. The opening of presents was the beginning, not the end.

Although I have focused on the topic of gift giving, I could similarly question dozens of aspects of what we believe to be tradition surrounding Christmas—writing cards, traveling long distances, helping with school or church activities, holiday baking. . . . Most of these traditions came about when the majority of families lived on one income. Today's Christmas remains the holiday largely orchestrated by women. They want to continue the same traditions as their mothers, who did not work outside the home.

The stress surrounding giving could be summed up simply. You feel unable to do as much as you want to do or feel you are supposed to do. This stress robs you of some of the joy you should be experiencing.

The solution is simple. Give yourself license to do less. Lower your self-expectation to a minimum level. If necessary, let your family know you feel a need to scale back so that you can enjoy the holiday more. You can do more if it happens that you find more time, energy, inspiration. Whatever you can do beyond your minimum will feel more joyful.

I could write pages on the topic of how to forge new Christmas attitudes, but someone already has. *Unplug the Christmas Machine* contains a few recipe and craft ideas, but the bulk of material covered is on the subject of changing attitudes. They offer several exercises to help the reader rethink through exactly what they find to be satisfying and unsatisfying about the holidays. The authors answer many commonly asked questions about how to deal with Christmas issues. Many readers would feel greatly liberated with a cruise through the chapters of this book.

If you can't find a copy at a bookstore, write to:

William Morrow & Co.
Special Sales
1350 Avenue of the Americas
New York, NY 10019
(212) 261-6500

The suggested retail price is $9 plus postage. They offer a 40% discount if you buy 10 or more. If you find a copy, and feel strongly about it, you (or a group of friends) could purchase several as gifts for family members as reading material for the coming year.

GIFT IDEA

Dear Amy,

If you are stumped for a gift for a couple who has everything (my parents, for instance), I've often found that they have sets of china, crystal and silver that

have been discontinued. They also have pieces missing from these sets. A unique and much-appreciated gift is to fill in these missing pieces. Two of the best places to find these things are:

Replacements Ltd.
1089 Knox Road
P.O. Box 26029
Greensboro, NC 27420-6029
(919) 668-2064

Walter Drake & Sons
Drake Building
Colorado Springs, CO 80940
(800) 525-9291

Susan Garrett
Webster, Texas

(Both companies accept phone orders and take credit cards. Delivery time varies from 10 days to 6 weeks. FZ)

GOOD WOOD

Dear Amy,

One day recently I went to a nearby high school to have the industrial education metals teacher do some metal work for me. He was busy at the time and I had to wait a few minutes. I walked to the woodworking lab and saw a truck bed about half full of wood scraps. I asked the woodworking teacher what they did with the wood scraps and he told me they sold them all for $5. I asked if I could buy $1 worth from him and he said, "Sure." I selected 50 pieces of hardwood . . . oak, walnut, cedar, and maple. They ranged from 12 to 48 inches in length and ¾ to 5 inches wide. I will use them for breadboards, and a variety of other projects.

Ken Cannon
Provo, Utah

CHARCOAL STARTER

Dear Amy,

We cut up Christmas trees and store them in boxes or bags for later use as a charcoal starter when grilling out-of-doors. The boughs burn great and have a more pleasant scent than commercially marketed chemical products.

C. Rieck
Forest Park, Illinois

FREE WOOD

Dear Amy,

Many of us heat, or supplement house heat with wood. Living on a suburban house lot creates a problem. We have no woodlot.

For the past several years I've gotten all of my wood "free." People around town take trees down from time to time. Generally the tree "experts" take the wood "to get it out of the way." But not always! So I've left notes in mailboxes and called neighborhood people.

The note simply says "I'll split your wood for you if you'll 'split it' with me."

It works! Many people are delighted to have their wood prepared for their fireplace. And this system has kept us warm just for the cost of our exercise.

Dave Shaub
Lake Bluff, Illinois

TIGHTWADDING

Dear Amy,

My 13-year-old son sat down to lunch in the school cafeteria. He took out his sandwich (in a washable container), other homemade items (also in washable containers), and finally a cloth napkin.

He turned to his friend next to him and sadly said, "My mom's tightwadding." The other boy replied, "Yours, too?"

It's an epidemic!

Cindy Kay
Topsham, Maine

THE MERITS OF COLD MEDICINES

Americans spend more than $900 million a year on cold and cough remedies. Amazingly, it has been known for some time that there is no evidence to prove that a great many have any effect at all.

Modern science knows of no substance to prevent the cold. This includes vitamin C, which has been extensively studied and may be as effective as a placebo. (Vitamin C and placebos often work because people believe they do.) Although it won't prevent a cold, recent studies indicate that vitamin C may shorten the duration of colds. But remember, megadoses can be harmful.

Colds are spread by sneezing, coughing, shaking hands, and handling contaminated articles. Therefore the best prevention is to avoid people with colds. I have found that once you have a school age child, colds are an inevitable aspect of life for all family members.

The primary reason why the cold continues to be an enigma is that there are more than 120 viral strains. Additionally we all bring a host of factors to the problem such as individual resistance and emotional well-being.

Most of the remedies we buy are actually directed toward suppressing symptoms rather than prevention or cure.

The over-the-counter cold remedies such as Dristan, NyQuil, and Contac combine several ingredients in a fixed combination. This "shotgun" approach forces the patient to take medications he might not need for his particular symptoms.

Most of these cold remedies contain similar ingredients. Antihistamines were developed originally for hay fever. Their use in cold remedies is unwarranted since there is no evidence to show

that they affect the cold. They do have side effects, the most common of which is drowsiness. People who feel they are getting some relief may have a cold and allergic reaction in combination, or may feel better because they are somewhat sedated.

Cold remedies contain small dosages of aspirin or acetaminophen, which is helpful in reducing muscle aches and fever. However, the dose is generally too small, and plain aspirin or Tylenol is cheaper and more effective.

The decongestants in cold remedies are also useful, but again the dose is too small. A decongestant is important for the child who is prone to ear infections since it can help prevent blockage of the eustachian tubes.

The time-release aspect of some cold medications is nothing more than a marketing ploy because, again, the dosage of the ingredients is too small to be effective. NyQuil does aid sleep because it contains an antihistamine and alcohol, both substances that produce drowsiness but are ineffective in symptom control.

If you want an oral decongestant look for a product that contains pseudoephedrine or phenylpropanolamine, or a combination. Sudafed and Sinutab-II are examples.

Decongestants in the form of nose drops or sprays are generally considered to be more effective than the oral type, but they can also be addictive if taken for more than two or three days.

In the same manner that cold medicines do, many cough medicines also use a shotgun approach by combining a number of ingredients in the hope that at least one will work.

The FDA has approved three substances as safe and effective. Of those dextromethorphan is the best. Romilar is an example. The downside of this particular drug is that taken in large doses it can produce a high. There have been reported deaths of teenagers who have overdosed.

Cough drops are no more effective than any piece of hard candy. A hot drink can also be helpful.

Vaporizers can also relieve cold symptoms; however, products such as VapoSteam or VapoRub provide little additional relief. *Consumer Reports* recently said that there is some evidence that breathing steam from a vaporizer may shorten the duration of the cold, but the particular vaporizer that worked cost about $100, and was probably not worth the cost. Breathing steam from a teakettle may cause burns and should not be done.

There is some disagreement among doctors if symptom relief is actually in our best interests. Some authorities believe you may actually prolong your cold by preventing your body from doing what it wants to do naturally to rid itself of respiratory infection. Coughing, for example, is an important function of your body to prevent infected mucus from entering your lungs. The supression of symptoms may be an act of postponement.

The best thing to do for a cold is to have a good diet, drink plenty of fluids, and *rest.* If your symptoms are severe enough to prevent rest some doctors would suggest you take some medication. If you do that, at least treat

the specific symptoms with pain reliever, a decongestant, or a cough medicine with dextromethorphan. To save money, seek out the generic or store brands that contain the specific drug you desire.

All the shotgun medications are clearly a waste of money. Even the medications that are known to work are expensive. Taking medications to make us feel better, even though we are going to get better anyway, is unnecessary in the majority of cases.

As a general rule the best approach to a cold is patience. It will probably last a week or two regardless. You should limit your contact with other people to try to avoid infecting others.

Your emotional well-being will also play a role in determining the length of your cold. Therefore give yourself a few days off to relax and to be "self-centered."

CHRISTMAS IDEAS

Dear Amy,

Ever since my children were small we have had an outing in the fall to gather fallen birch bark, small pine cones, and small pieces of spruce bush. From these three items one can make "to" and "from" cards one can purchase in a department store or card shop for approximately $1.99. By cutting the bark into pieces of 2″ × 3″ and gluing pieces of spruce and pine cones to the smooth side we have a festive card for our Christmas packages. You can write what you wish on the smooth side of the bark.

Karen B. Allen
Ellsworth, Maine

Dear Amy,

Cut circles of the same size out of Christmas cards. (A small juice can or silver dollar makes a nice size.) It takes eight circles to make one decorative ball for the Christmas tree or to hang in the window.

Fold one and use as a model. Make a triangle in the middle. Use this one to trace and fold other circles.

Glue four circles together using side folds to make the top and do the same to make the bottom. Then glue top and bottom together using the middle fold. To hang attach ribbon, string, or hook.

Carol Ordway
South Portland, Maine

Dear Amy,

Make your own vanilla to give away for Christmas presents. It is much cheaper than store-bought and we prefer real vanilla to imitation.

Here's how: Buy vanilla beans at your local health food store. Split the bean lengthwise without cutting it in half, and place in a tall narrow jar filled with white liquor such as vodka. It needs to age several weeks before you can use it. Also it will not be as dark as commercial vanilla. Just add more liquor as you use up the vanilla. Be creative with jar shapes and packaging.

Holly Moulton
Bath, Maine

THE SNOWBALL PRINCIPLE

Living paycheck to paycheck, or spending your final dollar, leaves no money to reinvest and no money to take advantage of bargains.

But when a portion of savings is reinvested in tools and skills which will save money or earn money the savings will compound, or snowball.

To demonstrate this concept I have created a simplified scenario that compares the spending habits of two couples over a five-year period.

The first couple, depicted in the column to the right, believes they deserve an occasional splurge. In contrast, the couple on the opposite page carefully reinvests surplus dollars. The first figure in each equation of the second scenario shows that this couple repeats the same saving effort from the previous year.

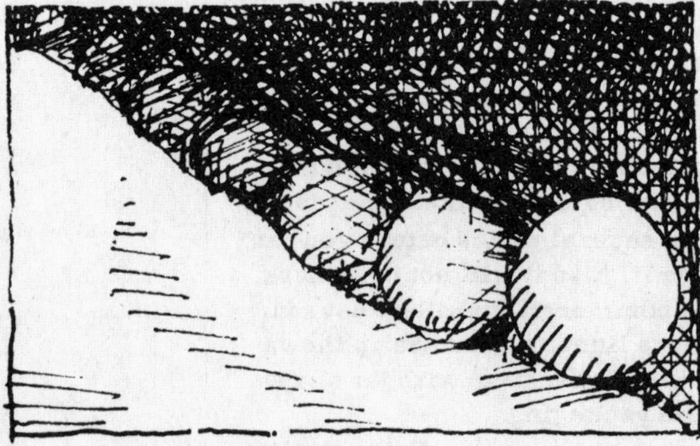

Year 1. Clyde and Bunni Smuckster have no long-term goals. At the end of the year they have $100.

$100 total savings

Year 2. Clyde and Bunni spend the $100 on a night on the town of dinner and dancing. At the end of the year they have saved another $100.

$100 total savings

Year 3. Clyde and Bunni spend the $100 to buy a small TV for the kitchen so that Bunni can catch all the soaps and get her housework done. At the end of the year they have another $100 saved.

$100 total savings

Year 4. Clyde and Bunni have a friend who needs to sell his entire Nintendo game setup to raise cash. They spend their $100 to pick up this "bargain." At the end of the year they have saved another $100.

$100 total savings

Year 5. Clyde and Bunni spend the $100 on a hotel weekend getaway. At the end of the year they have saved another $100.

$100 total savings

Clyde and Bunni live next door to the Albrights. They think "some folks get all the breaks."

Year 1. Craig and Susan Albright have goaled themselves to save up a down payment to purchase a house in five years. But Craig's income is modest and at the end of the first year they have saved only $100.

$100 total savings

Year 2. Craig and Susan put $50 in savings and spend $50 on cloth diapers. The weekly savings of $6 enables them to begin bulk purchasing sale items at the grocery store. The cloth diapers save the family $312 and the bulk-sale purchasing saves them $600.

$100 + $312 + $600 = $1,112 this year's savings
$50 + $3 = $53 last year's savings + interest
$1,165 total savings

Year 3. Craig and Susan put $600 into a three-year CD. The remaining $565 is used to purchase a used sewing machine, a used freezer, and a used chainsaw. By freezing bulk-purchased day-old bread and sale meats, as well as their garden surplus, they are able to save an additional $600 on their food bill. Susan uses her sewing machine to repair clothing and to make handcrafted Christmas gifts to save $200. Craig uses his chainsaw to cut up delivered logs and deadfall to save $300 on their heating bill.

$1,112 + $600 + $200 + $300 = $2,112 this year's savings
$600 + $54 = $654 last year's savings + interest
$2,766 total savings

Year 4. Craig and Susan keep their CD and put an additional $1,000 into savings. The remaining $1,166 is used to purchase a newer used car in excellent condition. The old beater car is sold for $200. This saves them $200 on gas and $500 on maintenance annually. Susan's sewing skills improve and she is able to earn an additional $900 by selling her handcrafted items and doing alterations.

$2,112 + $200 + $500 + $900 = $3,912 this year's savings
$600 + $54 + $1000 + $60 = $1,714 last year's savings + interest
$5,626 total savings

Year 5. Craig and Susan keep their $600 CD and leave $4,614 in savings. Craig uses $400 to purchase and fix up a utility trailer. With this he is able to haul home wood already cut and split for the same price as the delivered logs. With this time savings he hires out to clean garages and haul the contents to the dump. He gleans the "good stuff" and holds a yard sale. This effort earns $1,700. In a brilliant stroke of financial genius they spend the remaining $12 to subscribe to *The Tightwad Gazette* newsletter. The ideas they learn save $800.

$3,912 + $1,700 + $800 = $6,412 this year's savings
$600 + $54 + $4614 + $276 = $5,544 last year's savings + interest
$11,956 total savings

GIFT IDEAS

Dear Amy,

Make a glass cover for cookbooks to keep them clean while in use. You need a piece of glass about 8″ × 10″ and electrical tape (preferably red or green if making for Christmas gifts). Tape all four edges neatly. You can add holly and berry designs cut from the electrical tape in one corner.

Ann Davis
Andrews, North Carolina

Dear Amy,

The great story about your aunt giving you aluminum foil for Christmas gave me an idea. Why not purchase this year's Christmas gifts at the grocery store? I would be overjoyed to receive a month's worth of toilet paper rather than some useless item that will sit on my shelf or in a closet for the rest of my natural life. Most grocery stores have a gourmet or sugar-free candy section. Even an expensive sort of meat ready for the freezer to be enjoyed in the lean months of February when everybody will be cutting back to pay the fuel bills.

Chris Gernhart
Richmond, Texas

(I have two ideas along the line of practical Christmas gifts. One [different] aunt has given us a food basket for the past several years. It usually contains goodies that she knows I appreciate but am too cheap to buy. A ham, nuts, chocolate chips, etc.

The second idea I did for a grandmother who bakes hermits for us each time we visit. I made her a "Hermit Kit." This included nuts, raisins, a half gallon of molasses, brown sugar, flour, etc. I decorated the box, which weighed a ton, as if it were real packaging with the list of contents on the outside. FZ)

CALENDAR STRETCHER

Dear Amy,

Some friends of mine have a lovely summer home on the coast of Maine. On one of my visits a few years ago, I noticed that their kitchen calendar was odd. It had the word "November" crossed out and the word "August" written beside it. I asked about the calendar, and was informed that last year's September, October and November correspond on the calendar to this year's June, July, and August. Just cross out the old months and write in the new ones, adding also the 31st day to the new August. When they told me this I laughed. Now I pass along this fine idea that extends the life of a calendar by 25%.

David Westerberg
Chicago, Illinois

CALENDAR REUSE

Dear Amy,

Our calendar system (based on the Gregorian calendar) has 14 variations. If one were to save old calendars, just check the World Almanac's Perpetual Calendar listing to determine the years for which that outdated calendar would suffice.

T. Morse
Greenbelt, Maryland

TURNING DOWN THE DOOR-TO-DOOR SALES KID

I must admit I have not had to deal with this plague since I moved to rural Maine. Well, I bought one box of Girl Scout cookies because our local troop leader is a mother of five and I give her credit for filling an important niche. The story was something different living in a suburban area where there is a steady stream of short doorbell ringers selling overpriced goods. If you succumbed to your sense of civic guilt you might as well hang a flashing neon sign reading "Soft Touch." When a kid came selling $5 Christmas bobbles I decided enough was enough.

To deal effectively with the door-to-door sales kid you will need to have a convincing list of excuses. Make up a crib sheet and post it in an easily visible adult eye-level position just inside the door. This way you will be prepared if you are caught by surprise.

SALES KID CRIB SHEET

1. "I just bought one of those from the red-headed kid down the street . . . you know the one with braces?" (There is no such kid but details are convincing.)

2. "Sorry, we're on a diet." (Use this excuse only if they are selling something edible.)

3. Fumble in your wallet for a few minutes and then say "Gee, kid, sorry. I only have $100 bill. Maybe next time."

4. "Boy what rotten timing. My dog just ate my wallet." (This will click with her as she just that day told her teacher that *her* dog ate her homework.)

5. "I'm sorry. We are trying to save to buy a house." (This is fairly effective. I have found that even children will respect adults when they express a need to implement personal discipline.)

THE DOOR-TO-DOOR SALES KID UPDATE

I wrote a humorous article suggesting that it is acceptable not to buy items that kids are sent home from school to sell. Since then I have been on the other side of the door for the first time. Both my kindergartner and first grader brought home glossy flyers depicting goodies in fancy tins and wrapping paper . . . and they were overpriced. I read, pondered, and in the end finally decided that there was genuinely nothing I wanted.

In all fairness, schools raise funds in this manner because it happens to be a very effective method of involving every family, therefore probably raising a larger sum of money.

Since the fund-raiser was for the parents' group that sponsors many worthy events, why should I be a stick-in-the-mud over this?

First, it is consumerism—buying for the sake of buying and sometimes because we feel a little coerced. We feel that we cannot send our child back to school without at least one order. We also don't want our kids knocking on our neighbors' doors pressing

them to buy and I don't want my husband peddling them at work.

The manufacturing of most goods harms the environment in one way or another. The culprit is not the factory, but it is we who buy what it produces. Therefore we should think carefully about items we purchase.

Second, a portion of the money that we spend to help a worthy cause leaves the community. And I am concerned about those people who buy and can't afford to.

The parents' group in our community offers a few excellent alternatives. In the fall there is a potluck supper and auction. People who attend bring crafts, baked goods, and garden surplus. In this way you have the option to donate or bid for something. Our pumpkin brought $10. They also run a carnival in the springtime. Our church youth group "auctions" teenagers to do house and yard work. These types of events foster community spirit, keep all the money within the community, and are not consumer driven.

It was interesting that as I asked around I found several teachers and parents who shared my views. And, frankly, I didn't want to make waves any more than anyone else. I finally arrived at what I felt was my best choice. I simply donated money without buying anything.

NEWSPAPER KINDLING

If your town has a recycling program you will want to dispose of surplus newspaper in that manner. However, if you cannot recycle, or if you have a shortage of kindling and a surplus of newspaper, this is a terrific idea.

Starting with one corner roll a single sheet of newspaper into a long tube less than 1″ in diameter. Fold the tube into a *V*. Continue by alternating and folding over the underneath side until you have only 1″ ends left. Tuck these under so they are secure.

This type of newspaper kindling is so dense you will need to use crushed paper to start them burning. They burn hot enough to start a log burning without the use of wood kindling. About 10 will be enough.

If we do not pick up small sticks around our property, generally we make kindling by chopping scrap wood into smaller pieces, thereby reducing the heat value. If we make kindling from newspaper we increase the heat value.

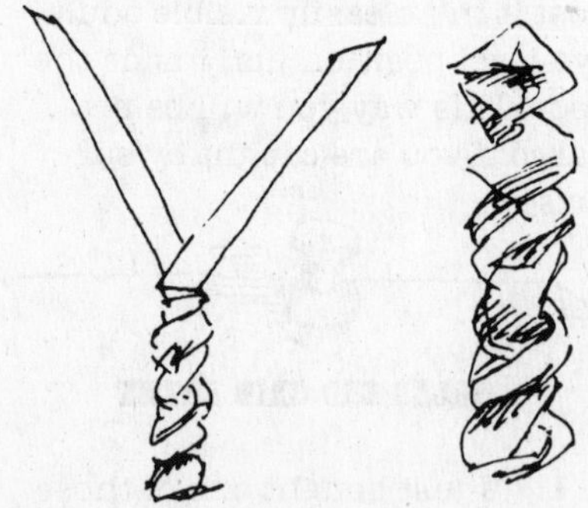

TIGHTWAD VALENTINES

Over the years Jim has been the lucky recipient of creative and artistic valentines that relied heavily on my graphic art background, including a pop-up valentine and a most impressive animated one.

These things provide interesting reading but lack applicability to those of average abilities. In truth, creativity and thoughtfulness supersede artistic ability. If your middle name is not da Vinci try one of the following.

- Bake a pie with strawberry or cherry filling. Cut a heart design in the crust.

- Make a very simple card with a meaningful or funny poem. Your middle name doesn't have to be Browning either. I was pregnant our first Valentine's day. I included a poem in a simple card:

Roses are red.
Violets are blue.
Within me beat
Two hearts for you.

(Maybe I should stick to art?)

- Why not complete the procrastinated task that has most annoyed your spouse, and then leave a valentine conspicuously in the area? I have a friend who papered the bathroom for his wife as a birthday present.
- Make a heart-shaped pizza, topped primarily with red items such as pepperoni or red peppers.

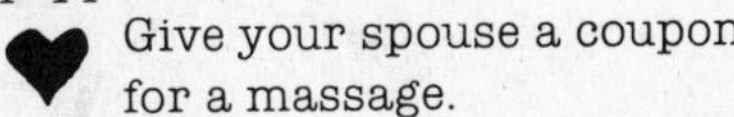

- Give your spouse a coupon for a massage.
- Make a heart-shaped cake by baking a round cake and a square cake. One side of the square cake must be of an equal length to the diameter of the round cake. Cut the round cake in half and combine with the square to make a heart. Frost to hide seams.

- Ambush your spouse as he or she comes home with a booby trap plastic bucket filled with small paper hearts, attached over the door, in such a way as to dump when the door is opened (see page 290).
- If nature cooperates, stomp out a valentine in a large area of snow. I tried this one year but was far too ambitious. We have a great view of our cornfield from the third-floor attic. My 50-foot valentine was not visible until I had stomped around it about 20 times. Every few laps I would run back to the house, across a distance of foot deep snow, up to the third-floor attic, to see if the valentine was visible yet. I exhausted myself and I am sure passersby thought the new neighbor was loony tunes. Before Jim arrived home, late afternoon shadows obliterated my creation.

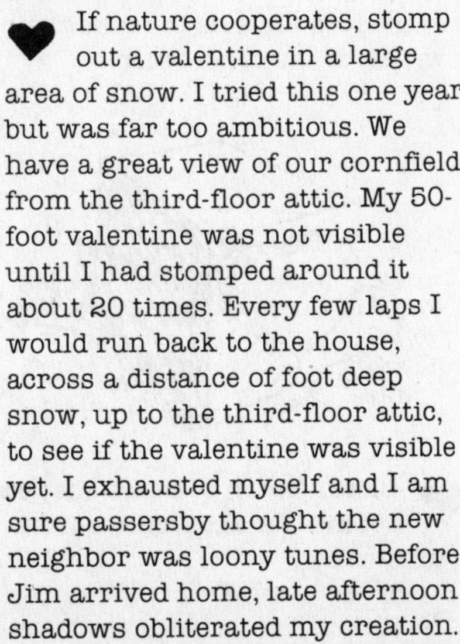

I suggest you try something no larger than 20 feet and be sure it

will be seen when your spouse arrives.

♥ Pick a bouquet of pussy willows or other winter growth, and tie it with a large red bow.

♥ Rent a romantic classic movie, especially one that you might have seen together when you were first dating.

♥ One year Jim (a fellow of less than average artistic abilities) made a card for me. He cut a heart design into an art gum eraser and stamped the entire cover of the card. This is a simple idea for kids to make their own cards for school also.

♥ Bake a batch of heart-shaped cookies (make a cutter from a tuna can).

EVERYTHING I ALWAYS WANTED TO WRITE ABOUT DATING, BUT WAS AFRAID TO SQUEEZE INTO ONE ARTICLE

In the 10 years I have known Jim we have had only one real argument. A few hours later he apologized and admitted that he had been dead wrong about the croquet rule.

Aside from this single shouting match we have had the occasional "stressful conversation" or "agreement to disagree," but generally we enjoy remarkable compatibility.

I have always believed that teamwork has been our greatest economic asset. It is about more than simply agreeing on how to handle money. We do not need to expend energy "working on our marriage," whatever that means. As a result we have maximum energy to devote to our common goals.

It is much like the biblical analogy of a team of oxen that is "unequally yoked." If the oxen work against each other they are ineffective. But pulling together they accomplish more than they would individually.

Compatibility is more likely to be found than created. A psychologist told me that whatever a relationship is in the beginning is what it will always be. In other words, people can modify their behavior to a degree, but sweeping changes are rare. While they may occur, they should not be banked on.

Since money is the most com-

mon marital problem, it occurs to me that people must be running amok in the selection process. Historically, we most commonly selected our soul mates through an economic bait-and-switch dating style.

Traditional dating has its roots in the Neanderthal era. The man demonstrated his ability to provide by bringing the desired mate (or her parents) gifts of furs, food, and other valuables. This tradition has continued until recently. The smitten spender (the man) demonstrated his economic prowess by paying for food, entertainment, jewelry, and other gifts.

He "baited" by sending the message that he could provide security and that he expressed love through money. It followed that if someone baited a mate with extravagant spending he was likely to attract a spouse who appreciated it. The "switch" occurred after marriage, when he or she balanced the joint checking account for the first time. If they were lucky they learned they were both tightwads, as Jim and I did. If they found they were both spendthrifts, they might be equally yoked but blissfully plowing off into the sunset . . . together but in the wrong direction. The third common scenario occurred when people found themselves in a "mixed marriage," or they discovered they had different economic styles.

In the past 10 years, the financial responsibility of the date has become more equitable, at least once couples get beyond the initial courtship. However, even when couples live together they tend to retain separate budgets, and the money never becomes "our money." In some cases after marriage couples may still keep separate accounts. It isn't until the state of "our money" occurs that couples develop a heightened awareness of economic incompatibility. When couples learn they have to make choices they may discover they wouldn't choose the same things.

The financial problems in marriage can involve more than a lack of sufficient funds, but also a difference in spending style. Even when there might be enough money, it can still drive a tightwad to the brink of insanity to see his spouse get little value for the dollar.

The issue of economic incompatibility may not come up until long after the couple has become emotionally hooked. But the signals are present from the beginning. They're just ignored or not looked for.

Our culture seems to frown upon the concept that we "choose" our marriage partners. Romance, we are told, is something that just happens. Early attempts to weed out a potential mate on the basis of incompatibility is "too cold and calculating," especially in relationship to money.

In reality, we fall in love with people we spend time with. It makes sense to look for the signals of all sorts of incompatibility during the first dates, before the emotional hook occurs, and not spend time with people who appear to have dissimilar values and goals.

Ignore social pressure to spend extravagantly on dates, and thereby send out the wrong message. If you want to attract a tight-

wad soulmate put out "frugal date bait." Instead of sending roses, give a flowering plant that you potted from your cuttings. Make your own chocolates. Invite her to dinner. Even if the meal is substandard, the right woman will love it.

What's the difference between putting out frugal date bait and being cheap? Lu Bauer, a CPA in Falmouth, Maine, who teaches courses on money and relationships, suggests that your dating style should be consistent with a whole life pattern. If you spend lots of money partying with your friends, and little on dates, you might rightfully be labeled "cheap." Largely it is a matter of thoughtfulness and style. Whipping out your two-for-one coupon at a cafeteria-style chain steak house may lack a certain class. Instead plan a modest but elegant picnic at your special private spot.

If you really want to separate the wheat from the chaff, plan a characteristically tightwad date, something that you enjoy and is a regular part of your life. It might be a date to go yard saling. You plan the route, and bring the homemade muffins and thermos of coffee.

While you are putting out your tasteful but frugal date bait, look closely at the reactions it brings. Look for it in the eyes. A spendthrift will appear to not "get it," and have a furrowed quizzical look. A tightwad will twinkle with delight.

When you are dating, don't worry about making a good impression. Make an accurate impression. Spend in a way that is consistent with your income and values. In doing so you increase your chances of attracting someone with whom you are most compatible.

Compatibility in all areas, not just spending, is a tremendous economic advantage.

THE KISS GIFT

Dear Amy,

Make a "kiss gift." Take a cardboard circle that is larger than the gift. Place tissue around the base to give it body and wrap the gift in tissue paper. Wrap the circle, tissue paper and gift in aluminum foil so that it looks like a

Hershey's Kiss. Run a piece of paper out of the top for a nametag and tape securely.

Mildred James
Greensboro, North Carolina

PHOTO VALENTINE

Dear Amy,

Last year I made my husband a card that is still on his desk at work. I made big letters out of construction paper for the words "I love you" and took a picture of our son holding each letter. I put them all together on a long cardboard card and underneath each picture wrote a short sentiment. *L* is for the lovely songs you sing, etc.

Jill Boyd
Seattle, Washington

A.M. VALENTINE

Dear Amy,

Get up before the family and write your Valentine's message on the bathroom mirror with lipstick.

Ruth Palmer
Glendale, Utah

SMOOCH CARD

Dear Amy,

Have Mom and all the children put on red lipstick. Take a plain piece of paper and have each person kiss it. Sign it if desired and frame.

Beverly Huff
Nashville, Tennessee

STUFFED HEART

Dear Amy,

I'll always cherish a red stuffed heart my mother gave each of her girls for Valentine's Day. The material probably came from a fancy gown or remnant. It is about 8″ at the widest part and can be stuffed with whatever you have. Mom sewed lace around and made a red tab with which to hang it. I have it in my bedroom with a fancy pin collection in it.

Lois Funke
Ontonagon, Michigan

(Or make a hanging from three hearts with different red-patterned material. Stuffing possibilities include cup-up nylons or the filling from an old baby quilt. FZ)

A SWEET HEART PACKAGE

When it comes to valentine exchanges at school, packages of 20 for $1 (on sale) are hard to beat, even though it seems uncreative. The problem with making your own is figuring out a way to make a lot cheaply and easily, and trying to do something that's at least as good as store

bought. It's a pretty tall order.

This little idea was sent in to me by a reader who made a heart package from an old greeting card. As I experimented with different cards I found many unlikely designs worked, such as Christmas cards. You see a small section of the original picture on the heart so it creates an abstract design. Trace the pattern onto lightweight paper. Make a template by transferring the tracing onto a lightweight piece of cardboard, such as a margarine box. An inexpensive way of making an erasable "carbon" is to cover a piece of paper with graphite, using the side of a No. 2 pencil. A template will save time if you are planning to make several hearts.

Fold up the cut-out heart package as shown. Glue the flaps where indicated. Secure with a ribbon.

As a suggestion for something to put in your heart try making these easy mints.

1 cup granulated sugar
4 Tbsp water
peppermint flavoring
red or pink food coloring
1 cup powdered sugar

Combine granulated sugar and water. Bring to a boil. Add flavoring, food coloring, and powdered sugar. Drop on wax paper quickly. (The first mints will be round, and as the mixture cools they become lumpier.)

By using different colors this recipe works for other holidays.

A BAKED BEAN HERITAGE

When Jim was a boy living in western Massachusetts, his fam-

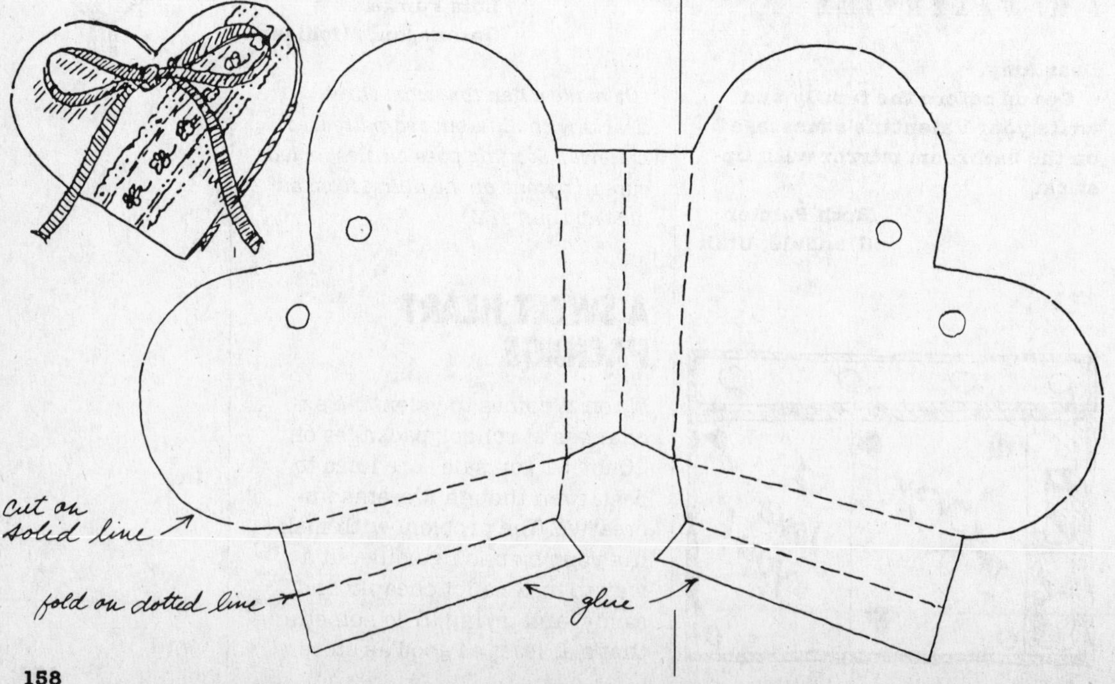

ily visited friends in Maine. During that trip they experienced a "bean hole supper" in which beans were cooked in pots buried in the ground along with hot ashes. The beans used at that supper were Jacob's Cattle beans. These attractive beans, appropriately named for their brown-and-white markings, look much like a dairy cow.

Jim's parents bought a package of Jacob's Cattle beans and brought them home. They planted the beans, and have eaten and replanted the surplus year after year for 30 years. When we moved to Maine, my father-in-law gave us some Jacob's Cattle beans, and now we grow them.

Dried beans are an excellent protein source, are nearly always less expensive than meat, and should be considered a staple of the tightwad diet. Because most of us are familiar with baked beans, they make a great dinner for the entry-level vegetarian.

When I married Jim I ate these scratch-baked beans for the first time, and loved them for their character and rich, dark flavor. You can use most types of dried beans in this recipe.

Maine Baked Beans

2 lbs dried beans (4 cups)
1 tsp. baking soda
1 medium onion
½ lb bacon or salt pork
¼ cup brown sugar
½ to ⅔ cup molasses
2 tsp dry mustard
½ tsp salt

Soak the beans overnight in cold water. In the morning pour off the soaking water and parboil beans with baking soda in fresh water until the skins crack when blown upon. Cut onion in quarters and put in the bottom of a bean pot or large casserole. Add parboiled beans. Put cut-up bacon or salt pork on top of the beans. Mix brown sugar, molasses, dry mustard, and salt with a pint of water. If necessary add more boiling water while baking. Bake at 300° for 6 hours or more.

This recipe makes the equivalent of six 28-oz. cans of B&M baked beans at $1.28 per can. The ingredients of the scratch beans (if you buy the beans) cost about $2 versus $7.68 for store bought. Even allowing a generous figure for electricity, scratch beans will cost well under half the cost of B&M beans.

We make this recipe in our two bean pots. It's hard to find old bean pots complete with lids, as the lids break easily. We've solved the problem with a little ingenuity. My grandmother gave us a bean pot without a lid. Shortly thereafter I found a smaller bean pot with a same-sized lid at a yard sale for 50¢. I bought the bean pot, saved the lid and resold the pot at my yard sale for 50¢. We now have a second bean pot that also lacks its original lid. Sometime earlier I broke my glass coffee perker. I must possess tightwad ESP, because I saved the seemingly useless glass top. We later found the glass top makes a nice bean pot lid if used upside down. (You didn't need to know this, but I think it's funny.)

We freeze the leftover beans in 1-cup size margarine containers to use in other recipes.

Although I recall eating mostly store bought baked beans, my own childhood is not without a baked bean tradition. My mother made two recipes that used baked bean leftovers:

Dunkin' Soup

2 cups baked beans
1 8-oz can of stewed or canned tomatoes
1 large celery stalk with leaves
1 chopped onion
salt and pepper to taste

Process all the ingredients in a blender. Heat to boiling and simmer 20 minutes.

We called this Dunkin' Soup because it was our tradition to eat it by dipping (dunkin') bread into the soup. As an adult, I no longer need all the carbohydrates I would get from eating the soup with bread, so I now enjoy it with a spoon. This recipe has become a favorite of my children.

Corn Pone

1 lb hamburger, browned and drained
⅓ cup chopped onion
1 Tbsp shortening
¾ tsp salt
1 tsp worcestershire sauce
2 cups canned tomatoes
1 cup baked beans

Sauté onion in shortening. Combine the remaining ingredients and place in a large casserole (we use a large cast-iron frying pan). Top with ½-inch layer of cornbread batter (recipe available in any basic cookbook). Bake at 425° for 30 minutes. Bake any remaining cornbread batter in muffin tins.

As with any good marriage, elements of Jim's family traditions have blended with elements of mine. But we experiment and add to our repertoire, thereby forging new food traditions. This is a soup recipe we have discovered and grown fond of:

Bean-Bacon Chowder

6 slices bacon, cut up
1 cup chopped onion
2 Tbsp flour
3 cups milk
2 medium potatoes, peeled
¼ tsp crushed dried thyme
1, 22-oz jar of baked beans (substitute homemade here)
¼ cup snipped parsley

Cook bacon and onion in a saucepan until bacon is lightly browned and onion is tender. Blend in flour. Add milk; cook and stir until bubbly. Dice potatoes; add with thyme, 1 tsp salt and ⅛ tsp pepper. Cover and simmer 12 to 15 minutes or till the potatoes are done. Stir in beans and heat through. Top with parsley. Serves six.

Spring

EASTER IDEAS

The commercialism surrounding Easter bothers me more than that which surrounds Christmas. Despite this a few foil covered bunnies have crossed our threshold.

I have worked out a few less expensive alternatives to the enormous pink plastic-wrapped baskets that crowd store shelves at this time of year.

Give smaller baskets. The smaller the basket the less needed to fill.

I have resorted to ridiculous lengths to create homemade baskets from recycled materials. Sane mothers reuse the same baskets from year to year.

Fill baskets with homemade edible items and inexpensive treasures. One year I made necklaces out of Froot Loops (purchased with coupons back when we lived in double-coupon territory) and marshmallow bunnies. I also collected all the freebies with coupons given to me by the Welcome Wagon lady. Many items ended up in Easter baskets.

Or do not fill the Easter baskets. Instead hide jelly beans for kids to find to fill their own baskets. A bag of jelly beans is comparatively inexpensive. The degree of difficulty will control the rate of sugar consumption. Do not do as my mother did. She would toss many beans in the toy box. The thrill of the hunt diminished when we were forced to clean out our toy box.

It is not necessary to purchase egg decorating kits. A cup of boiling water, a teaspoon of vinegar, and food coloring works as well. Professional paste food coloring produces better color.

My final thought is my most radical. Focus on the spiritual significance of the holiday.

HOW TO MAKE MARSHMALLOW BUNNIES

Clip the marshmallow as shown by the dotted line using a pair of scissors. Sprinkle confectionery sugar in cut places so it does not stick. To make eyes dot with a toothpick that has been dipped in red food coloring.

HOP, SKIMP, & JUMP

Dear Amy,

Sometimes by going through Las Vegas you can get cheaper fares when flying cross-country. For example, buy a round trip from San Diego to Las Vegas, and then a round trip from Las Vegas to your final destination. This is because Las Vegas is always having specials when the rest of the country isn't.

Jeannie Coulson
San Diego, California

FIX-IT LADY

Dear Amy,

My husband is not mechanical and so I am left to fix things or to have them fixed. I have repaired hundreds of things by trial and error. I fixed a Coleman lantern that would not stay lit. (It only had cobwebs in the air flow tube.) I also put a new belt and heating element in my Whirlpool dryer.

Most companies have 800 numbers you can call to talk to a serviceperson. Call 1-800-555-1212 for information or send a 19¢ postcard for more information.

I always order replacement parts for toys or to fix something cheap I got at a yard sale. All you need is the company name, toy name, or model number of the toy.

Fisher-Price offers a free Bits and Pieces Catalog of Replacement Parts:

Fisher-Price
636 Girard Ave.
East Aurora, NY 14052

Rachel Wiegand
Stanley, Virginia

50% SHAMPOO SAVINGS

Dear Amy,

Most shampoo instructions tell you to "lather, rinse, repeat." I've stopped "repeating" years ago and never noticed any difference in how clean my hair gets.

Eileen Mierski
Pittsburgh, Pennsylvania

JELL-O EGGS

Dear Amy,

Every Easter my mother takes a couple-dozen eggs and with a needle breaks a ¼-inch hole in the top of the eggs. She drains the eggs and rinses the shells before submersing them in boiling water for a few seconds. She then fills them with this mixture:

1 cup water
1 large box gelatin mixture
1 pkg. Knox gelatin
2 cups cold water

Dissolve the gelatin powders in one cup boiling water, then add the 2 cups cold water.

My mother sometimes lets this jell a bit, then pours in different colors to get striped eggs. She leaves them in the fridge till morning and we usually help her crack the eggs, which she serves with dinner. This turns out to be

fun and exciting for grandchildren, who don't know her secret and wonder how Grandma got Jell-O eggs. She saves the drained eggs and makes omelets or scrambled eggs.

Robin Lively
Idaho Falls, Idaho

DESPERATE MEASURES

Dear Amy,

When Ron and I were first married, March 1970, we had an income of $258/month; rent was $145. Those were extremely lean times. I kept track of all expenses as a matter of pure survival. We had a strict limit of $17 for food every two weeks. We wrote prices down as we went through the commissary, and if the total went up to $17.01 we put something back.

I sat in the dark (Ron worked nights) in order to save on electricity. We didn't buy magazines, newspapers, or clothes. We used our car only for him to go to work and to get food. We walked a lot. We gladly would have done without a phone but the Air Force insisted we have one.

Our apartment was furnished, so we asked if we could give the furniture back and drop the rent to $95. The landlord agreed to it and we made the eight-hour trip to Illinois to get my bed and a couple of chairs. To save money while we were gone we totally emptied the fridge, freezer, turned it off, and unplugged everything electric.

I was raised to use a towel once and throw it in the laundry, but when we got married, it quickly (1 week) became apparent this was nuts! We simply couldn't afford that luxury! And, even though I'd lived that way for three weeks short of 22 years, suddenly using a towel once, then washing it, seemed awfully wasteful, so I stopped and started using a towel for a week.

We lived in a tiny, rundown apartment—no balcony—but I strung lines over the bathtub to dry some things and would drape things over the outside back steps railing to dry while I read on the steps (to prevent them from being stolen). I've also been known to hand wash our laundry to save on water and electricity.

There are all sorts of measures you can take when you're financially desperate.

Pat Wagner
Columbus, Ohio

THREE PRINCIPLES OF USED ACQUISITION

A prerequisite for our dream home was the existence of at least one wood stove hookup, preferably in the kitchen. My great-grandmother's house had one of those black monster cookstoves with warming ovens, and my grandmothers both have small wood stoves in their kitchens. So in keeping with my "matriarch complex," I wanted one, too.

As it happened our kitchen had one such hookup and an empty space that cried out for a large cookstove. After several months of diligence we found a Glenwood F cookstove at the right price.

The location of the wood stove resulted from a strategy that I call "putting out the word." If you're looking for something, casually mention your search to

every soul you run into. Very often someone you know, or someone they know, has the very thing you want and would be willing to give it to you, or sell it for a reasonable price.

Putting out the word should not be confused with mooching. You are not asking for the shirt off someone's back. Instead you say, "I am looking for another good shirt. If you know someone who has one they might sell at a reasonable price, let me know." (Do not stare at their shirt while saying this.)

If someone has an item they are not using, such as a tool buried in a garage, or a piece of old furniture in the attic with at least 40 years of dust on it, let them know that you'd be willing to buy it for a reasonable price. You might also suggest a barter arrangement. Whatever the deal, always pay a fair price for a used item—though they'll often let you have it for free.

When you put out the word be sure to speak to the best scrounger you know. (In our case, it's my father-in-law. When you hit pawn shops and flea markets, speak up. And if your swap magazine runs ads for free, place a "wanted" ad.

In the case of our stove, Jim learned of it through speaking with a woman who ran the thrift shop. She had it stored in her garage in (rusted) pieces and would let us have it for $100, or $75 if we gave her dog a home, too.

We took the stove, but not the dog. I spent a few hours cleaning it with a wire brush, and applied stove blacking, and Jim replaced the fire brick. The stove is worth at least $500 today.

When we set the stove up we realized that,

even though the price was right, it was a smaller version than what we wanted. We still want a larger stove—a Glenwood E with warming ovens. Our plan includes a strategy called "trading up."

Most people know someone who has traded-up in housing. I know a man who acquired a handsome antique gun collection the same way. He bought a rifle in poor condition, restored it, and sold it. He used the profit to buy two more guns that needed work, restored those and so on.

We figure that if we bought a stove for $100 and sell it for $500, perhaps we could buy a larger stove for $500 in need of elbow grease. Ideally we could eventually own a stove worth $800 or more for an initial investment of $100, plus the cost of fire brick and stove blacking. If you need an item for a short period of time, or if you can't find

exactly what you want but need something to tide you over, you can get free use of an item by using a method I call "temporary ownership."

A new thing depreciates rapidly with its first ownership. A young couple might buy a new crib for $200 and sell it in two years for $50. The two-year-use of the crib cost $150. It depreciated by 75% of its value even though it's still functional and good-looking. (Multiply that cost by all the other short-term-use equipment and clothes you need for a child and you can needlessly spend many hundreds of dollars.)

As you become familiar with the used-stuff market you'll find a significant price range. That same crib might sell for $25 to $75. Shop around and buy items at the low end of the range—in other words, buy the $25 crib. After you've used it for your tribe, resell the crib. Even though the crib will be more worn, you'll be able to recoup your $25 because you bought on the low end of the price range. The use of the crib becomes free to you.

We've used the put-out-the-word strategy to acquire our first cookstove, which we plan to temporarily own until we can trade up when we find a black iron Glenwood E (or similar stove) with warming ovens. Using this example to illustrate ideas in my newsletter must be the ultimate example of putting out the word.

P.S. I used the hand-me-down crib as an example in this article. Before purchasing used baby equipment you should learn about current safety guidelines. You can receive free pamphlets on crib safety and tips for baby safety by writing to:

Consumer Products Safety
Commission
Washington, DC 20207

PUT OUT THE WORD

Dear Amy,

I recently tried your "put-out-the-word" strategy (as mentioned in the *Parade* article) and asked a friend where I might find an engine for my rototiller. He offered a complete tiller if I would just come and get it. It turned out to be a Craftsman 5 HP rear tine, self-propelled model! It needed a 50¢ flywheel key and now runs great. My friend did have a mower in need of a tune-up so I made his mower look and run like new in exchange for the tiller. Now we are both happy and I'm planning to do more small-engine repair for friends and neighbors after my initial success.

Lyle Merril
Logan, Utah

A GOLF TIP

Dear Amy,

Golf balls are getting more expensive each season, ranging from $16 per dozen for in-line balls on sale to as much as $30 per dozen for top-of-the-line tour balls. Many manufacturers of golf balls brag about their balls being durable, and several go to the trouble to print a guarantee on the packaging of the balls (sleeve of three) stating they guarantee their ball will not cut or split during the ball's lifetime. If they should, the company will replace the bad ball with three free balls.

Problem is, many golfers don't read the fine print on the package and never learn what a great guarantee they are offered. This season I have had six balls cut during play and have sent in all six using the guarantee. Now I have eighteen new balls.

Kevin Brown
Sheboygan, Wisconsin

QUICKIE CALL

Dear Amy,

I would like to point out a cost-effective procedure—the 1-minute phone call. Such calls are rare but on my recent phone bill 31 of the 58 calls cost less than a 1st-class letter. Some were calls to leave or pick up answering machine messages, but others had real-live participants who simply got to the point and said goodbye.

Try this exercise: Write down before the call what you really need to say on the phone. Time yourself reading it back. Can you stretch it to one minute? Probably not. Most of our phone talk is casual conversation that could be put into a letter.

There are many times when talk could not or should not be cut to the minimum, but you can be pointed and polite in one minute if necessary.

Ken Lundeen
New York, New York

KIDS' CAR SEATS

Dear Amy,

If anyone is planning to buy a child car seat at a yard sale or already has one that was handed down, they can write to the following address and request a current copy of "The Recommended Child Seats and Recalls." Enclose an SASE.

Center for Auto Safety
2001 S Street, NW
Suite 410
Washington, DC 20009

I purchased a car seat at a yard sale for $15. Upon checking the list I found the seat was listed under recalls. When I called the toll-free number they took my name and address and sent me a new redesigned one free of charge.

Dorothy L. Johns
Woodbury, Connecticut

STEEL WOOL PADS

Dear Amy,

After using a soapy steel wool pad, pop it in the freezer. It will thaw quickly for the next use and won't be a pile of rust next to your sink!

Susan Abbott
Windsor, Connecticut

TIME SAVER

Dear Amy,

You asked for time-saving helps. My neighbor and I exchange meals once a week. She cooks for me on Tuesday and I cook for her Thursday. We just do the main dish, adding the salad or whatever. Since she lives right next door, delivery is simple. We both enjoy our night off.

Lucy Scholand
Ypsilanti, Michigan

CONVERTING YOUR SPOUSE

I have hesitated to write this article because I cannot draw from personal experience. Although I might have implied it, I did not convert Jim. We were both spendthrifts with underlying tightwad tendencies . . . my tendencies being a bit stronger than his. Therefore, changing gears was a natural process for both of us.

I have observed many tightwad spouses who have struggled for years, or even decades, to change their spendthrift partners without success. In some cases they tried all the suggestions I have. The truth is that you cannot change your spouse.

Genuine change results from an inner willingness and cannot be imposed by others. I suspect that if a change runs completely against someone's character, the best you can hope for is a small degree of behavior modification.

As dismal as this sounds, consider spouse conversion to be a worthy pursuit. Many of my suggestions are proven sales or relationship strategies. Some are pure theory. With the exception of the first two, my suggestions are presented in random order.

In my experience men and women are equally as likely to be spendthrifts. My use of the gender-neutral "he" is for simplicity only.

1. Establish a financial goal that you both can agree on. Without a goal, saving money has no meaning, but with one you have a beginning point for encouraging change. The goal should be very specific and have a time period attached. By choosing a goal you show him how *he* can benefit by change.

2. Gather evidence. Know how much money you have coming in and where it goes. Record your spending habits meticulously. If your spouse will not participate, then you can at least show him how much is unaccounted for. Put together as comprehensive a proposal as possible before you call a meeting. Graphs and charts are not too extreme.

3. Always confront your spouse at a "good time." He should be relaxed and in a good mood. You may have to schedule a specific time. Do not confront in the heat of an argument.

4. When you discuss the problem stick with the facts. Do not label, accuse, or blame. Say something such as:

a. "We agreed that we would try to pay off our credit cards."

b. "This month you bought a $75 fishing reel."

c. "We only made an interest payment on our Visa card this time."

He may not agree that he is a spendthrift, but he cannot deny the facts.

The objective is to discuss the problem in a way that is easiest for him to hear. You want to maximize your chances to sell tightwaddery . . . not to be "right."

5. Be the leader. Your record of spending should show that you didn't spend on anything that could possibly be considered nonessential. If cutting on the food bill requires more cooking from scratch, and your spouse doesn't want to do it, then *you* need to learn to cook.

6. Request small changes rather than sweeping reforms. For example, request a waiting period of a month between when he tells you he wants to buy something and when he makes the purchase. Or convince the meat-and-potatoes spouse to have one meatless meal per month. When these changes have been accepted, increase the waiting time, number of meatless meals, or ask for new changes.

7. Give your spouse some freedom. Agree to a small amount of money that your spouse can spend on anything wanted . . . say $5, $10, or $25 per week. Determine a sum of money that fits into your budget. That discretionary fund is to be spent without comment or criticism from you. Give yourself a discretionary fund as well. Naturally, you will put yours into a savings account.

8. Show him. If an item goes on sale for which he paid full price a week earlier, point it out in a tactful way. If you discover something that works and saves money, show him. The gentle and regular sharing of information over time may win him.

9. Sometimes the person your spouse is least likely to hear information from is you. If this is the case in your marriage, get him to think it is *his* idea. Say to him "What do you think about . . . ?" Repeat this every few days. With any luck in time he will tell you about *his* new idea.

10. Be patient. Pushing too hard for change may cause your spouse to reject your wishes. My mother's favorite saying is, "You catch more flies with honey than with vinegar." Real behavior modification takes time. Hopefully you will be married for several decades. In the light of that, a transition that requires a few years may not be too long.

11. Leave copies of *The Tightwad Gazette* within the pages of his well-worn bathroom copy of the Sears, Roebuck catalog.

If you are single and think this is yet another article for married people that doesn't pertain to you, you're wrong. The very fact that large numbers of married tightwads have requested this article should be a red flag to you. Continue to weed out the candidates until you find one whose fiscal philosophy matches yours. Every good tightwad knows that an ounce of prevention is worth a pound of cure.

CONVERTING YOUR SPOUSE UPDATE

As a follow-up on my article "Converting Your Spouse," readers sent in the following suggestions. Contributors' names have been withheld to ensure future domestic tranquillity.

Single tightwads should note that fewer than half a dozen people shared success with conversions.

"In order to have any success in converting a die-hard spendthrift you first must understand the mental dynamics behind one:

1. They do not understand the concept of money. Period.

2. Like small children, they need instant gratification.

3. They are slow to realize that their money must be used to pay for life's necessities.

4. They don't understand that control over their money, in the long run, will give them more freedom and peace of mind.

5. Any attempt to make them responsible for money is perceived as punishment or an attempt to control their lives, and may backfire into another spending binge.

Coping suggestions:

1. Accept the things you cannot change, and change the things you can. Know the difference between the two.

2. Agree that purchases of over x-amount must be discussed.

3. Post your income and outgo in a place where it can be seen . . . either weekly or monthly.

4. Take care of necessities first, before discretionary funds are distributed. This seems like common sense to most, but spendthrifts get it backward. They buy 'wants' before 'needs.'

5. If you know a major expense is coming up, let them know well in advance there will be less discretionary funds available and ask for cooperation.

6. Make it clear that a savings account is not a discretionary fund and must be 'paid' like a bill. If necessary, set it up so that the spendthrift spouse cannot access it. Do not discuss how much is there, as it is frustrating for them to know that funds are available that cannot be spent without proving true need.

7. When there has been a spending binge do not retaliate with one of your own. This only proves to your spouse that the money was available all along, and your efforts to convert your spouse will go right down the tubes."

"I think it is an awareness process, so for phase one I tried to convince my husband that those

little things such as stopping at the market for a drink and a snack on the way home add up. I started casually asking about his day and if he stopped at the market. If he did I put the same amount as was spent in a jar. A month to 45 days later he wanted to buy some large purchases. I brought out the jar, explained what I had done, and had him count it. There was $80 in the jar. Phase one completed."

"I did not change my husband overnight. He came to our marriage with the idea that the key to financial solvency was to earn more money. He spent the first two years of our marriage pressuring me to get a better job, while many of our careless habits were eating away at our savings. Words were of no use because he felt it was beneath him to examine the food bill or live in a cheaper apartment. I slowly began to take control of areas I knew best, without discussion, as previous attempts made him angry and defensive.

"First I found a larger apartment with a savings of $100 per month. Then I began keeping track of our grocery bill and was able to show him how costs could go down.

"I didn't confront him with any 'I told you so's' and reminders of previous wastefulness, and soon he did internalize many of my money-saving ways. Now I have a quiet laugh when he expounds his thrifty principles, nearly all of which he learned from me!"

"My husband would never consider anything used. 'Someone else's junk' he called it. He had always been a stickler for 'if you're going to get it, get the best' philosophy. So I can't tell you how many top-of-the-line things we have lying around the house, which have since become obsolete, vastly decreased in value, or just plain useless.

"He hated mowing our 100′ × 100′ patch of lawn because it took so long with a push mower. Yet, the only riding mower he would consider was a 16 HP beast that mulched, vacuumed, plowed earth and snow, and tuned the car. New, they cost over $2,500, a bit beyond our budget. One weekend, after several summers of knee-high weeds, I looked in the classifieds, drove out with our pick-up, and returned with a used, reconditioned 8 HP riding mower for $350. It didn't look like much, but it got the job done. For the first few weeks he would have nothing to do with it and I took over mowing the lawn. Gradually his resistance faded, and now he even changes the oil in it.

"Next we wanted a Vermont Castings 'Vigilant,' a stove that burns coal and wood and costs $1,600 new. We found a classified that advertised one with considerable equipment for half the price. My husband, who was initially cynical, did the bargaining. After that I saw a subtle, but undeniable change in his attitude.

"Just recently, it was he who suggested we advertise in the wanted column to buy a used travel trailer. We found just what we wanted in excellent condition for a fraction of what they cost new."

CHEAP THRILL

Dear Amy,

I thought you might enjoy reading about how my husband and I entertained our daughter and her overnight guest. We created an elegant private dinner for two in a "rustic country inn" (our home).

We discussed the concept with the girls in the afternoon. We gave them an outline of the evening and reviewed table settings and helped them develop a menu based upon available foodstuffs suggesting traditionally appropriate relishes. We set a few ground rules as to the scope of services that could be requested (these had to be in line with what one would normally require of a restaurant staff). We explained that a distant relative had provided the dinner at no charge to the girls so that money was not the issue (no making menu selections based upon price). We also explained that the basis of all good manners is respect for the other party as a human being so that condescending behavior was nipped in its potential bud.

The girls dressed in an assortment of "dress-up" clothes, consisting mainly of cast-off lingerie and plastic beads, bracelets, and large hair ribbons. As maître d', Erik dressed in a tux with an outrageous multicolored tie, and I, as waitress, dressed in an evening gown and loaded up with every rhinestone I could find (earrings, necklace, rings, bracelets, hairclips, pins).

We set a table in Anna's upstairs room and provided:

a "linen" tablecloth (a white sheet) and napkins
candlestick (with a hurricane shade)
flowers (silk) with ribbon streamers across the table
an ice bucket on a stand (plant stand)
water in crystal goblets
a service table (also with cloth)
a handbell for service (this was a highlight)
music by Vivaldi

The arrival: a knock on the door, the maître d' opens the door, and welcomes the diners, exclaiming over the honor of welcoming them to the country inn and promising them an extraordinary evening. He introduces his wife, the cook and waitress. They are escorted to their table where the evening menu is presented in an embossed leather folder with each course described and listed in order (the girls prepared the menu inserts during the afternoon after the selections had been made, refined, and agreed upon).

The maître d' arrives with a towel over his arm and pours water and presents fresh hot rolls with maple butter; he assists the young ladies by using a pair of tongs and places the roll on the bread plate so the evening begins smoothly with no initial blunders (the individual butter knife is across the top of the plate).

When the girls are ready for the next course they signal by

using the handbell and a great flurry is created in answering their call along with some sort of anecdotal tale relating to the freshness or preparation of the next course. There is also a gushing of compliments.

Each course is served on an individual plate, and the main course is served at the table from service bowls. The silver platters and bowls are amazing in the candlelight (most of them are foil-covered pie plates with a ruffled edge).

Dessert arrives as a choice between a huge uncut chocolate cake and an assortment of cookies. Herb tea is served in the cups (liberally assisted by sugar and milk) and the maitre d' and waitress regale the guests with amusing stories of previous escapades at the country inn. The ladies are given a tour of the rest of the facilities and are chauffeur-driven home. (They take a ride down our long driveway and back up). The spell is not broken by any requests for dishwashing or cleaning up, but a timely bedtime is required. They awake the next morning to find the table, flowers, and menu still resplendent in the corner of the room.

This one evening showed up in the story writing of both girls in school and became quite a subject for discussion among the teachers. We did it for fun, but it was the teachers who pointed out the value of role-model learning of basic social graces.

Erik and I relearned a lot of the small points, and the entire evening paid off in a big way this summer when my parents treated us to an elegant seven-course dinner at a lakeshore resort. Our daughter, Anna, never skipped a beat.

Susan Davis
Bristol, Vermont

THE $64,000 QUESTION

Since the first page, you've been dying to know: How *do* you recycle a vacuum cleaner bag?

After extensive experimentation I have hit upon a method to get extra use out of a used bag. I unroll the glued bottom to open it. After it's emptied I reroll the end and staple it closed about 10 times to make an airtight seal. (Do not recycle a bag several times. A weakened bag could develop a hole and escaping dirt might damage the motor.)

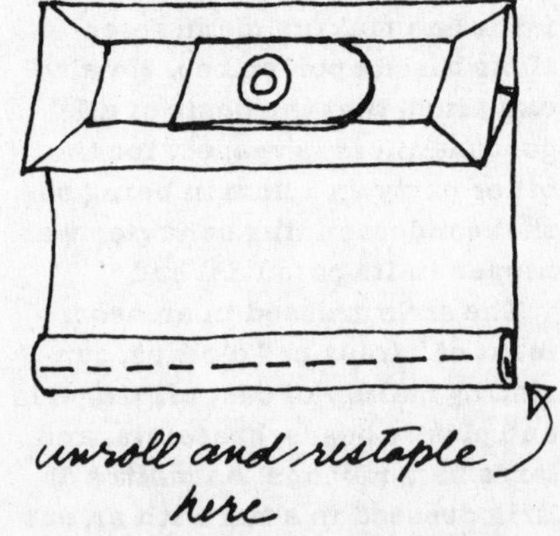

Is this nitpicky money-saving idea worth your time? I can recycle a bag in under five minutes including refilling the stapler. In theory I could recycle 12 bags per hour. The last time I bought bags they cost 85¢ each. So this effort is worth $10.20 per hour.

For me to net $10.20 per hour by working outside the home I would have to earn close to $20

per hour (figuring in child care, gas, taxes, etc.).

Granted, I do not spend my days recycling vacuum cleaner bags, but I do fill them with many ways to economize.

By learning how to optimize my time and resources I can create a tax-free income. I can elevate the standard of living of our family without working more hours outside the home.

It *is* worth doing. Not just the vacuum cleaner bags, but all the thousands of ways to save money. It *does* all add up.

THE $64,000 QUESTION UPDATE

I have recently learned that Kenmore makes a reusable cloth vacuum cleaner bag that fits our model. It sells for $9.99 through Sears. It only fits some models.

To learn if the manufacturer of your vacuum cleaner makes a reusable cloth bag call 1-800-555-1212 to see if they have a toll-free number.

A SUCCESS STORY

Dear Amy,

Last year my husband and I realized our dream. We purchased a rural home on 9 acres and were completely debt free. This was accomplished on my husband's income of less than $30,000.

After five years of marriage, my husband and I had buried ourselves in debt with the purchase of a second home. We soon came to the realization that there must be a better way to live. So we sold our home and moved into a one-bedroom duplex with two daughters.

After a year of saving all we could, we bought our third home. This time we had decided to set the unreachable goal of paying off our mortgage early.

We taped an amortization chart on the wall to show the progress each extra payment made. Raises, overtime, Christmas bonuses, and tax checks were all dumped on the principal as the years melted off our mortgage.

I began using coupons, mailing in rebates, packing lunches, and shopping at garage sales. We rarely ate out. Jeff and I agreed not to buy each other gifts. Jeff miraculously kept our junk vehicles running.

In four short years, despite skepticism of friends and family, we had paid off our $30,000 mortgage.

Some remodeling we did to the home increased its value from $48,000 to $62,000.

Just weeks after we paid off the house, we came across a home on nine acres that had been foreclosed on and was about to be sold at auction.

We immediately put our house on the market and it sold before the auction.

Never did we imagine we would be highest bidder at the auction with a $43,000 bid. The market value was almost twice that.

We were recently blessed with our fourth daughter, and look forward to many happy years on our "mini farm." We thank God for the opportunities he has made available to us.

Monica Stahlhut
Danville, Indiana

THREE INCOME TAX MYTHS

1. An income tax return is a good thing. Some people declare fewer allowances on their W-4 form, so that more money will get withheld so they will get a bigger tax refund. Part of the argument people use is they don't have the discipline to save on their own.

The problem with this is that the government gets the use of your money, interest-free. I know of one case where a couple's tax refund was delayed, and they didn't get their $1,500 until July. In this case some of the extra withheld money was in the possession of the IRS for 18 months.

2. It's foolish to earn more money because you'll be in a higher tax bracket. Some people think if they move up to a higher tax bracket all their income is taxed at the higher rate. Not so. If you are married filing jointly you pay 15% if your adjusted gross income is under $34,000. If your adjusted gross income is $35,000 only $1,000 gets taxed at the next higher rate of 28%. Earn to your heart's content.

3. You should not pay off your mortgage because you will lose your tax deduction.

The standard deduction for a couple is $5,700. In other words, you will take the standard deduction unless you have deductible expenses over $5,700. Aside from mortgage interest, itemized deductions include charitable gifts, medical and dental expenses, other taxes, moving expenses, losses from theft, etc.

Say your taxable income is under $34,000 and you are in the 15% bracket. You might think this means you could save 15% of your mortgage interest. But if your other deductions are below the $5,700 standard deduction, you only benefit from the 15% of the mortgage interest deduction that is above the $5,700.

And even then, you are still shelling out 85% of your mortgage interest. Conclusion: prepaying your mortgage principal remains one of the best "investment" strategies for the average homeowner.

If readers need last-minute tax advice, here are two sources:

1. Free tax clinics are held in many communities. Sponsored by the IRS, they are staffed by law school and graduate accounting students, who work under the direction of their professors. Call (202) 566-6352 for information.

2. If you want advice direct from the experts, call them at the IRS in Washington, D.C., at (800) 829-1040, or call your local IRS office.

ENVELOPE REUSE

Dear Amy,

I have a recycling method for business reply envelopes. Just insert table knife or other thin object, separate where it's glued, turn inside out, and reglue. To seal just lick the flap, tuck inside, and press down well.

John Etter
Hood River, Oregon

(John sent this idea in and it tickled me as the essence of tightwad ingenuity. I now look forward to junk mail

so I can reuse business reply envelopes. I have also used this idea to reuse 9" x 12" envelopes, closing with tape. FZ)

"I WAS A DISPOSABLE DIAPER MOM."

In the more than 20 years since the introduction of disposable diapers in the American scene they have become an unquestioned aspect of motherhood. However, researchers now believe that seven out of eight users suffer from "Disposable Diaper Parent Syndrome." The common symptoms include various types of distortion in perception. Users often have a mistaken sense of the amount of work involved in the cloth diapers (the archaic method) and an inability to grasp the cost both personally and to the community.

And is it a wonder? Our team of roving investigative reporters has uncovered a conspiracy by disposable diaper manufacturers to lure unsuspecting parents into their clutches. They provide large quantities of samples to new parents in hospitals. Coupons litter parenting magazines. Rebates and point systems further lure parents. Cloth diapers are promoted as unsanitary and are therefore against code in daycare centers.

Few parents have gone down the disposable diaper path and returned to tell their story. After an exhaustive search we have found one such parent. This former disposable diaper mom has granted an interview with *The Tightwad Gazette.* She has requested that her identity be concealed. She appears in silhouette and her voice has been electronically altered.

FZ: I would like to start by thanking you for agreeing to share your story with us. I appreciate how difficult this is for you to talk about. How long were you a disposable diaper user?

Ex–Disposable Diaper Mom: I used them for nearly three years.

FZ: Can you tell us how you first became involved with disposable diaper use?

XDDM: It was a combination of many things. Our washer was old and cranky and we did not have a dryer. I began working nights when our son was three months old, and my husband did not want to use cloth diapers. Later, when the baby was six months old I returned to daytime work. Most child care providers will only accept babies with disposables.

FZ: Do you recall how much you were spending on disposables every week?

XDDM: I spent a minimum of $10.50. The cheapest generic dia-

per is $8.47 a box. The infant size has 64. Most infants need to be changed 12 to 14 times a day, so I used more than one box a week.

FZ: And how much trash did the disposables generate?

XDDM: I filled a couple tall kitchen bags every week.

FZ: Wow! That much? But you can see why our nation spends over a billion dollars a year to landfill them. They make up a staggering 5% of our trash.

XDDM: Yes, that is why I switched . . . well, at first I switched to save money. When our twin girls were born I gave up daytime work. The cost of a toddler and two infants in day-care was prohibitive. At that point we also bought a new washer and dryer, so giving up disposables made sense. I couldn't see spending over $20 on disposables every week. Later I got to thinking about the environment . . . what I was passing on to my children. I hate using them now.

FZ: When you switched, how much did you spend on cloth diapers?

XDDM: I paid $6.00 to $9.50 a dozen for the prefolded Curity diapers. I bought eight dozen for the twins. So a mother with one baby would spend less than $50.

FZ: How long have the cloth diapers lasted?

XDDM: My girls are 18 months old now. Only two of the diapers have gone to the rag bag.

FZ: Since you are washing diapers for twins do you find this to create a lot of work?

XDDM: Hah! Mothers with one baby ask me this all the time. Actually, I don't feel it requires much more work than disposables.

FZ: I understand you have an unconventional method of cleaning your diapers.

XDDM: Yes, I soak them in the warm soapy water that comes out of my portable dishwasher. The way I see it any food particles in the water are basically the same as the material in the babies' diapers.

FZ: Dishwashing detergent is strong stuff. Doesn't it bother the babies?

XDDM: I am a nurse, as well as a mother of twins. If it caused a problem I wouldn't do it. I do add ¼ cup of vinegar to the wash to neutralize it. I wash them in Tide with bleach with cold water. I only run them through the washer's precycle. I have found it is not necessary to put them through the entire cycle.

FZ: My own method is also unconventional. It is recommended that cloth diapers be soaked in a disinfectant like bleach, Borax, or Lysol. I just soak the soiled ones in plain water and rely on a hot water wash and dryer to help kill germs. I do this because my husband is sensitive to bleach and I am also sensitive to certain detergents. Each parent eventually settles on the method of least work that suits their child's tolerance. How frequently do you wash?

XDDM: I wash a load every day; however, I wash that often because our apartment is small and we don't have room for laundry to sit around. Other cloth diaper moms I know with one baby wash only once or twice a week. I usually don't get around to folding them before they are used again.

FZ: What misconceptions did you have about cloth diapers?

XDDM: I thought they would be smelly but they aren't any worse than a bag of used disposables. If you add a tablespoon of baking soda to the soaking water it also helps.

FZ: How about diaper rashes?

XDDM: Much less, especially in girls. Disposables used to give my girls yeast infections. I have heard other mothers say that disposables gave their babies severe sores and they had to switch.

FZ: One final question. As a nurse, can you think of any reason that cloth diapers are less sanitary in daycare centers?

XDDM: Well, with a cloth diaper you have more contact with handling something wet. Since you also wipe the baby off I can't see that it makes any difference. Also the manufacturer recommends that you rinse disposables. Read the box. At any rate you should wash your hands after every diaper change. Then the centers claim it is unsanitary to store them. But disposables sit around in a trash bag. Why can't a soiled diaper be returned to a plastic bag in the diaper bag for the mom to deal with?

FZ: Thank you for sharing your story with us.

XDDM: I wanted to do this. If, through hearing my story, I can prevent at least one other mom the suffering of Disposable Diaper Parent Syndrome it was worth doing.

A few final notes.

In the years since I have been a cloth diaper user I have had difficulty determining even a rough figure of the savings in cloth diapers because factors widely differ . . . how frequently parents change their babies, which brands they purchase, and if they use coupons and rebates. They appear to be packaged in a volume to last about a week, regardless of the size of the baby. Bigger babies are changed less but their diapers cost more.

One also has to subtract the energy and detergent with cloth diapers. Even at a dollar per load twice a week I come up with a savings of $7.00 per week ($8.47 plus tax and cost of garbage bags minus $2.00 for laundering) or $364 annually. If it is made known that an expectant mother plans to use cloth diapers, she will receive them as shower gifts, as I did. Therefore, the purchase cost need not be a factor.

To "earn" that $7 tax-free savings a cloth diaper user will expend less than one hour weekly. The $1,000 or more savings by the time each child is trained can become capital for reinvestment.

NO SHAME

Dear Amy,

What is most important, I realize after reading your first issue, is that I need not, cannot and will not be ashamed or apologetic about my change in lifestyle. I have chosen this for our family and my husband will go along. How else can we achieve our dream of an outstanding education for our daughter?

Karen Richards
Solon, Maine

PLANT YOUR BIRDHOUSE

If you are better at gardening than carpentry—and you are a bird lover—grow gourds to use as purple martin houses.

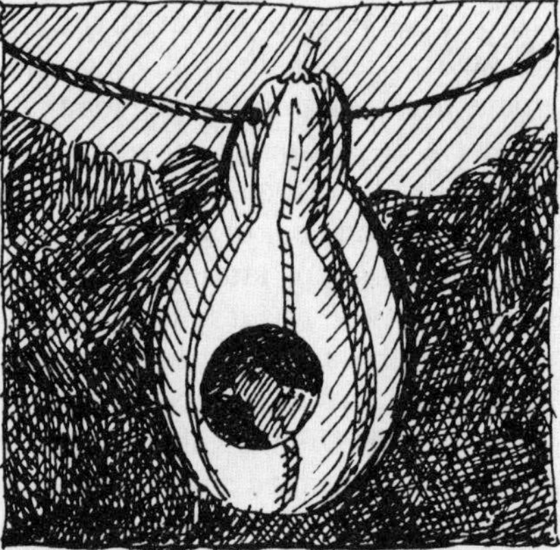

Grow large, round gourds that have short necks. Let them dry on the vine until midwinter. Pick, and cut a hole about 2 inches in diameter on one side. Let dry for another day, then sand the doorway's edges smooth. Clean the inside with a spoon. Drill holes in the bottom for drainage. Cut two more holes in the neck so that you can run a nylon cord through them.

Putting a teaspoon of sulfur in each birdhouse will help keep mites away and will not bother the birds. Sulfur can be purchased from Agway for $4.99 lb. Obviously, you would have to make a lot of birdhouses or have another use for the sulfur to make this purchase worthwhile.

Martins are colonial nesters, so in early spring, hang at least two or more gourd birdhouses at least one foot apart on wooden crosspieces fastened to a pole that is 12 to 20 feet high. The pole should be at least 40 feet away from trees or buildings, but not more than 90 feet from your home . . . martins like to be near human beings. Martins live in all states east of the Mississippi River and in several western states.

While writing this, I received the following information from reader M. Huckle of Tonganoxie, Kansas: to obtain a package of 15 to 20 gourd seeds, plus a 12-page book about growing and preparing gourds for purple martin houses, send $2 and a long SASE with two 29¢ stamps to: The Purple Martin Conservation Association, Edinboro University of Pennsylvania, Edinboro, PA 16444.

BUSINESS WEAR

Dear Amy,

In answer to a reader who requested ideas for saving on business clothes, I have a couple of suggestion. L'eggs and Hanes both sell "irregular" pantyhose through a catalog at about 60% less than discount stores. I have never found anything wrong with them.

She should be able to find beautiful, perfect designer suits, skirts, and tops for practically

nothing at secondhand or "consignment" stores. I frequented one store where I found several like-new Evan Picone women's suits for $20 each. My best buy was a beaded cashmere sweater for $10. The key is to find a store in a nice neighborhood that has the kind of clothes you like. Get friendly with the sales staff. They will call to let you know when something in your size has come in.

Katherine Kenward
Homewood, Illinois

SHEDDING LIGHT ON FLUORESCENTS

After I printed the address of a mail-order source for fluorescent bulbs in my newsletter, I received a few letters concerning their downside.

Common complaints about fluorescents include: they don't fit many residential light fixtures, they cost a lot, they don't give enough light, they don't provide instant light, and they "look funny." In fact, they are environmentally and economically sound. By understanding the limitations and the different options, most homeowners could find ways to use at least a few.

In researching this article I spoke with Owen Garner, an energy-lighting specialist from Conservation Lighting in Portland, Maine.

The average price for a quality fluorescent bulb is about $20. You should look for brands such as Osram, Sylvania, General Electric, Panasonic, or Philips.

Mr. Garner told me the bulbs sold by discount stores for about $8 are generally considered to be inferior. These bulbs do not last as long as they are supposed to, can cause radio and television interference, and light up slowly. When the quality $20-bulbs are sold for less by clubs, they probably have been donated for sale and can be sold cheaply.

Many on tight budgets will be hard pressed to fork over $20 for a single fluorescent bulb. But for every $20 investment you will save an average of $40 (and come out $20 ahead) in electricity and bulb replacements. Fluorescents used 2 hours per day will last for 7 to 10 years, and pay for themselves in 3 to 5 years.

The residential fluorescent industry is still in its infancy. For this reason, right now fluorescents are hard to find and have limited applications for home use.

Unless you know which bulbs you can use, purchasing bulbs in quantity through the mail is less than ideal. If possible, find a distributor who will show you the variety of options, and even lend you one to take home and try. This way you will learn how many and which bulbs you can use.

Each fluorescent is composed of a bulb (or lamp) and a ballast. The basic combinations include:

- All-in-one units (ballasts and bulbs are one piece).
- Screw-base adapters with replaceable bulbs.

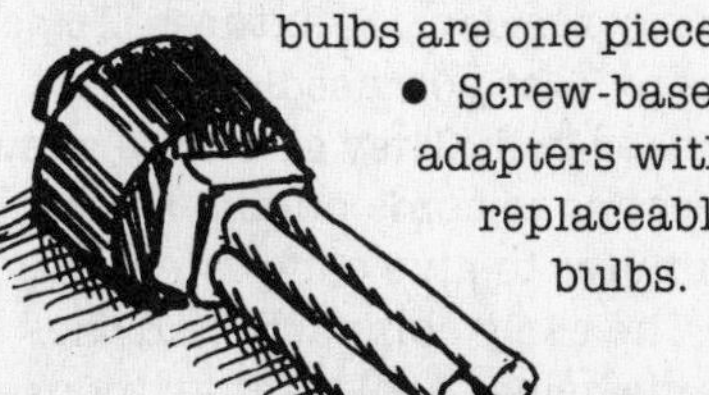

(Separate ballast and bulbs. The replacement bulbs cost between $3 and $8.)

- Hard-wire conversions. (Ballasts are permanently wired into existing fixtures, allowing them to accommodate larger bulbs.)
- Fluorescent fixtures (permanent ceiling or wall fixtures specifically designed to accommodate fluorescents).
- Lamp conversion kits. (The kits have a ballast that plugs into the wall. A plug from a table or floor fixture plugs into that. The fluorescent fits into a small screw-in adapter in the socket.)

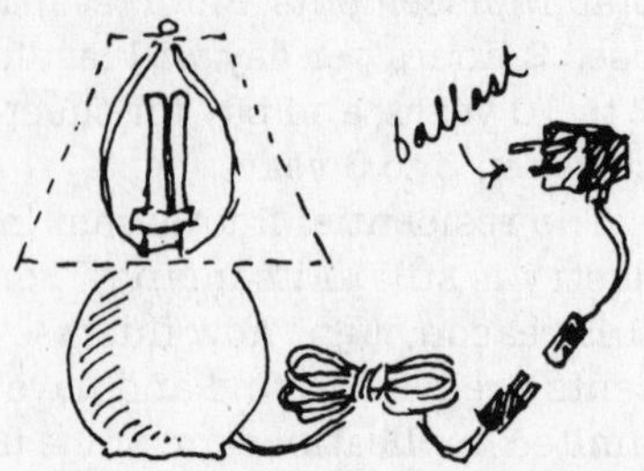

Compact fluorescents have two basic styles: either a twin tube (a design with two tubes) or a quad (a design with four tubes). Sometimes the tubes are encased in glass, making the bulb look like a large incandescent.

A 13-watt quad produces the same light as a 60-watt incandescent but has twice the length. It also has the bulky ballast near the bottom. These two factors make the lamps hard to use in many residential fixtures. To get more light you need an even longer bulb. They also take a few seconds to come on and a few minutes to give complete light.

The early compacts had the same bright cool light as industrial lighting. The newer soft white or daylight bulbs produce light that is very similar to an incandescent.

What about the "funny look"? It is true that fluorescents look different than incandescents. They look funny to us because we aren't accustomed to this bulb style. However, they are accepted in other parts of the world, where they have been used for some time.

Fluorescents do not work well in freezing temperatures, and cannot be used with dimmers.

Given all the limitations, fluorescent bulbs can be best used where instant or very bright light is not needed and the size or look of the bulb is not an issue. Because of the long payback time, look for uses where you have the greatest energy consumption, such as kitchens and hallways. For example, they work in a mounted ceiling fixture when the globe is at least 9 inches in diameter. If the fixture will accommodate two bulbs you can get ample light.

Fluorescents do not produce heat, so they will cut the energy consumed by air-conditioning (although incandescents help heat in the winter).

By far the most appealing aspect of the fluorescent is its positive environmental impact. Depending on the method of energy production in your part of the country, a single fluorescent bulb over the course of its life can prevent as much as 1,000 pounds of carbon dioxide and 20 pounds of sulfur dioxide from being released into the atmosphere.

After learning more we decided that we could use fluorescents in our home. We have a lamp conversion kit that will work with

our living-room floor lamp. We can use two quads in our kitchen fixture. We are using one in our bathroom ceiling light, which we leave on for a night light. We can also use them in our office, where aesthetics are less important.

If you can't find a local source for fluorescents you can mail order them from Seventh Generation. They'll sell just one. Including shipping, you can get a 15-watt quad for just over $20. Call: (800) 456-1197.

SHELL MAGNETS

Dear Amy,

I went on the theory "spend to save" and purchased a hot-glue gun and have started making gifts. People love my wreaths, but the best gifts are my seashell magnets.

I purchase the shells at a local craft store. The average price is 35¢ for the unique ones. A package of six small magnets costs under $1.

Take the shell and, using the hot-glue gun, place a small amount of glue on the shell and then place the magnet on the glue. Hold the magnet for a few seconds until it sticks completely to the shell. The whole process takes only seconds to make and the cost for a beautiful gift is minimal.

Judy McAtee
Dallas, Texas

RECYCLED GROUNDS

Dear Amy,

Recycle your coffee grounds by making the first pot of coffee the usual way. Then to make the second pot add only ½ the amount of grounds already in the filter. This allows me to have two pots of coffee at 1½ the amount of grounds. This has worked for me in all types of coffee pots.

Eileen Wells
Knoxville, Tennessee

SENIOR RESOURCES

If you are a senior citizen you have a wide range of discounts available from restaurants, schools, banks, clubs, etc. You should routinely ask for senior citizen discounts. The answer might be no, but it doesn't hurt to ask. Most of the time the answer will be yes.

In addition to these discounts you should investigate the benefits of organizations and services specincally for senior citizens. Here are only a few:

The American Association of Retired Persons
601 E St. NW
Washington, DC 20049

This has to be the best deal around for folks over 50. For a $5 annual membership fee you can get a variety of services.

The membership includes an annual subscription (6 issues) to *Modern Maturity.* The magazine features articles such as financial planning, retirement living, and travel. You also receive a bimonthly bulletin to keep you up-to-date on legislation that affects retired persons and contains information on AARP activities. They also offer a wide selection of

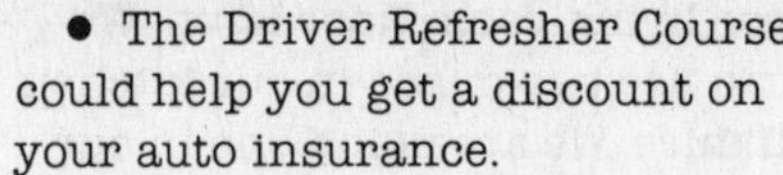

information guides on a variety of topics.

In addition, the AARP offers the following services:

- The pharmacy service has wholesale prices on prescription drugs, over-the-counter drugs, and medical supplies. Members mail in their prescription. It takes 8 to 10 days to receive the prescription. Their prices may not always beat your local pharmacy, so compare.
- Group travel programs are reasonably priced.
- The Automobile and Homeowners Insurance Program (from Hartford) is considered by some to be the best and most economical available.
- Their motoring plan offers low-cost road service from Amoco. This includes nationwide road service, free maps, and trip routing. They also offer sizable discounts for some major hotels and rental cars.
- The Crime Prevention Program helps seniors protect themselves from crime.
- The Consumer Affairs Program educates seniors about consumer goods and services.
- Income Tax Preparation Assistance is done by IRS trained volunteers.
- The Widowed Persons Service offers counseling.
- The Medicare Assistance Program helps seniors fill out Medicare forms and assists with related problems.

- The Driver Refresher Course could help you get a discount on your auto insurance.

The AARP has more than 32 million members and 4,000 chapters.

The National Council for Senior Citizens
1331 F St. NW
Washington, DC 20004-1171

This organization offers many similar services to the AARP. Their annual membership fee is $12 and they have a monthly newspaper for seniors.

The Golden Age Passport. If you are 62 or older and going to a federally operated national park, monument, historic site, wildlife refuge, or recreation area you can get in free with proof of age. This benefit extends to all persons traveling in the car with you.

Meals-on-Wheels. Good nutrition is your best strategy to combat rising medical costs. If you are having difficulty preparing meals, call your local Area Agency on Aging for information and to learn if you qualify.

Personal Emergency Response System. This is a small wireless alert system that must be kept in reach at all times. In emergencies the hospital or other help is alerted. Private companies charge a lot, but sometimes the service is offered as low as $15 by nonprofit organizations. Contact your Area Agency on Aging for more information.

In the front of most phone books there is a section for seniors that lists local resources. And don't forget to check with nearby colleges. Some offer free tuition for seniors.

TEENAGERS
ARE SO EXPENSIVE
NOWADAYS

MY TEENAGER PLAN

One reporter wrote a generally favorable article, except he seemed to express some cynicism that I would not be able to pull off tightwad parenting in 10 years or so, when I would have a handful of teenagers to deal with.

Guess what? I have a teenager plan currently being implemented.

I have heard the legends concerning the amazing amount of food they can consume. If their only option is the less expensive healthier foods this problem can be curtailed somewhat. Chips, soda, and cookies are expensive. Garden produce, potatoes, and oatmeal are not. The teenage metabolism speeds at a phenomenal pace. Allowing unlimited consumption of snack foods is like trying to fill a bottomless pit. The more you feed the metabolism the faster it goes. Therefore, limiting their options to cheaper, healthier (and less tempting) foods will help in cutting the expense.

The cost of food consumption is secondary to the teenager's lust for consumer goods, much of which results from peer pressure. We have taken a giant step to avoid peer pressure by moving to a rural area with few close neighbors. The pressures here are less than in an affluent community.

So far the "peer pressure monster" has only reared its ugly head when the kids take something for lunch and a classmate expresses a dislike for that item (such as pumpkin pudding or homemade dill pickles). I have given my best "march to your own drummer" speeches, but I still can't put pudding and pickles in their lunch boxes. Still, I have not given in to the expensive lunch box items that other children bring.

Dealing with their "externally generated desires" is different from their internal ones. In other words, sometimes their wants are not a result of peer pressure or commercials. Sometimes we are in a store and they see something they desperately want. I deal with this by asking, "Where is your money?" Usually they have none.

In our home any kid can do a job for a quarter at any time. Usually this is a 10-minute job. They do not get an allowance. By doing this they never get the idea that it is the duty of their parents to buy them more than the basics of food and clothing.

We start this policy as the kids reach the age of five or so. Although we are not within striking distance of businesses where they might get jobs when they are older, we will always have a long list of tasks for them around here. Even if the money eventually goes for something that I consider to be worthless, in exchange I get the value of having them understand money.

Current child psychologist wisdom says that children should do household tasks for no pay and also get an allowance so that they can learn how to handle money.

But if the money is not tied to a specific task, they miss the most important concept behind it. One must trade effort to acquire money.

Our children do tasks for no money on a daily basis. But I think it is important that they understand that a $5 plastic toy is equal to 20 jobs. They need a gauge to determine the value of money.

Surprisingly often, children are not willing to trade the effort to get the $5. They decide the hunk of plastic isn't worth the 20 jobs. And even though my first grader has money in his treasure box he is not willing to spend it on the more glamorous school lunches.

If your teenager wants the $75 sneakers and you want to buy the $15 pair, offer to chip in your $15 if he'll come up with the other $60.

Right about now all you parents of teens are laughing yourselves silly. I am aware that I am not going to be able to pull this off without rough moments. I don't imagine it will work perfectly. But my ideas are not untried theory. It is basically the same method my parents used.

Look for my teenager plan update in about 10 years.

GOOD GADGETS

THE WATER HEATER TIMER

These cost between $30 and $75. The cost difference reflects amperage capacity. Some are also digital. With an amperage of 4800 (about average) we bought a timer at the lower end of the price range on sale for $20. The installation requires a short length of wire and an hour's worth of time by someone handy. We have set ours to go on between 4:00 to 9:00 A.M. and 4:00 to 9:00 P.M. We haven't noticed any inconvenience. Friends who have installed them report a monthly savings on the electric bill of $10 to $15.

THE BATTERY RECHARGER

Is there anyone who doesn't have one of these yet? The cost runs between $11 and $20. The manufacturer claims rechargeable batteries equal between 65 to 150 regular batteries, depending on the size of the battery. Recharging takes 2 to 6 hours. Based on our own unscientific observation the charge seems to last about half the time as a disposable.

Rechargeables cost roughly 150% to 300% more than disposables. This initial investment deters many people, although the long-term savings are clearly substantial. The cost of the recharger and a pair of D rechargeables equals the cost of about eight pairs of disposable D batteries.

Keep separate containers for "dead" and recharged batteries near your recharger. The batteries need to be recharged in pairs, so recharge as soon as you have enough.

THE FUZZ AWAY

Remington manufacturers this gadget, which resembles an electric shaver. We broke down and bought one when the cost dropped to $7. It removes the "pills" especially common to syn-

thetic fabrics. Used in combination with my stain recipe, many a yard sale find has regained respectability.

"SPUDGATE" OR THE GREAT POTATO CONSPIRACY

An eternal mission of *The Tightwad Gazette* is to single-handedly wipe out the convenience food industry. In accordance with this we continue our series of investigative reports exposing the practice of the food industry to make inexpensive and healthful foods more expensive and less nutritious.

The focus of this article is the potato. Infinitely versatile, this humble food is completely natural, good-tasting and loaded with fiber.

The potato can lay claim to being the perfect tightwad food, because it is also very inexpensive. Depending on the season, area of the country, and type of potato a 10-pound bag of potatoes can be purchased for around $2.29, or 23¢ per pound. We buy 50-pound sacks for $3.90 each, or 8¢ a pound. A large potato the size and shape of a squashed baseball weighs about 8 ounces.

I sent Jim on a fact-finding mission to a large chain supermarket. Cleverly disguised, the potato spy posed as a regular guy just getting off work. His tools of espionage included state-of-the art pen and pad of paper. (He felt his bow tie camera might be too conspicuous.) Other than arousing the suspicions of a clerk stocking shelves, Jim's activity went unnoticed. He obtained prices for instant potatoes, potato chips, potato sticks, and frozen fries.

Acting on his own initiative Jim also made note of the high sodium content of these products.

An element of the conspiracy is the deceptive "standard serving size" on the nutrition panel. This is common to cold cereals and other convenience foods also. Many of the potato products list 3 ounces as a serving size. A 3-ounce potato is a tad larger than a squashed golf ball.

For purposes of comparison we will assume a 5-ounce potato (squashed tennis ball size) equals the suggested 3 to 3½ ounces of the frozen potato products, to account for any possible dehydration. We are also assuming the ½-cup serving size of mashed potato equals our 5-ounce potato.

Many of the potato products, such as au gratin mixes, contain elements other than pure potato —preservatives, salt, milk, or cheese, etc. Some are more expensive and some are less, but you have to add your own milk and butter. One prepared serving size does equal 5 ounces. We are giv-

ing the food industry the benefit of the doubt and call it equal.

Undoubtedly some will argue that it is unfair to compare potato chips and sticks to potatoes, since they are really a snack food (entertainment). Within the tightwad frame of reference, grocery shopping means expending money for nutrition. Besides it makes for more interesting reading.

To compare the chips we calculated how many 1/16-inch slices we could get from a 5-ounce potato and compared it to the weight of an equal number of chips. Potato slices get thinner as they are made into chips.

A plain uncompromised 5-ounce potato, purchased in a 1-pound sack costs about 7¢. The chart below indicates what this potato would cost after the convenience-food industry repackages it into the potato products we've researched.

We do use instant mashed potatoes in a pinch, because they are inexpensive. However, they lack the fiber of the real thing.

Oven-Fried Potatoes

A SUPERIOR ALTERNATIVE

Wash, but do not peel, one potato per person. Slice into 1/4-inch slices and soak in cold water for at least 20 minutes.

Melt four tablespoons of margarine on a cookie sheet. Drain potatoes and pat dry. Place potatoes on cookie sheet in a single layer, coating both sides with margarine. Salt and pepper to taste.

Place in a 425° oven and bake 20 minutes (or until lightly browned) on each side.

Save the surplus margarine on the cookie sheet for other uses. To save energy, prepare this when you are using your oven to cook something else for dinner.

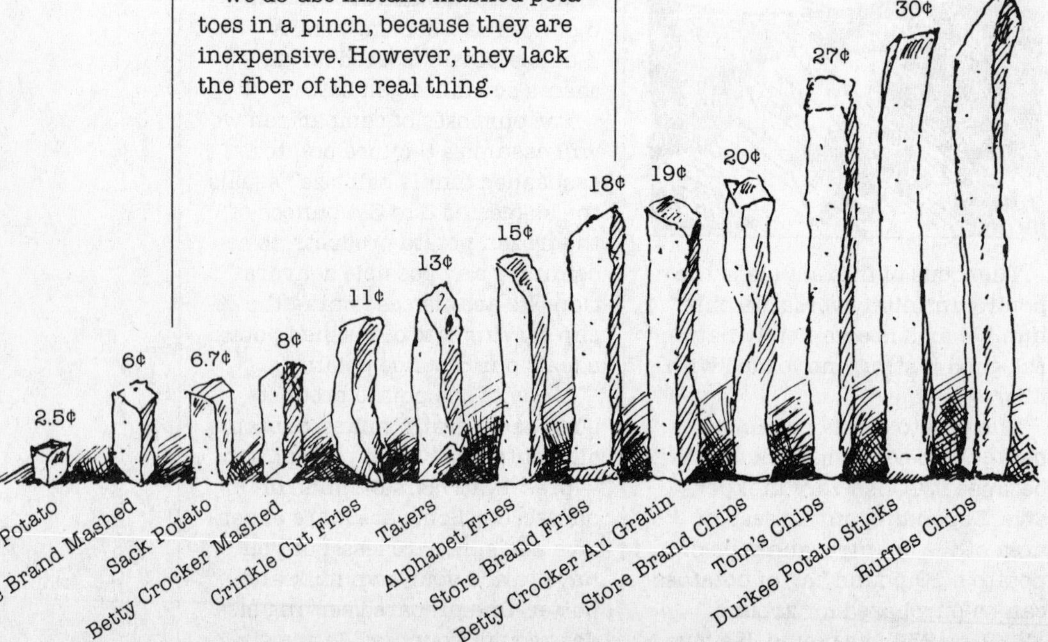

THRIFT SHOP THOUGHTS

1. There are four basic sources of used clothes:

a. Someone gives them to you. The selection is limited but the price is right. Always express thanks and keep what you can use.

b. Garage sales. These are the cheapest places where you can *buy* clothes—usually about half the price of thrift shops.

c. Thrift shops. They charge more for clothes, but they have a greater selection. Ask about specials. Some charge half price on colored-tag days. I have seen slacks as high as $5, but would plan to return if I knew the item would be half price another day.

d. Consignment shops. They offer the greatest selection, but the highest price. Items might be priced twice as high as a thrift shop. At $8 for a pair of kids' pants, one might do as well shopping sales at retail stores. However, consignment stores are a great source for adult business clothes. If you develop a relationship with the owner, he or she might help you find specific items.

2. Change your method of shopping. If you're used to retail you expect to find clothes in your size and your color wherever you shop. If you bring that attitude into the thrift shop you will be disappointed.

Instead of thinking about what a shop doesn't have, look at what it does have. You might really be looking for slacks but instead find a great blouse you can use.

3. Develop a notebook for your needs, especially if you are shopping for a large family. Record sizes and measurements for each family member. More than sizes, measurements are important because used clothing may no longer have the tag indicating size. If, for instance, you have a pants size, also write in the measurement of the waist and length of the inseam. Armed with a measuring tape and a notebook you won't need to bring along your child to try on clothes.

If shopping for an adult, you might also want to include color chips for clothes you hope to match. I have heard of someone who gets paint chips from a hardware store for this purpose. This practice falls into the "fuzzy-ethical" area for me. Instead I would suggest cutting a small square from the pages of a Sears catalog. If the match with the original garment isn't perfect indicate "lighter" or "darker."

4. Examine all clothing carefully for defects. Don't be put off by flaws. If an item is cheap enough it might be worthwhile to restitch a seam.

5. Don't be discouraged by poor-quality clothing you find. Look to the positive side. If something made it to the thrift shop and still looks respectable, it is likely to be a garment that will hold up well. New clothing is a greater gamble. Who hasn't had a new garment hopelessly pill, shrink, or fall apart after two or three washings? Even if a used item doesn't hold up, at least you didn't pay full price.

6. When you look at a used item, think of it as a new thing that's been washed 10 times. My

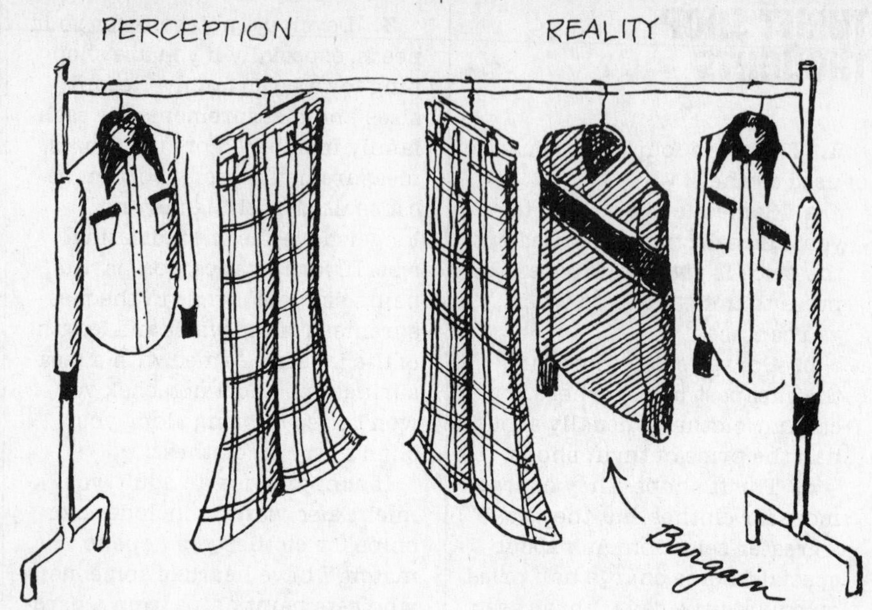

kids have had new clothes given to them. I would challenge anyone to go through their closets and pick out what they received new and what they received used.

7. Many of the same rules apply to used-clothing purchases as new: Buy classic styles. Know what colors and styles look good on you. Learn the signs of quality clothes. Learn which brand names hold up well.

8. When buying for kids, buy a few years in advance, and develop a storage system. It's unlikely that you will find everything you would need at one yard sale.

9. Know that there might be some things you won't find at a thrift shop. We've never been able to find tall men's shirts for Jim at thrift shops. We buy used clothing whenever we can, and expect to fill in around the edges with new stuff.

10. If you're trying to find things for a picky teenager, try to tune in to the subtleties of current trends. Hopefully you have successfully educated them since they were young. If not, you are going to have to make a case for the change.

There's good used stuff out there, and it ain't all plaid, polyester bell-bottomed pants and shirts with pointy collars.

THE (NOT SO) COMPLETE GUIDE TO TRASH PICKING

I do not have a lengthy and colorful career as a trash picker as some experts who have devoted decades to this calling. In fact prior to a year and a half ago my background was rather skimpy and I can recall only a few times that I gave in to the lure of the interesting-looking trash pile.

Fifteen years ago I lived in the Boston area. I strolled in the vicinity of the gates of Harvard University with a visiting aunt. She

had been a veteran city dweller of a more bohemian era. We passed a pile of what appeared to be discarded building materials from a remodeling project. My eyes strayed to a pair of old decorative iron shelf brackets still attached to a worthless chunk of board. My aunt, noting my hesitation, said "You want that? I'll get it for you." And she did. It was my first inkling that this sort of scavenging could be OK.

I don't recall committing the act again until a few years ago. At the time, Jim and I were living in a suburban area near Norfolk, Virginia. Our neighbor had spent the day cleaning out her garage and sheds, creating a huge pile in front of her house. It appeared to be the first time she had done so in recent decades. Pleased with her accomplishment she treated herself to a dinner out. Jim and I took note of her departure and decided that it was time to take our evening walk. It was a short one. We came home with a cooler, a few toys, two dozen canning jars, and our long-lost basketball.

Shortly thereafter Jim received choice orders to the Brunswick Naval Air Station, and we were lucky enough to get a government house while we looked for a home to buy. One evening as I read the Brunswick paper I came upon a remarkable ad for the "Spring Cleaning Season." (In other words, sanctioned trash picking).

Every year many towns in Maine, as well as a few other parts of the country, offer a week or two when residents can put out good, repairable, or very large items. These are left on the curb for about a week so that others might pick items they may have a use for. This effort helps to alleviate the problem of overburdened landfills. Additionally, when items are reused fewer goods are produced to replace that which is thrown away. World resources are conserved and less pollution results.

Naturally, I felt an obligation to do my part for the environment.

On opening day, as I revved the car engine in the driveway, Jim came out and pointed to our half-filled garage. We had moved from a larger home to a smaller one, and many things had never been unpacked. He cautioned me about getting too carried away. (Having known me for half a dozen years I am sure he understood the futility of his request.)

The Brunswick season got off to a dismal start. The first day I came home with only a small suitcase. But every few days I went out again and I sensed a building momentum. In the beginning I heeded my husband's words and brought home only very useful items. But my increasing success softened his stance. I began to bring home broken items that appeared to be repairable and discovered Jim possessed a wonderful ability to fix almost anything. Later I would scavenge more challenging projects for him. Little was thrown out again.

When the Brunswick season overlapped with the Bath season, a neighboring town, Jim was fully converted. Unlike Brunswick,

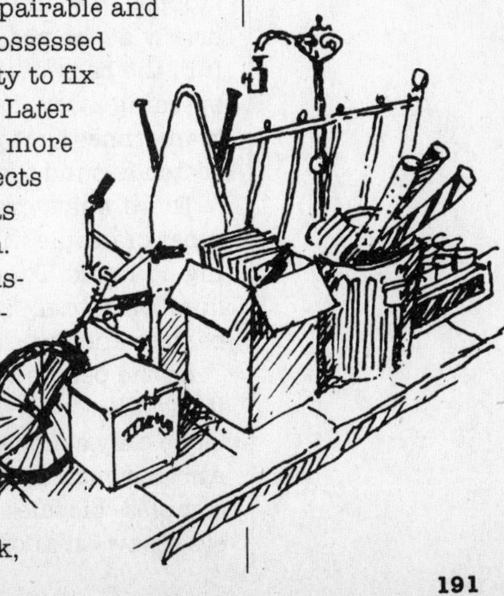

Bath's season started with a bang. You had to be out there the first weekend to get the good stuff. Jim came along for the first time. On the return trip our fully loaded Suburban resembled the Beverly Hillbillies on the move.

Aside from picking up enough items to jam our garage to capacity I learned a great deal.

We felt it a bit odd to hear our preschool cherubs exclaim "Yeah! We're going trash picking today." We quickly learned to substitute the more acceptable term "treasure hunting."

"When in doubt, throw it in" became our motto. If we were unsure we took it anyway. Later if we decided not to keep the item putting it out in our trash was a simple matter. On one occasion we came across a large oriental rug neatly folded in a trash bag. Rather than inspecting it on the spot to see if it had any salvageable parts we took it home. At home we spread it on the lawn to discover it was completely useless. We folded it up, put it back in the bag, and set it on the curb. Twenty minutes later a pickup stopped. A man got out, looked briefly at the rug, and then threw it in the back of the truck before speeding away. I wondered how many times that rug would hopscotch around town.

There was a great variety of types of people involved in picking up items. There were poor families driving 15-year-old beaters and yuppies in Volvos.

As the people varied, so did the items they collected. One man told us he only collected old motors. Another man had a buyer for any complete bicycles and lawn mowers. I saw an ancient Jeep so fully loaded inside and on top with small pieces of scrap wood that the passenger had to ride on the running board clinging for dear life. We collected a little of everything for a future yard sale.

Trash varies from town to town, neighborhood to neighborhood. The spring cleaning season in a community with older homes is more likely to yield antiques whereas a suburban community with ranches is more likely to throw out items for children. As a general rule affluent communities have the best trash.

We learned that if we found an incomplete item to pick it up, because another pile may yield the thing needed to make it complete. We brought home an excellent bicycle for our son needing only a new seat. The following day I went out with a wrench and stripped a good seat from a hopelessly rusted bicycle. A Fisher-Price record player without records was matched with records from another source. An old bureau was matched with a can of enamel paint from a separate pile.

We learned that a tremendous amount is discarded because people lack the imagination to envision what something could be—that many items are thrown out for want of a screw.

Our lives would be forever altered by this period of spring cleaning seasons. Since then yard sales and thrift shops pale by comparison. My concept of fun took on a whole new dimension. And a few friends questioned their relationships with us.

We had our yard sale—two actually. Between them we sold a total of $200 worth of things

we had picked up on a curb. We also kept a large percentage and are still using them.

If there are no communities in your area that hold this type of event, try to initiate one. Trash picking at the dump is usually outlawed. If you are there and see something of interest, speak with the dump custodian. I know of one individual who actually sneaks into the dump off-hours. He feels a need to respond to a higher moral cause. I have heard a prime trash-picking opportunity occurs in June. The Dumpsters behind the dormitories of affluent colleges hold wonderful finds. Dumpsters behind many businesses and factories offer year-round opportunities.

In many communities trash picking is illegal. If you feel strongly about maintaining your status as a law-abiding citizen, but spot an irresistible treasure in your neighbor's trash, it might be appropriate to knock on their door and ask to take it. You should also do this if you have any question that something was really meant to be thrown away. Children may accidentally leave sleds and bicycles near their families' trash cans.

Another method of trash picking to investigate is the free-for-the-taking pile that some dumps offer.

The most appropriate conclusion for this article is a partial listing of the items we brought home: a bucket of mixed nails, 3 working radio-control cars, 30 partly full quarts of paint, 2 tricycles, 3 floor lamps including 2 of 1920s vintage, 2 director's chairs, books, over 100 canning jars, 3 rolls of Christmas wrap, an antique ceramic crock, lumber, an antique bottomless egg box (sold as is for $5), a large rocker, plant stands, an ironing board, a fireplace screen, an antique school desk, an antique iron bed frame, a Rubbermaid trash barrel, a mirror from an old bureau (now providing ambiance in our attic), a doll's wooden high chair, a doll stroller, an applesauce mill, a broken brass bed with pieces missing (sold as is for $20), a wagon, flower pots, kitchen utensils and the complete works of Engelbert Humperdink, which we gave away free with every purchase at the yard sale.

CURBSIDE GLEANING

Dear Amy,

I am forever grateful to you for legitimizing "treasure hunting." I had never done it before. This year we were pressed for time, so I only devoted 6 total hours to the pursuit, all in Bath. We got:

A perfectly good barbeque minus the grill
A grill that miraculously fit into the barbecue
A nice bike minus the wheel
A nice wheel minus the bike: the result a nice bike for our son
A push mower that works perfectly, just the thing for our tiny lawn
A sled in perfectly good condition
15 canning jars
A plastic sandbox shaped like a turtle, ugly but sturdy
Men's downhill ski boots, German made, perfect condition
Downhill skis

A lovely art deco bread box
A terrific sturdy high chair

And we were hardly trying! I would add one piece of advice to your article. Many people treasure hunt primarily by scanning the piles from within their cars. The best way to find the good stuff is to park in the middle of the block, stroll around on foot and dig around in the piles to find what others missed.

By far the most common large item left out during pickup days are old water heaters. Do any readers have ideas about how to use these?

Brad Lemley
Bath, Maine

MAILBOX REVENGE

A small percentage of dim-witted rural teenagers play a sport called "mailbox baseball." The proper rules require a baseball bat, a vehicle, a driver and at least one passenger, a moonless night, and a country road lined with mailboxes.

The object is for the passenger to lean from the moving car and whack the boxes into scrap metal.

A similar game involves tossing small explosives known as cherry bombs into the boxes to achieve the same effect.

Mailbox baseball provides considerable entertainment for the teenagers for some curious reason. And it causes frustration and expense for the persistently harassed mailbox owners. Even the most diligent can't pound the damaged box back into some usable form more than a couple of times.

Corporate America is attempting to cash in by providing mailbox baseball defense systems. A recent ad depicted a bat-proof, bomb-proof mailbox made from space-age plastic that cost over $200.

Word of an ingenious (and less expensive) solution has reached the office of *The Tightwad Gazette*.

Buy a large mailbox and a standard sized mailbox (or reuse your damaged one). Remove the door from the smaller one. Set the large box on end and place the smaller one inside. Fill the cavity between the two boxes with concrete. Once dried, the very heavy mailbox must be bolted to a heavyweight post.

The originator of this solution has reported finding bits of splintered bats in the immediate vicinity of his box.

A large mailbox and a small amount of cement costs under $25, roughly the cost of one Louisville slugger.

No monetary amount can be placed on successful revenge.

A PIRATE BIRTHDAY

The creation of a great but inexpensive birthday party depends on the use of materials and resources readily available. You must be prepared to abandon ideas that do not work or cost too

much money. Often the best ideas result from finding yourself backed into a creative corner.

The fall our oldest turned seven we created a party that differed from earlier ones as it relied more heavily on Jim's abilities than mine.

The Theme: Our property, with all its interesting places, provided the perfect setting for a treasure hunt. Months in advance I planted the idea of a pirate party in Alec's head.

The Cake Design: I combined two flat sheet cakes to make one large flat one. I decorated it in off-white and brown frosting to look like a pirate treasure map. (This idea utilized my special ability to bake flat cakes resulting from poor rising.)

The Party Hats: In a precedent-setting move I did not provide some sort of hat or face paint for the guests. I was unable to find large sheets of inexpensive

black paper. The solution to spray paint newspaper hats black fizzled when I discovered all of our cans of black paint were empty. Rather than spending money I abandoned the idea altogether.

The Party Decorations: This is the better idea that came to me after finding myself backed into a creative corner. For earlier parties I had always made some type of paper decorations for the living room. The pirate theme stumped me for weeks. I presented my last-ditch idea to Jim, asking if he could build a pirate ship in the

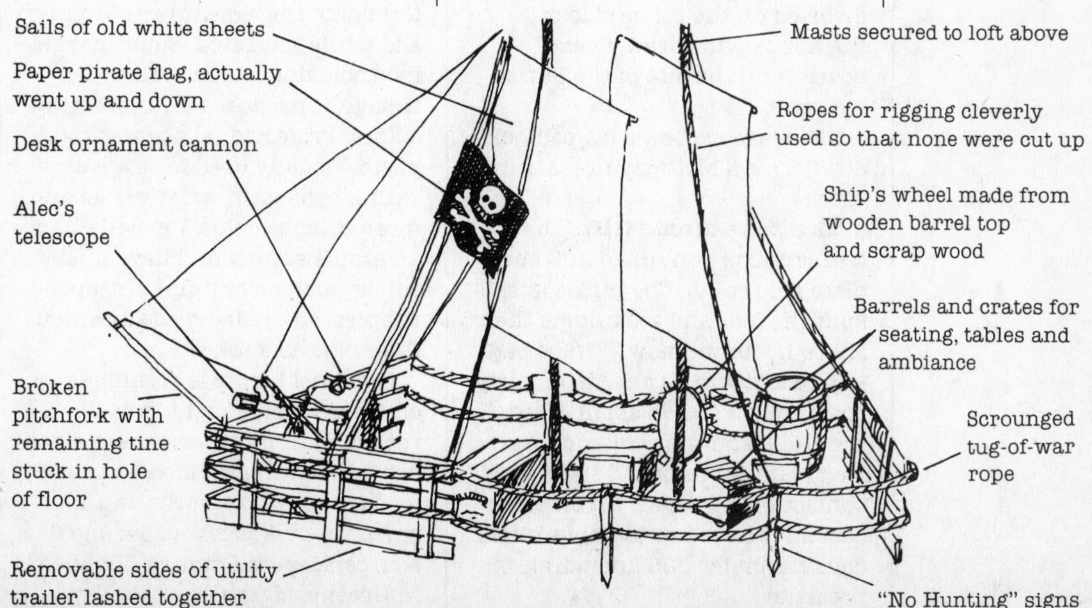

large open area of our barn from items we already had.

The morning of the party Jim went to work demonstrating that his wife was not the only parent with a creative knack. (See previous page.) The ship provided entertainment and a place to eat cake and ice cream.

The Activity: The treasure hunt. Jim scrounged a small wooden crate and added rope handles, hinges, a hasp, and a padlock (previously scrounged). I designed the treasure hunt consisting of pictorial clues on small hidden pieces of paper for the children to follow.

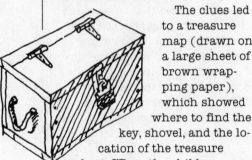

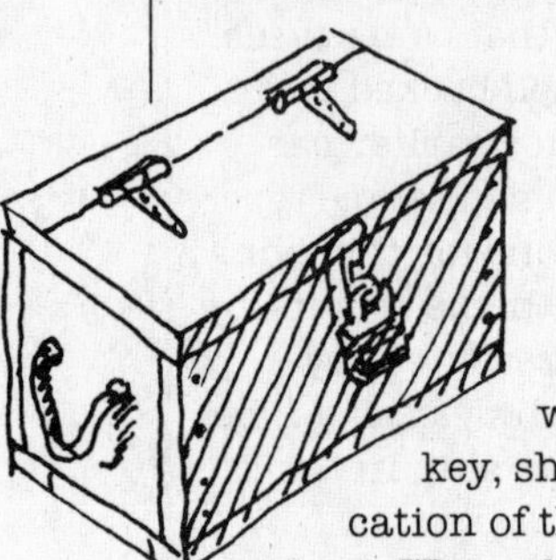

The clues led to a treasure map (drawn on a large sheet of brown wrapping paper), which showed where to find the key, shovel, and the location of the treasure chest. When the children were diverted on the other side of the house Jim threw a cardboard *X* on the site of the buried treasure.

The treasure box with padlock doubled as a birthday present for Alec.

The Take-Home Gift: The treasure box contained 300 chocolate gold coins. The pirate guests split the loot and took home their share in (brand new) Ziploc bags.

The Bottom Line: Alec's party cost under $10. We spent $6 on the coins and the remainder on ice cream, store brand soda, and confectionery sugar. On other occasions I have put together birthdays for under $25, including presents.

PLAY DOUGH

3 cups flour
1½ cups salt
6 tsp cream of tartar
3 cups cool water
3 Tbsp oil
food coloring

Mix dry ingredients together in a big cooking pot. Blend all liquids together in a bowl. Combine with dry ingredients and cook over medium heat, stirring constantly. Remove from heat when dough pulls away from the sides of the pot and can be pinched without sticking (about 5 minutes). Turn onto board or counter and knead until smooth and play dough consistency. Store in airtight container.

Note: The recipe suggests that you do not make double batches. The only reason I can see is that it is very hard to stir near the end of the cooking.

You can add food coloring with the liquid ingredients or carefully add while kneading. Supermarket food coloring works well although it produces uninteresting colors. Professional decorating pastes usually used for cake decorating produce a wider range and more intense color. I usually have an ample supply and have made colors such as hot pinks, deep purples, etc. I also made a camouflage blob as a joke.

Cream of tartar is significantly cheaper when bought in bulk rather than in supermarket-sized containers. Health food stores or food co-ops carry herbs and spices in bulk, such as our local source, Meyers Country Cupboard in Greene, Maine.

This play dough will keep well as long as a year. Occasionally I have made a batch that gets sticky after stored for a while. Maybe I didn't cook it long enough. If a little flour is kneaded in it will return to the original consistency.

If you plan to give these away as a gift (ages 3 to 10) find a nice recycled container and make a custom label with the child's name. If you aren't artistic, mimic a "punk" design.

I'M SAVING ALL MY FROZEN JUICE LIDS... BUT I DON'T KNOW WHAT TO DO WITH THEM.

New converts to tightwaddery write to me asking what they are supposed to do with all this stuff they've just started saving. After all, don't all self-respecting tightwads have an impressive stash of either egg cartons, styrofoam meat trays, toilet paper tubes, or frozen juice lids? My personal impressive stash currently includes 31 egg cartons. (The "Egg Carton Princess Crown" has long since lost its appeal.)

However, it's easy to get the basics of hoarding turned around. We don't save things for the purpose of throwing away less. We save things so that we *buy* less.

Christmas tree ornaments are the most common reuse for the frozen juice lid. Use a hammer and nail to pound a simple design and hang them with a ribbon. This is a better idea than buying more ornaments, but if you already have plenty, why bother?

Some parents like to glue magnets to the lid, put a picture of their child on the front, and put the lid on the front of the refrigerator. I don't like anything stuck to the front of my refrigerator so my inclination would be to throw the thing away before making a magnetized picture frame.

Kindergarten teachers have mastered the art of reuse, creating craft projects out of all sorts of things that are commonly thrown away. It's not that they can't bear to see stuff going to the landfill, but rather by doing so they need to purchase fewer craft materials, thereby stretching a limited budget. (Crafts for kids comprise the bulk of ways to reuse just about anything.)

If you do acquire an impressive stash, develop the habit of looking to it first for a solution. Say you have a table or appliance that is a bit wobbly due to uneven legs. Two or three stacked lids may solve the problem.

People who have limited space have to be selective hoarders, saving only the things they *know* they can reuse, or saving smaller stashes. Ask yourself, "Supposing I were to come up with an extraordinary reuse for the frozen juice lid. How many could I possibly need?" If the answer is 20 juice lids, then only save 20, and throw away the rest with reckless abandon.

THOSE PESKY JUICE LIDS . . .

When I launched a nationwide search for ways to reuse frozen juice lids, ideas poured in from all states of the union (give or take 25). We sorted through the mountain of unparalleled brilliance and have selected the most ingenious ones:

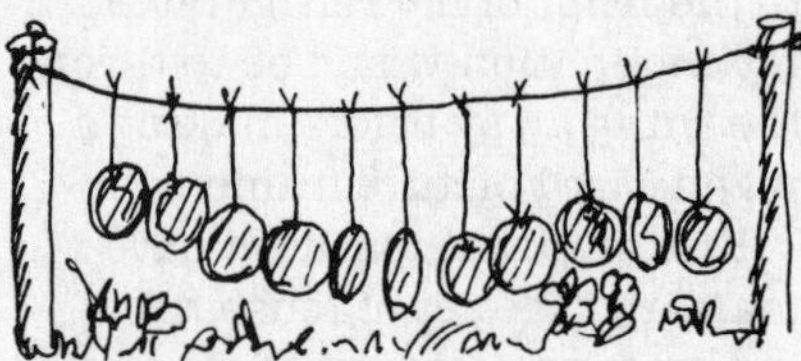

Garden Wind Chimes. Hang lids from a line close enough to clink together . . . to scare away birds. (Linda Sherman, Unadilla, New York)

Reflectors. Use to mark your mailbox or the end of the driveway where there is no streetlight. (Teresa Totaro, Powantan, Virginia)

The Flower Pot Aid. Punch holes and put one in the bottom of a flower pot to keep pebbles in. As it rusts the iron nourishes the plant. (Florence Meitzler, Kresgeville, Pennsylvania)

Coasters. Cover the bottom with felt. Spray paint or decorate if desired. (Judith Kopchak, Murfreesboro, Tennessee)

The Concentration Game. Glue stickers or pictures on lids . . . two of each type. Mix them up and put them on the table facedown. The children take turns finding matches. Mismatched pairs are turned over again and matches are kept until the end of the game. The child with the most matched pairs wins. (Dorothea Howard, Prairie Farm, Wisconsin)

Noisemakers. Nail 2 or 3 lids to a stick of wood, loose enough so that the lids rattle. (Louise Fernandes, Brookline, Massachusetts)

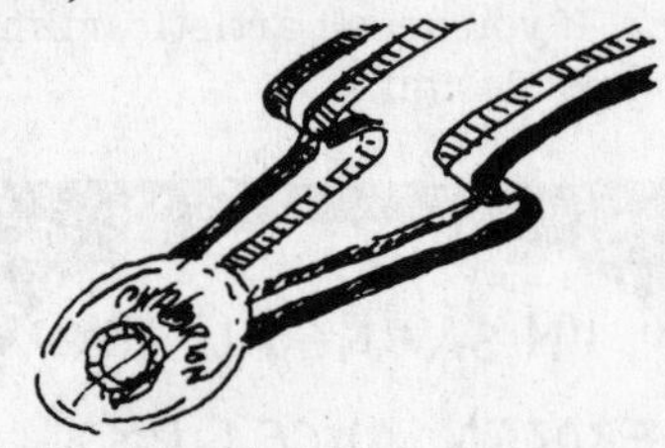

Medals of Achievement. Glue to ribbon to tie around the neck. To make them look more official add gold seal stickers, colored stars, and their name with small letter stickers. (Myra Koch, Merced, California)

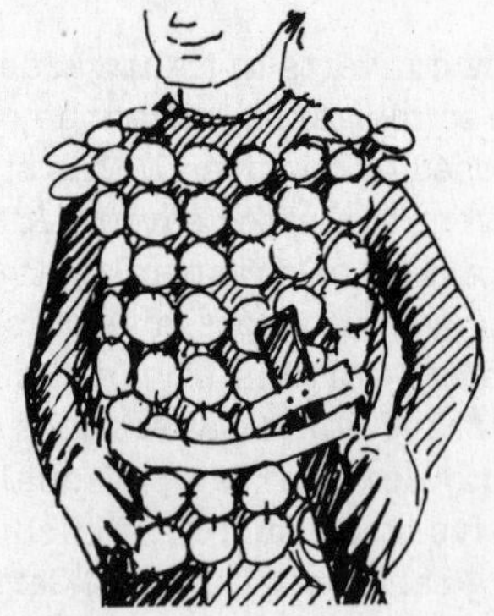

Suits of Armor. Poke holes near the edges and tie together. Start saving now for next Halloween's space warrior costume. (Barbara Winans, Dixon, California)

Toddler Entertainment. Give a stack to a toddler in a high-

chair. He tosses and giggles. Mom and Dad enjoy relative peace at dinnertime. (Tammy Naquin, Westwego, Louisiana)

When you're done with your lids, take them to the recycling center.

BUDGET WEDDINGS

Undoubtedly the cheapest way to get married is to see a justice of the peace and forgo the stop at Burger King on the way home. By comparison I have attended a wedding rumored to cost about $40,000. This lavish production lasted until 1:00 A.M., about five hours after the guests had suffered beyond their limit.

The vast territory in between would suffice for approximately 99% of the human race.

Weddings are one of the few experiences I feel justify financial investment. The objective is not to spend as little as possible or enough to impress royalty. Rather it is to spend enough to satisfy your reasonable expectations while not going into debt.

The traditional wedding leaves little room for creative budget slashing and fails to reflect changing demographics. Older established singles or couples marrying for the second time comprise a large percentage of today's knot-tiers. Often they pay the bills themselves. Standard wedding gifts of toasters and silver trays do not make sense. These couples already have household items or have formed strong ideas about the things they like.

Therefore my first budget wedding idea is:

The Contribution Wedding Gift: When my uncle married, a friend donated the use of a vintage 1920s Packard for transportation. A relative made a professional cake. I contributed a wedding invitation. Friends played music at the wedding and during the reception.

In other weddings I have attended, linens and silver serving pieces were loaned, centerpieces were made of winter greens, a grandmother's dress was altered.

Establishing this atmosphere of helpfulness depends largely on who will attend your wedding. If people know you plan to pay for this with your own limited funds, they will rise to the occasion.

Along with the contribution wedding gift consider:

The Potluck Reception: Before you gasp at this "tacky" suggestion let me make a case. Budget-catered meals tend to be very poor. Even the better ones offer only two predictable choices and rarely justify the cost. Conversely, wouldn't your guests prefer the opportunity to bring a covered dish that costs a few dollars to prepare rather than a $25 wedding gift?

I have seen four weddings with potluck receptions, including my own. My Yankee/Scotch family took it in stride. I suspect some of Jim's Ukrainian/Polish family politely masked their horror. In each of the four receptions the spread of food was diversified, interesting, and appealing and even superseded the catered meal at the $40,000 wedding.

Potluck, in this case, does not have to mean tuna casserole or

Jell-O in Tupperware. Guests will naturally bring their specialty. Some items may be transferred to more elegant (borrowed) serving dishes for a formal look, if needed.

Organizing who brings what will prove to be the largest obstacle. Solve this by including a note on the RSVP card saying: "We are planning a potluck reception. If you would like to bring a contribution as your wedding gift, please specify." Include a place for them to write in something. Also include a blank next to "I will call for a suggestion." Provide your phone number.

Other Receptions: Summer outdoor receptions, such as at your home or your parents' home, offer a cost-free location. Since they are not as formal, less expensive alternatives, such as paper plates versus rented plates, become acceptable.

Most churches have a hall with adjacent kitchen stocked with dishes and utensils. The women's group might also do the catering, serving, or clean-up for a modest fee. This option generally does not allow for dancing and alcohol.

In some parts of the country wedding receptions take the form of a tea or a hoedown. A sit-down meal is not necessary.

The Attire: Often bridal shops have display or discontinued dresses for as little as $100. This costs less than sewing your own or renting. Check classifieds for women selling their dresses, which have been worn only one time or not at all. (After the wedding recoup the cost by reselling.) Have your mother's or grandmother's dress altered.

For any member of the bridal party, strongly consider attire that can be worn again. Brides may wear a short white dress or white suit.

When my uncle married, his wife-to-be coordinated outfits with genuine flair. The men wore blue blazers and gray slacks. She reasoned that every man has these already in his closet. Each wore a matching tie and handkerchief. (A tuxedo rental costs about the same as a new jacket.)

For the right couple, yesteryear clothing (items from the '30s and '40s) can be purchased at thrift or vintage clothing shops.

The Rings: Window shop at a jeweler, paying attention to prices. Then go to a pawn shop and look for a bargain. (Only a true tightwad would find a pawn shop romantic.) The rings may not look brand new or come in a fancy box. But shiny new rings gain a used patina quickly.

Consider the heirloom engagement ring. check antique/bric-a-brac shops for estate jewelry. If you don't like diamonds don't buy an engagement ring.

The Invitations: I designed an unconventional invitation for my uncle. Since both are architects they agreed to a blueprint

invitation about 1′ × 3′ rolled and mailed in a tube. As it unrolled, the invitation read "Plans for a Wedding" with a portrait, then an invitation, directions on how to get to the reception, renderings of their home and church, a map, and a RSVP mailer to cut off. Although the postage cost more, the invitation cost nothing to produce.

A graphic designer might not step forward to offer an inexpensive invitation alternative.

Standard invitations, especially if you select something simple, can be comparatively reasonable. Shop for prices among many printers.

You might also purchase elegant stationery and hand write your invitations. This is suitable for a small group where an RSVP card might not be essential.

Flowers: If you opt for traditional flowers, at least spend the minimum—bouquets for the bride and maid of honor, corsages for the mothers, and a carnation for the men. Obviously some types of flowers cost less than others, especially if you pick flowers in season. Have a precise shopping list and get prices from several florists. Check for wholesale florists in your area.

If possible look to nature for other decorations. My sister in North Carolina planned her wedding when the mountain laurel were in bloom.

Often brides carry a single flower by itself, or in a prayerbook or Bible.

Silk flowers and other reusable accessories rival fresh flowers in price. Custom-made, they serve as permanent mementos or home decorations in the future.

The Cake: A bridal professional suggested having a smaller wedding cake supplemented with your own sheet cake.

Photography: A world of difference separates a professional wedding photographer and your amateur brother-in-law, both in quality and price. A professional photography package can cost about $500. This price makes the work of the amateur more appealing. If you do opt for the amateur have him take several rolls of film so that you have a selection to choose from when assembling your album. Odds are that you know someone with a video camera, too.

Bridal Party Gifts: Let wedding accessories double as the gifts. Bridesmaids and mothers can keep their silk flower corsages. The best man and ushers can keep their matching ties and handkerchiefs.

Negotiating: We are in a recession. Businesses that offer nonessential services hurt first. They may be more flexible to get your business. As one consultant told me, "Ask, ask, ask." If you have a professional service you might be able to barter. If you have a more personal relationship with the business owner you may be able to barter nonprofessional skills such as babysitting or housecleaning.

Whenever you barter hold up your end of the deal. If a business-person has a positive experience he will barter with others in the future.

Or have the vendor do only part of the service. One photographer charges less than half to shoot pictures only. Her clients assume responsibility for developing and album purchasing. To protect yourself you might have the photographer go one step further. Have her develop the film and give you a contact sheet.

One bride, whose financial circumstances diminished prior to the wedding, bought buffet items from a superb caterer and set up a buffet herself, reducing the cost of feeding the 200 invited guests from $8 to $3 each.

Bridal Consultants: If "budget wedding" strikes you as a contradiction in terms and you plan to spend several thousand dollars, professional help can be worth paying for.

One consultant charges a minimum fee of $500 or 15% of the budget, to be included in the total. Because she works regularly with suppliers she can steer you to the best values. You will very likely receive equal services for less than you can find on your own, making her services essentially free. Bridal consultants use vendors regularly, and in return they provide better service. She will help you evenly disperse your budget. As the coordinator of your wedding she'll free your mother or mother-in-law to enjoy the day.

GOOD STUFF THROUGH THE MAIL

Canning Information. If you garden but do not can you might want to rethink before time to order seeds in the spring. I find that people think it is more work than it really is. For a free newsletter called *Pantry* published four times a year send your name and address to Kerr Glass Manufacturing Corp., Attn. Dept. PRA,

THE FIVE-MINUTE COMPOST BIN

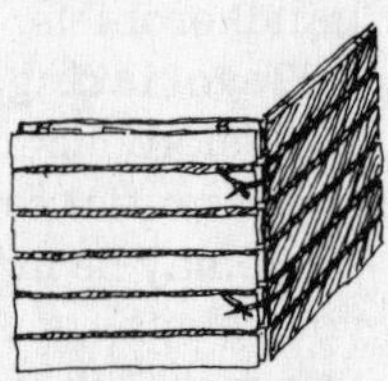

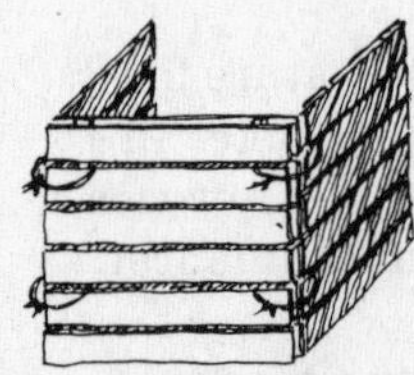

To construct this inexpensive compost bin you will need four wooden pallets and eight hangers. The pallets are usually free or can be purchased for a dollar. Simply wire the four together to form a square. When you wish to remove or stir compost open one side as you would a door.

P.O. Box 76961, Los Angeles, CA 90076. If you send $3.50 they will send you a 112-page paperback guide.

Junk Mail Relief. Send a letter to the Direct Mail & Marketing Association, 6 East 43rd Street, New York, NY 10017 requesting that your name (names) be removed from "all the direct mailing lists they service." This association has several hundred of the largest direct mailing organizations in its program. It will take about three months before you will receive junk mail relief.

A READER QUESTION

Dear Amy,

How do you reuse/recycle postage stamps?

William Cayce
Grand Rapids, Michigan

Technically, it's a federal offense to reuse any postage stamp, regardless of whether or not it has ever been through the postal system. Throw away those uncanceled stamps that come through the mail. The price of honesty is very small.

But what if you stamp an envelope, and decide not to use it, and you cannot reuse the envelope? The post office will accept the whole envelope with stamp and exchange it for a new stamp. They need to see the whole envelope to verify that the stamp has never been through the mail.

We get a large number of SASE's that we cannot use and frequently return them to the post office. I also use post office postcards for much of my correspondence. (I can fit more on them than a scenic or homemade postcard.) I also return any of these that I botch in the writing process.

CUTTING THE COST OF BAKING

As a general rule home-baked foods cost ¼ to ⅓ of the store-bought price. Exceptions include some packaged mixes, as well as some baked goods purchased on sale with double coupons. The cost of home baking can be further minimized using basic strategies.

Flour. For the past two years we have found white flour on sale for $2.88 for 25 lbs during the fall. This equals a 5-lb bag for 57¢, or about half price. (Flour in 25-lb bags generally costs more per pound than 5-lb bags.) Staples rarely go on sale, so when we see these deals we purchase in bulk. Last year we purchased 200 lbs. (Stores reserve the right to limit quantities, but we have never been challenged.)

To keep it from getting "buggy," flour (and other grains for long-term storage) needs to be frozen overnight. Then transfer to an airtight container. We use

clean trash barrels or 5-gallon buckets obtained from bulk food stores. This method is common practice in New England. Those in other parts of the country should check with their local Extension Service as I am not certain the method works as well in warmer climates.

Whole Grains. Whole-grain flour, oatmeal, and cornmeal cost more than white flour. But because whole grains combine with other foods to make a protein, they are a good value, so use liberally. Recently we purchased a 50-lb bag of oatmeal at 39¢ a pound compared to 80¢ per pound of Quaker Oats in a small carton. If these quantities are too much for your needs, try to bulk buy with other families.

Add a tablespoon of wheat germ to a cup of white flour as a substitute for wheat flour.

Milk. Use powdered milk in baking. When a recipe calls for cream or condensed milk mix powdered milk with half the water. Buttermilk also comes in powdered form and is almost as cheap as powdered milk. This is handy because it can be stored for a long time. Substitute "sour milk" (a cup of milk to a tablespoon of lemon juice or vinegar) for buttermilk.

One reader sent in the following recipe for sweetened condensed milk:

1 cup instant nonfat dry milk solids
⅔ cup sugar
⅓ cup boiling water
3 Tbsp melted margarine

Combine all ingredients in the container of an electric blender (or pour in a bowl and use electric mixer). Process until smooth. Store in refrigerator until ready to use. Yield: about 1¼ cups for 60¢.

The price of powdered milk rises and falls about a year behind the price of whole milk. Here in Maine whole milk prices are low and powdered milk prices are high. Therefore the difference between whole and powdered milk is temporarily only 40¢ per gallon versus the $1.50 per gallon difference of a few years ago.

Eggs and Oil. I group these two together because of the fat content. If you have a cholesterol problem, by all means throw out the yolks. Quadruple bypass operations cost a tad more than a few discarded yolks. The same applies to the use of the more healthy peanut and safflower oils. However, if your doctor looked at your test numbers, eyebrows raised, and said, "Whatever you are doing keep on doing it," then severe limitation of fats is not necessary.

Most egg substitutes are more expensive than throwing away yolks, as are powdered eggs.

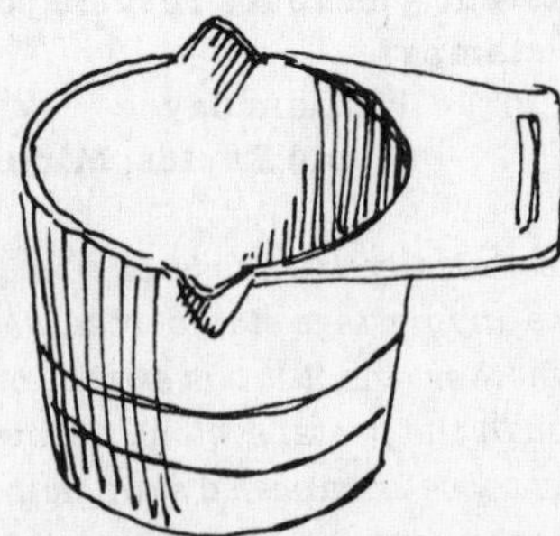

Mary Miller of Lakewood, Colorado, sent in this idea. Substitute one heaping tablespoon of soy flour (or powder) and one tablespoon of water for an egg in baking. She says she has never had a

recipe fail. We bought a pound for 99¢ (which yields about 45 heaping tablespoons) and tried it in muffins, pancakes, cornbread, cake, and even meatloaf. We could not detect any difference.

A heaping tablespoon of soy flour costs a tad over 2¢. An egg costs about 10¢ (if you pay $1.20 a dozen). For every egg you eliminate by substituting soy flour you would save a little under 8¢. This means if you substitute soy flour for a dozen eggs, this month you will save $1.

Soy flour is more versatile than eggs, since it does not require refrigeration and takes up less space. Those bakers who like to make up mixes for pancakes and waffles can make mixes with soy flour and powdered milk. They would only need to add water to make a batter. It would be great for camping.

Eggs and oil (or fats) rank among the most expensive and least healthy ingredients in baking. I have discovered, by accidental omission, that you can cut back on eggs and oil (or fat) without significantly changing the final product. Doing this will produce a slightly tougher muffin, for example. Sometimes this can be good for muffins that are too moist and fall apart. Since I always bake double or triple recipes, eliminating one egg is not a problem.

Margarine, shortening, and oil seem to be interchangeable in some types of recipes. On the average the price is comparable unless you buy one on sale and not the other.

Vicki Dely of Allison Park, Pennsylvania, wrote in that you can substitute unsweetened applesauce for oil in some recipes, especially cakes. I have been experimenting with this as well, and in combination with the soy flour.

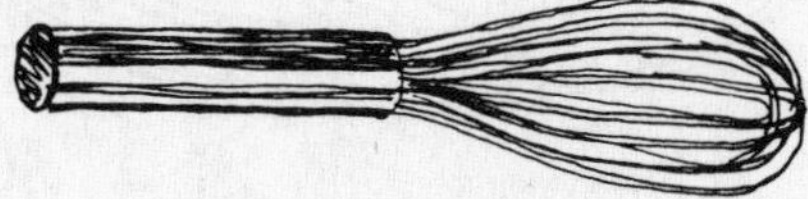

Substituting applesauce for fat works well when the taste might not compete with other flavors (such as cocoa) or where the fat content might not be critical. Our homemade stuff might be stronger tasting than store-bought applesauce. I liked the applesauce/soy flour combination in cornbread, but it produced a tough oatmeal cookie. I have had more satisfactory results substituting applesauce for half the shortening in cookies.

Depending on prices in your area, or if you make your own applesauce, you can save half or more on the cost of oil in your baking.

Sugars. You can also cut back on the amount of sugar in many recipes. If a recipe calls for brown sugar I may use half brown and half white. You can make brown sugar by mixing 1 tablespoon of molasses to 1 cup of sugar. This is not much cheaper, but works in a pinch. Bulk-purchased molasses is about 50% the cost of small bottles of the name-brand stuff.

Dot Platter of Imperial, Missouri, wrote:

"When shopping for sugar be sure to purchase baking soda. One can save half or more on sugar usage and cost when making pies, cobblers, fruit cakes, and fruit salads by using baking soda to neutralize the acid content in these types of dishes.

"For instance, if one uses ¼ to ½ teaspoon of baking soda in a fruit pie, only about half the usual amount of sugar is needed to get the desired sweetness."

This idea interested me because I frequently make fruit crisps. I put this idea to the "acid test." I made two mixed-fruit crisps of strawberries, apples, rhubarb, and blackberries. I added a teaspoon of baking soda and half the usual sugar to one crisp. The family and a couple of office workers taste-tested both. The crisp with the baking soda and half the sugar was slightly sweeter. Obviously one would have to experiment with different recipes to find the right amount to adjust the sugar and baking soda.

Many use honey because it is not refined. There is a difference of opinion as to whether one form of sugar is healthier than another. Honey can also be dangerous for infants, and any sugar in a sticky form (honey, molasses, raisins) is more likely to cause cavities.

Nuts. I seldom buy these because of the expense; however, they are healthy and therefore a good value. I substitute oatmeal in brownies and raisins or coconut in cookies.

Yeast. Try to find a source of bulk yeast, which costs about 7% of those little packets. If you do not buy yeast in bulk, baking bread may not be cheaper than buying bread at a thrift store.

Herbs and Spices can be remarkably cheap when bought at a natural foods store in bulk. The difference is so great I regard the little jars in grocery stores to be highway robbery. As an alternative look for an inexpensive brand called Spice Time, often found in 5 & 10 stores. In some cases you can save by growing your own herbs or drying orange peel.

Store Brands seem to be of the same quality as any name brand, so buy the cheapest on the shelf. Some stores carry a brand that beats all. Clabber Girl baking powder, which comes in a larger container, costs much less than other well-known brands. Again, you must investigate all the stores in your area.

Baking Powder. Make your own by mixing 1 part baking soda, 2 parts cream of tartar, and 2 parts arrowroot. This eliminates the aluminum found in commercial brands but the cost is roughly 25% more than the best baking powder price that I have, versus making the homemade version with bulk-purchased ingredients.

Convenience Foods. Food manufacturers design recipes that call for their products. The recipes are generally found on the product packaging (such as cold cereal boxes) or in magazine ads. They will drive up your baking costs. Avoid the recipe or try to find a homemade substitute. The same rule applies for recipes that call for a brand-name staple.

Saving on Energy. Baking double batches or baking two items at once can save almost

half the energy. You might be able to bake some items as the oven heats up (rather than when already fully heated) and turn the oven off a few minutes early, leaving the items in the oven longer. Do not do this for cakes and other finicky items.

Saving on Time. Establish a "baking center" by grouping baking powder, baking soda, salt, shortening, and other common ingredients in one area. Your baking utensils and measuring equipment should be within reach. I arranged my spices by alphabetical order. A friend has hers grouped together by the type of recipe for which they are used. Either method eliminates the "spice hunt." Preparing double batches saves half the time. Freeze the surplus.

Saving by Choice. Some foods cost more than others while offering little or no nutrition. Therefore, try to choose foods that are cheap *and* healthy. We gave up artificial sweeteners and now simply eat less sugar overall. Sugar is one of our last hold-outs —pumpkin pie just wouldn't taste right without it. But you can choose to make oatmeal raisin cookies instead of gumdrop or chocolate chip. Make carrot cake instead of chocolate. And you can bake fewer desserts altogether in favor of whole-grain breads, rolls, and crackers.

No food that offers little nutritional value is a bargain, even when it is homemade.

Learning to Bake. People have told me that they cannot bake. While mastery of the pie crust may elude some of us, overall baking is simple. It requires experimentation and practice. As a rule I follow recipes precisely the first time, and experiment in subsequent uses. Regard your first frustrating attempts as an investment that will reap future savings.

The Personal Cookbook. Develop your own cookbook to record experiments that work. Also write in recipes used frequently in double or triple batches and alter the amounts accordingly.

BAKING POWDER UPDATE

I gave a recipe on the previous page for a baking powder substitute that costs more than the cheapest commercial baking powder. The advantage was it had no aluminum. Some studies suggest aluminum might be hazardous to your health.

Later we ran out of baking powder, which jogged my brain to test a follow-up tip sent in by a reader: the arrowroot in the homemade version was unnecessary.

I tested this by making two half-batches of muffins—one with commercial baking powder and

one with the homemade, no-arrowroot version—and baked them in the same pan. There was no detectable difference.

Below are prices in my area:

Rumford baking powder (which has no aluminum) costs $1.79 lb.
Clabber Girl baking powder (which has aluminum) costs $1.25 lb.
Home version with 2 parts arrowroot, 2 parts cream of tartar, and 1 part baking soda costs $1.58 lb.
Home version with 2 parts cream of tartar and 1 part baking soda costs $1.34 lb.

The second home version is actually the cheapest of all, because you use less of it. Just 1/4 tsp of baking soda and 1/2 tsp of cream of tarter substitutes for 1 tsp of baking powder. Because you use 25% less, roughly $1 worth equals a pound of the other baking powders. (My calculations are based on store-brand baking soda and cream of tartar at $1.30 lb from a natural foods store.)

My Fannie Farmer cookbook says this version should not be mixed in advance, as it does not keep well. So keep cream of tartar in your "baking center" and add it, and baking soda, individually.

In using this idea I found that on-the-spot computing of odd amounts of baking powder (say 2½ teaspoons) became confusing. So I figured out all the possible baking powder quantities and the equivalent substitutions. I taped this information to the side of my baking powder box, where it would be handy to refer to.

CONTAINER GARDENING

Those of us who live in the country have the advantage of the big garden to help reduce our food bill. However urban or suburban dwellers with little or no space to garden can also supplement their food bills.

Of the many styles of small-scale gardening, container gardening lends itself well to the urban environment.

If you have a rooftop, fire escape, balcony, or patio

that is sheltered and sunny you have a place to garden.

The major advantage to container gardening is that containers can be moved to get maximum sunlight. Most gardens need a minimum of six hours per day. Some gardeners keep their containers on movable carts.

Almost any vegetable can be grown in a container, although you should look for the specific varieties that have been developed for containers.

Containers can include redwood tubs, stone planters, terracotta pots, and half barrels. However, since this is *The Tightwad Gazette* I encourage you to look for less expensive alternatives, such as apple boxes, bushel baskets, or laundry baskets with a trash bag liner. The best inexpensive solution is the 5-gallon bucket. Plastic containers will heat up more and tend to dry out the soil so extra care must be taken.

The 5-gallon bucket can be obtained free from many sources. A health food store or Dunkin' Donuts often has them for the taking.

Container gardens need more drainage than regular gardens. One author suggests drilling holes on the sides near the base, in pairs one above the other every 3 inches. If you have drainage holes in the bottom set your container on blocks off the ground. The bottom of the container should have drainage material, such as peastone gravel, deeper than side drainage holes or at least ½ inch deep for bottom drainage holes.

Soilless mixes, made up of peat moss, vermiculite, and perlite, work well in this application. This mix may become your greatest expense, so you will want to shop for price. The mix can be saved and reused from year to year. If you plan a large-scale operation you may want to learn to mix your own for the sake of economics. Any container must hold a minimum of 6 to 10 inches of soil or mix.

Use a slow-release nutrient to fertilize your garden. Make your own by soaking a handful of dried manure soaked in a jug of water. Not only is this inexpensive but ideal for the novice, as the nutrient is released slowly over a period of time.

To conserve water soak the soil not the foliage. Also water early or late in the day to prevent evaporation. Regular watering is critical. A surplus is better than not enough.

The Portuguese- and Italian-Americans who have settled in our urban areas possess the greatest expertise on urban gardening. Most of you will not be able to snag an expert and should find a book for additional information. A few titles are:

Vegetables by Derek Fell, 1982
Making Vegetables Grow by Thalassa Cruso, 1975
Square Foot Gardening by Mel Bartholomew, 1981

END SUBSTITUTE ABUSE

For years I have listened in silence to the malicious sneers, the wild and vicious accusations, the snickers, and the low blows. But

no more. It is time for someone to take a stand and defend against the onslaught of verbal attacks . . . to say with pride, "Dry milk has a place in this world, if nowhere else but in my cupboards!"

Yes, folks, this form of substitute abuse has been allowed to be unchallenged for too long. And I for one am an admitted long-term user of the stuff. Thus I have decided to bring this issue to the forefront of public awareness with this article to examine the attributes of dry milk.

Taste: I would quickly lose credibility if I tried to convince you that the taste of dry milk is indistinguishable from whole milk. I will say that *all* foods are an acquired taste. Chances are that the first time you tasted coffee, tea, diet cola, or wine you did not like them. In all likelihood one of those beverages is a regular part of your diet today.

Dry milk tastes best when chilled overnight and consumed with a meal. Until a few years ago we had been serving our children half dry and half whole. One evening we ran out of whole and served the children straight dry milk. When a child smacked his lips and said "I sure like milk," Jim and I looked at each other in amazed silence, mental gears turning in sync. We have never looked back.

If you wish to switch to dry milk for drinking, mix small amounts of dry to whole and gradually increase the ratio.

Economy: A gallon of whole milk costs $2.19 to $2.59 per gallon. Dry milk, when purchased by the 20-quart store-brand box for $7.00 costs $1.40 per gallon. Even with 100% dry milk use, milk and juice makes up 30% of our family's expenditure for food. A family that consumes a gallon per day could save $30 per month.

Think of it this way. Every time you finish a box of dry milk you have saved $5.

Health: Dry milk is 100% fat-free. Whole milk has a 4% fat content. By mixing half and half you can make your own 2% milk, which is often more expensive than whole milk.

It was once believed that dry milk was not good for children, who need the fat in their diet. Now you are more likely to pick up a magazine and read about the

growing problem of too much fat in the average child's diet. According to a current government survey it is now known that as many as one in four children is technically obese. The physician I consulted for this article verified that dry milk is absolutely healthy for children over the age of one. (Babies need breast milk or formula.) Children get ample amounts of fat, and often too much, in other parts of their diets.

According to current information children need two cups of

milk per day. Teenagers need three, adults need two, pregnant and lactating women need four. For reasons of health and economy it is not reasonable to allow unrestrained consumption of whole milk. It is easy to do simple math and determine how much milk your family should consume monthly. Including milk used in cooking, our family consumes about 10% over the minimum recommendation. Since we also eat cheese we are well within the guidelines.

Versatility: The attribute I enjoy most about dry milk is its many uses. By mixing with half the water you can make a mock cream that can be substituted for high-fat expensive creams in pies, quiches, and sauces. When a soup recipe calls for cream or milk, mix dry milk in powdered form with saved vegetable broth. If a batter looks too wet, dry milk in powdered form can be added. Vegetarian recipes often include dry milk to boost protein. To make instant hot cocoa mix ⅓ cup of dry milk, 1 teaspoon of sugar, and 1 teaspoon of cocoa to a cup of water. It requires two minutes to heat in the microwave.

Convenience: Think of dry milk as a staple. It does not go bad. We never have to make last-minute trips to the convenience store to buy ridiculously overpriced whole milk because we have run out. In fact we are now able to limit our shopping to one major monthly trip. (Whole milk die-hards can also do this by freezing jugs of milk.)

Rarely will you find absolutes in the pages of *The Tightwad Gazette.* I believe that each individual or family has their own priorities and values. Dry milk use is one exception. It may not be possible or desirable for you to switch your family to 100% dry milk consumption. However, you should at least use it for cooking.

Dry milk is a great bargain. It is not often that you find a food that combines economy, health, versatility, and convenience in such a perfect union. It has a place in every tightwad cupboard.

A RECIPE BREAKDOWN

One of the most frequent reader requests is for inexpensive recipes. Obviously you have to choose recipes that call for inexpensive ingredients. However, you can also learn to interpret an existing recipe to make it less expensive.

On the following page is a recipe for seafood casserole that I use frequently. I have included it in its original form and also shown the changes and choices. It was designed to be a time-saver recipe utilizing expensive ingredients. In the process of altering the recipe I made it less expensive but more time consuming. Counteract this by making double or triple batches and freezing the extra to eat on a busy day. Singles and couples can make single batches in separate smaller casserole dishes and accomplish the same result.

If you were to prepare this recipe with the most expensive ingredient options it would cost about $8.00. The way I prepare it, the casserole costs $1.81. Prepared without white wine would save another 40¢.

Mayonnaise or Salad dressing: Buy store brand for 99¢ per quart. You can make your own mayonnaise but the savings is marginal, and depends on the price of eggs.

Milk or wine: Wine is more expensive, but I like the flavor.

Topping: Make your own bread crumbs. Save all your crusts, cereal and cracker crumbs. Store in a bag in the freezer. Process in a blender or food processor.

Seafood: Tuna is the obvious choice. We stock up when it goes on sale for 44¢ per can.

Pasta: Use any pasta purchased on sale. We get it for 33¢ lb. I increase it by 2 oz. because the recipe makes too much sauce.

Mix-and-Match Seafood Casserole

6 servings

4 to 5 oz pasta
½ cup dry white wine or milk
½ cup mayonnaise or salad dressing
1 cup (4 oz) American cheese, shredded
1 10¾-oz can condensed cream of celery, shrimp, or mushroom soup
½ tsp dill
6 to 8 oz canned seafood (tuna, salmon, crab, or shrimp), drained
Topping (below)

Preheat the oven to 350°. Prepare the pasta, following the directions on the package; drain and set aside. Mix white wine with mayonnaise. Add the cheese, soup, and dill. Gently combine the noodles and the seafood with the moist ingredients. Pour the mixture into a 1½-quart casserole dish. Cover and bake for 30 minutes. Remove the cover, top with Topping, and bake for an additional 5 minutes. Serve hot.

Topping: Stir 2 Tbsp melted butter into 1 cup of soft bread crumbs. You can also try 1 cup of crushed corn chips, chow mein noodles, or french-fried onions, or ½ cup of sliced almonds.

Cheese: Use any mild cheese purchased on sale. We always buy it for less than $2 lb. Shredded is usually more expensive, but not always.

Condensed Cream Soup: costs 69¢ to $1.11 depending on the type. Instead I make a mock cream of celery soup that costs 15¢. Melt 2 Tbs. of margarine in a sauce pan. Saute 2 Tbs. chopped celery. Blend in 2 Tbs. flour. Add 1/3 cup dry milk powder and 2/3 cup vegetable broth. Add salt and pepper to taste. Cook until smooth.

CANINE CUISINE

After I requested ideas for inexpensive dog food, I received many letters, several of which had conflicting information. This diversity reflects the range of thinking among those who are knowledgeable about dogs.

In light of this I felt that experts needed to be consulted. This article is based on information from Dr. Gail Mason, a doctor of veterinary medicine and Maine's only board-certified veterinary internist. I also received input from two licensed animal health technicians, including Jody L. Burton of Vacaville, California. All of these individuals agreed with periodicals from the library.

Here are some points I learned:

Major pet food companies have done a great deal of research into animal nutrition. It would be very difficult to make a home petfood that duplicates the combination of protein, fats, and nutrients found in commercial petfoods. While your pet might seem to do well, in the long run it might suffer from a nutrition deficiency, obesity, and/or have a shortened life span. Although I didn't do a cost comparison, I questioned whether some of the home recipes would actually be cheaper because they called for expensive ingredients.

Dr. Mason says that you don't need to buy a super-premium dog food. Some of the companies that have put a long-term effort into developing good food are Purina, Pedigree Expert, ALPO, and Ken-L Ration. Reader Susan Ballard of Sloatsburg, New York, says she often purchases Purina on sale for $6.99 for 30 lbs. The coupons, often found on previous bags, will lower the price further, as low as $4.99. She also uses rebates.

People I know who breed dogs for show say they wouldn't use Purina. Because their dogs reproduce frequently, and because they want them to be in top condition, these owners opt for a dog food with higher nutrition (and higher price tag) than these ex-

perts felt was necessary for the average dog.

Stick with name brands. The term "guaranteed analysis" on the packaging is somewhat deceptive. It does guarantee some nutritional standard, but the standard is a loose one. For example, many generics and store brands include hooves and tails as a protein source, which is difficult for dogs to digest. Dr. Mason says some generic brands have been proven to be deficient in some nutrients.

A key way to save money on petfood is to not overfeed your pet. Obesity is one of the most common pet health problems. Begin by following the guidelines on the packaging and adjust as needed. Jody Burton says that you should just be able to feel your pet's ribs, but its backbone should not be too prominent.

A good dry food is generally nutritionally equivalent to a good canned food. Because dry food is cheaper, it is the tightwad choice. Dr. Mason advised against semimoist dog foods, which have dyes and additives to keep them soft. Dry food is better for the dog's teeth, as soft foods tend to stick to teeth.

A common tightwad practice one might avoid is buying in large quantities and storing for a long period of time. The vitamins tend to degrade during storage. So don't buy more than your pet might eat in a month, and store it in a cool, dry place such as a garbage can.

Pets do not need variety in their diet. Switching their foods to keep them from getting bored can actually do harm by upsetting their metabolism. Dr. Mason recommends Purina Puppy Chow for puppies, and then switching to adult food when they are grown.

Although Dr. Mason advises against homemade dog foods as the main part of the diet, she feels dogs can tolerate an occasional homemade snack.

Attempts to economize by purchasing low-quality food can backfire. Treating a common ailment, like pancreatitis, caused by feeding your dog too many fatty table scraps, can cost at least $150, not to mention the discomfort to your dog.

Our family has a dog and a cat because we feel pets would contribute to the quality of the lives of our children. In bringing the animals into our home we assumed a planned expense necessary to provide a reasonable level of care for them.

THICK TRICK

Don't cook down tomatoes to get thick sauce. Once they are prepared and ready to cook, just put them in the refrigerator overnight. In the morning, use your turkey baster to remove the clear liquid that has floated to the top. Voila!

Elaine Stalder
Harrisburg, Oregon

BOOK SMARTS

Before reading this article do the following exercise: count how many books you have in your home that you purchased new. Next count how many of those books you cracked open in the past year . . . or five years. My own tally works out to a couple hundred books purchased new that have not been read in over five years.

Jim and I were both readers B.K. (before kids) and brought our own libraries to the marriage. Now my John Updikes gather dust in the attic next to his Robert Ludlums.

Part two of the exercise is to inventory the books you use with regularity. These are the type of books you *need* to own. Based on my results these are the books I recommend for your library:

- A dictionary and thesaurus if you do any amount of writing.
- A general medical volume such as *The A.M.A. Family Medical Guide*. This provides useful information such as how to take a temperature or pinpoint the probability of a strange rash. It also helps judge when a child needs to go to the doctor in the wee hours of the morning.
- Cookbooks containing basic recipes, like Fannie Farmer or Betty Crocker.
- A basic home maintenance book, especially if you own your own home. If you are remodeling or renovating you should own a book on that subject as well.
- Books covering your special areas of interest, such as the spiritual book of your choice and books relating to your hobby.

Unless you are very lucky, you will not find these books at yard sales. Instead investigate used-book stores. If you are still unable to locate them and your need is pressing, purchase them new. You are likely to save more than the cost of the book.

The following new books I do not recommend:

- Fiction. Last year's best-sellers are soon forgotten and are available at your library.
- Children's books. No parent *wants* to read the same book to their child hundreds of times. If you bring home five library books weekly you will not exhaust your library's shelves before the child goes off to college. These books are also a glut on the yard sale market and can be purchased for a dime.
- Coffee table books. As a graphic designer I am a sucker for these, and the half dozen I have purchased are dusty. They are an attractive and expensive luxury. Stay away from mail-order books, especially the children's books that tend to be poorly crafted. I have responded to the free trial book offers and have found it difficult to cancel my membership. Then I had to pay postage to return books after

I opened the boxes. It was not worth the trouble. Book clubs, which offer free books if you buy two at the regular prices, are still more expensive than if you borrow all these books from the library. And you do not also have the option of browsing through the book before making a purchase.

Jim purchased a brand-new book called *How to Fix Damn Near Anything*. In horror I discovered a $15.95 price tag on the inside of the jacket. Upon interrogation he confessed that he purchased it at the thrift shop for 25¢.

This price difference typifies thrift shops and yard sales. Used-book shops, which have a more reliable selection, charge a little more . . . perhaps $2 for the same book. They will purchase your dusty library in exchange for credit. This allows you to weed out and rebuild a more relevant usable library.

Take advantage of the interlibrary loan system. Any library in the United States can borrow a book from any other library. In theory, as long as it is in print, it can be obtained for you in one to three weeks. You only need to provide the title and author. Some libraries offer this as a free service, while others charge a fee to cover postage. If it's free, bear in mind that it isn't free to the library. Especially if your library is small, don't abuse their generosity. If the book you want to read might be of interest to others, you can also ask your librarian if he or she would be interested in purchasing it.

Space, as well as money, is a precious resource. Before purchasing any new or used book leaf through the pages to determine the amount of information it contains that is of genuine value to you.

Ironically, the bookstore that raked in my hard-earned cash was located across the street from the Boston Public Library, a place I rarely ventured. Give yourself an inexpensive treat and plan an evening to wander through your own library and marvel at all that is free to borrow.

WHAT TO DO WITH . . .

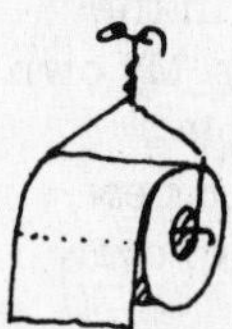

A Coat Hanger. Make a toilet paper holder. Such a contraption currently graces our yet-to-be-remodeled bathroom. Learn to create solutions to tide you over until you find an inexpensive alternative.

Broccoli Rubber Bands. Save these and cut in half to make two usable rubber bands. (Contributed by Polly Davis, Shirley, Massachusetts)

Butter Wrappers. Save by folding and storing in the butter compartment in your fridge. Then use when buttering cookie sheets, soufflé dishes, etc. before finally throwing away. (Contributed by Leslie Lee, Portland, Oregon)

Frozen Juice Lids. When our daughter was going through her medical phase, Jim pop-riveted a juice lid to a band of elastic to make a doctor's headband.

Watermelon Seeds. Dry and save to mix with bird seed. Musk melon seeds also work. The birds love them. (Contributed by Jim Spaulding, Northfield, Massachusetts)

Bread Bags. Cut in half; use the bottom half as an alternative to expensive sandwich bags. Use the original tab or twist-tie to close.

Old Towels. Fold and use in a clamp handle mop to clean floors. Especially good for corners. (Contributed by Ruth MacPherson, Belfast, Maine)

Potato Peels and Chicken Skins. Mix and fry in the oven (when baking something else). Makes a great treat for dogs, who need extra fat during the winter months. (Contributed by Carolyn Sue Marr, Otisfield, Maine)

An Old Sock. Make a toy for your cat. Sew over any hole and stuff with leftover quilt batting. Sew over the top. (Contributed by Kathy Closson, Wiscassert, Maine)

Old Roll-on Deodorant Bottles. Pry off the cap, rinse, and fill with tempera paint thinned with water. Replace the top. Let children paint with it.

Old Mattress Pads. Cut down to smaller sizes to make changing pads for children. Trim edge with bias tape. Smaller pieces can be used as filler when making potholders. (Contributed by Mrs. Richard Lunden, Haynesville, Maine)

Aquarium Water. Save to water your plants. It is tepid and contains algae and other organic waste, which is nourishing for both house and garden plants.

Cold Cereal Boxes. Make magazine holders for the publications you save. Cut diagonally as shown. (Contributed by Donna McKenna, Casco, Maine) It goes without saying that the cereal was purchased with triple coupons on sale.

Mesh Bags. The type that onions and frozen turkeys come in can be made into scouring pads. Just twist and secure with a rubber band . . . or one of those from broccoli. (This idea was sent in by many readers.)

Summer

THRIFT AND THE ENVIRONMENT

The tightwad bug bit me 10 years ago. A full 6 years would pass before I would fully grasp the profound relationship between thrift and the environment. Despite my ignorance, in the name of penny-pinching, I went about doing most of the right things anyway:

For the first five months after Jim and I married, while we lived near Boston, I rode a bicycle to work. (Pregnancy eventually forced me to abandon this.)

When Alec was born he slept in a crib from the Salvation Army. Within a few weeks we learned he was allergic to disposable diapers, and were forced into cloth diaper use. Despite having to cart soiled diapers to an expensive nearby laundromat they were less work than expected and cost-effective.

When Jim wanted to buy a new vehicle to replace his 12-year-old Chevy Suburban, I successfully argued for the purchase of a small, fuel-efficient car first.

The Navy transferred Jim to Norfolk, Virginia. During these 4 years of suburbia we yard saled with a passion. We came to regret most new purchases of the previous years.

We learned that buying in larger quantities and cooking from scratch would dramatically cut our food bill. We gave up soda and dabbled in vegetarianism.

Jim's parents were generous and brought cases of their home-canned garden produce when they came to visit.

Unlike our neighbors, we did not air-condition our whole house. We resorted to flicking on our small air conditioner to cool our bedroom only on the most sweltering of summer nights.

We hung laundry on a clothesline, took shorter showers, and convinced the landlord to insulate the attic. When I washed dishes I would fill the sink halfway. I baked more than one item at a time and put lids on all pots while cooking.

My passion for pinching extended to the reuse of everything possible. I was aware that many of my efforts would only save a few cents. (How much does a single Baggie cost, anyway?) I rationalized that it was a matter of attitude. If I took care with the small things, I would also pay attention to the larger things.

The military moved us again—this time to Brunswick, Maine. During our 15 months of house hunting, while we lived in a government house, I frequented the public library. It was my practice to scour the how-to shelves for books on a variety of topics that would help us to save more money.

During one of these hunts I found *Reuses* by Carolyn Jabs. The book is subtitled "2,133 Ways to Recycle and Reuse the Things You Ordinarily Throw Away." I checked it out of the library, thinking I would learn new ways to save money.

Instead I was more struck by the brief introduction and conclusion chapters that dealt with the environmental impact of the wasteful habits of our culture.

I was clobbered by facts such as: "Americans represent 5% of the world's population but produce half its waste," and "Each day we generate enough trash to fill the New Orleans Superdome . . . twice." Even more dramatic is the per capita growth of garbage. In 1900 the average person used 58 pounds of paper. In 1973 he used 639 pounds.

I got it. Our efforts to save more on purchases naturally resulted in less consumption of goods. Most of our efforts to cut our food bill, especially eating fewer convenience foods and more home-canned foods, produced less trash—about a third of our neighbors'. The purchasing of used items saved the energy and resources that would have been used to produce new stuff, and also saved space in our overflowing landfills.

The effort to save money on electricity and gasoline resulted in less energy consumption and reduced pollution.

I realized that economy and ecology are like two circles that overlap about 90%. The remaining 10% is the area where doing the right thing for the environment costs more. Buying organically grown food costs more. In most cases solar electricity is not cost-effective.

Sometimes doing the right thing economically is not good for the environment. For example, the use of coupons and rebates can make an overly packaged product less expensive than its equivalent prepared from scratch.

I have become aware of subtle transition in our lives. We've met our house-buying goal, and we have established a prosperous business to support us in Jim's retirement. We do not *have* to be tightwads anymore.

But having successfully blended the areas of economy and ecology in the 90% area, we have found we now have some surplus money, and this surplus gives us economic room to reexamine some of the areas within the 10%.

Not having to work away from home has significantly cut our driving. We can now afford the additional cost of recycled paper for the newsletter. I have even found myself hanging laundry in the attic while employing a room full of people downstairs doing our mail. I am making an environmental choice, and not the economic one.

The understanding of the relationship between thrift and the environment has given me the assurance that efforts to reuse and conserve could not be "too extreme."

People tend to think that environmental damage occurs because of sloppy practices of some factory out there. In fact, we consumers create the demand for what the factories produce.

I have also understood that one family making a supreme effort to

live entirely without any harm to the environment makes little impact. But the collective effort of the majority of the population to make smaller, seemingly insignificant changes can make a difference.

The environmentalist enjoys an economic bonus by adopting frugality. We tightwads, whether or not it is a prime motivation, get to wear the cloak of environmentalism, stand tall, and not let anyone tell us we're crazy.

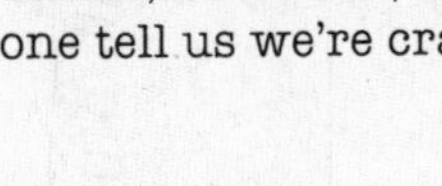

POPSICLE POSSIBILITIES

Summer is Popsicle season. It is the time of year when other neighborhood moms will thwart your attempts to economize. They give your children store bought pops—twin pops, Disney pops, Creamsicles—all of which cost between 10¢ and 22¢ when purchased by the box. Multiply that by the droves that will return to your house for reciprocal offerings and we are talking A LOT of Kool-Aid on a stick. Five per day could add up to $100 during the summer.

Fight back with homemade Popsicles, which are cheap and nutritious. Made from apple juice they cost about 2½¢ each.

OK. This is not exactly startling information and neither is the fact that the droves will not be satiated with such common fare.

So be resourceful. Consider any sweet or wet edible substance for Popsicle possibilities. Raid your cupboards for forgotten ancient commodities and combine them for dangerous new taste sensations. Treat this as another opportunity to use up leftovers. Here are a few ideas:

- homemade plain yogurt (especially what didn't set up well)
- homemade jam (especially what didn't set up well)
- left over Jell-O (especially what didn't set up well)
- juice or syrup left over from canned fruit
- juice left over from a runny berry pie
- fruit or chocolate syrup
- ice tea mix
- sprinkles and jimmies in thicker mixtures
- food coloring
- applesauce
- pudding
- cranberry sauce
- bits of fruit
- coconut

If you can leave the mold open and devise a way to prop the stick, you can make striped Popsicles. (Try aluminum foil for this.) Pour and freeze alternating colors. Tilting the mold will make angled stripes.

Every summer morning take a couple of minutes and create a variety. You will have a cheap and healthful alternative to satiate the thirsty droves.

POPSICLE MOLDS

A friend showed me an ingenious Popsicle mold. She has a surplus of small, neckless prescription bottles. She found that the childproof cap has an inner plastic circle that can be popped out with a knife. The inner plastic circle fits neatly on the top of the prescription bottle. She cuts a slot in the circle to hold a wooden Popsicle stick. These make a Popsicle that is less "klunky" than ones made in a paper cup.

Some might be concerned that the child would associate the prescription bottle with a treat. The labels can be removed or you can just not show the child the bottle when you remove the Popsicle.

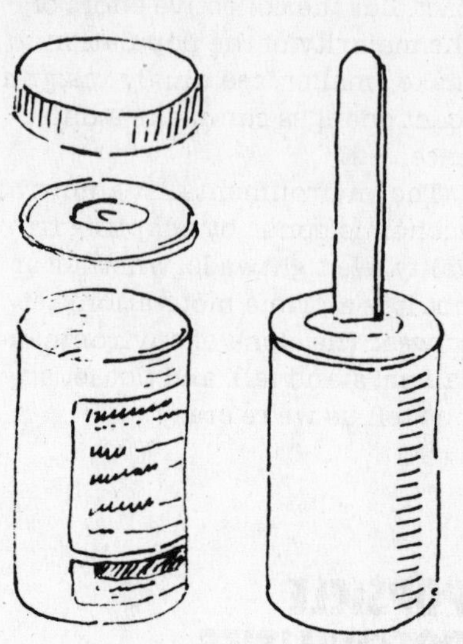

THE FRUGAL ZEALOT GOES TO HOLLYWOOD

It was 9:30 P.M. I was unwinding in a hot tub of water (one of the chinks in my tightwad armor), trying to come down after three consecutive days of interviews with the press (*Boston Globe*, *Christian Science Monitor*, and a tape interview for PBS radio). During this blissful relaxation I savored the thought that the craziness was at least at a lull. That's when the phone rang.

Jim brought the cordless to me and said, "It's for you. It's *To Tell the Truth.*" I said, "What?"

So there I was, standing on the bath mat, dripping wet, talking to Hollywood as Jim passed towels and a robe.

The woman on the phone told me her name and that she worked for *To Tell the Truth.* I said, "What?" After a few minutes of conversation she asked me if I would like to be on the show. I moved on to a more complex verbal expression. "Ah, come on, is this some kind of joke?"

It wasn't. A week and a half later I boarded a seven-something-seven that would propel me through the friendly skies toward my destination, one of the great capitals of consumer spending on the planet.

I should, at this point, interject that I do not have a high regard for most of television and that I am not sure which I loathe more, game shows or Teenage Mutant Ninja Turtle cartoons. The quality

of the newly revived *To Tell the Truth* falls somewhere between *Let's Make a Deal* and *Jeopardy.*

I went knowing that I was selected on the basis of my unusual profession rather than the merits of my message. I accepted the offer because I thought I would regret it if I didn't go. Having done it once I would not feel compelled to do it again.

Did I have fun? It was interesting to see how a show was put together, much as I expected it would be. But of my four days away I spent two very long days traveling and a full day in the studio. My one free day I was somewhat hotel-bound, as it was not within walking distance of anything. And I suffered from jet lag.

I observed several things in Los Angeles. One does not hail a cab as one might in an eastern city. One *calls* a cab (using a telephone). They are extremely expensive. A $20 fare is common. During an attempt to call the Mark Goodson office I bothered some poor woman three times before I finally called the hotel desk to learn I needed to dial a different area code. Los Angeles has three. And the trees are funny there.

I received $80 for food during my stay. I had vowed to try to bring back as much of this as I could. My goal was somewhat undermined as I was limited to the hotel café. I did eat or hoard all that was offered on the plane.

The evening after I arrived I ate with a fellow contestant, a 76-year-old woman from Idaho who counts moose for the forest service. I ordered a $10 turkey club and a glass of water. I learned how to make a white bread turkey sandwich look more substantial. Cut in quarters, corner to corner, stick in those fancy toothpicks, rearrange so that the four crusts face together to form an inner square and fill the square with potato chips.

From then on the only meal I paid for was breakfast. The café offered a $10 all-you-can-eat breakfast buffet. I ate all I could eat and smuggled muffins out in my pocketbook. This was good for the day.

I hadn't flown in about 10 years. I remember the old days when the movies were free. Now one pays $4.00 for optional headphones. I practiced lip reading. The very same movie was a cable TV option in my hotel room for $6.75.

The hotel included a few freebies. Every morning the daily paper, about the size of the Sunday paper here in Maine, was delivered to every hotel room. This struck me as a waste. They also provided us with trial-size soaps and Vidal Sassoon shampoo and conditioner. I verified my theory

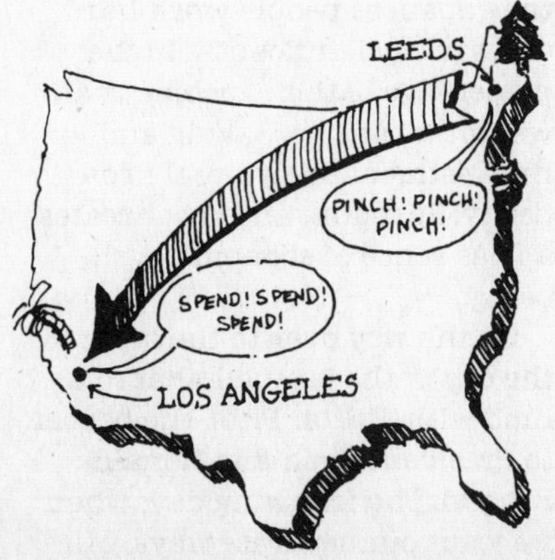

that my bargain brand shampoo makes my hair just as "bouncy and shiny." On my last day I realized that the maid would automatically replace anything that appeared to be used up. Therefore if I had hidden these items on a daily basis I could have brought home three of each.

The trip was my first time away from my children, and I wanted to bring home some West Coast treasures. This was the primary reason I ventured to Universal City (the studio theme park). After a lengthy cost comparison I determined that the airport gift shop, the hotel gift shop, and Universal City gift shop all sold loot for about the same elevated prices. My other shopping option was a $38 tour of the homes of the stars and Rodeo drive. Next time if I decide to buy something I will buy gifts in Maine before I leave.

I noticed another unusual occurrence in Los Angeles—25% to 35% of all people I saw in the airport, hotel, and theme park were Japanese. I was told they now own over half of all the real estate in Los Angeles. In all fairness their prosperity is deserved, as the Japanese people work hard and save a significantly higher percentage of their income than we Americans do. Saving and reinvestment spawn real prosperity. Spending and debt creates a false sense of economic well-being.

On the way over to the studio the day of the taping I shared a limo with Milton Pitts, the barber to President Bush and Ronald Reagan. The following day, when we went our separate ways, Milton Pitts gave me his business card and asked me to send him a newsletter. I mailed six to him, extras for any president or former president who might stop in for a trim.

To Tell the Truth did not let me give an address on the show, although I did squeeze "Leeds, Maine" into one of my answers. I had half a dozen people call for information and received even fewer pieces of mail. I got more mail from a paragraph that appeared in a newspaper in Anchorage, Alaska.

Kitty Carlisle, Orson Bean, and Vicky Lawrence correctly guessed that I was the true tightwad and so I came home with the minimum winning of $334 (plus $40 of my meal allowance).

TIGHTWAD ETHICS OR . . . MUCH ADO ABOUT A MUFFIN

Moments of great horror and pain permanently etch themselves into our memories. When we think back on these events we recall them with amazing clarity.

Such was the case when I read "The Letter" almost a year ago. While waiting in the church parking lot for my daughter to finish her Scout meeting, I browsed through the handful of mail I had just picked up at the post office. A woman wrote criticizing me for an incident of questionable ethics that I had recounted in my then-recent issue. I am sure that I rolled my eyes heavenward and smacked myself in the forehead. She was absolutely correct.

The letter referred to my account of a trip I made to Los Angeles, where I found myself stranded in an expensive hotel and the cheapest breakfast fare was a $10 all-you-can-eat buffet. I had taken one muffin more than I could eat from the buffet. Rather than leaving it behind to be thrown away, in an automatic-doggie-bag-mode I saved it for later consumption. I found it in my purse the following day, dried and crumbled. I never ate it.

Caught up in relating the sport of traveling cheaply, with my trademark humor I embellished my tale to a degree, and my choice of words might have led some to conclude that I had absconded suitcases of muffins. However, in hindsight, I admit that the single muffin was an ethical infraction.

In those awful moments, while reading "The Letter," my entire life passed before my eyes. But rather than the life of crime one might imagine, I saw an ironic contrast—my countless, zealous lectures over the evils of everything from "pilfering paper clips" to the "fudging of insurance claims."

I can offer no explanation for my oversight, except that sometimes, like those plain-as-the-nose-on-your-face typos, things become crystal clear only when someone points them out to you.

It was my hope that the "Smuggled Muffin Affair"—this smudge upon my otherwise spotless tightwad character—would fade into oblivion. However, it reared its ugly head when a journalist included it, against my vehement protest, in a magazine article, and as I predicted, someone wrote a letter to the editor about it.

I must also confess that I internally recall the "Smuggled Muffin Affair" with increasing frequency. Frugality appears to be gaining in acceptance in the '90s. I have found myself an unwitting "expert," and am interviewed on an almost daily basis by journalists and talk-radio hosts. In addition, readers from all over the country send me articles that document this trend.

I should be pleased. But I am also disturbed by what I see as a confusion concerning the ethics of frugality, as recent converts and scoffers alike grapple with this "new concept."

One radio listener called in, not to ask for my "nuggets of frugal wisdom," but to relate how cheap her brother was. It seems that when he invites her for dinner he has her bring the main course. And because his community has a per-bag charge on bags of trash, he drops his off in a community with free pickup service.

An article, which solicited thrifty ideas from area readers, reported such money-saving ideas

as phoning your mother-in-law when you know she's not home, and leaving a message on her answering machine, so that when she calls back, she pays for the long-distance call.

I met a woman who needed a business suit for a single occasion, purchased one, wore it for the day, and then returned it to the store.

Several people have written to me with pride about steaming and reusing uncanceled stamps . . . including one woman who happened to be the wife of a minister.

Because ethics often gets into fuzzy gray areas, no two people would draw the line in the same place. One situation might be clearly wrong, but change a single element of the circumstance and it might be acceptable.

So how do we sort it all out? The relationship between ethics and thrift can be summed up in one sentence. It is wrong to save money at the expense of others. Period.

Small, seemingly insignificant acts such as pilfering, swiping sugar packets, and steaming postage stamps, and fudging income taxes and insurance claims merely pass along your costs to other consumers. It doesn't matter if your boss pays you too little; the restaurant, the post office, or the insurance company charges too much; or if the government doesn't spend funds entirely on programs that you approve of. The collective impact of this raises the cost of living for everyone.

In my dealings with people, both professionally and personally over the past 15 years, I have been continually astounded at how few purely honest people there are. Nearly everyone, including the spendthrift scoffers who wouldn't stoop to stamp steaming, resort to questionable practices that they feel are justifiable.

People routinely make personal phone calls at work, or use their employer's copy machine for personal business. They "work under the table" to avoid income taxes. Or they accept food stamps and similar programs when they qualify but don't have a genuine need. If they see a clerk is undercharging them, they remain silent.

Beyond practicing sound ethics I see the importance of generosity or consideration for someone else, especially when their income might be less than mine. I believe in tipping when I receive good service. I will almost always dicker at a yard sale. However, I pay the set price if I buy something from a child, or from someone who appears to be raising cash due to lean times. And while I often make a sport out of seeing how well I can do Christmas on a small budget, I have "blown my budget" when a friend or relative was in need.

As individuals, our first economic responsibility is to ourselves and to our families. But meeting this responsibility also serves the larger economic community. We insulate ourselves from the possible financial pitfalls that could cause us to declare bankruptcy or make us dependent on some form of public assistance. Tricky ethical issues come up when we see ourselves as economic islands, separate

from the community . . . when we try to save money at the expense of others.

Through my own personal mistake I see another danger. When engaging in such activities we do damage to a worthy cause—one that we hope others will at least accept in us, even if they don't embrace it themselves. As frugality in the '90s takes hold, I anticipate a backlash of doubters who will look to find fault, and take cheap shots. By being consistently honest and generous in our dealings with others we won't give them any ammunition.

I might never have known about the recent letter to the editor, except that it was brought to my attention by a man with whom I have a business relationship. With folded hands and great solemnness he admitted that he agreed with the sentiment of the letter writer . . . as did I. Two days later, I chatted with this same man about my plan to hire a contractor to repair the cracked ceiling in our dining room.

"Hmm . . .," he said, "is there any way you could write that off as a business expense?"

A FRUGAL MEAL

Beans and rice are a staple of the frugal diet. However, dried beans usually require presoaking and/or lengthy cooking. Many opt for the more expensive canned version to save time. This reader has contributed a 30-minute energy-saving method. We tried it and were pleased to find it works perfectly.

Dear Amy,

In a large pan that fits inside a pressure cooker bring 1 cup beans to a boil, pour off water and add 2 cups fresh water plus 2 Tbsp oil. Place large pan into pressure cooker with 1½ cups water in the bottom of pressure cooker. Place smaller pan down in the bean and water mixture with 1 cup short-grain brown rice and 1½ cups water. Cover both pans with foil. Close pressure cooker and cook 30 minutes after the doodad starts rocking. Then drop pressure under running water and serve.

Flavor the meal however you like. I have enclosed a few suggestions:

Cumin and chili powder with pinto or kidney beans for a Mexican direction.

Curry powder with lentils.

Sage, basil, and bay with split peas or any other bean.

Tomato paste or sauce and Italian herbs with pinto, pink, or kidney beans.

Diane Gilman
Winslow, Washington

(This recipe fed our family of six with leftovers. Singles and couples can freeze the unflavored leftovers in meal-size portions. In subsequent meals try a different variation. FZ)

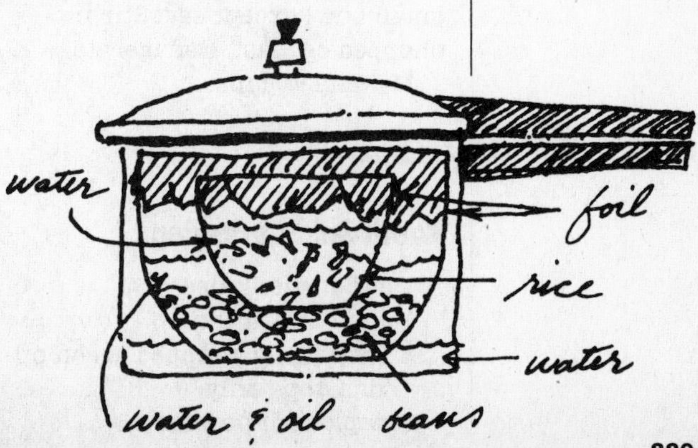

HOMEMADE SALAD DRESSINGS

Toss out those bottled-salad dressing coupons. You can save more by making your own.

The following collection of homemade salad dressing recipes cost 30% to 50% of bottled. For example, 16 oz of bottled name-brand dressing runs between $2.35 and $3.45. These home-made recipes cost between 45¢ (for the Italian) and $1.45 (for the blue cheese) per 16 oz.

Homemade dressings can be prepared in a matter of minutes, providing a healthy savings return for the time spent.

Thousand Island

- ¾ cup mayonnaise
- 1 Tbsp sweet pickle relish or finely chopped sweet pickle
- 2 Tbsp chili sauce or ketchup
- 2 Tbsp finely chopped green bell pepper
- 2 Tbsp finely chopped onion
- 1 Tbsp lemon juice
- ½ tsp granulated sugar
- ¼ tsp Worcestershire sauce
- 1 hard-cooked egg, chopped

Combine all ingredients in a small bowl except egg. Stir in chopped egg last. Refrigerate.

Makes 1⅓ cups.

Ranch Salad Dressing

- 1 cup mayonnaise
- 1 cup buttermilk
- 2 Tbsp finely chopped green onions, tops only
- ¼ tsp onion powder
- 2 tsp minced parsley
- ¼ tsp garlic powder or ½ to 1 garlic clove, finely minced
- ¼ tsp paprika
- ⅛ tsp cayenne pepper
- ¼ tsp salt
- ¼ tsp black pepper

Combine all ingredients in a small bowl. Refrigerate.

Makes 2 cups.

Sweet Tomato-y French

This is for fans of Catalina dressing.

- ⅔ cup ketchup
- ½ cup sugar (or to taste)
- ⅔ cup vegetable oil
- ½ cup red wine vinegar
- salt to taste
- 1 to 2 cloves garlic (or 1 to 2 tsp)
- 2 Tbsp finely minced onion

Combine all ingredients in a jar with a tight-fitting lid and shake. This can also be mixed in a blender, although the color becomes creamier rather than translucent. If preparing in a blender, mix all ingredients except onion. Stir in finely mixed onion by hand. Refrigerate.

Makes 2 cups.

Cucumber-Buttermilk

- 1 cup buttermilk
- ¼ cup grated cucumber
- 2 Tbsp minced green onions, white and green parts

1 Tbsp Dijon-style mustard
2 tsp minced fresh parsley
2 tsp lemon juice
¼ tsp dried dill
¼ tsp freshly ground black pepper

Combine all ingredients in a small bowl with a tight lid. Stir or shake well. Refrigerate.

Makes 1¼ cups.

Italian Vinaigrette

½ cup red wine vinegar
1½ cups olive oil or vegetable oil or a combination
2 large cloves of garlic, crushed
¾ tsp of salt
¼ to ½ tsp black pepper
1 Tbsp minced parsley
1 tsp dry mustard
½ tsp dried basil or oregano

Combine ingredients in a large jar with a tight-fitting lid. Shake well. The cost comparison is based on vegetable oil.

Makes 1 quart.

Blue Cheese

This recipe makes a large quantity and is very strong. For diehard blue cheese lovers only.

1 qt (4 cups) mayonnaise
1 cup buttermilk
1 cup small-curd cottage cheese
1 tsp worcestershire sauce
1 tsp garlic salt
1 tsp salt
4 oz. Roquefort or blue cheese, crumbled

Combine all ingredients in a medium bowl except crumbled

DO-IT-YOURSELF CROUTONS & SPROUTS

Croutons

4 slices homemade bread*
2 Tbsp Parmesan cheese
¼ tsp oregano
¼ tsp celery salt
¼ tsp garlic salt
2 Tbsp salad oil

Slice bread into ⅜" cubes and place in a bowl. Add seasonings and oil. Toss well to mix. Place on cookie sheet. Bake at 300° until crisp. Cool. Store in a glass jar. Costs about a third of store bought.

* or French bread from bakery thrift shop
Contributed by Ellen Marston, Brunswick, Maine

Sprouts

Place ¼ cup of mung beans in a quart jar and cover with tepid water. Cover with cheesecloth and tie securely. Soak overnight. Drain water off. Set in a warm dark place. Every day rinse with tepid water and drain. Place in a warm dark place again. Repeat four to five days or until sprouts are as big as you want.

cheese. Mix with electric mixer. Stir in crumbled cheese with a fork. Refrigerate.

Makes 1½ quarts.

—Salad dressing recipes from *The Oregonian*

HOW TO AVOID FEELING DEPRIVED

Our brass kerosene lamp gives off a warm glow, enough to provide the additional needed light for our dinner of hot cornmeal biscuits and refrigerator stew made of leftover bean soup and random freezer finds. The children, ruddy from outdoor play, consume without question. Jim's comment that the stew is good bespeaks the chancy nature of leftover cookery. I find myself curbing a smile. I would have the same strange satisfaction had the meal been less successful.

I have the same feeling when I adjust my ancient see-through sock so that the hole doesn't line up with my big toe. When I have time I'll darn it. I can afford new ones, but I have a secret quest to see how long I can make the old ones last.

The feeling occurs again when Jim completes a building project on the table saw that had been intercepted on the way to the dump, overhauled, and mounted on a curb-gleaned frame of a deep-fat fryer.

My attitude has undergone a complete reversal. A decade ago I enjoyed prime rib at the Ritz Carlton and purchased toys for nieces and nephews from F.A.O. Schwartz.

Even today, when excess would not stand between us and our goals, we still enjoy being frugal. In general, we prefer low-cost meals, used acquisitions, and free entertainment.

This attitude reversal lies at the heart of why we have never felt deprived while sustaining our lifestyle for so many years.

The feeling of deprivation will undermine any effort to pursue long-term disciplines.

The dieter will fail as long as he hates low-calorie food. The would-be athlete will fail as long as he hates exertion. The tightwad wannabe will fail as long as he views frugality as a lifestyle he has to endure, or was forced into by circumstance.

To overcome the feeling of deprivation consider the following three points:

First, recognize that you are engaging in the discipline out of choice. You decide to give up something so that you can have something else.

If you think "I eat leftovers because I *have* to," you view yourself as being deprived. Instead think "I eat leftovers because curbing my food bill is something I *can* do to reach my goal."

This attitude adjustment is like the question "Is the glass half empty or half full?" When you recognize that you are making a choice, attitudes change from deprivation to empowerment.

Second, as you cut back, give up expenses in the order of the ones that provide the least value for dollars spent. The order of elimination will differ from tightwad to tightwad.

In the beginning Jim and I ate out more. After a less-than-spectacular meal of stuffed lobster, we agreed to give up restaurant

meals altogether. We did not enjoy them enough for the cost. During one of my speaking engagements a woman told me her husband was a chef and loved to eat out. In their case they probably received sufficient value from restaurant meals to continue going out. They needed to find other things to give up first.

View giving up extras as transferring funds from one area of your life to another. I am the first to admit that there is nothing frugal about six kids and a 2,200-square-foot, 100-year-old farmhouse. To afford this we slashed expenses in the areas of food, entertainment, and clothing. Slashing your housing costs to spend more on food, entertainment, and clothing would be equally acceptable as long as you live within your means and are on track in pursuit of your goals.

To assess your values, constantly ask yourself if you received sufficient value for the money you spent. It costs $20 to take the kids to a fast-food joint. You could prepare the same meal at home for $2. Is the experience of the fast-food meal 10 times better than the home-cooked meal? Is the convenience worth $18?

Is the glass half-empty...
...or half full?

People commonly make the mistake of spending money on smaller items that are low on their priority list and, as a result, cannot afford the big things high on their list.

Real deprivation is not being able to afford the things that are high on your priority list. When assessing your values, think back to the concept of transferring funds from one area of your budget to another. Think about the trade-offs and redefine deprivation. Instead of being a matter of eating more leftovers or wearing used clothes, maybe deprivation is having to work a second job you hate, or stress from massive debt or not being able to afford another child.

When you give up the lower priority things first, hopefully your budget will allow you to keep the extras that genuinely give value to your life. However, if you find you still need to cut more, think back to your goal. The chef and his wife had been able to save to buy a home. They needed to measure the value of eating out in relation to the value of home ownership. If they are unwilling to give up the meals out, they need to admit that home ownership must be a lower priority for them.

Third, do not compare your economic situation to those of others. If you are trying to lose weight, it can be frustrating to watch a thin person eat twice as

much as you. Having a slow metabolism just means you have to work harder.

If your income is less than someone else's you will have to eliminate more from your priority list to achieve the same goal. Jim and I knew that we had to work harder than our parents and grandparents to afford a similar home. We had nothing to gain by bemoaning today's higher interest rates.

Wringing your hands over economic inequities merely wastes emotional energy that could be better used in a positive way to achieve your goal. Accept the givens in your situation and work with them.

Feeling empowered by recognizing you are choosing to scale down to reach a goal, eliminating expenses in order of least value received, and accepting the givens in your personal economic situation are aspects of "beginner tightwaddery."

Beyond this there is a higher plane of enlightenment . . . "the Zen of Advanced Tightwaddery."

You progress to a state of mind where you develop an aversion to "stupid expenditures," as defined within your personal value system. They become symbols of darkness that have been placed in your path to thwart your efforts . . . hence, my seemingly irrational disdain for Jell-O Pudding Snack Paks.

Likewise, you come to equate aspects of frugality (which our culture regards as deprivation) as symbols for past or future achievements. You know that you have gotten "it" when you discover you prefer refrigerator stew to prime rib, not because it tastes better, but because more than merely feeding your body it nourishes your soul. You know within yourself that these symbols represent a larger lifestyle that will enable you to acquire (or have enabled you to acquire) the things that are genuinely important to you.

And then when your cousin Wilbur waves a cigar in your face and says, "Eh, lighten up! Would it kill you to take them kids to McDonald's once in a while?" you can curb your smile, wiggle your toe to readjust the sock hole, and silently hold the knowledge that he has yet to reach your plane of higher enlightenment.

HOME HAIRCUTTING FOR BOYS

What I know about cutting hair I have learned from years of watching my own hair being cut. Still, I might never have started cutting my own children's hair if the first had not been born bald on the top with a long scraggly fringe around the edges. I trimmed it and he looked better.

I have learned to cut by trial and error—errors being made before the boys knew any different. I began with a one-length-all-over cut and gradually began to taper for a more traditional look.

Many mothers are closet haircutters with their own method. Mine is the scissors-and-comb technique, which does not require clippers. Before approaching this article I consulted *Scissors and Comb Haircutting* by Bob Ohnstad (You Can Publishing, 1985). The library has other books on home

haircutting. These books give a more detailed and intimidating approach. I do it a bit simpler, but the method is the same.

For tools you will need a sharp pair of scissors, a standard (not barber-style) comb, and a towel. I use a pair of barber-style scissors that I have owned forever. I would prefer the shorter-tipped precision scissors that hairstylists use but they cost about $50. A friend and closet haircutter uses Fiskars shears, which come in a variety of sizes at the sewing store. These can be obtained in a set for about $10. The main reason to use haircutting shears is that they are specially designed for that purpose, but other types will work. Traditional barber combs are for clipper cutting. Any regular comb will work with scissors cutting.

The most important rule of this style of haircutting is to cut in the direction of the grain of the hair. In other words, hair grows downward on the back of the head. Cut up and down (holding the scissors vertically), not across. If the hair grows forward on the top don't cut side to side. Cut correctly, the hair will lie like shingles on the side of the house. If you cut cross the grain you will see a horizontal chop line indicating that the layers of hair end in the same place.

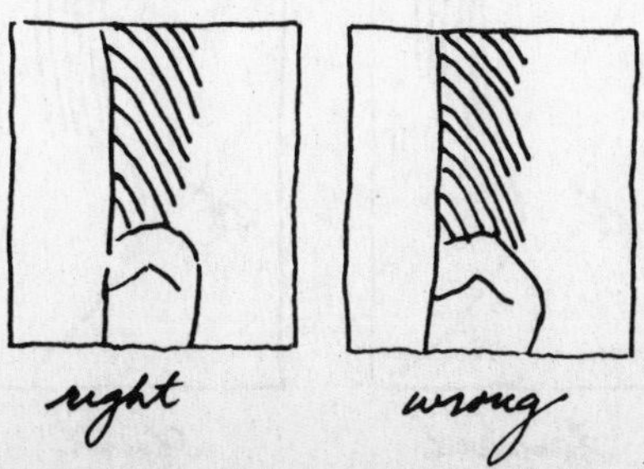

A simple beginner haircut is one with an equal length all over. I find that I can use the comb as a measuring tool. The inch-and-a-half height is about right for a preschooler. The height of the comb and thickness of my index finger is about right for an older child. As long as all the hair is cut to that same measure as pulled away from the scalp you can't go wrong. Continually comb and check for bits of slightly longer hair and trim to the same length.

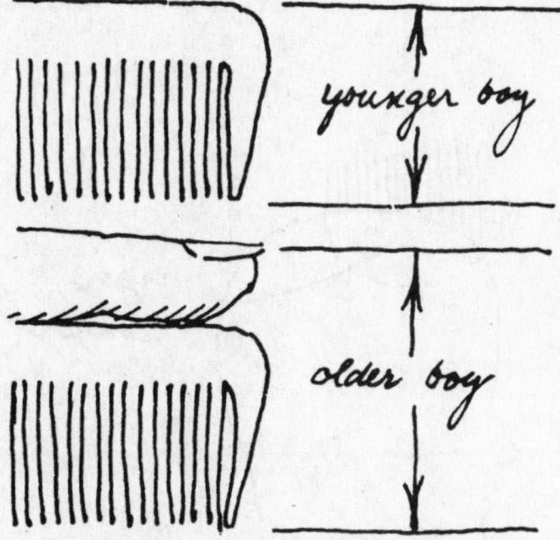

The equal-length-all-over cut tends to look short on the top and long on the sides. I simply vary it by tapering shorter on the sides and longer on the top.

After washing the hair I begin by cutting the crown to the comb

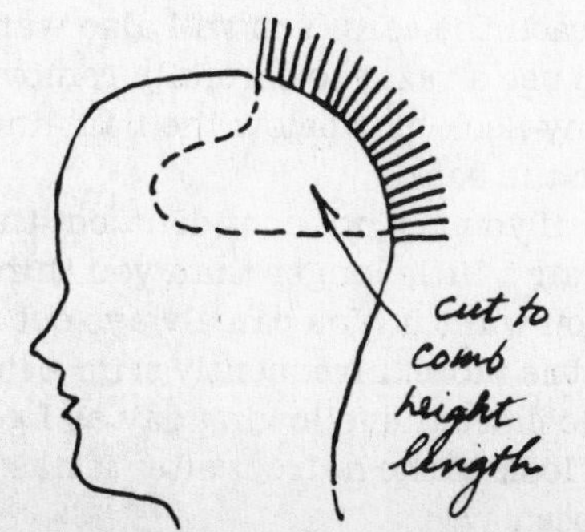

height. Next I taper the sides from comb height to about the thickness of my finger. Finally I taper the top from one comb height to about two comb heights in the front.

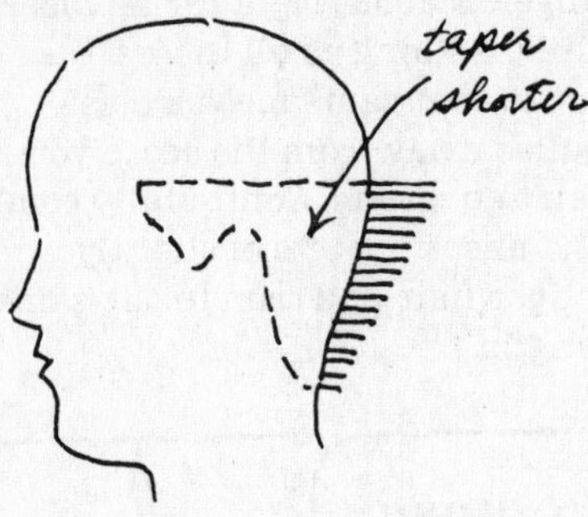

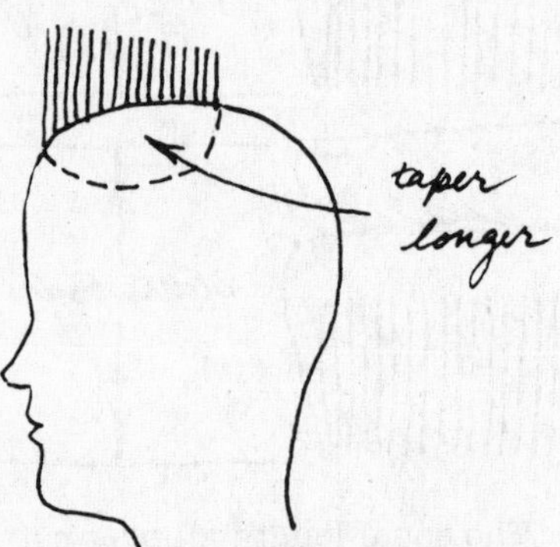

The last set is to trim the edges. Comb and cut hair flat against the head. Make sure the sideburns are of equal length. I comb the hair over the ears and trim just short enough so that it doesn't reach the ears. You will also want to use a razor to carefully remove any neck hair below the hair line in the back.

If you are not confident, cut the hair a little longer than you think you want it. You can always cut a little more. I frequently trim a little more the following day as I get a look at the haircut after it has dried.

Very young children won't sit long, and I will cut in stages over few days. With the most impossible toddler I measure out very small sections, holding the measured length between thumb and finger. As hair slacks I can follow his wiggle before snipping. This will not produce as good a cut as when you cut linear sections, but it serves him right.

We estimate that we save about $50 per year for each boy. I find that cutting my children's hair also saves me time. I don't have to chauffeur them to a barber when I can make the time. I can cut while watching TV at my own convenience and as frequently as I want. I can also get a more consistent, predictable look, rather than having a kid go from shaggy to whitewalls in a sitting.

A TRICK FOR CUTTING BANGS

After mastering a boy's haircut, I next attempted my daughter's bangs. Unlike Alec's slightly wavy hair Jamie has very fine straight hair. I found that no matter how careful I was, the blunt cut always seemed to look as though I had done it with pinking shears.

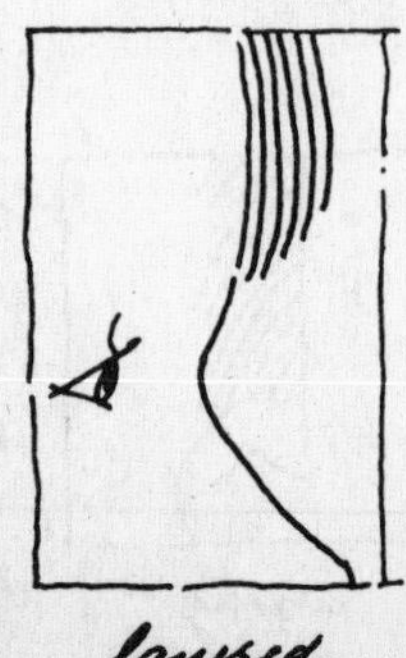

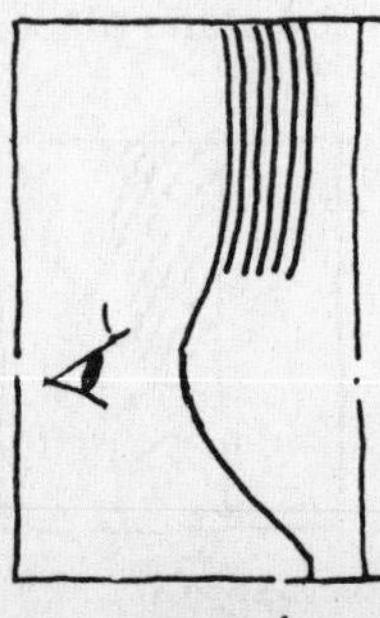

As I attempted to trim more the bangs got shorter, but not more even.

After several botches I realized why I had this new problem. Boys' bangs are not a true blunt cut—they don't end in the same place, but are layered.

I discovered a trick that works very well. After the blunt cut I separate out vertical sections. I then cut a slight angle as shown. It is important not to cut the bottom of the section as this establishes the hair line. When the hair lies down again it has a softer edge and any original imperfections are no longer visible.

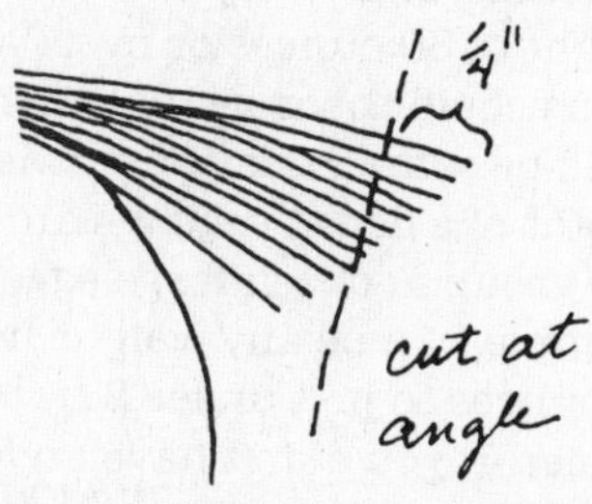

SOCK WISDOM

Dear Amy,

I'm a professional man, and I buy my socks 30 or 40 at a time. Seems like a lot to pay for socks all at once? Maybe so, but I buy them identical—all black poly-cotton. If one wears out beyond repair, I don't lose a pair . . . just one sock. And I save time (which is money) and bother by not having to match up socks. I just dump all my socks from one washline into one drawer. Any two I pick up will match! Using this method I haven't had to buy new socks since 1980 and expect the present batch to last another five years.

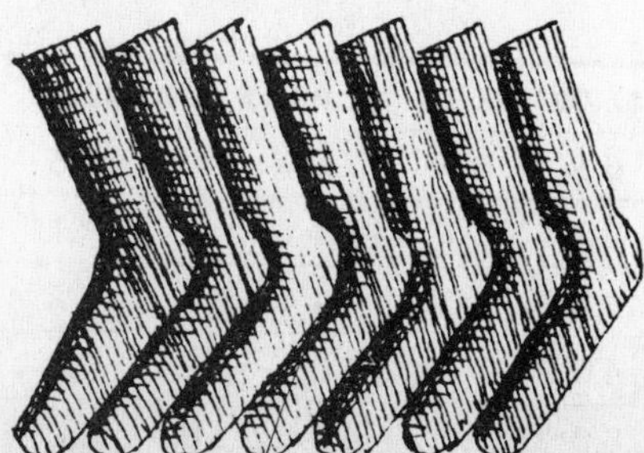

Willard Morris
Lanham-Seabrook, Maryland

PREVENTION

Dear Amy,

In my profession as a cardiac ultrasound technician, I've seen hundreds of people (including hospital employees) killing themselves, and costing them and us big bucks. Preventive medicine is definitely frugal. If everyone stopped smoking, for instance, I'd be out of work.

Diane Shaw
Turner, Maine

SYRUP JUGS

Dear Amy,

I reuse syrup jugs, with the little pop-up lids. My kids use them as canteens, particularly on car trips. Those with handles can be hung from a belt (with a hook) for hiking.

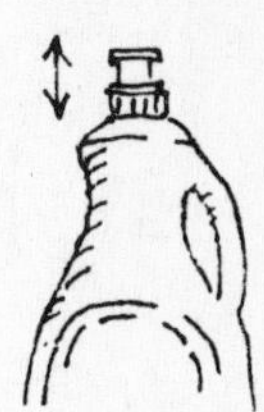

Jamien Morehouse
Rockport, Maine

FRUGAL INHERITANCE

Dear Amy,

Here's my scrapless method of using bath soap bars:

I use the soap until it's about ¼ inch thick or slightly thinner. Next time I take a shower I break

out a new bar. I use both bars to lather up, leaving some lather on the bars.

When I'm through showering, I press the small bar on top of the new bar (piggyback), and set them in the soap dish together. The lather dries bonding the two bars together for my next shower.

Each time I take a shower, the bond becomes firmer. When the double bar gets down to ¼ inch thick, I repeat the process with a third bar of soap. And so on, ad infinitum.

Theoretically some of the atoms in this soapy cycle will remain in my bar until my very last shower! When I am gone, my son can continue to use the bar as I have, reflecting that it has traces of the bar I used on the very first Earth Day, when I started recycling soap this way. And thus shall my zealous frugality be passed down from generation to generation as long as my descendents shall lather up.

Willard Morris
Lanham-Seabrook, Maryland

HOW TO COMPARE EGG PRICES

Did you ever wonder what size egg is the best value? OK, so I never did either. One reader sent

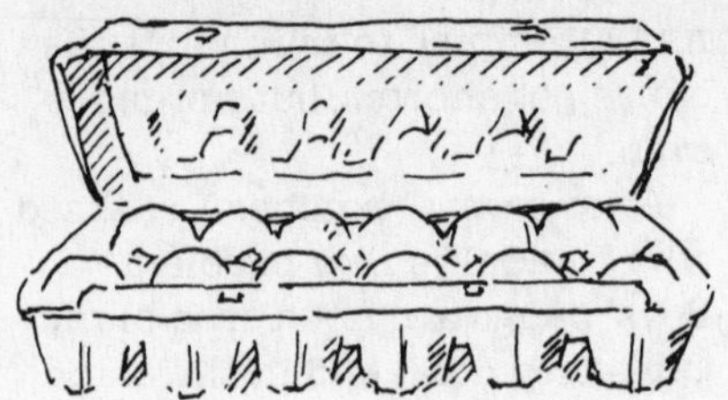

me a packet of material, and this one idea was something I hadn't thought about before.

Eggs are sorted by weight. Jumbo eggs are 30 ounces per dozen, extra large are 27, large are 24, medium are 21, and small are 18 ounces. The weight can exceed these numbers, but not be less. Jumbos can be a great hidden value, since they can be any weight of 30 ounces or over.

One could theorize that there could be some variation in the weight of a dozen eggs within a size group. A dozen large eggs, for example, can be any weight from 24 ounces to just under 27 ounces. If you didn't have anything better to do with your time you could take several boxes and hike the distance from the dairy case to the produce department to weigh them to find the best value.

(You can weigh bags of potatoes, carrots, onions, and heads of lettuce to find any that may be slightly heavier.)

	59¢	69¢	79¢	89¢	99¢	$1.09	$1.19	$1.29	$1.39	$1.49
SMALL	3.3	3.8	4.4	4.9	5.5	6.1	6.6	7.2	7.7	8.3
MEDIUM	2.8	3.3	3.8	4.2	4.7	5.2	5.7	6.1	6.6	7.1
LARGE	2.5	2.9	3.3	3.7	4.1	4.5	5.0	5.4	5.8	6.2
EX-LARGE	2.2	2.6	2.9	3.3	3.7	4.0	4.4	4.8	5.1	5.5
JUMBO	2.0	2.3	2.6	3.0	3.3	3.6	4.0	4.3	4.6	5.0

To determine the best values among different size eggs I have devised the chart on page 236, which shows how many cents per ounce you would pay at the common egg prices.

I have included prices for a dozen eggs from 59¢ to $1.49, but I don't want to perpetuate any myths that food prices are cheaper in Maine. We pay about $1 per dozen for large eggs if we buy from a local farmer.

A photocopy in your billfold might be a handy shopping aid.

A TIGHTWAD PARABLE

The philosopher Diogenes was eating bread and lentils for supper. He was seen by the philosopher Aristippus, who lived comfortably by flattering the king. Said Aristippus, "If you would learn to be subservient to the king you would not have to live on lentils."

Said Diogenes, "Learn to live on lentils and you will not have to be subservient to the king."

The Song of the Bird
by Anthony de Mello

TWO RECIPES FOR KIDS

Homemade Bubble Solution

Many readers sent in a variation of this recipe. Glycerin can be purchased at a drugstore. I recently purchased a 4 oz bottle for $2.25.

Several of the recipes specified Joy dishwashing liquid, perhaps because it is the best for bubbles. The longer you store the bubble solution the better it works. You will want to prepare it weeks (or even months) in advance for a special event.

9 parts water
1 part Joy dishwashing liquid
½ part glycerin

Giant Bubble Maker

Save coffee cans. Cut off tops and bottoms. Hammer the edges smooth. Dip cans in a pan of solution and wave through the air.

Have a contest for the biggest bubble, smallest bubble, and the bubble that floats the highest. (Contributed by Laurie Glendinning, Rohnut Park, California)

Homemade Finger Paints

1 envelope unflavored gelatin
½ cup cornstarch
3 Tbsp sugar
2 cups cold water
food coloring
dishwashing liquid
white shelfpaper

Soak gelatin in ¼ cup warm water and put aside.

In a medium saucepan combine cornstarch and sugar. Gradually add water and cook slowly over low heat, stirring until well blended.

Remove from heat and add softened gelatin. Divide mixture into separate containers for each color.

For each color first add a drop or two of liquid detergent and then add food coloring a drop at a time until you have the shade you want.

Store up to six weeks in the refrigerator.

CHEAP THRILLS

Dear Amy,

Sunday drives through the backwoods of Maine: in the past, when we found a sunny Sunday afternoon, we often drove out to gaze at wished-for farms (with or without attached barns) on back roads to get acquainted with our adopted state. Often we'd stop in antique shops and small restaurants and squander lesser or greater sums (depending on whether these businesses took Visa). Now when we have a sunny Sunday afternoon, we still go out for a drive, but instead of spending money we try to make some. It's amazing how many beer and soda cans and bottles are strewn along these otherwise beautiful country roads! In less than an hour we have found at least $5 worth, thus more than covering the cost of the gas we use for these trips in our 1984 Escort Pony, and additionally providing us with much self-righteousness in the thought that we're contributing to cleaning up the environment.

Carol M. Petillo
Springvale, Maine

Dear Amy,

Sometimes local high schools have night courses for adults, which meet usually once a week. They are noncredit but you can learn something. I paid $5 registration fee, and though I had to pay $15 for materials for one course, this certainly is inexpensive! One of the courses is introductory welding, which is a very useful skill to be familiar with. I already fixed one tool to make it work better, and plan to make another project.

Dana Morong
Madbury, New Hampshire

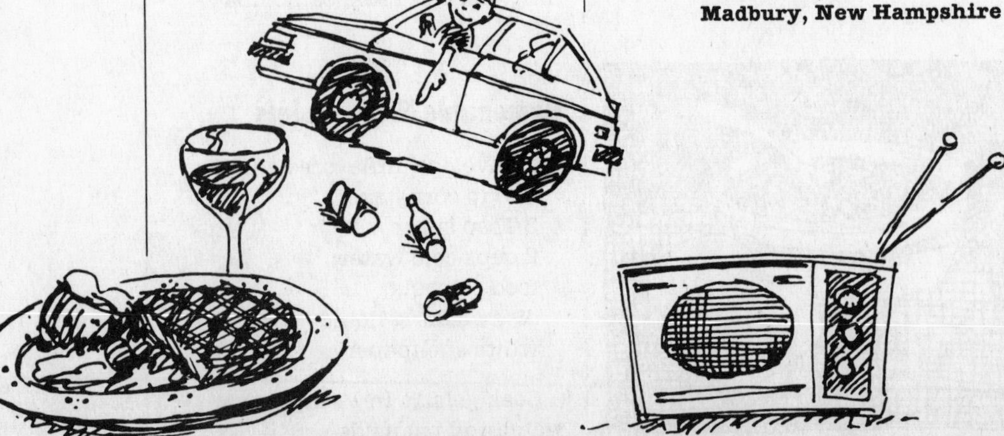

Dear Amy,

We live near enough to a college town to be able to enjoy an occasional free concert. Even a recital by music students is a delight. I hear of at least one free event each month.

As has been said before, public libraries are treasure troves of free stuff: information and entertainment. A favorite of mine is books on audio cassette. My husband and I like to listen and visualize Louis L'Amour while cozy in bed.

Westy Melby
Boone, Colorado

USED-CAR THEORY

Finding ways to economize on the cost of car ownership is becoming increasingly difficult as the newer cars are often too complex for the average backyard mechanic. Even a proper tune-up requires computerized equipment. As owners of new vehicles we have been hard pressed to come up with ideas other than the obvious, like buying oil on sale or keeping records of mileage and tune-ups.

Two readers, owners of older vehicles, have filled the void with lengthy submissions. I have gleaned the best of their ideas.

Dear Amy,

My philosophy of automobiles is to get a good model and stick with it, learning it, stripping it for parts as they rust out, and hauling the rust to a recycling place. Now I subscribe to a newsletter on that car, with useful tips from readers.

Get a good model, get the bottom welded up well, then rebuild the entire brake system (in some cases replace it entirely for safety).

There are four or five curved molded hoses that I got tired of paying crazy prices for (imported). By researching I found alternates (domestic), which are easier to get, less expensive, and work as well.

I spent $4 for a lens, used spare parts, and installed a third brake light in my car to prevent rear-end collisions.

Don't be cheap with engine oil, but replace whenever oil wears out: 5,000 miles for new cars and 3,000 to 4,000 for older cars. I buy several cases of quality oil when on sale (also filters). Those who try to go farther on worn oil only risk wearing the rings (and engine) thus burning more oil, lowering mpg, and polluting the air. Besides, old oil can be saved for recycling.

Every April remove the carpets and air them and the floor for a couple of weeks, to let the floor dry out. Water comes in on the boots in winter, then sets under the carpet and rots the floor in warmer weather. Also hose down the insides of the wheel wells until the water runs clear.

Dana Morong
Madbury, New Hampshire

Dear Amy,

The "turnaround" costs connected with replacing a car, including tag transfer, sales tax, expenses of selling, expenses of searching are likely to average

more than $200 through the decade. A car that is likely to go to the junkyard within a few months is probably a liability rather than an asset.

Purchasing a car when the appropriate opportunity (a good deal) presents itself is generally wise, even if it means selling a surplus car soon.

If your family owns "n plus one" cars, "n" being the number of drivers, so that there is a spare car, then a reliable mechanic may be willing to repair for less, because a rush is not required.

If there is a teenage driver in the household, the family generally cannot afford to own anything but compact cars too old to justify collision insurance, by reason of the higher premiums for liability insurance for heavier cars. However, if there are no young drivers, the heavy gas guzzler is likely to be the cheapest car for the family driving only a few thousand miles per year.

John Ewbank
Southampton, Pennsylvania

NEW-CAR THEORY

There seems to be a discrepancy in car ownership philosophy among the most frugal and expert. A new-car salesman told me never *ever* buy a new car. I have been impressed by letters from people who have never paid more than $500 for a car and have rebuilt engines in their basement. Conventional expert wisdom suggests that the two- or three-year-old car is the best value.

Just when I was feeling like a total clod for our two new purchased cars I received a letter from a reader. His theory of new-car ownership exactly reflects my husband's. The letter is very convincing, well written, and long. I have narrowed it down to the major points to save space.

I am convinced that the choice between the new car or old depends on how much you want to spend your winter weekends tinkering on a car in a frigid barn. The single drawback to a two-year-old car is the uncertainty of the care by the previous owner.

Dear Amy,

Two goals of minimizing cost per mile and beating inflation can be achieved by buying a good-quality car new, maintaining it carefully, and driving it for at least 10 years.

Don't wait until your old car dies and you have to rush out in a panic to buy a new one. Take your time and shop around. Get dealers bidding against each other.

When you find a good deal pay cash. Your frugal lifestyle has, of course, allowed you plenty of cash.

Drive your new car straight to an autobody shop for undercoating, or do it yourself with cans of 3M undercoating.

Proceed to the nearest tire dealer and buy a set of top-grade steel-belted radial tires. Now you have nine tires, including the spare. Set up a rotation scheme, rotating properly for even wear. In the year 2000 you'll still be driving on 1991-priced tires.

Most important advice! Change the oil and filter frequently, as often as twice as frequently as the manual says or when the dipstick is unreadable.

Change all fluids once a year.

Ask your service manager of your local dealership about the life expectancy of parts for your model, and replace parts before necessary to save money.

After seven to eight years get it repainted to give you good payback when you sell.

Here is my own experience:

In 1969 I bought a Toyota station wagon for $2,300. Ten years and 170,000 miles later I sold it for $1,000, still running fine and looking very handsome.

In 1979 I bought a new Saab for $8,700. It's going on its 12th year and some 170,000 miles, and I'm still driving it and expect to do so for some time to come.

Ed LaChapelle
Glennallen, Alaska

APPROACHING VEGETARIANISM

If you are like I was only a few years ago, you probably regard vegetarianism as some sort of peculiar diet bordering on a cult. People with that diet, I thought, ate all manner of weird-sounding foods—tofu, alfalfa sprouts, brewer's yeast, soy flour, wheat germ, miso. . . .

What I didn't realize was that I had eaten vegetarian meals nearly every day of my life. Many foods (without strange-sounding names) fall into a category of vegetarianism.

Vegetarianism is simply a diet that relies on the eating of plants as a source of protein. A vegan is someone who eats no protein from an animal source. A lacto-ovo vegetarian gets some of his protein from eggs and milk products but not from meat.

Meat contains all the amino acids necessary to make a complete protein. The protein that occurs in plant food is not complete in one source. But you can get all the necessary amino acids by combining different foods. It has been generally believed that the right foods must be eaten at the same meal. I have recently read that some nutritionists now believe the combinations do not have to occur within the same meal, just as long as you eat them the same day.

The diagram below shows which foods can be combined to make a complete protein. The solid line indicates combinations that usually combine to make a protein, whereas the broken line indicates combinations that work only some of the time.

Whole grains are grains that have not been processed. White flour and rice have had valuable nutrients removed and will not combine to make a protein. Legumes are any type of dried bean. Seeds include sesame seeds, sunflower seeds, and nuts. Milk products include cheese, yogurt, and ice cream.

Food combining may seem complicated, so remember: it's impor-

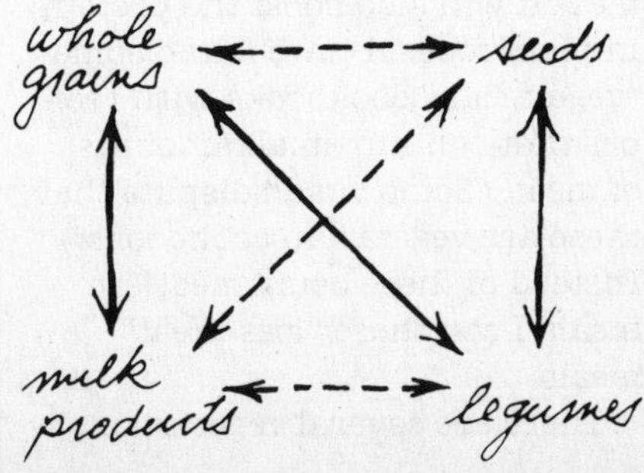

tant not to get too hung up on it. Many Americans were introduced to the idea of vegetarianism by Frances Moore Lappe's *Diet for a Small Planet*, published in 1971. Lappe spends almost the whole book emphasizing the importance of combining foods to create complete proteins. Many readers were left with the impression that vegetarianism was a noble but difficult art.

But in her latest edition, Lappe apologizes for mistakenly giving readers that impression. As she puts it, "If people are getting enough calories, they are virtually certain of getting enough protein." Researchers at institutions from Harvard University to the National Academy of Sciences to the American Dietetic Association now agree: if a variety of healthful foods are eaten, protein is not a problem.

Lack of vitamin B_{12} can be a problem for vegetarians who abstain from eggs and dairy products (vegans), and some nutritionists recommend a B_{12} supplement for them. But vegetarians who do eat eggs and dairy products (lacto-ovo vegetarians) generally get all the vitamins they need from their diet . . . again, if they eat a variety of healthful foods.

If you eat a small amount of meat it will also boost the protein in plant foods. I have found some "vegetarian" cookbooks with recipes that contain small amounts of meat. (Some would dispute that these are vegetarian cookbooks.) Instead of these being meatless meals I call these "less-meat" meals.

There are several vegetarian meals that are familiar to everyone. For example:

oatmeal and milk
baked beans and brown bread
peanut butter on whole-wheat bread
burritos made with refried beans (without lard)
corn chowder

So most die-hard meat eaters, without knowing it, have been eating vegetarian meals for years.

Meat is one of the most expensive foods we buy. It is also a food we eat far too much of. Animal fat contributes to high cholesterol and some studies also link it to higher cancer rates. Adults only need a few ounces per day, at most. New nutritional information suggests that we should treat meat more like a side dish rather than the main course. Learning to incorporate more meatless or less-meat meals in our diets makes sense from an economic and health standpoint.

Vegetarianism is also good for the environment for several reasons. Far less water is required to produce protein from plant sources than animal sources. The rainforest is being cut down to make room for grazing land. Meat requires refrigeration.

Eating less meat is another of those triple plays—something you can do that is good for your health, good for the environment, and good for your wallet.

Dried beans are cheaper than the least expensive meats purchased on sale in the family pack. You can even grow your own if you have ample garden space. Without incorporating some le-

gume meals in your diet you will never achieve the rock-bottom food bill.

I am not suggesting that we all make the great leap to a meatless diet, but we can all approach vegetarianism by beginning to include more whole grains, seeds, and dried beans in our diets while reducing the amount of meat we eat.

One reason we eat so much meat is that when we eat the standard meat-and-potatoes meal a five-ounce piece of steak seems the right size. "Disguise" the smaller (more appropriate) meat portions. Look for casseroles that combine small amounts of meat with dried beans, whole grains, seeds, or dairy products. Soups and stir-fry meals accomplish the same objective. You can also serve a small portion of meat along with legumes.

When you reduce meat consumption be sure that you increase the whole grains in your diet. We rarely make pancakes, waffles, muffins, biscuits, or bread without the addition of cornmeal, oatmeal, or whole-wheat flour. You can also add additional dried milk powder to boost protein in baked foods. These additions do increase the cost of your baking, but the decrease in your meat consumption will lower your food bill more. Likewise some meatless recipes call for expensive ingredients, including cheese and other exotic additions. Always do the math to determine if a recipe is truly economical.

When you feed your children breakfasts, they must have adequate protein or they will be lethargic midmorning at school. Breakfasts prepared from white flour without whole grains added (such as waffles or pancakes) will not provide adequate protein. I suggest you give your family milk instead of juice along with a whole-grain meal. Put the juice in their lunch boxes instead—it will keep better than milk.

We dragged our feet a bit in learning to eat more meals with legumes. The beans you buy in a can are not as cheap as the dried type. But the dried type usually requires presoaking and a lengthy cooking time. So our most common legume meal had been bean soup.

Then a reader sent us an energy-saving pressure-cooker method of preparing beans and rice. This can be prepared in about 30 minutes. Now we eat beans and rice when "someone" forgot to thaw meat for our supper. (Since Jim retired, the guilty "someone" is harder to identify.) Beans and rice have become our version of "fast food."

Rather than providing specific recipes I suggest that you get a cookbook from the library. Begin with foods that are familiar to you. In New England baked beans are common. Southerners like pinto beans. Those in the Southwest are familiar with Mexican bean dishes. Our family likes to eat bean soups. There is a 15-bean soup package at the supermarket in the dried bean section that is excellent. Lentil soups are a good place to start because lentils cook up quickly.

Many of the strange-sounding foods no longer sound strange to us. Things like sprouts and wheat germ have found their way into our pantry.

POOCH POTPOURRI

Homemade Dog Biscuits

3½ cups unbleached flour
2 cups whole-wheat flour
1 cup rye flour
2 cups bulgur (cracked wheat)
1 cup cornmeal
½ cup instant nonfat dry milk
4 tsp salt
1 envelope active dry yeast
¼ cup warm water
3 cups chicken broth
1 egg slightly beaten with 1 tsp milk

1. Turn oven on to 300°. Mix first seven ingredients with a wooden spoon in a large bowl.

2. Dissolve yeast thoroughly in warm water (110°–115°) in glass measuring cup. Add to dry ingredients.

3. Add chicken broth to flour mixture. Stir until dough forms.

4. Roll out dough until it is ¼" thick. Cut out bone shapes from dough. Place on greased cookie sheets.

5. Brush dough with egg glaze.

6. Bake bones for 45 minutes. Turn oven off. Biscuits should remain overnight to harden. Makes 30 larger bones at about 40% cheaper than store bought.

The Dog Biscuit Cutter

This recipe originally suggests that you cut bone shapes using a store-bought biscuit as a pattern. However my tuna can cookie cutter idea works for these, too.

You need a can that has a bottom that can be removed with a can opener. After removing both top and bottom shape cutter with two pairs of pliers starting at opposite symmetrical points.

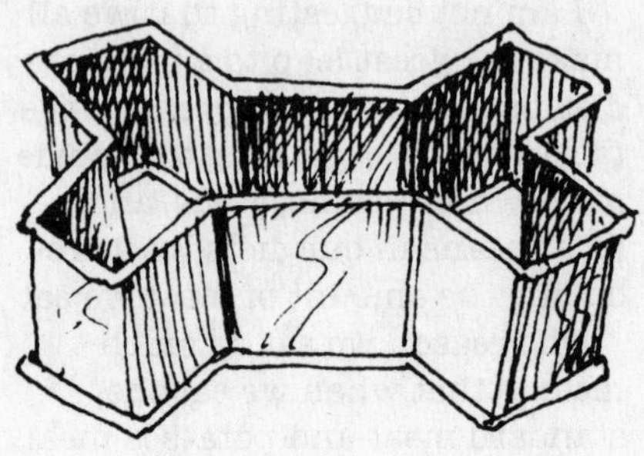

If you do not have a dog consider making these as a gift for someone who does have a dog, especially the hard-to-buy-for elderly person with a precious pooch.

The Pooch Poop Scoop

I developed this out of necessity as the new dog had trouble making the transition to a new home. I used a 20-quart dry milk carton cut diagonally as shown.

This size scoop works well for a shepherd. Use cereal boxes for beagles. Macaroni and cheese boxes for Chihuahuas.

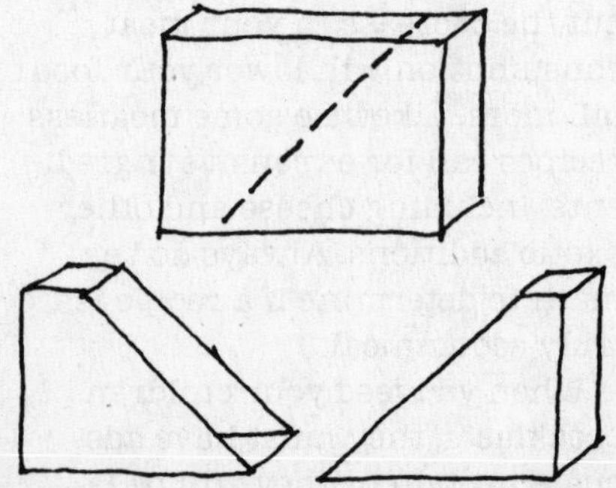

WHEELBARROW METAMORPHOSIS

Or How to Build a Wheelbarrow from Salvaged Materials

Plan 1. When you take your trash to the dump keep your eyes peeled for a discarded wheelbarrow with possibilities. When you spot one ask the dump custodian about it. He will scratch his chin and tell you to take it, as well as another you hadn't noticed. As it happens one will only have a salvageable tub and the other will be good except for a rusted out tub. Bring them both home and let them sit in your barn for several months as you wait for "a good day." This will allow you adequate time to mull your plan to combine the good parts to make one complete wheelbarrow.

Plan 2. By the time the good day arrives you will reject Plan 1. You will decide the wheelbarrow with the "good" tub isn't really very good. Take that wheelbarrow back to the dump. Plan to construct a new tub or body from salvaged lumber. Plan to use all the other parts from the wheelbarrow you kept.

Plan 3. When you disassemble the salvaged wheelbarrow you will notice that the handles are rather flimsy, being made of two pieces of wood held together with a thin metal bracket. You will scratch Plan 2 and make new handles out of salvaged two-by-threes. (This stage requires a little preplanning. First buy a pre-1900 house with attached barn and loads of junk in the attic including old bed springs with hardwood frames. Save the wood and discard the springs.) Shape two-by-threes with a draw-knife to make grips. Construct a new body from salvaged lumber and attach to the handles.

Plan 4. After attaching the wheel and axle you will notice that the brackets from the old wheelbarrow will not fit. You will be prepared, having saved brackets for some time from yet another wheelbarrow. When you go to dig those up, an hour-and-a-half's effort yields only one bracket. **Plan 4A.** Make wooden brackets from scraps of two-by-threes.

Plan 5. When you try to attach the legs from the salvaged wheelbarrow, they will be a little too long and not wide enough to fit the new plan. About this time your wife, and design consultant, will enter your workshop and second your idea to scrap the old metal legs, on the grounds of a lack of aesthetic appeal. Make new legs out of the remaining two-by-threes. (Note: this design utilizes only the wheel and axle from one of the original two wheelbarrows.) Finally, use your wooden wheelbarrow for a few jobs, and bark your shins several times. **Plan 5A,** move the legs back a few inches and to the outside of the handles.

TIGHTWAD PEEVES

An interviewer asked me if there was such a thing as being "too frugal." The answer to that question might be an article in itself, but there are a few common penny-pinching practices that don't wash with me.

The Dilution Solution. Your kid wants yet another glass of juice. You realize that all this juice drinking is driving you to financial ruin, so you decide to fool him. You dilute the juice and he's happy.

Why not do it? Junior should learn that all liquid need not have flavor. This practice will spawn a soda drinker of the future.

Instead tell him he can drink water. Or alternate letting him drink water one time and juice another.

The Paper Split. You've got one roll of two-ply toilet paper and two empty tubes. You separate the two plies and roll them each on the empty tubes to make two rolls of paper.

Why not do it? Because you have better things to do with your life! Besides, what's the first thing you do when you use toilet paper? You fold it, thereby making your one-ply a two-ply again.

Instead educate your family to use fewer two-ply squares.

The Syrup Switch. Your teenager is loyal to Mrs. Butterworth. You know the homemade stuff tastes just as good. For years you've been refilling the same Mrs. Butterworth's bottle. Even though the faded label is a dead giveaway she hasn't noticed yet.

Why not do it? Because you are allowing her to continue believing that brands matter, when in fact, taste preference is acquired.

Tell her to buy her own Mrs. Butterworth's with her babysitting money.

The Packet Swipe. You eat in a restaurant and fill your pockets with extra ketchup and sugar packets.

Why not do it? First, those things were intended for your use in the restaurant, not later at home. Second, what are you doing blowing your money in a restaurant in the first place? A whole cup of sugar costs about 20¢. You just spent about 20 times that amount for lunch.

The Stamp Steam. A letter comes to your home with an uncanceled stamp. You steam it off and reuse it. You figure it's only fair because postal rates just went up.

Why not do it? It happens to be a federal offense. OK, so a fleet of police cars won't converge on your home with sirens, blue lights, and a megaphone. But you're simply passing the cost along to others.

Seems like a better thing to do to aid the postal service in keeping future rates down would be paying for the services that you do use.

The Party Collection. You host as many Tupperware parties as possible to get the free gifts to give away as presents.

Why not do it? The salesperson is trying to make a living. If your friends are tightwads like you,

they won't spend. If they're spendthrifts they probably shouldn't spend, but will. (Not to mention that they're throwing away all those Cool Whip containers at home.)

The Card Shark. You send a friend a card, but you sign it in pencil so that they can erase your name and reuse it.

Why not do it? First they can't reuse it anyway because it requires an odd-sized envelope, which they can't replace. Second if you don't think your friend will want to keep the card, why send one at all? Instead send a thoughtful letter . . . using both sides of the paper, naturally.

A SUCCESS STORY

I receive wonderful letters from people. These are enormously important to me since, for the most part, my only connection with readers is through the mail. I wanted to share one particularly good one.

Dear Amy,

Thank you for what you are doing! After receiving my first issue, I promptly sent for all the back issues. When they arrived, I stayed up long past midnight reading every one. It has changed my life!

After receiving the first issue of my subscription, I did a lot of rearranging of my budget and, with some (I thought) severe belt tightening, managed to start saving $200 per month. After my *Gazette* Marathon, I redid my finances, and am now saving $600 per month . . . and my "belt" seems to have gotten lots looser in the process.

It is amazing the difference an attitude change can make in one's life. Before the *Gazette* marathon, I felt poor when I had to "do without" (and rewarded myself for my frugality with expensive clothes, food, and doodads). Now, I feel *smart* for finding fun, creative (and often better) alternatives for little or nothing.

I now shop the garage sales regularly and am finding *great stuff!* My job requires that I dress up every day for work. Recently at a garage sale, I found a beautiful navy wool suit in perfect condition for $5. When I wear it to work, everyone wants to know what special occasion I'm dressing up for. I just give 'em a model's pirouette and a smile.

I started a price book recently and am appalled at how much I've been spending (wasting!) on groceries. I never thought I had time to follow sales. I shopped at stores whose ambiance I liked. I budgeted (and actually spent!) $150 per month on food . . . and I'm a vegetarian! And I live alone! Now, after doing a little research, I discovered it's easier to be frugal. Instead of spending my Saturdays driving to expensive stores in ritzy neighborhoods, I stop by two discount supermarkets that are right on my way home from work, and on my lunch hour I hit the members-only outlet that's near my office. I not only save tons of money but also a whole day as well.

My plans have changed also. I can actually see a time when I'll have my (previously out-of-reach) paid-for little house on five acres in the woods, with a vegetable garden and fruit trees. I have some debts I'm paying off (from my prefrugal days), and when those are gone I'm going to

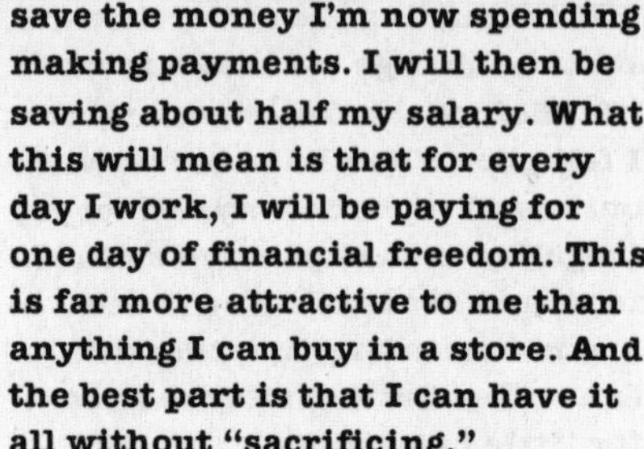

save the money I'm now spending making payments. I will then be saving about half my salary. What this will mean is that for every day I work, I will be paying for one day of financial freedom. This is far more attractive to me than anything I can buy in a store. And the best part is that I can have it all without "sacrificing."

Thank you for giving me control over my life and my future!

(Reader's name withheld by request)

TWO SIDES TO EVERY PAGE

Each month our computer printer spits out great stacks of paper for various reports. Not even four kids, feverishly coloring on one side, can hope to keep up.

The older ones have taken to making "books." Budding authors, you know. They want new paper that is good on both sides, so that their literary works won't be marred with the writings of another.

I've hit upon a simple solution. I fold six papers in half, with printed side on the inside. Then I staple them together on the open edge. Now their books have pages with two clean sides. And because our printer ribbon is so old, the printing on the inside of the pages is faint enough to barely show through.

THE TIGHTWAD CHECKLIST

Several recent magazine articles point to thrift as the new wave of the '90s. As with any trend, there will be those attempting to pass themselves off as genuinely thrifty.

Just how does one distinguish the practitioner of lifelong frugality from those drifting with the current fad? When visiting the homes of individuals in question use this handy checklist to record the telltale signs of a classic tightwad.

- ❑ A scrubber made from a mesh onion bag.
- ❑ A squirt bottle of homemade window cleaner.
- ❑ A new soap bar with a soap sliver adhered. (Any other soap-bit system is acceptable.)
- ❑ A bundle of old socks in the workshop to be used as grease rags.
- ❑ A pair of pantyhose minus a bad leg.
- ❑ A jug of vegetable broth in the refrigerator.
- ❑ A 20-quart box of powdered milk. (Used only for cooking is acceptable.)
- ❑ A roll of paper towels cut in half.
- ❑ Any overturned bottle in the process of draining the last bit out.
- ❑ A pencil less than three inches long.
- ❑ A marked-down crushed box of cold cereal.
- ❑ Any item repaired with a twist-tie, paper clip, or hanger.
- ❑ A shower curtain repaired with duct tape.
- ❑ An impressive stash of one of the following items: egg cartons, styrofoam meat trays, toilet paper tubes, or frozen juice lids.
- ❑ A screwdriver with a tip that has been reground several times.
- ❑ A started shopping list on the back of a utility bill envelope.

- ❑ A stockpile of 44¢ per can tuna.
- ❑ A started container of "refrigerator stew" in the freezer.
- ❑ An indoor clothesline or a wooden clothes-drying rack.

Any individual scoring 12 or more is likely to be a genuine tightwad, and can be trusted.

WHAT TO DO WITH . . .

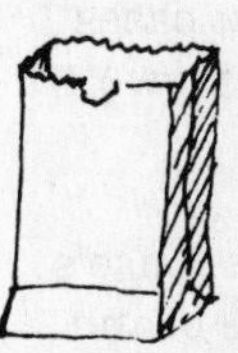

Brown Grocery Bags. These are now worth a nickel apiece. Many stores deduct 5¢ from your grocery bill if you bring back and reuse them for your groceries. This makes them too valuable for most any other types of reuse.

Cereal Boxes. Cut out flat sections and punch holes along the edges. Give them to your child along with a shoe lace. They can pretend they are sewing. A very nice set of these might make a gift for a three-year-old. (Contributed by Diane Meyer, St. Louis, Missouri)

Moth-eaten Sweaters. Make mittens from the remaining good sections. Trace a pattern from your hand. Place it on the sweater so that the sweater waist or cuffs become the cuffs of the mitten. Stitch two layers of the sweater on the sewing machine and trim. (Contributed by Eileen Donelan, Enfield, Connecticut)

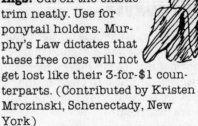

Old Knee-high Stockings. Cut off the elastic trim neatly. Use for ponytail holders. Murphy's Law dictates that these free ones will not get lost like their 3-for-$1 counterparts. (Contributed by Kristen Mrozinski, Schenectady, New York)

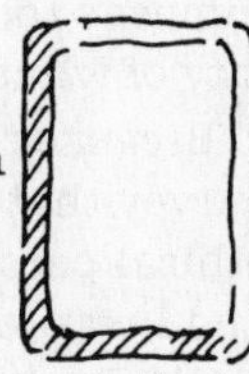

Holey Rubber Gloves. Cut the tips off the fingers to use for picking blackberries or raspberries. The gloves prevent your hands and arms from being scratched, but you can still pick the berries with your fingertips.

Styrofoam Meat Trays. Put them behind wall outlet switch plates for insulation. Trim to fit, and screw tightly for a snug fit.

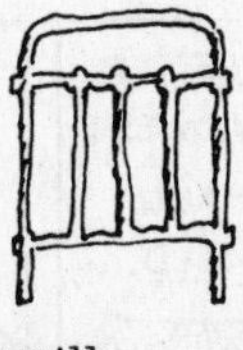

Coat Hangers. Use to make a hook to hold cookie cutters, canning jar lids, rolls of tape, etc. It can be hooked into an existing peg board. (Contributed by Jamien Morehouse, Camden, Maine)

Old Metal Beds. The head and foot boards can be reused to make great gates, especially around vegetable gardens. (Contributed by Dorothy Lockard, Greenville, Pennsylvania)

ETHICS II: THE SURVEY

After I ran an article on tightwad ethics, I received a higher-than-normal number of letters from readers pointing to ideas in the newsletter that they thought were unethical.

Clearly, ethics is a tricky area. As I wade through the uncharted waters of tightwaddery, I get letters from vast numbers of people who express opinions on things I have written or published. And frequently the opinions expressed are diametrically opposed.

I felt like I was the only person who was aware of this, so I offered a survey to the readers. My aim was to demonstrate the diversity of what people find ethical.

Because this was the sort of survey that only the most highly ethical person might respond to, and I wanted an accurate sampling, I requested that a few readers with low moral character respond as well.

I got over 1,000 responses. I was particularly interested/amused by those who answered "No to everything," and "Yes to everything." I also chuckled over the husbands and wives who responded separately with different answers. The possible answers were:

"Yes."

"Yes, but I wouldn't do it."

"No."

"No, but I would do it anyway."

I've also included a typical comment that best expressed the majority viewpoint (I included two comments in number 8 to reflect a fairly evenly split opinion). I have refrained from putting in my own two cents (but, in case you're curious . . . in most cases I agree with the majority view).

Is it ethical to:

1. Secretly switch your spouse's favorite, expensive name brand with store brand to see if they would notice the difference, providing that you eventually let them in on it?

76% Yes 6% Yes, but . . .
14% No 4% No, but . . .

"Yes, we both do this all the time."

2. Substitute another receipt to get a rebate if you lost the original receipt? The possible justification here is that you did in fact purchase the product and satisfy

FZ's World

WE LOVED YOUR NEWSLETTER. MY SON LIVES IN THE MIDWEST. AND I WAS TELLING HIM ALL ABOUT IT WHEN I CALLED...

HORRORS! DID I REALLY SAY THAT TO THE FRUGAL ZEALOT? SHE'LL THINK I'M A SPENDTHRIFT!
This says nothing important whatsoever.

BUT I CALLED HIM WHEN THE RATES WERE CHEAP!

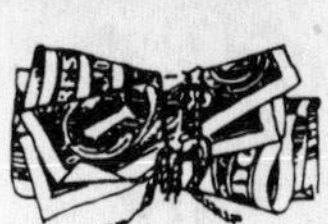

the manufacturer's intention.

70% Yes 5% Yes, but . . .
19% No 6% No, but . . .

"Yes, I bought the item."

3. Take all of the unused soap and shampoo from your hotel room?

76% Yes 5% Yes, but . . .
14% No 5% No, but . . .

"Yes, but not the light bulbs and rolls of toilet paper."

4. Offer half the asking price and show a wad of cash to encourage the sale when you are making a large purchase from a private individual? This assumes the seller does not appear needy.

72% Yes 12% Yes, but . . .
15% No 1% No, but . . .

"Yes, that's just good old Yankee trading."

5. Buy something from a pawn shop, knowing it is likely that someone under economic duress sold the item for a fraction of its real value?

76% Yes 15% Yes, but . . .
8% No 1% No, but . . .

"Yes, if the shops did not exist, those in need would have no way to raise quick cash."

6. Return a 10-year-old coat to L. L. Bean, to take advantage of the company's unconditional satisfaction guarantee?

12% Yes 10% Yes, but . . .
77% No 1% No, but . . .

"No, this violates the spirit of this guarantee. How can you be dissatisfied after 10 years?"

7. Buy toys for a fraction of their original price from a 10-year-old at a family yard sale?

66% Yes 9% Yes, but . . .
24% No 1% No, but . . .

"Yes, assume he prefers the money."

8. Take labels off thrift shop designer clothes and sew them onto new no-name clothes for your kids to wear? This assumes your kids know about it.

35% Yes 17% Yes, but . . .
45% No 3% No, but . . .

"Yes, if my kids were under extraordinary pressure from peers, I would see this as beating a stupid system."

"No, You're teaching your children false values."

9. Get Radio Shack's free battery card, and get a once-a-month free battery even though you never plan to buy anything from them?

63% Yes 11% Yes, but . . .
25% No 1% No, but . . .

"Yes, they were trying to bait you, and there were no strings."

10. To shop at a thrift shop if you have an average or above-average income? The possible objection is that you would be buying items that poorer people need.

95% Yes 2% Yes, but . . .
2% No 1% No, but . . .

"Yes, most thrift shops have too much merchandise. Profits go to a good cause.

SAVING MONEY ON YOUR MORTGAGE

One of the suggestions for an article that has come across my desk is the idea of "buying down the mortgage." I have seen a number of such articles in the past and was reluctant to add my entry. However, the subject recently hit home as we looked into our own situation and what it would take to pay off our mortgage early.

After we had lived in our house for 19 months, we sat down and figured some math. We had been paying $758 per month on a 30-year mortgage (plus taxes and insurance). That worked out to a grand total of $14,402 for the 19 months. Of that amount only $1,804 went toward the principal.

So, we knew this. But in a recent conversation with a friend about to sell her home, I learned that in 12 years she and her husband had paid off only $7,000 of their $39,000 mortgage. I got the feeling that she was completely surprised to find this out.

Most of the mortgages written now are of the 30-year variety. And it makes sense to get one. House buying is tough, and most of us struggle just to buy at all. But you should get one that doesn't penalize you for making extra payments. If your financial circumstances improve, and as inflation reduces the value of the mortgage, you should be able to make extra payments.

One of the common misconceptions about the mortgage is that you shouldn't pay off your mortgage because "you need the tax write-off." However, if you are in the 15% tax bracket you only save about $1.00 on income tax for every $6.66 you lost in interest.

What about investing, instead of using money to pay off a mortgage? In a conversation with an investment counselor, who consistently earned 15% to 20% on his investments, I asked what he thought of the merits of paying off the mortgage early. He told me that the average investor will not earn 9% or 10% on his investment. Therefore, paying off a mortgage early is a great investment strategy.

The exception would be the family with the mortgage at a very low interest rate of 5% or less. They will do better to invest surplus money in any one of a number of safe plans that yields 6% or more.

The chart on page 253 depicts the 30-year mortgage on $75,000 financed at 10%. This illustrates how much goes to pay the interest and principal year by year. Annually the mortgage costs nearly $8,000, but in the first year only $416.95 of the principal is paid off. It isn't until the 24th year that more principal is paid than interest. After 30 years the family will have paid back $236,944.32, and of that $161,944 goes for interest.

Every month the family pays $658.18 for their mortgage. If they were to round the figure up to the nearest hundred, or make payments of $700 per month, they would pay off their mortgage in 22½ years and save $47,944.32 in interest. If this same family set a goal to pay off their mortgage in 15 years they would need to increase their monthly payment by $147.77. By paying off this extra $26,598.60 ($147.77 x 12 months

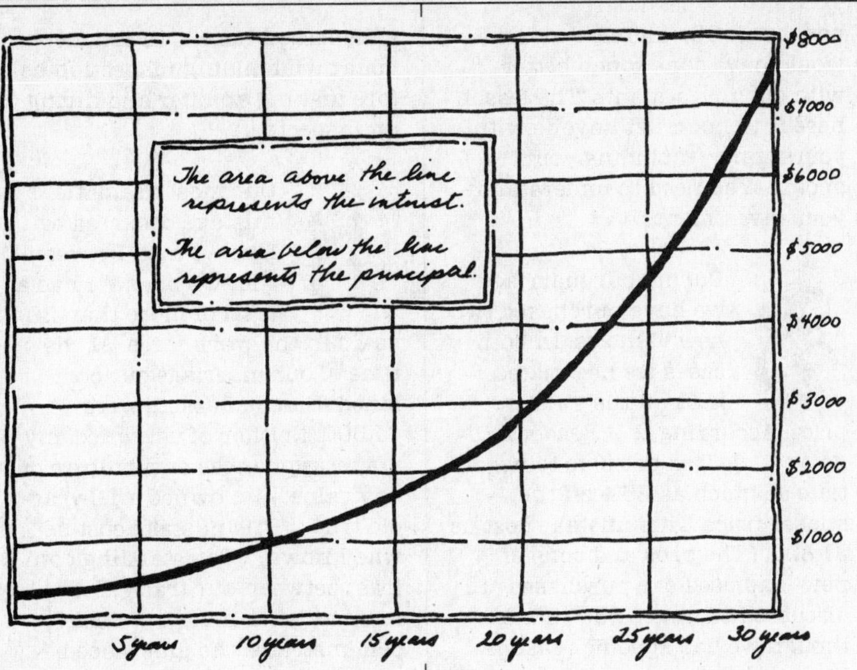

x 15 years) early the family would save $91,872.63 in interest.

In other words, after 15 years for every $1.00 paid early (of what the family would have to pay anyway) they would save $3.45. That's a hard investment strategy to beat.

SIX MISTAKES WE MADE

1 During the first year of our marriage my husband put our savings into a mutual fund account that he had since before we met. Because of a lack of knowledge and attention we bought many shares when the price had peaked. It was only after the shares dropped dramatically that we learned of the gap in the buying and selling price. After nine months of watching we decided to sell out when the shares had partially recovered. (We watched for an additional six months and the price never went higher.) This investment mistake cost us $1,500.

2 Apparently the pain of our earlier mistake was not severe enough, as we made a similar mistake five years later. This time our sizable nest egg was diversified in long term CDs and half a dozen funds. On the advice of our broker we bought into a fund that was tied to the stock market. Within 60 days the market crashed (Oct. '88). Our fund did not recover before we needed to liquidate. This mistake cost us $800. (At the time we invested, CDs were paying a very high rate. Had we

bought all CDs and no funds we would have done much better with our investments. The lesson here is to not trust anyone with your money, including your spouse. You need to understand your investments.)

During our marriage we have purchased two new vehicles. In both cases we negotiated 20% off the sticker price. According to a *Reader's Digest* article it is possible to negotiate as much as 25% off the sticker price. This mistake cost us $1,500. (The pros and cons of new- and used-car purchases are discussed on pages 239–40. Although we had specific reasons for our choice, it is still a frequent subject of debate in our household.)

We shopped for a set of secondhand bunkbeds for our children for several months and finally bought a new set that we liked. Within a matter of months they were trashed to the condition of most of the used ones we had seen. This mistake cost us $200. (Children are very hard on furniture, clothing, and toys. We usually try to buy used items, and I have regretted most new purchases.)

When our offer was accepted on an earlier house we hired a building inspector, who told us what any idiot with a pair of eyes could have seen (had they looked). An entire section of the house had no foundation. This mistake cost us $275. (The lesson here is to conduct your own building inspection before making an offer and hiring an inspector.)

Our most dramatic mistake occurred before we met. Between the two of us we had a total of more than 20 years in the work force. At the time of our marriage our combined financial assets were $1,500. Neither of us owned any major appliances or furniture of any value. Jim owned a 10-year-old truck. This mistake cost us . . . who knows? (The startling contrast between our track record before and after marriage clearly demonstrates the difference between a fun-oriented and a goal-oriented lifestyle.)

MILK JUG MAGIC

Milk jug plastic is lightweight and can be easily cut, making the jugs highly versatile. Many communities now have recycling programs to accommodate milk jugs. However, the reuse of the jug also benefits the environment because an object fabricated from a jug replaces another object that would be otherwise manufactured. All jugs and plastic scraps can eventually be recycled.

I have included a collection of possibilities.

Cut off the top to make a container to hold children's toys, such as Legos, Matchbox cars, Tinker Toys, etc. The handle makes them easy to carry. The

same idea makes a compost bucket or a clothespin holder.

Punch holes in the bottom to make an irrigation jug. Set into the ground near plants to be watered. This allows for slow watering without evaporation.

Cut off bottom at an angle to make a pooper scooper, a bailer, or a dust pan for the shop.

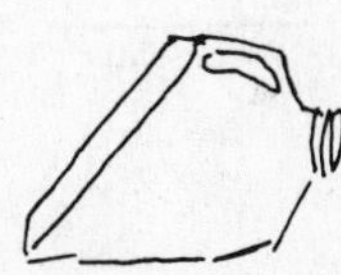

Cut as shown to make an Easter basket. Cut the ears out of extra side panels and staple on. Mark eyes and nose with a black marker. Glue on a cotton ball for a tail.

Cut out a flat panel to make a pinwheel. Tack to a dowel. Use markers and glitter to add color.

If you have an X-Acto knife you can also make simple stencils from the side panels. Or make holes with a paper punch to make sewing cards for children.

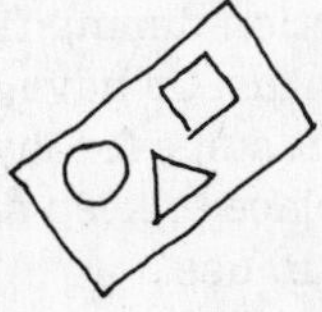

Filled with water and dark food coloring, or painted black, milk jugs can be stacked to make a Trombe wall. This functions as an inexpensive solar collector for a greenhouse.

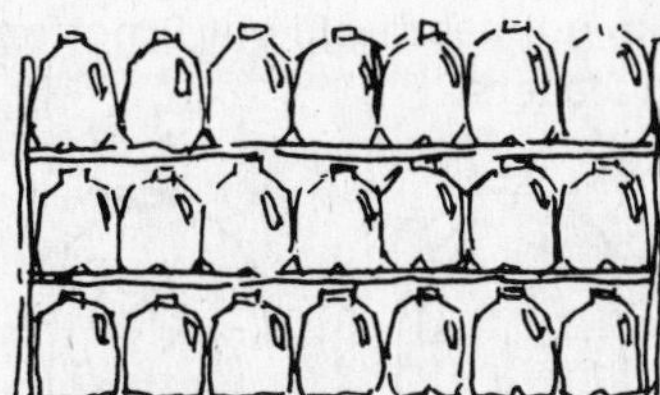

Cut the top and handle off to make a toilet brush holder.

Cut the bottom off to make miniature greenhouses. Remove the cap during the day. Or use to cover plants when frost threatens.

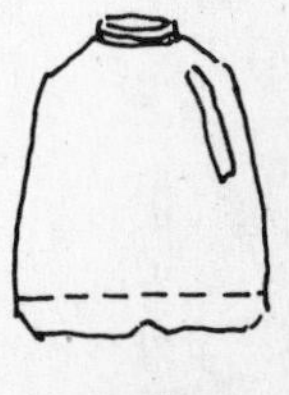

Fill with water and put in the toilet tank for a water saver. Or put in the freezer to fill the empty spaces (and improve the energy efficiency).

Fill with sand for weights in the trunk of the car for extra traction during the winter months. Or have a sand jug by the front steps for icy days. Leave cap in place to keep sand dry when not in use.

Cut large holes in the sides to make nonaesthetic but functional bird feeders.

Cut as shown below to make a mask for a small child. Painted black it makes a Darth Vader mask. I varied the theme to make a robot mask. Cut holes for the eyes the right size so that two spouts pop through tightly.

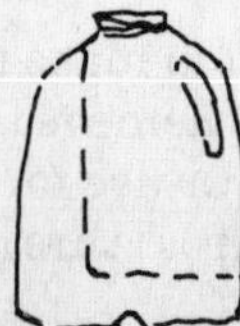

Empty milk jugs with screw caps can be used for buoys.

Cut as shown to make a container for seedlings and a collar to keep cutworms from plants.

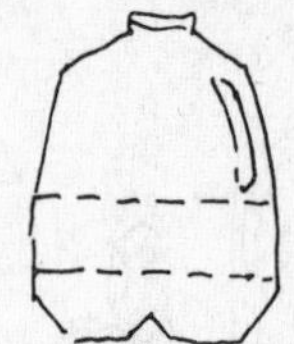

Cut off the bottom to make a megaphone for children.

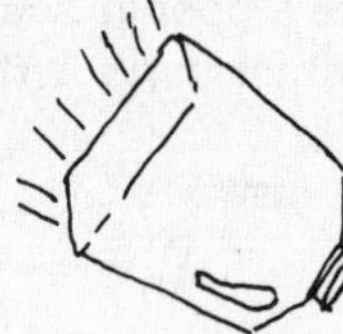

A COMMENT AND A QUESTION

Linda Van Atta of Scarborough, Maine, submitted this winning idea. She wrote a great comment as well as asked a great question.

THE COMMENT:

"My husband does the mechanical stuff and makes furniture, etc., while my knowledge is in things like growing plants, sewing, creative cooking (the kind you do when it looks like there isn't any-

thing to eat), organization, and cleaning. Sounds sexist, but it really isn't. We do what we do the best and help the other with the rest. And he does a lot of the cooking and some cleaning, too. Teamwork yields some good ideas and saves us money. We can do about anything we need to."

I agree with Linda completely and have always felt that teamwork and compatibility contributed greatly to our ability to save. Couples who often disagree or do not harmonize well expend energy resolving differences. This leaves less energy for working together toward a common goal.

THE QUESTION:

"How do you get your own house cheaply if you are financially responsible, but don't have a big credit history? We've promptly paid thousands in student loans but have been told these don't count. We pay cash, and make our money go much farther than the general public does, but from what we hear banks would rather lend money to people who live beyond their means."

Linda asks two questions. Several methods exist to obtain housing cheaper, such as a state-subsidized loan for low-income families, or buying a two-family house and renting half.

However, the most important aspect of her question concerns establishing credit, without which it is near impossible to get a mortgage, especially in these times of tightening bank regulations.

Establishing credit can be a common tightwad problem, as we like to pay cash for everything to avoid interest charges.

I consulted *Wealth Without Risk* by Charles Givens. He offers three basic strategies for rebuilding credit, which would also work for establishing credit (strategies 57, 58 and 59 in the book).

1. Get a cosigner on a loan to help establish credit. This could either be family or friends. Eventually you will qualify for credit on your own.

2. Get a secured credit card. Secured means that you have a deposit equal to the credit you want. Some banks put this into an interest-earning CD. After you have made payments for six months the deposit will be returned to you. The book offers three sources for secured credit cards.

3. Borrow $1,000 from a bank and put it into a secured savings account in the same bank. Because you cannot withdraw money from the savings account, the bank risks nothing. Pay back the loan with other cash. This costs you interest on the loan, but you earn interest on the savings account. You lose a few percent on your money in exchange for establishing credit.

The last two methods require that you have some savings. They can be attractive to the tightwad who does not want to lose interest money. Other parts of Linda's letter indicated that she and her husband possess remarkable savings ability, putting away a very large percent of a modest income. In our experience we found that large savings accounts impress loan officers. Banks look hard at

your ability to save and stay out of debt. Therefore I suggest they couple even a modest credit history with a proven savings track record.

BOOK REVIEW

For all you recently converted tightwads who have succeeded in your newfound restraint, but still feel the itch to part with a few dollars, I have a guilt-free justifiable spend for you.

And for those who have written asking if I would include tightwad recipes, those who are interested in healthful eating, and those for whom the term "sustainable culture" frequently finds its way into your conversation, this is a cookbook for you to add to your shelf.

The *More-with-Less Cookbook* came to my attention some time ago as mentioned in a letter from a reader. But I had not seen a copy until my sister gave it to me for Christmas.

Written by Doris Janzen Longacre, a Mennonite woman who passed away several years ago, the cookbook is in its 38th printing.

She devotes approximately one third of the book to the moral issues surrounding our American dietary habits in relation to the world food crisis, as well as basic nutrition and a general approach to food. Clearly written for the Mennonite people, the first third contains several biblical references. Regardless of your faith you will find the moral issues raised to be absolutely universal.

If this sort of message does not align with your beliefs (or you just want to get to the matter of how to spend less at the grocery store), then move directly to the remaining two thirds of the book. You will find simple and healthful recipes that rely on basic and inexpensive ingredients.

My two most frequent annoyances with many recipes is that they either call for convenience foods or expensive ingredients. As I flip through this cookbook I see many recipes that I can prepare without a shopping trip.

The author includes options to tailor recipes to your own pantry and ways to use up leftovers.

Many recipes contain white sugar, white flour, and red meat. The message is not abstinence but rather a strong suggestion that we attempt to limit these items and substitute more dried beans, whole grains, and fresh or home-preserved fruits and vegetables.

If you are a beginner into the voyage of more healthful eating, you will be quite comfortable with the majority of these recipes, as few call for tofu and sprouts.

You may be able to check out this book at a library. If not, look for it in either a Christian bookstore or a natural-foods store.

SAVING MONEY WHEN YOU HAVE NO TIME

The first year I published *The Tightwad Gazette* overlapped with Jim's last year in the Navy. Our dual careers put added stress on our family. We regarded his retirement date as the light at the end of our tunnel; a beacon signaling a return to more relaxed times.

The Mad Hatter lifestyle gave me a new respect for those who have asked, "But what if you don't have time to do all those thrifty things?"

Yeah, there is no doubt about it. Do-it-yourself furniture reupholstery, rebuilding car engines, rug braiding—many of the best skinflintian practices can be left for those with surplus time. However, investment of significant portions of time is only one of the three basic ways to save money:

1. Be more organized. This will save money as well as time. For example, at certain times of the year different types of merchandise go on sale. Purchasing a marked-down toy in January for a May birthday requires the same amount of time as paying full price at the last minute.

If you plan meals a day in advance you will not have to thaw a frozen piece of meat in the microwave. If you are going to replace your tires in six months, casually watch for a good sale.

Some methods of organization require a relatively small amount of initial investment time, such as setting up a grocery shopping system or organizing a way to pre-buy children's clothing as you run across it at yard sales.

Many forms of record keeping fall into this category, such as keeping a maintenance record for your car.

2. Scale down. Expect to do, have, or spend less. Eliminate the nonessentials. Eat out less. Make something last longer. Buy secondhand instead of new.

I recently bought a "new" handbag at the thrift shop for $1. I expended the same time as if I had bought one at a department store.

One would presume that the loss of surplus time has made our lifestyle more expensive. But we have resisted the temptation to scale up.

Back in my thumb-twiddlin' days I could spend a week preparing a birthday party. This spring we have had parties (if you could call them that) with little more than a cake, a few presents, and a promise for next year.

We've also had to pare down our repertoire of tightwad dinners and eliminate the multistep casseroles in favor of the simpler meals. While the common cuisine would not have excited Julia Child, we did not resort to convenience foods to jazz up meals. As a result our food bill has remained constant.

3. Do those time-consuming thrifty things.

Even those who feel they have little extra time to devote to activities that save money can rethink their use of this strategy.

Focus on using the time you do have on the ways to save that will give you the largest return for time spent. Make it a practice to record the hours spent on an activity and the savings return so that you can best determine the most profitable way for you to spend your time.

When Jim shopped for our Suburban, he contacted 22 car dealerships. Because his approach was organized he only spent an additional nine hours and saved $4,000 off the sticker price. However, he would not stop at 22 department stores to save a few cents on transparent tape.

Sometimes the return in time spent can be weighed by the quality of life achieved. I might spend an hour making a custom birthday card for a friend when I could buy one for $1.25. But a personalized card might have the equivalent impact of an expensive present. Likewise many tightwad strategies are worth doing because they are environmentally sound.

Money-saving activities can conflict with a need to spend quality time with family. Solve this by choosing activities that meet both needs. Our children like to help bake cookies, help plant the garden, or watch their dad build something. In the same way you can choose a personal hobby that will save money (rather than cost money).

Think about the spare minutes as small change that accumulates. Use those moments to accomplish small tasks. A list taped to your refrigerator will help to aid you. Also double up on activities. Have hand sewing to do when watching TV or talking on the phone.

Finally, be certain that you are not working more, to buy more conveniences, because you lack time. In other words don't moonlight to buy TV dinners. Often people fail to calculate how much extra they spend because they work more.

Recently an acquaintance's accountant told her that her part-time $5-per-hour job, when combined with other family income, netted only $2.48 per hour in take-home pay. Had she also factored in gas and commuting time, the figure would be less. Know your real hourly worth and bear that in mind when you think thrifty things aren't worth doing.

Of the three ways to save money, you may be only able to utilize one or two. But being busy does not have to mean spending more.

CHEAP THRILLS

"We worry that you and Jim aren't having enough fun." A relative stunned me with this observation and I replied, "Sure we have fun, like . . . ah . . . ah . . ."

I had to think over the years, way back to our honeymoon, to pinpoint the last shred of traditional expensive fun.

In the year since, I have prepared a better answer. Yes, we do have fun. But it is different from the fun we had when we were single. Somewhere our sense of fun became distorted and it now seems to be centered on conserving funds and working toward goals. Here are a few classic tightwad thrills.

Check out your neighbors' trash after they have cleaned out the garage and left for the evening.

Hold a yard sale. This surpasses the fun of purging by throwing things away.

Beat the supermarket at their own game by challenging yourself to see how much food you can bring home for the fewest dollars. If your sense of fun is greatly distorted, you might enjoy the spectator sport of watching spendthrifts go through the checkout line.

Summers in Maine offer many festivals and free concerts as a way to promote the various towns. They offer such things as bed races and parades. Avoid the temptation of purchasing cans of soda, expensive balloons, and cheap toys.

Gardening. There is something magical about planting seeds, and watching things grow all by themselves. Harvesting is the fun part.

A well-executed child's birthday party—not too much and not too little. The thrill is heightened when you have spent only a few dollars and some kid comes up to you afterwards and says, "This is the best party I ever went to."

Repair, renovation, or refinishing. The more gone the thing is the more fun to bring it back.

When your child catches his first fish, learns to ride his bike without training wheels, or jumps off the bus after his first trauma-free and glorious day of kindergarten and then spends 30 minutes telling you all about it.

CHEAP THRILLS FROM READERS

"I find crossword puzzles and jigsaw puzzles to be some of the cheapest entertainment available. Both provide hours of entertainment and are available for under $5." (Eric May, Racine, Wisconsin)

"The Premiere Dining Club coupon booklet provides two dinners for the price of one with repeat visits allowed. We eat out a fair amount and enjoy the sport of pursuing the greatest quality experience for the least money. We also only drink water in restaurants." (Jon Eberle, Redmond, Washington)

"I have a similar distorted sense of fun. When I get away from the computer or the mail desk I can usually be found fixing electrical appliances, rewebbing lawn chairs we salvaged from the street, or building shelves." (Joe Dominguez, The New Road Map Foundation, Seattle, Washington)

THE TIGHTWAD REFRIGERATOR

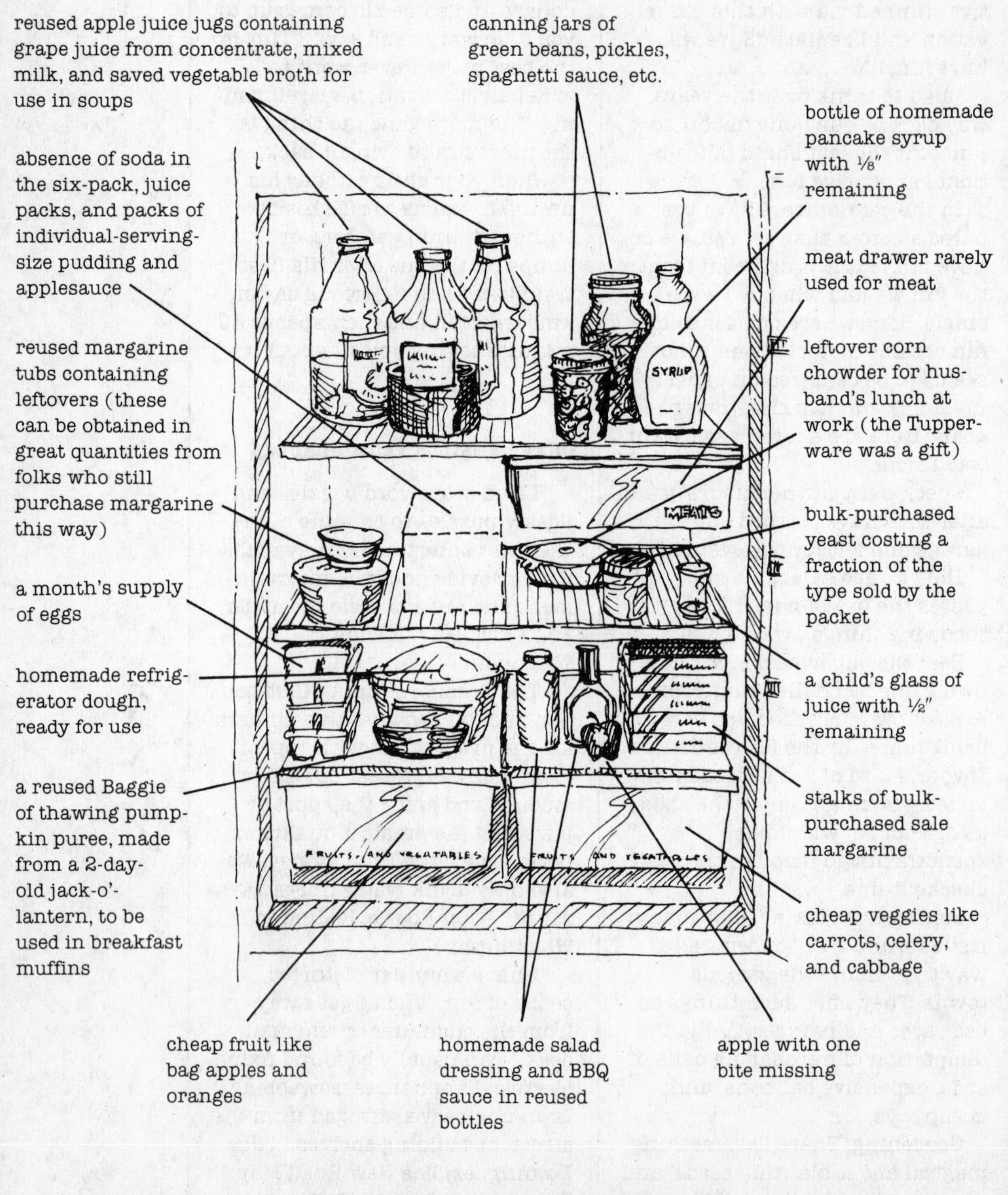
reused apple juice jugs containing grape juice from concentrate, mixed milk, and saved vegetable broth for use in soups
canning jars of green beans, pickles, spaghetti sauce, etc.
bottle of homemade pancake syrup with 1/8″ remaining
absence of soda in the six-pack, juice packs, and packs of individual-serving-size pudding and applesauce
meat drawer rarely used for meat
SYRUP
reused margarine tubs containing leftovers (these can be obtained in great quantities from folks who still purchase margarine this way)
leftover corn chowder for husband's lunch at work (the Tupperware was a gift)
MEATS
bulk-purchased yeast costing a fraction of the type sold by the packet
a month's supply of eggs
homemade refrigerator dough, ready for use
a child's glass of juice with 1/2″ remaining
a reused Baggie of thawing pumpkin puree, made from a 2-day-old jack-o'-lantern, to be used in breakfast muffins
stalks of bulk-purchased sale margarine
FRUITS AND VEGETABLES
FRUITS AND VEGETABLES
cheap veggies like carrots, celery, and cabbage
cheap fruit like bag apples and oranges
homemade salad dressing and BBQ sauce in reused bottles
apple with one bite missing

YOUR TIGHTWAD REFRIGERATOR MAY VARY.

HOMEMADE SHAKE & BAKE

Dear Amy,

This recipe equals 20 store packets at 25% of the price.

4 cups flour
4 cups crackermeal (or ground inexpensive crackers)
4 Tbsp salt
2 Tbsp sugar
2 tsp garlic powder
2 tsp onion powder
3 Tbsp paprika
¼ cup vegetable oil

Mix well and store indefinitely in the refrigerator in a covered container.

Ann Davis
Andrews, North Carolina

ABOUT SPACE

Dear Amy,

Do you save almost everything? If so, where do you keep it all? I like to save, but also believe if you haven't worn/used it all year (or five years) get rid of it. I am haunted by stories of people overrun by their own trash. Can you be frugal and neat?

Diane Shaw
Turner, Maine

Dear Diane,

Space, like time, energy, and money, is a precious resource. It is hard to be neat when your home is too full of too much. Organization is important to the conserving of time. Time is important to the conserving of money. In other words, the key is to balance all your resources for the maximum quality of life.

We have a large barn, sheds, and two attics. Space is not a precious resource to us. However, when I do save I make an effort to use those materials first. I design projects around what I have rather than deciding what I want to make and then buying materials. I do not save when I have a surplus or a steady supply of an item. When I purge I try to donate, hold a yard sale, or find someone who wants the items. I feel guilty about what I contribute to the landfill problem. I used to have a similar policy to yours when I was a single apartment dweller. Then I married a packrat. I discovered that saving stuff was more fun than saving space. For the true tightwad few thrills compare with that of making something from salvaged, saved, or leftover materials.

A REMINDER

Dear Amy,

If one isn't working in a coal mine, why waste water standing in the shower 10 or 15 minutes?

Marjorie Lunger
Williamsburg, Virginia

(Uh-oh . . . She's on to me. I am very guilty of using the shower as a creative think tank. This has resulted in some very good but expensively obtained ideas for the newsletter. FZ)

THE WHOLE KNEE PATCH

When a child rips the knees in a pair of jeans that otherwise has lots of life, I patch them. I gave up on conventional patches because no sooner had I patched them when the neighboring material would give out.

Now I patch jeans with "the whole knee patch" method.

This is time consuming, and I save the ripping for a time when I am watching TV or visiting with a guest.

Rip out the seam from the bottom to four inches above the tear. Make a new patch from a matching denim scrap that is wider than the pant leg and 5 inches high. Sew the top and bottom edge under ½ inch and then topstitch the patch over the tear. Resew the seams (double seam first from the outside, single seam from the inside).

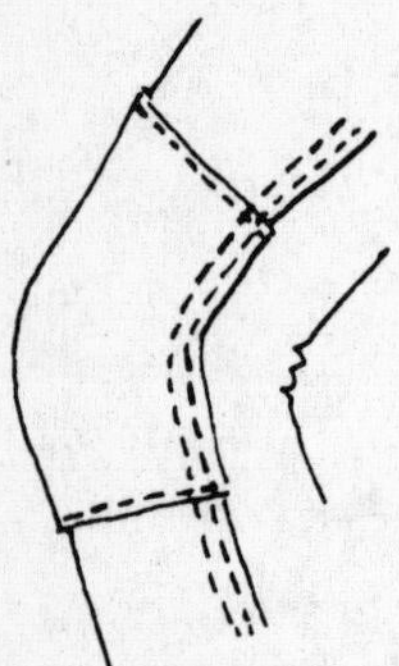

This patch will outlast the jeans.

Other uses for denim scraps:

- Sew strips to weave a seat for a wooden folding chair.
- Braid a blue jean rug.
- Make a blue jean patchwork quilt for a boy's room.
- Make trendy potholders with gold double topstitched seams
- Make a drawstring sack from a cut-off blue jean leg.

HOLDING A YARD SALE

While running errands on a Saturday afternoon you spot an obscure windblown yard sale sign tacked to a telephone pole on the other side of a busy street. Making great effort to backtrack, you read the sign, deduce the location of the sale, and head off into the unknown. No more signs appear to further guide you, and after 15 minutes of working your way through the suburban maze you luck upon the sale. You think . . . There are a few knickknacks on a table and a collection of 1970s vintage adult clothing in a pile next to it. The proprietor, lounging in a lawn chair, kills time, reading behind a newspaper. The newspaper drops down and you find yourself staring into your own face!

Just then you wake up in a cold sweat, your heart racing. It was only a dream—a nightmare of your own yard sale from hell.

How do you avoid sleepless pre-yard sale nights and the eventual bad yard sale? Think about everything you have disliked about the ones you have attended, and do not repeat the mistakes.

Ideally you want to hold a yard sale in a populated area, and an area where yard sales flourish. Generally an ad will not be essential unless you do not reside on the beaten path. If your location is hopeless, buddy up with a friend in a good location.

Although yard sales go on throughout the summer, the first sunny spring weekend day is your best bet. If you do not place an ad, and if you date your signs at the last minute, you have the

option of canceling in poor weather. Do not hold a yard sale on a holiday weekend.

Check to see if your town requires a license. (If you do not get one the Yard Sale Gestapo will not show up. This ordinance is designed to prevent the perpetual yard sale.)

As a graphics person I place a high priority on signs. Good signs have a distinctive quality of their own—something that makes them easy to recognize from the others. Make them all the same. It could be red lettering on cardboard, or tie a balloon to each sign.

The best and fastest method of sign making I have found requires cutting a stencil. Cut out the words YARD SALE in large letters (3″ to 4″) out of lightweight cardboard. Make a second stencil with a large arrow. Use spray paint for a fast job. Put YARD SALE on top and the arrow on the bottom. Use marker to hand write the date and location in the middle. Make half the arrows point one way and half point the other. This way you can place signs from either direction.

Placement of signs is critical. Recall your frustration in trying to follow poorly placed signs. Place on all the intersections near your home as far as the main road, whatever that is. Put your sign on the side of the road that you want your potential customer to turn.

Begin gathering stuff early. Have a designated yard sale carton and save items in it throughout the year. You won't know if you have enough until you see it all in one place. If your quantity of merchandise seems lean, buddy up with friends. If you learn a neighbor is planning a yard sale, hold yours the same weekend. You will enhance each other's business rather than being in competition.

People will buy nearly anything. During a yard sale my father held, a woman found a rock in our yard and bought it. Anything could be sellable.

In the same way that the retail business uses marketing strategies, so must you. No one likes to see tables of knickknacks and huge piles of clothes. Large items stop cars, so put those things near the road. Hang up as much clothing as possible. Lay out clothing for children according to size so that it is easy to see. Group similar items together. A box of odd hangers is junk. Simi-

lar hangers neatly bundled becomes good stuff.

When considering pricing, remember that your primary objective is to get rid of stuff, and not to make money. People expect to get a bargain. Generally sell things for between 10% to 50% of a comparable new item. Things that you want to sell the most should be priced lower yet. All items should be clearly priced.

Seasoned yard salers expect to negotiate. Hold firm if you think the item is already cheap enough. Negotiating should be considered at the end of the day rather than at the beginning. Encourage people to return late in the day rather than negotiate early. Do not agree to hold anything for anyone unless they pay first. Even the most sincere-looking person may not return.

After the yard sale put all remaining merchandise back in your yard sale box for next year.

The previous information will help relieve pre-yard sale stress. What of the guilt that leads to post-yard sale nightmares? Take down all of your yard sale signs and sleep comfortably with a clear conscience.

YARD SALE STRATEGY

Dear Amy,

I buy, fix up, and resell yard sale stuff. I just made $40 on two bar stools I got for $20 and sold for $60.

The selling trick is to save store flyers, cut out a picture of the item to be sold, and tape it to the item. Things sell faster when people are reminded of the original selling price.

I find buying things that can be fixed up pays better, as few people want to fix anything themselves. I can buy cheap and with a little paint and ingenuity make them look new.

Dottie Lawrence
Port St. Lucie, Florida

GREAT QUOTES

"You cannot bring about prosperity by discouraging thrift.

You cannot establish sound security on borrowed money.

You cannot keep out of trouble by spending more than you earn."

—Abraham Lincoln

"Junk is the stuff we throw away. Stuff is the junk we save."

—Frank Tyger
The Times, Trenton, New Jersey

WORD PROBLEMS

I have always been a mathematics midget. I am the kind of person who frequently cannot remember that 8 and 5 is . . . uh . . . 13? I married a math whiz. Jim can multiply 27 by 41 in his head and get it right. At least if he's pulling the wool over my eyes I'd never know.

One might think this union of opposites would have caused math atrophy. I have actually improved in recent years, but not because his genius rubbed off. Precision tightwaddery requires continual calculation. Also during my adult years the pocket calculator has become cheap enough to buy with pocket change.

Below are seven real-life word problems. The answers appear on page 268.

1. A heat gun costs about the same as a gallon of paint stripper, or $20. Presuming your electricity costs 9¢ per kilowatt-hour how long could you run a 1,000 kilowatt heat gun before you exceed the cost of the second gallon of paint stripper?

2. The postal service will update your mailing list with nine-digit zip codes for free. This will save .9¢ per piece of bulk mail. However the needed computer program would cost about $325. Presuming a constant monthly mailing of 1,500 how long would it take to recoup the cost of the computer program?

3. A local grocery store runs a special on ground beef: 75% lean costs $1.18 lb, 80% lean costs $1.58 lb, and 85% lean costs $1.88 lb. Presuming you plan to use the beef in such a way as to cook off the extra fat, and in a recipe where the taste difference is not critical, which sale offers the most lean beef per dollar.

4. You buy a battery recharger for $12 and two C rechargeables for $8. You send in for the $2 rebate with a 29¢ stamp. The manufacturer claims that a rechargeable C battery equals 150 disposables (which cost $3 per pair). How much could you save before needing to replace the rechargeables?

5. A 10-oz box of cold cereal costs $1.59. The same brand costs $2.19 for 18 oz. You have a 35¢-off coupon for that brand of cereal and your store offers double coupons. Which size box of cereal is the better value?

6. Generic oatmeal costs 57¢ lb. Assuming that a 1½-oz serving of oatmeal equals a 1½-oz serving of the cold cereal in the previous problem, how much would you

save over the course of the year if you fed your family of four oatmeal instead of cold cereal?

7. Blank address labels (1″ x 3½″) cost $10 per 5,000. Clear tape costs 69¢ for 12½ yards. Business-size envelopes cost 7¢ apiece on sale. The sender of the envelope writes small enough so that the two old addresses can be covered with one label each. You neatly slice the envelope end when opening so that it requires 4″ of tape to reclose. Is it cost-effective to reuse business envelopes?

WORD PROBLEM ANSWERS

1. A kilowatt-hour is 1000 watts consumed in one hour. Therefore a 1000 kilowatt appliance uses 9¢ worth of electricity in an hour. You could run a heat gun for 222.22 hours before using up $20 worth of electricity. A heat gun is not the best method of paint removal for every application, but much more economical than chemical stripper.

2. Using the nine-digit zip code would save $13.50 per month and the computer program would be paid for in 24 months. Since we would have to mail in a computer disk monthly it would take 25½ months to recoup the cost.

3. The 75% provides 10 oz of lean for $1. The 80% provides 8 oz for $1, and the 85% provides 7 oz for $1.

4. $431.71

5. The 18-oz box of cereal would cost .083¢ per oz and the 10-oz box would cost .089¢ per oz. That would be 8¢ and 9¢ per oz respectively if rounded off. Had the prices been closer, the bigger box would still be the better value providing the most cereal at a reduced price.

6. Using the .083¢ figure from the previous problem, the cold cereal would cost about 49.8¢ per day or $181.77 per year. Oatmeal would cost 21¢ a day or $78.01 per year. The oatmeal would save a family of four $103.76 annually.

Although 57¢ lb is a very good price we buy it for 39¢ lb in a 50-lb sack. Our children love oatmeal but will not tolerate it more than four times a week.

7. Labels cost .002¢ each (or .004¢ per envelope) and the tape costs .006¢ per piece of 4″ tape. The cost of reusing a business envelope is about a penny, or a savings of 6¢.

(There is no substitution for doing your own homework.)

BULK FRUIT PECTIN

When I mentioned that I learned I could buy bulk pectin to save money on jam making, readers asked me where to get it. Our local health food store buys it from:

Dutch Valley Food Distributors
P.O. Box 465
Meyerstown, PA 17067
(800) 733-4191

BABY-WIPE SOLUTIONS

Many readers have sent me directions on how to make homemade baby wipes using paper towels and a solution of baby oil and baby shampoo. I have always used old washcloths just as previous generations have done before manufacturers invented baby wipes and sold us on this as a "necessity." The cleansing solution may be superior to plain water, but I would prefer not to throw away the paper towels. Here is a letter from a reader that shares my views:

Dear Amy,

Baby wipes are very expensive. They run $3 to $4 for 80 in our area. These wipes are full of alcohol, fragrances, etc. that are potential irritants to the baby. Instead I "invested" in 12 one-color washcloths in a pack from our local department store ($2.99 for 12). These sit either in the bathroom or at the diaper changing table. I wet one just before the diaper change. Afterward I toss them in the diaper pail to be washed.

Patricia Hone
Apollo, Pennsylvania

However, daycare centers require that parents provide disposable baby wipes.

So if you must use them, the homemade version is certainly economical and worthwhile.

This baby wipe recipe was sent by Laurie Kenny of Portland, ME.

1 roll of Bounty paper towels or microwave paper towels
2¼ cups water
2 Tbsp baby shampoo or baby bath
1 Tbsp baby oil

Cut the roll of paper towels in half and remove the cardboard center. Mix the water, shampoo or bath, and oil in a plastic container (such as an old baby wipe container). Place half a roll in a container, put the lid on and turn upside down to let the towels thoroughly soak. When ready to use pull the towels from the center of the roll.

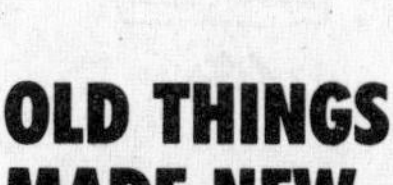

OLD THINGS MADE NEW

If you have a good relationship with a body shop you might be able to use it for more than getting a new paint job for your car.

Jim bought a used five-drawer filing cabinet. The paint job was pretty bad and I thought "Ugh, another obviously secondhand piece of office furniture for our already motley-looking office."

He took it to the shop that had just repainted our car. We were able to get the file repainted for $20. It looks brand new. And it certainly looked a long sight better than if we had attempted it with cans of spray paint.

My parents, who live in a different area of the country, had their medicine cabinet sandblasted and repainted by their body shop. I have heard of people getting their refrigerators repainted.

Obviously not all shops will be willing to be bothered or do it for such reasonable prices. I would not approach a chain shop with such a request. This shop accommodated us because we had two cars worked on, and we sent him more business. We were also will-

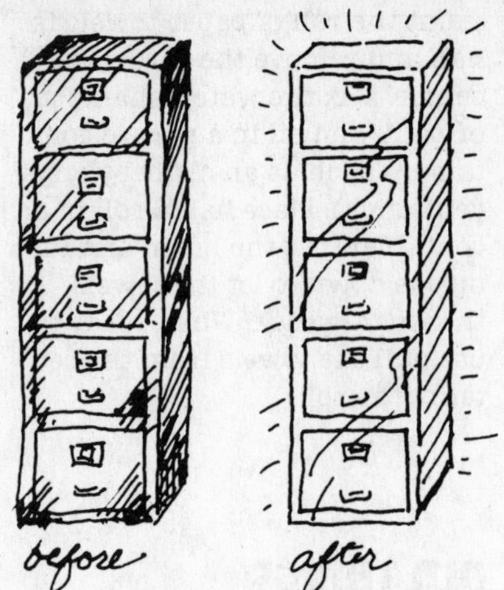

ing to wait until he had a slow time. My father told his shop to paint it when they were going to paint a car the same color as he wanted for the medicine cabinet.

If you need something repainted but do not have an established relationship, you might be able to negotiate in other ways. You might try to barter, for example.

THE USED-CLOTHING FILING SYSTEM

The growth of children occurs subtly enough so that we only notice it when their clothes appear to shrink between wearings. Typically I might begin to dress a two-year-old for church and suddenly all her dresses seem too short. On these occasions we go "shopping in the attic." I am able to locate the proper-sized dress within two minutes.

I developed my used-clothing filing system for kids when I had only two of them. As I collected yard sale finds and as relatives mailed hand-me-downs, going through the mountain of clothes for the next-sized wardrobe became a tedious task. During this sort, I would invariably discover that I had purchased yard sale clothes when I had sufficient hand-me-downs, or that clothing had become outgrown while in storage. I might also discover that I had failed to purchase enough of something.

Except for sneakers, socks, and some underwear I have never purchased new clothing for any of the children. (OK, once we bought Alec three shirts when he was a toddler.)

Currently my filing system is made up of 30 same-sized boxes. A smaller family could do the same with 4 or fewer boxes per child. The lidded boxes that the newsletters come in from the printer each month are ideal. I have marked each box with the size and sex . . . such as 5 YG (i.e., five-year-old girl), or 6 MB. Boys' boxes are on one side of a chimney and girls' on the other. I mark the boxes on the visible facing end with black marker.

I collect clothing years older than my oldest child. Alec is 9 and I have a box for a few teenage freebies that have come my way. However, I *buy* yard sale clothes only a couple years older than the oldest child. I don't buy too far in advance because free hand-me-downs might come along in the meantime. In addition, it can be hard to predict if your child will be a "slim" or a "husky."

At the same time I don't wait to shop for clothes six months in advance because I might not be lucky enough to find everything I need.

I seldom watch for clothes for younger children, as I know that there are ample hand-me-downs from an older sibling, and I am generally given enough things to perk up those tired wardrobes.

By having clothing sorted into same-sized boxes I can quickly gauge if I have too much or not enough clothes for a particular size. I have two full boxes of 3 YR B. Because one box of clothing is sufficient for a young child, I know I can sort the boxes, keeping only the best things. The dregs get donated to a thrift shop. (Some thrift shops sell poor-quality clothing for recycling.)

I graciously accept all clothing that is given to me. I sort later and may only keep a small percentage, depending on the quality of the used items and according to the things I need. I will keep things, even if I don't like the style, or if the item needs repair, when I have a shortage. I don't work on stains or repair clothing until I need to, as it is likely I will find better stuff in time.

I will buy things far in advance if I know they are

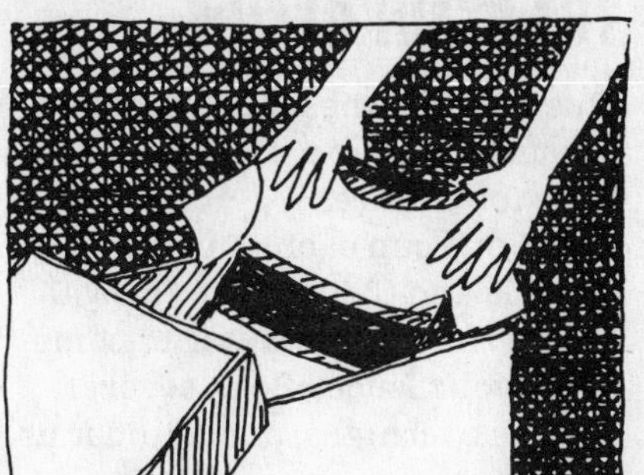

hard-to-come-by items such as pants, new shoes that turn up at a yard sale, or coats. I also try to choose items that are likely to be in style in a few years, such as Lee cords and crew-neck sweaters.

I store coats on a rack and shoes in separate boxes.

A used-clothing system such as this saves time, space, and money. I can "file" and retrieve clothes with a minimum of time. I never purchase new clothes or excess used clothes because I know exactly what I have. Because I don't keep more than I need, my system takes up a minimum of space.

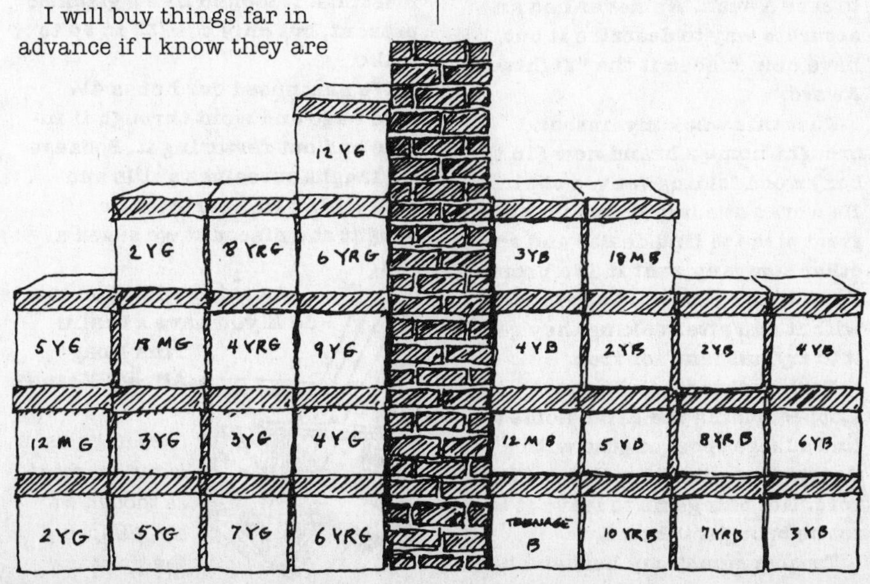

THE STAIN RECIPE

This recipe came from an expert, a woman who ran a used-clothing store for children.

Add one cup each of powdered Cascade and Clorox II to five gallons of the hottest water to come out of your faucet. Soak several articles overnight, and launder as usual.

This procedure will remove about 90% of the stains that do not come out with normal laundering. I do not use this recipe for delicate fabrics, or fabrics that are not color-fast. It is particularly good for removing food stains.

ON-THE-JOB SCROUNGE

Dear Amy and Jim,

We always used to get excited and "pat each other on the back" when we found or did something to save a buck. We never had an accurate way to describe it but have now dubbed it the "Tightwad Award."

Just this week my husband brought home a brand-new (in the box) wood folding canvas chair. He works at a lumber company (a great place to find deals) and another company sent it as a promo item. No one ever did anything with it and after asking they gave it to my husband for free.

Earlier this week Michael stopped during the drive home to find a large spool of cord with flagging tape in the middle of the road. Not being one to leave it to rot he brought it home.

To save money my husband has been making a couple of old-fashioned storm windows from cedar wood (scrounged from old pallets and "trash" at work). He happened to stop by to see a friend at work and noticed a couple of large window frames leaning against the Dumpster. He asked and learned they were going to the dump. So he threw them in the back of the truck and home he went. The other glass he needed came from stock windows at work, which had been ordered but not bought. A few weeks before inventory he asked his boss if he could take them off his hands for $2 each (they were worth $50). He needed three windows. When he went to pay he pulled out $5 and fumbled for several minutes looking for another $1 (knowing he had a $20 in his pocket). The boss, being impatient, said, "Oh, just give me the $5."

We have several wood (cedar) Adirondack chairs that Michael has made from free scraps from work. The only expense was the special screws and bolts. We made chairs for my parents at Christmastime. It looked like a gigantic present, but only cost $3 to $4 to make.

We purchased our house 4½ years ago and went through it inside and out restoring it. Because we taught ourselves skills and everything was bartered or bought at a discount we saved a ton.

Amazing what you can do if you have a brain!
Tina Hoag
Alfred, Maine

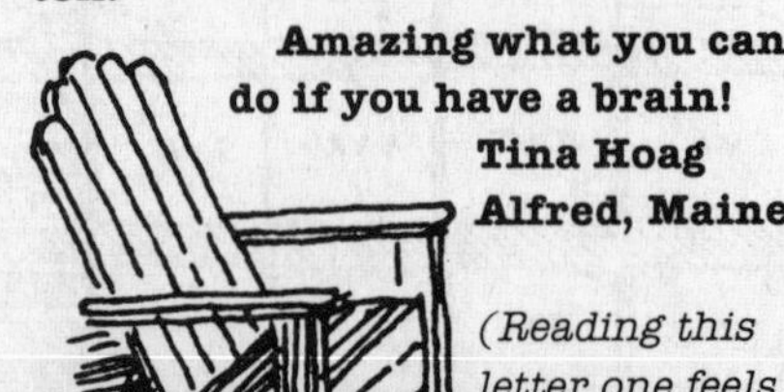

(Reading this letter one feels as though we are glimpsing the tip of

the iceberg at what this couple has learned to do. They combine a knack for scrounging, knowing how to ask if something is available, and acquired skills to save money. Every place of employment provides unique opportunities to scrounge, although we all wish we had his job. FZ)

WRITE THE MANUFACTURER

Writing a large and distant corporation concerning a product problem is similar to a man standing on the beach of a deserted island. When he throws out the bottle with the message inside he does not really expect a reply. If by chance one does come there is cause for celebration.

The first time I tried this I sent a letter to the manufacturers of the Snickers candy bar with a piece of wood taped to it. I had nearly eaten this. Snickers apologized for the "peanut twig" and sent me coupons for two free bags of candy bars.

My second successful attempt occurred this year. We purchased a "Magidoodle" as a Christmas present for our daughter. Within 10 days of normal use the screen was filled with lines resulting from cracks on the inside. I mailed it back to Ideal with a shameless attempt to extract their sympathy. I truthfully reported it was only one of two new Christmas gifts we had given our four children that year. Ideal promptly called me to ask if I would like a new Magidoodle. I maintained that I wanted my money returned. Although the product was not defective it did not deliver the durability one ought to expect from a $17 present. Ideal responded that it was not their policy to issue refunds, but they did send us a brand-new Magidoodle in the box, which we were able to return to the store without receipt.

Many years ago Jim broke a fishing reel spool. He wrote the manufacturer, Garcia Mitchell, and received no response. Six months later, while his ship was out on a cruise he was upset about a different matter. Making use of this anger he sent the president of Garcia Mitchell a "nastygram." He explained that he had already written, received no response, and was going to get rid of all his Garcia Mitchell equipment. A week and a half later he received an entire new reel and a letter of apology.

We are currently using this same strategy to get a response from Sony. We have been unable to get the part to repair our television for 18 months.

To learn who to write to, often you need only to look at the box

your defective product came in. If it does not provide the needed information, there are three sources you should consult. I have the 1990 *World Almanac,* which lists names and addresses of corporations, as well as the names of the company presidents. It suggests Standard and Poor's *Register of Corporations, Directors and Executives.* If you don't know the name of the manufacturer consult the *Thomas Register.* Both of these are available in most libraries.

The almanac also suggests a fairly lengthy list of pointers for writing such letters, such as including pertinent information like your name, address, phone number, dates of purchase, copies of paperwork, etc. They suggest that you do not send "nastygrams." (A lot they know.)

BIRTHDAY SAVINGS

Dear Amy,

• I make sure my charge card doesn't have an annual fee. Why would anyone choose one that does? I charge everything I *have* to buy—birthday presents, clothing, home and garden supplies, etc.—thereby allowing me to earn interest on my money in the bank till the bill comes in.

• There's always extra wallpaper left after finishing a room. I used to save the balance in case I needed to touch up. After many years and many rooms I have *never* needed the paper for this purpose; therefore, I now use the balance for wrapping gifts. I even use the vinyl stuff. This also makes your gift waterproof during inclement weather.

• Yard sales are the *best* places to get ceramic FTD's decorative florist containers (usually 50¢—someone else has already spent big bucks for this). But, it is almost impossible for you to use these again unless you use a styrofoam florist block and are very good at arranging cut flowers. Take it to a florist and tell them to fill it with $5 worth of flowers and deliver it yourself. You just saved $20.

• I bought a Craftsman ratchet wrench for only 10¢ (it was so rusty it didn't crank). I took it to Sears and got a brand new one in the package ($20 value)! Sears will accept your broken or destroyed Craftsman for a new one.

This birthday my dad's getting a brand new Craftsman ratchet (10¢); of course it's wrapped in only the best vinyl wallpaper (0¢). A floral arrangement for his desk at work ($5) that was of course charged on my Visa (earned 6%). A personalized card that I made on my computer (0¢). A chocolate Pepperidge Farm cake (wouldn't you know I clip coupons); I used a 20¢ manufacturer's coupon at a double coupon market ($1.09 after coupon). It's more expensive to buy a cake and frosting mix and bake it. You can be sure I use my birthday candles at *least* twice.

Cathy Levesque-Gilbert
Woonsocket, Rhode Island

(Cathy touches on two important points about credit cards. I am sure she knows this, and I want to be sure everyone else does. You have to charge at least $50 to recoup the 29¢ it costs to send in the bill. This is an excellent strategy for large purchases or combining many small ones. FZ)

'TIS THE SEASON . . .

. . . to do your Christmas shopping. It is the height of the yard sale season. By shopping now and hoarding in a very disciplined way you can save hundreds of dollars at Christmastime, as well as for birthdays.

Toys can be found in practically brand-new condition. Young entrepreneurs will often sell their wares for pennies, much to the dismay of the parents who bought them.

And don't overlook acceptable used presents for adults, such as collectibles, potential joke presents, or a special old book.

ELECTRICAL TRIVIA

Each month we receive an electric bill that shows the lump sum of our usage. Unlike other bills, like groceries, we do not get a breakdown, which might be of help in showing us where we need to make cutbacks. In short, we feel like we're "in the dark."

As someone who is not knowledgeable about such things, it was helpful for me to receive a free brochure from the electric company, which showed a breakdown of the average costs of using most household appliances. In looking this over I noticed that some of my appliances did not have the same wattage as their example. However, you can calculate the costs for yourself:

If you use 1,000 watts for 1 hour you've used 1 kilowatt-hour (or KWH). Your utility bill tells how much you pay for a KWH in your area. If you pay 10¢ per KWH hour you can run a 1,000-watt appliance for 60 minutes for 10¢. A 100-watt light bulb costs 1¢ per hour to run. A low-wattage appliance, like a sewing machine, might cost 1/10th of a penny to run per hour.

Appliances have the wattage marked on the bottom. And they don't all have nice easy numbers, so you need the equation:

$$\frac{\text{Watts} \times \text{Hours}}{1{,}000} = \text{KWH}$$

Example: a 1,400-watt hair dryer used for 2 hours a month:

$$\frac{1{,}400 \times 2}{1{,}000} = 2.8 \text{ KWH}$$

If your local KWH rate is 9¢:

$$2.8 \times 9¢ = 25.2¢$$

Appliances that go on and off to maintain a uniform temperature, such as an oven, water heater or freezer are somewhat harder to calculate. This has been something of a frustration for me as I would like to calculate how much energy I am using in baking, for instance . . . or how much it costs to take a shower. The challenge becomes greater with appliances such as ovens, which have several temperatures. In theory, you can calculate it. You would have to peer through your oven window and time how many minutes the oven coils come on during an

hour when it's set on 350°, for instance. In these cases I revert back to the brochure and trust their estimates.

If you know how to calculate energy usage you can also roughly figure comparisons between appliances.

If you're boiling water, boil the precise amount you need. If you have a hot-water kettle you can do this by pouring the premeasured amount in with a funnel.

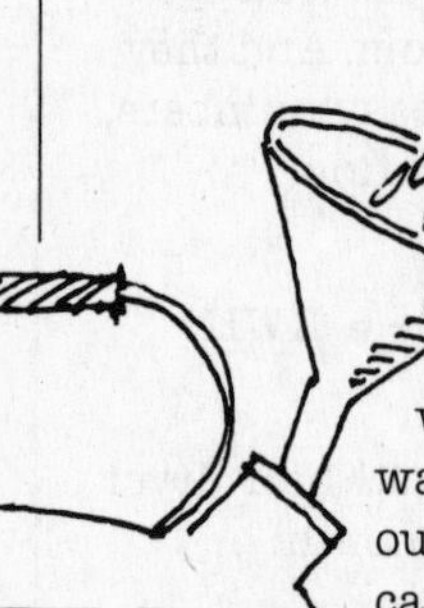

Don't heat water in the microwave. According to our calculations it can require 10% more electricity than boiling water on the stove.

When it comes to cooking solid foods, small appliances are the clear winner. In comparing a couple of recipes (scalloped potatoes and meatloaf) that could be prepared in an oven, a microwave, and a slow cooker, the slow cooker used about one fourth of the energy of the oven, and the microwave used one fifth the energy of the oven. In comparing cooking times of some other foods, the microwave uses less than one tenth of the energy of a conventional oven.

If you're baking something as well as using the range, put your pot on the surface unit that has the oven vent. The escaping heat will help warm the food. Not all ovens have these types of vents, but if yours does, take advantage of it.

Save electricity by turning the oven off 10 minutes early. Use the same idea for your dryer. Switch it to "air" during the last 15 minutes to take advantage of the hot air built up inside the dryer.

If you have a coffee maker or perker, keep a thermos or insulated carafe nearby. Pour the surplus into it instead of having the coffee maker rewarm the extra. Boil a large pot of water once, and store in the thermos, instead of boiling water several times in a day.

Here are a few more obscure bits of electrical trivia:

Set your water heater to 125°. It needs to be this hot to kill any bacteria in the water tank. Many water heaters are automatically set at 140°. If you don't have a hot water timer on it, do as Karen Godian of Phenix City, Alabama, does—turn the water heater off manually by throwing the switch on your circuit box.

Don't drain the hot water from your tub until it's cold. The heat will warm the bathroom. (Do not leave water in the tub if you have

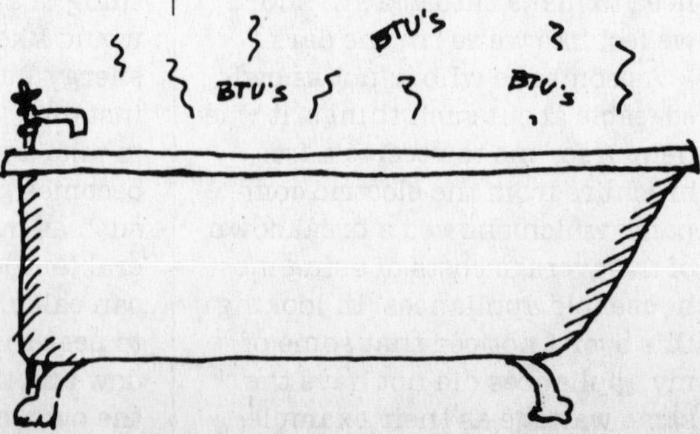

young children.) John Biel of Chesterfield, Ohio, sent me his impressive calculations to show that the equivalent to heat the bathroom with electricity would be worth about 35¢.

One reader wrote of a device called "Extra-Heat" made by Deflecto-o Corp., of Indianapolis, Indiana. It can be purchased for about $6 from a hardware store. It is installed in the dryer duct between the dryer and the outside vent. During cold weather the dryer heat can be diverted indoors. When the dryer is running it produces enough heat to keep a 30′ × 24′ room warm. They've used theirs for nine years, and have been very pleased with it. These devices are generally recommended for electric dryers only.

Low-flow shower heads are great energy savers. Not only do they use less water, but they also have an on/off switch so that you can turn off the water when lathering. Many electric companies offer these free as a part of their energy conservation program.

Use a 3-minute sand timer in your shower. Most people can finish in 6 minutes. Also use the timer to make sure your kids brush their teeth for 3 minutes. You can buy a timer specifically for the shower, with a suction cup, so that it sticks to the shower wall, from Coast Molding Inc., 7965 Dunbrook Road, Suite A, San Diego, CA 92126. Send a $4.95 check or money order. OR just get a regular timer and set it on the shower shelf.

Jim Spaulding of Northfield, Massachusetts, has installed a storage tank in the kitchen near the wood stove, where the temperature is often 80 degrees. The water is 40 degrees when it enters the house, and is prewarmed before it goes to the hot water tank.

In some areas of the country the power company offers a Time of Usage plan. The electrical rates are cheaper during off-peak hours. Here in Maine you have to use a very large amount of electricity to get the TOU plan . . . for example if you heat with electricity. I was unable to learn how the plans vary in different parts of the country, but readers have indicated they save as much a 40%.

HOME LITE

Dear Amy,

Today all of the margarine brands have added a reduced-fat product—⅓ less fat or "lite."

Instead I take a pound of regular margarine . . . usually store brand or whatever is on sale. After softening it slightly I gradually add skim milk as I beat it with my electric mixer. Adding the milk slowly, I can add about ⅓ cup of milk to a pound of margarine. The result is a light spreadable product that has increased in quantity by 50%, stays soft in the refrigerator, tastes the same, and has fewer calories.

Francis Perry
Troy, Maine

(If you prefer soft margarine, about three minutes of effort can save over $1. FZ)

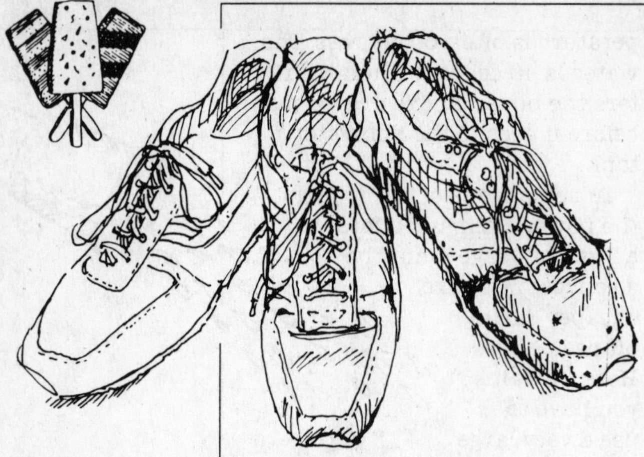

THE THREE-YEAR SNEAKER PLAN

I own three pair of sneakers—this year's sneakers, last year's sneakers, and the year before's sneakers.

The days that I plan to see anybody at all I wear this year's sneakers, such as when a reporter comes for an interview when I go to the women's quilting meeting at the church, or when I go shopping.

Most days I wear last year's sneakers. The soles have begun to separate from the uppers, and cracks in the suede reveal the colors of the socks I have chosen to wear that day. The purpose of wearing last year's sneakers this year is to keep this year's sneakers looking as good as possible well into next year.

When I garden, mow the lawn, paint the house, or do other very dirty work I wear the year before's sneakers. Not only do these sneakers have the cracks and sole separations but they are marked by paint splatters, grass stains, and garden dirt. The purpose of wearing the year before's sneakers is to keep last year's sneakers looking as good as possible well into next year.

My three-year sneaker plan ensures that I always have presentable footwear. I am able to purchase only one new pair of sneakers per year at a cost of $15 . . . $10 if I find a good sale.

When I buy new sneakers they become this year's sneakers, this year's sneakers become last year's sneakers, last year's sneakers become the year before's sneakers, and the year before's sneakers become history.

I have a similar blue jean plan . . . this year's blue jeans, last year's blue jeans, and the year before's blue jeans . . .

RAZOR EXTENDER

Dear Amy,

Here's how you can make a double-edge razor blade last longer:

a. Place the razor blade into a straight-sided drinking glass.

b. Apply finger pressure in the center of the blade.

c. With constant pressure move the blade side to side against the glass.

d. Do this ten times, then flip the blade over and do the reverse side.

Philip L. Masion
Seattle, Washington

BATTERY IDEAS

Dear Amy,

Many of your readers might not be aware of Radio Shack's generosity. At no charge, Radio Shack will give you a one-year battery card. Each month you can get one free battery. If your spouse gets one you can get 24 free batteries a year.

Deanna Rhoades
Auburn, Maine

(This is fine as long as you are aware that they offer this so that you will buy more of their merchandise. Be disciplined and stop only for the battery.

Because of the disposability factor I still prefer rechargeable batteries. FZ)

MARKER PALETTE

Dear Amy,

Take an old block of wood and drill holes in it to permanently secure the caps to children's

Magic Markers . . . transforming the block of wood into an artist's palette of sorts. Your children will not chew on the caps, lose the caps, or forget to put the caps back on. They just pull out the marker when they want to use one, and replace it when through. The markers don't dry out as quickly.

Suzanne Gage
Lincoln, Nebraska

REJUVENATING SECONDHAND TOYS

You might be a parent looking to fill in around the edges at Christmas, or a grandparent filling a toy box in anticipation of visiting grandchildren. Get it out of your heads that there is anything wrong with secondhand toys. You'll be way ahead of the game if your children (or grandchildren) become accustomed to them while still young.

Stores charge fantastic prices for a brand-new hunk of plastic. It hurts when that new toy is broken within a week, and you'll breathe a sigh of relief when a toy that was purchased for 25¢ becomes broken.

By the time any kid reaches kindergarten he'll be given 10 times his weight in toys. If the toys are not "reowned" they will take up space at the landfill. Meanwhile toy manufacturers use more resources to make and transport excessively packaged new toys. So if you're really just pinching pennies you can also claim environmental awareness.

If you're a dutiful tightwad you have been picking up "like new"

toys. But also develop an eagle eye for toys with rejuvenation possibilities. These items are overlooked by those with a lack of vision and, therefore, are your best buys.

- Fisher-Price toys are remarkably rugged, but they tend to show their wear as the stickers become soiled. These can be completely removed with nail polish remover or rubber cement thinner (always test first). The toys can be left plain or if you are very creative you can make new stickers. Wash toys with warm soapy water and a toothbrush. Scuff marks on plastic can be removed with scouring powder. An emery board or fine sandpaper will remove rough spots. If they are missing parts and the price is very cheap, take a chance. You may turn up what you need at another yard sale. (I got a record player at one and a bag of records at another.) If you do this you may have to hang on to the toy until next year.
- Wooden toys have great repair possibilities. I brought home a doll's high chair that was broken and in pieces. Jim fabricated new pieces out of an old croquet mallet handle with stripes sanded off. He then glued it all back together and refinished it. Shortly thereafter we saw an identical one in a secondhand shop for $18. Mine came from an interesting-looking trash pile.
- Plastic has an interesting property in that it can be screwed to a piece of wood. Therefore, a new wooden piece can be fabricated to replace or reinforce a broken one.
- Often game boxes are beat up even when the contents are new. These can be recovered with paper and rubber cement, or contact paper. I rejuvenated a Spirograph with new pens (on sale) and new paper.

• I generally avoid stuffed animals, because I know of no way to make worn ones look new. If it looks pretty good it can be dressed up with a new ribbon around the neck or other accessories.

• Metal wagons and metal Tonka trucks can be steel wooled and repainted with Rust-Oleum.

• A used bike comes a long way with a new paint job. If you consider doing a bike for a girl be aware that finding pink and lavender spray paints is just about impossible. You can add pinstripes and new accessories. Since this jacks up the price of my bargain I try to make these instead. I have made streamers and baskets. Colored ribbons woven into the spokes gives it a jazzy look.

• A poster with frayed edges can be trimmed with an X-Acto or utility knife. (Use a brand-new blade for best results.) It can also be ironed. (Again, test first.)

• My final suggestion is a long shot. Sometimes two broken toys can be combined to make one good one. I brought home a doll stroller that turned out to be irreparable. Before we threw it out I came across another. Between the two we were able to make a complete stroller.

When you take a chance on a toy in need of rejuvenation you should pay next to nothing for it. You may not be able to salvage your bargain. Try to use materials and paints you already have. If you buy new materials or tools, consider whether you will have other uses for them in the future. If you are a tightwad of extraordinary resourcefulness you will about 99% of the time.

ALTERNATIVE GLIDER

Here's a simple glider you can add to your bag of tightwad tricks to razzle-dazzle your child, niece or nephew, grandchild, or child of a visiting friend.

Fold any piece of paper on an angle as shown.

Fold up the folded edge about ½ inch, two times.

Curl the folded edge on the edge of a counter.

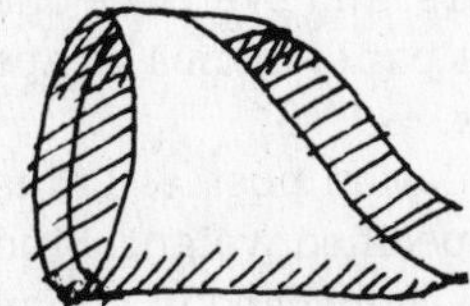

Tuck the ends securely together. Tape is optional.

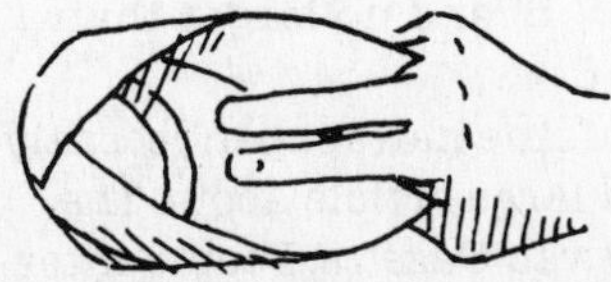

To fly this glider hold as shown, flip your wrist, and release.

POSTCARD POINTERS

I have learned to always keep a batch of postcards or 19¢ stamps around. Obviously, this saves a dime whenever I have to mail a short message.

If I need a speedy reply from someone who lives out of state, I usually cannot count on them writing me back quickly or at all. Therefore, rather than making a long-distance phone call, I send them a postcard in an envelope. The postcard is stamped and addressed back to me. I write the question on the card and write out the possible answers with boxes for them to check off. Works every time.

One reader (who did not want her name in print) sent me some Christmas postcards she had made from last year's Christmas cards. This saves on the cost of postage as well as Christmas cards. Just cut the "word side" off. Her personalized note was written in red and green marker.

You can make your own postcard out of any stiff card. Tightwads have sent them made out of file folders, and even one out of the front panel from a Grape-Nuts box.

A regulation postcard must meet a specified weight. Find a business reply card in a magazine, feel the thickness, and pick something a little heavier to be sure. It must be no smaller than 3½″ × 5″ and no larger than 4″ × 6¼″.

A Maine newspaper recently ran a large article about *The Tightwad Gazette.* People interested in a free issue were asked to send a 29¢ stamp. Of the 1,000 or more requests, only two were sent with a postcard. One stamp was hopelessly stuck on, but the other individual, Joyce Leo of Westbrook, Maine, neatly wrapped the stamp in plastic wrap and taped it to the postcard. Bravo!

THE PLASTIC JUG IRRIGATION SYSTEM

For many years we didn't own a lawn sprinkler. Before buying our first home we always rented and were too cheap to pay for the water to keep the landlord's grass green. Had we spotted one at a yard sale we would have bought it, but the purchase eluded us for years.

As a result, on hot days our children had been deprived and their backyard water fun had been limited to the spray of a garden hose dangling over a clothesline.

One summer my desire to remedy this deprivation blended with my mission to recycle plastic jugs. I conceived the plastic jug irrigation system. I had envisioned it as a lying down or prone model but my husband and father-in-law, the pair to whom I had delegated the engineering, got ambitious and constructed this design with a platform.

The first task was to find a jug with a neck size large enough to fit over the threaded end of a garden hose. A well-rinsed gallon bleach jug fit this criterion. A cut piece of old rubber-glove finger slipped over the end of the hose improved the "snugnicity."

Jim drilled a dozen holes in the bottom of the jug with a 3/32″ drill bit. The platform was constructed of 100% scrap wood. It needed to be 3 inches high so that the hose would have ample bending room.

A simpler version would be a prone jug with holes on the side.

Once it was assembled we ceremoniously turned on the spigot and waited with anticipation as the water level rose to the top and . . . TAH DAH!

Our wonderfully outrageous plastic jug sprinkler shot water jets heavenward in a seven-foot arched exuberance. (Your arched exuberance may vary depending on your water pressure.)

If this project exceeds your capabilities write to us. We have a few prone models available (rubber glove finger included). Send $19.95, plus $4.00 shipping and handling. Please allow six weeks for delivery. Offer good while supplies last.

A "BY THE GALLON" NONNUTRITIOUS COLD BEVERAGE COMPARISON

These figures are based on average prices of beverage type from a large chain grocery store, movie theater, and fast-food chain in our area. The prices were computed up to what the beverage would cost if purchased in gallon quantities.

Solar iced tea is made by hanging six tea bags in a gallon jug of water. Cover and set in the hot sun until it reaches the desired strength. Sweeten or add lemon to taste.

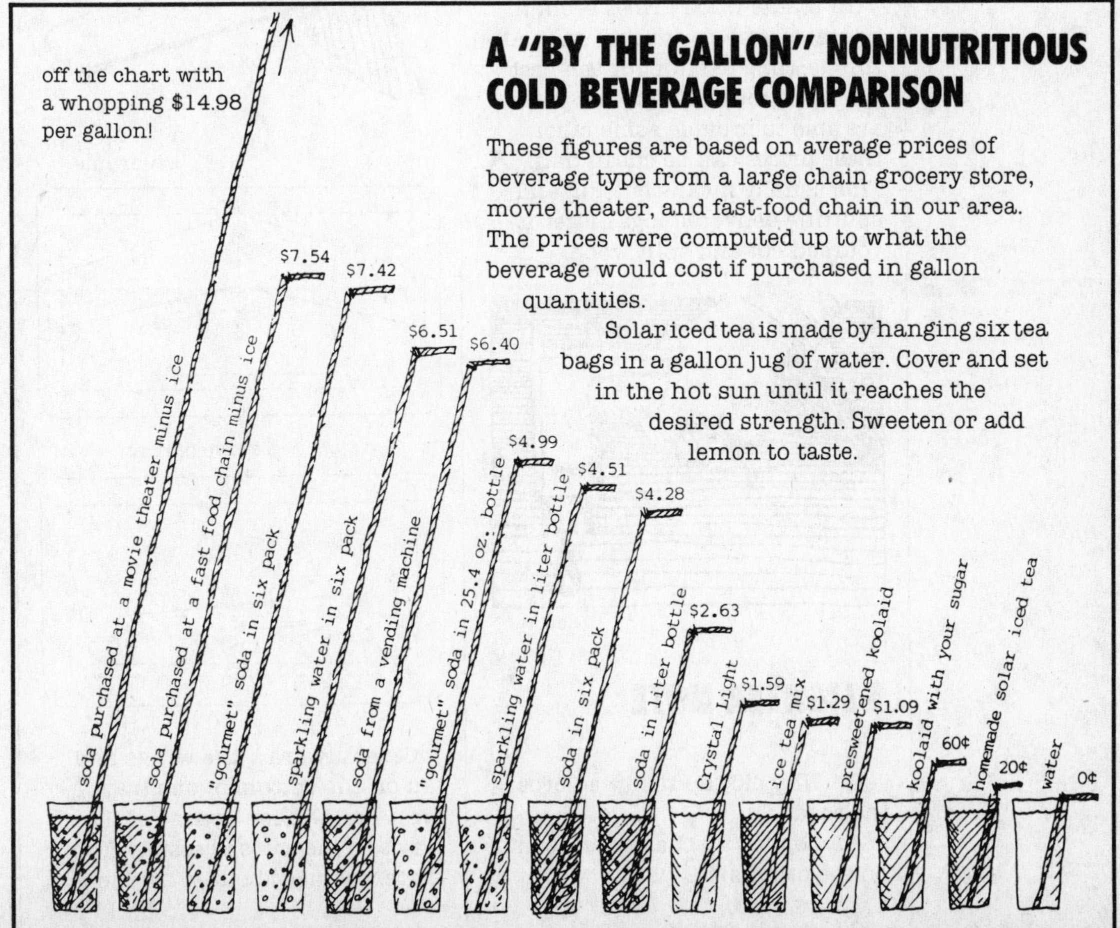

THINK HEAT

In our area heating oil prices drop more than 20¢ off-season. The dealers I spoke to had a difference of opinion as to when prices would hit bottom. It should occur sometime between July and early September. A summer fill-up of a 275-gallon tank can save as much as $55. Plan your cash flow to take advantage of this bargain.

Guessing exactly when to buy can be as tricky as playing the stock market. You will have to monitor prices for many weeks. What you should not do is get your first fill-up in November.

In Maine wood prices seem to be stable year-round, but as in all things, time to shop for the best price can mean savings. If you are able to provide some labor, these prices can be cut in half. This usually means cutting and splitting delivered logs or get-it-yourself cut and split wood.

A LIGHTER NOTE

Q. Why did the tightwad cross the road?

A. To pick up the deposit can on the other side.

THE MEAT TRAY GLIDER

To make this glider you will need two styrofoam meat trays. I used a 14¾″ × 8″ tray. The tray needs to be of the type that is ¼″ thick. You will also need a very sharp utility knife or X-Acto knife. The plans below are drawn to ¼ scale.

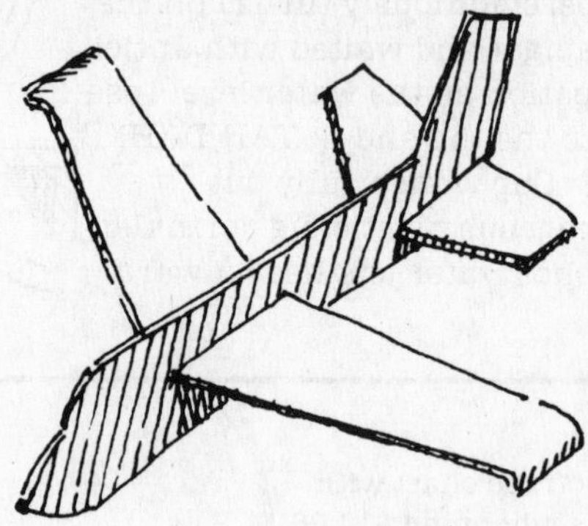

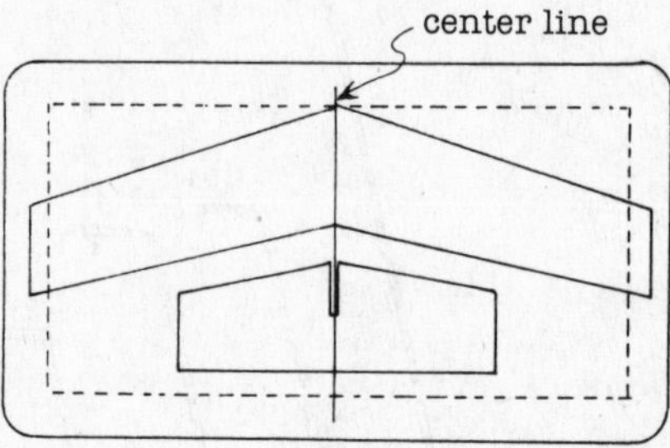

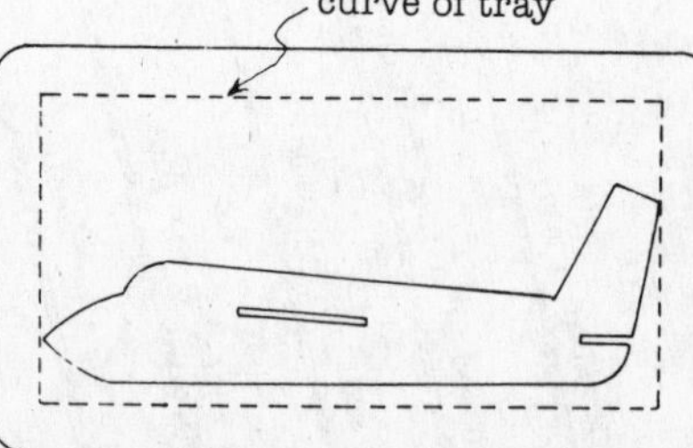

Carefully draw the wings and tail on the bottom of one tray. First find the center line of the tray and measure precisely from there. Include about ½″ of the

curve of the tray when planning the wings. This curve will give the glider lift. Cut all slots to match the precise thickness of the tray for a snug fit.

Draw and cut the body from the second tray and assemble.

The glider will need paper clips or a small nail in the nose to weigh down the front and help it fly level. If the glider still tends to arch up move the wings back farther.

To decrease the drag and further improve the glider's ability to fly, taper the front and back edges of the wing and tail with a knife or emery board. You can also warm the wing under warm water and bend up slightly on the center line. This will also help it fly straight.

A READER QUESTION

Dear Amy,

Would you please comment on Amway products? We have a friend who is trying to "save us a lot of money" by using the concentrated soaps and other products that he sells. I know there are other companies like Amway with the same claims. Do they really save money or is it a scam?

Nancy Schudalla
Boulder, Colorado

Dear Nancy,

No, it is not a scam, and you may or may not save money.

I have been familiar with Amway for over 20 years. Several friends, family members, and even a man I dated sold it.

One of Amway's good points is that its cleaning products are biodegradable and concentrated . . . two features that make them environmentally friendly. Another feature some people find attractive is that buying from Amway will probably save you time, since the products are delivered directly to you.

Because many of Amway's products are concentrated they are hard to compare in price to more familiar nonconcentrated products. However, about a year ago we did a cost comparison of several cleaning products. We found that the Amway products were generally cheaper than name-brand products, but that Amway could not compete in price with products that are on sale, purchased with a coupon, or that offer rebates.

I am not familiar enough with Amway products to comment on their quality, although my impression is that they tend to be good. I have heard more than one individual complain that they have a skin reaction to the laundry detergent, while the majority of people use it without problem. Also Consumer Reports *compared Amway's dishwashing liquid with name brands and found it about twice as expensive to use.*

Amway has now branched out into other products, like name-brand clothing, electronic goods, and food. As I cruised through their thick catalog with glossy, color photos, I noted that many of these items are things I would typically try to buy used, or in the case of the convenience foods, I would not buy at all.

In addition to Amway, Shaklee, and similar organizations, a number of buying clubs, like Consumer Buyline, have been making an appearance. Some of these other organizations charge a membership fee. In these

cases you have to calculate if your potential savings would justify the fee. Consumer Buyline guarantees to beat supermarket prices on food, with certain limitations. If you buy all your food from one source and don't like to watch prices, it may save money. But these organizations are not a good deal if you compare to buying food at several sources, making one trip to each place per month to pick up bargains.

As a general rule, no one source of goods has the lowest price on everything. You will always save the most money by diversifying. In keeping with this strategy, you'll want to consider Amway a possible source. When you plan a purchase, shop around for the rock-bottom price and then give your Amway distributor a call.

ENERGY SAVER?

Dear Amy,

I come from a long line of tightwads. My grandmother, an immigrant, took the light bulb out of her fridge because no one could convince her it wasn't on when the fridge door was shut.

Susan Day
Gloucester, Massachusetts

WEARERS BEWARE

Dear Amy,

Someone wrote asking about how to save on contact lens solutions. Contact lenses are not something to be tightwad about. Over the past several years I've treated countless serious eye infections caused by improper contact lens care. I've seen firsthand, people who have suffered permanent vision loss because they took shortcuts for the sake of saving a few dollars. If you want to save money on contact lenses wear glasses instead.

Toni Powell
Tacoma, Washington

(This letter went on to discuss contact lens care and potential problems at length. Use brands that your physician recommends, and follow directions precisely. Generics or name brands purchased with a coupon from a discount drugstore will yield the best savings. FZ)

MUSIC REQUEST

Dear Amy,

When my 16-year-old stepdaughter gave me her birthday list, she had listed more than 20 cassette tapes from her favorite music groups. Instead of buying them, I called a local radio station once or twice a day to request her favorite songs and then taped them. She got all her favorites, and all it cost was a few minutes a day and 50¢ for the tape (I bought top-quality cassette tapes at a clearance sale and paid $1.50 for three).

Kimberly Hill
Warren, Michigan

(After printing this idea in the newsletter many readers wrote that they thought the practice was illegal. I spent countless hours researching and consulting with the most expert sources in the country but was unable to come to any conclusion. There is no law that specifically addresses taping from the radio for personal use and it appears to fall under a fuzzy gray area of the copyright law called "fair use." Taping in from the radio for any business purpose is clearly illegal. FZ)

QUICKIE STREAMERS

As happens so often, I did something recently that struck me as normal and boring, and struck others as brilliant. When I made streamers for Jamie's seventh birthday party, I was surprised at how many staffers and mothers of guests had not seen these before.

My homemade streamers are quick to make, and only require 1½ sheets of 8½" × 11" paper to make a streamer that will stretch across a room.

The key to good party decorating is how much you do . . . not how perfectly you do it. Therefore you (or your kids), can work very quickly and use colored scrap paper, such as the notices the school sends home with your kids.

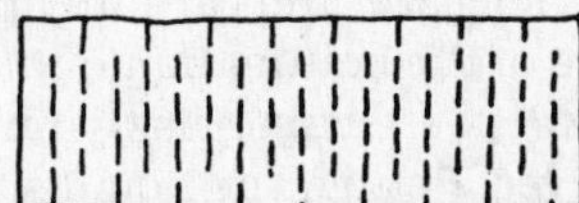

Cut one of the sheets of paper in half the long way. Cut the paper as shown below, leaving ¼" to ½" between cuts. Staple the end of this paper to the next one to make a long streamer.

When you stretch this paper it makes a streamer that looks like this:

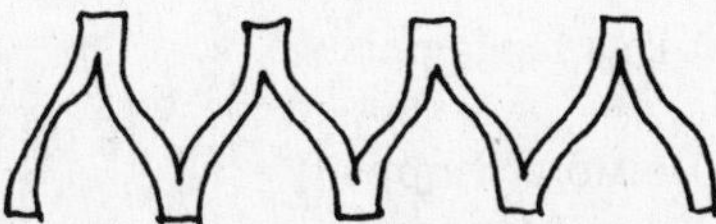

If you twist it, it looks like this:

You can make a more dazzling streamer (that uses up more paper) using the same idea, except you fold your half sheet of paper before cutting it:

When you stretch it out, the streamer looks like this:

AUGUST BARGAINS

Sylvia Porter's Money Book offers a calendar for bargains. Certain items go on sale during different months of the year.

Good buys for August include: air-conditioners, bathing suits, bedding, camping equipment, new cars, coats, drapes and curtains, fans, furniture, furs, gardening equipment, housewares, lamps, paints, rugs and carpeting, school clothes and supplies, tires, and towels.

Most of these items have other months when they typically go on sale. School supplies go on sale again in October. During one of these months you should buy enough to get you through the school year.

HOMEMADE WORCESTERSHIRE SAUCE

In response to a reader request, I asked if any readers had a recipe for worcestershire sauce.

We spent a good deal of time testing the recipes sent in, and now have several jugs in the refrigerator . . . a 10-year supply for us. Because of the required purchase of things many of us might not normally stock, because of the effort involved, and because most people use it in small quantities the cost savings was not significant. In some cases the homemade version was more expensive than commercial brands.

The best recipe, sent in by Edith Hallet of Brownburg, Indiana, is only slightly cheaper than commercial brands. Using her recipe we substituted ground spices for whole ones, substituted a few ingredients, and came up with an almost-as-good facsimile that costs about 25% of the commercial brands.

Original Worcestershire Sauce

Tie loosely in a cloth:

1 onion, chopped
3 Tbsp mustard seed
½ tsp red pepper pod
2 garlic cloves, crushed
1 tsp peppercorns
½ tsp cracked ginger
1 inch cinnamon bark
1 tsp whole cloves
½ tsp cardamom seeds

Simmer spices in a large, heavy pan with:

2 cups vinegar
½ cup molasses
½ cup soy sauce
¼ cup tamarind pulp or
6 Tbsp lemon

Mix in a cup and add:

3 Tbsp salt
½ tsp curry powder
1 anchovy, mashed
½ cup water

While spices are boiling, caramelize ½ cup sugar by putting the sugar in a heavy skillet and stirring over high heat. Move sugar back and forth as it starts to melt and brown. Lower heat. Move sugar continuously and keep chopping at it, breaking the lumps until it is almost black and soupy, not burned.

Take the spice bag from the sauce, squeeze, and carefully pour a little of the boiling liquid into the skillet, stirring briskly until dissolved. Return the liquid sugar to the large pan. Boil briefly. Pour into a bowl, replace the spice bag in the sauce. Place in a covered container in the refrigerator for 2 weeks. Stir from time to time. Strain and bottle. Keep refrigerated or process.

The Cheaper Version

Put in a large pot:

1 onion, chopped
(or 3 tsp onion powder)
3 tsp ground mustard
½ tsp red pepper
2 cloves garlic, crushed
(or ½ tsp garlic powder)
¼ tsp ground cinnamon
¼ tsp ground ginger

Add:

2 cups vinegar
½ cup molasses
½ cup soy sauce
6 Tbsp lemon juice

Mix together and add to pot:

3 Tbsp salt
½ tsp curry powder
½ cup water

Bring to boil and simmer ½ hour. While spices are boiling, caramelize ½ cup sugar using procedure given in original recipe. Cook another ½ hour. Store in refrigerator. Flavor will improve with age.

CHECKING UP ON CHECKING FEES

One of the ways that being poor costs money is when you have to pay a service charge on your checking account because you keep your balance below $500.

One of the ways that being stupid costs money is when you have to pay a service charge on your checking account because you keep the balance below $500 ... and you have money in your savings account.

Banks typically impose service charges on customers who allow their checking accounts to fall below $500. Robin Bullard Carter, a personal money management counselor, says her research indicates that these fees average about $10 per month for maintenance fees and/or per-check fees.

At $10, these fees would add up to $120 per year. So if your average balance is hovering just below $500, you are effectively paying 24% interest ... even more if your checking account balance tends to be lower.

So if you have money sitting around in a savings account drawing 4% to 5% interest, the smartest thing to do is to move enough of it to your checking account to boost it above your bank's minimum balance.

I would also add that at many credit unions there are no checking fees. Getting into a credit union may be worthwhile to you if you can't keep more than the minimum in a checking account.

(For more information on Carter's counseling services, contact her at Moneysense, 17 Graham Ave., Newbury, MA 01951, [508] 465-3282.)

HOMEMADE CRACKERS

This recipe came from *Yankee* magazine. The crackers taste something like Wheat Thins.

3 cups uncooked oatmeal
2 cups unbleached flour
1 cup wheat germ
3 Tbsp sugar
1 tsp salt
¾ cup oil
1 cup water

Mix ingredients and roll out onto two cookie sheets. (I use a plastic tumbler for this.) Sprinkle with salt, lightly roll again to press salt in. Cut into squares or diamonds. (A pizza cutter works well.) Bake at 350°. After 20 minutes begin checking. The outer ones are usually ready first. Remove crackers as they turn golden brown and hard.

THE CHEAP BIRTHDAY PARTY

Three years ago we celebrated Jim's 40th birthday. For lack of a better theme I designed a Cheap Party. (In this case, the word *cheap* is not to be confused with *thrifty.*)

I used household discards to make decorations and wrap. The same theme used for an office party would take advantage of available office waste, such as used computer paper.

All the presents Jim received cost under $1 and were either joke presents, yard sale finds, or homemade. In one case I finally found the time to make the curtains for his office that he had requested and provided the material for six months earlier. I also made up a standard collection of "Good For" coupons, which were all basically useless and funny.

THE CHEAP BIRTHDAY STREAMER

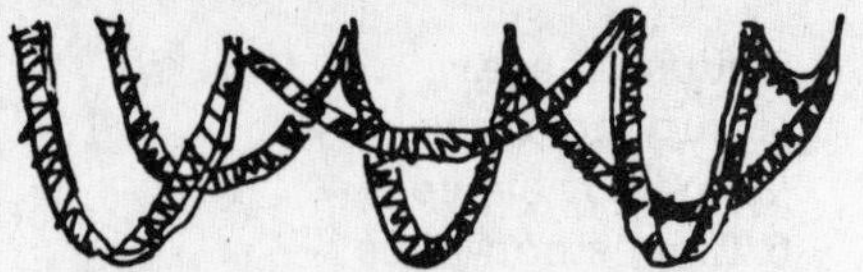

Paper chain made from sale flyer, newspaper, and brown bag . . . hung haphazardly.

THE CHEAP BIRTHDAY CAKE

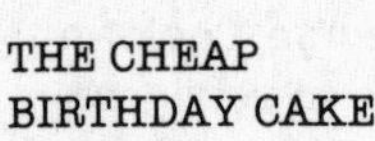

THE CHEAP PARTY HAT

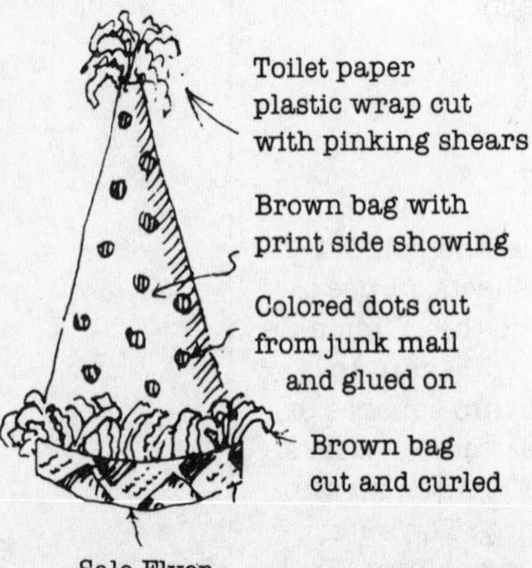

THE CHEAP (AND BEAUTY-FUL) BIRTHDAY DECORATION

THE CHEAP BIRTHDAY PARTY GAG

The Booby Trap Door

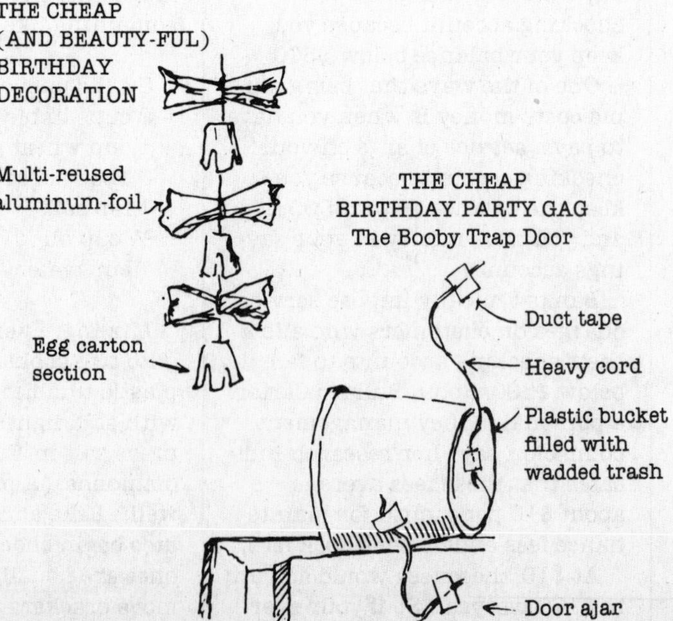

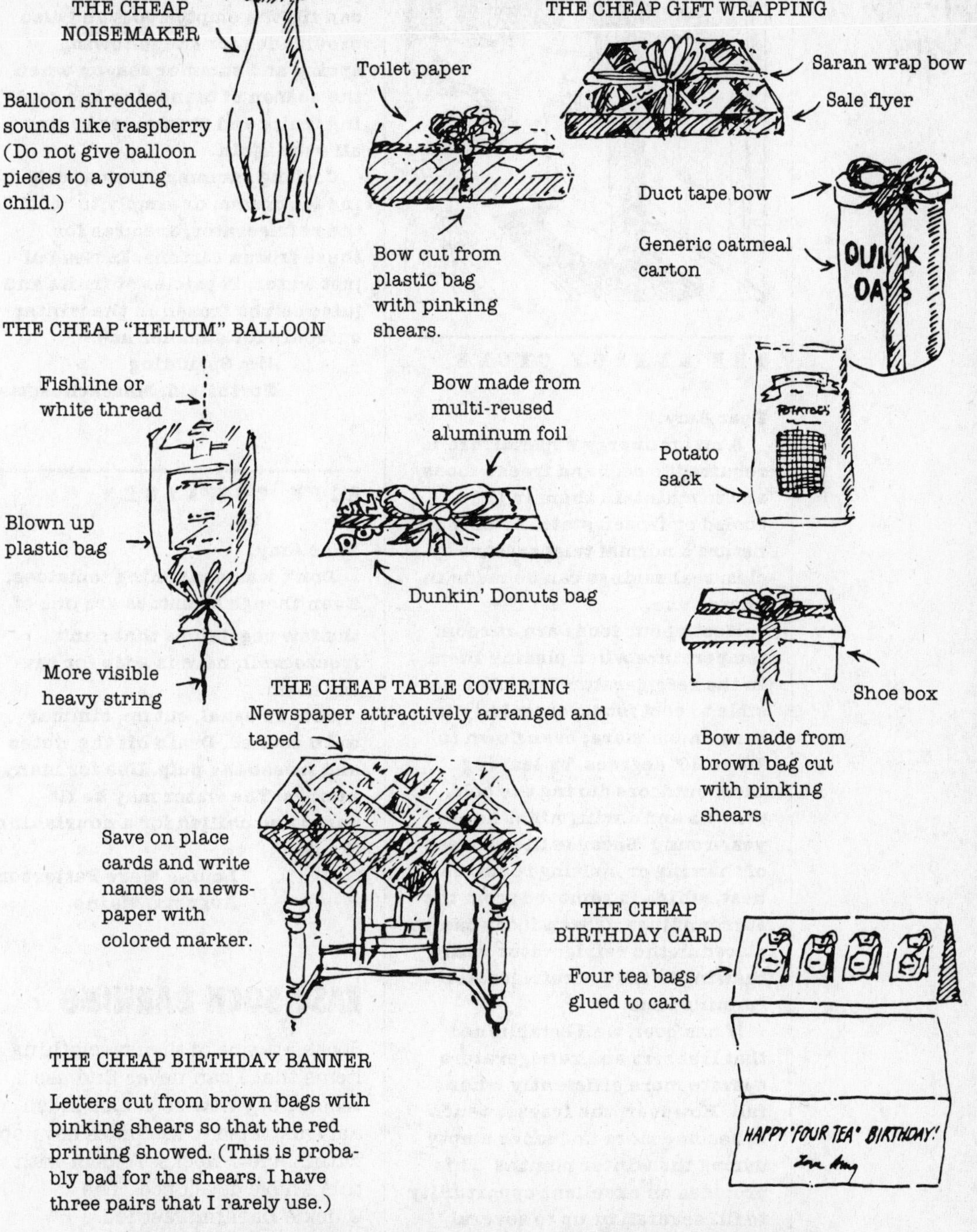

THE CHEAP BIRTHDAY BANNER

Letters cut from brown bags with pinking shears so that the red printing showed. (This is probably bad for the shears. I have three pairs that I rarely use.)

HAPPY BIRTHDAY!

THE ENERGY CYCLE

Dear Amy,

A major energy expenditure is required to cool and freeze foods and to maintain them in that cooled or frozen state. By using nature's normal temperature cycles, real savings can be made in energy use.

Most of our foods are at room temperature when placing them in the refrigerator. It's often possible to cool foods, especially in cans, much more, even down to 20° to 25° degrees, by leaving them outdoors during the cold months and during night hours year-round. Because the process of thawing or melting requires heat, which is removed from the surroundings, frozen foods can be placed in the refrigerator while thawing to reduce refrigerator running time.

If has been well established that freezers and refrigerators operate more efficiently when full. However, the freezer tends to become more and more empty during the winter months. This provides an excellent opportunity to fill several, or up to several dozen, milk or fruit juice cartons (not quite full) and freeze them during the cold winter months. Placed in the freezer, these cartons (sometimes well below zero) can fill the empty spots and also provide ice for the following spring and summer season when the season of blanching and cooling fruits and vegetables begins all over again.

Cooling summer drinks, making ice cream, or simply to "cool" the refrigerator, are uses for these frozen cartons. Instead of just water, Popsicles of fruits and juice can be frozen in the winter outdoors for summer use.

Jim Spaulding
Northfield, Massachusetts

RIPE TOMATOES

Dear Amy,

Don't waste ripening tomatoes. Even though tomatoes are one of the few vegetables that don't freeze well, here is a tip for saving them.

Peel as usual, cut up, simmer until cooked. Drain off the water and freeze the pulp. Use for many recipes. The water may be flavored and chilled for a nourishing drink.

Louise Ware Patterson
Augusta, Maine

EASY SOCK DARNING

Socks are one of the few clothing items that I can never find used. When I buy new socks for kids I am frustrated to see holes develop within a few weeks. To deal with this I have developed "The Quickie Darning Method."

To utilize this method one sock must be sacrificed. The ideal sacrificial sock would be one whose mate disappeared in the dryer

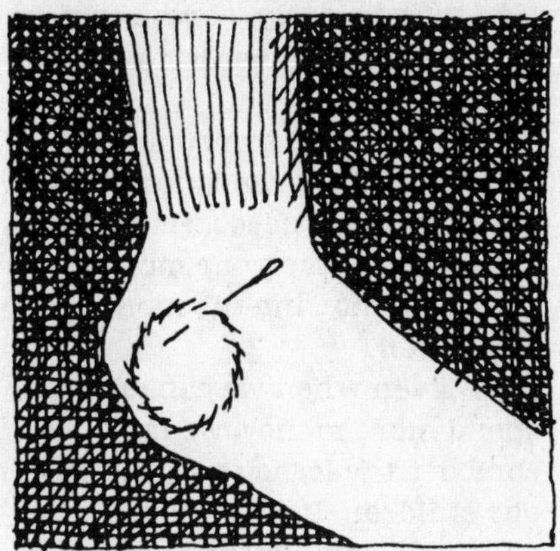

several years ago. (The Dryer Black Hole functions on the same principle as the Bermuda Triangle.)

Cut a circle from an unworn area of the sacrificial sock. The diameter of the circle should be about ¼″ larger than the diameter of the hole to be patched. Use a running stitch to sew the patch in place. Sew around the patch three or four times or until all edges are secure. The process requires only a few minutes.

WHEN YOU DON'T NEED TO BE A TIGHTWAD

It happens. There will probably come a time when you don't need to be a tightwad anymore. The scenario is most frequently played out by a couple who, after decades of pinching pennies, one day finds that the mortgage is paid off, all the kids have completed college, and they've saved a sufficient amount for retirement.

It happens because tightwaddery really does work. But tightwads can be confused as to how to let go of a lifestyle that has brought order and control to their lives and that they have come to enjoy.

The problem is that pressure to spend more increases from all sides. Friends urge you to "lighten up" and buy a sexy car to replace your sensible econobox. Kids' (or grandkids') requests for Sugar Zapper cereal can no longer be squelched with the statement, "We can't afford it." And you start to doubt yourself. You wonder, Does having more money really mean we have to waste it?

The answer is to understand that the tightwad life is not only about spending less . . . it's about spending in a way that reflects your values, and that should not stop if you have a billion dollars. Having more money simply means you can pursue your values in a larger and even more satisfying way.

Note: before abandoning tightwaddery, be sure you have touched all the economic bases. You need sufficient insurance, savings for current emergencies and for all future goals, and no debt whatsoever.

So if you've thought of all that, and still think you don't need to be a tightwad anymore, consider the following: these ideas reflect our values; they may reflect yours, too.

1. Spend in ways that are environmentally sound. Even billionaires need to wash out their Ziploc bags (or at least hire somebody to do it for them). Having surplus income does not grant you the right to be wasteful with the planet's limited resources.

Some environmentally sound

ways to spend money include making long-distance phone calls, hiring a contractor to paint your house, or going out to dinner.

2. If you live in an economically depressed area, buy locally, even if it costs a little more. For example, have a local craftsperson braid a rug for you rather than ordering one from a big mail-order house. This way, you know your money is going where it is needed.

3. Consider charitable giving. Think of it this way: if you're hungry and have a cherry pie, that first slice is very satisfying. The second one tastes good, too. But if you eat the whole pie your enjoyment will diminish with each piece you eat.

Spending all your surplus income on personal gratification can be just as unsatisfying.

I suggest sharing a slice of your pie. You could have a swimming pool put in even though you had previously decided it was a low priority for your family . . . or you could make an anonymous donation to the elderly woman in your community who needs a new water heater.

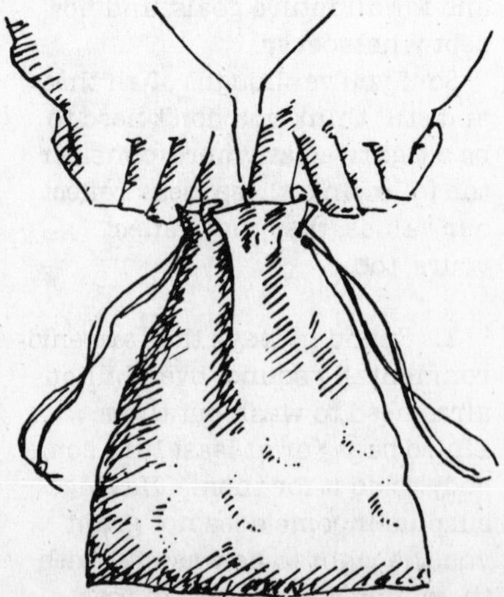

The recipient, someone who has insufficient funds to satisfy the most basic needs, gets maximum value from your money. You feel good knowing the money was spent well.

4. Even when we can afford to spend more money, we must also consider the legacy we pass on to our children. If we raise them in a lifestyle completely free of want, where everything is brand new, store bought, and expensive, we are raising children who know no economic boundaries.

In all likelihood, children raised in frugality will become young adults who spend as wastefully as children who are raised with excess. It's the nature of that stage of life—they are enjoying their first taste of economic freedom: extra money, no goals.

But children of frugality have an advantage. They grew up watching their parents fixing things, making Halloween costumes, and cooking from scratch. Those images were stored in their "mental banks." If needed, the information is there to retrieve in their adult years.

Because Jim and I were raised by thrifty parents, changing economic gears was a natural process for both of us.

5. Consider retiring early. We're conditioned to think that every breadwinner will work into their sixties. If our work creates extra income we raise our standard of living. However, we can choose to live well beneath our means and invest the surplus. When the interest from the investments equals our cost of liv-

ing, we reach financial independence.

This strategy is particularly good for singles or childless couples with a large amount of disposable income, and for people who don't like their jobs.

Even if you can't imagine saving up this much, you can increase your degree of financial independence by paying off all your debts and investing in tools, appliances, and other items that will make your life less expensive.

Once freed from having to earn a living, you can devote your time to doing things you find more enriching. You might choose to volunteer or have a low-paying but satisfying career.

The bottom line: spend money in ways that are consistent with your personal values. Don't let others pressure you into spending according to their values.

Think back to your original objective. In our case, we wanted three things—a large family, a large rural home, and time to enjoy our children and home. Our objective was not to amass the largest bank account possible.

I spend extra income in ways that enhance my original objective of achieving a quality family life. In the summer of 1991 we hired a company to put a new roof on our house. It would have been cheaper to do it ourselves, but it also would have taken an entire summer to accomplish given our current time limitations. So, for us, hiring roofers seemed consistent because it enabled us to spend more free time with our children.

Saving money is the means to an end . . . not the end itself.

The Tightwad Gazette II

Introduction

I know what you're thinking. "*The Tightwad Gazette II* . . . isn't that kind of like *Rocky II*?"

Interpretation: "All of the good ideas were used up in the original work. The sequel gets the leftovers." There are exceptions to this rule: The nine *Little House* books and the three *Godfather* movies come to mind. I believe you'll consider this *Tightwad* sequel an exception, too.

My new book is a compilation of about 80 percent of the articles from the third and fourth years of the *Tightwad Gazette* newsletter; my first book contained articles from the first two years. Although much of the work has the same character, there are a few differences, which resulted from changes in my life and in the outside world.

When I began my newsletter in June 1990, I had no journalism experience. I had a high-school-English background and had written reams of letters to grandmothers. I naïvely believed that if I could find a few thousand subscribers, between what I knew and what they knew we would never run out of ideas. Nine months later I had 1,700 subscribers. Since it was still hard to fill the "reader correspondence" page with good information from the very thin file of letters I received, the material continued to consist mostly of my own ideas, based on my own experience. At this time I was wearing all the hats in running the business. Jim, my husband, still worked for the Navy, and his long commute kept him away for twelve hours a day.

As we neared the close of the first year, the newsletter received extraordinary national publicity. A local reporter sold our story to *Parade* magazine, then we were featured as the sole guests on *Donahue*. At the time our business mushroomed to 40,000 subscribers, I was about to give birth to twins, my fifth and sixth children. Life became chaotic, despite the best efforts of my husband, who retired from the military and immediately stepped in to manage our business. At this point, the operation had a flock of "employees" (any friend or acquaintance who was willing to lend a hand) and was still run from the front parlor of our house. Our yard perpetually resembled a used-car lot.

Toward the end of the second year I was unhappy about the quality of our family life—we were

eating too many macaroni-and-cheese dinners at 8:00 P.M.—and the conditions under which we were operating our business made it difficult to produce my best work. I was fast approaching burnout. One night Jim and I collapsed on the couch, each holding a sleeping baby, and one of us (I don't recall which) said, "We both need a clone."

My clone turned out to be Brad Lemley, the very same writer who had sold our story to *Parade* and the namesake of my youngest son. Brad said the story he wrote about us for *Parade* had influenced him more than any story he had ever written. He became a card-carrying tightwad. We stayed in touch over the following year as an unexpected friendship grew out of the way in which we had changed each other's lives. Brad offered continuing support and encouragement and endless hours of over-the-phone idea-bouncing. Two years ago, he confided that he wanted to quit his newspaper job. He knew I needed help. In order to supplement his other writing, he needed two days of employment a week. I hired him on the spot. Imagine this: A real writer—someone who has written for national magazines and (golly!) has a college education—wants to work for the *Tightwad Gazette!*

Our plan was that Brad would help only with research, editing, and letter reading. I wanted to retain sole responsibility for the creative writing. But then, one day while I was banging my head against a computer screen to come up with a clever headline, he said, "What about 'Chalk Is Cheap'?" It was perfect. Over time our collaborative effort has evolved into a joined-at-the-hip writing style. We literally sit side-by-side, sharing one computer keyboard, often laughing until the tears come. I usually write the basic articles alone, then we refine them together.

When we discussed a potential clone for Jim, a perfect-but-unavailable candidate came to mind: Elaine Briggs, the owner of a small computer store, a friend, and a longtime subscriber. Word of our search traveled through the grapevine. Then one day Elaine appeared on our doorstep, announcing she *was* available and applying for the job. Elaine possesses exceptional business and computer skills, which keep our business running like clockwork. Most important, she brought to the job an unspoken understanding that her job is to make my job easier. With the addition of a capable manager, Jim could really "retire" to the full-time job of managing our household. We now eat real meals at reasonable times. We moved our business out of our front parlor, moving all the employees, mailings, noisy equipment, and the used-car lot to a ranch house four miles away. I still work out of my home office.

In addition to these two clones, we have six more full- and part-time workers. They sort incoming mail, fill orders, send out the monthly mailing, do bookkeeping, run errands, and occasionally offer creative headlines and article ideas. They've become our closest friends and extended family, with whom we've shared tightwad practical jokes, rubber-band shootouts, "pizza Fridays," and ruthless croquet games.

So, getting back to what I said

about sequels, *The Tightwad Gazette* is no longer a one-woman operation. This book has subtle differences that make it even more useful than before. Since I've had more free time to research, I've written a higher number of in-depth articles based on the expert opinions of others.

You'll also find much more participation from readers. For the past two years, I have had enough time to read some of the mountain of reader letters I received during the overload days, and many became the basis for articles. Previously when I asked readers for ideas on a specific subject, I would get only a handful of replies. Now up to 250 people respond when I ask for information. My network of newsletter readers (now about 50,000—not including the huge number of cheapies who read other people's *Gazettes*) is a frugal-ingenuity resource unparalleled anywhere in journalism. I've found that someone out there knows the answer to any tightwaddery question. If I'm wrong about anything, someone out there will let me know.

One feature this book has in common with the first is its "loose" structure. Because the material first appeared in a loosely structured newsletter, trying to shoehorn these articles and illustrations into a highly structured format would result in an organizational nightmare. Even more important, the looser structure makes the *Tightwad* books more readable. Most readers of the first book reported that it was fun to read. One reader offered the most astute observation. She found that this loose structure forced her to read the whole book rather than simply skip to chapters she thought would be relevant. As a result, she gained a broader range of information.

As you read this book, remember that the material first appeared in a newsletter, and that the very purpose of a newsletter is to address a need that is not met by the mainstream media. Traditional financial and consumer writers offer safe, halfway advice: They'll tell you how to feed a family of four for $84 a week (when it can be done for half that amount). The same writers tell you it's becoming increasingly difficult, if not impossible, for families to make ends meet. In fact, by adhering to this halfway advice, many families would not make ends meet. The *Tightwad Gazette* newsletter came about as a reaction to this traditional advice and the widespread belief that, financially speaking, life in the nineties is impossible. I knew that people could achieve the "impossible" with a little discipline and a willingness to do things that mainstream thinkers deem too extreme.

If you do not have difficulty making ends meet, you'll find that some of the material in the book does not apply to you. But you will find fresh ideas for saving money. Even if you do have trouble making ends meet, some of my ideas may seem too radical to you. It was never my intention to write about ideas that were 100 percent acceptable to mainstream America. This book explores the boundaries, and my intent is to present options, not to suggest that every idea is appropriate for everyone.

Finally, this is not only a financial textbook, it is also a celebration of the frugal life. While most

of the articles contain practical information, some are there simply to express what I have found: that tightwaddery is about not hardship and deprivation, but fun and creativity.

A READER'S GUIDE TO *THE TIGHTWAD GAZETTE*

A hardworking math instructor stood before a blackboard, demonstrating how to multiply large numbers. After she completed the third problem, a student raised his hand and said, "I suppose a few kids might need to know that 37 times 79 equals 2,923, that 16 times 81 equals 1,296, and that 46 times 59 equals 2,714, but I don't. I need to know what 83 times 22 equals. You're just not giving me answers that help me."

Obviously, the student didn't understand the instructor's teaching strategy. When she first began teaching multiplication to the class, she had students memorize multiplication tables. When they had mastered those, she proceeded to teach them how to use them to multiply larger numbers.

Because of the infinite number of combinations that could be multiplied, it wasn't practical to have students memorize beyond 12 times 12. Likewise, the teacher could not predict the multiplication answers her students might need to know in the future. So the instructor's purpose was to teach the *process* of multiplying by demonstrating specific examples. Once the students mastered the process, they would be able to solve every multiplication problem they encountered for the rest of their lives.

Teaching people how to save money through creative use of their resources is much like teaching multiplication.

A few problems are common to most people and can be solved with resources that are common to most households. For example, page 93's "Budget Bug Busting" presents seven inexpensive bug killers that can be made of stuff found in any household.

But in most cases, each of us is presented with unique problems, which we must solve with our own unique supply of resources. An example of this is the story on page 118 about how Jim made a sled for our twins using scrap lumber and old skis.

When you multiply the number of possible problems by the number of possible resources, the solutions are infinite.

Like the math instructor, I am from time to time confronted by readers who are frustrated that space was devoted to an idea or article that wasn't useful to them. In many cases, readers fail to see that he or she benefits from learning the process or from having a process they already know reinforced.

For example, when I wrote about making a Frankenstein Halloween mask from dryer-lint mâché, I thought a few readers might attempt to make a Frankenstein Halloween mask from dryer-lint mâché. Some might be inspired to make Halloween masks from other inexpensive materials. Others might be inspired to make other projects from dryer-lint

mâché. Most would learn a larger concept—that wonderful things can be made from the humblest of materials. A few readers, unfortunately, would not see any point in it at all.

The desire for "relevant tips" rather than "process" leads to a common observation among either older or single readers: that there are too many children's articles that "don't apply to me." Elaine, my business manager and an early subscriber, was the first to bring this up.

On the average, 12.9 percent of the total column space has been devoted to ideas relating to children of various ages. A high percentage of my readers have children, so to me this does not seem to be overdoing it.

No periodical is able to hit every reader right between the eyes with every article; that's the nature of publishing. In fact, many of the specific subjects that I write about are not relevant to *my* life. The mail-order prescription-drug article, the storage article, and the inexpensive travel-lodging article are a few of those that are not relevant to me.

But in each of these articles, the process—digging for the least expensive option—*is* relevant to me. And every once in a while I know that the lessons are getting through when a reader takes it upon herself to solve a problem. In a recent letter, Katherine Richardson Kenward of Homewood, Illinois, said she almost wrote to ask me if ground turkey at $1.18 per pound (the best price in her area) was a better deal than whole turkey at 49¢ per pound. But inspired by my many examples of nitpicky calculations, she decided to figure it out herself. She cooked up a whole turkey, deboned it, and weighed the meat. She learned that whole-turkey meat was 82¢ per pound. And she could make broth from the bones to boot.

When I decided to write about frugality, I made a conscious decision to approach the subject in a unique way. Some of my predecessors wrote about frugality as a collection of tips. But, like answers to multiplication problems, random tips are hard to remember and have limited application. Other predecessors wrote about frugality as a philosophy or process. Again, like learning about multiplication, general processes are hard to grasp and retain unless they are taught through specific examples.

So I've always worked for a balance of specific examples and process/philosophy. This way, even if the example isn't useful to every reader, the larger idea is reinforced.

Furthermore, tips alone are boring, as is process alone, but the combination tends to be far more interesting.

Finally: Sometimes, it's surprising to see what turns out to be relevant after all. We ran an article about making a hat by draping and molding sheets of newspaper over a kid's head, winding masking tape around the crown, and crumpling the paper up to form the brim. Elaine (a.k.a. Little Miss It-Doesn't-Relate-to-Me-I'm-Single) was so taken with my daughter's hat that she asked me to make her one, paper plume and all.

THE TIGHTWAD-PER-CAPITA SURVEY

Did you ever wonder if frugality is more acceptable in some parts of the country than in others?

We wondered if that could be figured based on our mailing list. Since our publicity has had an even distribution throughout the country via *Parade* magazine, *Donahue*, and several other national programs and publications, the notion didn't seem far-fetched.

We broke down our mailing list of everyone who had ever subscribed (over 100,000) and compared those numbers to the 1990 census. After a couple of hours of tedious work with a calculator, I came up with figures for how many subscribers we have per 100,000 people in each state.

Obviously, the Maine figure, and perhaps the New Hampshire and Vermont figures, reflects more local media coverage. Aside from that, we are generally more popular in the North than in the South. Beyond that, I don't see an obvious

TIGHTWAD GAZETTE SUBSCRIBERS PER 100,000

Maine	215.05	Rhode Island	50.03	New Mexico	36.36
New Hampshire	86.81	Iowa	49.46	New Jersey	36.15
Vermont	81.90	Ohio	48.08	Tennessee	34.31
Alaska	69.44	Missouri	46.26	Indiana	30.96
Wyoming	66.14	Montana	44.80	South Carolina	30.95
Washington	62.46	Illinois	44.68	Alabama	30.05
Nebraska	59.10	Pennsylvania	44.44	New York	30.03
Delaware	58.38	Georgia	43.80	California	28.67
Wisconsin	58.24	Virginia	41.53	Arkansas	28.50
Connecticut	57.60	North Carolina	40.57	West Virginia	26.54
Oregon	57.11	Maryland	40.00	Kentucky	26.38
Colorado	54.53	Michigan	39.59	Oklahoma	25.02
Minnesota	52.99	Florida	39.51	Louisiana	23.22
Idaho	52.55	Texas	38.57	South Dakota	22.84
Kansas	52.55	North Dakota	38.04	Washington, D.C.	22.74
Utah	52.47	Arizona	37.76	Mississippi	20.83
Massachusetts	51.92	Nevada	36.64	Hawaii	18.68

pattern. Why are we three times more popular in Alaska than in Mississippi? Beats me. Perhaps these figures demonstrate the popularity of *The Tightwad Gazette*, not a state's overall frugality.

In any case, to me by far the most revealing figure is that Washington, D.C., has the third fewest tightwads per 100,000.

POSTAL PRESCRIPTIONS

According to Joe and Dr. Theresa Graedon, who write a syndicated column called "People's Pharmacy," over the last decade prescription-drug prices rose at triple the inflation rate, which made the drug industry the most profitable in the nation.

You can combat these price increases by purchasing drugs through mail-order pharmacies.

Local pharmacies argue that they offer better service, but mail-order pharmacies also keep records of the drugs you have bought from them and have staff pharmacists available to answer questions.

As always, we ask you to compare for yourself. All of these companies will quote prices on the phone. And remember, ask your doctor to write "substitutions permitted" on your prescription so that you can get the generic equivalent. By law, these must be as good as the name brand and are often exactly the same medicine, made by the same company that makes the name brand.

I compared prices of several mail-order pharmacies with a large chain pharmacy in our area.

For the purposes of comparison, I requested the prices of four "maintenance" medications, the sort taken over a long period of time for chronic conditions. These were: Zantac, 150 milligrams, used to treat ulcers; Prozac, 20 milligrams, an antidepressant; Micronase, 5 milligrams, for diabetes; and Tenormin, 50 milligrams, for high blood pressure. All medications compared were in 100-tablet quantities.

Generally, a drug prescribed for a one-time use should be purchased locally, since you probably can't wait a week to receive it through the mail.

Below are prices for the

	Action	AARP	Family	Medi-Mail	America's	Local Chain
Zantac	$123.39	$126.85	$137.40	$138.95	$142.98	$148.21
Prozac	$162.99	$171.35	$182.97	$180.95	$187.98	$209.56
Micronase	$ 41.39	$ 41.60	$ 42.86*	$ 43.95	$ 50.00	$ 50.46
Tenormin	$ 73.39*	$ 69.95*	$ 75.24*	$ 76.95*	$ 77.79*	$ 78.69*

pharmacies I compared. (Ordering information follows.) Asterisks indicate that these companies offer a generic or alternative drug that is significantly cheaper.

The local chain pharmacy offers a 10 percent discount to senior citizens, which is not reflected in the prices listed. If you factor in this discount and the shipping-and-handling charge, the local chain pharmacy's prices become competitive with some, but not all, of the mail-order prices.

Action Mail Order Drug
P.O. Box 787
Waterville, ME 04903-0787
(800) 452-1976

Requirements: The written prescription must be mailed or the doctor must call.

Shipping and handling: 75¢ per order.

(Thanks to reader Kathryn Buck of Brunswick, Maine, for sending us information on Action Drug.)

AARP Pharmacy Service
P.O. Box 30047
Reno, NV 89520-3047
(800) 477-7407

Requirements: The written prescription must be mailed or the doctor must call. Anyone can use this service; you don't need to be a member of the AARP.

Shipping and handling: $1 per order.

Note: There are 13 AARP Pharmacy Service centers; call 1-800-456-2277 for the one nearest you.

Family Pharmaceuticals
P.O. Box 1288
Mt. Pleasant, SC 29465
(800) 922-3444

Requirements: The written prescription must be mailed or the doctor must call.

Shipping and handling: $1.50 per order.

Medi-Mail, Inc.
P.O. Box 98520
Las Vegas, NV 89193-8520
(800) 331-1458

Requirements: The written prescription must be mailed or the doctor must call.

Shipping and handling: $1.48 per order.

America's Pharmacy
6109 Willowmere Drive
Des Moines, IA 50321
(515) 243-6447

Requirements: For the first order, you must mail in the prescription. For subsequent orders, your physician may call.

Shipping and handling: $1.40 per order.

PIZZA FOR PENNIES

Jim can make two cheese pizzas for under $1 each in less than 20 minutes of hands-on time. How?

Our pizza dough recipe comes from a wonderful cookbook called *The Food Processor Bread Book* by the editors of Consumer Guide, published by Simon & Schuster. Unfortunately, it is out of print, but you may be able to get it from your library, through an inter-library loan, or from a used bookstore.

Bread dough made in a food processor requires no hand kneading. (A food processor is, in my opinion, a valuable tightwad tool.)

THICK AND CHEWY PIZZA DOUGH

½ to ¾ cup warm water (105 to 115 degrees F.)
1 package (1 tablespoon) dry yeast
1 teaspoon sugar
2 cups flour
1 tablespoon vegetable oil
½ teaspoon salt

Combine ¼ cup of the water with the yeast and sugar. Stir to dissolve the yeast, and let stand until bubbly, about five minutes.

Put the flour, oil, and salt into a food processor, and process about five seconds with a steel blade.

Add the yeast mixture to the flour mixture, and process about 10 seconds, or until blended.

Turn on the processor and drizzle just enough of the remaining water through the feed tube so the dough forms a ball that cleans the sides of the bowl. Process so that the ball turns around about 25 times.

Put the dough ball onto a 14-inch greased pizza pan or large cookie sheet. Cover with plastic wrap or a bowl, and let stand 10 minutes.

Pat the dough out so that it covers the pan, leaving a ridge on the edges. (Or, if you're feeling really adventurous, spin the dough in the air a few times.) Spread with pizza sauce, and add cheese and toppings.

Bake at 425 degrees for 15 to 20 minutes, or until the crust is golden and the cheese is bubbly.

We use the following recipe for homemade spaghetti/pizza sauce. We grow our own tomatoes and peppers, buy spices cheap from a health-food store, and buy tomato paste on sale, so the cost is only about 40¢ per quart.

If you have to buy the produce, this recipe probably wouldn't beat double-coupon-purchased sauce. But even if you can't garden, you might have a friend or relative who has surplus tomatoes. And top-quality produce isn't needed; we have purchased pepper seconds from a grower.

We have experimented with making tomato paste, but the required time to cook tomatoes down to paste thickness did not seem economical. Adding tomato paste to the sauce lessens the cooking time significantly.

Because you make large quantities at a time, this recipe is also a time saver compared to making sauce from scratch every time you need it.

SPAGHETTI/PIZZA SAUCE

12 onions
6 green peppers
1½ cups vegetable oil
1½ teaspoons black pepper
36 tomatoes, skinned
4 cloves garlic, minced
3 tablespoons salt
4 tablespoons sugar
2 tablespoons each: oregano, sweet basil, and thyme
12 bay leaves
5 12-ounce cans tomato paste

Grind (as you would with a meat grinder) onions and peppers, and simmer in vegetable oil. Add black pepper.

In a *large* pot place tomatoes, garlic, salt, sugar, herbs, and onion-pepper mixture. Bring to a good rolling boil. Add tomato paste last, one can at a time. Pour into canning jars and process in a pressure cooker for 25 minutes. Or sauce can be frozen. Makes 7 quarts.

WHAT TO DO WITH . . .

As you read these, keep in mind: You don't have to save every toilet-paper tube in the hope of finding a use for it, but if you have a need and a toilet-paper tube works, why not use it? The point is that you should look to the available materials you have before you spend money.

For example: Recently, I was framing several photographs with old wooden frames. I had everything but those tiny brads or diamond-shaped things used to hold the backing in the frame. The project lay unfinished for several days while I waited until I could get to the store. In the meantime, I spotted my huge collection of used X-Acto blades, which are too dull for doing paste-ups but fine for rougher cutting. These worked perfectly—even better than the brads—for securing my pictures in the frames.

The benefit of reusing things goes beyond monetary savings. In this case, even if I waited until I was running other errands, a special trip to a frame shop or hardware store might have required 15 to 30 minutes, depending on how many stores I needed to visit. It always amazes me that people don't think shopping is time-consuming.

Bread Bags. Use to make jump ropes by splitting the bag down the side seams to make a long piece of plastic. Braid three lengths together. When you get to an end of plastic, wrap another bag end around the first. Stagger joinings to prevent a clump. Make handles from duct tape. (Jean Trocchia, Vermilion, Ohio.)

Burned Cookies. Use a coarse grater to scrape off the burned bottom of the cookie. This works much faster and better than using a knife.

Six-Pack Plastic Rings. Use to make a volleyball net. Tie them together with twist ties. During the winter months let kids use a balloon for indoor volleyball. (Denise Muhlbauer, Carroll, Iowa.)

Bread Tabs. Use for stitch counters on knitting needles. Or use as a divider for index cards. Secure with tape on both sides. Use a permanent marker. (Dolly-Ellen Walters, Eagle River, Alaska.)

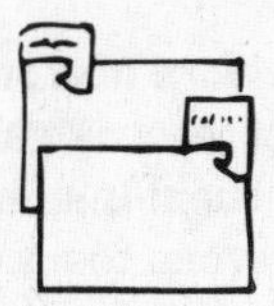

The Serrated Edge on Wax-Paper Box. Make a picture frame hanger. Cut into small sections, and bend into

needed shape. Nail onto a frame with two tiny nails. The serrated edge already has holes for nailing. (Jadie Henton, Lynnwood, Washington.)

Old Blue Jeans. Make coin purses out of the pockets for kids. Remove two pockets from pants, sew a zipper across the top, and stitch the sides together. (Laurel Craven, Fort Worth, Texas.)

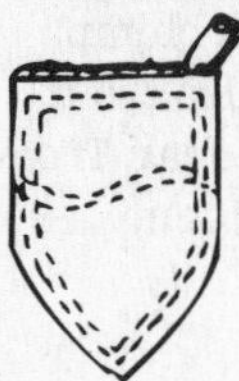

Old Shower Curtains. Make baby bibs. Clean and sterilize. Sew on bias tape for neck strings. Fold up bottom, sew to make a food-catcher pocket. (Sheryl-Anne Tumlin-Welch, Akron, Ohio.)

Magazine Stamps from Junk Mail. Use to make a piñata. Glue stamps to a balloon, and use toilet-paper tubes to make legs and head. (Sandra Sterner, Pittsburgh, Pennsylvania.)

Worn Tube Socks. If the toes wear out, first turn them inside out, cut off worn toe, and resew on a curve. Same sock, just shorter. (Judy O'Boyle, Kalispell, Montana.)

Old Credit Cards. Make several guitar picks from one card. Make softer picks from milk-jug plastic or plastic lids. (Rebecca Bryant, Russell Springs, Kentucky.)

Margarine Containers. Using a paper punch, make holes in the lid. This makes a great shaker container for cinnamon sugar to sprinkle on toast.

Milk Jugs. Use to get free hot water. Paint jugs a dark color, fill with water, and let them sit in the hot sun. (Linda Louden, Sierra Vista, Arizona.)

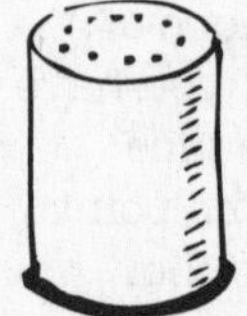

Film Canisters. Poke holes in the bottoms to make salt and pepper shakers for lunch boxes or camping trips.

Junk Mail. Save any large colored pieces of paper, such as the plain back of a brochure, for future art projects.

TO WASH, TO WAX, OR TO RUST

A friend told me his theory that waxing your car frequently would prevent rust. This seemed like worthy subject matter for *The Tightwad Gazette,* because rust kills cars, and new cars cost money. To check out his theory we devised the following test:

Ten years ago we bought three 1985 Plymouth Horizons. Car #1 was washed and waxed regularly. Car #2 was washed only. Car #3 was neither washed nor waxed.

Over the last decade we have taken great pains to insure that all three cars received equal exposure to the elements.

Today, cars #1 and #2 both have bodies in approximately the same good condition. Car #3, however, sits today a rusted-out hulk, a mere memory of its former self.

Our test results demonstrate conclusively that car washing by itself will greatly reduce a tendency to rust.

Only kiddin', folks.

There's a far tightwaddier way to gather information. Cite the research done by publications with more resources than we have.

In 1984, *Consumer Reports* took a survey (they didn't do the which-of-these-three-cars-will-rust-to-oblivion test either) of 3,303 car owners whose cars were at least eight years old or had traveled at least 100,000 miles.

Of snow-belt cars, 25 percent of those washed infrequently suffered significant rust, while only 8 percent of those washed frequently suffered severe rust problems.

But *CR* also discovered that of the frequently washed group, those that were also waxed often were not better off in terms of keeping rust at bay.

The *CR* engineers say that's because rust usually starts on the inside of the body. So keep your car washed, and be especially careful to rinse road salt off of the underbody and from under the fenders. An easy time to do this is when you are changing your oil: With the front wheels on ramps, the underbody is accessible for thorough squirting.

And, if you have time, a nice wax job looks good.

FIRE AND ICE

Dear Amy,

I put three pieces of charcoal in my refrigerator and three in my freezer. They are great at absorbing unwanted odors. After a month, I replace them with fresh ones and return the old ones to the bag for burning on the grill.

—Irene Hartley
Fowler, Ohio

TRASH 'N' TREASURE

Dear Amy,

Twice a year our church has a clothing exchange. One day, everyone may bring any clothes, toys, housewares, etc. that they don't need, and the next day they may come back and take anything they do need. No money changes hands; it's purely stewardship. On the first day, anyone who helps sort clothes (an all-day job) gets to take home things to try on that day; it's our "payment."

—Mary T. Lichlyter
Colorado Springs, Colorado

PICKLE-JUICE REUSE

Dear Amy,

I save the liquid from a jar of pickles when the pickles are gone. Then I buy a cucumber, slice it thin, and pack the slices back down in the pickle jar with its liquid. Cover, refrigerate for four days, and you have a jar of pickles for the cost of one cucumber.

—Claire Morgret
Elida, Ohio

CALCULATING YOUR C.P.M.

I've finally done something I've been meaning to do for years. I have always wanted to work out *and* write down the costs of various ingredients that I use frequently in baking so that I can easily calculate the savings of baking from scratch.

So here's my chart. I weighed a cup of each ingredient. From that, and the price per pound, I calculated the cost per cup. A cup has 16 tablespoons, and a tablespoon has 3 teaspoons, so I calculated those two quantities and rounded the cost to the nearest ⅒th for easy addition.

The important information here is the volume-to-weight equivalences. If your prices vary from mine (as they almost certainly will) you can use these equivalences to make your own equations. Then you, too, will be able to compute your C.P.M. (Cost Per Muffin).

The chart has two references to milk: dry milk powder for when you add it in dry form to your recipe, and liquid milk for when you add milk made from dry milk powder to your recipe. If you (heaven forbid!) use whole milk in your baking, the cost will be about 50% more, or 13½¢ per cup if you purchase milk at $2.19 per gallon.

The chart does not include the cost of eggs. If you pay 89¢ for a dozen, then one egg costs 7½¢.

For those who don't know . . . Soy flour makes a terrific substitution for eggs in baking, meatloafs, etc. A heaping tablespoon of soy flour and a tablespoon of water equals an egg. Once baked, there is no taste or texture difference in the final product. Look for it at natural-food stores.

Ingredient	Price Per Pound	Weight Per Cup	Price Per Cup	Price Per Tablespoon	Price Per Teaspoon
Flour	$ .16	6 oz.	6¢	4/10¢	1/10¢
Oatmeal	.40	4 oz.	10¢	6/10¢	2/10¢
Cornmeal	.30	6 oz.	11¢	7/10¢	2/10¢
Soy Flour	1.00	4 oz.	25¢	1 5/10¢	5/10¢
Sugar	.35	8 oz.	18¢	1 1/10¢	4/10¢
Brown Sugar	.38	7 oz.	17¢	1¢	3/10¢
Dry Milk Powder	1.74	3 oz.	33¢	2¢	7/10¢
Liquid Milk	.18	8 oz.	9¢	6/10¢	2/10¢
Margarine	.40	8 oz.	20¢	1 3/10¢	4/10¢
Shortening	.66	8 oz.	33¢	2¢	7/10¢
Corn Oil	.52	8 oz.	26¢	1 6/10¢	5/10¢
Cocoa	1.15	4 oz.	29¢	1 8/10¢	6/10¢
Baking Powder	.91	8 oz.	45¢	2 8/10¢	9/10¢
Baking Soda	.33	8 oz.	17¢	1 1/10¢	3/10¢
Cream of Tartar	1.80	8 oz.	90¢	5 6/10¢	1 8/10¢
Salt	.29	10 oz.	18¢	1 1/10¢	4/10¢
Raisins	1.05	4 oz.	26¢	1 6/10¢	5/10¢
Coconut	1.15	2 oz.	14¢	9/10¢	3/10¢

HOW TO DISSECT A PAIR OF PANTY HOSE

Hortense DuVall of Clinton, Maryland, swears by a product called Hosiery Mate, which the maker claims more than doubles hosiery life. The directions say that you should rinse between wearings and it will strengthen the fibers to prevent snags and runs. A 16-fluid-ounce bottle for $3.50 is good for 60 rinses. I am not familiar with Hosiery Mate, but because it costs less than a pair of hose, it does seem that it would save you money.

When it's time to retire a pair of hose, don't throw it away. Cut it up for other uses:

Use the elastic for a bungee cord or to replace stretched-out elastic in pajamas, or cover with cloth to make a headband.

Cut off the bad leg and wear the remaining good one-legged panty hose with another pair of one-legged panty hose. (Amazingly, some people have not heard of this oldest of tightwad tricks.)

Segments can be tied off at the bottom, attached to a trellis, and used as slings to support cantaloupe, eggplant, and other heavy fruits. This is useful in gardens with limited space where produce must be grown vertically. (Jill Finch, Irving, Texas.)

Put human hair (obtained in quantity from a barber) or dog hair into tied-off sections and place them around your garden. The scent keeps deer away.

Cut into loops to make filler for stuffed animals.

Cut in a spiral to make a thin strip that can be crocheted to make bracelets, headbands, rope—even a bikini. (Lorelle Becton, Philadelphia, Pennsylvania.)

Put onions into one leg of clean panty hose. Tie a knot between each one. Snip onions off as needed. No mess. (Kathy Takvam, Silver Bay, Minnesota.)

Cut off and wear over your head for a bank-robber or monster Halloween mask.

Lop off the toes. Put a "toe" on each foot before you put on a new pair to keep the toes from wearing through.

Lengths of panty hose can be used to tie many things. Because they're soft and elastic, they're perfect for tying up tomato vines.

NEW LIFE FOR OLD CARTRIDGES

Computers sometimes remind me of Barbie dolls: The expense isn't in the toy itself, but in the accessories.

Software, CD-ROM drives, modems, and other computer stuff all cost money, but for us, and probably many computer users, the biggest ongoing expense is supplying the printer with new cartridge-type ribbons. Both daisy-wheel and dot-matrix printers use them. Prices range from $3 to $32, with the average around $8.

Fortunately, there is an alternative to simply tossing and replacing cartridges. They can be reused.

Because of the great number of ribbon types, manufacturers, and distributors, it wasn't easy to compare costs. In some cases, it can be cheaper to buy a new ribbon than reuse an old one. This is especially true of one-time film ribbons, which cannot be reinked. This article, therefore, addresses reuse of the more common fabric ribbons.

There are two ways to squeeze more use out of a ribbon cartridge: re-inking and reloading.

RE-INKING (three methods)

1. Pry open your cartridge with a knife (test this on an old cartridge to see whether it can be opened and closed without damage), and drip a specially formulated ink directly onto the ribbon coil. This ink, called Ribbon Re-new, is sold by V-Tech Inc., 2223 Rebecca, Hatfield, PA, 19440, (215) 822-2989. V-Tech says if left overnight, the ink's wicking action will thoroughly coat the ribbon. One $4.95 bottle will re-ink a ribbon up to 30 times. The instructions recommend using 20 drops of ink, but reader David W. Carnell of Wilmington, North Carolina, found that only 10 drops work fine.

2. Re-ink your ribbon on a re-inking machine. These devices run the ribbon around an ink-filled spool.

The least expensive one we found is the EZEE Inker, a hand-cranked model offered for $39.50 plus $4.00 shipping by Borg Industries, Ltd., P.O. Box 508, Janesville, IA, 50647, (800) 553-2404. Borg sells motorized models too.

The most popular motorized re-inker among our readers was the MacInker, which sells for $69.95 plus $6 shipping by Computer Friends, 14250 N.W. Science Park Dr., Portland, OR, 97229, (503) 626-2291.

We bought a similar motorized machine from V-Tech for $63 (call them for shipping costs) and found it easy to use. The ribbon must run at a constant speed around the ink spool for at least fifteen minutes to get even coating, so we recommend the motorized version for all but the most patient.

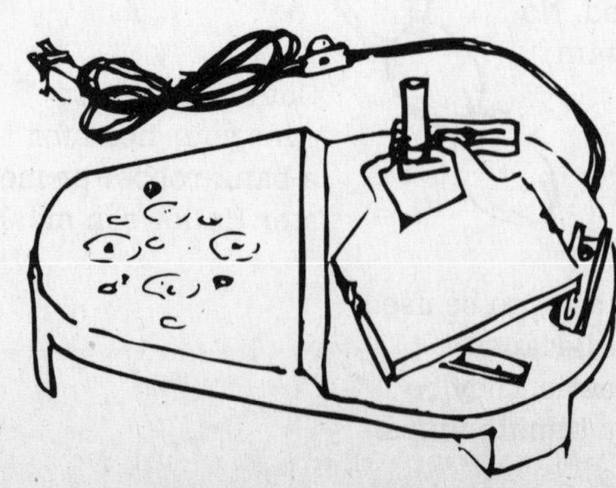

Remember:

You must use a lot of ribbons for a re-inker to pay for itself quickly (unless you are one of the poor slobs who has to buy those $32 cartridges).

3. If you are not the do-it-yourself type, mail your old cartridges to a professional re-inking company. The typical cost might be $3 per ribbon.

A note of caution: A reader who runs a computer-maintenance shop says that you must use specially formulated ink, like the kind sold by the companies listed here, or your printhead could be damaged. He also warns that if you let your ribbon get too worn, a pin from your dot-matrix printhead can catch in the frayed fibers and bend, so keep an eye on the ribbon's condition.

RELOADING (two methods)

1. You can pop a new ribbon into your old cartridge. V-Tech sells these, along with instructions, for about one quarter the cost of a new cartridge. Company president Gene Beals told us the process can be a bit messy, but what the heck—you end up with an essentially new cartridge (ready for a new succession of re-inkings).

2. You can send your old ribbons to a reloading company, but the savings drop off dramatically. One such company is Best Impressions, 1480 N. Cave Creek Rd., Suite 18, Phoenix, AZ, 85032, (800) 798-2345, which reloads ribbons for about 30 percent less than the price of their new ones.

Again, there are no cut-and-dried answers. You need to check all of the options and see what makes the most sense for you.

MAKING A SOLAR BOX COOKER

Across America, tightwads crank up their stoves to cook supper on hot summer days. As their utility bills roll in, they broil along with their chickens and mutter, "There must be a better way."

There is.

Solar cookers have been around for decades. But many of the early designs were expensive and needed almost constant tending. Then in 1976, Barbara Kerr, a Phoenix social worker and backyard tinkerer, fiddled with various solar-oven designs and came up with one that could be constructed in a couple of hours with common household materials and tools.

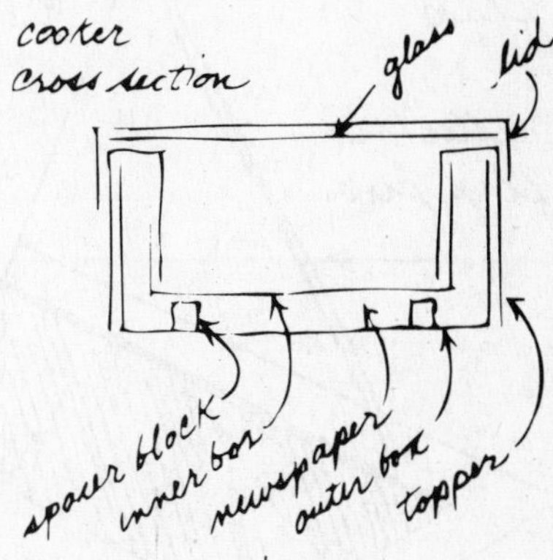

Her new design can reach 275 degrees F., hot enough to cook food or kill germs in water. It can cook almost anything that can be cooked in a conventional oven or on a stovetop. It can bake bread, roast chicken, cook stew, and steam rice, beans, potatoes, and other vegetables. The cooking time is about twice as long as by conventional methods, but there is less labor because there is no need for stirring or basting.

We got a set of plans and built one. Basically, you cover the bottom of a big box with insulating material such as crumpled newspaper. Put six small spacer blocks on the bottom of the box, and set a smaller box inside the big one. Fill

the space between the sides of the two boxes with more crumpled newspaper. If your boxes have flaps, use these to fold over and cover the insulated space. Or you can make "toppers," which are pieces of cardboard folded over the top of the insulated space; they cover the inside of the inside box and outside the outside box and are tied with string at the corners. Line the inner box and inside of the topper sides with aluminum foil adhered with nontoxic glue, so that the entire inside of the cooker is lined. Set a piece of glass over the oven. Make a cardboard lid that has a large, foil-lined reflector flap cut out of it that can be adjusted to catch the sun.

When building the oven, maintain the basic design, but modify to take advantage of materials you have on hand. In your resourcefulness, avoid using materials that might give off toxic fumes when heated, such as Styrofoam pellets and duct tape.

Your biggest expense will be the glass, so if you have a piece on hand—perhaps from an old storm window—try using that. We used old curtain rods for reflector-flap props. If you already have a dark, lidded pot, you'll want to make your cooker deep enough to accommodate that.

The ideal solar cooker is made to specific proportions. The inner box should be at least 18 inches by 22 inches, rectangular, and as shallow as possible while still being deeper than your pot. The ideal space between the inner and outer boxes is 1 to 2 inches.

Solar cookers can be used six months of the year in northern climates and year-round in tropical climates. (No one can accuse us of printing ideas that work best only in our geographic area.)

We have done some experimenting and like the idea, although this design seems a bit awkward. Because the oven lid and glass are not attached, it's a little clumsy to get food in and out.

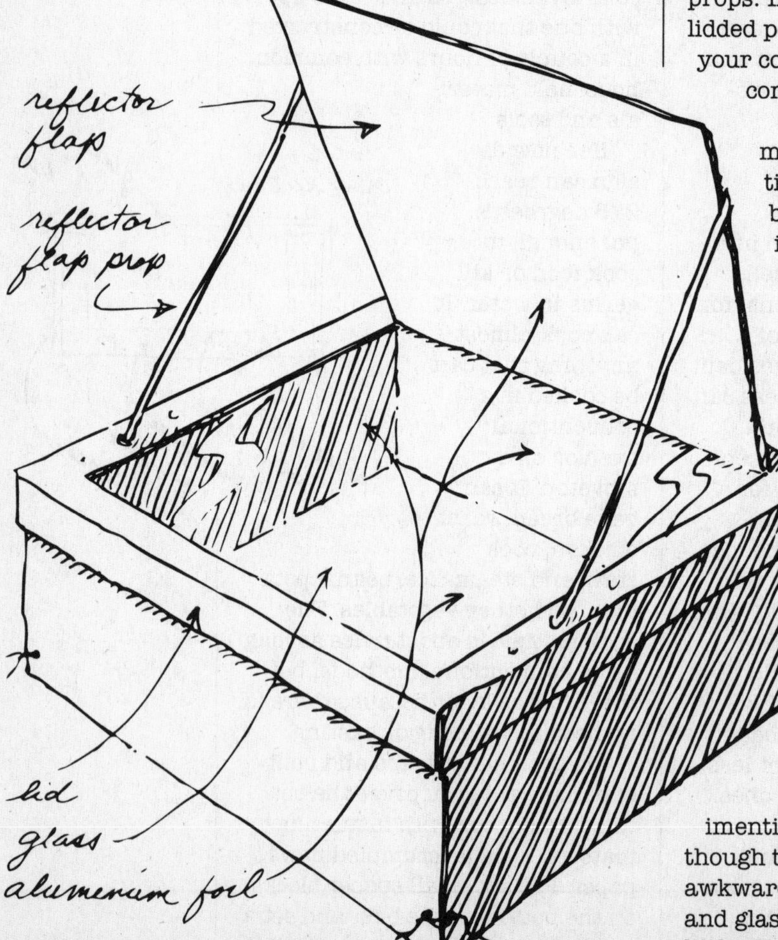

We plan to build a wooden oven with a hinged top and glass. However, I recommend trying this cardboard version first.

Some general tips:

Use covered pots with tight-fitting lids, except for breads, cakes, and cookies. The pots should be made of thin metal and be painted black. These can be set on a black tray to absorb more heat. Use flat black latex paint.

The golden rule of solar cooking is, "Get the food in early; don't worry about overcooking."

To keep foods hot after you lose the sun, add several bricks or large stones when you start cooking. These will help hold heat. To maximize heat retention, close the reflective lid and cover with a blanket.

Many foods can be cooked without moving the box to follow the sun. Just aim the cooker so that halfway through the cooking time the sun will be right in front of the cooker. For large quantities of food, or on partly cloudy days, you may have to move the cooker once or twice.

To bake cakes or bread, preheat the cooker for at least a half hour before adding the food.

I've tried to give you enough information to make a solar cooker on your own. However, you may feel you need additional resources. Kits and ready-made solar box cookers are available from these two sources:

Kerr Enterprises
P.O. Box 27417
Tempe, AZ 85285
(602) 968-3068

Plans for a cardboard model cost $2.85. Plans for a wooden model are $5.10. Kits cost $55 to $69. Ready-made boxes cost $72 to $85. Shipping is extra.

Solar Box Cookers International
1724 11th St.
Sacramento, CA 95814
(916) 444-6616

Plans for a cardboard model cost $5. A foldable, portable box with polyester window costs $50. Add 10 percent shipping for each item. SBCI's programs spread cookers throughout the Third World, where they can help sterilize water and stop deforestation caused by cutting wood for cooking fires.

Reader Michele Cahill of Carmichael, California, who cooks most of her meals in the cooker and "can't praise this idea enough," sent us the following list of cookbooks. All prices include postage and handling:

Eleanor's Solar Cookbook
by Cemese Publishers
7028 Leesburg
Stockton, CA, 95207

Cost is $10.

Solar Cooking Naturally
(Michele's favorite)
Sun Life Energy
745 Mountain Shadows
Sedona, AZ 86336
(602) 282-1344

Cost is $11.50.

Solar Box Cooking
by Sacramento Municipal Utility District
P.O. Box 15830
Sacramento, CA 95852-1830
(916) 732-5130

Cost is $5.

"HELP! MY FAMILY WON'T TRY STORE BRANDS."

Tell them this story:

As a teenager, Jim learned a valuable lesson about brand loyalty when he worked at Oxford Pickle Company for a few months in the mid-sixties. He personally oversaw the filling of jars of many pickle brands. Typically, after the workers had filled the order for Oxford's pickles, they would stop the line and switch the jars with labels for Cain's, Finast, or other name or store brands. The jar style, label, and retail price changed, but the vat of pickles was the same.

The practice remains the same today, according to our interviews with several supermarket executives and the Private Label Manufacturers' Association.

Although some stores have their own packaging plants, many store brands are packaged by name-brand manufacturers. For example, Safeway's store-brand green beans are packaged by Del Monte as well as 15 other companies. Safeway's store-brand cereal is made by Malt-O-Meal and Ralston Purina.

Does this mean that store brands and name brands are identical? Not necessarily. It all depends on the specifications each supermarket chain gives its suppliers. Most large supermarket chains specify that their store brands must be as good or better than the leading name brand.

If the products are of the same quality, why are name brands more expensive? Name-brand prices are inflated because of advertising costs, more complex packaging, the expense of handling coupons and refunds, and the "slotting fees" manufacturers must pay supermarkets to reserve a certain amount of shelf space.

Test marketing also makes name brands expensive. For example, in the 1970s, name-brand manufacturers spent big bucks to convince Americans to eat that weird, sour-milk stuff called yogurt. Only after the market was established did store-brand yogurt appear.

Are store brands always cheaper? On the average, store brands cost about 15 percent less, but that gap varies widely. With some products, such as baby food, the store brand and name brand cost almost the same. Other store-brand items, such as vitamins, toothbrushes, and English muffins, cost, on average, more than 30 percent less than name brands.

Who buys store brands? Almost everyone. A recent Gallup poll showed that 84 percent of those earning under $25,000 bought store brands. The figure was 90 percent for those earning $25,000 to $45,000, and 87 percent for those earning over $45,000.

What if you've tried store brands and really don't like them? Since each store sets its own specifications, you might try switching stores until you find store brands that suit you. If you can't switch stores, complain. It may also be that your store has improved its store-brand products since you last tried them. Supermarkets across the country have made dramatic improvements in store-brand quality in the last decade, and consumers are responding: 33

percent of respondents told Gallup they are buying more store brands now than they did a year ago.

Finally, remember that preference is an acquired thing. How do we know what a Cheerio is supposed to taste like, anyway? If you've eaten only General Mills Cheerios since you were a kid, then store-brand toasted-oat cereal might not taste right to you. Consider that if you had been raised on the store-brand version you might very well hold the unshakable conviction that General Mills Cheerios taste inferior.

AMAZING DISH-COVERY

Dear Amy,

The other day I read the directions on my box of dishwasher detergent. I was curious to see how much powder they recommend using, since in the past I simply filled the dispenser in the machine without thinking. It said to "Follow manufacturer's instructions, or use one tablespoon of powder." Talk about feeling stupid. By blindly filling the dispenser, I used about 6 tablespoons of powder. Now I use just 1 tablespoon, and the results are the same.

—Karen S. Phillips
Louisville, Kentucky

FREE WHEELER

Dear Amy,

I found a $39 designer stroller in the trash by the mall. One wheel was cracked. I popped it in the trunk and called the manufacturer's 800 number when I got home. For $2.50 and a little cleaning up, I now have a new stroller from a reputable manufacturer. I got the number from the free *Consumer's Resource Handbook.* For a copy, write to Consumer Information Center, Pueblo, CO 81009.

—Dawn Ward
Jackson Heights, New York

(Most major manufacturers have toll-free numbers. Another way to find them is by calling toll-free information at [800] 555-1212. FZ)

DRYER STRAITS

Dear Amy,

I am a retired appliance repairman (42 years). In that time I have fixed a lot of appliances that did not need a repairman.

Example: Your electric dryer runs but won't heat. Check to make sure both 30-amp. fuses or circuit breakers are okay. If one is out, the dryer could run but not heat, since it takes 220 volts to make the heating element work, but only 110 volts for the motor.

If it runs with heat but takes a long time to dry, check the vent pipe for lint.

—Tom Farmer
Monroe, Michigan

CHEAP-SCAPE

Dear Amy,

My training in school was in landscape architecture. I have come up with some ideas for inexpensive but effective ways to have a beautiful landscape:

1. Use what you have! If you

have too many rocks, edge with the larger ones, accent with the huge ones, and pound the little ones into a garden path.

2. Use native plants if you can. They will likely grow regardless of what you do to them. Some Forest Service areas permit harvesting plants by permit from public lands at very low cost.

3. Many plants are free! If you can learn to be patient, plant ground covers many times farther apart than the nursery suggests, then break off pieces as the plants grow, and fill in between the older plants. Ask friends for "shoots" from their plants that you like, take them home, and start new plants from them. Libraries have good books on propagating this way.

—Grant Collier
Flagstaff, Arizona

DO SWEAT THE SMALL STUFF

Which is cheaper to use—cloth or paper napkins? To research this pressing and complex question, I laboriously and tediously calculated . . .

(Across the country, thousands of readers' eyes glaze over and they think, "Egad! Another endless cost analysis that will yield a minuscule saving! What is it with this woman? This ranks up there with her riveting conclusion that using baking soda and cream of tartar is marginally cheaper than using baking powder, or that boiling water in the microwave versus on the stove may use an extra fraction of a penny's worth of energy, or that a ½-inch-by-1-yard hunk of duct tape is 3.2¢ cheaper than the same amount of clear tape. Get a life!")

So why should you sweat the small stuff? And why should I devote so much space to it in the newsletter? Because the small stuff is the essence of the tightwad life. Because it's where the action is! Because I'll run out of stuff to write about without it! Because:

1. There are more small strategies than big strategies. Think about it. How many ways are there to immediately save a huge wad of money? Five? Maybe ten? And of those that come to mind, how many are commonly known? Take prepaying your mortgage. Seems like every week I hear a TV financial reporter do a story on that idea. But there are thousands of small things you can do to shave a few cents off that most people don't know about.

2. There are more *opportunities* to use small strategies than big ones. How often do you buy a car? You do the small stuff every day, and the savings accumulate. If you discover that your dishwasher cleans just as well with 1 tablespoon of detergent as when you blithely dumped in 6 tablespoons, the cumulative savings over your lifetime is substantial. Once you figure something out, you *own* that information for the rest of your life.

3. Similarly, the time investment in figuring out this minuscule stuff actually yields a high "hourly wage." It might take you a total of five hours to make up a price book for comparison grocery shopping, but after several years of supermarket excursions, you may dis-

cover that your hourly "pay" for those five hours was over $1,000.

4. It's good training. It keeps you in the habit of thinking frugally, so that when one of those big financial decisions come along, you naturally attack it with a tightwad mind-set. You may find what I have found: that keeping my mathematical muscles toned by computing scotch-tape economies helps me make the right choices for life insurance.

5. Like most frugal writers, I could just throw one-liner tips at you, without showing how I arrived at those conclusions. But you need to know how I figured something out, because the variables in your situation are probably different. (Or—gasp!—I might even make a mistake.) And when I show you an

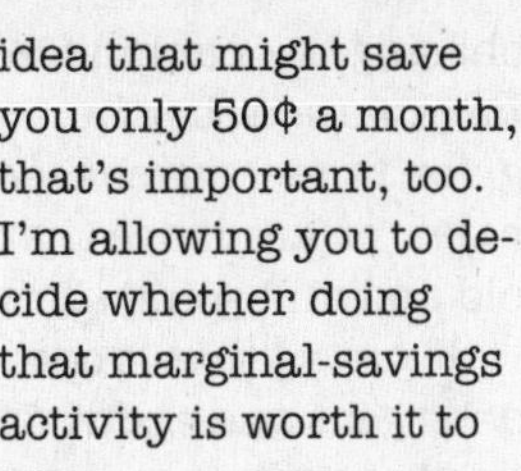

idea that might save you only 50¢ a month, that's important, too. I'm allowing you to decide whether doing that marginal-savings activity is worth it to you.

6. It's fun. If you are a real, genetically programmed, dyed-in-the-wool tightwad, you just love this stuff. So if your eyes didn't glaze over at the mention of another tedious calculation, if they actually widened with eager anticipation, let's forge ahead into the dark continent of napkin calculation:

Naturally, I could never wash a full load of cloth napkins, since I have only 30, but I figured the cumulative effect would eventually result in an extra load of laundry. So the best way to calculate it was as if I were washing a full load of napkins.

How many in a load? Theorizing that the material in cloth napkins was about the same type and thickness as in twin sheets, I used sheets as a basis for calculation. I figured out how many napkins equaled a sheet by comparing them two ways—by weight and by square inches (factoring in sheet hems; the napkin hems were negligible). I averaged those two napkins-in-a-sheet numbers and multiplied that by 8, which is the number of sheets I can wash in a single load. I concluded I could wash 200 napkins in a single load.

I didn't factor in the cost of pur-

chasing the napkins. All that I have were either homemade, given to me, purchased at yard sales, or are more than 12 years old and still going strong.

Figuring that it costs 12½¢ for detergent and about 4¢ for electricity to run a cold-wash cycle (based on information in a brochure from the electric company), I can wash 200 napkins for 16½¢. I hang my laundry to dry, but if I had to use my dryer, I would have to add 44¢ (for 60 minutes of dryer time to dry the eight sheets) to the total cost. If I had to pay for water (we have a well), I would have to figure that in. If I had to use a pay machine, the cost would be higher.

The cheapest paper napkins cost 50¢ per 120, or 40/100 of a cent each. Washing and machine-drying cloth napkins cost 30/100 of a cent each. Washing and air-drying cloth napkins cost 8/100 of a cent each.

If a family of four uses 12 napkins per day (one at each meal), paper napkins would cost $17.52 per year versus air-dried cloth napkins at $3.50 per year. So cloth napkins could save about $14 per year, or $140 per 10 years, or $1,400 per 100 years, or . . .

This trivial bit of information is yours to do with as you will.

DIALING FOR (INSURANCE) DOLLARS

Large, boring books have been written about the controversy over which kind of life insurance is better: cash-value or term.

Cash-value (which comes in several mutations: whole life, adjustable life, universal life, and variable life) is a combination of investment and insurance. Because it performs these two functions—*and* because insurance agents rack up five to ten times more in commissions selling this kind as opposed to term—it's expensive. Term, on the other hand, is pure insurance; it has no cash value. It costs more as you get older, but is far cheaper than cash-value insurance, at least until you reach retirement age.

Basically, I have come to the conclusion that for relatively well-off people, cash-value is a good deal because it offers attractive tax breaks. Others—generally, the young and not-rich—should get term. But the subject is much more complex than this and beyond the capacity of this newsletter, so plunge into one of those books. (One that is not so boring is *Winning the Insurance Game* by Ralph Nader.)

If you've decided on term, the next step is finding the least expensive policy. Start by calling:
Insurance Information, Inc.
23 Route 134
South Dennis, MA 02660
(800) 472-5800

As far as we can determine, this is the only truly independent source of information on term life-insurance rates (unlike other nationwide insurance price-quote

services, this one does not *sell* insurance). This company is recommended in two excellent books: *Scrooge Investing* by Mark Skousen and *Smart Money*, by Ken and Daria Dolan.

We called company founder Milton Brown (if you want to talk with him personally, call [508] 394-9117). He told us that the first step is to call. If you are not ready for a quote but just want more information, his company will send you a packet.

If you want a quote, you give your credit-card number, your age, the amount of insurance coverage wanted, and some other general information. Insurance Information runs this through a data base of about 250 companies. They deduct a $50 fee from your credit-card account and send you information on the five least expensive companies that they find. The search includes only companies that are rated "A" or better by A. M. Best, a firm that tracks the financial health of insurance companies. You can take this information to your insurance agent, or in some cases you can call the insurer directly to buy a policy, thus saving commission fees.

If you already have a policy, and Insurance Information cannot find one that saves you at least $50, they will send you the information they have found and will not charge you (Brown says of the 25,000 or so customers he serves annually, he only has to do this less than 1 percent of the time). In other words, if they can only save you $49 or less, you get the information free.

MIDNIGHT MAGIC

What can you do outside, on a late August night, with someone you love, that's free, fun, requires lying on a blanket, and if everything goes right, you see shooting stars?

Okay, name two things.

The second one is watching the Perseid meteor shower, which occurs annually from August 10–14, peaking on August 12.

Some visible meteors—also known, inaccurately, as shooting stars—fall every night, and there are about 15 recognized "showers" each year. But the Perseid shower has the advantage of happening in warm weather, and it's the biggest, with about 60 meteors visible hourly.

We watched the Perseid shower last year, and it's hard to say which was more exciting, the streaking lights in the sky or the kids' delight at this rare chance to be up in the middle of the night.

The best viewing time is after midnight, so check the weather forecast, lay out your blankets in advance, and set the alarm to wake the kids (this means no funny business).

BREAKFAST BREAKTHROUGH

I leaped a major hurdle in my development as a tightwad when I stopped going nuts for "bargains" (Wow! Double coupons will save me a buck on that box of Cheerios!). Instead I began comparing the cost of foods by the portion.

The breakfast-portion comparison below provides an excellent example of how much one can save by thinking this way.

When I began to compare breakfast costs, I ignored the 1-ounce-per-portion suggestion on the sides of cereal boxes and actually weighed the amount I thought I would eat. Therefore, I compared 2 ounces of cereal to two 4-inch pancakes, and so on. This works better than comparing by weight only, because most people eat a bowlful or plateful, not a certain weight.

In most cases, I basically compared a portion of grain-based starch. Clearly, it's a tad unfair to compare frozen breakfasts, which also contain meat, but I wanted to include them in the study—and besides, how much can that microscopic sausage be worth, anyway?

Obviously, all of these breakfasts would be supplemented with juice, fruit, jam, sugar, milk, syrup, and so on.

After I worked out my comparison, I rationalized that scratch breakfasts use some energy in cooking (a penny or so per serving), so I decided cold cereal would be a good value if I could get it for 7¢ or less per ounce (or about 14¢ a serving). So I went to the double-coupon store with a calculator in one hand and a fistful of coupons in the other and stood in the aisle with scores of cereals stacked to the ceiling and found almost none

that were cheap enough. As a result, we eat very little cold cereal.

People buy convenience breakfast foods because they think they're too busy to make scratch breakfasts. We're busy too. When we're truly short on time we rely on "fast" scratch foods such as oatmeal or a pan of corn bread.

When we have a bit more time, we make things like whole-grain pancakes, waffles, and muffins. If your kitchen is well organized, with your baking utensils and ingredients in one place, you can get a double batch of muffins into the oven in less than 20 minutes. (Then, take your shower while they're baking.) We always make extra and freeze the surplus for days when we don't even have time to make oatmeal.

Most of our breakfasts cost 10¢ or less per serving. If a family of four chooses breakfasts that cost 10¢ per serving over breakfasts that cost 25¢ per serving, it will save $219 a year.

- 2 ounces cornmeal (to make cornmeal mush)=4¢
- 2 ounces bulk-purchased oatmeal=5¢
- 2 4-inch scratch pancakes=6¢
- 2 scratch muffins=7¢
- 2 4-inch scratch waffles=8¢
- 2 pieces of french toast=8¢
- 2 oatmeal-raisin scones=8¢
- 2 2-inch squares corn bread=8¢
- 2 ounces store-brand oatmeal=9¢
- 2 4-inch Bisquick pancakes=10¢
- 1 egg and 1 slice of toast=11¢
- 2 ounces Quaker oatmeal=15¢
- 2 store-brand English muffins=16¢
- 2 ounces store-brand toasted-oat cereal=20¢
- 2 ounces Cream of Wheat=21¢
- 2 Eggo waffles=36¢
- 2 ounces Cap'n Crunch=41¢
- 2 ounces Froot Loops=42¢
- 2 store-brand doughnuts=43¢
- Carnation Instant Breakfast=43¢
- 2 4-inch pancakes from store batter=49¢
- 2 bakery-made cinnamon rolls=51¢
- 2 Pop-Tarts=82¢
- Great Starts microwaveable breakfast=$1.49

THE FRAME GAME

If you wanted to drop a wad of dough, acquiring ready-framed art would be easy—too easy. But like soup that tastes better when it has simmered all day, your home will feel more personal and to your liking if you take more time and acquire decorative items slowly.

Plus, you'll save your wad.

Relax with your blank walls. Work with the best that you have now. Think of the art, the frame, and where you hang them as fluid, changing as you find things you like better.

When I gathered the stuff I wanted to frame and my collection of frames—mostly found in the attic when we bought the house—I discovered only one obvious match of frame and art. So I looked harder for solutions. Here are a few I used or have learned of:

FRAME SOLUTIONS

Look closely at the yard-sale frames that have been overlooked

because of what's in them—like the framed, mildewed print I bought for 50¢. I discarded the print and put a picture of my great grandmother in the nice, old, wood frame.

Clean up older, varnished wood frames with a little denatured alcohol and linseed oil. The alcohol is a mild solvent that will redistribute the finish to minimize scratches.

Spray-paint frames with a paint you already have. I had several with odd colors that I painted with gloss-black paint. This allows you to group together frames of different sizes and styles in a single display.

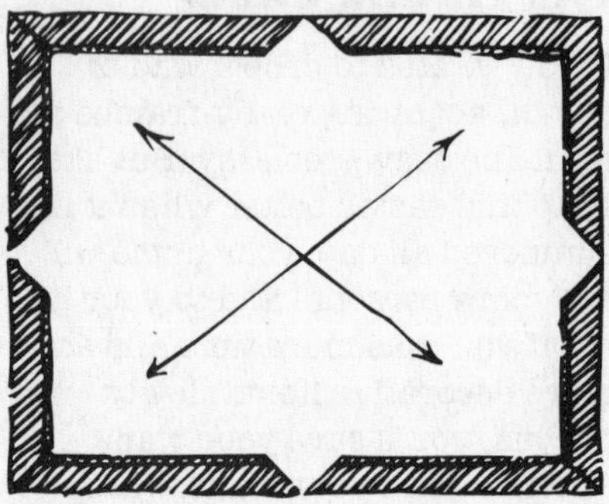

Cut down a large wooden frame to make a matching pair of smaller ones. Jim did this to an old 20-inch by 32-inch frame that I couldn't imagine ever finding art to fit. Don't cut down a frame that has antique value or that you care greatly about. This risky process requires skill and proper mitering tools. Or, as in my case, a husband with modest skills, Mickey Mouse tools, and great patience.

Reconsider those old, hopelessly chipped, ornate gold frames. These are made of gold-painted plaster molded onto a wood frame. The plaster will soak off, and the underlying frame may be attractive enough to refinish. Or it could be downright ugly, so only attempt this with a free frame. Don't soak frames in your bathtub and wash the plaster down the drain. You can buy a lot of frames for the cost of hiring a plumber.

When you disassemble an old frame, carefully save all of the parts (wire, eye screws, nails, backing, etc.) for reuse.

MATTING SOLUTIONS

A mat is a border between the artwork and the frame. Generally it is cut to fit the art, but a mat also allows you to resize art to fit an existing frame, without actually cutting the art. By floating the window over a larger piece of art, you can find a new, smaller composition.

At Vesper George School of Art in Boston, I learned that the ideal mat should have a beveled, cut-out window for the art to show through. The sides and the top should be of equal measure, and the bottom should be slightly wider (by about ½ inch). But being a purist gets expensive. You can break the rules as long as the results are pleasing to you.

Without going to a frame shop, there's almost no way to get that beveled cut. Instead use a utility or X-Acto knife when cutting a (non-beveled) mat. A drawing board and a T square can help to get things square. However, you can simply trace your frame on your mat and measure from those lines.

If you don't have mat board, cut the mat from very stiff paper, such as the inside of a brochure cover.

Skip the window. Trim your artwork and put it on top of a mat. Or use any piece of solid-colored or white paper backed with a heavier piece of cardboard. Sometimes the back side of the old art that was originally in the frame will do.

Spray-paint gray (not corrugated) cardboard to make a mat. Reader Tamar Fleishman of Baltimore, Maryland, suggests using the cardboard from a panty hose package. I tried this and found that even mat-finish paint didn't result in a completely even coat, but the glass hid the slight variation. Cut your window before painting.

Make a mat by covering cardboard with a solid-colored or small-patterned scrap of fabric. I made two fabric-covered mats: One scrap was from an old skirt, one was from the cotton couch-cushion covers I saved when I replaced them. I picked sections with little wear, and again, any imperfection was hidden by the glass.

Fabric can be folded around a precut mat and attached to the back side with a hot-glue gun. Instead, I coated one side of a mat with my handy and familiar one-coat rubber cement, which dries tacky. I pressed the glued side against the wrong side of the fabric. Using an X-Acto knife, I cut the fabric as shown so that I could fold it over and adhere it to the mat's back side.

Then, to give my artwork a visual breather from the fabric pattern, I made a smaller, heavy-paper mat so that it would create a quarter-inch inner border. This worked very well with a black-and-white photo and a black frame.

You can also make fabric frames by taking this method a step further: Use stiffer cardboard.

GLASS SOLUTIONS

If the frame you're using doesn't have glass, reuse other glass you already have.

I cut down large chunks of broken glass and old storm-window glass for frames.

Start with a clean, nonrusty glass cutter—if yours is rusty, buy another and store it in mineral oil. Using a straight edge, score the glass heavily—just once. Bear down hard; you should be able to see the line clearly and hear the scoring process.

Tap the scored line with the opposite end of the glass cutter. If this does not snap the glass, hang the glass over a tabletop with the scored line facing upward. Line up the score with the table's edge. Apply quick pressure downward on the overhanging glass. Wear gloves and protective eyewear.

ARTWORK SOLUTIONS

Now . . . what to frame? I like "real art," but I seldom like it enough to pay real-art prices, so I compromise.

Examples of nonreal but frameable art abound—like the art on calenders and note cards. I received two cards from the same series, from different people. These went in a pair of matched frames. Also, scrutinize magazines with elegant photos that could be cut out and framed. Sometimes the labels from cans and packages have vintage-looking art.

Look for items with a more personal interest. Our attic yielded some interesting old newspapers I plan to frame. Other old finds might include a section of lace or a quilted square.

Family photographs are excellent sources of inexpensive, personal art. Pictures of ancestors are more interesting than the steady stream of student portraits. (And your kids will forever cringe at toothless smiles, acne, and outdated haircuts. Dead people can't complain.)

Create your own artwork to fit the odd-size frame. You may feel you are not artistic enough to paint a picture. Try creating arrangements of pressed flowers. Take up calligraphy or cross-stitch.

Frame your child's art. Once under glass, you'll be amazed at how their brightly colored efforts resemble modern art. I've heard of one family that had a permanent "kid's art" frame and continually put new examples of children's work in this place of honor.

If you have a really wonderful antique frame and absolutely cannot find the right art for it, pop in a mirror.

FINAL NOTES

If you're unable to handle any one aspect of the framing process, ask whether your local frame shop would cut a mat, cut a piece of glass, or cut down a frame for you. You can still save some of the

material and labor costs. The do-it-yourself frame shops save a little money if you want a highly professional job.

Successful framing is marriage of art, mat, and frame. I experiment until I find a combination that I like, but before assembling it permanently and hanging, I leave it out a few days. Then, if I still like it, I finish the job.

A SMARTER STARTER

Save money—and avoid the charcoal-lighter-fluid taste. Next time you barbecue, use this free, easily made charcoal lighter.

Make holes around the bottom of a clean gallon can with a triangle-punch can opener. Then remove both of the can's ends. Use a nail or drill to punch holes on either side of the top, and attach a handle made of coat-hanger wire.

Remove the grill, and set the can in the barbecue. Put one or two sheets of loosely wadded newspaper (use the black-and-white sheets, since colors can release chemicals) in the bottom. Fill the can with briquets. Light the newspaper from the bottom through one of the punched holes. If you will need more briquets for your barbecue, pile them around the outside of the can.

When the coals are glowing, use tongs or a hot pad to lift the can from the barbecue. The lit coals will spread the fire to the surrounding ones.

We tried this, and it worked like a charm.

Gardener's Supply Company, an otherwise marvelous organization, sells a metal tube that does this job for $15.95.

According to the brochure from my electric company, most ovens cost about 28¢ to operate per hour. Charcoal briquets, when purchased at a wholesale store, cost about 10¢ per dozen. If you use the briquets conservatively—say, two dozen per meal, barbecuing chicken will cost the same, or less, than baking it in the oven.

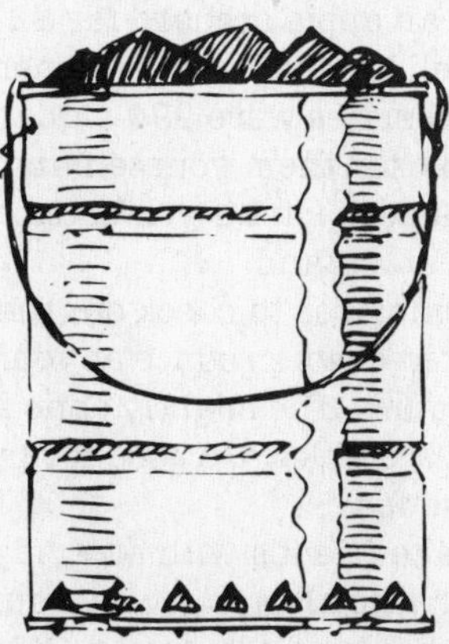

GARDENING ALTERNATIVES

Growing fruits and vegetables isn't a viable option for everyone. But during the harvest season there *are* ways to get produce cheaply.

Reader Lucille Ross of Springfield, Oregon, says her county has a "gleaner association." For $5 a month and two days of work a year, she can get free fruit, veggies, and nuts as well as bread from a local bakery. Check with your local county extension office to see if there is one in your community. You may need to meet income restrictions.

Some farmers throw away their seconds because supermarkets won't take them. Ask around to see if you can find a grower who is willing to sell these for a reduced price.

One man I met recently told me that surplus vegetables from a farmer's market are sold at auction in his area. He buys vegetables there more cheaply than he can grow them.

Check out the "U-Pick" places in your area. We can get "drops" from an apple orchard for $2 a bushel. In Maine this summer strawberries were 99¢ a quart if you picked them yourself and $2.89 per quart if you bought them at a stand.

Remember to check out the marked-down produce at your grocery store. The slightly gone fruits and vegetables are good for breads and soups.

Make friends with an avid gardener who always grows a surplus just in case of a bad year. Offer to help in the garden or to barter. Although most gardeners won't bring it to you, they are happy to share the surplus if you pick it yourself.

Cathy Millet, a reader from Bangor, Maine (a big city for these parts), was so successful in getting produce from alternative sources that she was able to freeze, can, and dry fruits and vegetables, even though she doesn't garden.

Always do your homework, though. Often there is little or no cost savings when you preserve produce that you have purchased.

NO PLAIN, NO GAIN

Dear Amy,

I laugh at the commercial extolling the virtues of "Top Job with ammonia." Why not just use plain ammonia and save yourself the expense?

I also laugh at all the expensive baby powders proclaiming their "100% cornstarch" contents. I buy regular cornstarch at the grocery store for a third of the cost and pour it into an old baby-powder container.

—Paula Ramm
Hoffman Estates, Illinois

(You can mix a cup of ammonia to a gallon of water for a strong cleaner. Use less ammonia when a milder cleaner is needed. Never mix ammonia with bleach. FZ)

THICK TRICK

Dear Amy,

Don't cook down tomatoes to get thick sauce. Once they are prepared and ready to cook, just put them in the refrigerator overnight. In the morning, use your turkey baster to remove the clear liquid that has floated to the top. Voilà!

—Elaine Stalder
Harrisburg, Oregon

LATE RATE

Dear Amy,

Resist the temptation to renew magazine subscriptions whenever they happen to expire. Many magazines offer special holiday gift rates. So I just call or write and give my husband a gift of a renewed subscription, and he does the same for me. I recently saved half the regular subscription rate on a popular golf magazine my husband enjoys!

—Carole Kline
Columbia, Maryland

CHEAP SHOTS

Dear Amy,

Our local health department gives free immunizations to anyone in our county. There are no income requirements. We filled out a couple of short forms, got shots, and were on our way in less than 15 minutes. No waiting room full of sick people, and best of all, it was free! I don't know if it is like this everywhere, but for anyone with kids, it is definitely worth looking into.

—Lisa Thompson
Shelburne, Indiana

GAS VERSUS ELECTRIC

When the day comes to spend big bucks for a new water heater, clothes dryer, or range, many of us simply go with what's familiar: If we're accustomed to gas, that's what we get; ditto for electric.

But there's a better way to make the choice.

Linda Watkins of Crofton, Maryland, sent me a fact sheet put together by the Baltimore Gas and Electric company. The company gathered information from a variety of sources to compile a "Cost of Operation" chart for home appliances. It's incredibly detailed. Did you know the average video-game system (not counting the TV) uses 9¢ worth of electricity a month?

I found the most interesting comparison to be the approximate operating cost per month for gas versus electric appliances. These costs are based on the national average of 9¢ per kilowatt-hour for electricity and 50¢ per therm for natural gas:

- Gas range/oven: $1.85
- Electric range/oven: $10.98

- Gas water heater: $14.32
- Electric water heater: $39.99
  (Based on a 30-gallon heater serving a family of four.)

- Gas clothes dryer: $2.00
- Electric clothes dryer: $9.90

These figures are averages and won't apply in all situations. But they do underscore a general rule that's good to remember: It is almost always a bad idea to make heat with electricity. Electricity is an expensive and precious source

of energy that should be used for what it's best at: tasks such as lighting and powering computers and small motors.

Of course, there are several variables you must take into account before chucking out your electrical collection. Gas may be relatively expensive in your area (if you are not on a natural-gas pipeline and must use bottled propane, your operating cost will almost certainly be greater than for natural gas), while electricity may be fairly cheap. And gas appliances require gas lines and venting; this adds to the installation cost. If there is still some life left in your electrical appliances, *figure out the payback cost* before getting rid of them.

For example: You sell your old electric range for $50. A new gas range, including taxes, delivery fees, and installation, costs $600. If a gas range saves $9.13 per month, it would take five years to make up your $550 out-of-pocket cost. You may decide that this is too long to make it worth the hassle of swapping for gas.

On the other hand, if you *need* a new stove, you'll find that gas ranges cost an average of $150 more than electrics, so you would make up the extra cost of the gas version in just 16 months.

Individual appliances also vary in efficiency, which is why it's essential to check the yellow "Energyguide" label on new appliances to see how they stack up. The figures above are intended to inspire you to compare between the Energyguides on gas and electric appliances—not just between those on electric appliances.

AVOIDING COUCH OUCH

Eleven years ago, Jim and I shopped intensively for a couch. We salivated over trendy, sand-colored, upholstered couches for several days before we came to our senses. Finally, one of us said, "This is nuts. The first time a toddler attacks one of these with a ballpoint pen, we're sunk."

So we opted for a different sort of couch. Though it wasn't my first choice aesthetically, we have never regretted the purchase.

We rationalized that the furniture style sometimes referred to as "crate furniture," manufactured by companies such as Cargo or This End Up, would withstand the toddler onslaught better than any upholstered couch. The style basically is a sturdy, exposed wooden frame with back, seat, and arm cushions. Usually viewed in a small mall store, crowded together with crate chairs, crate coffee tables, crate bookcases, and crate bunk beds, it tends to look a bit heavy. But as a single piece in our living room, the couch looks fine.

We found that this style offered many advantages:

1. An ink blotch, or any other damage, could easily be hidden by flipping the cushion over. (It was actually me, with a pen in my back pocket, who committed the first ink transgression.) Although upholstered couches have flippable seat cushions, the rest of the couch is vulnerable.

2. This kind of furniture is ordered to the customer's specifications, not picked out from a showroom floor. This allowed us to get precisely the dark shade for the cushion covers that we felt would hide dirt and blemishes

best—such as a navy blue (ink-colored) fabric.

3. When the covers get dirty on both sides, they are removable for cleaning. Although the manufacturer recommended dry cleaning, we learned we could wash them in cold water in our washing machine. the savings on the dry-cleaning bill more than offset any possible acceleration of fabric wear.

4. Kid grime could be washed off the wooden frame with Murphy's Oil Soap. Should the frame sustain any damage, we could easily sand out dents, scuff marks, or crayon doodlings and refinish.

5. When the covers wore out completely, we could buy new ones from the manufacturer for much less than we could hire someone to make them for us. (With my limited sewing skills, I figure I could make them myself and save about $1 per hour of work.) The manufacturer also sold replacement foam-rubber cushions.

With six active kids, our couch sees constant use; it's our most commonly sat upon piece of furniture. As a result, we wear out the covers every four years. After eight years we replaced the three foam seat cushions. With each replacement, we have an instant new couch. Aside from the financial savings, I feel a lot better about bagging up old seat covers to save for scraps and zipper scavenging rather than putting a beat-up couch out on the curb.

When we replaced covers the first time, we noticed this manufacturer had one disadvantage: It changes its fabric selection periodically, and our fabric had been discontinued. We realized that if we wanted to replace a single cover sometime in the future, it might not be possible. And now, having gone through two complete sets of covers (seats, backs, and arms), we realize that the seat covers wear out twice as fast as the back and arm covers.

But a solution was at hand. Shortly after we bought our third set of covers, the manufacturer sent us a $50 coupon good toward the purchase or more of their stuff. I suspect they wanted us to buy another big piece of furniture.

Instead, I brilliantly applied the coupon toward the purchase of three more seat covers of the same color as the set we just

bought. We plan to rotate the two sets of seat covers so that each set wears at the same slower rate as the arm and back covers. By doing this, we hope to extend the life expectancy of the entire set of covers from four years to eight years for little extra cost.

Now, let's suppose that you don't have the least inclination to buy a crate-style couch. What can you learn here?

First, whenever you acquire furniture, remember that the concept of a couch or chair with an exposed wooden frame and removable cushions, regardless of the style, makes sense. Other companies make wood-framed furniture. (I don't own any stock in Cargo, and there may be more reasonably priced manufacturers in today's marketplace.) We own an antique Morris chair, an oak armchair with cushions, that has the same advantage. Many current designs could be easily duplicated if someone had the right woodworking skills, a table saw, and a cheap source of materials.

Second, if you do have an upholstered couch and you have it reupholstered, remember that if one of your lovely new seat covers were to be damaged, you might not be able to find the same fabric again. Even if you do find it, dye lots vary—and couch fabric changes due to even the slightest wear, so a new cushion may not look right. So consider having at least one extra seat cover made at the same time. Then rotate the covers. If one is damaged, you'll still have a complete, matching set. If none is damaged, you will at least extend the life of the seat covers—and you might double the life of the whole reupholstery job.

BRINGING UP BABY—CHEAP

As soon as our fourth child outgrew them, I gave away and yard-saled most of the baby things I thought I would never need again.

Enter surprise twins. Suddenly, I had to come up with twice as much as I had just unloaded. So I employed all the baby-stuff tactics I had learned with the first four. Amazingly, when the twins reached their first birthday, I calculated that, aside from food and doctor bills, we had spent less than $100 on them.

Here are our basic strategies:

1. Buy used. When no longer needed, well-maintained items can be resold for the same price as you paid.
2. Subtly steer well-meaning relatives and friends from giving you cute outfits that will fit and/or look new for five minutes. Encourage practical gifts.
3. Borrow. Most people *don't* sell their stuff right away.
4. Graciously accept all the secondhand things people give you. Keep what you can use, pass on what you can't. This ensures a steady flow of used things.
5. Put off necessary purchases until you can find the items cheap. Avoid unnecessary items (this point covers

a lot of ground). Make substitutions, either short- or long-term, to achieve both objectives.

Although you have to acquire some things, often some items can substitute for others, at least temporarily. Here are some ideas:

Baby Shampoo. Use regular shampoo. Simply be careful to keep it out of baby's eyes.

Baby Tub. Wash infant in sink, or hold carefully in a bathtub filled with 2 inches of water.

Baby Wipes. Use old washcloths or cut-up old diapers.

Bottles. Babies can be nursed until a year old (or longer) and then taught to drink from a regular cup, without ever using a bottle.

Car Seat. There is absolutely no substitute for this. Some hospitals rent them for a nominal fee, say $1 per month, but in the long run it would be cheaper to buy a new one. A rental can serve until you find a used one.

Changing Table. Use a towel on a bed or bureau top—with baby-changing items in a nearby shoe box. I never owned a changing table.

Cloth Diapers, Rubber Pants, and Pins. Of the $100 we spent, $65 went to these. Rubber pants can sometimes be bought used, but diapers and pins generally cannot. We never use disposables, even for traveling. Sharon Fluet of Charlotte, North Carolina, says she discovered that cloth diapers could be used even in day-care centers. She says the directors of two separate centers told her that cloth diapers were permissible if she provided an adequate supply of diapers, pins, and plastic pants, provided an airtight container for the used diapers, and took the used diapers home daily. As she put it, "It can't hurt to ask!"

Clothes. If you don't get bag upon bag of free things from friends and relatives, you can find used things by the ton at yard sales, thrift and consignment shops. As long as babies have one good-looking public outfit, what they wear at home doesn't matter. In a pinch, pajamas can be worn in the daytime, and daytime clothes can be worn to bed. In warm weather, babies only need diapers and a shirt.

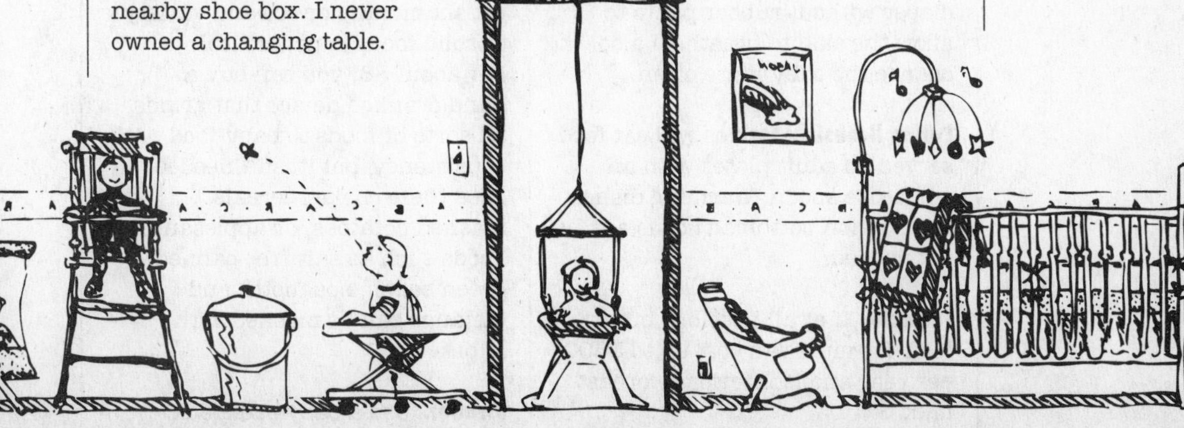

Crib. Use bedding in a bureau drawer on the floor for an infant. Put bedding in a playpen for an older child.

Crib Bumpers. Make a towel roll if you worry about bumped heads.

Diaper Bag. Use any sturdy bag: a duffel bag or backpack, for example. I often simply toss diapers, a bread bag (for wet diapers), and a wet washcloth in a Baggie into a plastic grocery bag for short trips.

Diaper Bucket. Real ones close securely to contain odors. But you can use a 5-gallon bucket that originally contained laundry detergent or drywall compound. Don't leave a bucket of water accessible to a small child.

Diaper Stuff. Shortening substitutes for petroleum jelly, and cornstarch substitutes for powders, but neither is necessary for every change. Some people swear by Desitin for diaper rash, but I remain unconvinced that it speeds healing. I use ointments and powders so sparingly that I never used up the samples I got in the hospital. When a rash is present I have found it's best to bathe the baby and put on a diaper without rubber pants to allow the skin to breathe. I also change the baby more often.

Eating Utensils. Babies will eat food served on adult plates with an adult-size spoon. Warming dishes and suction-bottomed bowls are not needed.

Formula. If at all possible, breastfeed. Formula can cost up to $800 per year and is inferior to breast milk.

Gate. Confine baby in playpen or crib, or close doors. If you need a gate for one doorway only, you can make one that hinges on the door casing.

High Chair. Use a baby swing, walker, or stroller, or hold the baby in your lap while feeding. Or buy the kind of seat that attaches to a tabletop for much less than a high chair.

Mobile. Babies soon tire of these and other entertainment devices. Instead, hold and entertain the baby yourself. The housework can wait a few years.

Pacifiers. All my babies thought these were projectiles.

Playpen. Use a crib or a baby-proofed room with doors or baby gates.

Shoes. Unnecessary (and perhaps even harmful) until the child begins to walk. Use socks and booties in cool weather.

Store-Bought Baby Food. As long as the babies are on breast milk or formula, they are getting adequate nutrition. So the timing (at six months or so) and variety of solid foods is not critical.
For about $8, you can buy a hand-cranked device that grinds all sorts of foods to baby-food consistency, but it isn't needed. Feed them cooked cereals, mashed potatoes, or applesauce. Foods such as salt-free canned green beans, spaghetti, and bananas can be mashed with a fork.

Stroller. Use a baby backpack.

Toys. Babies are happiest with pot lids and measuring spoons, and they are given more toys than they need.

Walker. Some doctors don't like these because of the potential hazard of kids toppling on stairs or thresholds and because they feel it can slow development. But my kids were happier in a walker than in a playpen and safer than on the floor. All walked between 9 and 12 months of age. Walkers aren't essential, but they substitute for many other things.

Wind-up Swing. All of my babies tired of this within a few weeks. Some babies hate it from the start. Buy only if used.

It goes without saying to always think about safety. Older used equipment, homemade toys, and unconventional substitutes may not meet with current safety guidelines. So educate yourself and use your head.

FROM READERS

We asked readers for their best frugal repair tips. Here are the best.

The Plastic-Stuff Fix. Melvin Tremper of Topsham, Maine, has a plastic "welding" technique that he's used to repair laundry baskets and other plastic items. First, he uses his hot-glue gun to seal the crack. Then, with more hot glue, he reinforces the repair with the flat plastic tabs used to close bread bags. He says since the tabs come in different colors, if you save them up, your collection should have some that match the object you are fixing.

Great minds think alike; before reading this, I attempted to fix the hole my dish drainer's foot had poked through its rubber mat using this exact same technique: I hot-glued a bread tab to both sides of the hole. However, the water and weight won out. I've put a juice lid over the hole until I can figure out something else.

Shower-Curtain Fixes. To save a favorite shower curtain that was tearing at the hanger holes, Shirley Jacobs of Tucson, Arizona, painted metal washers a complementary color and affixed them with Goop glue. Other possible hole reinforcers are plastic washers and scrap plastic (from milk jugs, plastic lids, etc.) cut into washers.

Joy Ramler of Greenville, South Carolina, saved her shower curtain by folding down the top, then sewing buttonholes through the doubled material about a half inch below the old holes.

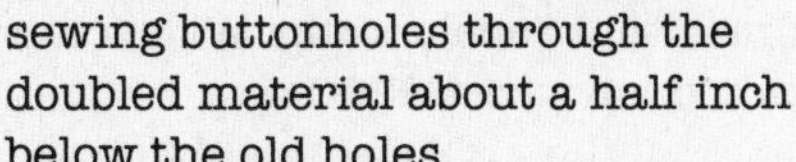

We noticed that our upstairs tub/shower curtain's end holes tore, while the middle ones held, so when we needed a new curtain for our downstairs shower stall, we just cut out the upstairs curtain's center section to use downstairs and bought a new curtain for upstairs.

I've wondered if hot glue could be used to fix shower curtains. I have used it to successfully repair the side seam that always splits in babies' rubber pants. So far, it seems to be holding up to washing.

The Laundry-Basket "Mesh" Fix. A plastic laundry basket that has a tear in its light mesh "weave" can be fixed by applying duct tape to the inside *and* outside of the torn area. The tape sticks to itself and holds the tear tightly.

Sneaker Fixes. The weak spot in running shoes is always where the upper is glued to the sole. I gave up on duct-tape repair and am experimenting with hot glue. This works better with porous materials such as suede and canvas rather than vinyl. Jane Ann Sayers of Elizabeth, Illinois, put inner-tube cutouts inside her tennis shoes after she had worn a hole in the sole.

The Car-Top Fix. When the vinyl top on the 1975 Oldsmobile that belongs to Tom Hoy of Scotland, South Dakota, began to tear due to time and moisture penetration, he sealed it with three coats of urethane finish. Not only did this seal the cracks, it gave the top a glossy finish that repels water. A new top would have cost $200.

Refrigerator-Door Fixes. Jean Fountain of Iowa City, Iowa, says that when the door handle of her refrigerator broke, she replaced it with a bolted-on leather-belt section. When that eventually broke, her husband removed the chrome oven-door handle from an old cookstove, sawed it to length, drilled it, and bolted it to the refrigerator. A new handle would have cost $58.

My grandmother's refrigerator repair illustrates the same concept: Do a quick fix until you can get a permanent one. When the door catch failed, she hooked one end of a bungee cord to the handle and the other to a hook on the wall behind the fridge. This held her over until a visiting handy relative took the door apart and fixed it for her.

The Toilet-Flapper-Chain Fix. Dick Bauer of Hartford, Wisconsin, used 25-pound test, braided, nylon fishing line to replace his toilet's broken flapper chain.

The Screen-Door Fix. Tracy Creager of Kettering, Ohio, also used fishing line—in this case, to "sew" a patch of screen material into a hole in her screen door. "It may not look as nice as a new screen, but it keeps the bugs out," she writes.

The Washer-Tub Fix. Kenneth Rondeau of Manchester, New Hampshire, had a ⅛-inch hole in the tub of his 14-year-old washing machine that seemed unfixable—until an appliance repairman told him about "metal-repair epoxy putty." He followed the package directions and reports that the $2.95 repair has lasted four months.

The Zipper Fix. Joanna Garber Miller of Jarrettsville, Maryland, writes that when she found the zipper on her consignment-shop jeans would not stay up, she threaded a paper clip to the top of her zipper pull. Then she opened the upper loop of the clip to make

a hook to loop over the jean-button's shank. She always makes sure that the open side of the paper clip is directed toward the inside of the fly, so it does not peek out.

The When-You-Can't Fix. Finally, keep in mind that you need not always repair something if you can find a workable substitute. The gas gauge on my friend's car broke two years ago and would have cost over $200 to fix. He simply got into the habit of resetting his trip odometer every time he filled up with gas. He calculated his car's mileage and discovered it went 400 miles on a tankful. So now he fills the tank every time the odometer hits 350. He has no need for the gauge.

THE PIZZA PLAN

Dear Amy,

I, too, am the mother of pizza fiends and have resorted to clever ways of satisfying appetites without going broke. I make pizza crusts four to six at a time, then "par" bake for 8 minutes at 350 degrees, cool and stack in a large freezer bag. I go to a local dairy that has a cheese outlet and pay $1.59 for ends of mozzarella or provolone—this amounts to a savings of over $1.00 over grocery-store brands. I buy at least 5 pounds at a time, go home, get out the food processor, grate it all, and spread it on baking pans to freeze. Then I put it in Ziploc bags and use as it is needed. It keeps for months and cooks up beautifully.

—Sarah Severns
Kensington, Ohio

OBEY OR PAY

Dear Amy,

Saving tip: Always obey the speed limit! Not only will this save you gas, stress, wear and tear on tires, brakes, etc., and reduce the chance of costly accidents, but a speeding ticket can be a penny-pincher's disaster! I should know: I got one, and now our auto insurance is going through the roof. "Bad driver" surcharges stay with you three to five years, and we're talking hundreds of dollars per year (not to mention the fine!).

—Alida Snow and Phil Carey
Bath, Maine

TANKS FOR NOTHING

Dear Amy,

I know a man who is a plumber and therefore has access to old hot-water heaters as he replaces them for people. He has taken several of them and hooked them up in a series at the side of his house

out of sight. All water coming into his home from the city supply is routed through these old heaters before it gets to his faucets indoors. He always has a supply of 300-plus gallons of fresh water on hand for emergencies. Here in California we are cautioned to have enough water for our family's use for 72 hours.

—Laurine Jones
Moraga, California

NOT FOR HAIR ONLY

Dear Amy,

I have used Breck Shampoo (full-strength) to remove grease, blood, grass stains, ink, etc. for at least 20 years. I have even used it to soak clothes (charred black from fighting a fire) overnight and then washed as usual and *no stains.* I buy a 16-ounce bottle for 99¢ less 50¢ to 60¢ with a double coupon. No more expensive prestain treatments for me.

—Barbara Blau
Bartow, Florida

COOL AT SCHOOL

Dear Amy,

My children felt deprived because other children were bringing box drinks or "Squeeze-Its" in their lunch boxes. In their school, thermoses are considered "uncool."

I found some colored cosmetic squeeze bottles on sale and bought some. They're the kind sold to use in travel for shampoo, etc. They have a pull-out, push-in top and are leakproof.

I started filling the bottles with juice, milk, or water and putting them in lunch boxes. I told my children they had their own reusable "Squeeze-Its." They haven't complained since.

The amazing thing is that their friends have started doing the same thing, and now it has spread through the school. My children feel like they started something.

—Deanna Beutler
Littleton, Colorado

RAGS TO RINSES

Dear Amy,

I restore limp but otherwise good-condition yard-sale clothing with a light rinse of starch. Makes it "new" looking.

—Alice Strong
El Monte, California

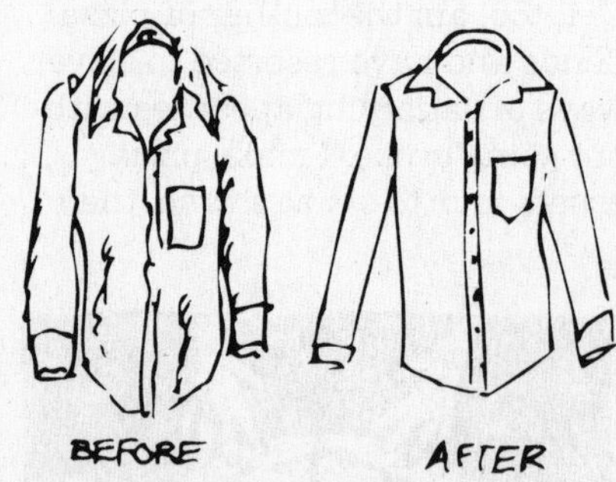

WRITE MAKES RIGHT

Dear Amy,

Keeping a record of monthly expenses is the best thing for reforming a spendthrift! It worked for me, and my husband (a firm believer in frugality) and I are thrilled! It makes me think about each expense.

For example, generally, after I pay our bills on the 15th of the month, I have $300 left over to get us through to the next paycheck. After just two weeks of recording and considering expenses, I paid our bills on May 15 and had over $1,300 left over. What a testimony to the practice of disciplined record-keeping!

—Kirsten Melton
Pleasant Hill, California

A LOFTY IDEA

Dear Amy,

I have noticed that the kids can get very excited over simple things. A prime example was a small backyard tree house I built in a willow tree. All I did was take a pallet and rest it into the crotch of the tree. I nailed it for security and put a piece of scrap plywood on top. My older boys almost lived there during the summer. Every day I had to go out and see what "improvements" they had made.

—Conrad Potemra
Poolesville, Maryland

(Conrad goes on to describe a sandbox he made from a used tractor tire—he set the tire on its side and enlarged the opening with a jig saw—and a swingset he made from old telephone poles. FZ)

ACTIVE AND PASSIVE TIGHTWADDERY

Three years ago, Neal, then five, tousle-haired and sleepy-eyed, stumbled into the kitchen and asked me for help with a stubborn blue-jean snap. As I stooped to fasten it, I had to chuckle to myself.

In what seemed like a previous life, I had patched the jeans with my whole-knee-patch technique I wrote about in the first book—a method where I patched pants by sewing on a large piece of good denim scavenged from the cut-off leg of another pair of jeans.

But Neal's pants had developed holes in the patches months ago, and not only did I lack the time to repair them, but I seriously wondered if I would *ever* have time to patch pants again.

These pants, previously worn by two cousins, a sister, and a brother, revealed as rich a history as any archaeologist could hope to find. And they demonstrate the two types of frugality—passive and active.

When most people think of thriftiness, all those active images come to mind. They imagine patching pants, baking bread, hanging laundry, and rebuilding car engines. It all sounds like so much hard work.

But most of frugality is about the passive stuff—it's not what we do, it's what we don't do. It's about letting pants go unpatched.

This idea is surprisingly difficult to get across. When photographers from the media come here, they want to take pictures of active frugality. After the first couple of shoots, we ran out of new examples of active frugality with sufficient "visual interest" to show

them. As a result, I've hung laundry on my attic clothesline for a dozen photographers.

But it always bothered me to do this, because I was afraid I was actually scaring people away from frugality—making it seem like it took tons of time and effort.

Instead, we suggested they shoot what we *don't* do. We told them they could set up the video camera across the street from McDonald's, and we'd pile all the kids in our Chevy Suburban and zzzooommm by. Or we could go to the supermarket, and they could position their cameras looking down the potato-chip aisle and capture that split second as we bypassed it.

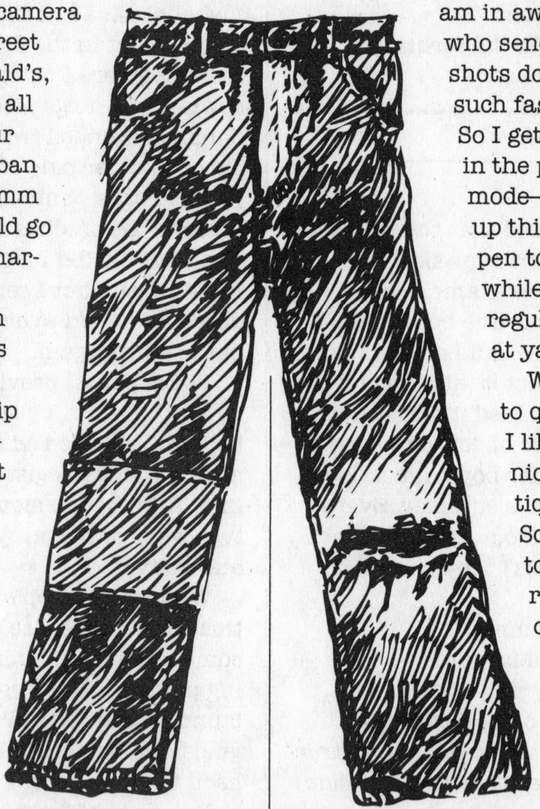

The photographers looked at us like we'd been eating too many bread-crumb cookies and sent us back to the attic to hang our laundry.

The frugal lifestyle encompasses both modes, and they are equally valid. However, each of us will make different choices based on what we like to do, what quality issues are important to us, and how much time and energy we have. Let's look at these factors, one by one.

I would much rather be working in the garden, with dirt squishing up between my toes, than buying cases of vegetables at the warehouse store. Because I like gardening, we employ active frugality to get our vegetables.

Conversely, I don't enjoy sewing enough to whip up matching Easter outfits for all eight members of my family (I am in awe of readers who send me snapshots documenting such fashion feats). So I get nice clothes in the passive mode—by picking up things as I happen to see them while doing my regular shopping at yard sales.

When it comes to quality issues, I like to have nice-looking antique furniture. So I am willing to spend hours refinishing a chair.

On the other hand, eating exquisitely prepared meals every day is low on my quality list, so we eat simply prepared, sometimes humdrum scratch foods rather than fussed-over dishes.

But I have learned that the most important factor in the active/passive question does seem to be time.

Within weeks of being notified we were going to be on the cover of *Parade* magazine, my obstetrician saw two blobs on the ultrasound screen and said, "Uh oh!"

We experienced the most wonderful/horrible year you could imagine. The number of our offspring increased by 50 percent as our fledgling business went from 1,500 subscribers to over 50,000. All that active-frugality stuff got tossed out the window.

Jim stopped baking bread and began buying it at the bakery thrift store. We postponed do-it-yourself renovations. I wrote letters less frequently.

I prefer to do active-frugality humdinger birthday parties that would blow any Hallmark-accessorized extravaganza right out of the water. That year, the kids were lucky just to pick the color of the frosting on a sheet cake.

Gradually our lives have begun to fall into place again. We hired a business manager and bought a separate building for our employees, while I still work from home. I hired additional research and support help to work directly on the newsletter. As a result, Jim has been able to fully retire from the workaday world. He now runs the home and takes care of the children.

We've found time for those active things again. Jim dug out his bread recipes, and I actually patched a pair of pants. The first time I went hunting in the attic for a piece of denim with a suitable shade-of-fade match, I found a cutoff pant leg with one of those holey whole-knee patches and chuckled to myself again.

BUY ALL THAT YOU CAN BUY—FROM THE ARMY

The focal point of the Second Annual *Tightwad Gazette* Barbecue and Croquet Tournament was a canopied smorgasbord table, which ranks as one of Jim's finest near-freebie achievements. He constructed it from a military-surplus parachute, a center pole, a 6-foot-diameter cable spool, tent stakes, and small poles cut from our woods.

The men in attendance—cowed and flustered by my no-mercy croquet style—huddled under it and made admiring comments. Although partly motivated by their fear of another game with me, they also gathered there out of sheer awe for Jim's creation.

"Sure, great," you mutter. "Her husband was in the Navy. Where do mere civilians get this stuff?"

Any civilians—or military personnel—over age 18 can buy surplus at military auctions.

We spoke with Lee Rude and Dale Guiou, who run the Defense Reutilization and Marketing Office (DRMO) at the Brunswick, Maine, Naval Air Station, and with Jim, the scrounging chief of our tightwad estate, who has been to these auctions both in Norfolk, Virginia, and Brunswick.

Military auctions sell anything that the Defense Department no longer needs. Once it has been offered to, and rejected by, other federal, state, and local government agencies, military surplus goes on the block.

The major exceptions are weapons and jeeps (sorry, the old "$50 surplus jeep" is a myth: The Department of Transportation won't allow military jeeps to be

sold because they cannot be licensed for public road use). And generally, items worth more than about $10,000 are sold through a nationwide "sealed bid" auction, which your local DRMO can also tell you about.

To find an auction, first locate the DRMO office nearest you. There are 142 of them around the world—including three right here in little old Maine. If there is a military base of any size near you, call base information and ask for the DRMO office. The people there will tell you when the next auction is. To get a complete list of stuff to be auctioned, ask to be put on their mailing list.

Typical items offered include chairs, couches, desks, bookcases, lawn mowers, bush hogs, garden tractors, refrigerators, stoves, computers, sound equipment, pickup trucks, and boats. Sometimes there's even stuff for kids, as the bases cycle toys, cribs, high chairs, and other items through their day-care centers.

Clothing—mostly uniforms—is generally sold by the crateload, and consequently usually bought by surplus stores rather than by individuals.

Along with this mundane stuff there is also a wide selection of exotica to excite the backyard tinkerer. Oddments Jim has seen include 55-gallon drums full of skis, broken-down tractors, barrels of outdated lubricants, automatic barnacle-scrapers, snowmobiles, ejectable fuel tanks from aircraft (these make great floats for docks), even the landing parachutes from an *Apollo* space capsule.

If you know what you're doing, these auctions can be a source of income. Guiou said one lady bought a gadget with the intriguing title of "titillating machine," for $85. "She had done her homework," he said. "It turns out this thing was part of a heating system for a large warehouse. She sold it for somewhere around $10,000."

While the Defense Department is to be commended for holding these auctions (it beats throwing the stuff away, right?), the items for sale can give you a disturbing peek at Taxes Down the Drain. Example: The Navy phases

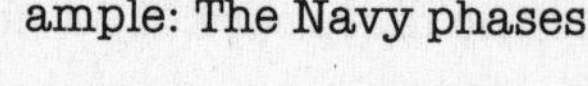

in—and phases out—an expensive new gun so rapidly that the expensive new gun-adjusting tools, in their perfect, watertight cases, never get used and get sold at auction. Jim says at the auction he attended, people bought these, threw away the tools, and kept the nice boxes.

There's a two-day inspection period before the auction. It's important to inspect stuff for two reasons:

1. Many items, especially those with motors, are probably busted, otherwise, another government agency would have snatched them. Inspection will tell you whether they can be fixed.

2. Items are not displayed on the auction block on the day of sale; the auctioneer will say only, "What am I bid for lot twenty-seven?" If you haven't inspected lot 27, you'll be stuck.

The government's goal is to get back 5 percent of its purchase price (hmmmm . . . 5 percent of a $600 toilet seat is . . .). At the last auction he organized, Rude says he got a 12 percent return.

Once you buy your titillating machine, automatic barnacle-scraper, or any other goody, you have five days to remove it.

Military auctions are like most other types of auctions: Some stuff goes cheaply, some seems moderate, and some overpriced. You must regard auction-going as a form of entertainment, with a great buy as a lucky by-product.

(Incidentally, the men at our barbecue learned there was no reason to fear my croquet prowess. The neat aspect of this game is that even a ten-year-old beginner can—and did—beat the likes of me.)

TRANSMISSION CONTROL

Dear Amy,

Last week, the transmission went out on my eight-year-old Subaru GL station wagon. I took it to my local mechanic, who is very good and trustworthy. He called back and told me that the only used transmission he could find would cost me $600. . . . I immediately began calling salvage yards in the area and in ten minutes located a transmission for my car, in a town 40 miles away, for $200.

My mechanic wasn't surprised. He said, "I don't have time to call around . . . and I don't have time to drive 40 miles." I drove the 40 miles, picked up the transmission, and had it installed in my car. I saved $400.

—Angie Lockhart
Eudora, Kansas

RUGS AND HUGS

Dear Amy,

My carpet needed cleaning. I rented the steam cleaner ($19) and bought liquid carpet cleaner ($5) and defoamer ($5). My two neighbors are elderly widows.

After I finished my carpets I had solution left, so I offered to clean their carpets. They were so pleased, and I was glad to do it. Each offered me $10. So my $30 went down to $10. My carpets were clean, and I felt good to do a favor. Both told me it would have cost $40 to have their carpets cleaned professionally.

—Susan Pannutti
Hillsville, Pennsylvania

LIPSTICK TRICK

Dear Amy,

I found a way to use that last stub of lipstick to make lip gloss. Put the lipstick stub with an equal amount of petroleum jelly in a small dish. Melt in a microwave about one minute, stirring a couple of times with a small stick. Keep in a small container. It works as well as the store-bought kind.

—Mary Steiner
Greenfield, Massachusetts

A PAIR OF REPAIRS

Dear Amy,

My husband just repaired our VCR tape player. It would start and then kick off . . . a small rubber band that ran to the counter had worn out and snapped. He put in a new plain brown rubber band that we get every morning on our newspaper. The last time this happened, about a year ago, he repaired it the same way.

The silverware basket in my dishwasher is plastic. One of the crosspieces in the bottom broke out, and the silverware handles would fall through. So I took a plastic trash-bag tie—the jagged slip-through type—and slipped it through both sides of the open space and strapped it tight. This has lasted at least two years.

—Shireen Eddings
Glendale, Arizona

WATT A SAVINGS!

Dear Amy,

Before beginning a tightwad regime, our yearly cost for electricity was $1,443.64. After:

1. Air-drying all of our clothes instead of using the dryer,

2. Using the air conditioner only when the internal temperature of the house went over 85, and

3. Being vigilant about turning off lights, our yearly bill decreased to $609.58—we saved $934.06!

—Kerry and Vernon Bassett
Clarksville, Georgia

SOLAR CLEANER

Dear Amy,

To clean gunky grills and oven racks: On a hot, sunny day place them in a dark plastic trash bag. Pour a cup of ammonia into the bag, seal with a twist tie, and leave out to cook in the sun. At the end of the day take out the grills and wash under hose water. Most of the crud will wipe off.

—Marian Hukle
Tonganoxie, Kansas

A is for apple-oatmeal bars. The recipe is from *Stories and Recipes of the Great Depression* by Rita Van Amber (Van Amber Publishers, P.O. Box 267, Menomonie, WI 54751):

1 cup oatmeal
1/2 teaspoon salt
1/2 cup butter
1 cup flour
1/2 teaspoon cinnamon
2 1/2 cups chopped apples
1/2 cup sugar

Combine the first five ingredients, and pat half into an 8-inch-by-8-inch pan. Layer on apples and sugar. Crumble remaining mixture on top. Bake 35 minutes at 350 degrees.

B is for barbed-wire wreath, which I saw in a (trash-picked) *Country Living* magazine. You don't have to buy craft materials to make one, but even better, you have an incentive to finally remove that camouflaged barbed-wire booby trap in the woods that you stumbled over in a slapstick-in-real-life style, tearing a hole in this year's jeans.

C is for credit-card insurance, which you don't need. Federal law protects you in case of loss or theft of credit cards. If you notify the issuing company immediately, you don't have to pay anything. Even if you don't make the notification immediately, your maximum liability is $50 per card on charges made after the loss or theft.

D is for defrost. Do it when the ice buildup in your freezer reaches 1/4-inch deep; doing it more or less often wastes energy.

E is for egg-carton bats, a Halloween decoration. Use a three-egg-cup section. Cut off the outer third of the end cups. String a rubber band, fastened by a small nail or pin, through the top of the middle one to make the bat fly. Paint the whole thing

black, and paint, draw, or glue on eyes. (Beth Vipperman, Fort Lauderdale, Florida.)

F is for film, which can be purchased cheaply in one of two ways: Buy outdated rolls from a photo shop, freeze, and thaw when needed, which we've done with great success, or get it by mail from a discount developer. Both Clark and York Color Labs sell three rolls of 100-speed, 36-exposure, 35mm film for about $6.10. We've also been happy with mail-order film developing.

G is for grocery-store scale, a great tool for saving on produce. When buying produce sold by the bag or piece instead of by the pound, weigh several to determine the heaviest. If a "5-pound" bag of fruit weighs 5½ pounds, you get that ½ pound free.

H is for hangers: classic tightwad raw material. Years ago I made a new "fastener" for an overall strap with coat-hanger wire. Using two pairs of pliers, the task required 45 while-watching-TV minutes, but I get a rush each time the overalls get passed down to another kid and I see my creation again. A new set of fasteners costs $2.50. Another way to get cheap sewing notions is by scavenging from yard-sale clothes.

I is for ice-cream sandwich, which the ice cream truck sold for 50¢, which the Navy commissary sold for 12½¢, and which we sold for 25¢ to our kids whenever the truck came by.

J is for the jar into which we put the ice-cream sandwich profits, along with deposit money from cans that we picked up along the side of the road, for a fund to go to the carnival.

K is for kaput, which is what an item must be, absolutely, before a tightwad will consider throwing it away.

L is for labeling. Put the family member's name on a glass, mug, towel, or other frequently washed item. Make the user responsible for deciding when the item needs cleaning, thus eliminating unnecessary washings. Reader Rosanne Dobbin of New York City suggests giving each family member a "unique" cloth napkin holder, so that the napkins can be used for more than one meal. Although paper napkins can also be reused, cloth napkins look better the second, third, or fourth time around.

M is for milk-crate toddler swing. Jim made one by cutting away two places for feet to come through. He then tied the crate securely to an existing swing. Once toddler Brad is belted in, it's impossible for him to fall out (his twin sister, Laura, doesn't like it). Milk crates are the property of the dairy, regardless of how you came by them, and therefore should be returned. This crate belonged to a dairy that went out of business years ago. If you don't have a "legal" milk crate, you can also make a toddler swing by scavenging the seat from a kaput indoor wind-up baby swing. (Since the elements will weather the seat, you shouldn't use one from a good swing.)

N is for nuts. I figure you'd have to be nuts to pay $4 a pound for something that only adds a bit of crunch to a cookie. At best, they are a healthful extravagance. Instead, I buy bulk, shelled sunflower seeds from a local health-food store. On sale, they are 89¢ a pound.

O is for oil-and-filter change. The cheapest local garages charge $15. Buying oil on sale for under $1, and filters for under $3, Jim can do a change for $7 in 15 minutes.

P is for poison-ivy relief. Once when severely afflicted, I was driven to a spending frenzy and bought every cream on the market. None worked. More recently I accidentally discovered, and later read in *The Doctor's Book of Home Remedies* by Rodale Press, that very hot water can provide relief. Submerse the rash in the hottest tap water you can stand. For the first few minutes the itching will intensify greatly. When the itching subsides you will be itch-free for a sufficient amount of time to, say, fall asleep.

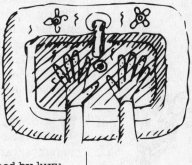

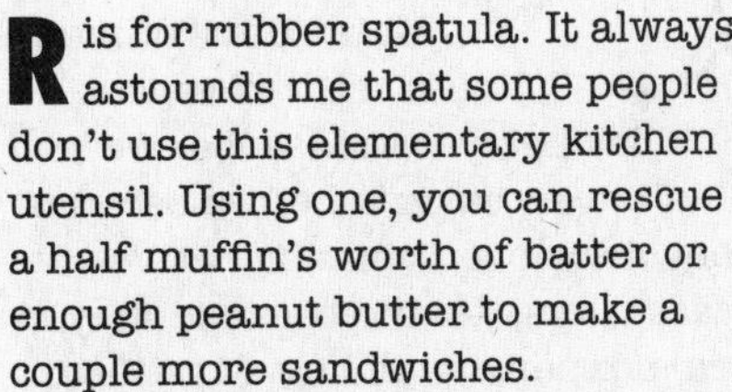

Q is for quote: "That most of us are considered poor is no disgrace, but does us credit; for, as the mind is weakened by luxurious living, so it is strengthened by a frugal life." Minucius Felix, third century A.D.

R is for rubber spatula. It always astounds me that some people don't use this elementary kitchen utensil. Using one, you can rescue a half muffin's worth of batter or enough peanut butter to make a couple more sandwiches.

S is for stamps, which you can buy by mail instead of wasting gas driving to the post office. The Postal Service pays postage both ways. Request a "stamps by mail" envelope from your local post office.

T is for thermos, which we religiously fill with ice water to take in the car every time we drive anywhere. When

the kids claim they are dying of thirst and must have a soda, we practice frugal rehydration.

U is for user's manuals. If you have a tool or appliance problem, check these first to save time and/or repair costs. Jim spent an hour trying to figure out the reason for the oil leak from the top of the gearbox on his Rototiller. Completely stumped, he finally consulted the manual and learned that it was *supposed* to leak—it's the overflow feature. You should keep all your manuals and warranties together in a file folder.

V is for vegetable storage. Root vegetables, like carrots and parsnips, can be stored in a cool, dark place in 5-gallon buckets of sand. Layer vegetables flat so that they don't touch each other. Scott and Helen Nearing, famous Maine environmentalists, stored vegetables in layers of leaves. We didn't grow carrots before because they grew poorly in our native Massachusetts and because they are inexpensive to buy. Mystified, our new Maine neighbors showed us their fine carrot crops and this sand-bucket method of preservation. We converted.

W is for whipped topping. Here's an inexpensive and relatively healthy recipe:

1 teaspoon unflavored gelatin
2 teaspoons cold water
3 tablespoons boiling water
1/2 cup ice water
1/2 cup dry milk powder
3 tablespoons sugar
3 tablespoons oil

Chill a small bowl. Soften gelatin in the cold water, then add the boiling water, stirring until the gelatin is completely dissolved. Cool until tepid. Place the ice water and milk powder in the chilled bowl. Beat at high speed until it forms peaks. While still beating, add the sugar, then the oil and the gelatin. Place in the freezer for about 15 minutes, then transfer to the refrigerator. Stir before using. Makes 2 cups for about 27¢.

X is for xenoJell-Ophobia. An irrational fear that strange convenience foods like Jell-O Pudding Snack Paks will invade your happy tightwad home. (Bet you were wondering what I'd come up with for *X*.)

Y is for yeast, one of the best bulk-buy deals. It costs $2.56 a pound when purchased in bulk from our health-food store, versus $23.29 per pound purchased in individual packets in the supermarket. Bulk-purchased yeast is usually sold in 1–2-pound bags. If you are afraid you won't use it all up before it goes bad, split the bag, and the cost, with a friend. Even if you *give away* half of it, you'll still save money.

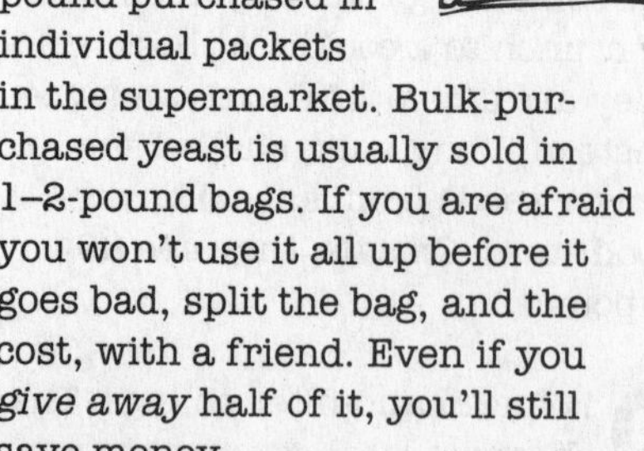

Z is for zero, my favorite price.

THE SUPERMARKET VERSUS THE STOCK MARKET

I have gotten a few letters from people who feel it's time for the newsletter to "graduate" to the big leagues, to discuss a really important, more intellectual topic: investing. They want my views on mutual funds, CDs, T-bills, IRAs, REITs, DRIPs, and so on.

They don't intend to be critical, but reading between the lines, the implication is that the information in the newsletter to date is unimportant, penny-ante, "women's" stuff.

I'm not closing out the option; I may write about investing in the future. But at the moment I have no plans to do so. Here's why:

1. I'm not qualified. Frankly, I sometimes wonder if anyone is. Experts seldom agree on even basic points. Examples: Charles Givens thinks whole-life insurance is always a rip-off. Some experts recommend prepaying your mortgage, but conflicting articles say the money could be better used for investing. These two issues, although somewhat complex, look like child's play compared to other areas of investing; among mutual funds alone there are over 3,000 to choose from.

2. The "right" investment changes constantly. When we were saving for this house, our CDs performed better than our mutual funds. Since then, the trend has reversed. Lately the two have just about evened out, and who knows what will happen next month? I much prefer the "timeless" quality of frugality. People tell me they save the *Gazette* in a three-ring 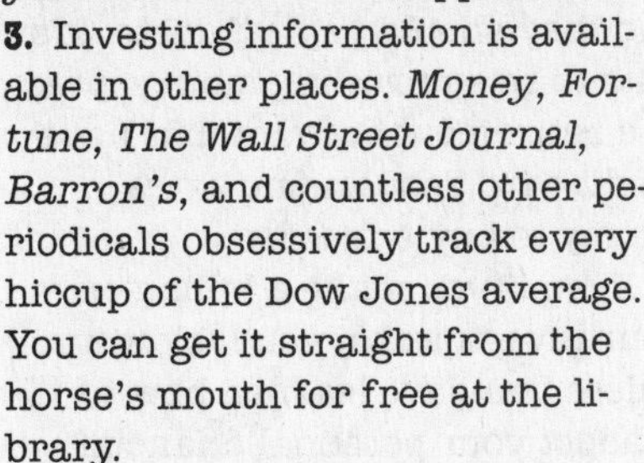 binder. The information in a two-year-old issue is still applicable.

3. Investing information is available in other places. *Money, Fortune, The Wall Street Journal, Barron's,* and countless other periodicals obsessively track every hiccup of the Dow Jones average. You can get it straight from the horse's mouth for free at the library.

4. Compared to investing, tightwaddery is more tangible. It's simple; I don't need to be a rocket scientist to track grocery prices in my price book. It's predictable; I know if I install a low-flow shower head I'll save money on my energy bill. It's quantifiable; I can always figure out something with a calculator, such as the cost of flushing the toilet. It's testable; I can put Desitin on one side and nothing on the other to see if it heals diaper rash faster (it didn't on my kids).

5. Most people need to do a more basic type of investing first. They

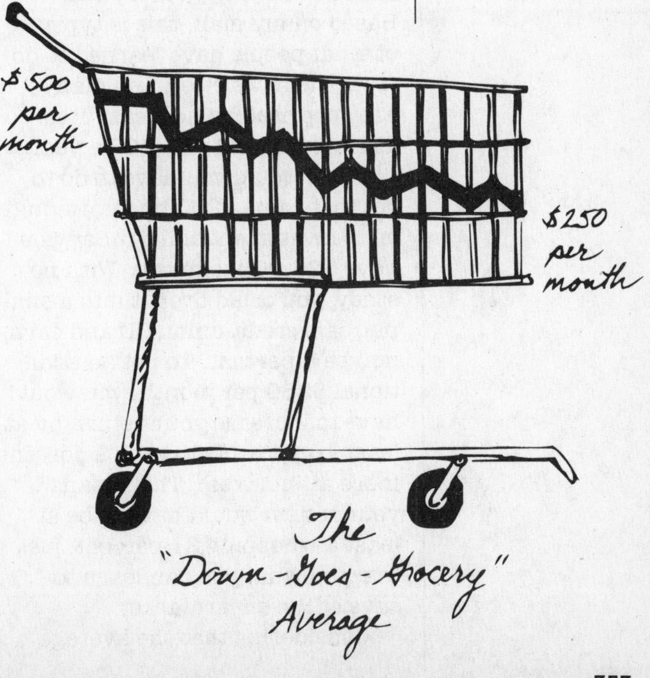

should put money into tools and maintenance that will save money, and they should pay off debts. It's nuts to be squirreling money away in a retirement account, but have credit-card debt and no extra money to buy a freezer.

6. Even if you make a killing on your investments, you'll blow it all unless you have learned how to conduct your personal financial life. It would be the same as getting a raise and never feeling it because your poor spending habits absorb the financial gain. Almost all of the financial giants, from J. D. Rockefeller to J. Paul Getty to Sam Walton, were tightwads *before* they made their money. That's how they got it to invest, and that's how they hung on to it.

But here's the clincher, the climax, the triple-whammy:

7. Tightwaddery gives you a great financial return for a similar investment of time.

Suppose you learn to save $250 a month on your grocery bill. Based on my mail, this is typical of what people have learned to do from the newsletter, and many are surprised by how easy it is. This works out to $3,000 a year.

What would you have to do to get that same $250 by improving your investment ability? Say you have $25,000 to invest. With no study, you could drop it into a simple, safe credit-union CD and earn maybe 5 percent. To net an additional $250 per month, you would have to increase your return by at least 16 percent (to net 12 percent more after taxes). This means your return would have to be at least a whopping 21 percent, just to equal what you can learn to save at the supermarket.

Considering that the average mutual fund lost money in the first six months of this year, anyone whose investments are doing this well is a financial wizard, is probably devoting a great deal of time to study, and/or is extremely lucky.

The supermarket doesn't require a huge amount of money, time, or luck. And it's safe (providing you can squeak by those Jell-O Pudding Snack Paks).

In short, there's nothing wrong with learning about investing—particularly if you own your home, are debt-free, have a financial surplus, and have mastered all the principles of penny-pinching. But in my experience, very few people have all of these bases covered. Until you do, it's incorrect to assume that investing is a superior pursuit to tightwaddery.

As long as the newsstands and airwaves are crowded with information about investing, I'm going to stick with what I write about best.

A BETTER BREAKFAST

Listen up, all you despisers of hot cereals! So you hate the pasty consistency of oatmeal? Try this hot-breakfast idea recently passed on to me by a friend.

Serve hot rice with milk and sugar. It was so successful, it became an instant addition to our breakfast repertoire. We tried it plain with brown sugar, and with cinnamon and raisins.

We buy store-brand, white, long-grain enriched rice in 5-pound bags for 27¢ per pound. At about 4¢ a serving, this is as cheap as cornmeal mush, which

was the cheapest breakfast we found in our "Breakfast Breakthrough" survey on page 24. And who could liken the consistency of cooked rice to that beige slime?

Rice, cooked from scratch, is quick to prepare. And leftover rice steams well, making an even easier breakfast.

THIS SPUD'S FOR YOU

One of our favorite cheap-and-easy meals is baked potatoes topped with chopped, steamed broccoli, cheese sauce, and a sprinkle of bacon bits. I can feed my entire family for less than a dollar with this complete, balanced dish.

In the fall, we get a 50-pound bag of potatoes from a local, independent market for $3.99. Stored in a cool, dry place, they last into the spring. Although we live in potato country now, even when we lived in Virginia we could get 50 pounds for $4.99.

Again, if this is more than you can use, *cooperate.* Split the cost with one or more friends. We frequently sell a small quantity of bulk goods at cost to singles, couples, and smaller families.

For the rest of the year, we buy 10-pound bags for around $1.50. This means that a large potato costs us an average of 3¢ to 5¢.

We grow and freeze the broccoli, so it is practically free.

We buy and freeze bacon when it is a loss-leader sale item at about 89¢ a pound. To get enough for one meal, I saw off about 1 inch from the end of the frozen slab with my multipurpose Ginsu knife (also cuts through nails and beer cans! Somebody gave it to me—I swear I didn't succumb to one of those TV ads). Bacon should not be considered a protein. Use it sparingly, and think of it as a condiment.

The cheese sauce is simple (no, don't buy Cheez Whiz and nuke it in the microwave). Melt 2 tablespoons of butter in a saucepan. Blend in 2 tablespoons of flour. Combine it with 1 cup of milk, and salt and pepper to taste. Cook until sauce thickens. Add a half-cup of grated cheddar cheese and cook until smooth. You can freeze any surplus. (Cooks of any experience will recognize this recipe as a white sauce with cheese added. Any basic cookbook will offer other white-sauce variations; many of them are potential candidates for toppers.)

To use the least energy, bake potatoes in your microwave. The only exception would be if you are already baking something else in your conventional oven; then it makes sense to toss in some spuds. When we use the conventional oven, we string three or four potatoes on a skewer. This radiates heat inside them and cuts about ten minutes off the cooking time. We skip the foil and/or butter coating.

I cut each baked potato in quarters (or in eighths for a small child) before adding the chopped broccoli, cheese sauce, and bacon bits.

Even if we had to buy the broccoli, we could make a one-potato portion for under 20¢.

Another potato-topper combination we like is chili topped with shredded cheddar cheese. We make chili in large quantities and freeze the surplus in meal-size containers.

To learn about other possible topper combinations, I sent an undercover agent to check out a Mr. Potato fast-food joint in a local mall. Along with the combinations I've come up with, it sells: chives and sour cream; pizza-style; onion, bacon, chives, and sour cream; cheese and mushroom; meatball sauce; sweet-and-sour chicken; and spinach soufflé. It shouldn't take too much imagination to replicate these in your tightwad kitchen.

Far more breathtaking than the multitude of combinations we found were the prices: a "Broccoli 'n Cheese" goes for $3.39, and a "Chili Tex-Mex" is $3.54.

Need I say more?

SPACE: THE FRUGAL FRONTIER

Stocking up on good deals and saving things for future use—what I call "organized packrattery"—are essential to successful tightwaddery.

This is easy for us. With a 2,500-square-foot farmhouse attached to a 4,500-square-foot barn (this doesn't include the two attics, the carriage house, and the icehouse), we even store stuff for other people: boats, furniture, even a pinewood derby track for the Cub Scouts.

But I know what it's like not to have this luxury. I've lived more than half of my adult life in tiny, Boston-area apartments. Most of the other half was spent raising a big family in small, suburban ranch houses. It wasn't as convenient, but we always stockpiled and saved stuff in these places too.

Think of it this way: Would you rent out your closet for $75 a month? That could be what you'd save by having the space to bulk-buy groceries, or to keep a craft box for money-saving projects, or to stockpile great yard-sale purchases of kids' clothes. Conversely, if you think you don't have space to bulk-buy, you can figure it's costing you $75 a month to store bronzed baby shoes, fourth-grade toothpick constructions, and Engelbert Humperdinck records.

So here are some strategies for people for whom space is a precious resource:

1. Get rid of what you *don't* need. Clothes that no longer fit, books that you bought on a lark and haven't read in ten years, toys

your kids have outgrown, and impulse-buy kitchen gadgets (when did you last use that fondue pot?) can all be sold at a yard sale or through a consignment shop or donated to a thrift shop (many thrift shops will even come pick them up). If you make a mistake, it's not the end of the world. What you sell at a yard sale can probably be bought at another yard sale for the same price.

2. Buy things that have multiple uses. Example: A teakettle can only boil water. A saucepan can boil water and cook dinner. Instead of buying a bike and an exercise bike, get a trainer, a device that lets you convert your bike into an indoor exercise bike.

3. Buy furniture that has built-in storage space. The conventional coffee table with legs has several cubic feet of wasted space underneath it. A flat-topped trunk makes a suitable coffee table with storage space. Other examples include beds with built-in drawers underneath and cabinet-style end tables.

4. Buy smaller. A compact microwave will handle 95 percent of your microwaving needs. The money and space you save will more than offset having to use your oven for the other 5 percent. Technical advances mean you no longer need refrigerator-size speakers for good stereo sound. Many tiny systems get top ratings.

5. Buy foldable furniture like sofa beds and flip-down desks. Use folding chairs, card tables, and army cots for company. Similarly, buy collapsible items; instead of rigid suitcases, buy canvas travel bags.

6. Buy items specifically designed to store compactly, such as drinking glasses or chairs that stack. One of the mysteries of the modern world is that most plastic food-storage containers are not designed to fit into each other for compact storage.

7. When saving things for future reuse, keep only the small, useful parts. One reader, a former tiny-apartment dweller, wrote of how he baked bread in a toaster oven (I presume he didn't have a conventional oven.) After several years he learned the heating element was the only part of this toaster oven that didn't last. So, whenever he spotted another toaster-oven of the same make at a yard sale, he would buy it but save only the element.

I have saved two sets of couch-cushion covers for the zippers. If I had a space limitation, I would cut off the zippers and discard the remaining worn material.

8. Customize your furniture to fit. You can do this two ways: build furniture to fit, or modify an existing piece. When we lived in one of those miniature urban apart-

ments, we shoehorned a nursery into a barely-bigger-than-a-twin-bed room by using both of these ideas. The room had a stairwell running under it, so there was this weird angle thing (see picture: Thank goodness I can draw) that chewed up a couple of feet of floor space. We bought a Salvation Army crib, cut off the two front legs, and bolted the headboard of the crib to the wall over the weird angle thing.

Then we converted the closet to a baby-changing table and diaper storage area. We built a wide, lipped shelf with foam padding for changing, and kept diaper stuff and baby clothes on lower shelves. The room then had enough remaining space that we were also able to squeeze in a drafting table and a small filing cabinet.

9. Keep track to avoid duplication. Perhaps the major cause of household clutter is ignorance about what you have; you can't find that hinge you scavenged from your ruined screen door, so you buy another, while the original still rests at the bottom of a clutter pile. Instead, you might keep track with a list of what's in your freezer, detailed labels on boxes of kids' clothes, and carefully categorized workshop storage containers.

10. Think square. A square juice

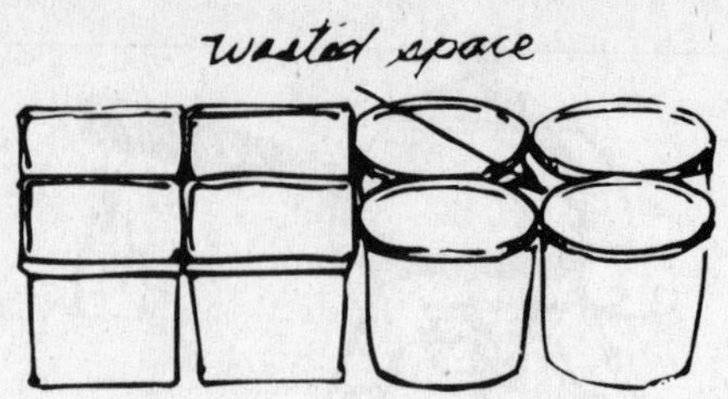

jug and square freezer boxes fit more efficiently into refrigerator and freezer spaces than do their round counterparts. Odd items can be stored neatly in (square) boxes, which can be stacked.

11. Keep the right amount on hand. Tuna fish is on sale every other week, so we never buy more than six cans. Peanut butter goes on sale more rarely, so we purchase four cases at a time. Don't keep more plastic bread bags, egg cartons, or toilet-paper tubes than you could possibly reuse.

Sometimes an overstock sneaks up even on me. Upon investigating why my daughter's closet was so jammed, I realized she had fourteen size-4 dresses (most of my children's clothes have been given to us). I plan to donate half to our church thrift shop.

12. Share ownership. An infrequently used item can be owned by a group of families, and the family with the appropriate space can store it. For example, the one family in the group with workshop space keeps the table saw, which all other families are free to use. Meanwhile, the family with attic space keeps the electric train set up, while the family with pasture space keeps the horse.

13. Barter for space. One of my staff asked if we could temporarily store an organ for her. In exchange she gave us 20 pounds of hand-picked wild blueberries.

In a barter arrangement that resembles shared ownership, you can allow a friend to use something you own—a canoe, for example—in exchange for storing it.

14. Think vertical. Generally, the space above anything is potential storage space. Examples include the closet space above your shoes or the space in the garage above your car. If you live in an old house with high ceilings, a lightweight aluminum ladder kept in a handy spot can help you reach high storage spaces.

One architect, Malcolm Wells, sometimes designs homes with a shelf 1 foot below the ceiling. Because this design element is carried throughout the home, you soon forget it's there.

15. Be creative in thinking about other possible spaces: the spaces under, behind, or between. A double bed, 6 inches from the floor, has 16 cubic feet under it. Use the basement space between floor joists by nailing up strapping to store fishing poles, car racks, tents, and lumber. Most couch backs taper away from the wall, leaving 6 inches of unused floor space.

16. Hang it all! Bikes can hang from walls or ceilings. Pots and kitchen utensils can hang on pegboard. Hang your basket collection on the wall, making an attractive grouping. One woman told me she attached a crib side to her bedroom wall and hangs wardrobe accessories on the slats.

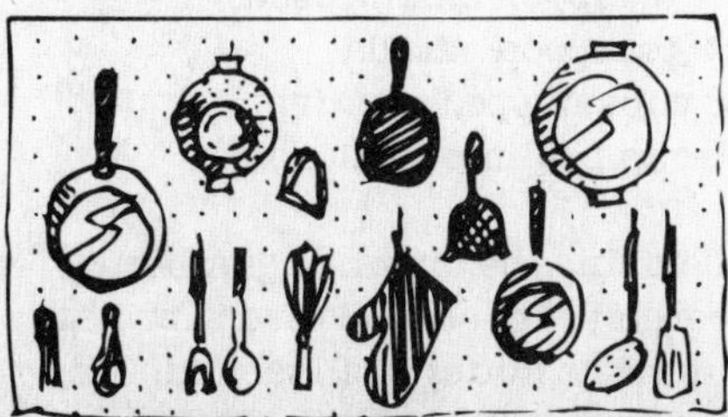

17. Store things in untraditional places. Your bulk food could be kept in the nearby living-room closet. You could keep your oil filters and cans of motor oil in that coffee table/trunk.

For many people, saving space is saving money. Smaller places are generally cheaper to buy, rent, heat, cool, maintain, and pay taxes on. The extra effort required to find storage space in cramped quarters can be amply rewarded by those savings.

FLUSHED WITH SUCCESS

Dear Amy,

I've discovered my mother-in-law is trying to save on her water bill by not always flushing. I am wondering just how much water is used per flush, and what it costs. Hope you can help.

—Kathy from Kansas

Dear Kathy,

To figure out how much water is used per flush: Remove the tank cover. Mark the inside of the tank right at the "full" level.

Turn off the tank intake valve. Flush the toilet. Refill the empty tank with a gallon milk jug or measuring cup. The amount needed to reach the mark is the amount used per flush.

To figure the cost per flush: Most water bills are figured in cubic feet. There are 7.481 gallons in a cubic foot. We have a well, and we only pay for the tiny energy cost to pump water. So I had an employee from a nearby town

bring me his water bill for calculating purposes.

It said he had used 1,700 cubic feet during the billing period, and the cost was $24.78. So the cost per cubic foot is:

$24.78 ÷ 1,700 = $.0145764

So the cost per gallon is:

$.0145764 ÷ 7.481 =.0019484

Rounding up, a gallon of water costs him 2/10 of a cent.

The average pre-1980 toilet uses about 5 gallons per flush. So, based on these figures, it costs 1¢ per flush. At 16 flushes per day (four each for a family of four) this is 16¢ daily, or $58 a year.

But water in Maine is relatively cheap. In Santa Barbara, California, which has one of the highest water rates in the nation, the cost is ½¢ per gallon, or 2.5¢ per flush. At that rate, 16 flushes per day would cost 40¢ daily, or $146 per year.

Another important cost to keep in mind is sewage fees. In many areas, these are based on water consumption rates, effectively doubling your cost per gallon.

Your own calculations may show that flushing is too expensive for you. Or you may be in a drought-stricken area and need to comply with water quotas. Or you may simply wish to save water out of environmental concerns. In any case, if you want to conserve:

1. Fill a plastic bottle halfway with pebbles, then fill it with water. Put the cap on, and place the bottle in the tank so that it is clear of the toilet mechanism. Experiment with different-size bottles so that you save the maximum amount of water and still get a good flush.

Some flush mechanisms allow you to lower the float ball by turning a screw.

2. Get a low-flush toilet. Sears sells one that uses 1½ gallons for about $100. Toilets are easy for a relatively handy person to install. If your water rates are high, this can pay for itself in a year. But be aware that the waste pipes in some older houses are pitched in such a way that at least a 3-gallon flush is required to avoid clogging. If you are unsure about your plumbing, consult a plumber who has plenty of experience with low-flush toilets before you install one.

3. Leave it. There is no refined way to phrase this, so let's just make up our own euphemisms: Some people allow "transparent" waste to collect between flushes, but draw the line, for esthetic, aromatic, and health reasons, at leaving "opaque" waste to accumulate. If you have young children or pets, I recommend flushing after each use, as they can be attracted to the toilet to play and drink, respectively.

BUT WHERE'S THE PRIZE?

Dear Amy,

Here's a Cracker-Jacks-ish snack that is quick, cheap, easy, and irresistible:

¾ cup packed brown sugar
¼ cup butter or margarine
3 tablespoons corn syrup
¼ teaspoon salt
¼ teaspoon baking soda
¼ teaspoon vanilla
8 cups popped popcorn
1 cup peanuts (optional)

Combine the brown sugar, butter, corn syrup, and salt over low heat until the butter is all melted. Cook without stirring for 3 minutes.

Add the baking soda and vanilla. Pour onto the popcorn and peanuts, and mix until evenly coated. Bake 15 minutes at 300 degrees. Break into pieces.

If you want a less sweet snack, use more popcorn. If you pop your popcorn in a saucepan, you can use the same oily pan to make the candy-coating mixture. The oil helps it slide right out.

—Lisa Smith
Cody, Wyoming

MAIL BAG

Dear Amy,

Did you know that you can use a small paper bag for a mailer? I was surprised to see one, and asked the post office if this was okay. They said yes. The maximum size allowable is 6⅛ inches by 11½ inches. The top can be folded down to meet length requirements, and stapled or taped.

—Laura Blyston
Crestline, California

CHECK OUT THE CHECKOUT

Dear Amy,

Now that the stores have electronic scanning and are trying to move people through the checkout as quickly as possible, I have found many errors. . . . For example, last week at Safeway I purchased bulk bridge mix marked at $2.99 a pound but was charged $3.09 at the register. When I questioned this, I received the item free because of the error.

At another store I was charged for three gallons of milk when I'd only gotten two. Also, coupons now have bar codes and are scanned. The scanners cannot always discriminate between a good coupon and an invalid one and will sometimes reject a good one, so baby-sit your grocery cashier.

—Pam Holcomb
Frederick, Maryland

(An article from the San Francisco Examiner, sent to me by reader Lesley Minearo of San Francisco, California, quotes a district attorney who estimates that there are millions of dollars in overcharges each year in Riverside County, California, alone. It occurs to me that there may also be millions of dollars in undercharges, too—in which case, one might feel ethically bound to report these errors as well. FZ)

TUX RELIEF

Dear Amy,

When both of my teenage sons (sophomore and junior) wanted to go to the homecoming dance, I talked them into going with me to several thrift stores looking (and hoping) for same appropriate clothing. By the end of our trek we had acquired two tuxedos in excellent condition and the exact sizes. We also found two cummerbunds. We borrowed shirts and broke

down and bought two black bow ties. Then, a year later, when the senior prom came up, my son tried on his tuxedo, and it still fit perfectly. While all his friends were scurrying around trying to come up with the money to rent their formal duds, my son had only to shake off the dust and dress. Each ensemble cost $15. An added bonus was overhearing a conversation he recently had with a friend. "Where did you rent your tux?" My son proudly replied, "I didn't rent. I own."

—Judi Manolas
Orlando, Florida

THE "WANTS" BULLETIN BOARD

You search thrift shops and scour yard sales, but you just can't find that elusive whatzit, so you break down and buy it new. When you tell a friend the sad tale, he slaps his forehead and says, "You should have asked me! I've got a whole bushel of whatzits in my attic that I've been trying to get rid of since 1947!"

Here in Leeds, we have a close-knit group of friends at work and at church who freely exchange goods and services, but the scenario above happens to us, too. Weeks can pass before our paths cross—and even then, our needs may not come up in conversation.

So here at the *Gazette*'s palatial office complex, we came up with this idea: a "wants" bulletin board. This could be used wherever folks associate closely enough to become friends—at the dorm, church, or teachers' lounge.

To participate, people post notices stating their names and what they want.

For the most part, these should be free exchanges between friends who know that "what goes around, comes around." However, valuable items may need to be purchased, bartered, or loaned.

Even if they don't have the item on hand, making friends aware of your needs magnifies your bargain-hunting power. If you post a notice that you need size-7 girls' pants, the yard-sale junkie in your group will probably ask you, "If I see them, do you want me to pick them up for you? How much would you be willing to pay?" Naturally, this type of exchange requires trust, but if you set the amount you are willing to pay low enough, even if you wind up with electric-green punker pants, you'll probably be able to resell them at your yard sale for the same price (or make a Halloween costume).

All "wants" need not be material. You might list a need for storage space, a ride, baby-sitting, or

information on where to get something inexpensively.

The board can also include items that you would be willing to give away, such as surplus garden produce, baby stuff, or the avocado oven range that you are replacing.

This can also work for borrowing, such as if you need a lawn mower for a use or two while yours is in the shop.

I would stress that the "wants" board works best for small (fewer than 20 people) groups who share a generosity of spirit and a love for bargains. If it doesn't work in one of your circles of friends, try it in another.

IS FRUGALITY BAD FOR THE ECONOMY?

I'm sort of a politics/economics junkie. Every weeknight I forgo *Wheel of Fortune* to tune in to *The MacNeil/Lehrer NewsHour* on PBS. The show's format includes a panel of experts on a given topic—who sharply disagree. When the topic is the recession, typically you can see a professor of economics from Harvard Business School duke it out with some guy who won the Nobel Prize for economics.

Though I'm not an "expert," one question I have been asked to comment on is "If I'm frugal, isn't that bad for the economy?"

It's true that plenty of economists believe we need to get that American consumer confident and spending again. This thinking, that we can spend our way to economic prosperity, leads some to believe that those people who don't spend money but save it instead, contribute to recession.

In fact, the reverse is true. Spending too much, and spending badly, got us into this mess. Frugality, in the long run, will get us out.

Here's why:

1. Former senator Paul Tsongas points out that business in America has suffered because of a lack of venture capital. Most businesses need capital to start up or to reinvest for greater productivity. This kind of borrowing is good debt, because in the long run it will create economic surplus.

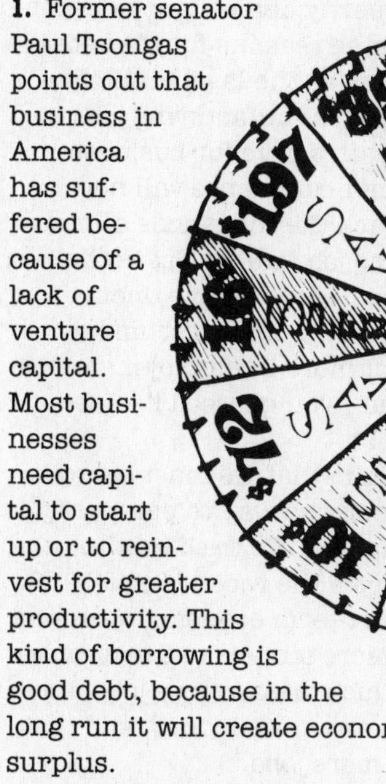

Currently, there is a shortage of capital for two reasons. First, Americans save very little money, and second, what is available is sucked up by the federal government to pay for overspending. Americans typically save 4 percent of their total income, compared to Germans, who save 10 percent and the Japanese, who save 18 percent.

2. The average American has huge debts. To ask him to spend more to get the economy rolling is silly. It increases his economic vulnerability.

If that American declares bankruptcy, we all pay for it in higher costs from companies that had to

eat the loss. If that person goes on public assistance, we all pay for it through higher taxes. And if chicken-hearted politicians are afraid to raise taxes, the government will have to borrow more money and . . . (see point #1).

3. The focus on spending our way to prosperity denies much deeper underlying reasons for the recession, such as the laws that make relocating manufacturing jobs to Mexico attractive for business. Consumer confidence will not bring back the thousands of manufacturing jobs we've lost in the last ten years. More people unemployed means the government pays out more unemployment benefits and—you guessed it—(see point #1).

To claim that we must borrow and spend our way to prosperity is shortsighted. We tried that to recover from the recession of 1982. The short-term economic gain was clear: More money was in circulation, which meant more jobs, and that meant more money, and that meant more jobs.

But this was a false "prosperity." The government "created jobs" through military buildup and expanding its own bureaucracy. Developers borrowed money to build office complexes when there was no market for them. Confident consumers bought CD players and snowmobiles on their credit cards. By trying to accelerate a recovery artificially, by going into debt on a government, business, and personal level, we eventually lost economic efficiency, because a larger and larger percentage of our money has had to be siphoned off to pay interest on our debt.

I'm not saying that debt is always bad. But debt must give you value; it has to save you money in the long run.

And I'm not saying you should never spend a dime. Clearly, some spending is essential for the economy. We all enjoy a higher standard of living because we understand the benefits of trading goods and services. Imagine if we all grew our own cotton to weave our own material to sew our own clothes. It's more beneficial to trade our labor with those in our economy who have learned to make clothing more efficiently. Even if everyone were a tightwad, there would still be an exchange of goods and services, but this exchange would be sustainable over the long term.

If you're not impressed by economic theory as expressed by a housewife from Leeds, Maine, I refer you to two books that say the same thing about our need to save to rebuild the economy. They are *United We Stand* by Ross Perot and *A Call to Economic Arms* by Paul Tsongas, which is available for a suggested $5 donation from the Tsongas Committee, 20 Park Plaza, Room 230, Boston, MA 02116. By the way, this is not a political endorsement of either of these men.

So don't rationalize spending because it's "good for the economy." And don't feel guilty about being frugal because it's "bad for the economy."

A healthy economy is made up of economically healthy citizens. If you make choices that are financially sound for you, they will probably be financially sound for the economy in the long run.

CREDIT CARD THEORY

At Christmas, Americans tend to go nuts with bank cards such as Visa and MasterCard, but, frankly, Americans tend to go nuts with bank cards for the rest of the year as well. The average American is carrying a $2,500 balance on 2.5 bank cards, or about $1,000 per card, and paying an average interest rate of 18 percent. This means that the average American is throwing away $450 annually in bank-card interest. And these numbers don't even include store credit cards. Ack!

Because of these grim statistics, some tightwads avoid plastic like the plague. But cards *are* handy. They serve as identification, allow you to make telephone transactions, and can save you in an emergency.

So carry a card, but be sure to carry the right one for you.

You can find it by picking up (at the library, of course) the latest copy of *Money* magazine—the best bank-card deals are near the front of each issue.

But keep in mind that the best card for you depends upon your situation. If, like all good tightwads, you pay off your balance each month, you need a card with no annual fee and a grace period during which no interest is charged. Once those needs are met, *then* you need the lowest interest rate you can find, just to protect you in the unlikely event that you carry a balance someday.

On the other hand, if you are a new convert to tightwaddery, chances are you carry a balance from month to month. If you do, your aim should be to transfer your debt to the lowest-rate card you can find, and don't worry so much about the annual fee.

Why? Suppose your average balance is $5,000. If

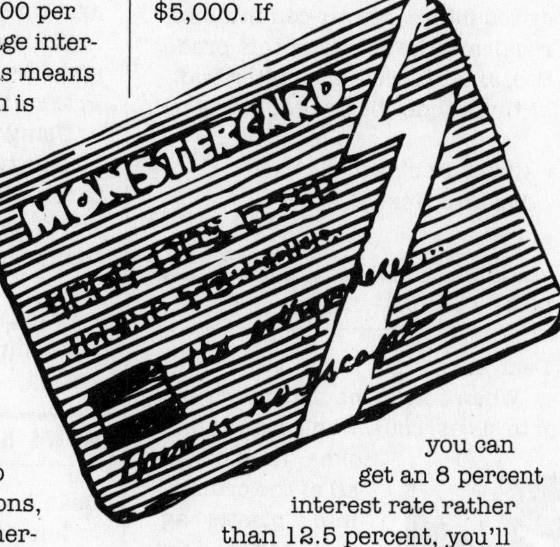

you can get an 8 percent interest rate rather than 12.5 percent, you'll save $225 per year. Most super-low-interest cards charge an annual fee of around $35, so the savings from the lower interest rate more than offset the higher fee. But keep in mind that once your balance drops under about $750, that lower-interest advantage disappears, and you'll be better off with a no-fee card.

Finally, let's explode a bit of tightwad credit card folklore. Some people like to buy everything with a credit card, reasoning that they profit because they can get free use of the money for up to 45 days. This looks like a better tip than it is: Remember, if you are getting 3 percent interest in your savings account, you must charge $77.33 to recoup the cost of the 29¢ stamp.

FILTER FACT

Dear Amy,

Instead of disposing of my disposable furnace and air-conditioning filters each month, I vacuum them and spray the clean filters with Endust. The Endust restores the dust-catching ability of the recycled filters. My air-conditioning repairman approves of this practice, and I recycle each filter two or three times before replacing it.

—Chuck Robinson
Bellaire, Texas

LOAF LESSON

Dear Amy,

When cutting homemade bread into slices, cut a whole loaf at one time. Then scrape all of the crumbs into a plastic bag that is kept in the freezer, and use when recipes call for bread crumbs.

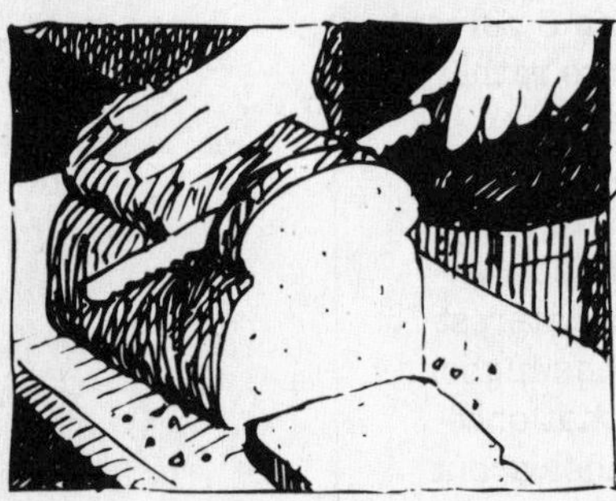

—Julie Watner
Gramling,
South Carolina

DEALS ON WHEELS

Dear Amy,

My car-buying strategy is to buy the least expensive model from a top-quality car maker, to look for cars with extras like sport trim or better upholstery (it's important to me not to have a car that feels "cheap"), to buy cars two years old or less, to buy through the newspaper (not dealers), to buy from owners who have maintenance records on the car, and to buy from people who seem trustworthy and are selling for good reasons. When I've been interested in a car, I've given the other party a deposit and taken the car to a mechanic (at my expense) after writing up a short agreement, which we both sign. . . . I also check *Consumer Reports* and *The Yellow Book of Used Car Prices* at the library. . . .

Using the method, I have bought two trouble-free, attractive cars. . . . It is worth the time and work, and a careful buyer can virtually eliminate the extra risk.

—Susan M. Kuhn
Washington, D.C.

MEWS NEWS

Dear Amy,

I use newspaper cut into strips for cat litter. It smells better, is cleaner, and can be changed often. First, you mix the strips with real litter, then use less and less litter, then just newspaper. It's good for eyes and lungs, because there is no dust.

—Mrs. Paka Hussey
Odessa, Florida

NOT MILK DUDS

Dear Amy,

I go into the grocery store and look at the expiration dates on the milk. Usually, there is milk that has expired the day before, that day, or will expire the following day. I ask a store worker to mark the milk down since it's expired or about to expire, and they cheerfully do so. I get half-gallon cartons, which sell from $1.50 to $1.89 for 25¢ to 50¢. Since the milk stays fresh for five days after the expiration date and the half-gallon cartons can be stored in the freezer, we always have fresh milk.

—Karyn Price
Rio Rancho, New Mexico

ONE PUMP OR TWO?

Dear Amy,

Most shampoo comes in a squeeze-type bottle or tube, leaving the portion control up to the user. With little ones and teenagers this can be expensive. Buy shampoo in bulk gallons and pour into pump-type dispensers for hand soap. Short hair: one pump. Long hair: two pumps.

—Jeannette Behr
Twin Falls, Idaho

BUDGET QUENCHER

Dear Amy,

A cheap alternative to juice: I buy store-brand lemon juice for $1.49 and make my own lemonade more cheaply than I can buy juice in any form. It's delicious and far superior to the cheapest lemonade powder mix. A quart of lemon juice will yield 2 gallons of lemonade. Mix ½ cup of lemon juice and ½ cup of sugar to 1 quart of water.

—Rebecca Novakovich
Cambridge, Massachusetts

THE FRUGAL FIXER-UPPER

The PBS TV series *This Old House* had a memorable episode a few years ago. Bob, the contractor, and Norm, the carpenter, had just finished renovation of the plus-200-year-old "Weatherby" house in Massachusetts. Here's the gist of their conversation:

Bob: We've finished her, Norm, and isn't she a beauty?

Norm: Yup. Though we did go a bit over budget.

Bob: Well . . . yes, the budget was $100,000, and we spent $200,000.

Norm: But isn't she a beauty!

As I watched, I cringed. *This Old House* inadvertently presents home renovation as discouragingly expensive. Many of their projects use costly, state-of-the-art materials and roar ahead quickly to meet the TV production schedule (which drives up costs).

But a fixer-upper doesn't have to mean financial insanity. Since my teenage years, I have consciously observed many renovations, noting what people did right and what they did wrong. Here's what I learned:

WHY GET A FIXER-UPPER?

By fixing up an old house, you can eventually own a home that is "technically" more than you can afford. Banks will rarely allow your mortgage payment to exceed 28 percent of your income—even if you prove you can handle more. But you can buy a fixer-upper with a small mortgage and put your surplus income toward renovation, eventually owning a more valuable home.

Usually, you can buy and fix up a house for less than it costs to build one or to buy one in good condition, particularly if you do much of the work. There are exceptions—like expensive top-to-bottom renovations of shacks. But if you do it right, you'll save money.

Fixer-uppers have other advantages over building new. You can more comfortably use recycled materials, and you don't have to be highly skilled to match existing old-house carpentry. Older homes usually have better construction and come with more land than newer homes.

WHO SHOULD BUY A FIXER-UPPER?

Because a fixer-upper is almost always an old house, you should appreciate old-house character: bumpy walls, sloping floors, and doors that don't quite fit. If you really want a new-looking house, don't buy an old house and try to make it look new. Not only will this be expensive, but you may destroy the architectural integrity of a historic building.

You'll need handyman skills, patience, persistence, and lots of time. In our case, Jim has the building skills, but I'm the one who loves the tedious work. If you or your spouse has a history of not finishing projects and you loathe this type of work, buy a home in good condition.

You should also have the imagination to see through grease-splattered walls, curling linoleum, and ancient crud and envision a cheerful kitchen.

HOW DO YOU SHOP?

Although most realtors are fine people, we found that many were hard of hearing. After specifically telling them we only wanted to look at older homes, we found ourselves being taken on frequent side trips to check out "a really interesting contemporary split level." We decided that shopping for fixer-uppers required a different strategy.

Unlike typical ranch houses, fixer-uppers vary greatly from property to property. Most drawbacks that are impossible or too expensive to change can be spotted by simply driving by, without time-consuming realtor-guided house tours. So, get copies of new listings that meet your criteria as soon as they come out and drive by the homes yourselves. Then arrange to have the realtor show you any that look interesting. We toured fewer than 10 percent of the homes we saw.

Because we looked at 176 houses in 15 months in a four-county area, we found we needed two important tools to save time and gasoline. We bought a book of area maps that showed street names. We also kept a notebook with the copies of listings taped to pages. Eventually we organized them by the town, in alphabetical order. When a realtor called we were able to tell him, in a matter

of seconds, whether we had seen a particular house, and we avoided looking at the same house twice.

We developed a relationship with one realtor in each county, and they eventually understood we were saving them time too.

Obviously, how long you persist in your hunt has to do with variables in your situation. You'll spend less time shopping if this is a home you plan to own for a short period of time. We were shopping for a home to live in for the rest of our lives, and few homes within our price range met our criteria.

WHAT SHOULD YOU LOOK FOR?

Location is the most important aspect of any house purchase. You can sink unlimited funds into your dream home, but you will never be able to move the pig farm located across the road.

The fixer-upper should be valued below other homes in the neighborhood. If you spend $200,000 renovating and the neighboring houses are worth $75,000, you'll never recoup your investment if you decide to sell. The purchase price should be so low that it plus the total cost of renovation is much less than the cost of a comparable home in good condition.

During your tour with a realtor conduct your own building inspection to look for obvious problems that might rule out the purchase. If everything seems okay, hire a building inspector who is familiar with older homes. He can help you locate problems, advise you about some costs, and recommend contractors for any needed estimates. The most diligent inspectors and contractors will miss a few problems, so your budget should have room for surprises.

Avoid homes that require major changes, such as complete alterations of floor plans. Only consider major changes when the property is either extremely cheap or has other unique advantages. Otherwise, it's easier to keep looking.

The ideal fixer-upper has never been "remuddled." While it's a joy to remove cracked floor tiles and rusty sheet-metal sink cabinets, it's sickening to tear out newly installed orange-shag carpeting and plastic "Colonial-style" kitchen cabinets (that you just paid extra for).

HOW DO YOU FIX IT UP?

After you buy the house, develop a detailed plan; know, basically, what you want to do, from start to finish, *before* you lift a hammer. If you need to do major work, a floor plan is a must. Know what you'll need a contractor for and what you can do yourself. Also know the sequence in which things need to be done; don't put down the kitchen floor before you figure out the room's layout.

An advantage to a fixer-upper is that you can live there during the process. However, there may be some things you need to do before moving in to bring the home up to a livable standard. In our

case, we repaired a gaping hole in the kitchen ceiling and had a furnace installed in the unheated ell.

You may want to deal with lead-based paint before moving in, particularly if you have children. In Maine, painting over most surfaces is considered to be reasonable abatement. Some "chewable" surfaces, such as windowsills, can be covered with duct tape until there's time for more extensive treatment. With adequate research you can learn how to remove lead paint from small areas with little risk. If you are planning any large-scale removal of interior paint after moving in, such as sanding floors, take the kids to visit relatives.

Once you are in the house, tackle the big eyesores first. Things like a thorough cleaning, hauling trash to the dump, a quick coat of paint on ugly walls, and mowing down brush around the property will provide the most improvement for the least money and effort.

Do small sections at a time. Big messes are overwhelming—especially if you're living in them. Instead, you'll need the feeling of accomplishment that comes from completing each small job—as small as painting a single window at a time.

Don't start any projects that you don't have the time, energy, or money to finish. This way, you avoid ending up with a perpetually gutted, unlivable house. And if something unexpected comes along (like a brilliant idea for a newsletter or uh-oh twins), remaining projects can be postponed for a year or two.

Allow *lots* of time to make decisions. Consider the landscape architect who planted grass in the new college's courtyard. He returned months later and designed walkways where the students had worn paths. Sometimes, you need to live in a place for a year or so before you know how to solve a problem.

In my pursuit of inexpensive solutions, I continually pore through magazines. I've noticed that the kitchens I like best are not the $30,000 renovations, but the ones based on simple solutions—refinished wood floors, original counters repainted, and simple, open shelves for storage. By doing this, I figure I can buy one or two strategic antiques for ambiance, and still save at least $27,000.

Always think of sources for recycled stuff, especially those that may already be in your fixer-upper. We found old, wide boards in our carriage house that we plan to use for countertops in our kitchen to match those in the pantry. If you need a door for a room, take it off a same-size doorway that doesn't need a door. Frequently, you can save money by waiting for salvage materials to become available.

Finally, don't do anything stupid. We saw an amazing number of botched renovations during our house hunt—like the mammoth brick fireplace that overwhelmed a tiny living room, a bedroom that could only be accessed by going through a bathroom, and a door that opened only partway because it banged against a counter.

Some people should be discouraged from tackling a fixer-upper. But the right person combined with the right house will result in great savings.

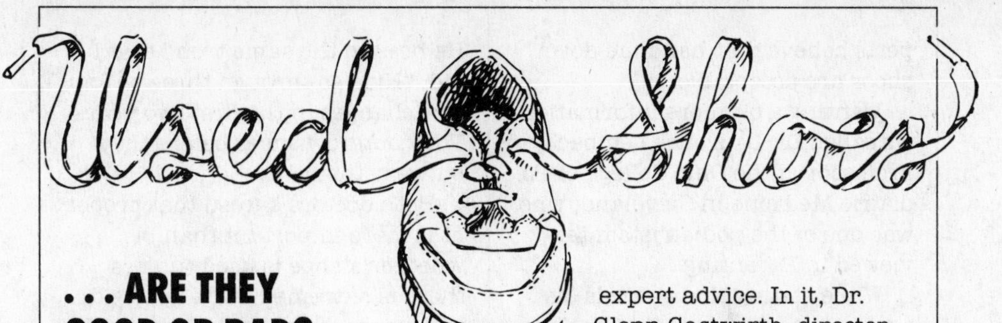

. . . ARE THEY GOOD OR BAD?

When we were on the Donahue show, we skillfully fielded questions from skeptical audience members. But I sputtered when, after discussing what my children were wearing, a guy stood and asked, "Aren't used shoes bad for kids?"

"Uh . . . uh . . . I believe there's a difference of opinion on that," was my less skillful reply. I *had* always heard that the "experts" say used shoes are bad for kids. I confess: *My* opinion was the only one I knew of that was different.

This black-and-white opinion, that all used shoes are bad for kids, has always been a mystery to me. Although it is logical that an extremely worn, hard-soled leather shoe could cause problems, it didn't seem possible that all used tennis shoes, flip-flops, slippers, sandals, and twice-worn patent-leather church shoes would cause lifelong foot problems.

I recently learned of an article in one of the parenting magazines that said that some experts believe that hand-me-down shoes are *not* bad. Filled with joyful exuberance that I might indeed be right, I sent one of my staff to the library to obtain a copy of this article. She returned with two articles, which expressed opposite opinions.

The June 1990 issue of *Parents* magazine contained the familiar expert advice. In it, Dr. Glenn Gastwirth, director of scientific affairs for the American Podiatric Medical Association, says that shoes mold to the individual foot, and shoes may become worn down in a way that is not outwardly visible. In addition, he says a natural bend develops in the shoe, and that bend might not be right for the next child. However, when I called him, he admitted that he knew of no studies showing that used shoes harm the feet.

He said the most important reason not to hand down shoes is that the only way to insure proper fit is with the help of a trained salesperson.

In other words, this doctor would not approve of a common, tightwaddy, new-shoe purchase method—trying on shoes yourself in a discount store. In his view, traditional, higher-priced shoe stores are the only option.

Just out of curiosity, we called a couple of shoe stores to inquire about the training procedure for clerks. The longest training course we found is two hours. A friend of mine, who was a shoe clerk for Sears, says her training lasted 60 seconds.

The second article appeared in *Parenting* magazine, in the June/July 1992 issue. This article, mainly about how to buy shoes for kids, devoted a couple of sentences to suggesting that some ex-

perts believe that hand-me-down shoes are acceptable.

Wanting a bit more information, we called Dr. Laurence Lembach, a professor at the Ohio College of Podiatric Medicine in Cleveland, who was one of the podiatrists interviewed in *Parenting*.

While stating that there is disagreement among professionals, Dr. Lembach said he believes that if a shoe is in good condition, and if it fits properly, it is okay to hand it down.

"Good condition," means that it is not badly worn along the outside edge of the heel or sole. He says a handed-down shoe may have "mild wear" on either side.

"Fits properly," means that there is about a thumb width between the end of the big toe and the end of the shoe (or a half inch for kids under two), and you cannot feel the bone or the little toe pushing against the side of the shoe.

He conceded that sneakers have much more give, and it's harder to get a good fit from a hard-sole leather shoe that laces tightly. In other words, choosing the type of used footwear, along with size and degree of wear, is also important.

Dr. Lembach practices what he preaches. He has six kids, and shoes are handed down within his family. He noticed the same trend that I did: "Kids go through three or four size changes in the first two years. They outgrow shoes before they outwear them."

Both doctors agreed that proper fit is more important than whether a shoe is used (unless there is extreme wear). So, rigid adherence to the professionally fit new-shoe advice could be *more* likely to cause problems. Financially strapped parents may be unable to replace expensive shoes soon enough. In contrast, I can replace a pair of shoes in minutes, as soon as they are outgrown. Each of my kids has a box with a large selection of used shoes for them to grow into.

Doctors, who are very busy, are the most difficult experts to interview, and often return my calls several weeks later. As I wrapped up this article, more opinions straggled in. One podiatrist said that suggesting used shoes were fine was "awful advice," while Dr. Dennis Wenger, an orthopedic surgeon at Children's Hospital in San Diego, said that I was "on the right track." The only exception he made was for shoes previously worn by a teenager or adult with severe bunions. He said the idea that new shoes are essential for proper foot development is "a myth."

So there you go. Pick your expert opinion.

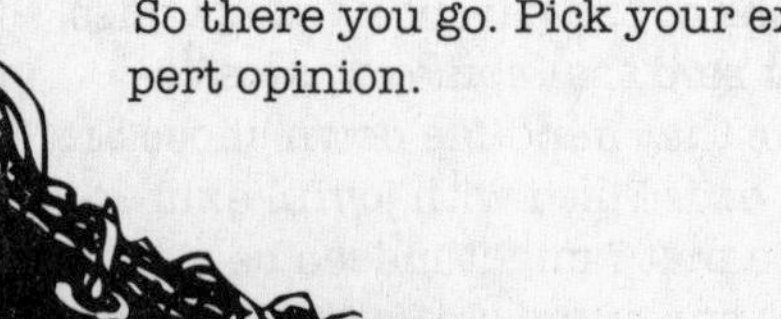

WRAPPING VERSUS UNWRAPPING: THE SLIPPERY TRUTH

One of the most ancient and respected bits of tightwad lore is that unwrapping soap several months before using it extends its life. The theory is that the soap dries out and therefore lasts longer. But is it true?

In the July 1992 issue of *Good Housekeeping*, Heloise addressed the question in her column (sent to me by reader Linda Bukvic of Williamsburg, Ohio). Heloise called the Soap and Detergent Association and was told that unwrapping soap does not prolong its life. In fact, the SDA stated that the wrapping protects the soap, and prematurely removing it could *speed up* the aging process.

I must admit that I have never unwrapped my soap to make it last longer, so I had no opinion one way or the other. But I suspected a conspiracy on the part of soap manufacturers to suppress this vital, soap-saving strategy—after all, they stand to sell more soap if it dissolves at an accelerated rate.

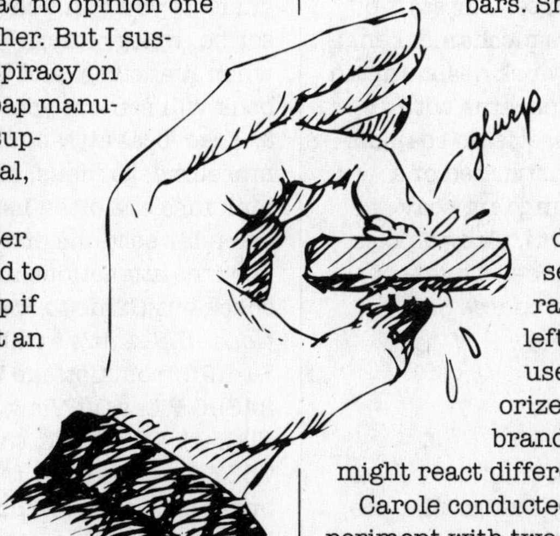

So I concluded that it was up to me, the dauntless researcher who ripped the lid off the cloth-versus-paper-napkin question, on page 20, to conduct the ultimate experiment to, once and for all, answer this critical question for tightwads everywhere. Yes, I would even fund the research myself and vowed to spend as much as $1 in pursuit of the truth.

I selected two bars of Coast soap that had been purchased in the same four-pack. I unwrapped one and put them both on my counter for several weeks. Then I unwrapped the second bar, put both bars in a glass loaf pan, covered them with water, and let them sit for two and a half days. I then precision-measured the remaining hard soap by shaping my thumb and index finger like a pair of calipers and squishing into the layer of goop. The measurement was the same for both bars. Finally, I scraped off the goop, and both bars appeared to be the same size.

I reported my findings to one of my staff, Carole, a longtime practitioner of unwrapping soap bars. She pointed to possible unscientific techniques in my experiment. Soap is not soaked in a dish, she observed, but rather used and left to dry between uses. She also theorized that different brands of soaps might react differently.

Carole conducted her own experiment with two brands of soap, Ivory and a facial soap with glycerine, both of which had been unwrapped for two months. She bought new soaps of the same brands. The unwrapped soaps did appear to be dryer, and weighed

½ ounce less than the wrapped soaps—even though all four bars were the 3-ounce size.

Using 120-degree water, she washed her hands for three minutes with each bar. She placed the bars on a rack to dry, turning them over when half dry. She repeated this process six times, for a total of 18 minutes of washing per bar. Both wrapped bars disintegrated after 18 minutes. The unwrapped bars disintegrated after 19½ minutes.

So, according to this experiment, unwrapping soap bars makes them last 7.69 percent longer. At 50¢ per bar, using 30 bars per year, our family of eight could save $1.15 annually.

But *wait*! Carole was prejudiced in favor of unwrapping soap, and she may have subconsciously washed 7.69 percent harder with the wrapped bars.

So watch for the unwrapping-the-soap-bar update: Our staff of *Tightwad Gazette* mechanical engineers is hard at work designing an experimental apparatus with robotic hands for precision soap dissolving, to be constructed of a trash-picked ceiling fan, scavenged bicycle parts, electronic gizmos, and four rubber gloves—wind-powered, of course.

FREEBIES

Actually, the only things that are truly "free" are those that would otherwise go to the dump—that's why the highest tightwad art, in my view, is legal trash picking.

Some of the offers below are government services—which taxpayers pay for eventually—so choose carefully. But as for the corporate freebies, if you feel at all guilty about accepting them, remember that some spendthrift (who's mocking your lifestyle) is paying inflated prices to finance these offers:

1. Do you wonder why your bank officer giggled when you asked for a loan? Maybe you need a free report on your credit status. Send your full name, addresses for the last five years, Social Security number, year of birth, and (if any) spouse's name to TRW Consumer Assistance, Box 2350, Chatsworth, CA 91313. Also include a copy of a letter or document that includes both your name and address, such as a bill. This prevents unauthorized release of your credit history.

2. Call *Consumer Reports* at (800) 234-1645 and request a trial subscription. You'll get a free issue and free copy of the latest buying guide. If you don't choose to subscribe, write "cancel" on the bill when it arrives, and the issue and book will remain yours to keep.

3. Free local attractions such as museums, gardens, and historical buildings are often listed in the calendar sections of newspapers. For free attractions nationwide, check out *Guide to Free Attractions, U.S.A.* It's available for $14.95 from Cottage Publications, 24396 Pleasant View Drive, Elkhart, IN 46517, (800) 303-7833, or get a copy from your library through interlibrary loan. For the same price, the same publisher sells *A Guide to Free Campgrounds.*

4. The federal government has dozens of free consumer booklets ranging from *The Student Guide: Financial Aid,* to *Understanding*

Social Security. To get the complete catalog, write S. James, Consumer Information Center-2D, P.O. Box 100, Pueblo, CO 81002.

5. Each month, the U.S. Postal Service sends an attractive poster promoting a new line of stamps to each post office around the country. We have a glossy, 2-foot-by-3-foot wild-animal-stamp poster hanging in five-year-old Neal's room that he loves. If you see one you like, ask your postmaster if you can have it when the office is through with it.

6. If you want to find loopholes in the tax law—or if you just can't get to sleep at night—bone up on tax law with free pamphlets from the government, including "Reporting of Real Estate Transactions to the IRS," and "Business Use of Your Home." Call (800) 829-3676.

7. If a flight is overbooked, you are usually offered a free round-trip ticket anywhere in the continental U.S. if you will give up your seat and take the next flight. You can increase the likelihood of getting bumped by casually striking up a conversation with a flight attendant over soda and peanuts and asking which times of the month or year the flight tends to be overbooked. In the future, fly at that time.

8. If you need to contact any large organization or company, start by calling toll-free directory assistance at (800) 555-1212. I have found this extremely handy. It's a rare large organization that doesn't have a toll-free number.

9. Many newspaper classified-ad sections and "swap" publications list "free-for-the-taking" items. We recently picked up a nearly new range this way that only needed a $15 repair. Other freebies I've seen offered include free firewood, pets, and lumber (there's usually a slight "catch" for building materials—you have to tear down a building to get it).

10. The Service Corps of Retired Executives, more widely known as

SCORE, is the consulting arm of the Small Business Administration. It offers free advice from executives, most of whom are retired, to small-business owners and to people who want to start a business. I have used this organization and found it quite helpful. They advise over the phone and/or on-site. To find the office nearest you, call (800) 634-0245.

11. After you get your prescription, ask your doctor if she has any samples of the medicine she's prescribed. Doctors are swamped with samples from drug companies and are usually glad to unload them. Aside from the savings, this is marvelously handy if it is 11:00 P.M. and 20 miles to the drugstore.

12. Your congressperson's local office hands out free calendars, listing a significant event from American history for every date of the year. When visiting his or her office in Washington, D.C., ask for free passes to the House and Senate galleries, and for the V.I.P. tour of the White House, which has shorter lines and smaller tour groups than the regular tour.

13. Some fairs offer free admission if you do some volunteer work. Maine's Common Ground Country Fair offers free admittance, a free, attractive T-shirt, and a free meal in exchange for four hours of work. You can choose your hours and type of work—anything from parking cars to shoveling you-know-what. Similar arrangements can be worked out with community theaters. You can get free admission for ushering or selling tickets.

WE ATE LENTILS . . . AND LIVED

Lentils are a cheap, filling source of protein, and because they don't require soaking before cooking, they are the handy fast food of the legume family.

The only problem is that many people find them bland at best, mealy and unappetizing at worst. So, to review lentil recipes sent in by readers, I assembled a panel of unrepentant carnivores and die-hard bean haters. I was seeking surefire recipes to excite the vegetarian virgins in your family.

While the vegetarian veterans around here enjoyed nearly all of the recipes received, this bean-hater panel narrow-mindedly rejected most of them. As it turns out, the only two recipes that received universal approval were not reader contributions but were developed by *The Tightwad Gazette*'s test kitchen. They both use a lentil-based meat substitute made of equal parts lentils and bulgur wheat (available from health-food stores). Simmer one part of this mixture with two parts water for 45 minutes.

LENTIL BURGERS FOR BEAN HATERS

2 cups cooked lentil-bulgur mixture
2 cups bread crumbs
1 cup chopped onion
½ cup chopped green pepper
4 tablespoons mixed Italian herbs (basil, oregano, thyme, etc.)
4 cloves garlic (or 4 teaspoons powdered garlic)
2 eggs (or 2 tablespoons soy flour and 2 tablespoons water)
½ cup milk

Mix the first six ingredients. Mix in eggs. Add milk and mix well. Chill ½ hour. Make into patties and fry 10 minutes per side, or bake on cookie sheet at 350 degrees, 10 minutes on each side.

BURRITOS

Combine 2 cups cooked lentil-bulgur mixture with ¼ cup taco-mix seasoning (purchased in bulk at a warehouse store, ¼ cup costs about 35¢).

Make tortillas as follows:

2 cups flour
½ teaspoon salt
¼ cup shortening
½ cup cold water

Combine flour and salt. Cut in shortening. Add water, mix until just combined. Divide into 10 balls and roll out flat. Fill with filling, roll up, and bake at 350 degrees for 20 minutes.

WHAT TO DO WITH . . .

A Crayon-Marked Blackboard. Use scouring powder to remove marks. We hung an extra child's blackboard in our pantry to write down shopping needs and things we want to remember to do.

An Egg Carton. Perfect for storing my 12 individually purchased jars of paste food-coloring. Usually purchased at a party-goods store, paste food-coloring can cost more than $1 per jar, but lasts longer and produces superior colors.

Jam Residue Left Inside Jar. Use for popsicle flavoring. Fill a popsicle mold with milk. Dump the milk into a jar that contains leftover jam. Tighten the lid on jar, and shake vigorously until the residue combines with the milk. Pour the milk back into the popsicle mold and freeze.

Ketchup Gunk in Empty Bottle. Pour ¼ cup hot water into the bottle and shake vigorously until the gunk combines with the water. Pour the water into your freezer container for leftover soup.

The Wrong-Color Liquid Foundation. Say you decide the shade you bought is too light. Buy a shade of the same brand that's too dark. Carefully combine small quantities of the two until you get the right shade.

Old Athletic Socks. Slit worn but clean socks lengthwise, and use for dish rags. The thick material is ideal for this use. Or cut a thumb hole and use as a mitten liner. (Maryann Lalley, Bartonsville, Pennsylvania.)

No-Longer-Needed Crib Sheets. Graduate them to car use. Crib sheets fit neatly over the backseat to protect it from spilled toddler drinks and crayon marks. (Denisha Tremain, Mesquite, Texas.)

Stuck Envelopes. When new envelopes have sealed closed due to moisture, heat in the microwave for 20 seconds. This will open them all or partway. (Miriam Watto, Marietta, Pennsylvania.)

Old Mylar Balloons. Cut the seams off and use the two pieces to wrap small gifts. Place the gift in the center, pull up the mylar, and tie with a ribbon. Can be used many times. (Monica Kingston, Geneseo, New York.)

Old Room Deodorizers. Disassemble, soak the inner absorbent pad with pine cleaner, and reassemble. (Brenda Evans, Winston-Salem, North Carolina.)

Juice Lids. Glue a piece of magnetic tape (cheaper than magnets) to the back and a child's picture to the front. One teacher uses these on a metal board to keep track of classroom jobs or assignments. Parents could use this idea to rotate household chores among family members. (Ellen J. Urbina-Martin, Jamaica Plain, Massachusetts.)

Milk Jugs. Make a toss-and-catch game by cutting milk jugs as shown. Toss homemade beanbags. Invented by reader's six-year-old son. (Marilyn Bruggema, El Cajon, California.)

A Turkey Net . . . that your Thanksgiving turkey came in. Wash it, run an old shoelace through it several spaces down. Use to keep bath toys so they will drip dry. (Sue Reading, West Jordan, Utah.)

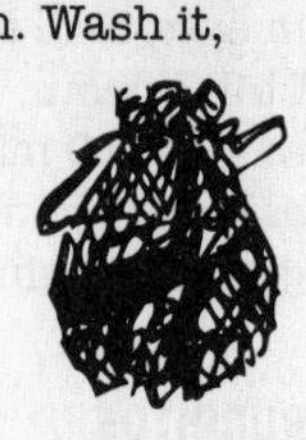

Musty Books. Put sheets of newspaper between some pages, and place the book along with crumpled newspaper in a suitcase or box. The newspaper will absorb the odor. (Denita Bradley, Knoxville, Tennessee.)

Six-Pack Rings. Acquire a large quantity from spendthrift friends. Tie them together with fishing line to make a hammock. Will last several seasons. (Jan Rusk, Roseville, California.)

Old Panty Hose. Use to make tiny pouches for fish bait, such as chicken liver. Helps keep bait on the hook. (Henry Howard, Smyrna, Tennessee.)

Old Kitchen Cabinets. Reuse them in the garage or workshop. (David and Cheryl Bernardi, Chicago, Illinois.)

Bacon Plastic. The plastic piece that comes in the bacon can be used to make stencils, such as for painting country designs on the walls.

GO WITH THE PRO

Dear Amy,

Please encourage readers to check the prices at their local janitorial-supply company (look in the Yellow Pages under janitorial supplies). Our local firm carries concentrated neutral cleaner, suitable for cleaning all surfaces including wood, for $7.70 a gallon. The label advises using 2 ounces of concentrate in a gallon of water. This works out to 12¢ a gallon of cleaning solution—a tightwad's delight!

—Rebecca Hodge
Raleigh, North Carolina

BIN BORROWING LATELY?

Dear Amy,

When visiting your local recycling center, spend a few minutes sorting through the magazine bins. You can find current or recent magazines, including some very interesting alternative publications. After reading these, I return them to the bins.

—John Raatz
Santa Monica, California

POSTAL PLEA

Dear Amy,

Here's an urgent warning to tightwads everywhere. As a new tightwad, my primary source of envelopes has become the return envelopes that come in advertisement/junk mail. There must be many tightwads who, like me, just throw a handwritten label over the printed address. However, postal workers have informed me it's important to put a label over those bar-code symbols on the bottom of the envelopes, too—because their computers will read the bar code and ignore my handwritten address label. I do know that some of my mail has seemingly been delayed or lost in the past year.

—Connie Boltz
Seattle, Washington

(By the time you slap two *labels on an envelope, chances are you are spending more on labels than if you bought new envelopes in bulk from a warehouse store. A cheaper way to reuse junk-mail envelopes is to turn them inside out, as explained in the first book. In any case, don't mark over the code with marker. This prevents the post office from printing its own bar code in that space and slows down the mail. FZ)*

THREE THRIFTY THOUGHTS

Dear Amy,

My sons don't like powdered milk, but they do enjoy it in a "purple cow." Fill a glass ⅔ with milk and ⅓ with grape juice.

If you have leftover salad, especially some to which dressing has already been applied, whir it in a blender with tomato juice, top with croutons and a few tiny cucumber bits, and serve as gazpacho.

After reading in your newsletter about the man who uses 1 square of toilet paper (yuck), I started using half of lots of things: shampoo, dish liquid, salt, and never noticed the difference.

—Marilyn Gibble
Lititz, Pennsylvania

CHANGE ON THE RANGE

Dear Amy,

To extend the lives of burners on an electric range, rotate them just as you would tires on a car. It evens out the wear.

—Nancy Deiter
Platteville, Wisconsin

WIPE THE WIPER

Dear Amy,

It is important to clean windshield wipers with vinegar and water in order to clean away the dirt and grime that accumulate. . . . I had thought my windshield wipers needed to be replaced, but after cleaning they were as good as new!

—Margaret Landsborough
Los Angeles, California

CREATIVE DEPRIVATION

At a yard sale I attended, a ten-year-old kid was barely visible behind a table piled with GI Joe paraphernalia. Along with about 30 Joe dolls, he was selling his Joe tanks, Joe bazookas, Joe rocket belts, and Joe you-name-it.

What struck me was what contempt he seemed to have for the stuff—he was practically giving it away. It was clear that this huge collection, which must have cost several hundred dollars to buy, was now an immense bore to him. When I commented to his parents about the good deals at their son's table, they just rolled their eyes as if to say, "That's kids for you."

Increasingly, I see this trend toward excess in children's lives. A friend, who has one child, says his son is so bombarded with toys from friends and relatives that "I don't tell him to clean his room—I tell him to shovel it out."

While we, as kids, might have been devastated to lose a favorite toy, kids today don't even bother to keep track of their stuff. When a friend found an $80 Game Boy, a hand-held video game, in his house, he was unable to learn whose it was. Six months later, the ten-year-old owner spotted her toy during a visit. She casually remarked, "Oh, I was wondering where I left that."

And the excess problem is not just toys. The average kid spends more than four hours parked in front of a TV each day. If there's nothing good to watch on TV (or cable), they have an unlimited supply of video movies and games.

As a result of all this stuff and stimulation, kids regard overload as a normal condition. Anything less—a walk in the woods, making cookies, or sitting in a classroom listening to a teacher—is boring.

In contrast, using a concept I call "creative deprivation" is, in my view, a healthier way to raise children.

The idea behind creative deprivation is that every event should have space around it, so that the event can stand out and be appreciated. A simple example is a frame around a picture, which provides a space to make it stand out from the busy wallpaper.

Until this century, the space occurred naturally. Entertainment and material goods were hard to come by, so they were appreciated when they came along. A child

cherished his few toys, and music was a special event, because it could only be heard when musicians were assembled.

The challenge of modern life is that we have to actively create the space. With mass production, toys are cheap enough to swamp even poorer families. With TV, videotapes, and video games, flashy entertainment can come into every home 24 hours a day.

That's why the best parents understand that their kids can have too much of a good thing. They place limitations on the stuff and stimulation. They are tough enough to slow down the flow of goodies.

Often, people think we refuse to avalanche our kids with toys because we're tightwads. But saving money is *not* the main reason. I just feel there's nothing sadder than a jaded eight-year-old.

Conversely, it's delightful to see a kid thrilled by a simple pleasure. During a rare trip to a mall a few years ago, we were shopping for a gift for one of our children, whose birthday falls in May—just before yard-sale season kicks in and just as I'm running out of the stuff from the previous season. To distract the kids while Jim went back to the store to pick up the gift and hide it in the car, we popped into an ice-cream shop and I ordered a junior cone for each child, which they consumed in complete silence, savoring every drip. I was very proud of my brood and their ability to enjoy these little treats.

Many parents, seeing their children appreciate junior cones, would buy them cones during each trip to the mall. Soon, seeing the kids' enthusiasm waning, they would assume they must wow them with banana splits. When those no longer produce the desired effect, they would move up to the jumbo deluxe sundae . . . and so on, until the kids became impossible to please.

But I see diminished appreciation as a barometer that shows when kids have had too much. Instead of moving up to the banana split, I decrease the frequency of junior cones.

While it's true I don't raise my kids this way to save money, saving is a natural by-product of creative deprivation. Not only do I save on the constant expense of the ever-increasing amount of stuff and stimulation, but when I *do* treat the kids, they get the same wow for far less money.

Creative deprivation does have a few rules. Limit the things kids don't need, but don't limit the things they do need—such as good

nutrition and parenting attention. Second, provide them with alternatives. Our kids have their own "office" in my office where they do artwork, a tree house they can build on with scrap wood, a playhouse in an attic, and a selection of Legos and other toys that demand creativity. If you limit passive entertainment, kids eventually get beyond the boredom and begin to be creative.

Incidentally, this insight of mine, while brilliant, isn't new. About 2,500 years ago, the Chinese philosopher Lao-tzu wrote:

> Guard the senses
> And life is ever full . . .
> Always be busy
> And life is beyond hope.

Finally, creative deprivation works for adults too. If you seem to need increasingly expensive thrills and gadgets to keep from being bored, I suggest you step off the merry-go-round. Though this might seem *more* boring at first, eventually you'll come to enjoy a game of checkers with your nine-year-old, trying a new bread recipe—or, one of Jim's favorites, watching the freezer defrost.

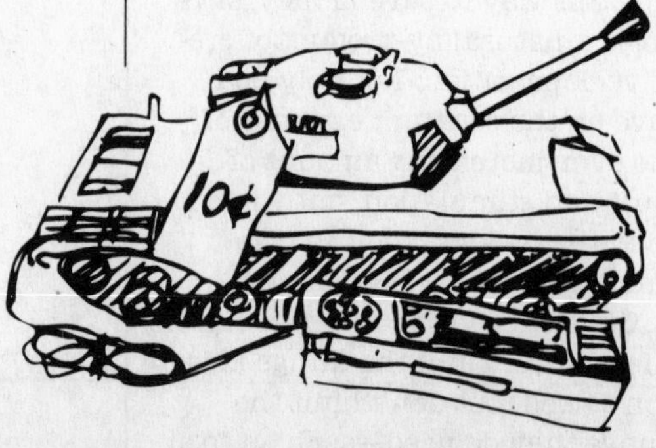

THE *X* SYSTEM

When you have several children and two or more are the same sex, it becomes difficult to keep their clothes straight at laundry-folding time.

One solution, which I read in an out-of-print thrift book, is to use a laundry marker to put *X*s in an inconspicuous place on children's clothes.

The oldest child is X, the next oldest is XX, and the next oldest is XXX, and so on. Every time an article of clothing is passed down, add another *X*.

Vicki Fisher of Clinton, Utah, uses a variation of this idea. She puts a tiny dot of acrylic paint on the inside of each article of clothing. Each time the article is passed down, she paints over the tiny dot with the color code for the next child.

Personally, I've developed a sixth sense, which allows me to detect even minute variations in white-sock size and sort accordingly. So to me, the attraction of the *X* system is that it would help my less gifted husband and kids to sort laundry.

LOW-COST COLOR

I had always suspected that paste-type food coloring, which is sold in party-goods stores, is cheaper to use than the liquid type sold in supermarkets. But I had never run a rigorous test to prove this. So when I was picked for classroom cookie duty recently, it seemed an excellent time to mix up a mountain of green frosting and settle the question.

Having used only paste food coloring for many years, I was surprised when I saw the high price of liquid coloring. A four-bottle box costs $2.29, or 58¢ for a bottle that contains 2 teaspoons, or 29¢ per teaspoon.

Paste colors last so long it had been a while since I'd priced those as well. The prices vary depending on the color. The average price is $1.79 a jar, which contains 6 teaspoons. Coincidentally, that also works out to 29¢ per teaspoon.

With this information, it was simple to compare them by making two large bowls of frosting and adding food coloring to each until we achieved the same shade of color.

To precision-measure the coloring, we used a chemist's 1/16-teaspoon measure. It took 1/16 teaspoon of paste to make a double batch of frosting turn medium green. In contrast, it took 7/16 teaspoon of liquid to make a double batch turn the same green. So the paste coloring costs less than 1¢ per batch, versus more than 6¢ per batch for the liquid.

The cost advantage becomes clearer when you consider how much you save when you buy four jars of paste colors for $7.16. The equivalent amount of liquid color would cost over $50.

In addition to their economy, paste colors are much richer than liquids and have a greater range of hues, including brown and black. The liquid red will make pink, but won't produce a true-red frosting, and combining liquid red and blue won't make a nice lavender.

If you wonder whether you'd ever use up the paste colors, keep in mind that they last for years. My mother-in-law, who used the colors conservatively when she decorated, had bottles that were 20 years old and still good. I, on the other hand, am not of the pastel-flowers-on-white-frosting school of decorating. A basic tenet of my cake-decorating philosophy is that liberal use of wonderful, rich colors goes a long way toward concealing my pitiful lack of skill.

Paste colors can be used for other things besides frosting. I use them to jazz up bland-looking homemade popsicles and gelatin. they make wonderful modeling-dough colors too: passion pink, canary yellow, brilliant blue. I've even mixed up military colors to create camouflage modeling dough.

SIX WAYS TO REUSE OLD BLUE JEANS

Workshop/Gardening Apron. Sew the front and back of jeans together as shown. Remove the inseam from the front section, and sew the legs together. Make neck and waist ties from surplus leg material. If you have one, sew on a D ring to adjust the neck tie.

Tote Bag. Each side is made from a leg section, with inseam removed. Bottom and handles are made from smaller jean sections. A "gusset" allows for easier flattening when the bag isn't in use. With extra reinforcement, this bag could be used in place of a $5 canvas grocery bag.

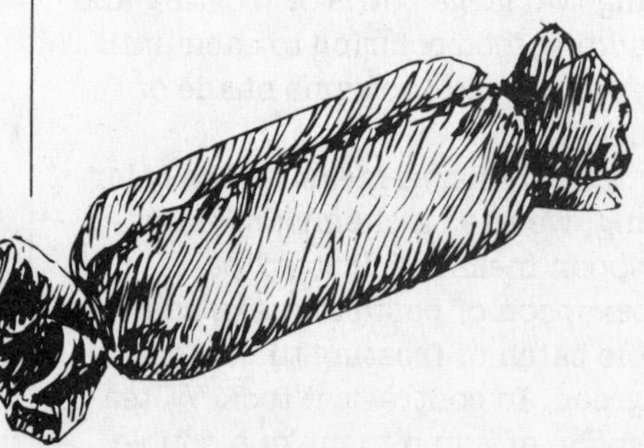

Neck-Roll Pillow. Hem cut-off sections of leg, stuff, and fasten with rubber bands.

The apron, tote, and pillow ideas were sent in by Tammy Aramian of Haywood, California.

Wall Organizer. Collect a variety of old denim jeans, overalls, and jackets with interesting pockets. Cut a piece of plywood about 2 feet x 3 feet, or to the size you wish your organizer to be. Cover all four raw edges of the plywood with a denim strip. The denim should overlap the front and back about an inch, or with enough material to tack in place. Select the pockets you wish to use, thinking about variety and visual interest. You might use an overall bib pocket, a designer pocket, a pocket with a hammer loop, or a ruler pocket from a construction worker's jeans. Cut them out larger than you need, and tack them on the board using carpet tacks. Overlap the sections so that the wood doesn't show, and turn under the edges to be tacked that will show.

Jeans Vest for Teens. Buy a vest pattern, or improvise from a vest you own. Cut inseam of two jean legs and iron flat. Cut front sections of vest from these, positioning pattern over the double seam any way you like. Use other material teen approves of for back sections and lining. Remove jean patch pockets and sew on vest fronts. Sent in by Michele Steinbacher of Harrisburg, Pennsylvania.

Purse. Turn jeans inside out, sew across just above the crotch, and cut off legs. Make a strap from surplus denim. Lace a bandanna or piece of fabric through loops. Sent in by Peggy Ham of Salt Lake City, Utah.

HOW TO SAVE ON FUNERALS

If you're like me, you're young, healthy, and have no plans to deal with death in the near future. You have no more interest in learning about low-cost funerals than I did. But so many readers requested information on this topic that I began to do research.

And then I became fascinated by this subject. Yeah, *fascinated.* I don't know when I've run across a subject like this—one that everyone needs to know about but nobody does. This lack of preparation could cost your family thousands of dollars in needless and hidden funeral charges. The average funeral costs $5,000, and you can spend as much as $20,000.

Yet, as I studied, I realized that some readers would tend to skip to other articles. So this article is divided into three sections:

1. For Those Who Don't Think They Need This and/or for Those Who Are Squeamish About Death:

Someday you're going to be blindsided by an unexpected death. You won't have had any discussions about it with your family. Your first instinct will be to let a nearby funeral home handle everything for you, because you don't know that there's any other way. That's how expensive funerals happen.

So . . . the resource I want you to file away for future use is:

Continental Association of Funeral and Memorial Societies
33 University Square, Suite 333
Madison, WI 53715
(800) 458-5563

Memorial societies are member-supported organizations that work on behalf of consumers to keep funeral costs low. There are over 175 of them in North America. The CAFMS can be contacted 24 hours a day and can provide you with the name of the nonprofit memorial society that's closest to you. To receive a pamphlet that describes the benefits of memorial societies and a directory of memorial societies nationwide, send a SASE to the CAFMS address.

Remember, this is a nonprofit organization run primarily by volunteers, and it provides a much needed service. Always send SASE's when you request information through the mail, and donations are appreciated.

To join your local society, you pay a lifetime membership fee of about $25. There may be an addi-

tional small fee if membership papers are filed at the time of a death.

Among their other services, memorial societies have negotiated in advance with funeral directors and come up with low-cost, no-frills "package deals." For example, a "cooperating funeral director" here in Maine will deliver the body to a crematorium and provide a container and a place to hold the service for $550. A traditional funeral costs a little more. Remember, though, that if you want something different from what is contained in the package, the memorial society may not be able to accommodate you.

Memorial-society members generally don't believe in open-casket viewing and makeup. They also don't recommend embalming, which is unnecessary in most cases. They encourage the use of inexpensive caskets and simple, personalized services.

Memorial societies can also inform you about other options, such as:

• Handling arrangements without use of a mortuary, if it's legal in your state.

• Where to get inexpensive coffins—simple wooden ones might cost as little as $200.

• Laws regarding home burial plots.

• Using cement slabs instead of a more expensive vault.

Since the nonprofit memorial societies are operated by volunteers, in some cases you may get an answering machine with several numbers you can call in an emergency. If you have difficulty reaching the service in your area, call CAFMS again.

Although we have provided this information for you to use in an emergency, that is *not* the best time to use these organizations. When you join a society, you'll be sent a "prearrangement" form that helps you plan *before* the need arises.

This is not a contract, but merely a way to express your wishes, and a beginning point for family discussion. The society will also provide "Living Will" and "Durable Power of Attorney for Health Care" forms for members who are concerned about death with dignity.

Note: Not all businesses using the title "memorial society" are nonprofit organizations, but these may save you money if there is no nonprofit society in your area.

Finally, there are some potential downsides to these groups:

• While the overall concept of memorial societies is great, your local memorial society may not be one of the best. Have an extended talk with the volunteer who runs your society to get a feel for the quality of the group.

• There may not be a funeral home with a cooperating director near enough to suit your needs.

• In response to the good work done by memorial societies, many funeral homes have taken it upon themselves to offer "budget" funeral packages. If you find such a home, participation in a memorial society may be unnecessary.

2. For Those Who Want More Information:

If you're interested in some in-depth reading, go to the library and check out *Dealing Creatively with Death: A Manual of Death Education and Simple Burial*, by Ernest Morgan. This is considered

to be the best book on the subject; at 170 pages, it tells you absolutely everything you could want to know about options in funeral and burial arrangements.

If you're not up for lengthy reading, a resource that might be helpful is "Funeral Information In-Home Seminar," by Dan Rohling, a former funeral director. This 60-page booklet is designed to be read in 1½ hours. It contains basic information on funerals and several worksheets including an obituary form, a vital information form, and a financial information form. It also includes a complaint form. If you have a problem with a funeral home, you can send Rohling the completed form and he will file it with the Federal Trade Commission for you.

I particularly liked the "Cemetery Pricing Survey," which lists all the questions you should ask—and most are questions I wouldn't have thought to ask. The questions are even phrased exactly as you should say them. All you have to do is read them aloud when you call for prices. Although some would think this is too basic, this simplicity would be very helpful if one were under stress. To purchase a copy, send $16 (includes shipping) to:

Funeral Information Service
3230 E. Flamingo Road, #287
Las Vegas, NV 89121

3. For Those Who Are Fascinated and Willing to Explore All Options.

If you're open to more "alternative" arrangements, you should read *Caring for Your Own Dead*, by Lisa Carlson. I am not the "alternative type" (I eat white sugar and give birth in hospitals), so I did not think I'd be receptive to this book. But I was extremely moved by three accounts she gave in which funeral arrangements had been made for less than $200. Within the context of these accounts, homemade coffins and hand-dug graves seemed loving and personal, rather than simply ways to cut some corners. The author makes a strong case that professionally arranged funerals tend to isolate you from the death, and that, in contrast, family participation is therapeutic. The book also lists regulations for different states and more specific information on other, more conventional, low-cost options. To order call Upper Access Press at (802) 482-2988. The softcover version costs $14.95.

Although I have never liked conventional funerals with their drawn-out, stressful ceremonies, I have further altered my thinking after having viewed this information. For the first time, I see the importance of writing down exactly what I would want. If my wishes weren't known, people might needlessly spend money on things I wouldn't like.

Also for the first time, the simplicity and practicality of cremation and scattering ashes seems very appealing. I like the idea of having an informal at-home memorial service at a later time, during which people may come in casual clothing and express their feelings to the family.

If all this stuff about cutting corners on funerals seems cheap and tacky to you, think about how the saved thousands could better be used. I feel it's better to spend money on the living—whether family or a charity—rather than for an expensive funeral.

HOW TO SAVE ON FUNERALS UPDATE

Another option that has been strongly recommended by several readers is donating your body to science.

Medical and dental schools in all states need bodies for anatomical studies. Many schools pay for transportation within the state. Most pay for cremation and will return the ashes on request. Reader Bob Balcomb of Findlay, Ohio, told me that by using this option, three funerals in his family have been "practically free."

It's always best to make advance preparations to donate your own body; many schools no longer accept body donations by relatives without such prior arrangements. Contact your nearby medical school, or get the address from the book *Caring for Your Own Dead* by Lisa Carlson, which lists medical schools in all states that accept body donations. The school will send you several forms to fill out and a Uniform Donor Card for you to sign and carry.

A final note: Carlson points out that many hospitals have a desperate need for organ transplants. Unlike donating bodies for study, organ donation can immediately save a life. Usually, corneas can be removed and the body can go on to medical-school study, but once a major organ has been taken from a body, medical schools usually don't want the rest of the body.

So, Carlson has specified on her Uniform Donor Card that her body be used for organ donation if possible; only if it's not needed for that should it be donated to a medical school. While organ donation may not be the absolutely cheapest alternative—because the family must still pay for final disposition of the body—it is probably the most compassionate.

PRETZEL VALENTINES

Every year I get pressed into sending "healthy" snacks to children's Valentine's Day parties at school. This year our stay-at-home dad will make heart-shaped pretzels, a variation on an animal-pretzel recipe sent in by David Westerberg of Middlebury, Vermont. Here's the recipe:

SOFT PRETZELS

1 package yeast
$1\frac{1}{2}$ cups warm water
1 tablespoon sugar
1 tablespoon salt
4 cups flour
1 egg

Combine yeast, water, sugar, and salt in a large bowl. Stir in flour. Knead on a table until the dough is smooth. Shape dough into heart or animal shapes, using water to "glue" two parts together. Place on a greased cookie sheet. Brush with beaten egg. Sprinkle with salt. Bake in a preheated oven at 425 degrees for 15 minutes.

TANGLE ANGLE

Dear Amy,

My small daughters took their Barbies into the bath, which made the doll hair tangle like a rat's nest. After trying to comb out the impossible hair, I decided to try hair conditioner on it. I let it sit for a while, rinsed it, and then was able to comb out the tangles. Although the doll hair doesn't look brand-new, I can now braid the hair or put bows in it.

—Matilda Carreras
Billerica, Massachusetts

OUNCE OUCH

Dear Amy,

I made a discovery. I purchased a jar of generic honey that read "32 oz. net weight." I put the honey in a syrup bottle that read "24 fluid ounces." I discovered that 32 ounces net weight of honey fits in a bottle that holds 24 fluid ounces of syrup. This showed me that the price of the generic honey was average and I made no savings. Read the labels and know the difference in measurements.

—Lisa DeReese
Alice, Texas

(Sixteen fluid ounces of water equals 16 ounces net weight. But 16 fluid ounces of oil, syrup, honey, or molasses equals 14, 20, 22, and 23 ounces net weight, respectively. When comparing same-size containers of these items, figure fluid ounces equals 114 percent, 80 percent, 73 percent, and 70 percent of the net-weight price, respectively. FZ)

CHEAP CHIC

Dear Amy,

I enrolled in a sewing class to learn to sew more complicated things and use fancy materials. The first thing I made was a party dress out of metallic fabric, very fancy, very chic. Last weekend we were invited to a benefit at the Chicago Lyric Opera. After quickly checking our coats (my ski parka and my husband's Colombo-style raincoat, both old) next to everyone else's furs, we went in to the fanciest party I've ever seen. I can't tell you how pleased I was when my friends commented on how nice my dress was (they didn't know I made it). Most of the dresses were probably worth over $200, while I spent $12 ($37 including the class).

—Katherine Richardson Kenward
Homewood, Illinois

FZ PHONE HOME

Dear Amy,

The telephone company in our area offers three levels of phone service. The first: You pay $9.36 plus 9¢ for each outgoing call. The second, for $14.61, gives you 65 calls per month, then you pay 9¢ for each additional call. The third, for $19.18, gives you unlimited calls. Incoming calls are free for all three levels. I use the first service because I only make 30 to 35 calls a month. This month my cost was $12.42. I saved $6.76. It seems like a little, but it adds up to $80 to $84 a year.

—Elizabeth Bissett
Huntingtown, Maryland

(We have a similar service in Maine. We switched to a more expensive service and saved money. Because we live 30 minutes from most places we shop, we make a lot of phone calls to compare prices. We save on phone bills, gasoline, and time. Factor in the money-saving aspects of using the telephone when figuring out which service works best for you. FZ)

BIRTHDAY BUCKS

Dear Amy,

Our two children had birthdays last month. They were pleasantly surprised that instead of the nice card their great-aunt usually sends each of them, they found $2 tucked inside a homemade card made from very old construction paper. Aunt Marg had selected cards at the local card shop, but when the lady added them up to $4.52, she sent the boys the money instead. The children were pleased with the $2 . . . and peeved when they calculated how much more money they would have received if other friends and family had been as clever as Great-Aunt Marg!

—Barbara Keltner
Medicine Lodge, Kansas

EEK—A LEAK!

Dear Amy,

We had a water trap spring a leak under an old sink. It was such an old model that we could not find a replacement. Following the suggestion of a plumber, we bought a pack of chewing gum. One stick, well-chewed, filled the hole, and then some tape wound around it held the gum in place. It cost approximately 10¢ and saved a $100 plumber's bill.

—Ward Schori
Evanston, Illinois

DELI DEALS

Dear Amy,

Many delis sell the end of a loaf of meat (some sell cheese, too) that cannot be reached by the electric slicer. After hand-slicing as much as possible, chop up the rest for German potato salad, scalloped potatoes, chef salad, or our favorite, potato soup!

—Karen Wilt
Ann Arbor, Michigan

(This is a great tip, which I've used many times. More recently it seems as if the stores are catching on. The last time I asked for cheese ends, the price per pound was actually higher than the price per pound of 5-pound bricks of cheese at the warehouse store. So remember to keep checking prices. FZ)

CUT A RUG

Dear Amy,

When I took up the wall-to-wall carpeting in the bedroom, I found that the area under the bed was like new, so I cut it out for an area rug. Binding is available at carpet or fabric stores and can be glued on.

—Sharon Cribbs
Jackson, South Carolina

THE FINE ART OF NEGOTIATION—OR HOW TO KEEP MORE OF YOUR CHEETOS

America is one of the few countries in the world in which shopping is a passive, "spectator" sport. In most other places, every purchase—whether of a piece of fruit or a home—is preceded by a long haggle. Jim, who has spent lots of time overseas, says some shopkeepers are actually offended if you don't haggle, because they enjoy the sport even more than they enjoy getting the full price.

In this country, somehow, the idea has developed that haggling is undignified, overly time-consuming, even unfair. None of this is true. The truth is that haggling is fun, need not take much time, and can benefit both the buyer and seller.

Jim and I are accomplished negotiators. This year, Jim got a new, $1,250 outboard motor at a boat show for $900 and a used Rototiller marked at $700 for $575, and I got a yard-sale "My Little Pony" marked at 25¢ for 10¢—I hope I wasn't too rough on the guy.

But for one of my readers, Daniel J. Mezick of North Haven, Connecticut, negotiating is his *life.* Mezick, a 35-year-old computer consultant, is addicted to negotiating. Virtually everything he owns is the result of haggling: He bought a complete aboveground swimming pool, with deck and filter, for $200; a top-quality $35 used coat for $5; and a Soloflex exercise machine for $90 that he sold six months later for $600.

Mezick has refined negotiating to a science. He has read books about it and even taken courses in negotiation. We called him and got these pointers:

1. Everything is negotiable. Most Americans haggle only over houses, cars, and yard-sale stuff (some don't even do this much). Mezick bargains for almost everything, including new retail goods such as shoes and motel rooms. The major exception is chain retail stores. The trick, he says, is to find the owner (generally, employees don't have the authority to haggle) and simply ask, "Would you take less?" The worst you'll hear is no, and you'll be surprised how often you'll hear yes. If you're negotiating with the owner of a small shop, you should do it discreetly, as he might be unwilling to let other customers know he is open to negotiation.

2. Negotiating is a human transaction as well as a financial one. Don't barge up and start haggling immediately. Chitchat, establish a relationship. This creates a bond between both parties; it also gives you a chance to assess the other person's character and motivation.

3. After this, gently guide the discussion to the item at hand. If you are the potential buyer, discuss it in a neutral way. Being too positive makes you seem overeager, but being too negative at this stage can lead the seller to dislike you and reject your offer.

4. Don't rush to discuss prices. As Mezick puts it, "The first one to name a price loses." This is because the person who names the price has given the other party the role of moving the price, and in negotiation, moving is everything.

5. Once you hear the proposal, never counter it immediately. "If you immediately counter a proposal, it makes the person think you didn't hear a word he said," says Mezick. By waiting and considering the proposal, you show respect for the other person and make him more receptive when you do respond.

(By the way, I used this technique with Mezick. When he sent me a letter offering to tell all about negotiating in exchange for a one-year subscription, I waited almost two years to call him back.)

6. When you *do* respond, give your reasons, *then* make your counteroffer. Most people do this the other way around, but the problem is that once the other party hears your counteroffer, he "shuts off" and does not want to hear your reasons. If you give your reasons first, the other party is *forced* to listen to them, because he is waiting to hear your counteroffer. Once he's heard your reasons, your counteroffer is usually more acceptable to him.

7. Suppose you go through this process and you still end up with a gap between what the buyer will pay and what the seller will take. Good negotiators bridge the gap with what Mezick calls "elegant currency." This is a noncash commodity that can "sweeten the deal" enough to satisfy both parties.

Example: The owner of a barber shop wants to buy your car. After haggling, you have a gap: He offers $2,000, you want $2,500. At this point, you might ask this barber to provide you with $500 in haircuts during his least busy days. This works much better for both parties than the usual "split the difference" route. You gain $500 in credit on something you really would have purchased out-of-pocket, and the barber's out-of-pocket expense is nil.

Mezick used this concept recently in a dispute with his auto-repair garage. He said he had been overcharged $300. He convinced the shop owner to drop $150 off the price and give him another $150 in repair credit.

While all of these concepts are important, the most important thing to remember about negotiating, says Mezick, is to *do it*, even if it makes you uncomfortable. Mezick describes his own personality as "extroverted, aggressive to the extreme," so haggling comes easily to him. If you are more the shy, introverted type, there is no easy answer, except, as Mezick says, "you have to be willing to climb out of your comfort zone."

Why should you do it? Mezick was very impressed with my concept of the "hourly wage" for various money-saving activities (for example, changing your car's oil and filter yourself saves $7 and takes 15 minutes, so it "pays" a tax-free $28 hourly wage. For more examples, see the first book). Negotiating, he says, can pay a higher hourly wage than any other activity.

Example: Recently, a junkyard Mezick visits frequently wanted to charge him $50 for a set of brake drums. He spread his arms wide and with a quizzical look said, "What? No preferred customer discount?" The owner immediately dropped $15 off the price. It took three seconds to say those five words; that works out to $18,000 an hour. Naturally, Mezick does not spend every minute negotiating, but he accumulates many hours worth of negotiation every year at a similar and sometimes better "hourly wage."

Because of the obvious value of negotiating, Mezick is making sure that his kids, ages eight, six, and four, all grow up skilled in the art.

He started them out early with this simple exercise: When each kid reached age three, he sat the child down and poured out a pile of Cheetos in front of the child, and another in front of himself.

"Would you like to play a game where you give me three Cheetos and I give you one?" he asks. The toddler agrees (toddlers agree to anything that sounds like a game) and soon discovers he's out of Cheetos. After what's happened sinks in, Mezick says, "Okay, let's play again, but this time *you* make the rules." The toddler considers and makes his own proposal, usually one that works to his own advantage. The parent makes a counterproposal, and the negotiation is on. The child is learning a crucial truth: You are better off if you don't let the other person make all the rules.

Interestingly, Mezick told me that the negotiation habit also eases family friction. His children constantly make deals with one another over disputes rather than running to their parents for mediation.

For those who think negotiating is unfair, here's my view: Everything in life is a negotiation. If you think that you never negotiate, you're wrong. Non-negotiators are, by their silence, saying, "You set all of the terms in this negotiation. I may accept it or reject it, but I refuse to seek a common ground that can meet both of our needs." While it's true that hustlers can fast-talk and cheat people, I find that honest negotiation is generally better for both parties than the silent, take-it-or-leave-it attitude that most people have.

My thanks to Daniel Mezick for his insights; but, as you might expect, I didn't get them for nothing. Mezick now has a one-year subscription to the *Tightwad Gazette* newsletter and a complete set of back issues—and I guarantee, we both feel we got good deals.

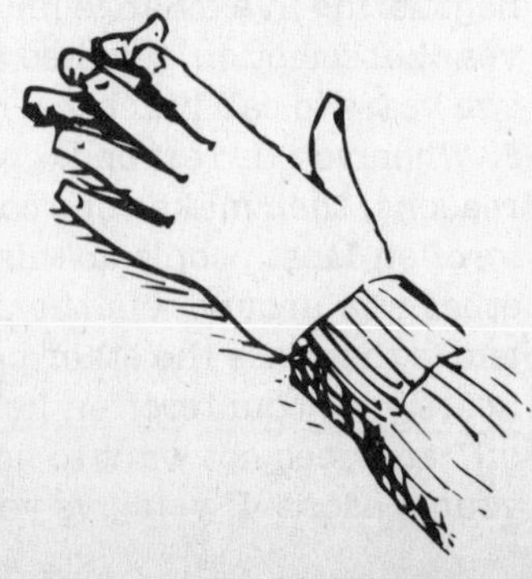

BUDGET BUG-BUSTING

Before you rush out to the home-and-garden store to arm yourself with your springtime bug-slaughtering arsenal, check out these clever, cheap, and safe bug-beating ideas from readers, and other sources:

REMEDIES FOR OUTDOORS

This idea for vanquishing fruit-tree bugs comes from the Berne (Indiana) *Tri-Weekly*:

2-liter plastic bottle
string
1 banana peel
1 cup sugar
1 cup strong vinegar

Slice banana peel into strips and insert them into the plastic bottle. In a separate container, combine sugar and vinegar. Pour this mixture into the bottle, then fill it to within 2 inches of the neck with water. Tie the string around the neck of the bottle, then tie the other end around the lower branches of a tree.

Fruit and black flies, yellowjackets, and other insects find the fermenting banana, sugar, and vinegar more attractive than the fruit on the tree. Once they fly in, they get caught in the sticky mixture and drown. This reportedly works so well that it can make spraying fruit trees unnecessary.

Several other readers sent their favorite concoctions for defeating garden pests:

Darcy Hutson of Tucson, Arizona, uses chopped garlic cloves and water in a spray bottle. She says to make the mixture extra-strong, boil tobacco and add the tobacco tea to mixture.

Rey and Sandy Naranjo of Albuquerque, New Mexico, make a garden spray from 1 tablespoon dishwashing detergent and 1 cup vegetable oil. They mix 1 to 2 teaspoons of this mixture with 1 cup of water and spray it on their plants.

Karen Hammond of Monroe, Georgia, waits for a day when the ground is dry and rain is at least a day away, then gently sprinkles a teaspoon of instant grits on each fire-ant hill in her yard. The worker ants carry the grits to the queen, who eats them. When she drinks water, the grits expand in her stomach and kill her. The remainder of the hill dies within a day.

REMEDIES FOR INDOORS

Glenda DeSantis of El Reno, Oklahoma, sent this method for ridding your home of fleas:

Fill a pan with soapy water (a true tightwad, Glenda reuses the soapy water from the dinner dishes), and place under a night-light in any room that you suspect contains fleas. Make sure it is the only light in the room. The fleas will jump at the light, fall in the pan of soapy water, and drown.

Michele Picozzi of Colorado Springs, Colorado, makes ant repellent by combining the following ingredients in a spray bottle:

$10^1/_2$ ounces water
3 ounces Tabasco sauce
$2^1/_2$ ounces Dr. Bronner's liquid peppermint soap (available at health-food stores)

Spray where ants enter the home.

Rhonda Barfield of St. Charles, Missouri, makes this "roach dough." It works because it creates gas when eaten. Roaches can't belch, so their digestive tracts explode.

$^1/_2$ cup sugar
$^1/_4$ cup shortening or bacon drippings
$^1/_2$ cup chopped onion
$^1/_2$ cup flour
8 ounces baking soda

Combine sugar and shortening. Add onion, flour, and baking soda. Mix in just enough water to make a doughlike consistency. Put small balls in plastic sandwich bags and place in roach-infested areas. You should probably keep them out of areas where children and pets play.

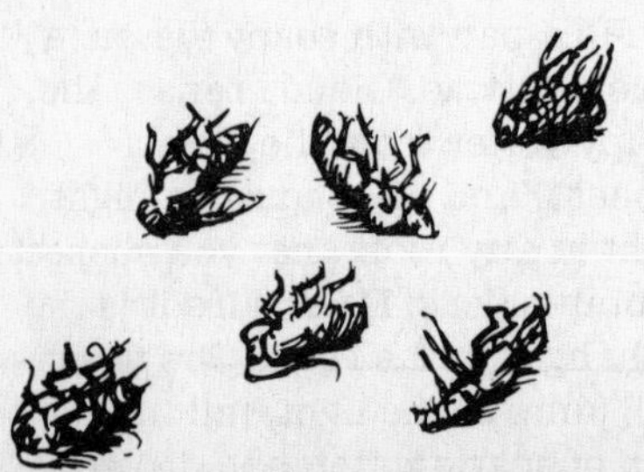

MIXES TAKE A BEATING

In my never-ending quest to shave more off my food bill, I read many books written by grocery-shopping experts. One surprising bit of information, which arose from three sources, was that some mixes and whack-'em-on-the-counter biscuits are cheaper than baking from scratch. But it wasn't until I read a more recent newspaper article suggesting that mixes were cheaper that I was finally inspired to get to the bottom of this apparent tightwad heresy.

To compare mixes to scratch baking, we bought the cheapest cake, biscuit, corn-muffin, and brownie mixes we could find at the supermarket, and for the purposes of calculation, we dropped their prices to the sale-price level. We also bought restaurant-supply cake mix (the chart price is based on a case that makes 24 cakes). And we tested whack-'em-on-the-counter biscuits as well.

We baked up each mix and its scratch counterpart, weighed them, and calculated the after-baked cost per ounce. The mix prices in the chart below include the cost of the ingredients you add at home (Example: 88¢ for the cake mix, plus 64¢ for eggs and oil equals $1.52).

As we baked and weighed, it quickly became obvious how the mixes-can-be-cheaper idea came about. If you compare only on the basis of *volume*, some mixes do indeed appear to be cheaper.

Scratch foods, however, tend to have more body and are heavier. Consequently, if you are interested in filling—rather than fooling—your family with baked

Baked Item	Weight Per Batch	Cost Per Batch	Cost Per Ounce	Taste Rating
Betty Crocker yellow cake mix	28 ounces	$1.52	.052	2
Restaurant yellow cake mix	38 ounces	$1.49	.039	3½
Scratch yellow cake	33 ounces	$1.05	.032	5
Jiffy biscuit mix (small box)	10½ ounces	.30	.028	1
Store-brand whack-'em biscuits	6½ ounces	.25	.038	2
Scratch biscuits	19 ounces	.30	.016	5
Jiffy baking mix (big box)	11 ounces	.10½	.009	2½
Jiffy corn-muffin mix	10 ounces	.38	.038	3
Scratch corn bread	24 ounces	.53	.022	5
Jiffy brownie mix	7 ounces	.40	.057	1
Homemade brownies	12 ounces	.35½	.030	5

goods, scratch is almost always cheaper.

Some would argue that mixes are quicker to make, but consider: To make a yellow cake from a mix, you combine four ingredients: mix, eggs, oil, and water. One from scratch takes eight ingredients: flour, eggs, shortening, milk, baking powder, sugar, salt, and vanilla. In my kitchen, it takes less than two minutes to add those extra items. (Presuming both cakes are equal, if it takes two minutes to save 47¢, that's like earning $14.10 per hour, tax-free.) In addition, by purchasing bulk baking goods, I save shopping time over buying individual cake mixes.

We also did a taste test. Six of our staff (including both those who grew up eating only scratch foods and those with a "mix" heritage) sampled everything. Our chart (above) contains a 1-to-5 taste rating. Because the scratch versions were the clear favorites, we gave those items a 5 and rated the mixes in comparison.

Scratch foods have at least two other advantages over mixes: They don't contain artificial ingredients, and they don't create nearly as much garbage as an endless succession of tiny mix boxes.

Our chart shows that Jiffy baking mix, when used to make biscuits, was the only mix we tested that was cheaper than scratch, although our staff did not like the taste as well. Its other disadvantage is that it has a white-flour base, and most of the scratch baking I do uses part oatmeal, cornmeal, or whole-wheat flour. I wouldn't be able to use these with a mix.

The only other way a mix could be cheaper than baking

from scratch is if you double a coupon or combine a coupon with a sale. For the mix price to be cheap enough, the after-baked cost per ounce has to be lower than the after-baked scratch cost per ounce. This is pretty complex, but if you really want to figure it out, wade through the following paragraph:

Multiply the cost per ounce of the after-baked scratch batch by the number of ounces in the after-baked mix batch. Then subtract the cost of ingredients that must be added to the mix batch. For example, to determine when a cake mix is cheap enough: Multiply 32¢ by 28 ounces, and you get 89¢. Subtract 64¢ (cost of eggs and oil) from 89¢, and you get 25¢. So if the box of cake mix costs 25¢ or less, it's a good deal compared to scratch.

Just to be sure, after we ran the above tests, we also got some more expensive mixes and some chocolate cake mixes and tested them as well. Surprisingly, the more expensive mixes turned out to be slightly more economical than the cheaper mixes (because they made heavier batches), but still were not nearly as cheap as scratch. The chocolate cake mix versus scratch showed a similar spread to the yellow-cake results in the chart.

WHOOPIE PIES

Usually when I make snacks I opt for healthier alternatives, but every once in a while I make these junk-food substitutes. The recipe is a little time-consuming, so I make these with the kids to get in a little quality time in the process.

Cookie ingredients:
1½ cups sugar
¼ cup shortening
½ cup cocoa
1 egg
½ teaspoon cream of tartar
½ teaspoon baking soda
1 teaspoon salt
2 cups flour
¾ cup sour milk*
1 teaspoon vanilla

Filling ingredients:
½ cup milk
2½ teaspoons flour
½ cup shortening
½ cup sugar
pinch of salt
1 teaspoon vanilla

To make the cookie: Cream the sugar and the shortening. Add the cocoa and the egg; mix well. Sift the dry ingredients. Add alternately with the milk to the sugar/shortening mixture. Add the vanilla and mix well. Drop by teaspoons onto greased cookie sheets. Bake 12 minutes at 375 degrees.

To make the filling: Cook the milk and flour until thick. Chill until cool, then beat well with automatic beater. Add the remaining filling ingredients, and mix well.

Pair off cookies by size; add filling to make sandwiches. Because they tend to be gooey, preserve them by wrapping individually in plastic wrap.

*Make sour milk by adding 1 tablespoon vinegar or lemon juice to 1 cup milk, then let milk stand 10 minutes.

WONDERING ABOUT WAREHOUSE CLUBS

Dear Amy,

What is your opinion of warehouse clubs? I notice that some items are cheaper, but others seem more expensive. Is there really any savings when you pay the annual fee?

—Roseanne Olejarz
Lombard, Illinois

You are right: Some items *are* cheaper, and some *are* more expensive than when purchased from other sources. Warehouse stores are cheap because they sell in bulk, have few employees, and have bare-bones "architecture" in their stores.

But other factors drive their prices *up*. Many don't take coupons, don't carry store brands or generics, and don't have loss-leader sales like traditional supermarkets.

So you must compare carefully. Unfortunately, warehouse stores make it difficult for you to compare. Unlike most supermarkets, they don't use unit pricing, and they carry products in unfamiliar (very large) sizes.

Another point is that warehouse stores carry bulk-purchase convenience foods and many other consumer goods that you don't need. I see people leaving them with cartfuls of dumb stuff—mirrored clocks, cases of juice packs, bushels of Lucky Charms cereal, and so on. People spend more than they should because "it's a good deal." At one point (years ago) we were bulk-buying fruit roll-ups until we came to our senses and realized that real fruit is cheaper.

Step one, then, is to make a price book. It is impossible to make an accurate comparison between stores unless you do this. I explain in detail how to make one in the first book, but basically, you use a loose-leaf notebook to record the lowest typical prices at various stores on goods you buy regularly.

To enter warehouse prices into your book, you'll have to do your own "unit pricing." It's simple and quick. Just take your calculator along, and divide the price by the units (pounds or ounces).

Don't sign up for a membership, which typically costs $25, until you do this. All of the warehouse stores in our area give you a one-day pass for free. If you buy anything, 5 percent is added to the purchase price.

Initially, we found that there were too few good deals for us to justify the membership fee. However, after we started our business, we found enough good deals on office supplies to make the fee worthwhile. If you aren't going to buy $500 worth of stuff per year, you would be better off getting the one-day pass with each visit and paying the 5 percent surcharge than paying a $25 annual fee.

After you've checked out the prices, chances are you'll find, as we did, that warehouse stores are a valuable part—and I emphasize the word *part*—of your overall shopping system. No single source has the cheapest price on everything. Know what items warehouse stores carry that have the cheapest price, and plan to stop in and get them once a month.

TAKE CHARGE OF CHARGES

One of the basic tenets of tightwaddery is to pay down your mortgage as quickly as possible—but how can you do it when you feel you don't have a cent to spare?

One answer is to chop out extra charges that you may be paying along with your mortgage payment, then use *that* money to pay down your principal. Much of this information comes from an interview we did with Marc Eisenson, who publishes a newsletter called *The Banker's Secret Bulletin.* (For a sample issue, send $1 to *The Banker's Secret,* Box 78, Elizaville, NY 12523).

Here are two examples of charges to examine:

1. Private mortgage insurance: Generally, if you make a down payment of less than 20 percent of the value of your house, you're required to buy private mortgage insurance. This insurance pays the lender if you default on your mortgage.

What the lender often *won't* tell you is that you don't have to keep the insurance forever. Usually, once you build up your equity beyond 20 percent of the value of your house, you can drop it. So ask your lender how much equity you need to be able to stop paying premiums. If property values have shifted in your area, you may also need to get an appraisal, which generally costs around $250 dollars.

The savings can be significant. According to the Mortgage Banker's Association, mortgage-insurance fees on a $67,500 loan average from $338 to $675 annually.

2. Property taxes and homeowner's insurance: No, you can't drop these, but you can pay them in a way that saves you money. If your down payment is less than 20 percent of the house's value, many lenders require you to put your property taxes and homeowner's insurance in escrow accounts, which you pay into monthly along with your mortgage payment. Some states require lenders to pay you interest on money in your escrow account, but the rate may not be as good as you'll get in another account. And some states don't require the lender to pay you a dime in interest.

So, contact your lender and ask whether you have enough equity to set up *your own* escrow account or can otherwise arrange to pay the property taxes and insurance yourself, and thus collect your own interest money. Again, the payoff makes the phone call worth it: Monthly payments of $250 at 4 percent interest would yield $65.73 annually.

Finally, Eisenson points out that the best time to explore these options is *before* you get the mortgage. When shopping for a mortgage (and if you can't plunk down at least 20 percent, which you really should try to do so that you can avoid all of these charges up front), be sure to ask the lenders when, exactly, you can drop the private mortgage insurance and pay property taxes and homeowner's insurance yourself.

TAKE THE PULSE

Dear Amy,

If the "pulse" (also known as rotary-dial) telephone service is cheaper each month than the "tone" (also known as touch-tone) signal, sign up for pulse and save $10 or more per year.

The usual concern with doing this is that you can't use automated answering machines—but you can! Use a "dual" phone with a "pulse/tone" switch when dialing long distance to any automated answering machine ("after the tone, press 1 for customer service, press 2 for account statements," etc.)

When you dial the long-distance call, use the pulse setting (you have to, if your signal is pulse), but when the machine answers, immediately switch to tone. It works perfectly!

—Steven P. Hill
Urbana, Illinois

(If you already have a dual phone, this is clearly a good idea. If you must buy one to do this, be sure to calculate whether the payback is worth the price of the new phone. FZ)

TRASH DANCE

Dear Amy,

As a high school teacher, I am routinely asked to chaperone the junior prom and the senior dinner dance. The students always do a fabulous job decorating the gym or cafeteria, but that night, or the next morning, all the decorations go into the trash. So, I always volunteer to help supervise the cleanup, and I scavenge as much as I can. I reuse the metallic paper, ribbons, streamers, bows, stars, bells, and plastic flowers for everything throughout the year. I decorate my classroom for the holidays, and I wrap and tie up boxes at home for Christmas. It makes me so happy!

—Anne Marie DeProspo
Hamilton, New York

USE THE RECYCLE CYCLE

Dear Amy,

Instead of washing your plastic bags in the sink, save them until you are doing your laundry. I turn them inside out and wash them with my white clothes. I use warm water, 1 teaspoon of bleach, and ½ cup of laundry soap. It seems to clean them better than washing them in the sink. It even cleans the greasy ones. I even wash the wrappers from store-bought goods so they are clean enough to be recycled. By washing our plastics we have reduced our garbage waste by half, which saves us $15 a month in garbage collection fees.

—Margaret Marsh
Hastings, Nebraska

PEEL A MEAL

Dear Amy,

Many of us either throw the stems of broccoli away or selflessly suffer through eating them. My coworker showed us that peeling the stems will make them amazingly tender. Now we like the stems better than the flowerettes!

—Carol Sabbar
Kenosha, Wisconsin

A CLEARER MIRROR

Dear Amy,

To make any mirror fog-free, you need not purchase the expensive antifog products. Simply use liquid soap; spread it on glass with a cloth to cover completely, then polish dry with another cloth. This lasts for a long time.

—Patricia Stark
St. Peter, Minnesota

SAVE THE SPOTTED TOWEL

Dear Amy,

I taught home economics for 27 years, and this recipe for homemade laundry pretreatment is one of the best tips I've seen:

½ cup vinegar
½ cup ammonia (sudsy or plain)
½ cup Wisk
½ cup water

Spray on grease or food spots, or dirty collars and cuffs. Wash garment as usual.

—Reader name withheld by request

PARLOR PAGES

Dear Amy,

The last time I got my hair cut, I asked my stylist what she did with the old magazines in the shop. She told me they were thrown out. I asked her if I could have them, and she said "Yes." Now, each month, she calls me, and I pick up 10 to 12 magazines for free! I clip coupons, find recipes, and read articles, all for no expense!

—Carol Foil
Barnwell, South Carolina

CURDS GO A LONG WHEY

Dear Amy,

Does everyone out there know that when you find a terrific price on cottage cheese you can stock up without worrying about the expiration date? All you have to do is store it in its own container upside down in the fridge. This week we opened up our last container from my last cottage-cheese spree. The expiration date on the container was more than four and a half months ago. All I had to do was stir it some, since it had separated, but it tasted fresh. Once opened, continue to store it upside down.

—Dora Winzeler
Waldron, Michigan

(To check this out, we called Kathy Gucfa, spokesperson for the United Dairy Industry Association. She said, "This is a fairly well-known household hint, and it does seem to extend shelf life, but there have been no studies or research to verify how long." We

called several other medical and dairy-industry authorities, but none would go on record as saying keeping cottage cheese inverted for months was either safe or risky—they just didn't know. It's clear that inverting does extend the shelf life to some degree. FZ)

SWF SEEKS SLIM, ATTRACTIVE FREEZER FOR COOL RELATIONSHIP

If you have a large family and a garden, you'd be crazy not to own a freezer. The largest available for home use costs under $500 and uses about $8 worth of electricity a month. It could easily pay for itself within a year. But does a freezer make sense if you are single, a working couple, or if you don't have a garden?

Yes, at least for certain lifestyles. To make my case, I only have to think back to my sorry past as an urban single and how not having a freezer made my life considerably more expensive.

I lived alone in the Boston area for over five years. Because keeping a car in the city is expensive, I always relied on public transportation and cabs. And I never lived anyplace that was convenient to a large supermarket.

If I used public transportation, I had to haul bags of groceries three blocks to the subway station, make a train change, catch a bus, and finally walk a couple of long blocks to my apartment. If I took a cab, it cost $5, plus a tip. If I walked, I might have to trudge up to 12 blocks with a pull-cart of groceries. I would be tired enough so that when I arrived home, the flights of stairs seemed like the Washington Monument's—my sundry apartments included third-floor, fourth-floor, and fifth-floor walk-ups.

The apartments' refrigerators generally had only slightly bigger-than-a-shoe-box freezers. So it was just as well that I was not inclined to lug home more—it would have rotted before I could eat it, anyway.

Because I had limited storage for frozen dinners, most meals I ate at home needed to be cooked from scratch after I came home from work—frequently after 7:00 P.M. I seldom felt like doing it.

Also, as an unattached single, I was far more susceptible to emotional valleys. If I had a bad day at work, there was no one waiting at home to cheer me up. So sometimes I was disinclined to go home to an empty apartment and fix a meal. Restaurant food was far more soothing. Like most spendthrifts, I felt I deserved this treat.

It was no wonder that I ate out so much, subsisted on convenience foods from high-priced neighborhood markets, and *never* bought food in bulk. In fact, I lived for two years in Boston before I made my first trip into a real supermarket.

I've recalled those years of late, mostly because of recent contact with New York singles in connection with my books. Food, they tell

me, is one of their toughest financial challenges. When I've asked why they don't cook up and freeze large quantities of food, they tell me that they want more variety than they could store in a refrigerator-top freezer. Likewise, many working couples and seniors who live in the suburbs can relate to the problems I've described.

But I've also been thinking of those years because Elaine, our business manager, has shown me how freezers can benefit singles. Because circumstances vary greatly, the feasibility of freezer ownership must be considered from case to case, but it certainly works well for her.

Elaine is in her midthirties and has lived alone for a good part of her adult life—but she's *always* had a freezer, even when she lived in a trailer. At first I questioned the economics of this, until I learned how she uses her freezer.

Elaine cooks up large quantities of food, such as lasagna, chili, or tuna casserole, repackages it in meal-size portions, and puts them in her freezer. She skillfully rotates them so that every day she has something different to eat. If she takes the portion out to thaw before she leaves for work, she can pop it into the microwave when she gets home. So even when she's tired, she has tasty, varied, inexpensive, home-cooked food in minutes.

Sears sells a dishwasher-size freezer for $200, which uses about $2.25 worth of electricity per month. I could have fit this size freezer into three of my four apartments. If using Elaine's strategy had prevented me from succumbing to two restaurant meals per month, the freezer would have paid for itself in a year.

This ability to avoid restaurants is the biggest money-saver for singles or working couples. Other, smaller benefits, which may not have paid for a freezer by themselves, are a welcome bonus. A freezer can enable you to:

- Eat a healthier, more varied diet.
- Use cabs efficiently. If I had purchased larger quantities of sale items, the savings on food would have more than paid for the fare.
- Store bulk grains such as oatmeal, cornmeal, or rice. Freeze them for 24 hours to kill off bugs, then they can be stored at room temperature in airtight containers for months.
- Save time and energy, by shopping less often and preparing meals in quantity (the time and hot-water savings on dish-washing alone are significant).
- Take advantage of garden surplus offered by family and friends. For Elaine, a rural single, this is a significant advantage. But it could have helped me in my urban days, too; one of my landlords let the tenants have small gardens. I never bothered. If I'd had a freezer, such a hobby might have seemed worthwhile.

As a final note, I don't recommend buying an ancient, inexpensive, used freezer. Freezers built within the last five years are far more energy-efficient and take up less space than older models. If buying new, look for a sale, and be sure to compare the yellow "Energyguide" labels.

SLASH YOUR TRASH

Frugality naturally creates less trash, but even frugal people can learn to generate less than they do. It's important, because trash disposal *is* becoming expensive. As of January 1993, we are charged $1 per bag to dump trash in Leeds. Readers Greg and Linda Stewart of West Lafayette, Indiana, report they save $160 per year by actively reducing their trash.

Here are some tips for saving on trash fees:

1. Buy used items. Secondhand items rarely come with packaging.

2. Omit convenience foods, most of which have excess packaging.

3. Eliminate as many disposable items as possible, such as paper plates, disposable diapers, and plastic eating utensils. Use a mug, soap, and brush instead of canned shaving cream.

4. If given a choice, buy products in recyclable containers. Milk in a recyclable plastic jug costs the same as milk in a nonrecyclable wax-paper carton.

5. Buy concentrated products.

6. Buy bulk foods. A 25-pound sack of flour produces less packaging waste than five 5-pound bags. Some bulk-food stores let you bring your own container—although this may not be the cheapest way to buy the actual item.

7. Bring your own bags when you go shopping. Decline the "courtesy" bags store clerks automatically give you with each purchase of a single item.

8. Participate in your area's recycling program, and develop an easy system to encourage your family to follow through. One interesting method uses an old chest of drawers—one drawer per type of stuff.

9. Reuse everything as much as possible. An old athletic sock makes a great dishrag. Ultimately you throw away one sock-turned-rag instead of both a sock and dishrag.

10. Compost your grass clippings, leaves, and food waste. Even city folks can compost banana peels by taking waste to community gardens.

11. Buy with durability in mind. Especially avoid junk toys that break easily.

12. Reduce your incoming junk mail. The average American adult is on over more than 50 mailing lists. Send a written request to Mail Preference Service, c/o the Direct Marketing Association, P.O. Box 9008, Farmingdale, NY 11735. This will eliminate most national catalogs and solicitations from national charitable organizations for five years. To remove your name from other mailing lists, request the removal in a short note, put it in the organization's business reply envelope, and mail it back.

13. Cancel magazine subscriptions

(if you can't recycle magazines in your area), and borrow from the library. Or share subscriptions.

14. Instead of throwing things away, give them away or put them in your "free" box at your annual yard sale. I've even put a too-used-to-sell baby swing in my front yard with a sign that said FREE, and someone carted it away within the hour.

15. Make the extra effort to repair things before you throw them away.

16. If you live in a rural area, you may be able to get a permit for a burn barrel to burn nonrecyclable paper. With our newly acquired permit, we have dropped our monthly trash production to one bag.

17. Compact your trash by flattening it, cutting or breaking it into smaller pieces, or filling hard-to-flatten containers with other trash.

18. Try to locate a scrap-metal dealer in your area. Nondeposit (or road-flattened deposit) aluminum cans can be worth as much as a penny. Save them until you have enough to make the trip worthwhile.

19. Grow and preserve your own food. Canning jars, freezer containers, and jam-sealing wax can be reused from year to year.

20. Think hard about whether you really need Magic Mushrooms room deodorizers and other consumer items of recent invention.

CHALK IS CHEAP

As summer approaches, lock up the Nintendo and let your kids enjoy colorful graphics *outdoors* with this sidewalk/street chalk. The recipe was sent in by Sharon Hankins Crosswhite of Julian, California. She says it lasts longer than the expensive store-bought type.

We tried this and found it easy to do and very cost-effective. Ten cups of plaster of Paris at a hardware store cost $2.29, and six jars of liquid tempera, each containing 4 tablespoons of paint, cost $1.69 (we also experimented with powdered tempera and found it made even brighter colors). This makes 27 sticks for 15¢ each, and they are big: We used a manicotti noodle tray as a mold, and made sticks 5 inches long, 1½ inches wide, and ¾ inch thick. In other words, for $3.98, you've got a lifetime supply of sidewalk chalk.

1 cup plaster of Paris (do not pack)
Almost ½ cup cool water
Liquid tempera (your kid's teacher may "donate" the tempera in exchange for a few pieces of chalk)
Margarine tubs or other disposable mixing containers
Disposable molds

Pour plaster into a container. Using a disposable stick, stir in *most* of the water. Add 2 to 3 tablespoons of liquid tempera, mixing well, especially at the bottom. Add a little more water so the mixture thickens, stir well, and pour into the molds. Sharon uses the plastic tray from manicotti noodles; you can also use paper cups or toilet-paper tubes with foil bottoms. Remove the molds after the chalk is completely dry.

THE NAKED TOOTH

I am a big believer in using the least amount possible; whether it's of laundry detergent, salt, shampoo, even bath soap. When it comes to toothpaste, my intuition has always been that those ads showing a 1-inch glob were leading us astray, so I was gratified to receive the following letter from Lisa Murphy, a dental hygienist of nine years' experience from Medway, Massachusetts:

"Toothpaste does offer flavor, fluoride (which is necessary if you don't have it in your drinking water), and slight abrasives. It may also contain tartar inhibitor or baking soda (for gum problems).

"But it is not necessary to use toothpaste. Proper flossing and brushing are far more important. In fact, while our patients were learning the proper strokes, we would recommend not using toothpaste, so that they could see what they were doing.

"If you use the proper stroke and brush for a total of five minutes (yes, *five* minutes), getting *every* tooth, you should be able to remove most of the plaque.

"If you do use toothpaste, ask a dental professional for a recommendation of what would best suit your needs. When you use it, all that is needed is ¼ inch on your brush."

I had a chance to try this idea out on my last book tour—I forgot my toothpaste. With a toothpasteless brush and glass of water, I performed dental hygiene while watching the news on TV. It worked great, and I also realized why most people—including me—have a hard time brushing for five minutes. It's hard to stand in front of the mirror for that amount of time watching yourself foam at the mouth. But I found I could watch TV brushing, swishing, and swallowing water for at least five minutes, if not longer. And my mouth did feel fresh and clean after brushing so thoroughly.

A TIGHTWAD TOY

This homemade toy is a variation of an idea one of my children saw on television. The original design called for a paper cup, which we didn't have. Instead my son improvised with a laundry scoop. He poked a tiny hole through the center of the "recycle" logo in the scoop-bottom. He knotted and threaded a 2-foot string through the hole. He made a ball from a wad of reused aluminum foil. He formed it so that the string end was secured inside the ball.

The younger children were entertained trying to land the ball in the scoop one time, whereas older ones competed to see how many consecutive times they could catch the ball in the scoop.

A BUDGET BURNER

"I'm looking for a tightwad way to make a camp stove," writes Sherri B. Saines of Marietta, Ohio.

Funny you should ask, Sherri. In our files we have a letter from Terri Ring of Lancaster, Pennsylvania, containing these instructions for making what she calls a "buddy burner":

1 empty, clean tuna can, label removed
1 empty, large coffee can
cardboard
paraffin

Cut the cardboard into a strip that is as wide as the tuna can is high. Roll it to fit tightly inside the tuna can.

Pour the melted paraffin over this. Cut a flap on the open end of the coffee can, and punch two holes on the opposite side of the can, near the closed end.

To cook, light the paraffin and place the coffee can over it. Place a pan on top to cook.

CHEAP SLEEPS

If I were going to travel a great distance with my family, I would, if possible:

1. Wait until summer.
2. Camp.
3. Stay with relatives who would love to host a family of eight (yes, I do have a few relatives who fit this description).

Obviously, travel is a low priority for me—going on a trip with six young children is more work than vacation.

But for those people who save their pennies so they can afford to travel and who don't like to camp, here are four alternative types of cheap travel lodging:

1. College dorms. Most dorms are empty during the summer, and several enterprising schools take advantage of that by offering overnight lodging.

For information, get *U.S. and Worldwide Travel Accommodations Guide for $12–$24 Per Day.* The 1993 edition is available from Campus Travel Service, P.O. Box 5486, Fullerton, CA 92635, (800) 525-6633. Cost is $14 postpaid.

Normally, I am unimpressed by the quality of many "save-money" publications, but this one is particularly well done. For each of the 700 colleges listed, the book gives the daily price for single and double accommodations; $12 to $24 is a typ-

ical single rate, with doubles usually less than twice that amount. But accommodations can run as low as $6 per night per person.

Along with prices, the book lists available dates (generally, Northern Hemisphere schools open their dorms to nonstudents in the summer months; Southern Hemisphere schools, such as those in Australia, open theirs during our winter), and what activities and attractions are nearby.

The quality of the accommodations varies greatly. Most rooms have two twin beds; the bathroom and showers are down the hall. But there are also some suites with private baths, or arrangements where two rooms share one bath. Most offer food service, and some have linen service.

The book suggests bringing sleeping bags for children; many colleges allow kids to sleep free in their parents' rooms. A small percentage of colleges don't allow children at all, so be sure to ask.

There is no central booking agency; make reservations by calling the schools directly. All necessary telephone numbers are listed in the book.

2. YMCA lodging. The same book also has a complete listing of YMCA accommodations: 43 lodging centers in 39 cities coast-to-coast, and 51 lodging centers in 26 overseas countries. Single accommodations average about $20, doubles around $35. Rooms for couples are widely available, and children are welcome, provided there is parental supervision.

You can call the YMCA's individually, but if you plan to stay in more than one and you know your itinerary in advance, you can book through the central New York office: The Y's Way, 224 E. 47th St., NY, NY 10017, (212) 308-2899. YMCA's also accommodate travelers on a drop-in basis when space is available.

3. Hostels. There are 6,000 hostels in 70 countries, including more than 200 in the United States. Many people think of these as "youth hostels" and imagine they are just for young people, but that is not the case. Many hostels have private rooms for families traveling together, and 10 percent of card-holding members of Hostelling International/American Youth Hostels are over 55. The price per person ranges from $5

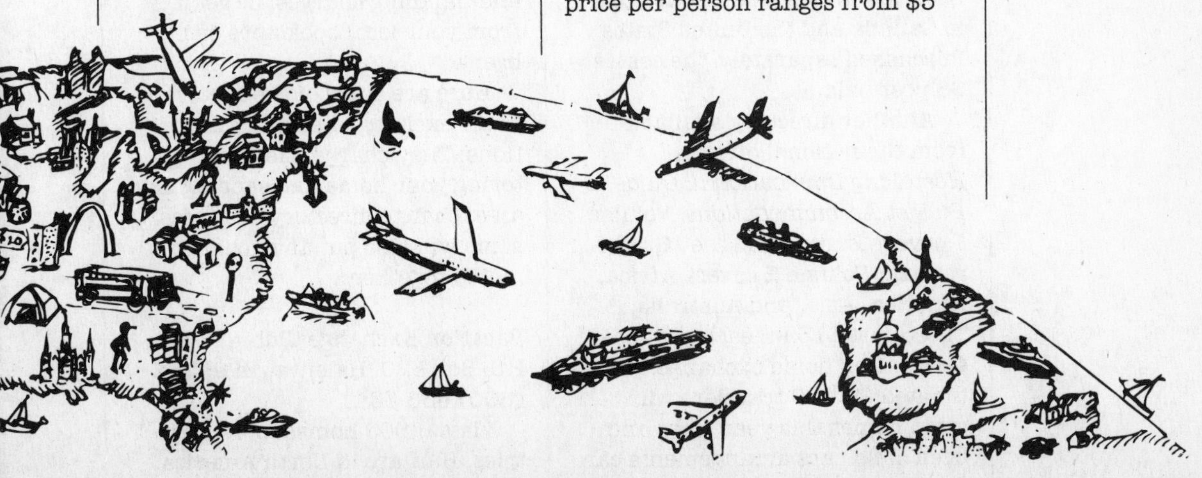

to $22, with the most common price about $10. Children often receive a discount.

Each hostel is unique, but they share some common characteristics. All have dormitory-style sleeping quarters and bathroom facilities separated for males and females. They have fully equipped, self-service kitchens and dining rooms. Most have a night curfew. You are asked to clean up after yourself.

A spokesman at Hostelling International/American Youth Hostels told us that most hostels will admit nonmembers, but those without cards must pay a slightly higher fee, and during busy times of the year in major cities, cardholders receive preference. Membership is $10 for those under 18, $25 for adults, $15 for those 55 and over, and $35 for families. To join, contact the national office at 733 15th N.W., #840, Washington, D.C. 20005, (202) 783-6161. This office can send you information directly or direct you to one of the organization's thirty-nine local sales outlets.

When you sign up, you'll get a free copy of *Hostelling North America,* which lists 260 hostels in Canada and the United States. Purchased separately, the cost is $8 post-paid.

Another directory available from the national office is *Hostelling International: Guide to Budget Accommodations.* Volume 1 covers Europe and the Mediterranean; Volume 2 covers Africa, America, Asia, and Australia. These cost $13.95 each post-paid.

4. Vacation home exchange. An estimated 20,000 travelers will swap homes this year. Cars and even child-care arrangements can also be swapped. Several clearinghouses publish lists of homes offered to swap.

As you might expect, this is a more complex lodging arrangement than the three listed above. Logistics must be worked out carefully, and you'll have more success attracting swappers if you live in Hawaii than in Nebraska (I've got nothing against Nebraska, but that's how it works).

But people who do this generally love it.

Because home exchange is a big subject with its share of pitfalls (such as the other party backing out just as you're ready to make the swap), it's worthwhile to read a book on the subject before you begin. One good one is *Trading Places: The Wonderful World of Vacation Home Exchanging,* by Bill and Mary Barbour. Along with everything you want to know about the nuts and bolts of home vacation exchange, it has a complete directory of more than 40 home-exchange clearinghouses. It's available for $9.95 from Rutledge Hill Press, 211 7th Ave. North, Nashville, TN 37219-1823. Call (800) 234-4234 for shipping-and-handling charges, or get it from your local bookstore or library.

Here are a few of the larger home-exchange-listing organizations. They charge a fee for registering your home and sending out an exchange directory. For a fee, some will also put an exchange match together.

Vacation Exchange Club
P.O. Box 820, Haleiwa, HI 96712
(800) 638-3841

Lists 6,000 homes in 40 countries. Half are in North America,

the rest are in Europe, Australia, and New Zealand.

Fee is $35.

Intervac/International Home Exchange
P.O. Box 590504
San Francisco, CA 94519
(415) 435-3497

Lists over 8,000 homes worldwide, 1,500 in the U.S. Membership is $45, but offers a free brochure.

Teacher Home Swap
P.O. Box 4130
Rocky Point, NY 11778

Exclusively for teachers. Has listings in 37 states, Canada, Virgin Islands, Germany, and Hungary.

GOOD TIMING

One of my he-man staffers has been bugging me for months to do an article about timing belts.

"Timing belt—is that a newfangled fashion accessory, kinda like a belt with a watch on the buckle?" I answered demurely, displaying my ignorance of both fashion and auto mechanics.

He scratched his tattoo, spat on the ground, and patiently explained that the timing belt connects the camshaft to the crankshaft. My eyes started to glaze over.

"Pull together some information and get back to me," I yawned, returning to my latest venture in dryer-lint mâché.

He returned with the book *Car Talk* by Ray and Tom Magliozzi with a bookmark in the appropriate chapter. He also suggested I interview Ray Fortin, owner of Autometrics repair shop in Brunswick, Maine, who has replaced hundreds of timing belts.

Turns out, the timing belt does indeed connect the camshaft, which opens and closes the valves, to the crankshaft. A durable timing chain (similar to a bike chain) used to do this, but today a more fragile rubber belt is often used because it's cheaper and easier to change.

In certain kinds of cars, if the timing belt breaks, it will severely damage the engine, because the pistons will smack into the valves, damaging the valves, the pistons, or both. Fortin says that generally, high-compression, 16-valve engines are most likely to incur damage if the belt breaks, but there are no hard-and-fast rules on this. Ask your mechanic whether your car is at risk for engine damage if its timing belt breaks.

Fortin says at least once a month he fixes an engine that was damaged by timing-belt failure. He told me that this is one of the most neglected areas of car maintenance.

Replacing a timing belt costs between $100 and $200, but if you have to open up your engine anyway to do other repairs, replacing the belt can cost as little as $30. Fixing a wrecked engine generally costs about $1,000.

While some types of cars' engines won't be damaged if the belt breaks, a broken timing belt *always* stops your car. If you've got one of these "invulnerable" cars, you might opt to take your chances, because these belts sometimes last more than 150,000 miles.

The timing belt is of particular

concern to my staffer because he had one snap in downtown Washington, D.C., during rush hour, and it cost a fortune in towing.

But the timing belt is just one of several parts that you might consider replacing *before* they fail because of the potential damage the failure could do to your car. Other such parts include brakes, belts, and hoses. Generally, these parts are easy to see, monitor, and replace.

Other parts to consider replacing before they fail are harder to get at. While the actual part cost may be low, labor costs for replacement are high. So if your engine has to be opened up for any work, use the opportunity to replace worn bearings, seals, and gaskets (make sure your mechanic charges by the hour, not by the standard part-replacement labor fee). Even if the part failure won't damage the engine, replacing it when it can be done cheaply often costs less than a tow.

The point is, you need to have a long, friendly, informative chat with a trustworthy mechanic who is specifically knowledgeable about your type of car. He can tell you when certain parts are likely to go (Fortin says, for example, that he's found that the timing belts on Subarus snap "like clockwork" at 70,000 miles) and whether it will be more expensive to wait until they do.

(By the way, I was just kidding about my staffer: He neither spat nor has a tattoo to scratch; he's a slender, well-mannered vegetarian.)

THE FEMME FRUGAL

"No, honey! Not supermaxi, round-edge, ultra-plus supers! I wanted ultra-absorbent, maxi-plus, super-thin regulars!"

Aside from fostering such marriage-testing experiences when hubby comes home from the supermarket, disposable tampons and napkins contribute to landfill problems and are overpriced (c'mon, how can a little cardboard tube, a wad of cotton, and a piece of string cost as much as a disposable diaper?). This has not gone unnoticed by my readers. I have a file labeled "feminine," full of letters from readers, that is impressively thick (partially because it contains a homemade sanitary napkin).

But I delayed writing about this subject until I found and tested a solution that seemed more workable for the average woman than cloth napkins, which must be soaked and washed.

The solution is the Keeper, a reusable rubber cup that replaces tampons. I learned of it through an article in *Garbage* magazine, through recommendations from readers, and from an employee who has used one for years.

The Keeper is accepted by the FDA and has a far lower toxic-shock risk than the 1-in-100,000 annual risk from tampon use.

Although the Keeper's initial cost is substantial—$37 postpaid—it is guaranteed for ten years, which works out to 31¢ a month. Compared to the cost of tampons, it would pay for itself in well under one year. (The com-

pany owner has used the same Keeper for 35 years.)

To try this out, I purchased five Keepers for staff and friends. All of us who tried it were very pleased. It works as well as a superabsorbent tampon, which means that if you use a napkin in conjunction with a superabsorbent tampon on days with heavy flow, you might use a napkin with this product as well. As you might imagine, removing a Keeper isn't as "neat" as removing a tampon, but this inconvenience is minor compared to the benefits.

So if this product is so great and has been available for decades, how come you've never heard of it before?

I asked the company owner. She told me that advertising is expensive and the company often does not recoup the cost of an ad. She added that she had tried to interest journalists in writing articles but with little success. She speculated that there were two problems: The "graphic" subject matter wasn't attractive to reporters, and women's magazines, which would seem to be the perfect place for a story, depend on advertising from companies that manufacture disposable feminine products and may be reluctant to publicize a product that might hurt those advertisers' business.

The Keeper comes in two sizes: A (after vaginal childbirth) and B (after C-section or before childbirth). Refunds are available if you aren't happy, although the company states that 92 percent of the women who try it are pleased with it. Order from The Keeper, P.O. Box 20023A, Cincinnati, OH 45220.

The Keeper seems to me to be the most appropriate option for most women, especially women who work outside the home. But if it doesn't appeal to you and you are willing to soak and wash them, consider nondisposable sanitary napkins. They are available through mail order for about $5 each. Write for information to Moon Pads, P.O. Box 166, Boulder Creek, CA 95006, or New Cycle, P.O. Box 3248, Santa Rosa, CA 95402.

Figuring that you would need a couple days' supply, this option is a bit steep.

I do have three lengthy, detailed sets of instructions on how to make your own cloth napkins. For free copies, send us a SASE. Write to *The Tightwad Gazette,* RR1 Box 3570, Leeds, ME 04263.

If you decide to stay with disposables, keep in mind that pads are generally cheaper than tampons.

In addition to these alternatives, I have personally conducted a nine-year study on the pregnancy/breastfeeding method to avoid the purchase of these feminine products. After thorough and intense calculation, I have determined that one cannot fully recoup the cost of children through tampon savings.

THE INCREDIBLE SHRINKING GROCERIES

An article from Pennsylvania's *Daily Intelligencer* newspaper, sent to me by reader Debbie Rodrigo of Line Lexington, Pennsylvania, confirms something you may have suspected: that many grocery-store foods are "downsizing." Although the package size remains roughly the same and the price stays exactly the same, the net weight of the food inside has shrunk.

The story noted the following as just a few examples of recent downsizing:

- A box of Hershey's chocolate-milk mix that once held 16 ounces now contains 14.5 ounces.
- Gerber's strained baby food has gone from 4.5 ounces per jar to 4 ounces per jar.
- Identical-size cans of Maxwell House coffee weigh 16, 13, 12, and 11.5 ounces.

There's nothing illegal about downsizing as long as the correct net weight is listed on the package.

Your best defense, then, is to depend upon unit pricing. If the store where you shop does not offer it, keep track of net weights and do your own unit pricing with a calculator.

WORK OFF THE WORKOUT

Dear Amy,

My friend Linda has found a good way to get a "free" membership in a local health club. She works a four-hour-per-week shift in the child-care room; the club provides child care there as a free service to members. She takes her kids along to play. This club is always looking for moms to do this in exchange for a membership, and so is another health club in town.

—Jan C. Kass
Davis, California

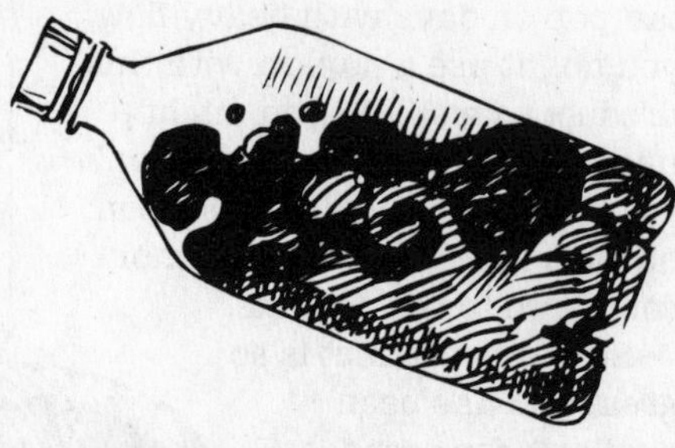

OCEAN IN MOTION

Dear Amy,

Here is a cheap toy for a preschooler: Make a "tidal wave" soda bottle. Fill it half with cooking oil and half with water colored with food coloring.

—Sherry Mayer
Greensboro, North Carolina

(Children lose interest in new things after about two days, whether the things are store-bought or homemade. When your child loses interest in this, you can reuse the cooking oil. We made a tidal-wave bottle and learned you should not shake it vigorously: This makes the oil permanently cloudy. FZ)

FOIL HEAT LOSSES

Dear Amy,

Here's an energy-conservation idea for those with accordion-style radiators. Put foil-faced insulation

board between the radiators and outside walls, with the foil side facing in toward the room. This reflects heat into the room that would otherwise radiate through the walls.

—Ellen Nagle Eggerton
Silver Spring, Maryland

(Because the expense is minimal and the installation is not permanent, this is one of the rare energy-saving ideas that is useful to renters. FZ)

ATTACK THE RACK

Dear Amy,

In our local paper, dry cleaners advertise that they will sell clothes for almost nothing. They will get rid of clothes left there for 60 days or longer. You just go into the dry cleaner, and there is a huge rack of clothes. Usually, they sell for what the dry-cleaning price was: $1 for a sweater, $2 for a coat, etc. I have bought a lot of clothes this way. It's worth checking into in other cities as well.

—Christi Kennedy
Shirley Clasey
Durham, North Carolina

SPECTACLE SAVINGS

Dear Amy,

Save big bucks by buying used eyeglasses frames at thrift stores. You can then have new lenses made for your new prescription and save a bundle—especially if you, like me, like to have a backup pair of glasses or have children who destroy frames. Or be really cheap and ask friends who are getting new glasses for their old frames. Since new frames cost from $30 to $100-plus, the savings can be substantial.

—Beverly Carlson
Carmichael, California

STALKING A GREAT KITE

Dear Amy,

The dead stalks of last year's goldenrod, ragweed, and various other species of medium and tall weeds make good frame members for a kite. For covering, we use ultrathin polyethylene film from dry-cleaning bags. This is the kind that can suffocate babies and small children, so use plenty of common-sense precautions to keep all pieces under control. To stick it on a kite, cut to the kite shape plus 1 inch all around. Fold the inch over the string, then hold it down with clear tape. The result is an ultra-lightweight kite.

—James R. Jenness, Jr.
State College, Pennsylvania

RUB-A-DUB TUB

Dear Amy,

When we moved into our house over 25 years ago, the surface of our bathtub was slightly rough and became stained after a while. I tried various cleansers, including the strongest ones, but nothing seemed to work.

Then I saw the craziest idea in the newspaper—and it worked!

Wet the surface, sprinkle it with cream of tartar, and rub this with the cut surface of a lemon. Then,

with some elbow grease, the tub will be as white as new within 20–30 minutes. I use two lemons and about ¼ can of cream of tartar on my tub, and it does not have to be done very often.

Today, I checked the prices for refinishing a tub. The range was between $225 and $250. One can buy a lot of lemons for that amount. The surface of the tub is still a little rough, but then, one is less likely to slip on a rough surface than a smooth one.

—Sally Weitlauf
Dayton, Ohio

CARPET TACTIC

Dear Amy,

Call carpet stores for carpet samples. When colors or styles change, carpet samples are usually thrown out. Samples can be used in cars, bathrooms, doorways, or cut to fit benches or chairs. Toss in washer to clean.

—Ann Williams
Rochester, New York

BAND AID

Dear Amy,

Never buy a band instrument from the companies that come to the school. We made that mistake with our first child, and one flute ended up costing us $816.00! This was with their handy-dandy payment plan that at the time did not seem like much, ha ha. With our second child, we have been shopping yard sales and already found several to choose from. Prices vary from $35 to $100 for a cabinet. Even if they need new pads and a cleaning, this is still quite a savings.

—Chawn Stiers
Cumberland, Ohio

FENDER MENDER

Dear Amy,

Even a minor car accident can require major amounts of cash for repairs. After our fender bender, we took our car to the vocational school. They saved us money by pounding out the fender and repainting. A body shop would have replaced the entire fender due to the high labor cost. At the vocational school, there was no labor charge. We paid only for the paint and parts.

—Dawn Hancock
Auburn, Indiana

SELECTIVE SQUEAMISHNESS

In the early years of my zealous frugality, I eagerly and naïvely offered money-saving ideas to the unappreciative. Usually, my suggestions would be rejected with such responses as: "I couldn't be bothered," or "My family wouldn't eat that."

I recall when I first identified a common reason for rejecting ways to save money. It's an attitude I call "selective squeamishness."

Seven years ago we lived in a suburb near Norfolk, Virginia. As I chatted with my neighbor, who was raking leaves in her yard, I

spotted a patch of scarlet among the brown leaves in her trash barrel. Propelled by my scavenger instincts, I zoomed in and saw a large, shiny, Delicious apple with two fresh bites missing.

Thinking she hadn't noticed this waste, I pointed out the apple to her. She casually responded that her four-year-old didn't want to finish it. So I helpfully offered my solution to this common dilemma. "You know what I do with an apple one of my kids doesn't finish? I save it in the refrigerator. Later, I cut it up, sprinkle on some apple-crisp topping, put it in the microwave, and presto-chango, he has his own apple crisp. He thinks it's a treat!"

I expected my neighbor would marvel at my resourcefulness. Instead, she recoiled in horror. "Ugh! I couldn't put her germy apple back in the refrigerator!"

My rejection radar went off. I dropped the subject and silently wondered if the fear of germs ever prevented my neighbor from exchanging kisses with her small children.

Since then, I've observed the same sort of situation time and time again. Americans are curiously inconsistent when it comes to squeamishness. We often reject "odd" or "germy" practices that are frugal, while happily indulging in equally "gross" activities that are expensive and wasteful.

As for "odd" ideas: When I was on *Donahue,* I demonstrated how the burned bottom of a cookie could be very easily scraped off with a grater. The audience emitted a collective "Eeeeew!" Yet I'd wager that this same group of skeptics routinely salivates over charred filet mignon.

On the same show, I explained how you could make a popsicle from jam-jar remains by adding milk, shaking, and pouring into a mold. The audience's groan made it clear they rejected my all-natural solution, apparently preferring to feed their children expensive popsicles made from unpronounceable ingredients.

People have expressed squeamishness over my practice of making soup from leftovers, yet if the same soup had been assembled from virgin ingredients, they would regard it as good home cooking.

As for "germy" suggestions: I've been taken to task for my "unsanitary" practice of trash picking. Although I draw the line at rummaging deep in trash barrels or taking things that are hard to clean, I feel quite comfortable carting away something from a pile that appears to be the result of a recent garage cleaning. Yet most people aren't squeamish about buying exactly the same stuff at a garage sale. I have been mystified by parents who throw away cookies their baby tosses on the floor. Yet the same parents let their baby crawl on the floor and pick up toys to chew.

The American public has been duped by advertisers to believe that a few invisible cooties in the toilet bowl are evil, threatening, and untouchable. But automatic, blue-tinged toilet-bowl cleaners—which may contain muriatic acid, paradichlorobenzene, and other caustic stuff and should be treated as hazardous waste, according to the Environmental Hazards Management Institute—are supposedly our salvation.

One of the most curious areas of germ squeamishness is secondhand clothes. Some people would never wear a yard-sale shirt, even after laundering it in germ-killing 120-degree water, yet blithely try on department-store clothing that dozens of people might have tried on before them.

I've encountered a few people who are squeamish about buying used sheets. Yet I'll bet these people don't take their own sheets when they stay in a hotel or at the home of relatives. Likewise, they don't give a second thought to using a cloth napkin in a restaurant.

Even people who feel comfortable with used clothes may take exception to wearing used undergarments. Although I have never purchased used underwear, I've swapped a bra or two in my time. Can you imagine the groans if I had advocated such a thing on a national talk show? Yet, think back to other talk shows that featured guests who had multiple sex partners. Although some audience members might have objected on a moral basis or because of AIDS, have you ever heard audiences groan over how "gross" such a thing is? It's fascinating that people who are squeamish about swapping bras are not squeamish about swapping spouses.

The fact is that germs are an unavoidable part of our lives. When we talk on a public phone, we are exposed to the germs of the person who previously used it. If we eat in a restaurant, we rarely wash up despite our recent contact with door handles, counters, booths, and chairs. When we purchase fresh produce, which may have been handled by many previous shoppers and clerks, we never feel compelled to sterilize it in 120-degree water. The simple act of breathing in a public place exposes us to germs of strangers.

Although some effort to minimize germ exposure is important, we also need to remember that we have immune systems designed to handle the majority of germs we encounter.

The things we regard as odd or germy are often unique to our culture. Many frugal practices I advocate are common in most parts of the world today and were common a generation ago in this country. In modern society our sense of squeamishness has become heightened because we are insulated from the most basic human activities—cooking, cleaning, and dealing with waste. Now convenience foods, disposable products, and mechanical devices keep us "from getting our hands dirty." But the price of squeamishness is high, both in financial and environmental terms.

So . . . next time an idea about saving money seems gross to you, consider whether you are merely being selective, and whether you accept a similar activity as okay. In other words, think before you squeam.

MIXED EMULSIONS

In every basement, just to the left of the tattered lawn chairs awaiting rewebbing, sits a stack of paint cans, left over from dozens of household projects. A new project arises, you scan the cans and discover that you don't have quite enough for this particular task. So you buy another can, use three quarters of it, and add it to the pile. Eventually, sick of the mess, you decide to take the whole lot to the dump, even though a lot of it is, technically, toxic waste.

There's a solution to this common dilemma. Mix it and use it!

In Snohomish County in Washington, solid-waste officials have been accepting old cans of paint from residents for the last three years. They mix the paint, seal it, and give it away—over 12,000 gallons so far. For an insight on how this can be done at home, we discussed the program with David Shea, project specialist for the Snohomish County Solid Waste Authority, and with Philip Morely, who ran a similar, larger project for the nearby city of Seattle.

The #1 rule of paint mixing is play it safe. Lead paint for residential use was banned in 1973, so if you have any paint that even *might* be older than that, don't mix it. Also, paints that say prominently on the label that they kill fungus and mildew may have high levels of pesticides and/or mercury and should be avoided, especially for interior use.

When it comes to mixing, combine latex with latex, and oil-based with oil-based—never latex with oil-based. But don't worry about mixing flat, semigloss, and high-gloss together. As Shea puts it, "We've found that paint is paint, and it generally comes out durable and looking good." If you mix interior and exterior grades and use it outdoors, you can lose some durability, but if you use the mixed paint for undercoats and "pure" paint for the final coat, you'll probably have good results.

In any case, paint mixing works. Shea says after distributing thousands of gallons, "We've never had a complaint."

Using mixed paint will require you to be a bit less picky about color—you won't be able to get precisely the shade you may want. But keep in mind that probably everyone you know has old paint and will be glad to donate it. Perhaps teaming up with friends and neighbors will give you the proper colors to at least approximate what you want.

In the past I've used this technique. I have several partially

filled cans of odd-colored paint that I trash-picked. I found that by combining latex paints I could make small amounts of good colors. I use them to rejuvenate the beat-up yard-sale furniture that we have in our children's rooms. I refuse to buy my kids good furniture until we're beyond the little-kid, furniture-abuse years.

Reader Joan Lovering of Scarborough, Ontario sent in another ancient-paint-revival technique:

"My tightwad son-in-law found that his four large cans of latex paint had settled to near-cement-like sludge after sitting in the basement for years. Inspired, he took a chance on using his wife's food blender, hoping for the best. To his delight, it worked wonderfully well. He salvaged all four cans of paint, thus saving at least $60. And the blender cleaned itself nicely with warm water and detergent."

Before publishing this idea we didn't run it by the Food and Drug Administration, so I can't give it my official endorsement. But clearly it will pose a serious health risk if this guy's wife ever finds out.

THE SLED SOLUTION

In March of '93 we had just weathered the "blizzard of the century." All of our sleds had long ago vanished under previous snowfalls, and we had been scooting Brad and Laura, the 20-month-old twins, around in cardboard boxes and a large plastic cooler. It never occurred to us to *buy* more sleds, knowing that ours would reappear with the spring thaw. But with this new, huge, wonderful snowfall, we felt we needed something that worked a bit better than the substitutes. Suddenly, Jim remembered the obsolete-but-not-antique wooden skis we trash-picked in the last book. He disappeared into his workshop. After two hours of the

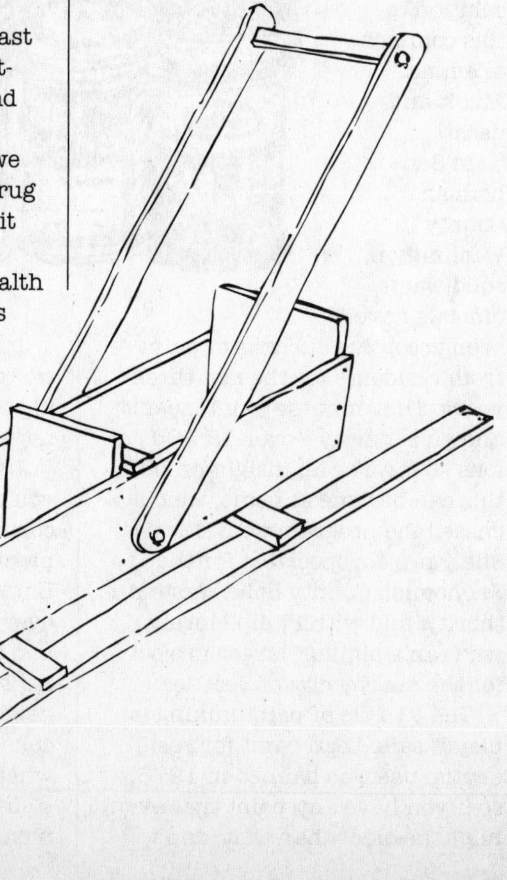

usual roaring, whacking, buzzing, and cursing, he emerged from a sawdust cloud bearing this contraption—a sort of double-stroller ski-sled, built entirely from salvaged materials. With this we were able to run the twins around our snowy driveway and push them down the small slope in front of our barn, much to their wide-eyed delight. Other ski-sled creations could be made in a similar way. Our original idea was to use the skis for a sled to haul firewood. I can also imagine four skis used to make a toboggan. If you build one, put a guard over the pointy tips, or use it on an uncrowded slope where collisions are unlikely.

You don't have toddler twins, you don't have old skis in your attic, you don't lose your sleds . . . why am I telling you about our double-stroller ski-sled?

Because this is yet another example of how being resourceful and creative with materials you have on hand, instead of spending money, can ultimately be much more fun.

SHARE—AND SHARE ALIKE

Many readers have sent me literature about SHARE (Self-Help and Resource Exchange). This nationwide, neighborhood-based, self-help food-distribution program is sponsored by a network of churches, community centers, unions, and other groups.

It works like this: You sign up one month in advance with a host organization and do two hours of community service. You then qualify to buy a package of groceries worth $30 to $35 retail for $14 in cash or food stamps. You have to pick up the food at a specified place and time. The SHARE program buys the food from wholesalers or directly from growers. This is not a government program or charity, and you do not have to meet income requirements to participate. One brochure I received provided a list of the contents of a typical food package. The monthly packages vary, but each contains 15 items including 6 to 10 pounds of meat, 4 to 7 pounds of fresh vegetables, and 2 to 4 pounds of fruits. I estimated the value of the list based on typical sale prices in my area.

5 pounds chicken-leg qtrs.	$1.50
1 pound ground beef	.99
1 pound fishsticks	1.49
1 pound pork sausage	.69
1 bunch celery	.99
3 cucumbers	.99
1 head lettuce	.69
2 pounds onions	.80
4½ pounds potatoes	1.12
1 pound tomatoes	.75
5 pounds apples	2.59
2 pounds oranges	1.00
1 cantaloupe	1.49
1 pound pinto beans	.50
1 pound spaghetti	.33
1 package frozen vegetables	.99
1 can fruit	.79
1 package "Touch of Butter"	.44
Total	$18.14

Our shopping style, as I've explained in "Let's Go Shopping with Jim," on page 228, allows us to get these prices regularly with no extra travel or effort. So SHARE would save us only $4.14 for two hours of community work.

Still, I think this is a good pro-

gram for many people, for a few reasons:

People who lack desire or have no transportation options, won't shop like we do. And our shopping style does require you to have enough money to buy in bulk. If you are really broke, this program can be a big help.

SHARE buys only nutritious food. It ensures that people with poor food-buying habits are getting some healthy food.

People who face hard financial times often isolate themselves. The community-service requirement forces people into the community, where they make friends and contacts and gain the self-esteem that comes from helping others.

To find the SHARE program nearest you, or to start one, contact:

SHARE U.S.A.
3350 E St.
San Diego, CA 92102
(619) 525-2200

SENSIBLE SUBSTITUTES

Many of the "nouveau frugal" are enchanted with making their own convenience foods—no matter how inconvenient the process may be. Take the time I tried a homemade Grape-Nuts recipe, which required making a dough, rolling it thin, baking it forever, and then running the concretelike chunks through a food processor. Not only did this require a lot of electricity and time, but I nearly burned out the motor on my food processor. I decided I would prefer to eat hot cereal.

In books I've seen about making your own convenience foods, many recipes have you jumping through hoops to replicate the recent invention of a manufacturer. Instead of eating tightwad versions of spendthrift foods, it's easier to switch your diet to simpler foods.

But here are some sensible homemade convenience-food recipes. The only possible exception is the homemade stove-top stuffing mix, which is the most time-consuming and yields the least savings. Personally, I'd rather boil some rice, but if your family loves stuffing, give it a try.

I've provided a cost comparison of each homemade product to its store-bought counterpart. These numbers are based on our own painstaking calculations—figured down to the cost of ⅛ teaspoon of salt (1/10 ¢).

By combining coupons and sales, you may be able to beat these prices. (If you use coupons to buy convenience foods, you should calculate the cost of preparing food from scratch and develop "rules of thumb for coupon use.")

But remember: Aside from cost savings, preparing foods from scratch has other benefits:

- Less packaging.
- No artificial ingredients.
- Staples require less space and shopping time than convenience foods.
- Homemade almost always tastes better.
- Homemade can be modified to taste or to meet dietary restrictions—such as reducing salt.

SEASONED SALT

8 tablespoons salt
3 tablespoons pepper
2 tablespoons paprika
½ tablespoon onion powder
½ tablespoon garlic powder

Mix all ingredients in a bowl, and store in an airtight container (an empty, store-bought spice shaker works well).

Durkee's seasoned salt: 98¢ for 3.5 ounces, or 28¢ per ounce.

Homemade: 14¢ per ounce.

TACO-SEASONING MIX

6 teaspoons chili powder
4½ teaspoons cumin
5 teaspoons paprika
3 teaspoons onion powder
2½ teaspoons garlic powder
⅛ to ¼ teaspoon cayenne pepper

Mix all the ingredients, and store in an airtight container. The homemade mix is twice as strong as the store-bought one, so add only half as much.

Old El Paso taco-seasoning mix: $4.95 for 1 pound, or 31¢ per ounce.

Homemade: 13¢ per ounce.

Contributed by Mary Jane Mandl of Lee's Summit, Montana.

STUFFING

6 cups cubed bread
1 tablespoon parsley flakes
3 tablespoons chicken-bouillon powder
¼ cup dried minced onion
½ cup dried minced celery (or fresh celery may be sautéed and added just before cooking)
1 teaspoon thyme
1 teaspoon pepper
½ teaspoon sage
⅓ teaspoon salt

Preheat oven to 350 degrees. Spread the cubes on a cookie sheet and bake for 8 to 10 minutes, turning to brown evenly. Cool. In a plastic bag or bowl, toss the cubes with the rest of the ingredients until well coated. Store in a tightly closed container in the pantry for up to 4 months, or in the freezer

for up to a year. To use: Combine 2 cups stuffing mix with ½ cup water and 2 tablespoons melted butter. Stir to combine thoroughly. Warm on the stove top or in a microwave. Stir again just before serving.

Stove Top stuffing mix: $3.45 for 6-cup package, or 57¢ per cup.

Homemade: 46¢ per cup.

Contributed by Margaret Gatz of Hiawatha, Kansas.

TOMATO SOUP

1 6-ounce can tomato paste
24 ounces milk (refill tomato paste can four times)
1 teaspoon salt or to taste
1 teaspoon celery seed

Put tomato paste in a small saucepan. Add the milk using the can, rinsing thoroughly. Add the salt and the celery seed. Cook on medium heat, stirring occasionally.

Campbell's tomato soup: 69¢ for a 10-ounce can, plus 11¢ for 10 ounces of milk equals 80¢ for 20 ounces, or 32¢ per cup.

Homemade: 21¢ per cup.

Contributed by "an appreciative reader in Boston."

ONION-SOUP MIX

¾ cup instant minced onion
4 teaspoons onion powder
⅓ cup beef-flavored bouillon powder
¼ teaspoon celery seed, crushed
¼ teaspoon sugar

Mix all the ingredients, and store in an airtight container. To use, add 2 tablespoons mix to 1 cup boiling water. Cover and simmer for 15 minutes. This makes a stronger soup than the store-bought mix, so you can use less.

Lipton onion-soup mix: 99¢ for 2 ounces, or 50¢ per ounce.

Homemade: 33¢ per ounce.

CHOCOLATE SYRUP

½ cup cocoa
1 cup water
2 cups sugar
⅛ teaspoon salt
¼ teaspoon vanilla

Mix the cocoa and the water in a saucepan. Heat and stir to dissolve the cocoa. Add the sugar, and stir to dissolve. Boil 3 minutes. Add the salt and the vanilla. Pour into a sterilized pint jar, and store covered in refrigerator. Keeps for several months.

Hershey chocolate syrup: $1.69 for 24 ounces, or 7¢ per ounce.

Homemade: 3¢ per ounce.

Contributed by Doris Schaefer of Corunna, Indiana.

CREAM-SOUP MIX

2 cups dry milk
1¼ cups cornstarch, or 2½ cups flour
¼ cup chicken-bouillon powder
2 tablespoons dried onion flakes
½ teaspoon pepper
1 teaspoon thyme (optional)
1 teaspoon basil (optional)

Mix all the ingredients, and store in airtight container. If the mix is made with cornstarch, add ⅓ cup mix to 1¼ cups water; if made with flour, add ½ cup mix to 1¼ cups water. This makes a concentrated casserole consistency. For soup consistency, double the water.

Store-brand soup: 64¢ for a 10-ounce can.

Homemade: Recipe makes ten 12-ounce batches at 18¢ per batch.

Contributed by Kathy Brown of Lakewood, Colorado.

SEASONED-RICE MIX

3 cups uncooked rice
¼ cup dried parsley flakes
6 tablespoons instant chicken or beef bouillon powder
2 teaspoons onion powder
½ teaspoon garlic powder
¼ teaspoon dried thyme

Mix all the ingredients, and store in an airtight container. To use, put 1 cup mix, 2 tablespoons margarine, and 2 cups water in a saucepan. Bring to a boil, cover, reduce heat, and simmer for 15 minutes or until the rice is tender. To more closely approximate Rice-A-Roni, substitute a cup of broken pieces of uncooked spaghetti for a cup of rice.

Rice-A-Roni: 89¢ per 1-cup box.

Homemade: 44¢ per cup of mix.

CALCULATING THE NET VALUE OF THE SECOND INCOME UPDATE

In the first book, I explored the idea that for many couples a second, smaller income may not be worth it when one considers the extra expenses that are incurred.

The second income could be a good idea, if: both incomes are low—say under $15,000; both spouses love their jobs; and/or the lower income provides medical benefits that are needed for a pre-existing condition.

But I received a letter that illustrates the possible economic benefit from going from two incomes to one. Linda Prentiss of Lake Ronkonkoma, New York, writes, "After leaving my art-teaching job last spring, I was worried that we couldn't make it on my husband's salary. Thanks to your newsletter, we are doing fine!"

She says she was making $13,000 gross, with no benefits. She realized the following savings by quitting and using the time she freed up to live more frugally:

Transportation:	$265
Clothing:	$200
Breakfast and lunch at work:	$720
Extra convenience food:	$2,080
Fast food:	$1,560
Day care (not tax-deductible in her case):	$5,000
Teacher supplies:	$200
Taxes and Social Security:	$3,380
Late fines, bank fees, and finance charges:	$720
Occasional housekeeper:	$100
Total:	$14,225

Prentiss says these are conservative estimates; her family has $2,300 more in savings than it had six months ago. As a further benefit, their lower income may help them qualify for more financial aid for their daughter's college education.

Certainly Prentiss could have avoided some of her work-related expenses. But most people in that situation do rely on meals out and convenience foods, so her example applies widely.

UNDER ONE ROOF

One of the most powerful frugal concepts is sharing. Whether it's tools, cars, or cookware, when more than one person or family uses it, money is saved.

Consequently, sharing makes a lot of sense when it comes to the biggest expense most of us face: housing.

That's the basic idea behind the more than 400 shared-housing programs in 43 states across the nation. With this country full of huge houses left over from the six-kids-per-family days and more and more people living alone (7 percent of the population lived alone in 1980, 12 percent in 1990), shared housing could be the wave of the future.

According to Margaret Harmon, codirector of the National Shared Housing Resource Center, there are two kinds of shared housing:

Match-ups. In these, homeowners share their homes with homeseekers who pay rent and/or provide service. For example, an elderly widow might share her home with a college student, who pays minimal rent, does some home or yard maintenance, and provides some companionship. Or single mothers may live together in a home one of them owns and share child-care duties.

Group-shared Residences. These involve a number of people living cooperatively in a single, large dwelling, usually rented. In the case of elderly or disabled residents, the home may be owned by a church or other sponsoring organization, and cooking, laundry, and housekeeping may be provided. Last year in Massachusetts, 230 people moved out of nursing homes and into shared housing.

Harmon says many young people work out their own shared-housing arrangements through newspaper classified ads, bulletin boards, and word of mouth. But older or disabled people, who may be more wary of potential problems and who may lack the time or energy to screen house mates themselves, often use shared-housing programs. These programs are sponsored by churches, housing authorities, social-service agencies, and other nonprofit groups. They carefully screen potential house mates to make sure they will be compatible.

To find the shared-housing program nearest you or to learn about how to start one in your community, call or write:

National Shared Housing Resource Center
431 Pine St.
Burlington, VT 05401
(802) 862-2727

A final note: According to a study done at Columbia University and St. Luke's-Roosevelt Hospital in New York, people who live alone are twice as likely to have second heart attacks and die from them as people living with family or friends. Another study at Duke University Medical Center found that unmarried heart-attack patients with no close friends were much more likely to die within five years than those with close attachments to family and friends.

In short, concludes the *Journal of the American Medical Association,* isolation and loneliness can actually be life-threatening. It

seems clear, then, that sharing housing and forming friendships and attachments could actually save lives.

THANK YOU, TANK GOO

Dear Amy,

I've learned that aquarium sealant works better on wet joints than anything else I've tried. I use Dow-Corning, 100-percent silicone rubber aquarium sealant, $2.79 at a pet shop. I learned by fixing a leak in my car trunk. . . . My repair has held up for six years. Later, after two different dive shops had failed to seal my diver's faceplate to the rubber part, I fixed it the same way.

—Leonce W. Many
New Orleans, Louisiana

GOOD-BYE, OLD FLAME

Dear Amy,

We've turned off the pilot light on our gas stove and use a flintless lighter. We've done this for at least ten years, and my husband estimates that we save $7 a month.

—Beatrice E. Lewis
West Newton, Massachusetts

SAVE A BUNCH

Dear Amy,

If you keep bananas in a closed plastic bag, they will keep at least two weeks on your counter. I experimented with this. I bought two bunches of bananas at the green, barely yellow stage. I put one in a closed plastic bag and one in an open plastic bag. By the end of one week, the open-bag bananas were

brown-spotted and almost at the banana-bread stage. At the end of two weeks, the closed-bag bananas were just starting to get small brown spots, and the stems still showed some green. Once the bag is opened and left open, the bananas ripen at a faster rate.

—Margie Jamison
Lynchburg, Virginia

MOM'S WATCHFUL EYE

Dear Amy,

When we received our copy of a bill from the hospital after our third child's birth, we discovered that the hospital had charged the insurance company twice for the birthing room (which added over $1,200 to the bill). Our in-

surance company has a hospital-audit program. If the patient finds an error that saves the company money, the patient receives 50 percent of the savings up to $500. After we followed the procedure required, the insurance authority issued us a check for $500. Not a bad return for a few moments of work.

—James and Ann Gallegos
Thoreau, New Mexico

COTTON TALE

Dear Amy,

This costume only cost me 50¢. I went to a garage sale, and they had a large, stuffed bunny for that price. I removed the stuffing . . . outdoors because of the mess . . . and cut out the face, hands, and feet. The costume was then ready for Halloween.

—Dianne Willis
Sterling Heights, Michigan

FOAM FOR FREE

Dear Amy,

My wife and I live in the Northern California foothills, where the temperature drops below freezing in the winter. I had some PVC water pipes to insulate. . . . I went to the local retail carpet business and asked if I could have some discarded foam pads from their Dumpster. They were happy to get rid of them. I cut the pads into strips about 2 inches or 3 inches wide. I secured one end of the strip to the start of the pipe with duct tape and wound the strip around the pipe, being careful not to overlap. When I reached the end of the pipe, I secured the foam with more duct tape and the pipe was insulated.

—David Stroble and Diane Hall
Nevada City, California

CAMP TIGHTOWADDIE

Dear Amy,

If you are unable (or unwilling) to spend money to send your children to camp, have some neighborhood mothers join you to make a neighborhood day camp. Two mothers form a team to take care of one afternoon's activities according to talent and interest: crafts on Monday, sports and contests on Tuesday, nature skills on Wednesday, cooking on Thursday, skits and songs on Friday. Friday evening can be a families-included barbecue (bring your own meat and a pot-luck dish), and the children display crafts and perform skits. If you are really brave, you could also include a Friday sleepover.

Moms meet a couple of months before to plan dates, activities, and pool resources.

—Colette Hymas
South Jordan, Utah

KITTY LETTER

Dear Amy,

After practically killing my cat, and running up a $300 vet bill, by using too many flea products, I bought a $6 flea comb. I combed my cat four times daily and got out an average of about 20 fleas a day for two weeks. Within a month of this, every trace of a flea was gone. Now I comb her one time a day, just to be sure. Nary a flea have I found.

—H. P. Peasley
Seattle, Washington

PERIODICAL PICK-UPS

Dear Amy,

I get free magazines from my local library. They keep magazines for one year only, and then put them out in the foyer for anyone who wants them. I go one step further and reserve particular magazines. They call when they've got them sorted and I go pick them up. I got a full year's worth of "Organic Gardening," "Mother Earth News," "Money," "Coinage," and "Bicycling," (for the husband) all for free.

—Janine M. Ott
Jacksonville, Arkansas

(We called our local libraries and inquired about their policies. Smaller libraries have little storage space and dispose of magazines far more frequently . . . they can't keep them a full year. We were advised to ask anytime we went in to see if any were available. The larger libraries keep magazines for 5 to 15 years. They suggested we call back in December to learn which publications would be available, and when. FZ)

BIDS FOR BIKES

Dear Amy,

In our small town, the police station holds a yearly auction of unclaimed bikes. These range from trikes to top-of-the-line racers. This year, we were able to get a midsize boy's 5-speed mountain bike for $25 (retail value, Sears catalog, is $149–$159). We also picked up a men's 12-speed in perfect condition for another $25 (approximate value $199 at Sears).

—Rhonda James
Fergus, Ontario, Canada

WEAR AND WASH

Dear Amy,

I make my washcloths from terrycloth garments bought at garage sales. I cut or rip the garments apart, cut in the right-size squares, round the corners a bit, and zigzag around the edges. After washing, the edges will need to be trimmed. If you end up with enough for two halves, sew them together. The seam through the center doesn't matter.

—Myrtle Usher
Ottosen, Iowa

CALCULATING PAYBACK TIME

Decaying leaves, sticks, and debris obscured the rusty remains of the trailer. Hardy vegetation had arrogantly sprung from the humus layer on the trailer floor. The pockmarked trailer sides, of beer-can strength, flapped loosely.

In a former life it had been a pop-up-tent camper-trailer, then it was

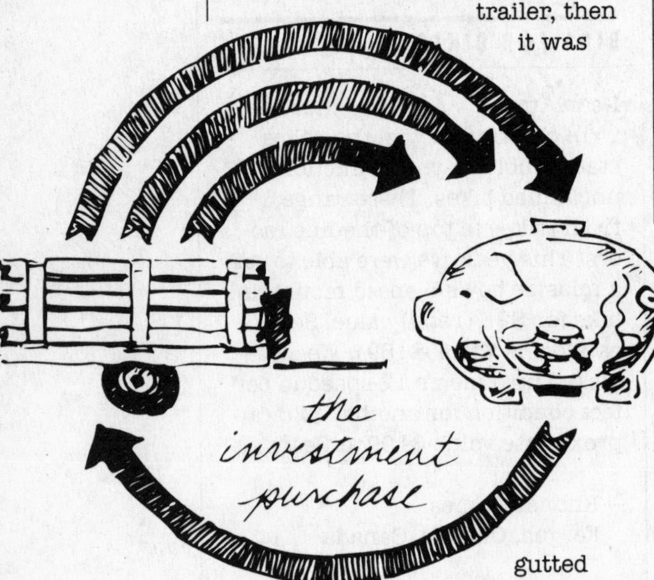

gutted and used for hauling wood, and finally, it was abandoned to the elements. Although free for the taking, it wasn't clear we were getting the better end of the deal.

But diligent scouring of the classifieds during the previous months failed to turn up a bargain utility trailer. So when we located this derelict, Jim's vision overrode his pride and he set forth to make something of the wreckage.

In the next days, Jim stripped away everything that didn't look like a respectable trailer, leaving only a sturdy skeleton of axle and frame. He spent $335 on mail-ordered wheels, sale-purchased, pressure-treated lumber, hardware, wiring, and lights. Up from the humble beginning miraculously arose a handsome utility trailer that became the envy of his coworkers.

We had an imminent need for a heavy-duty trailer to move our family's belongings over the 40 bumpy miles between our Navy house and our new pre-1900 farmhouse with attached barn.

By moving on weekends, the process took ten days. Renting a utility trailer of equal size would have cost $15 per day or a total of $150. During its initial use, nearly half of the cost of the trailer had been paid back.

In the last five years, the remaining cost of the trailer has been paid back in savings on delivery charges and the ability to haul free-for-the-taking items. We have bartered the use of the trailer, and it has saved us hundreds of hours of work.

A $335 utility trailer would not have sufficient payback for everyone. With each investment purchase, do the math to figure out whether it's worthwhile for you.

Calculating payback is a simple but often overlooked process and is a fundamental practice of successful tightwaddery. You divide the cost of the item by the savings per use to determine how many times you would have to use something to pay back the cost.

Example: A pair of hair-salon-quality scissors cost $14. A child's haircut costs $7. Two home haircuts will pay for the scissors.

You should also figure out how long the payback time is.

Example: If it takes two home haircuts to pay back the cost of

the scissors, and your child needs a cut every six weeks, multiply two haircuts by six weeks. The payback time is 12 weeks.

People often mistakenly assume that any investment that pays for itself is a good one. When figuring payback time, consider these points:

1. Factor in the life expectancy of the item you plan to buy.

Example: If the more expensive sneakers will last 30 percent longer than the cheap ones and cost 30 percent more, you are not gaining ground—and you would be better off using your money to invest in something else.

2. Similarly, consider how long you will need the item. If you are buying a tool you will only use briefly, try to buy it used so you can recover the cost when you resell it. Or you may find it's better to rent.

Example: Rent or buy used rather than new pump jacks to help you paint your house.

3. Generally, put your money in items that have the quickest payback time first.

Example: You estimate in your case the payback time on insulated windows is 20 years. You also can find many smaller investment purchases that pay back in 10 years that add up to the cost of the windows. The smaller purchases will pay for themselves two times in 20 years—and so you would save twice as much.

4. If a new product comes on the market that might save you money in the future, wait to buy it: The price may drop dramatically.

Example: You decide to buy a computer because your grade-school kids will need one when they get to high school. In the meantime you plan to use it to write letters to save money on your phone bill. But a computer that cost $2,500 seven years ago can be purchased used today for $250. Unless the item will give you immediate, significant payback, wait for the price to drop, for a great deal to come along, or for the technology to improve.

5. Consider the 90/10 rule. Sometimes for 10 percent of the money you can buy a tool that will do 90 percent of the job.

Example: You can buy a small, used, portable sewing machine for $50 that will do 90 percent of the sewing you need. Or you can buy a new, $500, whiz-bang sewing machine with all the attachments that will do 100 percent of the sewing. So you are paying $450 to get that 10 percent more.

Let's say you buy the smaller machine, and every two years you encounter a sewing job it cannot handle. If hiring a professional seamstress costs $45 per sewing job, the more expensive machine would take 20 years to pay for itself.

6. With great reluctance, I suggest you factor in time savings. People frequently and erroneously cite time savings as an excuse to buy expensive "toys." You can buy time-saving purchases to create more leisure time, but time-savers become money-savers only when you genuinely, absolutely have no spare time—and when you use the free time you gain to save money by doing something else.

Example: When we first moved to Leeds, Jim wanted to buy a riding lawn mower with snow- and garden-plowing capabilities. I resisted until I mowed our front yard for the first time. With our

push mower, that one small section required two hours—ample time for me to ponder how many hours I would have to spend every day to maintain the entire lawn. Mowing this way would have made it impossible for us to have a garden or do some renovations or other money-saving activities.

In cases like this, calculate the payback by transference.

We bought a used garden tractor for $1,600. The tractor frees up ten hours per week. If I use those hours to do home renovation instead of hiring an $8-per-hour contractor, then I can transfer those savings toward the cost of the tractor. It will pay for itself when I have completed 200 hours of renovations.

We feel economic triumph when we hitch our paid-for-itself tractor to haul leaves, brush, and garden debris around our 7-acre spread. The ultimate thrill for our little tightwads comes when, after the chores, we load them in the trailer and ride off, giggling and squealing, into the sunset.

TOYS FOR TIGHTWAD TOTS

As an experienced parent, I have noticed that for my kids the transition from "It's-the-greatest-toy-in-the-universe-thank-you-thank-you-Mommy," to "big deal," is about two days.

It's this rapid disenchantment that makes many parents swamp their kids with toys. One recent survey revealed that the average five-year-old has "cycled through" about 250 toys.

As an alternative, I was intrigued by the concept of a "toy library." There are more than 200 around the country. One opened two months ago in nearby Lewiston, Maine.

Its director, Anne Belden, says her nonprofit, volunteer-run facility is actually a combination of indoor play space and toy library. A family pays a $20 annual membership fee, and the kids, ranging from infants to eight-year-olds, can play in the library, which is located in donated space in a church. Belden says indoor play spaces are particularly needed in cold climates like ours, where snowed-in parents and kids can go a little nutty.

Kids can check out toys for two weeks. The Lewiston toy library has 300 toys, mostly donated.

To find out whether there is a toy library (with or without a play space) near you, contact: The U.S.A. Toy Library Association, 2530 Crawford Ave., Suite 111, Evanston, IL 60201, (708) 864-3330. The association publishes a national directory of member libraries. If you want to start one, Belden suggests visiting the nearest operating toy library for suggestions.

PRESSED-FLOWER PICTURES

Before I lose the male audience with this "woman's" article, let me say that I first became intrigued by pressed-flower pictures when a *guy* on my staff made one for Mother's Day about a year ago. His mother loved it. I realized this was a great tightwad endeavor for several reasons:

- Wildflowers are free and plentiful in rural and suburban areas. Cultivated flowers may also be pressed.
- Flower presses can be easily made from free materials.
- No special tools, materials, or talent is required.
- Pictures can be designed to fit in secondhand frames (I've got a box full of long, thin, rectangular frames for which this would be perfect).
- A variety of backgrounds can be used, including papers, matboards, and cloth, depending on what you have available.
- Pressed-flower pictures make great all-occasion gifts, and you can get a jump on Christmas by starting in the summer.

To learn more, I consulted four library books as well as spoke with a woman in my community, Joanne D'Unger, who has been pressing flowers since she studied botany in college ten years ago.

The familiar method of pressing flowers in heavy books is somewhat inconvenient. To prevent stained pages, you have to press flowers between facial tissues inside the book for 24 hours, remove the tissues, and press the flowers in the books with weights stacked on top for several weeks, meaning that you have a semipermanent pile of stuff taking up space. Then, Murphy's Law of Flower Pressing dictates, "If you've used your 'A' encyclopedia, your child will have to write a school paper on Albania." And after the flowers dry, you'll want to transfer them out of the books to some sort of file for safe keeping.

In contrast, Joanne's flower press consists

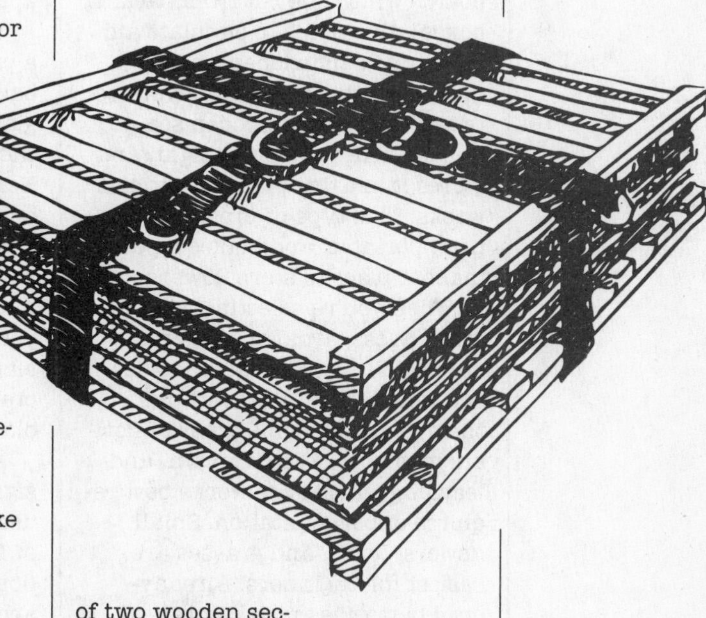

of two wooden sections made of glued-and-nailed-together slats (left over from a building project) in a style similar to the metal-rack type she used in college. You could also use discards like scrap plywood, oven racks, or our no-longer-needed homemade baby gate, which, if cut in half, would closely resemble Joanne's press.

To apply pressure, Joanne uses

cinch straps (that she trash-picked), but you could also use weights or bolts with wing nuts. If you use bolts, drill the holes through the center of the sides, as opposed to the corners, for even distribution of pressure.

Flowers have to be pressed between pieces of absorbent paper. Two authors suggest newspaper without colored ink. Joanne uses a plain, nonsmooth paper (which she scavenged from the trash at work) and has used the same sheets for many years. She places the paper sheets, with flowers, between layers of corrugated cardboard (which she cut from packing boxes); this helps to circulate air.

Joanne sandwiches many flower/paper/cardboard layers between the outside wooden sections, cinches the press tight, and stores it in a dry place for several weeks. This type of press is compact, portable, and makes a permanent place to store flowers.

When you're selecting wildflowers to press, avoid endangered species. Flowers along roadsides are usually fine, but don't pick them in parks. Some types of flowers may spot or turn brown, and learning which type works best requires experimentation. Small flowers, ferns, and grasses are easiest for beginners. Already-dead butterflies may be pressed and are suitable for making pictures as well.

Pick flowers in the middle of the day when they're the driest, and more than a day after the most recent rain.

When laying out flowers to press, curve the stems and press flowers to present both side and top views. Depending on humidity and type of flower, drying time can vary from two to six weeks. During the drying period, one book suggests, inspect the flowers to find and smooth any folded petals or remove any that have mildewed.

While you're hitting the yard sales in the summer, pick up inexpensive frames. If you're a beginner and planning to make gifts, you'll want smaller frames for two reasons: They require smaller, less complicated arrangements; and most people's homes can accommodate a sweet little picture, but giving any large piece of artwork is risky and may not be appreciated.

When you're ready to assemble a picture, choose a frame and background material. Trace the glass on the background, and cut the background to the right size. Next, lay out your pressed flowers on your background, using tweezers or a dry watercolor brush to position them, until you find a pleasing design. During this stage you'll want to avoid any coughing, slamming of doors, or whirlwinds created by careening three-year-old twins.

After you've settled on a design, carefully pick up each item, use a toothpick to apply a tiny dab of Elmer's glue to the back of the flower, and replace it in the arrangement. Once everything is glued, the finished picture can be framed. Be sure to use glass to protect the picture, and seal the back with tape to prevent problems from humidity.

To learn more about advanced techniques (such as for pressing bulkier flowers), design styles, and other applications for pressed flowers, consult one of those many books at your library.

TVP: A BAD NAME FOR GOOD FOOD

Who thought up this name, anyway? "TVP" sounds like an emissions control device, or maybe the knob next to "vertical hold" on your television. It doesn't even remotely sound like food—no wonder it's been around for 20 years and never really caught on. In fact, I had never heard of it until a friend, whose two daughters suddenly "went vegetarian" on her, introduced me to it. After some experimentation, I've concluded it is a reasonable product for people to explore.

TVP stands for "texturized vegetable protein." It is the same stuff that those convenience-food manufacturers sneak into your food to make it seem like it has more meat than it really does; it's often listed in the ingredients as "textured soy flour."

TVP is a staple food in many vegetarian households. But unlike tofu, brewer's yeast, mung bean sprouts, and other vegetarian mainstays with unique flavors and textures, TVP was designed as a substitute for meat, so mainstream families should find it easy to swallow.

All TVP is made by one company: the Archer Daniels Midland Company in Decatur, Illinois. Although it's made in America's heartland, ironically, TVP is much more widely used in Europe.

TVP comes in dry form in three sizes: flakes, granules, and chunks (kitty-food size). Before cooking it in any form, you reconstitute it by adding warm water.

Although TVP has little flavor of its own, it has a texture that is very difficult to distinguish from that of ground turkey or hamburger (You can trust me on this: I'm not the kind of person who oversells vegetarian dishes. I'd be the first to tell you that spaghetti with lentils just doesn't cut it). So TVP works very well in spicy foods, like spaghetti sauce and chili. When we made blander

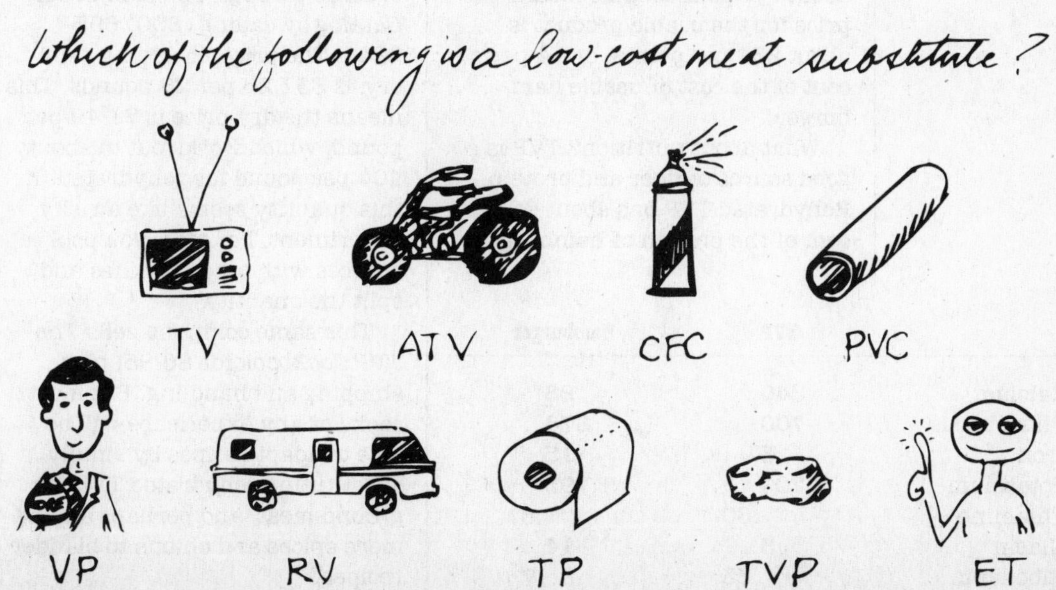

foods, like TVP gravy on biscuits, we decided we would add Worcestershire sauce in the future.

If you find you don't like it in meatless meals, try mixing it with hamburger. Instead of buying 85 percent lean ground beef at top dollar, you could buy bargain-priced 75 percent lean and mix it half-and-half with TVP; this mix would have a slightly lower fat content than the expensive hamburger.

Aside from any health benefits, the obvious advantage of TVP is its price. When we happen upon an amazing sale on ground beef, we can buy 75 percent lean for $1.19 per pound. We almost always fry and drain the meat before we use it in a casserole or spaghetti sauce. This means we're really buying 12 ounces for $1.19, which works out to $1.58 per pound of usable meat.

TVP, when purchased by the 25-pound bag from our local natural-food store, costs $21.50, or 86¢ per pound. But a pound of dry chunks, when rehydrated, weighs about 3¾ pounds. This means the price for the usable product is about 23¢ per pound, or 14 percent of the cost of usable hamburger.

What about nutrition? TVP is a good source of fiber and protein. Rehydrated TVP has about 60 percent of the protein of hamburger, and it has almost no fat. Here's how the vitamins and minerals in 400 grams of rehydrated TVP stack up with those in 400 grams of hamburger, in milligrams.

As you can see in the chart (below left), TVP has more of some nutrients and less of others.

But isn't this some kind of weird "chemical food"? No. TVP is a by-product of the process of making soybean oil. Although chemicals are used in this process, TVP has been repeatedly tested and has been found to have no trace of those chemicals. But if you're skeptical, you can buy organic TVP, which costs $1.05 per pound (of dry chunks) at my natural-food store.

How can you find TVP? Many natural-food stores carry the flake or granule types, but TVP chunks may have to be specially ordered for you. I recommend that you go to the extra effort of ordering the chunks, as these most closely approximate meat. If you cannot find a local source, TVP chunks can be ordered through *The Mail Order Catalog* by calling (800) 695-2241. The price, including delivery, is $37.25 per 25 pounds. This means the dry price is $1.49 per pound, which works out to about 40¢ per pound for rehydrated. If this quantity seems like a risky experiment, I suggest you pool resources with other families and split the quantity.

This same company sells *The TVP Cookbook* for $6.95, plus shipping and handling. But most cooks of any experience will be able to adapt recipes by simply substituting rehydrated TVP for ground meat, and perhaps adding more spices and onions to blander recipes.

	TVP	Hamburger
Calcium	340	28
Phosphorus	700	878
Iron	8	15
Potassium	2,200	1,795
Thiamine	.60	.61
Niacin	3	14
Riboflavin	.33	.7

A BOOK REVIEW

If you are in the market for a new appliance—or just want to learn how to make the ones you've got work better—I highly recommend *Consumer Guide to Home Energy Savings*, by Alex Wilson and John Morrill.

Unlike a lot of wimpy energy-efficiency publications ("Be sure to caulk those windows!"), this one goes into great detail on how to get the maximum energy savings from lightbulbs, furnaces, washing machines, water heaters—any appliance that uses energy.

Particularly helpful are the up-to-date, model-by-model listings of annual energy costs for various appliances. But I was also interested in the charts that help you maximize energy efficiency when you *use* your existing appliances—for example, the one below, which shows the most and least expensive appliances you can choose when cooking a casserole. The costs are based on 8¢ per kilowatt-hour for electricity and 60¢ per therm for natural gas:

	Temperature	Time	Cost
Electric oven	350	1 hr.	16¢
Toaster oven	425	50 min.	8¢
Gas oven	350	1 hr.	7¢
Frying pan	420	1 hr.	7¢
Crockpot	200	7 hrs.	6¢
Microwave oven	High	15 min.	3¢

To order, send $6.95 (California residents add 8.25 percent sales tax) plus $2.00 shipping to:

American Council for an Energy-Efficient Economy
2140 Shattuck Ave., Suite 202
Berkeley, CA 94704

CONTACTS BY MAIL

I have managed to stumble to the advanced age of 39 without needing corrective lenses. Readers who are not so fortunate have told me that contact lenses can make a big dent in a frugal budget, but some said they had heard that good deals are available from mail-order sources. So I plunged into research and discovered that the subject is both complex and controversial.

Cheryle Baker Dusinberre of Boiling Springs, Pennsylvania, sent me a newspaper clipping that indicated that the American Optometric Association didn't fully support mail-order replacement lenses. So I talked with Dr. Burt Dubow, chairman of the contact-lens section of the A.O.A., who cited these concerns:

- Consumers who buy mail-order contacts might skip regular checkups.
- A discount supplier might accidentally fill an outdated prescription.
- Any custom-made lenses, like torics, gas-permeables, or bifocals, should not be mail-ordered because they should be checked by your optometrist for any imperfections.

But Dr. Dubow said that if consumers have checkups, make sure their prescriptions are still good, and purchase daily-wear or extended-wear lenses (which aren't custom-made), mail-order lenses pose no problem.

In addition, Dr. Dubow confirmed what I had heard from other sources. Many optometrists are now offering replacement lenses at discount. If your optometrist isn't, try negotiating, using prices from mail-order suppliers to make your case. If your optometrist still won't budge, shop around with other optometrists.

Also check your warehouse club. Sharon Nelson of Auburn, California, said a pair of lenses that costs $150 through her optometrist costs $60.35 at Lens Express—but she found that the pair costs $36 at the optical shop at her warehouse store, Price Club. (Ironically, the mail-order suppliers have the same criticism of warehouse clubs that some optometrists have about mail-order suppliers: They are more likely to make mistakes and don't provide personal service.)

If you can't get lenses at discount prices locally and opt for purchasing them through the mail, consider these points:

Two discounters I surveyed, Lens Express and LenSmart, charge a three-year membership fee of $25, but their discount prices were still higher than those of other discounters who charge no membership fee. Although LenSmart offers no other benefits for this fee, Lens Express does; if you refer a friend who joins, you save $15 on your next purchase. Lens Express also may help you save on eye exams through an associated doctor. But the contact-lens industry is changing so rapidly, it may not be wise to lock into one discounter that long.

Shipping and handling fees vary considerably—from zero to $8.95—and may vary based on where you live in the country.

Most discounters quote prices for *pairs* of lenses, but we found a few that quote them for *individual* lenses. In the case of one catalog I inspected, this was only evident in the teeny-weeny print at the bottom of the page.

Lens Express guarantees the lowest price, which means it will "match any price at the time of order." In other words, the company's usual price may not be the

Mail-Order Company	Phone Number	Daily Wear	Extended Wear	Shipping
Lens Express ($25/3-year fee)	(800) 666-LENS	$45.90	$105.40	$8.95
LenSmart ($25/3-year fee)	(800) 231-LENS	$40.00	$84.00	$5.95
Contact Lens Replacement Center	(800) 779-2654	$49.00	$89.00	$4.50
Contact Lens Connection	(800) 695-LENS	$38.00	$98.00	none
Dial A Contact Lens	(800) 233-LENS	$19.50*	$89.00	$3 or $8
Contact Lens Supply	(800) 833-7525	$48.00	$93.00	$4.00
Prism Optical	(800) 637-4104	$45.00	$90.00	$5.00
Soft Lens Express	(800) 872-1880	$60.00	$148.00	$5.00

*Price is for a special offer of two pairs.

lowest, it's up to you to find a lower price, which Lens Express will match. A company representative told me the company would also adjust its price to compensate for its higher shipping charges and the membership fee. However, each time you place an order, you'll have to renegotiate.

By calling around each time you order replacements, you might locate a "special," as indicated by the asterisk (*) in the chart on page 136. At the time I researched this article, this company offered this price for a pair of lenses, but only if you bought two pairs.

This chart compares the prices of two specific types of brand-name lenses, from companies recommended by readers. All the prices are based on one pair of lenses. As you can see, no company offers the lowest prices on every type of lens, and there are over 100 types. You have to shop around yourself to find the best deal.

Finally, the bottom price isn't always the final consideration. Some companies may offer poor service and/or may not be well established. I omitted any company with a perpetually busy phone or that didn't return my call after I left a message on its answering machine. But I couldn't research the reliability of any of these companies.

Ultimately, you have to work out the best package of options for yourself. Some optometrists charge less for exams and mark up replacement lenses. According to Elizabeth Rhymer of Naples, Florida, these optometrists might not even release your prescription so you can buy lenses elsewhere. Other optometrists charge more for exams but sell discounted lenses or let you fill the prescription through a discounter. So in addition to factoring in membership fees and shipping, you may also need to factor in the cost of exams.

FLOWERS ARE FOREVER

Dear Amy,

Perennial flowers are a much better buy for the garden than annuals. You buy them once and they're there forever. While perennials are more expensive than annuals, there are ways to minimize the expense. Many can be started from seed. Others can be started from cuttings you take from the mother plant in the spring and fall. Still others can be divided in a couple of years. For advice, I specifically recommend *The Victory Garden Flower Book* by Bob Thompson and *The Perennial Garden* by Marilyn and Jeff Ball.

—Diana Bauer
Cincinnati, Ohio

DITCH PITCH TO SWITCH

Dear Amy,

I received a check in the mail for $75 to switch my long-distance carrier. I phoned my current carrier and asked them what pertinent questions I could ask the competition when I called to see if they had any similar plans to my current carrier. The service representative I spoke to was very honest and told me the competition probably had something similar, and although he could not send me a check for cash with the promise to switch like the competition, he

would credit my account for $75 if I mailed my check to their office. I could have switched, but then I would have had to pay new service fees. Instead, I spent 29¢ to mail in the competition's check and will get $75 credited to my account.

—Vera Ziegler
Bremerton, Washington

SCHOOL BUDGET CUTS

Dear Amy,

I admire those who can cut their own hair, but I can't. And I certainly don't trust my husband or two-year-old. My way to save money is going to a cosmetology school. Their prices on services are greatly reduced; I save $7 on a haircut. Having my hair just cut, and not dried/styled, has saved about $7 more.

—Dawn Hancock
Auburn, Indiana

SAUCE SAVER

Dear Amy,

I had found a bargain on a huge and slightly dented can of tomato sauce at a grocery warehouse. I really didn't know how I was going to freeze the sauce in usable portions with little waste after I opened the can. My mom told me to freeze the sauce in ice-cube trays and then put them in a freezer bag. It worked great. A homemade pizza takes us exactly five cubes. There is absolutely zero wasted.

—Melanie Wisdom
New Caney, Texas

SPEED DIAL

Dear Amy,

Often, radio stations have trivia contests where the first person to call with the correct answer is the winner. Many times, the questions aren't that difficult; the hard part is being the first caller. The secret: Dial the last number before they've finished asking the question. I've won two meals in the last month this way.

—Paul Stynsberg
Roseau, Minnesota

CHOO-CHOO CHEAPIES

Dear Amy,

In preparing a fourth birthday party for my rail-fan son, I remembered those little paper engineer hats they always gave to him on station visits. Thanks to the courtesy of the Amtrak representative, our guests had *free* theme-appropriate hats.

—Jill Zacharie
Alexandria, Virginia

BAGS IN A BOX

Dear Amy,

I used to feel that empty plastic grocery bags had invaded my pantries and closets. Now, I store plastic bags in an empty tissue box. It dispenses them one at a time and saves a lot of space.

—Name withheld by request
Peekskill, New York

GIANT FLOWER PRESSES?

Dear Amy,

Wood pallets (no deposit) are often available from stores, lumberyards, feed stores, etc. Ask the store manager if he/she has any no-deposit pallets for free. They can be used for:

1. Most obvious, storing things off the ground.
2. Firewood. Most pallets are hardwood and make great fires. We cut the 1 x 4 from between the rails and then cut the rails to the proper size for the wood stove.
3. Fences. Nail them together with a 2 x 4 along the top and use an occasional fence post to help hold the row up.
4. Tables and work counters . . . use your imagination.
5. Garbage and trash bins, to keep the neighborhood dogs out.

We have found pallets to be a great resource, especially for temporary-type projects when money is in short supply.

—Bob and Rusty Taylor
Poulsbo, Washington

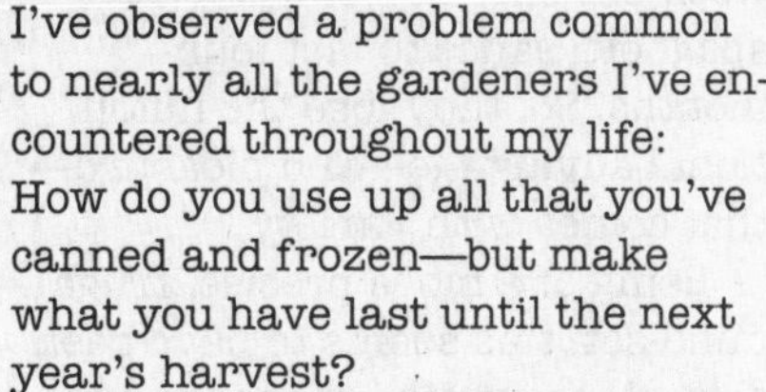

USE IT OR LOSE IT

I've observed a problem common to nearly all the gardeners I've encountered throughout my life: How do you use up all that you've canned and frozen—but make what you have last until the next year's harvest?

Home-canned goods last a couple of years, so ending up with extra isn't terrible—every once in a while you have a bad tomato year, and last year's surplus spaghetti sauce can be handy. But frozen vegetables should be used up within the year; they begin to lose their vitamins and develop a freezer taste if they're too old.

Throughout the year most gardeners, being unsure whether they have enough to last to the next season, buy supermarket fruits and vegetables. Then, as the new season rolls around, they find they have too much left over. So they have to throw away last year's surplus (or the year-before-that's surplus) to make room for this year's. As a result, money, effort, and energy are wasted.

Beans	49 qts	++++ ++++ ++++ ||
Cauliflower	10 qts	++++ ||||
Peas	27 qts	++++ ++++ ++++ ++++ |
Rhubarb	31 qts	++++ ++++ |
Spinach	46 qts	++++ ++++ ||
Strawberries	39 qts	++++ ++++ ++++

Of the gardeners who keep any records at all, most use a notebook system. They write in how much they freeze or can, and then throughout the year they make a mark every time they use something. This system, while good, doesn't insure the maximum use of garden produce. At some point, usually during the late spring, it becomes evident that their family has to

eat beet greens three nights a week but only has two jars of spaghetti sauce to last four months. So, they lose the nutritional advantage—and pleasure—that comes with variety.

Being of a more precise, frugal mind-set, this seems to have been a greater vexation to me than to others. If I didn't use my garden produce evenly throughout the year, my food bill would fluctuate greatly, and it would take me 12 months to know for sure whether it was going up or down.

So I decided I wanted a better system to schedule produce consumption. It would take into account that vegetables are harvested during different months, from June to October, so vegetables would be scheduled to last accordingly. I also wanted a system that would schedule canned and frozen-food consumption together—as opposed to a notebook by my freezer in the laundry room and another near the canned goods in the cellar.

So I decided to make up a calendar of sorts. First, I went through my freezer and canning shelves and recorded how many jars or packages I had of each fruit or vegetable.

Then I made up a time-line calendar, as shown below, on the backside of attached sheets of used computer paper. I listed the items vertically, in alphabetical order. I made horizontal spaces for the upcoming months. Noting the projected date of harvest, I divided the number of items by the number of remaining months. If I have 20 packages of spinach to consume in four months, I put five *X*'s in each month's space. If I have 13 packages of shredded zucchini to consume in five months, I alternately allot two and three *X*'s: 3 + 2 + 3 + 2 + 3 = 13.

Months of light consumption could be scheduled for the summer, since some fresh garden vegetables are available during those months. People who have small gardens might want to schedule their heaviest consumption during the winter months when supermarket produce gets most expensive.

This schedule is now taped up in our pantry with a pencil nearby. We look at it before planning our daily menu. When we use something, we circle the appropriate *X*. It took

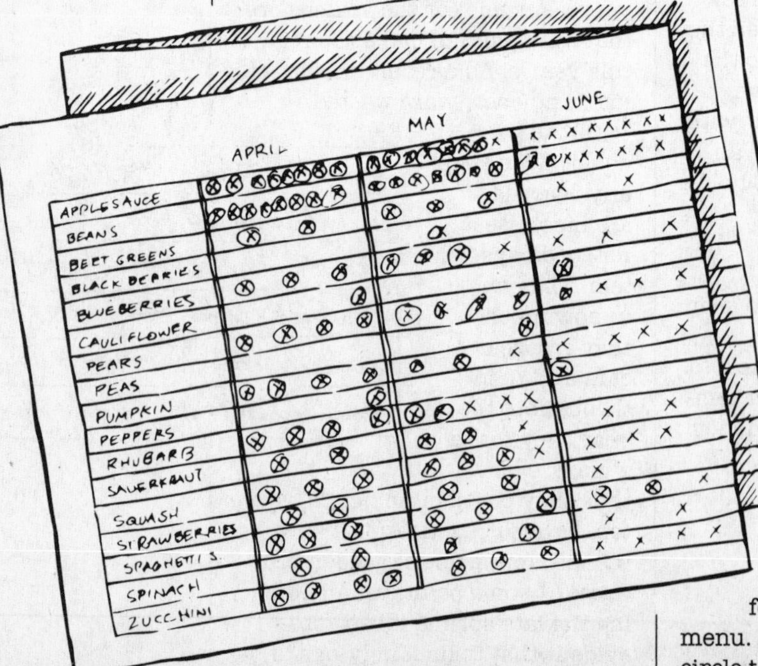

me about an hour and a half to inventory and make this schedule, and it requires no more than ten seconds a day to use.

I started my schedule in April, because that's when I devised this system. Next fall, after all of our garden is harvested, I will make a 12-month schedule.

This garden schedule illustrates a larger point. If you lack control over any area of your life—be it time, money, or other resources—design a system to manage it. Order will save you stress as well as money.

SAVE THOSE SEEDS

A dilemma that faces gardeners each year is whether to buy new seeds or take a chance on seeds left over from last year. Many gardeners, believing that seeds become much less viable each year, toss out all of the leftovers and buy a new batch "just to be sure."

But this isn't necessary, according to reader Pam West of Batavia, Illinois. She says that when she worked for one of the largest seed companies in the nation, one of her duties was to relabel the seed packages from the year before with the current germination information after the seeds were tested in the lab.

West wrote, "I was amazed to find out that in most cases, the germination percentage actually went up from the previous year, sometimes as much as 10 to 15 percent. So use those seeds from last year, and save your new seeds for next year."

According to *The Year Round Vegetable Gardener* by Anne Halpin, only onion seeds need to be purchased fresh each year. Here are the average storage limits for other varieties of seeds.

One to two years: corn, lettuce, parsley, and parsnips.

Three to five years: asparagus, beans, cabbage, carrots, celery, chicory, endive, okra, peas, peppers, radishes, and spinach.

Five or more years: beets, cucumbers, and tomatoes.

In *Square Foot Gardening* (a book that, incidentally, has been

recommended by at least a dozen of my readers), author Mel Bartholomew recommends storing seeds in airtight containers in a refrigerator. But even if you lack the room to store them in your fridge, there is a great chance they will be good next year if you store them in a cool, dry place.

If you don't want to risk devoting a large space in your garden to risky seeds, do your own germination test a few weeks before planting time. Sandwich ten seeds in a paper towel, and keep it moist. If at least seven sprout, your seeds are approximately as viable as new ones.

BUDGET PHILOSOPHY

Dear Amy,

I want to find out how to budget correctly. I've tried several methods but end up confused. Since my husband's and my income comes in sporadically, I have a hard time figuring out when I should start to figure; from the first of the month, or when all the income has come in, or when I pay monthly bills?

—Susan Sandoval
Elm Creek, Nebraska

Our personal budgeting system is so simple it doesn't seem like a budget, and I have often claimed that we don't have one.

Before I broached this subject, I consulted a couple of personal-finance books. Their systems seemed complicated and/or tedious. Sylvia Porter has four forms you need to fill out monthly. Likewise, readers have written to me about systems involving filling jars or envelopes with monthly expense money or even setting up an in-house checking system, which again seemed needlessly complicated. Conversely, many well-known personal-finance experts claim that budgets are like diets: Don't bother, because they don't work.

I'm in the middle. I do believe that every family needs a basic plan, but that plan should be extremely simple and flexible.

Early in our marriage, Jim and I spent an evening working out our plan. First, we pulled out our old bills and figured our average monthly fixed expenses: rent, insurance, utilities, and so on. Any bills that occurred annually were divided by 12, so that we knew how much to allocate for each month. Next, we estimated our nonfixed expenses: food, household expenses, clothing, gifts, transportation costs. By this point, we had accounted for every expense we could anticipate.

Then we subtracted our fixed and nonfixed expenses from Jim's take-home pay. If your income fluctuates wildly, base your monthly income on last year's after-tax income and divide by 12, and allow a huge amount for savings in case your income is less this year.

From this process, we determined we had a theoretical $500 per month surplus, or about 20 percent of Jim's take-home pay. Had this surplus worked out to less than 10 percent of our income, we would have done some refiguring.

By keeping a personal expense diary—a small notebook in which we recorded each expense as it occurred—we were able to make sure we stayed, on the average, within our budget.

It's easiest to keep records monthly, so start your records from the first of the month. Try to pay bills the same month in which they arrive, so that you know in which month to record the expense.

Budget gurus suggest putting 10 percent of your income into

savings each month, religiously, as if you were paying a bill. But this hard-and-fast rule "allows" you to spend the other 90 percent and doesn't challenge you to save more. It may also prevent you from paying off a high-interest debt or from buying an appliance that will save you money. They also insist on adherence to this rule whether your income is $10,000 or $100,000 per year.

Instead, I regard the budget as a beginning point only. Rather than seeing it as what you're allowed to spend, try to lower each area of the budget until you reach the point where it no longer feels comfortable, and then spend slightly more.

For example, we budgeted $200 a month for food, but over a period of years I whittled this to an average of $145 (back when we had three children). We only spent half of what we allowed for birthdays and rarely spent any of the money allocated for entertainment. By doing this in each budget category, we were able to increase our surplus to put into savings.

Additionally, sometimes you should overspend when it will save money in the long run. We average $180 a month for food (including school lunches and gardening supplies), but some months we spend $250 and other months we spend $100. The overspending occurs when we bulk-buy sale items or when we spend a lot for canning supplies during the summer months. If we have too many high months in a row, I figure out how much we should "underspend" this month to bring our average in line, and we eat from the items we have stocked up.

The physical management of our money was equally simple. We kept $1,000 in our checking account. Because we sought to spend as little as possible, our checking account naturally grew. When it grew to $1,500 we would transfer $500 into savings. We kept $2,500 in a savings account. When that grew to $3,500, we transferred $1,000 into an investment or paid off a debt. Some experts suggest keeping as much as six months' income in savings and liquid investments.

A question I've been asked is "How do you handle emergencies?" Plan your budget to include any expenses you can anticipate. If you drive an old car, figure on $1,000 per year for repairs. If you drive a new car under warranty, don't plan for any repairs. But if an unexpected fender bender occurs, pay for the repair, or the insurance deductible, with savings. Only dip into savings for emergencies or for buying something you can prove will pay for itself very quickly.

By deliberately living beneath our means we have *always,* I repeat, *always,* had enough money in savings for unexpected expenses. And because we always worked to save more than we had budgeted, even with emergencies, we saved an average of 21 percent of our income for seven years.

But everyone is different. Some people seem to need to put money into savings as if they were paying a monthly bill, or have it automatically withdrawn from their paychecks. For those with low incomes or little discipline, a more complicated and tedious system may be essential.

DARE TO DUMPSTER DIVE

As you become an accomplished tightwad, you find fewer and fewer new ideas that can significantly cut your expenses, so when you find one, you get excited. *The Art and Science of Dumpster Diving* by John Hoffman increased my awareness of a frugal frontier I had yet to explore.

Before I go any further, let me emphasize that I understand this subject crosses the line even for many hard-core tightwads; however, I am willing to risk the criticism. Dumpster diving can yield huge savings that may make a significant difference for some families.

In his book, Hoffman makes three basic points:

1. Americans are incredibly wasteful and throw away all sorts of good stuff.
2. Americans are snobby and afraid of germs.
3. Because of the first two points, the brave soul who is willing to poke his head into these forbidding urban caverns will be well rewarded.

Hoffman, who is now 29, writes with authority. He's a third-generation Dumpster diver (his grandmother took it up late in life) with over 20 years of diving experience. Much of what he owns, wears, and (yes, even) eats comes from Dumpsters. He now has a college education and a good job but continues to Dumpster-dive because he finds it a profitable, enjoyable, environmentally responsible pastime. The information in this article is based on both the book and a telephone interview we did with Hoffman.

Just as in Dumpster diving, where one must pick through the trash to find the treasures, it takes some effort to focus on the good stuff in the book. I had to ignore Hoffman's disrespectful attitudes toward authority figures, his profanity, and his slippery ethics (he has snipped locks on Dumpsters). And his tips on snooping for information and dealing with police are sure to offend all but the most ardent libertarian. At times, it seemed hard to find a single page without some offensive element.

But the saving grace of the book is that the guy is actually a skilled, entertaining writer, and I did learn a great deal. For example:

• If you dive consistently and well, you'll never have to buy any of this stuff again: manila envelopes, clothing, clothes hangers, boxes, houseplants, Christmas decorations, videotapes and audiotapes, furniture, candles, most toiletry items, books, magazines, newspapers, low-cost jewelry, and much more.

• The idea that Dumpsters are rat-infested is false, according to Hoffman. In 20 years of diving, he has seen exactly one rat. Even so, he keeps his eyes open for white powder sprinkled on a Dumpster's contents; it may be rat poison.

• The idea that Dumpsters are full of AIDS-contaminated syringes from drug abusers is also false, according to Hoffman. He has not seen a single syringe in the tens of thousands of Dumpsters he's inspected. (Nevertheless, be careful.)

• For food, Hoffman favors bakery and grocery-store Dumpsters, because the food is packaged or has been minimally handled. In an average week, about 50 percent of the food he eats comes from Dumpsters. Along with canned and packaged food, he salvages lightly bruised fruit and cheese with a tiny mold spot. Clearly, Hoffman is less squeamish than most people would be, but his hints about finding and using Dumpster food (he even includes two pages of recipes, such as "Bad-Banana Whipped Cream Substitute") could, at least, be valuable to people in dire economic circumstances. Any food that is questionable could be salvaged to feed to farm animals.

• Hoffman's other favorite Dumpsters are at motels (endless free soap), discount stores, wholesale florists (you'll be able to carry on multiple romances), candy stores, bookstores, toy stores, and garden stores (he planted his parents' orchard with discarded fruit trees).

• Madonna, the rock star, was once a Dumpster diver.

• The best time for diving is the early evening, because apartment dwellers put out trash after supper, and businesses put out trash at the end of the business day.

• Dress in nondescript, durable clothing. Wear gloves and thick-soled shoes. If using a car, bring a long stick with a bent nail on the end for poking and prodding. When on foot, Hoffman uses an antenna from a discarded CB radio for a prodding stick. His grandmother uses her cane. Bring a flashlight for night dives and a shoulder bag for finds.

• For sheer fun and variety, residential Dumpsters, such as those serving large apartment complexes, can't be beat. Hoffman also recommends hitting the Dumpsters of college dorms. As he puts it—and this is a sample of his prose style—"Lots of college kids are wasteful little pukoids." The day the dorms must be vacated is best, but fall, spring, and Christmas breaks are also hot.

• Diving success comes in "streaks." When you hit a good Dumpster, go through it thoroughly.

• When you Dumpster dive, you become invisible. People walk past you as though you don't exist. But

if you are approached, Hoffman suggests using the universally accepted excuse: Say you're "looking for boxes." You may actually need to scavenge boxes for the loot you hope to find.

Throughout the book, I appreciated Hoffman's concern for safety. He carefully explains specific techniques to avoid injury from common Dumpster hazards such as broken glass, deranged cats, aerosol can "mines," and Dumpster-lid-slam decapitation. He suggests avoiding actually climbing into Dumpsters.

And I enjoyed his hints on converting trash to cash through yard sales and other outlets. (Basic hint: Never reveal that the item came from a Dumpster. Hoffman supplies several vague, evasive answers you can use regarding the origin of your stuff.)

The book does have a few gaps. Hoffman spends little time discussing the legality of Dumpster diving, except to note that laws vary from city to city and that he's never been arrested.

To find out about laws in our area, I made a few calls to local police stations. The officers knew of no laws in Maine that prohibit Dumpster diving. The only legal problem they could imagine was if the Dumpster was located on private property and the owner complained; then, technically, you'd be trespassing. But even then, the police would merely give you a warning. The police in one town said they knew of several local people who Dumpster-dived regularly; it never occurred to these officers to stop them.

Furthermore, since shop owners pay for disposal, by removing things from Dumpsters you're saving them money. Hoffman routinely leaves a site cleaner than when he found it to avoid any ill feelings.

My personal experience with Dumpster diving had been previously limited to retrieving cardboard boxes. So I decided I needed to make a field trip (all in the name of research, mind you) to verify Hoffman's claims. My business manager, Elaine, and I paired up one evening (we called ourselves The Dumpster Divas) and drove a long distance to a city that shall remain nameless.

Most of the Dumpsters we found were located in the fronts of stores, and lacking Hoffman's bravado, we passed them up. The ones that were secluded contained mainly cardboard.

But just as we were becoming completely discouraged, we hit the mother lode. We found inexpensive toys still in their packaging, a case of dog biscuits, a case of "moist burgers" for dogs, a shrink-wrapped case of bottled juice in which one bottle had been broken, tuna-fish cans minus their labels, and several jars of Classico spaghetti sauce.

There was far more in that Dumpster, and most of it just as good, but as we were sifting and retrieving, a pickup pulled up. We were about to make a quick getaway when we realized that it was another Dumpster diver. We struck up a conversation, compared our loot, and he shared a valuable bit of information: "Never, ever, reveal your sources." Dumpsters divers are quiet about their hobby, not out of shame, but because it would be akin to telling everyone where the good fishing hole is.

As a result of my experience, I would add this to Hoffman's tips:

• If you wait until dusk, you'll feel braver about checking out less-secluded Dumpsters.

• Bring boxes.

• The buddy system is a good idea for women divers.

• Once we saw the actual food in impermeable packaging, we were more receptive to it than we thought we would be. However, we left behind the food in cardboard packaging.

I doubt, despite our success, that I will make Dumpster-diving a regular part of my life, simply because it is such a long drive from our country home to the nearest Dumpster. Hoffman suggests—and I agree—that diving works best when it's incorporated into an urban or suburban lifestyle. He checks his six favorite Dumpsters each day as part of his commute home from work.

If you are willing to sift through Hoffman's offensive language and opinions to glean the finer points of Dumpster diving, you can get his book by sending $12.95 plus $4.00 shipping and handling to:

Loompanics Unlimited
P.O. Box 1197
Port Townsend, WA 98368

With each book order, Loompanics sends a copy of its catalog of offbeat, dishonest, weird, and sometimes useful books.

DARE TO DUMPSTER DIVE UPDATE

My "Dare to Dumpster Dive" article attracted a spirited and generally positive response from readers. A listing of readers' great finds alone would fill a page. Even so, enough concerns were raised that I decided to lift the lid on this subject and rummage around a second time.

If you feel Dumpster diving goes too far, consider this scenario: You take your trash bags to your apartment building's Dumpster. As you make your deposit, you spot a $20 bill within easy reach. Do you take it?

This question illustrates an important point. Dumpster diving encompasses a range of activities. At the most cautious end, you can quickly check the contents of your apartment building's Dumpster whenever you dump your trash, and if you see some item that's right at hand, clean and useful, you snatch it. At the most daring end, you can rummage through dozens of Dumpsters nightly, taking whatever treasures, including food, they hold. And there are infinite gradations between those two.

Dumpster diving isn't a viable option for me because I live in a rural area. If it were, I would not approach it as aggressively as some, but I respect the hard-core divers. By helping to conserve natural resources, as well as tax dol-

lars to pay for landfills, I figure they're doing the rest of us a service.

At the same time, I feel we should respect the views of others who feel diving isn't socially acceptable. Some divers are becoming bolder about rummaging in Dumpsters in daylight or in visible areas. Although I don't feel diving is shameful, we should consider the discomfort other people may feel. Dumpster dive discreetly.

Several readers expressed concern about the legality of Dumpster diving. My original article pointed out that the police departments of several towns in Maine told me that there was no law against it. I've called several more law-enforcement officials since then. These sources confirmed that Dumpster diving is generally considered to be legal, with the following exceptions:

• If the container is on *clearly marked* private land, behind a fence, or locked up. However, most Dumpsters in "semipublic" areas such as parking lots are fair game.

• If the discarded items are outside the Dumpster, they should not be taken.

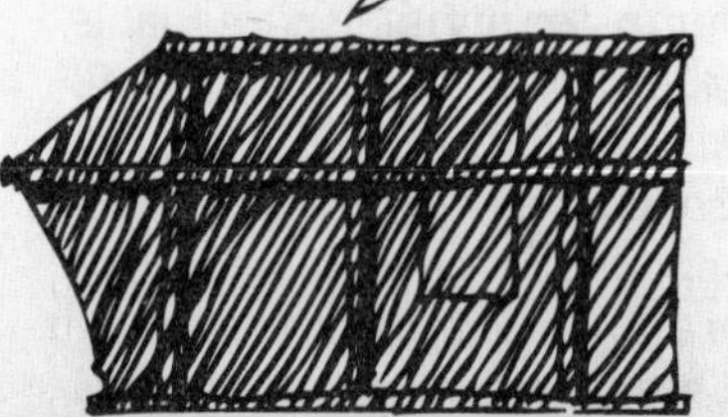

Dear Amy,
Your Dumpster article
changed my life...

• If you make a mess. Leave a Dumpster site cleaner than you found it.

One of the public officials with whom we spoke is Michael Adams, deputy district attorney for California's Santa Clara County. Because, by some estimates, there are hundreds of Dumpster divers mining the rich veins of discards behind the Silicon Valley high-tech firms, Adams has made a careful study of the legality of Dumpster diving.

"People have thrown this stuff away," he said. "The idea that people are stealing is not a prosecutable case." He said that by putting items in a Dumpster, the companies have "abandoned ownership."

Adams doubts that any municipality anywhere in the country could craft a law that specifically banned Dumpster diving under all circumstances. Nevertheless, four readers reported they knew of such towns.

A couple of readers brought up sanitation issues. Yet in some modern landfills, there are people who stand at a conveyor belt picking the recyclables from trash all day. If there really were a serious health risk, it wouldn't be allowed. If, as we did, you wear gloves and wash your finds immediately upon returning home, I feel you face less of a health risk than you would riding a crowded subway car during flu season.

Some readers questioned my confidence in foods with impermeable packaging. To learn more about the safety of packaged food, we called the National Food Processors Association in Washington, D.C., Spokesman Roger Coleman confirmed that although such things as broken glass, mold, and contaminants can collect under the rim of a jar, they can't get through a vacuum seal. He added that a dented or rusty can is safe as long as the can doesn't leak or bulge. As for the possibility that recalled food could end up in a Dumpster, Coleman said that supermarkets are extremely careful to return recalled items to the manufacturer.

Then why do businesses throw away good stuff? Frequently, it's because the labor costs to fix, reuse, or even give it away are too high. One former supermarket employee told me it was illegal for stores to sell canned goods with missing labels. His store tried to give these unlabeled cans to food banks, but none wanted them. It can also be illegal to sell goods with dampened labels (as happens when one jar in a case breaks). To prevent pilferage, many businesses prohibit employees from taking home good but unsaleable items.

There were also suggestions that the act of Dumpster diving itself is unsafe. Safety issues were among the reasons I promoted *The Art and Science of Dumpster Diving;* the book takes pains to discuss how to avoid hazards. I would rate Dumpster diving as less dangerous than using a circular saw. The key is simply to learn safety rules and apply them.

Finally, I'd emphasize that if I published only information that *no one* could find objectionable, this would be a very boring—and short—book. Our foray into Dumpster diving was a reflection of the fact that a wide range of people read my book and newsletter, and I need to provide information to readers who are willing to stretch the boundaries of the frugal life.

GREAT QUOTES

"Much ingenuity with a little money is vastly more profitable and amusing than much money without ingenuity."

—Arnold Bennett

"Those who have little, if they are good at managing, must be counted among the rich."

—Socrates 470–399 B.C.

"Beware of little expenses; a small leak will sink a great ship."

—Benjamin Franklin

WHIP UP A WALKWAY

Dear Amy,

In Seattle, the price for a single, round aggregate stepping stone ranged from $4.59 to $5.99. Since I needed five, I felt this was highway robbery. So I took a large bucket that is slightly wider at the top (5-gallon paint or joint-compound buckets work well). Buy one bag of concrete for $1.69 (total cost of the project). Mix the concrete right in the bucket to a 2-inch level. Let set for a couple of hours, but while still wet, press in aggregate stone if desired, or imprint a design (I used my children's footprints). Mist frequently with a water sprayer to keep the concrete from cracking. After two to three days, turn the stone out gently onto soft ground, so as not to break it.

—Marilee Thompson Duer
Mercer Island, Washington

BASKET CASE

Dear Amy,

When we moved from Massachusetts to Pennsylvania, we needed to bring our cats with us. Large plastic cat carriers in pet stores cost $40 to $60. They're nice, but seemed like a lot of money, especially if you need two.

I made a carrier of similar size by buying two large plastic laundry baskets. I flipped one basket over the other and used two bolts to fasten them together in the back. Then I tied them together securely in the front. The baskets could be separated and used for laundry after you reach your destination.

—James DeHulu
Edgewood, Pennsylvania

SEE SPOT GO

Dear Amy,

There is an easy way to remove stains off of white or lightly colored parts of a garment, where stains are always prominent. I've had great success renovating hand-me-downs and yard-sale finds for my toddler. It works great on garments that have bright patterns that would fade if I soaked or bleached the whole thing. Pour a little liquid bleach into the bottle's cap. With a Q-tip or paintbrush, dab a bit of the bleach on the soiled area. Within a minute, most stains are gone. Wash as usual. Use more bleach and leave on longer for stubborn stains.

—Rachelle Purcell
Peru, Indiana

(Based on my own tests and advice from experienced launderers, I would add that 1) be sure to rinse the bleach out immediately after the stain disappears, or holes can develop after a few washings, and 2) straight bleach can remove color from some fabrics. So reserve this tip for otherwise hopeless stains. FZ)

DISPOSAL AND PROPOSAL

Dear Amy,

What attracted my now-husband to me, and me to him, was that we always made use of what we had, or what was readily available. His first encounter with me and my junk picking was my ceiling fan, which he and I installed in my bedroom. When he asked where I bought it, I honestly told him that I found it down in the alley on garbage day. He then proposed.

—Jamie Bunch Elliott
Brinnon, Washington

I DREAM OF JEAN-KNEE

Dear Amy,

When I want a little more use out of old work jeans, instead of having to rip open and sew up seams, I just get my glue gun out and glue the patch on. My hus-

band is a welder, and his overalls are expensive.

—Penny Oberlander
Eagle Point, Oregon

HOLE-ISTIC REMEDY

Dear Amy,

I think I have discovered the ultimate in shower curtain solutions! I had one that lasted 17 years, and I finally got rid of it because it was so totally out of style. I don't repair; I prevent damage. When a shower curtain is new, I sew a strip of appropriate-colored heavy cotton duck cloth over the top 1½ inches of the curtain (folding the cloth over both sides of the curtain) and make buttonholes at the hanger holes. I have never had a hole tear. I am the mother of seven children, so this has been tested.

—Lynn Davis
Escondido, California

NO-MEAT FEAT

Dear Amy,

Here is a recipe you might enjoy. Even my husband, a diehard meat eater, asks for more:

LENTIL-RICE CASSEROLE

3 cups chicken broth, or use water and 1 tablespoon vegetable seasoning
¾ cup lentils, uncooked
½ cup brown rice, uncooked
¾ cup chopped fresh onion
½ teaspoon sweet basil
¼ teaspoon oregano
¼ teaspoon thyme
¼ teaspoon garlic powder

Blend all together in a casserole dish. Bake, covered, for 1½ hours at 300 degrees. During the last 20 minutes, you may top with ½ cup grated cheddar cheese, if desired.

—Christina Parli
Springfield, Ohio

(We tried this recipe, and Jim rated it a "9" on the 1-to-10 lentil scale. Because of the lengthy cooking time, plan to bake other items at the same time or use your solar cooker or crockpot. FZ)

BEATS A DEAD MOUSE

Dear Amy,

My brother and I have the perfect cheap—oops, I mean thrifty—cat toy. Place any object that will rattle (paper clip, pen top, etc.) into an empty 35-millimeter film canister. My cat Martha loves hers, although several have mysteriously disappeared beneath the entertainment center.

—Michelle Stanton
Medina, New York

CHEAT SHEETS

Dear Amy,

When it's time to change the sheets on the beds, if I changed them the week before, I just turn them around so the unused end is now at the top of the bed. It works well on the beds of children who aren't tall enough to touch the bottom portion of the sheets.

—Shelbey Dutter
Kalispell, Montana

THE CHILI CHART

It's always interesting to examine how widely the costs can vary when you purchase or prepare a particular dish in different ways—in this case, chili. Whenever I do one of these charts, I'm reminded of how there can be such a huge difference in the food bills of two families who eat almost identical meals.

Using the same basic recipe, we costed out several versions. We calculated it using the most expensive ingredients we could find at the supermarket, including canned kidney beans. We also used the cheapest store-bought ingredients, and substituted 2½ cups of cooked dry kidney beans for the 40 ounces of canned beans. We substituted rehydrated TVP (see page 133) for the hamburger. We calculated another version made with TVP and homegrown ingredients (peppers, onions, tomatoes, and dried beans).

Here's the recipe we used:

HOMEMADE CHILI

1 tablespoon oil
1 cup chopped onions
1 cup chopped green pepper
1 pound hamburger
1 40-ounce can kidney beans
1 28-ounce can tomatoes
1 6-ounce can tomato paste
1 tablespoon chili powder

Heat oil in a large skillet. Brown onions and peppers. Add hamburger and brown well. Add beans, tomatoes, tomato paste, and chili powder. Add ¾ cup water and simmer, covered, for one hour.

Some observations:

• If you spend an hour making 12 cups of homemade, dry-bean, hamburger chili and packaging it in meal-size freezer containers, versus buying microwaveable chili, even if you factor in energy usage, you will earn $10 per hour, tax-free, for your time.

• Hormel's microwave chili in individual-serving containers is so expensive that it's cheaper to buy chili from Wendy's.

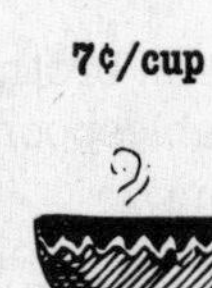

• Making homemade chili from the most expensive store-bought ingredients is more expensive than buying canned chili.

• It's worth your time to cook up dried beans. A store-brand, 40-ounce can of cooked kidney beans costs $1.15. The same amount of beans cooked up from dry costs 25¢, based on 42¢-per-pound beans at a wholesale club. It takes about 5 minutes of hands-on time and 30 minutes of cooking to prepare beans in a pressure cooker.

• Having a garden is not essential to making huge savings on your food bill. Compared to microwave chili, you save 87¢ per cup by making scratch chili with the cheapest store-bought ingredients. You save only 13¢ more per cup by using homegrown ingredients.

• If you use a coupon to buy store-bought chili, the final cost should be less than 3¢ per ounce, as compared to hamburger chili made with dried beans, and less than 1¢ per ounce as compared to hamburger chili with homegrown ingredients.

"ARE BREAD MACHINES A GOOD VALUE?"

This question was posed by reader Heidee Lindsey of Fremont, California, and it's a good one to explore. My mail tells me that many beginning tightwads are buying or considering the purchase of these gadgets, propelled by a vague notion that "it will pay for itself."

People think this because they know homemade bread is cheaper, but they think the traditional, hand-kneaded bread is too time-consuming to be worthwhile. Because it takes five minutes to make bread using a bread machine, people presume it's a money-saving device.

To research this question, my crack investigative staff mooched machines from acquaintances, girlfriends, and brothers-in-law (you didn't think we'd *buy* one, did you?) and put them through a grueling series of trials. Bread machines cost between $99 and $199. *Consumer Reports* recommends the Sanyo Home Bakery, which costs $140, so we used that cost as the basis for payback calculations.

Before we go any further, let's talk about the positive aspects of bread machines:

• You make one loaf at a time, so you can have freshly baked bread every day.

• Bread machines make bread that tastes better than store-bought—although our staff unanimously agreed that this bread is not as good as traditional homemade bread.

• Bread machines require no exertion, which is important if you have physical limitations.

• You don't have to be home while your bread is baking; you can put in the ingredients, set the timer, and the machine will mix, knead, and bake, and shut off automatically.

In short, if you demand fresh, homemade bread every day, and cannot or won't make it yourself, a machine could be a worthwhile luxury.

But if you're buying a bread machine to save time or money, think again. Our calculations show

it's doubtful a bread machine will accomplish either of these goals.

THE MACHINE VERSUS TRADITIONAL HOME-BAKING METHODS

Let's look first at time savings. It takes five minutes to load ingredients into a bread machine and push the appropriate buttons to make a single loaf.

In contrast, when using the hand-knead method, you can bake four loaves at a time. Although you must be around for a few hours as the bread rises and bakes, the actual amount of hands-on time required, based on our careful timing of three cooks of average ability, is 25 minutes for four loaves, or 6 minutes, fifteen seconds per loaf.

However, a bread bucket, which features a hand-cranked dough hook, will save some time. We

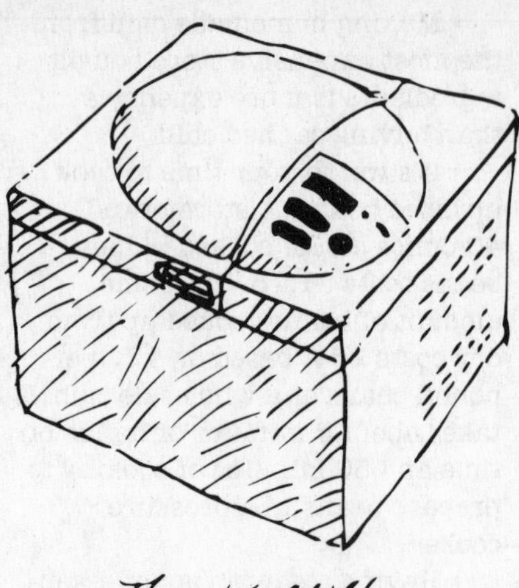

The Welbilt Bread Machine

timed three breadmakers using a bucket. Each was able to make four loaves with 20 minutes hands-on time—or the same 5 minutes per loaf required by bread machines.

Although it does take some muscle, one bread-bucket user I know is in her fifties, another is under 5 feet tall, and they have no trouble. (Think of it as a tightwad exercise machine: If you have a hard time doing this, you *need* the exercise.) Because these buckets last for decades, you should be able to dig up a used one. Of the five bucket users I know, four procured theirs secondhand. The average yard-sale price is about $3. New buckets cost from $20 to $45.

Aside from time saving,

the bucket method is neater than hand kneading.

You can make bread in a food processor, one loaf at a time, and this would take five minutes per loaf. Or you can buy frozen dough, which requires one minute per loaf of hands-on time.

So, if you have a freezer to store extra loaves and have reasonable physical capabilities, a bread machine doesn't save time.

Does it save money? The same ingredients are used however you make bread, so the only possible savings would be in energy usage.

Including preheating, an oven will run for an hour to bake four loaves of bread. At 8¢ per kilowatt-hour, it costs 16¢ to run an oven at 350 degrees for one hour, or 4¢ per loaf.

Finding out how much energy bread machines use proved to be extremely difficult. The machines come with wattage information, but they run intermittently during the cycle. We called all of the manufacturers, and none would tell us the cost of running their machines. We called Underwriter's Laboratories, which among other things, tests products for energy usage. The UL representative was not allowed to give us this information and suggested we call the manufacturers. Finally, one of my staffers ran the machine, carefully noting every time the machine went on and off during the cycle, and computed the energy usage as about 3¢ per cycle. This figure is the same as I have read in other sources.

So using a bread machine may save you 1¢ per loaf over other methods of home baking. If you have a gas oven, it won't save anything.

THE MACHINE VERSUS THE STORE

Let's suppose you'll make bread only if you have a bread machine. Compared to store-bought bread, will a machine pay for itself?

Most store-bought bread weighs 19 to 22 ounces. Frozen dough makes 14-ounce loaves. Bread machines vary in the size loaf they make. Most bread recipes make two 1½-pound loaves. Because of this variation, we calculated the figures based on an "ideal" loaf of 1½ pounds and added in energy cost where applicable. The homemade and bread-machine prices are based on

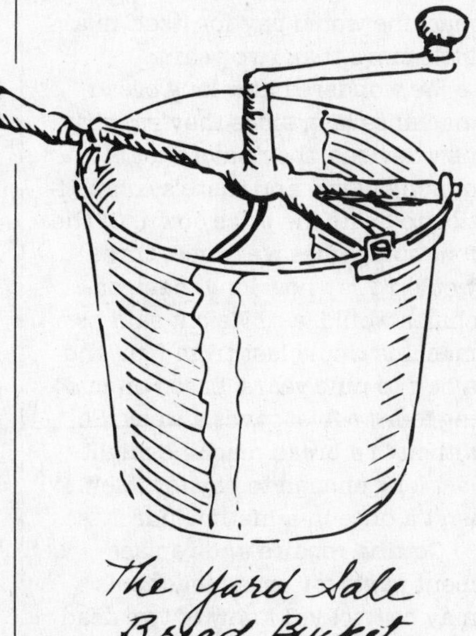

sale-priced ingredients. We used bulk yeast from a health-food store, which costs $2.00 per pound. If you use those little packets of yeast, figure another 15¢ per loaf. All the prices are for a whole-wheat loaf, which contains two thirds white flour and one third whole-wheat flour.

Supermarket	$1.49
Wholesale club	$1.46
Frozen dough	$ .68
Thrift store	$ .57
Homemade	$ .27
Bread machine	$ .26

Bakery thrift shops are common throughout the country. Without making a special trip, or perhaps by cooperating with friends, most people can buy day-old bread and keep it in their freezer.

So if a bread-machine loaf saves you 31¢ over a thrift-shop loaf, you would have to bake 451 loaves to pay back the cost of the machine. At four loaves a week, the machine would pay for itself in a little more than two years.

We wondered how long bread machines last, since they're fairly new devices, they have a lot of moving parts, and there's competition to bring the price down. Of the four companies we called, three wouldn't say how long their machines would last. Welbilt said its machine would last from four and a half to nine years, based on making four or five loaves a week. So although a bread machine might last long enough to pay for itself, it isn't a once-in-a-lifetime purchase.

Getting repairs and replacement parts for bread machines may be tricky; I know of two dead machines. In one case, the needed replacement part is no longer available. A second machine lies dormant because the owner decided the cost of getting his repaired was too high.

A further disadvantage of the bread machine is that it eats up a square foot of precious counter space. In contrast, a bread bucket stores easily in a cupboard.

IN CONCLUSION

As long as you have no physical limitations, a bread machine isn't a true time- or money-saver. Those people who want homemade bread should use traditional methods. With a little planning, traditional bread-making can fit into a busy life as easily as the bread-machine method.

Finally, making bread by any method is not essential to the tightwad lifestyle. Our bakery thrift shop is conveniently located near our printer, and we buy 15 loaves at a time. If we made bread, we would spend five minutes to save 30¢, which is like earning $3.60 per hour. In addition, our family consumes homemade bread at a significantly faster rate than storebought—11 loaves versus 7 loaves a week—so it's hard to keep up. We make bread when we can, but when life gets hectic, it's among the money-saving activities we skip.

By the way, for those really lazy folks out there, you can now buy gourmet bread-machine mixes. A mix that makes one 1½-pound loaf costs between $3.50 and $4.95.

WOODEN REINCARNATIONS

Wood is great stuff. Compared to concrete, metal, and glass, it is easy to reuse. Somehow, it's deeply fulfilling to disassemble some hideous and/or no-longer-needed wooden item and create just the thing you need.

Sources are everywhere. Frequently people discard or give

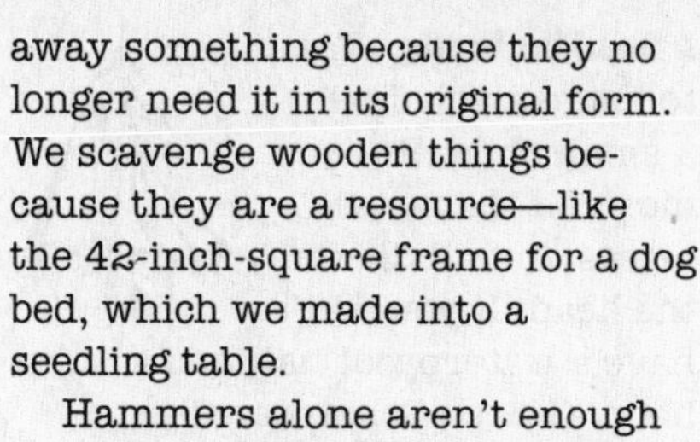

away something because they no longer need it in its original form. We scavenge wooden things because they are a resource—like the 42-inch-square frame for a dog bed, which we made into a seedling table.

Hammers alone aren't enough for most disassembly operations. But if you get a flatbar . . .

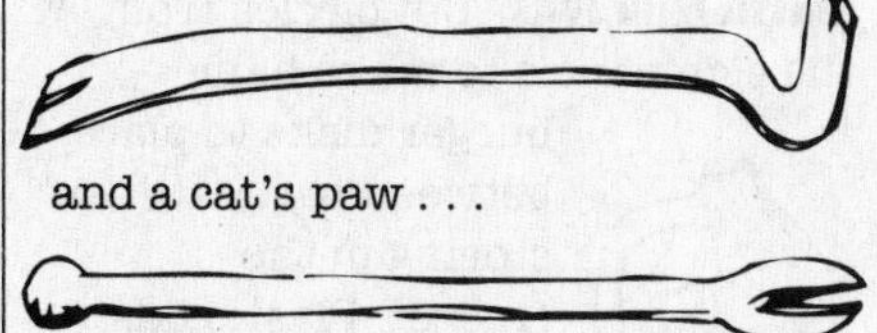

and a cat's paw . . .

you can take apart nearly anything. Wood is like wrapping paper: It gets smaller with each incarnation.

The examples on this page are taken from real life.

dog bed
seedling table
poorly-constructed paint-stained work bench
workshop storage with paint stains cleverly hidden on underside of shelves

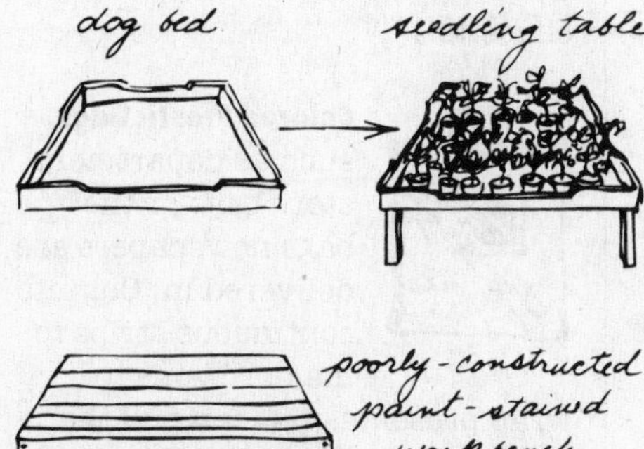

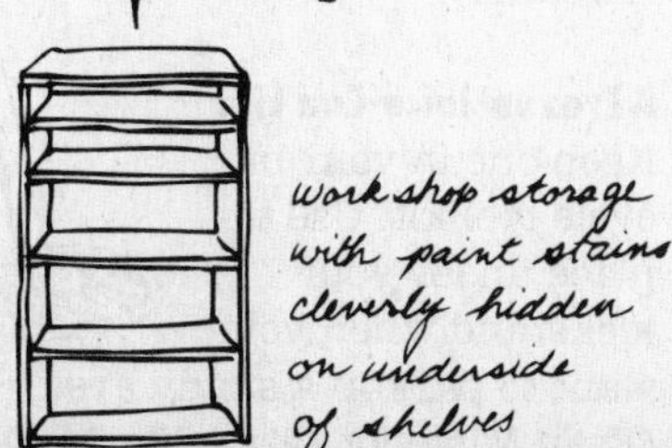

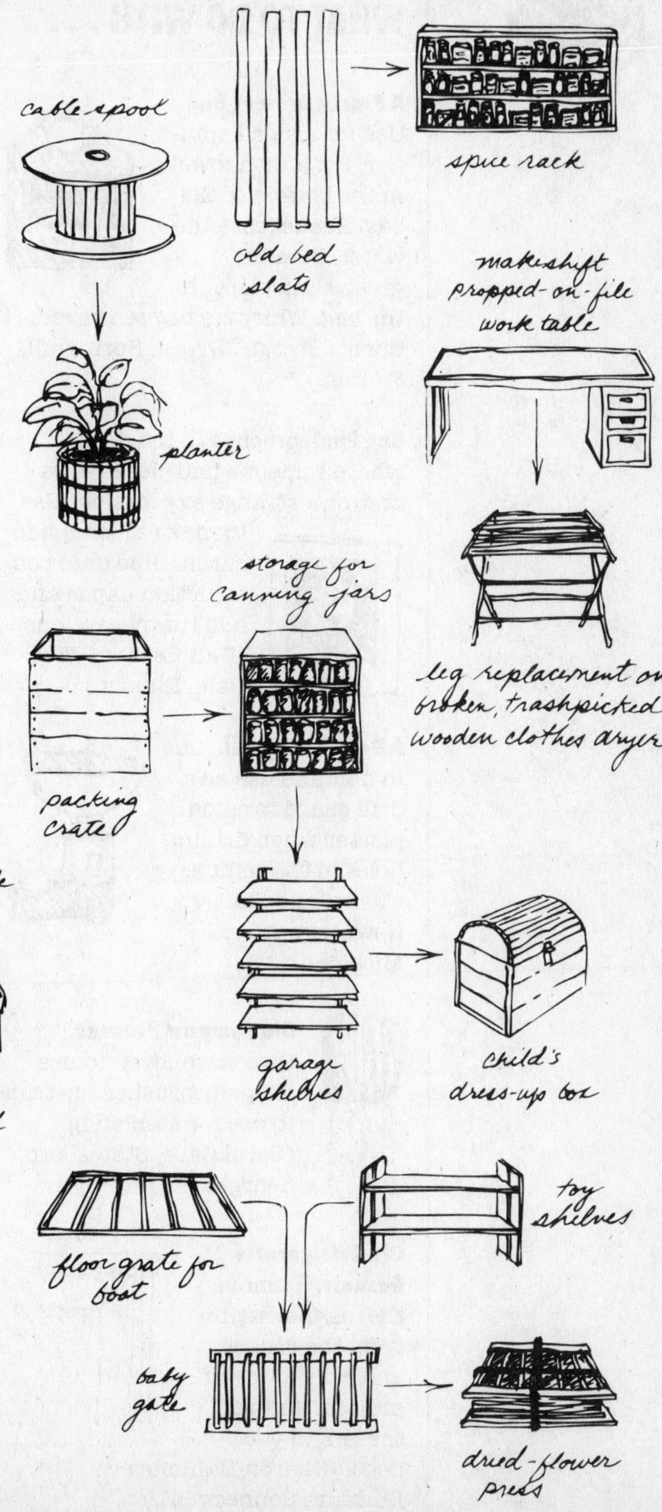

cable spool
planter
old bed slats
spice rack
makeshift propped-on-file work table
leg replacement on broken, trashpicked, wooden clothes dryer
packing crate
storage for canning jars
garage shelves
child's dress-ups box
floor grate for boat
toy shelves
baby gate
dried-flower press

WHAT TO DO WITH . . .

A Plastic Grocery Bag. Use for a salad spinner. Put a dish towel in the bottom of the bag. Shake loose the water from the greens and place in the bag. Whirl the bag ten revolutions. (George Silvera, Springhill, Florida.)

Bad Photographs . . . the ones where someone had closed eyes and/or a strange expression. Use to make all-occasion cards. Glue onto construction paper and add funny captions. (Gail Bedard, Wood Dale, Illinois.)

A Dead Volleyball. Cut in half and use as a drill guard to catch plaster when drilling holes in the ceiling. (Maxel and Stacey Newberry, Ithaca, Michigan.)

Old Compact Brushes. Give to children to use for paintbrushes, or trim to use for stenciling. (Carol Case, Statesboro, Georgia.)

Old Refrigerator Gaskets. Remove the magnet strip from the gasket, and save for craft projects. Snip off the length you need. (Sharon Dahlmeyer, Durham, Connecticut.)

A Dead Umbrella. Use to make a poncho for a small child. Remove all the metal pieces. Cut a hole for the head. If you don't have a waterproof hat, add a hood. (Karen Schneider-Chen, Seattle, Washington.)

Plastic Milk Jugs. Cut circles from the side panels to make hamburger disks to place between patties when storing in the freezer. Plastic lids also work. (Ginger Player, Williston, Vermont.)

Old Inner Tubes from bike tires. Use to make rubber stamps. Slit up the middle and lay flat. Draw and cut out simple designs. Glue pieces onto wooden blocks. (Denise Augusto, Shelburne Falls, Massachusetts.)

Colored Plastic Bags, such as department-store bags or the bags newspapers are delivered in. Cut into continuous strips to make ribbons to wrap presents. You can pull the edges to create a ruffled effect. (Norma Kelly, Huntsville, Alabama.)

A Frozen-Juice-Can Lid. Keep one in your bicycle tool kit. Use to place under your kickstand when you want to park in a sandy area. (Fran Misterly, Citra, Florida.)

IF YOU DREAD IT, SHRED IT

Around August each year, your garden begins to crank out more zucchinis than you can eat, and friends stop answering the door when they see you staggering up the walkway with a double armload. Eventually, as you fall further behind in production, the zucchinis grow to baseball-bat proportions, with tough skins and huge seeds. The dilemma is worsened because your garden is producing so much *other* fresh produce that you can barely keep up with the hoeing and canning.

I handle this problem by waiting until I have a pile of these overgrown zucchinis. I get out my food processor and start slicing, shredding, and filling Ziploc bags. These bags go into the freezer to be saved for baking during the more tranquil winter months.

When shredded zucchini thaws, it is very watery. If the recipe calls for milk, I frequently combine this juice with dry milk powder and use it for the milk in the recipe.

Shredded zucchini (as well as shredded yellow summer squash) gives a wide variety of baked goods more moisture, fiber, and nutrition. I use it in muffins (zucchini-pineapple or zucchini-raisin), brownies, pancakes, and quick breads. Shredded zucchini is interchangeable with common baking ingredients like pumpkin purée, applesauce, mashed bananas, or shredded carrots. Because zucchini has little flavor, I usually add spices like cinnamon, nutmeg, and dried orange peel, or combine it with a more flavorful fruit or vegetable. A recent experiment, a zucchini-blackberry crisp, was extremely successful.

WALLPAPER SOLUTION

Personally, I like white walls. They are classic, go with everything, and paint stores don't have to custom-mix the color.

But some people love the look of wallpaper. For them, here's an idea from reader Sara Brown of Longview, Washington. She makes incredibly cheap wallpaper that isn't wallpaper at all.

For a floral effect, paint a wall a base color in latex paint. Then take about 1 cup of that base color and add a small amount of another color—for example, add a little white to a blue base color to make a light blue. Add water to thin down the light blue. Then wet the feathers of a cheap feather duster, shake it out, and dip it in the tinted color. Practice on some cardboard first, then touch the wall in a random pattern (not rows) to make a floral pattern.

You can mix in other colors. As long as you begin by mixing with the base colors, they will go together. Other objects can be used as "daubers" to create different effects: crumpled newspapers, sponges, bristle brushes, and

broom ends. For kids' rooms, use handprints, or cut sponges into shapes and "rubber-stamp" the walls.

Sara's technique has clear financial advantages. Wallpapering a 12-foot-by-15-foot room costs about $18 for the sizing (stuff that's painted on to make the walls receptive to the paper) and $107 (at discount prices) for the required six double rolls of wallpaper, for a total of $125. In contrast, primer and top-quality paint to do the same-size room, including enough extra paint for this wallpaper-look technique, at a cost of less than $35.

A further advantage is that Sara's technique can be done solo by anyone who can wield a paintbrush. A quality wallpapering job is extremely fussy. A friend told me he and his wife nearly got divorced after they attempted to paper a bathroom and argued about the acceptable tolerances for error. If one factors in the savings in avoiding divorce proceedings, this technique could be worth thousands of dollars.

A DEAL TO DYE FOR

Dear Amy,

Here's a "tightwad" way of getting the most out of prescription glasses.

I have to wear mine all the time, and sometimes I just *want* new frames. When this happens, I take my old glasses to the optical shop and ask them to dye the glass dark so I can wear them for sunglasses. It costs about $10.

—Paulette Fordan
Ellensburg, Washington

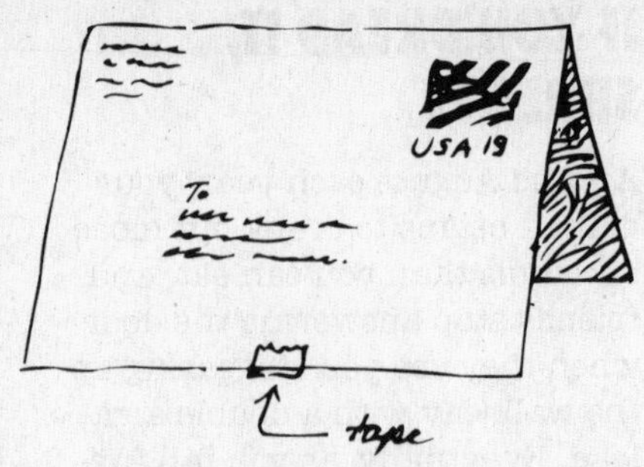

RETURN TO SPENDER

Dear Amy,

I used to send stamped, self-addressed envelopes (5¢? plus 29¢) when I requested responses. That meant sending a letter, too (4¢?), in an envelope (5¢? plus 29¢). Double postcards (sold by the post office) cost 38¢, a savings of 34¢ round trip, not to mention the amount of paper saved. You can make your own double postcards too, out of card stock and two 19¢ stamps.

—Malcolm Wells
Brewster, Massachusetts

(Double postcards look like two regular post office postcards that are attached at the top. To reuse, the recipient simply tears off the used side or flips the used side from the outside to the inside. FZ)

TAP TIP

Dear Amy,

I was medically advised to drink lots of water but grew weary of the chlorine taste from our tap water. I bought bottled water and investigated water filters.

Then I remembered what I read in an aquarium guidebook. I filled two jugs with tap water and didn't

cork them. The chlorine evaporates out, and after two days I had tasty water. This method has served us well for two years now.

—Edgar and Denise Isaacs
Pittsville, Maryland

A FRUGAL LESS-ON

Dear Amy,

I find frugal ideas pop up in the strangest places. For instance, I was in the park, walking the dog, when I spotted a tiny yellow scrap of paper saying "Less is more." I took the paper home and propped it in the kitchen alcove, and the cogs in my brain started whirring. This is what I came up with:

LESS junk food, MORE nutrients.
LESS car trips, MORE exercise.
LESS sweets, MORE weight loss.
LESS possessions, MORE space.
LESS self-pity, MORE happiness.
LESS presents, MORE appreciation.
LESS waste, MORE conservation.
LESS TV, MORE conversation.

I have since learned that the "Less is more" card comes from a packet of low-tar cigarettes. Less tar is more flavor. So the mystery of the inspiring card is solved.

—Mrs. M. Lockyer
Camberley, Surry, England

NO COVER CHARGE

Dear Amy,

My sister made seat covers for her Volkswagen bug from old Levis that she bought at the thrift store. These wear like iron and haven't been replaced in ten years. With a little creativity she added pockets for sunglasses, etc.

—Erin Quinn
Las Vegas, Nevada

NO-TOIL OIL

Dear Amy,

Most of us pitch the plastic bottle after putting oil in our car, but did you ever think about the oil left over in the bottle or can?

I saved 45 oil bottles until I made a "dripper." Out of 45 bottles, I got ¾ of a quart. Based on this I calculate 60 containers would give you a quart.

That's a lot of oil when you consider it frequently ends up in the water table.

Here's how to make a dripper: Drill one ⅝ inch hole in a garage stud on an angle. Drill four or five one inch holes in a 1½ inch pipe. Place the pipe in the stud with the holes up, and put a screw through the stud until it snugs the pipe. You're all set.

—John T. Cant
Blauvelt, New York

SAVINGS ON DISPLAY

Dear Amy,

Many stores, especially pharmacies, get many product displays every year, only to throw away later. I have a Dr. Scholl's rack for my LP's. A four-foot-tall Scotch tape rack is now an office basket. A brass and wood display holds my houseplants. I am hoping to bring home a bamboo-looking Hawaiian Tropic suntan lotion display to use for kids' books, stuffed animals, or an open dresser.

—Venus Weir
Albuquerque, New Mexico

PITCH AND SWITCH

Dear Amy,

We needed a picture framed. To get it matted and framed at a local framing store would have cost nearly $100. One day I was in a discount department store and they were selling matted/framed posters for $15.99. This was exactly the size I needed for my picture, so I swapped the poster for my picture and got exactly what I wanted for $15.99.

—Ruth Campbell
Rockaway, New Jersey

PINCH SITTER

Dear Amy,

A few years ago I joined a baby-sitting co-op. Participating parents were initially given 30 coupons (printed by one of our members). A coupon was worth one hour of child care, and this was how we paid each other. We used the co-op to grocery shop, clean house, or have an evening out. Members were free to specify if they wanted to baby-sit during the daytime, evening, or weekends. One could always say "no" on an occasion that wasn't convenient. Our once-in-a-while meeting allowed us to meet new neighbors and keep up with how many coupons members had accumulated.

—Patty Kimmel
Clarksville, Tennessee

CHEAP AND DIRTY

Dear Amy,

I needed some dirt to fill a hole in my yard. I thought: Where can I find some free? Who takes out dirt and can't put it back? Of course, the cemetery. They were glad to let me have all I wanted—free!

—Bill French
Muscatine, Iowa

YOU DON'T HAVE TO BE A SOCKET SCIENTIST

GreenPlug sounds too good to be true. Plug this gadget, which is about the size of a pack of cards, into your wall socket. Then plug an appliance into it, and bingo: Your appliance works as well as it ever did, but it uses less power. As a bonus, says the company's literature, your appliance will last longer.

I was skeptical—at $35 (the local hardware store's price), would it pay for itself?

I'm no socket scientist, so we called Bill Howe. He is a re-

searcher at E-Source, an independent energy-efficiency information service in Boulder, Colorado. Howe has done extensive tests on GreenPlug, and was generally positive about it. "It is a viable approach," he said.

GreenPlug saves energy two ways. First, if you receive high voltage in your home, GreenPlug reduces it to the minimum needed to run your appliance. Second, GreenPlug varies the amount of power it sends to your appliance's motor, depending on the load the motor is handling.

Howe says the payback time on a GreenPlug varies from 1 to 12 or more years. You're most likely to have a short payback time if all of the following apply to you:

1. You have high voltage. The voltage delivered to homes varies around the country from about 104 to over 130 volts. GreenPlug drops this to 106 volts, which is sufficient for all appliances.

Your utility company can give a ballpark estimate of your voltage. Or you can use a voltmeter (all electronics-repair people have them). If you live in a rural area, it's likely that you have high voltage, because utilities boost the power to send it down long, rural lines.

We interviewed several experts to determine whether running a refrigerator at 106 volts would prematurely wear out the motor. Opinion varied. A couple thought it might, most did not know, and several said it would be extremely unlikely.

2. Your utility rates are high. The national average is 8¢ per kilowatt-hour.

3. You use it on a constantly running, energy-*in*efficient appliance. Generally, 1978 to 1985 refrigerators are the best bet. If yours is older, you will probably do better in the long run if you buy a new one.

One of the worst criticisms leveled at GreenPlug came in a November 1993 *Consumer Reports* article, which asserted that in some cases GreenPlug could make your refrigerator use *more* energy. But in my conversations with the makers of GreenPlug and with representatives of several utilities that had tested it, I learned that the device tends to make a refrigerator run a bit colder, and you don't realize energy savings unless you adjust the thermostat to bring the refrigerator back to its original temperature. I called *CR*'s researcher, Ed Growth, and learned that *CR* had not adjusted the thermostat, which makes its conclusions suspect.

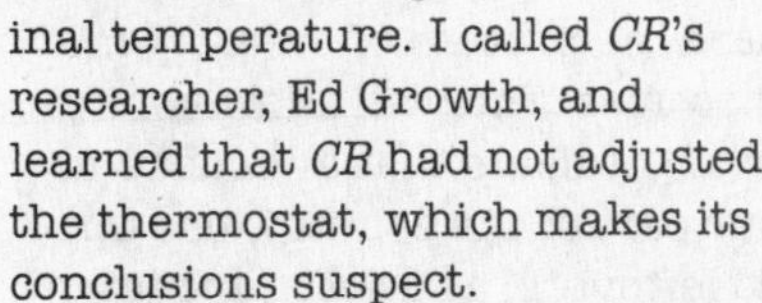

The maker claims that GreenPlug will help many motors run cooler and thus prolong an appliance's life. Though Howe hasn't done long-term testing, he believes that claim could well be true.

Using his voltmeter, my handyman husband, Jim, determined that our household receives 121 volts. That, plus the facts that we pay 12¢ per kilowatt-hour and have a 1982 refrigerator, has persuaded us to get one of these devices.

CREATE A BREAKFAST MUFFIN

As you read *The Tightwad Gazette*, you may notice that I don't print many recipes. Running recipes would be the easy (that is, lazy) way to fill the book, but blindly following recipes won't help you save the maximum amount on your food bill. Over the years, I have collected and created recipes that use foods that are cheapest to me, but you can't count on my pumpkin-blueberry muffin recipe to be a money-saver in Tucson, Arizona.

So instead of sharing a single muffin recipe, I wanted to share the process of *creating* muffin recipes. This will allow you to use ingredients that are cheap in your part of the country, use up odd leftovers, and accommodate dietary restrictions.

So I made a big chart to compare the various components in 30 muffin recipes. Although no two are the same, the recipes all combine a grain, milk or juice, egg, a fat, a sweetener, baking powder, and salt. These basic ingredients are often combined with spices, fruits, vegetables, and/or nuts.

I studied these elements, came up with a formula, and made numerous batches over a period of weeks to make sure it worked. Now I've memorized the formula. I no longer need to refer to a recipe to make any kind of muffins, which saves me time.

The quantities listed are for a single batch of 12 muffins. To save energy and time, I always make a double batch. If your oven is large enough to allow ample air circulation, the tins can be placed side by side. If you have a small oven, place tins one over the other, and swap positions after ten minutes of baking.

To make muffins, combine dry ingredients, and then mix in wet ingredients until just combined; the batter should be lumpy. Grease muffin tin and fill cups two thirds full. Bake in a preheated oven at 400 degrees for 20 minutes (give or take 5 minutes).

The following ingredients are required:

Grain: Use 2 to 2½ cups of white flour. Or substitute oatmeal, cornmeal, whole-wheat flour, rye flour, or flake cereal for 1 cup of the white flour. Or substitute 1 cup leftover cooked oatmeal, rice, or cornmeal for ½ cup of the white flour and decrease liquid to ½ cup.

Milk: Use 1 cup. Or substitute buttermilk or sour milk (add a tablespoon of vinegar to 1 cup milk). Or substitute fruit juice for part or all of the milk.

Fat: Use ¼ cup vegetable oil or 4 tablespoons melted butter or margarine. Or substitute crunchy or regular peanut butter for part or all of the fat. The fat can be reduced or omitted with fair results if using a "wet addition."

Egg: Use 1 egg. Or substitute 1 heaping tablespoon of soy flour and 1 tablespoon of water. If using a cooked grain, separate the egg, add the yolk to the batter, beat the white until stiff, and fold into the batter.

Sweetener: Use between 2 tablespoons and ½ cup sugar. Or substitute up to ¾ cup brown sugar. Or substitute up to ½ cup honey or molasses, and decrease milk to ¾ cup.

Baking Powder: Use 2 teaspoons. If using whole or cooked grains or more than 1 cup of additions, increase to 3 teaspoons. If using buttermilk or sour milk, decrease to 1 teaspoon and add ½ teaspoon baking soda.

Salt. Use ½ teaspoon, or omit if you have a salt-restricted diet.

The following ingredients are optional. Additions can be used in any combination, up to 1½ cups total. If using more than 1 cup of wet additions, decrease the milk to ½ cup:

Dry Additions: Nuts, sunflower seeds, raisins, coconut, and so on.

Moist Additions: Blueberries, chopped apple, freshly shredded zucchini, shredded carrot, and so on.

Wet Additions: Pumpkin purée; applesauce; mashed, cooked sweet potato; mashed banana; mashed, cooked carrot, and so on. If using ½ cup drained, canned fruit or thawed shredded zucchini, substitute the syrup or zucchini liquid for all or part of the milk.

Spices: Use spices that complement the additions, such as 1 teaspoon cinnamon with ¼ teaspoon nutmeg or cloves. Try 2 teaspoons grated orange or lemon peel.

Jellies and Jam. Fill cups half full with a plain batter. Add 1 teaspoon jam or jelly and top with 2 more tablespoons batter.

Topping: Sprinkle cinnamon sugar on the batter in the tins.

Nonsweet Combinations: Use only 2 tablespoons sugar and no fruit. Add combinations of the following: ½ cup shredded cheese, 3 strips fried-and-crumbled bacon, 2 tablespoons grated onion, ½ cup shredded zucchini, 2 tablespoons Parmesan cheese. Spices could in-

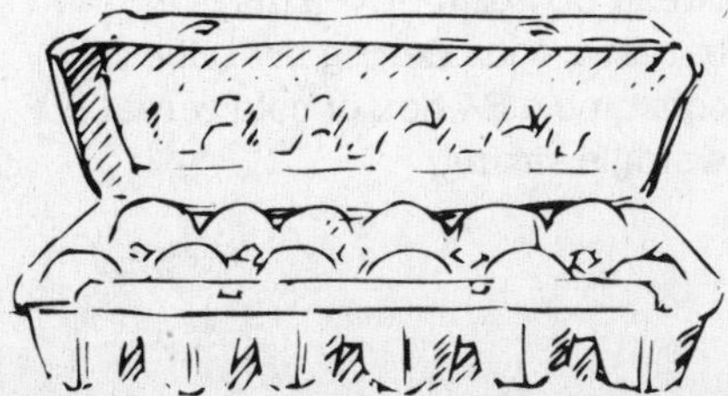

clude a teaspoon of parsley and a pinch of marjoram.

All this may seem a bit complicated to follow first thing in the morning. So, once you learn the possible variations, copy the following list of ingredients into your personal cookbook.

2 to 2½ cups grain
1 cup milk
Up to ¼ cup fat
1 egg
Up to ½ cup sweetener
2 teaspoons baking powder
½ teaspoon salt
Up to 1½ cups additions

Even including the "brain work" of creating a new recipe, I can get muffins in the oven in 20 minutes, and I take my shower while they're baking.

Muffins are a mainstay in our household; we eat them about twice a week. If made with nutritious ingredients and served with juice or milk, they make a hearty breakfast. Leftover muffins become snacks or are hoarded for future lunch boxes. Those who don't have six children can freeze the extra muffins for future breakfasts.

Though the cost varies depending upon the ingredients, I can make muffins for an average of about 4¢ each, including the cost of electricity to bake them. A breakfast of muffins costs our family between 50¢ and 60¢. This is a bargain, considering my tribe can consume a $4 box of cold cereal in a single sitting.

SAWDUST MEMORIES

Dear Amy,

Our neighbor had hired the tree company to cut down and mulch some trees. My husband asked the workers if they needed a place to dump the mulch (which they often do to go empty to the next job). They said, "Yes," and he had it dumped in our yard. We had enough to mulch our entire long driveway, and then some!

—Mimi Bock
West Palm Beach, Florida

PICKUP TRICK

Dear Amy,

We live in a rural area, but our nearest neighbors are only about a mile away. We discovered that we each had only about one barrel of trash per week, so we decided to share a trash pick-up service, which is the same for two to three barrels. We take our barrels to their driveway, and both barrels are emptied there. This saves us $6 per month.

—Greta Goforth
Loveland, Colorado

(To be completely ethical, I would check with the trash hauler to make sure this is okay. FZ)

ROLL REVERSAL

Dear Amy,

To use toilet paper for facial tissue, wrap the outside of the roll with wide tape and pull out the cardboard tube. Pull the tissue from the inside. I then put the roll

inside a square, pop-up Kleenex box with the bottom cut out. Then pull the toilet paper through the slot. The box makes it look nicer than having a roll of toilet paper on the nightstand.

With toilet paper, you can take the exact amount you need: one, two, or more squares.

—Leanna Hawley
Hales Corners, Wisconsin

THE GREAT LATE RATE

Dear Amy,

When going to the ballet, play, or symphony, buy "rush" tickets. These tickets are usually sold 15 minutes before the performance. In Atlanta, rush tickets are $5 for the ballet and $12 for the symphony. Normally, these tickets sell for $37.

—Walter Dowis
Atlanta, Georgia

CHEAPER BY THE DOZER

Dear Amy,

Construction yards, brick companies, and lumber mills often have back areas where the public can pick through perfect-condition supplies and haul them away for next to nothing. I landscaped my entire yard with new brick costing from 10¢ each to nothing. Let people building those fancy new houses pay for your projects. The companies are glad to let you have their leftover materials in these days of rising dumping fees.

—Lindsay Amadeo
Chanhassen, Minnesota

VOLUME DISCOUNT

Dear Amy,

Thinking about a set of encyclopedias for your children? Do not, I say do not, buy a brand-new set.

Five years ago, we bought a six-year-old set for $50 out of the newspaper. They were perfectly adequate as my sons went through their high-school years.

I'm selling them at my next garage sale for $35.

I have a friend who signed a $2,000 contract for a set at the same time I bought mine.

—Anne Husk
Vista, California

LUMP IT AND LIKE IT

Dear Amy,

Since I sometimes need only ½ pound of ground turkey or two chicken legs, I don't freeze them in large, hard-to-divide lumps. I'll put the small amount of meat in the bottom of a bread bag, tie it off with a twist-tie, and then continue moving up the bag this way.

—Claudia Tomkiel
Carlisle, Pennsylvania

(We do this. To avoid putting a long, greasy bag back into the freezer, we cut off each section as we need it. If using thin bags (for example, produce bags from the supermarket), double the bags to avoid freezer burn. FZ)

BE A SMART FISH

When Meg Downey of Boca Raton, Florida, sent me the following tip, it sparked an ethics debate among my staff. It's a perfect example of a type of ethics situation with which many people struggle.

"For a small fee (usually reimbursed) you can change telephone companies to take advantage of their generous offers. One month, I used Company A and got $35 in free calls (usually, you must sign up for at least two months). After 60 days, Company B offered the same deal, so I switched. Company C had a comparable offer, so I switched again after two months. All of the companies reimbursed me for the switch-over fees. I got $110 in free services over six months."

Based on letters from other readers concerning situations I have previously printed, I know many would think this is unethical. I don't, and here's why:

If you put a worm on a hook to try to catch a fish, would you think the fish was stealing if it snatched the bait without getting hooked?

Likewise, large businesses utilize highly sophisticated marketing strategies to separate you from your money. The companies (fishermen) know they will lose a small amount of money (bait) to a small percentage of savvy consumers (smart fish), but they are willing to take that loss because they will gain (hook) the business of a larger group of not-so-savvy consumers (stupid fish) in the long run. The small loss (a worm or two) is factored into their plan.

The success of such marketing is clearly evident just by looking at the stupid stuff most Americans buy. In fact, you could just as easily argue that it's unethical for businesses to utilize such sophisticated strategies to get your money.

I don't think smart marketing strategies *or* smart shopping strategies are unethical. I figure that's just part of free enterprise.

If a grocery store offers loss-leader sale items to lure you in, hoping that you'll spend lots of money on other products, it's ethical for you to buy the loss-leader items and nothing else.

If a time-share-condo company lures you to a sales pitch by offering a FREE CHEVY BLAZER, it's ethical for you to go, never intending to sign up for a condo, and accept the free jacket with the word *Chevy* printed on it. (This was a real offer.)

If a company offers you coupons, it's fair for you to combine these with sales and rebates to get free products and still not become a loyal customer.

Some readers have argued "What if everyone took advantage of the companies this way?" All successful businesses carefully monitor the profitability of their marketing strategies, and they withdraw any offers that lose money. As long as companies continue these offers, rest assured that they are still hooking customers.

So don't feel guilty about being a smart consumer. It helps to keep businesses more competitive and therefore to offer you lower prices in the end. And by taking advantage of the freebies that successfully lure naïve consumers, you may contribute to that company's withdrawing the offer, and consequently to sparing a few stupid fish from getting hooked.

NO STRINGS ATTACHED

Jim saw a television ad for a $9.95, solid-plastic replacement blade for a grass string-trimmer. The ad claimed it worked just as well as the string, but once you bought one of these you wouldn't have to buy the string anymore.

This commercial got Jim thinking, and he devised a way to make his own. He designed a plastic blade that could be cut from the lid of a plastic, 5-gallon bucket, the kind that holds paint or drywall joint compound.

Rotate the "tooth" shown at right around the bucket top, tracing around it each time with a felt-tip pen, until you have drawn a three-point star. It is easiest to cut out with a stationary jigsaw or band saw, but a hand-held saber saw also works well. If the lid has a natural curve or warp, cut the blade so that it curves up.

Measure the spindle of your trimmer, and bore a hole exactly that size in the center of this star. Use two large-diameter washers (at least 1½ inches) to hold the star on the spindle.

As you use this, remember: This is *not* a string trimmer, which stings if it hits your leg. This thing will *cut* your leg.

But, on the plus side, Jim has used this to mow down brush that string could never conquer, including a patch of half-inch-thick raspberry canes.

This idea is particularly good to use on older trimmers, many of which are prone to hopeless string tangling. And string trimmers with broken or missing spools are dirt cheat at yard sales; this is an easy way to revive them. But note, this blade won't mount on trimmers with nondetachable spools. Although we've found these blades won't break easily even if you whack them against a boulder, in time we did manage to break one. But it was no big deal. Jim can make a new blade in a couple of minutes.

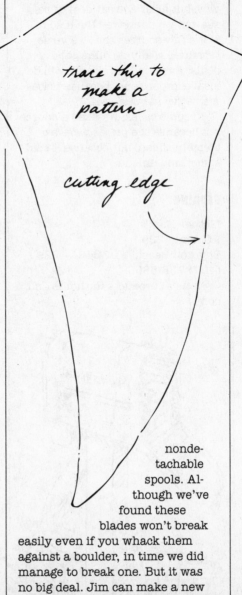

trace this to make a pattern

cutting edge

MAIL TO THE CHEAP

When I asked readers to send me their favorite mail-order sources, I was skeptical. I have always believed that although there are some good deals through the mail, generally you can do better shopping locally if you wait for a sale.

By and large, I still feel that way, but after a great deal of research, we narrowed the field to just a few sources that we've determined really do offer good deals. Even so, you should still do local comparisons, because prices may vary in your area.

In some cases, we liked a source not because the prices were extremely cheap, but because it sold something unique.

BEDDING

Mother Hart's
P.O. Box 4229
Boynton Beach, FL 33424-4229
(407) 738-5866

Natural products for home and body.

BOOKS

Christian Book Distributors
P.O. Box 6000
Peabody, MA 01961
(508) 977-5050

Twenty-five to 50 percent off Christian books and tapes.

Dover Publications
31 East 2nd St.
Mineola, NY 11501
(516) 294-7000

Amazing books and stuff for kids, like cut-and-assemble medieval castles.

Edward R. Hamilton Bookseller
Falls Village, CT 06031-5000

Discontinued books up to 90 percent off.

COMPUTER SOFTWARE

Reasonable Solutions
1221 Disk Dr.
Medford, OR 97501
(503) 776-5777
(800) 876-3475

"Shareware," inexpensive computer software.

HERBS AND SPICES

Let's Spice It Up, Inc.
P.O. Box 15
Highwood, IL 60040
(708) 433-6309 inside Illinois
(800) 659-6302 out-of-state

These prices beat my best local prices on herbs and spices by 25 percent.

HOSIERY

Legg's Brand Inc.
P.O. Box 748
Rural Hall, NC 27098
(919) 744-1790
(800) 522-1151

Fifty percent off name-brand hosiery.

POSTERS

Giant Photos, Inc.
P.O. Box 588
Rockford, IL 61105
(800) 826-2139

Posters and prints at reasonable prices.

RESTORATION SUPPLIES

Van Dyke's
P.O. Box 278
Woonsocket, SD 57385
(800) 843-3320

Hard-to-find parts for antique furniture restoration.

SCIENCE SUPPLIES

American Science & Surplus
3605 Howard St.
Skokie, IL 60076
(708) 982-0870

Optics, chemicals, science equipment—amazing stuff that makes great presents for older kids.

SEWING AND CRAFT SUPPLIES

Bee Lee Co.
P.O. Box 36108
Dallas, TX 75235
(214) 351-2091
(800) 527-5271

Kieffer's
P.O. Box 7500
Jersey City, NJ 07307
(201) 798-2266

TOOLS AND HARDWARE

Northern Hydraulics
P.O. Box 1499
Burnsville, MN 55337
(800) 533-5545

Constantine
2050 Eastchester Rd.
Bronx, NY 10461
(718) 792-1600
(800) 223-8087

Harbor Freight Tools
3491 Mission Oaks Blvd.
Camarillo, CA 93011
(800) 423-2567

VETERINARY SUPPLIES

UPCO
3705 Pear St.
St. Joseph, MO 64502
(816) 233-8809

R. C. Steele
P.O. Box 910
Brockport, NY 14420-0910
(800) 872-3773

Up to 50 percent savings, $50 minimum purchase.

WALLPAPER

American Blind and Wallpaper
28237 Orchard Lake Rd.
Farmington Hills, MI 48334-3765
(800) 735-5300

Style Wall Coverings
P.O. Box 865
Southfield, MI 48037
(800) 627-0400

THE PANTRY PRINCIPLE

Generations of thrift writers have passed down certain "helpful household hints" for so long that they have become a sort of "Gospel According to June Cleaver." We hear them over and over and don't stop to wonder whether they really work.

Typical is the admonition to plan meal menus 30 days in advance and shop accordingly, never daring to veer from this carved-in-stone schedule. At the very least, we've been told, you should plan meals seven days in advance, working with what's on sale that week. You can even buy a computer program to prepare a shopping list based on your long-range meal plan.

WALLY, BEAVER, IT'S THE 17TH! WIENER-WRAP NIGHT!

Because I am the Grande Dame of Frugality and the World's Most Organized Human Being (read with tongue in cheek), people often assume that I plan meals days or weeks in advance. Wrong. In fact, planning meals far in advance is entirely backward. You should never decide first what you want to eat and then go out and buy it, because:

- Your predetermined plan probably will not coincide with what's on sale, or with the very best sales;
- Stick-to-your-list thinking doesn't allow you to take advantage of the unadvertised deals;
- During the course of your long-range-plan period, you may discover you need to use up a perishable or clean out the leftovers from your crammed freezer.

Long-range planning probably evolved as the solution for the individual who habitually stops at the supermarket or fast-food restaurant on the way home from work to pick up the evening meal. This pattern is apparently pretty common, which is why people panic and empty store shelves before a snowstorm.

Although I agree that the long-range plan is better than the panic plan, it is far from the best solution.

A far more logical method is called the pantry principle, and Jim and I have successfully used it for years. (I first read about this

concept in *Cut Your Food Bill in Half* by Barbara Salsbury and Cheri Loveless [Acropolis Books, 1983].)

Many families use this idea to some extent, but in my opinion, few take it far enough to save the maximum amount of time or money.

The basic premise is that you stockpile your pantry (and/or kitchen, freezer, basement, closet, and/or the space under your bed) with food purchased at the lowest possible price. The sole purpose of grocery shopping becomes replenishing your pantry, not buying ingredients to prepare specific meals. This is a subtle but important distinction.

To put the pantry principle into action, Jim and I scan the sale flyers each week for good deals. When the rock-bottom sale occurs, we inventory our supply and decide how much to buy. Unlike many families, we'll buy flour even if we have 20 pounds left—if the price is right.

Bulk-buying is not just for large families in large homes. Singles in tiny apartments can stockpile in accordance with their needs and available space.

We stockpile larger quantities of food that goes on sale less frequently (over time, you develop an instinct about this). Although we do most of our shopping once a month, when sales occur we make a point of picking up the items while doing other errands or by coordinating efforts with a friend. Because we buy in quantity, we don't have to take advantage of every sale.

Occasionally, we miscalculate and completely run out of 29¢-per-pound chicken. Nothing will induce us to pay 69¢ per pound. We simply don't make chicken meals until we replenish our chicken supply. Instead, we eat other sale-purchased meals. By having a full pantry, we never need to plan our meals weeks or even days in advance.

Depending on your family's preferences, perishables may be handled differently. If you want to eat only fresh produce, you will have to shop for it every week. We buy fresh fruits at the beginning of the month, and as we run out, we gradually shift over to our supply of dried, frozen, and canned fruits and juices. If the fruit stand on my yard-sale route has good deals, I'll make a special stop. But I don't believe we'll die if there isn't fresh produce in the house.

Our meal planning works like this: Jim and I alternate washing the evening dishes. We have a rule that whoever washes the dishes plans the next evening's meal. During that 30-minute period, the designated meal-planner considers what type of meal we haven't eaten in a while, what we have a surplus of, what we need to use up, what the weather will be like (so we can make hot meals on cool days, and vice versa), what our schedule will be, who will be home, what garden vegetables are ripening, and so on. These and many other factors cannot possibly be known 30 days in advance.

Planning meals 24 hours in advance is ideal because many of our foods need to be thawed or dried beans need to be soaked. Meals to be prepared in a solar cooker or crockpot must be ready to begin cooking in the morning. And thawing foods in advance saves electricity because there is no need to

microwave frozen foods. Although we have a repertoire of short-notice meals, the selection is much smaller.

A final note: This general concept applies to many areas of the frugal life. During the summer I stockpile yard-sale items I might need to replace during the remainder of the year, including lunch boxes, backpacks, sneakers, and clothing. I stock up on yard-sale toys for birthday and Christmas presents, and on sale-purchased gifts that would be suitable for my children to take to another kid's birthday party. Jim stocks up on sale-priced motor oil and oil filters, film, bolts, and hot-glue sticks.

When an unexpected need arises, we "go shopping in the attic." Consequently, we almost never make an emergency trip to the store. Whenever people complain to me that "I don't have time to do all of that frugal stuff," I wonder if they waste time running off to the store every time they run out of something. The pantry principle is one of many frugal practices that saves both money and time.

AVOID ANTI-SEPTIC PRACTICES

According to the U.S. Census Bureau, 22 percent of American homes use septic systems. According to several septic-system pumpers we interviewed here in Maine, at least 50 percent of people with septic systems don't know how to take care of them.

This can be expensive. Replacing a failed septic system generally costs about $4,000 and can cost as much as $10,000. On the other hand, properly maintaining a septic system costs only about $50 a year—plus a little common sense.

To research this, I spoke with septic pumpers, the local extension service, EPA Small Flows Clearinghouse (which specializes in septic-system information), and health-department officials in several states. I also read three books and six magazine articles. I was thorough because a great deal of information on septic-system maintenance is just folklore and anecdotes, and I wanted the informed, scientific viewpoint.

A septic system consists of two parts: a tank and a leach field. The solids settle to the bottom of the tank. The liquid drains from the top of the tank into the leach field, which is made of buried gravel.

Septic systems fail because the tank fills with solids, and these overflow and clog up the leach field. You'll know your system has failed if bad-smelling water leaks out above the ground, the plumbing in your house backs up, or both.

There are two basic things to remember if you want your septic system to last: Don't put the wrong things in it, and have the tank pumped at regular intervals.

These things should *not* be flushed or poured down the drain:

- Grease. To work properly, septic tanks need bacterial action to break down solids. Grease interferes with that biological action. Small amounts won't hurt, but dumping a pan full of hamburger grease into the kitchen sink is really rough on the bacteria.
- Colored toilet paper. The dyes in colored paper are also difficult for bacteria to digest.
- Garbage-disposal waste. This brings in more solids and grease. Use a compost pile.
- Excessive water. "A lot of people move to the country from the city, take an hour-long shower, and wonder why their system fails," says Steve Davis of Minot, Maine, who has pumped tanks for 20 years. "Septic systems won't take water continuously."

Aside from the shower, the other biggest wastewater producer in the average household is the washing machine. To make matters worse, its water contains harsh detergents that can block the septic tank's bacterial action. Davis says routing your washing machine's wastewater into a "dry well"—essentially, a hole filled with gravel—can extend the life of your septic field.

But note: All household wastewater aside from toilet water is known as "gray water." Laws vary on how gray water can be handled. In some areas, it *must* be routed into the septic tank. Check with your local codes-enforcement office before engaging in any creative plumbing.

Even if you follow all of the rules above, you must have your tank pumped at regular intervals. Some pumpers told us it should be done every two or three years, others said every three or four years. Ask around for an honest, reliable pumper, and when he arrives, ask his advice, based on what he finds in your tank. In Maine, pumping out a tank generally costs around $200. If it's done at four-year intervals, that works out to $50 a year. If you are lucky enough to have a place to dump the stuff, such as a big field, and local laws permit this, the pumping fee can be as low as $50, or $12.50 per year.

Try as I might, I was unable to find any independent source who believed additives could make pumping unnecessary. As far as I could learn, only the additive companies are making these claims. (And one company's additive package does say that you will still need to pump). The additive companies were unable to cite any independent studies to support their claims, whereas the independent sources said all the studies they had read indicate the additives were of little use, and that some could be harmful.

And even if it worked, the economic advantage of an additive is dubious. A spokesman for Rid-X, one of the best-known additives, told me that his product costs $48 annually. At that rate, it's generally cheaper to have your tank pumped.

Although most septic systems should be pumped every three years or so, it's possible to go much longer, depending upon many variables. Again, the best way to find out is to ask an honest pumper. In Maine, I've found that most pumpers are so busy they have little incentive to fabricate a short interval.

HOMEMADE GOO

Stephanie Sloan of Renton, Washington, sent in a recipe to make a substance that is like a cross between Gak and Silly Putty. I made up a batch of the stretchy stuff and let my children play with it. It provided hours of hilarious entertainment. It doesn't leave a residue or stick to anything but itself and will stretch to seemingly unlimited lengths. Its "disgusting" qualities make it a natural for Halloween entertainment.

8 ounces white or carpenter's glue
$^3/_4$ cup water
food coloring (optional)
1 teaspoon 20 Mule Team borax
1 to 2 tablespoons water

Combine the first three ingredients. In a separate bowl, combine the last two. Add the borax mixture to the glue mixture, stirring until a "blob" forms. Remove the blob from the mixture. Add a new batch of the borax mixture to the glue mixture. Repeat the process until the glue mixture is all gone. Knead all the blobs together. Store in an airtight container.

BEYOND BREAD-TAB EARRINGS

While I am a leading authority on frugal food and kid's clothing, and I know a dozen uses for dryer-lint mâché, inexpensive jewelry strategies are not my strong suit. So I asked readers to help. I specified that each idea had to be for something that Diane Sawyer would wear on prime-time TV.

About 75 readers responded. Most included samples. To narrow the field, I assembled a panel of seven staffers (of varying ages, tastes, and sexes) to judge the samples. Aside from fashion appropriateness, we also considered durability, how commonly available the materials were, price of materials, and how easily they could be made (we were particularly seeking ideas that required no talent or special skills).

Most of these jewelry ideas will require that you buy findings, stickpins, clasps, pin blanks, jeweler's pins, and/or a strong, clear-drying glue. This stuff is available by the bagful at craft shops and is surprisingly cheap. People who are allergic to inexpensive metal would need to buy gold or silver earring backs. A pair of needle-nosed pliers is also needed in making some of this jewelry.

One general idea first: Readers suggested picking up jewelry cheap from various sources and remaking it into new jewelry. Beth Dodd of Gainesville, Texas, pointed out that single earrings can be made into pins. Colleen Washburn of Newport News, Virginia, talks to the manager of an everything-for-$1 store and asks to buy broken jewelry. She buys a bagful for $1 and then repairs or remakes the pieces. Sherri Spare of Parsons, Kansas, picks through bargain bins for $1 jewelry. She paints the pieces with clear nail polish to prevent chipping and fading. Regard cheap or free jewelry from any source as raw material for your projects.

By far the most common idea that readers sent me was "button earrings." Any large buttons with a loop in the back can be made into very inexpensive earrings.

These might be metallic, mother-of-pearlish, or colored buttons. Many samples were surprisingly elegant. Susan Coy of Spring, Texas, wrote that she uses wire cutters to snip the loop off. She gently sands the remains of the loop smooth and attaches the earring back with glue. If you use pierced-earring backings, place them off-center so they don't twist or turn and so they set lower on your lobe.

Lona Lockhart of Roxboro, North Carolina, pointed out that craft stores yield a variety of other items from which earrings can be made. Silk rosettes come in a range of colors. You can also find satin hearts (usually used for sweatshirts), tiny bows, and glass rhinestones. She uses hot glue to attach these to earring backings.

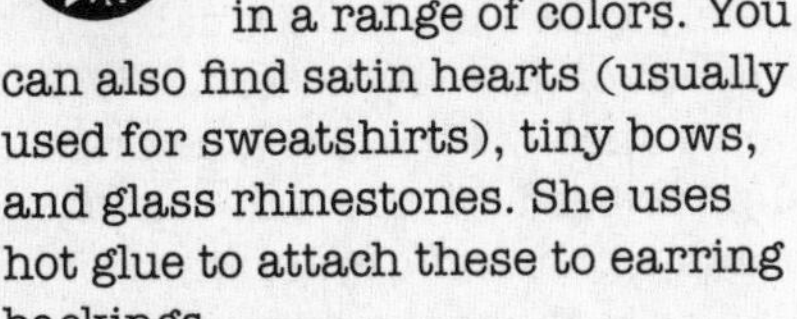

As a testament to how easy earrings are to make, ten-year-old Monica Madson of Minnetonka, Minnesota, sent in some of the loveliest pieces we received. She strings small, iridescent beads on jeweler's pins. She then bends or loops the pin ends to attach them to the earring findings.

Kathy Littman of Santa Rosa, California, sent me earrings made by the same method; however, she buys old necklaces at yard sales and thrift shops and takes them apart to salvage the beads.

All of these earrings can be made in fifteen minutes and cost between 15¢ and $1.

Susan Meyer of Beverly Shores, Indiana, sent me bracelets made from an unlikely item. Brass fishing swivels, which are used to attach fishing lures to the line, can be purchased in department or sporting-goods stores in bags of nine for about 47¢. She ties a swivel with a 1-inch section of gold wire, strings one to three beads on this wire, and attaches the other end of the wire to the next swivel. By continuing this procedure, she makes a chain. When it reaches bracelet length, you can attach the ends or add bracelet clasps. The samples she sent had wooden and stone beads.

Larrisa Stretton of Webster, Massachusetts, sent me her version of a pin she saw in a catalog for $29.95. She cut a small heart, about 1 1/2 inches high, from white cardboard. Then she glued a selection of tiny buttons, beads, bows, lace, and silk rosettes to completely cover the cardboard, being careful to retain the overall heart shape. These items were white, gold, pink, or clear. I had seen this idea once before using all tiny gold items including tiny lapel pins (such as Masonic or high school ones). Larissa prefers Tacky brand glue. Finally, she glues a pin blank on the back.

One reader sent a necklace made from 50¢ worth of black, blue, and silver "six-strand" embroidery floss. You could also use leftover yarn.

To make one, wind a total of 8 yards of floss around a large book or the back of a kitchen chair. Twist this big circle of floss tightly or loosely, depending on the style you want. Thread three 18-inch strands of floss through each of the loops at the ends of the twisted floss. Braid these strands tightly, and knot the ends of the braids.

Thread a tapestry needle with floss, and wind floss very tightly over the place where the braided and twisted floss joins together, overlapping each by about ½ inch. Knot the necklace in the center. Tie together the ends of the braided floss to form the necklace.

Debbie Sailer of Sooke, British Columbia, sent in a method of making beads from glossy magazine pages. As it happens, a staffer had recently picked up a 1950s crafts-from-trash book at a yard sale, and this idea was in it. I have been experimenting with this and have become addicted. To fully appreciate how nicely this idea works, you'll have to try making beads from several different pages. The final look of the beads depends on the color and composition of the art or photo of the magazine page. The beads have a Southwestern look. Part of the uniqueness of this technique is that ten or so beads that you make from a single page are "of the same family," meaning they look alike yet are individually unique.

To make these beads, cut long, triangular strips from a magazine page. I use an X-Acto knife (this tool is a must for crafts) and a metal ruler to do the cutting. You can also draw guidelines on the back side of the page and cut with scissors. At the wide end, the strips should be no wider than 1 inch (the width determines the final size of the bead). Cut the wide end so it has a shallow point. Starting at the wide end, tightly roll the strip on a small nail, making sure to get the strip rolling straight from the start. Once the strip is completely rolled up, dab a small amount of glue on the end so it won't unroll. When the glue dries, slip the bead off the nail. Coat the beads with acrylic craft spray or shellac to make them weatherproof. The beads can be used to make a necklace by alternating them with other types of beads on a colored string. To make earrings, I would make dangling clusters of four or five beads per earring ring.

Jewelry making is an area in which my readers have taught me a great deal. I have very little personal need for jewelry and have relied on two pairs of earrings and a few pins to get me by. But from now on, I'll poke through those piles of yard-sale baubles and beads with a more discerning eye.

WANTED POSTERS

Dear Amy,

I was chatting with the manager of our local video store, and he volunteered that they regularly throw away the promotional video-release movie posters they get from the studios after about two weeks. I asked if I could have one (for a children's movie my kids love), and it made the perfect birthday gift. Since then, I've gotten several more and used them as gifts at birthday parties.

—Maria Hylton
Evanston, Illinois

TWO-MINUTE WARMING

Dear Amy,

After years of feeling cheated by not being able to get that last little bit of solid antiperspirant deodorant out of the container, I finally decided it was time to try.

I dug all the remaining stuff out of the container with a knife and put it in a glass custard cup. I put it in the microwave for two minutes. Using a spatula, I scraped all the melted antiperspirant into an old container and let it cool. Four used-up antiperspirant containers filled a recycled container half full.

—Sally Ryan
Black Hawk, Colorado

THE SUN ALSO DEFROSTS

Dear Amy,

I live in Vermont, where there's often frost on the car windows from October to April. To shorten both the length of time I must scrape snow/frost/ice from my window and the time I must run the defroster prior to driving, I always park my car facing east. This allows the warmth of the rising morning sun to melt most, if not all, of the snow/frost/ice from my car's biggest window.

—Susan DuBois
Montpelier, Vermont

GET WELD SOON

Dear Amy,

A friend had a little bicycle just the size I needed for my son, only one pedal was broken off. Having it welded was the only way to fix it. After several frustrating trips and phone calls to welding companies (minimum charge, $15 to $40, one- to three-week backlog), I had a brainstorm. I called the welding department of our local technical college, and they were happy to fix it for me. A welding student did a super job in ten minutes, no charge! We wrote them a letter!

—Stephanie Sloan
Renton, Washington

MARKER MAGIC

Dear Amy,

To reuse a highlighter pen, remove either the felt tip (the retaining pin must be pushed out) or the end plug, and add water. Better yet, add water mixed with food coloring. You can even make your own custom colors.

—David Stennes
La Mesa, California

PICKUP PICK-ME-UP

Dear Amy,

The rusted wheels on our 1985 Chevy truck made it look dated and shabby although it functions well and is in good shape. We looked into replacing them and found, to our horror, it would cost $400.

Then we stumbled across a $5 can of "wheel spray paint" from an auto-parts store. Not only do we have "new wheels," but the whole truck looks more than presentable. Although this is only a cosmetic change, it extended the life of the truck in our eyes . . . my husband can't drive a broken-down-looking vehicle because of his business.

—Janet Steddum
Raleigh, North Carolina

WASH AND CARE

Dear Amy,

This is a good idea if you know college students. We get a night of free baby-sitting for our two children (which would cost us $6 an hour for at least four hours) in exchange for letting the students use our washer and dryer. They provide their own soap, etc.

—Linda Smith
Davis, California

THE FRUGAL BALANCE

Almost every time I give a speech or talk on a radio show, I hear a comment like this:

"My wife and I do many of the things you suggest to save money. Of course, we're just not as . . . er . . . well . . . as extreme as you are."

The notion that I am somehow too extreme is also reflected in a question journalists often ask: "Can you be *too* frugal?"

This sounds like a simple, yes-or-no question, but it actually requires this long answer:

Most people think of frugality only in terms of saving money. Under that narrow definition, the answer would clearly be "Yes, you can be too frugal." But if you look up *frugal* in the dictionary, you'll find it isn't defined specifically as having to do only with money. It's defined as "not wasteful," "economical," or "thrifty." These terms can apply to the expenditure of *any* resource.

All of us attempt to achieve the highest quality of life possible by balancing four basic resources: money, time, space, and personal energy. Because these resources are interconnected in an intricate way, frugality must encompass more than money; we must manage these four things in relationship to one another.

When people think of frugality run amok, they're usually reflecting on situations when these resources are out of balance and this imbalance hurts the quality of life.

There are limitless examples that I could discuss to illustrate this point. Let's focus on a common one that people sometimes mention to me: pack-ratting.

Typically, someone might say to me, "Yeah, my sister Thelma is really frugal. You can't move in her house because of all of the bread bags, Styrofoam meat trays, juice-can lids, egg cartons, broccoli rubber bands, and toilet-paper tubes. But I just can't live that way. I guess I'm not the tightwad type."

My response is that Thelma isn't being "too frugal;" rather, her frugality is out of balance. Her pack-ratting may save her money in small ways (if you have 600 bread bags in the closet, you don't need to buy plastic bags), but it costs her more in other ways:

• Because Thelma has to move piles of things to finish a sewing project, she wastes time and energy. Because she can't find her one good pair of scissors, she wastes time. Because she has to buy more buttons when she can't find the ones she saved, she wastes money.

• Because Thelma has limited space, she can't stock up on good deals on nonperishables at the supermarket. Instead, she buys only a few days' supply of food at a time and therefore wastes more time, energy, and money.

• Because Thelma has so much stuff saved, she rents a larger house—in addition to renting space in a storage locker. Aside from spending more money for rent, she also pays more to heat the larger space. Because she has to work overtime at her K mart job to pay for these additional expenses, she wastes more time and energy.

The result of this lack of balance is that Thelma's quality of life is diminished.

In contrast to Thelma, a shrewd, successful frugal person constantly monitors how much is stored, never keeping more than the maximum amount of bread bags or Styrofoam meat trays that might be needed at a given time.

Pack-ratting, with organization and precision, is a huge money saver, especially when more valuable things are stored away.

We have an abundance of children's clothing, lumber, hardware, and nonperishable food. However, I have exactly eight Styrofoam meat trays and four bread bags, and I can still move in my kitchen.

It's possible someone like Thelma may save more things than she needs, but because she has a surplus of space, stacks of meat trays might not cause her to be out of balance. Although she might not be saving money by keeping them, neither is she wasting other resources. It's also important to note that this lack of balance isn't a problem associated only with frugal people. Spendthrifts are frequently out of balance. If Thelma's brother doesn't have time to enjoy his new bass boat because he has to work overtime (at a job he hates) to pay for it, then he is out of balance as well. But people who aren't frugal can achieve balance. They might love their jobs, make loads of money, and spend a lot to buy

things from which they derive great value.

In observing both the frugal and nonfrugal, this lack of balance is usually indicated by an expression of unhappiness or frustration about some aspect of their lives—when they complain about not being able to pay bills but aren't making adjustments in their habits. Regardless of their spending style, I don't worry about people when they and their families are clearly happy with the choices they've made.

When someone labels me "too extreme," it's usually because they've flipped through my books, picked out some obscure idea that doesn't work for them, and made a judgment about me. But I've never had a journalist come to my home, observe the obvious harmony, and write that I'm "too frugal." Although their values might be different from mine, they can't find fault with our choices.

Because we all have different amounts of money, time, space, and personal energy and different ideas about what constitutes quality of life, we each must find our own frugal balance.

If you think about frugality as I do, asking the question "Can you be too frugal?" is like asking "Can you be too happy?"

WHEN TO USE A COUPON

All of the books I've ever read on coupons focus solely on how wonderful they are. I have never read one that helps you figure out when coupons cost you money.

In many instances, a little quick in-the-aisles math will show whether a name brand with coupon will beat the price of a store-brand equivalent.

But the waters get murkier when you use a coupon to buy a convenience food. When does the convenience food become cheaper than making the same item from scratch? To learn this requires that you make the scratch item, weigh or measure it, and carefully add up the cost of the ingredients used. When the final cost of the convenience food combined with coupons falls below this price, you should probably use the coupon. (I say "probably" because many of these foods are highly packaged, highly processed, and lack the nutrition of the scratch versions.)

Unfortunately, no one ever takes the time to figure this out. So I decided to break some ground in the Wonderful World of Coupondom and provide you with a list of rules of thumb. Because there are thousands of products at your supermarket, this list is incomplete. To be really accurate you should figure prices based on ingredients available to you, but if you don't want to take the time, this list should help.

Many of the prices on my list are based on previous articles I have written. In many cases, the recipes appear in my books. I've provided a per-ounce figure as well as a per-package figure. I rounded the numbers to the nearest penny, which accounts for any discrepancies.

Here's how low the price with coupons must be for each of these products to be a good deal:

Baked beans: 1¢ per ounce or 33¢ per 28-ounce can.

Cake mix: 2¢ per ounce or 25¢ per 15-ounce box.

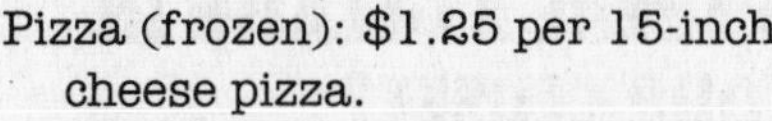

Chili: 4¢ per ounce or 54¢ per 15-ounce can.

Chocolate syrup: 3¢ per ounce or 72¢ per 24-ounce bottle.

Cookies: 40¢ per pound for sugar cookies and 60¢ per pound for oatmeal cookies.

Hot cocoa from mix: 7¢ per 1-cup serving or $1.12 per 16-pack box.

Chicken Tonight: 4¢ per ounce or 99¢ per 23 1/2-ounce jar.

Cold cereal: 7¢ per ounce (as compared to other breakfast options).

Corn-muffin mix: 3¢ per ounce or 22¢ per 8 1/2-ounce box.

Cream of mushroom soup: 4¢ per ounce or 43¢ per 10 1/2-ounce can.

Frosting: 3¢ per ounce or 48¢ per 16-ounce can.

Granola (without nuts): 6¢ per ounce or 48¢ per 8-ounce box.

Hamburger (or Tuna) Helper: 75¢ per box.*

Jell-O Snack Paks: 2¢ per ounce or 35¢ per pack of four 4-ounce containers.

Jelly and jam: 3¢ per ounce or 42¢ per 16 ounces (as compared to homemade with homegrown fruit).

Microwavable pancakes and waffles: 10¢ per 2-ounce serving.

Microwave popcorn: 2¢ per ounce or 8¢ per pouch.

Onion-soup mix: 33¢ per ounce or 66¢ per two-envelope package.

Pancake syrup: 3¢ per ounce or 66¢ per 24-ounce bottle.

Pizza (frozen): $1.25 per 15-inch cheese pizza.

Popsicles: 3¢ each or 60¢ for a 24-count box (as compared to homemade from apple juice).

Pudding snack packs: 7¢ per ounce or 44¢ per pack of four 4-ounce containers.

Ramen noodles: 5¢ per ounce or 17¢ per package.

Rice-A-Roni: 28¢ per cup. Box contains 1 cup.

Italian salad dressing: 3¢ per ounce or 45¢ per 16-ounce bottle.

Tomato soup: 5¢ per ounce or 53¢ per 10 1/2-ounce can, as compared with homemade from tomato paste.

Seasoned salt: 14¢ per ounce or 49¢ per 3 1/2-ounce container.

Spaghetti sauce: 45¢ per quart (as compared to homemade with homegrown vegetables).

Stove Top Stuffing: 46¢ per cup or $2.76 per 6-cup package.

Taco seasoning: 14¢ per ounce or 21¢ per 1 1/2-ounce package.

TV dinners: 50¢ per dinner.

Yogurt with fruit: 14¢ per 8-ounce container (as compared to homemade with a tablespoon of jam added).

*Recipe from *Cheaper & Better* by Nancy Birnes.

IS THERE A GELATIN IN YOUR CLOSET?

When most people think of gelatin, they're really thinking about Jell-O: They don't know there's any other way to make a gelatin dessert. I never buy Jell-O because it's basically nothing more than unflavored gelatin, sugar, and Kool-Aid powder. In short, it provides no nutrition other than an insignificant amount of protein from the gelatin.

Instead, we buy bulk, unflavored gelatin for $5.33 a pound at our health-food store and use this to make our own fruit gelatin. This is by far the cheapest way to buy unflavored gelatin; a four-packet, 1-ounce box of Knox unflavored gelatin costs 95¢, which works out to $15.20 a pound. Unflavored gelatin keeps indefinitely, so there is no advantage to buying smaller quantities.

A tablespoon of unflavored gelatin combined with a cup of cold liquid and a cup of boiling liquid will make solid gelatin. You can make your own version of Jell-O by using Kool-Aid for this hot and cold liquid. This will cost about 18¢ per four 1/2-cup servings. A box of Jell-O makes the same amount, but costs 44¢ a box. Royal gelatin is 33¢ a box.

I prefer to use fruit juice to make a healthier gelatin. Apple juice, for example, with a little food coloring (brown gelatin doesn't cut it) works well. At a cost of 32¢ for four 1/2-cup servings, this is still cheaper than Jell-O or Royal gelatin.

Obviously, it's easier to just drink juice than make gelatin out of it. But fruit-juice gelatin is a handy way to suspend frozen fruits (like blueberries, strawberries, or blackberries), which are hard to convert to "lunch-box food." I can make pies or crisps to use up my supply of berries, but my family has to eat lots of sugar and fat to get a little fruit.

Fruit gelatins are a form of lunch-box fruit that I can make using a little sugar and no fat. I also use fruit gelatin to suspend overripe banana chunks.

After some experimentation, I've progressed to a speedy method to make fruit gelatin that uses frozen fruit (which we either grow or pick from wild bushes) and no juice (which I would have to buy). Here's how I do it:

I thaw a quart of frozen berries and whiz it in a 5-cup-size blender. If I'm using blackberries, I then strain out the seeds and pour the thick, pulpy juice back into the blender. I add 2 tablespoons of unflavored gelatin and 1/2 cup of sugar and fill the blender with hot water. I blend this mixture, pour it in a bowl, and chill.

Blender gelatin has one important advantage: The gelatin always mixes completely. I find if I simply stir the mixture, my gelatin might have chewy gelatin "seeds."

Blender gelatin also becomes foamy, and as it jells, it tends to separate to form a light-colored foamy layer and a dark, clear layer. These layers are interesting if we're making parfaits.

Aside from using less fat and sugar, fruit gelatins require much less energy and time to make than other scratch desserts like pies and puddings. And, for some reason, homemade gelatins seem to hold up better in lunch boxes on warm days than Jell-O does.

Another quickie lunch-box treat is "jigglers" or "Knox blocks," a sort of gelatin finger food. To make them, simply double the amount of gelatin or add 1 tablespoon of gelatin per cup of liquid. Combine in a bowl using a whisk. Recently I made jigglers with lemonade and pink food coloring. I poured 6 cups of gelatin/lemonade mixture into a 9-inch-by-13-inch Pyrex baking dish and chilled it. Once jelled, this can be cut into cubes or, for fancier shapes, cut with cookie cutters. These were hugely successful with my kids and made fashionable, fake-looking, sort-of-healthy lunch-box food.

FACTORY FINDS

Dear Amy,

My husband gets our firewood (oak, untreated) for $10 a truckload from leftovers at a local log-cabin manufacturing plant. I get new material (many pieces over 1 yard) for $2 per large box from remnants from a local sewing factory. These make great curtains, pillows, and kids' clothes. Check your local factories. Many have materials to be given away.

—Cynthia Hale
Clay City, Kentucky

SMEAR TACTIC

Dear Amy,

A plastic surgeon friend said to use Crisco shortening on my dry lips rather than anything else. It works well!

—Tina Schneider
Oceanside, California

MICKEY MISER

Dear Amy,

As soon as you make your plans to visit Disneyland/World, shop at garage sales for souvenirs. I was able to stockpile Disney hats, T-shirts, coin purses, waist bags, and stuffed characters for $4.70. The retail for these items was $114.05. These were doled out over the course of the week as the "I wannas" struck.

—Kathy Gervasio
Mendham, New Jersey

FIND IT AND BIND IT

Dear Amy,

Since I love trying new ideas and foods while cooking, I have ended up with at least a dozen cookbooks that I use for only a few recipes. Now, I go to the library and check out cookbooks instead. I look for and copy recipes that I like or will use, insert them into a plastic sheet protector, and organize them by category (i.e., seafood, salads, chicken, etc.) in a binder. I also use this idea to keep track of home projects, articles, crafts, etc. I'm on my fifth binder, and my total cost so far is less than one cookbook.

—Deborah Holtzer Potter
Vineyard Haven, Massachusetts

CITRUS SYRUP

Dear Amy,

After making the candied orange and grapefruit peels (see page 198), I found that you can use the syrup in which you boil the peels on pancakes and waffles . . . the peels give it a nice flavor. This brings the cost of the candied peels down to the energy cost of using the stove.

—JoAnn Sprague
Three Lakes, Wisconsin

KILL A WATT

Dear Amy,

A friend of mine discovered a unique way to cut down on her electric bill. Instead of having her high school–graduate son pay rent, she made him pay the electric bill. Once it became his responsibility, he ran around turning off lights and appliances that weren't being used. Her bill was cut by almost 30 percent! She not only saved energy, she taught her son a valuable lesson.

—Robin McFetridge
Jonesboro, Georgia

DECIDE TO DIVIDE

Dear Amy,

When your physician prescribes medicines, ask what milligram sizes the medication comes in. If he, for example, plans to order 5-mg. tablets and the medication also comes in a 10-mg. size, and the cost is the same, ask him if he will prescribe the larger size. Then cut them in half. Tablets are often scored and easy to break in half.

—Harriet Reisman
Port Jefferson, New York

(I asked my physician about this, and he agreed it was a good idea because the larger sizes may cost the same or only slightly more. There are a few exceptions to this practice. Coated tablets should not be broken. The coating makes the medication dissolve more slowly, often when it reaches the lower intestine. A broken, coated tablet would release the medication too quickly. And don't do this with unscored tablets, unless you have the device mentioned in the following letter. FZ)

SPLITTING PAIRS

Dear Amy,

I use a pill splitter for dividing both scored and unscored pills of any size. Theoretically, it could also be used to halve each half. This is useful for people with arthritis, unsteady hands, or poor eyesight.

—Beatrice Slamavitz

(A pill splitter costs $4 at drugstores in my area. FZ)

GOWN ABOUT TOWN

Dear Amy,

We celebrate our wedding anniversary by donning our wedding outfits and doing something cheap but fun. This year, we rode the bus and stopped at a garage sale. I also wore it to teach preschool the day we learned the letter *W*. Kids came from the other classrooms to gasp. Tim and I decided I'm having too much fun with my wedding dress to sell it. The ad would read: Wedding dress, size 8, worn just 7 times, $50.

—Mary Nelson-Smith
Billings, Montana

LUCK-KEY LUGGAGE

Dear Amy,

My wife, Carolyn, found a used, Samsonite, hard-shell, 26-inch luggage piece with wheels at a thrift store for only $7 (comparable new retail pieces are $90 to $120). The only thing wrong with it was there was no key to the locks. Carolyn merely called Samsonite at (303) 373-2000 and gave the name of the model, located inside the suitcase. The rep sent her two free keys.

—Don Reeves
Nashville, Tennessee

HOMEWARD BOUND

Dear Amy,

In my car's glove compartment I keep a spiral-bound 6-inch-by-9-inch notebook and a small stapler.

When friends and relatives give me directions to their homes, I staple them into my book.

We travel a lot, and this handy idea saves us phone-bill money.

—Louise Cady Fernandes
Lexington, Massachusetts

PACK IN THE BOX

Dear Amy,

Don't buy those outrageously priced boxes to store clothes. Go to your grocery or liquor store and ask for the boxes they are throwing away. The liquor-store boxes have convenient, built-in compartments to store breakable items.

—Sharon Dahlmeyer
Durham, Connecticut

THE 95¢ QUILT

My first exposure to quilting occurred when I moved to Leeds six years ago. Here, women from ages 25 to 85 gather twice a month at the church to make quilts to raise money.

The quilts are beautiful, but I was surprised to find they are made from all new materials. Lois Hathaway, a professional quilter and instructor, told me why:

- Maine laws restrict the sale of quilts with used batting.
- Used fabrics may not be as durable as new ones, and so are not desirable in quilts for sale.
- Used fabrics are more time-consuming to work with, so they aren't cost-effective for quilts to be sold. There is generally a limited amount of the same type of fabric, it's harder to find the grain, and it may be hard to identify cotton/synthetic blends (these stretch more than 100 percent cotton does when sewing).

My theory is:

- Quilting from used fabrics may have fallen out of favor when frugal quilters attempted to use garish fabrics from the sixties and seventies . . . big green polka dots, purple polyesters, and orange plaids.

But Lois agreed that used materials *can* work well in quilts for personal use—and that the original purpose of patchwork quilting was to use up leftover fabrics. A quilt made from used fabrics also has an appealing sentimental value: Each time you see it, you'll remember "those were Brad's toddler pants, that was my maternity top," and so on.

And, naturally, sewing with scraps is a money-saver. Professionally made quilts cost a minimum of $200. New fabrics alone cost $50 to $100. But by using secondhand materials, you can easily make a quilt for under $5.

To learn more I visited 82-year-old Louise Grant, one of the few quilters in my area who sews with scraps. Although she uses no secondhand fabrics, she makes quilt tops from factory scraps, fabric-shop samples, and extra material from other quilters. She also buys scraps and partially completed quilts from an antique dealer, who obtains them when cleaning out attics. Louise has about ten quilts in progress, awaiting scraps to finish them.

As we chatted in her fabric-crammed workroom, I came to understand her feeling about quilt making. She knows that using scraps won't produce the most beautiful quilts conceivable, as compared to using entirely new and expensive materials. Instead, she enjoys the challenge of using the discards of others to make the most attractive quilt that she can within that limitation.

Quilting from scraps means that you accept what one of my art teachers termed "accidental quality." The results aren't always perfect, but you kind of like that. Accepting this less-perfect result is actually liberating. Louise says

she doesn't "fuss" about combining different prints and colors. And it's obvious that making a quilt from near-free fabrics is less intimidating than making one with a $100 investment.

Although you can make totally random designs, Louise suggests settling on a basic design and color scheme and sometimes having a lot of one common, plain fabric to separate printed fabrics. She showed me a variety of examples of how using this method produced attractive quilts that looked "planned." To illustrate one solution, here's how I recently completed my first quilt for—get this—95¢.

Four-year-old Rebecca and eight-year-old Jamie share a double bed in their Pepto-Bismol–pink room (the supreme act of maternal love is to let kids choose their room color). I gave them a set of dark pink sheets (which were given to us). Unidentified culprits soon cut a hole in one pillowcase and stained the bottom sheet with play makeup.

These ruined sheets and an old, torn, store-bought, twin-size comforter became the beginning of the girls' new quilt. I decided to cut up the ruined pillowcase and sheet to make patchwork pieces and use the one good sheet for the quilt backing.

I thumbed through a stack of *Country Living* magazines specifically looking for examples of quilts made with scraps. Then, after doodling on graph paper, I designed a square that would be easy for my first quilt, consist of 50 percent pink fabric, and lend itself to the randomness needed for used fabrics. The shaded areas represent the solid-pink fabrics and the white areas represent printed fabrics. I designed it so that when the squares were sewn together, they would create diagonal patterns across the quilt, as shown below.

I purchased four items of cotton clothing with a variety of pink flowery prints for a total of 85¢ at yard sales. I sacrificed a stained, pink-printed dress and a pink-printed blouse that I didn't like, providing two free items. I cut all of the items at the seams and

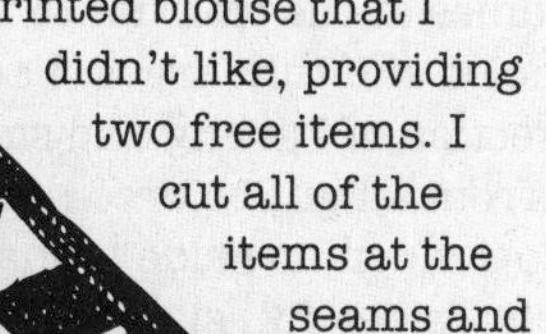

pressed the sections flat. Using cardboard templates for the square and triangle pieces, I marked and cut this fabric.

I machine-sewed the squares. No two pieces of printed fabric were alike in each square. This ensured I would have fewer leftover pieces and I could make future repairs with fabric that didn't match precisely.

I used up many of my spools of odd-colored thread to sew the squares, and "borrowed" pink thread for the more visible top stitching from a friend with whom I have a mutual-mooching relationship. I bought a ball of embroidery cotton for 10¢ at a yard sale to "tie" the quilt.

The old comforter required special preparation. The batting in store-bought comforters is rolled under at the edges before it's sewn, making a bunchy edge that is hard to work with when re-covering. I slit the edges and pulled this batting out flat. I also smoothed out lumpy batting and used batting scraps (from the ladies at the church) to repair holes and thin areas. I added a section of batting and scrap fabric (from a light-colored baby comforter) on one side to make the comforter full-size.

When assembling the layers of sheet, old comforter, and quilt top, I duct-taped corners to the floor to assure there were no wrinkles while I pinned it. Then I trimmed, tied, and hemmed the layers.

I had enough remaining pink material to make a new pillowcase and a matching, ruffled throw pillow.

This project required roughly 60 hours spread over six weeks. A "cutting wheel" (looks like a pizza cutter), knowledge of time-saving techniques, and experience would reduce these hours significantly.

After completing this quilt, I did some research to determine whether used fabrics really are cheaper than other options. I am working on my next quilt (design shown on page 188), which needs 3-inch square pieces almost exclusively. I used this dimension for my calculations:

A yard of fabric (36 inches by 45 inches) would yield 180 3-inch squares. You can buy a yard of dirt-cheap remnant material for $1.25 at a fabric store.

I went to a nearby bedding-factory outlet and bought ½ pound of sheet-fabric trimmings for $1. This yielded 196 squares. Because these were long strips there was some waste, but not as much as with smaller pieces. So purchasing fabric this way roughly equals 92¢ per yard.

I bought a boy's size-14 dress shirt for 25¢ at a yard sale. This yielded 90 squares—plus buttons. So purchasing fabric this way roughly equals 50¢ per yard, even less for adult-size clothing.

I went to a nearby thrift shop that has some boxes of quilt scraps containing both new and used fabric. I picked out what I could use in this next quilt and bought 3 pounds (half of a grocery sack) for 50¢. Because these are smaller pieces there will be far more waste. Figuring there will be a pound of waste and that ½ pound of fabric roughly equals a yard, I got 2 pounds, or 4 yards of usable fabric for 50¢. So buying fabric this way roughly equals 13¢ per yard.

But the great advantage of quilting from scraps is that you

can use clothing that is torn, stained, and otherwise unusable, as long as the fabric isn't too worn, so the material is free. In addition, once people learned I'm now working on a blue quilt, I've had two offers of free blue fabric.

Prices will vary depending on the resources in your area, but remember that sale-purchased new fabric will probably not be the cheapest.

The real surprise to me was not how cheaply quilts could be made, but that this is an ideal hobby for people with limited time and space. Because you sew a few squares at a time, quilt making can be squeezed into the tiny chunks of time we all have. Then all the pieces can be stored in a small box until the next fragment of free time. The handwork can be done while watching TV. I found it was stress-relieving to sew at the end of a one-step-forward-two-steps-backward type of day. This is a terrific example of a productive hobby that can be combined with quality family time. My children were fascinated. I discussed the process and design with them. They helped iron squares and clip threads, and ten-year-old Alec is working on his own quilt design (for me to sew).

I also learned why quilting can become a lifelong hobby; the combinations of designs, colors, and patterns are unlimited.

I made a quilt with minimal knowledge, but a stack of library books on quilting techniques and designs will be useful and a source of inspiration for most beginners. They can, however, be overwhelming. As I did, you should choose simple designs for your first venture into quilt making.

I'M DREAMING OF A TIGHT CHRISTMAS

During a rare speaking engagement I briefly addressed our culture's tendency to wrongly associate frugality with poverty. I pointed out that because frugality is incorrectly perceived as "poor person's behavior," many people are embarrassed about being frugal.

As I chatted with audience members after my speech, a woman said my comment was exactly right. She admitted that last Christmas she had spent more on her nieces and nephews, because they were from an affluent family, than she had spent on her own children.

Her story powerfully illustrates the fact that many frugal people allow themselves to be pressured into overspending during the holidays. Readers frequently tell me that they have similar problems at the workplace: pressure to chip in on birthdays, to buy candy bars to support the soccer teams of coworkers' children, and to exchange holiday gifts.

If you give in to the pressure to buy expensive gifts despite your wishes, understand why you are doing this; and why you lack the courage to say no. You may believe people perceive inexpensive gifts as signs that you are "poor,"

"cheap," and/or "thoughtless." Self-esteem becomes entangled with gift giving.

In addressing the perception of being "poor," consider that inexpensive gifts are often a sign of different values and priorities. You *can* afford the expensive gifts, but you prefer to spend your money on things that have a higher priority for you. Or you prefer to work fewer hours so that you can have more quality time with your family.

If you fear people will think you are "cheap" or "thoughtless," ask yourself if you would be happy with the quality of the gift you're giving. If you buy yourself expensive goods from Bloomingdale's, people will justifiably feel that it's inconsistent for you to buy them bargains from the dollar store. In contrast, if you always seek out bargains for yourself, others will be far more likely to accept them as presents from you.

Having a clear vision of your financial goals and making sure that frugal gifts are consistent with your whole lifestyle provide the self-esteem that's essential in dealing with those who make expensive demands of you.

Once we gain the confidence to say no, we further desire that our coworkers, friends, and family will accept, and perhaps even adopt, frugal gift giving themselves. There are two ways I know to achieve this:

THE UP-FRONT PLAN

Talk about it.

Your first inclination may be to hold the discussion on Christmas day, since everyone is in one place, but that isn't the best time. People could easily interpret what you say as a rejection of what they just gave you. Bring it up at a graduation party, a summer reunion, or some gathering that's at least a couple of months from Christmas.

You may be surprised to find how receptive other people are to the idea. Many people feel that Christmas is too commercialized, but they believe *other* people like it that way.

If you all agree that gift-giving has gotten out of hand, the next step is to decide on an alternative.

Many of these may sound familiar, but you can use this list as a tool to guide the discussion.

1. For acquaintances and friends who have become distant geographically, you might simply decide to exchange cards rather than gifts.
2. Draw names within families or between extended families, rather than buying for and receiving from everyone.
3. Shift to "household" gifts, rather than gifts to everyone in a household.
4. Try alternative gifts. Make a rule that only food can be exchanged. Suggest more swapping of services such as baby-sitting. Money that would be spent on gifts could be used to take a family trip or donated to a charity.
5. Set a spending limit, say $5, and then challenge yourselves to see how wonderful and creative you can be within that price range.

It's important that this talk be an exchange, not a lecture. Make it clear that all comments are welcome, and no point of view is "right."

As you move toward a decision,

it's also important to emphasize that it need not be permanent. If one of the strategies doesn't work, try a different one next year.

THE COVERT PLAN

If it's too late to discuss the problem with your family this year, or if you are sure the discussion would be fruitless, try *showing* them.

Although extravagance has seldom been a problem in my family, if it were, I would regard frugal gift giving as my mission to show others how much more fun inexpensive gifts can be. Here are some examples of my successes:

When Jim visited the home of a distant Navy friend during the summer, he was surprised to see the clever tag I made to go with our Christmas gift, "Jim's Homemade Wild Grape Jelly," still prominently pinned to their bulletin board. My mother has kept my homemade Christmas cards on display in her home for months. One aunt, who watched my delighted kids open their top-quality yard-sale presents as I whispered the cost of the gifts to her, laughed and said, "Gee, next year I'm doing all my shopping in Maine."

If you choose the covert plan, consider these points:

1. To successfully convert people, your gift giving must be excellent. Gifts that are inappropriate or poorly made will fail. Frugal gift giving usually requires more time and/or thought. Let your desire to prove your point drive your efforts. If those on your gift list think inexpensive equals inferior, make an extra effort to "bowl them over" with your cleverness.

2. Start slowly. In some families, where extravagant, commercial holidays are deeply entrenched, change can require several years. One friend, who can afford the extravagance of her family but dislikes their lack of imagination, has still continued to spend in the expensive tradition but has also begun to sneak in clever, homemade gifts, a first for her family. Each tiny success will slowly erode their prejudice.

3. Provide information. Although it's generally considered tacky to divulge the cost of a gift, it's essential if you want to educate the receiver. I *always* tell my children, usually at a later time, that a toy came from a yard sale. I tell them how much I paid and how much the new equivalent would have cost. If a friend thinks my homemade gift is store-bought, I "accidentally" let it out of the bag that I made it. If she really loves the gift, I might also share how easy the gift was to make, how much the materials cost, and offer a set of instructions.

4. Be confident. Never apologize for the "humbleness" of your gift. Don't even let the thought enter your mind. If you think giving your children gifts from yard sales is a sign that you are "poor," they will pick up on your feeling and believe the gift is inferior. This is also true when giving to adults. The way you feel about the gift will, to some degree, be reflected by the recipient.

In attempting either the up-

front plan or the covert plan, it helps to explain why you want to save money. If you choose the up-front plan, this reason should be a part of your discussion. If you choose the covert plan, frequently mention your financial goals to those around you. If you let everyone know you are saving for a down payment on a house, what reasonable person could fault you?

But if others still see your frugal gift giving as "poor," "cheap," and/or "thoughtless," use . . .

THE BUZZ-OFF PLAN

It's unreasonable for others to expect you to spend in accordance with their values.

And it isn't written anywhere that the cost of your gift has to match the cost of theirs. In some cases, both parties can be comfortable with the "inequity."

But even if you do encounter hostility, consider this to be their problem, not yours. If everyone had the courage to ask for a change, Christmas could be transformed from a marketing opportunity to the holiday it was meant to be.

WRAPPING IDEAS

When you buy wrapping paper on those wide, wide rolls, it's easier and less wasteful to use if you cut through the entire roll one third of the way down, using a sharp razor blade or bread knife. The smaller roll is then just right for wrapping smaller boxes, and the larger roll is perfect for shirt boxes, and so on. (Muriel Kupper, Downers Grove, Illinois.)

Wrap awkward-shaped gifts in a Rudolph bag. To make one, take a brown paper bag. Fold down the top, folding in the sides so the top is triangle-shaped. Cut antlers out of brown paper, and tape or glue to the bag. Add eyes and a red nose with crayon, marker, or even a red pom-pom. (Vicki Fisher, Ogden, Utah.)

Use leftover trick-or-treat candy from Halloween for gift-decorating presents. You can make a neat bow from gum sticks . . . leave them in the wrappers, put a small dab of Elmer's glue on the centers, and arrange in a star shape. Put an old button in the center. (Donna Watkins, Lucedale, Mississippi.)

Make a simple, decorative box from any kind of heavy paper, such as old greeting cards, wallpaper, or old calendars.

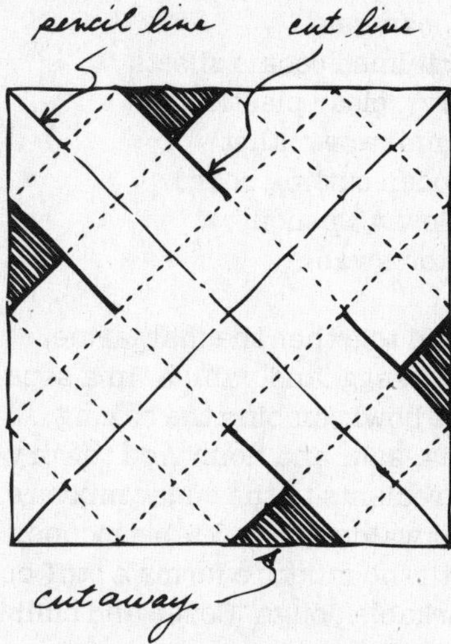

Cut the paper to a perfect square. To establish the center point of the paper, draw a pencil line from corner to corner on the reverse side. Fold a corner to the center point. Fold this fold line to the center point, lining it up with the pencil line. Repeat with the other three corners.

Cut the paper on the fold lines as shown.

To make the box, fold the corners of the two wider sides to the center point. Then fold the remaining two corners in to the center point. A dab of glue under each corner will secure the box.

To make a matching box to fit inside, repeat the process with a paper square that is ¼ inch narrower and shorter than your first square. If making boxes from greeting cards, use the "word side" for the inside box. (Jackie Wood, Gordon, Georgia.)

Enhance your scaled-down gift giving through creative "mystery wrapping." This is an especially good strategy if a family member has an annoying talent for guessing what's in a present before he unwraps it. For example if you're giving him a new belt, you could wind up the belt, put it and three marbles in a glass jar, and wrap. Or you could insert the belt into a long wrapping-paper tube and wrap. You could bend a coat hanger into a circle, wind the belt around the circular hanger, and wrap the present so it looks like a doughnut.

Cut an apple in half vertically, dip in acrylic paint, and stamp it on the inside of a cut-up paper bag. Then paint on brown seeds and green stem. Other fruits, such as lemons or oranges, could also be used. (Shawn Philley, Colville, Washington.)

FOOD FOR THE FESTIVITIES

All of the recipes in this section will make terrific gifts. You could make gift baskets with a selection of goodies. Decorate small bags with ribbon and "glitter stars," and include a homemade ornament.

In each case we tested the recipe and figured the cost (including energy for baking) and the preparation time to help you decide whether you want to try it.

STAINED-GLASS COOKIES

The original recipe, which came from a library book, frustrated my crack recipe tester so much that we initially rejected it. But her failed cookies so fascinated my children that I decided to experiment and alter the recipe to make it work. After many attempts, I finally had success.

This is a wonderful project to do with children. However, it's a bit finicky. I strongly suggest you try one cookie first, to be sure your oven times are the same as mine.

The recipe requires about 2 hours (less if you don't have help from kids) and makes about 20 cookies for $2.41.

You will need:

½ cup softened margarine
1 cup sugar
1 egg
1 teaspoon vanilla
½ teaspoon baking soda
½ teaspoon salt
2½ cups unsifted flour
1 pound assorted colored hard candies
2 foil-lined cookie sheets
heavy, clear plastic bag
hammer or mallet
wooden cutting board
yellow #2 pencil
cotton swab

Blend together the margarine, sugar, egg, and vanilla. In a separate bowl combine the baking soda, salt, and flour. Add the dry ingredients to the sugar mixture. Add water, about 6 tablespoons, until the mixture forms a stiff but workable dough. Cover and chill for 1 hour.

Unwrap and sort candies by color into separate bowls. One at a time, put each bowl of candies into the plastic bag and crush with a mallet. The final texture should include granules and small chunks. Return crushed candies to their separate bowls.

Preheat the oven to 350 degrees. Flour your hands, and roll a small piece of dough into a rope exactly the thickness of a pencil. Shape the ropes into holiday designs on the cookie sheets. Chanukah designs could include a dreidel, a Star of David, or a menorah. Christmas designs could include a Christmas tree, a star, a bell, or even a stained-glass church window.

If you want to make cookie ornaments, shape with a loop on top. For strength, this loop should be made from the middle of a long rope that forms a larger design—not added on afterward. To be sure that your loop doesn't close

up during baking, test the size with the pencil. The loop hole should be slightly larger than the eraser tip. To join the ends of the dough pieces, dab with a wet cotton swab.

Prebake the cookies for 10 minutes or until lightly golden. Remove them from the oven. Fill the cookie sections with crushed candy. The depth of the candy should be the same as the thickness of the dough. Although you can mix colors for special effects, avoid mixing "color opposites" like red and green or yellow and purple, which, when blended, turn brown or gray.

Bake about 4 minutes, watching carefully. Remove cookies as soon as the candy melts. The candy can be lumpy or smooth, depending on your preference, but it should not cook until it bubbles.

At this point you can leave the cookies plain, or you can further decorate them by immediately pressing uncooked candy chunks into the melted candy. In this way you can add "colored lights" to your Christmas trees.

Let the cookies cool completely before carefully peeling them off the foil. If your cookie loop breaks easily, you might not have prebaked the dough shapes long enough. If you want these to work as ornaments, the final cookie should be so hard that only a kid would want to eat it.

BISCOTTI

These cookies have a grown-up taste that would go nicely with a special tea. My kids were excited only about the ones that were dipped in chocolate. The recipe requires 45 minutes of preparation time and yields 16 ounces for $2.32. A pound of Stella Doro biscotti costs $3.84, and a pound from a specialty shop costs $20.

½ cup sugar
¼ cup margarine
2 eggs
1 teaspoon almond extract
¼ teaspoon anise extract
1¾ cups flour
½ cup ground almonds
¼ teaspoon salt
1 teaspoon baking powder

Mix the first five ingredients with a mixer. Combine 1½ cups of the flour, ground almonds, salt, and baking powder. Add to the egg mixture, beating well. Stir in remaining ¼ cup flour. Cover and chill for two hours. Coat two sheets of heavy-duty plastic wrap with cooking spray. Divide dough in half and shape each half into a 12-inch log using the plastic wrap. Remove the wrap and transfer the logs to a cookie sheet coated with cooking spray. Flatten the logs to a ¾-inch thickness. Bake at 350 degrees for 20 minutes. Put the logs on a wire rack to cool. Slice diagonally into ¼-inch slices. Lay slices flat on a cookie sheet, and bake at 300 degrees for 15 minutes. Turn the slices over, and bake an additional 15 minutes or until dry. Once cooled, the top edge of the cookies can be dipped in melted chocolate chips. (Monique Van Hoek, Charlottesville, Virginia.)

CANDIED ORANGE PEEL

This is classically tightwaddy, as its main ingredient is something that is usually thrown away. Assuming the peels are free, it costs 52¢ to make 20 ounces. If you figure in simmering time but not drying time, this requires 1½ hours. These are pleasantly bittersweet.

Peels from 3 large oranges or grapefruits
¾ cup water
2 tablespoons corn syrup
2¾ cups sugar

Cut the peel on each fruit into quarters. Pull the peel off in these quarter sections. Slice peel into ¼-inch-wide strips. Put them in a 3-quart saucepan (not aluminum), and add water. Bring to a boil, reduce heat, and simmer 15 minutes. Drain. Boil the water, syrup, and 2 cups of the sugar. Keep stirring until the sugar dissolves. Add the peels. Simmer 40 minutes, stirring occasionally. Remove the peels with a slotted spoon, then put on a rack over a baking pan. Drain for 5 minutes, separate peels, and dry for another hour. Toss the peels into a plastic bag with the remaining sugar. Allow to air-dry 3 more hours, then store in an airtight container. Keeps one month, or can be frozen.

TOFFEE

Candy making scares some people, so this simple, delicious recipe might be a good way to begin. You can make 1¼ pounds for $2.20. Almond Roca, which tastes almost exactly the same, costs $3.99 for 7.05 ounces. Preparation time is 21 minutes.

1 cup chopped walnuts
¾ cup packed brown sugar
½ cup butter or margarine
½ cup semisweet chocolate chips

Butter an 8-inch square pan. Spread the chopped walnuts in the pan. Heat the butter or margarine and sugar, and boil over medium heat in a 1-quart saucepan, stirring constantly. Do this until the mixture darkens and just begins to smoke, about 7 minutes. Immediately pour the mixture over the walnuts. Sprinkle the chocolate chips evenly over the hot mixture, and put a cookie sheet over the top to hold in the heat so that it melts the chips. Spread the chocolate with a knife. If desired, sprinkle ground walnuts on the melted chocolate. Score into 1½-inch squares while still warm. Refrigerate. Break into squares when cool.

CHRISTMAS CHEESE BALL

A plain, 12-ounce cheddar ball from Hickory Farms costs $3.99. This recipe makes an 11-ounce ball for about $2.80 and requires 20 minutes of preparation time. If you mass-produce these using a food processor, you can save more time. The festive look and tangy taste make this recipe a winner.

2 ounces cream cheese, softened
1 teaspoon minced onion
2 teaspoons chopped pimento
dash garlic salt
2 tablespoons mayonnaise
¼ cup chopped green pepper
8 ounces grated cheddar cheese
½ cup chopped walnuts

Combine the first seven ingredients, and form into a ball. Roll the

ball in the chopped walnuts so that the outside is completely covered. (Cindy Alldredge, Allen Park, Michigan.)

WHOLE-WHEAT CRACKERS

If you're making cheese balls for gifts, you might want to bake a batch of homemade crackers to go along with them. This recipe, a personal favorite of my recipe tester, is similar to a recipe I published a few years ago, except it's less crumbly. It requires 35 minutes of preparation time and makes 20 ounces for about 88¢. A 12-ounce box of Nabisco Wheat Thins costs $2.79.

1½ cups whole-wheat flour
1½ cups white flour
¼ cup sugar
1 teaspoon salt
½ teaspoon baking soda
½ cup margarine
¾ cup buttermilk
¼ cup wheat germ

Sift the first five ingredients together. Add the margarine and process in food processor. Add the buttermilk, and process until it forms a ball. Set it aside for 10 minutes. Cut the dough into four parts. Grease cookie sheets and sprinkle them with wheat germ. Roll each dough piece out on a cookie sheet. Sprinkle with salt. Cut into diamond shapes with a pastry wheel. Bake at 350 degrees for 20 to 25 minutes. Cool and put into a covered container.

PUPPY CHOW (FOR PEOPLE)

A staffer made these for us last year, and I asked her for the recipe for publication. If you don't have double coupons, the Crispix cereal will be the expensive ingredient. This recipe requires 20 minutes and makes 8 cups. Without coupons, the recipe costs $3.94, or 49¢ per 1-cup gift.

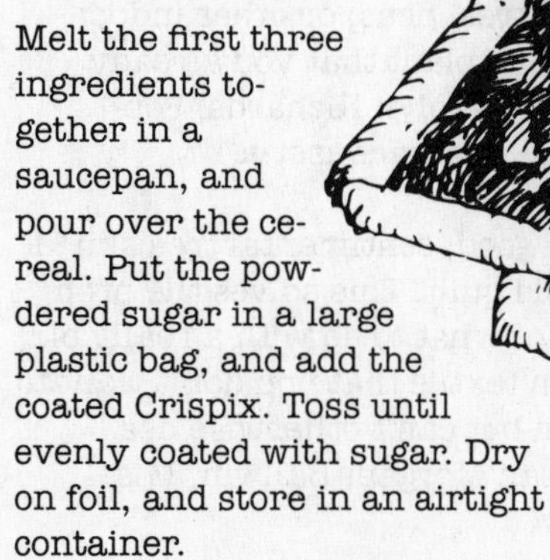

1 cup chocolate chips
1 stick margarine
1 cup peanut butter
8 cups Crispix cereal
2 cups powdered sugar

Melt the first three ingredients together in a saucepan, and pour over the cereal. Put the powdered sugar in a large plastic bag, and add the coated Crispix. Toss until evenly coated with sugar. Dry on foil, and store in an airtight container.

SOUTH OF THE BORDER SALSA

A quart of homemade salsa, a huge bag of taco chips, and a 2-liter bottle of soda make a flavorful and appreciated gift.

4 cups canned tomatoes with juice
1 large onion, diced
1 small, fresh jalapeño pepper, seeds and all, minced fine (adjust the amount depending upon the spiciness desired)
¼ teaspoon garlic powder
Salt and pepper

Cook all the ingredients in a large saucepan for 20 minutes. Pour into hot, sterile quart jars, and seal. Process in a pressure canner for 25 minutes. (Peggy West, Cleveland, Ohio.)

TREES FOR FREE

Residents of college towns should note that students leave for home between December 10 and 15 and leave the curbs strewn with perfectly good, discarded Christmas trees waiting to be rescued and recycled. (Corinne Kinane, Syracuse, New York.)

There's no law dictating that a Christmas tree must be a dead evergreen. You can decorate an orange tree, ficus, or other indoor treelike plant that you already own. (Carolyn Richards, Pepperell, Massachusetts.)

A good, sentimental tree skirt is an old quilt. This solves the problem of what to do with a really old, worn textile that you don't want to pitch but can't otherwise use. (Susan Morgan, Ballwin, Missouri.)

In some areas, the U.S. Forest Service sells a permit for about $8 that allows private citizens to select and cut one Christmas tree from a national forest. Forestry experts advise taking small trees that are within 10 feet of another small tree, as this "thinning" can help the forest. (Valerie Campbell, Calhan, Colorado.)

If you get all gooey about the ritual of tree decorating, this idea may seem *too* efficient, but you can save lots of time, energy, and money by buying an on-sale artificial Christmas tree, decorating it with lots of sale ornaments and lights, and storing it, complete with decorations, in the basement. Protect it with two garbage bags: one over the top, the other pulled up from the bottom, and seal the seam with duct tape. (Andi Hart, Camas, Washington.)

NOT NECESSARILY HALLMARK

This is a well-known tightwad tip, but it bears repeating just in case you don't know it: You can cut off the front half of a used Christmas card to make a Christmas postcard.

Kids enjoy making cards. Just supply them with green construction paper, gold paint, and red glitter. But they may tire before they produce the desired volume of cards. You can mass-produce their artwork as follows: Have the kid draw a picture on a Styrofoam meat tray, pressing hard enough to make an impression. Then use a hard-rubber roller (available at art-supply stores) to roll ink on the meat tray. Lay a piece of paper over the inked tray, and rub lightly with a spoon.

Paste a wintertime picture of your home on a piece of plain paper, leaving a 1-inch margin at the bottom. Using calligraphy, write something like "Holiday Greetings from the Swartz Family." Photocopy the card onto some colored paper (white paper might give better results with some photos). Then fold and trim to fit the envelope. (Ron Swartz, Sharon Springs, New York.)

GIFTS FOR GROWN-UPS

Make a jewelry purse for frequent travelers. As I made samples to test this idea, my small daughters were quick to claim them. Cut one 13½-inch and one 11-inch circle from paper to use as patterns. Cut two circles of each size from lightweight fabric. Cut a 5-inch circle from a piece of noncorrugated cardboard or, if you want the purse to be washable, use the plastic lid from a margarine tub. Stitch the "right sides" of the large fabric circles together with a seam that is about ¼-inch from their edges, leaving a 1-inch gap in the seam. Do the same with the small fabric circles. Turn the fabric circles inside out, press, and hand-stitch the gaps closed.

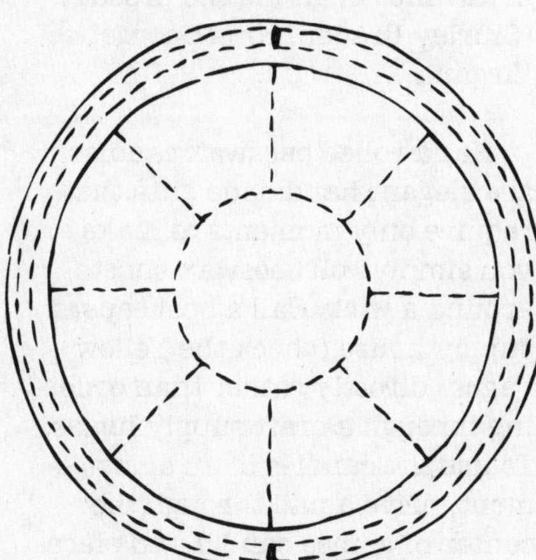

Place the two fabric circles on top of each other with the cardboard in between and pin to secure all three pieces. Sew around the cardboard circle. Fold the 11-inch paper circle into eighths, and use the fold marks as a guide to divide the smaller fabric circle into eight sections. Mark the sections with pins. Sew eight seams from the edge of the cardboard circle to the edge of the smaller fabric circle.

Sew two seams around the larger fabric circle, one about ½-inch from the edge, and the second ½-inch inside the first. Cut two slits between these two seams on opposite sides of the purse. (To prevent fraying, these slits can be coated with "Fray Check," or you can sew buttonholes in these places before the larger fabric circles are sewn together.) Using a large safety pin, thread two drawstrings through these slits.

When the drawstrings are pulled, the purse has an area in the center for large pieces of jewelry and eight pockets for earrings and other small items.

If you have extra fabric, you might stitch some matching drawstring bags to hold shoes. (Meg Winfield, Columbia, Maryland.)

Copies of old photographs, such as grandparents' wedding pictures or Mom and Dad's baby portraits, make wonderful gifts for grown family members. Photo stores can charge as little as $3 to make a negative, and 30¢ for each 3½-by-5-inch copy. Extra touches, such as sepia toning, can cost a bit more. If you don't own family heirloom photographs, borrow them, and make an extra photo

for the lender to show your appreciation. These can be given for years, as you work back through parents, grandparents, great-grandparents, and so on. (Karen Humiston, Sheboygan, Wisconsin.)

Check to see if local, nonprofit agencies are offering items. For instance, a local group raising money to renovate low-income housing is selling cedar ornaments at $5 each. A purchase like this contributes to a good cause and provides a gift that could be given to a boss, and so on. (Joan Brown, Lake Lotawana, Missouri.)

For elderly relatives who find shopping difficult, stock up on the foods and products they like as they go on sale throughout the year. At Christmas, you'll have collected enough to fill a carton, which you can decorate for their Christmas present. While it is not an "exciting" present, it is sure to be appreciated. (Camille Hawthorne, Munchen, Germany.)

Make a homemade bird feeder: Take a hardwood branch that is about 12 inches long and 3 inches in diameter. With a drill or hole saw, cut two holes about 2½ inches apart as shown. About ½ inch below the large holes, drill another hole about ½ inch wide. Cut two ½-inch dowels, or twigs, about 6 inches long, and insert them into the ½-inch holes. Glue into place. Cut the top of the branch at a slight angle so water will run off. Put an eye bolt in the top center of the log, thread with cord, and hang from a tree.

Fill the two large holes in the bird feeder with birdseed mixture. Be sure to include this recipe with your gift:

2 cups shortening
1 cup peanut butter
1 cup cornmeal
1 cup oatmeal or flour
1 cup birdseed

Melt the shortening with the peanut butter in a large saucepan. Add the cornmeal and mix well. Add the birdseed and mix well. Pour into a rectangular baking pan or cupcake pans, and let set overnight. Pack into holes in the bird feeder with a spoon or your hands. Can be made months in advance of giving the present. (Shirley Braden, King George, Virginia.)

Hand-rolled beeswax candles are elegant handmade gifts that require only moments to make . . . you simply roll beeswax sheets around a wick. Call a beekeepers' supply house (check the Yellow Pages) directly rather than ordering through a craft-supply house. To use the candles in an arrangement, drive a nail through the center of a juice-can lid and place on a table with the nail up. Press candle on the nail to secure it. Arrange several candles together, and put the flowers or greenery around the base. (Sharon L. Crow, Klamath Falls, Oregon.)

For a "homemade" gift that requires only shopping skills, put together your own version of the

overpriced food baskets sold by Hickory Farms and similar companies. For example, there is a gift pack with five 2-ounce packages of flavored coffee for $18.99. At a gourmet coffee shop, they can be purchased for $1.49 each, totaling $7.45. At the grocery store, they can be purchased for 99¢ each, totaling $4.95. Use decorative baskets or tins, and fill with gourmet coffee, homemade spiced-tea mix, homemade cookies and candies, mixed nuts (bought in bulk), and/or home-canned jam or jelly. Add some fresh fruit and a personal touch, such as a homemade Christmas ornament. (Angela Birchfield, Warner Robins, Georgia.)

Certificates for services are always appreciated. "One night of baby-sitting" is common, and a welcome gift to parents. More creative alternatives include "One year's worth of mending," which is especially appreciated by college students. Other ideas could include snow shoveling, changing oil, or home repairs. (Jody Grage Haug, Seattle, Washington.)

The Lentil-Rice Casserole (page 151) works well as a gift. Put raw ingredients in a 1-pint canning jar. Put a pretty piece of fabric over the top before screwing on the band. Make a label that says "Tightwad Casserole" and provide cooking instructions. (Kirsten Melton, Pleasant Hill, California.)

A hot-glue gun is a gift that every young parent should have . . . handy for toy repairs, Halloween-costume creation, and general crafts. (Dr. Richard Sonnenfeld, San Jose, California.)

If you own a camcorder, make videotapes of your adult children. Each year, give them a videotape featuring them and their families. (Joyce Bant, Hazelhurst, Wisconsin.)

Have a contest to see how many gifts a husband and wife can buy for each other for $10. Requires ingenuity, and makes for a special Christmas morning. (Vivian Walker, Markham, Ontario, Canada.)

Make it a rule that only consumable, "festive" items can be exchanged. Examples (many of which are homemade): flavored salad vinegars, honey, spices, candies, and fancy jams and jellies. You may also specify that less exotic items are okay, such as cotton balls, soda, tissues, soaps, pens, lightbulbs, and so on. Add quips such as "Do you know how to tuna guitar?" to a can of tuna. (April Passofaro, Prior Lake, Minnesota.)

Give a "soup of the month." Make a double batch of some special soup once each month, and give half to the gift recipient. This gift enhances your own menus as well. The same idea could be used for breads. (Pat Miller, San Antonio, Texas.)

If the recipient has freezer space, make several batches of slice-and-bake cookie dough, which can be frozen in rolls and wrapped attractively. This allows the recipient to have cookies after the holiday glut has passed. Recipes can be found in *The Complete Make-a-Mix Cookbook* by Eliason, Harward, and Westover. Order it

through interlibrary loan. (Rebecca Novakovich, Cambridge, Massachusetts.)

If you have an excess of family photos, recycle them into mini photo albums made from 5-inch-by-7-inch pieces of construction paper. Put yarn through holes punched in the left side, and add clever captions. (Wanda Owen, Wexford, Pennsylvania.)

For a gift for a grandparent, have a child put her hands on a copy machine at the edges of the markings for a regular-size sheet of paper. Either put a photo of the child between the hands, or leave blank if you have a photo you want to paste in. A note under the photo or just a signature with the date and/or age of the child finishes the gift. If these are given each year, they can be collected into a notebook. (Mary Lou Fisher, Redmond, Washington.)

Make a bead-and-fabric necklace: Get a piece of cotton

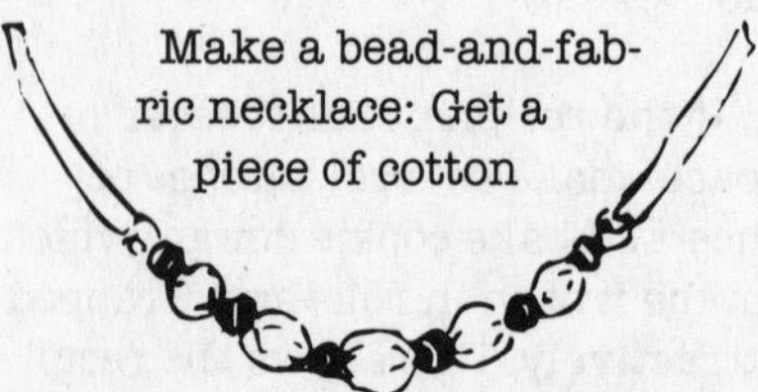

or cotton-blend fabric, 36 inches by 3 inches. Fold in half lengthwise. Sew down the long edge with a ¼-inch seam allowance. Turn inside out. Alternately insert large beads into the tube, and string smaller beads on the outside of the tube. Make about 8 inches of beadwork. Adjust all to the center of the strip. Knot each end of the beadwork. Tuck in a half inch of each end of the fabric tube, and stitch closed. (Rhonda Monden, Moore, Oklahoma.)

GIFTS FOR KIDS

This Christmas section would not be complete without a plea for restraint when it comes to toy buying, which is where Christmas becomes the most crazy and materialistic. So here's a letter that makes some excellent points:

I am approaching my first tightwad Christmas with three sons (ages thirteen, ten, and five) who have seen only spendthrift Christmases. I was worried about how well my resolve would hold out as the shopping season approached, so I went into the boys' rooms and made lists of last year's gifts (those that were still around), writing down the cost of each and estimating the time each had been played with. Some (jigsaw puzzles and board games) proved to have been good buys. Unfortunately, in other cases, my estimates showed that my husband had worked more hours to pay for a toy than my children had played with it!

Armed with last year's list, I made my first Christmas-shopping trip last weekend. After slowly touring every aisle of one of the largest toy stores in Wichita, my cart held only two modest gifts. I looked at everything, considering

the probable play value of each item. I discovered there really are not many good ideas in toys and games. In many cases, the good ones have been around since my childhood. I am no longer worried that I will spend too much this year. Rather, I am worried that it may prove hard to find gifts that meet my new criteria. (Jane Kelly, Wichita, Kansas.)

Begin stockpiling yard-sale toys in May. New-looking toys selling for less than one tenth of their original cost are common at yard sales. Also, for older kids, check out the used sporting-goods stores that are popping up all over the country.

A month or so before Christmas, take books you no longer need to a secondhand bookstore. Trade them for "new" children's books. (Marie Davies, St. Louis, Missouri.)

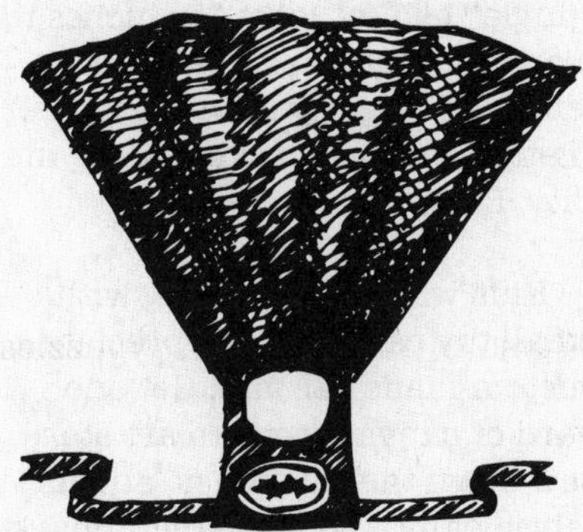

Make a superhero cape from fabric scraps. Cut two chest pieces, then cut out pieces for the logo. Adhere the logo to the front, chest piece with fabric glue and a zigzag stitch. Make two long strips for tying on. Attach these when you are sewing the chest pieces together. Attach the cape at the shoulders. (Cindy Alldredge, Allen Park, Missouri.)

Make an Indian teepee. Cut triangular shapes for the height wanted. Sew together, making a casing at each seam. Put PVC pipe through for poles, about a foot taller than the top of the fabric. Tie poles together at the top, and secure with hot glue. Paint on Indian designs if desired. Similar teepees sell in catalogs for $59.95. (Cindy Alldredge, Allen Park, Missouri.)

One of the best kid-gift concepts is "gathered presents." Assembling these requires skilled scrounging and advance planning, but they make wonderful, creative gifts. These include:

Doctor's office: Bag (black canvas or vinyl purse with white cross and "M.D." written on it), eye dropper, syringe (no needle), small scissors, adhesive tape, swabs, cotton balls, tongue depressors (cleaned popsicle sticks or ask your doctor for a few) bandages, gauze, small cups, plastic gloves, sling, mirrored headband, name tag, stethoscope (can be made from wire coat hanger, black electrical tape, adhesive tape, and a juice-can lid), X ray (black paper with a white drawing of skull or bones), small skeleton model, skeleton chart (copy from reference book), eye chart, clipboard, prescription pad, office-hours sign.

"Crimebusters": Magnifying glass, flashlight, gloves, binoculars or periscope, camera, decoder, invisible writing pens, handcuffs, I.D. with badge, signs for office, attaché case, small tool

kit, safe, crime-scene reports, evidence bags, money, CRIME SCENE — DO NOT CROSS banner.

School: Chalkboard, chalk, eraser, pointer, spelling tests, report cards with envelopes, write-and-wipe calendar, markers, roll book, bell, flag and stand, U.S.A. map, puzzles, whistle, clock, hall pass, stamps or stickers that say "excellent," "well-done," and so on, awards, reward jar with treasures, red pen, pencils.

Crafts: Feathers, sequins, construction paper, yarn, beads, colorful macaroni, mini-clothespins, paints, markers, dowels, confetti, glue, scissors, pipe cleaners, doilies, buttons, pom-poms, moving eyes, metal brads, idea book, carrying case.

Other possible gathered-present themes include: café, office, travel, veterinarian, learn-to-read, and theater. (Debra Posthumus-Forbes, Kalamazoo, Michigan.)

Make Christmas "treasure boxes." Cut long strips of the colorful Sunday funnies, and put in a box. Bury within this assorted candies, and, for girls, a pretty lipstick holder, a pink, folding comb, inexpensive, colorful earrings, and other small yard-sale treasures you've collected over the year. This is a nice idea for mailing to distant relatives, when you don't know their children well enough to know what they like. (Laura Henning, Flushing, New York.)

Metal riding horses on spring frames are often inexpensive at yard sales because they have worn paint. You can repaint one with a variety of colors . . . you can even paint it to match the colors of the child's favorite "My Little Pony." (Lauren Wahl, Miami, Florida.)

Babies love a simple Christmas rattle made from a large, metal "jingle" bell (at least 1½ inches in diameter) attached to a short length of brightly colored ribbon. (Letty Bernard Steckler, Morgan City, Louisiana.)

Kids who enjoy playing with small toy cars might appreciate a custom-made car mat. Get one yard of canvas from an art store, sew down the raw edges, and use fabric paint and permanent markers to make streets, stores, Dad's work, our house, the library, the local sports stadium and McDonald's (for spendthrift families) or the thrift shop (for frugal families). (Mary Nafis, Chino, California.)

HOLIDAY TRADITIONS

If your child constantly asks "How many days until Christmas?" try this variation of a Cherokee ceremony for children: Tie knots in a rope, one for each day remaining until Christmas, and hang it on the child's doorknob. Each night, untie one knot. This can become a much-loved family tradition. (Jennifer Pounds, Dawsonville, Georgia.)

Ask older children to take on a service project, such as helping in a food drive for the homeless, in place of a gift to their parents. On Christmas, have them report on what they did as they open their gifts from the parents. (Sharon Ditto, Hixson, Tennessee.)

Insert "work chores" and "fun chores" into red and green balloons. Examples: "Help clear the table, and share a favorite Christmas memory," "Serve the dessert, and kiss the neighbor on your left," "Take extra chairs back to the kitchen, and tell about your best Christmas ever," and "Relax, put your feet up, and take a nap." Blow up balloons and tape them overhead at Christmas dinner. Have long, curly ribbons hanging from each one. After dinner, each diner pulls a ribbon, bursts the balloon, reads the note, and does what it says. Children and adults both love this, and it can become a family tradition for Thanksgiving as well. (Jean L. Winteringham, Farmington, Michigan.)

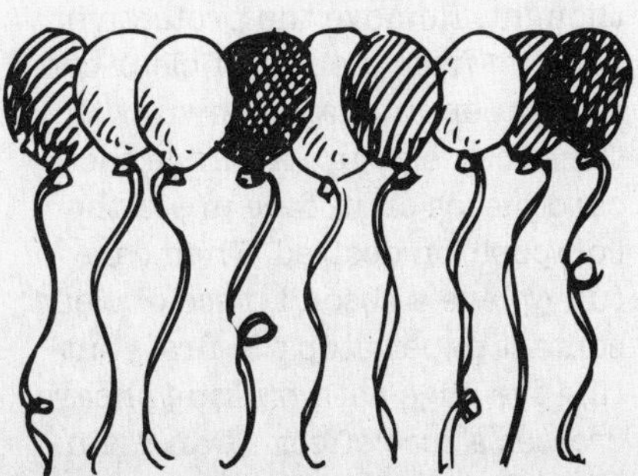

Make an Advent candle from 11-inch to 12-inch candles, which can be purchased on sale for as little as 20¢. Mark them into 24 sections with acrylic paint, then number each section, starting with 1 at the top and 24 at the bottom. Each night at dinner, burn down one section. (Vicki Fisher, Ogden, Utah.)

For families with several young children, pick up inexpensive gifts at yard sales . . . a typical price is 25¢. During the holiday season, allow kids to do special chores in exchange for "Mommy money." Just before Christmas, set up "store," setting out gifts you have preselected for one child at a time. The kids come and buy using "Mommy money." Little kids enjoy earning and giving gifts, older

kids enjoy saving money, and parents enjoy the extra help they get from kids. (Susan Dransfield, Nampa, Idaho.)

A homemade "Christmas Book" can be made from yard-sale stuff, including a three-ring binder covered with a scrap of Christmas fabric. Put dividers inside labeled: STORIES, RECIPES, GIFTS TO MAKE, DECORATIONS TO MAKE, and so on. Cut out stories, recipes, and craft instructions from Christmas magazines purchased at yard sales or fished from recycling bins, and put them in their proper places in the book. Get the book out the day after Thanksgiving, and use it regularly up until the big day. (Vickie Jackson, Lubbock, Texas.)

DECORATIONS FOR THE HOME

The decorative border on some Christmas cards makes a perfect mat for framing holiday photographs. Just cut out the center of the card with an X-Acto knife so that the border remains intact, then trim the edges so it will fit in a yard-sale frame. (Karen Jones, Lovettsville, Virginia.)

Luminarias, made with paper bags, sand, and candles, can be difficult to light in windy weather. Gallon plastic milk jugs, cut off so that they are about 8 inches high, provide a similar look, but with more manageability and safety. (Carol Leppert, Erie, Michigan.)

Luminarias can also be made of tin cans. Fill a can with water

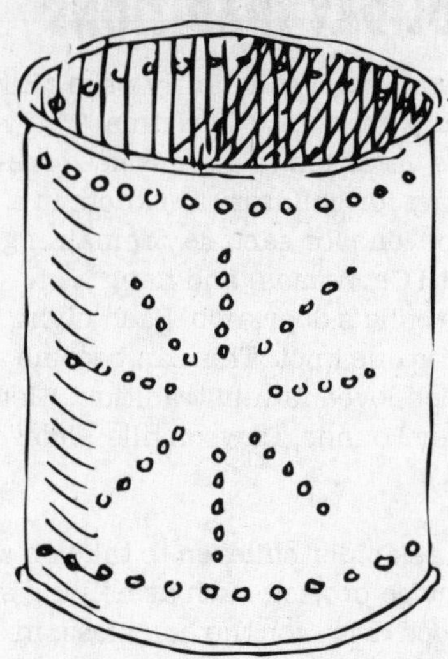

and freeze, then punch holes with a hammer and nail to form a picture or abstract pattern, such as a Christmas tree, snowflake, or Star of David. The frozen water inside keeps the can from bending as you punch it. (Jay-Niles Memorial Library, North Jay, Maine.)

You can add sparkle to old-fashioned pomander balls by alternating the cloves with silver studs . . . the kind kids stick on jeans. (Ruth Sutton, Porterville, California.)

Christmas placemats can be made with old Christmas cards. Choose the part you want to show . . . either the cover, the inside scripture, or a warm, handwritten thought. Remove the protective backing from a sheet of clear contact paper, and lay it down with the sticky side up. Arrange the card pieces on it, face up, in the composition desired. Then carefully place a second piece of clear contact paper atop the first. Cutting the edge with pinking shears creates a nice effect. (Dan Steinbeck, Canton, Missouri.)

Children who are too young to light Chanukah candles can "light" the candles on a menorah wall hanging made of felt. The "flames" are attached with Velcro backing, so that one more can be stuck on each night. Ready-made, store-bought versions of this cost $25, but materials for a homemade version are under $2.50. (Celeste Leibowitz, Brooklyn, New York.)

Make an Advent calendar from poster board, construction paper, and glue. You can make a Christmas-tree shape of green paper, and cut pictures from holiday catalogs or Christmas cards. (Barbara Durmick, Alexandria, Virginia.)

Here is an inexpensive Christmas potpourri:

peels from 2 apples, dried and broken up
1 cup or less orange peel, dried and broken up
2 tablespoons whole cloves
1 cinnamon stick, broken into small pieces

Mix and store in a jar or paper bag. Simmer in a pot for a wonderful aroma. (Rene Miles, Lake Jackson, Texas.)

Use what you have, creatively. For example, collect a half-dozen stuffed bears, tie inexpensive plaid ribbon around their necks, and arrange them on a cleaned-up child's sled to make an attractive indoor display. (Jane R. Gilson, Denville, New Jersey.)

Make decorative "snowflakes" from six-pack rings. You can obtain these without buying the soda by speaking with the vending-machine stocker at your place of business or the manager of a convenience store.

To make one you'll need 20 six-pack rings, a small stapler, thread, and white yarn or narrow ribbon.

Place two rings together, and staple together at points 1, 2, and 3. This makes one "pair" with a "front and back section." Repeat until you have ten stapled pairs. Fold the end of each of the 20 rings, and staple at points 4, 5, 6, and 7.

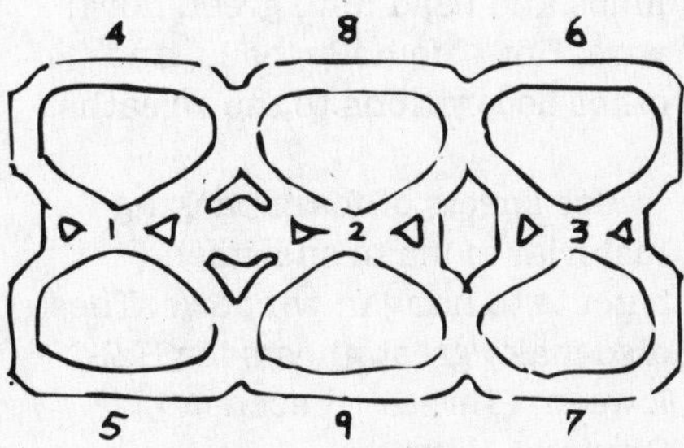

To attach the ten pairs together, staple point 8 in one pair to point 9 in another. Attach both the front and back sections in this way. You now have one long piece.

Run a piece of thread through one end of front sections. Repeat with the back section on the same end. Pull these threads tight to form the center of the snowflake. To complete the snowflake, staple the remaining points 8 to the remaining points 9.

These can be left as is or decorated with "spray snow." Hang with yarn or ribbon.

By cutting the rings and experimenting with different combinations, you can make different sizes and designs. (Norma Kelly, Huntsville, Alabama.)

Make "grapevine" wreath ornaments from the hanging branches of weeping willow trees. Gather branches while they are still soft and pliable, wrap them to form a circle and fasten with wire. Set them aside for a few days to dry, then decorate with a small bow. Small ones can be used to decorate wrapped packages, larger ones can be hung on the wall. (Christine Summers, Levittown, Pennsylvania.)

Beat-up artificial Christmas trees can be recycled into permanent wreaths . . . just remove the limbs and bend onto green floral wire. Hot-glue holly, bells, and other decorations to the wreaths.

Use sheets of foam packing material to make snowmen cutouts to hang in windows. These also make great ghosts for Halloween. (Teresa Huebener, Ottumwa, Iowa.)

Put several mason jars on a sill, and stuff an equal length of inexpensive twinkle lights in each jar. (Mary Christensen, Larson, Wisconsin.)

Pine-cone Christmas trees are an excellent project for large groups of children. Spray-paint large pine cones green, then have kids decorate them with glitter and top them with stars. (Larada Lynn Read, Oxford, Georgia.)

EASY AND INEXPENSIVE ORNAMENTS

Recycle scratched glass ornaments. Remove the metal neck and hanger. Soak the whole ornament, inside and out, in bleach for 5 to 15 minutes. Use a cotton swab or child's toothbrush, if needed, to carefully scrub the inside. Rinse it, dry it, and stuff it. Use feathers, tinsel, potpourri, confetti, or anything colorful. Replace neck and hanger. The outside can also be decorated with feathers and lace. The sample sent in to me is attractive enough to make a nice gift. (Fran DeChane, Eastpointe, Michigan.)

Make woven hearts: Cut two 7-inch-by-2-inch pieces from different-colored paper or felt. Fold each piece, round the end, and cut strips as

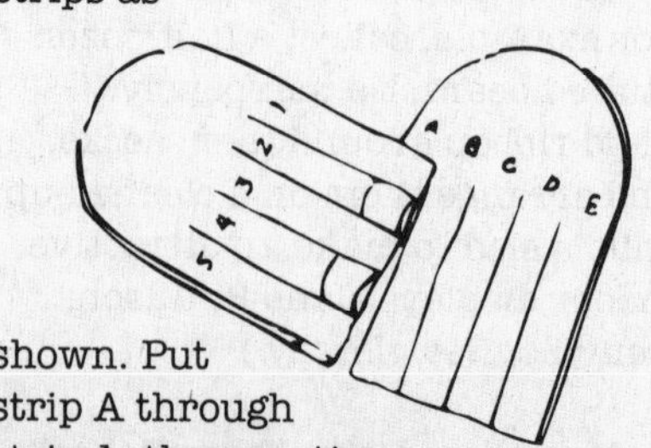

shown. Put strip A through strip 1, then continue in an "around, through, around, through" pattern. Slide strip A up

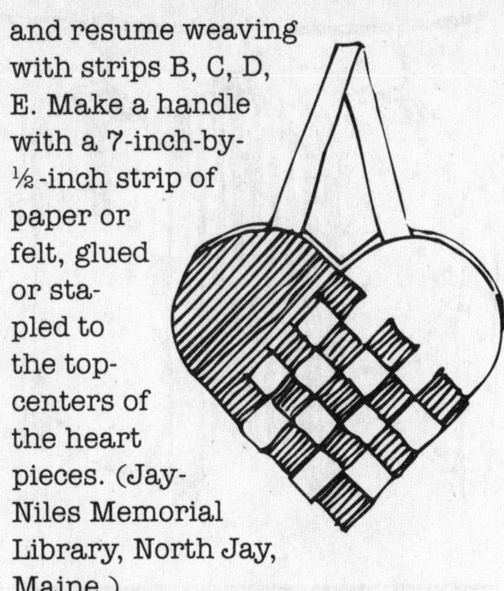

and resume weaving with strips B, C, D, E. Make a handle with a 7-inch-by-½-inch strip of paper or felt, glued or stapled to the top-centers of the heart pieces. (Jay-Niles Memorial Library, North Jay, Maine.)

Glitter stars are among the simplest ornaments to make, yet they are strikingly pretty. Use white craft glue (such as Tacky, Sobo, or Elmer's, which works best) in a bottle with a tip. Simply "draw" a star shape on wax paper. (Aluminum foil worked better for us.) The shapes can be solid or a ¼-inch line. Don't try to make the star shapes too perfect. Sprinkle the glue with glitter, making sure it is completely covered. Let the stars dry for 4 to 24 hours, depending on the type of glue. Carefully peel the wax paper or foil away from the back, working in from each point. Hang on your tree, or use to decorate presents. Use this same idea to make hearts for Valentine's Day. (Rhonda Cliett, Belton, Texas.)

Put a cheap paper plate and water in a blender, and process on "liquefy" for one minute. Press the pulp into a cookie mold, and let dry until hard. Decorate with gold glitter, and hang from a loop of gold thread or an ornament hanger. (Barbie Murray, Sterling, Virginia.)

The pattern to make this paper dove comes from *Better Homes & Gardens* magazine. Start by making this pattern out of cardboard:

Fold a heavy piece of white paper in half. Line up the top edge of the pattern with the fold, and trace. Cut out the paper bird. Glue the two halves of the head together with a drop of white glue . . . put on a paper clip to hold it together as it dries.

Once dry, insert each wing through the slot from the inside outward, as shown. Make a hole in the bird's back, and hang with a loop of string.

AFTER THE HOLIDAYS . . .

About a month after Christmas, visit any large cemetery. You'll find the caretakers have piled big heaps of ornaments and decorations ready for trash pickup. It's easily possible to collect several bags of decorations. If you have a problem with this hint, ask yourself this question: Why is a landfill a more sacred and respectful destination than your home?

This seems incredible to those of us who live up north . . . but apparently, in Southern areas, the weekend after Christmas is the best time of year for yard sales, as that is when many people get rid of unwanted gifts. This is an excellent time to pick up brand-new gifts for next Christmas.

Save gifts that you cannot use to give to someone else next year . . . for example, if you don't drink and are given liquor, pass it along next Christmas. Be sure to put a tag on it noting who gave it to you, to avoid major embarrassment. (Anna Weisend, Cleveland, Ohio.)

PICTURE PERFECT

Dear Amy,

I have a tightwad *perfect* gift suggestion when you are the mothers of the bride and groom. Moms get together and swap pictures from birth—match age to age—Cub Scout to Brownie, cheerleader to Little League, whatever. Place in a collage and have a *keepsake* gift for the couple.

—Deb Palka
Peoria, Illinois

A FINE LINE

Dear Amy,

I don't use clothespins to hang up my shirts. Instead, I hang them on plastic hangers, and put the hangers on the clothesline. I can fit more clothes on the line this way, and taking them down to put them away is much quicker.

—Ellen J. Urbina-Martin
Salem, New Hampshire

ISN'T THIS GRATE?

Dear Amy,

Our grocery store sells blocks of cheese for about $3 per pound. The same store has a salad/taco bar, which features, among other items, grated cheddar cheese. The items in this salad bar sell for $1.99 a pound. Most of the time, when we want cheese we want it in grated form, so buying our cheese from the salad bar saves both money and the work of grating.

—Susan Schubel
Fredericksburg, Virginia

SCRAP HAPPY

Dear Amy,

For cheap or free fabric, contact a custom drapery shop. My husband installs draperies, and the drapery workroom has tons of remnants from lace to heavy fabrics. This has been a big savings on dresses and craft materials for my family.

—Marlene Albers
Katy, Texas

WEAR AND SPARE

Dear Amy,

I used to feel that waiting a week to ten days, then doing six to eight loads of laundry, was cost-efficient (because the loads were full) and energy efficient (my energy, that is) in that I would save on trips to the various areas where the folded clothes were kept. But I suddenly realized that if you wash more frequently, you can have fewer clothes and need less storage. In my limited-storage home, that's a larger saving.

—Lynn Golson
Tucson, Arizona

(I realized this years ago. Because I wash every day, it's possible for a boy to squeak through a school year with two good pairs of jeans. FZ)

EARN DOCKET CHANGE

Dear Amy,

By appearing in court to "explain" a traffic violation, you can save money.

I neglected to renew my tags, and the original fine was $133 (stated on the ticket). In court I explained this was an oversight. The judge reduced the fine to $75. That saved me $58. It would have been a greater reduction if I hadn't been five months expired. *Oops!*

—Kathleen Sconce
Evans, Washington

NEWS YOU CAN USE

Dear Amy,

Encourage your local paper to start a reader exchange. Our weekly town paper just started one, and it has been a big hit. People can call in their requests for hard-to-find items or offers of free items. People call in their replies, which are printed the following week. We already have acquired some nice things for free.

—Kimberly Frodelius
Solvay, New York

UNITED WE SAVE

Dear Amy,

I wanted to make my own price book for over a year but could not seem to make myself spend the time or effort. Finally, I made up a list of regular grocery items and then photocopied the list and distributed it among friends. Each person did a price survey of a different store in our area in the same week. I compiled the results and distributed these to each participant. Now I have a price book, and it took only one week to put together!

—Eve Burch
Claremont, California

VAPOR VALUE

Dear Amy,

To get "free" distilled water, save gallon jugs and use water from your dehumidifier during the summer months. Use it for your iron or vaporizer.

—Amy Guenterberg
Madison, Wisconsin

TEST-TUBE TIGHTWADDERY

Jim's guffaw boomed from the laundry room where he was changing Brad's diaper. "Come on, Amy, don't you think bread-bag plastic pants is a bit over the edge?" Although my long-suffering husband of 12 years has become used to such oddities, it still caught him off-guard to unsnap his son's pants and read "Butter-Top Wheat Bread."

This particular experiment came about because our plastic-pants supply was low and our bread-bag supply was high. I had remembered the early disposables, which were held with pins, and wondered if a slit-open-and-flattened bread bag could work with cloth diapers in the same way. It did work reasonably well. Although I've never used the idea again, I've always known it could serve in a pinch.

Scoffers will rightly accuse me of being nutty if I ever advocate bread-bag plastic pants as a permanent solution. However, I proudly defend my actions in the larger context of tightwad scientific experimentation. The person who is willing to try new ways of doing things will have some failures, but also have infinitely more successes than the person who is unwilling to try at all. It's the constant, creative experimenting—"tweaking" to make adjustments—that helps you save an extra 5 percent or 10 percent more than the less adventurous tightwads.

But often people don't experiment because:

- They figure that Heloise, or I, or some other domestic genius must have already figured out the best way. But in consumer reporting, complex information is often distilled into very simplistic answers that work only for the average person in an average place with average resources. It's a sure bet that you don't fit that description.
- They have complete faith in the way they've always done things. But think back to all those

scientific facts that have been disproved: The world is flat, the earth is the center of the universe, and man can't fly. Given that these immutable facts have been disproved, how do we know that freezing panty hose makes them last longer, anyway?

• They're afraid they will be ridiculed if their experiment fails. But don't think of ideas that didn't work as failures. When Thomas Edison was asked about his 1,000 failed experiments in an effort to perfect the lightbulb, he said he didn't regard these experiments as failures, he had merely learned 1,000 ways it wouldn't work.

I see this experimental mindset in "black-belt" tightwads who send me all sorts of unconventional ideas. However, one failing I frequently observe is a lack of true scientific methodology—specifically, the failure to test the idea against a "control group." To be purely scientific, you need to compare results of the experimental method to the results of the conventional method.

One experimental-versus-control-group test I plan to try involves an old tightwad theory: If you put iron-on patches on the inside knees of new pants, the pants will last longer. Although this sounds logical, I have wondered whether it would make sense for yard-sale pants in good condition. If I buy these pants for 50¢, would it be worth it to iron on $1.25 worth of patches?

In the past, I've found that though the patch holds up, sometimes the area around a patch wears faster. So I plan to iron a patch on one knee and see how much longer the patched knee lasts compared to the unpatched one.

Like Edison, I've tried experiments that didn't work. I wondered if small amounts of leftover casseroles could be saved in a muffin cup to make "leftover muffins." It didn't work.

I knew you could substitute a heaping tablespoon of soy flour and a tablespoon of water for an egg when baking, and I knew you could substitute an equal amount of applesauce for cooking oil in baking. So I wondered what would happen if I used soy flour *and* applesauce in a drop-cookie recipe. The cookies, after a much longer-than-normal baking time, just sat there and got harder; they never expanded and melted the way regular cookies do.

I concluded that in most baking, recipes need some fat to work.

But I have also had successes. Last year I made sauce from the small, sour apples of neglected, nearby trees. The resulting dark applesauce was so sour the children wouldn't eat it. So I tried the applesauce in place of pumpkin purée in pumpkin pie. Applesauce pie was a great success.

Similarly, one day Jim started making bread-crumb cookies (from the first book) and realized he hadn't allowed enough time in his schedule to bake them. So he spread the chocolaty dough in a Pyrex cooking dish and baked it. The result was respectable bread-crumb brownies.

Aside from determining whether an experiment actually works, I often note how long an idea took to execute and whether that justifies the savings. For example, I experimented with methods to repair torn plastic pants. Hot glue worked, but melted when the pants went through the dryer. Then I successfully stitched the tears on the sewing machine in seconds. But I also learned that if tears are due to long-term aging, within a few wearings the pants will simply tear again next to my repair. In contrast, I've learned it *is* worthwhile to stitch ragged diapers; it takes a minute, and they last for another year.

Sometimes before you actually invest money and time in an experiment, you might gather data for months. When his household knives became too dull to sharpen with his diamond-dust rod, a friend embarked on a search for a cheap alternative. Each time he visited a friend or relative's house, he asked how knife sharpening was done there. He *tried* the method on the spot and judged how well it worked.

After a year (during which the toughest meat his family ate was hamburger/TVP meat loaf) he determined that the only sharpening tool that met his exacting standards was a $75 motorized gizmo. But he noticed the stone it used was of the same grit as a $2 grinding wheel for an electric drill. He bought a wheel and tried it on his dull knives. It worked perfectly. (If you try this, hold your finger on the blade to make sure it does not overheat. This could make the blade lose its "temper.")

Of course, there are a few areas where you should not experiment. Readers keep asking for a homemade contact-lens solution or, at least, a method for using less store-bought solution. And other readers have sent me a few ideas. But, sorry, I can't recommend creative ocular hygiene. Stick to the wide range of everyday activities with which you can experiment safely.

Finally, you ask, what's this about freezing panty hose? Supposedly, if you freeze new panty hose, they last longer. Since *The Tightwad Gazette* has a blue-jeans-are-fine dress code, it would take me years to test this theory. But it could be done by purchasing two identical pairs of panty hose, freezing one pair, then cutting one leg off each pair, combining the remaining prefrozen and not-prefrozen hose to make one pair, and then wearing them to see which leg lasts longer.

But what if your office desk tends to snag one leg more than the other? Then forget cutting the legs off: Buy two pair, and wear prefrozen and not-prefrozen hose on alternating days.

But does the freezing technique work differently on different brands? And does it matter if it's winter or summer?

If anyone figures this one out, let me know.

HOP, SCRIMP, AND JUMP

My daughter Jamie reminded me of the amazing entertainment possibilities of scrap paper when she taught herself to make an origami hopping frog. Although this works best with a 3-by-5 index card, she amused her siblings for a good hour making scores of frogs from scrap paper. I couldn't step anywhere without squishing one. She learned that the smaller the frog, the bigger the jump. One ¼-inch frog hopped as high as a flea.

If an hour's worth of free kid entertainment doesn't impress you, think back to how long your children really played with those "Happy Meal" toys.

A parent, with practice, could entertain birthday-party attendees with a repertoire of a few dozen origami creations, as well as provide take-home gifts for nearly nothing. Special origami papers are nice, but not necessary. For advanced origami, you'll want to check out a library book.

In the meantime, save those abundant lime-green school notices, and on the next snow day show your kids how to make hopping frogs.

As you follow the directions, note that a line of dots means to fold up to make a "valley" and a line of dashes means to fold down to make a "mountain."

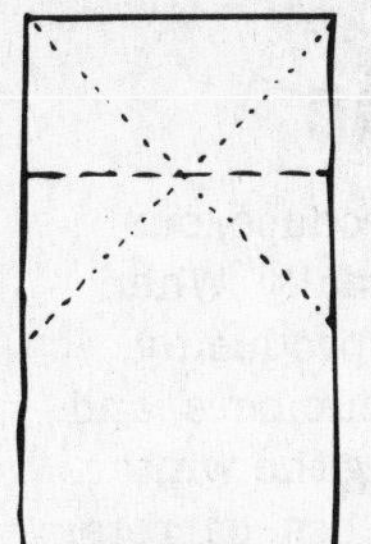
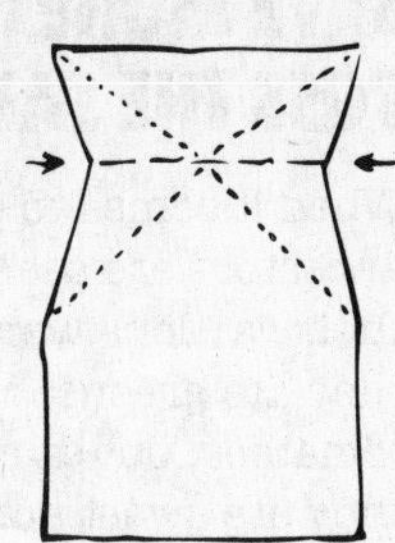

Fold and reflatten paper.
Push in at the sides, and fold down to make a triangle shape.

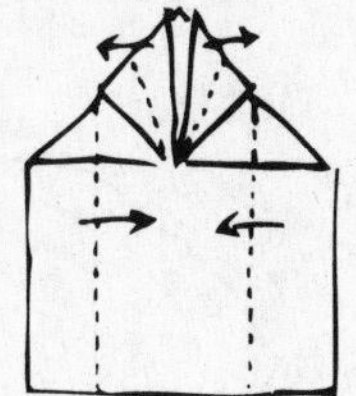
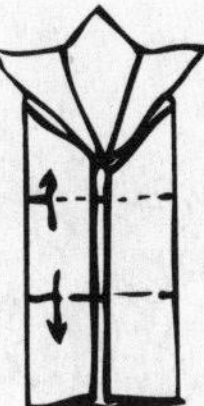

Make folds as indicated. Then turn over and draw eyes and a nose.

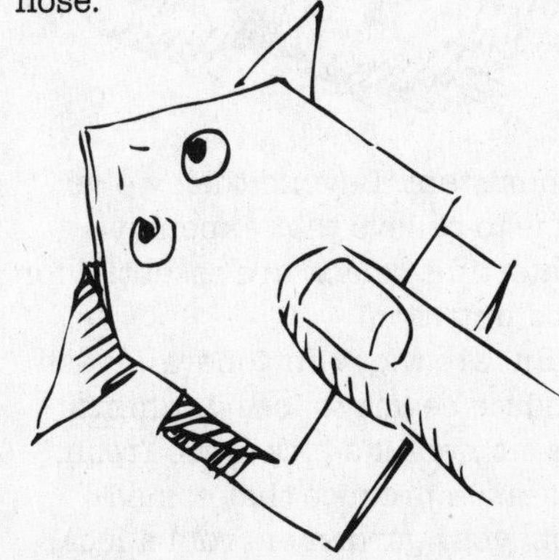

To make the frog jump, push its back down and slide your finger off. Hold frog races and jumping contests.

SAVE MONEY; TOSS THE SALAD

When it comes to produce, our ancestors ate seasonally. When their gardens were producing, they ate greens, cucumbers, and tomatoes, but during the winter they ate sweet potatoes, carrots, and butternut squash because these would keep without freezing or canning. Now, with modern transportation and food preservation, seasonal eating is almost nonexistent. Beyond this, we've come to believe that expensive wintertime salads are essential for good nutrition.

But are they? In general, fresh produce begins to lose vitamins the moment it's picked. So fresh, in-season produce that comes from your garden or from a local grower is superior. But the so-called "fresh" produce shipped from Florida and Mexico in January is often six to ten days old by the time it gets to the market. According to the produce manager at a large chain supermarket, produce can sit on the shelf for another ten days before it's sold. Then, it may reside in your refrigerator for seven more days. In short, store-bought "fresh" produce can be almost four weeks old before it's consumed.

So the question is: How does fresh supermarket produce, which loses nutrition through aging, compare to canned and frozen vegetables, which lose nutrition through processing? There are many variables, but in one study, conducted by the University of Illinois, flash-frozen green beans lost 17 percent of their vitamin C content due to processing, but seven-day-old fresh green beans picked from the same vines at the same time lost 60 percent. According to registered nutritionist Liz Ward, home-canned foods also retain most of their nutrition, but commercially canned foods, which generally have added sodium, are regarded as the least nutritious alternative.

It's true that some fresh produce can be consumed without the cooking that would cause some further loss of nutrients and fiber. But given the possible age of fresh produce, processed and cooked vegetables can still have equal, if not superior nutrition.

Then where did we get the idea that we need to eat salads all year long? Most of us are recalling our mothers' admonition to eat dark green, leafy vegetables to get vita-

min A. So, lucky for us that they ship all of that iceberg lettuce north, right?

Wrong. Iceberg lettuce is a "head" lettuce, not a leafy lettuce, so it's not a good source of vitamin A; a serving provides only 2 percent of the Recommended Daily Allowance of A. In fact, it provides so little nutrition overall that it's never a good value. Leafy lettuces are better, providing 20 percent of the R.D.A. of vitamin A. Spinach provides 35 percent.

But dark green, leafy vegetables aren't the only sources of vitamin A. Deep yellow and orange vegetables and fruits (except citrus) are even better. The real vitamin A powerhouses are carrots, at 330 percent of the R.D.A. per serving, and sweet potatoes, at 520 percent per serving. Other candidates include cantaloupe, tomatoes, butternut squash, pumpkin, and apricots, which provide between 30 percent and 140 percent of your daily need for vitamin A.

Vitamin C also has its share of mythology. While an orange provides 110 percent of your daily need for C, you don't need to eat citrus fruit every day. Look at the amount of C provided by other produce: A serving of tomato has 40 percent, potato has 50 percent, cabbage has 70 percent, cantaloupe has 90 percent, cauliflower has 110 percent, kiwi has 115 percent, a bell pepper has 130 percent, strawberries have 140 percent, and broccoli—wow—provides 240 percent!

(These percentages are based on a broad sampling of fresh supermarket produce and are intended only as a general guideline. Nutrition calculation is a fuzzy science, as actual nutrition may vary due to many factors.)

The nutritionists I interviewed all agreed that the exact form of produce (fresh, frozen, canned, or dried) was a minor concern. Instead, they stressed volume and variety. Eat a minimum of five servings of fruits and vegetables daily, including some that are high in A and C. Eat cruciferous vegetables (cauliflower, brussels sprouts, cabbage, and broccoli) several times a week. Several studies have shown that these help to prevent cancer.

So, you wonder, just what is the cheapest way to buy fruits and vegetables? Because of the variables in season, region of the country, and type of produce, I can't offer hard-and-fast rules. You need to do the homework by calculating the cost per serving. For example, notice how many meals you get from $1 worth of frozen broccoli versus $1 worth of fresh. Also compare how many servings you get from a head of cabbage versus cauliflower, and lettuce versus frozen spinach. Vary your strategy accordingly. The bottom line: Although fresh, green salads *look* more nutritious than cooked vegetables, they may not be. If you prefer them to sweet potatoes, or if you prefer fresh over cooked, you can opt to pay a premium price for them in the winter. But if you want to save money and still eat nutritiously, shift your diet to frozen out-of-season produce and to fresh, low-cost winter vegetables. Your family may balk for a while, but most people come to enjoy a different food as it becomes more familiar. And it won't become familiar if you don't serve it.

SHOOT, I FORGOT

Dear Amy,

In response to your article on winter vegetables . . .

People forget about sprouts. They are very easy to grow at home, take only a few days, are a perfect substitute for lettuce in sandwiches and pack a powerful nutritional punch. A creative sprouter can grow a wider variety than is available at the supermarket. Sprouting how-to's can be found in vegetarian cookbooks.

—Madeline Sobel
Westport, Connecticut

DAYS OF OUR SOAPS

Dear Amy,

I always mark the date on certain products. I stick on a piece of masking tape and mark the first day of use on it. It gives me incentive to beat the number of days I can make the product last. Examples: dish soap, dishwashing detergent, shampoo, and so on.

—Suzette J. Lucas
Hightstown, New Jersey

RETURN TO VENDOR

Dear Amy,

Although I've taken steps to decrease my junk mail, I still get some. If the mail contains a new business-reply envelope marked "postage paid," I sometimes stuff all the junk mail (including the used envelope it came in) into the envelope and send it back to the company. I *never* hear from them again!

—Virginia Scharf
Adamant, Vermont

(Living in an area where I must pay to dispose of trash, this idea is especially appealing. And what a thoughtful gesture: That company saves money by taking you off its mailing list. FZ)

FROM-SCRATCH PATCH

Dear Amy,

In "Test-Tube Tightwaddery" (page 214) you talked about denim iron-on patches, which cost about $1.25 to repair two knees. You can make your own iron-on patch from a scrap of fabric and Wonder-Under fusible webbing. It costs about $2.50 per yard (20 inches wide) . . . or as little as $1 per yard on sale. You iron the Wonder-Under to the fabric scrap, cut it out, pull the paper off the Wonder-Under, then iron the patch to your pants. It works great for appliqués, too. Other manufacturers make a similar product, but I find that Wonder-Under works the best.

—Cindy Cousineau
Appleton, Wisconsin

PRIME CUT RATE

Dear Amy,

I have discovered an excellent way to get high-priced meats at a 75 percent savings. Every Monday at my local supermarket, the meat department marks down all the meat dated for the following day. I buy in quantity and freeze that day. Sometimes stores don't display marked-down meat in the meat case . . . you must ask.

—Erin Goodwin
East Bridgewater,
Massachusetts

HOW TO CUT YOUR DRY-CLEANING COSTS

When I requested tips on saving money on dry cleaning, I expected the result would be a short article. But there was more to learn than I imagined. I soon had a two-inch stack of letters from readers.

I concluded that it is possible to save on dry cleaning, but that one must be careful. Many of the tips readers sent seemed risky, so I ran them past Norman Oehlke, director of information services at the International Fabricare Institute, and a dry cleaner for 35 years.

He pointed out that among the tips were several common myths. You may disagree with some of his conclusions, but I felt it was important to include the "official" viewpoint:

Myth #1. "Dry cleaning will wear out clothes quickly." No. According to a University of North Carolina study, dry-cleaning solvents will not damage fabrics. Soil is what prematurely wears fabrics.

Myth #2. "Most fabrics were around long before dry cleaning was invented, so consumers have been duped into believing they can't hand-wash 'dry-clean only' clothes." No. It's true that dry cleaning has been around only since the 1800s, when Parisians used kerosene, benzene, and gasoline to remove soil from clothes, but many fabrics have been developed since. In some cases the fibers may withstand hand-washing but the dyes will not. Fabrics that were not preshrunk and some interfacings and linings may not fare well when exposed to water.

But it's true that a 1984 FTC ruling allows manufacturers to list only one laundering method on garment tags, and most choose the more cautious method. Oehlke says that if the garment says "dry-clean" instead of "dry-clean only," there is a slightly greater chance it will withstand home laundering. But because of the range of types of fabrics, it's impossible to give concrete rules as to ones that can be hand-washed. Even among wools, some can be hand-washed and some can't. You can ask your dry cleaner for an opinion, though. It's also wise to test the garment in an inconspicuous place for colorfastness. This, however, may not determine whether the garment will shrink.

Myth #3. "You can use solvents, such as lacquer thinner, to remove spots." No. Any solvent residue remaining in the clothing will make your clothes more flammable, and fumes in your clothes aren't good for you. Likewise, you shouldn't use professional dry-cleaning fluid. Dry cleaners have methods to remove the solvents after they clean the clothes. Instead, use the spot removers sold in drug and department stores designed for "dry-clean only" clothes.

Myth #4. "Instead of dry-cleaning, simply have garments pressed and save two thirds the cost." No. Oehlke says the heat from pressing, as well as from fluffing clothes in a hot dryer, could set dirt and stains in clothes that haven't been cleaned. Not all dirt is visible.

Myth #5. "Women get charged more than men for cleaning shirts, so specify that your shirt is a man's to save money."

This one may actually have some truth to it. Oehlke says dry cleaners press a large volume of shirts on a shirt-pressing machine. This machine will accommodate only a certain size range. Any smaller (or much larger) shirt, regardless of gender, must be hand-ironed, which costs the cleaner more money. Along with being smaller, women's shirts tend to have more pleats, darts, ruffles, and delicate fabrics than do men's. In short, he says it's the extra labor that causes the price difference, not a gender-based price gouge.

On the other hand, several readers told me that a Chicago television station did an intensive investigation and found that many Chicago-area cleaners charge far more for shirts labeled "women's" than for those labeled "men's," though the shirts were exactly the same. I tried to track this down but was not successful; apparently, this investigation took place several years ago. Other readers told me that they personally knew of instances in which women were overcharged for shirts that required no extra work to clean or press. The bottom line: If you find a cleaner who seems to be overcharging you for no reason other than gender, ask the manager why you can't have the man's rate. (I don't recommend saying that the shirt is a man's. As our mothers correctly pointed out, two wrongs don't make a right.)

Myth #6. "All clothing that goes to a dry cleaner is dry-cleaned." No. Men's cotton shirts for example, are laundered. Ruth Miller of Valatie, New York, a dry cleaner for eight years, pointed out that about 35 percent of clothes brought to a dry cleaner don't need to be dry-cleaned.

Myth #7. "Same-day cleaning and clothes left at a 'drop shop,' which sends them for cleaning elsewhere are subject to extra charges." Oehlke said this isn't generally true, although there may be exceptions. Check just to be sure.

Myth #8. "Budget dry cleaners, which charge by the pound or offer very low prices, and do-it-yourself machines at laundromats do just as well as expensive dry cleaners." No. Depending on the method, your clothes will receive little or no finishing, nor expert stain removal. But if the lesser service meets your needs, the savings can be significant. Sally Kirby

Hartman of Norfolk, Virginia, says her off-price cleaner charges $1.79 per piece, no matter what it is. The full-service cleaner charges $7.50 for a dress and $8.85 for a coat.

Oehlke's general advice is to follow the manufacturer's instructions, unless you're willing to risk ruining the garment. Obviously, as a professional, he tends to stick to the industry's viewpoint.

So let's move on to the tightwad mind-set. If you buy a blouse for 25¢ at a yard sale, you are more likely to "wash dangerously." As Jane Paulson of Seattle puts it, "Since most of us reading this publication buy our clothes at thrift stores, laundry roulette is a game we can afford to play."

Reader after reader reported success with home laundering "dry-clean only" clothes, and very few cited ruined garments. They generally suggested hand-washing or using the gentle cycle with cold water and mild detergent, then laying the garment flat to dry.

By *far,* the most common suggestion we received was "Don't buy stuff that needs dry cleaning." Obvious, but it bears repeating: When you buy, take the laundering advice into account.

Here are some of the tips from readers with which Oehlke agreed:

1. Wear underarm shields to protect clothing from perspiration. (Debbie Halvorson, Somerville, New Jersey.)

2. For men's silk ties, spray with a fabric protector. If you get a spot, simply wipe it off with a damp cloth. Fabric protectors work best on tightly woven fabrics like silk, chintz, etc. (Joyce Whatley, Atlanta, Georgia.)

3. Compare prices for a suit versus a blazer and skirt. Sometimes it's cheaper to have individual items cleaned. (Lisa Romano, Cedar Grove, New Jersey.)

4. A down coat can be washed alone, using the gentle cycle, in cold water with Woolite. Rinse several times. Place in the dryer with a pair of clean sneakers. (Linda Krupa, Fairport, New York.)

5. Leather-goods stores sell something called "Suede Bar and Brush" for about $4.50. This makes suede jackets look new. Cleaning by professionals costs from $25 to $40. (Margaret Maloney, Casper, Wyoming.)

6. Use a non-terrycloth dishtowel as a press cloth when ironing hand-washed "dry-clean only" fabrics. Iron when fabrics are still slightly damp, except for wool, which should be dry to avoid shrinkage. Use lower temperatures for silk, higher for linen. Rayon needs medium, and wool can take medium-high. (Lori Stahlman, Fort Collins, Colorado.)

7. You can have clothes dry-cleaned, but press them yourself. The pressing of a professional cleaner can be approximated with pressing boards, sleeve rolls, and so on, from a sewing-supply store. (Janet Campbell, Houlton, Maine.)

8. Or if you're brave, wash wool blazers and skirts in Woolite and cold water, then have the dry cleaner press them. This can save two thirds of the cost over dry cleaning and pressing. (Linda Bennett, Farmington Hills, Michigan.)

9. Some cleaners will accept competitor's coupons. Look for specials in newspapers, coupons in telephone books, and "entertainment bargains" books. (Hedwig Blaser, Lakewood, California.)

10. Many cleaners offer a small amount per wire coat hanger that you return. (Dawn Katzoff, Orem, Utah.)

11. Point out and identify various stains to your dry cleaner. Food, blood, and mud require different chemicals. (Albert Gatica, Atlanta, Georgia.)

12. If a woman's suit needs cleaning, consider having only the jacket cleaned. Hand-wash the skirt, which is easy to press yourself. Again, this depends on your confidence that the skirt can be hand-washed, (Nancy Roebke, Stuart, Florida.)

13. Avoid buying "dry-clean only" clothes that are worn next to the skin. Layers of clothing, such as a T-shirt and dress shirt, catch the perspiration that would soil a suit. (Betty Alsberg, Astoria, New York.)

14. If you sew your own clothes, buy ¼ yard of extra fabric and wash the fabric before cutting out the material. This way you know delicate fabrics will survive home laundering. (Deborah Ronnie, Tucson, Arizona.)

15. Dry-clean only the parts of clothing that require it. Remove zip-out linings, belts, and detachable collars. Some cleaners charge $2 just to clean a belt. (LaDonna Jewson, Wasaba, Minnesota.)

16. Avoid buying "dry-clean only" clothes with pleats, beadwork, and other adornments that drive up pressing costs. (Sandy Croslow, Vincennes, Indiana.)

17. Check your pockets. Forgotten money is treated as a tip by dry cleaners. Oehlke says the common industry practice is to keep small change, but to return any paper money. (Frederick Young, Newton, Massachusetts.)

THE GREAT MOTOR-OIL DEBATE

We received about 50 letters in response to our newsletter solicitation for readers' experience with synthetic motor oil.

There was a wide range of opinion. Much of it was positive. For example, a reader said his salesman-father's synthetically lubricated 1980 Chevy was nearing 300,000 miles when he sold it. He changed the oil twice a year, or about every 12,000 miles.

But other readers reported excellent luck with high-quality, standard mineral oils and had also accumulated impressive mileage. Because top-quality standard oils are about one third the price of synthetics, they can be changed (by the car owner) three times as often for the same price.

Confronted with these diverging viewpoints, we called the Society of Automotive Engineers, *Nutz & Boltz* (an automotive consumer newsletter), the American Automobile Association, the technical editor of *Star* (the magazine of the Mercedes Benz Club of America), the technical director of Blendzall Corp. (which makes racing-car oils), and representatives of Amsoil and Mobil 1, the two largest synthetic-oil manufacturers. We also reviewed articles and surveyed technical data.

The result? There's no dispute that synthetics lubricate somewhat better than regular oils. But most of these experts questioned whether the average motorist would see a benefit that justified the extra cost.

It's true that synthetics cost no more if you extend the drain interval beyond what your car

manufacturer recommends, but most of these experts agreed this is a bad idea. *Any* oil will still accumulate acids, condensation, and dirt. The experts added that although the base stock of synthetic oils lasts longer, the additives in both kinds of oils wear out at about the same rate.

Further, extending the intervals of oil changes will almost certainly void your car's warranty. Amsoil says you can extend the interval to 25,000 miles and guarantees to replace any parts that have failed as a result of poor lubrication, and they say they have never had a claim. Skeptical experts pointed out that it would be difficult to establish that a specific part wore out due to the oil's condition. Thus, it might be impossible to prove your claim. David Solomon, editor of *Nutz & Boltz* and a former "direct jobber" for Amsoil, said that he personally diagnosed engine failures that resulted from poor lubrication when customers followed the 25,000-mile recommendation. He added that he didn't know whether Amsoil honored the claims.

To add one more note of caution, reader Stanton Sittser of Gresham, Oregon, said several years ago he exactly followed a synthetic-oil maker's instructions to change the filters and oil, except he changed the oil every 20,000 miles instead of every 25,000. The engine failed at 51,000 miles. His mechanic said it was no wonder, as the oil he drained was like mud.

On the other hand, there *is* evidence that drain intervals can be stretched with synthetic oil, particularly if high-quality air and oil filters are used and changed regularly. The synthetic manufacturers are quick to provide their own "conclusive" test studies to "prove" this (the experts I consulted were skeptical of these tests). Solomon, former owner of an oil-analyzing company, said analysis of 1,000 synthetically lubricated engines showed that, at 12,000 miles, still-viable oil was the rule, not the exception. But it's important to note that Solomon was the only knowledgeable, independent source that I could find who supported extended change intervals. He recommends changing synthetics at 12,000 miles or once a year, whichever comes first. He endorses only Redline oil.

Now, suppose you decide to use synthetics *and* change your oil at the car maker's recommended intervals because, though it costs more, you feel your car will last longer. The experts we interviewed knew of no independent studies that conclusively prove that your engine will last longer. They agreed that synthetics may marginally extend the life of your car, but there's no way to know whether this benefit will offset the extra cost of the oil.

Likewise, it's uncertain whether the improved gas mileage, which is claimed by some synthetic-oil makers, would offset the cost. Some readers said they got better

mileage with synthetics, and others said their mileage was the same. Either way, one expert pointed out that some standard oils also improve gas mileage.

There was also disagreement between these experts as to whether synthetics and standard oils could be mixed, and whether it was a good idea to switch an older car to synthetics.

One area of universal agreement was that synthetic oils are particularly beneficial in extreme cold (like Alaska), in extreme heat (like Death Valley), and in industrial applications (like pulling house trailers). But most passenger cars aren't exposed to these conditions.

The bottom line? If experts who live and breathe cars can't agree on this one, I can't make a final determination. At the very least, a good case can be made for either high-quality standard oil that is changed every 3,000 miles, *or* synthetic oil that is changed at the car manufacturer's maximum recommended interval (usually, about 7,500 miles). If you follow the latter course and you change your own oil, using synthetics will cost about $250 more every 100,000 miles. Because this extra cost, spread out over several years, is fairly low, even one of the skeptical experts used synthetics to hedge his bet.

David Solomon is a certified master mechanic in every aspect of auto repair with an impressive list of credentials and 30 years of experience. I don't know enough about auto mechanics to endorse his publication, but if you would like a free sample, write to:
Nutz & Boltz
Butler, MD 21023

STUBBORN DIAPER PINS

Dear Amy,

I use cloth diapers on my baby. I used to stick pins in a bar of soap to lubricate them so they would slide easier. But the bar of soap broke up after a few months. I figured there must be a better way. So I melted paraffin in a tuna can and now stick the pins in the hardened wax. When the wax breaks up, I remelt it.

—Lorie Slater
Pittsburgh, Pennsylvania

(Stubborn pins can be enough to discourage people from using cloth diapers. I solve the problem another way. I run the pin under my hair, along my scalp. The natural oil lubricates the pin. FZ)

FREEZING RAIN CHECKS

Dear Amy,

Living in a tiny one-bedroom apartment, I found everything else was scaled down to size, especially my freezer, which is one of those tiny, flimsy, tin ones inside

the refrigerator. I learned to go to the grocery stores on the last day of a sale and get a rain check for frozen sale items that they were out of and I didn't have room for. Then, a week or so later when I have more freezer room, I go back and pick them up. Some rain checks are good for 30 days.

—Jon Juliot and Tina Triebs
Eau Claire, Wisconsin

A FARE TO REMEMBER

Dear Amy,

For urban dwellers, many employers now offer transit subsidies for employees who use public transportation, but it may be up to the employee to investigate it. For example, I receive a check for $15 per month from my employer, which must be used for mass-transit costs. Also a group of employees in my office teams up to purchase large quantities of mass transit passes and receives a 5 percent discount.

—Lori Kier
Philadelphia, Pennsylvania

FLIGHT OF THE TIGHT

Dear Amy,

My husband and I love to backpack in the West but seem to have less and less time to drive. Now, we call our travel agent with the dates and ask for the cheapest flight *anywhere* west of, and including, Denver. We also ask for the cheapest mileage-included rental car. When we've found a cheap flight, we can almost always find a wonderful backpacking venue within a half-day's drive. We have flown for less than it would have cost to drive.

—Kathryn Paul,
Bloomington, Indiana

METER MATTERS

Dear Amy,

You once wrote that you really couldn't get an exact wattage use on a bread machine. You might try checking at a utility company and asking for a "check meter." It is an actual meter in a "box." You plug an appliance in it and voila: exact usage. We did this on an old freezer and were horrified at what it was costing. We replaced it.

—Valaree Stodola
Shellsburg, Iowa

(I am aware of these, however when I called my utility several months ago, they didn't know such a thing existed. You can buy your own [through a mail-order company], but the cost exceeds that of a new freezer. FZ)

WINNER TAKES ALL

Dear Amy,

Never, ever refuse anything that someone wants to give to you . . . even if you have to haul it directly to the dump. If you say no, they may never offer anything to you again . . . and next time, they might have something quite useful or valuable that could be sold at a garage sale. Some things that people have given me over the years include: two bushels of zucchini, a workshop cabinet, a metal shelv-

ing system, a deluxe baby buggy, 50 pounds of carrots, stone-tumbler equipment, a microscope, six Styrofoam coolers, a terrarium, countless broken tools, and a 9½-pound lobster that was breathing its last.

—David Currier
Orlando, Florida

QUICK QUIP

Dear Amy,

I came across this recently and thought you'd enjoy it:

Sign in store window: Use our easy credit plan . . . 100 percent down, nothing to pay each month.

—Henra Trent
Irving, Texas

100-YARD STASH

Dear Amy,

Birthday gift wrap is expensive, and you don't get much of it. So during the Christmas season I look for 100-yard rolls of Christmas paper that would double as all-occasion wrap. I usually get one roll for adults and one for children.

—Pam West
Batavia, Illinois

(Great tip for those after-the-holidays sales. FZ)

LET'S GO SHOPPING WITH JIM

Whenever I discuss our frugal accomplishments, nothing impresses people more than the fact that we feed our family of eight for under $180 a month. To be specific, from January 1992 through December 1993, we averaged $175.60 a month.

This figure represents only the cost of food and gardening and canning supplies. We never eat out or buy hot lunches at school. It doesn't include things like toothpaste and toilet paper. I figure it this way because comparing "grocery" budgets has become extremely difficult as you can now buy motor oil in the supermarket and snacks in the autoparts store. In theory, you could artificially lower your grocery budget by eating out more, buying school lunches, and buying personal-care items in the drugstore. By defining the food budget as the cost of feeding a family, you can compare more precisely.

Our monthly budget for personal-care and cleaning supplies is about $25. We also spend $30 to feed a big cat that requires an expensive diet, and a big dog.

We achieve our low food budget through a combination of scratch cooking, gardening, semivegetarianism, *never* wasting food, and other strategies (17 in all; see the first book).

But if I had to list one tactic as the most crucial, it's smart shopping. By using our price book to compare deals at local stores, we realized it's possible to buy many foods for half of what most people pay, if we buy them at the right place and the right time.

For most of our 11-year marriage, Jim has done the grocery shopping. In the early days, it was because the stores were on his commuter route. Now it's because he's the "homemaker."

So let's go shopping with Jim and see how our system works. We followed him on September 6, 1993. Jim went, as usual, to Lewiston/Auburn, a metropolitan area of 30,000, to do our big, once-a-month, stock-up shopping expedition. This is where our closest supermarkets are located, 15 miles or 30 minutes away. As usual, he took the two-year-old twins, Brad and Laura.

This trip always takes place near the sixth of the month so that it coincides with dropping off the *Gazette*'s newsletter paste-ups at the printer. A basic principle of the frugal life is to combine errands. *Never* make a special trip.

The first stop was Myer's Country Cupboard, a natural-food store in the small town of Greene, which is about midway between Leeds and Lewiston/Auburn. Myer's specializes in bulk natural food; it's where we get nearly all of our spices. But we didn't need spices that month. Jim bought cocoa, soy flour (which we use one tablespoon at a time as an egg substitute in baking), and sunflower seeds.

The next stop was Marden's. This "surplus and salvage" chain sells everything from aluminum siding to odd lots of food to zippers. On Saturday, the fourth, I had stopped by (it's on my yard-saling route), scouted the offerings, and bought a box of "Maizoro" (Mexican-made) sugar-frosted cornflakes. The price worked out to 5¢ per ounce, about one fifth the usual price for sweetened cold cereal. I had taken it home and tested it on my kids, and they were pleased to find it just as disgustingly sweet as the more popular brands. So Jim bought 18 boxes, a six-month supply for us. This was our first purchase of presweetened cereal in five years.

The next stop (after dropping off the paste-ups) was the Country Kitchen Bakery Thrift Store. Jim bought twelve 20-ounce loaves of bread at 50¢ a loaf.

Then he headed to Shop 'n Save. This New England supermarket chain is remarkable for its large selection of high-quality store

brands. Everything Jim got there was on sale or a store brand.

Finally, Jim got the big-ticket items at Wholesale Depot, a warehouse store. He bought a lot of tomato paste because it was spaghetti-sauce-canning season.

The price book is handy when deciding whether to buy something at a supermarket or a warehouse store. For example, supermarkets usually beat warehouses with "loss-leader" sales, particularly on meats, but flour and cheese usually cost less at the warehouse. A 25-pound bag of "Robin Hood" flour is $5.98 at Shop 'n Save, versus $3.88 at Wholesale Depot. Mozzarella cheese is $11.90 for 5 pounds at Shop 'n Save, versus $8.99 at Wholesale Depot.

Altogether on this trip, Jim spent $124.77 on food items. Clearly, the list of items purchased doesn't represent a balanced diet; it's simply what we needed to buy that month. We were loaded with garden surplus. We already had some fruits and meats, and bought more at supermarket sales in the middle of the month. These later-in-the-month excursions are always combined with other trips.

We also shop by cooperating with friends. If anyone within our circle of tightwads finds a great deal, he or she calls around to ask, "Do you want me to pick some up for you?" Such relationships will help your budget.

Although I've provided a list of our prices (unit prices are rounded to the nearest penny), don't use these as your guideline. Maine prices tend to be slightly higher than those in many areas of the country. And we have since purchased some of these items for less. We recently found tuna at 39¢ a can; we bought a lot.

Because of odd great deals that pop up, and because our surplus waxes and wanes, our actual monthly outlay for food over the past two years has ranged from $89.43 to $296.59. But the average is under $180.

You may have noticed Jim didn't use coupons. An effective coupon shopping system relies on access to double-coupon stores, a large number of free coupons (usually obtained by collecting a dozen Sunday-paper inserts from friends), and shopping at several stores each week to combine coupons with sales. We don't have double-coupon stores, and only 16 big-city newspapers with coupon inserts are sold in our town of 1,700 people each week (most people buy the local paper, which has no coupons). By calculating the true savings, I've found I usually can't recoup the cost of the paper through coupon use.

I do agree that coupons can be beneficial, but be careful of overuse. Two coupon experts, who have appeared on national television demonstrating amazing shopping trips with savings up to 95 percent by using coupons, shared their real grocery-bill averages with me. Both spend more on groceries for smaller families than I do.

Now, here is the point that I want to emphasize about our shopping system. Many people resist frugality because, as they put it, "I don't have time to drive all over the state hunting down bargains." We have carefully kept track of the total amount of time we expend on shopping per month. The major expedition

chronicled above takes four hours, including nonshopping errands. The side excursions we make during the rest of the month easily take less than two more hours. So we do a month's worth of grocery shopping in under six hours. Although we shop this way because of the distance we drive to large stores, it's an excellent strategy for people with limited time.

Finally, for those who are wondering how Jim handles the challenge of shopping with toddler twins, the answer is: immobility. He keeps one twin in the backpack and the other in the kiddie seat of the cart at all times. He stays near the center of the aisles and extends his arm fully to take things from the shelves. "As long as my arms are longer than theirs, we won't have any problems," he says.

Myer's Country Cupboard	Cocoa, 1.78 pounds at $2.18 per pound	$3.90
	Soy flour, 1.93 pounds at $1 per pound	$1.93
	Sunflower seeds, 2.18 pounds at $1.39 per pound	$3.03
	Total	$8.86
Marden's	Sugar flakes, 18 boxes at 50¢ per 10-ounce box	$9.00
	Total	$9.00
Country Kitchen Bakery Thrift Store	Whole wheat, six 20-ounce loaves at 50¢ per loaf	$3.00
	Oatmeal, six 20-ounce loaves at 50¢ per loaf	$3.00
	Total	$6.00
Shop 'n Save	Macaroni and cheese, 8 boxes at 25¢ each	$2.00
	Dry milk, 20-quart size	$8.49
	Tea bags, 100	$2.29
	Brown sugar, 2 pounds at 59¢ per pound	$1.19
	Tuna, 5 cans at 53¢ each	$2.65
	Powdered sugar, 2 pounds at 59¢ per pound	$1.19
	Celery, one bunch	$ .59
	Bagged apples, 3 pounds at 33¢ per pound	$ .99
	Total	$19.39
Wholesale Depot	Raisins, 6 pounds at $1.42 per pound	$8.54
	Shortening, 6 pounds at 76¢ per pound	$4.58
	Tomato paste, 36 12-ounce cans at 69¢ each	$25.14
	Brown sugar, 4 pounds at 56¢ per pound	$2.24
	Powdered sugar, 4 pounds at 56¢ per pound	$2.24
	Ketchup, two 40-ounce bottles at 4¢ per ounce	$2.98
	Salt, 5.5 pounds at 36¢ per pound	$1.97
	Shredded mozzarella, 5 pounds at $1.80 per pound	$8.99
	Cream cheese, 6-pack at 87¢ per pack	$5.25
	Colby cheese, 2 pounds at $1.99 per pound	$3.99
	Monterey jack, 2 pounds at $1.93 per pound	$3.86
	Onions, 10 pounds at 39¢ per pound	$3.98
	Flour, two 25-pound bags at 15¢ per pound	$7.76
	Total	$81.52

PEANUT-BUTTER SNACKS

Dear Amy,

I have a quick and easy recipe that my kids love in their lunch boxes:

½ cup honey
½ cup peanut butter
¾ to 1½ cups dry milk

Combine all the ingredients and roll into small balls. Roll the balls in coconut, sunflower seeds, or nuts.

—Teresa Duncan
Marion, North Carolina

(This was a big hit in my home. If it seems too sweet, you can experiment with less honey. FZ)

BUDGET BREW

Dear Amy,

While stationed in Germany, we found that European coffee is ground almost to a talcum-powder fineness, which makes it possible to use much less. Now I buy extra-fine grind and regrind it to a powder at home before using it in my machine.

—Ruth Campbell
Comox, British Columbia

HAIRDO-IT-YOURSELF

Dear Amy,

I'm proud to announce that I've mastered giving myself a permanent. A year ago I would have sworn I would *never* get it, but I shut myself in the bathroom early one Saturday morning and really set myself to the task. Once you decide you *will* learn to handle hair, end papers, and rods, you will get it.

—Beth Wright
Union City, Tennessee

(When I was at a book-signing I was approached by a handsome, 50-ish couple—the kind who look like they have a yacht and a summer home. The wife proudly told me she saved money because her husband had learned to give her a permanent. Her husband blushed, but his wife looked wonderful. FZ)

AX THAT TAX

Dear Amy,

My son recently bought a new truck at a city dealership. The dealer charged him at the sales-tax level within the city, though we don't live in that city. A friend of my son's worked at the dealership and caught this error. She then figured out the correct sales tax for the area where we live. She found that the dealer had overcharged him $156. The dealer had to pay us back the money. We were told that dealers do this everywhere.

—Mona Breaux
Livingston, Louisiana

ROWS OF ROSES

Dear Amy,

When my sister was married last year, I took the half-dead roses from her bouquet after the ceremony. At home, I rooted them by cutting off the heads, making a clean cut on the bottoms, dipping the fresh-cut bottoms in a rooting hormone, and putting them in a pot that was half Perlite and half soil. I kept these moist until rooted and then planted them in a shaded location in my garden. This year, on her first anniversary, my sister received a gift that could never be replaced: 12 rose bushes from her wedding bouquet.

—Kimberly Hill
Warren, Michigan

FEE FREEBIE

Dear Amy,

When moving to a new home or apartment, investigate using the former dweller's phone number. This will save you the $40 to $50 usual hookup fee for telephone service and instead cost you less than $10. The phone company will call the former dweller to ask permission (because if he moved nearby, he may still use the same number). You will have to put up with wrong numbers for a short time.

—Judy Davies
Mystic, Connecticut

(Undoubtedly, phone company policies vary around the country, and you should check with your local company. I called mine and learned their policy:

The regular installation charge is $44.75. If you know the previous tenant well and just want to change the name on the account, the charge is $6.74.

But if you don't know the previous tenant, and your move doesn't coincide with the end of the billing cycle, there's a third option. For $18.70 you can get a transfer of service: You keep the old tenant's number but you can specify when this bill ends and when yours begins. By doing this, you can't get stuck with his unpaid bills.

These last two prices apply only if you plan to keep the exact same service options that the previous tenant had. FZ)

GAIN SOME GROUND

Dear Amy,

Adjacent to our backyard is a large, vacant piece of land. I approached the owner last fall about using a portion of it in the spring for a garden. He was willing, because I would be clearing it of weeds and he wouldn't have to worry about the city weed ordinance for the part I cleared. Now I have a garden of over 1,000 square feet and lots of fresh vegetables every year.

—John Mauro
Wheat Ridge, Colorado

THREE STEPS TO A FRITO-FREE CHILD

After "How do you pronounce Dacyczyn?" perhaps the most frequent question I get is "Don't your children feel deprived?"

Because I'm asked this so often, my antenna is always up looking for signs. I even interview my kids on this subject. The fact is, our children rarely complain of any gap in material goods.

The objections are so rare that when they arise, they surprise me. Such was the case when Neal, then five, asked, "How come we don't have 'good food' like other people?" I pressed him for specifics and learned he wanted store-bought snacks in his lunch box like most of his kindergarten classmates had.

Many frugal parents would give the simple answer "We can't afford it," presuming small children can't comprehend the complexities of money. But this unfortunate response leads children to conclude that their family is "poorer" than other families who do buy those things, and therefore frugal alternatives are second-rate.

I do believe children can understand, and I explain why our choice is "smart." Here's how I handled this situation:

Step 1. I had a conversation with Neal to explain:

1. If you do the math, you find it's not worth the money. I pointed out real fruit costs 25¢ to 50¢ per pound, while fruit-chewy things cost about $5 per pound. So, pound for pound, we can buy ten times more apples than Shark Bites. If he had wanted juice boxes, I might have explained that the juice inside costs 10¢, and the package costs 20¢. Then I would have asked him whether he would throw two dimes in the trash. I might also have used a calculator to show that over the school year, one juice box per day times three kids would add up to $100 wasted.

2. Store-bought snacks often have artificial ingredients and less nutrition. Although fruit-chewy things are made with some fruit juice, they're so overprocessed that the nutrition label shows an almost total lack of vitamins. I ex-

plained that children need good nutrition to do well in school. (Subsequently, Neal noted he was the smartest in his class in math, and he theorized his homemade snacks were the key. It was tempting to let this slide, but I did explain that the relationship might not be so direct.)

3. Store-bought snacks are usually worse for the environment. We had a kid-level conversation about the trees that are chopped down to make packaging, the pollution produced by factories, and the mountains of trash that result when people throw this stuff away. I said even recyclable trash requires energy to recycle. Kids learn about "saving the earth" in school, and they need to know their family's behavior does make a difference. I told Neal that the "dump guy" said he couldn't think of another family that brought as little trash as we do. I said we could be proud of that.

4. Without discussing the finances of a specific family, I stressed that people who buy store-bought snacks aren't necessarily "richer" than we are. The children he envied might have been from families that are deep in debt, whose parents work multiple jobs to keep up with their bills, or perhaps even receive public assistance. I explained that some families make different choices; they spend money on lots of little things to make them feel good for a short time now, instead of saving for something bigger that will make them feel good for a long time, like a nicer house or a parent who can stay home with children.

Step 2. I improvised. Although I always try to make sure that our frugal alternatives satisfy the children, if a kid raises an issue, I step up my creative efforts. In this case, I made an extra effort to create homemade snacks with a higher "wow" factor, such as fruit-juice jigglers, whoopee pies, cinnamon rolls, popcorn, trail mix, pies made in tiny aluminum pie tins, and so on. Victory occurred when Neal reported a friend asked to taste a jiggler.

I am one mom with six kids, so I have to focus my attention on the specific areas in which the kids express concerns. Neal has never fretted over his yard-sale clothes, but he does care about his snacks. So I spend more time on snacks than clothes.

Children don't need exactly what their friends have, as long as they feel that they have some things that are as good.

Step 3. I asked him to earn it.

Usually, steps 1 and 2 work for my children, and they worked with Neal for a year. But he raised the question of store-bought snacks again the next year. I repeated steps 1 and 2, but I knew this alone would not satisfy him.

So, I had Neal do a special 15-minute chore to earn 25¢. The next time I was in the store, I bought a small bag of corn chips with his quarter to put in his lunch box. Neal was excited about the chips but has not asked for them again in the year or more that has transpired.

When I shared the corn-chip story during a radio interview, a woman called in and said having kids earn money for food, even junk food, was near-abusive. "After all, it cost only 25¢," she said. I argued that it wasn't the

question of a single bag of chips. We're establishing a pattern of dealing with money that we hope will carry us through the age when their wants escalate to stereos and cars.

Having children earn money for extras not only saves the parents money; it also provides these benefits:

1. It slows their rate of consumption by 90 percent. Kids rarely want anything enough to work for it, and if it's not important enough to them to work for it, why should I?

2. It empowers them. Kids gain the ability to satisfy their wants on their own. Most children get what they want by whining, complaining, and making their parents feel guilty, and this pattern continues through the teenage years. My children *never* whine for anything.

3. It teaches children that money is the relationship of effort to stuff. A six-year-old can understand that taking three buckets of food scraps to the compost pile equals a bag of corn chips. This is a very important concept, one that has escaped many adults. By always being paid in increments of 25¢, my children can easily compute the relationship of effort to stuff.

4. It teaches them, early on, one of life's most important lessons—that what they covet isn't worth their hard-earned money. Jamie didn't ask for a school lunch until the third grade. Our school-lunch deal is that we will split the cost with the children. After careful consideration, she chose a pizza lunch. When she got home that day, I asked about her lunch. She shrugged and said, "I like Dad's pizza better." She hasn't bought any more lunches.

5. If they use their own money to buy toys, they take better care of the things.

6. It teaches them to save. As your children get older, they will sock away money for larger items. Alec, who is ten, recently saved $14.50 and bought a well-made toy crossbow with suction-cup darts (to be used only with adult supervision). Although he could have, he didn't spend a cent on store-bought snacks. Alec got his bow within days of when Neal got his corn chips. I asked Alec if he would rather have his bow or 58 bags of chips. "The crossbow!" he exclaimed, as if this were obvious.

These strategies have been part of our kids' lives from the start. But if you're making a transition from a spendthrift way of life, it's important to sit down with your older children and explain the new rules. Point out that it's okay to express a want, but begging and whining will be treated as misbehavior.

If these three steps fail—your child doesn't accept your explanation, is not satisfied with creative frugal alternatives, and is unwilling to work for the stuff he wants, remember that families are not democracies, and that you should stand firm. You are the adult and are better able to judge how your money should be used.

20-20 TELEVISION

It always amazes me how many people have come to regard cable TV as a necessity. I can think of only one situation in which it might be needed: if the reception in your area is so poor, it seems to be the only way your picture can rise above "fuzzy blob."

But if this is your situation, there may be other options. You can put a big antenna on your roof, but this is impractical for those who are transient or live in apartments. So I was pleased to learn about a bit of "intermediate technology" that could solve the problem: powered rabbit ears, also known as amplified indoor antennas.

There are several varieties, ranging in price from about $30 to over $80. How to choose?

Start by heading down to your local Wal-Mart or Radio Shack and buying the cheapest set of powered rabbit ears you can find. Powered versions can be identified because they brag about their levels of "db gain" on the box. Be sure to keep the receipt. Try them out. If they don't work well enough to suit you, return them and buy the second-cheapest set, again, keeping the receipt.

Keep going through this process until you find some that meet your needs. One of my staffers who did this discovered that a set called Recoton TV500 improved his reception by about 50 percent, allowing him to double his available channels (from two to four). These cost $29.

We talked with Frank Rodriguez, the antenna's inventor. He said Recoton boosts the signal "gain" about ten times as much as a nonpowered indoor antenna and draws less than 1 watt per hour. At the national average of 9¢ per kilowatt-hour, it would cost less than 6¢ a month to operate.

Though my staffer settled on the Recoton, we aren't recommending any particular brand. The point is to "seek the minimum level" or find the cheapest satisfactory solution.

POST-JERSEY PJ'S

You can make toddler pajama pants from hubby's old knit or velour shirts. Reader Alicia Lopez of Torrance, California, says they can be completed in 30 minutes or less.

Turn the shirt inside out and lay it flat. Use a pair of your toddler's pants as a pattern and trace onto the shirt allowing extra for seams and the waistband.

Cut the two pant legs out. Sew up the side of each. Put one leg inside the other, right sides together. Pin and sew the crotch.

To finish, sew waistband down, to form casing for elastic, leaving a 1-inch opening for insertion. The elastic can be scavenged from old panty hose.

SWAP TILL YOU DROP

Reader Carol Parker of Oakland, California, writes, "I would like to join a bartering network. How do I know which ones are legitimate and legal?"

Back in my graphic-design days I joined two trade exchanges, also known as bartering networks. I observed a curious contrast: some members thought these were a scam, other members loved them. After some thought, I've come to some conclusions about exchanges.

First, some facts. A trade exchange is a group of businesses (usually between 300 and 3,000) that trades goods and services. When one business sells to another, it's credited with "trade dollars," which have the same value as cash dollars and can be traded with any other member. Typically, exchanges charge an annual fee of $100 to $800, and collect a 10 percent cash or trade-dollar fee on all transactions.

This modern form of trade exchange has been around for 15 years, and there are over 150 nationwide. Over time, exchange owners have learned better methods of operation. If you had a poor experience ten years ago, you might fare better today.

Frugal people are attracted to trade exchanges because they're accustomed to saving money through informal swaps with friends. But a trade exchange is actually a miniature economy. One of the major ways in which it differs from personal barter is that trade dollars are reported to the IRS as earnings. Like cash, trade dollars spent in the operation of your business are tax-deductible, but trade dollars spent for personal use aren't. So when you spend 100 trade dollars at a hair salon, remember that you paid Uncle Sam (about) $25 in cash for taxes. You must also factor in materials and exchange costs. Don't think of exchange goods and services as free.

Although most exchanges are legal, some have serious management problems. If you're considering joining an exchange, learn the following:

- Whether there have been any complaints filed with the Better Business Bureau or the National Association of Trade Exchanges (27801 Euclid Ave., Cleveland, OH 44132; [216] 731-8030).
- How many members it has. A good exchange will show you a directory of all members. Call several members for references.
- How long it has operated.
- Whether it complies with IRS laws.
- Whether members trade 100 percent. A 50 percent cash/50 percent trade-dollar policy may mean members aren't confident they can spend trade dollars.

An exchange, like any business, is only as good as its owner. If the owner creates trade dollars out of thin air for personal use, inflation occurs. Members become overloaded with trade dollars and are unwilling to accept more. When

you call members for references, ask how easily they can spend their trade dollars.

Any exchange that meets all the above criteria is probably first-rate. However, don't discount one that doesn't. A "lesser" exchange can be beneficial under the right circumstances.

Beyond determining whether the actual exchange is good, decide whether your business is right for an exchange. Consider an exchange if:

1. You own a service business or sell a product with a minimum 40 percent profit margin. If you have a small profit margin, you won't recover out-of-pocket cash costs.

2. Your business has slow times. A business that's *always* busy should avoid exchanges, as real cash is easier to spend than trade dollars. But if your hair salon is slow on Wednesdays, or if your carpentry business slows during the winter, you can specify that you'll accept trade dollars only at those times.

3. Your business is in a heavily populated area. Exchanges in large cities offer dramatically better trading opportunities than those in small cities.

4. You offer something many people want. If you're a hypnotherapist, there may be few members who want your services. You may not recoup your membership fee.

There are also personal qualities that lead to successful trading, such as:

• A yard-sale mentality. If you can always find a bargain at a yard sale, you'll like exchanges. People who prefer the predictable selection of department stores will be disappointed.

• Realistic expectations. Some businesses acquire more trade dollars than they can use. I knew one member who amassed thousands of trade dollars to pay for a house addition, only to find that the building contractor dropped out. If you're saving for a large trade, work closely with the exchange and the other business to avoid nasty surprises.

• An awareness that "lesser" exchanges primarily trade services rather than goods. The better exchanges have an abundance of goods; lesser exchanges have few or none.

• Creative trading skills. Some businesses allow employees to use trade dollars as a benefit or bonus. My baby-sitter agreed to accept trade dollars as payment. I made the arrangements, and she got haircuts at a member salon.

Clearly, trade exchanges are more complicated than dealing with cash. So why would anyone bother? Because the exchange funnels work to you that you might not get otherwise. Exchanges are good for new businesses, as word-of-mouth from members may eventually bring in cash customers.

Initially, I belonged to a poorly run exchange, then I joined a lesser exchange. Even so, I successfully traded for a pawnshop microwave and VCR, restaurant meals, auto repair, furniture refinishing, chair cushions, upholstery cleaning, dental work, hair care, new encyclopedias, a clown/magician for a birthday party, and small items for gifts.

To learn whether there is a trade exchange in your area, look in the Yellow Pages under "barter and trade exchanges," or contact N.A.T.E.

FASTER THAN A SPEEDING BREAD MACHINE

Our favorite complement to quick-but-humble leftover soup has been popovers because of their speed, tastiness, and elegance. But move over, popovers. Sarah Severns of Kensington, Ohio, sent me this recipe for "Cuban Bread." Aside from eye appeal and great taste, it has one remarkable feature that sets it apart from other yeast breads: It takes only an hour and 15 minutes from start to finish.

5–6 cups all-purpose flour (you can substitute whole-wheat flour for 1 or 2 cups)
2 tablespoons dry yeast
2 tablespoons sugar
1 tablespoon salt
2 cups hot water (120–130 degrees)
1 tablespoon sesame or poppy seeds

Mix 4 cups of the flour with the yeast, sugar, and salt. Pour in hot water and beat 100 strokes, or 3 minutes with a mixer. Stir in the remaining flour until the dough is no longer sticky. Knead 8 minutes.* Place the dough in a greased bowl, and cover with a damp towel. Let rise 15 minutes. Punch down. Divide into two pieces. Shape into two round loaves, and place on a baking sheet. Cut an *X* ½ inch deep on top with a sharp knife. Brush with water, and sprinkle with seeds. Place on the middle shelf of a *cold* oven. Place a cake pan of hot water on the lowest shelf. Heat the oven to 400 degrees. Bake 40–50 minutes until deep golden brown.

*If your food processor has a dough blade, you can avoid the hand-kneading: Combine dry ingredients in the processor. As the machine is running, drizzle in water until the dough forms a ball. Spin the ball 20 times.

WHAT TO DO WITH . . .

Gunky White-Out. Instead of buying expensive White-Out brand thinner, thin it with a few drops of nail-polish remover. (Chris Rogers, Madison, Illinois.)

Empty Match Folders. Make into sewing kits for traveling. Needles and pins can be stuck into bottom fold. Various colors of thread can be wrapped around the back of the folder. (Wanda Good, Mount Joy, Pennsylvania.)

A Band-Aid Box. Make a soap holder for showering when camping. Poke drain holes in bottom. Attach a string to hang around your neck. (Carolyn Marck, Seattle, Washington.)

A Milk Jug. To make a great berry-picking bucket, cut the top off a gallon-size jug, put a strip of rope or cloth through the handle, and tie it around your waist. Can also be used to carry clothespins or nails. (Sally Kirby Hartman, Norfolk, Virginia.)

Newspaper. Dampen and use in place of masking tape when painting windows.

A Record Player that spins but doesn't play. Use for art projects. Place paper plate in the middle, and hold markers or paintbrushes against the spinning plate. (Mary Kay Carney, Minneapolis, Minnesota.)

A Paper Clip. Use as a "buttoner" if you have arthritis in fingers. Mail-order version costs $4.49. (Abraham Landsman, Madison, Wisconsin.)

A Dead Lawn Mower. Remove engine and bolt a board to the base. Use for carting heavy items. (Charlene Rasmussen, Milwaukee, Wisconsin.)

Carpet Scraps with attached foam padding. Fold with foam side out. Clamp with a clothespin to make a touch-up paintbrush.

Dented Ping-Pong Balls. Put them in boiling water to pop the dent out. (Peter Baylies, North Andover, Massachusetts.)

Soda-Can Tabs. Use to make replacement clips for elastic bandages. Clips aren't sold separately. Attach two tabs with a rubber band. (Leonard Duane, Newport, Maine.)

Margarine-Tub Lids. Make playing-card holders for children. Place two lids with flat sides together. Staple together in the center and put a sticker over the staples. (Sue Quinlan, Rosemont, Minnesota.)

Old Socks. Make a mop head for the old clamp style mops. Stitch toes together and clamp as many pairs in the mop as will fit. (Gertrude Roll, Forestville, New York.)

Old Metal Shower-Curtain Rings. Use to make homemade space-saving hangers. Put the ring over the neck of a hanger, then hang a second hanger from the ring. (Robin Gauthier, Halifax, Massachusetts.)

Marker Caps from kids' dead markers—the long kind. Use to make pencil extenders, so you can use too-short-to-hold pencils. (Theresa Stafford, Albany, Georgia.)

Styrofoam Peanuts. Use as bean-bag-chair refill after original Styrofoam pellets pack down. Some nursery and grammar schools have beanbag chairs and might appreciate your donation. (Debbie DeLost, Santa Ana, California.)

LAUNDRY QUANDARY

When we buy laundry detergent, Jim and I usually don't strain our brains. Years ago at a warehouse store, we bought the 4¢-per-load, weird-brand powdered detergent in the 50-pound bucket, but it irritated the kids' skin. So now we buy jumbo boxes of 12¢-per-load, name-brand powdered detergent at the warehouse. We've always bought powdered because sometime in my early tightwaddery I determined that, on average, the per-load cost was about half that of liquids.

But last year a rare thing happened. I found myself in possession of several high-value coupons and rebates for liquid detergents. So I ventured into the detergent aisle at a local supermarket to see if these would bring a liquid down to a competitive price, and I realized why so many readers have asked for an article on this subject.

Unlike powdered detergents, only two off-brands of liquid detergents had loads-per-container information on their labels. Most label instructions say to add a "capful," but only 5 out of 24 brands said how many ounces were in a cap. The caps vary in size because the detergents vary in concentration. The stores offer a per-quart unit price, but this is useless when trying to compute price per load.

So, without a calculator (I was cursing myself for not bringing it) I tried to figure the loads per bottle by guessing that the cap looked like, say, a ¼ cup measure. After ten dizzying minutes I found one brand, with coupon, that I guessed would equal my regular warehouse price.

Back at home, I learned that even this calculation was flawed. The caps to liquid detergents have an inner rim that extends down into the bottle, so you can't accurately compare cap sizes in the store. In short, it's near impossible for shoppers to make an informed choice.

Why do manufacturers go to such lengths to muddle the number of loads per bottle? We called several and got weasel-worded responses. So we were surprised when a Procter & Gamble representative told us frankly that if the information were listed, "People would find that liquids are generally more expensive."

So, why bother with liquids? Some people prefer that they can easily be poured directly on stains, and people with exceptionally hard water may find that powders don't dissolve completely. Finally, if you can calculate the cost per load, there are cases in

which liquids can be cheaper than powders.

So, since the manufacturers would not, I decided to provide you with a way to calculate the cost per load for liquid detergent. At first I tried to do this by simply buying various detergents and measuring how much the caps hold. But after finding many confusing, odd measurements, I decided to call the manufacturers themselves. I learned that they're in the process of concentrating their products. This makes the situation even more confusing for a number of reasons:

- The manufacturers use the terms "concentrated" and "ultra" inconsistently. "Ultra" usually means the product is concentrated, but not always. Fab Ultra has been concentrated and is now called Fab Ultra Power. So it's hard to figure out whether you're buying the old regular product or the new concentrated one.
- None of the "with bleach" versions say they're concentrated, although many clearly are.
- Even if you call the manufacturers to get information on cap sizes, you can't be certain that the representatives are always right. When I called Dial Corp. to learn cap sizes for Purex, the representative didn't even know that Purex was available in Ultra Concentrated.
- The manufacturers are downsizing differently. Colgate-Palmolive is downsizing from 4-ounce to 3-ounce caps. Lever is downsizing from ½ cup to ¼ cup, but their "with bleach" version is ⅓ cup—which results in an odd-ounce size. Procter & Gamble has the most confusing measures. Their representative told me their caps hold 98 milliliters, except for their Tide "with Bleach Alternative," which holds 125 milliliters, but she didn't know how many ounces these numbers equaled. So, unless you know how to convert ⅓ cup to ounces, and milliliters to ounces, you can't figure ounces per load.
- In this downsizing process, some manufacturers are staying with the old 32-, 64-, and 128-ounce bottles, while others are changing to 50-, 100-, and 150-ounce bottles.

I also observed other potential fiscal hazards.

- The cap sizes often aren't exactly what the manufacturer claims. I amplified the disparity by dumping four caps of water from each brand into a Pyrex measuring cup. I found, for example, that 4-ounce caps from different brands could vary by ½ ounce. This sounds insignificant, but if you compared 128-ounce bottles,

this difference would equal 4½ loads, or about $1 of detergent.

• The "fill lines" in the caps are a problem. In some cases the words "fill line" or the line itself could not be seen without holding the cap up to a bright light. Some caps didn't have the words "fill line" or an actual line; I presumed I was supposed to fill to where the "ridge design" ended. The fill lines varied from ⅛ inch to ⅞ inch from the rim of the cap. So, one could easily use too much detergent.

• It's hard to get all of the detergent out. Liquid-detergent bottles have a recessed plastic-spout-thing into which the cap screws. Because it's recessed, the spout can retain between 1 and 3 ounces of detergent. You could get this out by filling the bottle with water, shaking, and dumping the water into your washer, but chances are many people wouldn't realize so much is still in the bottle.

Given these problems, I have three solutions to offer:

• If you're a math wizard who loves to combine sales, coupons, and rebates, you might regard an evening spent in the detergent aisle with a calculator to be a thrill. If so, you'll need the specific cap sizes:

Arm & Hammer's "double power" PowerFresh is 2 ounces.

Colgate-Palmolive's "Ultra Power" versions of Ajax, Fab, and Dynamo are 3 ounces. The unconcentrated versions are 4 ounces. This company deserves credit for being the only major manufacturer that prints cap sizes on the labels—though you must hunt for this on the back of the bottle.

Dial's Ultra Purex is 3.5 ounces. The unconcentrated Purex and Purex "with Bleach Alternative" are 4 ounces.

Lever's "Double Power" All, Wisk, and Surf are 2 ounces. The "with bleaching action" versions are 2.7 ounces. The unconcentrated versions are 4 ounces.

Procter & Gamble's Bold, Cheer, Era, Gain, Ivory Snow, Solo, and Tide are 3.3 ounces. Its Tide "with Bleach Alternative" is 4.2 ounces. These products are usually labeled "Ultra" and/or say "Super Concentrated" on the cap.

To calculate ounces per load, first determine your after-sale, after-coupon and/or after-rebate cost (remember to factor in postage). Divide that by the number of ounces in the bottle to determine the price per ounce. Multiply that by the ounces per load to determine the cost per load.

Because you can often get a better deal using a coupon or rebate on a smaller product with a higher unit price, you'll have to do this calculation with several bottle sizes in each brand that you're considering.

• If you're not a math wizard but still want to use your coupons and rebates to buy name-brand liquids, try to get them for half price. We found that the cost per load for name-brand liquids varied from 18¢ to 28¢, so at half price they cost the same as powders. Also investigate store brands, which cost as little as 12¢ per load. We found one on-sale off-brand called Xtra that cost 9¢ per load.

One reminder: Ignore the manufacturer's suggested retail price printed in the flashy starburst on the label; it usually varies from the store's actual price.

• There are about 25 brands

available in my area, and each comes in three or more bottle sizes. Of these brands, there are seven different cap sizes. This is simply ridiculous. If this makes your brain hurt, simplify your detergent shopping by boycotting any detergent, be it liquid or powdered, that doesn't include loads-per-container information on the label, and report this decision to the manufacturers. Here are their numbers:

Arm & Hammer: (800) 524-1328
Colgate-Palmolive: (800) 338-8388
Dial: (800) 457-8739
Lever: (800) 598-5005
Procter & Gamble: (800) 846-7669

"WHOOPEE, WE CAN SPEND AGAIN!"

Roseanne is in its seventh season on TV, but old shows are syndicated nightly in our area. I caught few of the weekly episodes when they first ran, but I'm catching up, fast-forwarding through the past 6 years of the Connors' lives. A fascinating aspect of this show is that it's one of the few sitcoms featuring a family with financial problems. Specifically, the show's creators have perfectly depicted the feast-or-famine spending style of most American families.

Dan is frequently unemployed, and Roseanne works dead-end jobs. Money is tight. When an unexpected lump of money not only allows them to catch up on bills but actually yields a surplus $50, Dan and Roseanne vow to save it. But Roseanne secretly purchases a $50 bottle of perfume, while Dan secretly buys a $50 bell for the boat he is building in the garage. Another show was devoted to their misadventures when their power was cut off because they couldn't pay the bill. Yet, in good times, there is always money for beer, soda, and bowling. When the family goes to the mall and daughter Darlene wants money, she holds out her hand. Dan and Roseanne oblige.

You may feel that your income isn't cyclical because you don't have seasonal, iffy employment like Dan, a building contractor. But there are many kinds of employment cycles. For some, the cycle is annual. For others, it is linked to the performance of the national economy, which may take a decade to shift from boom to recession.

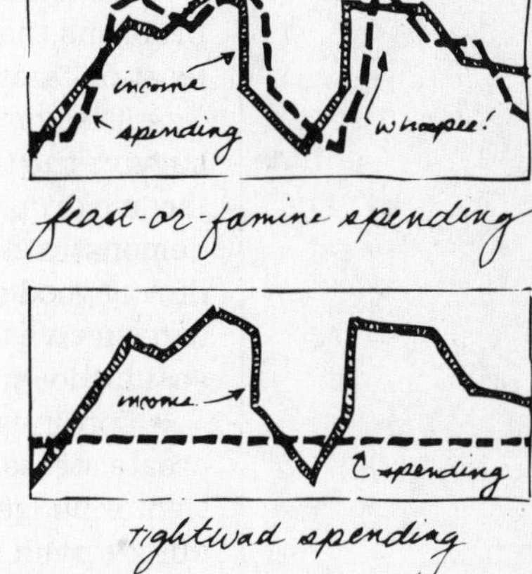

In any case, at the first sign of a personal economic improvement, we celebrate. We saw this whoopee-we-can-spend-again syndrome during the 1993 Christmas-shopping season. With November and December reports that the economy was improving, retailers experienced an "up" Christmas. There was a direct relationship between the drop in unemployment figures and the rise in gifts under the tree. In fact, frugality and bad economic times are so closely associated that I can actually gauge the severity of a drop in the G.N.P. by the boost in the number of media inquiries I get.

People spend lavishly during good times because they believe

that it's better to have splurged and gone bust than never to have splurged at all. Even the semiresponsible admonition to always save 10 percent of your income essentially endorses the constant contracting and expanding of family expenditures.

But surprisingly, life is easier and more enjoyable if spending, particularly in "lifestyle" areas (food, gifts, clothing, entertainment, and so on.) always stays, on average, at a modest level.

Let's look at some of the problems that arise from the feast-or-famine spending style.

• It leaves you with little to survive the times when your income drops. If, as my chart demonstrates, you save money during good economic times, you can survive the bad, often without scaling down your lifestyle.

• Continually changing rules create stress. Adjusting to a tighter budget is hard for parents, but it's even harder for kids. And their unhappiness, moping, and arguing make the unemployed parent feel guilty and inadequate. Kids are happiest when the rules are constant. If their allowance changes from 50¢ to $5 and back to 50¢, the happiness over the $5 allowance will be more than offset by the unhappiness over a return to 50¢.

• Although some frugal activities can be quickly adopted in times of famine, others can't. A garden might take a year or two before it produces well. It might take more than a year to stockpile enough yard-sale clothes so that you rarely have to buy new again. It takes time and patience to convert uncooperative family members. Many skills, from bread-making to oil-changing, require much practice before you can perform them quickly and skillfully enough to make them practical.

• When frugality is practiced only during unemployment, it acquires a stigma. Family members associate meatless meals and yard-sale clothing with bad times. Often, the terror of unemployment isn't about not having enough to eat or losing a house, but about having to do all that "low-class" penny-pinching stuff. Conversely, when frugality is practiced even in good times, the family learns to enjoy it and stretch the possibilities with their creativity.

A tightwad tends to be fearless in an uncertain economy. He knows that as long as there is enough money for basic needs, he can live quite happily without luxuries. He knows that there will always be Christmas because he can create it from nothing. He knows he can wring more miles from his old car. He knows he can feed his family well from his extensive repertoire of hamburger recipes. Most important, he doesn't feel like a victim of economic circumstances beyond his control. While he might dip into savings for a period of time, his lifestyle need not change. He is in control.

To some, constantly cruising along at a spending level that's near the bottom of the family's cyclical income level sounds like a life of permanent deprivation. But if there is one thing I would like to hammer home, it is a *new* definition of deprivation. True deprivation has nothing to do with a lack of stereos, restaurant meals, flashy toys, Caribbean vacations, and similar consumer items. To

me, a worse kind of deprivation is a lack of security—the constant nagging feeling that the tiniest downturn in one's income, or the smallest domestic disaster such as a blown engine or broken window, can wipe you out.

We don't place much value on this feeling of security in our culture because it doesn't have an ad campaign on TV, it's not promoted by our political leaders, and it doesn't surround us with lots of visible stuff with which we can easily impress our neighbors. But anyone who has lived without security and then slowly, patiently acquired it knows that it's more satisfying to own than any consumer gadget.

If you feel your economic circumstance is good now—possibly it has improved with the economy—this is not the time to abandon frugality. It may be a good time to fix the roof or replace the dying car, but it isn't a good time to raise everyone's expectations. If there's anything we know for sure, it's that there'll be bad times again.

A BOOK REVIEW

Even black-belt tightwads can go all squishy and overspend when it comes to car repair. If the guy in the greasy overalls says your venturi is cracked, and you have no idea what a venturi is, you'll hand over the credit card rather than display your ignorance by asking, "My what?"

But take heart. Catherine McClintock of Fort Collins, Colorado, says *Auto Repair for Dummies* by Deanna Sclar (Ten Speed Press, $17.95) has lifted the veil surrounding automotive ailments. We obtained a copy and were also impressed. It contains over 400 pages of car-repair and maintenance information written specifically for people who "have never held a wrench." You'll want to read it cover to cover, as you would a mystery novel. It'll be fascinating to finally understand the purpose of weirdly named car parts.

This book includes everything from "How to Open the Hood of Your Car" to the location of the idle stop solenoid. "The what?" you ask. That's the point. This is explained in everyday language. You are guided through basic maintenance such as changing the oil and flushing the radiator, up through minor repairs such as replacing radiator hoses, all the way to fairly difficult tasks such as tune-ups and repacking wheel bearings.

There are tons of excellent illustrations, and it's even spiral-bound so it'll lie flat next to you while you're under your car. Catherine wrote, "So far, I've changed my oil and spark plugs, flushed my radiator, checked my hoses, belts, and fluid levels, and cleaned my battery terminals. And I've learned an awful lot about how my car works."

Our only criticism is that the book was last updated in 1988, and automotive technology changes quickly. But if you're driving an older car, even the small percentage of dated information would still be relevant.

Try to get the book through interlibrary loan before you buy. It's still in print, but you'll probably have to have a bookstore order it for you.

MUSIC FOR A SONG

One of my favorite nuggets of tightwad wisdom came from Darrell Schweitzer of Strafford, Pennsylvania. He said, "Make friends with compulsive upgraders." He was referring to computer buying, but the concept applies broadly.

New technologies are often underdeveloped and expensive, so if you wait a few years, the quality improves as the price drops. But technology junkies stampede to buy the newest high-priced gizmos—and dump their old

equipment for ridiculously low prices. So, if you're patient, you can either buy new stuff once it is better and cheaper, or buy used stuff from compulsive upgraders.

Stereo equipment typifies this basic concept. CD players were first marketed ten years ago by Sony for $900. Today, a CD player with superior sound (but that is less durable) costs $100. Similarly, the earliest CDs were of low quality just when LP quality reached its peak.

Unlike turntables, CD players offer convenient operation and are nearly maintenance-free. The CDs themselves are "unscratchable" and should last forever. Because most people didn't replace their needles and balance their turntables to achieve optimum sound, early CD players did seem like a vast improvement. Consequently, CDs have almost completely snuffed out the LP market, which now comprises less than 2 percent of music sales.

But are CDs always better? Richard Lenhert, assistant editor of *Stereophile* magazine, told me that if you plan to spend less than $1,000, a new CD player will probably sound better than a new turntable. But if money is no object, a high-quality turntable will unquestionably deliver superior sound.

Further, some purists in the music industry feel that CD technology is flawed. They say that because the CD reproduces music through a digitizing process, it doesn't capture the subtleties of the LP. It's similar to the difference between a photograph, which has gray tones, and a magazine reproduction of a photograph, which is comprised of tiny black dots. Singer Neil Young, the most vocal critic of CDs, calls the last decade "the darkest time ever for recorded music." Many musicians and nearly all grunge bands insist that their music be available on LP.

Realistically, CD technology probably does suit the average ear and the average budget. And given that so little new music is available on LP, it's also a practical choice for those who desire the newest recordings.

So if you've already made the transition to CDs, look for bar-

gains. Used CDs cost $8 to $10. If you want state-of-the-art CD quality, consider mail order. Our business manager, Elaine, joined BMG Music Service and buys only during buy-one-get-two-free sales. This brings the price of each CD down to $7.50. Be very sure to read all of the fine print in any mail-order club's literature.

But if you haven't made the jump—and here's the real point of this article—you can take advantage of one of the best yard-sale opportunities of our time, as compulsive upgraders are dumping their LP's. Duane Corpe of Mount Vernon, Iowa, reports that he bought a half-dozen for a total of $1.50. My uncle, a 45-ish baby boomer, finds records from his favorite artists of the sixties and seventies for 25¢. To preserve these LPs, he records the music on a cassette and then listens to that. (For a thorough discussion of LP- and cassette-preservation methods, read "Fair Play," published in *Stereo Review* magazine, July 1992.)

But note that the unbelievably low-priced LP may be a short-lived phenomenon. Due to increasing scarcity, many LPs are becoming collectors' items and some in mint condition can be worth hundreds of dollars. (For a thorough discussion of collectible LPs, read "Where's the Value in Vinyl?" published in *U.S. News & World Report*, December 1993.)

Aside from the cheap LP, used turntables are a bargain, especially if you already own one. If you're unhappy with the sound quality, try a little maintenance before you decide to heave it. If your needs are modest, yard sales may also offer some bargains. A friend failed to sell a clean, new-looking turntable at his yard sale for $10. Since our turntable died at the hands of reckless toddlers, he traded his to us for five bags of our frozen berries. Although purists would shudder at our acquisition (because lower-quality turntables can be hard on LPs), it suits our needs. Our music-listening experience consists largely of breaking out old Doris Day and/or Bing Crosby Christmas music once a year. Otherwise, *quiet* is music to our ears.

The yard-sale LP strategy can be either a way to postpone your entry into the world of CDs or a permanent solution. If you do plan to switch to CDs, there's a good argument to be made for waiting to pick up used CDs and CD players as upgraders dump these within a few years. But be cautious. While some people set prices realistically, others try to recover part of their inflated purchase price. If a seller argues a ten-year-old CD player "is worth $250 because it cost $900 new," be aware that the sound quality may be worse than that of a new player costing the same amount.

In short, if you're resisting the expense of those space-age-looking disks, you're not "out of it." Many people continue to listen to LPs for reasons of a nostalgic preference for vinyl, because their favorite oldies are not available on CDs, because they believe the sound quality is better, or because they can listen to really good music for a fraction of the price.

Music is like movies, books, magazines, and fashion: It's much cheaper if you wait a couple of years. So if anyone laughs at you for being hopelessly behind the times, don't get mad, get friendly.

SAFETY-PIN UPHOLSTERY

If you have mediocre sewing skills or little time, sewing cushion covers with zippers seems like a daunting challenge.

One solution is safety-pin upholstery. I have never tried it for a six-cushion couch, but it works well for furniture with only one or two cushions. It can be used as either a temporary or permanent solution.

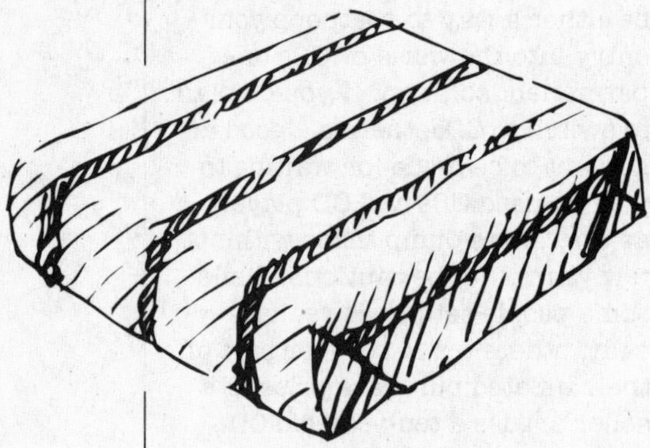

Safety-pin upholstery requires medium-size safety pins (a minimum of six per large cushion) and a piece of heavy fabric. Very simply, you wrap your cushion with the fabric in the same way that you would wrap a box with wrapping paper.

Ideally, the fabric should be large enough to overlap as you wrap from front to back, but if you happen to have material that isn't quite large enough to overlap and the old cushion covers are sturdy, you can fold it under and pin it to the old cover. The side-to-side dimension needs to be only large enough so that it can be wrapped under and securely pinned. In any case, wrap and pin front to back first, so that the folds are concealed on the sides. Using this technique, there will be no visible raw edges.

If you use this as a temporary solution, use the same fabric you hope to sew into real cushion covers someday. While waiting for something nicer to turn up, I have also used temporary fabrics: a surplus scrap of lightweight canvas, old drapes, and a torn bedspread.

Like real cushion covers, this pinned fabric can be removed for washing and quickly replaced.

Safety-pin upholstery has one final advantage. If I change my mind about the cushion fabric (as may happen when I find a better bargain rug) I can reuse this material elsewhere.

INSTANT ANALYSIS

When, back in 1990, I first wrote about our family's use of instant powdered milk, whole milk was very expensive in much of the country: $2.50 or more per gallon. At the same time, store-brand powdered milk in the 20-quart-size box was as low as $1.20 per gallon. But in more recent years, due to government regulations, whole milk prices have dropped to as low as $2.00 per gallon in many parts of the country, while powdered milk has climbed to $1.80 per gallon. With these skimpy savings, I wouldn't fault any tightwads for drinking whole rather than powdered milk.

But a couple of years ago Claudia Tomkiel of Carlisle, Pennsylvania, mentioned a third alternative: noninstant powdered milk, purchased in 50-pound-sack size,

which she claimed tasted better than the instant variety. I promptly called local bulk-food sources and found it cost about the same as instant at that time, about $1.60 per gallon. Unimpressed, I disregarded the idea. More recently two other readers including Jane Moran of Meadville, Pennsylvania, wrote with similar information, only these readers also listed their per-gallon prices: from $1.00 (picked up at the factory) to $1.54 (from a bakery-supply company) per gallon. With the recent price increases of instant powdered milk, this became more interesting. Additionally, Jane maintained it tasted far better than instant (which she felt had a "burnt" taste) and was only slightly less rich than 2 percent milk. We made some and we agree: It does taste better than instant powdered milk.

Noninstant powdered milk comes in low-heat and high-heat varieties. This refers to the processing method. Low-heat is slightly more nutritious and slightly more expensive, but the taste is the same.

While noninstant milk is harder to mix, it *can* be done successfully in a blender or with a mixer. Mix 2¾ cups of powder (about 1 pound) to 2 cups of water, let the bubbles evaporate, and then add enough water to equal a gallon.

Like instant, noninstant tastes better if it sits overnight. So keep one jug of newly mixed in the back of the refrigerator while drinking from yesterday's mixed.

Many people wouldn't want to keep a 50-pound sack of anything around, but families who drink a lot of milk might. If this intrigues you, first buy a small quantity of noninstant milk from your local health-food store. (Purchased in small quantities, it will probably have a higher per-gallon cost than whole milk.) If you like it, try to find a cheaper source. A 50-pound sack for $75 equals $1.50 per gallon.

Our local price for noninstant milk is still about $1.60 per gallon. But people who live in the West and Midwest will do better because that's where most of the milk is produced. Contact large producers of dairy products near you to see whether they make noninstant milk and whether you can buy direct. If not, contact bulk-food sources: food coops, health-food stores, and bakery suppliers.

Finally, remember that powdered milk of either kind isn't just for large families. Singles, couples, and small families tend to buy milk in quarts because gallons go bad before they can drink them, so they pay even higher prices for milk. Powdered milk is also a good choice for people whose milk consumption is very limited and for those who primarily use milk for cooking, on cereal, and in hot drinks.

GIZMOS AND GIMMICKS FOR THE NOUVEAU FRUGAL

In the spring of 1991, just after we were featured in *Parade* magazine and on the Donahue show, over 200 feet of mail was delivered to our house. In June of that year, I delivered a set of twins (with, to be precise, exactly four feet). Even with additional help, months would transpire before we began to make a dent in the reader mail.

Along with these letters came a mountain of promotional materials for all sorts of money-saving enterprises: how-to videos, financial-freedom cassettes, vegetarian cookbooks, budget planners, haircutting kits, shop-at-home services, frequent-flyer promotions, toilet-tank water savers, multilevel-marketed everything, computer financial organizers, powdered-milk substitutes (hmmm . . .), toothpaste-tube squishers, flavoring and extract samples, fuel-economizer doohickeys, superinsulated water-heater wraps, coupon pouches, and, perhaps the most unusual, a toilet-to-bidet conversion kit.

I piled all of this stuff in boxes, planning to sort through it someday. I thought if I ever ran out of ideas for the newsletter, this stuff would make handy subject matter. Over time the pile grew . . . and grew . . . and finally it just grew dusty.

Occasionally, I tried to dig through it, but found that much of the promotional literature was too tiresome for a mother of infant twins to absorb on four hours of sleep. I developed an aversion to anything that rolled frequent-flyer miles, phone services, and credit cards into one promise-to-save-you-a-fortune program.

Well, the twins got bigger, and I got more sleep. With my new alertness, I began to spot some of these same products and services in the mass media. When a reader asked about one, I would tack the letter to my bulletin board, making it a priority to research. In most cases, when I overcame my aversion to tiresome literature, I found the analysis interesting. Sometimes I saw that readers could have learned the answers on their own. Other times researching the value of a $100 product required $200 worth of phone calls. Much of what I was able to learn could not have been obtained had I not been with "the media."

The $12 Banana Hanger

As I complete four years of publishing, I've begun to understand that along with increased interest in saving money, the 1990s have seen whole industries spring up to satisfy the newly frugal, many of whom have yet to kick their old habit of buying stuff. Now they can buy money-saving stuff to satisfy the craving without guilt.

They're attracted to easy ways to save money that require only that they sign up for a new gimmick or buy a new gizmo.

Thrift and environmentalism go hand-in-hand. Along with the money-saving gimmicks and gizmos, there's a whole mail-order line of "environmentally responsible" products. Some products are sound but come with a higher price tag than equivalent products you can purchase locally (a push mower is a push mower). Other products you don't need at all, like a rubber necktie made from an old tire (no kidding). These products, like those marketed to the frugal, satisfy our craving to consume without the guilt; we can feel good about buying anything with "Save the whales" silkscreened on it.

The media has recognized the interest of the newly frugal and that there's a huge collection of new products and services to bring to their attention. And indiscriminate product plugs are an easy way to fill airtime or column space. With all of this careless plugging of products, a scam or two is bound to slip through. Unfortunately, people believe "If it weren't true, they wouldn't be allowed to say it on television."

Albeit clunky, let me take a literary detour here and give you an inside view of the media.

I've made dozens of television appearances, and no one ever asked me to verify anything I planned to say. Most talk shows and news spots are hastily assembled. In some cases, I've arrived with barely enough time to catch my breath and clip on a mike.

As both the subject and writer of many articles, I can offer a unique perspective on the print medium. Most of the stories written about me have contained at least one error or misrepresentation. Even when reporters are extremely careful, mistakes happen. Often when I research questionable money-saving offers, I call reporters who previously wrote favorably of them to learn whether they had received any complaints. Invariably, they admit having had too little research time and say they simply trusted what was told to them—or they presumed that, since the gizmo had been plugged elsewhere, *someone* had done the necessary homework. And sometimes they weren't too concerned about letting their readers know they had goofed.

So you shouldn't blindly trust any media report you hear or read anywhere—including in *The Tightwad Gazette.* End of detour.

With the proliferation of talk shows, books, magazines, and newsletters, and these sources all interviewing each other, there has been far too much slipshod product and service promotion geared to the nineties money-conscious consumer.

There's also been a sort of subtle subversion in the thrift publishing business, a kind of "I promoted you in my book, you should promote me in your newsletter" feeling. I feel like a heel for not cooperating, but I didn't ask for their plug, and their book contains the same information that can be found in free library books.

Sometimes the product is given a blanket endorsement even though it isn't good for everyone in every circumstance. There's a lack of effort to analyze and quan-

tify the benefit. In other cases the product might have some possible benefit—like a $12 banana hanger (a gizmo to hang a bunch of bananas on so they won't spot). But often people could improvise: Why not screw a cuphook into the underside of your cabinets?

A lot of this stuff you don't need at all. One birthday, Jim had a *Tightwad Gazette* coffee mug made for me. We realized there would be a market for such mugs among our most enthusiastic readers. Similarly, marketing whizzes have told me I'm missing out by not selling *Tightwad Gazette* buttons, decals, bumper stickers, and T-shirts. It's been suggested that I should sell *Tightwad Gazette* price books with blank pages (even though mine is a scavenged insurance-rate notebook). There was even a lucrative offer from a well-known calendar company that wanted to sell *Tightwad Gazette* tear-off thrifty-tip-a-day calendars. We never debated; all of these things were counter to our philosophy.

I could easily devote every issue to the promotion of semi-good products, although I personally get excited by little of this stuff. I could likewise devote each issue to debunking dubious products and services. I limit my efforts to ones that seem to be taken seriously by the media.

But in both cases, see this for what it is. This is America, the land of the entrepreneur, and there is nothing wrong with people spotting a trend and trying to make money. Just be aware that some of this stuff is useful.

Most of it is not.

DON'T PUT ALL YOUR CONFETTI EGGS IN ONE PAPER-SACK EASTER BASKET

So far, I've managed to collect only three long-handled FTD flower baskets from yard sales to use for permanent Easter baskets, but I seem to be acquiring children faster than I can acquire baskets. When you have six kids, every basket must be identical so that everyone is happy. Hence, I'm still making "disposable" baskets. But I enjoy surprising the kids with something new each year.

As my family has grown, the baskets have had to be quicker to make. So when Cheryl Tomski of Littleton, Colorado, sent in directions to make Christmas baskets using standard grocery sacks, I saw easy Easter-basket possibilities.

Cheryl's baskets were made from large grocery bags. I used lunch-size bags to make Easter baskets.

To make one, roll down the rim of a bag to within 2 inches of the bottom. Roll down a second bag to within 3 inches of the bottom, and tuck it into the first bag, so that its rim rests on the first rim. (To make the larger baskets, you would repeat this procedure until you've combined three to four bags.)

For a handle, cut 6 inches off the top of a standard grocery sack to form a paper circle, and fold in fourths to make a band 1½ inches wide. Glue the raw edge down. Put the basket inside this circle as shown.

To attach the nested bags together and the handle to the bags,

I used small dabs of hot glue because this was quick and easy. But if you have a bit more time—or aren't producing six baskets—you can enhance the "baskety" look with yarn. Lace it in and out of the rims and around the handle by poking holes in the bags with an embroidery needle. The basket can be spray-painted or otherwise decorated.

As for what to put in your paper-sack baskets, try confetti eggs. They're used in Mexican Independence Day celebrations but are great for other holidays. These colorfully dyed, confetti-filled eggs are free to make, won't cause cavities, and take up lots of space in sparse Easter baskets. When a child smashes an egg on his or someone else's head, it explodes (the egg, not the head) in a surprisingly dramatic shower of colored shell and confetti.

Obviously, confetti eggs require less time to smash than to make and clean up. (Pick an easy-to-vacuum place for this activity.) But it's fun to surprise kids with these at least once.

To make the eggs, first poke a tiny hole in one end and a ½-inch-diameter hole in the other end of a raw egg. Blow the egg out (saving the yolk and white for tomorrow's scrambled-egg breakfast).

Rinse the egg shells, and dye them as you would regular Easter eggs. (You don't need to purchase egg-dying kits. Add food coloring and a teaspoon of vinegar to a cup of boiling water.)

While the dye dries, make confetti by cutting up colorful paper or magazine pages into ¼-inch squares. Or ask a copy shop for paper punches from its hole puncher. Use a funnel (make one from a roll of paper) to put the confetti in the eggs. Glue a piece of tissue paper over the large hole in the egg.

I used this idea when I needed wacky and dramatic props for an appearance on the David Letterman show. Dave loved it.

AVOIDING THE PRICE-BOOK HASSLE

In my first book, I wrote about the price book, a small, loose-leaf binder in which you record the lowest prices at various stores in your area, so you'll know which store generally has the best price on a particular item, and when a sale price really is a bargain.

While scores of readers have told me that the price book led to major savings, several have said they were hassled by management as they wrote in their books. Lisa-Anne French of Yarmouth, Maine, recorded prices in ten stores and at five of them was confronted by angry managers; some accused her of working for competing stores. She asked what one should do in this situation.

Curious, we called two Maine assistant attorneys general. They theorized that stores do have a legal right to ask people to leave; after all, the stores are private property. But, they said, if you explain what you're doing, refuse to leave, and are physically ejected, you might go to a private attorney to see whether you have a case.

We also called two local supermarket chains. Neither had any policy regarding customers writing down prices. A representative suggested telling the store's manager what you'll be doing *before* you begin.

In any case, I never had this problem. I think it's because I never went to every store in my area and jotted hundreds of prices in one intensive effort. I spent almost *no* time standing in aisles, conspicuously scribbling.

- First, I gleaned prices from my sales slips and from products in my cupboards with prices marked on them. I jotted down prices from sale flyers for a month. *Then* I went to the supermarket to fill in the gaps resulting from the few products that never went on sale. I did make a special trip to record prices from the warehouse club, but there was a limited range of items to record. Because I gathered prices as I shopped, I probably didn't look like an undercover supermarket spy.
- I buy few convenience foods, paper goods, or cleaners, so I need to keep track of fewer than 100 items. I didn't record prices of items I don't buy.
- Some items need not be included in the price book, either because I've memorized the best price or because I have developed a price guideline for an entire product group. For example, I won't pay more than 7¢ an ounce

for cold cereal. So I don't have a cold-cereal page at all, much less a separate page of prices for each type of cereal.

- I generally record only the lowest sale prices at the supermarkets. The only regular retail prices I record are for items that seldom go on sale, such as flour, and the few store brands we buy.
- Because we primarily buy only sale items from supermarkets, and because sale prices are similar from one supermarket to another, I was less interested in comparing supermarkets. I focused on comparing supermarket sales to the prices at other places that have few or no sales: warehouse clubs, the military commissary, farmer's markets, "damaged-goods" stores, discount department stores, U-pick farms, food coops, and health-food stores.
- After I gathered several prices, I would record a new price only if it was lower than what I had seen before.

As a final note, remember that through keeping a price book you gain a general sense of where you should shop for each item, but far more important, you learn the bottom price. It doesn't matter where you buy it, what matters is the price you pay.

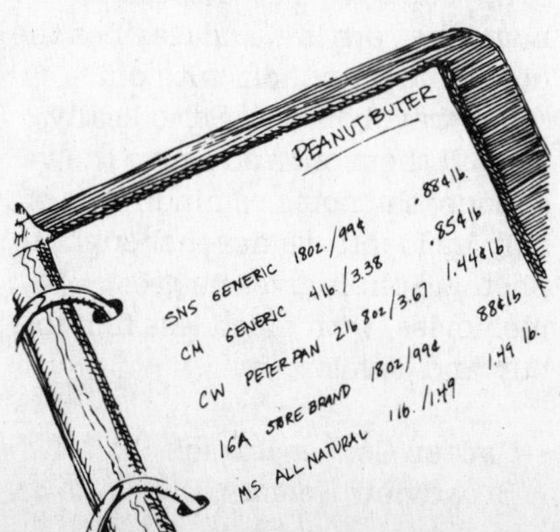

COPY CAT-ALOG

Dear Amy,

I use all of the gift catalogs that come in the mail to study to see what I can copy cheaply. A microwave bacon "fryer" that cost $35 and could be used only for that purpose was recreated with a package of wooden chopsticks that cost 99¢ and one of my microwavable bowls. I have made fun chocolate pizzas that looked even better than the ones in the catalogs (and I found that pizza stores will sell, very cheaply, or even give you the box to put it in). My next year's grandkid project is to copy a catalog's "doorway puppet stage" ($39.95) made from some fabric and a tension rod.

—Gail Jackson
Blue Springs, Missouri

TOYS FROM TEENS

Dear Amy,

Looking for toys but don't want to spend a fortune? Try the local junior high or high school. These kids have outgrown their "baby" toys and are on the prowl for real money. Ask to put a note on the bulletin board or in the school paper, and be specific. I have gotten: 20 GI Joes for 25¢ to 50¢ each, an entire set of Castle Legos (retail $60) for $10, and a Little Tykes sink, stove, refrigerator, plus a huge box of play food for $25. Be sure to get the parents' permission.

—Julie Edgar
Manassas, Virginia

IGNORE THE STORE

Dear Amy,

Here's a neat technique used for a wedding shower given for a fellow tightwad. We knew that many guests would be unable to spend much for shower gifts, but that other guests would prefer spending a lot more than necessary. So we issued an invitation with the following request: "Please bring a gift that cannot be purchased in a store." This encouraged homemade gifts and provided noncrafty guests with the possibility of buying gifts in creative places. The bride-to-be received many personal gifts made especially for her as well as a few garage sale items, plants, and other unique gifts. We didn't force frugality on the guests, we simply encouraged it along with encouraging creativity.

—Jill Tammen
Lakeland, Minnesota

SAND SAVER

Dear Amy,

For years, in late spring or early summer, I've gathered road sand spread by the town during the winter. I scoop it from along the side of the road and put it in 5-gallon plastic buckets. I recycle it by spreading it where necessary during the following winter months. Three buckets full of sand have been sufficient for my 40-foot, double-width driveway and walk for one winter.

—Rudi Smith
Brunswick, Maine

DOUBLE BUBBLE

Dear Amy,

Our local florist will reinflate those mylar balloons for about 75¢, so I get several uses from the same balloon for family occasions.

—Carolyn Pollock
Hunt, New York

PHRASES, NOT PHOTOS

Dear Amy,

Neither my husband nor I particularly enjoy taking pictures on vacation . . . and we often forget the camera. His habitual note-taking (he's a reporter) has ended up reducing our desire for photos. At the end of each day of our trip, he makes concise notes about what we did . . . places we ate, sites we saw, people we met, etc. Once home, he rewrites and clarifies the notes and puts them with our other travel diaries. Periodically, we pull them out and relive the vacations, the notes reminding us of silly incidents we never thought to photograph. It gives us great memories, with much less film to buy and develop.

—Colleen Cooper Russell
Broadview Heights, Ohio

HOW TO MOVE INEXPENSIVELY

Moving can cost thousands of dollars. How cheaply you can move depends on how much advance notice you have, how far you're moving, how much stuff you have, how healthy and strong you are, and how resourceful you're willing to be. If all of those factors are in your favor, a move can be almost free.

The following ideas are from over 250 letters from newsletter readers about their experiences with inexpensive moves.

LIGHTEN THE LOAD

By far the most common suggestion was to get rid of possessions. Scrutinize your belongings as to whether you need them at all, and if so, how easily they can be replaced. A professional mover can charge up to $1 per pound to move items, so you don't want to pay $1 to have a 50¢ can of beans moved.

Lighten the load by having a yard sale, taking books and magazines to libraries, and taking clothes to consignment shops. You might be better off giving an old piano to a piano dealer. Eat up your food during the months prior to your move. If you're moving locally, this is a good time to have your TV repaired, rugs cleaned, and furniture recovered. Have the stuff delivered to your new home.

PACKING MATERIALS

A professional moving company would charge you over $500 just for packing materials, yet this is the one part of your move that can be achieved almost for free. You will need to buy only packing tape and felt markers.

Free boxes can be found in abundance at a variety of places. Check liquor stores for boxes with compartments, copy shops for photocopy-paper boxes, supermarkets for fruit, egg, and gallon-water boxes, schools in late summer for book boxes, paint stores for paint boxes, and hospital loading docks for supply boxes. Dumpsters behind furniture stores are good sources of cardboard corners for large furniture and boxes for pictures and mirrors. Appliance stores have large pieces of cardboard to tape to furniture. And you saved the box

and packing your computer or stereo came in, right?

Having boxes of a uniform size is helpful for longer moves, because you can pack the truck more tightly. You can buy new boxes and resell them to the moving company when you're done, or buy used ones from moving companies. Keep your eyes open for people just moving into your neighborhood, and ask them for their boxes. Trash piles in military housing are good places to look. Put out the word to your friends and coworkers. Another source is Paper Mart (800-745-8800).

Don't use newspaper for packing, as the print will come off on your stuff. Get an end roll of unprinted stock from your local newspaper. You'll also want to scavenge Styrofoam peanuts, Styrofoam blocks from office-equipment stores, and bubble wrap and shredded paper from hospitals and offices. Use your towels, sheets, and blankets. If you don't have enough, it might be cheaper to buy thrift-shop blankets than to rent blankets. Padded envelopes are good for small pictures.

Some items don't require boxes during shorter moves. Leave clothing in bureau drawers. Pack soft unbreakables in trash bags. Tie books in bundles. Remember to pack stuff in stuff—like in your washer.

PACKING TIPS

Pick up free brochures on packing tips from moving companies. Some companies even offer free packing classes.

In the weeks before your move, gradually begin packing the stuff you don't use every day. Certain items should be packed last—like the microwave and vacuum cleaner (so you can vacuum your old house last and your new house first). Don't fill large boxes with very heavy items. Pack dishes upright for less breakage. Mark all boxes with the contents and room destination. If disassembling anything, put small parts in a Baggie and tape to the larger item.

SPECIAL EQUIPMENT

If you're moving yourself, rent a hand-truck or borrow one from a supermarket, a lumberyard, or an employer. If you're moving with a trailer or pickup, you'll need a tarp and rope. Also consider renting a back brace.

THE MOVING-DAY LABOR

The second most common suggestion from readers was to get your friends to help you actually carry the stuff. To ensure their willingness, volunteer to help when they move in the years prior to your move. When they help you, be considerate. Have all of your packing accomplished before they arrive. Give them plants, food, and other items you can't take with you. To avoid overworking them, consider rounding up both a packing crew and unpacking crew. Provide a meal and beverages as a thank-you.

If you can't find friends, consider sources of inexpensive labor: workers through temporary and unemployment agencies, college or high school students, and teens from local youth groups or Scouts. One reader successfully hired men from a halfway house for recovering alcoholics.

THE WHEELS

If you're moving yourself, try to borrow a pickup, van, or truck, and/or a utility or horse trailer. Be sure to fill the gas tanks before returning borrowed vehicles. For longer moves, readers bought trucks, trailers, and even school buses. If you shop carefully, these can be resold after the move so you can at least break even.

TRUCK RENTALS

If you're renting a truck, do some research and compare many options. It's generally cheaper to rent midweek, midmonth, and not during the summer. It'll probably be cheaper to get a larger truck to make one trip than to rent a smaller truck and make several trips.

Because of seasonal "gluts" of trucks all going in the same direction, you'll save if you go in the reverse direction. So if everyone goes south in the winter, you could save half the rental cost if you move north at this time. If you're moving "against the glut," you have negotiating power. Get prices from several rental companies, and see if you can get one to bid lower. Also check with the national and local offices of the same company; sometimes prices are different.

It may be cheaper to return the truck to the point of origin or to pay a friend to come with you and drive the truck back. You may save by dropping the truck off in a larger distant city rather than a small nearby town.

You might be able to get an AAA discount if you're a member, and you may save a little if you rent a manual-transmission truck. Remember to verify the odometer reading with the company before leaving and to fill the gas tank before dropping the truck off.

HIRING A MOVING COMPANY

This is your most expensive option, and the one that requires the most research. Moving companies vary in how they charge; it's usually some combination of distance, weight, and labor. Get a firm quote in writing, and ask about any hidden charges, deductibles, or deposits. Make sure that their insurance is for full replacement value.

You can save if you pack your own stuff, but the mover probably won't insure it. The stuff might be insured anyway under your homeowner's policy. Either way, it'll probably be cheaper to pack yourself and replace a few damaged items. Transport your most valuable breakables

with you in the car. If the movers pack, watch them: Without supervision, they'll pack up your trash. Break down your furniture in advance. But avoid companies that insist on breaking *everything* down; some furniture, particularly any antiques, will never be the same again.

If you need just a few items moved a long distance, see if you can get your stuff on a truck going the same way.

If you're moving locally, small local movers will probably be cheaper. These "three guys and a truck" outfits often charge solely by the hour, so make sure that you have everything completely ready to go before they come.

Be sure the moving company knows the fastest route.

UNCONVENTIONAL OPTIONS

If you're moving a long distance, it can be cheaper to move some things through the post office—especially books that go book rate. Get prices from UPS and bus companies too. In this case, someone will need to be at the destination to pick up the packages.

Some readers were successful in finding independent truck drivers with empty loads who were willing to move stuff.

Some realtors offer discounts with certain moving companies and may even provide free use of the realtor's van. When choosing a realtor, be sure to inquire about this.

IF YOUR EMPLOYER IS PAYING

See if it will pay you to move yourself. The military has such provisions, and we found we could "earn" a little by moving ourselves. Many large companies may have similar policies. Save all your paperwork to be sure you get reimbursed.

MISCELLANEOUS TIPS

Baby-sitters are cheaper than movers, so find a place for your children away from the moving-day hustle.

If you're driving a long distance with a pet, it's worth the 50¢ to get a pet tranquilizer from your vet.

Before you move, get a credit history from your utility companies so that you won't need a deposit at your new destination.

Remember to make provisions to save during lengthy trips. Pack a cooler of food and drinks. Camp or stay with friends and relatives whenever possible.

Keep all receipts together if these would be applicable for income-tax deductions.

A great advantage of moving yourself is that you can afford to leave a full rented or borrowed truck in the driveway for several days while you do messy work such as replacing the carpet, sanding and refinishing the floors, repainting the whole interior, or simply a major cleaning. It's tiring, but these things are much more efficiently done in an empty house.

And remember the "Natural Law of Moving." The number of things you lose while moving is directly proportional to the number of things you find that you had thought you lost in the last move.

THE TWILIGHT PHONE ZONE

Although it seems like a worthy subject for my books, I've hesitated to tackle long-distance telephone service for several reasons:

• Virtually every one of the hundreds of long-distance companies that has sprung up since the 1984 AT&T breakup uses a different billing method.

• Virtually every customer has a different calling pattern.

• Whatever conclusions I publish could be obsolete within months, as rates change and new plans are offered frequently.

• If you bounce around from plan to plan to get the cheapest rates, switching fees could eat up any savings (unless you are taking advantage of a special).

• The few dollars you save by switching to a small company may not be worth the tradeoff in poorer service.

• It's easier for me to predict that you'll save money by making a touch-up paintbrush out of a carpet scrap and a clothespin than by switching phone services.

However, the subject of long-distance phone rates isn't completely hopeless either. An organization called the Telecommunications Research and Action Center (TRAC) has taken on the daunting task of monitoring the ever-shifting world of long-distance calling plans.

The TRAC periodically produces charts that compare the monthly cost of different plans for different usage patterns.

Studying the chart, we came to these conclusions:

• The companies that offered "friends and family" type plans were the cheapest if you made most of your calls to other plan customers, but I personally feel this is impractical, and the savings were not great.

• AT&T was never the cheapest in any category, but the extra expense was not great.

• This is an area of your budget in which you can legitimately throw up your hands and stick with whatever you have now, especially if you don't spend a lot on long-distance calls. But if such calls are a splurge you work into your budget, and you spend as much as $50 per month, it's possible that the information in the TRAC chart could save you as much as $10 a month. To get one, send a long SASE and $2 for the residential information chart or $5 for the business chart to:

TRAC
P.O. Box 12038
Washington, DC 20005.

THE CROCKPOT TROUBLESHOOTER CHART

The problem: Although your Rival crockpot heats up it doesn't seem to cook the food thoroughly anymore.

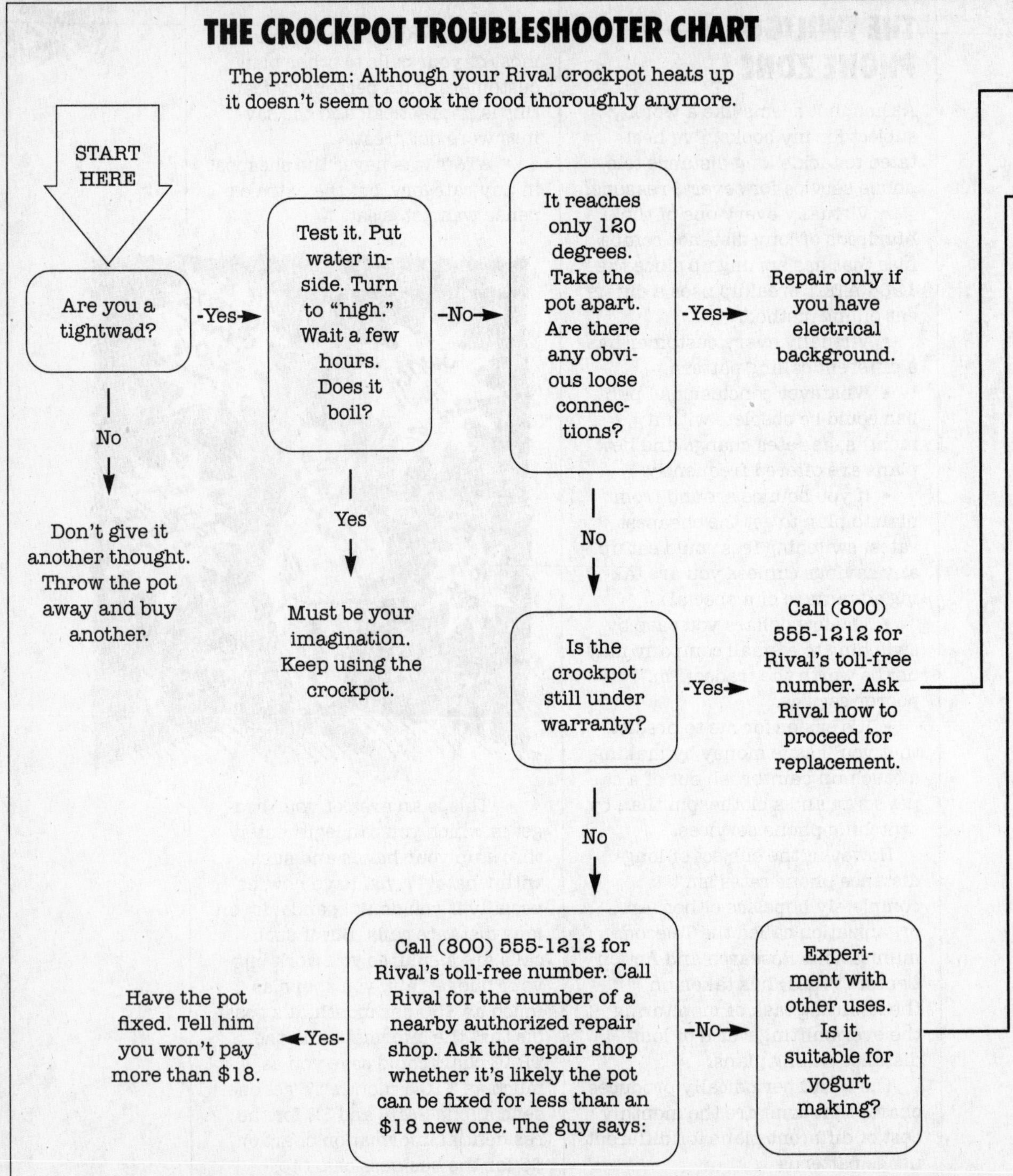
START HERE
Are you a tightwad?
-Yes→
Test it. Put water inside. Turn to "high." Wait a few hours. Does it boil?
-No→
It reaches only 120 degrees. Take the pot apart. Are there any obvious loose connections?
-Yes→
Repair only if you have electrical background.
No
Don't give it another thought. Throw the pot away and buy another.
Yes
Must be your imagination. Keep using the crockpot.
No
Is the crockpot still under warranty?
-Yes→
Call (800) 555-1212 for Rival's toll-free number. Ask Rival how to proceed for replacement.
No
Call (800) 555-1212 for Rival's toll-free number. Call Rival for the number of a nearby authorized repair shop. Ask the repair shop whether it's likely the pot can be fixed for less than an $18 new one. The guy says:
←Yes-
Have the pot fixed. Tell him you won't pay more than $18.
-No→
Experiment with other uses. Is it suitable for yogurt making?

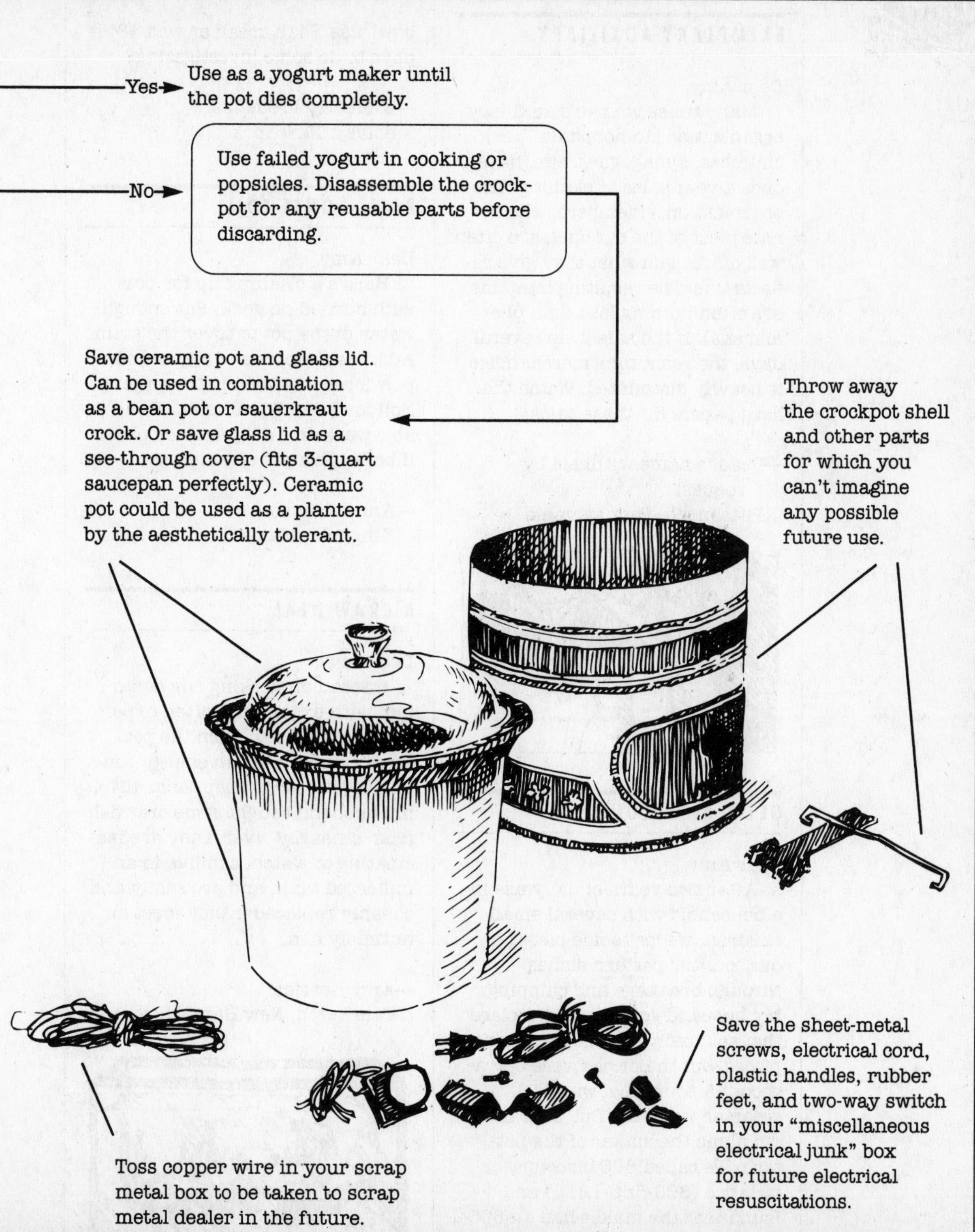
Yes
Use as a yogurt maker until the pot dies completely.
No
Use failed yogurt in cooking or popsicles. Disassemble the crock-pot for any reusable parts before discarding.
Save ceramic pot and glass lid. Can be used in combination as a bean pot or sauerkraut crock. Or save glass lid as a see-through cover (fits 3-quart saucepan perfectly). Ceramic pot could be used as a planter by the aesthetically tolerant.
Throw away the crockpot shell and other parts for which you can't imagine any possible future use.
Toss copper wire in your scrap metal box to be taken to scrap metal dealer in the future.
Save the sheet-metal screws, electrical cord, plastic handles, rubber feet, and two-way switch in your "miscellaneous electrical junk" box for future electrical resuscitations.

EXEMPLARY AUXILIARY

Dear Amy,

Many times women's auxiliary organizations to hospitals, churches, synagogues, etc., have once-a-year sales of clothing. The organization's members, who donate most of the clothing, are often well off . . . and what they give reflects this. The resulting bargains are often nothing less than phenomenal. If the sale lasts several days, the remaining merchandise is heavily discounted. Watch the local papers for these sales.

—Reader name withheld by request
Pittsburgh, Pennsylvania

GET A DISH-COUNT

Dear Amy,

After two years of daily use in a household with several small children, we lost some pieces of our country-pattern dishes through breakage and chipping. My husband got a lead on a place that sold individual replacement pieces, but the prices were outrageous! A soup bowl was $15, a creamer was $22! But their list did name the maker of the pattern. We called 800 directory assistance (800-555-1212) and found that the maker had an 800 number. Direct from them, a soup bowl was $4, a creamer was $8! It pays to do some investigating!

—Kimberly Frodelius
Solvay, New York

BOIL, DON'T TOIL

Dear Amy,

Here's a cleaning tip for pots with burned-on gook: Put enough water in the pot to cover the stain. Add 2 tablespoons of any brand of powdered dishwashing detergent. Boil for 15 to 30 minutes. This also works for dirty burner plates if boiled in a pot of water.

—Anna Johnson
Kingfield, Maine

A CRAW DEAL

Dear Amy,

Instead of stocking our aquarium with exotic (and often expensive) tropical fish from the pet store and running an energy-consuming heater to keep them alive, my husband caught some crawfish from a nearby river. They are fascinating to watch, can live in an unheated tank, and are easily and cheaply replaced if they meet an untimely end.

—Amy Berrier
Tamworth, New Hampshire

STORM THE DORMS

Dear Amy,

If you live near a university that has family/student housing, you can find excellent deals at yard sales there at the end of every semester, especially in May. Student families sell off much of their households very cheaply, or even leave hard-to-sell items out for the taking. (After all, you can't take everything back to Korea very easily!) Check it out!

—Frank and Shoshonah Dietz
Austin, Texas

IT MUST BE SPRIG

Dear Amy,

When a recipe calls for parsley, just use the leaves from celery. It works great.

—Emile Taylor
St. Louis, Missouri

MANURE MANEUVER

Dear Amy,

We live in a city with a very active fairgrounds and horse track. When fertilizing time comes for our gardens, we just load up some boxes and bags and a couple of shovels and head for the barns. The hands are more than happy to get rid of the piled manure. I compost it to make sure it doesn't burn the vegetation. Even in the city, a person can find manure for the taking.

—Mary Beth Frampton
Tulsa, Oklahoma

NO MORE TEARS

Dear Amy,

We've made the switch to cloth diapers. It's been much more doable since we began to use nylon pants instead of vinyl ones. The nylon ones are nearly indestructible. The vinyl ones often got holes after just a few uses. We also found out that the larger-size nylon pants still did not leak. We skipped medium and went right to large, thus reducing the investment.

—Dorothy Miller
Eaton, Colorado

BOOKS IN BULK

Dear Amy,

I live in the New York metropolitan area, and there are quite a number of publishing companies here. Many have company stores open to the public for brief periods during the month. In the case of one children's publisher, the prices are 25¢ to $2 per item, or a savings of about 75 percent. Sometimes the items are not just books, there are board games, household utensils, and school supplies. Readers in other parts of the country could check their Yellow Pages to see what's available.

—Ellen Peixoto
Waldwick, New Jersey

TUNA-CHEDDAR CHOWDER

A soup called "tuna-cheddar chowder" may not sound particularly tempting, but this is actually one of the best soups I know. It is delicious and has an appealing orange-gold color.

2 carrots, shredded
1 onion, chopped
¼ cup butter or margarine
¼ cup all-purpose flour
2 cups chicken broth
2 cups milk
1 6½-ounce can tuna, drained and flaked
½ teaspoon celery seed
½ teaspoon Worcestershire sauce
¼ teaspoon salt
1 cup cheddar cheese

In a large saucepan, sauté the carrots and onion in the butter until the onion is transparent. Mix in the flour. Add the chicken broth and milk. Heat and stir constantly until thick and bubbling. Add the tuna, celery seed, Worcestershire sauce, and salt, and heat through. Add the cheese and stir until it melts. Serves 4.

REFUNDER BLUNDER

On December 28, 1993, NBC's *Today* show aired a segment called "The Great Coupon/Rebate Scam." It showed a November police and postal-inspection raid of a refund swap meet in New York State. Thirty-six people were detained, and authorities confiscated enough evidence to fill a 2-ton and a 20-ton truck. Arrests are anticipated pending further investigation.

As I watched this, I was disturbed. When I researched refunding for an article that appeared in my first book, I focused solely on whether refunders saved as much as they thought. This story indicated that some aspects of refunding commonly believed to be legal may not be.

To research this I spoke to postal inspectors; the IRS; assistant district attorney David Nutter, who had successfully prosecuted a refund fraud case; and the Coupon Information Center, which represents 25 major manufacturers and gathers data for prosecutions.

Bud Miller, the CIC operations manager, said that based on his organization's 1991 study of 250,000 refunds in a three-state area, he estimated $324 million worth of refunds, about one third of all refunds submitted annually, are fraudulent in some way. He said that all of the people arrested so far owned stacks of refund newsletters, and that he believes most of the fraud occurs through newsletter transactions. Although refund newsletters have been around for more than 15 years, it's only been in the last 2 years that manufacturers have learned how extensive fraud is.

Although no one knows exactly how many newsletters exist, one recent refund book listed 24 of them. The largest has 23,000 subscribers. The newsletters inform their readers of refund offers available and publish ads for people to buy, sell, and trade coupons and refund materials (proofs-of-purchase, receipts, refund forms, and combinations of these three things called "complete deals.")

Refunders typically buy only

name-brand products and save all proofs-of-purchase (POP's) and receipts in organized filing systems. In the future, when a refund is offered, they already have the necessary POP and receipt. In addition, they trade their surplus complete deals or individual refund materials through ads in newsletters, at swap meets, in local clubs, and with "refund pen pals." Theoretically, a group of ten refunders who all buy different products could trade their surplus and increase their refund income tenfold.

Because this refund activity had occurred openly and has been promoted in books, newsletters, and videos for 15 years, most refunders believe it's perfectly legal. But is it?

In December 1993, refund-newsletter publisher Ellen Biles of Norcross, Georgia, was convicted on four counts of refund fraud and later sentenced to 21 months in prison. Two counts of fraud involved the submission of three refunds for the same offer. She was entitled to only one refund. The other submissions were fraudulent because she violated the one-refund-per-household rule and because she submitted refunds for products she didn't actually purchase herself. The third and fourth counts on which she was convicted were for selling complete deals to an undercover postal inspector. This was fraud for several reasons, including that this was simply a way to evade the one-refund-per-household rule, and the purchaser couldn't honestly represent to the manufacturer that she knew the product had actually been purchased.

The trading of proofs-of-purchase and complete deals is generally illegal because most refund forms state or imply that you must buy the product to be entitled to the refund. Of the 138 forms we collected locally, 119 indicated you must buy the product yourself.

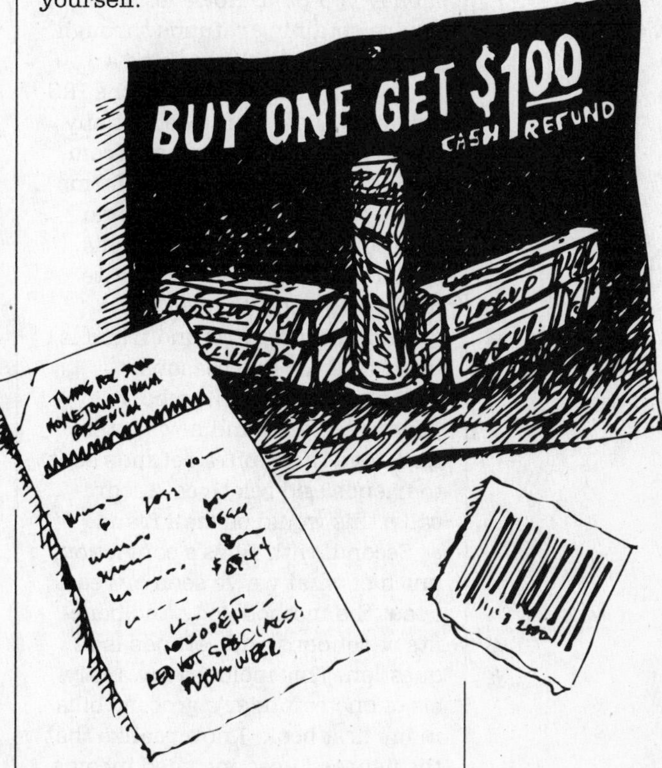

What if the form doesn't require that you be the original purchaser? An attorney for the postal service said he didn't think submitting this refund would be illegal. But Nutter said the manufacturer's intent is still clear, and he believed such a case could be successfully prosecuted. Unless you're certain you could pick your own prosecuting attorney, it might be wise to avoid this activity.

Trading through newsletters presents other problems: You could be trading with others involved in blatant fraud, and you

could be receiving counterfeit materials.

Further, refunders have been led to believe that all refund income is tax-free. Refund income is generally tax-free because you're getting back part of the money you paid. However, if you're obtaining refunds through trade, you're really making a profit. If fraud is involved, the IRS wouldn't allow you to deduct any business expenses. Income from selling coupons and refund forms would also be subject to income tax. Coupons and refund forms sold to others within your state might be subject to sales tax.

Understanding refund fraud is important for two reasons.

First, many people who've never read a refund newsletter also have their extra refunds sent to friends and relatives. Technically, this would be mail fraud.

Second, with Biles's conviction, much of what we've seen or read about the methodology and benefits of coupons and refunds is in question. This includes my analysis of one refunder's grocery bills in my first book; I now realize that the figures I used included income from traded complete deals.

Most large libraries and bookstores have pre-1994 library books on coupons and refunds that indicate that trading complete deals is legal, that all refund income is tax-free, and that you can save up to 80 percent on your grocery bill by using this system.

Further, over the years, most of us have read magazine articles or seen programs on TV demonstrating "the amazing shopping trip": A coupon queen buys $200 worth of groceries for $10. In most cases, the coupon queens were also refunders, and because some of the most valuable coupons can be obtained through refunds, some of the coupons used on these trips were probably obtained through complete-deal trading. Unfortunately, these demonstrations contributed to a widespread belief that grocery-shopping magic can be worked with coupons.

In April 1994, the Postal Inspection Service declared war on refund fraud. They began an intensive effort to educate manufacturers on the magnitude of this practice and consumers on the legal consequences of engaging in it.

Refunding itself is not illegal, but ever-increasing form limitations and the 1994 legal understanding will make refunding more time-consuming and considerably less profitable.

I don't want to discourage anyone from sending in refunds. Many people consistently get certain products for free by combining sales, coupons, and refunds. I want people to do the math, as very often I find combining these three things does *not* result in a good deal. Most important, when you send in a refund, scrupulously adhere to the limitations on the refund forms.

OUTLET GASKET UPDATE

In my first book, I published an unattributed reader tip to use Styrofoam, or polystyrene, meat trays to make outlet gaskets that are similar to the ones you can buy at hardware stores. Installed under outlet covers, these seal out drafts. Some 2½ years after the

idea was published in my newsletter, the criticism has been raised that this could be a fire hazard.

Before originally publishing this idea, I consulted my husband, Jim, who was a Navy electrician for 20 years. He reasoned that it would be safe because you can buy similar foam gaskets. After extensive research, I am not convinced he was wrong. But it does fall into a gray area. If you read my first book and used this idea, it's important that you have all the information to make an informed choice.

Store-bought gaskets are made of a variety of foam materials, although we found none that were of meat-tray-like polystyrene. Some, but not all, store-bought gaskets have the Underwriters' Laboratories approval seal, which indicates they meet safety standards.

Both polystyrene and UL-approved gaskets smoke, melt, and burn when exposed to heat. Unlike paper, polystyrene tends to melt and shrink away from a heat source; we could not get it to burn with a hot soldering iron. We put four different brands of UL-approved gaskets to a match test. One burned but went out when I removed the match. Two burned independently after three seconds of match time. One brand and the polystyrene burned independently after one second of match time.

This did not surprise UL communications director Holly Schubert. "We don't test to see if they'll withstand the heat from a match flame," she told me. "We test to see if they'll perform well under circumstances they would be exposed to in an outlet."

It's important to note that a UL approval indicates only that a product meets a safety guideline, but products that have not been tested could be equal or superior. Some electrical products don't require approval, but the manufacturers have them tested anyway for marketing purposes.

I asked William King, director of the Electrical Engineering Division of the Consumer Product Safety Commission, whether homemade polystyrene gaskets violated the National Electrical Code. Because the wording is so vague and because gaskets aren't addressed, King believes the interpretation would be up to local authorities. (UL agreed with this assessment.) If there had been many fires associated with any kind of gasket, it would have come to his attention. Thus, the CPSC has no official position on polystyrene gaskets.

While there are flammable materials in electrical boxes, King prefers that consumers don't add more. He was surprised to learn that some UL-approved gaskets were flammable. King personally believes that it's better to have ample air circulation in electrical boxes, since faulty wiring would heat up more in a tightly sealed space. Thus he had concerns not only about gaskets, but about child safety caps, which also block air flow.

Homemade polystyrene gaskets have not been tested by UL, and my flammability test is far from scientific. But it seems to me that polystyrene gaskets aren't dangerous as compared to some UL-approved gaskets.

So should you use gaskets at all? We end up with two "expert" opinions: the UL stance that even flammable gaskets are safe

enough to earn its approval, and King's belief that putting anything flammable behind the switch plate or restricting air circulation within an electrical box may not be a good idea. In cases where experts disagree, I can only present their opinions and let you decide.

WEALTH, POVERTY, AND FRUGALITY

I was 11 years old when I began to understand wealth.

Our family had just moved into our third home in my brief memory. It was a large, Cape-style house with outbuildings on 74 acres. The homes I had known before were also large. Our family had a garden, drank either powdered milk or farm milk, took box lunches to school, ate oatmeal for breakfast, and wore secondhand clothes. For a brief time, I felt some discomfort about not having white go-go boots like some of my classmates. But then I noticed that kids who always had the latest, new clothes frequently lived in small houses. I concluded that people who lived in small houses had new clothes, and people who lived in big houses had secondhand clothes.

My simplistic view of the world had plenty of exceptions. I knew a few families who lived in large houses and also had new clothes, and people who lived in small houses who had secondhand clothes. But the general idea is true. People who put their surplus money into short-term extravagances rarely build the same wealth as those who put their money in things with lasting value.

Although I figured this out at 11 years of age, the majority of American adults don't understand this basic idea. We still think that frugality has to do with being "poor," and that wealth and frugality are mutually exclusive terms. Overcoming this misconception is crucial to achieving a successful frugal life.

The fact is that income level has very little to do with whether a person chooses frugality. Many poor people aren't frugal, and a surprising number of wealthy people are.

Although this idea for an article has been kicking around in my brain for some time, two recent pieces of mail prompted me to write it.

A nonsubscriber wrote the following in reference to her occasional purchase of junk food: "I found if I try to be too thrifty or too cheap, my kids have a 'poor mentality' . . . in other words, thinking of themselves as being poor instead of thrifty. So I do make allowances once in a while for 'comfort food.' "

Grrrr! In her view, she has to give her kids the occasional Twinkie, like the other kids have, instead of an inexpensive alternative, or they'll have low self-esteem.

About the same time, I came across an article entitled "Why You're Not As Wealthy As You Should Be" by Thomas J. Stanley, Ph.D., who is the chairman of a research firm called Affluent Market Institute. The author began to study wealthy people 20 years ago and made an amazing discovery: People who live an affluent lifestyle are seldom wealthy. Affluent-lifestyle people spend all of their money on extravagances and have nothing left over.

Wealth, on the other hand, is not how much you earn, it's how much you accumulate. Stanley discovered that the typical wealthy person lives in a middle-class house, marries once and stays married, owns a small factory, chain of stores, or service company, and lives his entire life in one town. His money is seldom inherited. Dr. Stanley estimated that 80 percent of American millionaires are first-generation rich. Instead, the wealthy person typically acquires money through hard work and self-discipline. And he is a compulsive saver and investor. It simply isn't his nature to spend money frivolously because it wouldn't be a good investment.

He is someone like the late Sam Walton, the founder of Wal-Mart, who was a billionaire *and* well known for owning an old pickup and ancient office furniture.

A financial advisor I know confirms this distinction between affluence and wealth. Referring to her wealthiest clients, she says, "You couldn't pick most of them out of a crowd."

This makes it clear how the confusion between affluence and wealth arises. We *see* the behaviors of affluent people, and this becomes our only clue as to how the "rich" behave. We don't see the behaviors of the truly wealthy. A goose-egg diamond ring stands out. A ten-year-old suit and a healthy bank balance don't.

Dr. Stanley observed, as I have, that most Americans are confused about the relationship between frugality and wealth. This confusion has a profound impact on how Americans spend. Because we think frugality has to do with being poor, we see it as an admission of economic failure. We think only poor people go to thrift shops, only poor people bring home a good find from the dump, and only poor people cut their kids' hair.

Because we don't want to be seen as economic failures, we spend our money the way we mistakenly think the wealthy do—usually on day-to-day extravagances. We feel good because, briefly, we've made people think we are wealthier than we are. If we do it often enough, we may even fool ourselves along with our neighbors.

It is true that most wealthy people buy a few more luxuries than do poor people, but the total percentage of income they spend on extravagances is extremely small. Consequently, a person with a low income and a wealthy attitude would live as modestly as possible to create a maximum surplus to save and invest.

Poor people often remain poor because they spend any surplus in-

come on short-term gratification. Therefore, buying Twinkies is more likely to be the behavior of a person with a poor mentality than of a person with a wealthy attitude.

The point isn't that big houses are better than little ones (actually, little ones are usually more frugal), or that used clothing is always better than new, or that no one should ever buy Twinkies. Neither do I mean to imply that we should all strive to be wealthy. And certainly, many poor people are frugal and many wealthy people aren't.

What I do see is that many people are ashamed of being frugal. When we're pressured to spend on gifts at the office, we have a hard time saying no. When our relatives snicker at our thoughtful homemade gifts, we feel bad. When our up-to-the-eyeballs-in-hock obnoxious neighbor picks on us for owning an ancient car, we cower in embarrassment.

Likewise, when dealing with coworkers, neighbors, and relatives, I've found that if you explain your financial goals and the choices you must make to reach them, people seem more understanding. Who could object to your desire to save money to send your kid to college?

To be successful and happy in the frugal lifestyle, we have to be proud and confident in our choices. We must have a clear view of our goals, and we must understand the tradeoffs we're making. If we do this, we'll feel no shame about being frugal. Instead, we'll understand that we have a wealthy attitude.

The Tightwad Gazette III

Introduction

It's hard to believe that it's been almost seven years since that fateful night when I woke Jim up and said, "I have this idea for a home-based business—and I don't think it's bad!"

There was nothing in that small moment that provided a clue about the amazing years that were to come. After all, waking up my long-suffering husband at two A.M. with my latest brainstorm was nothing new, and a fair number of my ideas had fallen somewhere short of genius in application.

But the success of the newsletter—and these books—has been overwhelming. Though subscriptions rose and fell, the newsletter has had as many as 100,000 subscribers, and the *Tightwad Gazette* books I and II have collectively sold 475,000 copies. I've been interviewed about 750 times, including three *Donahue* appearances. I won the *Dateline NBC* Challenge by helping a family chop its grocery bills, survived an appearance on *Late Night with David Letterman*, and was even rendered in one of those little stipple drawings on the front page of *The Wall Street Journal.*

The financial success we've enjoyed—combined, of course, with frugality—has allowed us to retire early, which is why this will be the last compilation of articles from the newsletter. Closing down a successful business (i.e., killing the golden goose) is a mystery to most people, but I prefer the luxury of freedom from a job to the luxury of material goods. All along, I have pointed out that both earning and saving money should be means to an end, not ends in themselves. The "end" that I plan to pursue for the next several years is being a full-time mom to my six kids, and helping them realize—just as I have—that dreams can come true if you have the courage and determination to pursue them.

I also feel that, with the information in this volume, I have explored most of the ways in which the average American family can save money. If I have not covered a specific idea, I have at least provided a model that should allow you to figure it out for yourself. Magazines can plug along for decades by, essentially, repeating the same old articles, but I have always refused to do that.

And while most people might think a life of book tours and media opportunities is glamorous, it isn't all it's cracked up to be. It

was a minor thrill to meet folks like Danny DeVito, John Travolta, Tom Selleck, Glenn Close, and George McGovern—I even traded autographs with Gene Shalit and was smooched by Richard Simmons—but to be honest, I had more satisfying exchanges with people like the limo driver in Cleveland who told me all about how his company economized on cleaning supplies. While I've been happy to have the opportunity to disseminate my ideas, I never wanted to be famous. I look forward to regaining my anonymity, so that I can once again go to yard sales without the proprietor saying, "Hey! Aren't you the Tightwad Lady? Harry, bring the camera!"

But as I close out this part of my life, I will always treasure a fat file that I've kept, labeled "Success Stories." This three-pound collection consists of testimonials from readers who have followed the principles set forth in the books and newsletters and found that they really do work. They tell of conquering mountains of debt, buying a home when it had once seemed impossible, passing on important frugal values to their kids, and even turning back from the brink of divorce to a happy marriage.

I will also savor memories. One moment in particular that stands out occurred at a book signing somewhere in a month-long blur of cities. I felt a tap on my shoulder. I turned, and there was a woman. She said, "I just wanted to tell you that you changed my life." Then she walked away. She didn't want to take any of my time, or even ask for an autograph. She just wanted to tell me that. The exchange was so brief that I remember nothing else about her. Yet that woman has stayed with me as a mental symbol of all the unknown people who have been affected positively by *The Tightwad Gazette.*

I want to thank all those who have contributed to the success of *The Tightwad Gazette.* Its strength has always been the readers—not only have they encouraged me, but much of the content of the newsletter and books is based on their good ideas. Thanks also to the team of staffers who handled the everyday duties of running the business. This group changed over time, but in the last few years has included Pam Barker, Holly Wise-Copland, Blanche Hill, and Francis Page. A special thanks goes to my staffer Brad Lemley, who shared in much of the writing and researching during the last four and a half years. Were it not for his help, ideas, and especially his good humor, *The Tightwad Gazette* would have had a much shorter run.

Finally, I want to thank my family. Jim assumed all the duties of house-husband, has been an enthusiastic supporter of my work, and has patiently listened to a series of two A.M. brilliant-article-idea briefings. The children, Alec, Jamie, Neal, Rebecca, Brad, and Laura, who now range in age from thirteen to five, endured far too many television and magazine photo shoots, not to mention having a mother who was often so lost in a creative stupor that she could only be reached by waving a hand before her eyes. As much as I have enjoyed the last seven years, I hope to slow down the passage of time as I watch them mature to adulthood. I am grateful that frugality—and my readers—have given me that option.

DROWNING IN RISING EXPECTATIONS

The idea that the baby-boom generation has fewer opportunities and must struggle harder than previous generations is believed by millions of Americans. Specifically, they believe that it's almost impossible to afford kids on a middle-class income anymore.

A major reason I started the newsletter was that I believed this was false. It seemed to me that boomers were victims of their own inflated expectations, not the economy, and if they didn't live so extravagantly and planned better, they could easily afford what they really needed. But I lacked the statistics to back up my belief.

So now I am indebted to Karl Zinsmeister, an Ithaca, New York, writer and the editor in chief of *American Enterprise* magazine. He sent me some fascinating information, which will be included in an as-yet-unnamed book. His basic premise is that we are more fortunate today than we realize. Understanding this can be a great help to tightwads wrestling with the notion that "it's not fair."

First, why is this idea that boomers are worse off so prevalent? Zinsmeister says politicians can get lots of mileage from convincing people that they are hurting, and that a particular political plan will bring back opportunity. And news stories thrive on finding villains and victims. Stories built along these lines are more interesting than "gosh, everything is great" stories.

There have even been news stories that present statistics to back up the idea. Typically, a 1991 front-page article in *The Washington Post* stated that, adjusted for inflation, "young families with children suffered a 24% decline in median income between 1973 and 1987."

This information, says Zinsmeister, is just plain wrong. It's based on a statistical error in the way the figures were computed, and it's based on the idea that modern families are the same as those of the past. But families were, on average, 13 percent smaller in 1990 than they were in 1970.

When you correct those mistakes, a different picture emerges. A 1991 federal study found there was actually a 20 percent inflation-adjusted *increase* in the average family's income between 1973 and 1989. And when you factor in non-income "benefits" such as health care, which are about twice as generous as they were 20 years ago, you find that the real rise in family income is about 30 percent.

So why do people "feel" poorer than their parents? Zinsmeister says it's mainly because we have come to expect more. For example:

- The average American now

consumes twice as many goods and services as he did back in 1950. (Going back to 1928, when our grandparents were having children, the number of consumer durables bought annually per person has gone up ten times.)

• The number of motor vehicles per adult is 50 percent higher than it was in 1950. One reason is that it takes one *fewer* month's worth of family income to buy the average car now than it did then. Cars are cheaper to run, too. Today's biggest Ford, the Lincoln Town Car, gets the same mpg as Ford's smallest car did in 1975.

• Now, every year, 16 million Americans go to foreign countries other than Canada or Mexico. In 1950, the number was 680,000.

• Per-person spending on hobbies and home recreation has gone from $403 in 1950 to $1,149 in 1991, adjusted for inflation.

• In 1960, purchasing a refrigerator cost a family 145 hours of labor. Today it costs half that. As for what to put inside, in 1960, Americans spent 15 percent of their incomes on groceries, versus 7 percent today, and there are 12 times more items to choose from at the supermarket.

• In 1990, 42 cents of every food dollar was spent on restaurant meals—twice the amount spent by the previous generation.

• Only about 25 percent of the parents of baby boomers went to college. Half of all of the boomers themselves got to go, and by 1992, 62 percent of high school graduates chose and were able to go on to college.

Even if a boomer concedes all of the above, he'll still contend that housing prices have shot out of sight, and it is far harder for him to afford a house than it was for his parents. Although this is true in a few areas of the country, Zinsmeister says that, adjusted for inflation, the average price of new houses climbed 21 percent over the last 25 years, which is less than the rise in median-family purchasing power. And the price of existing houses—"used houses"—actually declined, adjusting for inflation. After factoring mortgage, utility, insurance, and other expenses, a Harvard University study found that home ownership is about 15 percent more affordable than it was in 1980.

The reason people feel priced out of the housing market, argues Zinsmeister, is because they want houses that are so much bigger and "better." Though the average family is smaller, the average modern, new house is twice as big as the average one built just after World War II. More than 75 percent of new houses have central air-conditioning, up from just 34 percent in 1970. Almost half have more than two bathrooms, up from 16 percent. In 1970, 58 percent of new homes had a garage; now 82 percent have them.

All of this would be pointless if boomers could not afford these places, but they can: 57 percent of married couples under 35 owned their homes in 1989, up from 43 percent 25 years ago.

And what about health care? Although this expense is rapidly escalating, the insurance of most families is paid for by employers. Thus, average out-of-pocket medical expenses have risen only slightly, from 5 percent of income in 1980 to 6 percent in 1990. And while health care costs are on the rise, that's because we expect more:

organ transplants, high-tech testing, cancer cures. Health care was cheaper when people died easier.

The one area in which boomer families have a legitimate beef, says Zinsmeister, is in taxes. Since 1948, the federal-tax-and-Social-Security bite for the median family of four has risen from 2 percent to 25 percent of income. (Taxes for people without dependents have stayed roughly the same.) As bad as this seems, it doesn't completely offset the gains in family buying power. Further, we probably do get at least some money-saving services from the government, even if indirectly. For example, previous generations bore more direct financial responsibility for helping elderly or unemployed relatives. Today these services are paid for with additional taxes.

You might argue that the boomers earn more only because women have gone to work, unlike the stay-at-home moms of the previous generation. But Zinsmeister's figures point up a fact that I've been stressing all along: If you are willing to live like people did in the 1960s, you can be a stay-at-home parent, too. Today's second income is often consumed by child care, extra taxes, and luxuries that our parents happily did without.

Zinsmeister's arguments are based on statistical averages. You might respond that they are interesting but they *don't* apply to you. You've examined your situation, and despite your hard work, you really are worse off than your parents were at your age.

I would respond that even if there is a financial inequity, complaining about it wastes emotional energy. You could use this same energy to be even more creative than your parents were. For example, our family expenditure for food and clothing is almost the same as what my parents spent for these items 25 years ago, and this *isn't* adjusted for inflation. There are many ways to save money today that didn't exist when I was a kid: yard sales, warehouse stores, and energy-saving appliances, to name a few. I feel that today it's easier than ever before to be a tightwad.

Zinsmeister's point, however, is that a great deal of modern complaining is baseless. There is more wealth, more luxury, and more opportunity. If you doubt it, sit down and have a long talk with your parents and grandparents.

MACARONI MIRACLE

In a newsletter article, I mentioned that we buy store-brand macaroni-and-cheese dinners for 25¢ each. Catherine Kenyon of Berwyn, Illinois, responded that at her local health/bulk-food store, she can buy the same kind of cheese powder that comes in the little packets in these dinners. She wondered if, at $4.46 a pound, it was cheaper to make macaroni-and-cheese with this stuff and bulk-purchased macaroni.

I admit, it seems hard to believe that the little boxes of macaroni-and-cheese could possibly be a good deal. Every tightwad has an instinctive distrust of convenience foods that come in tiny cardboard boxes.

So we checked it out. A 7.25-ounce box of macaroni-and-cheese contains 6 ounces of macaroni and 1.25 ounces of cheese powder. It is commonly sold as a loss leader for 25¢, but we have gotten it as cheaply as 20¢.

An equivalent amount of bulk-purchased elbow macaroni costs 12¢, and an equivalent amount of bulk-purchased cheese powder costs 36¢, for a total of 48¢.

I don't know that the cheese powder in macaroni-and-cheese dinners is the same as you would buy in a health food store. But with the exception of artificial coloring (and it probably contains less than the average hot-pink-and-purple Dacyczyn birthday cake), the ingredients don't appear to be "fake" food.

In short, the 25¢ box of macaroni-and-cheese is one of the few exceptions to the general rule that convenience foods cost more. I am the first to admit that this is probably not the most wholesome, nutritious meal imaginable, but we have found that by tossing in a can of tuna fish, it makes a satisfying last-minute meal.

THE KIDS' CLOTHING INVENTORY

I spend about $50 annually to dress six kids; that's an average of $8.33 per kid. This amount covers everything, including snow pants, boots, jackets, and mittens, which are essential for our cold climate. I buy clothing primarily for the older children, and to replenish the worn-out hand-me-downs for younger children.

Some of the clothing my children wear was given to our family. Socks and underwear are often purchased new, with a rebate. But well over half of what they wear comes from yard sales.

The kickoff of yard-sale season here occurs during Memorial Day weekend. During the next three months, I hope to buy most of the clothing our kids will need for the following year.

Managing the wardrobes of six children cannot be done without incredible organization. I found this difficult even when I had fewer children because I always shop a few years in advance. (Shopping in advance is essential if you hope to achieve the near-100-percent-secondhand wardrobe.) In the past, I wasn't quite organized enough. I bought duplicates of things I already had and overlooked a few gaps in my kids' wardrobes. Both mistakes are potentially costly, so I decided to be even more organized. Here's how:

I spent several hours in preparation in April. I went through my kids' bureaus and closets, and my clothing file (a box-storage system described in my first *Tightwad Gazette* book), and inventoried the contents. I tallied only school clothes, shoes, and outerwear, because there is always a way to improvise the rest of their apparel. Thus my inventories for the oldest boy and girl were more thorough than the ones for younger siblings.

Then I made up a chart for each child. Jamie's is shown at the bottom of this page. The first column shows clothing from her bureau that I anticipated will still fit the next school year, and the next two columns show clothing from the attic into which she'll grow. In categories with multiple items, like pants, I marked an *X* to indicate each item. In categories with only one or two items, I made specific notes as to the color and condition of the item. This will let me know that a borderline-worn-out coat can be replaced if I find a bargain, or if the colors of snow pants and a winter coat clash.

The purpose of making this chart becomes clear if you look at Jamie's shoe inventory. Previously I had bought four pairs of sneakers that ranged from size 5 to size 6½. They were great sneakers, most cost under $1, and she or one of her younger sisters will wear them someday. But this past year Jamie ran short of size 1 shoes. I want to ensure that gaps and unnecessary surpluses don't happen again.

In making an inventory, I saw that the manufacturers' sizes can vary dramatically. The shoes that fit Jamie are marked from size 2 to size 5. Additionally, the tags in used clothing are often faded or missing, making the sizes hard to identify. Thus I made notes as to the measurements in pants and shoes, the two items for which fit is most critical. I measured the waist in pants from side to side (which is really half of the waist size) and down the inseam. My measure for Jamie is size 8 (11 inches by 22 inches). I measured shoes from heel to toe. Her shoes are size 2 (8¾ inches). Boots generally have this same shoe measure, except any L. L. Bean–style or other bulky boot, for which you need to allow another inch. When shopping, I will rely more on my measurements than on tags.

Pre-buying pants is a bit tricky, since it's hard to predict how quickly children will sprout in a

JAMIE	SIZE 8	SIZE 10	SIZE 12
SHIRTS, WINTER	XXXXXXXX	XXX	XXXXXXX
SHIRTS, SUMMER	XXX XXXX	XXXXX	XXX
SCHOOL PANTS	XX XXXXXXX	XX	XXXXXXX
SKIRTS	XXX	X	XXXX
DRESSES	XXXX X		XXX
LT. JACKET	LT. BLUE		
WINTER COAT	BLUE & GREEN / PINK		
RAINCOAT	GREEN & NAVY		
SNOW PANTS	PURPLE		LAVENDER
SNEAKERS	BLACK & PINK (2)	BLACK (3) WHITE (2½)	WHITE (5) (5½) (6½) (6½) (6½)
DRESS SHOES	LEATHER WEAVE (2) BOAT (5)	WHITE SANDALS (2½)	
BOOTS	BLUE (4)		GREY (5)

year. Most kids will grow between 1 inch and 4 inches per year, and half of that growth will be in their legs. Thus I try to have a supply of pants that are at least 2 inches longer than the child currently wears; 4 inches longer is better. So, while Jamie is size 8 now, I will buy size 10 and size 12 clothes this summer.

Naturally, when pre-buying pants, you run some risk that the kid will chunk up or slim down. But I've found kids generally remain husky, thin, or average through their childhoods, and anyway, if I guess wrong, I can resell the pants for the same price at a yard sale.

Wanting to forever resolve the mystery of pants and shoe sizes, I went through my extensive supply of kids' pants and shoes—toddler-sized through young-teenage sized—and measured each item. Although the measures for each size varied, I determined an average.

The clothing inventories give me a clear picture of what I need to shop for, but they are too cumbersome to refer to while I'm shopping. So I use them to make up a list of needs for each child. I put this information in a small spiral notebook. I also copy in my lists of pants and shoe sizes. I then file away my detailed inventories in case I need to refer to them.

As in the past, I will yard-sale with a tape measure and a list of sizes (now my list is far more precise).

At the sales themselves, I generally pay 25¢ per item of children's clothing. I pay more for new-looking shoes, coats, and snow pants. I pay more for next year's needs, and less and less the further in the future the kid will wear the item. For example, one summer I paid $3 for L. L. Bean–style boots for then ten-year-old Alec. I paid that much only because it was August and he needed them for the following winter. But I would never pay more than 25¢ for a shirt he'll wear in four years.

Making up a clothing inventory required less than an hour per child. Considering the money I'll save by avoiding gaps and surpluses, it was time well spent.

PANTS (waist and inseam measure)
Size 2 = 8½″ × 11½″
Size 3 = 9″ × 14″
Size 4 = 9″ × 16″
Size 5 = 10″ × 17″
Size 6 = 10¼″ × 18″
Size 7 = 10½″ × 20″
Size 8 = 11″ × 22″
Size 10 = 12″ × 24″
Size 12 = 12½″ × 26″
Size 14 = 13″ × 27″

SHOES (heel-to-toe measure)
Size 8 = 7″
Size 9 = 7¼″
Size 10 = 7½″
Size 11 = 7¾″
Size 12 = 8″
Size 13 = 8¼″
Size 1 = 8½″
Size 2 = 8¾″
Size 3 = 9″
Size 4 = 9¼″
Size 5 = 9½″
Size 6 = 10¼″
Size 7 = 10¾″
Size 8 = 11″
Size 9 = 11¼″

A BOOK REVIEW

The blurbs on the back of the book are enough to set any frugal traveler's heart pounding:

Paris for $199!

Mexico City for $99!

Hong Kong for free!

The book is *The Insider's Guide to Air Courier Bargains,* by Kelly Monaghan. After reading it and speaking with the author on the phone, I am intrigued.

Courier travel grew out of a need companies have to transport stuff from country A to country B quickly. For lots of reasons, often the cheapest, fastest way to do this is to send it as passenger baggage. Freelance couriers give up their baggage allotment in return for a cheap fare.

It works like this: You start by calling around to the various courier companies. Monaghan's book lists dozens, which are concentrated in New York, Miami, San Francisco, and Los Angeles, though more cities are becoming courier take-off points each year. (If you don't live in one of these cities, figure out a way to get to one cheaply; call the companies about a week before you arrive.) Let them know when and where you want to go and return, and they'll tell you if they need a courier for those trips.

If you find an opening, you pay for it immediately. The prices vary widely, but tend to be about 25 percent of full-fare coach. Super-cheap or free flights happen when the courier company is desperate and needs couriers in the next day or two. If you are willing to go to a strange place on very short notice, this could be for you.

Then you go to the airport on the right day and meet a courier company representative, who gives you your ticket and some paperwork that must accompany the shipment. You fly to your destination, meet another representative of the courier company, hand him the papers, and hang around until stuff clears customs. The return flight works the same way.

Most arrangements require that you stay for a specific period of time. A week is typical, but it can be up to 30 days. You are responsible for your expenses during your stay. It's possible that you and your spouse can both travel as couriers, but you might not be able to travel on the same day.

Monaghan's book answers the inevitable question, "Will I be smuggling drugs?" He says reputable courier companies carefully screen the packages you transport. It simply isn't a problem.

"The first time you do it, it's like playing James Bond," Monaghan told me. "After that, it's just another boring way to get from one place to another."

This concept is obviously ideal for the adventurous, single tightwad with a flexible schedule who lives near a large city.

The book costs $14.95, plus $3.00 shipping and handling. Call (800) 356-9315, or write:

The Intrepid Traveler
P.O. Box 438
New York, NY 10034

(Or check your library.)

HOW DOES YOUR FOOD BUDGET COMPARE?

Terry Lepire of Aurora, Oregon, sent me a newspaper clipping that includes a "Cost of Food at Home" chart issued in November 1993 by the USDA. I was fascinated, as I have always wondered if there is a way to accurately compare food budgets, given the varying sizes and ages of members of different families.

So I sat down with my calculator and was stunned to find our family not in the "thrifty" plan, but in the "low-cost" plan. After I moped around for several days, an employee double-checked my math and started laughing. The USDA chart, he said, "doesn't list the *monthly* budget, it lists the *weekly* budget!"

Oops.

The government figures food costs the same way I do. This chart indicates the cost of food only, and presumes that all the food is prepared at home—no restaurant meals. It shows the average of what people actually spend. It's not a recommendation.

According to the "thrifty" plan, my family could be spending $149.40 per week. We spend $41.53—just 28 percent of that. For laughs, we computed that under the "liberal" plan we could spend $282.10 per week!

I absolutely do not expect all my readers to duplicate what our family does, although some have reported they spend less than we do. But this chart does offer some way for you to compare. You should easily spend less than the "thrifty" plan.

This chart also shows us one of two things: Either the federal government is totally inept at gathering numbers to make charts, or Americans are totally clueless at the supermarket.

Or both.

		THRIFTY PLAN	LOW-COST PLAN	MODERATE-COST PLAN	LIBERAL PLAN
Child	1–2 yrs	$13.50	$16.40	$19.10	$23.10
	3–5 yrs	$14.50	$17.80	$22.00	$26.30
	6–8 yrs	$17.60	$23.60	$29.05	$34.40
	9–11 yrs	$21.00	$26.80	$34.40	$39.80
Male	12–14 yrs	$21.80	$30.40	$37.80	$44.50
	15–19 yrs	$22.60	$31.40	$39.00	$45.20
	20–50 yrs	$24.30	$31.10	$38.70	$46.90
	51 years up	$22.00	$29.50	$36.20	$43.40
Female	12–19 yrs	$22.10	$26.30	$31.80	$38.50
	20–50 yrs	$22.00	$27.30	$33.10	$42.30
	51 years up	$21.70	$26.50	$32.60	$39.00

BAGMAN AND RIBBON

Dear Amy,

Here's an idea for extending computer-printer-ribbon life. Pop out the cartridge after each use and place it in a Ziploc bag. With less exposure to the air, the ink stays useful longer. I haven't done a scientific experiment, but it seems to extend the life about two times.

—Katherine Malm
Austin, Texas

GUNK GETTER

Dear Amy,

When drains get sluggish, use this tested, inexpensive remedy:

1. Pour 1 cup of baking soda into the drain.
2. Follow the soda with 1 cup of vinegar.
3. Pour a pot of boiling water down the drain and follow through with the plunger.

This is safer, cheaper, and better for the environment than store-bought remedies, and it won't harm the septic system.

—Jan Mitchell
Salinas, California

(In some cases, boiling water alone is enough. FZ)

HANGOVER REMEDY

Dear Amy,

I don't have room in my house for a clothesline, so I came up with a "clothes bar" to hang over the tub. Drill holes through the ends of an old broom handle. Bend two wire clothes hangers and put the hook end through the holes. Hang this on two plant hooks screwed into the ceiling over the tub. I dry skirts, socks, pants, towels, etc. by hanging them on plastic hangers on my bar.

—Susan Hutchens,
Luquillo,
Puerto Rico

TURNIP AT SCHOOL

Dear Amy,

Investigate enrolling in a Master Gardener program offered through the county extension office in 45 states. You are taught every aspect of gardening by experts, and it is free. All you have to do is volunteer time back to the community on completion of your education.

—Beth Burrows
North Bend, Washington

GET IT FOR FEE

Dear Amy,

It may pay to buy a TV or VCR that was abandoned at a repair shop by its previous owner. I bought two VCRs this way. Generally, you are only charged for the cost of the repair.

—David Kaplan
Glen Head, New York

(One of my staffers recently bought a superb Hitachi stereo cas-

sette deck for $25; it had been abandoned at a repair shop. This buying strategy does not apply only to stereo equipment. Any place that repairs or services anything generally has some items around that the owner did not reclaim and can be purchased cheaply. FZ)

SAVE A PILE

Dear Amy,

Avoid the spendthrift mistake we made of having our new carpet professionally patched after a hot coal from the fireplace burned an unsightly hole in it. A 2-inch square patch cost us a hefty $75! I watched the repair and saw that all it took was an X-Acto knife, a scrap of our carpeting, and a hot-glue gun. We were really kicking ourselves after that one!

—Paula Ramm
Marysville, Ohio

DISCOUNT DUET

Dear Amy,

My neighbor and I save money by having our carpets cleaned, septic tanks pumped out, and furnaces cleaned at the same time. I start by calling a service company and asking if they will take $10 off if we both have the service performed at the same time. They agree, because they get two jobs and don't have to travel far for the second. This would probably work for other kinds of services as well.

—Deborah Maier
Copley, Ohio

HOME SUITE HOME

Dear Amy,

One time you asked for ideas for seniors. Here's one: We have put out the word to our scattered family and friends that we are available to sit with their house and pets. So far we have spent five lovely weeks in a new house in Florida with two cats; time in Kansas City with a young lady; and in the fall we are going to Arizona to sit with a dog and enjoy another new house. We will probably travel to Arizona on our railroad pass. This is a good way to travel and avoid the high motel charges. And it is fun.

—M. Helen Weaver
Ozawkie, Kansas

LOW-CHARGE NO-CHARGE

Dear Amy,

A great static eliminator is simple to make. Mix 1 part fabric softener and 20 parts water. Put in a spritzer bottle and spray just the amount that is needed. Works great and is much cheaper than commercial products.

—Elaine Hodgman
Ludlow, Massachusetts

CHEAPER CHOCOLATE

Dear Amy,

I'm fond of chocolate sprinkles on ice cream but find them prohibitive in cost. The supermarket has only tiny bottles (even so, it's synthetic chocolate). The cost figures

out to about $9 per pound! Then I discovered that a local franchised steak house with an ice cream bar is glad to sell them to me by the pound, at their cost: $1.66.

—Isadora Becker
Ithaca, New York

DENTED, DATED, AND DISCOUNTED

When we first moved to Maine, we were told to check out the wonderful salvaged-foods store in a nearby town. We went, with our price book in hand, and noted that the prices weren't as good as had been indicated. The convenience foods cost more than making foods from scratch. Other deals didn't beat buying loss-leader-sale items at supermarkets, or regular-price items at the wholesale clubs. As a result, we buy only a few items there regularly.

On a recent trip to Vermont, we visited another salvage store that had truly astonishing deals, but I was suspicious as to whether all the salvaged foods met state regulations. I called Vermont's health department and learned that this state, like many others, has no regulations governing the sale of these items. This store is located just over the border from highly regulated Massachusetts. Massachusetts has salvage stores like the one near me—the deals are unremarkable.

It occurred to me that this pattern probably holds across the country. If the deals in the salvage stores in your state seem paltry, check the situation just over the border, or in other states that you may visit regularly. The best deals are likely to be found in a store in an unregulated state that is just over the border from a highly regulated state, because the salvaged goods may be transported over state lines for resale.

Highly regulated states may prohibit the sale of any processed food that lacks a label. Such states may also require a special license to repackage foods that have damaged packaging. For example, if a clerk cut the inner bag in a cereal box when he opened the case, an unlicensed store couldn't repackage the cereal and sell it for a reduced price. (Incidentally, as I noted in *The Tightwad Gazette II*, a spokesman for the National Food Processors Association stated that

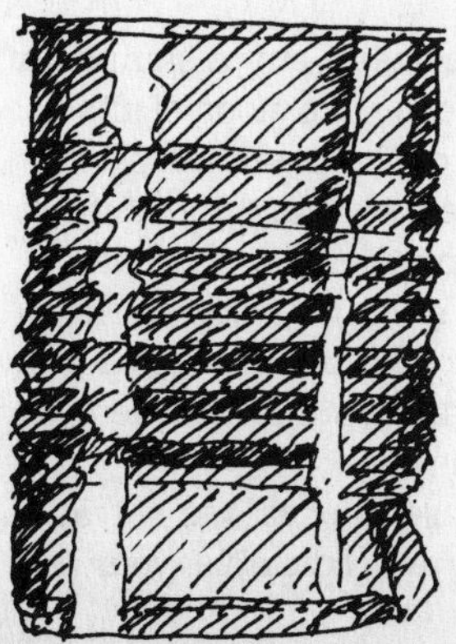

dented or rusty cans are safe as long as they don't leak or bulge.)

Oddly enough, even highly regulated states don't generally restrict the sale of outdated foods—that decision is made by individual stores. Consumers erroneously call the date on the packaging the "expiration date." Instead, this is a "recommended sell-by" date. While you probably wouldn't buy milk that's a week past the sell-by date, other products like canned goods and hard cheese would still be good beyond the date. Many foods that are outdated might be stale or have lost some nutritional content, but they aren't a health hazard.

With all this in mind, what might you find in an over-the-border salvage store?

Salvage stores specialize in damaged and discontinued items, such as cans battered in transit. The most remarkable deal we've found are "mystery cans." One store has a large bin of dented, unlabeled cans selling for 10¢ each, or $3 per box. Jim dropped the per-can cost to 5¢ by artfully fitting 60 cans in a box. The contents of the cans are guaranteed to be for human consumption; they are mostly vegetables and fruit.

We had only spotty success in determining the contents by comparing codes. So we just avoided small cans (less value) and large cans (probably pumpkin puree or tomato sauce, which our garden produces in quantity).

Mystery cans have become a major source of entertainment for our kids. They take turns choosing a can and guessing its contents. Once we open the cans, we plan meals to use them up, and this has resulted in some creative tightwad meals. On one occasion, we opened one can of baked beans and another of kidney beans. I combined these with some of our own leftover scratch baked beans and a few sliced hot dogs to create a tasty bean medley.

Aside from the cans, this store also sometimes sells cheese that's outdated by a few weeks. We've spent as little as 50¢ per pound for mozzarella and 75¢ per pound for cheddar. We found powdered milk at a $1-per-mixed-gallon price. A $1.39 bag of potato chips sells for 33¢. Oreo-like cookies sell for 50¢ a pound—the same cost as scratch cookies. We found good deals on canning supplies as well. While we can always find 33¢-per-pound spaghetti and macaroni in our area, other types of pasta cost more. This salvage store had a variety of cheap pasta—we even found lasagna noodles that weren't too badly broken.

Shopping in salvage stores is similar to other alternative strategies. You must:

• Bring your price book. Even in this good salvage store, most of the prices didn't beat other strategies.

• Look carefully at everything on the shelves. Salvage stores may have only a single unit of some products, like just one can of bug spray.

• If uncertain, buy a sample to test. We were suspicious of the freshness of the potato chips. We bought one bag, found the chips to be good, and then bought more.

• Even at salvage-store prices, nonnutritious foods should be purchased sparingly and hoarded as special treats.

• Because the deals in salvage stores are unpredictable, your sav-

ings will also be unpredictable. Go several times. Note the time and gas required for this out-of-the-way trip. Calculate your true savings as compared to other strategies. If the trip takes an hour and you save $20, you've netted a nice "hourly wage."

THE DRAPE ESCAPE

When poring over the Sears catalog in my quest for curtain ideas, I observed pages of "window treatments" featuring multiple layers of floral drapes, shades, and sheers, finished off with the latest styles of valances, ruffled swags, and tasseled tiebacks. You could easily spend $150 on one window. If you tried to duplicate this look for less by sewing the curtains yourself, it would still require lots of time, skill, and money.

So I turned to my stack of (trash-picked) *Country Living* magazines and found hope. Half of the windows featured had no curtains at all, and the rest had "minimalist" curtains. The simplicity appealed to me. Newsletter reader and interior decorator Sharon Cribbs of Jackson, South Carolina, expressed the same view. She wrote that most windows today are "overdressed" and suggested concentrating on simple treatments that use less fabric.

Whatever your taste, the first step in selecting a window treatment is to focus on your needs. Window treatments serve a variety of purposes. They hold in heat (only window quilts do this well), block out sunlight when we wish, provide privacy, and are decorative. Rather than spending your money satisfying a preconceived idea of what window treatments are supposed to look like, carefully assess your needs and preferences.

In our case, our home is secluded, so our privacy needs are minimal. I don't want to hide our nice woodwork, and to me curtains should be the background to our nice possessions, not the focal point of our rooms. I needed only ground-level privacy for one bedroom and a bathroom. So I sewed "café" curtains, which require little material or effort to make. I made these from white given-to-me sheets and hung them on trash-picked hardware; this window treatment was practically free.

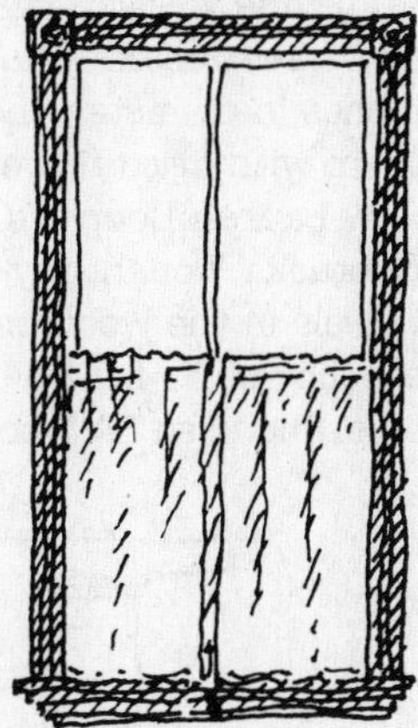

Readers who have greater needs for privacy and/or decoration have sent me a variety of ideas.

A decorative solution that uses little material is the "swag" style. It's simply a long piece of fabric that's draped over the window. The fabric is 18 inches or more wide, and the length, or the dis-

tance the swag hangs down, is optional. Swags are frequently combined with sheers or blinds and held by a bracket at each upper corner of the window. A pair of brackets typically costs $10 to $25. Readers offered cheaper hardware alternatives:

• Debra Meyers of Watertown, Connecticut, suggested draping the material over a nail and adding a grapevine wreath. These are easy and free to make. She made hers 7 inches in diameter and decorated them with dried flowers and ribbon.

• Lauren Bopp of Omaha, Nebraska, bought toy-truck wooden wheels in the woodcraft section of a hobby store for 25¢ per pair on sale. She used 5¢ wooden spools

for spacers, and attached the spool/wheel combination to the window casing with a long screw. The wheel can be painted with wall or metallic paint, or stained. The cost per pair is 35¢.

• Jackie Stevens of Lake City, Florida, bought bicycle-storage hooks for $1.47 a pair. She wrapped the material around the hooks so they wouldn't show, and to create a pleasing effect.

• Merrilee Malcolm of Lawrenceville, Georgia, bought coat hooks for $2.50 a pair. She bunched the swag material and used rubber bands to make fabric "rosettes" to attach the swag to the hooks.

• Susan Abbott of Windsor, Connecticut, hammered a nail into the molding, leaving most of the nail showing. She bought inexpensive dime-store earrings, bent or removed the posts, and superglued the earrings to the nail heads.

Aside from alternative hardware, readers offered ideas for alternative fabrics:

• Julie Angotti of Madison, Wisconsin, pointed out that long cur-

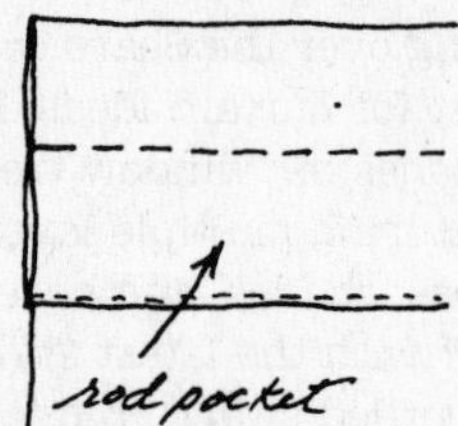

tains are easily made from twin sheets because the wide hem makes a handy rod pocket. You simply sew a straight seam through the center of this hem. Because you haven't cut them, they can be used as sheets in the future.

• Kim Connell of Yarmouth, Maine, suggested using either muslin or fabric from a mill store. One such store near me sells strips of sheet material that would be perfect for swags.

• Paula Martindale of Warner, New Hampshire, sent a magazine photo of a window decorated simply with a white, 48-inch square tablecloth

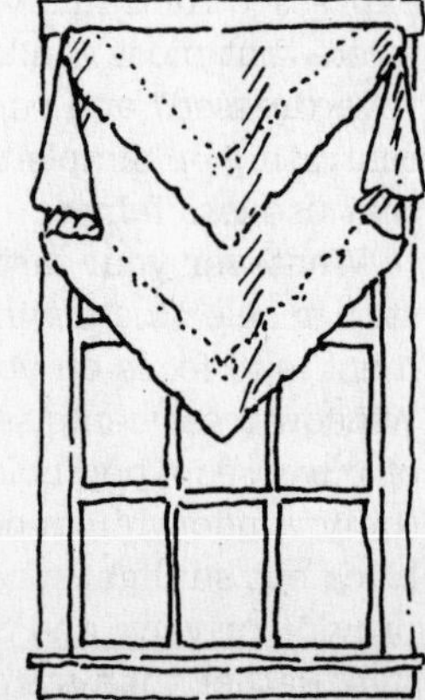

with decorative cutwork. This was hung over a rod and tacked on the inside of the window frame.

• Belinda Ford of Bad Kreuznach, Germany, says her husband

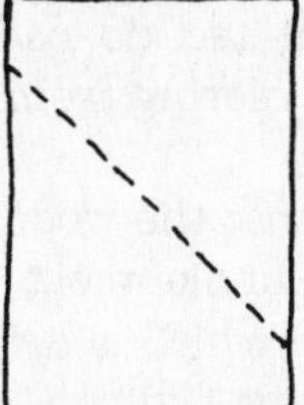

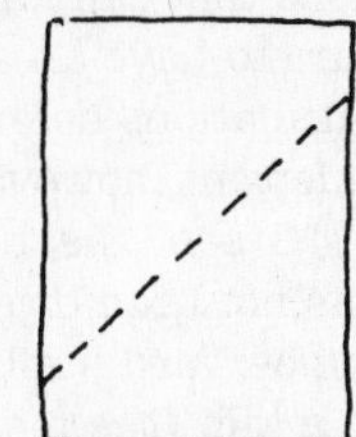

found dozens of discarded white tablecloths. She cut two cloths at an angle to make two pairs of diagonal curtains. She sponge-painted a border on these.

• A reader from Tucson, Arizona, sewed together small pieces of fabric to make curtains with a patchwork design.

• Earlene Giglierano of Iowa City, Iowa, suggested using cheesecloth, which is commonly available for 20¢ per yard. She saw this used in a magazine with lovely results.

Other readers offered these miscellaneous suggestions:

• Cindy Burns of Waco, Texas, duplicated the new, fashionable look of wide, expensive rods. She simply used her old thin rods and slipped a wide piece of poster board in the rod pocket.

• Mary Richardson of Saint Paul, Minnesota, needed miniblinds for her many odd-sized windows and found custom-made blinds were too expensive. She purchased standard-sized blinds at a discount store that were slightly wider than she needed. She cut a little off each side of the blinds, rounding the corners to make a "factory edge." Using a hacksaw, she cut the top rail and bottom bar. These came with caps that would cover the sawed edge. Each blind required one and a half hours to complete. Yard-sale blinds could be modified in the same way.

• An unusual privacy solution for a small window, such as in an entryway or bathroom, came from Denise Casey of Fayetteville, Georgia. She used Rubbermaid's clear contact paper to create a frosted look. Using a piece slightly larger than the window, she positioned the contact paper with a straight edge against the edge of the pane, smoothed it with a ruler wrapped in a washcloth, and cut the remaining three edges with an X-Acto knife. For this technique to look like real frosted glass, there should be no bubbles or uncovered glass showing around the edges.

One solution that no reader suggested is the un-curtain window treatment. Sometimes instead of decorating with fabric, decorate with a collection of things. Most frequently people do this with hanging plants. Simple shelves attached to a window frame can hold your plants, colored bottles, or other collectibles.

WHERE THERE'S A MILL THERE'S A WAY

A growing worldwide demand for lumber combined with stricter environmental regulations has pushed lumber prices through the roof. Even here in Maine, where timber is abundant, lumberyards were recently selling an 8-foot spruce 2-by-4 for almost $4. Fortunately, there are alternatives.

Perhaps the best is getting rough-sawn, green lumber directly from a small sawmill. Patsy Hennin, founder of a house-building school called the Shelter Institute in Bath, Maine, says such lumber is from 15 to 50 percent cheaper than what's available at lumberyards, but Jim has realized larger savings. He bought 12-foot 2-by-12s from our local sawmill for $7.92 each. The best regular-lumberyard price was $17.39, so he saved 65 percent.

"Rough-sawn" means that the wood has simply been sawed—it has not subsequently been run through a planer, which makes wood smooth to the touch. As the name implies, it has a rough texture, but it is perfectly good for most applications. When we've used it for flooring, we've smoothed one side with a relative's planer.

Rough-sawn lumber can provide double savings. Not only is a rough-sawn 2-by-6 cheaper than a planed one, it is also larger, because it hasn't lost ½ inch in width and breadth to the planer. This means it may work in applications that call for a 2-by-8. (Be sure to have an architect do load calculations before veering from a blueprint, however.)

"Green" means that the wood has not been dried, unlike most lumberyard lumber, which is dried in a kiln (the marking "kd" on lumber stands for "kiln-dried"). Hennin notes that green wood is only half as strong as dried wood, but that the wood will dry on its own in from one month to one year, depending upon the climate. To air-dry it, it should be stacked under a cover with "stickers" (strips of wood about 1-inch square) between the pieces to allow air to circulate. As the wood dries, it will shrink about 3 percent in width, depending upon the type of wood.

While these independent sawmills are small, not all are rustic. An increasing number are computerized and can cut wood to extremely fine tolerances.

To find them, call your county extension agent for a list of small sawmills in the area. When you call the mills, in addition to asking about prices, be sure to ask about what is available—small sawmills often don't keep much stock on

hand. If the mill does not have what you need, it will have to be custom-cut.

For those who have their own trees, two other options deserve brief mention:

• Portable-sawmill operators will actually bring their rigs to your site, where they will fell, limb, drag, and cut your wood. These can be found in "shopper" type newspapers, the Yellow Pages, or by asking around at sawmills and lumberyards.

• For the ultimate do-it-yourselfer, there are "guide" attachments that convert a chain saw into a hand-held sawmill, allowing you to cut boards from logs. You'll find ads for these in woodworking and back-to-the-land magazines. The Shelter Institute has a subsidiary called Woodbutcher Tools, which sells two models: the Granburg Mini-Mill for $85, and the Haddon Lumbermaker for $63.50. For a free information sheet and list of shipping charges, contact:

Woodbutcher Tools
38 Center Street
Bath, ME 04530
(207) 442-7938

SAVE A WAD OF DOUGH

For his Sunday-morning birthday breakfast, Neal requested homemade doughnuts. So, Saturday night Jim whipped up a double batch of whole-wheat refrigerator dough. The next morning he made powdered-sugar and cinnamon-sugar doughnuts with some of the dough.

Sunday night Jim left town for two days, just as I was deathly ill with a cold. I didn't feel like cooking for my ravenous children, so Monday night I made tomato soup from tomato paste and milk (this quickie recipe appeared in *The Tightwad Gazette II*) and a dozen

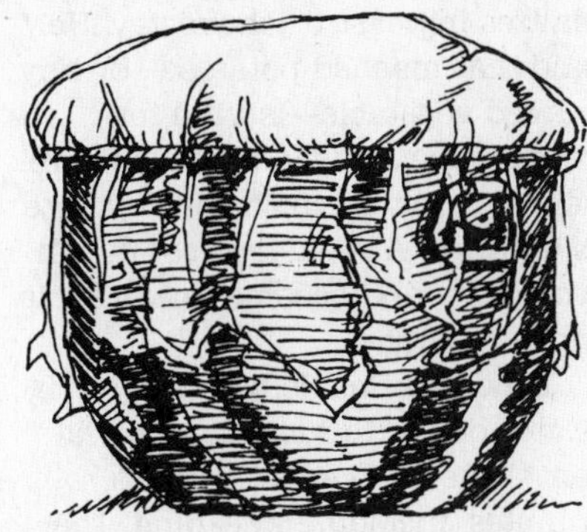

"cloverleaf" rolls from the same batch of dough. While I was at it, I rolled out and baked breadsticks for lunch boxes.

Thursday afternoon Jim used the remainder of the dough to make a dozen cinnamon rolls. Three of these went into lunch boxes the following Monday.

In short, refrigerator dough is extremely versatile and convenient. It's ideal for smaller families and for busy people who like fresh bread daily. You could make a large batch of dough on the weekend and use just a little at a time over the week.

The multipurpose refrigerator-dough recipe appears in all pre-1986 editions of *The Betty Crocker Cookbook.* (In some editions the recipe is called Potato Refrigerator Dough.) Jim has a version of the recipe that includes potato flakes.

Refrigerator dough includes mashed potatoes. To save time, Jim gets out potato flakes and other required ingredients to make 2 cups of mashed potatoes, then adds

the separate ingredients directly to the double batch of refrigerator dough.

What's the purpose of the mashed potatoes? We asked Lloyd M. Moxon, author of *The Baking Book* and a microbiologist who specializes in yeast biochemistry. He said that mashed potatoes—or any pureed vegetable—is vital for refrigerator doughs because it preserves moisture in the dry climate of a fridge. A regular yeast dough would dry and become unworkable more rapidly.

Making a double batch of refrigerator dough (a four-loaf equivalent) takes Jim exactly 19 minutes, including kneading. The dough is stored in a greased, covered bowl in the refrigerator. It's ready for use in eight hours, and lasts up to five days. (We've stretched this a few days and made sourdough-tasting rolls.)

The Betty Crocker Cookbook has directions for an amazing number of variations: brown-and-serve rolls, crescent rolls, pan biscuits, cloverleaf rolls, fantails, and Parker House rolls. Variations on other pages include raised doughnuts, hot-cross buns, and balloon buns. But this dough can be used in virtually any configuration, including braids, hamburger rolls, or sticks. It also makes a moist, heavy loaf suitable for toast and some types of sandwiches.

USED NEWS

Dear Amy,

We have many elderly people in our building who have difficulty disposing of their newspapers. A week's worth of papers is heavy, bulky, and hard for them to handle. We worked out a barter arrangement with our neighbor. She keeps her newspaper until she is finished with it—usually the day it is delivered. When she is done reading it, she brings it down the hall to us. We, in turn, get the complete newspaper for free. This saves us $13 a month.

—Sally Ennes
Independence, Missouri

HOW TO KNIT-PICK

Dear Amy,

I watch yard sales for buys on yarn. One problem with this yarn is that the label is usually missing, so you don't know if the yarn is wool or synthetic. A good way to test the yarn is this: Light the end of a piece of yarn with a match, then blow out the flame. If the residue is ashes, it's wool. If there is a little hard ball, it's synthetic.

This way you won't mix incompatible yarns when knitting afghans.

—Ann Zawistowski
Walpole, Massachusetts

KILL TWO BIRDIES . . .

Dear Amy,

The tightwad way to aerate your lawn: Wear your golf shoes while pushing your lawn mower. It works! I heard about this from a neighbor. I've tried it and it does open up the clay soil so the grass roots can grow and receive the water better.

—Jackie Steinberg
St. Peters, Missouri

LOW LIGHT

Dear Amy,

An inexpensive light box can be made this way: Obtain a piece of Plexiglas from your local hardware store. Remove one of the leaves from your dining room table and put the Plexiglas on top of the opening. Place a lamp (without the light shade) under the table.

—Maria Hester
Friendship, Maryland

HAVE RUN, WILL RAVEL

Dear Amy,

A dab of nail polish stops runs in swimsuits. After about 25 wearings it might need to be reapplied, so check periodically.

—Debbi Heffern
St. Louis, Missouri

TYPO TIP

Dear Amy,

I use a Brother electronic typewriter and go through a lot of correction tape. During an idle moment, I tried to rewind the lift-off correction tape that I had just replaced on my typewriter. I noticed there was a lot of space left on the tape that could still be used for corrections. With a little patience, I rewound the tape and placed it in my typewriter. It works just fine the second time around. The tapes cost about $4.

—Laurie Spangler
Roanoke, Virginia

XEROCKS-BOTTOM PRICE

Dear Amy,

I need to make a lot of photocopies, and at 7¢ per copy (the cheapest price in our town) it was becoming very expensive. I found out that my copier store would charge me only 3¢ a copy if I bought my own paper. I was able to buy a 500-sheet package of Xerox paper from Wal-Mart for $3.48 plus tax. I figured that the copier store was charging me $20 for the same amount of paper. The people at the copier store were very nice. They loaded and unloaded my paper into the machine without complaint.

—Bonnie Andreani
Shawnee, Oklahoma

RETURN TO FENDER

Dear Amy,

While driving home from work one day this past winter, I failed to negotiate one of our infamous Rhode Island potholes. Needless to say, I lost one of my hubcaps. Upon doing some research, I found that new ones (plastic, no less) cost $90 each! Well, I had to buy it; then I got the idea to take off all my hubcaps, put my phone number and the word "reward" on the inside of each one, and put them

back on. Now if I lose another one, at least I'll provide the motivation for someone to return it for an amount far less than the $90 cost of a new hubcap.

—George Hadley
Lincoln, Rhode Island

GENIUS FLY TRAP

Dear Amy,

During canning season, I always get clouds of fruit flies in my house. I finally found the answer, thanks to the extension office's gardening expert. Take a plastic bag (a bread bag works great). Put banana peels, peach pits, rotten fruit, or whatever attracts fruit flies in the bag. Set it on the counter, wide open (cut the bag shorter if necessary). In a few hours, shut the bag with a twist-tie and throw it away. Repeat until the fruit flies are gone. Last fall I got rid of 99.9 percent of my fruit flies this way.

—Vicki Fisher
Clinton, Utah

SOAK AND SAVE

Dear Amy,

I love the stain-removal recipe (*The Tightwad Gazette I*) but I find the ingredients quite expensive to make each time I buy a garment at a yard sale for 25¢. To reduce the cost, I reuse the solution over and over. I keep it in a kettle in my cupboard, which enables me to reheat the solution on the stove.

—Donna Henderson
La Habra, California

SERIAL BOWL

Dear Amy,

My husband enjoys bowling through the winter months in our small town. We have found that for a small sign-up fee, he can bowl as a substitute almost every week. The regular for whom he is bowling is responsible for paying that night's fees. Also, this is a good time of the year to check with bowling alleys for used balls, bags, and even shoes. My husband brought home a used ball and bag for $15.

—Debra DeWitt
Edgerton, Wyoming

MADE TO FADE

Dear Amy,

I have found that if you add a squirt of dishwashing soap to the recipe for sidewalk chalk (in *The Tightwad Gazette II*), it cleans up more easily. This is important since we live in rental properties.

—Kym Reid-Reynoso
Boise, Idaho

NOT PALTRY POULTRY

Dear Amy,

The Hardee's in our area sells all its fried chicken for 25¢ per piece after 9 P.M. If you purchase only breast pieces, that's a pretty good deal. Sometimes my husband picks this up for his next day's lunch.

—Kristin McCoy
Mineral Point, Wisconsin

FOCUS BEFORE YOU FEAST

The diet-book author and the TV talk show host surveyed a banquet table of exquisitely prepared foods. The TV talk show host said that looking at the food made him hungry and he wanted to load his plate with some of everything.

The diet-book author, using this situation to demonstrate the premise of her book, had the TV talk show host do a mental exercise. She asked him to walk away from the table, close his eyes, and blank out the image of the banquet. Then she asked him to think about precisely what foods would satisfy him.

After a moment, the TV talk show host decided what he would like to eat. When he returned to the banquet table, the diet-book author instructed him to select the food he had imagined. From the vast bounty, the TV talk show host prepared a humble roast beef sandwich with mayonnaise and lettuce on a bulkie roll. Walking away from the remainder of the banquet, he began to eat his sandwich and admitted that it, alone, would satisfy him.

Had this diet-book author conducted the experiment with the studio audience, each individual would have selected different foods, or combinations of foods, and in different quantities.

The diet-book author's theory was that people often eat just because it's there. When we choose food this way, we will eat more, probably until we accidentally happen to consume the one item we really wanted in the first place. If, however, we can identify what food, and exactly how much of it, we need to feel satisfied, we will probably eat less.

The larger point is that, whether it is at the banquet table or the mall, you must decide what you want *first; then* look at the options. If you are confronted by options before you are firm about what you want, you'll be swayed.

As obvious as this sounds, a lot of people don't get it. In *Your Money or Your Life,* authors Joe Dominguez and Vicki Robin report that:

- 53 percent of groceries and 47 percent of hardware-store purchases are "spur of the moment" spending.
- When 34,300 shoppers in malls across the country were asked the primary reason for their visit, only 25 percent said they had come to look for a specific item.
- 70 percent of all adults visit a regional mall weekly.
- The number of U.S. shopping centers has grown from 2,000 in 1957 to more than 30,000 today. There are now more shopping malls than high schools.

Can you imagine what would

happen if all of these shopping-addicted adults blindly approached that banquet table and ate the same way they shop? It would be a carnage of Jell-O, taco chips, deviled eggs, potato salad, cheese dip, and those funny triangle things on the ends of toothpicks.

All of this points up the fact that there are two sides to frugality:

The glamorous side is the innovative and interesting strategies to get more for your dollars. Virtually everyone, including spendthrifts, is interested in getting more stuff for less money. They want to know how they can gorge at the banquet just as they've always done, but for, say, 50 percent of the money. Because there are hundreds, even thousands of such strategies, I tend to focus on these in the *Gazette*.

But the other side is about wanting and buying less. This unmagical aspect often disappoints people. They balk when they realize that achieving the lowest budget means they might also have to do without soda, designer suits, and first-run movies.

They need to understand that sometimes they're buying/eating just because it's there, not because they've determined it will bring sufficient satisfaction.

If people approach the banquet table with a clear vision of what they want, they will likely eat less and still feel quite satisfied, if not more satisfied.

Both aspects of frugality are important. If you buy something for half price and buy half as much, you've spent only 25 percent as much as the person who doesn't use either strategy.

SLACKS AX TAX

Anna L. Meenan of Cherry Valley, Illinois, wrote to say that for upper-income tightwads, donating used items to a charity to get the tax deduction will probably net a greater return than selling them at a yard sale.

To check this out, we called Barbara Shuckra, a public-affairs officer for the IRS, and Captain William Greenaway, administrator of the Salvation Army store in Portland, Maine. I also talked to John O'Malley, the CPA and tax consultant for our business, and Stephen DeFilippis, a member of the board of directors of the National Association of Enrolled Agents.

For this strategy to work for you, you must itemize your deductions and, as with any deduction strategy, your total deductions must exceed the standard deduction for you to save any money.

If you do itemize, obtain a list of the value of various items from your local nonprofit thrift shop (the shop to which you donate *must* have nonprofit status). Salvation Army stores will give you an IRS-approved document that lists the "high" and "low" thrift-shop prices for various types of clothing.

These amounts serve as your guideline for what you can deduct. Use them to determine if you could save more by donating to the shop, or by selling clothing at yard sales and consignment shops. For example: You can deduct between $15 and $60 for donating a man's suit. To be safe in the event of an audit, Shuckra suggest choosing a value in the middle. If you're in the 28-percent bracket and figure the suit's value is $35, donating it will

save $9.80 in taxes. If you are in the 15-percent bracket, it will save $5.25.

Even if you determine that consignment shops or yard sales will yield more, unsold clothing can still be donated. This is a good strategy if you lack storage space to stockpile yard-sale goods, or don't have the time or a good location in which to hold a yard sale.

O'Malley reminded me that there are some catches to this strategy. If your income is very high, you begin to lose deductions. In 1994, a couple filing jointly with an income over $111,800 would not get the total benefit of the deduction for the suit.

DeFilippis pointed out that if your noncash contributions exceed $500, you have to list your contributions on IRS Form 8283 and include it with your tax return. You need not list every pair of socks—"men's clothing" is sufficient—but you should have a list of every item in your files. He even recommends taking and filing a photo of your donated clothes.

You must have a receipt for deductible charitable contributions over $200, so be sure to get one when you drop stuff off. This receipt should list each item, although the thrift shop won't assign a value to the items; that's your job.

Finally, while I think this is a useful idea, keep in mind that you can often get the best value from your stuff by giving it to friends and relatives. Because what goes around comes around, giving things away ensures a steady stream of incoming clothes and favors. This is also the least time-consuming method, since buying and selling or donating (and getting the tax deduction) require time. Giving and receiving don't.

CRACKING THE DRESS CODE

The dress code here at *The Tightwad Gazette* is pretty lax—we all generally dress as if it's a day off. But having labored in the trenches of corporate America, I know that it can be challenging, and expensive, to dress up every day.

Some women, particularly those in urban areas, have written to me that they have had excellent luck getting top-quality business clothing at yard sales, thrift shops, and consignment shops. Because I'm tall and live in a rural area, I haven't been so lucky. After years of searching for outfits that I could use for speeches and book tours, I finally gave up and bought a $49, medium-quality suit at a discount store.

My need for business clothes is so minimal that I can get by with my Spartan wardrobe, but I know

my one-suit strategy won't work for most businesswomen. So here's a plan sent in by Patty Paulman of Randolph, New Jersey, for getting a month's worth of different business outfits at minimal cost.

Start with these nine pieces: two blazers, three tops, and four bottoms. Make sure that the blazers and bottoms all coordinate. This is easier if you choose solid colors and limit the number of patterns.

For example, Patty has a black blazer and a black-and-white checked blazer that match various shirts and slacks. The tops are blouses, sweaters, shirts, and T-shirts.

These combine as follows to make 24 different combinations:

Blazer #	1	1	1	1	1	1	1	1	1	1	1	1	2	2	2	2	2	2	2	2	2	2	2	2
Top #	1	1	1	1	2	2	2	2	3	3	3	3	1	1	1	1	2	2	2	2	3	3	3	3
Bottom #	1	2	3	4	1	2	3	4	1	2	3	4	1	2	3	4	1	2	3	4	1	2	3	4

WILL A DISHWASHER SAVE MONEY?

Calina Clarkson of Colorado Springs, Colorado, writes that she is curious about the cost of using a dishwasher versus washing dishes by hand.

I've known people who have purchased a dishwasher specifically because they believed that it would pay for itself in hot-water savings. This idea is supported by some consumer articles that have vaguely suggested a dishwasher will save you money. But these articles presumed that when hand-washing you rinse dishes under a running faucet, and they didn't factor in the cost of buying and maintaining a dishwasher. In fact, whether you would save depends on many variables. Let's use my situation as an example.

Most energy-efficient dishwashers use between 8 gallons (for china) and 14 gallons (for pots and pans) of water per cycle. I wash dishes by hand and rinse them in a dishpan. I use about 5 gallons for the breakfast dishes and about 7 gallons for the evening dishes (including all dishes accumulated after breakfast). If we used a dishwasher, we would run at least two loads per day and so would use about 6 more gallons of hot water per day.

The three energy experts I called agreed that the average cost of electrically heated hot water is about 1¢ per gallon at 8¢ per kilowatt-hour. (About 1¢ worth of natural gas will heat 5 gallons of water.) With our latest rate increase, we now pay 14.6¢ per kilowatt-hour, including tax. We have a well, so we don't have a water bill. So the extra hot water would cost us 11¢ per day.

In addition to the extra hot water, the energy to run the dishwasher could be another 4¢ or 8¢ for two loads.

We use $1.50 worth of liquid dishwashing detergent each month, or about 5¢ worth each day. A staffer says he needs to use 2 tablespoons of cheapo dishwasher detergent to ensure clean dishes; this amount costs 3.5¢ or 7¢ for two loads. So dishwasher detergent would cost me an additional 2¢ per day.

Various manufacturers and trade associations say that the average life span of a dishwasher is 11.5 years. The first repair averages at 8 years and costs $60. This means the purchase and mainte-

nance costs of a $400 dishwasher averages $40 per year.

So, in my case the extra cost of buying, maintaining, and using a dishwasher versus washing by hand would be $116.75 annually.

Compared to a frugal wash-by-hand method, a dishwasher doesn't save money. But does it save time? I believe so, but the amount is highly variable.

In some households, the cleanliness standard dictates that dishes must be clean enough to hold surgical tools, so when hand-washing, each item must be laboriously scrubbed and then rinsed under running water.

In my home, the standard is that dishes must not have visible food particles or be greasy. Thus we employ the speedier "dish-swishing" technique for washing and rinsing.

To determine how much time we would save with a dishwasher, I did all other related dishwashing activities first—putting away left-overs, washing countertops, scraping dishes, etc. After I assembled all of the dishes in one place, I timed how long the washing required. I repeated this experiment several times. I found that my actual dishwashing time was about one third to one half of the total after-meal cleanup—less than 30 minutes total each day for two washings. (Smaller families would use far less time.)

Because a dishwasher does save time, then it could, indirectly, save money. If I spend an extra 182½ hours per year hand-washing dishes and save $116.75, then my "hourly wage" would be about 64¢. Because there are other tightwad tasks that "pay" better, a dishwasher can be justified as a frugal purchase only if you are diligent about using the time you save profitably, not if you would use this time to watch a little TV.

Another point to consider is that dishwashers take up space enough to store a few 50-pound sacks of oatmeal. It seems to me that the same people who say they don't have enough time to be frugal also say they don't have enough space.

Some people think that because a dishwasher uses hotter water it kills more germs, so they will save money on their medical bills. A spokesman for the Centers for Disease Control said this was an improbable leap of logic. Germs are *far* more likely to be spread through the air or through hand-to-hand contact than by less-clean dishes. (I later theorized that since washing by hand also results in cleaner hands, this might offset the germ-killing benefits of hotter dishwasher water.)

Jim and I aren't planning to get a dishwasher. We don't mind washing dishes, partly because we use the time to watch the news on our small kitchen TV.

And within a couple of years the kids will assume this job. But my primary reason has more to do with aesthetics than frugality. I prefer not to put another modern appliance in my old-fashioned kitchen.

In short, if you already have a dishwasher, I won't discourage you from using it. If you don't have one, you should consider the variables in your situation carefully before getting one.

AVOID DEPTH CHARGES

Dear Amy,

To help stop water waste, I put a small piece of electrical tape on the bathtub to mark an appropriate water level for each child. Older ones get higher levels.

—Carla Matthews
Emmett, Idaho

NO-SPENDING CAP

Dear Amy,

I lost the gas cap off of my car. The next time I was at the gas station I asked if they had gas caps for sale. The clerk brought out a box of forgotten caps and let me choose one to fit my car for free. There was a large selection. I felt that I had donated mine to someone else, so I was happy to take him up on the offer.

—Dee Ann Dorman
Brookfield, Wisconsin

BUDGET BUMPER

Dear Amy,

I bought my daughter a used bicycle. It had a high bar between the handlebars. I was afraid she might fall and hurt herself. My husband suggested I get some pipe-insulation foam, which costs $2 for a big package. It was split along the side so we just had to cut the length. A friend saw it and said she paid a lot more for something very similar at the bike shop.

—Denita Bradley
Knoxville, Tennessee

MUSICAL SCORE

Dear Amy,

I decided at the beginning of November that I wanted an upright, second-loved piano for Christmas. I told everyone I knew that I was looking for one, that I had a very limited budget ($100), and, most important, that I would move it. I actually found *two* free pianos! One was in rough shape, but the other was in very good con-

dition and needed only a few repairs. After a week of coordinating the truck and the muscle, we moved it on New Year's Day. I am now negotiating with the piano tuner and repair guy to bring the cost within my $100 budget. So tell your readers to ask everyone they know if they're looking for something. You will never know what's out there if you don't ask.

—Carole Normandin
Gardner, Massachusetts

SWINGING WITH THE REIN

Dear Amy,

Here's a fun idea our kids love! Save an old horse from the spring-mounted-horse riding toy. Get some rope and string it from a tree branch. Makes a fun swing and extends the life of the toy. If the horse is plastic, make sure it is not cracking.

—M. L. Carson
Gainesville, Florida

I CAN DIG IT

Dear Amy,

We recently had our septic tank pumped and were charged $90 for the pumping and $30 to locate it and dig the dirt off the lid. They told us that next time we can do the digging ourselves (since we now know the location) and save ourselves $30. When buying a house, it would be worth asking where it is.

—Celia Byrnes
Crawfordsville, Indiana

FILL, FREEZE, AND FIT

Dear Amy,

A man the same size as my husband gave Bobby a pair of new boots. Bobby didn't wear them often until he got a new position at his job and had to dress up. One boot was a little too tight. Another man at his job gave him the solution: Put a garbage bag in the boot, fill the bag with water, and freeze. It worked. It stretched the boot just enough to fit comfortably.

—Cindy Burns
Waco, Texas

BOARD OF EDUCATION

Dear Amy,

My twin girls love to play school. For their ninth birthday they wanted a larger (classroom-sized) chalkboard. We found that they were outrageously expensive. My husband bought a sheet of plywood and some chalkboard paint at the hardware store for about $20. The same size chalkboard would have been about $200 if we had bought one. It hangs on the wall in their playroom and playing school is so much fun now!

—Beth Cape
Royston, Georgia

NOT STIFFED ON STARCH

Dear Amy,

My husband likes all of his shirts heavily starched. Instead of using the spray cans of starch, which cost 87¢ for 22 ounces, I mix 4 tablespoons of powdered

starch with 4 cups of hot water. Using a good spray bottle, I spray on the starch (shaking it often) and iron the garment as usual. One can of store-bought starch costs 87¢. An equivalent amount of homemade starch-spray costs 10¢.

—Pam Hoyer
Warrensburg, Missouri

BEAMPOLES

Dear Amy,

My neighbor built a pole barn out of used utility poles. Our local electric company gives the poles away for a onetime charge of $1. You must sign a contract that you won't hold them responsible for any damage, etc. The poles can also be used for landscaping and other uses.

—Mike and Cathy McDermott
Kokomo, Indiana

FLAPJACK SNACK

Dear Amy,

Kids love PPRs (Peanut-butter Pancake Roll-ups). I take pancakes left over from breakfast, spread them with peanut butter and a little honey, roll them up, and cut them in half. They stick together pretty well—good use for extra pancakes.

—Rose Sabel-Dodge
Portland, Oregon

HOW MUCH DOES IT REALLY COST TO RAISE A CHILD?

Now and then, in the midst of the daily mix of murders, muggings, and plane crashes, the newspapers run a story that's *really* scary. It's the latest government report on the cost of raising an American child.

A newsletter reader from Boca Raton, Florida, sent me an article from the April 1, 1994, issue of *The Wall Street Journal*. It says the U.S. Department of Agriculture determined that "the typical baby born to affluent parents in 1993 could cost as much as $334,600 to raise to age 18." The reader asked, "Are these costs real?"

To learn more, we called Mark Lino, the USDA economist who computes these numbers. He said that the figure cited in the *WSJ* is the maximum amount spent by the most affluent families, and that it assumes 6 percent annual inflation for the next 18 years. In other words, it's the USDA's highest kid-cost figure.

He went on to explain that the USDA bases its numbers on a survey of the spending habits of 20,000 families. He said all of its figures are based on the cost of raising the second of two children. And he said "to age 18" means from birth until the day before the child's 18th birthday, so it does not include prenatal or college expenses.

He also gave us a figure for a family-income range that is more typical of *Tightwad Gazette* readers and it was almost as scary as the "affluent parents" figure. He said it will cost families with taxable incomes of from $32,000 to $54,100 an average of $132,660, in 1993 dollars, to raise a child born in 1993. Add 6 percent inflation and the total rises to $231,140.

Each year we are both terrified and mystified by these USDA numbers, so I decided to dig into this further. I found that the USDA computes some of its numbers in a unique way that may not really reflect the cost of an extra child. Further, I found that when you consider the spending habits of a tightwad family, it's possible to come up with a dramatically lower number.

I want to make it clear that I am not coming up with an alternative number to refute the USDA number. All situations are different, and unlike the USDA, I can't do a detailed survey of the spending habits of 20,000 tightwad families. All I hope to show is that it is possible to raise a kid for much less than the USDA number would have us believe.

I'll use the real-life "Smith" family for my example. They are frugal friends of mine who already have one child, an eight-year-old son.

Kids cost more as they get older. According to the USDA's figures, the amount spent during a child's eighth year approximately represents the average cost per year over 18 years. So what the Smiths spend on their son now can provide clues about how much they would spend on another child.

The USDA figures costs in the following categories:

• Housing. The USDA figures per-kid housing costs by dividing the family's average monthly housing costs by the number of people in the family. A different, and perhaps more realistic, way to compute this number would be to determine how much housing costs would increase with an additional child. The Smiths already bought a three-bedroom ranch house with a yard because they didn't want to raise their son in an apartment. Based on other families in their neighborhood who live in homes of the same exact layout, the Smiths know they could raise three children in their 1,000-square-foot home. So their extra-child cost would be only for yard-sale furniture and utilities. This could easily be as little as $50 annually.

• Transportation. The USDA estimates that 40 percent of a family's transportation costs are work related. So they divide the remaining 60 percent by the number of people in the family to arrive at the per-kid transportation cost.

But the Smiths already have two cars, and each has a backseat, so an extra kid's transportation expenses would be zero when he accompanied the parents on family outings. Naturally, the Smiths

would make some special trips to shuttle the new kid around to doctors, schools, sports, etc. Annually this might cost an extra $50 in gas and maintenance.

Once every three years the Smiths take a plane trip to visit relatives. A ticket costs $400, so the annual average for the new child's ticket would be $133.

Transportation total: $183 annually.

• Food. The USDA says it costs an average of $1,316 to feed a kid annually, ranging from $870 for a 1-year-old to $1,750 for a 17-year-old.

Using the USDA chart on page 127, the Smiths determined that they can feed their family for 62 percent of the "thrifty" plan. This means the Smiths now feed their eight-year-old for $567 a year, so this would also be the annual average for the second child.

• Clothing. The USDA says this average annual cost is $603, ranging from $450 for a 1-year-old to $850 for a 17-year-old.

Through yard-saling, clothes-swapping, and other strategies, the Smiths spent $40 this year to dress their eight-year-old.

Some people claim that it's impossible to find good teenager clothing at yard sales, but I haven't found that to be the case. My 13-year-old Alec is a big kid, and I have had good luck stockpiling 25¢-per-item teen-sized clothing for him to wear in three or four years. The adult Smiths spend less than $50 apiece annually for clothing, and there is no reason that a teenaged Smith would cost more. So we'll put the annual clothing budget at $50. If, as teens, the Smiths' kids want something fancier, they will have to earn the money themselves.

• Health care. The USDA pegs this number at $470 annually, which covers the portion of insurance paid for by parents and any out-of-pocket costs for medical and dental bills. We accept this number as reasonable; indeed, this is one area in which people usually don't waste huge amounts of money.

• Child care and education. The USDA says this cost is $545 per year. As a result of making frugal choices and some creative job juggling, the Smiths have always had one parent at home. Thus they have never and would never pay for child care. Their son is in public school, as their next child would be. While the Smiths' son did go to a private nursery school, they probably would not do this again with another child.

As kids get older they need to buy school supplies or may want special lessons. So we'll estimate these costs to average $100 per year.

• Miscellaneous. Entertainment, personal care (such as haircuts and toothpaste), and school activity fees are all extremely variable. The USDA figures this to amount to $761 per year. The Smiths cut their son's hair. They spend less than $40 per year on presents, and $50 per year on entertainment for their son. Throw in some toothpaste, soap, laundry detergent, Q-Tips, etc. and the annual total is $110. Let's be generous and assume there is $60 worth of stuff we can't track down—we'll call the total $170.

So the average annual cost of raising this younger of two tightwad children would be $1,590. But

one factor that the USDA did not consider was the dependent income-tax exemption, which was $2,350 in 1993. The Smiths are in the 28 percent tax bracket, so their new kid would save them $658 annually in taxes, bringing the net cost to $932. Multiplied by 18 years, the cost is $16,776. Assuming 6 percent inflation, the total becomes $28,682, or about 12 percent of the USDA figure.

When looking at your own situation, you may find that our estimates are lower than yours. The point is that, at 12 percent of the USDA figure, even if we have forgotten some expenses and underestimated by a huge 100 percent, raising this second kid would still cost far less than what the USDA estimate indicates.

I'm not necessarily recommending that all of my readers rush off and produce another kid, but whenever one contemplates such a major step, it's handy to have accurate information.

TREND REVERSAL?

I get a great deal of mail, mostly from women, telling me that by applying the lessons of the newsletter they have been able to achieve their goal of quitting their jobs and staying home with the kids.

It turns out that these women are part of a nationwide trend. According to a study by Richard Hokenson, chief economist for the Wall Street brokerage firm of Donaldson, Lufkin and Jenrette, the percentage of women under age 30 in the workforce peaked in 1989 at 75 percent, after years of marching steadily upward. By early 1992 it had dropped to 71 percent. Since then it has crept back up to 72 percent, but Hokenson says indicators are that the long-term trend will continue downward.

"Honey, I'm home... for good!"

He said it's possible that this is happening because more and more women are realizing what was revealed by a Labor Department study: About 80 percent of working mothers' income is absorbed by job-related expenses such as child care, clothing, transportation, and meals away from home.

This return-home trend explains an economic puzzle: Why didn't lower interest rates boost housing sales? Hokenson says it's because families didn't move. Instead they refinanced and used the money they saved to allow Mom to stay home with the kids.

It has never been my position that all moms should stay home, but I do feel that one of the great values of frugality is that it can allow moms—or dads—who want to stay home with the kids to do so. I asked Hokenson if he had any figures regarding whether more fathers are leaving the workforce and minding the kids, but he said he has no data on that.

LEARN BEFORE YOU BURN

In *The Tightwad Gazette* I wrote an article about how to compute whether wood or oil provides cheaper heat. At the time (1990), oil was peaking at $1.20 per gallon due to the Gulf War. That same year we got a terrific deal on wood: $60 per cord. We have a furnace that can burn either wood or oil, and at the end of that year I determined that burning wood saved us a lot of money.

But last fall Jim and I spent part of a weekend stacking maple firewood in our cellar. As I did this, I had time to wonder whether this wood, which cost $80 per cord, would provide cheaper heat than oil, which last year averaged 75¢ per gallon. The potential savings in the heating season ahead were not nearly so obvious as they were in 1990.

To help me fine-tune my ability to choose one or the other, I needed to know, precisely, the heating value of the maple. By making phone calls and going to the library, I was able to locate no fewer than eight different charts that listed the heating value of different species of wood. They agreed 100 percent on the "rank" of the wood species. Maple, for example, has more heat value than elm, which has more than pine. But they disagreed by as much as 25 percent about just what the heat value of a single species is. A cord of maple, for example, was listed as having the same heat value as between 132 and 188 gallons of oil. This difference would be enough to throw off any analysis.

As I investigated further, it appeared that the high figures represented oven-dried wood with a zero water content and the low figures represented air-dried wood with a 20 percent water content. I called Andrew J. Baker, a chemical engineer with the U.S. Forest Service's Forest Products Laboratory in Madison, Wisconsin, and he said that firewood stored under cover for a year generally dries to the 12 percent to 20 percent moisture range. He said you can tell if it has achieved this level by checking the ends—they should be cracked.

So, assuming that you are a true tightwad and you have taken care to let your wood season properly, here is the list of gallons-of-oil equivalences per cord that appears to be the most relevant. It is from the U.S. Department of Agriculture and assumes a 12 percent moisture content. In cases where there are several varieties within the

species (such as black oak, scarlet oak, water oak, etc.), this list shows the average of that species:

alder—125	hickory—206
ash—171	magnolia—149
aspen—117	maple—164
basswood—113	oak—202
beech—195	pine—142
birch—190	redwood—114
butternut—116	sassafras—140
cedar—116	spruce—119
cherry—152	sweetgum—158
cottonwood—111	sycamore—149
Douglas fir—146	tamarack—161
elm—152	tupelo—152
fir—115	walnut—168
hemlock—139	willow—118

Multiply these figures by 173.41 to get the equivalence in cubic feet of natural gas.

Basing my calculations on maple's 164-gallon equivalence, we would have to buy $123 in oil (75¢ × 164) to get the same heat we'd get from a cord of the wood. That seems to indicate that, at $80 a cord, maple is a good deal.

But it might not be for you. A final calculation has to be made based on the efficiency of your oil or gas furnace versus the efficiency of your woodstove.

According to the manufacturer, both wood and oil burn at the same level of efficiency in our furnace, so we can do a straight comparison like the one above.

But the efficiency of woodstoves ranges from just 20 percent for old Franklin types to over 75 percent for modern, airtight versions with catalytic combusters. Depending upon age, technology, and upkeep, the efficiency of oil furnaces ranges from 60 percent to about 82 percent; for gas, from 65 percent to over 95 percent.

If you don't know the efficiency of your stove or furnace, contact the manufacturer. Then determine the difference in their efficiencies and use that to calculate the actual difference in cost.

For example, supposing I have, as in the above example, determined that I would have to buy $123 in oil to equal $80 in wood. If I have an old oil furnace that is 65 percent efficient, and a new, high-tech woodstove that is 75 percent efficient, the 15 percent greater efficiency of the woodstove means that, for purposes of comparison, I can subtract 15 percent from the price of the wood. Wood, then, actually costs $68 per cord. Wood becomes an even better deal than my original calculation indicated.

As with all energy questions, there are, of course, other variables. Nadav Maline, managing editor of *Environmental Building News* in Brattleboro, Vermont, told me that if the ductwork of your furnace is leaky, or is uninsulated and runs through a cold space, your furnace may be far less efficient than its rating indicates.

Also, I have noticed an interesting behavioral effect of woodstoves. They tend to draw people away from cold parts of the house and toward the stove itself. So a woodstove does not necessarily have to crank out the same number of Btu's as a whole-house furnace to keep your family warm.

The bottom line is that it's a mistake to assume—as many people do—that wood is always a cheaper source of heat. While wood can be a good deal, you won't know for certain until you calculate all of the variables in your particular situation.

NO-GAIN OCTANE

Lisa Demick of Dublin, Ohio, asks, "How does one figure out which gasoline is the best deal? Is it ever an advantage to spend more for the higher octane?"

There is a "you-get-what-you-pay-for" notion that the more expensive "premium" gas will improve your mileage, give your car more power, and/or be better for your engine, so the extra expense is worth it.

Consumers haven't acquired this idea by accident. The ads of many oil companies have implied this. In fact, in 1992, Public Citizen, a consumer advocacy group founded by Ralph Nader, awarded Amoco the Harlon Page Hubbard Lemon Award, which is its award for the most misleading ad of the year. This ad suggested that cars with over 15,000 miles on the odometer—which includes most cars that are over a year old—could benefit from higher-octane gas, though automakers dispute this claim for all but a very few models. According to Public Citizen, the Federal Trade Commission cited Sunoco with making similar misrepresentations about higher-octane gas.

For the real story, I talked with David Solomon, editor of the *Nutz and Boltz* automotive newsletter, and William Berman, national environmental director for the American Automobile Association, and I did some library research.

First of all, Solomon and Berman said that higher-octane gasoline has no more power than low-octane gas. Higher-octane gas simply ignites less readily than the low-octane kind.

High-octane gas is needed in some kinds of engines. In these engines, the cylinders compress the fuel/air mixture so much that the resulting heat (pressure makes heat) can make the mixture explode prematurely—before the spark plug has a chance to ignite it. This premature ignition is "knocking" and it sounds like little metal balls rattling around inside your engine. It also means lost power, bad mileage, and, in some severe cases, engine damage. High-octane gas resists exploding prematurely.

But the chance that your car truly needs it is slim. Only 10 percent of the cars on the road were manufactured to require an octane that's higher than regular unleaded, which is 87 octane. Berman said that 20 percent of the gas sold in the United States is premium grade, so many drivers may be buying premium unnecessarily. That, according to Public Citizen, translates to about $3 billion in waste, or $95 wasted per vehicle per year.

Generally you should use a higher-octane gasoline only if your owner's manual specifies it.

There are also some rare cases in which cars begin to knock persistently and need higher-octane fuels as they age. But before you treat the symptom, try to cure the disease. Knocking can be due to a correctable carbon buildup. Solomon suggests trying a gas additive that can strip away carbon. He likes Redline SI One. Berman said several gasolines, notably Texaco's System 3, claim cleaning abilities, so you might try one of these.

If this doesn't work, try a tune-up. The average motorist uses 560 gallons of gas a year. If a $65

tune-up gives you the ability to run on regular, you will save about $112 on gas, for a total savings of about $47.

Berman believes that these steps will almost certainly solve any knocking problem, but if it persists, consult a mechanic.

If your car doesn't require high-octane gas, using it will not improve your mileage. In fact, it can actually *decrease* engine performance. GM Research and Development Center researchers say many premium gasolines are refined from lower-volatility (less readily combustible) feedstocks. The average car can't vaporize these heavier gas grades. They simply push the unburned gas out into the exhaust, wasting it and increasing emissions. This causes poor combustion, stalling, and hesitation. If you remain unconvinced, simply try filling up with various grades of gas and then calculate your miles per dollar.

One final consideration: Even if you're paying for high-octane gas, you may not be getting it. Berman said that, according to a government survey, when you get gas from a pump marked "premium," there's a 10 percent chance you're getting a lower grade. Some states now test octane levels; others have "hit-or-miss" programs; and a few have no regulations or testing regarding octane levels. "When you buy premium in those states, you have no idea what you are getting," Berman said.

A TIME-SAVER OF SORTS

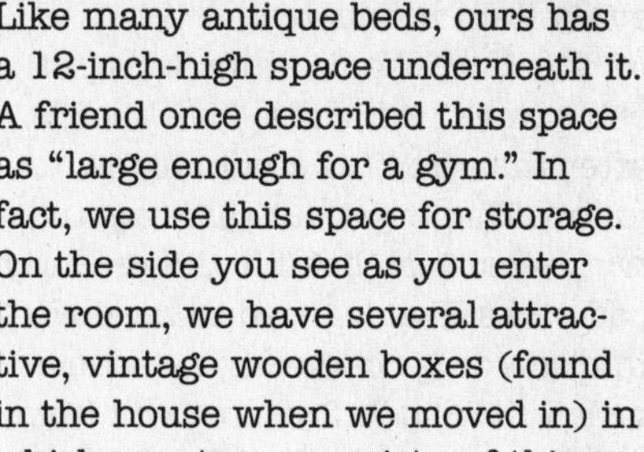

Like many antique beds, ours has a 12-inch-high space underneath it. A friend once described this space as "large enough for a gym." In fact, we use this space for storage. On the side you see as you enter the room, we have several attractive, vintage wooden boxes (found in the house when we moved in) in which we store a variety of things.

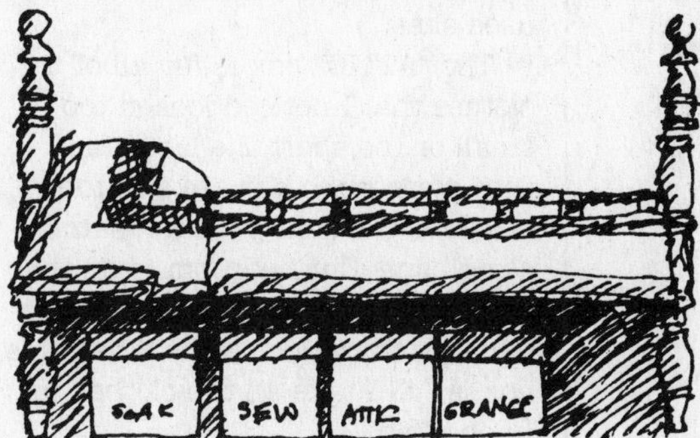

On the side you don't see, we have my time-saver four-box clothing-aid system. These four lidded cardboard boxes, marked "SOAK," "SEW," "ATTIC," and "GRANGE," are here because I sort the family's laundry on our bed and they serve as temporary storage for clothes that shouldn't go back into drawers and closets.

The "SOAK" box is for clothes that need to be soaked in the Clorox II/Cascade stain remedy given in the first *Tightwad Gazette* book. When this box is half-full of stained clothes, I know I have enough to make it worthwhile to mix up a batch of the stain recipe.

The "SEW" box is for any clothes that need mending. Once every couple of months, a rare intersection of two moods occurs: 1) I'm at a loss for something to do, and 2) I feel an urge to be pro-

ductive. When this happens I have a sewing afternoon and repair every item in this box.

This box also contains a bag of our unmatched socks. I sort socks after the rest of the laundry is folded. Then I get out this bag and try to find matches for the recently odd socks. I've learned to be slow in discarding odd socks, as sooner or later a match for most will turn up. (A sock can be lost for years if accidentally folded up in a seldom-used sheet.)

The "ATTIC" box is for all of the clothes that I noticed looked too small or too short the last time they were worn but are still too large for the next younger, same-sex sibling. Our bedroom is on the first floor and my clothing storage is in the third-floor attic. When this box is full I take all the clothes up in one trip.

The "GRANGE" box is for all the clothes outgrown by my youngest children and the adult-sized clothes we don't want to keep. I donate these to our church's thrift shop, which is run out of our town's grange hall. I'm happy to do this because we buy some clothes at the grange. When this box is full, I put it in the car to be dropped off on our next trip by. Before we moved to Leeds, this box was labeled "YARD SALE," and full boxes went into the garage, where we kept items to be sold at our next yard sale.

By putting the clothes into these four boxes as I sort laundry, I am assured that the clothing in my children's drawers is mended, has no stains, and is the correct size.

A FLUFFY FILLER ARTICLE

Jim and I each brought a pillow to our marriage. As our family grew, we acquired additional bedding from yard sales and older relatives who were breaking up households. But we've never seen pillows at yard sales or been able to get them from other cheap sources.

Which is too bad, because pillows are surprisingly expensive—from about $10 to $60 retail. We've reluctantly bought cheapo pillows for about $5 at a salvage store as we have needed more. Thus we've always had exactly enough pillows, unless company visits.

During one winter's flu season, then-two-year-old Brad got sick on an old fiberfill pillow. When I washed it, it came out in a trapezoidal lump. When I tried to pull it back into a rectangle, the casing material ripped.

After several months of making up Brad's bed with this mutant pillow, inspiration struck. I ripped it open, removed the fiberfill, and discarded the old casing. I shredded the fiberfill into marshmallow-sized fluffy pieces and filled up a white pillowcase (we have an impressive pillowcase surplus from the above-mentioned relatives). I also added some leftover batting scraps from quilting.

Once the pillowcase was full, it took just a minute or so to machine-stitch the end closed. Because a pillow needs to be shorter than a pillowcase, I folded and pinned the 4-inch hem inside before stitching. The result is an ever-so-slightly lumpy but quite serviceable pillow.

Flushed with this success, I recalled an old kid's comforter in our attic. Like most colored store-

bought comforters, this one became badly faded and pilled after a few washings. Also, the batting had become too matted to ever be reused in a quilt. Yet it always seemed like too much raw material to throw away, so I had saved it. Now, as I began to take it apart, the old threads tore easily. It yielded enough batting, once shredded, to make a second large pillow.

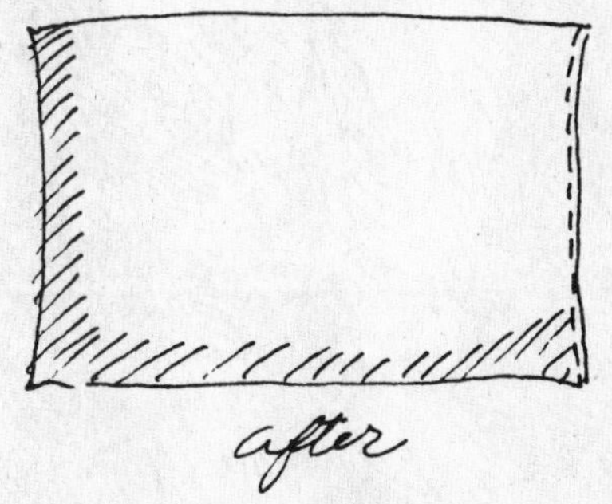

Making these two pillows from free materials required about 90 minutes, mostly in the shredding. It's a perfect activity for idle hands while watching TV. In addition to saving at least $10 on pillows, I was also able to avoid our $1-per-bag trash fees by not discarding the old pillow and comforter.

ROTTEN-BANANA IDEAS

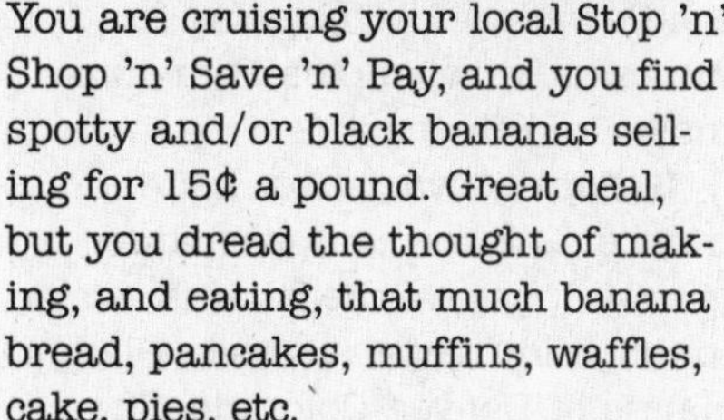

You are cruising your local Stop 'n' Shop 'n' Save 'n' Pay, and you find spotty and/or black bananas selling for 15¢ a pound. Great deal, but you dread the thought of making, and eating, that much banana bread, pancakes, muffins, waffles, cake, pies, etc.

But go ahead and buy them, because there are other ways to use this fruit, ways that are low in fat and sugar.

Bananas that can't be used immediately can be frozen. There are two ways to do this, depending on how you plan to use them.

• Bananas to be used in a frozen state: Peel and freeze whole, or sliced in a bag.

• Bananas to be used in a squishy state: Place bananas directly in the freezer without peeling or putting in a bag. To use, thaw completely, then cut off the tip and goosh the liquidy banana out. This sounds rather gross, but it's very convenient, because you don't have to mash the banana to use it.

Some frozen-banana recipes:

1. Banana "milkshake." In a blender, combine 3 frozen bananas, 4 cups of milk, a teaspoon of vanilla, and ¼ cup of sugar (optional). To make it even colder, add up to 6 crushed ice cubes. Maria Veres Homic of Austin, Texas, suggests that frozen bananas, with or without milk, make great "shakes" when combined with almost anything: other fruit, juice, coconut, yogurt, jam, cocoa powder. For creative tightwads, the possibilities are endless. Health-food stores and restaurants call these drinks "smoothies" and sell them for $2 to $4 a serving.

2. Popsicles. Same as above, except use thawed banana and add a little yellow food coloring to increase "wow" factor. Pour into molds and freeze.

3. Popsicle variation. If item number 2 is too complicated for you, simply peel the banana, wrap in foil, and freeze, suggests Gladys Harris of Denver, Colorado. She says this treatment improves the flavor and texture of overripe bananas.

4. Banana "ice cream." Debbie Mason of Virginia Beach, Virginia, combines frozen bananas with just enough orange juice to keep the mixture blending. For variety, she adds other fruits. She tops this with homemade granola.

5. Fruit salad dressing for those who like a banana/peanut butter combination. Combine 1 soft banana, 1 tablespoon lemon juice, ¼ cup peanut butter, ½ cup mayonnaise, 3 tablespoons milk powder, and ¼ cup water.

6. Banana toast. Frances Strauss of Victoria, British Columbia, suggests this simple recipe: Mash one limp banana and mix well with 2 eggs and 1 teaspoon cinnamon, or blenderize all ingredients. Dip bread slices into mixture and fry on both sides in oiled pan. Serve with fruit puree or syrup.

SLEEPWEAR SAFETY

Following a newsletter article about making pajama pants from hubby's old knit shirts, a reader wrote that she believed there's a law that says all children's sleepwear must be flame resistant. I investigated and found information that can be useful in helping parents choose both flame-resistant and cheaper sleepwear for their kids.

In 1972 the Consumer Products Safety Commission established flammability standards for children's sleepwear. These mandated that manufactured sleepwear be either polyester (which is naturally flame resistant) or, if a natural fiber, it must be chemically treated to be flame resistant. The standards govern only what can be manufactured and sold, not what parents can dress their children in for bed. They were passed at a time when most childhood burns from garments involved sleepwear and when about 60 deaths in the United States annually resulted from sleepwear fires.

In the years since the standards were established, the CPSC has gathered new data that indicates it can be safe to dress kids in certain kinds of flammable sleepwear.

The data shows that almost all sleepwear burns occurred when the children were playing before going to bed or after getting up in the morning. And almost all of the burns resulted from nightgowns, robes, and other flowing garments, which are more likely to come in

contact with fire. The point here is that children's clothing doesn't catch fire in bed. In keeping with this fact, there has never been a standard mandating that sheets and blankets be flame resistant.

Over the last two decades, sleepwear burns have declined so that they now make up only 8 percent of all garment burns. While the standards have contributed to the decline, the CPSC also attributes this to fewer fire hazards within the home. Cigarette smoking has declined in the last 20 years, and many fire hazards, like fireplaces, space heaters, gas stoves, and cigarette lighters, have developed improved safety features.

With this new knowledge, the CPSC staff is proposing to amend the standards to allow skintight pajamas and infant sleepwear to be made from fabrics that aren't flame resistant.

Upon learning all this, I asked CPSC spokeswoman Kathy Kaplan if a child who wore a T-shirt while sleeping was at more risk than a child who wore a T-shirt while playing. She said the risk would be exactly the same.

What does this mean for frugal parents selecting sleepwear for their kids? First, the common tightwad strategy of using an adult-sized cotton T-shirt for toddler sleepwear should not be considered absolutely safe. T-shirts are flammable and on a small child are loose and flowing.

Kaplan also said parents should assess the fire hazards in their home. In some homes, like mine, the fire hazards are almost nonexistent, so the flammability of sleepwear isn't a concern. However, parents in homes with hazards should choose sleepwear carefully. In the most hazardous situations one might even avoid flame-resistant gowns and robes, which still result in nearly all of the sleepwear burns.

In short, it's reasonable to assume that whatever is safe for your child to wear while playing is safe for your child to wear while sleeping. This can save you money, as it increases the sleepwear options for your children. Although most of my kids wear yard-sale-purchased traditional sleepwear, my older boys have been wearing no-longer-presentable sweatpants and correct-sized T-shirts.

BUDGET BUBBLES

Dear Amy,

My daughter's craft teacher gave me a great recipe for homemade bubble soap that's cheaper than the one in *The Tightwad Gazette* because it contains corn syrup instead of glycerin. Mix it ahead of time for best results:

6 parts water
2 parts Joy dishwashing liquid
¾ part corn syrup

This recipe costs 18¢ per cup, compared with 26¢ per cup for the glycerin recipe.

—Lori Evesque
Paw Paw, Michigan

AGED AD ADVANTAGE

Dear Amy,

I just bought a high-grade 6-foot picnic table (bolted instead of nailed) through the *Want Advertiser*, a classified-ad publication, for

$35. But I did not find it in the latest copy. I perused one that was a month old. Lots of items go unsold, and then you are in a stronger position to bargain.

—Susan Elliott
Milford, Massachusetts

OVER-CAPITOL-IZED

Dear Amy,

American flags that have been flown over the Capitol in Washington can be purchased very inexpensively from your senator or congressman. All flags come with a

certificate noting the date flown and, if requested, a person's name or special occasion. These make particularly nice and very special presents.

—Betsey Surmeier
Kensington, Maryland

(I wrote for and received an order form from my congressman and found that the least expensive option was a 3-foot-by-5-foot nylon flag for $6.76, plus $2.46 for postage. I called three suppliers in my area and found they charge from $28 to $31 for a 3-by-5 nylon flag.

Flags from your senator or congressman are available in both nylon and cotton, and range in size up to 5 feet by 8 feet. FZ)

POWDER YOUR JOES

Dear Amy,

I use instant, nonfat, powdered milk as a creamer in my coffee and tea. I pour it directly from the box. It does not dilute the flavor of the coffee, has no fat, and is inexpensive. It is far superior to the "creamer" products.

—Carol Collins
Greenville, South Carolina

CAN'T BEAT THIS WRAP

Dear Amy,

In order to save a substantial amount on waxed paper, aluminum foil, and plastic wrap, we buy the large, restaurant-sized boxes from our local restaurant-supply store. We just finished up a box of aluminum foil we bought six years ago for $10!

—Tina Hornsby
Allentown, Pennsylvania

(Warehouse stores also sometimes stock these big rolls. FZ)

SCOTCH ON SCOTCH

Dear Amy,

When I had a professional service clean stains from our sofas, I asked if they would spray my just-washed camping coat with spot

protector, as long as they were here. They did, and at no charge. I have priced cans of Scotchgard at $6.50, so now that I know about this, I'll have more items clean and ready to be zapped by them the next time I need the upholstery cleaned.

—Heidi M. Wright
Albuquerque, New Mexico

WORDS FOR WEAR

Dear Amy,

Have you ever mentioned "hand-me-ups"? We old parents wear our college kids' castoffs and work clothes. When anyone compliments our apparel, I mention it and no one has ever heard the term before. When my daughter moved out of her first rental home to get married, I got so many clothes my closet rod broke.

—Anne Hanna
Laurel, Maryland

SWEET AND LOW COST

Dear Amy,

Make your own brown sugar by taking 1 cup of white sugar and mixing it with 2 tablespoons of molasses. It tastes good on your oatmeal and in baked goods and is much cheaper. By our figuring, 2 pounds of the bargain brand of brown sugar costs $1.92, and 2 pounds of this homemade version costs only $1.00 (using bargain-brand white sugar at 35¢ per pound and molasses at $1.79).

—Clare Jones
Ogilvie, Minnesota

(The savings in this strategy is highly variable. We stock up on brown sugar when it hits 38¢ to 50¢ per pound. In our case, making our own brown sugar could cost slightly more; however, we use this strategy when we're out of brown sugar. FZ)

THE LEAST YEAST

Dear Amy,

I have enjoyed making "Cuban Bread" (from *The Tightwad Gazette II*). It is one bread that everyone loves, and it is quick and easy for me. However, I discovered that I needed only half the dry yeast called for in the recipe; that is, 1 tablespoon instead of 2. The bread does not taste as "yeasty," and the loaves turn out just as large.

—Carolyn C. Smith
Burlington, Connecticut

HANGER IN THERE, BABY

Dear Amy,

I had a baby daughter recently, and told my mom to put baby-clothes hangers on my shower list. She told me just to bend my wire ones, and it worked great.

—Nancy Waletzko
Zimmerman, Minnesota

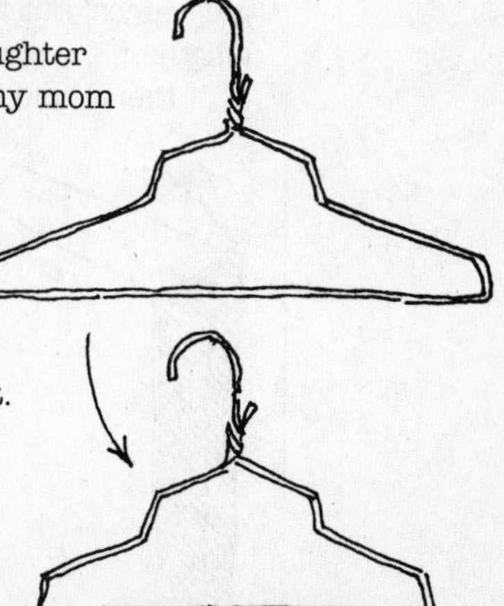

THE TUBE THAT BINDS

One of our best yard-sale finds was the *Reader's Digest Fix-It-Yourself Manual*, purchased for 25¢. Like all Reader's Digest books, it has excellent graphics and tells you just about everything you need to know about the subject. I thumbed through it and immediately found information I could use:

Months earlier, the covers had come off my 14-year-old, flour-dusted, batter-splattered *Fannie Farmer Cookbook*. I had been mystified as to how to reattach the covers of this essential hardcover book. The *Fix-It-Yourself Manual*'s book-repair section revealed the tightwaddy trick: a simple brown-paper tube.

You start by cutting a rectangle of grocery-bag paper that's slightly longer than the spine, and a ½ inch more than twice as wide. Form a tube and glue together the overlapping edges. Cut the tube to the length of the spine.

If there's old backing on the spine, remove as much of it as possible. Apply white glue along the spine and let it dry. Glue the "un-overlapped" side of the paper tube to the spine with white glue and smooth it down.

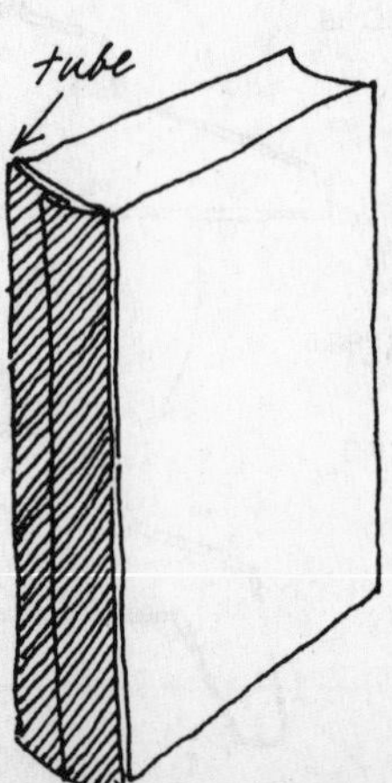

The manual then explains how to recover the spine and reattach the covers. The process involves gluing a cardboard strip to the exposed side of the tube, then gluing a piece of "book cloth" (available from bookbinding supply stores) over the strip and onto the covers.

But since I didn't have this special kind of cloth and don't care about the appearance of this book, I took the simple route: I used duct tape, pressing it firmly onto the tube and overlapping it onto the covers by about 1 inch to hold them in place. I also opened the front and back covers and pushed a strip of duct tape into the crease between the covers and the first and last pages.

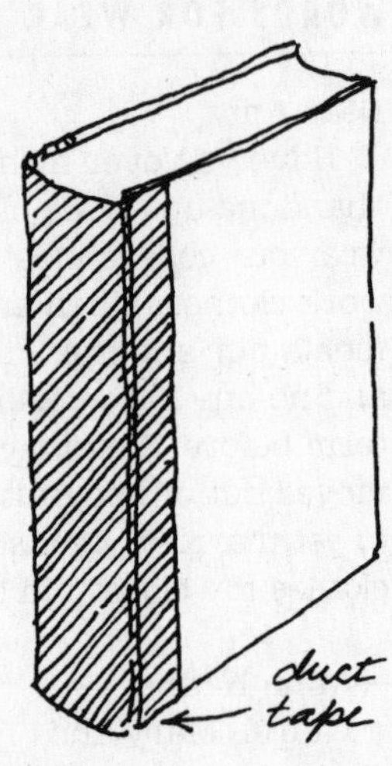

This entire process took just 10 minutes, not including glue-drying time, and I look forward to another 14 years of flour-dusting and batter-splattering my favorite cookbook. Further, when my *Fix-It-Yourself Manual* expires someday, I now know how to revive it.

TOWARD SNEAKER IMMORTALITY

Whenever I point out that I spend less than $50 annually to dress six kids, frugal friends say that it generally seems possible, except when it comes to shoes. Even one pair of new, cheapo $10 sneakers per kid would put me over budget.

The secret is that I get their shoes at yard sales along with the rest of my kids' clothing. Last summer I picked up 16 pairs of shoes and sneakers and 3 pairs of boots, all in good-to-brand-new condition, for a total of $9.05. I'll concede that this required "power yard-saling," in which I hit at least 20 yard sales on each of 10 yard-sale days throughout the summer, but the point is that it can be done. This footwear comprises a small percent of my total haul, but if I bought only shoes, it would still be worth my time.

Getting yard-sale shoes has a couple of advantages aside from simply saving money. When my mother visited recently, she noted that the kids had many pairs of shoes lined up in their closets, and that if I were buying new shoes, they would have fewer pairs.

In addition to this, a new $10 pair of sneakers usually lacks style and quality. The brands I find at yard sales include Nike, Reebok, Etonic, and New Balance, which would cost anywhere from $25 to well over $50 new and would have that brand-new look for just a few weeks. My kids are not concerned if their shoes were previously owned, but they do prefer certain styles, and I can almost always accommodate them.

Kids are rough on sneakers. After a few months, these excellent-condition yard-sale sneakers can start to look ratty, and yard-sale season is over by then. So along with buying inexpensive sneakers, I also need to make them last and look good longer.

My first step is having the kids follow a strategy similar to my adult "Three-Year Sneaker Plan" outlined in *The Tightwad Gazette.* They reserve their best-looking sneakers for school and other occasions when they need to be presentable. As soon as they get home from school, they change into their "play" sneakers, which are often the "dress" sneakers that were worn by an older same-sex sibling. Because the kids want to have good-looking sneakers to wear to school, they are happy to do this. In the summer my kids like to go barefooted, which happens to save wear on both sneakers and socks.

The second step is to continually refurbish sneakers for optimal appearance. Once you learn a few tricks, you can also visualize the possibilities in an old pair of sneak-

ers in a yard-sale "free box." Some basic tips:

• You can hand-wash vinyl sneakers by briefly submersing them in warm soapy water and scrubbing with an old toothbrush. Scuffs clean up beautifully with scouring powder and a damp cloth.

• Replace old laces with new ones. In a pinch, I've scavenged newer, snazzier laces from sneakers I purchased for a child to wear in future years. At the least, dirty laces can be added to your bucket of Clorox II/Cascade stain remover (see *The Tightwad Gazette*) while you soak other clothes.

• When Velcro fasteners become loaded with fuzz, hair, and dried grass, they look dirty and no longer adhere. Pick out this stuff with a sharp tool. Clip off all loose threads from the Velcro stitching and hand-sew any places it has become loose.

• Black leather or vinyl sneakers (as well as black patent-leather shoes and any black details on white sneakers) are easily spruced up with black permanent marker. In one yard-sale "free box" I found an excellent pair of black high-top sneakers. The only flaw was that the original owner crossed paths with some spray paint, leaving fine speckles of white. The black marker covered these perfectly.

• After the paint wears off white leather sneakers, I had thought they were hopeless. But a newsletter reader alerted me to a spray paint called Sneaker White Refinish by Kiwi. It enabled her to get an additional six months wear out of her old sneakers. We picked up a 4.5-ounce spray can for $2.98. It yielded enough paint to cover two pairs of badly worn, size-8 high-tops. The product lasts longer if used sparingly on lightly scuffed sneakers. You have to mask off any stripes and logos, but the paint covers the sides of the rubber soles nicely. (As a comparison experiment, I also painted a sneaker with regular flat white spray paint and another with gloss white. Neither produced a satisfactory finish.) Because the Kiwi paint costs about $1.50 per major overhaul, I would use it only for light touch-ups. This paint is a little hard to find but it's sold in some sporting goods stores.

• The downfall of vinyl sneakers occurs when they begin to crack where the toe bends. Once this happens the sneaker can deteriorate rapidly. The process can be slowed with Shoe Goo, a clear, flexible shoe-repair glue sold in sporting goods stores. I force a little glue under the crack while it's still small.

• Any top-stitched stripes that have become too loose or frayed to glue back into place can be removed altogether.

• Holes in the cloth tongue can be resewn. A fabric rim at the top of the shoe that has become separated can be repaired with a combination of gluing and sewing.

As a final note, if I were going to buy new sneakers for a boy, I would buy black high-tops for three reasons: black is easier to maintain than white; black sneakers can double for "dress shoes" in a pinch; and high-top sneakers are terrific for concealing those slightly too-short slacks.

CREATE A DINNER CASSEROLE

When confronted by an odd collection of leftovers, the typical tightwad response is to make them into leftover soup.

But Maria Kleinberg of Sterling Heights, Michigan, offers another alternative. This universal casserole recipe can use up a wide variety of ingredients, with impressive results.

1 cup main ingredient
1 cup second ingredient
1–2 cups starchy ingredient
1½ cups binder
¼ cup "goodie"
Seasoning
Topping

Main ingredient suggestions: tuna, cubed chicken, turkey, ham, seafood.

Second ingredient suggestions: thinly sliced celery, mushrooms, peas, chopped hard-cooked eggs.

Starchy ingredient suggestions: thinly sliced potatoes, cooked noodles, cooked rice.

Binder suggestions: cream sauce, sour cream, can of soup.

"Goodie" suggestions: pimiento, olives, almonds, water chestnuts.

Topping suggestions: potato chips, cheese, bread crumbs.

Thoroughly mix your combinations of the above ingredients. If it seems dry, add ½ cup milk or stock. Place in buttered casserole dish and bake at 350 degrees for 30 to 45 minutes.

In the Dacyczyn household we routinely concoct casseroles. We almost always use a white-sauce variation as a binder because it's cheaper than sour cream or canned soup. This can be found in any basic cookbook. The "goodies" are optional, as they are generally expensive foods.

DRIVE THE FREE WAY

As a general rule, the cheapest way to go from one city to another is by car, particularly for a group of people, or for one person with stuff to transport. But what if you don't have a car or, for whatever reason, you would rather not use your own car?

An excellent alternative is the "drive-away" car. Several companies with offices throughout the nation offer the use of a car free of charge to make a long-distance one-way trip.

Jinx Smith, owner of the A-1 Automovers office in Phoenix, Arizona, told me that it works like this: People who want their cars driven somewhere contact their local drive-away agency. Frequently these are retirees who will fly to their seasonal vacation homes and want their car to be there when they arrive. They pay a fee of about $300 for the service.

Meanwhile, potential drivers call these agencies to find out if a car

is available to be transported to the place and at the time they desire. If so, the person fills out an application to prove that he is a safe driver, puts down a deposit of about $200, and, at least at some agencies, he must also provide a reference from both the departure and destination cities.

To ensure that he uses the car solely for transportation between two cities, the driver is given a time limit. For example, from the East to West coasts, the trip must be completed in eight days. He also must not exceed the allowed mileage by more than 10 percent. The drive-away agency pays for the first tank of fuel; generally, the driver must pay for the rest. It is also the driver's responsibility to deliver the car to a specific address in the destination city.

If you consider this idea, be sure to carefully compare the costs of the gasoline and lodging against budget plane, train, and bus fares.

Drive-away companies can be found in the Yellow Pages under "Automobile Transporters and Drive-Away Companies."

SURPRISE PIES

Dear Amy,

My family does not care for cooked carrots, but carrots are often cheap and are high in vitamins. I now use well-cooked carrots to make "pumpkin" pie. My family loves it. I use four big carrots for a pie, and milk in place of sweetened, condensed milk.

—Lois Snyder
Peru, Massachusetts

SOFT-SERVE ICE BEANS

Dear Amy,

To cook beans quickly: Soak beans overnight. Drain. Then freeze in whatever quantity you choose. (I usually do some of 4 cups and some of 2 cups.) Freeze the beans. When you cook them, they will soften easily in about 20 minutes. The reason: When they are frozen, the water expands and breaks some of the cellulose strands that hold the cells together. This is the same action that occurs when you cook beans for hours. You can shorten the cooking time even more by putting frozen beans in a pressure cooker.

—Susan Burke
Santa Rosa, California

TIGHTWAD TURNOVERS

Dear Amy,

I have another way to use Jim's "Refrigerator Dough" (page 19). I make something my family calls "Bunches of Bunches" (family joke, don't ask). I take about ¼ cup of the dough for each person, roll it out into a circle, fill with a variety of ingredients, roll it up, and pinch the ends together. Bake in a 400-degree oven for 15 minutes. It's a good way to use up leftovers. The kids can even make up their own, using the "smorgasbord" method. Our favorite combination is ham, cheese, and broccoli.

—Kelly Miller
Virginia Beach, Virginia

GUTLESS WONDERS

Dear Amy,

As a first grade teacher, I have been interested in putting together a collection of puppets, but at $10 to $30 apiece the cost seemed prohibitive. I found a solution by buying stuffed animals at yard sales and thrift stores, making 4-inch incisions in the bellies or rear ends, and taking the stuffing out. Puppets seem to have far more play value than stuffed animals do.

—Kelye Stowell
Bellevue, Washington

DUCT TAPE 101

Dear Amy,

The University of Texas at Austin has evening "informal" non-credit classes on a whole range of subjects. Last year I began teaching a one-evening, three-hour course on frugal living, and I use material from *The Tightwad Gazette* as backup support.

—Janet L. Lewis
Austin, Texas

("Adult education" or "open university" programs are common in many cities throughout the country. Other readers who are black-belt tightwads might consider developing a curriculum and offering their services to teach a frugal-living course. FZ)

KEEP TABS ON GRIME

Dear Amy,

I use plastic bread tabs to get really stuck crud off pans (i.e., meatloaf remains in a bread pan) while doing dishes. They work, and don't scratch Teflon surfaces.

—Kim Jaworski
South St. Paul, Minnesota

MORE HANG TIME

Dear Amy,

With all six of us bathing once a day and my husband showering twice daily, and each of us using a fresh towel each time, we were generating a lot of laundry.

So we have installed a special towel rack in our bathroom with a peg for each person's towel. I brought out our store of towels, and everyone got to pick their own personal towel for the rack. The only rule was that everyone had to pick a different color so we could tell them apart.

This rack has cut our towel laundry from ten loads a week to one.

—Elizabeth Case
Belfair, Washington

MONEY-BACK KNACK

Dear Amy,

Most big-ticket items are sold with a guarantee. But many small-ticket items are also sold with guarantees that most people ignore because they figure it would be too hard to collect. The usual catch is that you must have the purchase receipt. Well, I simply have a file for such receipts, and about once a year I cull it for ones that are no longer useful. Recently I returned about 35 sprinkler heads that were of inferior quality and very clogged after one season, and got my money back. About four years ago my wife bought two washable throw rugs with rubber backing that had five-year guarantees. Imagine the surprise at the department store service desk when we came in with two frayed rugs and sales receipts from 1990!

—Jonathan Kennedy
Lancaster, California

MORE HANG TIME II

Dear Amy,

I used to hang shirts on the line with hangers, but they would blow off. My father-in-law solved the problem. He put a length of chain on the end of one of the lines. Now, I hook the hangers in the links. I can hang a lot of shirts in a small space, and they stay put until I take them down.

—Phyllis Wamack
Mt. Victory, Ohio

MOTEL SICKS

Dear Amy,

My husband needed arm surgery. The hospital was one and a half hours away over mountain passes. He needed to stay for 27 days. I stayed in his room for 20 days. If I had stayed in a hotel room across the street, it would have cost $68 a night, or $1,360 for 20 days. If your hospital does not allow this, maybe it's time to change their attitude.

—Thea Lou Seese
Mt. Shasta, California

A TALE OF TIGHTWAD TRANSFORMATION

Whenever *The Tightwad Gazette* examines everyday family life, the family that is examined is mine. Readers have, over the years, become intimately acquainted with how we live our frugal, happy life. Aside from little snippets that appear in reader letters, they generally don't get a peek into the lives of other readers.

I, however, frequently do see into the lives of these others, as people write to share the changes they have made in their lives. We have their letters in a fat file that we've labeled "Success Stories."

Readers say that what they've learned from *The Tightwad Gazette* has allowed them to, among other things, keep their homes despite a job loss, avoid bankruptcy, pay off huge credit-card debts, and/or cut their food bills in half.

I've refrained from publishing any of these letters because I

didn't want to appear to be patting myself on the back. But the downside of never highlighting success stories is that skeptical readers may not understand that the basic ideas in the newsletter work for others, and so could work for them, too. In short, I've been explaining the method, but I've never shown that the method works for anyone but us.

So I decided, just for once, to make an exception and highlight one successful reader's experience. Karen Lee of University City, Missouri, sent me a typical success story. Her letter is unusually rich in detail and outlines some of the basics that just about anyone can do to make a start.

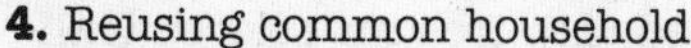

She begins her letter by pointing out that, when she first came across my book and newsletter, she was "a miserable spendthrift, in debt, and a working mother." My book inspired her to "do the math" and discover that her working outside the home caused her family to simply break even, and sometimes even lose money. So she quit her job and incorporated many basic lifestyle changes that produced immediate results, such as:

1. Making school lunches every day.

2. Cooking from scratch. She also figures the cost of meals and records it on the recipes, next to each ingredient, with the total at the bottom. This allows her to record price changes of the ingredients.

3. Going to garage sales. She had never done it before, although she had shopped at thrift stores. She noted that thrift-store merchandise is usually priced higher than yard-sale stuff, so she keeps track of the stores' sale days and goes then.

4. Reusing common household items, including Ziploc bags, aluminum foil, and bread bags.

5. Using a price book for purchasing groceries. She also uses it to track prices of yard-sale merchandise and school supplies.

6. Using a freezer.

7. Buying in bulk.

8. Setting up and using a pantry under the basement stairs. Her husband made it from scavenged shelves, along with screws, nuts, and bolts that he already had or had scavenged.

9. Using the library much more. Children who met reading quotas at her library received the following, at no cost: a swimming party, a sleep-over at the library, a mini-circus with trained animals and birds, a carnival with horses and

pony rides, coupons for free fast food, a pizza party, a paperback of choice, and coupons for nearby theme parks.

10. Buying kids' shoes used.

11. Being more creative about birthday parties. For her daughter Christy's tenth birthday, Karen made pizza dough, used homemade sauce, had the guests top their individual pizzas, and then baked the pizzas in metal pie plates. The kids then ate a scratch cake decorated with frosting colored with paste coloring. Finally they watched a rented video and had a sleep-over. For the ninth birthday of her other daughter, Cassie, they went to a public-school-sponsored flea market. Each guest was given a small amount of money to spend. What they bought ended up as their party favors. Then they came back home for scratch cake.

12. Having her kids make economic choices. Karen and her husband provide what she calls "the basics of life," while her daughters figure out ways to come up with their own extras. If her kids want to buy something, they either work for the money or sell something of theirs.

13. Entertaining themselves, spending little or no money. Examples: free concerts, parks, garage-sale board games. They are also active in church activities.

14. Gardening.

15. Cutting her family's hair.

Karen goes on to list the benefits that she now enjoys as a result of making these changes:

1. She doesn't have to deal with the stress of working outside the home and putting her kids into child care.

2. Her family eats better, healthier, cheaper food. Their food bill has gone from $81 to $38 a week and continues to drop.

3. They are greatly reducing their consumer debt, incurred during her working years. She and her husband, Rudy, "no longer wake up in the middle of the night in a cold sweat . . . on those nights when we could get to sleep."

4. They enjoy family activities that they didn't have time for before.

5. She has learned how to cook (at age 38!).

6. Her kids have set new lunch trends at school. She says other kids try to trade store-bought granola bars, fruit snacks, and pudding cups for her girls' pineapple muffins, pumpkin bread, homemade granola, and oatmeal-applesauce bars. As she puts it, "This got so bad I had to pass out recipes to other mothers and make a rule about no trading."

7. Her girls learned quickly about cost and value. Now when they want to buy their own books, they get them at garage sales or at a specific, extremely cheap thrift store. After they've read them, they sell them to the used-book store for as much or more than they paid. If they want a brand-new outfit, they use their birthday money (from relatives). They keep their clothes, books, and toys nicer so they can sell them to the appropriate resale shop. And they can always do jobs around the house to earn money. They do not get an allowance.

8. Her daughter Christy no longer asks, "Are you babysitting me tonight?" and "When can we have an appointment?" Karen says that when she worked, she actually had to make appointments with

her girls and write their names in her appointment book.

9. Karen and her daughters will be able to drive to Florida this month and see Karen's mom.

10. They are happier and life is fun.

DISCONCERTING CONCERT

A brief note to add to your "We've Got a Long Way to Go" file:

Nancy Hallock of Delmar, New York, sent me a clipping from the *Albany Times Union* newspaper. It's a column by Fred LeBrun in which he contrasts the aftermaths of the Woodstock festivals of 1969 and 1994.

He writes that after the original Woodstock 25 years ago, "for the most part the ground was littered, after 500,000 passed through, with what is traditionally considered garbage and trash. . . . Very little useful gear, belongings, or food was purposely discarded. Waste not, want not was still ingrained and passed down to the great-grandchildren of the Depression."

But, describing the more recent Woodstock event, he writes: "I stopped counting at 200 the tents left standing and abandoned at Woodstock '94, a fraction of the total, many of them brand new, the boxes they came in ground into the clay alongside. Thousands of sleeping bags were strewn about, muddy and still wet but otherwise whole and reusable after a good cleaning. Duffel bags full of clothing, backpacks with keys and books, just left behind." He theorizes that the participants found it "too much work to lug all that wet stuff back again. So they left it. Mommy and Daddy will buy another."

It's a grim story, but there is, at least, one hopeful note. "By early afternoon and with the roads reopened, the locals were on the scene in growing numbers with pickups and vans, doing their own heavy-duty recycling."

Sounds good to me, I'll meet you the day after the closing of Woodstock III in the year 2019.

SKINFLINT SKIN CARE

When it comes to a "skin-care regimen," there are three basic approaches:

1. Using a vast variety of expensive astringents, toners, clay masks, scrubs, wrinkle creams, and other stuff, the benefits of which are heavily promoted by manufacturers.

2. Using homemade, "tightwad" alternatives to such products, such as cornmeal scrubs and banana/honey/egg-white masks, the benefits of which are heavily promoted by authors of numerous budget skin-regimen books.

3. Using a few basic, inexpensive products.

Personally, I follow number 3, but I'm the first to admit that I'm no expert and maybe I *would* look more "radiant" if I "sloughed off" those dead skin cells.

Some investigation led me to a book that has all the answers. It's *The Look You Like,* written by Linda Shoen (Marcel Dekker Inc., 1989). It was sponsored by the American Academy of Dermatologists and answers 500 questions about skin and hair care.

The bottom line? Shoen says

whole ranges of products that are marketed for skin care offer little or no benefit, and their "tight-waddy" alternatives are no more useful. In fact, the author expresses concern about home-made alternatives, which, she feels, are more apt to cause problems. Some of the ingredients used can be allergenic or irritating. These concoctions may also lack the preservatives necessary to control contamination by bacteria and fungus.

First, let's look at the products we don't need:

Scrubs. Also called exfoliators, these are designed to remove dead skin cells with a mild abrasive. They come in the form of abrasive cleansers, special sponges, or pumice stones. Homemade/alternative advocates suggest using oatmeal, baking soda, cornmeal, or sugar. The truth is that there is little evidence that these do more than can be achieved with a wash-cloth—the results are more psychological than anything else. If you use them too frequently, too vigorously, or have dry skin, scrubs can irritate your skin.

Masks. Traditional masks are made of clay products. They are said to help minimize wrinkles, improve texture, shrink and unplug pores, stimulate circulation, and smooth and refresh the skin. But the actual benefits are few. They may make your skin feel better, but only for a few minutes to a few hours. Clay masks do have some cleansing ability, but so does soap. Some "masks" marketed for people with dry skin are actually just lubricating films that have the same effect as moisturizers. As for the homemade masks, most of the ingredients are more effective when used in your muffins.

Astringents. Also called toners, fresheners, or clarifying lotions, these are supposed to be applied after cleaning your face to remove oil, or between cleanings to "refresh" the skin. Suggested cheap alternatives include witch hazel, cucumber, rubbing alcohol, and peppermint. One of the supposed benefits of astringents is that they "shrink" pores. Actually, they irritate your skin so that the area around the pores swells temporarily, making the pores appear to shrink. While astringents do remove oil, they don't stop your skin from producing more oil. Actually, astringents provide the same benefit as washing with soap and water. If you have extremely oily skin, you can use an astringent pad at times when it's inconvenient to wash, such as when at work. Because astringents contain alcohol, which dries the skin, people with dry skin should avoid them.

Wrinkle creams. There's no proof that any nonprescription cream, lotion, or gel will remove wrinkles. (The only topical product that appears to be of benefit is retinoic acid, which must be prescribed by a doctor.) Because wrinkles are primarily caused by exposure to sunlight, the best product to prevent them is a maximum sunblock cream, SPF 15 or higher.

Now, let's look at products that are useful:

Cold creams and cleansing lotions. These products are beneficial for removing makeup, especially the waterproof type. These are also useful for cleaning if your skin is too dry for frequent washing with soap and water. If you have oily skin, follow these with soap and water.

Soap and water. With the exception of the above uses for cold cream, soap and water are adequate for most cleaning. The choice of soap depends on skin type and personal preference. For some people, regular bath soaps are fine. Soap for oily skin is more efficient at removing oil, and soap for dry skin is less efficient. However, a moisturizing bar is not a substitute for a moisturizer. Bar soaps clean as well as expensive liquid facial soaps.

Moisturizers. Also called emollients and lubricants, these are said to speed cell renewal, improve "microcirculation," or retard aging. They don't. Instead, they do make dry skin smoother and softer by putting a film of oil on your skin to hold in the natural moisture. If your skin is oily, you may not need a moisturizer. If you do use a moisturizer, it need not be expensive. The September 1994 *Consumer Reports* magazine reveals that the cheapest moisturizers are among the most effective. Inexpensive body lotions may be harsher but can be used if your skin doesn't react negatively. Petroleum jelly also works, but it doesn't accept makeup as well as other kinds of moisturizers.

In short, despite the hype, you don't need a lot of money—or a lot of bananas—to have healthy skin.

THE PIE CHART

Pie-making is a "grandma skill" that I was determined to master. Even once I had, I still found making pies to be a bit time-consuming. I've found three ways to save time:

1. Draft help. I've taught Alec to make pies. He made his first lattice-top strawberry-rhubarb pie with almost no supervision when he was just ten years old.

2. Practice. People get discouraged by slow early attempts. Speed comes with practice.

3. Mass-produce. As with other frugal activities, you can save hours of labor if you do a lot all at once. In pie-making, for instance, much of the work is in the cleanup, and cleanup time is the same for 1 pie as it is for 12; I have made as many as 12 at one time.

Apply this basic system to the type of pie that is cheapest for you to make. I'll focus on pumpkin pies, because pumpkins are my free resource.

Crust mass production. Crust-making was my biggest stumbling block in learning to make pies. My humble

goal was a crust that wouldn't fall apart when I lifted it into the tin. For years, I would ask every successful pie-maker what the secret was, and each offered a different answer. I finally found that the

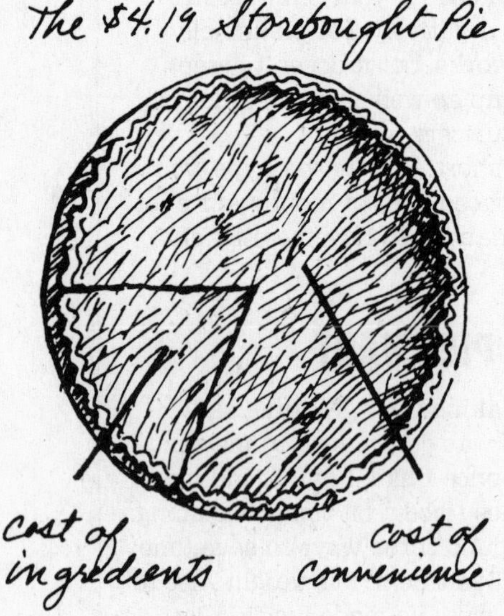

trick was to avoid overmixing the dough. I do this by mixing the dough with two knives in a scissor-action until the pieces are the size of small peas. It should also be just moist enough to hold together. I use Fannie Farmer's basic recipe and Crisco shortening, though I know others who have had success with oil or lard.

I always make enough crusts for at least four one-crust pies. I either use them all immediately or I freeze the surplus as one-crust-portion balls of dough. You could also put the crusts into aluminum pie tins and freeze them. My grandmother has rolled out crusts, covered them with plastic wrap, rolled them up on empty paper-towel tubes, and stored them in her freezer.

I also have a bag in my freezer for pastry scraps. When I accumulate enough scraps, I make a tough-crusted quiche. (Rerolled dough is always tougher.) When I clean up my pastry surface, I scrape up and save the excess flour and dough bits to be used in my next batch of muffins.

Recently I made six one-crust pie crusts in 30 minutes, including cleanup time; that's five minutes per crust. The cost per crust was about 8¢. The cheapest ready-made frozen crusts we could find were 63¢ each.

Pumpkin puree mass production. We grow our own pumpkins and butternut squashes. When we harvest them in the fall, our freezer is already packed full, but they will store for many months in a cool, dry place. We lack the perfect place to store them, so they begin to develop soft spots by midwinter—about the time our freezer begins to empty out.

So that's when I crank up the pumpkin-puree factory. I cut the slightly soft pumpkins into big chunks with an electric knife. I cut up the harder squashes by whacking my big knife through them with a mallet. Then I cut the peel off the chunks, and cut the peeled chunks into 1-inch pieces. I fill my largest pot with pieces, fill the pot halfway with water, cook until soft, and drain. I puree the cooked chunks in my food processor, but you could also use a potato masher or a blender. Some people find it easier to bake or microwave raw, seeded pumpkin halves until soft, then scoop out the flesh. I freeze the puree in pint containers.

Last year I put up 16 pints in two hours of hands-on time. Throw

in another hour for gardening and handling time, and it takes about 15 minutes to produce a pint of pumpkin puree. A store-bought pint (a 16-ounce can) costs about 80¢.

Pie mass production. In the spring my freezer is emptier still, allowing me to store even bulkier items, so that's when I crank up the pumpkin-pie factory.

With six crusts and the proper amount of puree thawed, it takes me another 15 minutes to make pumpkin-pie filling, fill the crusts, put all six pies in my large oven, and clean up. (I bake pumpkin pies before freezing to help them "set up." Fruit pies can be frozen unbaked.) I use a standard recipe, except instead of evaporated milk I use either whole milk, or powdered milk made with half the usual water. The pie assembly requires 2½ minutes per pie.

A relative who worked in a school cafeteria collected a large quantity of used, tiny aluminum pie tins for me. I wash the tins and use them to make little pies for lunch boxes. I've made as many as 64 of these at a time.

Pie storage. I put the cooked, cooled pies in the freezer, uncovered. Once they are frozen, I wrap them in plastic wrap and stack them in the freezer. The little pies stack nicely in bread bags.

Pie economics. The bottom line is, how much time does it take, and how much money do you save, by making your own mass-produced pies as compared to buying them? The following costs-per-pie include the cost of baking in an electric oven at 12¢ per kilowatt-hour. The "hourly wage" figures are based on a comparison to a store-bought 9-inch pumpkin pie that cost $4.19.

1. Store-bought crust and store-bought puree: costs $2.09 and requires 2½ minutes per pie. Hourly wage: $50.40.

2. Homemade crust and store-bought puree: costs $1.54 and requires 7½ minutes per pie. Hourly wage: $21.20.

3. Homemade crust and home-made puree: costs 74¢ and requires 17½ minutes per pie. Hourly wage: $11.83.

These figures show that even extraordinarily busy people should consider making pies with ready-made components rather than buying a premade pie. But don't let these hourly wages confuse you. Strategy 3, the one with the lowest hourly wage, still saves you the most money per pie.

DIRECTORY RESISTANCE

If you want to list your phone number in the Yellow Pages, you have to fork over a hefty fee. But in the white pages, it works just the opposite way—it costs extra to have an *un*listed number. The fee is $1 a month in my area.

Two readers offered a way to get a free "unlisted" number: give the phone company a listing name that's not your real name.

Anthony Willett of Annandale, Virginia, says his family is listed under his wife's maiden name. He says an unexpected side benefit is that the sales calls always ask for someone with his wife's maiden name. (The Willetts' reply: "She's not here.") They also throw away, unopened, all mail that comes addressed to the wife's maiden name, reasoning that a junk mailer

picked the name out of the phone book.

Another reader, who asked to remain anonymous, made up the name of a fictitious "roommate."

Sally Pelletier, customer service representative for my local phone company, said most phone companies allow customers to choose any name at all, even a fictitious one, for their listing, as long as they give their real name for billing.

Pelletier could think of only one possible hazard of this practice. In an emergency (such as when a person is rendered unconscious or killed), police can quickly submit a subpoena to the phone company to get the person's number if it's unlisted in the traditional way. She said if the number is under a fake name, the police would have no way of learning the person's phone number, unless he carried it along with his other identification.

WHAT TO DO WITH . . .

A soda bottle. Make a drip catcher for a cooler that has a spout near the bottom. Cut bottle diagonally. Then cut a horizontal slot in bottle to fit over the vertical spout. (Marliss Bombardier, Great Bend, Kansas)

Bread tabs. Use to mark various electrical cords in remote places, such as behind the entertainment center. (John Cant, Blauvelt, New York)

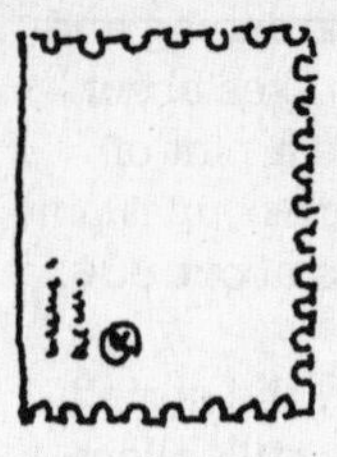

Blank stamps that come on the end of a sheet of postage stamps. Use to label jars of homemade jelly. (Martha Farley, Evanston, Illinois)

Old magazines. Make a booster seat by taping a stack together and covering with fabric. (Marie Rippel, Grayslake, Illinois)

Old baby gates. Use for drying rack for sweaters that need to dry flat. Simply place over tub. (Debra J. Brock, Rialto, California)

A dead refrigerator. Remove adjustable shelves and drawers. Discard fridge. (Be sure to remove door first.) Reuse shelves and drawers for garage storage by mounting on wall. (Bonnie Finch, Pueblo, Colorado)

Fruit peelings and apple cores. Save in a bag in freezer. To make house smell great, put some of each type of peeling in a saucepan, cover with water, add a little cinnamon, and simmer. (Sheri Youngquist, Newark, California)

Squeeze containers that white glue and mustard come in. Use for cake decorating. The tips can be cut with a sharp knife to make different designs. (Maria Ferris, Bernville, Pennsylvania)

A large plastic toy-store bag. Use to make disposable painting smock for child. Cut head and arm holes. (Barbara Kaloydis, Fenton, Michigan)

A wine cork. Use to replace missing handle on pot lid. Attach with a screw. (Anne Hedian, Rockville, Maryland)

A milk jug. Cut off and discard bottom third. Use as a microwave splatter-shield. (Jean Fountain, Iowa City, Iowa)

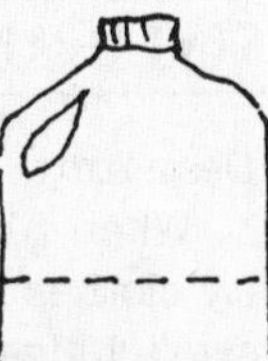

A mesh onion bag. Use for storing cookie cutters. Dirty cutters in an onion bag can go on top shelf of dishwasher for easy cleaning.

Plastic tubing. Use to replace a missing handle on a lunch box. Attach by threading line through the tubing.

Old blue jeans. Make carrier for snow chains. Cut off pant legs to "shorts" length and sew legs closed. Put one chain in each leg. Make handles by putting rope or webbing through belt loops. Store gloves, tighteners, etc. in pockets. (Dorothy Jones, Seattle, Washington)

Old T-shirts. Cut into long strip 2 inches wide. Stretch this so that it curls to make a cord. Crochet into hot mats, doormats, and even baskets. Use colored shirts to create designs. (Heather Jack, Thomaston, Maine)

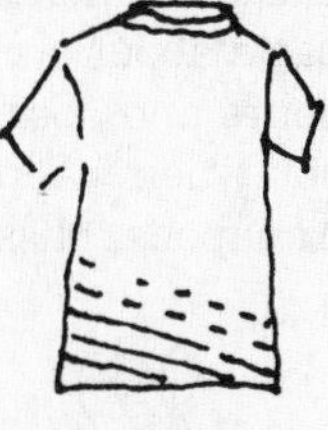

Used dryer sheets. Use as backing for embroidery instead of buying "stabilizers." Depending on the project, the sheets can be left in place or cut away. (Mary Frances Jablonskis, Westchester, Illinois)

Plastic bags of all types. Collect in burlap bag and use as an archery target. Plastic bags will stop the arrow, but allow it to be removed easily. (John Matejov, Story, Wyoming)

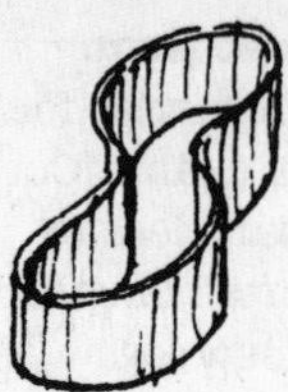

Broccoli rubber bands. Use for a jar or bottle opener. Place band on lid and twist. (Beverly Kendall, Seattle, Washington)

Bubble wrap. Those who spend their days on their feet can use sections for insole cushioning. Lasts about six hours and doesn't pop when walking. (Trish Luthro, Annapolis, Missouri)

Holey rubber gloves. Cut into sections, these make great rubber bands, which can be custom-cut for specific uses. Fingers make small ones, cuffs make large ones. (Norma Tabbi, Amherst, New York)

Dried-up oil-based paints in paint-by-number kits. If you don't have turpentine on hand, try a little vegetable oil. Adding too much will make the paint too thin. (Valerie Smith, Chicago, Illinois)

EYE A PEEL

Dear Amy,

I took this idea from restaurants that sell potato peelings as appetizers. Scrub your potatoes well and peel with a knife, trying to get large pieces. Place peels in a bowl and add salt, pepper, garlic, and onion powder. Grease a cookie sheet and place the skins on it. Bake in a hot oven at about 400 degrees for eight to ten minutes or until done. Remove from oven, sprinkle with grated cheese, then return to oven just until cheese melts.

—Sarah Flemming
Gulfport, Mississippi

REVEAL APPEAL

Dear Amy,

When I hit a sale that has quality clothes in one of my children's sizes, I give the party "my card" (one half of an index card with my name, number, and "Garage Sale" written on it). I ask them to please give me a call the next time they are having a sale. You would be surprised how many "sneak previews" you get this way.

—Kris Jergenson
Hokah, Minnesota

ALL ON ABOARD!

Dear Amy,

If you live near a college or university, utilize their "ride board." It's usually hanging in the student center. Students hang cards indicating where they desire to go, or where they are driving. When I drive out of town, I share the gas expense with someone who needs an inexpensive mode of travel. I have met several wonderful babysitters by taking college students along when we drive to Grandma's house, three and a half hours away.

—Julie Minasian
Evanston, Illinois

STANKLESS STEEL

Dear Amy,

Many "kitchen gadget" stores carry a stainless-steel bar, which costs about $10, for a cook to use to rid his or her hands of pungent smells. I have found that *any* stainless-steel item does the trick. After working with garlic, onions, or fish, I rub my hands over a stainless-steel spoon under running water and the smells are gone!

—Jennifer Eldredge
San Rafael, California

LOW-PAY SPRAY

Dear Amy,

Do you like the convenience of spray-on cooking oil such as Pam but hate the price? Pam costs $2.69 for 6 ounces and contains only vegetable oil, grain alcohol, and lecithin. On sale, I can get a half-gallon (64 ounces) of vegetable oil for $2.69. I mix 5 ounces of oil with 1 ounce of vodka (because it is fairly odorless, tasteless, and clear), shake well, and spray. Use either a recycled Pam pump bottle or a purchased small spray bottle. It works like magic. My 6-ounce bottle cost me 49¢ to make.

—Penny Rapp
Louisville, Kentucky

(Some readers have suggested using plain oil in a spray bottle. Others have suggested adding some liquid lecithin from a health food store, but this raises the price considerably. Results may vary due to differences in spray bottles and the quality of ingredients. Try plain oil first and add other ingredients if you don't get satisfactory results. FZ)

CURE FOR SMALL BOX

Dear Amy,

When my husband needed to mail a new, small appliance recently, he took the item out of its original box, turned the box inside out, and taped it back together. He then had a plain cardboard box that was just the right size. The item came with plenty of padding, which we simply left in the box to cushion it.

—Maria Veres Homic
Austin, Texas

WALL-TO-WALL VOILA

Dear Amy,

We save big bucks on carpet cleaning by using our wet-dry shop vacuum instead of renting a commercial carpet cleaner, which costs $18 for four hours in our area. We buy the liquid carpet cleaner sold for the rental machines and mix according to label directions. Using a garden watering can with sprinkler head, we wet down the carpet lightly with the mix, then vacuum immediately with the shop vacuum set on "wet pickup." This works quite well.

—Cindy Kroon
Hartford, South Dakota

SOFA, SO GOOD

Dear Amy,

I work in an upholstery shop. I have learned that there is an awful lot of waste in this business. Through the years, people from the elderly down to Boy Scouts have asked for remnants for crafts and miscellaneous items. We ask them to bring by a paper bag, and when we are actually cutting, we conveniently drop scraps into the bag. The scraps range in size from 2 inches by 2 inches to 18 inches by 18 inches (we do this only when the customer does not want the scraps). All shops may not do this, but it doesn't hurt to ask.

—Mary Manly
Jacksonville, Florida

CLEAN YOUR PLATE

Dear Amy,

I am a dentist. I advise my patients to clean their removable partial dentures and complete dentures by soaking them overnight in vinegar and water and brushing them with baking soda in the morning. Obviously, this is cheaper than using Efferdent.

—Rose Mathews
Scottsdale, Arizona

REPOSE AND REPOSITION

Dear Amy,

I just purchased a new mattress and box spring—a major purchase, so I want it to last as long as possible. In the past, I've never been able to recall which way to turn it next. The mattress has four possible positions, so I marked the corners 1, 2, 3, and 4 with waterproof markers. I only have to see that the next number is in the corner near my pillow.

—Kathleen Hendrix
Goleta, California

(Another way to remember: "Spin in the spring, flip in the fall." FZ)

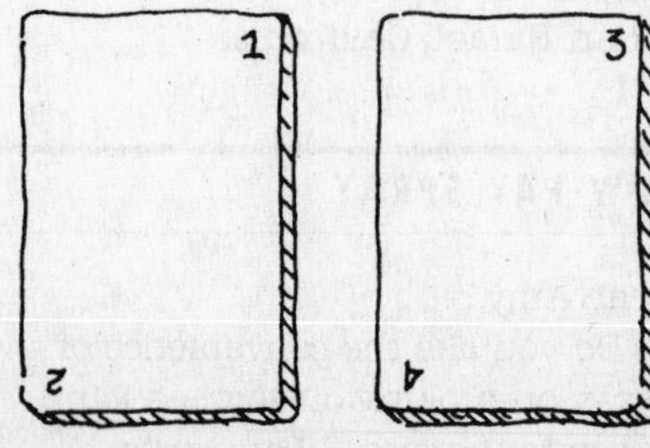

THE CLOVE COMPARTMENT

Dear Amy,

In place of sweet, sickening car air fresheners, I use cloves in the ashtrays. Any health food store that carries bulk items will have cloves. An ounce costs about 25¢. I have put cloves into each of my car's ashtrays for about 31¢ total. It is long lasting and very aromatic.

—Steven Lavender
West Palm Beach, Florida

ROUND ROBIN REDUX

Dear Amy,

With our six children spread all over the United States and in foreign lands, we used to use the "Round Robin" method of correspondence (explained on page 236) to keep in touch. For the past couple of years we have successfully used a variation; admittedly it's a little more expensive, but it's still reasonable and much more timely. Ours is the "Radiating Robin," and we, the parents, are the hub. The kids mail us a letter on the first Sunday of each month. We then make six photocopies of each and mail a set to each individual within the next week. I had a copy shop run off labels with the kids' addresses to make mailing easier.

—Gail Jackson
Blue Springs, Missouri

IMAGINING HOLIDAY PERFECTION . . . OR TRY IT, YULE LIKE IT

If I were the master of the universe, I would change all of the rules for holiday gift-giving. In my tightwad utopia, I would decree the following:

- Gifts shall not be given simply for the sake of giving a gift.
- Gifts shall be given only according to each individual's resources and inspiration.
- If an individual receives a gift from someone for whom he doesn't have a gift, no one shall care.
- The merits of a gift shall be based on thoughtfulness, cleverness, and appropriateness, not on the amount of money spent or whether it came from a store.
- If an individual is a regular recipient of a gift from a close friend or relative, it shall be acceptable for the recipient to suggest a gift idea that would be free and easy for the giver.

I am not the master of the universe, so the world will probably never be as I would like. I am, however, the "benevolent boss" of a much smaller realm: a company called *The Tightwad Gazette.* While we have no company policy on gift-giving, I've encouraged certain attitudes among my handful of employees. In the aftermath of one company party, I sat and viewed the explosion of wrappings, reflected on the gifts, and glowed. I thought, "This is the way everyone's Christmas should be." So, I want to share the specifics of what everyone did:

During the previous fall, I had suggested something that Elaine, our former business manager,

could do for me for Christmas. My great-grandmother knitted mittens for us every Christmas when we were young. I failed to appreciate them completely back then, but had become nostalgic for them in my adult years. A few years ago I came into the possession of a pair of child-sized mittens my great-grandmother had begun more than 25 years earlier. Although all the yarn was there, one mitten was only half finished. Elaine is an excellent knitter, so I asked if she would complete the mittens for me as my Christmas gift. She was pleased at my suggestion because it was an easy gift for her to give. So I received the completed mittens, and Elaine's work is indistinguishable from my great-grandmother's.

Elaine had a special relationship with my then five-year-old daughter, Rebecca. For Becca's previous birthday, Elaine had made matching yellow aprons for them to wear when cooking together at the office. Before Christmas, Becca wanted to make a present for Elaine. So I helped Becca make a pastel drawing of her and Elaine in their matching aprons, baking cookies. This was made to fit into an existing secondhand frame, which Becca and I also refinished. The picture now hangs in Elaine's office.

David, who ran our addressing machine, pleased and surprised us with simple, wooden, cut-out and painted ornaments of his own design, frugally wrapped in small brown bags.

I collect old blue-and-white dishes. Pam, a multipurpose employee, bought a lovely, large blue-and-white antique teacup at a yard sale as a gift for me. The cup has a rural scene painted on the outside; inside is a painted dog that resembles our own dog, Charlie. I love it.

In contrast to those of us who dress primarily for economy and comfort, Holly, our Generation X data-entry person, dresses far more stylishly. It has become an employee joke to tease Holly by asking her for fashion advice. Holly's husband works for a men's clothing store, and with his employee discount she was able to purchase several pairs of marked-down, loud-colored plaid socks for $1 each. She gave these as joke presents, and naturally we pretended to have complete faith in her fashion advice and wore them to work for weeks.

Frances, who opens our mail, came to me a month before Christmas and asked me if she could barter a few cuts of her home-grown beef, which she had in surplus, for newsletter subscriptions she could give to people on her list. The swap would have messed up our company bookkeeping, and the bartered cost of the meat exceeded the amount we customarily pay. So I declined and reminded her that in addition to a Christmas bonus, employees are entitled to give away a certain number of free subscriptions. But I also subtly indicated that surplus beef makes a nice gift. We enjoyed ten pounds of her beef last winter.

Many of the adults gave our children yard-sale finds. Brad was thrilled with his recorder and tooted around the house for hours. Becca received an enormous pile of yard-sale jewelry from Elaine. Elaine, a lover of books, bought Jamie, my lover of books, a stack from a library-book sale. Pam picked up some coloring books at yard sales, which had just a few pictures already colored and some odd pencil markings. She carefully cut out the colored-on pages, erased the pencil markings, and gave my kids the like-new books. Alec received a new football-shaped soap-on-a-rope from a yard sale, and a carpenter's apron from a mail-order source which had discounted it to $1.

Blanche, another mail opener, gave our children a selection of small gifts she had purchased from a salvage store. She gave other employees homemade wreaths and craft items she had purchased at discount from a relative who makes them.

Pam likes old comic books. When Elaine went into the comic book store she found used ones for 25¢ each, and she bought a pile for Pam.

Frances is an excellent cook and gave various coworkers homemade jams, salsas, and pickles. Frances also made "jelly-bean prescription jars." The jars are filled with variously colored gourmet jelly beans and include "instructions." Each color is designated with a special cure that is relevant to the recipient, such as "Green is good for memory improvement."

Elaine gave Jim a volume of "Far Side" comics and another of "Doonesbury." These used books were slightly worn, but the jokes were still good.

One of the downsides of my minor-celebrity status is that I get spotted when I go to area yard sales. This is a problem, as I find it difficult to negotiate while blushing. As a joke present, Jim made me a pair of "anonymous glasses." He popped the lenses out of an old pair of sunglasses and then covered the frame with a huge rectangle of black felt. He cut tiny holes for me to see through. Then, because I have a tendency to lose earrings, he attached large brass fishing lures to the sides.

While I've highlighted some of the successful gifts, as with all gift-giving, there was, undoubtedly, a gift or two that missed the mark. But part of the pleasure of frugal gift-giving (and receiving) is that when the wrong gift is given, it's comforting to know that little or no money was wasted.

My situation may seem unique, but it really isn't. Every business, and every family, has one or two people who set the tone, either by domineering, or by (my style) gentle, kindly, unrelenting persuasion. I wish you success in persuading the people in your own "realm."

AN ITCHING, BURNING QUESTION

I have often written on the cost advantage of used shoes. People usually raise two objections to them. In *The Tightwad Gazette II,* I quoted experts who cast serious doubt on one of these objections: that used shoes can structurally damage feet. The second question concerns the possible spread of athlete's foot.

To check this out, I talked with Dr. Donald Greer, a professor in the department of dermatology and pathology at Louisiana State University. Dr. Greer might rightly be regarded as "Mr. Athlete's Foot." He has conducted several in-depth studies on the subject, and has been recommended by the National Institutes of Health as a leading authority.

He said that while it's theoretically possible to be infected by an athlete's foot fungus in a used shoe, "the probability is almost nil." And, he told me, a couple of simple precautions can eliminate even the remote chance of infection.

Dr. Greer said four conditions are needed for athlete's foot to develop: natural susceptibility (and no one knows what causes this), warm temperature, high humidity, and occlusion (being covered up, such as by a fairly airtight shoe). He said natural susceptibility is perhaps the biggest factor—if by age 30 you've never had athlete's foot, it's very unlikely you'll get it. If you are susceptible, chances are far greater that you'll reinfect yourself with your own shoes than with someone else's shoes.

He added that athlete's foot is quite rare in children, and so the spread through kids' used shoes is even more unlikely.

Dr. Greer said the organisms that cause athlete's foot can live in shoes, but only as long as the shoe remains relatively damp, as could happen over long periods in the humid Southeast. Once a shoe is completely dry, the athlete's foot fungus dies. This factor indicates why rented bowling shoes, which may swap owners within an hour, are sprayed; but why, at least in Maine, there are no laws governing the treatment of used shoes to be sold in thrift shops.

If you have any doubts about used shoes, Dr. Greer recommends these precautions:

- Run canvas sneakers through the washing machine and dryer.
- Spray the interior of leather shoes with a disinfectant such as Lysol, then dust with a drying powder such as Desenex.
- A tightwad alternative in dry climates is simply to unlace the shoe, pull back the tongue, and leave in the sun or in a hot, dry place.

Dr. Greer said he couldn't give any specific recommendations as to the length of drying time because there are too many variables. My guess is that any used shoes that have been sitting in the blistering sun on a summertime yard-sale day will be plenty dry enough.

THE PANTRY PRINCIPLE UPDATE

In my "Pantry Principle" article in *The Tightwad Gazette II,* I explained that to save the most money and time when buying food,

you should shop to replenish your pantry, not to make specific meals. That article prompted Karen Buckwalter of Palmyra, Missouri, to ask: "What must the tightwad pantry include?"

Because people have different needs, resources, and preferences, I can't prescribe "musts." Instead I offer this list of what's in our pantry and freezer as a general guideline; it's complete except for a few foods we purchase specifically for holidays and birthdays. It's as important to note what's *not* on this list as what's on it.

Baking supplies: Baking powder, baking soda, salt, cocoa, yeast, coconut, sunflower seeds, soy flour, eggs, bulk-purchased gelatin, cornstarch, vinegar, paste food coloring, colored sprinkles.

Breads: Whole-wheat loaves, bagels, English muffins, saltines. (We make other breads.)

Cheese: Parmesan, cream, and hard cheeses when the price drops below $2 per pound.

Cold cereal: Any cereal when price drops to 7¢ per ounce, frequently corn flakes, rarely presweetened cereal.

Condiments: Catsup, mayonnaise, mustard. (We make jams, pickles, and relishes.)

Fats: Corn oil, olive oil, margarine, shortening, no-stick spray.

Fruits: Apples, bananas, raisins, and, occasionally, other fresh fruits when on sale. Canned pineapple and other canned fruit as it turns up in "mystery cans" from the salvage store (see page 13). (We grow strawberries and acquire blackberries, blueberries, and pears from a relative.)

Grains: White flour, whole-wheat flour, rye flour, oatmeal, cornmeal, rice, popcorn, wheat germ.

Juices: Orange, apple, grape, lemon.

Legumes: Peanut butter, dried beans, dried peas, lentils.

Meats: Chicken parts, ground beef, ground turkey, whole turkey, tuna, ham, pork shoulder, bologna, hot dogs, bacon, salami, kielbasa, and other meats when sale price is low enough. (The article on page 105, "I Wouldn't Steer You Wrong," details my basic guidelines for meat purchases.)

Milk: Dry milk, whole milk.

Nonnutritious beverages: Tea, ground coffee.

Packaged dinners: Macaroni-and-cheese.

Pasta: Spaghetti, macaroni, and other pasta when the price drops to 33¢ per pound.

Seasonings and flavorings: A large selection of herbs and spices, wine and sherry for cooking, bouillon, soy sauce, Worcestershire sauce, artificial vanilla extract, maple extract.

Sweeteners: White sugar, brown sugar, confectioners' sugar, molasses, honey, corn syrup.

Vegetables: Onions, celery, potatoes, frozen french fries, instant mashed potatoes, tomato paste. (We grow a wide range of other vegetables.)

GET A PIECE OF THE AUCTION

I generally buy used household items at two places: yard sales and estate sales. In terms of saving money, yard sales are a better use of my time. But in terms of entertainment value, estate sales win hands down.

An estate sale is an auction of the contents of a home, usually of someone who has died. Because most people who die are older, their household effects frequently include antiques and collectibles. For this reason the term "estate sale" is generally synonymous with "antique auction."

Although some of these auctions offer only a selection of antiques from several estates, a true estate sale will include merchandise ranging from the very valuable to the very useless. In between you may find rakes, vacuum cleaners, and bedding—stuff that is rare at yard sales.

Ads for estate sales appear in the Sunday paper and include a partial listing of items to be sold. On-site sales (sales at the house instead of another location) generally have more nonantique items, but not always.

Having attended the auctions of several companies, I've found that it's hard to pick a good auction by reading ads. That's because it's the auctioneer, rather than the specific merchandise, that determines the quality of the auction. Some are more entertaining, more knowledgeable, and have more talent for putting together a good event. Attend sales of several companies before deciding if there's enough fun and/or savings to make this activity worthwhile for you.

I view estate sales

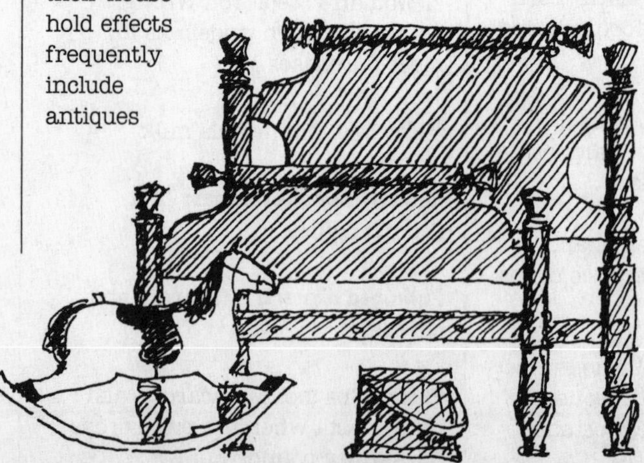

primarily as entertainment. I attend a dozen a year and purchase less than one item per sale. So to avoid hefty babysitting fees, Jim and I go separately, each with our auction buddies (good friends who enjoy old things and share a sense of adventure). We share the cost of gasoline and bring a "bag dinner." By doing this, we feel no disappointment when we come home empty-handed—we've had a good time for free.

When you go, arrive early to get a bidding card with your number and to preview the sale. Carefully inspect the merchandise for quality and condition, and note the item's lot number when similar items are to be sold. At this point, make a mental note as to the top price you'd pay for the item—you don't want to decide this during the bidding frenzy. Also learn the sales terms. For instance, some auctions tack on a 10 percent buyer's premium to the price you've bid.

It's a good idea to attend several auctions before you bid on anything. Not only will you get a good feel for how it's done, but you'll also get a sense of the price things bring at auctions and how common certain kinds of merchandise are. For instance, you might see an old treadle sewing machine sell for $50, which seems like a steal until you discover that every other sale has a $50 treadle machine. It's more likely a beginner will regret buying than not buying, so be slow to bid.

There's no surefire strategy to "psych out" other bidders. Just stick to the top price that you've already determined.

As for the merchandise offered, I've observed four categories:

Antiques and collectibles. Because about half of auction attendees are dealers, steals are rare. Generally, dealers will not bid more than 80 percent of any item's retail value, and their presence ensures that few valuables will sell for less than 50 percent of the retail value. Exceptions can occur when nondealers bid the price higher than this range.

So think of estate sales as a source of wholesale-priced antiques. A small oak table might

sell for $35 at an estate sale, $60 at an antique shop, and $90 at an antique show. However, since I'm extremely slow to buy antiques, I primarily view the sale of antiques as educational and entertaining. It's educational because I learn about the value of antique furniture, which will help me make more intelligent purchases, from whatever source, in the future. And it's just plain entertaining to see a Civil War diary sell for $675.

Nonantique valuables. These may include appliances, boats, and snow blowers; however, you'll more often find good-quality used furniture circa 1940 through 1960, before the scourge of particleboard overtook middle-class furnishings. Because most people attending these sales are seeking antiques, this stuff can go surprisingly cheap. One of my auction buddies purchased an "inoffensive," quality maple bedroom set, including a bed frame, full-size mattress, and box spring, a writing table, and two bureaus for $280. I've never seen any furniture remotely this nice at a yard sale.

If you're blessed with "unique" tastes, you can really clean up. Ugly furniture goes breathtakingly cheap. I've seen a massive, ornate, solid-mahogany sideboy sell for $50. Formica dinettes with chairs go for $10.

Box lots. A true estate sale in which the entire contents of the house are sold will have boxes of common household items such as bedding, tools, books, and kitchen utensils, as well as loads of stuff representing the worst of American taste. (You gotta wonder how anyone who owned a Chippendale highboy also decorated with "string art" and starburst clocks.) This stuff usually sells last, when the crowd has thinned dramatically, or at the "preauction." Often, whoever bids a dollar gets a whole box of stuff. Within this category I've seen merchandise exceed yard-sale prices, but I've also seen a garbage bag full of sheets sell for $1. If you want just one item in the whole lot and you don't win the bid, you can privately approach the buyer with an offer. Jim bought a 16-quart pressure canner for $6 this way.

The truly amazing. These antique and nonantique items reveal a side of human nature that boggles the mind. I've seen an 80 percent complete 1940s homemade airplane, in parts, that wouldn't sell for $1, but individual parts sold for a total of hundreds of dollars. A trunk of miscellaneous items sold for $2; a locked, unopenable one sold for $20. In one sale a large, rare wooden bowl sold for $150. The next bowl, identical except for a splash of original blue paint on the underside, sold for $300 (at which point the auctioneer yells to his helper, "Hey, Charlie, get out the can of blue spray paint!").

Like I said, estate sales are great, cheap entertainment, with the occasional bargain thrown in.

EEK! ANTIQUES?

After just reading about estate auctions, I imagine many readers are wondering, "What's so tightwaddy about antiques?" In fact, some antiques can be economical.

Many people think of antiques as what the Queen Mother lives with; all Chippendale, candelabras, and crystal. Or they think it's all like what's featured in *Country Living* magazine—severely countrified kitchens crammed with so many Indian baskets, painted firkins, spinning wheels, quilts, duck decoys, and crocks of wooden spoons that no grandma could turn around in one, much less bake a pie. When you price these smaller antiques, you know this look could be achieved only by spending a small fortune.

But there is a range of antique furniture that does make economic sense. It generally dates from 1875 to 1925. It was the middle-class furniture of its day. It's solid wood, and sometimes shows signs of use. It's appealing, but it was made to be lived with, not just collected and admired.

Even within this category there are exceptions for reasons of impracticality and price. For instance, antique sofas may be uncomfortable, bed frames may be of an odd size, and dining chairs may turn to kindling after a bit of abuse by children. And there are a few raging collectible trends, such as mission oak, that have pushed prices into the stratosphere.

The exceptions aside, these modest antiques can make sense for the following reasons:

• When comparing furniture of equal craftsmanship, antiques are frequently cheaper. It's true that many smaller antiques far exceed the price of their new counterparts, and so I seldom buy these things; instead I pick up look-alikes and collectibles at yard sales. But often the larger the antique is, the more competitive the price is when compared to new, quality furniture. At estate sales, large antique bureaus in good condition average $300. A same-sized but lower-quality bureau costs about $350 at Sears. A bureau with quality and aesthetic appeal equal to that of an antique can cost $750 at a contemporary furniture store.

Antique prices vary depending on the month, the affluence of the community, and the region of the country (although a West Coast auctioneer that I called told me that prices there are similar to what we see in the Northeast).

• Antiques appreciate in value, so if you ever change your mind, you should be able to sell the item for what you paid, if not more. Any minor wear and dings you've added won't matter. As witnessed at estate auctions, even quality contemporary furniture depreciates in value, and furniture of medium quality depreciates even more radically.

• Contemporary furniture will almost certainly look dated within a decade or two. The antiques my grandparents purchased in the 1930s look even better today.

• Often good antiques can be priced low because they require refinishing or repair. Sometimes hiring this work isn't cost-effective for dealers. Yet many visionless buyers will overlook these pieces.

Predicting how much refinishing or repair might be required isn't always easy. Sometimes an evening's worth of work increases the value of a bureau by $100. In cases where I guessed wrong, my hourly wage dipped to 73¢.

• Antiques provide entertainment as you hunt down hard-to-find items; we have casually searched for specific pieces for years. Because many antiques are unique, you have to educate your-

self about types of wood, construction, styles, and prices. But most important, it takes time to learn what you really like. Holding out for affordable treasures has always paid off. In the meantime, we've made do with scavenged furniture and had fun poking around antique shops and attending auctions.

Finally, if you don't love antiques, don't buy them. While they can be fairly economical if purchased intelligently, they aren't the cheapest way to furnish a house. Creative scroungers who aren't picky about aesthetics can furnish a house for free. But if you have already determined that you are going to own quality furniture that you love, antiques are an option to explore.

ETCH AND CATCH

Carol Stutts of Berea, Kentucky, alerted us to a unique method of saving on your automobile insurance and, as a side benefit, greatly reducing the chance that your car will be stolen.

It's simple: Using a kit (available by mail from Automark Corp.), you etch your car's federally registered vehicle identification number (VIN) onto each of its windows. In a study conducted in a high-theft area of Southern California, 6,955 vehicles were etched. Statistically, 133 of these vehicles should have been stolen during the next 18 months, but only 15 were stolen.

This works because when a valuable car is stolen for resale, the thief pops in a new dashboard vehicle identification number tag from a same-model junked car that he's purchased. Having to replace all the windows as well makes the operation too expensive. Medium-aged cars are often stolen for sale to "chop shops," where they're disassembled for parts. Chop shops don't want cars with etched glass because the doors, a valuable replacement part, become worthless for resale.

However, etching may not prevent the theft of an old car. These are usually stolen only for joyriding or for use in the commission of a crime. In this case, the thief plans to ditch the car within a few hours.

Because of the success of etching, several states have passed laws requiring car insurance companies to give discounts on the "comprehensive" portion of car insurance to car owners who etch their glass. Some insurance companies also have their own policies regarding discounts for etching. Call your state insurance commissioner and/or your insurer to find out whether your state and/or insurance company participates in these discounts. Automark will also be happy to provide you with up-to-date copies of legislation from states that require the discount.

The etching process isn't complicated. A kit comes with eight stencils, each of which is preprinted with your car's vehicle identification number. You peel off the backing and stick one on the bottom corner of each window in your car. You apply the etching gel and wait one minute. Then you peel away the stencil and the window is etched. The kit includes a decal warning crooks that identification numbers have been affixed to the windows, and it contains a certificate to send to your insurance

company verifying that you've etched your windows.

The regular price of the kit is $24.95 plus $2.50 shipping and handling, but *Gazette* readers get a discount. If you mention that you read about the kit in *The Tightwad Gazette,* the price is $11.95 plus $2.50 for shipping and handling. (If you order two or more kits, the total shipping charge is still just $2.50.)

Order from:

Automark Corp.
4323 Poplar Level Road
Louisville, KY 40213
(502) 452-9500

Along with your name, address, and number of kits desired, be sure to send the VIN(s) of your vehicle(s). You'll find it on your registration, or on a small metal plate on your dashboard.

Be aware that some automakers have begun etching car windows at the factory. Also, some glass companies, military bases, insurance companies, and police stations offer free etching. Check your windows and call around before ordering a kit.

BAG TO BASICS

Dear Amy,

All my life, I've loved my mother's Christmas wreath. It wasn't until I was an adult that I discovered she'd made it out of clear plastic bags and a wire coat hanger!

Start by snipping off the hook of a hanger and shape the remaining part into a circle, covering the joined ends with electrical or duct tape. Then cut about three dozen plastic bags into strips about 4 inches wide by 8 to 10 inches long. Tie the strips to the wire and fluff out the ends. Try to squeeze as many as possible onto the wire (but don't stretch the plastic in your effort to keep the knots small). The result is a fluffy, shimmery, silvery wreath, which you can then decorate with ribbons, ornaments, or whatever.

—Rebecca Nguyen
Alexandria, Virginia

ST. NICK TRICK

Dear Amy,

Take your own camera to the mall when your kids visit Santa. I've found that the Santa booths always allow you to take your own pictures. This tip saved me $7 per photo.

—Kim Lenart
Denton, Texas

BUDGET CUTTING GIFT

Dear Amy,

Here is a gift kids can make. Taking into account the interests of the recipients, collect these from newspapers: crossword puzzles, word games, cartoons, or bridge or chess problems. Make booklets of construction paper folded crosswise and sewn together through the centers. Paste clippings on pages; put solutions on the last pages.

—Mary B. Licari
Ft. Washington, Maryland

PHOTO FINESSE

Dear Amy,

While organizing my mother's "picture drawer" into albums, I decided that I would love to have some copies of these photos for myself and as gifts. But professional copies of old photos are very expensive if there are no negatives. So I lightly taped my favorite photos to a piece of typing paper and took them to a local copy shop to be reproduced on a laser copier. I was very impressed with the results. The charge was about $1.70 a sheet.

—Janet Bayless
Camdenton, Missouri

TIDEPOOL TIDINGS

Dear Amy,

Using twine, I tie a real, large, dried starfish to the top of my Christmas tree for a beautiful, inexpensive, natural "star."

—Sherry Brooks
Westlake Village, California

CHRISTMAS TREE CONES

Dear Amy,

These holiday treats taste good and look pretty:

6 pointy ice-cream cones
Lots of small pieces of candy, such as M&Ms, red-hots, sprinkles, etc.
2 cups powdered sugar
3 tablespoons soft margarine
1 tablespoon milk
3 teaspoons green food coloring
1 teaspoon vanilla

Mix sugar, margarine, milk, food coloring, and vanilla until creamy. Stand cones on plate or pan. Spread frosting all over cones with a butter knife or spatula. Stick candy on trees by pushing into frosting.

—Catherine Chavis
Florence, South Carolina

GOOFY GIFTS

Dear Amy,

My relatives and I give each other "goofy gifts." The rules are simple: It can't cost over a dollar, it must be clean, and it should be totally useless and/or as tacky as possible.

Garage sales and flea markets are the main sources. The trick is to turn your mind at garage sales to finding the worst thing, not the best. It's lots of fun to see the shock and amazement on the faces of the sellers, as they think, "I never thought *that* would sell!"

Through the years, we have exchanged stuff like beer-can bedroom slippers, tacky ashtrays, a

leather chewing gum dispenser, and several things we have yet to figure out.

Several of my friends have now joined my list, and some of the gifts get given again. It has turned out to be one of our favorite parts of Christmas, and we can't wait to see what will turn up next.

—Muriel Kupper
Downers Grove, Illinois

YANKEE SWAP

Dear Amy,

When family gift-giving becomes overburdened because there are too many kids or money is tight, a "yankee swap" is a creative alternative.

Each person brings one wrapped gift and puts it into a large container (we used a wicker laundry basket). Then everyone draws a number. Number One chooses a gift from the basket and opens it. Number Two then picks a gift, opens it, and can either keep it or swap it for Number One's gift. Number Three picks a gift, opens it, and can swap with Number One or Two, and so on. This keeps going until everyone has picked, swapped, and kept, amid laughing and joking.

—Nancy Wilson
Warren, Maine

(How about combining "Goofy Gifts" and "Yankee Swap" to make the gift-exchanging ritual even funnier? FZ)

'TIS THE SEASONING

Dear Amy,

I grow herbs and dry them. Then I package the herbs for friends and family as gifts. People who cook love to receive them. If you mail them, they are very lightweight for shipping.

—Laura Lipinski
Seven Valleys, Pennsylvania

FROM CHIPS TO STRIPS

Dear Amy,

I recycle Mylar popcorn and potato-chip bags into ribbon for wrapping and decorating packages. Just wipe out the inside of the bag with a damp cloth, then cut a long strip from it by spiraling around the bag. You now have a ribbon to curl like any other curling ribbon. Be sure to curl it so that the shiny side is facing out.

—Ellie Pett
Elmhurst, Illinois

THE UNMAGICAL TIME-MANAGEMENT METHOD

Because readers know that we have six kids and do time-intensive frugal activities such as gardening, canning, and quilt-making, they apparently feel there's a magical strategy that we've hit upon to squeeze more hours out of the day. "How do you manage your time?" and "Can you describe your typical day?" are among the most frequent questions I'm asked.

But the answer is that magical

strategies are few. Like saving money, most of saving time involves the making of choices.

In response to the requests to share a "typical day," I must say our lives vary quite a bit from day to day. However, there is a basic pattern:

We get up at 7 A.M. Jim makes breakfast while I prepare lunch boxes. Within an hour the six children are all out waiting for the school bus.

Then the houseperson (once it was always me, now it's usually Jim) divides the day into two parts. The morning is devoted to the routine household maintenance without which our lives would be completely chaotic. Each day the houseperson washes breakfast dishes, washes and hangs one or two loads of laundry, vacuums the downstairs, makes our bed, and generally picks up. Every two or three days a mountain of clean, dry laundry gets folded, floors get damp mopped, and bathrooms are cleaned.

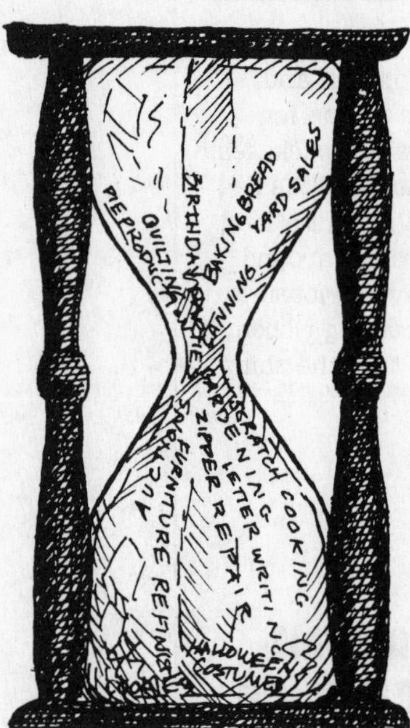

The houseperson compresses these boring activities into the morning so that the afternoons are freed up for more satisfying activities. These might include lawn work, gardening, cleaning the workshop, refinishing furniture, writing letters, home-renovation projects, Halloween-costume making, or baking cookies.

Jim usually makes supper. We alternate washing dishes. Aside from a continuation of the afternoon activities, our evenings consist of helping kids with homework, Scout-related activities, paying bills, giving baths, and occasionally going to estate auctions.

Sometime around 9 P.M., Jim and I crash and watch an hour or two of TV before going to bed. I may or may not be working on a project while watching TV.

If this routine doesn't sound remarkable to you, I agree. It isn't. If there's any "magical strategy," it's to be found in what we *don't* do. For instance:

- I don't blow-dry my hair and put on makeup, except on special occasions. I spend about the same time grooming as does my husband.
- I don't commute to a job.
- I don't have a spotlessly clean house, although it is generally tidy.
- I don't clean my children's rooms for them. They clean their rooms daily and aren't allowed to do anything else until their rooms "pass inspection."
- I don't prepare meals that would impress Martha Stewart.
- I don't chauffeur my kids to several places each day. If they want a friend over I will provide transportation two times a month. They are allowed one outside activity at a time.
- I don't insist on 24-hour togetherness with Jim. For example, he does the grocery shopping alone because my coming with him wouldn't speed up the process. Similarly, I yard-sale alone, attend school events alone, and sometimes even visit far-away relatives alone.

• I don't micromanage my kids' appearance. By age four, they choose their own clothes and dress themselves each morning. And I don't do complex hairdos—my girls have simple, straight hairstyles.

• I don't read more than one book a day to children.

• I have few volunteer commitments to organizations. Jim is a Scout treasurer but has no other commitments.

• I don't give my children a bath and shampoo each night. They get a bath as needed, or a minimum of once a week.

• I don't have an hour-long bedtime ritual for kids. Once I announce "Bedtime!" everyone is in bed in less than ten minutes.

• I don't drive my kids to get professional haircuts. Home haircuts save time as well as money.

• I don't read the newspaper every day. I occasionally read parts of the Sunday paper.

• I don't read novels, although I like them. I do read nonfiction when the information applies to work or to a personal project.

• I don't stop what I'm doing every time a child "needs" something. I say, with firmness, "I'm busy and can't do it now."

• I don't prepare sit-down lunches, although our family always eats breakfasts and suppers together. I will fix a sandwich or warm up leftovers for small children, and I make sure there's a selection of snacks and lunches that are easy for older kids to get for themselves.

• I don't socialize a lot, unless I'm combining it with a productive activity.

• I don't spend hours on the telephone. I average less than one social phone call per week, and even then I might wipe down kitchen cabinets at the same time.

• I don't watch TV during the daytime unless I'm doing a monotonous project at the same time.

• I don't work out . . . enough.

• I don't entertain my children. We place limits on television and leave them to their own devices after that.

• I don't have relatives who live nearby, so I don't spend time with them on a regular basis.

Within this group of "I don'ts" are things that others cannot duplicate easily. They are offered only as an explanation. Other "I don'ts" do provide genuine value to the lives of those who choose to do them. And there are some "I don'ts" that I could—and maybe should—make more time for. But I've arrived at these because they work best for myself and my family.

About half of these "I don'ts" others do because they feel it's part of "good parenting." But by omitting some of these I can include other activities that double as quality time with my kids. They have fun, learn, and feel accomplishment when they help me with my projects. Typically, when I was canning carrots one fall, five out of six of my children offered to help with washing, peeling, chopping, and filling jars. The other child, Alec, was helping Jim with a woodworking project in the workshop.

Further, I believe my kids benefit more from having a chaos-free home life.

There's an interesting parallel between those who claim they don't have enough money and those who claim they don't have enough time. In most cases, those who are short of cash are spending money on nonessentials. People

who claim they don't have enough time are usually choosing to give time to nonessential activities. In each case, it would be more truthful to say that they are *choosing* to spend money/time on other things.

The choices that you make won't necessarily be the ones I've made. But what's important is that whatever time-management strategy you use, you do it consciously. In my experience, most people who feel incredibly harried haven't made conscious, deliberate decisions about what is valuable to them and what isn't. Rather, they allow their time to be monopolized by whatever someone else demands of them at the moment, or whatever project happens to strike their fancy at a given time.

Successful time management means setting your own agenda and sticking to it. You can be flexible, but you must be willing to say "no" if there are too many obstacles between you and your goals.

PARSIMONIOUS PURCHASE POINTERS

Peggy Beals of Marshfield, Massachusetts, offers the following "Test for Value." Before making a purchase, she asks the following questions:

1. Can we do without it?

2. Does it do more than required?

3. Does it cost more than it's worth?

4. Can we do what it does with things we already have?

5. How often will we use it?

6. Where will we store it?

7. Will using it be more work than we're apt to want to do?

8. How many ways can we use it?

9. Have we checked with people who own one and with consumer ratings?

10. Would I be smarter to resist, and put the money toward another goal?

Peggy says this test has prevented her from buying a pasta machine, a bread-making machine, a word processor, joining a book club, and subscribing to several magazines.

While few purchases would pass all ten questions, it's safe to say that a wise purchase should pass eight or nine of them. Further, I would like to add another point:

11. If the item does not satisfy these criteria, can I at least resell it for the same price I paid?

This point means that it might be sensible to buy a secondhand item at a good price even if it does not measure up on points 1 through 10, because if you decide the item isn't worth keeping you can always recover your investment. Items in this category include expensive toys and sporting equipment for fickle kids, and marginal tools and kitchen gadgets for adults.

YOU CAN CAN . . . CHEAPLY

There's no shortage of written information out there about canning. Dozens of books and magazine articles give lengthy, specific explanations about how to can various vegetables, fruits, meats, and seafoods.

In this article we won't repeat any of this basic information, so it's essential that you pick up a comprehensive guide with the latest USDA recommendations.

One that I have read and highly recommend is *The Ball Blue Book: The Guide to Home Canning and Freezing,* which is available for $3.50 plus $1.00 shipping and handling from the Alltrista Corporation, Consumer Products Company, Consumer Affairs Department, P.O. Box 2729, Muncie, IN 47307. You can also write to the same address and sign up for a *free* lifetime subscription to Ball's excellent twice-yearly canning newsletter, *Consumer Newsline.*

Another up-to-date book is *The Kerr Kitchen Cookbook: Home Canning and Freezing Guide*, which is available for $3.50 plus 50¢ shipping from Kerr, P.O. Box 67961, Los Angeles, CA 90076. Kerr also has a newsletter free for the asking from the same address.

In this article we'll cover the tightwad angle on canning. Specifically, we'll dispel some myths and pass along some time- and money-saving pointers.

First, the myths:

• "Canning is difficult, tedious, and time-consuming." Several times I have run into modern, hip, '90s-type folks who have learned to can and they always say they are amazed at how easy it is.

People assume that canning must be difficult simply because it's unfamiliar; most of us are a generation or two away from anyone who's done it. But watching a pressure gauge isn't rocket science. If you can drive a car, you can can.

As for "tedious and time-consuming," canning can seem that way because you are generally processing a great deal of food at one time. But as you use that food day after day, you'll find it is actually a time-saver. For example, rather than making spaghetti sauce from scratch dozens of times in a year, you can cook up a year's worth of ready-to-use spaghetti sauce in just a few hours. If you're canning carrots, you'll do the same washing, peeling, chopping, and cooking that you would do over and over during the year. Canning is just one more simple step.

dial-type pressure gauge

• "Canning is not economical." I have actually read this statement in "How to Can" books. The assumption is based on buying all of your equipment new and does not factor in that you'll reuse the same canner, jars, and rings year after year.

The reality is that when you're

canning free food such as surplus garden vegetables that would otherwise go bad, the only cost per quart is 7¢ for the lid, an insignificant energy cost, and the amortized cost of the canner, jars, and rings (which can be near zero; more on this later).

Naturally, the savings depend on what you're canning. Assuming the produce is free, and comparing home-canned to store-bought equivalents, the "hourly wage" for canning rhubarb jam is $15, but for canning pears it's just $1. The difference is in the time required to prepare the fruits.

In addition, canning can be an energy saver. The energy required to pressure-can 7 quarts of green beans is about the same as is needed to cook a single pot of fresh beans.

• "Canning is dangerous." It's important to acknowledge the danger of botulism in improperly canned food, but it's just as important to keep it in perspective. According to the Centers for Disease Control, in 1992 (the most recent year for which statistics are available) there were just 17 cases, and 1 death, resulting from food-borne botulism nationwide. ("Infant botulism" is more common, but it's a separate disease that infants can get from eating foods that are harmless to adults.)

Botulism outbreaks are most frequent in Alaska, Washington State, Oregon, and California, apparently because the *Clostridium botulinum* spores are more common in the soil there. Nonetheless, canners in all states should follow the rules to the letter. When they do so, canning is quite safe.

• "Canning is just for country folk with big gardens." It's true that it's seldom economical to can regular-price supermarket produce. But enterprising urbanites with some initiative can often buy cheap produce through informal arrangements with produce managers, can get it by U-pick and "gleaning" programs, or can even get it free from gardening friends. For example, I bought a bushel of "drops" at a U-pick apple orchard for $4. This made 21 quarts of applesauce. Including the lid, the cost of each quart was 26¢. That's about half the lowest price for store-bought applesauce.

• "Canning is only for people who love to cook." Kelly Frey of Readfield, Maine, loves to cook and hates to garden. Her friend loves to garden and hates to cook. They've worked out a deal in which Kelly cans her friend's garden produce and they each keep half the jars.

• "Canning is unnecessary for people who have freezers." Every canner I have ever known has also had a freezer. One reason is that many people, myself included, prefer the taste of certain canned foods, such as canned string beans, over their frozen counterparts. Home-canned foods are far better tasting and more nutritious than their store-bought counterparts.

Also, canning is a flexible method of dealing with surplus. Sometimes, after your freezer is full, you may come across an unexpected windfall—say you are offered four leftover turkey carcasses from a church supper. You could cook up the carcasses and can the resulting soup stock.

Further, compared to freezer food, canned food is more "immedi-

ate"—it doesn't need to be searched for and exhumed from the bottom of a freezer and it doesn't require thawing.

Another great advantage of canned foods over frozen is that they make wonderful, much-appreciated gifts. Home-canned salsa is great under the tree; frozen stuff is harder to give away.

Having dispensed with these myths, here are some tightwad tricks that we use.

• Get equipment cheaply. Avoid buying new jars and equipment. Because canning isn't as common as it used to be, chances are if you "put out the word"—either by asking friends or by taking out a free ad in a "shopper" publication—you will be able to get most of what you need for free. To buy some time in this process, try to borrow equipment as you need it.

Jim located our first pressure canner for $2 in a thrift shop and our second at an auction for $6 (it's handy to have two so we can do twice as much at once). Older canners generally use a dial-type pressure gauge; many extension service offices have equipment that tests these for accuracy. Also, if a canner has missing or defective parts, you can get replacements by mail order from the manufacturer. Jim got a new gasket for one of our canners for $8. That's a heck of a lot cheaper than a new, sale-priced $60 canner.

I also trash-picked an "applesauce mill." We even made our canning shelves from scavenged lumber and old bricks we found.

There's also no need to buy canning jars. We got virtually all of our canning jars free, some from older relatives who no longer used them and another 200 from trash-picking.

You can also use quart-sized mayonnaise jars, as these take the same-sized lid and ring as the canning jars made by Ball or Kerr. The USDA says these are fine for water-bath canning but tend to break in a pressure canner. However, every canner I know says that mayonnaise jars break no more often in pressure canners than the "proper" jars.

applesauce mill

There are two basic types of jars. One is the glass-top jar, which requires a disposable rubber ring. The USDA no longer recommends these, as it's difficult to tell if the jar has sealed. The other, called a "dome lid," uses a screw-on metal ring that holds a flat metal lid in place. This lid has a rim of rubber on the underside.

You can reuse the rings indefinitely if you remove them from the sealed jars and store them in a dry place so they won't rust. Removing the rings also allows you to put up hundreds of jars with just a few dozen rings.

In most canning, the only part that needs to be replaced is the lid. We watch for good deals on these and have found them at salvage stores. Some tightwads claim to

successfully reuse the lids; they say they simply remove them carefully to avoid denting them. But I don't reuse lids, and experts and manufacturers specifically advise against doing this.

It's common for canners to seal jars of jam or jelly with wax instead of a lid. This can be frugal, as the wax can be reused for years, but the USDA also now advises against this.

Some canning requires supplies like spices, pickling salt, alum, or sugar. It goes without saying that you'll look for deals on these things as well.

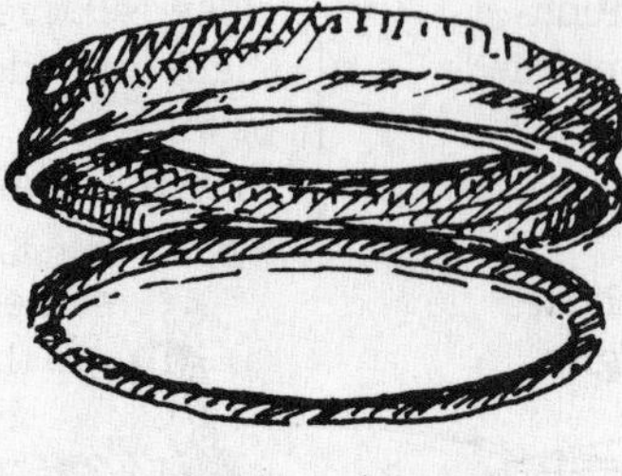

dome-type canning jar lids

• Use the right-sized jar. Canning jars come in small-mouth and large-mouth quarts, and small-mouth and large-mouth pints. Small lids generally cost 7¢ each, and large lids usually cost 9¢. The obvious tightwad choice is to use small-mouth quarts whenever possible.

I use small-mouth quarts for all canning aside from jams and pickles. For these I use pints, because we just don't use quarts quickly enough.

• Save on energy. For foods that can be either pressure-canned or water-bath canned, we choose pressure-canning because it's so much quicker. Green beans, for example, can be pressure-canned in 25 minutes, versus three hours for water-bath canning. (The USDA no longer recommends water-bath canning for green beans.)

• Cut small, pack tight. The more food you can pack into a jar, the more efficient and economical the operation becomes. Unless you are willing to laboriously pack long foods like carrots and string beans into a precise, puzzlelike configuration, you'll be able to pack in another 15 percent if you cut things into small pieces so that they pack tightly. To test this, pack a jar with large pieces, empty the jar, chop the same pieces smaller, and refill. Be sure to remain within the official "headroom" guidelines, however.

• Use the hot-pack method when possible. Food shrinks during cooking, so filling jars with precooked foods instead of raw foods will save on jar space.

Finally, it's a mistake to think of the advantages of canning strictly in economic terms. While it can save lots of money, it also has psychological value. There's a great satisfaction in transforming the bounty of a garden into row upon row of canned fruits and vegetables. In my view, this is reason enough to give canning a try.

A TALE OF TIGHTWAD TRANSFORMATION UPDATE

Readers express their success with tightwaddery in a variety of ways. The following doodling appeared on the bottom of a letter from Jodi Peterson of Bloomington, Illinois.

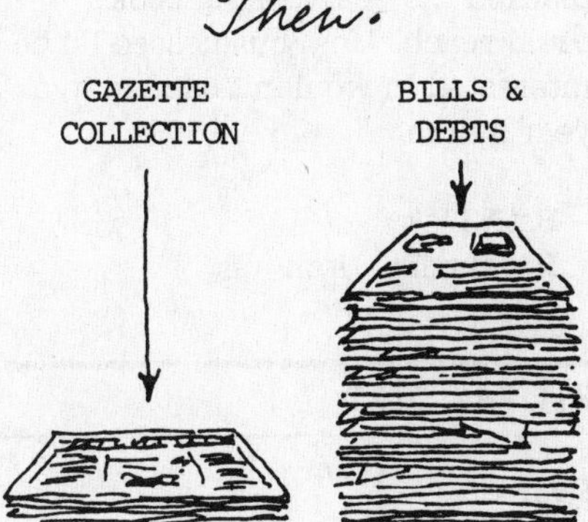

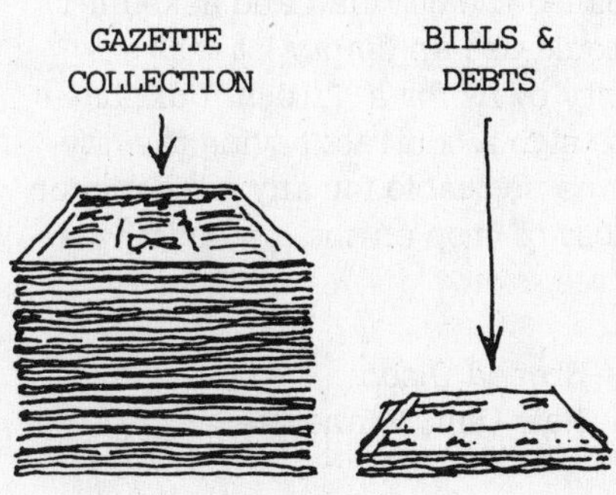

PAINT FOR KIDS

There are few more enjoyable activities for kids than painting pictures. Here are three recipes for kids' paints. The first two are from Rhonda Langley of Dayton, Oregon, and the third is from James and Earlene Giglierano of Iowa City, Iowa:

- Mix 1 teaspoon water and 1 teaspoon dishwashing liquid with ½ teaspoon liquid food coloring.
- Mix evaporated milk with enough food coloring to achieve desired hues. This paint is glossy when dry.
- Mix ⅓ cup powdered laundry starch with ½ cup cold water. Add 6 cups of boiling water, stirring constantly. Cool slightly. Divide into individual paint cups. Add food coloring, stir, and add more coloring until you achieve the desired shade. For prolonged storage, cover and keep in refrigerator.

To make each of these recipes even cheaper, I recommend the use of the paste-type food coloring sold in party-goods stores. It offers a far better range of colors and costs about the same per ounce as the liquid type, but it is much more concentrated, so it's cheaper to use.

PAINT FOR GROWN-UPS

Having recently had our house painted, I was astonished at the high price of quality latex paint. You are lucky if you can get it for $15 a gallon.

So I was intrigued by information one of my staffers gleaned from a back issue of *Organic Gardening* magazine. It's a recipe for whitewash, the stuff that used to cover practically every house, barn, and fence in America.

The mixture could not be simpler. Combine 10 pounds of ground limestone with 5 quarts of water, stirring until you get a smooth paste. A paint stirrer attached to an electric drill might make this easier. Then thin it until it is the consistency of milk.

For better, more durable cover-

age, add 1 pound of calcium chloride (available at farm-supply stores) dissolved in 1 gallon of water to the paste before you thin it.

The magazine says that one gallon of either mix will cover about 200 square feet of wood.

Unlike paint, whitewash bonds better to a wet surface, so start by scrubbing the surface to be painted with water. The stuff reportedly looks thin and fairly transparent when painted on, but is more opaque when dry.

I have not tried this, so I cannot vouch for how well it works. But in 1987, when this recipe ran in *Organic Gardening,* it cost just 30¢ a gallon. Even if today the price has zoomed to 50¢ a gallon, I'd say it's still worth a try, particularly on barns, sheds, and other buildings where you can tolerate a less-than-perfect finish.

FEELS LIKE A DEAL

Dear Amy,

The expensive carpet that our local carpet store installs is guaranteed 100 percent—even if the customer simply dislikes the color once it is installed. We let the store know that we would be interested in buying carpet that had been pulled up. We got beautiful carpet that was less than two weeks old, because the couple that bought it didn't like the way it felt on their feet. It normally costs $30 a yard. We got it for $6 a yard.

—Diane Rambo
Modesto, California

REACH OUT AND RECYCLE

Dear Amy,

I live about an hour from Salt Lake City. I wanted an SLC phone book, but I didn't want to purchase one at an outrageous price. So I waited until phone-book replacement time, went to the book recycling bin at the grocery store, and plucked the best-looking book I could reach. Most businesses I'd be interested in wouldn't change in a year's time.

—Beth Lisk
Harrisville, Utah

HIT PAY DIRT

Dear Amy,

I live in town, and our house is on a half-lot. That doesn't give us any room for a decent garden. I called the city hall and asked if I could use an empty lot that the city owns for a garden. I did have to sign a contract saying the city was not liable for any accidents or loss of crop on the lot, but it was free.

—Brenda Olson
New Ulm, Minnesota

DO THE WRITE THING

Dear Amy,

While in the hospital last month, I had a truly wonderful nurse. I wanted to do something special to express my appreciation. Instead of a gift, I wrote a letter to the director of the hospital, with copies to the nurse and her supervisor. I praised her work and positive atti-

tude, and suggested she be considered for a raise or promotion. The cost of this "gift" was under $1 for stamps and stationery, and it took no more time to deliver than a plant or candy. It occurred to me that a note to my principal from an appreciative student or teacher would have been far more welcome than many of the small gifts I received when I was teaching school.

—Karen Taylor-Ogren
West Trenton, New Jersey

SAVE BUCKS ON BUCKETS

Dear Amy,

Our community had a wonderful tightwad event this year: a toxic-waste turn-in and paint swap. Toxic wastes were safely disposed of and people acquired paints that others could not use, all for free! I brought home enough oil-based stain to completely restain our deck, and a brand-new can of paint, which I used to paint a bedroom. In addition, I got enough paint thinner to clean up the staining mess, two new paint-roller covers, an unopened tin of tile grout, and enamel paint to do the window trim in a bedroom.

—Tamara Kittelson-Aldred
Missoula, Montana

TAKE GREAT PANES

Dear Amy,

One of my favorite sources of bargains is the local demolition company. I got enough glass for a 6-foot by 6-foot greenhouse/porch addition on our house for $82. They also have everything to build with, as well as wooden carousel horses, hospital beds, marble pieces, and stained glass.

—Mrs. H. Smith
Mead, Washington

VASE VALUE

Dear Amy,

I recycle vases that come with floral bouquets by bringing them back to the florist's shop for reuse. I've also brought several from friends. The florist, in turn, sent a free bouquet to my aunt, out of state, when she was in the hospital.

I also save bags and hangers and return them to the local cleaners. In return, they give my husband a discount.

—Donna Ott
West Dundee, Illinois

USE FOR JUICE

Dear Amy,

While walking I spotted some beautiful oranges still on the tree. I knocked at the house and was told I could have some, but they were sour. I took some home anyway and juiced them. They were similar in taste to lemons, so I made "lemonade." My kids liked it. I also made frozen pops with it, which they are still enjoying. Other possibilities are key lime or lemon meringue pie, or orange marmalade. I thought I would pass this along for your Southern readers, because sour orange trees are fairly common in the South.

—Lynette Wayne
Middleburg, Florida

RUMMAGE FOR RUFFLES

Dear Amy,

Instead of making doll clothes for my two daughters' baby dolls, I buy "newborn" baby clothes for almost nothing at rummage sales. Usually the dresses that are all lace and ruffles have been worn only once or twice, and are my daughters' favorites.

—Joyce Eveler
Jefferson City, Missouri

A NEW WAY TO LOOK AT USED THINGS

It is strange, and sobering, to contemplate the odd beliefs that lurk in people's minds.

I ran into one such belief as I was being interviewed on a radio show. A listener called in and said, "I remember reading about you in *Parade* magazine, and I agree with everything you were saying . . . except for one thing: I couldn't believe you give your kids used toys for Christmas. Do you really do that? Kids *need* new toys on Christmas morning."

I responded by explaining that our kids do, frequently, get one special, new toy on Christmas morning. However, I also disputed her basic premise: that kids have a basic need for new stuff and will somehow be damaged if they don't have the experience of receiving new things.

The idea that kids—or adults, for that matter—have a basic need for new stuff is one that many people hold. Like this caller, even people who support the basic concept of frugality often still believe that people need some new things to be happy.

One reason this belief is so pervasive is that until fairly recently, the quality of used merchandise was poor. I remember, as a kid, going to the thrift shop in the small city of Fitchburg, Massachusetts, and finding the clothing selection truly pitiful. Thirty years ago there simply wasn't as much good used stuff floating around. Yard sales were just beginning, and people generally held on to their things until they got pretty ragged.

Because new stuff really was significantly better in those days, it

was trotted out with great fanfare: "Look, honey, a *brand-new* bike from Santa!" By their enthusiasm, our parents taught us that new is better.

But then came the great boom in production, and the subsequent buying frenzy, which continues right up until the present day. A more recent development is the imposition of trash disposal fees, which make people very reluctant to throw away anything that someone else would take. The result is that in the 1990s there are tons of superb, used items available out there.

But the old attitude lives on. Even frugal parents who bring home yard-sale toys for their kids still give them only new toys for Christmas. The new merchandise is given with more honor and enthusiasm, even when the quality is the same. Kids *learn* that new is better, and their parents mistakenly conclude that this preference is "natural."

For the past 13 years I have been conducting what amounts to a social-science experiment to determine what would happen if kids were raised without receiving the message that new is better. Because I don't regard new stuff as superior, without consciously doing so I have offered used things to my kids with the same enthusiasm as new stuff. I also take my kids to yard sales and let them spend their own money.

The result: When I tell a three-year-old that I need to buy him a widget, he responds, "Need to get it at a 'Arrrd sale.' " When I tell a five-year-old that some people believe kids need new things to be happy, she giggles and rolls her eyes like she thinks I'm telling her a preposterous fairy tale. When I ask a ten-year-old if he thinks many other kids at school wear secondhand clothes, he responds, "I don't know. How can you tell?"

In other words, when children haven't been taught the faulty distinction between used and new, they don't presume that new stuff is better.

Conversely, it's also wrong to assume that used is always a better value. Each has benefits. Here are some guidelines:

THE ADVANTAGES OF NEW

- Sometimes you simply can't find exactly what you want used. This is why I usually buy each kid one new toy for birthdays and Christmas. For instance, Alec got a new Erector set for his birthday. While we find a lot of good used things for him, secondhand toys that come in sets of many tiny pieces are rarely complete. Similarly, expendable merchandise such

as lumber and fabric can be found used, but not always in the quantity or type you need.

• Sometimes new technology is so superior it isn't cost-effective to buy used things. For instance, most refrigerators and freezers should be purchased new because their old counterparts are energy-inefficient and therefore more costly in the long run.

• Sometimes the used alternative is simply overpriced, based on its life expectancy. Jim, who needs to buy tall-sized clothes, found thrift-shop flannel shirts for $5, but the elbows were worn. Instead, he went to Sears and bought new ones for $14.

THE ADVANTAGES OF USED

• Sometimes you can get the identical used item for significantly less. Jim hit the jackpot at a yard sale when he found a large bucket of Legos (including the miscellaneous wheels, hinges, and so on) for $1.50. This was a $100 value. Occasionally I wonder if people think my kids accept used toys because they're naïve. Actually, they're smart enough to figure out that this wealth of Legos is better than any $1.50 new toy.

• Sometimes used things are better for the environment. A friend bought a like-new $67 L. L. Bean jacket for $1 at a yard sale. He likes the savings, but he's also pleased to realize that if no one bought this jacket, it would have gone to the landfill and a new jacket would be made from virgin materials.

• Sometimes used things are more aesthetically pleasing and comfortable. This is part of the reason people value antiques so highly. Some manufacturers actually "distress" new furniture, to give it that worn, lived-with look. But it never really looks like a real antique. No one has yet figured out how to duplicate the honest, comfortable attractiveness that an object acquires through years of actual use.

• Sometimes, used things can give you important clues about their durability, whereas with a new item you simply have to guess. I know if I buy good-looking clothes at yard sales, they'll still look good after several washings.

• Sometimes used items are made better. At yard sales I buy older kitchen utensils with wooden or metal handles. I like them better than the new ones, which usually have plastic handles.

• Sometimes used things are more fun to acquire. I enjoy the "sport" of used-stuff acquisition. Anybody can grab something off the shelf at Wal-Mart, but it is an enjoyable challenge to hunt down, find, and bargain for a used item.

So both new and used items have their places in a frugal household. The important point is that your choice between them should be determined by the *actual value* to you, rather than some vague idea that one or the other is better, or necessary for good self-esteem. Of all of the big, sweeping frugal guidelines, understanding and appreciating the value of used stuff is one of the most important to master—for you, and for your kids.

AN AIRTIGHT CASE FOR FAMILY PACKS

Usually, the cheapest way to buy meat is through loss-leader sales at the supermarket. When buying hamburger and chicken, the two tightwad mainstays, the best deals are generally on the large "family packs." I have encountered many singles and couples who feel they can't take advantage of these because they can't eat that much. The fact is that these packs are too large even for a family of eight.

Here's how we handle it: When hamburger goes on sale for $1.19 per pound or less, and when chicken goes on sale for 39¢ per pound, we buy 20 to 30 pounds and individually wrap meal-sized portions.

The first step was purchasing a humongous, $7.99, 2,000-foot roll of 12-inch-wide clear plastic wrap from a warehouse store. One could make the argument that free bread bags are cheaper, but this wrap costs just 4/10ths of a cent per foot and allows a stretched-tight wrap that gives good protection from freezer burn. If this quantity is too much for you, we found that store-brand plastic wraps are 6/10 of a cent. (But be aware that name-brand wrap costs as much as 2 3/10 cents per foot.)

Next, if the chicken is in large pieces, Jim cuts it into small ones, removing the thighs from the legs, for example. Then he removes the skins (too much fat) and backs (too much bone), saving them in a big pot. He fills the pot with water to cover, and simmers it on the stove while he continues to work.

He then pulls out an 18-inch length of wrap, deposits a pound of hamburger (weighed on our kitchen scale) or a meal's worth of chicken pieces in it, and wraps it. Then he rotates the package 90 degrees and deposits it in the center of another 18-inch length of wrap. He folds this around, creating a double-wrapped, airtight package. When putting them in the freezer, he spreads them out as much as possible, to facilitate quick freezing. Once they are frozen, he gathers them into a single location in the freezer so they can be found easily.

After the chicken skins and backs are thoroughly cooked and cooled, we fish out the skins and bones. We chill the broth, then remove and discard the solidified fat. This broth and meat make several soup meals.

We discard the bones. Then we use the skins and other ookey soft stuff to make treats for our dog. Our vet says he's slightly underweight, so the chicken fat is good for him. To make the treats, I put a golf-ball-sized blob in the bottom of a bread bag, tie it off, add another blob, tie it off, and so on. I freeze these. To use, I snip off a section of the bread bag and thaw.

SOURDOUGH SIMPLIFIED

Ever since he was a kid, my staffer Brad has been in love with the taste of sourdough bread. When he was 13 years old, he lived in Alameda, California, and whenever his family would cross the Bay Bridge to visit San Francisco, they would buy a huge, crusty loaf of famous San Francisco sourdough. Brad ate at least half of it himself.

Brad has since learned how to replicate that bread. He has made over a hundred loaves of it, and relatives who come for dinner always clamor for more. Unlike other recipes for sourdough bread, which require the tedious creation of "sponges" and often call for added yeast, Brad's method is very simple.

Along with its distinctive taste, sourdough bread has a unique attraction for tightwads—it's the cheapest bread you can make, consisting only of flour, water, and salt. Brad's 24-ounce loaves cost 20¢ each.

The first step is to make a starter. The simplest way is to mix 1 tablespoon of yeast with 2 cups

of chlorine-free water (allow your tap water to "air out" in a jug for a couple of days) and two cups of white flour. Combine these in a glass, plastic, or earthenware container—not a metal one. Cover loosely with plastic wrap and allow this mixture to sit at room temperature for at least 48 hours, until it foams and develops a pleasantly sour smell. Cover with plastic wrap and refrigerate. You can also get starter from a friend who makes sourdough. (The sourdough books warn that if the starter turns orange, pink, or any other strange color, you should throw it out. In years of sourdough baking, Brad has never had that problem.)

To make two loaves of bread:

5½ cups flour (you can substitute whole wheat flour for 1 or 2 cups)
2 cups starter
1 tablespoon salt
1 cup water

Dissolve the salt in the water in a mixing bowl. (Some sourdough cookery books say you should not use a metal bowl, but Brad has used his metal KitchenAid bowl for years.) Add the starter, and then the flour. Stir, then knead into a ball. (Brad uses the dough hook on his KitchenAid.) Cover with a damp towel and let rise *overnight* at room temperature. The next morning, punch down risen dough and divide in half. Shape each half into a round loaf, make an X-shaped slash on each top, and place the two loaves on a greased baking sheet. Cover with a damp towel and allow to rise at room temperature for about four more hours. Place a pan of water on the bottom rack of the oven and pre-

heat to 400 degrees. Bake for 35 minutes.

Each time you remove some starter, you must "feed" it. Just add back 1½ cups water and 1½ cups flour, stir, cover loosely, and return starter to the refrigerator.

You'll notice that the rising times seem extraordinarily long compared to yeast baking. Brad sees this as an advantage. With yeast breads, you may have just a 15-minute "window" in which the bread has risen to the right size for baking. Sourdough bread is far more forgiving. The first "window" is about two hours long (depending upon how warm the room is). If you should happen to miss that, just knead the bread again and allow to rise again. The only effect will be that the bread is somewhat more sour and the texture is finer.

Brad uses his starter, fresh from the fridge, for weeks at a time. Eventually the loaves he makes start to rise a bit more slowly. Whenever this happens, he just leaves the jar of starter out at room temperature overnight to speed its fermentation.

You need not confine your efforts to loaves of bread. Brad uses this bread recipe to make homemade pizza. He allows the dough to rise once, divides it in half, and rolls it out to make two pizzas.

Troubleshooting tips:

- After this story ran in the newsletter, readers reported varying success with their starters. After much correspondence and experimentation, we determined that the variety of yeast used for the initial starter was crucial. So if your starter doesn't work, make another batch with a different brand of yeast.
- Sourdough baking is generally less predictable than yeast baking. Accepting the fact that sometimes rising times need to double or triple is part of the adventure of sourdough. As with yeast baking, temperature is crucial; if you set your dough over a pan of warm water, it will rise much more quickly.
- Brad believes one reason his sourdough is so successful is that he bakes twice a week, so his starter is fed frequently. If you are an infrequent baker, you'll need to drain off some starter and feed it at least once every two weeks to keep it alive.
- Don't feel bound by the notion that the initial rising must double the volume. Brad often lets the initial rising quadruple the volume. He feels this makes better bread.
- The starter separates in the refrigerator. This is normal. Always stir it well before using, and stir it well again when feeding.

GREAT QUOTES

"Budgeting is the art of doing that well with one dollar which any bungler can do with two."
—Arthur Wellington, British soldier and statesman (1769–1852).

"Economy is the art of making the most of life."
—George Bernard Shaw (1856–1950)

"Any fool can waste, any fool can muddle, but it takes something of a man to save, and the more he saves, the more of a man does it make of him."
—Rudyard Kipling (1865–1936)

LET'S GARDEN WITH JIM

A newsletter reader from Manhattan, Illinois, asked, "How do frugal people garden? I always feel that by the time I buy my seeds, seed potatoes, tomato plants, fertilizer, and insect killers, I could have bought a whole lot of vegetables."

In response, I can't speak for all types of gardeners and gardens. Jim uses a basic system that works well for our situation, and we have determined that it is, indeed, a money-saver.

First, some statistics: We have four garden plots totaling about 8,700 square feet. We spend an average of seven hours a week over our four-month season to garden and process the food. We grow about 95 percent of the vegetables we eat.

To estimate the economy, I'll use exact figures from our 1994 gardening year. Jim spent $108 on gardening supplies and gas for the rototiller. It's difficult to calculate the amortized cost of the rototiller itself, which we bought used for $575. We don't know how many years it will last, and we also rototill gardens for a few other people, and get some benefit when favors are returned. In any case, a rototiller isn't necessary for smaller-scale gardening.

We froze or canned 317 quarts of food from our garden. In addition, we stored away a hard-to-measure quantity of unprocessed foods such as dried beans, carrots, beets, pumpkins, and squash. We also ate and gave away an unknown quantity of fresh food during the summer. I conservatively estimate we grew about 500 quarts of food. So, not including the cost of the rototiller, each quart cost about 22¢, plus about 8¢ per quart of processed food. It's clear, then, that gardening *can* save money.

Figuring the "hourly wage" for gardening is a bit trickier. Assuming, very arbitrarily, that a quart of store-bought vegetables costs $1.00, our gardening efforts are worth $2.91 an hour. But we feel that the improved taste, nutrition, and quality family time we spend together in the garden boost the value higher.

Further, the main thrust of our gardening style *isn't* to gain the highest hourly wage. We grow cheap stuff, such as carrots and cabbage, to have more variety and because we like them. It's conceivable, then, that by gardening more selectively you could have a higher hourly wage, or by gardening under less than ideal circumstances or gardening less frugally you could have a much lower hourly wage.

Here are some strategies to make gardening more profitable:

• Buy gardening supplies cheaply. All of our tools were purchased secondhand or acquired for free. We borrowed a rototiller until we found a used one.

• Shop around for the best price on seeds. Jim found that Fedco seeds were about half the price of the major seed companies. (For a catalog, send $1 to Fedco, P.O. Box 520, Waterville, ME 04903. Their

seeds are suitable for gardens in the northern half of the United States.)

• Grow from seeds whenever possible, as they can cost one tenth the price of nursery seedlings. If you have a short season and a light-filled south-facing window, you can start your seeds indoors. But trying to extend the season outdoors with hoop houses, row covers, "Wall-o'-Water" protectors, and other devices drives up the price of gardening considerably.

• Choose the right vegetables. Get varieties that do well in your climate. If your time and space are limited, bear in mind the expense of the store-bought counterpart—potatoes and carrots tend to be cheap to buy, but lettuce and strawberries are expensive. Choose vegetables based on their yield as compared to the space and effort required. A large, sprawling brussels-sprout plant may yield enough for just one meal, while bush beans and lettuce require comparatively little effort and space for the yield. Keep in mind how they will be preserved—carrots can be stored for months in sand, so although they're cheap to buy, I still think they are worthwhile to grow.

• Don't buy garden paraphernalia, particularly the obscenely overpriced stuff in catalogs. Egg cartons can be seed starters, plastic milk jugs can serve as mini greenhouses, and scavenged lumber and old windows can make cold frames in regions that get little snow.

• Design your garden based on your space. We use the row method, but those with minimal space will get higher yields from the square-foot gardening method, outlined in the book *Square Foot Gardening* by Mel Bartholomew.

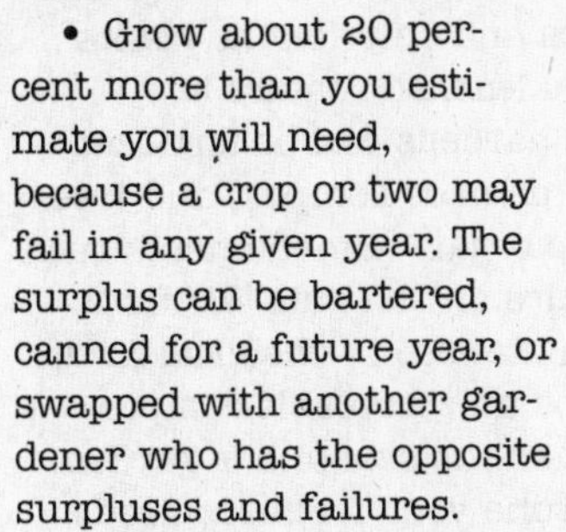

• Grow about 20 percent more than you estimate you will need, because a crop or two may fail in any given year. The surplus can be bartered, canned for a future year, or swapped with another gardener who has the opposite surpluses and failures.

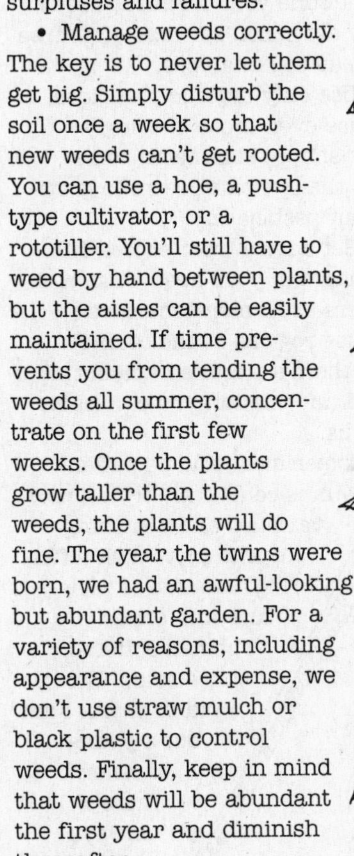

• Manage weeds correctly. The key is to never let them get big. Simply disturb the soil once a week so that new weeds can't get rooted. You can use a hoe, a push-type cultivator, or a rototiller. You'll still have to weed by hand between plants, but the aisles can be easily maintained. If time prevents you from tending the weeds all summer, concentrate on the first few weeks. Once the plants grow taller than the weeds, the plants will do fine. The year the twins were born, we had an awful-looking but abundant garden. For a variety of reasons, including appearance and expense, we don't use straw mulch or black plastic to control weeds. Finally, keep in mind that weeds will be abundant the first year and diminish thereafter.

• Fertilize inexpensively. Because our soil is so rich, Jim uses just 40 pounds of 10-10-10 fertilizer each year. He gets it from the local farmers' co-op for less than $8. He waits until the plant is firmly

rooted and doing well, then hand-sprinkles and hoes in a circle of fertilizer around it. He does this just once and only for the plants that he's learned require it. Smaller gardens can be fertilized with homemade compost and free or cheap organic amendments such as manure or fish guts. We find our minimal use of chemical fertilizer to be an acceptable compromise given the size of our garden. To fine-tune your fertilizer needs, many extension services offer free or cheap soil analyses.

• Use only organic pesticides, and use even those sparingly. We've simply eliminated some crops that we can't seem to grow without pesticides.

• Get advice from successful gardeners in your area. Chat with farmers at farmers' markets. Because regions of the country vary, there's a limited amount of useful information you can learn from us.

• Experiment and be patient. Jim is constantly trying new varieties and switching crops to plots with differing amounts of moisture and shade.

Thomas Jefferson once said, "Though old in years, I am but a young gardener." There's always more to learn, and if your first year was dismal, you at least know now how *not* to grow certain items. Keep asking, trying, and refining, and eventually you'll succeed.

WHEEL SHARP TIP

Dear Amy,

As a quilter, I use a rotary cutter for speed-cutting my pieces. I used to have to replace the blade at least once for each quilt. At $5 per blade, it's expensive to use. Then I found that I could sharpen it with my sharpening stone. Keeping the blade in the cutter holder, I hold it at a 30-degree angle while sharpening. The Olfa blade has numbers, so I can keep track as I rotate and sharpen each section.

—C. Dong
Wayland, Massachusetts

RATE REDUCTION

Dear Amy,

It pays to keep your auto insurance company advised of your driving habits. The premium on the car my husband drives was cut 5 percent when I told them he carpools to work. The company cut 14 percent off the annual premium for my vehicle when I informed them I no longer worked full time and had become a stay-at-home Mom.

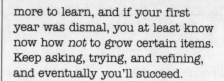

—Diane Ogle
Kent, Washington

UNDER ONE CONDITIONER

Dear Amy,

My husband and I use inexpensive hair conditioner in place of shaving cream. A little bit goes a long way, and it does not dry your skin like soap often does.

—Barbara Davis-Pyles
Seattle, Washington

FIND YOUR MARBLES

Dear Amy,

You can easily make heart-shaped cupcakes. Line the muffin pan with paper baking liners. Place a small marble in each cup between the liner and the muffin tin. Pour in batter, filling halfway, and bake as directed.

—Nancy J. Martin
Wyoming, Michigan

HOT WASH, COLD RINSE

Dear Amy,

I learned from a former boyfriend, a health inspector, that rinsing dishes in hot water has no bearing on the cleaning process. I rinse in cold water I collect in jugs while waiting for the dishwater to get hot.

—Deann Landers
Georgetown, Texas

(Or you could simply fill your rinse-water dishpan as you wait for the water to get hot. FZ)

IT SAVES TO ASK

Dear Amy,

If you don't see something at a garage sale, ask. I've bought a pitchfork that the owner brought out from a shed after I asked. Sometimes other garage salers hear the question and know where you can find the item.

—Jan Jacquet
Olympia, Washington

APPROVAL OF STAMP

Dear Amy,

Don't buy gummed and sticky address labels. I invested $5.95 in a rubber stamp, which can be reused, possibly indefinitely, with a few drops of ink. I ordered mine through a mail-order house.

—Nancy Brockmeier
Yorba Linda, California

(The Tightwad Gazette *can testify to the durability of these self-inking stamps. We bought one for our business nearly five years ago. Every once in a while we add a little more stamp-pad ink to its reservoir. We know that this one stamp has been used tens of thousands of times since then. FZ)*

READ THIS ARTICLE AND SAVE $150,000

The Guinness Book of World Records contains two interesting facts: The weight-loss record is held by a woman who lost 917 pounds; as you read on, you find that this same woman holds another record—the highest weight ever for a woman. She weighed 1,200 pounds.

I'm sincerely happy that this woman lost weight, and I don't mean to make light of a serious medical problem. However, I instantly saw her situation as a way to illustrate a hard-to-grasp flaw I routinely see in advertising, in consumer reporting, and even in the way tightwads discuss saving money. In each case, they emphasize the amount a strategy theoretically could "save" without focusing on the amount that was actually spent or might have been spent.

It's important to understand this flaw because sometimes to "save" the most, you have to spend the most. In the case of this woman, she was able to lose so much only because she weighed so much in the first place. Further, at the time of publication she still weighed 283 pounds, so whatever strategies she used may not apply to those of us who struggle with 10 unwanted pounds.

If this woman wrote a diet book and marketed it on the claim that she lost 75 percent of her weight, you'd immediately conclude she must have weighed a lot before the diet. Unfortunately, when fuzzy claims are made about how much *money* can be "saved," we don't always grasp the implication.

The term "saving money" can mean one of two things:

- In the tangible sense, we "save money" when we literally put money in the bank.
- In the theoretical sense, we "save money" when we use one strategy versus another. In this case, to use this term responsibly we must specify the comparison strategy and, at best, give specific numbers to show how we arrived at the claim. The following are examples of how I have seen the term "saving money" misused in the theoretical sense.

First, let's pick on advertisers. Long ago, advertisers learned they could get a consumer to spend money by claiming he could save money. This commonly occurs when a store has overpriced merchandise and then marks it down "on sale," thereby appealing to the consumer's lust for spending and his need for feeling that he is saving money. Amusingly, one advertiser turned this around to his advantage. In a pre-Christmas ad, a low-cost jewelry shop said a competing shop had marked up its diamonds and then advertised customers could save 50 percent at its sale. Typically, an overpriced $2,000 diamond was marked down to a more reasonable $1,000. The low-cost jeweler said you could buy the same-quality diamond in his shop for $750, although you wouldn't, ahem, "save" as much.

The same strategy can be used when marketing save-money ideas. Say, for example, an author writes a book on how to renovate a house cheaply. In it, he shows how a ranch house can be fixed up for $10,000. But this isn't sufficiently sensational to sell books, since most people with common sense know how to do this. So he finds a brain-dead home renovator who spent $50,000 to fix up a similar house. He can now market his book on the claim that he saved 80 percent on the cost of home renovation. Although he does reveal how he arrived at his savings claim in the book, you have to buy the book in order to learn this. For this author to increase his savings claims to 90 percent, he just has to find a $100,000 home renovation.

Second, let's pick on consumer reporters. Sometimes consumer reporters throw out a statistic that a product or strategy could save X percent, or X amount of dollars without specifying the basis of their claim. They may do this because it's a fast way to express an idea. Unfortunately, the claim may be misleading.

For example, a magazine contained this typical claim about coupons: "By combining coupons and rebates you can save up to 60 percent of your grocery bill." As usual, nowhere attached to this claim were the other important pieces of information. For this statement to have any meaning, we must know the amount of the grocery bill either before or after the coupons are deducted.

Personally, I "save" about 1 percent on my grocery bill by using coupons. Because my percentage of savings is so much smaller, this might lead you to assume I'm not a very good shopper. But I spend $190 a month to feed a family of eight. I challenge anyone to show me how coupon use can save me 60 percent and knock my food bill down to $76 a month. In researching this previously, I know that such claims are based on extremely high starting grocery bills.

As an example of how focusing on "coupon savings" instead of spending is misleading: I buy store-brand cold cereal only when it goes on sale for $1 per box. Instead, if I apply a $1 coupon toward a $4 box of name-brand cereal in a double-coupon store, I would spend $2. In this case, to "save" 50 percent on cereal I'd have to double my spending.

Now it's occasionally possible to get name-brand cold cereal for free by using coupons and rebates. If the *only* cold-cereal option I had was a $4 box, it would be fair to say that if I got a free box I "saved" $4. However, since store-brand cold cereal can be purchased for $1, my true savings would be only $1.

Although coupon use can save money, after a certain point the only way you can increase your "savings percentage" is by increasing your after-coupon grocery bill.

Third, let's pick on tightwads. Sometimes out of simple enthusiasm we quantify the value of a bargain by focusing on a theoretical savings rather than on the amount we realistically would have spent. For example, a tightwad acquires ten free movie posters discarded by the local video store. Since large posters at Wal-Mart cost $5, he claims that by picking up these free posters he "saved" $50. In this case, the savings claim is misleading since he wouldn't have purchased ten $5 posters in the first place. As tightwads, we all delight in such freebies, but even if we collected 1,000 posters, it wouldn't result in more money in the bank.

In contrast, another tightwad claims she saves $7 each time she cuts her son's hair. Since she doesn't want her son to have a ponytail, one way or another he must have a haircut. Her only other option is a $7 haircut. In this case, her claim is accurate.

To be honest, I'll bet you could find a time or two when I have specified the value of a strategy in terms of a savings rather than the amount spent. But overall I do laboriously and tediously give a basis for any claims I make about money-saving strategies.

By focusing only on a theoretical savings, you may buy products you don't need, use too many coupons, or expend a lot of energy running around picking up free movie posters. In short, thinking about saving money in this way is nothing more than fake frugality. To "save money," in the tangible sense of putting money in the bank, you have to focus on the amount of money you actually spend.

To me, the basis of this article is pretty obvious. Yet, I am amazed at how often I see intelligent people get the "save money" concept backward. Surprisingly often, for example, reporters try to strong-arm me into quantifying the value of my book by asking, "If people used every idea in your book, how much could they save each year?" And what a great marketing opportunity it would be for me to enthusiastically gush, "If you buy my $12 book and use every idea in it, over the year you could save $10,000!"

But making such a claim would be unrealistic and misleading. Instead, I make my point by responding, "Gee, I dunno. That depends on how stupid those people were last year." We both laugh, and then I redirect the conversation to a discussion of how little money we spend on specific areas of our budget.

Oh, yeah, about that tip on saving $150,000: Don't buy a Rolls-Royce.

READ THIS ARTICLE AND SAVE $150,000 UPDATE

After the previous article ran in my newsletter, Patty Furlong of Mt. Pleasant, South Carolina, sent me what may be the best illustration of all. It's a joke she found in *The Best of the Good Clean Jokes* by Bob Phillips (Harvest House, 1989):

A man staggered into his house panting and exhausted. "What happened, honey?" inquired his wife.

"It's a great new idea I have," he gasped. "I ran all the way home behind the bus and saved fifty cents!"

"That wasn't very bright," replied his wife. "Why didn't you run behind a taxi and save three dollars?"

BOXES FOR BONBONS

Dear Amy,

I usually give homemade candies as gifts for all occasions. I solved my packaging dilemma by purchasing 50 white Chinese-food containers for $3, or 6¢ each. We decorate them with markers or rubber stamps and ink. Preprinted boxes sell at Hallmark for 69¢ each!

—Jeanne Buchanan
San Mateo, California

RETREADS RECONSIDERED

When Nancy Kish of Monroe, Connecticut, needed a new set of tires, she carefully researched all of the options and decided that in her case, retreads were the best value. I investigated and concluded that retreads are a worthy option to explore.

The information that follows is based on industry literature, and on my talks with Ken Collings, the manager of the Federal Tire Program; Dana Arnold, an environmental protection specialist with the EPA; David Van Sickle, director of automotive engineering for AAA; Rene Therrien, owner of a tire retreading shop here in Maine; and Harvey Brodsky, managing director of the Tire Retreading Information Bureau.

The technology of retreading has improved dramatically. Years ago, new treads were simply vulcanized onto old tires. Since then, retreading has evolved to a computerized business that uses the latest manufacturing technology.

A huge number of vehicles use retreads. In 1993, truckers purchased 16 million retreads and just 11 million new tires. Retreads are widely used on school buses, U.S. mail trucks, private delivery vehicles, even aircraft; about 80 percent of commercial jets use retreads.

Still, average motorists remain skeptical. When people see hunks of tread littering the sides of highways, they assume these peeled off of retreads, "proving" retreads aren't durable.

But when Probe Scientific Laboratories of El Paso, Texas, sampled roadside tire pieces in several states, it found that about two thirds were from nonretreaded tires and a third were from retreads. Further, research indicates that these tire treads ripped loose because the tires were underinflated, overloaded, or were mismatched dual truck tires, *not* because of the type of tire they were.

Recently the magazine *AAA World* raised another possible objection to retreads: that the buyer has no way of knowing whether the original casings are identical, and that mismatched

brands could affect a car's handling. But the experts we interviewed, including a spokesman for AAA, told us that this effect would be noticed only in high-performance cars taken to "the edge" of their capabilities. They also said that this loss of handling would be no greater than what results when one tire has a pound or less air pressure than another, and that it would be unnoticeable in trucks.

So, are retreads cost-effective? It depends.

The benefits of retreads may be negligible for the average passenger car. Although car retreads are about one third cheaper than new tires, the casings of car tires aren't as sturdy as those of truck tires. So while you might expect 36,000 to 40,000 miles from a new car tire, a retreaded one may be good for only 25,000 to 30,000 miles. Based on that assumption, and on prices in our area, we determined that the cost per mile for each kind of tire was about the same.

Nevertheless, retreads can make sense for cars driven in pothole-strewn areas where tires are torn or punctured before they are worn down. They may also save money on an older car that might not outlast new tires.

The obvious savings begin when you move up to tires for larger vehicles, such as pickup trucks and full-sized vans. In these tires the casings are far more durable, so you can expect to get as many or even more miles from retreads as from new tires. Further, retreaded truck tires cost about half as much as their new counterparts. For example, a mounted, balanced, new tire for a three-quarter-ton truck costs about $120. A mounted, balanced, retreaded version costs approximately $60.

If you are teetering on the question of whether retreads are worthwhile for you, consider that retreads are the environmentally responsible choice. According to the TRIB, while it takes 7 gallons of crude oil to make a new passenger tire, a retread requires only 2.5 gallons. Further, retreading significantly slows the flow of tires into overcrowded landfills.

The best way to find out who sells retreads in your area is to call or write:

Tire Retread Information Bureau
900 Weldon Grove
Pacific Grove, CA 93950
(408) 372-1917

You can also find retread dealers under "Tires—Retreads" in the Yellow Pages.

Look for a dealer who buys from a retreader who belongs to either the American Retreaders Association and/or is an A-rated member of the National Tire Dealers and Retreaders Association. You should also insist on a warranty that's at least as good as the one offered for a new tire.

Nancy Kish researched—and rejected—one other cheap tire alternative: used tires from a junkyard. These are removed from wrecked cars. She found them to be roughly a third cheaper than retreads.

I called several junkyards and found that a typical used passenger-car tire costs from $5 to $30, depending on its condition. I also called several tire service centers and found they charge an average of $9 to mount and balance a tire.

So it's clear that used tires can have the cheapest initial cost; they could cost as little as $14 each for the poorest-quality used tires. But they have no warranty, are sometimes hard to find, may be aged or damaged in ways that aren't obvious, and require two errands: first to the junkyard, then to the tire shop. Van Sickle, our expert from AAA, agreed with all of these observations. He said he "wouldn't touch them with a 10-foot pole."

PROM 'N' AID

According to *Your Prom* magazine, the average cost of a prom date is $1,058: $585 for the girl and $473 for the guy. As in all areas of spending money, people mistakenly believe that because the average spending habits of most people are so high, getting by with much less is simply impossible. Some expenses, like tickets, are fixed, but letters from several readers prove that most prom costs can be beat.

FOR GIRLS

Kimberly Barbour of Wilmington, North Carolina, wrote that her daughter was thrilled with her consignment-shop prom dress, which cost $10. (Her daughter insists that anyone who pays mall prices is "like, a total dweeb!")

Judy Burkhardt of Wall, New Jersey, bought a pink Jessica McClintock gown that originally cost $100 for $5 at an end-of-the-season sale at Marshall's, and then saved it until the next season.

One teen, of West Alexandria, Ohio, wrote that after much fruitless prom-dress searching she realized that she already had the perfect outfit—in her mother's closet. She borrowed her mother's elegant evening dress, along with her matching shoes, purse, and gloves. She added her own necklace and had to buy only earrings. The total cost was $6.50.

Merrie Hallman of Livingston Manor, New York, sent a precise breakdown of the cost to outfit her daughter. A basic black gown from an auction cost $5. Two yards of fabric to update the bow on the dress cost $12. Black patent-leather shoes from Fayva cost $8.

Sale-priced fancy stockings cost $2.50. A comb with matching fabric flowers from a craft store cost $5. Gloves and shoe clips were donated by her grandmother for no cost. So the total cost of her daughter's outfit was $32.50.

FOR GUYS

In *The Tightwad Gazette II* we published a reader letter in which a mother related how she outfitted her two sons for $15 each. She bought thrift-shop tuxedos and cummerbunds. She borrowed shirts and bought new black ties. Each ensemble cost $15 and still fit a year later.

Another reader, who asked to remain anonymous, wrote that she makes corsages for her son's dates. She buys florist's tape and ribbon to make bows. She substitutes quilting pins and recycled wire for their professional counterparts. She either uses a flower from her garden or buys a single flower and uses greenery from her houseplants. For presentation, she buys a plastic see-through salad container from a deli, places the corsage on a bed of Easter grass or exotic paper cut in strips, and ties a ribbon around the container.

MINOR MIDASES

Dear Amy,

Our bank offers "junior savings accounts." The kids get incentives all year long because if they make a deposit they can get a gift.

Just before Mother's Day they get a free mum plant for depositing money. Other holidays also yield gifts.

During the year they have received a special day at the movie theater, which included popcorn and a prize (like a Frisbee or squeeze bottle). We get coupons every few months for free french fries, discounts at the skating rink, free breakfasts, and so on. Aside from the freebies, the children are learning to save money.

—Julie Schulte
Dubuque, Iowa

GRASS ACT

Dear Amy,

Here's a cheap thrill for kids: When we mow our lawn (we live on a farm and have 2 acres to mow), we cut a "maze" in the lawn for our kids to play in. They love running along the paths and trying to beat one another to the end. We've done this all summer and they have yet to tire of it.

—Valaree Stodola
Shellburg, Iowa

TOWELS WITHOUT SCOWLS

Dear Amy,

As a lifeguard/swim instructor, I'd like to suggest a free source of towels. At the end of the outdoor swim season, the lost and found often has some wonderful but "not matching" towels. Of course, this is after reminding the users to review the lost and found for their missing items.

—Ebie Morris
Villa Park, Illinois

A GOOD IDEA, I TINK

Dear Amy,

We like to play with Tinkertoys, but we needed more sticks. Using a hacksaw, Mom cut a dowel the lengths we needed and put slits in the ends.

—Heather Melton
Lucas, Texas

(I used this idea because the yard-sale Tinkertoys I purchased were short on sticks. Jim used the band saw to make more from ¼-inch dowels. It took him 40 minutes to make 64 sticks; the dowels cost $1.91. FZ)

LABOR AND SAVOR

Dear Amy,

We give a frugal baby shower that we call a "casserole shower." We give it about three weeks before the baby is due. All the guests bring a casserole as their gift. The mom-to-be just puts them in the freezer until the baby arrives. Then, during those hectic postpartum days, she just has to pop a casserole from her freezer into the oven and dinner is ready! These showers are fun, easy, cheap, and a godsend if you're the mom-to-be!

—Jane Kiel
Kalamazoo, Michigan

TAGS FOR TOGS

Dear Amy,

I use homemade, numbered cardboard markers on the hangers holding my office clothes to indicate whether the garment can stand another wearing or is due for washing. I can tell at a glance whether I have enough ready for my work week, and as I usually handwash these garments separately, it allows me to wash them more efficiently.

—Deirdre Angus
British Columbia

PUNCH AND MUNCH

Dear Amy,

The cracker recipe [in the first *Tightwad Gazette* book] is great. But instead of cutting them, use a comb to "dot" them and break apart when done. You can also sprinkle them with onion or garlic powder, powdered cheese from macaroni-and-cheese in a box, or sugar and cinnamon.

—Pam Ristaino
Lindenwold, New Jersey

READ 'EM AND WEEP

Dear Amy,

For my parents' 35th wedding anniversary, I got the idea to write letters to all of the people who were in their wedding and to some of their close friends, asking them to send a card and their well-wishes. Everyone wrote back, many with letters that included a recounting of funny things that happened during that time. I wrapped the letters like an ordinary present and when my parents opened it, they were so surprised! My mom tried reading the first letter, but became so choked up she had to hand them over to my father, who finished reading them aloud to the family. What fun it was watching the smiles on their faces!

—Jan Chase
San Jose, California

WHAT'S CHEAP, DOC?

Dear Amy,

Check with your local hospital to see if they have an in-house printing department. We use the hospital for much of the printing needed for our business. They are happy to do it to fill their excess capacity. The cost is less than half of what we used to pay a commercial printer.

—Barbara J. Durflinger
Benton Harbor, Michigan

ROLL OUT THE SAVINGS

Dear Amy,

I normally buy the single rolls of 1,000-sheet toilet paper, which sell for 50¢ to 60¢. Today I went to the local paper products factory in my town and purchased a case of 72 rolls of the same kind of paper for $14.25. This is about 20¢ per roll. These were "seconds"; they were not perfectly round, but are quite usable.

—Karyn Price
Kissimmee, Florida

(While you may not have a paper factory in your town, many factories do sell directly to customers at wholesale prices. It's worth a phone call. FZ)

KEEP UP APPEARANCES

Dear Amy,

My husband's white gym socks lose the elasticity in the tops before the bottoms wear out. I buy elastic "thread," wind it into the bobbin of my sewing machine, and stitch around the cuff about three times to restore the elasticity.

—Carolyn Pollock
Hunt, New York

CREATE A BREAKFAST MUFFIN UPDATE

In *The Tightwad Gazette II* I published a sort of universal muffin formula. This was one of the most well-received articles I've published. Well, I've found an improve-

ment on the technique I suggested for using cooked grains (such as leftover oatmeal, rice, or cornmeal mush) in muffins.

In the original article I passed along a common cookbook suggestion: If you're adding cooked grain, you should separate your egg, add the yolk directly to the batter, beat the white until stiff, and fold it into the batter. I assume this was suggested to offset the heaviness of the cooked cereal.

Personally, I found beating egg whites to be too laborious at 7 A.M. So, despite frequently having several small containers of leftover cooked cereal jammed in my freezer, I've tried to find other ways to use it up.

I've experimented and found that I could use cooked cereals in my muffin batter with the aid of my blender. First, I mix all of the dry ingredients in a big bowl. Then I put all of the wet and moist ingredients in a blender. These could include: cooked grain (about ½ cup per batch), egg, milk, honey or molasses, peanut butter, pumpkin puree, applesauce, and/or banana. I've even added unused cookie dough and pastry scraps. I don't blenderize any moist ingredient that I want to retain its original texture, such as shredded zucchini.

Another possible addition to your blender of wet stuff could be small quantities of unappealing dry leftovers, such as broken cookies, cornbread, muffins, or bread crusts. This stuff is hard to crumble in a blender alone, but it blends easily with wet ingredients.

After blending, I mix the wet stuff into the bowl of dry stuff.

I make a final adjustment to the batter by adding more liquid or flour.

The blender seems to whip up the egg sufficiently as well as helps to quickly combine hard-to-mix-in moist stuff.

If you still have a hard time working muffins into your busy morning routine, I have a final suggestion: Premix your ingredients the night before. Put your dry ingredients in a large bowl and cover. Put your wet and moist ingredients in a separate bowl or blender jar and put that in the refrigerator. Also, pregrease your muffin tins. In the morning it's a simple matter to combine the two bowls of ingredients to make your muffins.

I WOULDN'T STEER YOU WRONG

Three newsletter readers asked the following questions about meat:

- Linda Linden of Kettering, Ohio, asked, "Could you write down some of your 'rules of thumb,' such as the prices that you generally pay for meat?"
- Robin Mertz of Edgewater, Maryland, asked, "I have been toying with the idea of purchasing a steer and having it slaughtered for my family's consumption. Have you researched the cost to pur-

chase meat in this manner versus store-bought?"

• A reader from St. Paul, Minnesota, asked, "Shopping for chicken is frustrating. It can be bought in at least six different packages, all with different combinations. Are boneless breasts really that much more expensive when you consider all the bones and innards you throw away from the other packages?"

All of these questions come under the larger topic of my "protein philosophy."

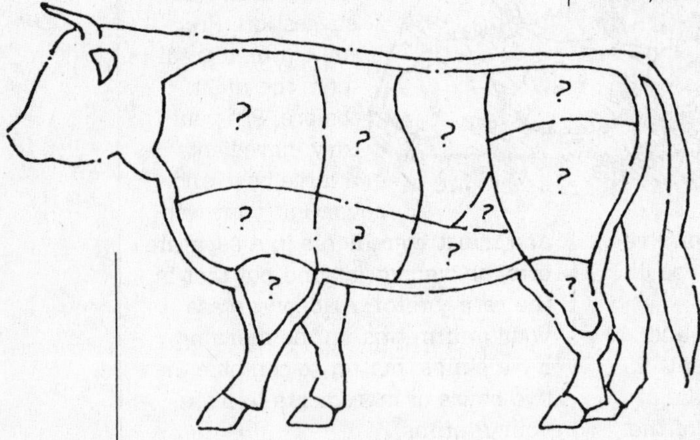

Before going further, let me emphasize that this philosophy is mine. Meat consumption is a subject surprisingly loaded with political, environmental, and health beliefs. Our "less-meat" meals might not meet with the approval of vegetarians or hard-core carnivores. So you can make different choices based on your beliefs, health restrictions, or personal preferences.

That said, there are three basic ways to compare meat prices:

• Keep track of the prices of all the various cuts of meat. Unfortunately, there are too many types to track easily, and there are variables within each type, such as how much bone or fat are included. But simply purchasing meat on sale won't necessarily reduce your food bill either—filet mignon and lobster go on sale, too.

• Calculate the cost per gram of protein. *Sylvia Porter's Money Book* (Avon Books, 1976) has a chart to help you do this. It shows that because hot dogs have more fat and filler, chicken, even when it costs more per pound, could provide more protein for less money. But this method has two flaws. First, it's the most complicated way to compare meat costs. Second, we don't need to track our protein consumption, because most Americans eat far too much anyway. The average American eats over 100 grams of protein per day. The recommended daily allowance is 55 grams, and studies have shown that we need as little as 30 grams daily.

• Calculate the cost per portion, or the cost of one meal for your family. This is the simplest method, and the one that reflects the way people really eat. For example, a one-serving portion might be 4 ounces of turkey, but just 1½ ounces of cheese. So though the turkey costs less per pound, the actual cost of the meals might be the same.

When I was first trying to reduce my food budget, I tried and rejected the first two methods. Instead I began to pay attention to how much each type of protein meal cost. When we bought a pork roast, we would eat a meal and

then package the leftovers into family-dinner-sized portions. If the roast yielded four family dinners, I would divide the price of the roast by 4 and use that number for comparison with other protein sources.

From this I developed price guidelines, which with inflation have gradually risen over time. To answer the first question, we now pay up to 69¢ for with-bone meat and $1.19 for boneless. We often buy meat that costs much less than this, and just a couple of times each year Jim splurges above this price range.

By limiting ourselves to these prices, we still have plenty of variety. I detailed the types of meat in our diet on page 66, "Pantry Principle Update."

My guidelines largely eliminated the following meats from our diet: seafood, chicken breasts, most cuts of beef, deli meats, and pork chops.

It's true that the low-cost meats we've chosen aren't always the ones with the least fat and preservatives. Neither are we eating 100 percent organically raised meats. But we feel our choice is reasonable because we eat less meat than most American families. We usually use it as an ingredient rather than as a main course, and we average one pound per dinner for all eight of us. Further, we remove the skin from chicken and drain the fat from ground beef.

We use this exercise to keep us on the frugal-meat course: When we buy or are given a rare expensive cut of meat, we consider if the extra cost is worth the extra pleasure. For example, if sea scallops cost ten times as much as turkey, we ask "Did we enjoy this ten times as much?" The answer is almost always no.

To answer the latter two readers questions specifically:

When you buy a whole steer, you'll probably pay the wholesale price. This is less than the regular supermarket price for the same cuts of meat, but more than the supermarket's loss-leader prices. A supermarket sells some things below wholesale because they make it up when customers buy overpriced potato chips.

The problem with buying whole or half steers is that you lose the option of choice: You must buy the more expensive steaks to get the ground beef. But even if you would buy the steaks anyway, the steer may not be the best deal. To be sure, you must haul out your calculator and price book and determine if the cuts from the whole steer are as cheap as the sale prices you can get on the cuts at the supermarket.

To answer the last question, the amount of waste in cuts with fat, bones, and skin varies among types of meat, but it's fair to say that the waste might be about one third of the total weight. So if boneless costs one third more, it's about the same price as with-bone. The only reliable way to know is to buy both types and count how many meals you get, including soup stock.

FOR SALE BY TIGHTWAD

Our newsletter solicitation for readers' "For Sale by Owner" experiences received a large and, to me, fascinating response. We got 188 letters, and the consensus was overwhelmingly in favor of the FSBO route versus selling through a real estate agent.

In all, 130 readers said they had successfully sold their own homes, while just 10 said they had tried to sell on their own and failed. We also received a number of letters about readers' success with "compromise" strategies such as bargaining for a lower agent's commission. And we got a surprisingly small response, just six letters, from real estate agents warning that owner-selling is an awful idea.

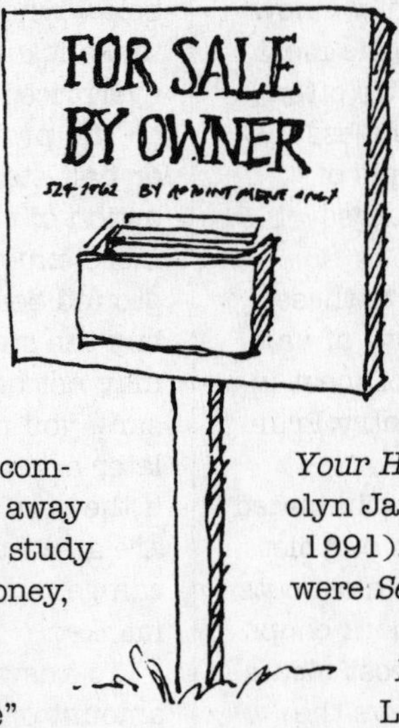

Clearly, these letters are not a scientific sample of house-selling experiences across the nation, but I found them compelling. The lesson I took away was: If you are willing to study and invest some time, money, and energy, selling your own home can be one of the highest "hourly wage" activities a tightwad can do. Readers who supplied dollar figures said they saved from $3,500 to $31,000 by selling their homes themselves. At the least, many readers suggested, it makes sense to give owner-selling a try for a month or two before turning the task over to a real estate agent.

Our research revealed that owner-selling isn't rare. According to the U.S. Department of Commerce, in 1993, 29.4 percent of all single-family-home sales and transfers were conducted by the owner. (Although the real estate industry argues that the total drops to 10 percent if you subtract sales between family members.)

And the savings can be substantial. Say you sell your house for $140,000. The average agent's commission is 6 percent, so the approximate cost of using an agent is $8,400.

While selling your own home can be an excellent idea, it can have pitfalls, and it is important to educate yourself. This article will provide a basic outline of what readers said they did to sell their homes, but we can't cover the whole topic in this limited space.

So the first step is reading one or more of the many books on the subject. The one most highly recommended by readers is *How to Sell Your Home in the '90s* by Carolyn Janik (Viking Penguin, 1991). Also recommended were *Sell Your Own Home* by Warren Boroson, and *For Sale by Owner* by Louis Gilmore (Simon & Schuster, 1989). These, and others, should be at your library or available through interlibrary loan.

The next step is to ask around for a local lawyer who specializes in real estate. Make contact and tell him or her your plans. (Usually, this first consultation is free.) Some readers have never used an attorney, relying instead on advice from their bank or other sources, but most felt that having an attorney on your side is crucial to avoid mistakes. The attorney can guide you through the whole sales process.

Now, you need an appraisal. You can pay $200 to $400 for a professional one, but many readers got one free from their local real estate agents. To avoid an ethics violation, "be up front about the fact that you plan to sell it yourself, but point out that you would consider their company in case you are unable to sell it," said Linda Courtney of Worthington, Massachusetts. One plan that made sense to me is to get five such appraisals and use the middle one to price your house. You can also attend open houses and review recent property sales information at your county recorder's office.

The next step is to spruce up your property. Eliminate clutter, paint with neutral shades, buy potted plants for your porch, mow the lawn twice a week if necessary, and clean, clean, clean.

The next step is marketing, and it is here that the advantages of FSBO really shine. As a reader from Salt Lake City, Utah, put it, "Realtors don't care which houses in particular they sell, as long as houses are sold. They will spread their resources and energy over as many houses as possible and let market forces do the rest. An owner-seller cares about selling her house in particular. She can concentrate resources and energy on it."

Readers' marketing strategies include:

• Make an excellent, handmade sign that includes your phone number (and "By Appointment Only" if you don't want random visits). Put them up on your street and, if possible, on any heavily traveled streets nearby. Attach a small box to hold flyers.

• Print a flyer to hand to people who tour the house, and to put in the box on your sign. Many readers sent copies of their flyers, and some were absolutely gorgeous. Nancy Tague of Baker, Louisiana, produced the best one I saw. It was printed on eye-catching orange paper and included, along with the usual nuts-and-bolts information, the house's history, a complete floor plan, photographs of the front, back, and sides, a description of nearby amenities and attractions,

and a month-by-month breakdown of gas, electric, water, and sewer bills.

- Put out the word. A surprising number of readers sold their homes through word of mouth. Rebecca Gumina of Rocky River, Ohio, said that through this strategy she got visits from the doughnut shop manager's brother, church members, relatives of neighbors, and her daughter's soccer coach.
- Advertise creatively. Along with an ad in the newspaper, advertise in unusual places and publications. Sharon Jonah of Highland, Michigan, sold her home through an ad in the local hospital's employee newsletter. "Any major employer within a few miles of the house is an ideal place to find potential buyers," she wrote.
- Have an open house. Sunday afternoons are best.
- Try to sell in the spring or summer, if possible.

For any of these marketing strategies to work, people need to be able to reach you. If you are not home for much of the day, you'll need to have an answering machine to field calls. Change your outgoing message so that it mentions that you are, indeed, the people who are selling a house.

Prepare for the fact that up to half the calls you'll get will be from realtors trying to get your listing. They may also say they've got the "perfect buyer" for you. But be aware: If you sign a contract and the realtor doesn't provide this buyer, you'll have to pay him a fee even if you attract a buyer on your own later.

Arrange visits at a time that's convenient for you. For safety, arrange to have a companion with you during house tours. Have a stack of purchase agreements (available from any title company or office-supply store) on hand in case anyone makes an offer.

When people visit, point out nice features that they might otherwise miss, but generally leave them alone; you want to give them the chance to mentally arrange their furniture in your living room.

Avoid verbal dickering. If someone asks, "Would you take . . . ," you should always answer, "I'll consider any offer that I receive in writing," and hand them a purchase agreement to take.

Any formal offer should be accompanied by a check to demonstrate seriousness; $1,000 is a good number. The check isn't cashed; it's held by the title company or closing attorney and usually voided at closing. You should also ask for some evidence, such as a loan preapproval, to indicate that the buyer can come up with the money.

Most potential buyers expect a counteroffer. Many readers said they appreciated not having a realtor as a go-between in this process. As with the original offer, the counteroffer should be made in writing.

The closing itself is generally handled by the title company or an attorney.

Again, I emphasize that this is just a general overview. You may approach the whole process differently.

There is, in fact, a new kind of owner-selling that seems to be catching on. The book *How to Sell Your Home in Five Days* by William G. Effros (Workman Publishing, $14.95) outlines a method to attract many potential buyers quickly and get them bidding

against each other for your home in that short period. To anyone who has spent six months trying to keep a house spotless for showings, Effros's five-day plan may have real appeal. Effros says he's sold 100 homes this way, always at market value or above. Effros successfully demonstrated his method for CNN. As it happens, I was interviewed by the same CNN journalist who did his piece, and he agreed, to his amazement, that the method did work.

All of the above is not to say that readers had no negative comments. Among the ten readers who had failed FSBO experiences, one said she got tired of giving tours to people who were "not serious." Another felt that prospective buyers were reluctant to talk business with owners.

But the vast majority of the general comments were positive, and informative. For example:

• "I am a former real estate salesman," wrote Richard Bachler of Peoria, Arizona. "We were taught that 'laymen' can't possibly sell their own homes without professional help. Hogwash!"

• "Over the last 12 years, we have bought and sold six homes: three with the help of a real estate agent, three we sold ourselves. Let me tell you, the houses we sold ourselves went much more smoothly than the houses we listed with an agent," contributed Erin Tolli of St. George, Utah.

• "Brokers will say, 'Buyers will discount the price because they know you aren't paying a commission.' The truth is, if you have a saleable house, you will get market value," wrote Ann Crowley of Beverly, Massachusetts.

• "My only caveat would be that owners must realize that it takes more effort than just sticking a 'For Sale' sign out on the front yard," cautioned a reader from Colorado Springs, Colorado. "Professional realtors are correct when they say that people who do just this are likely to fail."

• "We hired a retired real estate agent on a consulting basis," wrote Jenny Beatty of Monkton, Maryland. "This cost less than $200 and was invaluable."

• And, finally, a comment from Kathy Lloyd and Drake Barton of Clancy, Montana, points out that the benefits of owner-selling are not just financial: "An advantage of FSBO is that it promotes self-sufficiency, and sidesteps those who would try to convince us we can't handle our own affairs."

LOOK FOR FRUIT LOOPHOLES

When I was a kid, the local supermarket always had a bin full of imperfect produce, such as brown bananas and grapes that had become separated from their bunches.

But as more and more of the big chain supermarkets strive for an upscale image, less-than-perfect foods have become difficult to find—they just seem to vanish.

Or do they?

Gloria Whitelaw of Wilmington, North Carolina, struck up a conversation with the produce manager at her local store. He told her to come in on Tuesdays, Thursdays, and Saturday mornings and she could have all of the overripe produce she wanted.

"So, every other day I've been

coming home with literally bushels of peaches, tomatoes, green beans, bananas, limes, apples, kiwi fruit, mushrooms, etc.," she writes. "He charges me a dollar or two for a cart full. We've never eaten so well, and I am stocking the freezer and pantry."

To see if Gloria's experience has widespread applicability, I had one of my staffers visit seven supermarkets in and around his hometown. In each, he casually sidled up to the produce manager and asked what happens to overripe fruits and vegetables.

At two of the upscale supermarkets, the PMs informed him that all overripe produce goes immediately to the local food bank.

At another, equally upscale place, the PM told him that it's strict company policy that all dated produce gets thrown out. "We used to give it to a pig farmer, but he stopped coming," he said.

At another relatively posh market, the PM directed him to a wheeled cart full of 11¢-per-pound spotted bananas in an obscure corner of the produce section. As my staffer loaded up (he eventually peeled and froze them), the PM informed him that this cart appeared irregularly, and that there were no private backroom deals made.

At a considerably lower-scale market, the PM told him that "we order carefully, so there's no waste." At another market of a similar economic stratum, the PM was only mildly encouraging. "We may have something, but it would be very rare," he said. "I'll keep you in mind."

My intrepid staffer was about to give up when he decided to swing by the lowest-scale market in his area. Here, he hit the jackpot. The PM informed him that she had private arrangements with several individuals to buy large quantities of outdated produce. While she did not offer the kind of prices cited by Gloria, she did say that she generally sold the stuff for less than half of its usual retail price.

As my staffer reflected on his survey, he realized that the important factor here was probably not so much upscale versus downscale as it was chain versus independent. Chain supermarkets, even those with as few as three stores, generally have cast-in-stone policies against backroom deals of any kind. One-of-a-kind mom-and-pop stores, while free to set up creative side deals, are often too small to have any produce section at all. So the optimum place to get a backroom deal is a store that is similar to the last store my staffer visited—large enough to have a good-sized produce section but not part of a chain.

Finally, Laura Smith of Maple Valley, Washington, points out that she's found a similar phenomenon in meat sections. "Your friendly butcher makes his hamburger out of the roasts and steaks that he didn't sell after they're a few days old," she writes. "See if you can make a deal with him to buy them at hamburger prices. Also, chicken and turkey parts are generally tossed after a few days; if you can get him to sell them to you, go for it."

So, next time you go to the market, strike up a conversation. You may be pleasantly surprised.

SCRATCH 'N' SPIFF

Dear Amy,

If your glasses have plastic lenses and are scratched, try spraying them with Lemon Pledge, spreading it gently over both sides of each lens, and then wiping with a soft cloth. The furniture polish fills in some of the scratches and improves your vision without the purchase of new glasses.

—Anita Puzon
Poulsbo, Washington

GOT TWO COVERED

Dear Amy,

My husband and I receive full family health insurance coverage from both of our jobs. My employer will refund a portion of the premium that they would pay if the employee can show that he or she is covered by the spouse's insurance.

—Julie Doerr
Watsonville, California

BIG BUCK SAVINGS

Dear Amy,

Every year, deer are hunted and killed, taken to processing plants, and not even picked up by the hunter! It is illegal in many states to sell deer meat, so the plant processor sells the deer for the butchering fee alone, which in this area is around 40 cents a pound. Venison can be eaten alone, mixed half and half with beef hamburger, or ground with beef fat to make a less lean ground beef. If you don't care for the flavor, you can disguise it in chili, stews, and casseroles.

—Cathy White
Idabel, Oregon

TAKE A LAPSE

Dear Amy,

To reduce the cost of membership in a warehouse club, we intentionally allow our membership to lapse each year, renewing it several months after it has expired. So, for example, if we allow three months to elapse before renewing, in effect we reduce the cost of membership by 25 percent. Naturally, we time our purchases to maximize the time period between membership renewals.

—Patrick Kearney
Shippenville, Pennsylvania

ODD ADVICE

Dear Amy,

In "Get a Piece of the Auction," (see page 68), you mention making a mental note of the top dollar you'd pay. My husband and I attend several auctions and have noticed most people's "top dollar" is even money. Example: If the bid is $700, and your "top dollar" bid is $725, you are likely to get it. This concept works well for sealed bids, too. We got an answering machine for a sealed bid of $10.28. The only other bid was for $10 even.

—Judy J. Nelson
Gilmore City, Iowa

BUYS IN THE 'HOOD

Thought I'd pass along my greatest yard-sale find, which happened just yesterday. At my very first stop in a wealthy Mobile neighborhood, I purchased eight complete six-piece place settings plus serving dishes, cream and sugar bowls, etc. of brand-new Mikasa china for $20. I asked the owner why she was selling it and she told me they buy new china about once a year and she was tired of that color. I stopped at a department store later that day and priced the china. It sold for $130 a place setting. I am still in shock. With all of the other china she included in the set, it was about a $1,400 value.

—Jeanetta Seay
Chatom, Alabama

SOAP CRAYONS

Take one cup of laundry soap and add 30 to 40 drops of food coloring. Add water by teaspoonfuls until soap becomes liquid. Stir well. Pack soap into ice cube tray. Set in a sunny, dry place for two days. Crayons will become hard and great for writing in the sink or tub.

—Julie T. Offutt
Louisville, Tennessee

OLDER BUT MISER

The high school in my town allows any adult resident to attend classes with the kids free of charge, as long as there is room in the class. I took a class in pottery. I had a lot of fun and made some pieces that I used for Christmas presents.

—Linda Bodnar
Windsor, Connecticut

HELP FOR WEARY WIPERS

Dear Amy,

My thrifty husband has a way of making our windshield wipers last for "one more rainy season." He lightly sands the edge of the brittle rubber with sandpaper, and once again they're like new!

—Kathleen Balge
New Berlin, Wisconsin

AVOID THE TRAPEZOID

Dear Amy,

Regarding your reconstruction of a "mutant" pillow ruined by washing (see page 38), next time you wash a pillow, take the time to "tie" it with yarn, running the yarn through both the inner casing and fill, just as if you were tying a quilt. This keeps the polyester from shifting. Then clip the yarn when you are done.

—Jessica Ayers
Cassopolis, Michigan

WOW KNOW-HOW

Once when I inventoried my supply of kids' clothes before yard-sale season, I had then nine-year-old Jamie try on a pair of respectable-looking boots. She agreed that they would be satisfactory for the following winter. However, six months later she informed me that she now wanted green L. L. Bean–style boots like most of her classmates had. She also decided that the boots she had previously approved were slightly too big for her.

Although I felt no parental obligation to satisfy her change of tastes, I did want her to have boots that fit properly. So before we headed to a retail shoe store, I suggested we hit our church's thrift shop. It offers clothing at yard-sale prices; however, the selection of footwear is so poor that I guessed I'd have a better chance of converting Donald Trump to frugality than I did of finding suitable boots for her there. But as we browsed, Jamie plucked a pair of plum-colored L. L. Bean–style boots from the shelf and exclaimed, "I want these kind of boots . . . only green!" Amazingly, these boots were exactly Jamie's size, in great condition, and cost just 25¢. Although she wasn't interested in the boots, I bought them anyway.

Once home, I attempted to "sell" these boots to my disinterested daughter. "Look, these boots are almost exactly what you want. Do you think I should spend $25 to buy new boots for you?" My daughter's response was revealing: "Mmmooommm! I didn't say *'new,'* I said *'green'*!"

By her own admission, the only difference between the boot alternatives was the color. So I offered my counterlogic: "Okay, plum-colored boots cost 25¢ and green boots cost $25. Are green boots a hundred times better than plum-colored ones?" She admitted they weren't and quite contentedly wore the plum-colored boots for the rest of the winter.

This story provides an example of a crucial tightwad test for value: examining the ratio of satisfaction-to-price between two or more alternatives. Put another way, it's important to examine the "cost per

wow," or CPW, when making purchase decisions. The point should always be to get the most wow for the smallest expenditure of money.

The concept applies to nearly every purchase. Suppose you have the choice of a $600 camping vacation or a $6,000 luxury cruise. You

evaluate how much you would enjoy each vacation on the 1-to-10 wow scale. The camping trip would rate 5 wows, and the cruise would rate 10 wows. This means the camping trip would have a $120 CPW as compared to the $600 CPW of the cruise. Although you would enjoy the cruise twice as much, you would get only a fifth of the value. If you go camping, you'll have funds in reserve to purchase other things that are also relatively low-cost per wow. So you wind up with 40, 50, or even 60 wows for the same $6,000 that would have yielded 10 wows if spent on the cruise.

Mastering this value test requires a somewhat different thought process than many people use. Most people will buy the more expensive alternative if they 1) like it more, and 2) can afford it. These two criteria don't include the question of whether they receive sufficient value for the money they spend. And it's not always enough to go further and vaguely consider if the purchase was "worth the money." Using the 1-to-10 wow scale enables you to make more precise decisions.

I also use the 1-to-10 wow scale as one of many ways to determine how important financial and/or time-usage decisions are to other family members, especially with kids whose feelings are hard to read. Some kids express themselves in a way that leads you to believe all of their wants are a 10, while others lead you to believe every desire is a 1. By asking them to place a number on their wants in conjunction with asking them other questions such as "Would you pay for half of it yourself?," I can determine how important the want is to the child and make decisions accordingly.

For example, over the past years I've often felt that our family was devoting too much time to Scouting activities. (At one point there were about 12 commitments during a two-week period.) I was unsure if the children were enjoying it enough to warrant the hassle of hurry-up dinners and ferrying them around. When I asked them, I learned that Scouting is an 8 for them, so we decided to stick with it. Had I learned it was a 3, I would have suggested the kids drop out.

Here are some other pairs of options where I concede the expensive alternative may be nicer but it fails my personal CPW test:

- In-theater movies versus a $1 rented tape at home.
- Restaurant versus home-cooked meals.
- Retail merchandise versus good-but-not-perfect yard-sale stuff.
- Cable TV versus broadcast TV.
- A new car versus continuing to drive a five-year-old one.
- A kid's haircut at a salon versus one at home.
- First-class versus coach airline travel.
- Real maple syrup versus homemade "maple" syrup.
- A magazine subscription versus old freebies from the library.
- New CDs versus yard-sale purchased LPs.

However, there *are* some cases where more expensive options do pass the 1-to-10 wow-scale test.

- Given my family's size, my home is several times better than a house that might have cost half as much.
- Given the needs of our business, a $1,800 new computer is

more than twice as good as a $900 used one.

• Given my tastes and the fact that it could remain in the family for generations, a $200 antique empire bureau from an estate auction is more than four times better than a beat-up $50 yard-sale find.

Two final points. No one can dictate, or even guess, what wows another person—it's best simply to ask directly. And sometimes, with time, our feelings about wows can change. I asked Jamie about the effect of not wearing green boots all winter. She said that once she had the plum-colored boots she began to notice a lot of other girls had plum-colored boots as well.

POWER YARD-SALING

Articles I've written in which I refer to yard sales have prompted letters from newsletter readers. A few doubted that I was finding clothing as cheap as I claimed (from free to $1 per item). They hadn't seen *any* clothes that cheap at yard sales. Others, noting that I said I went to more than 200 yard sales per summer, questioned the payback on my time and gasoline.

So I thought it might be useful to discuss my yard-sale techniques. Finding good deals requires going to a lot of yard sales because the merchandise is unpredictable. But to ensure a high payback, I use certain strategies to save time and gas.

In my area, yard sales are held for up to three consecutive days, generally from Friday to Sunday. I've experimented with going on various days and have been most successful on Saturdays. This allows me to hit some sales on the first day (good stuff goes early) and some on the last day (leftovers go cheap).

On Friday, I pick up the newspaper from Lewiston/Auburn, the metropolitan area of about 30,000 where I go to yard sales. The classifieds list from 50 to 100 sales. The ads are arranged by town but are otherwise listed randomly, and so are hard to work from on yard-sale day. In addition, I'm unfamiliar with most of this area's complex sprawl of streets.

So on Friday night I get out my city map. Using a pencil, I circle the street names and write in the street number(s) next to the circles. By doing this I can easily see where the yard sales are clustered and how to drive the most efficient route possible. Although I bring the newspaper with me, I seldom refer to it during the yard-sale day. Since I rarely go with another adult and must navigate as well as drive, I can easily fold the map small enough to reveal one section at a time, and can hold it with my thumb pointing to the next sale. Before I yard-sale again, I will erase all my markings. One map will last through the summer.

I always take our 1983 Plymouth Horizon as opposed to our Chevy Suburban; the Horizon uses less gas and is easier to park and turn. It's also our least valuable car, and so the best candidate to subject to the stop-and-start rigors of yard-saling. In the last several years, I had to return with our Suburban just once, to pick up a free-for-the-hauling bureau.

Yard sales start between 7 and 9 A.M. I plan to arrive at the first sale by 9, unless I know that many yard sales at the beginning of my circuit are open earlier. So-called

early birds arrive before the advertised time hoping to get the good deals. The rudest may even stop in the day before the sale or at 6 A.M. I prefer to go to more yard sales to offset my politeness disadvantage. On a few occasions when I've accidentally arrived early, I've been turned away, or found that all the merchandise wasn't unpacked yet and my preplanned route didn't allow me to return at a later time. It's true that a lot of the good stuff, particularly furniture, goes early, but proprietors are less likely to negotiate in the early morning, whereas they'll announce "Make any offer" later in the day.

Your route will depend on geography as well as the type of stuff for which you are looking. New suburban developments generally offer more stuff for kids, but have only '70s Sears-style household decor items. Older neighborhoods tend to yield interesting near-antique junk. Affluent areas may consistently offer neatly displayed name-brand clothes—with higher, nonnegotiable prices. Moderate-income neighborhoods seem to have more jumbled piles of clothes for 10¢ to 25¢ per item, and these have yielded good-looking clothes.

Aside from my map, I bring:

- A measuring tape and my kids' clothing inventory (as discussed on page 6.)
- Snacks and a Thermos with a cold drink. If I'm traveling with a child, I make sure these are especially appealing snacks.
- Paper bags and a blanket to hide finds with gift potential.
- A pocketful of coins and dollar bills, because I can make purchases faster if I have the correct change.

• A lightweight jacket and other clothing that will accommodate unpredicted cold or hot weather.

Although I have never been this organized, I've also thought I should bring a large selection of working batteries to test suspicious electronic stuff.

Though I travel faster alone, I often take one child at a time. It's a way for me to do one-to-one quality time. I also want my kids to get used to yard-sale prices, so they experience sticker-shock in retail stores. Each child must swear to keep mum if I find a gift for a sibling.

If you have to bring toddlers along and you want an early start, try this: Dress them in sweatsuits for bed the night before. Pack a portable breakfast. In the morning, put the groggy kids in the car without changing their clothes. Give them a breakfast once they're fully awake.

Although some people will simply pass by "boring-looking" yard sales, I stop anyway since I've already invested time locating the sale. I've learned that *any* sale can yield surprise finds.

The one type of yard sale I avoid is the perpetual yard sale—those that appear to be permanently set up in garages. Because these people are more interested in making money than in getting rid of stuff, the prices are higher and less negotiable. In addition, the merchandise has already been picked over. I keep a list of addresses of the suspect garage sales so I won't waste time going there again. Similarly, flea markets have become a sort of communal perpetual yard sale. They offer so few good deals that I seldom stop at one.

Once I arrive at a yard sale, I don't dawdle. I look very quickly at every single item. If I don't find anything I want, I can complete a single yard-sale stop within 60 seconds. But if the merchandise looks more promising, I'll look more carefully. I poke through every "free box" item by item. These have yielded such things as a rechargeable battery, an unopened bar of soap, an air mattress, old sneakers with new laces, a handful of Legos, measuring spoons, and a bag of Band-Aids. One box was full of girls' tights and socks; I carted away the entire box.

When it comes to *buying* stuff, I usually negotiate unless the merchandise is already so cheap that negotiating would seem rude. There are several techniques you can use. If I am the only buyer at the sale, I may refrain from actually picking up the item (which would indicate a greater degree of commitment). Approach the proprietor and ask, "Would you take $5 for the garment bag over there?" Depending on the original price, my offer could be 10 percent to 50 percent off. If she says "No," it's my choice to pay her price, negotiate further, or walk away. If the item is marked much too high for a yard sale, I always walk away, rationalizing that I'm doing my part to keep yard-sale prices low.

If a child wants to buy something, I have him negotiate as well. Proprietors rarely turn down a child, and some give items to kids for free. If my child is shy, I'll co-negotiate by saying, "My son would like to buy that telescope over there. Would you take $1 for it?"

Is power yard-saling worth the time and gas? This can be easily figured by comparing yard-saling to department-store shopping. If I

spent five hours going to yard sales, I subtract the one hour I might have spent doing the same shopping in retail stores. If I used $2 worth of gas to go to yard sales, I subtract the 50¢ I might have spent in gas to make a special trip to the retail stores. If the stuff I brought home from my yard-sale day might have cost $75.00 retail, I subtract the $10.00 I spent at the yard sales as well as the $1.50 extra used for gasoline. So, in theory, I spent four hours extra to shop at yard sales and saved $63.50. In this case, my tax-free hourly wage would be $15.88.

People who aren't shopping for children and who already have all the household stuff they need probably won't do this well. I always do this calculation and know my hourly wage is rarely below $10, and often it's much higher. Jim actually does better because he buys tools.

An article about yard sales would be incomplete without pointing out the sheer fun and thrill of the hunt. And when I return home, my children all gather around to see if I brought them anything—a "new" shirt, a 10¢ jar of beads, or maybe some trinket from a free box. Bringing them something regularly reinforces the concept that good things come from yard sales.

FREQUENT-BUYER MILES

Fritzi Griffis of Tucson, Arizona, writes, "In your first book I noticed a newsletter reader's comment: 'Why would anyone pay a fee for a Visa card?' Well, we do, $50 a year, and so far it has paid for itself and more." Fritzi says she uses one of the many "affinity" credit cards that give you one frequent-flyer mile for every dollar you charge.

I have an aversion to affinity cards. The deals are complex and constantly changing, and I've always figured that the payoff, if any, is probably too small to warrant tedious calculating and comparing. But enough people have written extolling the virtues of credit cards that are linked to frequent-flyer miles that I decided to study this further.

Here's the deal: Generally, you have to accumulate 25,000 frequent-flyer miles to get one free round-trip ticket anywhere in the continental United States. In her postcard, Fritzi states that in 1994, by using her affinity card, she earned 11,987 miles. In other words, her $50 fee put her about halfway to the goal of a ticket that could cost as much as $700 (that's about the upper limit for purchased flights that have the same kind of restrictions that frequent-flyers must obey). So it does look like a good deal.

But the catch is that she had to rack up $11,987 in credit card purchases in that year. Fritzi explains that her husband is a consulting engineer who travels often, and he uses the credit card to cover business expenses.

This unique circumstance—the ability to use the card for business costs—can, clearly, make these

cards worthwhile despite their high fees ($50 is about the cheapest fee you'll find, and they range up to $100 annually). But if you're frugal and use your credit cards strictly for personal business, you need to do some analyzing:

First, decide where you would like to travel and learn the lowest price on round-trip airfare there. Then dig out your credit card statements from last year and total up the dollar amount spent during the year. If you could have used the card more—say, for groceries or gasoline—add on your estimated annual expenditures for those categories. What you're trying to calculate is the maximum amount of your normal purchases that you could make annually with the credit card.

Suppose you come up with a total of $5,000. Divide 25,000 by that figure and you discover that you'd have to pay 5 years' worth of $50 fees to earn one airline ticket. So if the ticket you want costs more than $250 and you would probably buy it anyway, the card could be a good deal.

But before you plunge ahead, I would add several cautions:

1. Obviously these calculations assume you'll pay off your balance each month. Affinity cards generally charge high interest rates. Carrying a balance will make them considerably more expensive.

2. One study revealed that people spend 23 percent more when they use credit cards instead of cash. Be sure you have the self-control to spend no more with the card than you would with cash.

3. Be aware that the airlines can change the rules; they can boost the required miles and/or the annual fee.

4. Airlines "black out" popular travel dates and restrict seating for frequent flyers. Make sure you can fly when you need to.

The bottom line is to do the math. Griffis has, and continues to do so. "I think this has been well worth the $50," she says, "but you can be sure we will continue to evaluate this investment more than once a year, since we also have a free Visa through our credit union."

REVIVAL BY REMOVAL

Sometimes what makes an item of clothing look secondhand is not what it lacks, but what it has. Simple clothes seldom look dated—it's the faddy add-ons that give them away. When you understand this you realize that updating these clothes can be as simple as "taking it off."

Often secondhand clothes are missing the belts, and the empty belt-loops are a dead giveaway. I simply remove these. Recently I carefully removed the loops on a pair of girl's slacks because my daughter Jamie never wears belts.

I have successfully removed the fancy embroidery stitching from the "designer pockets" on '70s jeans by carefully picking it off from the inside with an X-Acto knife. If the pants are faded, I test a small area to see if the design will show after the stitches are removed.

I was given a dress I liked except for a large lacy collar. Using a small pair of scissors, I cut off every bit of visible lace at the neckline seam. I always get compliments on this dress.

Although more sewing skills are

required, you can update a big, pointy, circa-1970 shirt collar if the collar is made with two sections of fabric. By removing the outer section you leave behind a "Chinese-style" collar.

My daughter Laura had a jersey with two sets of three decorative gold buttons. One of the buttons was lost. I simply removed all the buttons.

I bought a 25¢ sweatshirt for Jamie that had beads and sequins sewn onto the front. These began to come off and were annoying her. So one night I carefully removed all of this adornment.

Other excesses like epaulets, Davy Crockett fringe on suede jackets, pom-poms, and the like can also be easily removed.

SUSPEND THRIFT

Dear Amy,

Some insurance companies allow you to suspend the collision and liability portions of your auto insurance if your car is not in use, even if just for a week. While on vacation this year, we suspended coverage on both cars and saved $65. Just ask your company if they have this feature.

—Karen Collier
Southington, Connecticut

DEALS FROM THE DEAN

Dear Amy,

A real find for us has been the Purdue University Surplus and Salvage Barn. Whenever they update equipment or furniture, the old stuff is taken there to be sold. We have gotten solid oak library chairs for $10, dorm armchairs with oak frames and cushioned backs for $5 each, and metal cabinets that normally sell for well over $100 for $30. They also sell unclaimed items from the lost and found. These usually include good ten-speed bikes that students leave behind at the end of the year. Other tightwads who live near universities might check to see if this is available to them.

—Jo Holmes
West Lafayette, Indiana

PARSIMONIOUS PAGES

Dear Amy,

I keep a tightwad journal in my organizer. Each day I enter even the most minor frugal triumph: an aluminum can found in the park, grape jelly discovered dirt cheap, avoiding using the car by biking for errands, etc. When I need a "pick-me-up" I reread a few months of my journal. It really helps!

—Denise Yribarren
Mesa, Arizona

STOCK-UP MARKET

Dear Amy,

Our lot is too shady for gardening, but I get fruits and vegetables for canning another way. There is a farmers' market downtown on Tuesdays, Thursdays, and Saturdays. I wait until almost closing time to go. I then go to the booths that have the best prices and offer to take a bushel or two for about half the price they are asking. I figure they can't hold the food much longer, and they really don't want to pack it up again, so they usually agree.

—Susan Arkles
Jackson, Michigan

WASTE-FREE PASTRY

Dear Amy,

When baking an apple pie, there is no reason to waste anything. I use the extra dough to make mini-cinnamon rolls; and I make snacks from the peels by coating them in oil, sprinkling cinnamon and sugar on top, and baking at 250 degrees for an hour or more.

—Marilyn Bruggema
El Cajon, California

HOSE SPRAY CAN YOU SEE

Dear Amy,

We have no water (truck delivers), so living in the desert, I really conserve and watch the H_2O! For drip irrigation of plants, garden, or whatever, I take an old garden hose, measure where I want the water to drip out and make slits in those places. But the water will spray all over, so the key is to take used soda cans and cut a hole in each end wide enough for the hose to go through. Then slide the cans over the hose to cover the slits. The water squirts into the can and slowly drips out just where you want it.

—Monica Thomas
Yucca Valley, California

AA-OKAY

Dear Amy,

Our local photo center sells used AA batteries for 10¢ each. They come out of the "all in one" disposable cameras and last as long as new batteries.

—Denise Cox
Callahan, Florida

THRICE AND EASY

Dear Amy,

A home perm kit is supposed to provide just one perm, but I get three perms out of a kit. My hair is short and thin, so I need only one third of the solution each time. I have been doing this for three years, and it works great.

—Grace Hallas
St. Johnsbury, Vermont

100-YARD-SALE DASH

Dear Amy,

Our homeowners' association (which includes about 80 percent of the city) has a ban on garage sales, except on the first Saturday in May and the first Saturday in October. On these two days, people come by busloads to the "Mill Creek Garage Sale Saturday." This has advantages to both buyers and sellers: 1) No advertising is necessary for individual sellers. 2) Sellers get more foot traffic because whole neighborhoods are having sales on the same day. 3) Buyers can garage-sale shop more efficiently because of the large number of homes joining in the "garage sale fever."

—Kimiko Rhoten
Mill Creek, Washington

INTERIOR DECLARATION

Dear Amy,

After renting a one-bedroom apartment, I spread the word among my coworkers that I would take *anything* for free. I've received a single bed (my couch), a wooden coffee table (my desk), a glass coffee table (my TV stand), a loaned TV, a small dining room table with four chairs, a double bed, an armchair, a bookshelf, two lamps, two plants, two end tables, one TV table, six bottled-water crates, one trunk, numerous plant cuttings, one coffee maker, one automatic can opener, one roll-around vacuum, one spice rack, food, dishes, hangers, clothes, and a framed painting. It's amazing! I now have a furnished apartment and it cost me *nothing*! Ask and you shall receive, and receive, and receive.

—Sherri M. Felton
Germantown, Maryland

GUIDE AND PEEK

Dear Amy,

I briefly borrow my neighbor's TV magazine each Sunday. I just write down the few programs I am interested in and a brief description so I can record them on the VCR. Then I return the magazine to her, saving either the cost of the Sunday paper ($1.25) or *TV Guide* (which is 80¢ at the grocery store).

—Naomi A. Fowler
Ringgold, Georgia

(It goes without saying that this reader seeks opportunities to return this favor. FZ)

THE MARCH OF A DIFFERENT DREAMER

Fifteen years ago, while freelancing in a Boston design studio, I became friends with Nancy, another graphic designer. At that point, our lives seemed similar: We lived in the same city, had the same occupation, and we both married in the early '80s.

Nancy and I stayed in touch and managed to see each other every few years. Each time we met, I marveled at the different roads we had taken. About the time my third or fourth child was born, Nancy was still pondering whether she would *ever* have a child. When I told her Jim and I were saving for a New England farmhouse in which we hoped to live for the rest of our lives, she shuddered—she couldn't imagine living in the same place forever. Just as I was feeling disenchanted with graphic design, Nancy's career flourished. The job that had been an empty experience for me was meaningful for her.

I last saw Nancy about four years ago. We again compared notes on how different our lives were. Nancy had decided not to have children. Feeling pressure to take yet another "grown-up" step in life, she and her husband had been shopping for a house. After months of indecision, she realized she didn't want to own a house either. She was content with their small apartment, which enabled them to have a streamlined, uncomplicated life. She went on to confide that she really wanted to save for a one-year trip around the world with her husband. She told me they had been squirreling away money but had not made huge lifestyle changes; for example, they still sometimes ate in restaurants.

The conversation then turned to my odd career direction, and, as many people do at a similar point in conversations with me, she described herself as "not frugal" in an apologetic tone. She felt this way not only because her goals were different, but also because she used fewer frugal strategies than Jim and I did. I leaned toward her and said, "But what you just told me five minutes ago is the essence of frugality."

My point was that although our goals were vastly different, we had both stripped away the expectations of others and had decided to generate surplus income to pursue our dreams. Jim and I had less disposable income, so we had needed to use every strategy possible. Nancy and her husband both had good-paying careers and no children, so they would need to use

fewer strategies to accomplish their goal.

Neither did I think it "spendthrift" of her to spend a good chunk of her life savings on this one temporary pleasure. Replacing their savings would be easy since their ability to generate more income was high and their personal expenses would be few. And since both of them couldn't imagine their lives without working, spending money wouldn't result in a painful tradeoff of having to work to replace the money.

There's a reason why I have chosen to relate this story. On my book tours I occasionally bump up against two reactions that concern me. The gentler response comes from those who, like Nancy, apologize for not being frugal. This response is strange coming from people who clearly have adequate resources for all their needs. The second response is a criticism. During a radio interview, the editor of a competing thrift newsletter called in and accused me of being a "thrift terrorist," because the ideas I publish "aren't really appropriate for Middle America."

Both of these responses are based on the same incorrect assumption: that all people should be frugal in the same way, regardless of their circumstances. Everyone's goals, resources, talents, values, and "frugal comfort zones" are different, and there are many legitimate ways to be frugal.

Further, it's incorrect to assume that certain frugal ideas are appropriate for upper-class Americans, others for the middle class, and yet others for low-income Americans. If I've learned *anything* in six years of publishing, it's that no two people agree on what is and isn't an acceptable idea. For instance, in some parts of the country, furnishing a home with curbside finds is socially acceptable only for the lowest-income groups. Yet this practice is considered to be "chic" in New York City by people of all income groups.

My readers fall into a variety of categories. I support all of these choices:

- Some have ample economic resources and modest goals. These readers may choose to use a more limited range of frugal ideas.
- Some have modest resources and are facing desperate circumstances such as unemployment, house foreclosures, and/or bankruptcy. For these people few ideas would be "too extreme," and it would be shortsighted of me to withhold ideas that might not be acceptable to everyone in "Middle America." I want to provide them with the "black-belt" techniques their situation demands.
- Some readers have ample resources and still want to use the black-belt strategies. It's perfectly legitimate to find hard-core frugality a worthwhile lifestyle for noneconomic reasons, such as enjoying the challenge, preserving the environment, or passing on frugal skills to kids.

In other words, I'm an easygoing person. Most people spend money in ways that I wouldn't, but the only time I think of people as "spendthrifts" is when:

- They have spending habits that are making them or their families unhappy, or may make them unhappy in the future, *and* they complain rather than making the lifestyle changes required to improve their lot in life.
- They have wasteful spending

habits yet they carry no health insurance, declare bankruptcy, or fail to pay child support.

In short, it's my job to provide the range of strategies from which you can choose. It's not my job to determine which or how many frugal strategies you should use, or what to apply your surplus toward. Those are *your* choices.

Nancy did take her yearlong trip around the world, returning in the fall of 1995. Interestingly, she wrote me to say that the experience made her more frugal, as she and her husband had been forced to adhere to a tight budget to avoid having to return early. Not only does frugality vary from person to person, but we can adjust it individually day to day—that's one of the wonderful things about it.

KEEP YOUR PORTIONS IN PROPORTION

Unless you've been living in a cave, you've seen that the old "Basic Four Food Groups" nutritional recommendations have been scuttled. The new recommendations are found in the USDA's "Food Guide Pyramid."

The notable aspect of this pyramid from the tightwad perspective is that, with the exception of the pyramid's peak (fats, sweets, and oils), the more you are supposed to eat from a category of food, the cheaper those foods tend to be. The following costs are based on the tightwaddiest alternatives from the various groups:

- Bread, grains, rice, and pasta cost from 15¢ to 50¢ a pound, or about 2¢ for a slice of homemade bread.
- Vegetables cost from 20¢ to $1 a pound, or about 5¢ for a 1-carrot serving.
- Fruits cost from 30¢ to $1 a pound, or about 10¢ for a 1-banana serving.
- Milk costs from $1.40 to over $2.00 per gallon, or about 9¢ per 1-cup serving; cheese costs about $1.60 a pound, or about 20¢ per 2-ounce serving.

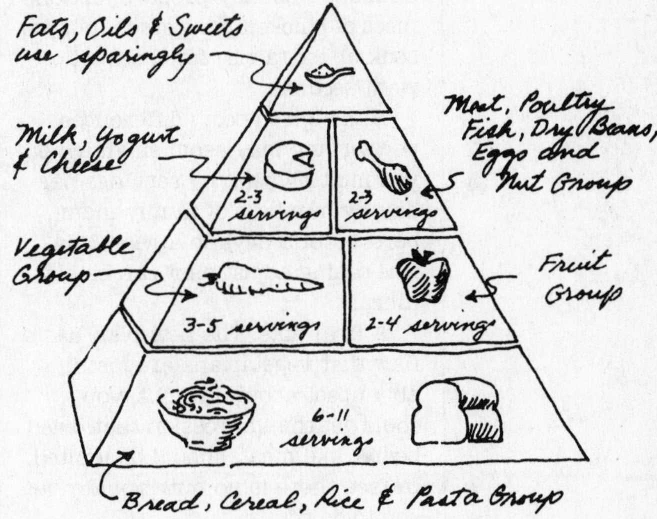

- Meats, dried beans, and peanut butter cost from 50¢ to several dollars per pound. At $1 a pound, meat costs 25¢ per 4-ounce serving.

It has been said to me, "I don't understand. I eat the same foods and pay the same prices as you; why is my grocery bill higher than yours?" The reason may be because there's a third variable: the proportion of foods from different groups that are consumed.

A common health-and-budget mistake people make is to serve a big slab of meat accompanied by tiny dollops of vegetables and rice. Others make choices that aren't

unhealthy but are needlessly costly: Dieters often eat endless salads and restrict their consumption of grains, and parents with young children often allow unlimited consumption of juice or fruit.

In my home we tend to hit these USDA minimum numbers on average. If a child has had juice and two servings of fruit in a given day and asks for more, I'll suggest he eat popcorn or a muffin instead. At dinner we usually prepare just one piece of chicken per person, but we cook up extra rice for those who want seconds.

Although the cost differences per serving may seem small, when you multiply that by servings per day, by numbers of family members, by 365 days in a year, this fine-tuning adjustment can be significant.

A final note: The new plan has a flaw that vegetarians are justifiably upset about. From it, you could get the impression that dried beans, like meat, should be limited. In fact, there is no nutritional reason to do so.

SHIFT AND SAVE

Many parents who have "done the math" have come to a startling realization: When child-care and transportation expenses are subtracted from take-home pay, their "good" jobs actually pay very little.

Cherise Harper, a graphic artist from Middletown, Pennsylvania, came up with a solution that works well for her. After her first child was born in 1993, she persuaded her boss to allow her to work three 12-hour shifts each week instead of the usual five 8-hour shifts.

"In the last two years, there have been no 'cons' to this schedule," she writes. "I pay less in child-care and travel expenses and have more quality time with my daughter." The benefits to her employer were longer office hours three days a week, computers that were not as tied up during the day, and the ability to have "rush" jobs completed at night without having to pay overtime. If a 12-hour day seems too long, another possibility is four 10-hour days per week.

Cherise believes many employers would be open to reasonable agreements such as this to keep reliable, responsible workers, and statistics from the U.S. Labor Department bear out her claim. The number of full-time workers with flexible schedules was 12.1 million in 1991, up from 9.1 million in 1985—all part of a general movement toward offering more "family friendly" work hours.

Cherise writes that the key is presenting the idea in the right light; you should point out that it's beneficial to the employer as well as the employee. She adds, "Sometimes the most difficult part of changing your schedule is asking!"

DIAPER DO'S AND DON'TS

In my book *The Tightwad Gazette,* I wrote about the savings (at least $7 a week) and the minimal labor (about 30 minutes a week) involved in using cloth diapers. Since then, several readers have offered additional information or asked questions that I didn't originally address. What follows is based on reader input, my ten years of experience, and information from Gerber, a leading maker of cloth diapers.

WHAT TYPE OF CLOTH DIAPER TO BUY

I used standard "prefolded" diapers. These have layers stitched together, with extra material in the middle. After washing and drying I piled them in a stack. If you're really lazy you could store them loose in a laundry basket. I also found that nylon pants last longer than plastic pants.

Rose Ann Kirsch of Springview, Nebraska, asked, "What do you think of preformed diapers with Velcro and elasticized legs?"

There is a variety of new diapering systems with different price tags. Some readers have said that contoured cloth diapers with Velcro wraps make cloth diapering easier, as no pins are needed. Some prefolded diapers also have Velcro fasteners. I never used these because they cost more and I was skeptical about how well they would work.

Catherine Washburn of Baltimore, Maryland, confirmed my suspicions. She bought contoured flannel diapers and Velcro wraps but found it was "a big mistake!" The wraps cost $11 to $15 each, compared to $1 a pair for new nylon pants. Since you'll need several sets of wraps or pants as the baby grows, this can add up to a big difference. She also discovered that the wraps leaked much more quickly than the nylon pants.

Another drawback: Her son learned how to remove the wraps at 11 months of age. In comparison, none of my six kids ever undid a pin or was hurt by a pin that came unfastened. And in ten years of diapering, we poked a baby just twice. If you put your hand between the diaper and the baby, you can't poke the baby. If you rub the pin along your scalp, it picks up natural oils that let you push the pin easily through the diaper.

Catherine found she disliked contoured diapers' lack of versatility. In contrast, a prefolded diaper can accommodate a child of any size if you vary the folding, as shown on page 130. A single folded-in-half diaper will accommodate a tiny infant. Two of the same diapers can be used for a toddler.

Catherine has since returned to prefolded diapers, pins, and nylon taffeta diaper pants.

HOW TO ACQUIRE CLOTH DIAPERS

Many people don't buy cloth diapers because they are put off by the "high" initial cost. But even if you bought 50 new diapers (about a five-day supply) at $1 each, they would pay for themselves in seven weeks. And there are ways to get diapers cheaply or for free:

- While you're pregnant, let family and friends know that you plan to use cloth diapers on your baby. With luck, you'll get diapers and paraphernalia as shower gifts instead of $20 baby outfits that

will fit for two weeks. Also "put out the word," as you may know parents who have diapers they no longer need.

• Deborah Collier of Fairview, North Carolina, buys "discard" diapers from diaper services. These companies sell diapers that are a little stained or slightly frayed for "rags"; however, Deborah picked out 50 acceptable ones for 40¢ each. Laura Boynton of Bellingham, Washington, bought used diapers by the pound from a commercial laundry.

• Look for diaper stuff at yard sales. I found a shopping bag of diapers for $1, and nylon pants at a children's consignment shop for 25¢ each.

HOW TO WASH CLOTH DIAPERS

Christina Stone of Ann Arbor, Michigan, wanted directions on washing diapers, and asked specifically, "Do you rinse the messes in the toilet?"

Elizabeth Case of Belfair, Washington, hunted through parenting magazines and baby books and "couldn't find answers to even basic questions about cleaning diapers."

It's hard to track down laundering guidelines because systems vary depending on several factors. For instance, during our "diaper years" we lived in five different houses. The varying proximities of the changing area (i.e., bed or top of freezer), bathroom(s), and laundry room dictated my systems. Individual "squeam" levels also vary widely. Nevertheless, offering some guidelines would be useful.

Elizabeth quizzed other moms and came up with a regimen that works well. The following washing system is based on both Elizabeth's and my experience, and on recommendations from Gerber.

1. Choose a diaper pail. Any 5-gallon bucket will work, but it should have a lid that can close tightly. Though it's rare, a toddler can drown in a bucket of water just as he can in a toilet, believe it or

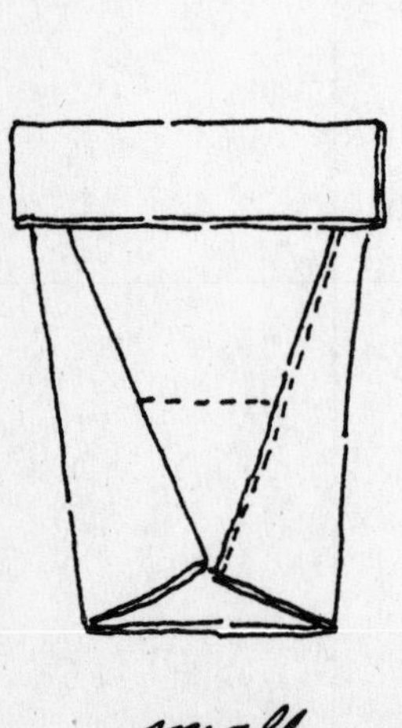

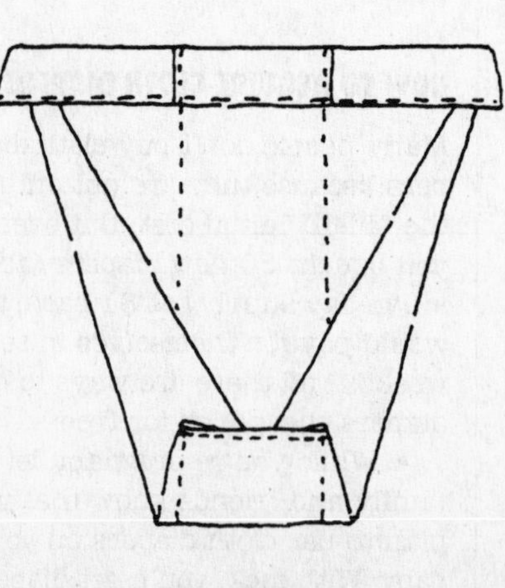

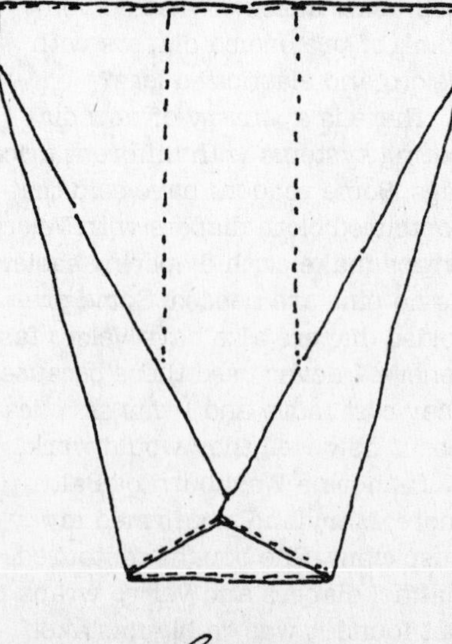

not. I always used 2 buckets so that I could collect enough diapers to make a full laundry load.

2. Fill the pail three quarters full with water. To control odors you can add ¼ cup of borax, but this is optional.

3. Put wet-but-not-soiled diapers and nylon pants directly into the pail to soak.

4a. Remove as much of the solid material from soiled diapers as possible. Some of it will just fall off the diaper into the toilet. Many parents remove solid material by holding the top edge of the diaper firmly, dipping it in the toilet, and flushing. You can also soak soiled diapers in a separate bucket for a few hours to make "sticky" solids fall off easily with a little swishing or rubbing. Once the solids are removed, transfer these diapers to the regular soak bucket. Dump the water from the "soiled" bucket at the end of each day. Wash your hands after handling diapers.

4b. If having to swish soiled diapers is all that's keeping you from using cloth diapers, you might try a compromise strategy: disposable diaper liners. These let you remove solids more easily, though you must still remove the material from the liner because it isn't flushable. I know several cloth-diaper moms who like liners, but I dislike the expense and disposal aspects.

5. When the pail becomes full after one or two days, tote it to the washing machine and pour it all in, including the yucky soak water. Set the machine on "spin" to spin out the soak water.

6. When the machine is through spinning, add your regular amount of detergent. Avoid detergent with bleach or softeners that can irritate the baby's skin. Wash diapers on a regular-length, medium-load, hot-water cycle. Dry on a line or in a dryer.

7. Rinse out the diaper pail in the bathtub. Refill with water.

HOW TO PROLONG CLOTH-DIAPER LIFE

Rose Ann also asked, "Do you have any ideas on how to prolong the life of cloth diapers? My first son is not yet two and he's got some pretty ragged ones."

According to Gerber, using bleach, or detergent with bleach or softeners, will prematurely wear out your diapers. Although bleach is a disinfectant, you can also kill germs with white vinegar or borax added to the wash, heat (hot water, hot dryer), or sunlight (air-drying).

Nylon pants age prematurely in a hot dryer, so air-dry them. An extremely hot dryer will also prematurely wear the diapers.

Regardless of how you care for them, diapers will wear out. As the stitching in the prefolded diapers comes apart, these diapers will "tangle" inside-out in the dryer and can be difficult to make right again. I periodically resewed these seams and around any ragged edges. Each diaper required only a few seconds (and a few feet of odd-colored thread) to repair, but this extended the life for many months. If I was diapering with two diapers, I often used a still-absorbent-but-too-ragged-to-pin diaper on the inside and a good diaper on the outside.

ALES BY COMPARISON

Angela Spicer of Davisburg, Michigan, asked, "Can you tell me if it's cheaper to make your own beer at home?"

Her inquiry led us to our files, where we found a letter from Joan Harris of Albuquerque, New Mexico. She wrote, "We have found that home brewing doesn't provide us with the cheapest possible beer, but for the price of a cheap beer and a little effort we get premium quality beer. Plus it's a fun hobby."

For some precise numbers, I spoke with Karen Barela, president of the American Home Brewer's Association in Boulder, Colorado, and Tim Tardif, owner of Beverage World in the nearby town of Lewiston, Maine. He sells both home-brewing supplies and a wide range of bottled beers.

First, you need equipment. For $27.50, Tardif sells a basic home-brewing kit that consists of a bottle capper, a sanitizing agent, an instruction book, a hydrometer, a plastic bucket for brewing, and an air lock. Another onetime expense is non-twist-top bottles, which cost $2 for 48 at a redemption center. Caps cost 2¢ each.

But Barela points out that an industrious scrounger could assemble his own better, cheaper system. She says plastic fermentation buckets can be difficult to sanitize, and the best choice is a 5-gallon glass bottle such as is used for a water cooler; these can often be found used. She says plain bleach is as good a sanitizing agent as the stuff sold specifically for that purpose. A $2 air lock and a $12 bottle capper can fill out your kit. She says a hydrometer, which measures alcohol content, is optional.

Tardif says a home brewer can make a batch of "basic beer" (similar to Budweiser or Miller) that yields 48 bottles for about $14.50, which equals $1.81 per six-pack. To make a beer that approximates the taste of the most expensive imports requires more expensive ingredients. The cost works out to $3.31 per six-pack. For the purpose of comparison, the bottled beers Tardif sells range from $2.56 to $14.65 for a six-pack of 12-ounce bottles.

Depending upon the process you use, it might take you three to five hours of hands-on time to brew and bottle a typical batch. At this point, I could calculate a theoretical hourly wage for you; however, since beer is a luxury item, and there are variables in costs, making such a claim would be iffy. It's fairer to say that beer-making is a low-cost hobby.

Barela says "almost anyone" can make beer, it is simply a matter of following a recipe. You can get a set of basic beer-making instructions for free from the American Home Brewer's Association, P.O. Box 1679, Boulder, CO 80306. You can also request information on the home-brewing club that's nearest to you. There are over 500 nationwide. Barela said the best book on the subject is *The*

New Complete Joy of Home Brewing by Charlie Papazian (Avon, 1991), which is widely available.

Incidentally, home brewing was federally legalized in 1978. You can make 100 gallons per adult per household, or a maximum of 200 gallons per household per year.

FIX-ITS FROM READERS

Fix-it solutions are unique to circumstance. Each involves an item in need of repair combined with a specific resource. For instance:

The rubber-glove fix. Lynn Wright of East Greenwich, Rhode Island, repairs holes in rubber gloves by cutting a small piece from the cuff end, turning the glove inside out, and using "super glue" to patch the small piece over the hole. The glove must be dry. She says it never leaks in that spot again.

The waterbed fix. Carol Everett of Meadville, Pennsylvania, had a hole in her waterbed. She applied a 1½-inch square of Shoe Goo over the dried hole-area and let it dry uncovered.

The clothes-dryer-door fix. Robin Jackson of Lafayette, Georgia, wrote that her dryer's door no longer stayed closed and a replacement latch would have cost $70. Instead, her husband screwed on a latch from an old screen door. It works great.

The overstuffed-chair fix. Sharon Carr of Brookesmith, Texas, stopped the stuffing hemorrhaging out of the arm of her overstuffed chair with an iron-on patch. Then she tacked place mats of complementary colors on the worn spots on the arms. "The chair actually looks dressier than before," she says.

The on/off-switch fix. When the switch on her TV wasn't working properly, Cathy McSweeney of Plano, Texas, sprayed it with Cleaner Degreaser, a $4.99 product sold at Radio Shack for cleaning electronics. She saved herself a $40.00 repair charge.

The cheese-cutter fix. Mel Hanson of Milwaukie, Oregon, says that if the wire on your cheese cutter breaks, you can replace it with guitar wire. Ask your guitar-playing friend to save a correct-thickness wire for you.

The sneaker-lace fix. Pam Lenza of Staten Island, New York, says when the plastic tip comes off laces, you can repair it with trans-

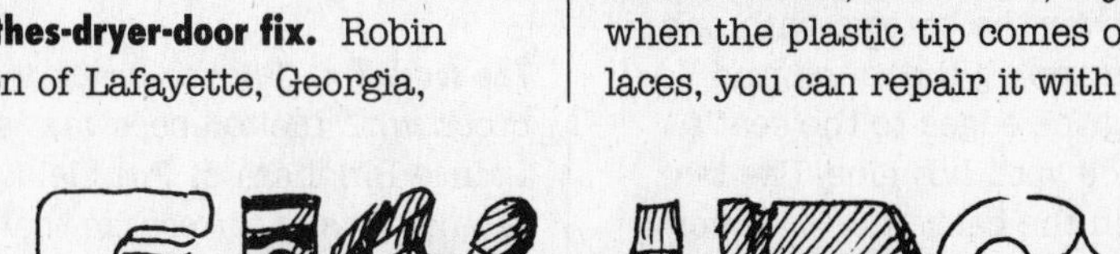

parent tape (not "magic" tape, which isn't sticky enough). Simply wind it around the end of the lace several times.

The sofa-cushion fix. Edna Musso of De Bary, Florida, suggested that if you absolutely ruin a sofa cushion on a sofa that backs up to a wall, you can remove the upholstery from the back to use in making a new cushion cover. Replace the fabric on the back with something compatible.

The wooden-knob fix. When the screw no longer holds in a wooden knob, such as on a bureau drawer, Linda Corssmit of Greenwood Village, Colorado, suggests fixing it with a wooden match. Coat the match with white glue, insert it in the knob hole, and break it off flush. Replace the screw and let dry. *(FZ note: I tried this and it worked.)*

The high-chair fix. Dabney Nunley of Phoenix, Arizona, lists these steps to replace the torn vinyl covering on the back and seat of a high chair. First, remove the screws that hold the back and seat to the metal frame. Cut three pieces from a vinyl tablecloth—if you use a rectangular cloth, you can be left with a usable square cloth. Cover the bottom with one piece, wrapping it around and securing the edges to the seat's underside with hot glue. Use two pieces on the back (one to cover the cushion, the second to make the back look finished). Reattach to chair.

The scorched-Formica fix. Instead of replacing the whole countertop, Betty Garman of Lititz, Pennsylvania, points out that a carpenter (or you, if you are experienced in Formica work) can carefully cut out the damaged section and replace it with a piece of butcher block.

The silverware-drainer fix. Julie Dennis of Portland, Oregon, says if the bottom of your dishwasher's silverware drainer has broken out, use a long embroidery needle to thread dental floss in a crisscross pattern across the bottom.

The eyeglasses fix. If your eyeglasses or sunglasses keep coming unscrewed at the arm hinges, screw tightly and apply a thin coat of clear nail polish. Once it dries, they won't become loose again, says Linda Mientkiewicz of Waterford, Pennsylvania.

The cat-scratching-post fix. Theresa M. Lemire of Iowa City, Iowa, says you can recover a deteriorating scratching post by removing the old carpeting and winding the post tightly with sisal twine.

The sagging-headliner fix. Use upholstery twist pins to reattach the cloth liner that covers the interior of a car's roof, suggest Don and Gail van den Berg of Waxhaw, North Carolina.

The crock fix. Fill the crack in a crock with melted beeswax, says Laurie Bingham of Pittsfield, Maine. This is for crocks that hold items at room temperature; it's not for Crock-Pots.

The nicked-appliance fix. Marcia Lanphear of Collegedale, Tennessee, says you can touch up white kitchen appliances with

white correction fluid. She says it is durable and matches well.

The scratched-woodwork fix. Fill in with a crayon and buff away excess with a cloth, suggests Dawn McFadden of Calhoun, Georgia.

The vacuum-cleaner fixes. This one is from my own experience: When the cord-retracting spool inside our vacuum cleaner broke and stopped retracting, Jim snipped off all but about 6 inches of the cord and added a new male plug. We now use the vacuum cleaner with a heavy-duty extension cord, which has an advantage: it's longer than the original cord, so we can vacuum farther without moving the cord.

This one is from one of my staffers: When the connection between two metal sections of his vacuum cleaner's hose became worn and too loose to stay together, he put a metal, screw-adjustable pipe clamp around the female end. By carefully tightening the screw, he made the female end small enough to get a good friction fit.

WOOL-AID

Dear Amy,

I have a safe, easy way to liven up yard-sale wool sweaters. Kool-Aid (and generic equivalents) will dye wool to a variety of brilliant colors. Wash and rinse the sweater in room-temperature water, using dish soap. Fill a big pot with room-temperature water. Add two or three packages of Kool-Aid (from the small packets that don't contain sugar). Wring out the sweater and add it to the pot. Slowly bring pot to simmer, simmer for 10 minutes and cool down. The water should be colorless. Rinse in water that is the same temperature as the sweater. The Kool-Aid is absolutely colorfast. I have been told that Kool-Aid also works to dye cotton, but the colors are not as intense as with wool.

—Elaine Brannen
Fairfield, Iowa

(Elaine sent samples that are quite lovely. At 10¢ a package for generic Kool-Aid versus $1.99 for Rit Dye, the savings are significant. FZ)

FAREWELL, TWO ARMS

Dear Amy,

Pullover bibs for small children can be made very inexpensively from used sweatshirts purchased secondhand. Leave the front, complete with its design, and trim off the sleeves and back. Finish the rough edge with a zigzag.

—Jeannette Paulson
Grand Rapids, Michigan

CHEAP CHOPS

Dear Amy,

If you live near a university, check to see if students produce or package food in any of their courses. I buy top-quality meat at discount prices at the Iowa State meat lab. When we lived near Penn State, we got great honey, cheese, and ice cream.

—Katherine Jackman
Ames, Iowa

ALMOST-FREE A-TO-Z

Dear Amy,

If you need encyclopedias, you should check with your local library first. Our library buys a new set each year and sells a five-year-old set each year. I was able to buy a five-year-old set for $20.

—Martha Bisacchi
Lake Village, Indiana

ROD AND ROLL

Dear Amy,

While painting my pantry recently, I needed an extension rod for the paint roller. I discovered that my broom handle unscrewed and fit the roller perfectly.

—Charlotte Baillargeon
Hinsdale, Massachusetts

NO-SHOWS AND UH-OHS

Dear Amy,

Our pizza place sells "mistake" or unclaimed pizzas at or below half price. We can buy a large pizza for $2 or $3. Usually during their busiest hours, like Saturday evenings, you can stop and pick up a cheap pizza.

—Corine Sandifer
Nashville, Tennessee

CORN-BROCCOLI CASSEROLE

This casserole does a wonderful job of absorbing our abundance of mystery-can corn. Yellow squash, zucchini, cauliflower, and a wide variety of other vegetables can be substituted for the broccoli with impressive results. This one-dish supper can be made in about 15 minutes of hands-on time if you are using preshredded cheese and frozen broccoli. If you use fresh broccoli, it should be steamed al dente first.

1 can corn, drained
1 can creamed corn
1½ cups shredded cheddar cheese
4 eggs, beaten
3 cups frozen broccoli, thawed and chopped into ½-inch chunks
1 small onion, minced
⅔ cup milk
1 sleeve saltines, crushed
2 tablespoons margarine, melted

Preheat oven to 350 degrees. Combine first seven ingredients and ¾ cup of saltine crumbs. Pour into 10½-inch metal-handled frying pan or large casserole dish. Combine remaining crumbs with margarine and use to top casserole. Bake uncovered for 40 minutes, or until firm. Serves eight.

CUBBIES CONQUER CHAOS

Betty Cotter of Wakefield, Rhode Island, saw a magazine photo of me posing before a set of "cubbies" that Jim built. She wrote to say it was a great idea and suggested that I mention it.

We built them because we had a huge problem with storage of coats, gloves, snow pants, boots, schoolbooks, backpacks, and lunch boxes. Multiply these by six kids and you get the picture.

We used a combination of scavenged and leftover lumber; Jim estimates they could be built with about $25 worth of new lumber. We recycled hooks we already had (a quirk of our pre-1900 house was that each closet bristled with dozens of coat hooks) and used leftover white paint.

I won't launch into construction details. I'll assume readers will modify the basic idea based on their skills and available space and materials. However, it's useful to discuss how we arrived at the measurements.

The total width of the unit was based on our available space—the distance from a corner to a window in our laundry/mud room. We divided this into six equal spaces of about 12 inches each.

Each cubbie has three levels: the bottom shelf for boots, the middle section for coats and snow pants, and the top section for books and lunch boxes.

The depth of the cubbies was determined by the length of a teenager's boot—about 12 inches deep. The height of the middle section was determined by the placement of the coat hook: It had to be low enough for a small child to reach and high enough to hang snow pants or a long coat of an older child, so the hook is 42 inches above the floor. The top section had to be tall enough to accommodate a standard 8-inch-tall lunch box. Add an inch or two here and there, and the total height is 57 inches.

Aside from neatening up our lives, the cubbies proved to be a time-saver. We spend less time looking for misplaced schoolbooks and winter gear.

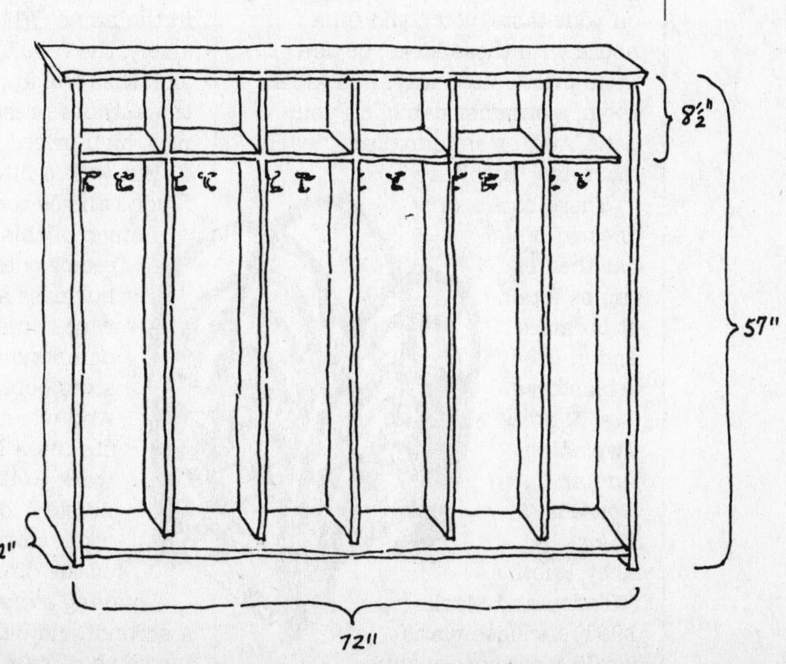

STICKS AND STONES MAY GRACE MY HOME

When it comes to finding low-cost furniture and household accessories, most tightwads have already discovered yard sales, flea markets, and auctions. These sources generally offer items suited for those with mainstream tastes and modest-to-average budgets.

If you have adventurous tastes or a thinner wallet, there are other alternatives. The following four books explore untraditional furnishings and accessories made from free or low-cost stuff.

Many of the ideas are whimsical or weird, depending on your point of view. For example, it takes a unique turn of mind to attach a wooden sled to your kitchen's ceiling and hang saucepans from its slats, as suggested in *Found Objects.* Depending on your taste, you could fill a house with these ideas, or use them in a limited way: in a kid's room, a summer cabin, on your patio, and/or as temporary "early marriage" furniture.

These books, or ones with similar themes, can be found at libraries and in used-book stores.

• *Making Twig Furniture and Household Things* by Abby Ruoff (Hartley and Marks, 1991) includes plans for 35 pieces of furniture and household objects ranging from a love seat to a small twig-and-bark basket. But beyond the individual project plans, this book's value is in telling the beginner all about finding, cutting, storing, bending, and assembling twigs into useful objects.

A houseful of twig furniture—or even a single, large piece—might be too much for a contemporary decor, but any home could be complemented by small pieces such as twig planters, picture frames, or a magazine rack.

• *High-Tech* by Joan Kron and Suzanne Slesin (Clarkson Potter, 1978) is as far away from twig furniture as decorating gets. The style uses industrial hardware, furniture, and materials in the home. When used exclusively, the result is a cold, uncozy look that will appeal to few. And the authors presume you will buy new, high-priced stuff.

But with a little imagination, you can see the frugal angle: much of this stuff is available free or cheap at going-out-of-business auctions, restaurant-supply stores, demolition sites, or Dumpsters behind businesses. And when the items are used in a limited way, they work well. Examples include old steel lockers for kids'-room storage, a factory light for the dining room, piled-up paving stones for an end table, a secondhand bakery pie-case for a medicine cabinet, hung-on-the-wall

bicycle baskets for vegetable storage, a wallpaper hanger's table for a desk, geological survey maps for art, and stainless-steel hospital dressing jars for kitchen canisters.

- *Found Objects: A Style and Source Book* by Joseph Ruggiero (Clarkson Potter, 1981). "Found objects" are anything you can get for free, and so they encompass natural items, industrial discards, and everything in between. This book celebrates the beauty of these items and shows you how to work them into your home. Some of the odder ideas will make you chuckle and/or scratch your head, such as an oil drum converted into a chair. You may also be amused to note just how lovely a bowl of rocks looks on a $1,000 coffee table.

But the basic concept of decorating with found objects is quite valid. The book depicts how you can use a weathered clam basket for a magazine holder, a gnarled tree trunk topped with glass for an end table, new-but-vintage-looking can labels and seed packets for framed art, a wooden nursery flat for a lap table, and a terra-cotta chimney-flue liner as an umbrella stand.

- *Nomadic Furniture* by James Hennessey and Victor Papanek (Pantheon, 1973). This was popular in the groovy '70s and some of the "modern" ideas look dated today. And a few ideas, like the kids' cardboard car seat, don't meet current safety standards. But many of the ideas will work in '90s homes.

The premise is that this stuff is lightweight, recyclable, and/or easy to take apart and move, but much of it also happens to be cheap or free. Examples include the cut-from-one-sheet-of-plywood desk, a basic cardboard-cube structure that supports up to 400 pounds, a chair made from an old mattress, a bureau made from scrap wood and plastic tubs, and a simple three-legged collapsible table made with tied-together dowels or broomsticks.

Unlike the previous books, this one stresses innovation rather than choice of materials. Therefore, when looking through it, consider possible cross-over ideas with the other books. For example, the three-legged table could be a very stylish permanent end table if made with birch-twig legs and neatly tied jute.

Although these books are diverse in style, the common lesson is that if you can accept the unconventional, you'll save money when furnishing your home.

NO MORE CULTURE SHOCK

Though the steps required to make yogurt are fairly simple, success has eluded some of the finest frugal cooks that I know. Their attempts, and mine, have too often yielded (at worst) failed batches or (at best) yogurt that's runnier than store-bought. Other batches were too tart or had an odd texture. And it bugged me to keep buying store-bought yogurt for starter, particularly when the success of the homemade batches was so inconsistent.

But the economic advantage of homemade yogurt is clear. Here in Maine, a quart of milk costs from 35¢ (from powdered milk) to 52¢ (from a $2.09-per-gallon jug), while a quart of store-brand yogurt costs $1.39. Even factoring in other ingredients, homemade yogurt costs less than half as much as store-bought. A two-quart batch can be made with 15 minutes of hands-on time, which makes the hourly wage over $7. And homemade yogurt can be made less tart than store-bought.

So I decided, once and for all, to solve this yogurt mystery. I started by comparing all the yogurt-making articles and recipes I could find. These 25 sources suggested a boggling array of ingredients, proportions, preparation methods, batch sizes, and troubleshooting tips, and many declared themselves to be magic "never-fail" recipes.

To compare them, I made up a big chart that breaks down these variables, and I converted the recipes to uniform measurements and batch sizes.

Then, over two months, staffers and I tested the different variables by making two separate batches at a time but altering one variable in a batch. To ensure our findings weren't anecdotal, we also interviewed Edward Yaghoubian, director of dairy food research for the National Dairy Board. Here's what I learned:

THE STARTER

Yogurt begins with "starter"—plain store-bought yogurt with the words "Live Cultures" on the container's label. Yogurts that were heat-treated after incubation have dead cultures and won't work as starter.

Dannon is a well-known brand with live cultures. Although recipes may specify its use as the starter, Yaghoubian said no one brand is better than another.

You can have a continuous supply of cheap starter by "chain yogurting." Use starter from a previous batch that's less than five days old. Subsequent batches may become increasingly runny. Yaghoubian said that's because over time, other microorganisms enter the yogurt and start to overwhelm the yogurt cultures. Most sources say you can chain-yogurt up to four times.

Eventually you'll need fresh starter. To avoid purchasing store-bought yogurt for starter every few weeks, I checked out other options.

I investigated dried yogurt starter sold in health food stores. Since this has an unlimited shelf life, I wondered if it would be cheaper than buying a 45¢, 1-cup container of yogurt. But I found that dried starter costs 65¢ per quart of yogurt.

Then I tried an option I'd read about: freezing commercial yogurt

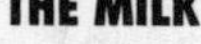

in ice-cube trays, storing the cubes in a Ziploc bag, and thawing for use. Each cube equals about 2 tablespoons. I found that previously frozen starter works as well as never-frozen starter.

Most recipes call for from 2 to 4 tablespoons of starter per quart of milk. We compared using 2 versus 4 tablespoons and found the resulting yogurt was identical. The smaller amount is the obvious tightwad choice. Two tablespoons of store-bought yogurt cost 5¢.

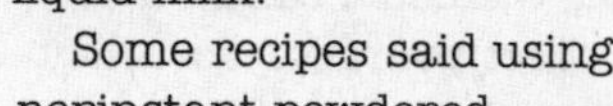

Some sources say tart starter results in tart yogurt. Yaghoubian disputes this, emphasizing that the most critical variable is incubation time. However, in our comparison test, the tart starter did produce a tarter yogurt.

By buying starter yogurt at the cheapest unit price (usually quarts), freezing it in cubes, and chain-yogurting, the starter cost can be as low as 1¢ per quart.

THE MILK

The recipes called for milk in many forms: whole, low-fat, skim, instant powdered, noninstant powdered, evaporated, or some combination.

Yaghoubian said any of these will work, but milk with a high concentration of milk solids yields a thicker yogurt that is more similar to store-bought. You can achieve this by adding ½ cup of powdered milk to a quart of liquid milk.

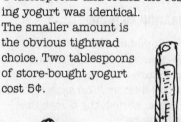

Some recipes said using *non*instant powdered milk was the "trick": either using it exclusively or for the added ½ cup of powder. (For details on this product, see *The Tightwad Gazette II.*) Yaghoubian said there is nothing special about noninstant powder that would yield better yogurt. It's about twice as dense as instant powder, so adding the same half-cup will make a thicker yogurt. But

when we added the same weight of each to two batches, the resulting thickness was the same. In some of my experiments, the taste was the same; in a few cases the instant seemed to make a tarter yogurt.

PREPARATION METHODS

Most recipes require heating the milk to 180 degrees, then letting it cool to about 115 degrees. The most sophisticated equipment you'll need, then, is a candy thermometer. (Test yours for accuracy by measuring boiling water; it should read 212 degrees.) Yaghoubian said preheating kills off microorganisms that might compete with the culture, and it breaks down the milk proteins, which leads to a tighter curd and a better yogurt.

Interestingly, some sources said that not boiling the milk was critical, whereas others, like my *Fannie Farmer Cookbook*, said the milk should be boiled for one minute. In my boiling/nonboiling comparison tests, the result was the same.

The most tedious aspect of yogurt-making is watching the thermometer as you wait for up to an hour for the milk to cool. But you don't have to stand over your stove the entire time. You can:

- Time how long it takes for your milk to cool. When making subsequent batches, set your timer to ding a few minutes before that period has elapsed.
- Make yogurt when you'll be doing other small tasks in the kitchen. Each time you complete a task, recheck the thermometer.
- Make your yogurt an hour before you go to bed. Take the cooling milk with you into the living room while you watch TV.

After the milk drops to 115 degrees, whisk a half-cup of the warm milk with the starter. Then add this mixture to the pot of warm milk and whisk again. Undermixing can result in a failed batch, so mix well. Despite common belief, vigorous mixing won't kill starter.

INCUBATION METHODS

The milk-yogurt mixture should incubate *undisturbed* at a constant temperature of about 115 degrees for 4 to 12 hours. The longer the incubation period, the tarter the yogurt will be.

You can use any container, such as a pan or bowl. I use quart-sized canning jars with lids. I use a jar to measure out my quart of milk before heating it, and the tall quart jars use little space in the refrigerator.

There are two basic forms of incubation: insulation-only, or providing an outside heat-source.

Insulation-only methods include putting mixture directly in a Thermos or a specially made insulated container for yogurt-making, or wrapping jars in a towel and placing them in a small cooler, or wrapping jars in a quilt.

Yaghoubian said that providing a constant, correct temperature is crucial. And as my friends and I recall the failed batches we've made over the years, we suspect they resulted from using an insulation-only method or an outside heat-source that was insufficient. So, I recommend a method that provides constant, reliable heat from an outside source. You can:

- Place jars in a pan of water, cover with a towel, and place near a warm radiator.

• Place in a gas oven near the pilot light.

• Preheat electric oven to lowest setting. Turn the oven off, turn the oven light on, and place yogurt in the oven overnight, as suggested by Nancy Jensen of Logan, Utah.

• Place the jars on a heating pad set to "low" and cover them with a towel, as suggested by Ann Stephens of Pittsburg, California. I've been using this method, with a large inverted soup pot over the top for extra measure.

If you're having failures, experiment with different methods of incubation before you change other variables. A staffer had been getting batch after batch of runny yogurt using her yard-sale purchased yogurt maker. When she switched to the heating-pad method, which had a 100 percent success rate in all our testing, she made her first successful batch of thick yogurt.

THE FZ PREFERRED METHOD

For quick reference, here's a recipe that consistently produces a quart of thick yogurt:

Before making yogurt, put 2 tablespoons or a frozen cube of starter in a small glass, cup, or bowl, and allow to warm to room temperature.

Put a quart of milk in a large saucepan. Blend in ½ cup of milk powder. Heat the milk to 180 degrees and cool it to 115 degrees. Add a small amount of this warm milk to the cup of starter, whisk, add this mixture to the saucepan of milk, and whisk again. Pour this into a quart jar, screw on a lid, place on a heating pad set on "low," cover with a towel, and cover that with a large soup pot. Incubate for eight hours.

You can make double and triple batches; but to efficiently chain-yogurt and to avoid old, tart-tasting yogurt (yogurt grows slightly tarter each day in the refrigerator), don't make more than your family will eat in five days.

Several sources pointed out that you can make "yogurt cheese" by lining a colander with cloth, plopping in the yogurt, and draining (in fridge) overnight.

And remember that all failed and too-tart yogurt can be used to make popsicles and in cooking.

IN CONCLUSION

Through all of this, I've concluded that the reason there are so many recipes and theories out there is that everyone's situation is unique. If you don't succeed using the guidelines above, experiment as we did.

This investigation has changed our diet. Due to the expense, we had given up on buying store-bought yogurt years ago. Now yogurt has become a regular part of our diet again.

WHAT TO DO WITH . . .

Scorched ironing-board cover. Make potholders and oven mitts from unscorched parts. (Karina Millet, Greenville, Ohio)

Bread tabs. Make ties that allow balloons to be reused. Slit a tab, put the twisted end of an inflated balloon in the slit, wrap it around the tab once, and put the end in the slit again. (Maureen Melton, Lucas, Texas)

A plastic audio-cassette case. Use as a windshield scraper. Take apart and insert fingers in the clear "pocket" part for good grip. (Helen Darinsig, Port Carbon, Pennsylvania)

Leftover flat root beer and other soda. Use to make gelatin. Combine 2 cups with 1 packet or tablespoon of gelatin granules. (Joan Ayers, Elkton, Maryland)

Dead umbrellas. Use the fabric to repair snowsuits and nylon jackets. (Carolyn Hoppe, Little Rock, Arkansas)

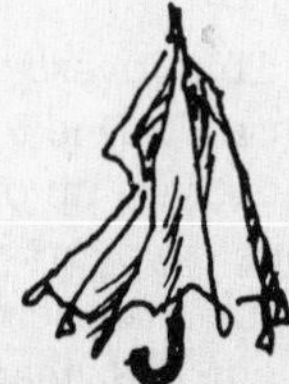

Styrofoam cups. Use to make party-favor hats. Place cups upside down on a cookie sheet. Place in a warm oven until the edges curl up and outward. Decorate with ribbon and tiny flowers. (Name withheld by request)

Dad's old T-shirt. Use to make superhero cape. Slit up the front, leaving the neck intact. Depending on the desired effect, the child can put his arms through the sleeves or not. (Vicky Grist, Buxton, North Carolina)

A refrigerator magnet. Place over keyhole on car door to prevent it from freezing. If already frozen, heat key with match or lighter. (Meg Winfield, Columbia, Maryland)

A milk jug. Make a disposable dish for a dog who chews dishes. Cut the jug off below the handle. (Marilyn MacLachlan, Morganton, North Carolina)

Dental floss. Use to resew ripped stitching in loafers and sneakers. [FZ has used this tip.] (Fran Hulette, Lawrence-ville, New Jersey)

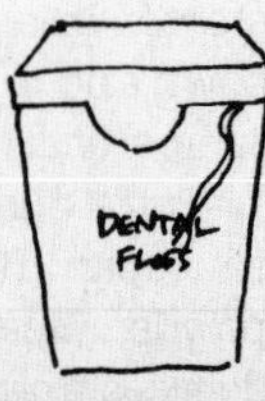

Old chain belt. Make a paper-towel dispenser by fastening it to wall with cup hooks. (Barb Carlson, Randolph, Vermont)

WATTS AND WAIT

Dear Amy,

We have been using the "time of use" program offered by Wisconsin Electric for a few months now, and recommend it highly. When we began the program, the electric company gave us a wired-in type of timer for the water heater and paid an electrician to install it. They also provided an appliance timer for no extra charge.

—Christine Henkel
Oak Creek, Wisconsin

(These programs, which offer reductions during nonpeak hours of up to half off the normal rate, are becoming common at utilities around the country. It's worth a call to your utility company. FZ)

A NEW WRINKLE

Dear Amy,

To increase my chances of winning local prize drawings in stores, I fold my tickets several times in interesting ways to make them more susceptible to being drawn. So far I have won a bag of groceries, a $10 gift certificate, a large Christmas stocking, and a small propane bottle.

—Teresa Busse
Klawock, Alaska

SPHERE, ROVER

Dear Amy,

I can't bring myself to buy new tennis balls for our dog to play with. I went to the local racquet club and asked if they had any old tennis balls that my dog could have. They showed me bins and bins of "dead" balls that had lost their bouncy newness and said, "Take all you want."

—Linda Bukvic
Williamsburg, Ohio

LOW-PRESSURE TACTIC

Dear Amy,

Air is the main cause of freezer burn. Here's a way to almost completely remove the air from food to be frozen in Ziploc bags. Place food in bag and almost seal the bag up completely. Place a straw in the corner and suck all of the air out of the baggie. Then, while still sucking, remove the straw and quickly seal the last section. Then place the baggie in the freezer.

—Christine Sunda
Centreville, Virginia

BOYS TO WOMEN

Dear Amy,

I was having a hard time parting with the money for some new winter boots. Out of desperation, I tried the boys department. I found the same style, and it fit my wider foot nicely—at half the price of the women's version.

—Michele Giesen
Boulder, Colorado

DIPLOMAS AT A DISCOUNT

We've all seen the terrifying statistics. The annual cost of tuition and room and board at the average private college has now passed $16,000. Public schools run around $8,000.

To compound the problem, college costs have increased at more than twice the rate of inflation since 1982 (9 percent versus 4.4 percent). At this rate, costs for a child born in 1995 would be $75,000 annually for the average private school, and $38,000 for public school.

Articles written on the subject generally conclude that you should invest large chunks of cash in mutual funds starting from the year the child is born. At this point, with a sinking feeling, you turn to the comics page.

Don't get me wrong. I feel that saving for a child's education is crucial, and I do not want to let anyone "off the hook" about this basic parental responsibility. And the invest-early-and-often-in-mutual-funds strategy does make sense.

But, as with every other financial decision in life, it pays to think more creatively.

Each of the following options requires careful consideration. Though we have called and confirmed the accuracy of addresses and telephone numbers, I can't vouch for the quality of the services offered. Like any other major money-saving ideas, you need to do research to see if one or more of these fit your needs.

Go to a free college. Readers have sent us information about two tuition-free colleges: College of the Ozarks, Point Lookout, MO 65726, (417) 334-6411; and Berea College, College Post Office 2344, Berea, KY 40404, (606) 986-9341. Both are highly rated academically, but have, as you might expect, fairly restrictive entrance requirements. An admissions director at College of the Ozarks told us that if a student qualifies for a Pell Grant, he or she has virtually a 100 percent chance of acceptance; otherwise, only about 1 in 20 appli-

cants gets in. And Berea College requires that 80 percent of the student body come from the Appalachian region.

Parents work at college. Parents who are employed by colleges often get reduced or even free tuition for their children. This can make it worthwhile to take a pay cut to land a campus position. Marcy Werner of Coral Gables, Florida, writes, "My husband teaches at the University of Miami and we all go free. The same applies to families of secretaries and office workers. Some schools even have reciprocal arrangements with other colleges."

Students work at college. There are many jobs that students themselves can do. Tanya Christman Kuntz of Grand Forks, North Dakota, highly recommends the position of dormitory resident advisor. At the University of North Dakota it pays $192 per month plus free room and board.

Students work outside college. More than 900 schools offer "co-op education" courses, in which formal study alternates with real-world, career-related work. It can tack an extra year or so on your college experience, but the work phase can pay up to $7,000 annually.

Do "distance learning." It's estimated that 100 American colleges and universities offer degrees entirely by "distance learning." This includes instruction by satellite, cable, audio cassette, video cassette, mail, computer conferencing, fax, and/or electronic mail. Tuition tends to be low, and you avoid the huge expense of moving to a distant college. Written tests are monitored by "proctors," sometimes at local high schools.

Reportedly, the best book on the subject is *College Degrees by Mail* by John Bear, Ten Speed Press, (510) 559-1600. Other books include *The Independent Study Catalog* and *The Electronic University*, both from Peterson's Guides, (800) 338-3282.

Mind Extension: The Education Network is a 24-hour cable network that offers degrees such as a BA from Maryland University College or even an MBA from Colorado State University. Videotapes are also available by mail. Call (800) 777-MIND for details.

For free booklets such as *Is Home Study for You?* and a directory of home-study-accredited schools, contact the National Home Study Council, 1601 18th Street NW, Suite 2, Washington, D.C. 20009, (202) 234-5100.

Go to a junior college. Roughly half the students entering college today go to junior colleges, which generally have far lower tuitions. It's become increasingly popular to go to a junior college for the first two years and then transfer to a four-year school for baccalaureate and graduate degrees. Be sure to thoroughly research transferability of credits before you enroll.

Go to a college with a high quality-per-dollar rating. Each year, *U.S. News & World Report*, *Money Guide* magazine, and *Lovejoy's College Guide* (all available through interlibrary loan) rate America's best college buys.

Get financial aid. There are two general categories of aid: outright gifts and cheap loans. These come from federal and state governments, private industry, and fraternal and religious organizations.

Because this is such a huge subject, it pays to read one or more books about it. The consensus among our readers and the financial-aid officials we interviewed is that the best books are published by Octameron Press, P.O. Box 2748, Alexandria, VA 22301, (703) 836-5480. Write them for a free brochure.

Octameron's flagship publication is *Don't Miss Out: The Ambitious Student's Guide to Financial Aid* by Robert and Anna Leider. We read a copy of the 1995–96 version and were very impressed. It's comprehensive (did you know there are generous scholarships available for former golf caddies?) and makes this confusing subject quite understandable. At $7 plus $2 shipping and handling, it's an excellent investment.

Over 1,200 colleges offer academic scholarships to students who have a B average and SAT scores of 900 and above. Most of these awards aren't based on financial need. Octameron's *The A's and B's of Academic Scholarships*, edited by Debra L. Wexler, lists 100,000 scholarships available at these schools.

Two more comprehensive books are *Cash for College: The Ultimate Guide to College Scholarships* by Cynthia Ruiz McKee and Phillip C. McKee Jr. (Hearst Books) and *The Scholarship Book* by Daniel J. Cassidy (Prentice Hall).

Go off-hours or off-season. Many colleges reduce tuition rates for evening, weekend, and summer classes.

Be a smart high-school senior. Many high schools now offer advanced-placement courses that allow students to enter college with several hours of tuition-free credit. Some colleges offer free on-campus classes for high-school seniors.

Go for three years. Popular in Europe, three-year baccalaureate degrees are catching on in the United States. For example, at Albertus Magnus, a liberal-arts college in New Haven, Connecticut, 80 percent of the freshmen signed up for a three-year bachelor's-degree program. It cost 17 percent less than the four-year program.

Take an equivalency test. ACT/PEP (American College Testing/Proficiency Examination Program) tests are offered by over 800 colleges and universities. They cost from $45 to $140 and are worth from three to eight semester credits per test. You can take them through your school registrar's office, or contact ACT/PEP directly at P.O. Box 4014, Iowa City, IA 52243, (319) 337-1363.

The CLEP (College Level Examination Placement) tests are similar. Call (609) 771-7240 for information, or call College Board Publications at (800) 323-7155 to order *The College Board Guide to the CLEP Examinations.*

Many colleges also offer "challenge" exams, in which you take the final examination for a particular course and get credit for it if you pass.

Do the military thing. Go through the four-year ROTC (Reserve Officer Training Corps) program and in your junior and senior years you'll receive $100 a month. The Montgomery GI Bill pays veterans up to $400 per month for 36 months. To qualify, soldiers, sailors, or airmen must contribute up to $1,200 into a special fund while they are enlisted. For more information, call (800) USA-ARMY.

Do the early-tuition-payment thing. Many states offer prepaid tuition plans—you pay at today's tuition rates and the state ensures it will be sufficient for the date your child enters a state university. Make sure you can get a refund if your child wins scholarships or goes to school out of state. The admissions office at your school of choice will have details.

Carefully match the student with the school. A newsletter reader from Boulder, Colorado, offers an important point: "If your child is unhappy because of an inappropriate situation, the costs in poor grades and making arrangements to transfer will outweigh the tuition you saved."

Peggy Beals of Marshfield, Massachusetts, puts it even more forcefully. "People who would never buy a lottery ticket or put their money in stocks and bonds without a careful study of track records will blow thousands to get their darlings into the most prestigious college that will accept them."

Peggy recommends a year or two in the workforce learning about "reality," or a couple of years in junior college, before spending the big bucks on expensive colleges. "It takes tough love to be firm with these youngsters as they devour college catalogs and dream of some faraway school, dorm life, beer parties, and no parental killjoys nagging them. Being realistic hurts parental pride, but it is kinder in the long run for everyone involved."

BRAIDERS OF THE LOST ART

Like quilting, rug braiding is an old craft that was developed to use up leftover material or to recycle old garments. And like quilts, braided rugs have become expensive; a kit to make a 3-foot-by-5-foot rug costs about $100, and buying a hand-braided rug this size might cost $300. But if you make a rug the way our grandmothers did, it can cost very little.

I spoke with three area braiders: hobbyist Donna Tretola, rug-braiding teacher Nancy Young, and professional braider Anna Smith. I also read several articles.

Space limitations prevent me from covering more than the basics. A library book would be useful for detailed information. I was told the best book on the subject is *The Braided Rug Book* by Norma M. Sturges. It's available from Lark Books at (800) 284-3388.

Ideally, braided rugs are made only of wool fabric. Unlike other fabrics, it's extremely durable, naturally repels dirt, is heavy enough to lie flat, and yet remains soft. Sources of wool include plaid skirts, winter coats, shirts, uniforms, and mill ends. White fabrics can be dyed to achieve hard-to-find colors. Since pure wool comes in a limited range of colors, many braiders also use 80 percent blends.

First, machine-wash any recycled garments; it doesn't matter if they shrink. Cut or tear the wool into strips. As there is a fair amount of waste in each garment, it saves space to do this in advance. Roll the wool into balls for storage.

The optimum width to cut strips is about 2 inches. Cut thicker wools into narrower strips and thinner wools into wider ones. Hand-baste or machine-sew them end-to-end to make longer strips.

Fold the strips with raw edges inside: narrow strips into quarters, wide strips into sixths. Test before cutting to ensure that the final

folded strips are uniform in thickness.

Experienced braiders fold as they braid. Beginners may prefer to baste or press the strips closed. Some braiders use Braid-Aids, small, metal devices that fold the strips as they are fed through. But they cost $7 each, you need three, and they don't work well with used fabric, as the joining seams get caught in them.

Braid the folded strips and join the braids in a circular pattern to form the rug. Originally, braids were hand-sewn together, but in the 1940s a faster and stronger technique was developed: lacing through the braids, not the fabric, with a blunt needle or a Braidkin, a flat, curved tool that costs about $1.50.

"Hit-or-miss" rugs are easiest for beginners, and the most economical, since you don't need a specific quantity of certain colors. For the most pleasing effect, stick with a small range of colors, such as blues and greens. Rugs with planned designs are more challenging. You need to braid a little and lace a little to anticipate color changes. Change colors by adding new-colored strips, staggered one at a time. Depending on the colors and your preferences, you might add one new color per 6 inches of braid, or one new color per row.

Finish the rug by tapering the strips, braiding them to a point, and sewing this on.

As for economy, braided rugs are extremely cheap. Over the years, Donna has spent $20 on her hobby, has made 15 rugs, and has enough material left over to fill two large trunks and a huge basket. Once people learned that she braids rugs, they began to *give* her their wool castoffs, and she was given thread by a relative. Nancy buys unsaleable garments by the pound from thrift shops. A 3-foot-by-5-foot oval rug might require from five to seven full-length winter coats, or 9 pounds of strips.

The biggest expense is the thread to lace the braids together. Although some articles suggested using carpet-and-button thread, twine, or kite string, my sources said these won't hold up for more than five years. A stronger but more expensive thread is six-ply linen (or three-ply for small rugs). A 3-foot-by-5-foot rug requires 225 yards (or 4 ounces) of six-ply thread. Mail-ordered, this quantity costs $12. Anna uses waxed six-ply linen/nylon, purchased in quantity from a local discount source. Her thread-cost is $3 for a rug this size. Nancy uses beeswaxed Nytex, purchased through a shoemaker.

Ask local braiders for their sources of low-cost thread.

Aside from ovals, braided rugs can also be round or heart-shaped. Rectangular rugs can be made by sewing together parallel lengths of braid and leaving the ends ragged. This shape would complement contemporary decor.

These three braiders agreed that a 3-foot-by-5-foot oval rug might require a total of 50 to 60 hours of work, or about 2 hours per night for one month, done while watching TV or visiting.

It might seem that braiding rugs saves a small amount of money for the time spent, particularly when compared to purchasing machine-made versions. But hand-braided rugs are more durable; they can last 35 years in highly trafficked areas and indefinitely elsewhere. Two rugs in the entryway of Donna's home were ten years old and looked almost new.

Also, hand-braided rugs are much more attractive and can be made in subtler designs and to match any color scheme. They can be made larger or smaller as needed. They are easily repaired. If you lack fabric to finish your rug, you can still use it until you find more. And unlike other types of rugs, braided rugs have two usable sides: an everyday side and a "company" side.

Rug braiding interests me because over the last ten years I haven't found any rugs I've liked at yard sales. From now on, I'm going to save all of our old wool garments, and maybe I'll make one of those rectangular rugs for our living room someday.

FREEZER FIGURES

Gricelda Chavez of Upland, California, writes, "My husband and I are looking to buy a freezer. What size do you recommend for a family of four? Is upright better than horizontal?"

Freezers are sized by the cubic foot. We have eight people in our family, and we own a 23-cubic-foot Kenmore freezer, the largest of the standard sizes. Because we have an 8,000-plus-square-foot garden, we fill it right to the brim at the end of summer, but even at its lowest it's at least half full. We can a lot of foods specifically because we don't have room in our freezer.

On the other hand, friends of ours, a couple with one eight-year-old son, have a 14-cubic-foot freezer. They freeze some produce from their 600-square-foot suburban garden, and also freeze garden surplus from friends (us) and bulk-purchased meats. Their freezer has never been more than two thirds full, and they concede they could probably get by with a somewhat smaller model.

So a good general rule is to buy a freezer with about 3 cubic feet per person in your household; less if you don't garden, more if you garden intensively or have a neighbor who hunts moose.

As for the upright-versus-chest question, the 1995 edition of *The Consumer Guide to Home Energy Savings* says the typical annual energy cost for a 15-cubic-foot chest is $35; for the same-sized upright it's $44 (based on the national average of about 8 cents per kilowatt-hour).

When it comes to which brand to buy, go for the best price. One effect of efficiency standards that were imposed in 1993 is that there are no longer significant differences in efficiency between brands of new freezers of comparable sizes.

When freezer shopping, be sure to buy a manual-defrost model. These consume 35 percent to 40 percent less energy than automatic defrost versions. Auto-defrost freezers also tend to dry foods and cause freezer burn.

Due to large advances in freezer efficiency in recent years, this is one of the few areas in which I recommend you buy new rather than used.

OWN TO RENT

Sandy Croslow of Vincennes, Indiana, wrote to us about the success she and her husband have enjoyed as live-in landlords. "This can be a wonderful way to buy a first home," she wrote. Because the Croslows are also CPAs, we called Sandy for details.

They moved to Vincennes in 1987, in debt "up to our ears" from a business failure. They researched the rental market and found there was a shortage of housing for college students. Then they "ran the numbers" (both realtors and CPAs can do this for clients), calculating all factors, including the mortgage payment, property taxes, rents, utilities, and depreciation.

Ultimately, they put $3,000 down on a $50,000, four-apartment Victorian home (housing is cheap in the Midwest). Rent from the other three apartments equaled $875 and their mortgage payment was just $500. This allowed them to save for their "dream home," a single-family dwelling on ½ acre where they moved last year. They still own the Victorian and operate their CPA firm from it.

Sandy says banks favor live-in landlords. They typically ask 10 percent down from live-in landlords versus 20 percent down from absentee landlords.

She says a key to success is carefully screening tenants. "In my experience, the only people who get into trouble doing this are those who are so desperate to rent that they'll take the first person who comes along."

CHECK THE CEREAL NUMBERS

Mary Ellen Wobbecke of Cleveland Heights, Ohio, sent me two curious articles, each addressing the rising cost of cold cereals.

The first made these points:

- Of the 150 cold cereals the reporter surveyed, the average retail price was about $4 a pound. (Compare that to the retail price of cereal's raw ingredients: Rice, oats, wheat flour, cornmeal, and *sugar* cost from 15¢ to 40¢ a pound.)
- It's estimated that 15¢ of material and 15¢ of labor go into a $3 box of cereal.
- A 1992 survey of advertisers showed that 67 percent of a cereal's price is spent on marketing.
- Despite the above, in 1994, cold-cereal retail sales in this country exceeded $8 billion, a 5.7 percent increase from 1993.

A bizarre reaction to spiraling cereal prices was detailed in the second article. Congressmen Sam Gejdenson of Connecticut and Charles Schumer of New York have asked Attorney General Janet Reno to launch an antitrust investigation of the biggest cold-cereal producers. Representative Schumer, who confesses he can gobble a whole box of cereal for dinner, told the Associated Press that high cereal prices make his "blood boil."

This struck me as strange. If name-brand cereal is too expensive, why should the government get involved? Why don't consumers *stop buying it*?

Speculating that the congressmen had overlooked this obvious solution, I called Scott Kovarovics, legislative assistant to Representative Gejdenson. He shot down my idea. Cold cereal, he essentially said, is a necessity.

"Look at modern lifestyles. People don't have time to make pancakes or waffles, bacon and eggs. It isn't something you can just give up, it's something more and more people have come to tremendously depend upon," he said.

He added that generics aren't the whole solution. "You have to have time to search high and low for the generics, squint at prices, make the calculations. People just don't have time to do that."

Kovarovics said they suspect name-brand companies of colluding to keep generics off the shelves. However, they know of just one case that might support this theory. His office's main concern seems to be simply that the cost of this "necessity" is too high.

My reaction:

- If the name-brands are colluding to keep generics off the shelves, it's worthwhile to investigate that.
- But it's silly to say people don't have time to comparison shop. Unit pricing is now the norm in most stores, thereby making squinting and calculating obsolete.
- And I don't believe cold cereal is a necessity for busy Americans. Even if they lack time on hectic weekdays, they can make and freeze muffins, pancakes, and waffles on weekends and microwave them later in the week. A huge batch of granola requires ten minutes of hands-on preparation.

In our house, we eat cold cereal less than once a week, and it's always either a $1-per-18-ounce box of store-brand, on-sale, stockpiled cornflakes, or homemade granola. And if I had to eliminate any breakfast that we generally have, cornflakes would be the first to go. Two hours later, I'm always hungry again.

FIRST-CLASS IDEA

Dear Amy,

When mailing in camera film in the provided envelopes, it states on the envelope that you need two stamps. But that doesn't mean you need two first-class stamps. You need one plus a 23¢ stamp. You save 9¢.

—Margie Walter
Munising, Michigan

(This applies to all first-class mail. Up to one ounce is 32¢. Each additional ounce or fraction of an ounce is 23¢. For example, postage on a 2½ ounce letter is 78¢. FZ)

TANK USED

Dear Amy,

During some recent plumbing problems with the toilet, the fixture itself actually broke. A new toilet would have cost a minimum of $75, but our local plumber sold us a used one for $30. It was in perfect condition, clean, and worked properly. The previous owners got rid of it simply because they wanted a fancy $300 toilet. The plumber went on to explain that plumbing shops often have these used toilets and that people simply need to ask.

—Jan Kingston
Beaverton, Oregon

GLOVE CONNECTION

Dear Amy,

I wear rubber gloves when I wash dishes. I'm right-handed and the right glove is usually the one that gets a hole first. Instead of throwing away both gloves, I save the left ones for my left-handed friend, who saves the right ones for me.

—Cathy Sylar
Kelseyville, California

SPOUTING WISDOM

Dear Amy,

You can make a wonderful lid with a pouring spout from any canning jar. Take an empty, round salt box and, using the lid from the canning jar as a guide, cut out a circle from the top of the salt box. Place this new lid onto the top of the canning jar, screw on the ring, and you have a pouring spout on your jar. I use mine for dried parsley, basil, and my own cinnamon-sugar mix.

—Ellie Pett
Elmhurst, Illinois

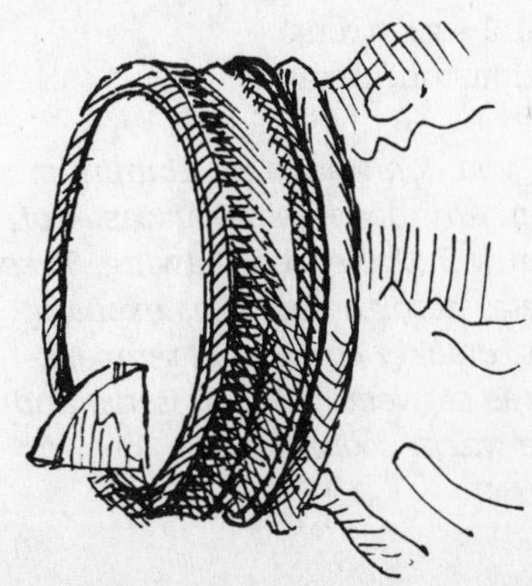

CHEAP DATES

Dear Amy,

Never buy a calendar. You can always get one free from a bank, just for the asking.

—Nancy Graham
Keokuk, Iowa

SHE THAWED IT THROUGH

Dear Amy,

There is a new product called Miracle Thaw that advertises you can greatly reduce the amount of time needed for thawing frozen foods without using the microwave. Then I read an article in the local newspaper that said all this item consisted of was a sheet of aluminum with a Teflon coating. I decided to try a test with my good, heavy, anodized aluminum pans. Much to my surprise, the ice cube in the pan melted in less than a minute at room temperature while the control ice cube just sat there. Now, I thaw things faster with my aluminum pan (I still use the microwave in an emergency) and saved myself the $19.95 plus shipping and handling.

—Jill Armstrong
Houston, Texas

(If you don't have an aluminum pan, any heavy steel or cast-iron pan will also speed thawing. These metal items act as heat exchangers, quickly equalizing temperatures between the cold items and the warm room. FZ)

RESCUING LOST SOLES

Dear Amy,

I found a pair of shoes in perfect condition in an unlikely spot: the local shoe-repair shop. The owner was selling shoes that had not been claimed in over a year. There was quite a large collection.

—Kathleen Layman
Whittier, California

TASTY TATERS

Dear Amy,

Here is a homemade recipe to replace those expensive "shake and bake" potato recipes that are becoming so popular:

1 cup flour
1 cup cracker crumbs
1 tablespoon salt
1½ teaspoons sugar
2 teaspoons Italian seasoning (combination of basil, oregano, and garlic powder)
1 tablespoon oil

Mix and store in refrigerator. Put a small amount in a plastic bag. Shake together with potatoes cut into ½-inch to 1-inch chunks. Put ¼ cup oil in baking sheet or cast-iron skillet. Bake coated potato pieces in skillet at 350 degrees for 30 minutes or until they brown.

—Terry Zimmer
Courtland, Virginia

CLEAN-SLATE RATE

Dear Amy,

In 1990 my son had an at-fault auto accident. For the next three years he had to pay surcharges on his policy. Last fall at renewal time, his insurance company tried to charge him again. He sent a check for $10 to the local motor vehicles department and received a copy of the last three years of his driving record. When it arrived, sure enough, he had a clean record and his insurance company immediately lowered the premium $300 a year.

—Mrs. William Laurent
Mountainside, New Jersey

CARD TRICK

Dear Amy,

If you want to make your own cards, don't buy card stock. I priced it at $13.00 a pack! The stationery store clerk suggested 8-inch-by-5-inch unlined index cards; a pack of 100 costs $1.85! They are made of the same card stock. Fold them in half, decorate any way you like, and you have wonderful, sturdy cards.

—Kimberly Mendoza
Rockledge, Florida

MUTUAL MOOCHING

A couple of years ago we solicited older readers of the newsletter for recollections of the Great Depression. Their tales of hardship and deprivation were memorable. Most moving were the stories of how neighbors came through for each other. Cooperation was often the key to their survival.

As I read, I couldn't help but reflect on how much times have changed. Today, suburban neighbors seldom cooperate and help each other. In fact, they often don't know each other. Generally, each house is a self-contained unit. On a street of 20 homes with 20 families, there are 20 weed-whackers, 20 gas barbecues, and 20 *Lion King* videos, though each of these is used only a few hours per year.

But cooperation can work as well in the 1990s as it did in the 1930s. Once, I asked a fellow who helped Vietnamese refugees get established in this country how they became so successful so quickly. After all, most arrived here with no money and couldn't even speak English. He said that, aside from their frugal diets, their key to success was cooperation. They shared virtually everything, even housing and cars, and pooled the money they saved to start businesses.

I suspect a major factor in our transition to a more solitary, uncooperative culture is the breakdown of communities. Our society has become more transient, and we don't invest in short-term relationships. And because every family has an entertainment center rivaling the technology of NASA, we don't leave our homes long enough to chat with our neighbors across

the fence. Mass production has made goods more affordable, and so while sharing is economically beneficial, it's not a necessity. And we are a less patient bunch of people; we want to be able to use that router immediately when the whim hits us, rather than waiting for our neighbor to return home so we can borrow his or get ours back from him.

We're all aware of this trend away from cooperation, and we all complain about it. But what should we *do* about it? The key is recognizing that when cooperation doesn't occur naturally, we have to *cultivate* it.

First, *offer* goods and services to others. Start by asking such things as, "I'm going to the bakery thrift shop, can I pick up something for you?" Whenever we moved into a new area, I would scope out my new neighbors in this way. Some were cool to these offers, whereas others immediately understood that this is how the game is played and accepted.

Second, if a new neighbor offers you a favor, accept it when feasible. When my offers were consistently and curtly turned down, I stopped offering. I became aware that if someone made me an offer I couldn't accept, I should at least say, "No, thank you, but let's stay in touch. Maybe I can do something for you sometime."

Once the first exchange occurs, the relationship can proceed to surprising levels of trust and benefit. But this can occur only if both parties abide by certain rules of engagement:

- Start by offering something small and "safe," such as surplus from your garden. Offering larger or more valuable goods and services in the beginning intimidates people; they don't want to feel deeply indebted to a stranger.
- Reciprocation is crucial. If you've accepted a favor or two, actively look for ways to return them. You might even say, "You've been so helpful. Let me know if I can do something for you."
- If you borrow something, return it in the same condition it was in when you received it—or better. Clean it, fill the tank, sharpen it, and so on. If damage occurs, always make good on it by replacing or repairing it.
- If you offer a service, do it well. Offer to do only those things that you're good at. The fact that you're doing it for free doesn't excuse lateness or sloppiness.
- If someone turns down several offers, stop offering. Some people are simply uncomfortable with accepting favors of any kind.
- Be patient when reciprocation doesn't occur; don't keep a scorecard. In many cases, you might never look for reciprocation, such

as when you do favors for an elderly person.

• But if someone accepts many of your offers and *never* reciprocates, even when it seems appropriate (you babysit her kids but she is always "unavailable" when you need a sitter), consider redirecting your favors to those who understand that cooperation is a two-way street.

Cooperation can take place at many levels, and these levels tend to correspond to the level of friendship.

The most basic and common level is to mutually *offer* small goods or services. This level occurs between new neighbors and acquaintances. It can be useful, but the financial impact tends to be small.

Mutual mooching starts when either party feels free to *ask*, politely, for small favors from the other, such as asking a friend to pick up milk for you when she goes to the store. You might precede your request by saying, "If it's inconvenient, please feel free to say no." Or you might wait until you've performed a large favor (helped paint their house) before you ask for a small favor (borrowing a tool). This level usually occurs between friends and family members. It's far more efficient, because it's hard to guess and make offers that fit a friend's needs.

At the next level, either party feels complete freedom to *ask* for even large favors. This generally occurs only between black-belt tightwad friends who have a very open understanding of the economic benefits they both enjoy from the relationship. When a friend asked if I had a spare bicycle for his seven-year-old, I was delighted. It meant that our friendship had progressed to where we could ask each other for a wide variety of useful goods and services.

At this level, the concept of shared ownership is introduced. For example, we pooled resources with two other families to buy staging for house painting.

The ultimate level is the one those Vietnamese immigrants enjoy—shared ownership of even large, expensive items such as houses. This is unfamiliar to many Americans, who have a long-standing tradition of independence and privacy. But I do know of two small families who purchased a home together and had a successful, harmonious life for many years. And, in any case, a sharing arrangement like this seems *very* sensible for the growing number of single-parent families. For instance, two (or more) single mothers could share a household. If they worked different shifts, they could also eliminate child-care costs.

Cooperation-and-friendship is a chicken-and-egg thing. Often cooperation comes out of friendships. But cooperation can also be a way to initiate and build friendships.

CLEAN AND LEAN

Ground beef is a tightwad mainstay. We seldom eat it in the form of hamburgers, but we frequently add it to casseroles and other dishes. It's convenient to cook, tastes good, and can be purchased on sale for as little as 89¢ a pound.

Unfortunately, the cheapest

ground beef tends to have the highest proportion of fat. So I was interested in a handout from the Minnesota Beef Council sent to me by Linda Erdahl of Proctor, Minnesota. It explains an easy method to greatly reduce ground beef's fat content:

The first step is browning the beef over medium heat. If the recipe calls for them, you can also add onion or garlic at this time. Then use a slotted spoon to place the beef "crumbles" on a large plate lined with three layers of paper towel. Blot the top of the beef with a paper towel. Let sit one minute, blotting with an additional paper towel. (Apparently due to fears of contamination, the Beef Council advises you to use paper towels that are white and nonrecycled. This seems overcautious to me, but use your own judgment.)

Then place the beef in a strainer or colander and pour about 1 quart of hot tap water over it, stirring while the water pours. Drain for five minutes and use in recipe.

The fat reduction accomplished by this method is impressive. A 3-ounce cooked portion of 70-percent-lean ground beef has 18 grams of fat when fried in the form of a patty. But the same portion, fried into crumbles and then blotted and rinsed, has just 6.1 grams of fat.

The Beef Council reports that less than 10 percent of the meat's protein, iron, vitamin B_{12}, and zinc are lost in this process.

Remember that it doesn't take much ground beef to make a satisfying addition to a casserole. We find that one pound of uncooked ground beef—which cooks down to considerably less than a pound—is about the right amount for a family of eight.

Since you can never have too many recipes that use browned and crumbled ground beef, I thought I would share a Rice-A-Roni-style concoction of Jim's that our family enjoys.

1 pound ground beef
1 medium onion, chopped
1 cup rice
8 ounces spaghetti, broken into
 1-inch pieces
4 tablespoons margarine*
4 cups broth, or water and bouillon
salt and pepper

Brown beef and onion in a large skillet. Drain (and rinse if desired). Brown rice and spaghetti in margarine. Add in beef, onion, rice, and broth. Cover and simmer for 20 minutes, or until rice and spaghetti are fully cooked. Season with salt and pepper.

*You can use no-stick spray and reduce the margarine, or substitute olive oil.

DISCOUNTS FROM DIXIE?

About 60 percent of the furniture made in the United States is made in North Carolina. Because of this, hundreds of outlet stores cluster around Hickory, North Carolina. Many people travel long distances to shop there and there are even packaged shopping tours. The outlets also take phone orders and ship to customers nationwide. The average saving, it's claimed, is about 50 percent.

You've probably heard of this before. It's been touted in many major-city newspaper articles, in save-money books, and on *Oprah* when Kate Gladchun, author of *The Fine Furniture and Furnishings Discount Shopping Guide*, appeared as a guest.

I had never pursued this because new furniture holds little interest for me. Secondhand furniture (including some antiques) usually costs less and holds it value better than even wholesale-priced new furniture.

But sometimes new furniture is the best option, such as when I decided to replace our creaky hodgepodge of dining room chairs. I've never found eight secondhand matching chairs I've liked. I even called a restaurant supplier and learned that sturdy commercial chairs, even used, cost $100 each. And antique chairs wouldn't survive six kids.

So in July of 1995, when I visited relatives in North Carolina, I tested the strategy as I looked for chairs. For many reasons, I narrowed my search to casual-looking "thumb-back" chairs with a woven seat.

To compare prices, you should first shop locally and collect manufacturers' names and model numbers. Then you need to find North Carolina outlets (manufacturers don't sell directly to individuals) that carry those items. To find the outlets, you can order Gladchun's book, or call the Chamber of Commerce in Hickory. I got more accurate and complete information by calling the manufacturers directly. I got their numbers through directory assistance.

Before leaving, I did phone research and shopped extensively in Maine. During my trip, I visited the Hickory Furniture Mart, a 12-acre complex of outlets. I also went to the Mart's clearance center and a dozen other stores in Hickory and surrounding cities.

My conclusion: The North Carolina furniture-buying strategy isn't all it's cracked up to be.

Why? First, this strategy may pose an ethical dilemma. Many people might feel it's unfair to view merchandise and collect buying information from local merchants. After all, the merchants aren't reimbursed for providing essential elements of long-distance shopping. In an interview, Gladchun told me that if people are uncomfortable doing this, outlets will send customers photocopies of catalog pages. But few people would feel confident buying furniture based only on viewing photocopies. Although you can return shipped furniture, you're out the shipping fee and must also pay up to a 30 percent "restocking" fee.

Further, most of the North Carolina outlets carry only high-priced name-brand furniture: Lexington, Drexel-Heritage, Henredon, and so on. So even the discount prices may still be too high for average pocketbooks. Even the clearance

center's prices seemed steep; it sold no chairs for under $100.

In addition, when shopping for under-$100 chairs, I found that *no* price tags contained model numbers, and few even listed the maker's name. Store owners in North Carolina and Maine were evasive when I asked for this information. Two gave me false information.

I finally acquired manufacturer names and numbers for two different thumb-back chairs, called many stores for prices, and found that the lowest prices from North Carolina weren't impressive. A Maine store's sale price for an unfinished thumb-back was $59, versus the North Carolina shipped price of $64. A Maine Pier One Imports store would order the other, finished thumb-back for $66, versus the North Carolina shipped price of $64. Interestingly, Pier One Imports told me that if they stocked this chair, the retail price would be $89. They can offer better deals on ordered furniture, while prices on stocked furniture must reflect in-store overhead. I realized then that while in this latter case I would save $16 on eight chairs ordered from North Carolina (not factoring in my phone bill), this was only because a North Carolina store was willing to make a better deal. Each store has identical chair costs and shipping costs. In theory, a Maine store should be able to give me the same deal.

thumb-back Chair

As we needed to take our trailer anyway, I hoped to buy in North Carolina to save the shipping costs. But I could find no North Carolina stores that stocked the chairs that I wanted—all had to be ordered and shipped to me. I could have brought the chairs home myself only if I had given the stores several weeks' notice.

The few under-$100 stocked chairs I could find in the North Carolina outlets cost the same or more than I could have paid at home. For example, a made-in-Thailand white-and-clear-finish Windsor chair sold for $60 in North Carolina. This same iffy-quality chair sells in discount department stores nationwide for as little as $29.

Although I didn't comparison-shop larger, more expensive types of furniture, the *Columbus* (Ohio) *Dispatch* did and found similar patterns; local sale-priced furniture often cost less than shipped North Carolina furniture.

On a separate note, shipping charges varied depending on stores' policies. Chairs, which are compact and lightweight, cost about $5 to ship to Maine through UPS. Some stores ship only through trucking services and this can cost $15 per chair.

Though I wasn't impressed, I can't say this strategy never works for anyone. If you like and can afford new, expensive furniture, and what you want never goes on sale, you might find North Carolina shopping worthwhile.

Gladchun's book can be ordered by sending $19.95 to Resources, Inc., P.O. Box 973, Bloomfield Hills, MI 48303-3440.

DISCOUNTS FROM DIXIE? UPDATE

A few months after the previous article ran in the newsletter, we took delivery of ten chairs made by a North Carolina firm, and we are delighted with the deal we made.

Here's how we did it. After we decided on the brand we wanted, my staffer Pam said she would ask her husband, who owns a building-supply store, if he could order the chairs we wanted directly from the North Carolina manufacturer. Her husband simply called and placed an order. The shipped price to him was $50 per chair. He resold them to us for $55 each. Ordered through Maine's Pier One store, they would have cost us $66 each. The normal retail price is $89.

This seems like a good place to plug a good company. My chairs are the Homestead model made by Builtright Chair Company, P.O. Drawer 1609, Statesville, NC 28687, (704) 873-6541. This company makes casual hardwood dining room chairs (Builtright calls them "kitchen chairs"), rockers, and barstools.

Based on my extensive search, I believe these may be the best hardwood chairs available for the money. Builtright chairs have a unique, tension-fit frame construction that requires no glues, pins, or nails and virtually never loosens up. I have Builtright chairs that have seen daily use for 15 years and are still perfectly solid. The chair I bought has a natural seagrass seat that resists stains and can be easily cleaned.

Another unique feature is that the seat of each chair is a separate screw-on unit. These are well made and far superior to those I've seen by other companies. Builtright sells replacement seats for about $10. The company has been around for 55 years, so it will probably still be in business when you need to replace your old seats.

Builtright also sells much cheaper chairs than the ones I bought. Their slat-seat "Carolina" chair sells for $35 retail, and they say—quite sincerely, I believe—that it is the best chair for the money sold anywhere in the world.

If you're in the market for chairs, write Builtright for the name of the store nearest you that stocks their chairs. If there's no such retailer nearby, you can engineer a deal through a retailer (one that could conceivably sell furniture, such as a furniture, hardware, or department store) just as we did. Builtright will mail you a flyer that illustrates their line of chairs.

A REASONABLE REGISTRY

For a tightwad, it's frustrating to be asked to buy wedding gifts through a registry at an overpriced department store. So I was pleased to receive a letter from Angela Henson of Southgate, Kentucky, about a refreshingly practical solution.

She says she didn't want to subject her wedding's guests to the expense of a traditional registry, but people kept asking her mother what she wanted.

"So my mother finally had me make a list of everything I could think of that I needed," Angela writes. "Because my household items included one set of old dishrags and a Papa Smurf glass, I

deduced that I needed everything. I wrote down everything from buckets and brooms to cookware to towels. The only thing I requested in a specific pattern was Corelle dishes in Morning Blue.

Angela says that whenever a guest asked what to buy, her mother simply pulled out the list. The person would look it over and decide what he or she wanted to buy, and her mother would check off the item.

"People kept telling her how sensible I was, and how wonderful it was to be able to

pick an item and shop for it wherever they chose instead of being forced into shopping for expensive items at expensive stores.

"The list was extremely successful. I got everything I needed, and then some. The most wonderful thing about this is after seven and a half years of marriage and two beautiful daughters, I still use all of these wedding gifts daily. I haven't yet had a need for china, and can't really see a need for it in the near future!"

SUITE DEALS

There are several ways to save on hotel-room rates. You can sometimes negotiate a good deal directly with the hotel. Or you can have your travel agent dig up a hotel that's having a special.

But one of the newer and more interesting ways to save is to book your room through a hotel discounter. Valerie Smith of Chicago, Illinois, sent me a *Chicago Tribune* article about these organizations, which have expanded dramatically in the last few years. They buy hotel rooms in bulk, cheap, and pass the savings on to customers. The *Tribune*'s independent survey found room rates averaged 30 percent below the regular rate.

Discounters include:

RMC Travel Centre; books rooms for hotels in over 100 American cities: (800) 782-2674.

Quikbook; serves 21 cities: (800) 789-9887.

Hotel Reservations Network; serves 20 cities: (800) 964-6835.

Accommodations Express; serves ten cities: (800) 444-7666.

Central Reservation Service; serves Miami, New York, Orlando, San Francisco: (800) 950-0232.

We received information from Quikbook and RMC Travel Centre that listed the regular rates and their discount rates for various hotels. To learn if the discounts were real, we called 15 hotels and asked them for their room rates. We found that when calling expensive hotels, the discounts were significant. But when we called economy hotels, we were told their regular rates were much less than the discounter stated; their regular rate was about the same as the discounter's rate.

Wendy Galfund, marketing director for Quikbook, said that happens "occasionally" because discounters can't keep up with all of the low-rate specials offered by moderately priced hotels.

I called a local travel agent to discuss hotel discounters with her. She said they seem legitimate and she had actually dealt with some. But she added that to be on the safe side, she would work only with those discounters that allow you to pay the hotel directly. Quikbook, which claims to be one of the largest discounters, is among the services that operate this way. Other services require you to pay the discounter in advance.

One often-asked question is: Will I be given a room in the basement? The discounters with whom we spoke said the rooms they book are as good as the ones the hotel books directly with its customers. "The hotels know that if they give our customers bad rooms, we can drop our affiliation with them," said Galfund. She said that since discounters fill rooms that would otherwise go empty, hotels don't dare threaten their relationship with discounters.

Hotel discounters may be like coupons. The one that gives you the biggest "discount" may not be the one that gives you the lowest price, and other hotels that don't work with discounters may offer better deals. So if you consider using a discounter, verify the regular room rate with the hotel and compare the price offered with that of other hotels in the area.

THIS ARTICLE WILL KEEP YOU IN STITCHES

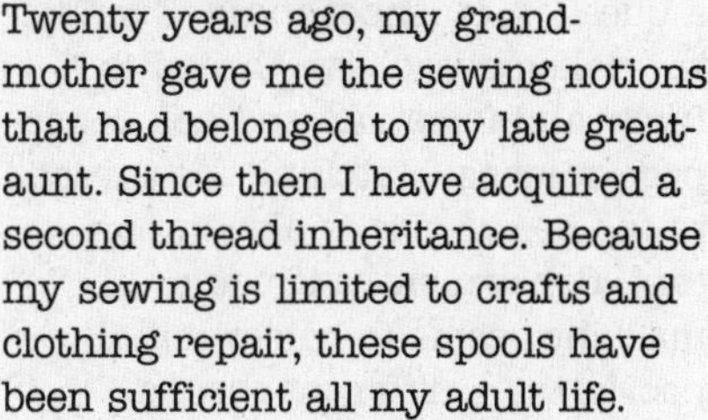

Twenty years ago, my grandmother gave me the sewing notions that had belonged to my late great-aunt. Since then I have acquired a second thread inheritance. Because my sewing is limited to crafts and clothing repair, these spools have been sufficient all my adult life.

But I've been trapped in a time warp. The wooden spools have stamped-on prices of 15¢ to 50¢. You can imagine my sticker shock when I found that a spool now costs $2.50. Yet I've seen bins of thread selling for prices that harked back to my old spools' stickers.

So I decided to unravel the thread mystery. I interviewed David Coffin, associate editor of *Threads* magazine, and Lois Hathaway, a local quilter.

Thread varies tremendously in price depending on quality. Department-store 2/$1 spools are usually poor-quality 100 percent polyester and generally should be avoided. This thread can literally melt when ironed.

Some people economize by using large cones of "serger" thread for regular sewing. At $1.25 for 3,000 yards, this seems like an amazing deal compared to those 400-yard/$2.50 spools. But serger thread is much thinner than regular thread, as a serger uses several strands at a time, so it probably won't hold up to any real stress.

There are different types of quality thread. Silk and 100-percent cotton are the best but cost the most. Cotton-covered polyester and 100-percent polyester cost less but can serve well if you know what to look for. Although there's a

lot to be said about the type of thread needed for certain applications, quality mostly boils down to a question of smoothness. Even to the naked eye, cheap thread is fuzzy and irregular and will cause poor stitches. Matching the thread to the needle size is also important. Consequently, if your machine seems to be sewing poorly, try a different thread before you take it into the shop.

Instead of buying poor-quality thread, economize in other ways:

- Stock up during sales. Ask to be put on your fabric shop's mailing list so you'll be notified of upcoming sales. With luck, you'll get thread at half price, or about .3¢ per yard.
- Look for thread at yard sales. Make sure the quality and thickness suit your needs.
- Use up low-quality thread in less-critical applications, such as hand-stitching a hem.
- Revive old thread. Cotton can dry out with age, become brittle, and break easily. *Threads* contends it can be remoisturized by placing it in your refrigerator's vegetable bin.
- Remember that exact color-matching is critical only for top-stitching. Otherwise, you can use a thread with the same color value (lightness or darkness); a neutral gray blends with many colors.
- Buy large cones of thread in a few basic colors. If you can't find them locally, they can be mail-ordered from Home-Sew, P.O. Box 4099, Bethlehem, PA 18018, (610) 867-3833 (a free catalog is available on request). A 6,000-yard spool of Coats & Clark cotton-covered polyester thread costs $13.35, or a little more than .2¢ per yard. In other words, compared to $2.50/400-yard spools, 400 yards of this thread costs 90¢.

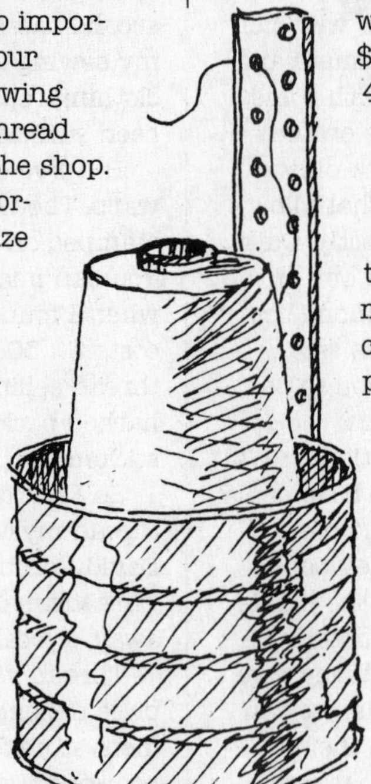

Most people think large cones require a $10 adapter or stand to feed the thread to the machine. Smaller-sized cones can be simply placed in a wide-mouthed canning jar.

Jacqueline Cannizzo of Shaker Heights, Ohio, offered a simple solution for larger cones. Tape a plastic paint stirrer to a jar or can large enough to accommodate the cone.

Place the cone inside and pull the thread through the top hole in the stirrer. Adjust the can's position to maintain proper tension on the thread.

A VIN-WIN SITUATION

Dear Amy,

My husband etched the car windows with the vehicle identification number (as explained on page 166), and we've told a number of people about it. We got a substantial discount on our car insurance for making the effort. Be prepared to plead your case when you call your insurance company headquarters. Don't give up at the first

"I never heard about this." Persist. Ask for the supervisor, then the supervisor's supervisor. Get their 800 number right away and call back on that number to save toll costs.

—Lou N. Overman
Manteo, North Carolina

COMBO COOLER

Dear Amy,

Instead of buying Snapple (or similar) drinks, I mix homemade iced tea with juice. Cheaper, delicious, and not so sweet.

—Dianne Meier
Des Moines, Washington

WASH AND WALK

Dear Amy,

I wash yard-sale shoes, even leather ones, in the washing machine, then let them air-dry, stuffed with newspapers. This has not ruined a pair of shoes for me yet, though I couldn't guarantee it couldn't happen.

—Katie Jackman
Ames, Iowa

CATS ON CAMPUS

Dear Amy,

If you live near a college of veterinary medicine, or a community college that teaches veterinary technicians, they may do routine vaccinations, dentistry, neutering, and spaying at very reasonable cost. The work is always done by a licensed veterinarian. If your animal is ill or needs surgery, try to have it referred there.

— Julie Pinochet
Lexington, Virginia

GET GRATIS GROUPER

Dear Amy,

We took a deep-sea cruise and there were 35–40 people from all over the States on the boat. We all could fish. After docking, many people left the boat with the main large ice chest filled with the day's catch. We were the last off the boat and were offered numerous wonderful fresh fish to take home. The captain said many customers leave without their fish because they are vacationing and can't bring their catch along with them. It was his practice to give away the unwanted fish to whomever wanted them. If you live near a harbor where boats run charters, it might be worth asking about.

—Deborah Chalk
Chimney Rock, North Carolina

BUDGET-TRIMMING IDEA

Dear Amy,

Our barber is a talented lady, and one day I asked her if she cut women's hair, too. She said, "Of course!" I reasoned that if a barber can do a good job with thinning, short men's hair, then he or she should be able to do equally well with trimming thick, long hair like mine. I was right. I've had all sorts of good cuts from her now at $8 each. The only thing she can't do are treatments that require a sink for washing hair, so on haircut day I wash my hair just before leaving the house and arrive at the shop still dripping. She trims it and can even blow-dry it.

—Elizabeth Case
Belfair, Washington

MARINADE AID

Dear Amy,

For an economical, tasty stew, buy a cheap grade of beef roast, cut it into small pieces, marinate these in pickle juice for three to four days in fridge, then simmer them with veggies until cooked. Very tasty, and a lot cheaper than buying "stew beef."

— Jerry Sass
North Anson, Maine

REVIVE YOUR SPIRITS

Dear Amy,

Turpentine and mineral-spirit thinners/cleaners can be reused if they are kept in a tightly closed jar and the particles are allowed to settle to the bottom. You can then pour off the top of the jar's contents through a cheesecloth into a clean jar to reuse the product.

—Maxel and Stacey Newberry
Ithaca, Michigan

SPRITZ AND SAVE

Dear Amy,

We found a way to make our charcoal last longer. After grilling, we spray the coals with water and leave them in the grill. By the next time of use, they have dried and are ready to use again. (Add more if needed.)

—Patti Layman
Cherry Valley, California

THE YOUNG AND THE DEBTLESS

"I am praying that you get a big response to your 'Generation X Supersaver' inquiry, because if everyone is like the people I am surrounded by, I feel we will be in dire straits in the next century," wrote Nancy Oberdorfer of Brooklyn, New York.

"Thank you for requesting letters from your twentysomething readers. I've often wondered if we are the only ones you have!" contributed Kim Hainsworth of Lomita, California.

I have good news for both of you: We received 103 responses to our newsletter request for letters from tightwads who are in their 20s. It was extremely heartening to read so many upbeat stories of success and hope from young sin-

gles and couples. While rampant consumerism and maxed-out credit cards have hit this generation harder than any other, clearly there are many brave souls who have escaped and are doing well.

It's important to focus on people in this generation because they are the least likely to take frugality seriously, yet, ironically, they receive the greatest benefit if they practice it. Even if you are not of this generation, chances are you know someone who is, and can pass this article along to him.

I know the advantage of early-adulthood frugality from personal experience. The fact that Jim and I saved $49,000 in seven years on our annual income of under $30,000 a year is widely known. But what's not so well known is that we squirreled away $20,000 of that during the first 18 months we were married. This "pre-kid" period in marriage is often squandered, but it's actually a golden opportunity because:

• A couple, or single person, is free to live in a small, cheap, "kid-unfriendly" apartment.

• With no child-care concerns, both husband and wife have maximum freedom to work and earn.

• The earlier that money is saved and invested—whether in a home, a chest freezer, a mutual fund, or any other investment—the greater the return. Once you get ahead, life becomes cheaper, and you tend to continually get even farther ahead. You earn interest instead of paying interest, and the spread between the two increases daily.

Most of the young people who wrote to me had grasped and exploited these concepts, and told of impressive financial accomplishments:

• On an income of $18,000 a year, Shenan Ott of Stafford, Virginia, and her husband saved $5,800 a year, and recently purchased a home.

• Though she has never earned over $15,000 a year, Melissa Hitsman of Orlando, Florida, had saved $32,000 by the time she reached age 30.

• John Wood of Aurora, Illinois, saved $20,000 in three years while working as a teenager at a grocery store.

• At 28 years old, on a $35,000 annual income, a North Carolina couple (who requested anonymity) have paid off their mortgage on an owner-built house appraised at $75,000. They own two cars and have a small amount in savings.

Given these fairly obvious advantages, why is Gen-X frugality uncommon? Our respondents offered their theories:

"We were raised in the first wave of the MTV culture. The pressures of the heavily marketed view of life are manifested everywhere," wrote a newsletter reader from Eugene, Oregon.

"We are a generation that, while young, was blared at, sold to, and assaulted with images of plenty."

"Everyone wants to live as they did before they left their parents' houses: cable TV, fancy foods, new cars, and many fancy electric devices," contributed Jennifer Palmer of St. Paul, Minnesota. "They don't understand/remember how their parents lived when they first began without those niceties."

Aside from these observations, note that in previous generations couples didn't marry until they "could afford to," i.e., until the man earned enough money to support a family on his income alone. With the advent of the woman in the workforce and easy credit, today's dual-income couples can create a false affluence. They live it up for a few years before having children, believing they can easily sustain the debt and workload after they have children. When the children come and a parent wants to stay home with them, they feel "trapped" and "betrayed" by society, though they are actually victims of their own miscalculation.

But now for the good news. Clearly, the virtue of thrift has been successfully communicated to at least a few of these young people. I was interested in their comments about *why* they were different from their peers. Day after day, the most common criticism I get is that "once they get out of the house, your kids will become major spendthrifts to compensate for their frugal childhoods." These respondents prove otherwise. They are frugal, they say, because they were raised that way.

"I was home-schooled from the age of 11 and did not attend junior high or high school, and so missed out on a lot of the 'commercialism imprinting' that I think happens to teenagers in school." (Name withheld by request, Orlando, Florida)

"I was raised by my grandparents and learned many of my thrifty traits from them." (Kim Hainsworth, Rancho Palos Verdes, California)

"Having grown up under the influence of the Masters of Frugality (Depression-era family members), I was eager to practice all I had learned when I married in 1985. The best gift my parents and grandparents ever gave me was advice: 'Waste not, want not'; 'A penny saved is a penny earned'; 'Well, when I was growing up. . . ' " (Melissa Yell, Hesperia, Michigan)

"My parents raised me to be frugal. I never knew any different." (Deborah Burton, Crown City, Ohio)

What specific strategies did the Gen-Xers use to achieve their enviable positions? They sent along hundreds of details about their lifestyles and, actually, there was very little that was unique about the savings strategies they listed. It proved a point I've made all along: There are very few strategies that are unique to seniors, singles, or any other subgroup of society. The basics of frugality—yard-saling, bulk buying, scratch cooking, negotiating, doing it yourself, writing down expenses, and so on—work for any group.

Finally, if you're a Gen-X tight-

wad but your financial accomplishments are less impressive than those I listed earlier in this article, don't despair. Those were some of the most amazing we found in over a hundred letters. As I read most of the letters, it occurred to me that if a reader's accomplishments seemed unremarkable, that's perfectly normal. As people who are just beginning adulthood, the results of frugality are not as evident at this stage as they will be in 10 to 15 years. Rest assured that by the time a Gen-X tightwad hits 40, the net-worth gap separating him or her from other 40-year-olds who have similar incomes will be unmistakable—and gratifying.

LIFESTYLES OF THE FRUGAL AND OBSCURE

During my second book tour I had the good fortune to stay with newsletter readers Marie and Mike Davies of St. Louis, Missouri, who own and operate a bed-and-breakfast called Lehmann House. It proved to be the most pleasant aspect of an otherwise grinding month for me.

The Davieses are thirtysomething parents of four young children. Both chemists, Marie left her job when she realized that after subtracting job-related expenses she netted $500 a month. She then investigated the bed-and-breakfast industry as a home-based business option.

Shortly thereafter, they purchased their 20-room, 7,500-square-foot brick Romanesque Revival fixer-upper/mansion on a historic city square. With their remaining limited funds, they renovated the foyer, library, and dining and living rooms enough to be presentable and completely renovated a few rooms to let out. The revenue from these rooms is being used to renovate more rooms.

As an old-house enthusiast, I was fascinated to stay in this house-in-transition and note how they were solving problems similar to ones I face in my home.

Although I could share many aspects of the Davieses' lives, of particular interest were the strategies they're using to furnish this vast home in the elegant style that is expected of bed-and-breakfasts. They have succeeded by using many strategies I've written about before, and a few that were new to me.

- Estate auctions. They've purchased furniture such as four oak dining room chairs for $100 and a burled-ash chest of drawers for $180. Once, when Mike didn't like the pair of

Eastlake chairs Marie bought for $25 each, they resold them for $100 each.

• Flea markets. Although they find that many items are overpriced, flea markets have been good sources of old photographs and other framable items for $1 each or less. They also buy old frames, and will pay $2 to $5 for framed art. Marie picks up china serving pieces for the dining room for as little as 50¢.

• Yard sales. These are also good sources of pictures, frames, and serving pieces. Marie buys coffee makers, sometimes just for the glass carafes, and juice pitchers for $1 to $3 (juice and coffee are available on small tables outside guest rooms). She buys old books for their library. When selling, Marie likes group yard sales, as she finds other participants will let her keep what they don't sell.

• Dumpster diving. Marie scouts nearby Dumpsters regularly, taking particular note of when people move. She found a mirror, originally attached to a dresser, which fit onto their sideboard. Mike was able to reassemble a maple rocker that he found in a pile of pieces. They've also found an antique steamer trunk, living room side chairs in need of reupholstering, pieces of marble for vanity tops, claw-foot tubs, lumber, and paint.

• Building suppliers. This source has provided useful temporary fixes. During my stay I peeked under a floor-length lacy tablecloth in my room and was amused to find not an elegant table but rather a table made from a fiberboard circle and dowels.

• Bartering. Marie has traded her sewing skills for an iron bed and a ceremonial kimono (which hangs on a guest-room wall). They traded an over-the-mantel mirror they couldn't use for a serpentine-front dresser and a hall runner, and they traded surplus building materials for a marble-topped foyer table.

• Helping people move. Marie has found that when she helps people move, she is conveniently poised to receive unwanted excess, which has included an antique upholstered side chair, a 6-foot pantry shelf, an antique treadle-table sewing machine, and general household items.

• Offering to buy. Marie often tells friends she would be willing to buy an item if the friend should ever think of parting with it. In some cases the owner, months later, has offered to sell the item, and the price was quite cheap. Once, Marie bought a picture for $5 because she liked the frame. Sometime later, a knowledgeable visitor mentioned that this rare, long, narrow picture was worth $150.

• Storing people's stuff. Marie stores large items for people if they let her use the items. Since the storage is free, the owners understand that any minor dings the item might suffer are a fair tradeoff. Marie is storing/using a baby grand piano, a sofa, an oak hall tree worth $1,000, a mahogany chest of drawers, a chandelier, and a refrigerator.

• Work for discounts. Marie works part-time for a renovator supplier. Aside from the wage, she gets an employee discount. This has enabled her to buy reproduction supplies, such as plumbing fixtures, for 10 percent over what her employer pays.

• Negotiate for discounts. Marie

told her paint store's owner that she was renovating a 20-room house and boldly asked for a contractor's discount. He agreed.

• Doing it themselves. Marie loves to sew and has made many accessories, including shower curtains, dust ruffles, Austrian shades, and curtains. People give her material, but she also buys yard-sale sheets and lace and discount fabric. Mike is generally handy and has done some light construction. Marie refinishes both woodwork and furniture. Mike bought a beveled-mat cutter, which enables him to do professional-looking framing when he puts together art and old frames.

As my weekend ended, I concluded that I'd had the rare experience of "meeting my match" in Zen-level, black-belt frugality, and had picked up a trick or two I plan to use in my home.

THE ANSWER FOR A GRIDDLE

When we visited my sister a few summers ago, Laurie made pancakes for breakfast. Upon observing the bottleneck created by making pancakes in a single pan for 13 people, Laurie commented that she did have a huge black-iron griddle, but she gave up on it because food always stuck to its surface. Like many people, she was unaware that her problem could easily be remedied by properly seasoning the pan.

Black-iron cookware (pans, popover pans, Dutch ovens, griddles, and so on) are excellent cooking utensils. If seasoned and well maintained, the cooking surface is almost nonstick, and so requires just a small amount of fat to prevent foods from sticking. But black iron must be treated differently from other types of cookware.

A new iron pan, which is gray, must be seasoned before use and will eventually darken to black. Used iron pans that have been poorly maintained, even rusty ones, can be revived through the same process.

If you're reviving an old pan you may want to remove excess crud and scaliness. It's normal for black iron to eventually develop a bumpy texture or buildup on the outside of the pan. Generally this should be left alone. However, an antique-dealer friend who specializes in black iron removes extreme buildup for aesthetic reasons. She places the pan in her oven at the self-cleaning temperature for two and a half hours. The heat makes the buildup flake off.

If you do the previous step, there will be a fine residue of rust on the pan. Similarly, a neglected pan may have rust. Remove this with fine steel wool and hot water. If you use soap, use mild hand soap, not strong dishwashing detergent. Rinse well.

From this point, new and in-need-of-reviving pans are seasoned in the same way. Coat the inside of the pan with vegetable oil or short-

ening and place in a 250-degree oven for 30 minutes. Remove the pan from the oven, wipe off the excess oil, and return it to the oven for another 30 minutes. Then turn the oven off and leave the pan in the oven overnight. You may need to repeat this step if seasoning a new pan.

This seasoning process draws the oil into the iron. As you cook, the pan will continue to absorb oil from the food, thereby replacing oil lost through use and washing. If the pan does seem to lose its nonstick quality, you can reseason it, but you shouldn't need to do this more than once or twice a year.

Once the pan has been seasoned, it needs to be treated differently from other cookware. Never soak an iron pan in hot, soapy water, as this will soak the oil out of the metal. If you cook a greasy food, such as bacon, you might be able to simply wipe out the pan with a paper towel. The remaining residue is good for the pan. Any food that sticks can be lightly scrubbed out. But avoid heavy scrubbing, which will remove oil from the surface.

If the humidity in your home is high, you may need to take steps to prevent the pan from rusting again. Some people immediately towel-dry their black iron after washing. If your pan is used infrequently, you can coat it lightly with oil before storing it.

When you're scouting black iron through secondhand sources, make it a habit to look for the maker's name. "Griswold" is *the* name in antique black iron. It's highly collectible; a piece of Griswold iron may have resale value beyond its yard-sale price.

SHOULD YOU GIVE IT A DRY?

Tracy Andrews of East Douglas, Massachusetts, wrote that while she enjoys her food dehydrator, she wonders about its economy. Her question: If you factor in the cost of purchasing fruit to dry, and the cost of buying and running the dehydrator, is it a worthwhile product?

I asked four dehydrator owners for their experiences and opinions, did a little reading, and interviewed Scott Reinhard, a spokesman for American Harvest, a leading maker of dehydrators.

Electric food dehydrators dry fruit, vegetables, meats, herbs, and flowers. The versions produced by American Harvest cost from about $29 for the 300-watt Snackmaster to $169 for the 1,000-watt Gardenmaster. They usually come with a couple of trays; additional trays cost extra.

Making "specialty foods" such as dried fruit, fruit leather, and beef jerky are among the most common uses, but these aren't generally money-savers. If you buy fresh bananas to make dried banana chips (to convert a cheap-to-buy food into an expensive-to-buy food) you're simply spending additional money on electricity to get the same food value. Avid backpackers are the only people who might save money doing this, as they have an ongoing need for lightweight fruits. But generally, unless you have a free or cheap fruit source (such as apple-orchard "drops"), this type of drying is purely recreational.

A more interesting question from the tightwad perspective is whether dehydrating homegrown

vegetables is a valid method of food preservation compared to canning or freezing.

Dehydrating does have advantages. Dried food is more compact. Eleven quarts of tomatoes, when dried, fit in the same space as a number 10 can. The storage of dried foods is simple: in paper bags in dry climates, in airtight glass jars in humid climates. Some sources contend that dried foods retain more vitamins than canned or frozen foods.

But disadvantages include:

• Dried vegetables have limited uses. Once reconstituted, they are generally suitable only for soup. To reconstitute some dried vegetables, such as green beans, you must pressure-cook them, or simmer them for up to four hours (thereby offsetting any nutritional gain from drying). Only a few vegetables, such as dried tomatoes, can be used in their dried form. Some people blenderize dried tomatoes into a powder and add this to soups. One how-to-dry book pointed out that some vegetables, such as carrots and onions, are so cheap to buy year-round that drying them may not be economical.

• The capital investment can be high, particularly for large-scale preservation. The Gardenmaster comes with four trays, and additional trays cost $12.50 each or $325.00 for 26 more trays. So this investment can cost up to $494.00. That's about the same as a new chest freezer, but freezers preserve a wider range of vegetables, as well as bulk-purchased meats, bread, and so on. The cost of canning equipment can be quite small. Our two pressure canners and hundreds of jars, all secondhand, cost under $50.00.

• The operating expense can be high. The Gardenmaster dehydrator requires ten hours to dry 30 trays of ⅜-inch-thick tomato slices. So, at 8¢ per kilowatt-hour, the energy would cost 80¢. I sliced up ten varying-sized garden tomatoes and measured their required drying area by laying them on a 1-square-foot area—the same size as a Gardenmaster tray. Then I crushed these and filled up quart canning jars. My ten tomatoes would fill three trays or two quart jars. So, you can can five tomatoes in a quart jar for 10¢ (for the lid and a little electricity). It also costs 10¢ to keep that five-tomato quart frozen. You can dry 100 tomatoes for 80¢ or five tomatoes for about 4¢. On the surface, then, the cost of drying seems lower. But Reinhard says the drying time is the same for 1 or 30 trays. So if you're drying 40 tomatoes (12 trays) or less at a time, it costs more than freezing and canning.

That's important, because few gardeners would have over 40 ripened tomatoes at once. Those who do might choose to use most of them to make ready-to-eat foods like spaghetti sauce, rather than rehydrating tomatoes to make sauce at later times.

A reader from Farmersburg, Indiana, has seen commercials for electric dehydrators and wonders if there are more economical methods. Solar drying is an ancient form of food preservation, predating electrical dehydrators by thousands of years. It was common until the invention of home canning and is still common in many parts of the world.

Herbs can be bundled and hung for air-drying. Some foods can be strung on thread for drying. Otherwise, food needs only to be laid out on a clean, smooth surface such as a cookie sheet or butcher paper. For better air circulation, you can make wood-framed racks of cheesecloth, nylon, or stainless-steel mesh (do not use Fiberglas, copper, galvanized steel, or aluminum). Put cheesecloth over foods that might attract bugs.

Library books and magazines such as *Mother Earth News* and *Organic Gardening* can provide plans for more complex solar-drying structures, such as boxes with many removable racks.

But solar drying has disadvantages. Sunlight destroys some vitamins. It works best in warm, dry climates because the drying might require several hot days.

Laura Vlaming of Gurnee, Illinois, asked for a recipe to make fruit leathers (or roll-ups). My mother makes them from her own blueberries. She simply purees fresh berries, puts the puree on a special fruit-leather tray, and dries it in her electric dehydrator. This makes excellent, hassle-free fruit leather. She stores the leather, rolled up, in plastic wrap.

You can also make fruit leather in the sun or in your oven. Tape plastic wrap onto a cookie sheet and spread the puree on it ⅛ inch thick. To sun dry, two or three hot dry days are required. (Bring the tray in at night.) When the leather is tacky, place it in a 120-degree oven for an hour, then cool and store. You can also dry fruit leather in your oven at 150 degrees for 6 to 12 hours, though a lot of electricity is needed.

In summary, an electrical food dehydrator may be fun to use, but it probably has too few cost-effective applications to justify a large initial investment. Solar drying might be a better option if you want just a few dried foods. If I found a dirt-cheap dehydrator at a yard sale, I might buy it. But even then I would use it only for free or cheap fruits and a few tomatoes.

DON'T MAKE A TRIPLE-PAY

The rent-to-own business has expanded dramatically in the last decade. It's grown from 2,000 to almost 7,000 stores nationwide.

But rent-to-own has another, more dubious distinction. According to a fascinating article in *Business and Society Review,* it's often a huge rip-off.

These stores rent TVs, stereos, furniture, appliances, and other items. If you pay the rent long enough, you get to keep the item. Sounds good. But the article states

that rent-to-own customers routinely pay from two to four times as much as they would if they paid cash outright. As an example, it cites a 20-inch Zenith TV offered at a Roanoke, Virginia, rent-to-own store at $14.99 a week for 74 weeks, or $1,109.26. The same TV sold at Sears in the same city for $329.99, or less than a third of the rent-to-own price. If a customer put aside that same $15.00 a week, he could buy the TV at retail prices in 22 weeks.

COLD REMEDY

Dear Amy,

I get motion sickness when I fly, but I don't like taking medications that are costly and/or can make me sleepy. So I use plastic, refreezable ice cubes. I put them in an insulated lunch bag in my purse, and when it's takeoff or landing time I take a few out and hold them in my hands. It stops my nausea, and there are no side effects. I learned this trick from some flight nurses when I was being flown to a bigger hospital for a premature delivery. It really works. My husband and friends have tried it and it works for them, too. It works with other kinds of nausea as well.

—Cindy Warntjes
Boyden, Iowa

(I prefer to personally test out unusual tips such as this, but I decided to take Cindy's word for it instead of subjecting myself to "Egg Scrambler" amusement park rides. FZ)

À LA CARTON

Dear Amy,

I make egg-carton lunches. I simply fill the 12 spaces with small food items such as raisins, tiny cheese cubes, grapes, animal cookies, small crackers, etc. Each space does *not* need a different item; I double or triple up on favorites. I cover with a napkin and add a rubber band if we're traveling. We take these to the zoo, as car lunches, or just as a fun kid's lunch.

—Carolyn Marck
Seattle, Washington

(Bacteria can't survive on a dry surface, so be sure to use very dry egg cartons. FZ)

EVERLASTING BASKET

Dear Amy,

My husband, a fisheries biologist, came home with a "fish basket." It looks just like a round laundry basket, and that's exactly what I use it for. To give you an idea of its sturdiness, it holds 73 pounds of fish. I can almost guarantee that it will last a lifetime. I've had mine eight years and it

looks new. They do not fall apart like those ordinary, flimsy-plastic laundry baskets. He paid $10.25 for it at a commercial fish house.

—Laura McKenna
Greenville, North Carolina

PART SMART

Dear Amy,

I have a friend who did the most creative, tightwaddy thing that I have heard of in a long time. Her 1982 car was undrivable after an accident. She purchased another 1982 car of the same model. The first car was towed to her house, where she and her father removed and stored all of the usable parts. She now has hundreds of dollars worth of spare parts that fit her car, should she need them.

—Carolyn R. DeBliek
Indianapolis, Indiana

PACKAGE BENEFITS

Dear Amy,

I've found that people will pay double or triple the going garage-sale rate for a toy in its original box. A couple of years ago, I began pitching Christmas and birthday toy boxes into the attic. Toys the kids had outgrown were sold at my last garage sale in their original boxes, and you should have seen everyone snap up those toys! Those not in a box were passed up countless times.

—Marcia Noyes
Kingwood, Texas

AN ARTICLE OF INTEREST

If you're a new convert to frugality, you may be mired in credit card debt. Because credit cards such as Visa and MasterCard typically carry high interest rates, it's crucial to pay off these debts if possible. But if you can't do it immediately, you should at least lower your interest rate; this will allow you to pay it off more quickly.

An innovative way to do this comes from Joyce Bant of Hazelhurst, Wisconsin. She points out that credit-card-issuing companies are in stiff competition now and offer introductory interest rates as low as 5.9 percent if you switch your balance to their card. These rates are offered only for the first six months, but if you can't manage to pay off your balance by then, simply switch to another company that offers a card with a similarly low introductory rate.

How do you find these companies? Check your junk mail. A staffer says he receives at least three credit card solicitations a month. Read through them carefully and save the ones that offer *all* of the following:

- A low introductory interest rate.
- No annual fee, or an annual fee that is low enough that you'll still come out ahead due to the better interest rate.
- No other special restrictions that prevent you from using this plan to your advantage.

A SANER DRAINER

(Read the following with Andy Rooney inflection.) Have you ever noticed that the rubber trays that go under dish drainers are too darn narrow? Wet cups and glasses drip beyond the edge of the tray. Why is that, anyway? For years, we had a folded dish towel permanently positioned alongside the drain tray to catch these drips. And another thing: The drainer feet eventually make indentations in the tray; these indentations fill with water, and within a couple of years the water rots holes in the tray. Don't you hate that? (End of Andy Rooney inflection.)

Vexed by this situation, I told Jim about an expensive solution sent in by a reader, and without telling me, Jim had a sheet-metal shop custom-make a stainless steel drainer tray for (yikes!) $32. But after I got over the shock, I had to admit that I liked this idea.

Although the payback time is quite long (you can sometimes find replacement trays sold separately for $5, although the color might be different), I found I simply liked this drain tray better because it's wide enough to catch drips from cups and deep enough to have additional room to put a row of small cups behind the drainer.

If you like this idea, you'll have to measure your sink area carefully, as yours might be different from mine.

Our custom-made tray is 20 inches wide and 22 inches long. It has two metal pipes welded to the underside, a large one in the back, and a smaller one in the front, to give the tray a slight pitch (our sink unit is slightly higher than the adjoining counter section). Others might need just one small pipe or rod in the back. The tray has a ¼-inch lip that runs around three sides, and it tapers on its "sink side" because our sink isn't as wide as the tray.

Since we've had our tray we've noticed how common trayless drainers are at yard sales. Jim bought one recently. Then it occurred to me that our silverware holder was also too small for our needs. So I took the holder off this yard-sale drainer and now have two on the one in the kitchen.

These two modifications greatly ease our dishwasherless life.

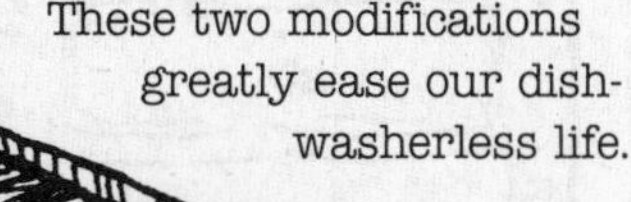

FUNDAMENTALS OF FURNITURE FUSION

Norm Abram, the head carpenter for the *This Old House* series, has his own show: *The New Yankee Workshop.* In each episode he demonstrates how to build a piece of reproduction furniture that he designed based on studying originals. I admire Norm for his skill and sense of design. But I also have to admire his workshop, crammed with every conceivable, expensive woodworking tool.

Although many people own (or can borrow) basic woodworking tools such as a table saw, drills, and clamps, they lack the tools and skills to turn a table leg or make a dovetailed drawer. Further, quality hardwood is so expensive it's usually cheaper to buy used furniture.

But years ago, I spotted an intriguing make-your-own-furniture method that does not require exotic tools. A magazine photo featured a blue-painted garden bench that was made from parts of unrestorable furniture. Since then, I've looked at junk furniture with a different eye.

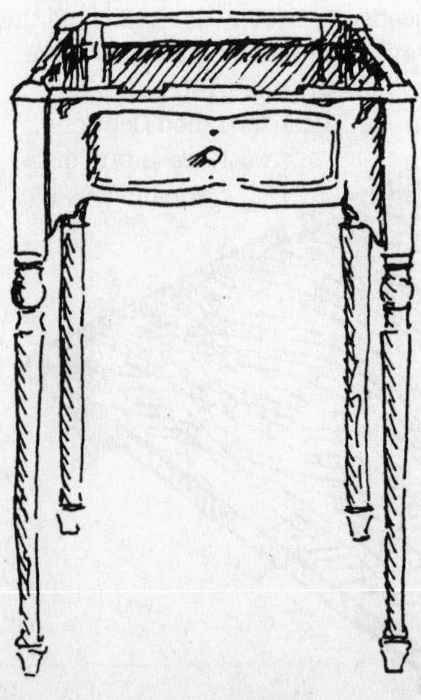

For instance, I spotted a junked sewing table donated to our church's thrift shop. It was missing both the tabletop and the machine. The sides of the table had buckled and broken veneer, and one side had a cutaway place that had accommodated a piece of the sewing machine. I didn't like the scalloped-cut sides or the fake-drawer/flip-out compartment. But the table did have four nicely turned legs and I could envision them as part of a smaller, Sheraton-style bedside table. I knew that the church deacons would simply cart the table to the dump, and so I asked and they let me have it for free.

A few months later I was at a sort-of flea market and found three small dovetailed drawers, complete with wooden knobs and broken veneer, for $3. I picked out the best drawer and offered $1 for it. The seller accepted.

Now, having several of the critical components for my table, I presented the project to Jim and asked if he had enough same-thickness pieces of wood to glue together a tabletop. He returned from our barn loft with a large shelf made from a single, knot-free pine board (he had scavenged the

shelf for the metal folding brackets attached to its underside). He also found a hardwood, dark-stained table leaf that fit none of our tables, to make into new table sides.

Jim began by working on the drawer. He unscrewed the knobs and then used a heat gun to remove the veneer from the drawer's face. Then he sanded the remaining glue off the underlying wood surface.

He disassembled the table, which was primarily held together on the inside with metal brackets. We planned the overall size of the table based on the size of the drawer. It would be just wide enough so that the drawer would clear the inside brackets and just deep enough to accommodate the depth of the drawer.

Jim made new, straight-bottomed sides and a back from the table leaf. Using the old sides as a guide, he used his table saw to duplicate the edge-cut that fit into a groove in the table legs. He made a new face to fit around the

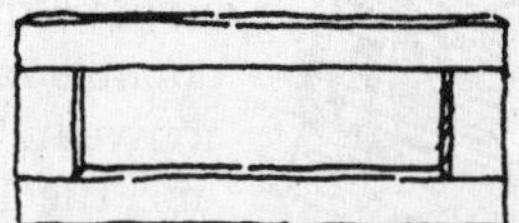

drawer front by gluing together four strips of wood. He made drawer rails and stoppers (so that the drawer didn't slide in too far).

Jim cut a tabletop from the scavenged shelf, making it large enough to overhang by an inch all the way around. Then he used his router to make a gently rounded edge.

Once all the elements were finished, he sanded them. The assembly of the table was simple. The sides and legs screwed together easily. He attached the top to the table using blocks on the inside screwed to the sides and to the top.

As you can imagine, at this point the table looked a bit hodgepodge due to the various types, stains, and finishes of the wood used. We solved this by duplicating a new style I've seen at furniture stores: combining paint with natural-finish woods. I left the knobs and top natural, and painted the remaining parts of my table an indigo blue, the dark-blue shade commonly found in Oriental carpets.

Our new table goes nicely with our country furnishings. The joy in such an effort is not just the finished project, but also in the process of making something attractive from items that would have wound up in the burn pile at the dump.

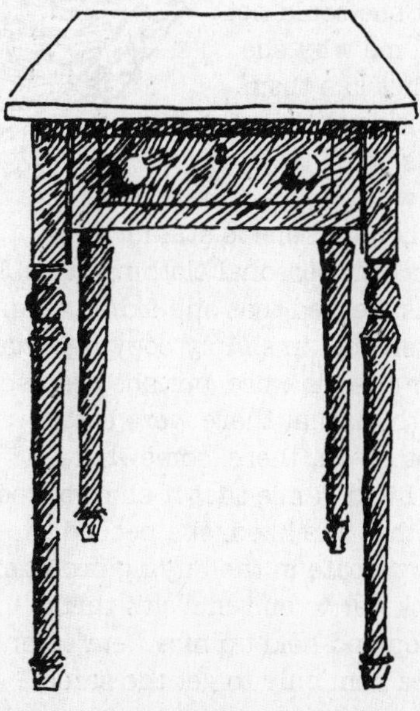

RETAIL REVELATION

For the 13 years during which I've been a frugal parent, I've heard one pessimistic prediction more often than any other: "Once your kids are teenagers, they won't wear secondhand clothes." But after watching the television series *My So-Called Life,* I concluded that, in the 1990s, teenager clothing demands can be met with two flannel shirts and a baggy pair of jeans.

Even so, I feel compelled to report the tiniest wrinkles in my frugal life, so readers will know we're "real." When Jamie was ten, I picked up subtle signals that she was dissatisfied. She would shrug—her polite way of saying No—at about half of the used clothing I brought home for her. The items were good-looking and similar to those worn by her peers, yet she could not tell me why she didn't like them.

It's not that Jamie was being too "picky." How she looks is important to her, and she is still forming her own personal clothing style. I was pleased that she didn't seem interested in simply copying what her friends wore, but she seemed to think that there were better clothes out there, somewhere.

I told Jamie that if she wanted clothes she liked, she needed to participate in the buying process. I took her to our church's thrift shop and held up nice item after nice item only to get the same shrugging response.

I then recalled a letter in my file from Jean McGrew of Coral Gables, Florida, who wrote that she made regular "scouting" trips to the mall with her daughter. Once her daughter showed her the styles she liked, Jean was able to watch for these things at secondhand sources. So I decided to try this with Jamie.

Jamie and I visited the major department stores in our area: Ames, Porteous, Sears, J. C. Penney, and Wal-Mart. We also visited T. J. Maxx, a discount store that carries unsold clothing from trendier stores, in faraway Portland, Maine.

Because neither of us had ever shopped the retail market for kids' clothes, we both were surprised to find the selection of clothes was fairly limited. We even checked with clerks to verify that this, indeed, was it. And, in an odd bit of tightwad serendipity, our maiden scouting trip occurred during a questionable fashion year. To me, the 1995 "fall collection" looked like *The Brady Bunch Goes to Colorado:* an abundance of faded denim combined with "retro" prints and busy stripes that evoked the childhood fashion memories I had tried to suppress.

Carefully guarding my reaction, I held up awful item after awful item and said, with the straightest face I could muster, "How about this, honey?" Jamie not only shrugged, but grimaced as well. And when she peeked at price tags she winced involuntarily.

Jamie didn't even like some of the fashions I felt were passable. She did like the simple jeans, the flared jean skirts, and the dark, solid-colored turtlenecks, but we commonly find these through secondhand sources for 25¢ to a dollar.

Our final stop was the Salvation Army, a store in which we rarely shop because the prices are higher than at other secondhand sources. Jamie picked out a flared stonewashed denim skirt with pastel-blue-and-pink flowered lace on the hem. It had a $2.99 blue price tag on a green-tag 50 percent-discount day. I could have returned and bought it on a blue-tag day, but I felt that buying the skirt on that day was a lesson at a bargain price.

I suspect that Jamie had believed there was a whole world of wonderful new clothes out there that I wasn't letting her see. Our excursion showed us both that although thrift shops have a higher percentage of ragged, weird clothes than department stores do, the percentage of clothing that appealed to Jamie was about the same in each kind of store.

After our trips, Jamie asked to look through the "ten-year-old girl" box of clothes in the attic again. This time she picked out a few items that she had passed over the first time.

I know, I know, this sounds a little too much like a *Leave It to Beaver* conclusion, but that's what actually happened.

REAL TIGHTWADS EAT QUICHE

My staffer Brad and I brainstormed article ideas by comparing the commonly served meals in our homes. The similarity ended when I listed quiche and he said his family never made it because it called for "so many eggs." He thought a quiche used 8 or more eggs and was surprised to learn that a 9-inch quiche is usually made with only three or four eggs, and that a quiche this size will serve at least four hungry adults.

It's true, however, that quiches can be very high in total fat. Aside from eggs, a recipe might also call for heavy cream, fatty cheese, and bacon. And don't forget the crust: A 9-inch pastry crust has 8 tablespoons of shortening, each tablespoon having 12 grams of fat. So one sixth of a quiche might have most of the fat you should eat for a day.

On the plus side, quiches are simple, elegant, and versatile. And because eggs provide a complete protein and contain all of the vitamins except C, quiche served with a high-vitamin-C food makes a very nutritious meal. Finally, depending upon the ingredients you choose, quiche can be reasonably frugal: A 9-inch one costs us an average of $1.25. We eat quiche about once a month, and make it only when our freezer contains a surplus of cooked rice, pastry scraps, or leftover vegetables.

So this article will have two parts: first, a "universal quiche" recipe, and second, how to work quiche into your life if you're trying to eat less saturated fat.

THE UNIVERSAL QUICHE

Crust. Use a standard pastry crust. Some recipes suggest prebaking this before filling to prevent sogginess. I don't. Instead, I prepare the crust, then prepare the various components of quiche, and then assemble the quiche all at once just before putting it on a lower shelf in my preheated oven. You can also make a rice crust using 2 cups of cooked rice, 1½ ounces of grated cheese, and one egg. Combine the ingredients, pat into a Pam-sprayed pie tin, and prebake at 425 for 15 minutes or until just firm.

Eggs. Use 3 or 4.

Cheese. Most recipes call for 1 to 2 cups (4 to 8 ounces) of a grated hard cheese. I use about 1 cup. You can use Swiss, cheddar, feta*, Monterey Jack, or Gruyère*. Or use from 2 tablespoons to ½ cup of Parmesan or Romano. Or use a combination of these. Some softer cheeses, such as mozzarella and American, will not set up well.

*Ha ha. Only if you have a free or cheap source of these items.

Milk or cream. Use 1 to 2 cups of milk, half and half, cream, evaporated milk, or powdered milk made with half the usual water. You may also use part sour cream, cottage cheese, or yogurt.

Filling. Use 1 to 2 cups of a combination of meats and/or vegetables. Meat possibilities include crisply fried and crumbled bacon, or pieces of crab*, lobster*, shrimp*, tuna, chicken, or ham. Use virtually any cooked or steamed vegetables, but squeeze out excess liquid. Don't be afraid to take risks. Once I made a sauerkraut quiche that was very tasty.

Seasoning. For a basic quiche, use up to 1 teaspoon of salt (bearing in mind the saltiness of the other ingredients), ¼ teaspoon pepper, and a dash of nutmeg. If you're a bit more adventurous, experiment with other seasonings such as chives, Tabasco, tarragon, dry mustard, Worcestershire sauce, cayenne pepper, sherry, parsley, paprika, dill, garlic, onion powder, lemon juice, basil, and/or oregano.

To make the quiche: Prepare the crust in a 9-inch pie plate. Grate cheese and prepare the filling ingredients (sauté, cook, chop, crumble, etc.). Beat eggs, milk, and seasonings together until just combined. Spread filling ingredients in crust, top this with grated cheese, and cover with egg/milk mixture. (If you've made too little egg/milk mixture, mix up slightly more. If you've made too much, toss the surplus in tomorrow morning's universal muffin recipe.) Bake for 10 minutes in an oven preheated to 425 degrees. Then turn the oven down to 350 degrees and bake for an additional 45 minutes, or until it's done. The quiche is done when it's golden brown and slightly puffed, and when a knife inserted comes out clean.

FAT REDUCTION STRATEGIES

- For filling, use vegetables and little or no meat.
- Reduce the total amount of eggs and cheese and increase the amount of filling. For instance, one Weight Watchers recipe uses just 2 eggs, 1½ ounces of cheese, 1 cup of cooked spinach, and ¾ cup of onion.
- Choose the nonfat milk options.
- Eat just one-eighth slice of quiche and serve it with low-fat foods such as soup, raw vegetables, and/or unbuttered bread.
- Choose the rice crust. Or use a pastry recipe that uses oil instead of shortening. Use (bulk-purchased) olive oil so that you at least use the right kind of fat.

REAL TIGHTWADS EAT QUICHE UPDATE

The previous article's exploration of the frugal advantages of quiche prompted a number of readers to point out that we neglected to mention "crustless" quiches. These generally have a cup of either flour or Bisquick (or a homemade Bisquick substitute, see page 193) added to the filling to stiffen it. If you are time-pressed or pastryphobic, this is a good alternative. Crustlessness can also help to lower the fat content, as a pastry crust has 96 grams of fat versus no grams for a cup of flour.

Judith Pratt of Hillsboro, New Hampshire, sent us this recipe:

1 cup plain yogurt (milk, cottage cheese, or other substitutions are possible here)
¼ cup water
2–3 eggs, slightly beaten
1 cup flour
½ cup grated cheese
¼ cup chopped, cooked meat
¼ cup chopped, cooked vegetables
Seasoning to taste

Preheat oven to 425 degrees. Mix all ingredients thoroughly. Pour into a greased 9-inch pie plate. Bake for 30 to 35 minutes or until set.

And Brenda Olson of Fremont, Michigan, sent along this recipe for a low-fat potato crust:

In a 9-inch pie pan, stir together 3 tablespoons vegetable oil with 3 cups of coarsely shredded raw potato. Or you can spray Pam in the bottom of a pie pan and omit the additional oil. Press the grated potato into a pie-crust shape. Bake at 425 degrees for 15 minutes or until just beginning to brown.

Remove from oven, add quiche filling, and bake.

Brenda says this is thicker than a pastry crust, so it is best to use just 2 or 3 eggs in the quiche. She adds that she often makes more than one crust at a time and freezes the extras after baking, which allows her to make quick meals in a pinch.

A MYSTERY DISSOLVED

In *The Tightwad Gazette II,* we ran a letter from a reader who had made an amazing discovery: Her dishes got just as clean when she used one tablespoon of detergent in her dishwasher instead of her customary six tablespoons.

That letter prompted Deann Polanco of Austin, Texas, to write to us about information in her new dishwasher's manual. It said: "The amount of detergent to use depends on the water hardness." Hardness is a measure of the concentration of minerals, primarily calcium and magnesium, in water.

Then it listed the following recommended measurements:

- Soft water, 0 to 3.5 grains per gallon, 1 tablespoon of detergent.
- Moderately hard water, 3.6 to 7 grains per gallon, 2 tablespoons of detergent.
- Hard water, 7.1 to 10.5 grains per gallon. fill cup.
- Very hard water, 10.6 grains and over, detergent alone may not be enough, water softener recommended.

Deann then called her water company and asked about hardness. She was told that water in her area ranges from 6 to 8 grains per gallon. "So, although I need more than the person who wrote the original letter, I need a lot less than I had been using, and it was so easy to get the water hardness information from our utility company." If you are on a well, you may be able to get hardness information from your cooperative extension agency.

I was curious about whether this tip also applies to the use of laundry detergent, so I called Jane Meyer, consumer affairs director for the Soap and Detergent Association in New York City. She said that, yes, the amount of laundry detergent needed also varies according to hardness. The recommended amounts listed on the box are for average water conditions. If your water is unusually soft or hard, you can vary the amount you use accordingly.

But she also noted that there are four other variables to consider: size of load, dirtiness of load, duration of agitation, and water temperature.

So when it comes to detergent, don't fall into the habit of simply filling the dishwasher cups or filling up and dumping the plastic scoop that comes with your laun-

dry detergent. Due to water hardness and other variables, each load of dishes or laundry is different. With a little research and experimentation, you should be able to adjust your detergent "dose" so that you always use the minimum amount that gets the job done properly.

ACQUIRE A POSITIVE RENTAL ATTITUDE

Surveys show that rental shops are used by only about 8 percent of the population. Yet a recent trip to a tool-rental shop reminded me of the surprising array of equipment available for rent.

For more information, I interviewed Charlie Marks, manager of Taylor Rental of Brunswick, Maine, one of the larger shops in this area. He said that you should call your local rental shop even if you don't know the name of the tool you need. Just describe the task you want to perform and the rental shop personnel will suggest tools. After a friend, equipped with only hand tools, spent an hour removing just 2 square feet of old vinyl flooring, he called his local rental store and asked, "Do you have a power tool that can handle this?" Sure enough, the store had a gadget called a "stripper." The $33-a-day tool saved about 80 hours of work.

Other items commonly rented by homeowners include stump grinders, pressure washers (to strip paint and remove mildew from siding), small-animal traps, pneumatic nailers, concrete drills and saws, hand trucks, pumps (for flooded cellars), generators (for power outages), and power edgers (to cut a slice in a lawn at the perfect depth for installing now-popular "invisible" dog fences).

If you are adventurous, rental places can lend you some serious equipment. For example, Marks has a $30,000 backhoe that rents for $200 a day. "We give you instruction. Everything we have can be operated by the average person," he says.

Marks says it is perfectly okay for several people to share one rental. "It happens all the time," he says. "One guy rents a chipper and it goes down the whole block."

And full-service rental places rent more than just tools. Taylor Rental, for example, rents beds, cribs, and high chairs, as well as odd items like karaoke machines and a "dunk tank" (which is used when, for example, students pay to throw a ball to dunk the principal).

Some other advantages of renting:

- It can save space. You might not want to have a cement mixer around forever.
- It can allow you to judge if a gadget is worth buying. We've wondered about how well paint sprayers work and have been researching the pros and cons; it might be useful to rent one to try for ourselves.
- It can help you postpone a major purchase while you're shopping for a hard-to-find item in the secondhand market. If you've been unable to locate a used utility trailer but need to move a piano today, try renting.

While renting is terrific for seldom-used items, you should still consider other options that may be even cheaper:

- Borrow whenever possible

(and allow others to borrow from you).

• If you will use a tool several times, it can be cheaper to buy. A Makita drywall screw gun costs $11.55 a day to rent and about $150 to buy, so if you'd use it for more than 13 days, you should buy it.

• You may be able to buy a tool secondhand, use it for the one occasion that you need it, and then resell it for the same price you paid.

DRIVE A BARGAIN

Dear Amy,

Make friends with several area car mechanics and used-parts dealers and let them know you are looking for an older, high-mileage car in good condition. We did this and bought a 90,000-mile 1986 Olds for $2,500. It is loaded and in great shape. As long as it lasts 18 months to 2 years and can be sold for $1,000 or more, we come out ahead. My goal is to pay $60 or less a month to own a car.

—Kenneth T. Podell
Glenside, Pennsylvania

HEAT BY THE SEAT

Dear Amy,

During the winter I like to keep the heat set as low as possible to save utility costs. I find when I work actively around the home I am comfortable with a lower temperature than when I work at my desk or read. Instead of turning the heat up, I place a heating pad turned on low behind my back whenever I sit for a time in a chair. I always wear a top and a sweater, which serves for a time as insulation. (Heating pads should not be used on infants or invalids.) I have saved a lot on heating bills.

— Judy Hedrick
Altadena, California

HECK OF A DECK

Dear Amy,

People have often accused me of not playing with a full deck, and I guess they are right. I cleaned out the drawer with playing cards the other day and found we have a whole lot of cards that don't make up a deck. I used to throw these out, but I had an idea: Why not combine all of them and use the deck for crazy eights only? We've played it a couple of nights in a row, and laughed so hard we almost cried. So what if the deck has only three queens? It has seven threes, which allows player 1 to play a three of spades and player 2 to play a three of spades on top of it, which we find awfully amusing.

—Melissa Hunter-Kilmer
Vienna, Virginia

CUT THE MUSTARD COSTS

Dear Amy,

My husband loves gourmet mustard, a holdover from our spendthrift days. Instead of buying those 3- to 10-ounce jars for $2 to $12, I have learned to make my own. I simply take ground mustard powder, purchased in bulk for $2.39 a pound. One-half pound makes a total of 32 ounces of prepared

mustard. You start by mixing the powder with water, wine, or beer to get the proper consistency; then you can add horseradish, honey, jam, pepper, herbs, spices, and/or coarsely ground mustard seeds to taste.

—Susanna C. Moulton
Chicago, Illinois

FANTASTIC PLASTIC

Dear Amy,

I sew, and have wanted a cutting mat for some time but was unwilling to pay the very high prices at most sewing-supply stores (from around $39 for a small one to $99 and up for larger ones). Then I came across fluorescent light panels at a hardware store. These are the large, translucent plastic rectangles that cover fluorescent tubes in fixtures and dropped ceilings. One side is hard and textured, but the other side is smooth and slightly pliable, like the pricey "self-healing" cutting mats. They are 4 feet by 2 feet, much larger than the sewing cutting mats, making them perfect for laying out most garment patterns. Best of all is the price: $2.97. I found mine at Home Depot, but they can be found at similar prices in any large hardware or home-supply stores.

—Laura C. Hartog
Oakland, California

TO COIN A FACE

Dear Amy,

A birthday gift for children ages five to ten: On colored paper, make a face. Use quarters, dimes, nickels, and pennies Scotch-taped on the paper. Do the outline in pennies, the smile in nickels, the nose with dimes and the eyes with quarters. Total cost is under $2. Wrap flat in a shirt box. This was a winner with our four boys.

—Marian Nordquist
Moscow, Idaho

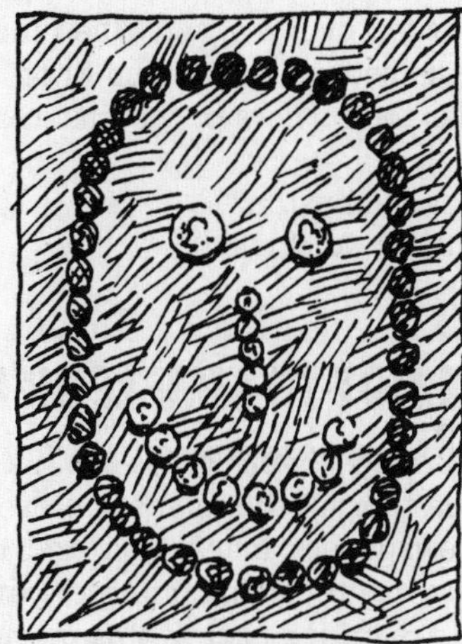

(This strikes me as a great in-a-pinch gift idea for those last-minute party invitations. FZ)

FILL OUT AND FILL UP

Dear Amy,

Send in those evaluation forms at restaurants and stores! I've sent them in critiquing restaurants (both positively and negatively) and received coupons for free meals. After sending in an evalua-

tion to our local juice bar, they asked me to be their mystery shopper. I get two free smoothies a week. I just have to send in quality-control forms every week.

—Susan Reese
Irvine, California

TOP-KNOT TIP

Dear Amy,

I can almost always find good used top sheets at garage sales, but not fitted sheets. I recently found a way to easily convert a top to a fitted sheet. Tie a knot in each corner of the top or flat sheet. When making the bed, just tuck each knot under the corners of the mattress.

— Joan Johnston
Milford, Michigan

THE NOT-SO-SIMPLE LIFE

"Voluntary simplicity" is the hot media topic of the moment. Dozens of newspapers, magazines, and TV shows are reporting on Americans who are taking part in this movement.

Voluntary simplicity is about scaling down—deliberately owning less and working less so that you can focus on what's really important to you, be it your spirituality, your family, or a social cause. And it isn't new. Throughout history, figures such as Christ, St. Francis of Assisi, Gandhi, Thoreau, and 1960s back-to-the-landers have advocated a life of fewer possessions. It was first called "voluntary poverty" but in this century gained its more palatable name.

Is it the same as tightwaddery? Tightwaddery can differ, as people may use it to acquire even more stuff for less money. But, in general, tightwaddery overlaps broadly with voluntary simplicity. Scaling down is a common theme in my newsletter, in my life, and, judging from my mail, in the lives of my readers.

Because of the obvious overlap, I received many calls during one particular media-blitz period. In one case I had a long conversation with a harried talk-show producer who was trying to ascertain if I'd be a good guest to appear with "simplicity authors."

But as the conversation progressed, I felt this possible appearance slipping away. I pointed out that living simply often means working less, and most people cannot do that unless they employ money-saving strategies, and these are not always simple. The producer seemed frustrated as she couldn't see how my not-so-simple strategies would fit into her show on simplicity. In a subsequent conversation with a simplicity author, I learned that she, too, felt people were often frustrated to learn that transitioning to a simple life might require some complex strategies.

Both she and I noticed that people seem to want simple, easy answers to complex problems. We've seen this before. In the 1980s, get-rich-quick gurus proliferated because they suggested wealth could be yours by (simply) adopting a new attitude about success and employing a few (simple) techniques. Similarly, new diet plans sold books as long as they offered new (and simple) strategies, like eating more grapefruit or drinking more water. But their simple solutions rarely worked.

(The sheer numbers of "Gutbuster" exercise gizmos at yard sales prove the point.)

Then *The Tightwad Gazette* came along in 1990. When I stated that, for example, it was possible to eat well for less money, I interested many people looking for simple answers. But some of these people seemed disappointed to learn that achieving a lower food bill requires not-so-simple lifestyle changes and learning new skills.

There are simple strategies out there, but many are so simplistic they're inherently flawed, such as: "Shop only in the perimeter of the store—the expensive foods are in the aisles." Unfortunately, so are the items needed to cook from scratch.

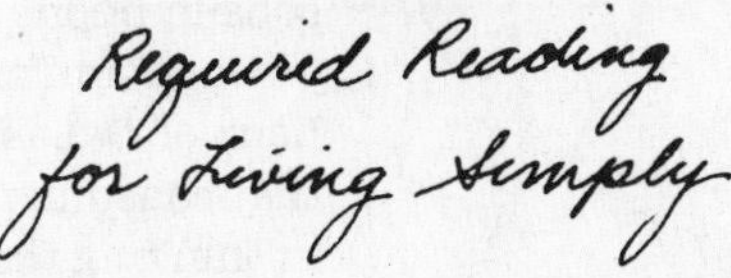

Even basically good strategies, when offered too simplistically, can be flawed, such as: "Buy in bulk." Unfortunately, the big sizes aren't always the cheapest.

Some simple strategies really do work, such as: "Buy cheaper cuts of meat." Unfortunately, even this may have a not-so-simple aspect of getting your family to agree to it.

Simple answers may help you save a little on your grocery bill but will not achieve the 50-percent savings that is common among my readership.

People are attracted to simple answers because they want to skip crucial steps that require brainwork. But real brainwork is required to become an excellent shopper and do-it-yourselfer.

Upon learning that frugality/voluntary simplicity often means learning new skills and working harder at certain tasks, people question, "Then what's so simple about 'voluntary simplicity'?"

The answer: People forget that working at a job isn't simple either. Particularly for parents, jobs create stress as employees try to meet the demands of a client or boss; these demands often compete with the immediate needs of the family. It's this competition that is complicated.

Frugality may not always be simple, but it's definitely more "family friendly." It might seem simpler to buy vegetables than to grow your own. But it isn't simple if you have to press a suit, put on makeup, drop the kids at a sitter, and commute 45 minutes to a job you dislike to earn money to buy vegetables. In contrast, an at-home parent who gardens may not be tending to his child continually, but if the child skins a knee, the weeding can wait. The frugal parent may not be working less, but he or she probably enjoys the work

more and isn't bound by a corporate schedule.

Learning to manage your money well may be the most important step on the path to a simpler life. Using simplistic strategies, even the good ones, won't provide enough financial leverage to allow you to give up a job. To gain an overall simpler life probably means doing some not-so-simple things.

I summed up my explanation to the TV producer this way: Remember when you learned to ride a bike? That wasn't so simple. In fact, if I had to explain in an interview how to ride, it would sound even more complicated. It would be easy to conclude that walking is simpler than biking. But walking is a much slower method of transportation than biking, so if you walk, everything else in your life must be compressed to compensate for the extra transportation time. So, if you put in the necessary time and effort to learn to ride, it will ultimately seem simple and simplify your life.

WHEN BIGGER ISN'T BETTER

A recent study by the Marketing Science Institute in Cambridge, Massachusetts, yielded information that tightwads should note: Large packages encourage consumers to increase the amount of a product they use.

A Harvard Business Review article sent to me by Ann Gilson of Port Angeles, Washington, reports that consumers who purchased large containers of Creamette spaghetti, M&M's, Diet Pepsi, Crisco Oil, or Mr. Clean ate more, drank more, and poured more than people who bought smaller containers of the same products. Wharton School marketing professor Brian Wansink said that's because consumers know they got the product for a lower unit cost and thus feel justified in using more.

His study also revealed that people use more of a product from a full container than from a half-empty one. As for products that recommend an amount to use, such as household cleaners, instructions are ignored 70 percent of the time.

Some people, understanding they use more if a product comes in a large package, avoid bulk packaging altogether. Others might "trick" themselves, by putting bulk-purchased items into smaller containers. But my advice is simply to be aware of the human tendency to overuse bulk-purchased items and modify your behavior accordingly. Understand that unit savings that come from bulk buying can easily be canceled by overconsumption.

On a similar note, John Kleinhenz of Dallas, Oregon, pointed out that consumers are often mistaken in thinking that the big sizes are always the cheapest. For example, he observed that a 4-pack of toilet paper cost 68¢. In the very next display, the exact same toilet paper, packaged in 12-packs cost $2.28. Three 4-packs would cost $2.04. He's found this with milk, toothpaste, and other items. Jim and I have noticed that five 5-pound bags of flour can cost less than one 25-pound bag of flour. These scenarios occur for both on-sale and regularly priced products.

MYSTIFIED BY HOMEMADE MIXES?

A newsletter reader from Cambridge, Massachusetts, has a few recipes that call for Bisquick and asked for a homemade version. Her request leads to the larger topic of the usefulness of homemade mixes. Recipes for these are commonly published in thrift books, women's magazines, and extension-service bulletins. So this article offers a "biscuit-baking mix," and some recipes for using it, but will also explain why I don't use homemade baking mixes.

To make homemade biscuit-baking mix: Combine 10 cups of flour, ⅓ cup of baking powder, and 1 tablespoon of salt. Mix this with 2 cups of shortening using a pastry blender, food processor, or two knives. Place in a sealed container. It will keep for one to six months at room temperature during cool, dry weather. Otherwise, refrigerate. Use as you would Bisquick. Some of the simpler examples:

Pancakes: Combine 2 cups of mix, 1 cup of milk, and 2 eggs.

Dumplings: Combine 2 cups of mix with ⅔ cup of milk.

Waffles: Combine 2 cups of mix, 2 tablespoons of vegetable oil, 1 egg, and 1⅓ cups of milk.

There are many varieties of homemade biscuit-baking mixes. A few call for oil instead of shortening. Some suggest the addition of 1⅓ cups of powdered milk. When using the mix, you add water instead of milk.

This homemade mix could be handy because some recipes do call for Bisquick, and because it would be convenient for camping.

But there are reasons why I don't use this or other homemade baking mixes. There are two basic types: universal mixes, such as the above biscuit-baking mix, and master mixes, which when combined with other ingredients make a variety of baked goods. Makes-one-thing mixes—and there are dozens of them—make just one thing or offer minor variations (such as a brownie mix that also makes peanut butter brownies). Each type has its disadvantages:

- The universal mixes don't save much time compared to using regular scratch recipes. For example, one master mix is a combination of seven ingredients. To use it to make yellow cake, you must combine five ingredients: the mix with four other ingredients (including sugar, an ingredient that is also in the original mix). But a scratch yellow cake recipe uses just eight ingredients. When making waffles with the biscuit-baking mix, you must add oil, thereby negating the time savings of adding shortening to the baking mix and saving you only the "work" of measuring salt and baking powder. Baking requires many steps, from recipe-reading to cleanup. These mixes may save you only a 30-second step in the process, but the rest of the steps are the same.

• Most universal mixes use shortening. But when I bake I prefer to use oil because it's healthier as well as easier to measure and combine.

• Like convenience foods, homemade mixes take up more space than staples alone. Your kitchen probably has several permanent containers of staples. If you use the ingredients in these containers to make several large containers of mixes, you could easily end up doubling the total amount of space required for baking supplies.

• The shelf life of the universal mixes and some makes-one-thing mixes is shorter than that of the uncombined ingredients. The baking powder, for example, loses some of its effectiveness over time when combined with other ingredients. Most of the makes-one-thing mixes are for desserts, which I usually prepare less than once a month, even with six kids. So some of these mixes might go bad before I would use them.

• Baking from scratch each time allows me to add varying types of whole grains, reduce fat, use up leftovers, and otherwise alter recipes. I never make plain white-flour-only pancakes, for instance. Although I could make up mixes using part whole grains, I would need a mix container for each type of whole grain that I commonly use.

• You may save more time, space, and/or electricity simply by preparing standard recipes in large batches and freezing the surplus. For example, rather than using a pastry mix each time I make a pie or quiche, it's quicker to make a triple batch of pastry and freeze the surplus.

If you disagree with me (it's allowed, really) and you like these mixes, look for Nancy Birnes's book *Cheaper and Better: Homemade Alternatives to Store-Bought Goods* at your library. She offers a "Biscuit Baking Mix" with 15 recipes, along with many makes-one-thing mixes.

Finally, you might want to add another recipe that calls for Bisquick to your repertoire. Kelley Reep of Gardener, North Carolina, sent this recipe for a delicious, easy dish.

PIZZA CASSEROLE

1 pound ground beef
2 14-ounce jars pizza sauce
3 cups mozzarella cheese, shredded
1½ cups Bisquick-type mix*
2½ cups milk
3 eggs

Cook and drain beef. Spoon beef into a 9-inch-by-13-inch baking dish. Top with pizza sauce and cheese. Combine Bisquick, milk, and eggs. Beat until smooth. Pour batter over casserole, covering evenly. Bake at 400 degrees for 30 to 35 minutes. Serves 8.

Kelley often stretches this by adding 1 cup of presoaked TVP (texturized vegetable protein; see *The Tightwad Gazette II*) along with the ground beef.

*If you don't want to mix up a big batch of biscuit-baking mix, you can make the required amount by combining 1¼ cups flour, 2 teaspoons baking powder, ½ teaspoon salt, and ¼ cup shortening or oil.

MAIL TO THE CHEAP

It's time once again to peruse some of the mail-order sources sent to us by readers.

Our research shows that these companies have at least the *potential* to save over local sources. Be sure to compare carefully, and take shipping and handling charges into account.

An asterisk (*) indicates that a company offers lower prices than a company I listed in my previous books.

APPLIANCE PARTS

Culinary Parts Unlimited
80 Berry Drive
Pacheco, CA 94553
(800) 543-7549

Parts for 35 brands of small appliances, including discontinued models up to 25 years old.

AUTOMOBILE/TRUCK PARTS AND ACCESSORIES

J. C. Whitney & Co.
P.O. Box 8410
Chicago, IL 60680
(312) 431-6102

Over 55,000 parts and accessories at low prices.

BIBLES

American Bible Society
P.O. Box 5656
Grand Central Station
New York, NY 10164
(800) 322-4253

Bibles available in hardcover for $7.00, paperback for $2.50.

BOOKS

New World Books
2 Cains Road
Suffern, NY 10901
(914) 354-2600

Up to 30 percent less than publisher's price on new books.

BULK FOODS, HERBS, AND SPICES

Glenn's Bulk Food Shoppe*
6411 West Morgan Avenue
Hutchinson, KS 67505
(316) 662-2875

Natural foods, including bulk pectin.

San Francisco Herb Co.*
250 14th Street
San Francisco, CA 94103
(800) 227-4530

Atlantic Spice Co.*
P.O. Box 205
North Truro, MA 02652
(800) 316-7965

A sister company to the San Francisco Herb Company, it offers the same prices and cheaper shipping to those east of the Mississippi.

CASSETTE TAPES

Roxan, Inc.
5425 Lockhurst Drive
Woodland Hills, CA 91367
(800) 228-5775

Blank video and audio cassettes.

CHECKS

Artistic Checks*
P.O. Box 1501
Elmira, NY 14902
(800) 224-7621

Discount mail-order checks.

CLOTHES

The Working Man
Antioch Wholesale
P.O. Box 140204
Nashville, TN 37214
(615) 883-1530
Used, reconditioned uniforms from rental companies.

Just My Size
P.O. Box 748
Rural Hall, NC 27098
(800) 522-9567
Large-sized women's clothes and lingerie.

DIAPERS

Dundee Direct
1440 North Expressway
Griffin, GA 30223
(800) 522-3388
Cloth diaper "seconds."

GREETING CARDS

The Current
The Current Building
Colorado Springs, CO 80941
(800) 525-7170
Half-priced greeting cards.

MUSICAL INSTRUMENTS

Elderly Instruments
1100 North Washington
P.O. Box 14249
Lansing, MI 48901
(517) 372-7890
New and used acoustic and electric instruments and supplies.

Musician's Friend
P.O.Box 4520
Medford, OR 97501
(800) 776-5173
New and used instruments and accessories.

SOFTWARE

HG Shareware
P.O. Box 515
Eagle Creek, OR 97022
(503) 637-3334
2,300 programs at 99¢ per disk.
"Shareware" often involves additional payments to the program's author.

Surplus Direct, Inc.
P.O. Box 2000
Hood River, OR 97031
(800) 753-7877
Sells older versions of commercial software at a discount.

Public Software Library
P.O. Box 35705
Houston, TX 77235
(713) 524-6394

VETERINARY SUPPLIES

Jeffers
P.O. Box 100
(353 West Inez Road)
Dothan, AL 36302
(800) 533-3377
Offers a complete line of pet, horse, and livestock supplies.

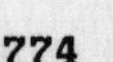

TAKER'S DOZEN

Dear Amy,

I am a commercial real estate photographer and I prefer to use 35mm film in 12-exposure rolls. I have discovered that when I load the film, I must make sure that the film is in the roller "teeth" or guide rail. When it is secure in both the top and bottom and it has one turn on the take-up roller, I close the back of the camera, advance the film one frame only, and click the shutter. Now I am ready to begin taking pictures, even though the film counter shows the dot *before* frame one! I always get one or two extra pictures per roll, but am charged for only 12 or 24, depending on the roll that I used.

—Jackie Steinberg
Saint Peters, Missouri

HEATER BEATER

Dear Amy,

Our electric company mailed us a chart showing the average cost of operating appliances. I noticed that a king-sized waterbed heater costs an average of $8.65 a month to operate. Three years ago, we put egg-crate foam on the waterbed, at a cost of $15. This allowed us to turn off the waterbed heater. Based on electric-company estimates, I am saving over $100 a year, and I recovered my investment in the first two months.

—Dabney Nunley
Phoenix, Arizona

SACK TACTIC

Dear Amy,

Lately I have seen paper lunch bags in pastel colors at K mart, 50 for under $1. I have used these as gift bags for smaller gifts in place of "real" same-sized gift bags that sell for $1 to $2. I wrap the gift in a piece of tissue paper, put it in the bag, fold down the top edges, punch two holes in the folded part, and tie a ribbon. The ribbon can be recycled or made from a spool of nicer ribbon bought at a fabric store on sale.

—Carol Harrison
Asheville, North Carolina

A COLOR-FOIL IDEA

Dear Amy,

Make foil-covered candy do triple duty. After Christmas, when the red, green, gold, and silver candy is heavily discounted, purchase what you need for New Year's Day (gold and/or silver), Valentine's Day (red), and St. Patrick's Day (green).

—Karen Jones
Lexington, Virginia

PAY NOW, SAVE LATER

Dear Amy,

Don't wait for self-employed persons to send a bill. I've found that most of them will charge less if offered payment at the time of job completion; or ahead of time, for that matter, if they can be trusted. I've talked to a plumber, a carpenter, and a construction worker, and all agreed this is true. I am self-employed as a tax preparer and have found this to be true in my business as well. If I have time to think about a bill, invariably it will be for more money. This is hard to prove, but I believe a considerable amount of money could be saved over a year using this strategy.

—Jean Doeden
Worthington, Minnesota

SAVE SOME BREAD

Dear Amy,

A money-saving technique I use because our household is only my husband and myself: When I buy bread, I put two slices at a time into fold-lock-type sandwich bags, put all the bags back into the wrapper, and freeze it. For toast or a sandwich I just remove what is needed at one time. It thaws in no time, and the remainder stays frozen without freezer burn. I found a store-brand box of 500 sandwich bags for 99¢ and have been reusing the bags for three years. I do bagels, muffins, and cake the same way.

—Frances Hohl
Pearl, Mississippi

SHOP AND SHAVE

Dear Amy,

When my husband expressed interest in a "foil" razor, I looked into it as a possible gift. My first stop was the mall razor store. The salesman helped me sort through the necessary features (cordless) and the unnecessary ones (bells and whistles) until I found a model that was suitable. The salesman sensed I was looking for a bargain and pointed out a rack in the back of the store that had the model I wanted for less than 50 percent of the retail price. He explained that the only difference was that it came in a blister pack instead of a gift box. Further, all their razors were 20 percent off. I did compare to discount stores, but no one came close to that price.

—Amy Butler
Alpharetta, Georgia

FOUR-WATTS FOR WHAT?

Dear Amy,

Four-watt bulbs, which can be used in night lights, are sold at Christmas time in big bins at 10¢ each without the packaging. Stock up then for the whole year. Even better, wait for the half-off after-Christmas sale. The normal sale price is two for 99¢.

—Wendy Howell
Camano Island, Washington

CHEAP SUITS

Dear Amy,

Casinos in Las Vegas, Atlantic City, and other places give away free used decks of cards. They are great gifts.

—Edgar Wunsch
Woodmere, New York

DEAR DESPERATE . . .

I have gotten several letters that start like this:

Dear Amy, *help!* I'm desperate!

The letters go on for several pages describing the writer's deep financial hole. Often, bankruptcy is looming.

These letters are hard to read. They are filled with genuine pain. They usually sum up with: "I know you're busy, but please write and tell me what to do."

With about one million Americans filing for bankruptcy annually, desperate financial circumstances are, sadly, becoming common. So I thought I would address the special concerns of those who are deep in debt. But often their past mistakes aren't easily fixable, so I also hope I can keep some people from winding up in similar straits. Here are the mistakes/factors that commonly create serious debt—and some ideas on how to get out:

• Obviously, some people just don't earn enough money. It's possible to support a family on under $20,000 a year, but only if you've made all the right choices during the previous years. Frugality is a powerful tool, but it has limits; you can chop your food bill by 50 percent but not by 99 percent. If your income is very low and/or your debts are high, it may make more sense to pour your energy into making more money than into hanging laundry.

• Some people deceive themselves about their overall spending habits. Their letters to me highlight some of their frugal activities (such as baking bread) but omit others (such as their long-distance-calling habits). It's like pointing out the places on a sinking ship that are not leaking. If these people kept a daily log that included all expenditures, no matter how small, they would soon discover where the leaks are and how to patch them.

• Some people abuse credit cards. Sue McCann of Arnold, Maryland, sent me an article about the sharply rising bankruptcy rate in her region. It quotes a bankruptcy attorney who has handled 800 cases and says that improper use of credit cards is the primary reason for his clients' plight.

Obviously, credit cards themselves aren't the problem, it's people's attitudes toward them. Studies have shown that people spend 23 percent more, on average, when they pay with a card rather than with cash. For too many people, paying with a credit card just does not feel like really paying.

If you have problems controlling your use of these cards, visualize pulling the equivalent amount of cash out of your pocket and counting it out, dollar by dollar, before you actually charge a purchase. Those in truly desperate circumstances should stop using their cards altogether.

• Some people don't plan for

their lives to change. Couples may base their debt load on two incomes, but when they have children their expenses increase and their ability to work profitably decreases. Others plan their finances on their current income (which often represents their highest earning potential) and presume they'll always earn the same amount. But history shows us that the economy keeps changing; whole industries vanish while others are created. Everyone should assume their lives can change and spend accordingly.

• Some people marry spendthrifts. Money is the most divisive issue in marriage, so it's not "unromantic" to carefully note his or her spending habits and discuss financial goals *before* marriage. If you're already married, spouse conversion is difficult but possible. An article on this subject appeared in my book *The Tightwad Gazette.*

• Some couples divorce, failing to consider the huge financial impact, particularly when child support is involved. The couple ceases pulling together toward a common financial goal. It's costly to maintain two households, and two frugal parents can raise their kids for much less than the amounts listed in court-mandated support payments. One reader who endured a particularly messy divorce reported that her lawyer fees alone exceeded $12,000. While divorce is sometimes the best alternative, it's often worth the effort to make it work. Only 5 percent of divorced couples get counseling before they split. Counseling fees could easily yield more than the hottest mutual fund.

• Some people have enormous medical bills. According to Gail Merrill, director of education for the Consumer Credit Counseling Service of Maine, this is often a major factor driving families into bankruptcy. While there's no way a family of modest means can easily pay a $150,000 medical bill, Merrill said that in many cases, a more frugal lifestyle could have yielded enough money to buy health insurance and avert disaster. A cheap, high-deductible insurance policy is *much* better than no insurance at all. Further, live right; a high percentage of accidents and illness are completely avoidable.

• Some people have killer debts from buying new cars. In his book *How to Live on Nothing,* Edward Romney puts it in perspective: "New-car prices are now so high that having two new cars is only for the very wealthy." If you're an affluent tightwad and can pay

cash, some new cars may be as cheap as used in the long run. But if you're broke, carefully selected used cars are best. They're cheaper to buy and have lower tax and insurance costs.

• Some people won't abandon cable TV. This may seem like a small point, but to me, cable TV is a sort of barometer. Anyone who is deep in debt and spends $25 a month for cable clearly hasn't "gotten it." A frequent excuse is that "we can't afford any other entertainment, so we feel this one expense is justified." Deeply indebted families should not only cancel cable, but might also sell their TV and use the time they free up for frugal activities or a money-making hobby. They must maximize their use of time to get ahead.

• Some people are unwilling to resort to extreme measures. Once you've covered all of the normal frugal bases, start thinking radical: one or no cars, sell your too-expensive house, ban long-distance calls, limit showers to two minutes, eat less (a good idea for many adults), work opposite shifts from your spouse to avoid child-care costs, and/or move to a cheaper part of the country.

• Some people don't take responsibility for their situation. They blame it all on a spouse, the recession, unexpected bills, and so on. But most financial problems are due to poor decisions and a failure to plan ahead. If they won't own up to past mistakes, it's unlikely they'll change their behavior in the future. It's crucial to honestly confront past mistakes. Then sit down with your family and develop specific plans for doing better.

• Some people have a negative attitude. They view frugal behaviors as restrictions forced on them rather than choices that improve their situation. Eating beans and rice should give you a warm, victorious glow rather than a feeling of deprivation. When money is extremely tight, this can be difficult, but it's crucial.

• Some people see no value in frugality, as it is "too little, too late" to help them. It's true that many tightwad strategies won't get you out of debt overnight, but they *can* help you feel less deprived as you marshal resources to pay down your debt. Rather than suffering because you "can't afford to go out for pizza anymore, don't have new furniture, and can't afford new kids' clothes," you can learn equally good alternatives: homemade pizza, scrounged-and-spruced-up furniture, and yard-sale clothes.

Finally, if you're in a desperate financial situation, contact your local Consumer Credit Counseling Service. The CCCS is a nonprofit group that helps people avoid bankruptcy. As Beckie J. Rogers of Redkey, Indiana, puts it, "They deal with bill collectors for you, and you don't have to worry about nasty calls, getting sued, etc. You make a weekly payment to them instead of sending money to your creditors. CCCS is paid for by creditors; you are charged only for stamps and envelopes. They are a respected organization and can usually get a creditor to lower or even drop the interest rate. It was our first step out of debt and got us started using a budget." To find the CCCS office nearest you, call (800) 388-2227.

GET A WHEEL JOB

Frugality can take time, and a way to gain time is to get your kids to help with chores efficiently. An ongoing hassle in our home has been the equitable distribution of kids' chores. For example, when the four oldest kids put their laundry away, they must also either put away upstairs linen or downstairs linen, or help one of the five-year-old twins put away their clothes. They would complain, "I helped Brad last time!"

I resolved this by making a "job wheel." Using cereal-box cardboard, I cut out 3-inch and 4-inch circles. I marked these into fourths. I wrote a child's name in each section of the larger wheel and a chore in each section of the smaller wheel. I drew arrows to indicate the turning direction. My junk drawer failed to yield a brass fastener, so I attached the wheels with two buttons and string. Now, every time I finish folding laundry, I turn the wheel.

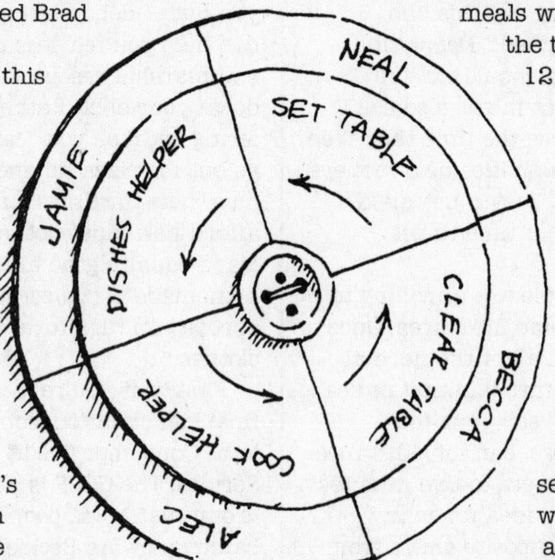

It worked so well that I also made a dinner wheel. In the past, the four oldest kids had rotated setting and clearing the table. However, we hadn't eased them into dish washing or dinner preparation yet. So this wheel's jobs are setting the table, clearing the table, helping a parent with the dishes, and helping a parent prepare dinner. The dinner-helper job follows the dishwasher-helper job because the next night's meal is planned while the dishes are washed and the child can help choose the meal he'll help prepare the next day. Although few parents require children to help prepare meals, I feel this is important so that they learn to cook and may eventually relieve the parents of this job altogether.

Jim was able to prepare meals without help by the time he was 12.

As the kids get older, the twins will be added to the wheel. If you already have older children, the parents and children could be given sections on the wheel and alternate doing adult-type tasks.

Even though these wheels required them to take on additional chores, the kids were quite agreeable, because at last they felt chores were fairly assigned. I also find that when assigning overwhelming tasks to children (such as washing dishes for a family of eight), it's best for the parents to work alongside them. This way the children have a more pleasant experience, and by observing our efficiency they learn how to accomplish tasks quickly.

THE GOLDEN AGE . . . IT'S YOUNGER THAN YOU THINK

Many people are aware of "senior citizen discounts" but think you have to be 65 to get them. "Not true," says Harriett Harrow of Austin, Texas.

"As my husband's 55th birthday approached," she writes, "I researched 'senior' discounts that kick in that early, wrote off for brochures and discount cards, and presented him with all of this information (in rhyming scrapbook form!) as a novel birthday present any tightwad would love. The discounts are offered by banks (no-fee accounts, cheaper safety deposit boxes), grocery stores (10 percent off purchases every Wednesday), bus trips (15 percent off Greyhound regular-price fares), rail travel (in Scandinavia), hotels (some offer twice the standard AARP or AAA discounts), retailers (10 percent off all purchases every Tuesday), haircuts ($2 off at Supercuts), and more. Most discounts are unadvertised—you have to ask! I now always ask every establishment I frequent if they offer special discounts or services to those 55 and up, and I'm often pleasantly surprised!

"P.S. All these discounts made my husband feel a lot better about growing a little older!"

A COOKBOOK QUERY

A newsletter reader from Atlanta, Georgia, writes, "I'm adding my voice to the chorus that I am sure implores: 'Can you please give us a tightwad cookbook?' "

This reader is correct in that we do often get requests from readers for a cookbook. We have discussed writing one, but we realize that doing it really well would be an enormous undertaking. Even if I were to start today, the publication date might be years away.

In the theoretical meantime, how should you fill this gap in your life? In various places in my books I've offered different strategies. The following pulls those strategies together, and offers some new ones:

• You should have a collection of various types of cookbooks. My shelf of cookbooks is over 3 feet long. I don't think I paid retail for any of them. Some were gifts, some were free "review" copies, and some came from used-book stores and yard sales. Most cookbooks have some useful recipes. Your collection should include a few basic books, such as *The Betty Crocker Cookbook.*

When considering books, flip through them and reject ones that lean heavily on convenience foods or exotic ingredients. Specifically look for older cookbooks. These tend to have simpler recipes, such as a chocolate cake recipe that calls for cocoa rather than chocolate squares.

• Select recipes that call for ingredients that are inexpensive to you. Refer back to page 66, "Pantry Principle Update," in which I listed the staples I buy. These are likely to be cheap in your area, too. But because there are regional cost differences, there's a limited number of recipes that are universally cheap to everyone.

• Rather than choosing a recipe and buying the ingredients required, decide what you need to

use up and work from there. On one occasion when I worked at a church supper, I was the only helper who wanted to take home the huge container of leftover cooked carrots. This led me to look for recipes for carrot bisque—a recipe that would use up and disguise a lot of mushy carrots.

• Compare recipes for similar dishes from several cookbooks to get some sense of how much recipes can be successfully varied.

• When you're trying a recipe for the first time and you have all of the ingredients, follow the directions exactly. If you don't like the result, you'll know the recipe is at fault and not your variation. For instance, after I made stuffed tomatoes I found that the recipe called for too much thyme. So I noted in my book to use less next time. When I've tried similar recipes in the same book I've also given them a star rating, so that years later I'll recall which I liked best.

• If you lack a few ingredients for any one recipe, try combining elements of different recipes, such as when I created corn-broccoli casserole (see page 136) from recipes in two books.

• Substitute for ingredients you don't have, as I detailed in "Have-It-Your-Way Seafood Casserole" in the first *Tightwad Gazette* book. If a recipe calls for cream of celery soup, make a white sauce with sautéed celery.

• Make your own cookbook from a loose-leaf binder. Use it to record your experiments, and to copy in recipes from the *Tightwad Gazette* books and other sources. This allows everyone in a multiple-cook household to make the same "family favorite" recipes, and it's handier to have all your favorite recipes in one place.

• Experiment. Food is central to your life, and you will cook nearly every day. Learning to cook is a lifelong process. You should try new recipes regularly; at least once a month. Many of our experiments have become my family's regular favorites.

A final point is that most of the recipes our family uses are for basic dishes that can be found in any number of cookbooks.

DIET, YOU'LL LIKE IT

The weight-loss industry has grown to $32 billion annually. Clearly, many dieters believe they need the aid of clinics, health club memberships, appetite suppressants, expensive healthy foods (fish and fresh salad), and/or expensive "crutch" diet foods (diet sodas, diet shakes, NutraSweet, Weight Watchers frozen dinners, and so on).

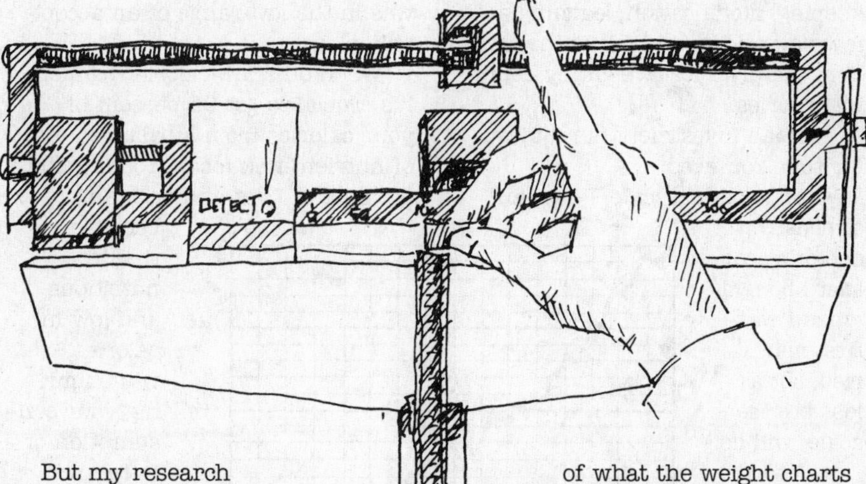

But my research has convinced me that those who want to lose weight can almost certainly do so without spending extra money. Further, if you've mastered frugality, you already possess the parallel skills required.

We interviewed several experts, including John Foreyt, an obesity specialist and director of the Nutrition Research Clinic at Baylor College of Medicine. Foreyt said that despite all the theories, weight loss boils down to one principle: You must use up more energy than you take in. While it's true that genetic factors can make weight loss tougher for some people, if losing weight is important enough to you, you can overcome your genes.

Weight loss is a fairly precise science. To lose a pound you must eat 3,500 fewer calories than you burn. Most adults use about 1,500 to 2,000 calories daily. If you create a daily deficit of 500 calories through eating less and/or exercising more, you should lose a pound a week.

Which brings me to *my* story.

In my early 20s I hit 163 pounds. This was at the upper end of what the weight charts said was acceptable for my height (5 feet, 8½ inches), but I was definitely "chunky." By jogging three to five miles daily my weight dropped to 148, where it stalled. For me, exercise alone wasn't enough. I switched to more moderate exercise and joined Weight Watchers. In four months I lost another 15 pounds. Over the next ten years, despite four pregnancies, my weight stayed between 133 and 138.

But after the birth of the twins five and a half years ago, I'd never dropped below 140 and had averaged about 145. At various times I'd casually tried eating less and exercising more, but I never lost

more than a pound or two. Then, in the spring of 1995, my weight edged up and I was startled one morning when it was over 150. I determined to get serious. I was pushing 40 and wanted to conquer this last unresolved area of my life.

So I decided to use the same skills I had learned from tightwaddery. Like saving money, losing weight can be achieved through unremarkable means. It's about self-honesty, precision, record-keeping, modification, learning a few new tricks, and follow-through. Very simply, I lost weight by counting calories.

A small investment is required for this. You need:

- An accurate scale. I own an expensive doctor's scale that I bought when I was first married, but a less-precise scale will do.
- A food scale (or even a postal scale) to measure food in ounces.
- Measuring cups and spoons to measure food by volume.
- A calorie guide.
- A small notebook to record what you eat. A piece of paper folded in eighths also works as a weekly record; use one section to record each day.
- A piece of graph paper to plot out your progress.

Next, set a daily calorie maximum for yourself. If you need to lose a significant amount of weight, are pregnant or nursing, or have medical problems, discuss this with your doctor.

Otherwise, the calorie maximum you choose is somewhat optional. Most diets are designed at 1,200 calories for women and 1,800 for men. Diets below 1,000 calories for long periods aren't advisable without medical supervision, and diets of 1,500 calories may be too much for many women to lose weight. I chose 1,000 calories and I took a multivitamin. Both Foreyt and a weight-loss physician told me this was in the low range of an acceptable plan.

When on a low-calorie regimen, it's crucial to get 95 percent of your calories from a balanced diet of nutrient-rich foods. You'll tend to eat a lot of fruit and vegetables because they're nutritious and low in calories, while limiting your consumption of fatty and sugary foods. Because protein is important when dieting, I ate the same moderate amounts of meat, eggs, yogurt, and cheese as usual.

150
145
140
135
130

Each day I began a new page in my notebook with the date and my weight that day at the top. Throughout the day I wrote down what I ate. I didn't weigh and measure my food before each meal, but instead weighed sample portions of, say, granola, to get an idea of what a 1-ounce portion looked like. I worked out my calorie count before supper and adjusted supper and my evening snack accordingly.

I tallied the total calories each night.

By keeping a notebook I found it very simple and useful to refer back to previous entries, as many of our frugal meals repeat themselves. Eventually I made a one-page calorie list of foods our family commonly eats. In many cases I just estimated as well as I could. I also figured out how many calories were in certain scratch foods by adding up the total calories in the ingredients, noting the volume the recipe made, and doing simple division to determine the calories in a single portion.

Exercise is important while dieting. It burns calories and helps prevent the loss of muscle tissue. Although my life does include some exercise, such as 8-mile bike rides, and physical labor, such as 12-hour house-painting days, it remained about the same as before I dieted.

The result: I lost 20 pounds in 16 weeks. Foreyt said that my rate of loss was excellent. At first you lose weight a bit quicker; then you should lose about a pound a week. If you lose faster than that you'll lose muscle tissue as well.

Foreyt staunchly believes that counting calories, combined with exercise, is the best weight-loss method. People are attracted to diets that save them the work of counting calories, but they will do best if they don't try to skip this brainwork step. Foreyt agreed with my observations about the drawbacks of the following popular weight-loss methods:

- Counting fat grams. Foreyt said he tried having his patients do this because it seemed simpler than counting calories. But he found these patients didn't lose weight consistently, because some foods, such as sugar, are high in calories but low in fat.
- Exercise alone. Foreyt said this doesn't always work. If you exercise, you'll build muscle tissue, and muscle burns more calories than does fat. But a five-mile jog won't help you burn more calories all day long. Your metabolism quickly returns to normal after you stop exercising. Whether they realize it or not, people who maintain weight "through exercise alone" are still balancing the calories they eat with those they burn. In fact, it's amazingly hard to exercise away high-calorie foods. For example, a cup of pudding has about 400 calories. A 150-pound person would need to run about an hour to use up these calories. Most people would find it easier to skip the pudding.
- Relying on "crutch" foods. Diet soda, sugarless gum, Equal, and low-calorie prepackaged foods are a big part of many informal diets and are often used in combination with formal diets. When I was on Weight Watchers, I constantly consumed crutch foods. Because my stomach became used to being fed something frequently, I became obsessed with food and sometimes found myself actually daydreaming about it. By dieting without crutch foods, food eventually became less important to me, almost "utilitarian." I was hungry during the first week while my stomach adjusted, but I chanted my mantra: "Hunger is good." After that, I seldom felt very hungry.
- Eating prescribed, daily portions of certain foods, such as fruit, milk, or fish. Many formal diet programs require this, while others rely on prepackaged diet foods (such as shakes and frozen

dinners) in combination with portions of regular foods. Although this seems simpler than counting calories, it results in the following three problems:

1. It can be more expensive. Some diets require that you eat fish twice a week but limit potatoes to three times a week. They might require a daily citrus fruit, even if your freezer is full of homegrown broccoli, which has much more vitamin C.

2. It's less flexible. Some foods are "illegal," such as pizza made with homemade dough. When I was with Weight Watchers, I could eat English-muffin pizza or Weight Watchers frozen pizza, but since the plan had no provision for homemade pizza dough, eating it was "cheating." This made eating with others difficult. Once I had a family, following a Weight Watchers diet meant either eating different foods than my family or switching everyone over to my diet. In social situations I would have to conspicuously abstain from parts of meals or ask my host to prepare something special for me. But during my calorie-counting diet, I went on vacation for nearly two weeks, went to our annual company picnic, ate at seven birthdays, had overnight houseguests on four occasions, and went to a church supper and an ice-cream social. A couple of people noted when I passed up a second helping, but few people suspected I was trying to lose weight.

3. It doesn't accommodate cravings for specific "illegal" food. When I followed the Weight Watchers diet, I craved illegal foods and binged on several occasions. But counting calories allowed me to eat a few sweets each week yet remain within my limit. Similarly, I've found that I'm rarely satisfied eating "rabbit food" but feel better if I eat the equivalent amount (or less) of calories in a baked potato or muffin. Foreyt said that on the ideal diet, no food is forbidden.

Finally, the problem with myriad diet plans isn't the diet itself, but how to get off it without regaining the weight. This is particularly true of diets based on prepackaged meals and protein drinks. Dieters don't know how much they must eat of regular foods to maintain their desired weight. But if you've kept a record of your calorie consumption, through calculation and experimentation you should be able to pinpoint the number of calories you need to maintain the desired weight.

In the year since I lost this weight, I have easily maintained my weight. I weigh myself every few days. If I find my weight has crept up a pound or so, I simply revert back to the diet for a few days.

One last note: A hidden cost of losing weight is that you may need to replace some of your wardrobe, but this need not be costly. In fact, losing weight can be one of the best tightwad strategies to improve your wardrobe. The secondhand market has a much better supply of clothes for thin people, possibly because people get rid of clothes when they gain weight. Also, thin people almost always look good no matter what they wear. In contrast, some larger women compensate by spending more on hair, nails, and wardrobe. In my case, many of my clothes simply fit better. I had also kept many of my slim clothes, so my wardrobe actually expanded dramatically.

DO YOUR HOMEWORK

Dear Amy,

We saved thousands of dollars when we purchased our home by knowing what the previous owners had paid for it. I merely went to the county assessor's office and asked for the "green sheet." This was a copy of the tax information on the house, including the history of sales of the house. You can also ask for tax information on nearby addresses or similar houses to find out what is a reasonable selling price. Knowing what the current owners paid for it gave us the nerve to offer far less than the asking price. I'm sure we would never have gotten our house for the price we did without knowing this information.

—Debbie Huber
Danville, Illinois

FAMILY FREEBIES

Dear Amy,

Call area attractions you'd like to take your family to and ask if they have any "free to the public" events scheduled or regular "free admittance" times. Our local museums usually charge no admission on the first Monday after each new exhibit opens, and sometimes on school holidays. When my kids were little, the zoo was free on Monday morning before noon. It doesn't hurt to ask!

—Mary T. Graupman
Rochester, New York

EGGSTRA SAVINGS

Dear Amy,

Many people don't take full advantage when eggs go on sale because they don't know that eggs can be frozen. Lightly mix 1 cup of raw eggs (about five large ones) with 1 teaspoon salt and store in an airtight freezer container. Thaw overnight in refrigerator. Properly frozen, eggs will keep for up to six months. Three tablespoons of egg mixture approximates one large-sized egg. They taste good scrambled, in omelets, or in baking.

—Eileen Herman
Seattle, Washington

UNDERFOOT, UNDERPRICED

Dear Amy,

I bought a beautiful 100 percent wool oriental rug by asking a local rug cleaner if he had any that had never been picked up. I had several to choose from and paid only the cost of cleaning.

—Patricia Wyatt
Sunnyvale, California

CHEAPER CHECKUPS

Dear Amy,

I save $50 every other year by creatively scheduling "annual" dental checkups. My dental insurance requires that I pay nearly the entire cost of the first dental visit in any calendar year to satisfy a deductible. The cost of a second dental visit in a calendar year is covered (almost entirely) by insurance. My "annual" checkups are early January and late December of even years (1992, 1994, etc.). The dentist gets the same volume of visits, but I pay less out of my pocket.

—Bob Kastner
Niantic, Connecticut

RENTED, DENTED DEALS

Dear Amy,

Check rental stores for cosmetically damaged or otherwise unrentable items. From two different stores we bought two major-brand color TVs with remotes that work perfectly for $50 each. One had the adjustment-knobs door broken off, the other had a broken rabbit-ears antenna holder (easily fixed). Both were only about a year old. Rental shops frequently have cosmetically damaged or dirty items that they sell *cheap*. They also throw away many repairable or very dirty items. Check their Dumpsters or ask them to call you to unload freebies.

—Anthony K. Colbert
Fort Worth, Texas

SAY IT WITH CARDS

Dear Amy,

I hate using money for flowers when someone dies. Instead, I make up cards and mail one every one to two weeks for several weeks or months. This way, contact is maintained. I've had many people comment to me how much they looked forward to the cards during their time of adjustment.

—Mary Ann Weaver
Paw Paw, Michigan

STU-DENTAL DEAL

Dear Amy,

The local community college offers dental examination, cleaning, fluoride treatment, and X rays, all for $8. The students working on you are usually very thorough because they are being graded and must complete several cleanings in order to graduate.

—Ruth M. Kennedy
Lindenwold, New Jersey

DETERGENT SOLUTION

Dear Amy,

A way to save on dish soap: Fill a small spray bottle with a couple of teaspoons of dish soap and then fill with water. Use one or two squirts for washing. This works great for handwashing one or two items or filling a dirty pot to soak.

—Joan Lasche
Rochester, New York

MINT HINT

Dear Amy,

My husband used a leftover Christmas candy cane to stir his coffee. It gave the coffee a nice minty flavor. It would be good stirred in any hot drink. Then put it in a container for the next time.

—Linda Bukvic
Williamsburg, Ohio

EQUITY IN THE HOME

When we needed to do something about a window that had a broken glass and a rotted section of sash, Jim's first response was to price a new window. He discovered a replacement would cost $150. He decided to fabricate a new wooden-sash section and replace the glass himself.

That situation caused me to wonder why Jim's first inclination had been to entirely replace the window rather than repair the old one. When I asked him about it, he reminded me that while he would enjoy making the new wood section, he loathes glazing (applying putty to hold in a new pane). In fact, he hates it so much that on a few occasions, I later discovered, he had taken a whole sash with a broken pane to a glass-replacement center and paid an extra $5 to have the glazing done there.

Suddenly, I realized that the only reason window-glazing had been Jim's job was because, as a man, it was a skill he'd happened to pick up. I suggested that he teach me how to glaze, as it looked like something I would enjoy and do well. So Jim did a splendid job making a new wooden section from scrap lumber and I happily glazed the window.

Around this time, I happened to catch a talk show (I was sick with the flu) on which couples were squabbling over the allocation of housework. A situation common to two-income couples was presented: The wife did all the housework in the evening while the husband watched television. But another situation was presented in which a husband would come home from his full-time job and was expected to do the housework that his stay-at-home wife should have been able to complete.

Although suggestions were offered, none was as effective as the method Jim and I use. So I felt a discussion of gender roles, and how they relate to frugality, was in order.

Modern families have abandoned the traditional gender responsibilities . . . to some extent. This has usually been the result of changes in the traditional man-as-sole-breadwinner pattern, like dual-income families and stay-at-home dads. But it's still an area of some confusion that often results in poor use of time and therefore dependence on a whole range of expensive luxuries such as restaurant meals and hiring out for cleaning, lawn care, and simple carpentry.

First, let's tackle the allocation of chores on a day-to-day basis. Although it seems obvious to me, it's a solution that wasn't presented on that talk show. Very simply, each spouse must contribute the same number of hours each day to productive activities that directly contribute to the well-being

NAILS
Draw a line from each item to the person who uses it.

of the household. How you do this depends on the wage-earner structure of your family.

If your family has two full-time wage earners, and you work the same hours, each spouse must share in the housework during evenings and weekends until it's completed. If one spouse works just part-time, he or she must take on additional housework equal to the hours of extra work put in by the full-time spouse. By working during the same hours, it's easy to see that the share of the work is equal. If a wage earner works a night shift, then instead of working during the same hours each day, the spouses must agree to put in the same *number* of productive hours every day.

If your family has one wage earner, the stay-at-home spouse should expect to work an equal amount of time at home, from the time the wage earner leaves until he or she returns. Any remaining work, including giving kids baths and helping with homework, must be shared equally. During these nine or more hours, the stay-at-home spouse should be able to complete the basic housework and meal preparation, even with caring for young children.

I've been amazed at stay-at-home moms who claim that doing this much is nearly impossible. Few people have as many children as we have, have a larger house than we have, or take on as many do-it-yourself tasks as we do. As a former navy wife, I successfully tended to all the household needs of my family when Jim was away for months at a time, even when I had three preschoolers. Nowadays, we find basic housework (washing dishes, vacuuming, laundry, and so on) can be completed in half a day. Only then do we move on to less essential but still productive tasks, such as weeding the garden, volunteer work, sewing, writing letters, and spending quality time with our children.

If you are a stay-at-home spouse and your daily activities include chatting on the phone, reading romance novels, watching TV (without doing a productive activity simultaneously), etc., you shouldn't expect your spouse to share in the housework when he or she arrives home.

Now that Jim is the stay-at-home spouse, he does for me what I once did for him. It's rare that I come home and find that basic housework has not been completed. When I do come home to an enormous pile of unfolded laundry, I know that he has been busy doing other tasks we both agreed were of a high priority. In fact, we often strike a bargain in the morning: If he'll make wooden "treasure boxes" for kid-gifts, I'll fold laundry when I get home.

(After this article ran in my newsletter, a few readers objected to these points. Some argued that they didn't complete basic housework because they felt that spending their days giving their children most of their time was more important. In response, I would point out that if the wage earner must come home and do basic housework, he or she has less time to give to the children. Others argued that personal time for reading or chatting on the phone was essential in helping them survive the grueling reality of the stay-at-home role. In response, I would point out that being a stay-at-home parent is a *privilege* that many working parents desperately want but have yet to achieve. So, frankly, I have little patience for either sentiment.)

Second, aside from fairness, it's simply more efficient to allocate chores based on each individual's abilities and preferences rather than gender stereotypes.

But what often happens is that, even though we are in the 1990s, jobs still tend to be allocated by traditional gender roles. Frequently readers write to me: "We can't buy a fixer-upper because my husband isn't handy," or "We can't save on our food bill because my wife doesn't like to cook." But the majority of house-painting and renovation on our house has been done by women, either by me or by a crew of female carpenters. And since we've been married, Jim has done most of the grocery shopping and cooking. I've known women who could repair their own motorcycles and a man who taught himself to use a sewing machine because his wife just didn't have the knack for it.

So if your wife avoids a task she intensely dislikes, strike a deal. Teach her to change the oil in the car and have her teach you how to bake bread.

And as for the chores no one likes, a reader summed up the best advice: "You should each do what you like best, and split the rest." There are certain tasks that neither of us loves to do, such as cleaning bathrooms and washing dishes. We're each responsible for cleaning one of the two bathrooms, and we trade off washing the evening dishes.

If I had to list factors that contributed to the financial success of our family, somewhere near the top would be "teamwork."

WAR AND PEAS

Caroline Johnson of Garner, North Carolina, sent me a newspaper clipping that really caught my attention. It told of a single mother who was "struggling" to feed two sons, ages two and four. She worried that her $388 in food stamps wouldn't see her through the month, and her cupboards at home were bare.

This mother's inability to feed her family had several causes. But in reading the story, it was clear that this family's biggest problem was picky eating. The mother preferred sodas and salty snacks. And since she "hates to waste food," she bought microwavable dinosaur-shaped pasta and sugary cold cereals like Apple Jacks for her picky young sons, because they refused to eat cheaper or healthier foods.

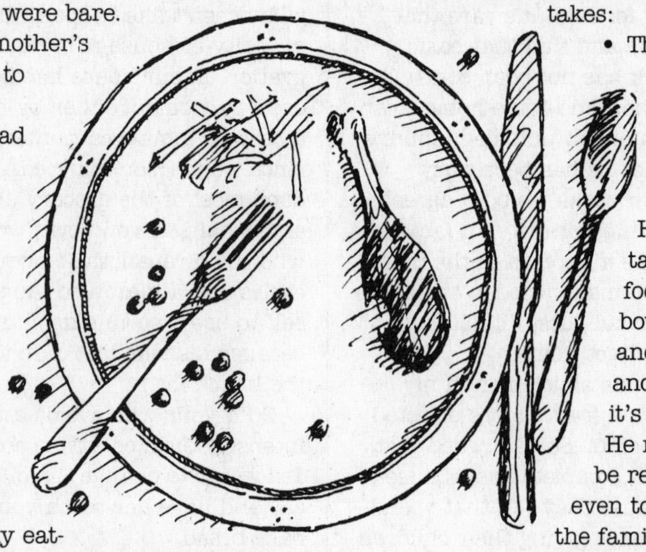

Although this story was about a welfare recipient, picky eating occurs regardless of family income. It drives up your food bill, as you either throw away uneaten food or buy more expensive foods to accommodate the picky eater.

Many people regard overcoming picky eating as impossible. But food preferences are largely an acquired habit, and like all habits they can be molded for the better or worse. One of the major reasons our food bill is low is that we have conquered picky eating. We have instilled in our children the "habit" of eating (and, usually, enjoying) the food that is set before them. If you want to chop your food bill, you must conquer pickiness, too.

Picky eating often results from one or all of these parental mistakes:

• The child has not been given enough limits. He dictates what food is bought, and when and how it's served. He may not be required even to sit with the family at mealtimes. He is allowed to eat snacks shortly before or after meals, even when he didn't eat the meal.

• The child's eating has become the entire focus of the meal. The parents continually nag, threaten, or play "down-the-hatch" games. The child learns he has power to manipulate his parents' emotions by being picky.

• One or both parents are picky eaters. They often make negative remarks about meals, or about other foods they think are "disgusting." The child learns that disliking foods is normal. Because of the parents' limited preferences, the child isn't exposed to a variety of foods.

The solutions take a variety of forms, from gentle to firm.

Ellyn Satter, a registered dietitian and family therapist, authored a useful book on this topic called *How to Get Your Kid to Eat . . . But Not Too Much* (Bull Publishing, 1987). She espouses a common professional approach, which I would describe as gentle. If you do at least this much, you'll conquer most of the dinnertime problems.

Satter says that as parents you should choose what food is purchased and selected for meals, how it's prepared, and when it's served. *Never* prepare a special meal for a picky eater or allow an older child to do this for himself. *Never* plan meals around what you know he'll eat. The child must come to the table and sit through meals, but he decides which foods and how much he wants to eat. Whether he eats or not, don't allow him to eat again until the next meal or scheduled snack (which consists of nutritious foods also selected by you). Continue to put some foods on his plate he dislikes, but don't pressure him to eat.

I believe Satter's method can work, but it isn't the most economical way, because wasting food is an acceptable option. The child isn't required to finish his meal, including any seconds he requested. And when one child doesn't eat something, it can have a "domino effect" that magnifies the waste. For example, when Alec, my oldest child, expressed a dislike of mushrooms, his younger siblings also decided they didn't like mushrooms—before they even tried them.

Satter believes that if kids come to the table hungry and are allowed to choose, they'll discover peas are pretty good, sometime in the next ten minutes or ten years. Although I have occasionally observed this in children, I've also seen kids stubbornly hang on to an irrational dislike forever. They refuse to eat sliced beets but will eat julienne-cut beets. Sometimes they decide to dislike a previously liked food as a way to express individuality. Some foods just require practice to like.

Satter believes you should respect your child's individual preferences. I believe that this is like the many situations when your child can override his preference for the greater good of the family. By eating everything, he respects the parent's effort in preparing the meal, he adheres to the family's no-waste ethic, and he participates completely in a shared meal, which I believe contributes to family unity.

Satter believes that pressuring kids to eat generally produces pickier eaters. This has not been my experience.

So here's my "firm" method, which I suspect would never be approved by any modern professional. I agree with Satter until the point where she states that the child gets to choose what he'll eat at meals. We require our kids to clean their plates.

Most children eat well until they are two. Then their growth slows and they require less food. They also begin to challenge authority by not eating foods they already like. Until a kid seems mature enough for firmer measures, we only encourage finishing and put much less food on his plate than I think he'll eat.

When the child reaches two and a half, we begin transitioning him to an understanding that he must

clean his plate. I start by gently reminding the child to eat. Occasionally I may help by feeding him a few spoonfuls. Then he receives mild praise for finishing.

At some point he will simply refuse to eat, even though he hasn't eaten for several hours. I tell him he will be disciplined if he doesn't, and remind him of this a few times during the meal.

If, after everyone else has eaten and left the table, the child still refuses, he is disciplined. The key point here is that the child has been warned but has not controlled my attention throughout the meal. It's crucial to be 100 percent consistent in following through with discipline.

The form of discipline depends on the child's age, what is effective for this child, and what type of discipline is accepted in your home. Discipline can provide a choice for your child. If you tell an older child he can't watch TV for a week unless he eats the fish sticks, you've given him the options. In the rare case when the fish sticks will truly make him ill, he can opt not to eat, and you haven't caved in. But the right discipline is almost always effective.

With each of our six kids we had from one to six showdowns that led to discipline. Sometimes the episodes occurred over foods a three-year-old liked but decided not to eat that day. Other times they balked over certain foods they disliked. I respected their dislike by giving them very small portions, but they had to eat that portion.

Once kids accept that they must eat some foods they don't like, it's not traumatic. Without prodding, they valiantly work their way through the small portion as if it were any other undesired task I ask of them. Frequently this occurs as they continue to chat and laugh. In our home, we revere the ability to eat disliked foods just as we revere other skills. Later, I might hug a child and say, "You did a good job eating the turnip. I know it's not your favorite."

It doesn't work to have the child sit for hours until he eats. Small kids eventually fall asleep. Older kids miss their school bus. Pokey eating (chewing a bite of oatmeal for an hour) is treated the same as not eating.

Because it's a given that the kids will eat at mealtimes, we've found it isn't necessary to schedule snacks to ensure hunger at supper. We discourage snacking within an hour of the meal, and the kids must ask for permission, but I let them choose their snacks because almost all of the food in the house has nutritional value. I place limits only on juice and some more-expensive foods I'm saving for lunch boxes.

Kids, like parents, should not

make negative comments about foods. I resolved the previously mentioned mushroom problem by leaning toward Alec and whispering, "If you say one more bad thing about the mushrooms, I'm going to fish around in the casserole and find you a few more."

It's commonly believed that forcing kids to eat will cause obesity. In a telephone interview, Satter said she knew of no studies that confirmed this. I believe asking your kids to eat ¼ cup of peas when they haven't eaten during the previous two hours won't make them fat. My kids all tend to be lean—in the 90th percentile for height and 75th percentile for weight.

What are the results of each method? With Satter's method, she says school-age kids may still eat a limited number of foods. If you don't pressure them, they will gradually accept more.

With my method, all my kids eat 100 percent of the meals set before them without problems, and they like 95 percent of the foods offered. Neal, who once loathed asparagus, now "almost" loves it. Jamie's onetime dreaded food, bean soup, is now like any other to her. Many mealtime guests have watched in amazement as our children ate.

Parenting isn't an exact science. If my method doesn't work or feel comfortable for you, use Satter's method.

Is cracking down on picky eating mean? I consider it to be a tough-love kindness. The short period of discipline required to conquer this problem seems like a worthwhile tradeoff to gain 15 years of harmonious mealtimes.

WAR AND PEAS UPDATE

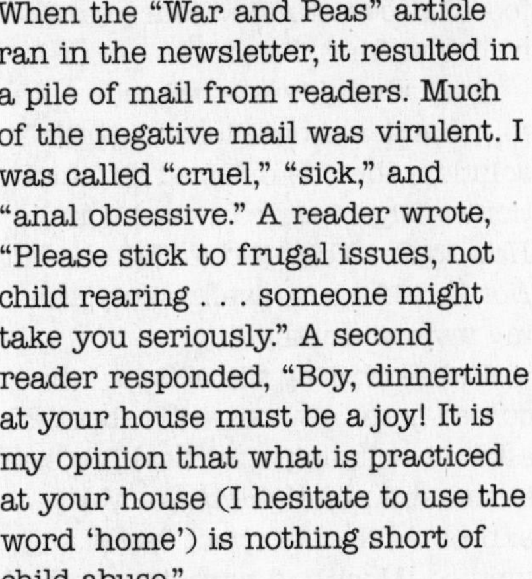

When the "War and Peas" article ran in the newsletter, it resulted in a pile of mail from readers. Much of the negative mail was virulent. I was called "cruel," "sick," and "anal obsessive." A reader wrote, "Please stick to frugal issues, not child rearing . . . someone might take you seriously." A second reader responded, "Boy, dinnertime at your house must be a joy! It is my opinion that what is practiced at your house (I hesitate to use the word 'home') is nothing short of child abuse."

But the positive comments outnumbered the negative ones and were often just as charged with emotion. Readers said the article was "fabulous," "profound," and "the only way to go." Marlene Yanchus of Wilkes-Barre, Pennsylvania, wrote, "Bravo! Finally, a parent who doesn't take orders from children!" Karen Poulson of Los Angeles, California, said, "Everything we serve has a nutritional purpose. Just as we do not allow children to take medication at will, they may not choose what they eat at mealtimes." Vicki Robin, president of the New Road Map Foundation, a group that promotes frugality, wrote, "The latest issue is great. I continue to refer all people who are economic hostages of their children to you."

Obviously, people have differing—and very strong—opinions about what constitutes good parenting. Further, although my system was common a generation ago and works beautifully for my family, I know that it isn't generally accepted by modern child-rearing professionals. That's why, although I have always believed that picky

eating is one of the chief reasons that Americans spend too much on food, I procrastinated four years before writing the article.

And when I wrote it, I took care to present a professional, "gentle" solution, the one outlined by nutritionist Ellyn Satter in her book *How to Get Your Kid to Eat . . . But Not Too Much,* as well as explaining my own method.

Before writing the article, I discussed both methods with about 25 adults (including a medical professional and non-tightwads). Most expressed doubts about Satter's method. Most had parents who had used a clean-your-plate system, and/or they used it with their own kids. Only one objected strongly to my method. Had I presented Satter's method alone, I believe that *many* parents would have disputed the article.

Some readers suggested I was too compulsive in worrying about the cost of a small portion of peas. But picky eating often begins with small amounts wasted and can increase to where as much as one third of the food on the child's plate is wasted, even when the child is allowed to choose what's put on his plate. I know, because I have seen this. Parents often tell me that their food bills are out of control because their older children refuse to eat low-cost foods. They sigh and regret they weren't firmer when their kids were young.

It's also significant that in over 400 pages, Satter's book didn't devote a single sentence to the cost of wasting food. When I asked her about it, she indicated that she didn't feel it was an important issue.

While child abuse is a serious problem, I feel our culture has become so oversensitized to it that some have begun to use the term indiscriminately. I have, for example, been accused of "child abuse" because I dress my kids in yard-sale clothing. By my discussing discipline at the dinner table, people presumed that Jim and I do it constantly and that all of our mealtimes are tense and grim. But, as the article stated, I disciplined each kid an average of three meals. This means that from ages 3 to 18, each child will eat 16,422 meals in which he is not disciplined and food is not wasted.

Mealtimes in our house are *happy* times, precisely because the expectations are clear, and we are free to get beyond constant battles over food and talk and laugh together as a family.

A WHISKER'S DIFFERENCE

A newsletter reader from Bellevue, Washington, asks, "Have you ever done a study comparing electric razors versus shaving with a blade?"

No, but now's as good a time as any. All comparisons below are based on a man who shaves daily. Women (usually) shave less often and will have to adjust the figures accordingly. As you'll see, there are too many variables to give unequivocal guidelines.

Electric razors (priced at a discount department store in nearby Auburn, Maine) cost from $35 to $169, and, according to *Appliance* magazine, last an average of four years. A Norelco representative told me that the heads of their razors should be replaced annually, at a cost of about $25. Jim, who has a light beard, says he once had an electric razor that today would cost about $75. It died after six years and he never needed to replace the heads. So the annual cost of using an electric razor might be as high as $67.25, but Jim's annual cost was the equivalent of $12.50.

As for blade shaving, store-brand one-piece disposable razors cost $1.39 for 12. Used carefully, one razor can last a month, so this is a year's supply. Jim uses a $1.59 can of shaving gel each month. So his annual cost for blade shaving is $20.47, but this cost could be lowered.

Canned shaving cream is not the only option. David Sumner of Muncie, Indiana, wrote that he uses a free shaving mug (an old coffee cup) and a $5 brush. The shaving soap, he said, costs $1 per bar and lasts much longer than a can of shaving cream.

To this, I would add a couple of black-belt tightwad comments from my male staffers. First, you need not use special "shaving mug" soap. Any hunk of bath soap will work. And if you shower every day, you may not even need shaving cream at all. The purpose of the cream is to make whiskers wet and soft, but a hot shower has virtually the same effect. Immediately after showering, dry everything but your face and shave with no cream. You may be surprised at how well it works, particularly for men with light beards. And there is no annoying soap goop to rinse off.

Use a mug-and-brush and the annual blade-shaving cost drops to under $5.00. Use no shaving cream at all and the annual cost is $1.39.

So those in pursuit of all-out economy should probably opt for some variation of blade shaving. But given that the annual cost variation may be fairly small, and that men shave every day, I feel this matter should be left up to personal preferences.

TOYS FROM TRASH

The following is a collection of toys made from everyday objects.

Meat-tray blocks. Make building blocks from meat trays by cutting off the rounded edges, leaving only the flat part. Cut slits in the trays ¼-inch wide (or the thickness of the tray) and as deep as you want. Cut trays into circles, squares, and triangles. Kids can use these to build a variety of structures. (Sent in by Julie Lewis, Decatur, Arkansas.)

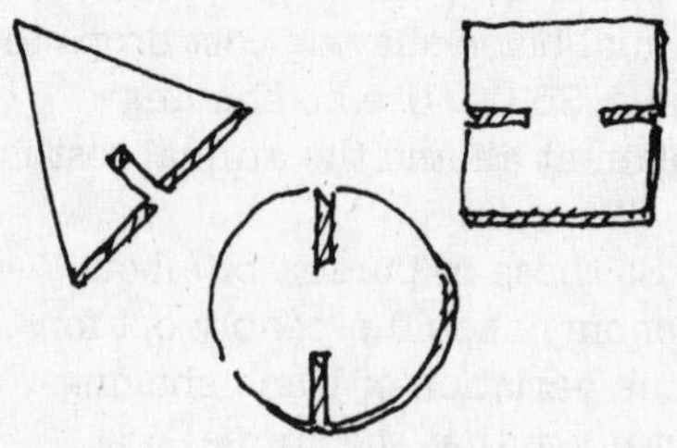

Hockey game. You need the bottom of a large box, markers, small round and flat objects such as checkers or poker chips, and small rulers. Draw on the playing lines and cut out two holes on the opposite sides of the box to make goals. Use the round object for a puck and rulers for hockey sticks. (Sent in by Susan Finley, Albuquerque, New Mexico.)

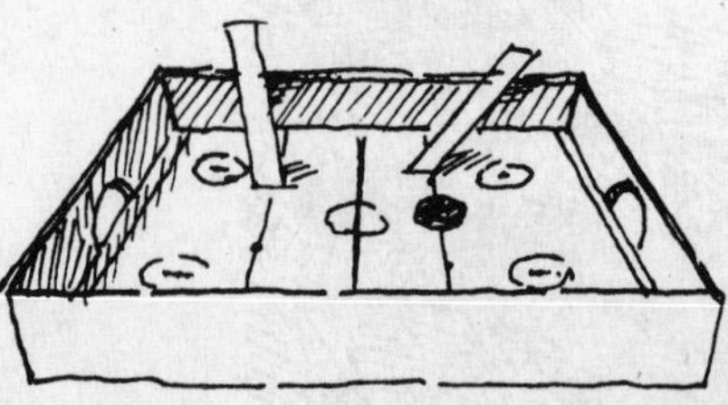

Box easel. Cut the corner off a sturdy, appropriately-sized box. To attach paper, use tape or push pins. (Sent in by Earlene Giglierano, Iowa City, Iowa.)

Pull toy. You need five large soda bottles, four washers, a piece of string, and a coat hanger. Remove the hard-plastic bottom from four bottles. Cut off the rounded inner bottom, turn it around, and reinsert it into the plastic bottoms (certain brands, like 7-Up and Pepsi, work best). Make four holes in remaining bottle and make holes in the four plastic bottoms. Cut the hanger to make two axles and assemble the pull toy. Put a washer on each end of the axles and bend the wire end so that the washer can't come off. Poke a hole through the cap, thread the string through it, and screw it back on the bottle. (Sent in by Ruth Palmer, Glendale, Utah.)

Ribbon dancer. Advertised on TV for $12.95, this can be easily made. Tape an 8-foot crepe-paper streamer (party leftovers work fine) to the end of a dowel or paper-towel tube and let the kid swirl it around as he/she dances. Can also be made using a paint stirrer and more than one streamer. (Sent in by Sharon Mitchell, Camillus, New York.)

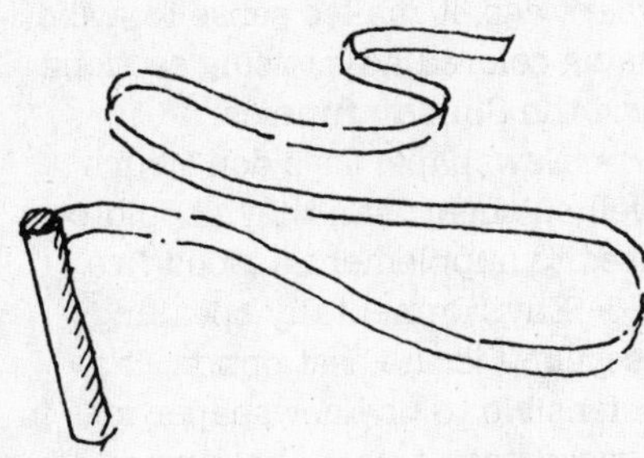

Skip it. Toy stores sell a version of this for $13.95. It helps a child count. To make one, you need a plastic coffee-can lid, masking tape, a tuna can, and 3 to 4 feet of twine. Cut away the inside of the plastic lid, leaving a hoop. Wrap the hoop with masking tape so that it won't chafe. Poke a hole in the bottom of the tuna can, knot one end of the twine, thread it through the hole in the tuna can, and tie the other end of the twine to the hoop. The child puts the hoop over her ankle, swings the can in a circle so she can skip it, and counts herself.

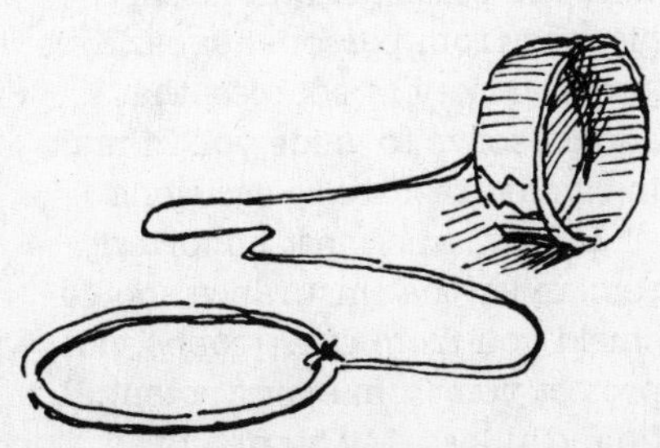

Flickers. Bread tabs can be used to make interesting projectiles. Break the tab as shown. Place tab on fingertip. Use your thumb to hold finger back as you flick the finger forward. The bread tab will sail surprisingly far—about 20 feet. The tabs work best on smaller fingers, so your ten-year-old may accomplish this better than you; and it does pinch a bit. Encourage kids to shoot at a target rather than at each other. These entertained the Dacyczyn children for hours.

Giant loom. Back in the '60s, we made pot holders by weaving nylon-stocking loops on little square frames. The same idea can be enlarged. Cut a square frame from a piece of plywood, put finishing nails around the sides about ¼ inch apart, and weave loops cut

from the bodies of old T-shirts. The resulting squares can be used for placemats, chair seats, blocks for a rug, pillows, hot mats, etc. (Sent in by Lita Wallace, Boise, Idaho.)

HOT OFF THE PRESS

A frugal way to supplement a dwindling woodpile is using rolled-up newspapers as logs. A 10-inch-high bundle of newspapers can put out as much heat as 18 pounds of coal. But some people are discouraged from trying this, as they have heard or read that: The newspapers must be rolled on an expensive, mechanical roller; to burn properly, the "logs" should be soaked in water and dried; and inks in newsprint emit toxic chemicals when burned.

We read a few articles on this subject, did some experiments, and called environmental groups that had studied toxicity in newspaper inks. We learned that:

- Mechanical rollers yield a slightly tighter log that burns a bit more slowly than a hand-rolled log, but the difference is small. So just hand-roll a 2-inch-high stack of papers as tightly as possible. Secure with coat-hanger wire, which can be fished from the ashes and reused.
- Soaked logs take up to three months to dry, yet there's no appreciable difference in their burning quality compared to unsoaked logs.
- Though chemicals used in colored inks contain fewer toxic heavy metals than they did ten years ago, it makes sense to avoid using colored advertising sections and the Sunday funnies.
- Newspaper logs don't burn well on their own; they should be used to supplement a wood fire.
- Environmentally speaking, recycling is the best option. It's defensible to use newspaper logs in a woodstove to help heat your home, but newspapers should be recycled rather than burned in a heat-wasting fireplace.

INSURANCE PHILOSOPHY

Insurance is a complex subject. We've covered aspects of it in previous *Gazettes*, but thumbing through some huge books on insurance has persuaded me that we can never cover all of the specific ins and outs. Consequently, I thought it would be useful to write about insurance *philosophy*. So here are some general ideas, gleaned from personal experience and a variety of sources, that should serve to guide you in making smart insurance decisions.

1. First, and most important, remember that insurance should shield you from catastrophe, not protect you from every potential financial loss. My staffer Brad was chuckling the other day

because he bought a $19 calculator at a local store and the clerk tried to sell him a $6 service contract to go with it. (A good rule of thumb: *Never* buy a service contract.) If you try to insure everything to avoid going broke, you *will* go broke from the cost of insuring everything.

2. When it comes to areas of your life where insurance is essential, such as for your home or medical care, set the deductibles high. As in point number 1, your goal should not be to pay nothing in the event of misfortune, but simply to avoid unbearable financial pain. What "unbearable" means is an individual decision that each family must make. But keep in mind that the savings that come with high-deductible policies can quickly grow into a substantial emergency fund. Always have an agent quote you rates for a wide range of deductibles.

3. Comb through existing policies and cancel unnecessary coverage. In reviewing our auto insurance policy, I found that we were covered for the cost of a car rental in the event our car went in the shop. But we would never have used this because we have two personal vehicles and a business vehicle; and it's an expense we can afford, anyway. So we canceled this part of the insurance and saved a little money. Make sure you understand every provision in every policy.

4. Shop around. Price differences of over 100 percent for precisely the same coverage are common. You can compare rates on the phone, though Bob Millar, an independent agent we interviewed, pointed out that agents have considerable discretion in pricing policies, and in some cases can offer you a better rate if they meet you in person and get to know you. Don't forget to call independent agents; to some extent, they can do the comparing for you. But be aware that extremely low rates may indicate that a company is shaky and/or has a bad payout record. A reputable independent agent is probably the best source of information on the trustworthiness of a particular company.

5. Shop around again. Every few years, rates change, so you should do your phone survey at least once every three years.

6. Get discounts. Breaks on premiums are offered for all sorts of things: marriage, graduating from a driver's course, not smoking, having several policies with the same company, having antitheft devices in your car, and so on. Agents may not list these for you, so be sure to ask.

7. Think term. Unless you are wealthy, term life insurance is generally a better deal than whole-life. Whole-life combines insurance and tax-sheltered investing, and the investment component is usually a good deal only for those who are in the highest tax bracket *and* have already put the maximum allowed in other tax-sheltered retirement accounts. So most people should stick with term insurance, which is cheaper, and invest the surplus in other ways.

8. Change your insurance when your life changes. Once a car is over five years old, it often makes sense to drop collision and comprehensive coverage. As children leave home, your need for life insurance may decrease or vanish.

9. Don't rely solely on your agent's advice to save money. Even

good agents tend to overinsure tightwads, because they are accustomed to providing coverage for average, debt-ridden, on-the-financial-brink Americans, not disciplined people who have stashed substantial emergency funds. *You*, and not an agent, are in the best position to decide if your coverage is adequate.

MIDWIFERY: A BIRTH OPTION TO EXPLORE

Although I've written before on how to spend less on infant care, Andrea Sims of Providence, Rhode Island, suggested what could be the biggest baby-related saving strategy of all: having a certified nurse-midwife (CNM) handle the birth. Andrea writes, "Women's and Infants' Hospital in Providence, Rhode Island, estimates the hospital cost for a mother and baby attended by a CNM at $2,000. For a mother and baby attended by an obstetrician, the hospital estimates the cost at $3,400."

To learn more, I called the American College of Nurse-Midwives (ACNM) in Washington, D.C., and received a large packet of information. I also interviewed Deanne Williams, director of professional services for the ACNM, and Mary Gabay of Public Citizen, a consumer-research group.

A CNM is a registered nurse who has completed a graduate-level midwifery program and passed an examination administered by the ACNM. There are over 4,000 CNMs practicing throughout the United States, and in 1993 they attended nearly 5 percent of all U.S. births. They can provide the following: prenatal care, labor and delivery care, postpartum care, well-woman gynecology (including breast and pelvic examinations and Pap smears), normal newborn care, family planning, medication and/or vitamin prescriptions, preconception care, and health maintenance counseling. In general, they charge less for all of these services than an M.D. would. Service by CNMs is covered by most private insurance companies and by the federal CHAMPUS and FEHBP programs.

About 95 percent of CNM-attended births are in hospitals, where doctors are immediately available in case of complications. But some CNMs also attend home births. Like doctors, CNMs carry professional liability insurance.

Along with the financial advantages, many women prefer this alternative because they feel CNMs are generally more attentive and more oriented toward natural childbirth. A Public Citizen survey revealed that CNMs are much more likely to walk with laboring patients, give them fluids, and suggest alternative birthing positions than are OB/GYNs. I've had six kids with five different OB/GYNs, and in one case a midwife also happened to be present. Although

my experience is just anecdotal, I agree that a few OB/GYNs were annoyingly inattentive, but the midwife seemed like an angel to me, offering a level of support that I had never experienced from an OB/GYN.

The study also found CNMs' success rate with vaginal births after a previous C-section is 68.9 percent, far better than the national rate of 24.9 percent.

Several studies have backed up the effectiveness of CNMs. An article in the *American Journal of Public Health* judged by birthweight and newborn-health-index scores that "mothers and babies have distinctly better outcomes when births are attended by midwives, either in or out of hospitals." In 1992, Kaiser Permanente, a California HMO, reported that CNMs managed 70 percent of the low-risk patients there and had lowered the C-section rate to 12 percent, compared to the national average of 23.5 percent. The success rates of CNMs may be at least partially due to their tendency to specialize in low-risk births, but Public Citizen's survey revealed that 87 percent of CNMs also co-manage high-risk patients with obstetricians.

Williams told me that in England, where the infant mortality rate is lower than it is in the United States, the Royal College of Midwives has about 36,000 members, while there are only about 3,000 OB/GYNs. Midwives handle over 80 percent of births in England.

To find a CNM, look in the Yellow Pages under "Midwives," ask if one is associated with your local hospital or clinic, or call the ACNM at (202) 728-9860.

THE MATCH GAME

Ever since we moved to Maine seven years ago, I've wanted to get cross-country skis for our family. We need an outlet for exercise during the long winter months, and we are ideally situated, surrounded by countless acres of snowy woods and fields.

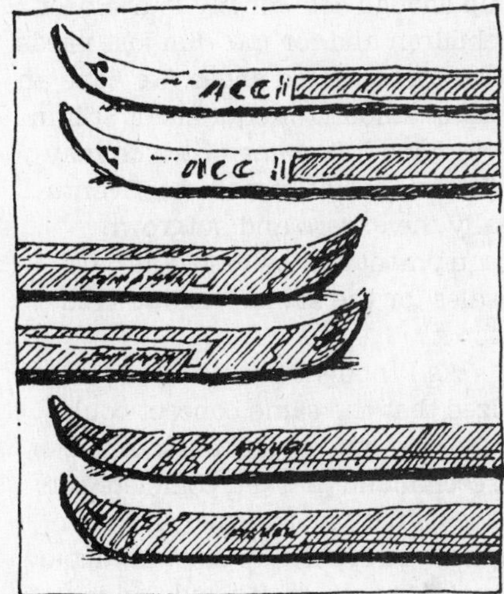

So I began to look for skis at yard sales. I found that the minimum price for a complete outfit (skis, shoes, and poles) was $25—cheaper than used-sporting-goods-store prices, but still much more than I wanted to pay. Sold individually, unmatched ski equipment was much cheaper, say, $1 for a pair of shoes. But the problem was that there are about three types of bindings. This, compounded with the need to buy for six family members, kept me from purchasing anything for fear I could never use it.

Finally, in the summer of 1995 it occurred to me that my approach to the problem was wrong—unmatched stuff was so cheap that

I could afford to take some risks. I began to buy *all* of the inexpensive unmatched equipment I found at yard sales (eventually I made an inventory to avoid buying duplicates).

By the end of the summer I had spent a total of $50. Then we began to look for matches, and to swap bindings from one ski to another when needed. We matched up enough sets for my four oldest children and for me. Jim just needs the correct-sized shoes. We have an equal amount of equipment still in our barn loft, some of which may fit someone at some time. Eventually the excess and outgrown equipment can be resold at yard sales for the same price we paid for it.

As I thought about this, I realized that the same concept could apply to other purchases. In the secondhand market, complete sets are usually more expensive than pieces of broken-up sets. In fact, a major reason stuff winds up in trash-pickable piles is that it is missing some part. But some risk-taking, hoarding, and imaginative combining can yield big savings.

Examples:

- Last summer, I trash-picked a small lampshade for which I did not have a lamp. An hour later I found a shadeless yard-sale wall lamp for 10¢. The combination made a perfect reading light over Alec's bed.
- People often don't buy an individual article of clothing because they don't have anything to match it. But if the item is cheap enough, it's worth the risk. If you don't buy the first item, you won't have anything to match the second item when it comes along.
- We often buy up makes of small appliances that are similar to the ones we have. For instance, we often see blender base-units without jars, and jars without base-units, at yard sales. We've found if we always buy items from the same maker, they'll match. We've replaced two jars, and recently replaced the base-unit.
- Children's games often have missing pieces. The game Mousetrap, for instance, is worthless if it lacks a single piece. You can get spare parts directly from the manufacturer. But if a game is very common, it's generally cheaper to buy a second game with missing pieces to make one whole game.

HEARTBREAKING HINT

Dear Amy,

I've found that chocolate candy in the shape of hearts, bunnies, pumpkins, etc. can be purchased after the holidays for up to 90 percent off. These are easily broken into chunks or melted down for use in recipes. Calculate the cost per ounce to be sure it is cheaper than buying baking chocolate.

—Nancy Melough
South Windsor, Connecticut

FIT FOR A QUEEN

Dear Amy,

After buying a "new" queen bed at an auction, I looked for bedding at garage sales. I found that you can use king-sized sheets and cut off enough to make two pillowcases.

—Barbara Janish
Scotland, South Dakota

BUT NOT THE *GAZETTE*!

Dear Amy,

I have a small business that requires me to ship my product. I bought a $70 shredder and now have all the packing material I'll ever need by shredding all of my unwanted mail, newspapers, and catalogs.

—Susan Stone
Los Lunas, New Mexico

A WORD ABOUT CURDS

Dear Amy,

Your yogurt article (see page 140) mentions "yogurt cheese" made by draining yogurt in a coffee filter or a cloth-lined colander. I've found that a pinch of salt stirred in before draining greatly improves the flavor. Also, the liquid that drains out is whey, which is very nutritious. I've used whey instead of milk as the liquid in muffins and other baked goods.

—Karen Lee
University City, Missouri

FROM DOGS TO HOGS

Dear Amy,

My kids love "Pigs in a Blanket." I stir up half a batch of biscuits, roll them out, cut them into thin strips, and wrap the strips around hot dogs. Half a batch is enough for a package of ten hot dogs. I bake them at 400 degrees for 12 to 15 minutes.

—Jeannette Kiper
Forest, Ohio

ZAP DOGS

Dear Amy,

Instead of dog treats, microwave hot dogs sliced into small pieces until you have little shriveled treats. Freeze in Ziploc bags and use for rewards, training, etc. An animal trainer told me these are more nutritious than commercial treats, cheaper, and dogs love them!

—Karen Yochim
Sarasota, Florida

BEYOND THE PALE

Dear Amy,

Last year we bought a $20 gallon of paint for $2 at a yard sale. It was very light blue. Our local paint store colored it for us to a lovely dark gray, at no charge. The man there said that if the paint is light in color, he could tint it to almost any color we wanted.

—Lynda F. Ward
Searsport, Maine

(Your paint store may not provide free tinting, or may refuse to do it to paints they don't sell. Check this out before stocking up on yard-sale paint. FZ)

BUDGET BRIDGE

Dear Amy,

We have a 30-foot-wide creek and needed a "cheap," very sturdy bridge. The city was widening a street about two miles from our home and I noticed that they were putting in new power-line poles. I called the electric company, and they gave the old poles to us free and even delivered them free. We used cheap landscape timbers for the deck of the bridge.

—Linda Fiedler
Arlington, Texas

A DYE TO TRY

Dear Amy,

My daughter and I came up with a new twist for your homemade play-dough recipe [given in the first *Tightwad Gazette* book]. We were low on food coloring, so we used Kool-Aid instead. It is spectacular. It makes a great color, and it is the best-smelling play-dough we've ever had. We used three packages per batch of dough. You can add it to the dry ingredients, or to the liquid before mixing.

—Patty Wheeler
Waverly, New York

DON'T DESPAIR, REPAIR

Dear Amy,

I recently spilled bleach on a favorite black shirt. I took some black fabric paint and rubbed it on the spot. This covered it perfectly. You can also salvage yard-sale and hopelessly stained kids' clothes the same way. This works best if rubbed in rather than brushed on. I got the paints on sale for 49¢ for 2 ounces. Only a few drops are needed for each repair.

—Cynthia Linkous
Amherst, Ohio

THE CITY TIGHTWAD AND THE COUNTRY TIGHTWAD

Recently, I was amused by a suggestion that I write a "city" version of the *Gazette* to complement the current "country" version. While the specific suggestion was new, this sentiment has been expressed before. I'm often seen as a "rural tightwad," someone who saved all her money by gardening, canning, and squirreling away bulk-purchases in a large house and a big barn.

The truth is that although I grew up in rural areas, I've lived most of my adult life in cities and suburbs. I went to art school in Boston, and I lived in either Boston or neighboring Cambridge until I was nearly 30. Then Jim and I lived in suburban areas of Virginia and Maine. We moved to the country when we bought our current home in 1989.

None of the money we saved to buy our house was saved when we lived in the country. This is important to understand. Many people have said to me, "Gee, I try to be frugal, but it's harder because I live in the city." But frugality is not necessarily easier in the country, the city, or the suburbs. Each setting has advantages and disadvan-

tages. To save money, you must exploit the advantages and minimize the disadvantages.

Living in a city has numerous pluses for tightwads, including:

• Cheaper transportation. Mass transit, and being within walking or biking distance of many amenities, make it possible to get by with one or even no cars. Even if you choose to own a car, it does not have to be a top-notch, reliable one, because you aren't so dependent upon it. However, if you do own a car, it will cost you more to park and insure it.

• More resources for cheaper goods. A downside of living in Maine is that there are only two major supermarket chains here, and real price wars are unknown. Conversely, where my father-in-law lives in Massachusetts, a half-dozen grocery chains compete for a slice of the market. Stores there typically slash prices and offer double and occasionally even triple-coupon sales. This can hold true for other consumer goods. For instance, there are literally hundreds of consignment and thrift shops in the Philadelphia area; so many that there's actually a guidebook devoted to them. In contrast, there are only about five such shops within a 30-minute radius of my home. I've found that everything from gas to consumer electronics is cheaper in cities.

• More cheap housing options—if you're flexible. Single people and couples without kids who are willing to live in small spaces and/or less-desirable neighborhoods can have very low housing costs in the city. Singles, in particular, can exploit the phenomenon of "group houses" and live in relatively elegant—albeit crowded—homes for minimal rent. Studio apartments are roomy enough for two-career couples before kids come along. Few people would opt for these living arrangements permanently, but the city does offer more of these short-term, low-cost housing options than can be found in the suburbs or the country.

• Better trash. A resourceful New Yorker can furnish an entire apartment from stuff that has been discarded. A San Francisco antique dealer told me that her best supplier was a trash-picker. Trash disposal in cities is expensive and inconvenient. This leads urbanites to leave good stuff out on the curb.

• Free cultural entertainment. The Washington, D.C., area is perhaps the best example, with several gigantic, free Smithsonian museums that would require years to fully explore. But most cities offer at least some free or inexpensive entertainment: free outdoor concerts, free days at the children's museums, street entertainers, and large libraries with a variety of programs and offerings.

The country offers different advantages:

• The ability to garden. This can lower food bills, though even in the case of our family of eight, gardening saves us only about $500 a year. We also have greater access to pick-your-own orchards and farms.

• Cheaper family-type housing and cheaper land. Our house and barn on seven acres cost $125,000 in 1989. Though it was a great deal, even for here, a comparable property near a large city could cost well over $250,000. And housing in rural Maine is very expensive compared to some other rural areas. In the Midwest, in particular, country ranch houses go for as little as $30,000.

• More utility options. Building a solar home, or heating with wood that you cut and haul yourself, can dramatically lower heating costs. Similarly, a well and septic system can cost less in the long run than city water and sewer service . . . *if* the systems are maintained properly.

• The ability to stockpile. Food, clothing, lumber, and furniture that are purchased cheaply can be set aside for later. I stockpiled when we lived in city apartments, but I can definitely store much more now.

• More lifestyle freedom. Theoretically, cities are bastions of tolerance and individuality. But my experience is that practicing black-belt frugality has been easier since we moved here, because our family is more isolated. If my kids lived in the city or suburbs, I think the fact that they never eat junk food, aren't swamped with toys, and don't own a Nintendo would seem odder and less comfortable to them than it does in the private world we have here. Although they see junk food in school, they are not confronted by material excess once they come home.

What about the suburbs? The 'burbs combine both the advantages and disadvantages of city and country life, but they do have some frugal advantages all their own:

• Better schools. Inner-city schools are often so poor that parents who can afford it tend to send their kids to private schools. Schools in the country can be either good or bad, depending on the particular district. We have been happy with our school, but also know that the incidence of parents resorting to home-schooling in other rural Maine communities (indicating a dissatisfaction with public schools) is significantly higher than it is in our district. While there are certainly exceptions, suburbs generally have the best public schools.

• Access to yard sales. When Jim and I lived in the city, we never encountered yard sales, so they were not part of our saving strategy. Now that we live so far out in the country, going to yard sales requires conscious effort and a lot of driving. However, when I lived in the suburbs I could find more than enough yard sales within a few blocks.

• Low cost of keeping a car in combination with many resources. While there are many resources in the heart of larger cities, it can be inconvenient to get to them if you are relying on public transportation. In the country, while we have cars, it is often inconvenient to drive far to get to the resources.

• Carpooling. This is generally a suburbs-to-city phenomenon, as it's unlikely that two country people

would work for the same employer on the same shift. So though many ruralites commute over an hour to a good-paying job, I know of just one man in my area who carpools.

One last point: Despite all of these dissimilar advantages, frugal behavior generally should not change depending on your location. City, suburban, and country people should all cook from scratch, negotiate, sew, cooperate, buy used, cut their children's hair, "do-it-yourself," and so on. Most *Gazette* articles apply no matter where you live . . . which is why I have no plans to start a "city" edition.

ADVICE OVER AIRWAVES

When a friend's car began making a chicken-bone-in-a-garbage-disposal noise and lost 90 percent of its power, he was in a quandary. The car had 166,000 miles on it, a slow brake-fluid leak, and a fair amount of rust, so it seemed likely that this engine problem spelled the car's demise. There was a small chance that it would be cost-effective to fix it, but if he took it to a mechanic, he'd have to pay for a diagnosis of the problem; chances are, all he would learn was that it should be junked.

Then inspiration hit. The success of the National Public Radio show "Car Talk" has spurred the creation of local versions. Sure enough, each weekend, a local radio show called "Auto Answers" is hosted by one of the top mechanics in Portland, Maine. My friend called the host and together they figured that the problem was a blown valve-cover gasket. My friend spent $300 to get it fixed, and has since put another 20,000 miles on the car.

Reader Nancy Dietz and her husband have extended this concept into other realms. Not only do they call the auto repair show in Baltimore, Maryland, they also regularly quiz the host of their local "Garden Club" radio show.

In fact, as Nancy writes, "for over a year now, we have been taping the gardening program each Saturday. During the week, I type up notes from the show on our computer in alphabetical form, from 'Acid Soil' to 'Zoysia Grass.' There are now over 70 pages in the computer that my husband and I can refer to. I feel as if I'm getting a degree in horticulture at no cost!"

Aside from cars and gardening, common themes for local call-in shows include home repair, medical treatment, pet care, and investments. Such programs are usually on "all-talk" AM radio stations. For a listing,

...AND THE DRIVE SHAFT'S CONNECTED TO THE...

check your Sunday newspaper or call the station directly. While you can get advice free from other sources, radio shows are unique in that, generally, the hosts are not trying to sell you something. And don't worry about getting through. Unlike national shows, local shows are generally desperate for callers, and a line is usually open.

CHECK UP ON CHARITIES

Kim Strom of Coeur d'Alene, Idaho, asks, "What are your thoughts on large charitable organizations such as CARE, Children's Defense Fund, St. Jude's Hospital, etc? Is there any way to find out who gets the most value for my dollar?"

Kim's question applies not only to big charities like the ones she lists, but to any organization or person that accepts donations. It's a real dilemma for tightwads. While frugality will naturally create surplus funds, and most of us understand the moral obligation to give, will the recipients of our money use it as wisely as we would? It's a question with which I personally wrestle.

Here are some of the methods that Jim and I use to ensure the money we give is put to the best use:

• Never give to a person or organization you don't know. Early in my urban life, a clean-cut young man approached me with a convincing story about how he had just run out of gas and had no money. I believed him but was carrying almost no cash. The following day, not recognizing me, he approached me again with the exact same story. I also worked in an inner-city convenience store and recall selling to some panhandlers who were carrying serious amounts of cash. Following these experiences, I never again gave money to strangers, no matter how honest or down-and-out they appeared.

Similarly, there are many fake charitable organizations that use names similar to those of legitimate organizations, and that use telemarketing techniques and door-to-door sales pitches to raise money.

So play it safe. If you want to help a street person, give directly to a shelter. If you give to an organization, check it out first. Get material, in writing, that satisfies you before you give. Make checks out to organizations, not to individuals, and mail the check in. Don't give out your credit card numbers to strangers. Don't make commitments over the phone.

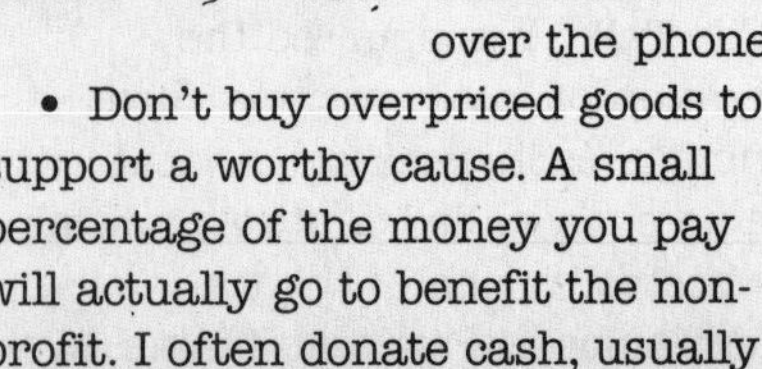

• Don't buy overpriced goods to support a worthy cause. A small percentage of the money you pay will actually go to benefit the nonprofit. I often donate cash, usually

a smaller amount than the cost of the item being sold, directly to the organization.

- Give to local organizations. You are more likely to know the work of the specific organization and/or personally know the individuals who run it.

- Give directly to people you know personally. In my case, I prefer to help elderly individuals, because regardless of financial mistakes they might have made in the past, they are often unable to change their current circumstances. In contrast, I rarely encounter "needy" young people who are doing everything possible to improve their current situations.

Giving to people you know personally can be tricky. In one case, I learned of a specific need in my community and made arrangements with a local organization to operate as a go-between so that the recipient would not know that the help came from an individual.

- Give something other than cash. I always save my deposit bottles for Scouts and other organizations conducting bottle drives. I give baked goods and other items to local fund-raiser auctions. While I could sell outgrown clothing at yard sales, I prefer to donate ours to our church's clothing center, which resells it at yard-sale prices. High school auto shops need used cars (this can be a smart option when a car is worn out and unsellable; most school auto shops will provide you with a form that allows you to take a tax deduction for the car's fair value). Also remember to give of your time. Meals on Wheels needs drivers, Habitat for Humanity needs builders, and schools need classroom and field-trip helpers.

- When giving to large organizations, check them out first. The leading evaluator of national and international charities is the National Charities Information Bureau.

Dan Langen, NCIB's director of public information, told me that his organization, which has been in operation since 1918, collects information on over 400 charities. The NCIB evaluates many factors, including the charity's specific purpose, the makeup of its board of directors, and the percentage of contributions that actually goes to programs rather than to fund-raising or administration. (NCIB says at least 60 percent of funds should go directly to programs.)

All of the information is distilled into the NCIB's *Wise Giving Guide.* I received a copy of the winter 1995–96 issue and found it quite impressive. It contains a listing of 200 charities that meet all nine of the NCIB's standards for quality. The current copy of the guide is available free on request from NCIB, 19 Union Square West, New York, NY 10003, (212) 929-6300. The NCIB is now also on the World Wide Web at http://www.give.org.

Another source of information on large charities is the Philanthropic Advisory Service of the Council of Better Business Bureaus, 4200 Wilson Boulevard, Arlington, VA 22203. The group's website is http://www.bbb.org/bbb. Its publication *Give, But Give Wisely* is free with a self-addressed stamped envelope.

A final point: I have come to understand that almost no individual or group uses money as carefully or efficiently as I do. If I held everyone up to my own frugal standards, I might never give any

money. Further, there's a limit to how much I can find out about how my contribution will be used. Ultimately, for a tightwad to make a contribution, there comes a time when he or she must simply swallow hard, sign the check, and hope for the best.

ECONOMIC RE-PRESSION

Dear Amy,

Pressed powder compacts often fall apart before they are half used. I salvage them by breaking up the remaining chunks, adding a small amount of rubbing alcohol, and mixing to a paste. As the alcohol dries, a solid cake forms again. The drying takes a few hours, but hands-on time is only a couple of minutes.

—Kathy Kritzberg
Santa Cruz, California

TIGHTWADS IN TAFFETA

Dear Amy,

A local high school recently held a consignment sale for prom dresses. For every dress sold, $25 went to the donor and $5 was kept by the school for the prom fund. It was a great way for people to get money for used dresses, and it was a bargain for the buyers.

—Laura Schenk
Newton Lower Falls, Massachusetts

SALING WITH THE RICH

Dear Amy,

My yard-sale secret is to hit the sales in expensive neighborhoods. These people rarely go to yard sales themselves, which means they are not always aware of yard-sale prices. Sometimes, the prices are very high, but I offer less and say, "I usually see these for $2 at yard sales." More often, they assume yard-sale prices are even lower than they actually are (or they don't care) and I find wonderful bargains.

—Kathleen Clary-Cooke
Centerville, Oklahoma

LOSERS TAKE ALL

Dear Amy,

A group of friends has found a frugal and fun alternative to expensive weight-loss clinics. The "Chubby Buddies" meet once a week, not just to weigh in but to share our mutual experience. Everyone puts a dollar in the "piggy" bank and the buddy that loses the most weight takes it home at the end of the month. The $25 prize may not be the lottery jackpot, but it sure is fun.

—Sarah Severns
Kensington, Ohio

BUDGET BABY BYPASS

Dear Amy,

A Cooperative Method of Natural Birth Control by Margaret Nofziger [Book Publishing Co., 1991] is a short, well-written book explaining how to use fertility awareness to avoid pregnancy. I've found the method easy and empowering. I found the book in the public library, so the only cost is the price of a basal body thermometer (about $7).

—Eve Abraham
Columbia, Maryland

SHOWER POWER

Dear Amy,

Instead of buying distilled water (which protects against mineral buildups) for my iron, I collect rainwater and it serves the same purpose.

—Lori Buckley
Grayslake, Illinois

PAGES FOR PENNIES

Dear Amy,

Library sales are a huge help to my family's home-schooling budget. This fall we are studying composers, art history, and American history. We selected books on these subjects and took home a shopping cart full of literature, much of it priced at 25¢ per book.

—Diane Gasaway
Troy, Ohio

ORANGE YOU THRILLED?

Dear Amy,

I love orange marmalade but don't have the patience to follow usual recipes. So I cut up an orange with the skin on and place it in the blender with about 1 tablespoon water. After blending, pour into a pan along with ½ cup sugar and boil for 15 minutes. Cool and refrigerate. Keeps for several weeks.

—Lois Venzke
Streamwood, Illinois

(If possible, use an organic orange for this recipe. Otherwise, be sure to scrub the orange peel thoroughly. FZ)

PERM YOUR PRESENTS

Dear Amy,

If you cut strips of wrapping paper, you can curl it with the edge of a pair of scissors, just like ribbon. Be careful, as it tears if you're too rough. This is a gorgeous topping for a gift.

—Sheri Youngquist
Newark, California

MOM TARTS

Dear Amy,

Here's a quick homemade "toaster pastry" recipe that's better and cheaper than store-bought. Make a pie crust. Roll it out flat on a cookie sheet. Score with a knife into squares. Bake until almost done. Spread with jelly or preserves. Bake about three minutes longer. Top some squares with other squares, jam-sides touching. Yum!

—Mary Swerens
Dunkirk, New York

PARSIMONIOUS P.S.

Dear Amy,

When I start a letter to my son, I leave it out on the kitchen table. I encourage my daughter, younger son, and husband to each add a paragraph. If a grandmother or aunt stops by, I have them add a note. It keeps our son up to date with all his favorite people and all for the price of one postage stamp.

—Lynda F. Ward
Searsport, Maine

E-MAIL BONDING

Dear Amy,

Many people are using E-mail these days. They communicate through computers via Prodigy, America Online, or even free networks. We know people all over the country and exchange Christmas cards each year. This year, we are having a rubber stamp made up with our computer address on it, which we'll use to stamp each Christmas card. This will allow those who are "on-line" to send us E-mail anytime they wish. This will save a lot of money on phone calls and it is quicker than the mail.

—George W. Hadley
Lincoln, Rhode Island

SAVING LACE

Dear Amy,

When we get used little-children's shoes, they almost always need new shoelaces. I've not been able to find shoelaces for little shoes, so I take a long, flat nylon lace, cut it in half with a diagonal cut, and then melt the end with a match or candle flame. This makes it pointed, so it goes through the holes.

—Mrs. Wendell Filbrun
Hamilton, Ohio

SAVING SOFTLY

Dear Amy,

We live in a high-altitude area of North Carolina. We have a great deal of rain. The dehumidifier runs almost constantly. Our washer is close by. We empty the water collected into our washer. It's nice soft water in which to do your laundry.

—Shirley W. Craft
Sapphire, North Carolina

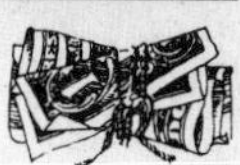

A PROCLIVITY FOR PRODUCTIVITY

Imagine you're on a tropic isle. Sipping a "Coco Loco," you recline on a beach chair and watch the gulls lazily wheeling overhead. The azure sea, warm as bathwater, laps at your toes. There is absolutely nothing to do, day after day, but relax on this white-sand beach. Sure, it has cost you a bundle, but you are living out the fantasy that's promoted in dozens of travel ads.

There's only one problem. You don't get it. "What," you wonder, "is the big deal?"

The scene described above actually happened to me. When I was in my early 20s, I visited the Caribbean island of St. Thomas. I saw sun worshippers similarly reclining and inert and simply could not fathom the attraction of it.

To live a successful, frugal life, you should develop a very critical attitude toward what seems to be our new, national goal: lying around doing nothing. Being busy, being productive, doing things that improve your family's long-term prospects should not be seen as drudgery to be endured until you reach the cherished goal of utter inactivity. The happiest and most successful people I know have realized a crucial truth: The *act* of doing things is more fun than doing nothing. If this is not your current attitude, you should work to acquire it.

If an efficiency expert followed Jim and me around for a day, he would find that most of our time is filled with productive activity: making pies, refinishing furniture, painting bedrooms, sorting clothes, yard-saling, cutting hair, and so on. We enjoy the fact that each of these tasks helps us financially; but there is also a satisfaction that comes from being absorbed in the task itself.

Wise people throughout the world have long understood this. Playwright George Bernard Shaw said, "The secret of being miserable is to have the leisure to bother about whether you are happy or not." Former British prime minister Margaret Thatcher said, "Look at a day when you are supremely satisfied at the end. It's not a day when you lounge around doing nothing; it's when you've had everything to do and you've done it."

Similarly, in stories in *People* magazine and *60 Minutes,* gracious-living guru Martha Stewart said that she doesn't enjoy nonproductive activities such as playing games and sailing. She washes her car or does a craft for fun. We can debate the relative usefulness of covering lampshades with moss,

but the point is that Martha Stewart is a professionally successful person, and preferring productivity over leisure is a hallmark of successful people.

If you remain unconvinced—if your dream is still to loll endlessly on Aruba's sands—it may be because you have approached your work or chores around the house incorrectly. Here are some keys to enjoying a life of productive activity:

• Plan. One reason people find their activities unrewarding is that they are nagged by the notion that they are doing the wrong thing. They can't concentrate on painting the hall because they feel they should be canning beans.

Scott and Helen Nearing, the famous New England homesteaders, began each day by surveying the weather to determine if they should work indoors or outdoors. Then they made a precise schedule of the day's activities. Similarly, before we go to bed each night, Jim and I each decide what we are going to do tomorrow. Secure in the knowledge that we are doing the right thing at the right time, we are able to concentrate on it. (Incidentally, if the beans are ripe, can them now and paint the hall later.)

• Understand your own clock. Mike Harper, a management consultant and author of the book *Hope Is Not a Method*, points out that people's internal clocks differ, and their energy peaks at different times. Morning people should tackle their most daunting tasks early in the day; afternoon people should begin with simpler chores.

• Do what you like to do. As I pointed out in "Equity in the Home" (see page 238), as much as possible Jim and I divide up chores on the basis of what each of us prefers to do. Jim likes to cook, can, and garden. I like to refinish furniture, paint, and tackle big cleaning tasks. We split the chores that neither of us enjoys.

• Involve the family. Increasingly, "quality time" with kids is seen as doing what the kids want to do: playing video games, cruising the mall, etc. But quality time can just as easily be centered around productive tasks. Our kids make baked goods, pick strawberries, and help with painting. Involving kids in household chores can be fun, teaches them responsibility, (usually) increases the amount of work that gets done, and imparts skills that they will need to get along on their own. Above all, it gives kids the right attitude about productive activity. Those who learned the pleasure of productivity as children tend to go on to be productive, happy adults.

• Do it well. If you resolve to do a task to the best of your ability, you will find that you enjoy it more. This is true even when doing something well requires more time. For example, replacing a zipper on a jacket is a time-consuming challenge for any seamstress. Some hope the task will go quickly so they can move on to "fun" activities; when the job takes longer than planned they become frustrated. I approach the same task knowing that it will be time-consuming and that each seam may not come out right the first time. But ultimately, it's satisfying to replace a zipper and have it look as good and function as well as the original.

• Reflect on the basis of happiness. In his 1951 book *How to Stop Worrying and Start Living,* Dale Carnegie lists many cases of people who pulled themselves out of despair simply by being productive. For example, he tells of a man who lost two daughters to disease and saved himself from insanity by going from room to room in his house and compiling a list of 242 items that needed attention; everything from broken storm windows to leaky faucets. He spent over two years fixing them one by one, and he also joined the school board, attended adult-education classes, and collected money for the Red Cross. "I am so busy now," he said, "I have no time for worry."

All of this is not to imply that tightwads should never goof off. But I have found that a distinguishing characteristic of successful frugal people is that they tire rather quickly of nonproductive activities and long to do something that shows concrete results. If you follow the recommendations listed above, you should find your definition of "fun" expanding to include activities that provide you and your family with long-term benefits.

You may not go as far as I would, but if you at least see some sense in the following statement, you are on the right track: I would—honestly—rather scrape paint off my barn than lounge around on a Caribbean beach.

GARDEN-FRESH YEAR-ROUND

One of the most intriguing methods of boosting a garden's productivity is using a cold frame. It's an enclosure made of wood, cinder blocks, or hay bales and topped with glass or Plexiglas. It extends the season in both directions, allowing earlier planting and later harvest.

Until recently, I had thought of cold frames as aids to extending the spring seed-starting season. But Eliot Coleman's book *Four-Season Harvest* (Chelsea Green, 1992) points out that the real advantage of cold frames comes in the fall. He writes, "Only the harvest season, not the growing season, needs to be extended."

The distinction is important because extending the growing season more than a month or two is a difficult technological feat, while extending the harvest season through the whole winter is easy with a cold frame; it simply protects plants in their dormant state. In Harborside, Maine, where lows can hit minus 20 degrees, Coleman harvests 18 kinds of vegetables from his cold frames up until spring.

The cold frame is among the simplest handyman projects. Don't use costly, kiln-dried lumber. Lacking large pieces of used lumber, my staffer Brad built three cold frames from rough-sawn, green, 2-inch-by-10-inch hemlock he bought at a local sawmill for about one third the price of equivalent kiln-dried lumber. He used 3-inch screws for assembly; three at each corner. He avoided having to cut tricky bevels by assembling the frame upside-down on a flat sur-

face. When flipped right side up, the uneven edges are on the underside and are buried in the soil when in use. Coleman recommends nailing 1-inch-thick scrap pieces to the bottoms of cold frames; as these rot, they can be replaced.

The challenge of the tightwad cold frame is finding inexpensive materials for the top. Articles in *Mother Earth News* and other publications blithely recommend "old storm windows." These may work in some climates, but around here the weight of snow tends to break them. Further, storm windows don't shed water properly; it pools around the crosspieces. If you are very lucky, you may be able to find used tempered glass (such as from a salvaged sliding-glass door) or Plexiglas for a reasonable price.

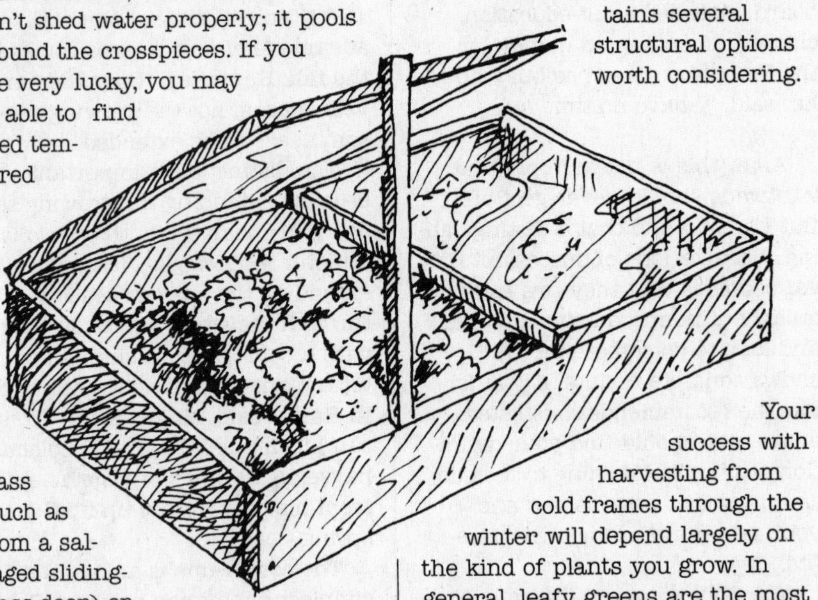

Probably the best choice among new materials is a space-age transparent polycarbonate called Polygal. It seems expensive—the best price we could get is $1.85 a square foot. But this is only one third the price of new tempered glass (which is what Coleman uses). Further, it is guaranteed to lose less than 6 percent of its transparency in ten years, and it is 200 times more impact-resistant than regular glass. Its double-layered, air-channel construction means it has about twice the insulating ability of regular glass. To find a distributor in your area, call (800) 537-0095.

Because Polygal is so light, you should enclose its edges with a wooden frame to lend it weight and rigidity. This frame should be open at the bottom to allow rain and melting snow to run off. If you live in an area with high winds, use hinges to attach the Polygal's frame to the cold frame. Coleman's book, available at libraries, contains several structural options worth considering.

Your success with harvesting from cold frames through the winter will depend largely on the kind of plants you grow. In general, leafy greens are the most cold-hardy plants. Coleman says in his area, any of the following can be planted in the late summer and harvested right through until the following spring: arugula, claytonia, Italian dandelion, kale, kohlrabi, lettuce, parsley, radicchio, scallion, sorrel, spinach, Swiss chard, and sugar-loaf chicory. A cold frame filled with straw can even overwinter root crops such as carrots.

In the late spring and early fall,

a cold frame can be a bit fussy to use. You must be sure to prop it open by early afternoon on sunny days to avoid overheating. Place a thermometer inside and make sure that the temperature inside does not exceed 80 degrees. In the depths of winter simply leave it closed, except when harvesting. Brush off snow, but don't worry if it accumulates for a week or two while you're away. Remember, the plants are dormant.

I've seen elaborate watering systems proposed for cold frames, but it's generally simplest just to water with a mister attached to a hose. Once the plants stop growing in winter, no further watering is required.

Should you use cold frames? If you build with new materials, a 4-foot-by-8-foot cold frame will cost about $75. A cold frame this size might grow 50 heads of lettuce. So you would have to figure that a cold frame might take a year or two to pay for itself. But for those who love fresh, homegrown produce and who enjoy gardening, cold frames are a reasonable investment. They allow those with little gardening space to extend their season and get two harvests where they previously got one.

Our situation is somewhat different. With our 8,000-square-foot garden, Jim and I don't need to maximize our land's productivity. Further, our garden space is often on the other side of a 3-foot snowbank, so fetching food from a cold frame for supper could be a bit of a chore. However, fresh is nice, and we may place a few cold frames next to our house so that we can have a small quantity of greens for wintertime salads.

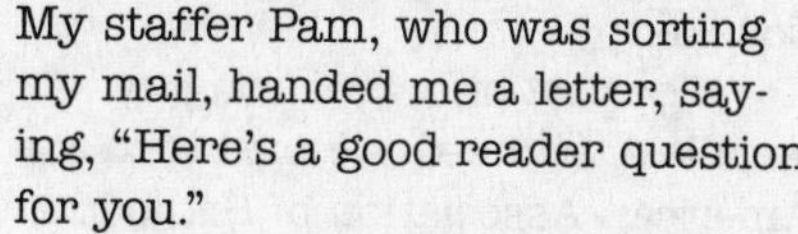

THE STRAIGHT TOOTH

My staffer Pam, who was sorting my mail, handed me a letter, saying, "Here's a good reader question for you."

Suzanne Johnson of Lawrence, Kansas, asked, "Have you considered an article on dental braces? It's a major expense that seems to have become an acquired need. Are we depriving our children by refusing to spend $3,000 for cosmetic corrections? It's hard to stand firm when half the eighth-grade class seems to have braces."

After reading this, I turned to Pam, smiled broadly to exaggerate my crooked-toothed overbite, and said jokingly, "Geez, why do you suppose she's asking *me* this?" Kidding aside, I realized I could offer a unique perspective on this question.

I grew up in a home with modest financial resources, and spending money on nonessential dental care was never considered by either child or parent. To be perfectly honest, it was something to which I never gave a thought. I'm living proof that it's possible to be successful and happy despite having an imperfect smile. Like Suzanne, my initial reaction to this expense is that the notion that everyone must have perfect teeth is a bit misplaced.

I also feel it's important to distinguish between a child's desire for braces and her desire for better-looking teeth. Braces were despised when I was a kid, but nowadays they are less obtrusive and some kids actually like how they look. Braces are much too expensive—not to mention painful—to be used solely as a fashion accessory.

However, persuasive arguments can be made in favor of braces. Consider:

• The cost of braces roughly parallels the need. According to the American Association of Orthodontists, minor corrections can be achieved for as little as $1,500. Corrections for the most serious medical or cosmetic problems can cost up to $5,000. Due to improved materials and techniques, the cost of braces has actually increased much more slowly than the inflation rate.

• Unlike the temporary benefits derived from designer clothes and trendy haircuts, braces are an "investment" purchase. When you consider haircuts, nail care, makeup, and wardrobe, most women spend at least $1,000 annually on temporary improvements to their appearances. A $2,000 orthodontist bill, spread out over 60 years, is just $33 annually.

• In many areas of our budgets, tightwads can spend far less than everyone else while achieving the same level of quality. But braces are an either/or thing. You can't "do-it-yourself" with paper clips, rubber bands, and duct tape. When there are no economical options and I determine that the benefit is worth the cost, I shop for the best price and don't sweat it any further.

To sum up: If affording braces for a minor cosmetic problem means making difficult financial trade-offs for the family, I think it is appropriate to ask the child if she is willing to forgo store-bought clothes, allowances, and family vacations. Is she willing to take on more housework and give up after-school activities so that her parents can work overtime to earn the money required? An eighth-grader is old enough to peek into the family ledger to gain a clear understanding of what the entire family must give up to accommodate her desire. If she's unwilling, it isn't that important to her.

On the other hand, if the child has a fairly serious, noticeable cosmetic problem, I feel it can be appropriate for a frugal parent to insist that the child get braces even if he doesn't want them. Boys, in particular, are often completely oblivious to their physical appearance, but as adults they will thank their parents for making them wear braces. In either case, make sure the child understands the hassle and possible pain involved in braces. For some people, braces can involve months of soreness to gums and teeth—even to the point of tears. Braces also require special care in brushing, and avoiding certain types of food.

One of my children does have a minor cosmetic problem and does want braces. I said yes.

HAVE A BLOCK PARTY

Wooden blocks are among the best toys for young children. They're simple, durable, and foster imagination and coordination.

I find that commercially made wooden blocks, which can sometimes be purchased at yard sales, are usually too small to make the impressive structures kids enjoy building. Larger blocks are obviously a possible do-it-yourself project, but how, exactly, should they be made?

David G. Fielder of Akron, Ohio, provided the answer. He wrote that short pieces of 2 × 4 can always be found around building projects. With the builder's permission, take these home. The thickness and width are already fine, so they need only be cut to length and sanded.

David's block sets (he's made 12 so far) consist of three sizes. First is a square, the second size is twice that long, and the third size is three times that long. That makes them 3½ inches long, 7 inches long, and 10½ inches long respectively. The fact that they are all based on the same basic 3½-inch unit is important because it makes many structures possible.

David says he tries to provide at least 20 blocks of each size in a set, and perhaps a few extra of the smallest size. These can be made with a handsaw, but a circular saw makes the job much easier. Easiest and most accurate is a radial-arm saw, or a motorized miter saw (commonly called a chop saw). Virtually all carpenters have one or both of the latter saws; beg, borrow, or barter access (and ask for a lesson—these are serious tools).

Sand by hand or with an orbital or belt sander.

For variety, I would also add "ramp" pieces in several sizes. These are made by cutting some of the basic-sized blocks diagonally (safest for older kids). You can also use a coping saw, scroll saw, or jigsaw to cut a semicircle out of the longest side of the longer blocks to make arches. Finally, you can cut 1½-inch-thick dowels in 3½-inch, 7-inch, and 10½-inch lengths to make columns.

INCREDIBLE BULK

Dear Amy,

To buy in bulk, don't be afraid to contact manufacturers directly. I saved 33 percent (includes shipping) off the price of some specialty honey for gift baskets . . . delivered to my door! All I did was call and inquire about buying a case of 12 and they were glad to help.

—Heidi and James Kushlan
Harrisburg, Pennsylvania

CHEZ CHEAPSKATE

Dear Amy,

Work in a restaurant or get friendly with someone who does. My college roommate worked in a high-class steak house. Every night she'd bring home a steak not cooked to order, or a cracked lobster, or broken crab legs, which they were not allowed to serve to customers. We also got day-old pastries and slices of cake that didn't cut prettily or had smeared icing. The restaurant was closed on Mondays, so on Sunday nights we got whatever vegetables and salad fixings remained on hand. Our grocery bill was negligible and our friends were envious when we'd moan about being tired of eating lobster.

—Karen M. Campbell
Sacramento, California

PEANUT POINTER

Dear Amy,

It is important to recycle the Styrofoam peanuts that are often used for packing these days. Contact your local private mailing service (such as Mail Boxes U.S.A.) and ask if they accept them. Some services will give you a discount in return for giving them your old peanuts.

—Gloria Pomykala
New Kensington, Pennsylvania

REBIRTH OF THE BLUES

Dear Amy,

To rejuvenate worn denim garments, we buy RIT denim dye and use it in an entire wash load of denim items. They come out looking like new.

—Linda Santa Maria
Phoenixville, Pennsylvania

DELIGHTFUL DISCARDS

Dear Amy,

A friend of mine cleans houses for a living, and her clients include at least one landlord. Renters will sometimes move out and leave their units a blessed mess, abandoning furniture, housewares, and especially clothing. Sometimes the tenants owe back rent, so they leave quickly and quietly and don't take anything they can't fit in their cars. (Using a U-Haul might attract attention.) In addition to her hourly wage, my friend gets her pick of what is left behind. If you are interested in this kind of work, check city/county records for rental owners and solicit their business by phone or mail.

—Elizabeth Case
Belfair, Washington

CROWNING ACHIEVEMENT

Dear Amy,

You mentioned the savings you can get from student dental assistants cleaning your teeth. Well, we are fortunate to have a full-fledged dental school here that trains both

future dentists and orthodontists. I recently got a crown that would have cost $500 for $135 by signing up with the University of Texas Health Science Center Dental School. You pay fees for the materials used.

—Janet Whitehouse
San Antonio, Texas

LOW-TECH LOAVES

Dear Amy,

If I make homemade yeast bread, I use my Crock-Pot. You can order a metal canister insert for bread or cake baking from the manufacturer for $9. You have to do the mixing yourself, but otherwise it works as well as a bread machine.

—Deborah Black
Grandview, Missouri

SLICK OIL TIP

Dear Amy,

In your newsletter you wrote that one reason you do not use homemade mixes is that the recipes call for shortening. I, too, prefer to use oil and have made my own biscuit mix for years. I substitute two thirds the quantity of oil for the amount of shortening called for in the recipe. In fact, I do this for all my baking. I entered a batch of my scratch biscuits at the local county fair and won first place!

—Nadine Bryan
Sidney, Ohio

WEED IT AND REAP

Dear Amy,

A plant that is nutritious, free, and abundant is the dandelion. It is very good for everyone to eat and contains many vitamins.

—Robyn Quaintance
Sidney, British Columbia

(Pick these from your own yard to be sure they have not been sprayed. All parts are edible. They are less bitter if picked before they flower. FZ)

WATER WORKS

Dear Amy,

I used to shampoo and condition every day. Then I read a "star's" hint in a magazine. She shampoos every other day with some expensive product, then just washes with water on the other days. Tried it. Works great.

—Kathy Terrill
New York, New York

BISECT YOUR BIRD

Dear Amy,

When buying a frozen turkey and you don't want to or can't use it all at one time, ask the meat cutter to saw it in half or quarters. They will do this for a few cents, or sometimes for free.

—Bish Wolf
Lebanon, Pennsylvania

BATTERY BONANZA

Dear Amy,

Many hospitals are sending patients home overnight with cardiac, respiratory, and brain-wave monitors. These are battery run; 9-volt, C, and AA cells are the most common varieties used. Frequently, new, industrial-grade batteries are used, and are thrown away after a single overnight use. They are mine for the asking at the local hospital.

—Jeffrey P. Hazzard
Valrico, Florida

PUREE SAVES THE DAY

Dear Amy,

I have been using your suggestion to replace half the fat in cookies with applesauce. When making some cookies, I didn't have applesauce, but I had pumpkin puree. I used that in place of half the fat. The cookies were delicious! Pumpkin puree is cheaper for me than applesauce.

—Laurie Lentz-Marino
Belchertown, Massachusetts

SWINGING INTO SPRING

Dear Amy,

As springtime approached last year, my husband and I began pricing gym/swing sets. To purchase even a kit plus lumber was way out of our budget. While driving through a nearby town we noticed one in someone's backyard that was exactly what we had wanted. It was clearly no longer being used (the beautiful lawn around it gave that away). We got our courage up and knocked on the door. We offered to remove the set, fill the holes, and reseed their lawn. The owners agreed. We saved about $500.

—Francine Fazio
Schenectady, New York

GOING WITH THE GRAIN

Here's another universal recipe, and I hope it helps put to rest the silly notion that frugal eating cannot be healthy. This "Universal Pilaf" represents state-of-the-science nutritional excellence; it is low in fat and cholesterol and high in fiber, vitamins, and complex carbohydrates. Depending upon the options you choose, it also ranges from extremely to moderately cheap.

My thanks to Andrea J. Albert and David E. Gurzynski for sending it in. They say these proportions make a meal for two with leftovers for lunch the next day. For my family I would at least triple the recipe.

Grain: One cup of uncooked brown or white rice, bulgur, couscous, or other favorite grain.

Fat: Two tablespoons of olive oil, butter, vegetable oil, or other favorite oil.

Base vegetable: Two to three cloves of diced garlic and one of the following, cut up: one small onion, three shallots, or one small leek (white part only).

Liquid: Two cups vegetable broth, chicken broth, cooking water from boiled vegetables, or water.

Meat or protein (omit if using the pilaf as a side dish): From ½ to ⅔ cup skinned chicken (may be diced and boned or left whole), tuna, cooked white or red beans, white fish, hamburger, or cheap steak cut into cubes.

Additional vegetable: About ½ cup frozen or fresh peas, cut-up carrots, frozen corn, green peppers, celery, and/or any other favorite vegetable except for leafy greens and potatoes.

Seasoning: Salt, pepper, chervil, parsley, whatever works well with chosen ingredients.

Directions: Heat fat in a large cast-iron or nonstick skillet. When hot, add the base vegetables and fry until golden and translucent. Add the meat and brown (but if using tuna, don't add it at this point). Add the grain and fry for a minute or so to coat it with the fat. Add the liquid and bring to a boil (add tuna now). Add the other vegetables, season, stir, return to a boil, lower the heat so it just simmers, and cover. Check it often; if using whole grains, it will take up to 40 minutes to cook, while white rice takes only about 15 minutes. Don't stir too much. When the liquid is completely absorbed, it is done. Stir, season to taste, and serve.

INVESTIGATION 101

Most people know how to research timeless questions such as how to lay tile or do upholstery: Simply read library books. But judging by my mail, many people are stumped when it comes to researching "new deals." These deals—discount grocery offers, phone deals, and network-marketed doodads—supposedly save you money; others are touted as income opportunities. Each type can cost you money if you don't do proper research. But because they're new, you can't learn about them in library books.

Sometimes I do investigate such offers and publish the results, but there are too many to report on them all. And I don't like to devote space to bad deals that few people would hear about anyway.

In such cases, readers have to

do their own research. So I thought I would pass along a few basic consumer-research methods. Many of these are also useful for digging up other sorts of information, such as answers to safety, legal, or health questions.

When investigating, gather several kinds of information, such as: the company's history, what consumer reporters have written about it, whether certain claims the company makes are true, and so on. This information can be gathered from a variety of sources. Here are some we typically use:

• The Better Business Bureau. I usually call the BBB first, because whenever my research ended after a single call, it's been when I found the BBB had received complaints. But no record of complaints is not necessarily a sign of a good company. For example, if a bad company has been doing business in that BBB's area for less than a year, it may not have received complaints yet. BBBs can also tell you a company's history and the type of business it does. To find a local BBB, call information in the town where the company is located. If there is no BBB in that town, ask the operator for the nearest branch. Some BBBs charge a small fee for information provided over the phone but will give you the same information free if you write.

• The company itself. Call the company and ask questions! It's crucial that company officials provide a satisfactory answer to every question you have. If they refuse, give contradictory answers, are never available to take your call, or simply can't make a good case for their deal, odds are it's a bad risk.

Also, ask companies for all the free literature they'll send you. Often if you read all the fine print and do the math, you can determine if the deal is bad. If it looks good, keep investigating. And *don't* rely solely on the information and references of happy customers provided by the company.

• On-line resources. Subscription-based on-line services offer a wealth of information. CompuServe, for example, gives you access to complete texts of articles from some 400 magazines and dozens of major newspapers over the last several years. Some large, well-financed city libraries provide similar access for free. Smaller libraries may offer stripped-down versions. Basically, you enter a keyword or words, such as "affinity credit cards," and every article that contains those words is listed; you then select the ones you want to read. Two caveats: There's often a fee. CompuServe, for example,

charges $1.50 per article retrieved. And be aware that most consumer reporters lack the critical tightwad perspective. For example, when I wrote about telephone debit cards, I read dozens of articles that raved about the potential savings, but *none* that explained when these cards would cost more to use than calling cards. Negative reviews are generally more reliable than positive ones, perhaps because a negative story requires more careful research to avoid lawsuits. An exception to this is *Consumer Reports,* which tends to be extremely thorough and accurate whether its conclusions are positive or negative. All articles, regardless of their accuracy, can provide other leads, such as names of experts or companies that offer similar deals.

- Reference librarians. They can help locate experts to verify the claims of a company. These claims might include medical or nutritional benefits, scientific facts, or the feasibility of a marketing plan. Librarians can tell you the names and addresses of industry associations, which periodicals track this industry, government sources, contacts in major corporations, and so on. Many of these have toll-free numbers. You need not travel to the library, as reference librarians will field queries over the phone. As an example of just how specialized experts can be, before running a bird-feeder idea I called the National Bird-Feeding Society. If an expert can't answer your questions, ask for suggestions of who you might call.

Investigations usually require both time and money, but how much depends on how thorough you want to be. In most cases, if a deal is bad, only a few phone calls are needed to become sufficiently skeptical to pass on it. It can take a lot of work to definitively prove a deal is either bad or good. Weigh your time and research expenses against your potential savings or investment.

If, for whatever reason, you are disinclined to investigate, simply walk away. In the 16 years that I have been a tightwad, I've rarely seen a new, nationally marketed, ongoing deal that was genuinely amazing. Great deals are usually local and/or limited, such as the odd great find at a yard sale, salvage store, or in the freebie section of the classifieds.

RELOCATION CALCULATION

It's common knowledge that housing is cheaper in some parts of the country than in others. This insight leads many people who want to get ahead to consider moving from expensive-housing to cheap-housing areas.

But often these people hesitate. Why? Because they believe that salaries in these cheap-housing areas are correspondingly low. Consequently, they believe that one region is no more affordable than another. In fact, this is not true. Some regions of the country are *much* more affordable than others.

To make a state-by-state comparison we obtained a 1990 Census Bureau report on median house values. These figures are based on estimates homeowners put down on their census forms and tend to be lower than market prices. We also obtained a 1993

Bureau of Labor Statistics survey that details average per-worker income, which includes all workers covered by unemployment compensation. The terms "median" and "average" are different, but a Census Bureau statistician told us that for the purposes of our comparison, it's valid to compare the two. As far as we could determine, these are the best state-by-state numbers available.

We divided the median house value by the average annual pay and came up with a ratio and a ranking. Theoretically, the lower both of these numbers are, the more affordable the state is.

There's a lot of variation in housing affordability because housing prices vary widely; but salaries don't. For example, we have friends in California who have been unable to buy a home there and are considering a move to Michigan. The chart indicates that they might lose $1,208 in annual income, but could save $134,900 on the cost of a home. So this would be a very wise financial move for them. Although Maine is relatively unaffordable, moving

	MEDIAN HOUSE VALUE	AVERAGE ANNUAL INCOME	INCOME/ HOUSE RATIO	RANK BY STATE
Alabama	$53,700	$22,786	2.36	11
Alaska	94,400	32,336	2.92	30
Arizona	80,100	23,501	3.41	36
Arkansas	46,300	20,337	2.28	7
California	195,500	29,468	6.63	50
Colorado	82,700	25,682	3.22	33
Connecticut	177,800	33,169	5.36	47
Delaware	100,100	27,143	3.69	39
District of Columbia	123,900	39,199	3.16	32
Florida	77,100	23,571	3.27	35
Georgia	71,300	24,867	2.87	27
Hawaii	245,300	26,325	9.32	51
Idaho	58,200	21,188	2.75	21
Illinois	80,900	28,420	2.85	26
Indiana	53,900	24,109	2.24	5
Iowa	45,900	21,441	2.14	3
Kansas	52,200	22,430	2.33	10
Kentucky	50,500	22,170	2.28	6
Louisiana	58,500	22,632	2.58	17
Maine	87,400	22,026	3.97	41
Maryland	116,500	27,684	4.21	43
Massachusetts	162,800	30,229	5.39	49
Michigan	60,600	28,260	2.14	1
Minnesota	74,000	25,711	2.88	28
Mississippi	45,600	19,694	2.32	8
Missouri	59,800	23,898	2.50	14
Montana	$56,600	$19,932	2.84	25
Nebraska	50,400	20,815	2.42	12
Nevada	95,700	25,461	3.76	40
New Hampshire	129,400	24,962	5.18	46
New Jersey	162,300	32,716	4.96	45
New Mexico	70,100	21,731	3.23	34
New York	131,600	32,919	4.00	42
North Carolina	65,800	22,770	2.89	29
North Dakota	50,800	19,382	2.62	18
Ohio	63,500	25,339	2.51	16
Oklahoma	48,100	22,003	2.19	4
Oregon	67,100	24,093	2.79	22
Pennsylvania	69,700	26,274	2.65	19
Rhode Island	133,500	24,889	5.36	48
South Carolina	61,100	21,928	2.79	23
South Dakota	45,200	18,613	2.43	13
Tennessee	58,400	23,368	2.50	15
Texas	59,600	25,545	2.33	9
Utah	68,900	22,250	3.10	31
Vermont	95,500	22,704	4.21	44
Virginia	91,000	25,496	3.57	37
Washington	93,400	25,760	3.63	38
West Virginia	47,900	22,373	2.14	2
Wisconsin	62,500	23,610	2.65	20
Wyoming	61,600	21,745	2.83	24
Average of all states	79,100	24,803	3.19	

here from even less affordable Massachusetts made the difference in our being able to buy the house we wanted and still live on one income.

In viewing the chart, there are a few points to bear in mind:

• I ranked the states in affordability based on the ratio of income to house value. In a few cases, the ratios in two or three states were the same, although the incomes and house values varied. In these cases I gave the higher-income states a better rating, assuming that you're always better off earning more money.

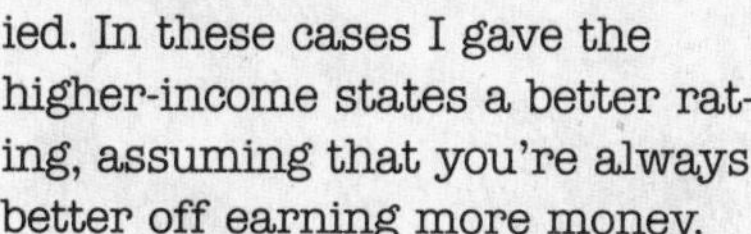

• The fact that we are dealing with average numbers for entire states leaves out the important differences between cities and rural areas. For instance, our chart indicates that New York has a high 4.0 ratio, but that number is pushed up because of New York City; rural New York State is probably approximately as affordable as neighboring Pennsylvania.

• In our comparison we're assuming that your income and your housing costs are the two biggest factors in your financial picture. Obviously, there are other factors. Utilities costs, local taxes, and insurance can vary widely from state to state. Consumer goods and groceries are less variable.

• The differences in average annual pay in your particular profession may vary more widely than does overall average pay. Further, there may be far fewer employment opportunities in certain professions in one state versus another. It's seldom a good idea to move unless you actually have a job lined up.

• Moving is in itself expensive, so if you plan to move to gain an economic advantage, try to do it just once.

• People whose incomes would not vary regardless of where they live, such as retirees and owners of mail-order businesses, should pay more attention to the house-values column. The ratio of income to house values is of little importance to them.

Given these points, this exercise is intended to provide a rough guideline for affordability and is in no way a substitute for the thorough research required before you pack your bags.

APPROVAL, THEN REMOVAL

Dear Amy,

I called our city hall about an abandoned house, hoping I could remove the small plants for landscaping. They gave me five addresses and told me how to contact the owners. While three declined, the two who gave permission owned old farms. I got rose bushes, bugle vines, hydrangeas, and enough of a fieldstone retaining wall to make a walkway.

—Annette Weber
Eden Prairie, Minnesota

A GRATITUDE ATTITUDE

Dear Amy,

During all our years of scrimping and saving, I resented being poor. Then, *The Tightwad Gazette* entered our life. We began doing many more frugal things, but the real change was in my attitude. It hit me after I dropped off a boot at the local shoe-repair place. One year before, I had dropped off the other boot because it was coming apart. At that time, I felt sorry for myself that I was having to repair five-year-old boots rather than buy new ones. But this year was different. As I walked home, I felt triumphant that I was making it through one more year with these boots. The burden of always wanting things has been lifted, and I feel good about what we do have. So thank you from the bottom of my heart.

—Laura Honan
Whitewater, Wisconsin

GOOD CUP, BAD CUP

Dear Amy,

I honestly didn't know that I didn't need to put dishwasher detergent in both cups for the regular wash cycle! Unless my machine is set to a prewash cycle, such as pot-scrubber, detergent placed in the open cup is wasted. It's amazing what you learn when you *read the manual*!

—Name withheld by request
Bakersfield, California

BUT HOLD THE MUSTARD!

Dear Amy,

This is a fun snack idea my kids like, and it is also a use for overripe bananas. It's called a banana dog. Spread peanut butter on a bun or bread, place the whole peeled banana on the bun/bread, and eat like a hot dog.

—Lori Kimbley
Bellevue, Nebraska

FRUGAL FUNGI

Dear Amy,

My grocery store sells huge bags of "tarnished" mushrooms very cheap. I buy the bags and sauté the mushrooms, sliced, 2 cups at a time, in 1 tablespoon butter or oil for about 3 minutes. I freeze them immediately in little bags. The mushrooms are very flavorful (no comparison to canned!) and make a frugal gourmet addition to soup, casseroles, etc.

—Ruth Laura Edlund
Bellevue, Washington

CHART SMARTS

Dear Amy,

For wrapping some of our gifts, we use obsolete aviation charts. They are often very colorful and unique. We have always gotten positive responses from the receivers. I'm a commercial pilot and am required to update my charts many times per year. Any active pilot should be able to supply you with obsolete charts.

—Stephen Craven
Edgewood, Kentucky

(Stephen sent a sample, and he is right—the charts do have an appealing, technical look. Older children, in particular, would appreciate these as wrapping, wall art, or for study. FZ)

SOAK FOR SUCCESS

Dear Amy,

I have five small, active children. It seems that every load of laundry includes dozens of stained items. I used to spend a lot of time pretreating and scrubbing spots. Now I just throw them in, turn the washer on, let it run for a few minutes, then turn it off and let everything soak for 15 to 20 minutes. They come out just as clean (except for tomato-based stains, which still need a good scrubbing). Saves pennies on pretreatment and lots of time.

—A grateful reader
Huntsville, Alabama

FROZEN ASSET

Dear Amy,

Keeping yeast in the freezer will prolong its life nearly indefinitely. Make sure it is in a well-sealed, moisture-proof container.

—Tammy Janelle
Caledonia, Mississippi

THE UNEMPLOYMENT OPPORTUNITY

Back in 1990, when I had been publishing the newsletter for just three months, I got a call from a man who said, "You should send copies of your newsletter to the New Road Map Foundation in Seattle. Your ideas are similar to theirs." I followed his advice. That was the start of a friendly relationship I've had with the foundation's founders, Joe Dominguez and Vicki Robin, ever since.

At that time, their ideas were available in a cassette-tape program. Since then, the same material has been published in a book called *Your Money or Your Life: Transforming Your Relationship with Money and Achieving Financial Independence* (Penguin, 1992). I weaseled a "review copy" of the tape program and spent a day listening to Joe while scraping paint off my porch.

His personal story is fascinating. Years ago, while employed as an investment counselor on Wall Street, he realized he was tired of working hard and spending his money on things that meant little to him. It occurred to him that if

he stopped spending in this way he could save the difference and become financially independent. He experimented with lowering his budget to the minimum level that felt comfortable to him. He began investing the surplus in supersafe treasury bonds. When he had saved about $100,000, this yielded an annual income of about $6,000, which happened to be the same amount he could live on. He quit his job in 1969, at the age of 31, and has lived on the same $6,000 per year ever since. To do this, he now shares housing and transportation and buys high-deductible health insurance. In the last 25 years he has devoted his time to working on various causes that are important to him. All of the proceeds from his tapes and books have been distributed to various causes through the foundation.

It was then that I first understood that financial independence wasn't exclusively for the super-rich—that it was possible for at least some frugal people with average incomes. But I doubted that it could apply to us. "What an amazing concept," I wrote back to Joe, "if you don't have kids." I pointed out that, at that time, we had four small children, and a year earlier we had bought a large fixer-upper that would consume most of our surplus cash for some time. Jim would be retiring from the military the following year and it was likely our income would be smaller. It had taken us seven years to save $49,000 at a time when we had relatively few expenses. We'd be hard-pressed just to pay off our mortgage early, much less save for an early retirement.

But since then, I've realized that financial independence is possible for a surprisingly broad range of people, including us. It's important to realize this, since the first, crucial step in achieving financial independence—or FI, as Joe and Vicki refer to it—is believing that you *can* reach it.

I'll concede that given the "strikes" we had against us, FI was possible only through a financial fluke. Within a year of its founding, the newsletter gained phenomenal national media coverage, and with the resulting income we were able to pay off our mortgage and could have just barely survived on Jim's pension, making us technically financially independent. In the last few years, we've saved for large future expenses.

I'll also concede that a great many of my readers have so many strikes against them that achieving FI early is very unlikely. While virtually any reader can put frugal strategies into practice, financial flukes are exceedingly hard to come by.

Nevertheless, FI is very relevant to some readers. I frequently encounter people who could achieve FI . . . and don't realize it. If at least some of the variables below describe you, you might be a candidate:

- You have no children, or your children will be grown by the time you are in your forties.
- You don't have excessive debts.
- You have a significant amount of disposable income. Single people with average incomes can achieve FI in five to ten years.
- You have low-cost housing, such as a paid-for, low-maintenance ranch house.
- Your work offers an early retirement option. Downsizing cor-

porations often offer attractive early-buyout deals, and military people can retire and receive a pension after 20 years.

• You have a financial windfall, such as an inheritance (it happens).

• You and your family members are reasonably healthy. Unfortunately, people with expensive preexisting conditions who receive medical coverage through their jobs may need to work simply to keep the coverage.

• You're young. Even if many of the above variables don't describe you, if you start early, you can overcome many obstacles.

Of these variables, not having children seems to be the one most crucial for achieving FI at a young age. As an example of one FI success story, I just received a letter from a 40-year-old single reader (who requested anonymity) from Phoenix who'll retire in December. Her net worth is nearly $180,000. Over the last few years she has saved 52 percent of her income.

Although families with children have achieved FI, it's far more rare. If you have kids and an average income, you can still shoot for retiring early; say, in your 50s.

Another with-kid option is achieving an increased freedom from the need to earn money. Consider my staffer Brad. Brad was the journalist who sold the story about us to *Parade* magazine, converted to tightwaddery, and then a year later came to work for me part-time. Frugality enabled him to leave his newspaper job (which he disliked) and build a successful freelancing career. This allowed his wife to quit her job (which she disliked); she's considering new career options. Recently, they paid off their mortgage. With one school-aged child, they now need about $15,000 per year to get by. Although not yet FI, Brad can be very selective about the freelance assignments he accepts. This in-between phase of *increased* FI is an option for virtually anyone.

FI through frugality is an important concept for anyone who ever said or thought, "I make so much money I don't need to be frugal." Typically, such people save 10 percent of their income and blow the remainder. They're assuming their desire to work and ability to generate income will be the same until they are 65. Striving for FI is a way to anticipate that these variables are likely to change.

Still, some people are cool to the idea of FI because it would be "boring." Work is the best part of their lives—either because they love

their work or because their home life offers little to keep them busy. The work-till-you're-65 thinking is so deeply ingrained in our culture that the question most frequently asked about my retirement is, "But what will you do?" Others assume I'm going to immediately gear up for another career. But with six kids, a huge house, a gigantic garden, many hobbies, and numerous volunteer opportunities, I will never be "bored." I can't imagine any job could be so attractive as to lure me into an away-from-home commitment anytime in the next decade.

Joe and Vicki point out that most who achieve FI have fewer at-home commitments than I do, and devote their newfound free time to a variety of volunteer jobs. They say that, given the hard work and discipline needed to achieve FI, they have never met anyone who achieved it and then sat around doing nothing.

In my view, the point of aiming toward FI isn't necessarily to never again work for money. Rather, it's to acquire the freedom to choose when, where, what, and how much work you do. I often reflect on something Vicki once said to me that seemed to sum up so much: "I buy my freedom with my frugality."

The Last Issues

TENDING TO GOALS

Ask most people what their goals are, and they'll say something like, "Well, I'd like to have a nicer house, and maybe some kids, and own my own business." I feel that this is why many people were attracted to my "American dream" story. Clearly, I was someone who had gotten what I wanted, and a lot of people wanted to find out how I did it.

The short answer is: through frugality. But the larger answer is that Jim and I set specific goals, and frugality was a tool that we decided we'd need to achieve those goals.

I admit, on the surface, an article about goals seems to be a bit of a yawn. But if everyone agrees that goals are important, then why is there so often an obvious gap between what people believe and what they actually do? Think about it. How many people do you know who are not significantly better off—or closer to their goals—today than they were ten years ago?

The reason for this gap is that there is a big difference between goal setting and goal achieving. People often don't realize that there is a very precise process they can go through to achieve their goals.

The process that Jim and I went through to save for and buy our home classically illustrates most of the key components of goal achieving:

- Settle on one goal or a few main goals. As I said in my premiere issue, I wanted a large family, a large pre-1900 house in the New England countryside, and I wanted to do this without resorting to day care. If, like me, you have more than one goal, be sure they're compatible: It's unlikely you can be a high-powered lawyer *and* a stay-at-home parent.

- Regularly discuss your goals with your spouse and children. Within the first few dates, I learned that Jim was open to the goals I wanted. I would *not* have continued the relationship if he had been dead set against them. It's no exaggeration to say that during the first seven years of our marriage, our goals, and particularly the home we wanted, were our most common conversation topics. We also involved our small children in our dream. We would point out nice homes and say, "If we save our money, someday we'll own a nice home like that."

- Do thorough research. We had mistakenly assumed that banks would allow us to carry the largest mortgage we could prove we could afford, which was more than most people could afford, since we were thrifty. When we learned about the 28-percent-of-your-income rule and did the math, we were shocked to discover that without a down payment, we could afford only a $70,000 house, which in most of New England is a nice house trailer. Then, living in Virginia, we began to subscribe to a magazine that featured homes for sale in New England. Suspecting that even this didn't give us a clear enough idea, we took a trip and

visited Realtors to look at houses in different parts of New England. We gained a feel for which areas were more affordable.

- Set a time frame to meet your goal. For us, this was determined by Jim's military service. Six years after we were married, Jim's final assignment before he retired would be to shore duty, and he managed to be transferred to Maine. This would be our first opportunity to buy a permanent home, and we resolved to have enough saved by then. Setting a date to shoot for is essential. If you don't, it's likely you'll drift for years without achieving your goal.

- Adjust your behaviors to meet your goals. After our scouting trip, we returned to Virginia in shock. We realized that, given our current savings rate, we wouldn't be able to afford a home that met our minimum-goal standards in most parts of New England. Moderate frugality wouldn't do; we needed to be more "extreme." I spent a week combing through our budget and tried to figure out every possible way to save more money. It was then that I devised my price book and many of the strategies I teach today. By learning the amount of money we would likely need and setting a time frame, we were able to establish the needed savings rate. If your goal is to complete a volume of work—say, remodeling your home—you can similarly set a finish date and a schedule by which you'll accomplish smaller remodeling tasks.

- Allow for a margin of error. Because we didn't know where Jim would be stationed for his final assignment, we couldn't precisely determine how much money we would need—some areas are much more expensive than others. Consequently, we saved with the most pessimistic scenario in mind. Even if you can be more precise, you should still factor in unexpected setbacks. Whether you are saving money or accomplishing a volume of work, seize every opportunity to do so ahead of schedule. I've found that many people who don't achieve their goals blame unforeseen circumstances, but establishing a cushion to deal with the unforeseen is part of the process.

- Don't expect goal achieving to always be comfortable—sometimes discomfort is necessary in the short term. After Jim got stationed in Maine we didn't find a house immediately. So we reluctantly moved into government housing while we shopped for the next 15 months. We soon realized that good buys were snatched up quickly and we would have to look at every possibility as soon as it came on the market. So every couple of weeks we packed up the kids for a marathon day of house drive-bys. We checked out 176 houses this way. It wasn't always fun or easy on the children, but it was worth it in the long run. Similarly, when I'm working on house-renovation projects, I often simply grit my teeth and plow through the boring or difficult parts, knowing the result will be worth it.

- Be prepared to take advantage of luck. There's a saying—"Luck is when preparation meets opportunity." In our case the preparation was having enough saved, being extremely familiar with house prices, and having forged a relationship with several Realtors. The opportunity was the extremely rare offering of a house that met or exceeded all of our desires and was in our price range. A Realtor tipped us off to this house before it had even been listed; we were one of three couples who made offers. We knew it was a good deal and offered full price with no contingencies.

Having said all this, let me address a few reasons why people don't set goals. Some people fear the failure of not meeting their goal. But even if you don't achieve your goal on schedule, you'll be better off for having more money in the bank or having more work done. Younger people may have no goals because they don't yet know what they want. But it's important for them to work toward the "unknown goal." Odds are that they will figure out what they want and, by being more financially secure or having more skills, be in a better position to achieve it.

A natural progression in life is that younger people have larger goals, while older people, having accomplished (or abandoned) most of their major life goals, have more modest ones. Nevertheless, setting and achieving goals is, in my view, an essential, lifelong pursuit.

Having achieved my big goals, I am now happily focused on smaller ones. We have a series of house-renovation projects planned for the next couple of years, and as my kids grow older, I want to spend more time helping them discover what they want to do with their lives and how to achieve the goals they set for themselves.

A HOME COMPUTER: TOOL OR TOY?

As my husband and staffers will attest, I'm not exactly a computer whiz. It took me two years to figure out how to do a "block move" in Wordstar, and the term "on-line" always makes me think more of laundry than cyberspace.

I make no apologies, however. While I agree that computers are needed for many business applications, I remain unconvinced that many people need them for personal use. Techies in my acquaintance agree that there are zillions of ways that messing around with computers can waste time and money but few that can truly make the average person's life significantly better.

So what follows is, I think, one of the rare levelheaded looks at the pluses and pitfalls of the computerization of America. This information is gleaned from books, inter-

views with experts, and reader letters we have received over the years.

We've gotten several letters from readers who say, essentially, "We're wondering if we should get a computer. Everyone seems to have them these days, and they are supposed to be very useful."

If you are "wondering" about the usefulness of a computer, you don't need one. Tightwads should get a computer for the same reason they would get anything else: because they have researched its capabilities and determined they really *need* it. In other words, they encounter many situations in daily life in which not owning a computer is a serious problem, and they can't get around it through borrowing, using school facilities, using a calculator, and so on.

For example, we had no justifiable use for a computer until we started the *Gazette*. I produced the first three issues on an electric typewriter, but if you have ever tried to wrap words around art with a typewriter, you'll appreciate how tough it was. After careful research, we bought the least expensive computer that could handle this job.

If you decide that you definitely need a computer, the next step is to determine exactly what you will use it for. This is a step that many people skip, and they end up overspending. The truth is that many uses for home computers, such as tracking your grocery bill, planning your garden, and creating kids' artwork, can be accomplished at least as quickly using old-fashioned paper and pencil.

Without question, one task at which computers excel is word processing. If you need one just for this, get a dedicated word processor. Brother makes an excellent one (model WP7550 J) with a 14-inch screen and an ink-jet printer that sells at department stores such as Service Merchandise for under $400. The other word-processing possibility is a used pre-486 computer. These are quite cheap; you should be able to spend less than $300. Ask around; it's likely one or more of your friends have a "starter" computer in storage. Or look for them in a "shopper" publication, and bargain ruthlessly. There's a glut of these things on the market; a good negotiator could persuade someone to *give* one away.

As for printers, one of the great bargains in the used market is the daisy-wheel printer. We use one to print my newsletter. These print supercrisp type and are mechanically extremely simple and durable. Granted, they cannot print graphics, but think: How often will you really need to print computer-generated pictures? On those rare occasions, we take a disk to Kinko's, a nationwide photocopy center, and use its state-of-the-art printer.

If you must have graphic printing capability, ink-jet printers are usually cheaper than laser-based ones. Marcie Funchess of Hurst, Texas, writes that her husband's company, Amerijet (800-555-2538), offers refills for *all* ink-jet printers, both color and black-and-white. "I am now refilling my HP 560 color cartridges for $1.11 apiece instead of paying $27.99 a cartridge at the store," she writes. George Funchess told us that the Canon BJC-4100 printer, which retails for about $320, is among the easiest to refill.

As your needs become more sophisticated, so will the features

and price of your computer. To the question "Which brand is best?" there is no hard-and-fast answer. But, again, I'd emphasize that the first question should be not "What should I buy?" but rather "What do I need to do?" Let all of your decisions flow from that question.

If the only reason you can come up with is that your kids will need a computer for schoolwork, explore other options first; for example, many schools offer computer access. In any case, wait until your kids are in high school. I do think a good case can be made for a home computer for college-bound students. A staffer's daughter is an honor student who hopes to go to medical school. A home computer would make her more competitive when applying for scholarships and better prepare her for college. Her father brought home an old computer from his business, and Jim shopped around and obtained the program she needed for $125.

The bottom line: Depending on your needs, a computer can be a bona fide tool or a nice toy. I'm not opposed to owning toys. I have a TV, a VCR, a boat, and so on. But I do object when people, including some on the financial edge, spend thousands on a computer and rationalize it as a tool when in fact it's more of a toy. So honestly evaluate your true need and ability to buy a computer before plunking down your money.

SHOULD YOU TAKE THE HIGHWAY?

In the previous article, I wrote about the usefulness, or lack of it, of a home computer. This article, about going on-line—or, as the media pundits put it, merging with the information superhighway—is really Part II. We just couldn't get it all in one issue.

The criterion for going on-line is similar to the one for buying a computer: You must have something specific you need to accomplish, and you must determine that venturing into cyberspace is the most cost- and time-effective way to do it. Otherwise, surfing the Internet just for kicks can be an expensive hobby.

Most people go on-line by subscribing to one of the commercial services such as America Online, CompuServe, or Prodigy. Typically, these services charge about $10 a month, for which you receive five hours of connect time; there's an additional charge for extra connect time. Be aware that, particularly in rural areas, there may not be a local number that you can call to get connected, so each time you log on you'll be racking up long-distance charges.

Lynette Wood of Bridgeport, Connecticut, suggests that you can reduce your fees on America Online (which is the largest on-line service) by becoming an on-line teacher. "You don't have to teach a class so much as be available for a homework room or to answer questions in your area of knowledge. Then your AOL bill goes down, you have fun, learn from the 800 other teachers on-line, and add an extra area to your resume." Teachers receive credit in their accounts. Go to keyword AAC (Academic Assistance Center), and request information on becoming a teacher.

There are many other ways to avoid on-line expenses. If you're

associated with a business or school that is on-line (and these days that includes nearly all of them), find out if you can get an account through the organization. You may even be able to do this through your public library—the one in the nearby town of Brunswick offers all library-card holders free text-only Internet access from their home computers.

As far as I can determine, going on-line has only two truly useful advantages.

First, there's E-mail. This is a letter-writer's dream come true. You type a letter, and with a few mouse clicks it's instantly sent on its way to the recipient's E-mail address. Note that E-mail isn't always *received* instantly, but wending its way through the tangled electronic web of the Internet usually takes no more than a couple of hours. Warren Crescenzo of Vineland, New Jersey, suggested an interesting alternative if E-mail is all you need. A company called Juno is offering free E-mail service, which is supported by advertising. Call (800) 654-JUNO for more information.

Second, there's research. You can find out almost anything you want to know, in a hurry, by going on-line. But I would emphasize that, unless you are in an information-intensive profession such as magazine freelance writing or high-finance investing, the services of a local research librarian should fulfill all of your research needs.

The one kind of information that you can get only on-line is "real people" advice that draws from an international group. For example, you can "chat"—that is, have a typewritten conversation—with other people, or you can "post" questions about obscure matters and get answers from others who read it.

There are many kinds of affinity groups that meet in cyberspace. Increasingly, readers tell me about ones devoted to swapping frugal tips and strategies:

Mary Lynne Ashley of Reston, Virginia, created the Unofficial *Tightwad Gazette* Fan Club Home Page at http://users.aol.com/maryfou/tightwad.html.

Doris O'Connell of Bethlehem, Connecticut, told us about two other groups; one is at http://pages.prodigy.com/Tightwadding-frugal-living. The other is at http://pages.prodigy.com/ASCD29A.

Another, called Frugal Corner, is at http://www.best.com/spiner/frugal.

And there is a newsgroup about frugality called misc.consumers.frugal-living.

Each of these Web sites contains "links" that can take you to related sites. At a friend's house, I did a little surfing on these sites and found them interesting but not indispens-

able. Readers who will miss their connection to other frugal people when I retire might find that these can help fill the gap.

However, Web sites have downsides. While they are usually monitored by a leader who periodically removes any bad information that's been posted, you might read that information before it's pruned. For example, I know of one case in which a scam was repeatedly added to and removed from one Web site. Some sites have a rule that users can't promote their businesses, but some do anyway.

Also, the letters that are posted are seldom edited for quality. Some are too vague, too narrowly applicable, or of doubtful value in some other way. The letters I published represent the top 5 percent of all those I received.

In short, in certain applications and used prudently, cyberspace has things to offer. But the loudest voices telling us *everyone* must be on-line tend to come from those individuals I call "techies." Some people are so enamored of new technology that they haven't thought hard enough about the cost versus the usefulness. Most people—myself included—don't have an overwhelming need for this.

TAKING SIDES ON SIDING

Since our 2,500-square-foot, turn-of-the-century Victorian house with attached barn received its handsome, two-tone paint job four years ago, we've gotten lots of compliments. Even strangers have stopped to tell us how much they like it.

Given this, I'm stunned when someone will say, "Now, all you've got to do is put up vinyl siding and you'll be all set!"

From their perspective, I guess, it seems logical. After all, I'm a tightwad, and we've all been told over and over that vinyl and aluminum siding (collectively called "substitute siding") will save money.

The fact is that I'm an old-house purist. I don't like vinyl siding, and even if it did save money, I wouldn't use it. Furthermore, I've always wondered whether, given the huge cost of installation, it really saves much, if anything.

So I was fascinated by an article sent in by Suzannah Talton of Newburn, North Carolina. In it, a group called the Rohm and Haas Paint Quality Institute suggests that maintaining a quality paint job can be cheaper than using substitute siding, even if you hire out the painting.

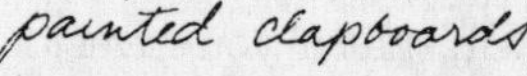

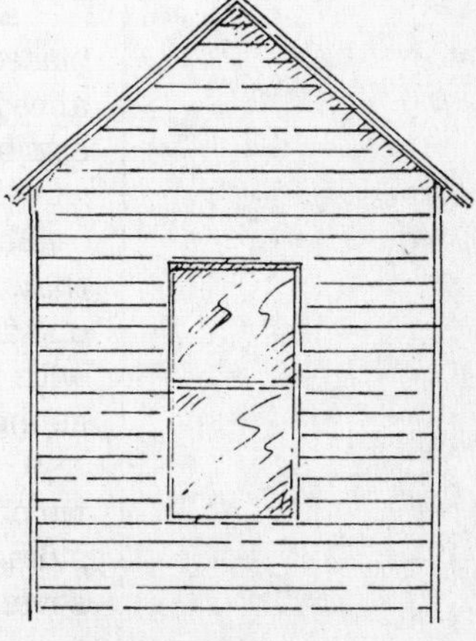

substitute siding

Suspecting a bias (since this is a paint-industry group), we obtained information from the Vinyl Siding Institute, which contends vinyl siding is cheaper in the long run.

Aside from industry groups, it appears that only historic preservationists have written on this issue. But these folks are also biased—they dislike substitute siding for the same reasons I do.

The only objective information I could find was a September 1992 article in *Decorating Remodeling* magazine. It said that, on new construction, substitute siding is about 25 percent cheaper than clapboards. But this doesn't address the question of whether you should install substitute siding over existing wood clapboards.

The reason this question remains unresolved is that there are simply too many variables, such as quality of materials, climate, and contractor fees, to definitively conclude that one alternative is cheaper than the other. Since I can't definitively answer this question, all I can do is list points to consider.

I admit I'm a teeny-weeny bit biased, so in the interest of a balanced article I'll list every positive attribute of substitute siding:

- It's maintenance-free.

Hope you can remember all that. Now, some of the potential disadvantages. Most of these deal with vinyl rather than aluminum siding, as vinyl is more popular:

- In the four cost comparisons we obtained, installing substitute siding over clapboards costs two to seven times as much as hiring a house to be repainted. Paint advocates maintain that if you invest the money you might have spent on substitute siding, you can use the interest to hire a crew to repaint your house every five to ten years and never touch the principal. Your situation will vary; get several estimates from painters and siding installers, and do the math.
- Preservationists agree that whenever possible, the original materials should be maintained. Brian Conway, an architectural historian for the state of Michigan, told us that some houses built as recently as the 1940s are approaching historic status. Substitute siding adds an extra layer that changes the overall look of the house. Windows often take on a recessed appearance, and trim and architectural details may be covered over or removed. Further, original clapboards are imperfect and so have a different character from too perfect substitute siding. Altering the look of a historic house can lessen its resale value. For the last 20 years, substitute-siding removal has become a common part of house restoration, and in certain historic neighborhoods grants are available to defray the cost. Certainly, some siding jobs are better than others, but those that least alter the look of the house require fussier (and more expensive) installation.
- Critics of substitute siding maintain that it prevents moist air from migrating out of the house and so promotes rot. The Vinyl Siding Institute says ventilation holes on the undersides of the vinyl "clapboards" allow plenty of ventilation, though a U.S. Department of Agriculture study disputes this. Critics also suggest that substitute siding is more likely

to hide moisture leaks and insect problems.

• The average homeowner probably lacks the skill to install substitute siding but can paint his own house. When the choice is between contractor-installed substitute siding and homeowner painting, paint is far cheaper.

• Substitute siding is easily damaged. A friend's vinyl-clad home has some rippled siding; it melted when the previous owner put a hot barbecue grill near it. Also, vinyl siding can break on impact in cold weather, and aluminum siding dents easily. Yet it can be difficult or even impossible to make a color-matching repair, because vinyl siding fades and because manufacturers may discontinue styles and colors. Rich Gottwald, technical director of the Vinyl Siding Institute, conceded that vinyl siding does fade and it can be difficult to make a good-looking repair.

• Substitute-siding colors are limited to a few shades, mostly pastels, so such houses have a sameness about them. In contrast, an interesting paint job can increase a house's value.

• Although substitute siding is sometimes touted as a source of insulation, the Federal Trade Commission states that substitute siding alone has negligible insulation value. You can tack insulation to the house's exterior before installing substitute siding, but experts agree there are much more cost-effective ways to save energy.

• Manufacturers' warranties do not cover problems stemming from damage or poor installation. The installer may offer a separate warranty, but these businesses are often short-lived.

• Substitute siding may not eliminate the need to paint. Better-looking siding jobs don't cover original wood trim and other details. Scraping and painting window trim is often the most laborious aspect of house painting.

Given the above arguments, the U.S. Department of the Interior contends that maintaining the original siding is usually the more economically sound approach, particularly if you wish to preserve the architectural integrity of your home.

Now, it isn't enough simply to present arguments against substitute siding. A major reason people are attracted to it is that painting their homes has become an endless ordeal. Some homes, for example, peel badly after just one year. To get more life out of a paint job, you should:

• Use a top-quality paint. Field tests by the Paint Quality Institute showed a top-quality acrylic latex paint lasted ten years, while an ordinary latex paint lasted only three to four years. On our house we used Benjamin Moore brand exclusively. It's perhaps the most expensive paint on the market, but it's consistently rated among the best by *Consumer Reports* magazine.

• Make an effort to diagnose your specific paint problem. Improper preparation and application, lack of a vapor barrier, incompatible paints, and so on all cause specific problems. Research this by talking with painters and paint dealers and/or reading magazine articles.

• Keep your scraper sharp. I suspect it's the scraping, rather than the painting, that most people dislike. A key reason might be that people don't sharpen their scraper

blades, and working with a dull blade *is* frustrating. We sharpen ours with a bench grinder, but a file also works well. When I do this, I actually find scraping satisfying.

- Realize that painting isn't all-or-nothing. Paint holds up unevenly due to many factors. When we assess our home, it's clear that some areas that are subjected to excessive moisture will need to be repainted every three or four years. The paint on our shingled barn will last many times longer. By tending to the few bad areas each year, we can greatly extend the entire paint job. Some people repaint one side or section of their house every year. I know seventy-year-olds who are still able to maintain large homes this way. By sticking with a quality stock-color paint, we've found that the touch-ups match perfectly.

In conclusion, I concede that people may not share my feelings about architectural purity and my affinity for house painting. But those things aside, the more important point is that people should not assume that substitute siding will be a good investment.

CONSIDER THE ALTERNATIVE

Amanda Wittig of River Falls, Wisconsin, writes: "Some years ago, I began reading and learning all I could about preventive and alternative medicines. I have put into practice much of what I've learned over the past three years, and our family is, in general, a much healthier group. I realize this is a controversial subject. But people need to realize there are alternatives to dragging family members to doctors and then filling them with medicine."

Amanda is right: Alternative medicine, which includes acupuncture, homeopathy, herbal and vitamin therapy, guided imagery, and other fields, is very controversial. But it is also being taken more seriously and is increasingly popular. In 1992 an Office of Alternative Medicine was established at the National Institutes of Health, and a 1993 Harvard study said one third of Americans use alternative therapies.

But how do you separate the wheat from the chaff? One of the most helpful and respected books on the subject to date is *Natural Health, Natural Medicine* (Houghton Mifflin, 1995) by Dr. Andrew Weil, a Harvard-trained M.D. who has made a lifelong, exhaustive study of which alternatives work and which don't. Weil is a professor at the University of Arizona School of Medicine and is widely regarded as the leading spokesman for alternative medicine.

I like the fact that Weil is not antimainstream. He contends that the typical drugs-and-surgery regimen of American medicine can be very useful, especially in life-or-death emergency situations. He says alternative systems *comple-*

ment mainstream medicine, in that they are often the best choice for less serious conditions . . . they can be gentler, safer, and cheaper.

I also like the fact that Weil provides the reader with specifics. Most of the book is a listing of various maladies such as insomnia, colds, ear infections, et cetera, each followed by recommendations for specific dietary changes, herbal dosages, and other natural therapies.

I'm not a doctor and don't feel qualified to say much more about this subject. But Dr. Weil's book is an illuminating read.

THE THIRD WORLD VERSUS DISNEY WORLD

A reader in Illinois sent the following letter, which I liked so much I am reprinting it in full:

Dear Amy,

This at first sounds like an expensive idea, but I suggest traveling abroad in order to save money! Well, maybe you would not have to go 'abroad.' Mexico may do just as well.

My husband and I met when we were both Christian missionaries in Uganda, East Africa. As a young nurse there, I learned many lessons, including:

- How to live without electricity or running water.
- That a hot shower could never be taken for granted.
- That I could grow to love and appreciate beans and rice and other simple, made-from-scratch meals.
- That letters can reach out and touch someone better than a phone call.

Above our dining room table is a framed photo of a smiling Ugandan woman collecting water to carry home to her family. That photo helps me remember our friends overseas who have much less than we do but who are joyful.

It also reminds me that it's okay to drive a 1981 car, to buy our clothes and toys at garage sales, and to eat oatmeal for breakfast.

Many mission agencies and nonprofit organizations offer one- or two-week service projects in developing countries away from the beaches and resorts. A taste of the Third World can go a long way in helping a person live a simpler but more full life.

—Dawn Getz
Champaign, Illinois

To Dawn's excellent letter, I would simply add that her experience is far from unique. Many people have told me that traveling to and living in Third World countries was the most important factor in their decision to live frugally. Personally, I have not done much international travel, but if I ever do, I would be much more interested in traveling to some of these countries than in visiting typical upscale tourist destinations.

THE 95¢ QUILT UPDATE

In my second book (see page 490), I wrote about how I had been making quilts from scrap and recycled materials for as little as $1 per quilt. Since then, I've made two more quilts with uniquely tightwad twists.

First, I made a quilt to use up the cut-off parts of holey jeans and (mostly) bright-colored corduroy pants. I used the three-dimensional

cube pattern, which consists of three diamond-shaped pieces. I used lighter denim on the left side of the cubes, darker denim on the right, and corduroy on the top. When cutting out the corduroy diamonds, I made sure the ridges always went in the same direction. I assembled each three-piece cube, then laid them out so the various colors were evenly dispersed. I sewed the cubes into rows, then sewed the rows together. Though this quilt had some purple and pink (from girls' slacks), the strong geometric pattern and bright solid colors made it look great in a boy's room.

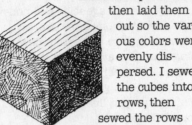

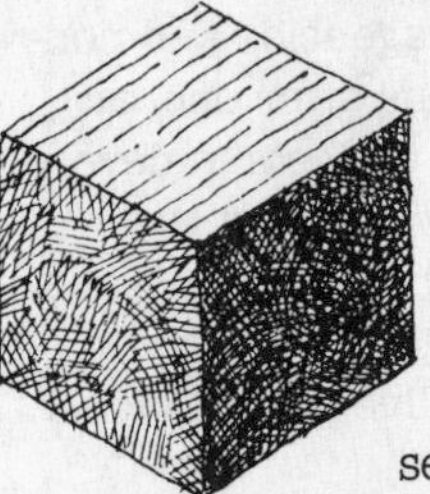

Heavy fabric does have a downside: The individual pieces can't be small, so there's more waste. Also, heavy fabric tends to make a heavy quilt unsuitable for warmer climates.

For the second quilt, I wanted to try the technique of sewing fabric scraps on precut squares of interfacing (which serves as a sewing surface only and doesn't provide strength). But I had resisted this, as it would require buying interfacing. Then one day I realized I could instead use squares cut from too-worn-to-repair cotton sheets. I thought I was an amazing genius until one day I looked at the flip side of an old quilt top and saw that the maker had used cloth Domino sugar bags—apparently interfacing had come to be used as a substitute for old cloth.

Sewing scraps onto precut squares versus sewing scraps together has several advantages. It's fast, as you sew scraps onto the square and then trim all the scraps at the same time. The completed blocks have a more uniform size, making the final assembly easier. And precut blocks enable you to make certain types of designs.

A common design made this way is the "crazy quilt." Various-shaped scraps are seemingly randomly sewn on (right sides together and ironed over, so the seam is hidden), starting from the middle and working outward in a roughly circular pattern.

However, I discovered that the diagonal-block design is extremely fast, easy, and uses up very tiny pieces of fabric. In this design you precut strips of fabrics to the same width. You sew the first scrap on a diagonal. The next strip is sewn over the first (right sides together, ironed over, so the seam doesn't show), and you proceed until you complete the square. Trim the strips to the precut square.

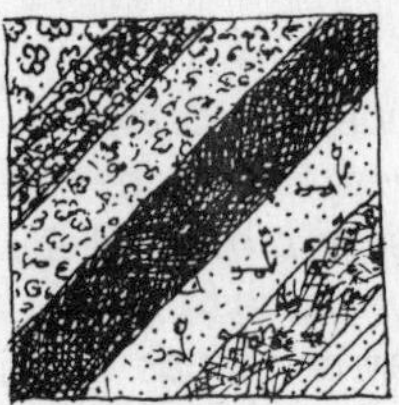

This basic design can accommodate variations. I used a solid red diagonal in the middle in combination with red printed fabrics. You could also vary the fabrics, corner to corner, from dark to light. I've seen this design used where the maker simply stayed with a basic color (such as blue prints), and it was still successful.

At this rate, I'm cranking out just one or two quilts a year—for reasons more to do with available sources of fabric than with my

available time. I tend to work in spurts when I find fabric scraps that will work with one of my quilts-in-process. Early on, each quilt-in-process is claimed by a child, who shares in the excitement of watching it being made.

FILL THE EMT HOURS

Dear Amy,

My husband and I are volunteer firefighter-EMT's with our local department. In New York this requires 110 hours of training, and the benefits of this are many. The first, obvious one is saving lives and helping the community. Then there's the great people you meet. And being an EMT has made me a better mother, because I can determine if a problem is a real emergency. But there are other perks. Anytime there is a large gathering of people, medical and/or manpower help is needed to ensure safety. Examples of such events include county fairs, air shows, concerts, et cetera. Usually, you can get free admission for yourself and your family and a meal voucher as well. It's very nice to be able to give something other than money—it's much more personal.

—Laura Power
Galway, New York

SAVE . . . DON'T SHAVE

Dear Amy,

Another alternative to "A Whisker's Difference" (see article on page 796 about reducing shaving costs). About four years ago I decided to grow a beard to save money and help our environment. I

use a hair/beard clipper that I obtained for free and a straight razor without soap. Since both items will last indefinitely, my annual cost has become 36¢ for electricity. It is also less time-consuming than completely shaving.

—Anthony Krebs
Rapid City, South Dakota

HIT C ECONOMICALLY

Dear Amy,

A piano tuner told us that our 90-year-old upright piano wasn't worth the $60 tuning fee. My husband is a musician and has an electronic chromatic tuner, which cost much less than $60. He was able to tune the worst keys himself, using the wrench he uses to tune his hammered dulcimer. While not a professional job, it's good enough until we can afford a decent piano. And now, when a key goes out, he can get it in shape fairly easily.

—Cynthia DeGrand
Columbus, Ohio

CAFFEINE-FREE DELICACY

Dear Amy,

You can take ground barley, put it on a cookie sheet, brown it until

it is almost burned, and it makes a good, Postum-like drink. I understand you can also use other grains the same way.

—Erma Thompson
West Jordan, Utah

SHOT SELECTION

Dear Amy,

Many larger stores that offer photo-processing services will refund the price of any developed picture that you don't like. Call around to find out who in your area offers this goofproof policy, as many don't advertise it. When your photos come back from developing, sort through them, choose those that you don't want (eyes closed, blurry, bad angle, et cetera), and return them to the photo counter. In our area we get a credit of 12¢ to 15¢ for each returned picture.

—Denise Hackney
Ann Arbor, Michigan

ELEMENTARY TIP

Dear Amy,

A friend told us that we need not replace our failing 52-gallon electric hot-water heater if it was not leaking. All we had to do was empty the tank, remove the two heating elements, take them to our local plumbing-supply store, buy replacements, and install them. The elements cost $21 for both.

—Christine Burton
Media, Pennsylvania

DISCLOTHESURE

Dear Amy,

When buying clothing at a store, ask for a discount if you notice the garment has a slight flaw. I have received discounts in regular department stores, outlet stores, and discount clothing stores. The secret is to find the manager, tell him or her you would like to buy the item but it has a flaw (point it out). Ask "Could I have a discount if I buy it?" Let the manager be the first to name the discount. I usually expect 10 percent to 20 percent off, but my best success was with a pair of Reeboks at an outlet store. They were normally $45, marked down to $30. There was a slight smudge of dirt on one toe. I found the manager, and he suggested half off! I got a $45 pair of shoes for $15!

—Jill Amos Gibbons
Alexandria, Virginia

LATTE FOR WORK?

Dear Amy,

I used to buy a $2 cafe latte every morning on my way to work. But I've found it's very easy to make. Just microwave ½ to ¾ cup of milk for one to two minutes, then mix with ½ cup strong coffee. The cost is 16¢ a cup.

—Alice Tao
Irvine, California

NO CREEPY, JUST T.P.

Dear Amy,

I have used your storage-under-the-bed idea and found an extra advantage. When my daughter was afraid there were monsters under her bed, I told her there was no room for monsters because of all the toilet paper under there.

—Elizabeth Rippee
Richland, Washington

PARSIMONIOUS PLAYPEN

Dear Amy,

In the cooler months, or even in the summer when it is not filled with water, our cheap blue kiddie pool serves as a "kid corral." We put a blanket in the bottom and fill it with miscellaneous toys. The kids sit inside and play while we do yard work, refinish furniture, et cetera. Our two children are very young, so this is an ideal way to keep them safe and within view.

—Terre Kimmel
Ft. Hood, Texas

REDO THE MATH

Dear Amy,

As a home-schooler, one of the best money-saving ideas I've come up with is a method for making workbooks reusable. I purchase plastic page protectors (100 for $7), cut my workbooks apart at the binder, and then put the workbook together in a three-ring binder.

Then washable markers can be used and the answers can be wiped off, leaving the expensive workbook usable for my next child. This can be quite a saving, because some of our workbooks cost more than $30!

—Lucie Dufendach
Kokomo, Indiana

FORGO THE PHOTO?

Trudy Mills of Gardnerville, Nevada, writes, "I have two children in school, with two more to come. I was shocked by the cost of school pictures. Buying them seems to be somewhat traditional for most families, including mine as a child. I do like to have a nice yearly portrait of the kids to help record their growth and changes through the years. But with large families, especially, the cost must be prohibitive. Our school even does two sets of pictures, one in the fall and one in the spring. What does your family do regarding school pictures?"

I'll respond to Trudy's last point first. Recently, I've noted that many schools (not ours, fortunately) have begun taking photos twice a year. This is ridiculous. Rather than a fifth-grade photo, do we really need early-fifth-grade and late-fifth-grade photos in our albums? Parents in at least one school in Maine rose up as a group and demanded that the second picture-taking session be dropped. The principal complied. I urge

tightwad parents everywhere to follow suit. If you don't succeed, at least *don't* buy the second set.

As far as what our family does, if a child wants a school picture, we always buy the cheapest package deal. If the child doesn't want a picture, we don't buy any at all. Because just one shot is taken, school photos are often unflattering. My kids agree that, more often than not, they dislike their school photos. We have an impressive accumulation of bad photos, never out of the package, still in our paper-junk drawer, that are years old. You *can* be a good parent and not buy a school picture.

UH OWE!

As we pursue our frugal lifestyles, tightwads can sometimes get discouraged when we look at the extravagant spending patterns of others. We ask ourselves: Is everyone really making that much more money than I am?

The answer: No—everyone is deeper in debt than we are. Kim Telley of Peoria, Illinois, sent me an eye-opening Associated Press article about the extraordinary spiral of credit-card debt that has gripped many Americans. For some reason, perhaps because I get so many positive letters from happy, successful tightwads, I'd gotten the feeling that Americans are becoming at least somewhat more responsible about money. I have even read several articles about how frugality is a hot, growing trend. But the fact is that things are getting far worse in a big hurry. Consider:

- The average household has four credit cards with outstanding balances of about $4,800. That's up from two cards and $2,340 just five years ago.
- As of last fall there were 376 million Visas and MasterCards in circulation, up 80 percent from five years ago.
- Consumers owe $360 billion on their credit cards, double the level in 1990.
- Credit-card debt comprises one third of all consumer loans—that's up from less than one fourth a decade ago.

The lesson to take away from these statistics is that, for the first time in history, you can no longer accurately assess a person's financial status simply by observing how he or she lives. Now much of the middle class is living affluently—and careering toward disaster. My staffers and I can think of instances where we were mystified at how someone was doing better than we were—and then within a few years we discovered that the person in question carried two mortgages or even went bankrupt.

Consequently, it's important for tightwads to focus on their own financial lives and feel no sense of failure if they don't keep up with

the apparent wealth of their friends and relatives.

A DIFFERENT SPIN ON WASHERS

There are lots of common-sense ways to save water: installing low-flow showerheads and low-flush toilets, careful landscaping, shutting off the faucet while brushing teeth, and so on. But one often overlooked alternative is the use of front-loading washing machines.

Front-loaders have been the standard in energy-conscious Europe for decades. In this country, I've read a number of vague references to how they can save, but in typical tightwad fashion, I wanted hard numbers. After some digging, I found those numbers . . . but before I get into that, some basic information:

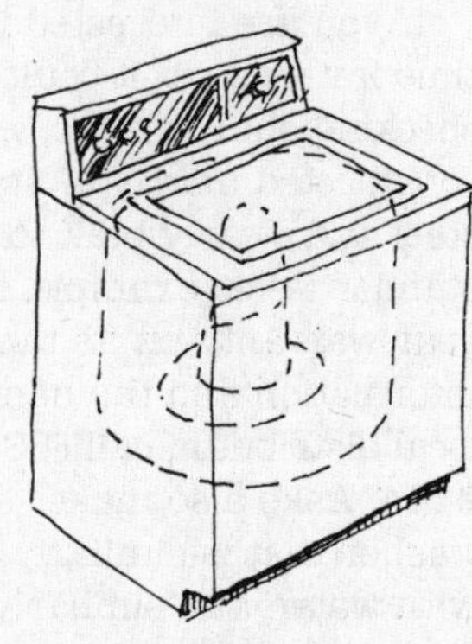

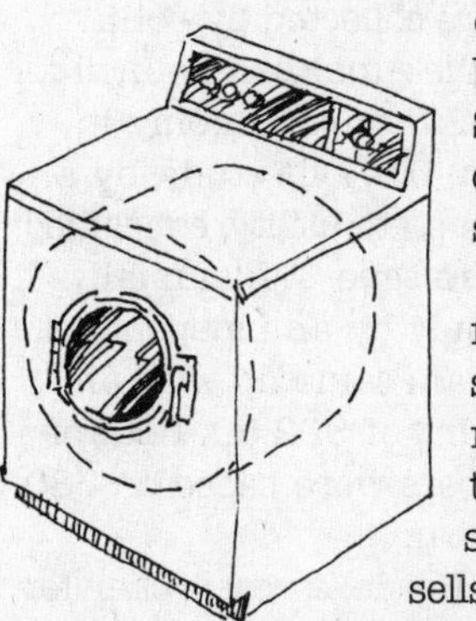

Unlike the typical American top-loading machine, front-loaders feature a horizontal drum that lacks a central agitator. (Actually, a more technically accurate term than "front-loader" is "horizontal axis" machine, since at least one model loads from the top, through a trap door in the drum's side—but we'll stick with the more common term in this article.) They save money in several ways:

- They use less water. Front-loaders use from 11 to 15 gallons per load, compared to 40 or more gallons for top-loaders. This represents a saving in water bills, sewage bills, and water-heating bills. The savings are significantly higher if you heat your water with electricity rather than natural gas.
- They use less detergent. Because they use about a third of the water consumed by a top-loader, they also use about a third of a top-loader's detergent requirement.
- They shorten drying time. The typical top-loader spins clothes at about 700 r.p.m. Front-loaders usually spin faster; one made by Asko, a Swedish company, spins at 1,500 r.p.m. A sales representative for a store that sells Asko washers contended that this can cut drying time in half.
- Most of the company officials and others that I interviewed contended that front-loaders make your clothing last longer, though none could cite a specific study to prove this.
- Finally, *Consumer Reports* has concluded that front-loaders get clothes cleaner.

Front-loaders do have a couple of disadvantages:

- They are more expensive than top-loaders. A typical high-quality top-loading machine costs

from about $450 to $600. Front-loading machines run from about $800 for domestic models up to $1,200 for top-of-the-line European models such as the Asko.

- Some sources say they have somewhat smaller capacities than the larger top-loaders, although an Asko salesman told us that front-loaders can be packed more tightly and still clean well, so he contended the capacities are roughly equal. The comparison studies we looked at were based on the assumption that the capacities of the two kinds of machines were about equal.

Two research studies on the savings of front-loaders versus top-loaders were collected by John Morrill of the American Council for an Energy-Efficient Economy in Washington, D.C. One study, by a Washington state utility, concluded front-loaders save $72 annually. Another study by an independent research team came up with an annual saving of $92.30. Both of these numbers were based on 380 loads per year.

Richard Heede, a researcher for Rocky Mountain Institute, an environmental-research group, estimates the average savings from using front-loaders is about $65 annually.

So these three numbers average out to $76. If you add in Morrill's estimated annual dryer-energy savings of $25 to $30, this works out to an annual savings of about $100, which means you would recoup the extra cost of a front-loader in three to seven years.

Note, however, that the savings can be much smaller or larger. If, like us, you get your water from a well, have a septic tank, wash in cold, and hang everything to dry, your saving with a front-loader would be almost nil. But if you pay for municipal water and sewer, wash in warm or hot water, and always use an electric dryer, the payback time could be under two years.

Which front-loader should you buy? Heede says that though there are a couple of American-made front-loaders on the market now, your best bet may be to wait for a Maytag version, due to be released by year's end. A Maytag spokesperson told me it will be available wherever Maytags are sold.

If you are interested in a lifetime investment, it could be worth checking out the Asko, which is constructed mostly of stainless steel and clearly built to a higher standard—for example, it has a 25-year warranty on its tank. For information and the name of a local distributor, call (800) 367-2444. Asko also makes a dishwasher that is similarly frugal with water, and similarly expensive up front.

THE POSTAL PRINTER

More and more people are starting home-based small businesses. But it can be expensive to project a professional image on the typical start-up's shoestring budget.

So I was interested in a letter from Scooter Marriner of Artas, South Dakota, about a deal offered by the United States Postal Service. The USPS will print your return address on envelopes in business

(#10), enclosure (#9, which fits inside a #10), and small (#6¾) sizes. These envelopes are already stamped with first-class postage. You have to order at least 50, delivery can take four weeks, and the USPS generally does not print logos. But the price is usually lower than that offered by printing companies, even factoring in shipping charges.

Here's the math: The cost for 50 printed, stamped #10 envelopes from the USPS is $19.20, plus a $3.20 shipping fee, or $22.40 total. This equals 45¢ per envelope. Subtract the 32¢ postage, and the cost of each printed envelope is 13¢. Bulk purchasing drops the price: If you buy 500 #10 envelopes, the cost is $176.40, plus a $5.20 shipping fee, or $181.60. This equals 36¢ per envelope. Subtract the postage, and the cost per printed envelope is 4¢.

The latter price, in particular, was lower than the price offered by printers in our area. Be sure to call around and get your own estimates before taking advantage of this offer. For information, call or write:

Philatelic Fulfillment Service
Center
United States Postal Service
P.O. Box 419208
Kansas City, MO 64141
(800) 782-6724

SCRATCH BACK-TO-BACK

Recently, at least two respected national magazines have suggested that a clever way to save on midweek airline fares is to employ "back-to-back" ticketing. It works like this: You buy two round-trip tickets, each of which encompasses a Saturday-night stay. Then you use only the departing "leg" of the first ticket, and the return "leg" of the second. Because midweek fares sometimes cost more than twice as much as stay-over-a-Saturday-night fares, this can save money.

But I was surprised to see these recommendations, because a couple of years ago, at the suggestion of a reader, we researched back-to-back ticketing and concluded it was a bad idea. Why? Technically, purchasing an airline ticket is a contractual arrangement between you and the airline. When you buy it, you are obligated to meet the restrictions. If you look carefully at many tickets, they specifically ban back-to-back ticketing. Several airline-company representatives told us that if they find out that you are employing this practice, they will yank your ticket—and if you happen to be 3,000 miles from home when this happens, that's your tough luck. One representative told us that he knew of several instances in which this had actually happened.

We further checked this out with an official of the Federal Aviation Administration. He said that back-to-back ticketing is not illegal, but he confirmed that the airlines are within their right to yank your ticket if they specifically ban the practice and they discover that you are using it.

So *don't* use back-to-back ticketing. Stick with legitimate ways of reducing airfare, such as comparison shopping, using frequent-flier miles, and staying over on a Saturday night whenever possible.

FREE FROM THE M.D.

A couple of times in previous issues, we have mentioned that you can sometimes avoid having to purchase a prescription; just ask for some of the free samples your doctor receives from pharmaceutical companies.

But it turns out that free drugs are just a small part of the bounty that pours into doctors' offices. Rebecca Rogers, a licensed practical nurse from McBee, South Carolina, writes that, if her experiences are any indication, doctors truly receive an embarrassment of riches. "I work in a family practice/general-care doctors' office. In our office we have received hundreds of educational videos and books, as well as hand lotions, baby formula, diapers, Ensure (by the case), Pedialyte, thermometers, bandages, baby bibs, paper cups, toilet paper, latex gloves, syringes, antacids, aspirin, Tylenol, Advil, Children's Motrin, Metamucil, condoms, thousands of Post-it–type notepads, pens, pencils, stickers and toys for kids, trash bags, and enough cardboard boxes to go around the world. Also, some vaccines are shipped in Styrofoam coolers with dry ice." Rebecca reports that she used the dry ice to make "spooky fog" on the front porch at Halloween.

Rebecca reminds us not to overlook prescription samples, which pile up quickly and which doctors are glad to give away so that they can free up the storage space. "I personally have discarded hundreds of outdated birth control pills and other medicines because they had passed their expiration dates." You should never take outdated medicines, she says, but these could have been given away and used before they expired.

My experience is that while doctors will sometimes offer samples, don't expect it. Generally, the doctor does not personally handle the incoming flood of samples and may not be aware of what's on hand. But if you ask, and your request is passed on to the nurse, you may find that all or part of your prescription can be filled from office samples.

CLOSE ENCOUNTERS OF THE THRIFTY KIND

Longtime readers have realized by now that I think birthday parties are important. We manage a friends-over party every two years per child. I work hard on them because I enjoy creating a memorable event for such a large group of kids. I also see them as a highly visible way to demonstrate creative frugality.

The year Neal turned nine, he had a UFO-theme sleepover party. This one is worthy of a write-up because it wowed a hard-to-wow age group and many elements could be duplicated by other parents. Because of the strong design possibilities, other parents could even improve on what I did, using different resources and game ideas, for instance.

Although I do just a little each day, I need about ten days to execute a good party. This lead time allows me to brainstorm with others, research, experiment with ideas (and readjust for failed ones), and make decorations. It never comes quickly; it's a jelling, building process.

To begin, our whole family brainstorms together. In this case, we wrote down everything we could think of related to UFO's . . . colors, sounds, materials, activities, and so on. We voiced any ideas, no matter how "stupid," as these can trigger others' ideas.

Next, I inspected every corner of our home and barn looking for UFO-like raw materials, especially ones that were metallic or offered some sort of lighting. I came up with Christmas lights, used scraps of metallic and mylar gift wrap, a jumbo roll of aluminum foil, and three trash-picked Mylar window shades.

Neal and I went to the library and checked out UFO books. I also cruised through salvage, party, and craft stores to look for cheap resources and expensive ideas that I could duplicate.

To decorate, I completely emptied our project/guest room of all furniture so it would look UFO-sterile. I hung the three shades together to block windows. We put up strings of blue and green Christmas lights. I made Mylar stars for the ceiling and walls and hung metallic decorations from the ceiling with thread. I covered the top of my project table with foil (salvaged after the party). It looked iridescent with the lights.

Once decorated, I thought the room needed something more. So I made a 4-foot by 8-foot mural of the planets on some black paper that's normally used to control garden weeds (lightweight tar paper could also work). I used plates to draw various-sized circles and colored them with ancient pastels (art chalks), using encyclopedia pictures for reference (the trick to making them look spherical is leaving a shadow on the same side of each planet). The kids drew "billions and billions" of stars and comets. The project took about an hour and a half and looked so good we hung it in Neal's room after the party.

As for the actual party, we had a marshmallow fight (it's a thematic stretch, but we explained it's a "Marshian" game) and played a panty-hose–helicopter game—*very* silly and alien-looking). A valiant try but not awesome was the UFO we dangled from the highest loft in the pitch-black barn, made from Christmas lights, a circle of metallic rigid insulation, a disposable cake plate, aluminum foil, and egg cartons.

The most successful activity was making UFO's from store-bought "moon pies" (a.k.a. marshmallow pies). We used leftover salvage-store–purchased colored-foil–covered Easter candy (chocolate kisses and tiny peanut butter cups), as well as gumdrops, tiny M&M's, and Quaker Oats' version of Froot Loops (a free sample). The candy was "glued" to the moon pies using chocolate frosting (Jim and I manned the frosting bags) or attached with toothpicks. Although I presented the kids with a prototype so they would get the idea, each created a unique UFO.

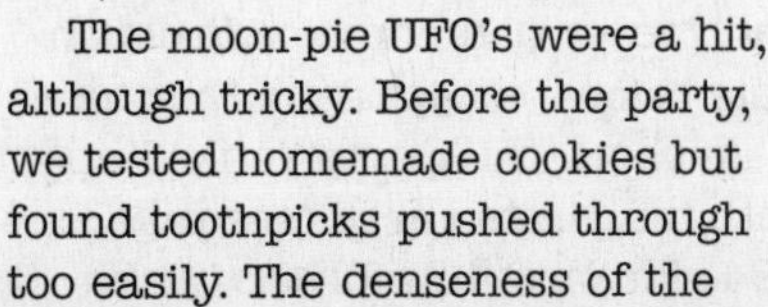

The moon-pie UFO's were a hit, although tricky. Before the party, we tested homemade cookies but found toothpicks pushed through too easily. The denseness of the

moon pie makes this project work. They should also be refrigerator-chilled to make them more dense. In terms of looks and stability, the only successful UFO feet were made of three sets of two toothpicks pushed into a single gumdrop "landing pad." Parents may want to help on this part. The feet are best attached midproject (after heavy construction is completed) and flared slightly outward. If attached with toothpicks, some harder candies, like jelly beans and kisses, need to be prepoked with a harder-than-a-toothpick object (such as a large needle).

These UFO's served as an activity, and they replaced birthday cake. They could be made in advance for a younger kid's party.

The kids ate their UFO's and ice cream ($1 per half gallon from a salvage store) on blue-plastic (disposable but reused) plates on the foil-covered table. We sprang for store-bought green drinks in plastic bottles (11¢ each). Green lemonade was provided for refills.

By chance, we had a photo shoot earlier that day (for the August 1996 issue of *Family Fun* magazine), and the magazine brought intensely green goo (see page 478) for a prop. This entertained the sleepover guests far into the night as well as turning their hands faintly Martian green.

For breakfast, Jim made doughnuts (see page 597). The boys stood in line to dip them in chocolate sauce and sprinkles or shake them in a bag with confectioner's sugar. One boy commented that he had "never had homemade doughnuts before, except from the store."

In short, this party ranked up with the pirate party (see page 194) for most fun for the buck.

THE PUFFY PANCAKE

Barbara Sunamoto of Vancouver, Washington, sent us a wonderful recipe for a dish she calls a giant pancake. We call it a puff pancake, because it puffs dramatically when baked. This is cheap and quick yet elegant enough for guests. It is excellent served with syrup or preserves.

2 eggs
½ cup flour
½ cup milk
¼ teaspoon nutmeg
5 tablespoons butter*
Peeled, thinly sliced apples (optional)
2 tablespoons confectioners' sugar (optional)
2 tablespoons lemon juice (optional)

Preheat the oven to 425 degrees. Blend the eggs in a blender until foamy, then add the flour, milk, and nutmeg, and blend well. Melt the butter in a heavy ovenproof skillet or a 9-inch by 13-inch baking dish in the oven. When the butter is melted, swirl it to coat the pan. Put a layer of sliced apples on the bottom if desired, then pour in the batter all at once. Bake for 15 to 20

minutes until puffed and golden. Sprinkle sugar over all (if using apples, you may substitute cinnamon and granulated sugar), and cook one minute more. Sprinkle with lemon juice if desired, cut into wedges or squares, and serve.

*Barbara says she has used 3 tablespoons successfully.

PRINT HINT

Dear Amy,

I had hoped to buy four floral-type prints for our newly redecorated dining room but just couldn't afford them. I went to the Victoria's Secret shop at our mall and bought bath bubbles that come in those beautiful envelopes with floral designs. I already had four matching frames with mats the right size. I painted the frames gold and inserted the envelopes. The framed pictures turned out beautifully.

—Kathy Haubner
Cincinnati, Ohio

GO AHEAD, BAKE MY WAY

Dear Amy,

Here's a way to save even more time and energy with muffins. Bake a double batch in a 9-inch by 13-inch cake pan. You can cut the "muffins" into 15 pieces. These are easier to split, they can be baked two pans (four batches) at a time, and there are no muffin pans to grease or wash and no papers to buy. We use glass baking pans because they are much easier to grease and clean.

—Lisa Reese
Mosinee, Wisconsin

EXERCISE IN FRUGALITY

Dear Amy,

I gained 30 pounds in 18 months on a new job where I cannot bike to work. Exercise books advise getting off the bus a couple of stops earlier each way and walking the remaining distance. Instead, I decided to walk the five miles to and from work three days a week. This is a good plan for people who live in areas where mass transit is available but expensive. In my case, it eliminated the need for a health club, I get great ideas about work and home while I walk, and I'm spending $15 per month less on transportation.

—Mary Campbell
Annandale, Virginia

FEEL GOOD OIL OVER

Dear Amy,

If you have dry skin, buy a cheap brand of olive oil. Put it in a small dispenser bottle—it can be a small dishwashing-liquid bottle. Keep it in the tub or shower. While you still have some moisture on your skin, apply the oil. You will feel as though you have new skin.

—Jean Keiter
Tucker, Georgia

A KNOCKOUT PUNCH

Dear Amy,

For a different summer drink, a children's party punch, or punch for the most elegant wedding, try this amazingly simple and low-cost recipe:

1 package unsweetened strawberry Kool-Aid (or generic)
1 cup sugar (or less)
1 6-ounce can frozen orange juice
2 quarts water

I have used this for all sorts of occasions, and everyone raves over it but can never figure out what's in it.

—Karen Lancaster
Alvy, West Virginia

FIGHT FRIZZ FRUGALLY

Dear Amy,

I wasn't blessed with the kind of hair that looks good no matter what cheap shampoo I use, so I must buy a quality salon shampoo and conditioner. But even so, I've found a way to be frugal. First, I purchase the products at cosmetology schools, where prices tend to be discounted. Second, one local school has a program where you can bring back your empty bottle for refilling at half the price. It's also environmentally friendly, since I never throw away the bottles.

—Mauri-Mac Heath
Franklin, New Hampshire

R. F. DEALS

Dear Amy,

In our part of the country there are a lot of farm auctions. The best reason for us to go is a small item that appears near the end of the sale listing: miscellaneous lumber. I have seen huge stacks go for $5.

—Paul and Vesta Romine
Ligonier, Indiana

(At an estate auction, a part-time antique dealer told me he often finds his best deals in antiques and collectibles at farm auctions. Estate auctions are heavily attended by dealers, so great deals are rare. Farm auctions are attended by those wishing to buy farm equipment, so other types of merchandise go very cheaply. FZ)

TUITION INTUITION

Dear Amy,

In graduate school, one thing that really helped me maintain the right perspective on things was to break down my tuition payments and figure out how much tuition I was paying per class per week. It's so easy to make that big payment before the quarter begins and then just forget about it. I divided out my tuition by the number of weeks, and the numbers told me that it was as though, when I walked into a classroom, I was handing a $100 bill to the professor. This was motivation to me to get everything I could out of every class (and, certainly, never miss a class unless there was an emergency) and to do each assignment thoroughly and completely.

—Carol Blair
Chicago, Illinois

TRANSPORTABLE TREAT

Dear Amy,

A good way to use up birthday cake and make a good lunch-box dessert: Slice a piece of cake through the middle, and then flip over the frosting side, making a "sandwich" with the frosting in the middle of the cake. Slides into a plastic Baggie without a mess.

—Annette Graham
Huntsburg, Ohio

FOOD, FUEL, AND FRIENDS

Dear Amy,

My elderly neighbors can't get out as much as they used to, so now they go with me when I shop, and they pay for the gas. Not only do I get my fuel paid for, but I get good company as well. I started doing this when I called them when it snowed this winter and figured (rightly) that they might want to get some things at the store but might be hesitant to go out themselves. I started going to the store for them. Then, when the weather turned better, they started going with me. Everyone benefits from this arrangement.

—Deborah Lange
Seattle, Washington

LITERARY LEGACY

One fall day when Rebecca was six, she asked if I would do something special just with her. She had noticed that many of her siblings had enjoyed special events and trips, either with the school, with Scouts, or with a parent. For instance, when I visited my grandmothers in Massachusetts, I took the twins into Boston to see the sights and eat lunch at McDonald's (calm down, we used coupons).

I spent a day considering options that would provide a similar "wow" but cost little or nothing. Then I asked if she would like me to read a "chapter book" just to her. She liked that idea.

So we began reading the Laura Ingalls Wilder "Little House" series. I have the same well-worn hardcover set that I read as a kid. Every evening, we would snuggle under an afghan in my bedroom and read a couple of chapters. The revelation was not that Becca enjoyed this but that the ritual soon became *my* favorite time of the day.

The frugal fun of reading to children seems, on the surface, *way* too obvious a subject for an article. But I asked various people about their families' habits and have concluded that reading longer chapter books to kids is an option often not explored by parents, and the pleasure of it was a huge surprise to me.

Like most parents, I read "kiddie" books to my children, particularly when the older ones were small. After we moved to Leeds, several things made this difficult to continue. We don't have a town library, and though we pay the $20 annual fee to borrow books in

another town, returning them is so inconvenient that I usually have to pay late fines. While we have a stash of yard-sale kiddie books, it frustrates me to read the same ones over and over. And it became almost impossible to read books with six kids crammed on our couch, including wiggling toddler twins who would grab at the book from both sides. I had to hold the book at arm's length, jerking it from side to side so they couldn't reach it. So call me a bad mother, but I gave up on the daily ritual.

In contrast, reading chapter books to one child at a time has been a great pleasure. The older children read independently and so weren't interested in joining us. We tried to include the four-year-old twins, but their attention span was too short.

So Becca and I read through the eight books in the "Little House" series and moved on to other books. These included one of my childhood favorites, *Little Britches* by Ralph Moody, an autobiographical story set in turn-of-the-century Colorado (this was homogenized into a Disney movie, but the original book is rich in gritty real-life details). The following spring I began reading the "Little House" series again—to Brad and Laura, who, six months later, were mature enough to sit through a single chapter. And then nine-year-old Neal asked if he could sit in on Becca's reading.

In the summer, it stays light in Maine until almost 9:00 P.M. The kids and I both have outdoor things we do in the evenings, so our readings became less frequent. Once we began the descent into the cold, dark winter, the readings picked up again.

I've thought about why this reading has been so successful for us:

- I recognized that there's a window between the ages of four and eight when kids are old enough to understand chapter books but not old enough to read these books themselves (although one parent I asked said she read chapter books to her kids when they were older and younger than this age).
- Chapter books provide a continuing story. We were drawn back to reading them each night, just to find out what happened next. The characters in the stories become almost like friends. And unlike kiddie books, we don't have to decide on a book to read each night.
- One chapter book provides the same amount of reading entertainment as 20 or more kiddie books. This means fewer books to acquire—even at yard-sale prices, this is significant. We also have fewer books to store.
- I use age-appropriate reading material. There's a good reason why the Laura Wilder books are

American classics: The language is simple enough for young children to understand, yet the story line is interesting. Becca and I started *Rascal* by Sterling North, a story about a boy and his pet raccoon, but the grown-up prose was too difficult for her. Similarly, the original version of *The Swiss Family Robinson,* with its flowery, dated writing style, is too challenging for young children, but we did well with a condensed version.

- In my case, it has helped to choose books that interest me as well. When the kids have brought home kiddie books from the school library, I've found that some were well done, but many had such shallow story lines that reading them felt like a chore.
- I've enjoyed selecting books that, because they are set in less affluent times or cultures, help the kids acquire the frugal perspective. Sometimes, I'll stop the narrative so we can talk about passages that I think are valuable. We paused to discuss how, when Laura Ingalls's family moved, it took just a couple of hours to pack all their possessions in a covered wagon, and when Laura was four years old, her only toy was a corncob doll. When eight-year-old Ralph Moody worked for other ranchers, he was proud that all of his earnings went to buy a cow and other necessities for the family. The fact that these stories are based on the lives of real people helps the kids appreciate the relative affluence of their own lives—even if their mother is the country's most famous tightwad.

Aside from these points, I've found chapter books can be handy when kids have a lot of time on their hands and little access to other entertainment, such as during long car rides, camping trips, and after-dark power failures.

Having loved these books as a kid myself, it's an enormous pleasure to see they have the same capacity to enchant my own children. Kids love rituals, and "chapter-book time" is definitely one worth exploring.

P.S. A funny but irrelevant aside: About the time I began to read to Becca, Jamie asked if I would give her a chore so that she could earn money. So I told her she could have the "chore" of reading kiddie books to her twin siblings. She would get a quarter for each book read as long as the book averaged more than one sentence per page. The happy arrangement was short-lived, as the twins soon tired of Jamie's entrepreneurship—they became bored with the reading. Then, for a while, the twins' interest in reading inexplicably revived. I discovered Jamie had offered them a "cut"—she had paid them a nickel apiece for each kiddie book they would allow her to read to them.

RAIN-BARREL ECONOMY

While gardening is a money saver, the "hourly wage" (the savings per hour invested) is fairly low, and it gets considerably lower if you must use expensive municipal water.

Upscale garden-paraphernalia catalogs sell plastic "rain barrels," which collect water from downspouts, for as much as $69. But Michele Ankuda of Hastings-on-Hudson, New York, sent an elegant, cheap alternative.

Start with a plastic 40-gallon trash can with a secure-fitting lid,

which can be purchased on sale for approximately $9. With a sharp knife, cut a rectangular hole in the lid that's the same size as a cross section of downspout. It's important to keep the lid on the can when collecting water, to protect small kids and pets.

Purchase an *S*-shaped piece of downspout. When you need water, attach this piece to the downspout so the flow is diverted into the trash can.

When it's full, or if you don't need water, reattach the straight piece. Both the straight and curved sections can be friction-fit onto the downspout, or you can drill holes and use a nail to connect the sections.

To use the water, dip in a watering can, siphon with a hose, or attach a spigot to the side of the trash can.

John Wright, manager of Water Wiser, a water-efficiency clearinghouse in Denver, Colorado, told us that roof-runoff water is perfectly safe for garden use. He also told us that the national average municipal water-and-sewer rate for 4,000 gallons in 1994 was $18.58. At this rate, it would take 48 fillings for a 40-gallon $9 trash can to pay for itself.

This did not seem like a good payback rate to me. I figured it would take forever to fill the trash can.

But if you do the math, you discover that a roof sheds a surprising amount of water. In a 1-inch rainstorm, 688 gallons of water are shed by the roof of a typical 24-foot by 46-foot ranch house. If it has four downspouts, each would deliver, on average, 172 gallons in that storm.

If this ranch house were in a region with only 11 inches of rainfall a year, a barrel under one of its downspouts would be able to fill 48 times in one year.

All of the previous calculations assume that none of the water would be lost to evaporation or spillage. As a practical matter, probably a fair amount would be lost that way, but friends of mine who have used rain barrels do say it is surprising how quickly they fill.

A natural question might be, "Is roof-runoff rainwater suitable for drinking?" Scott Chaplin of the Rocky Mountain Institute told me that, given the right variables, such as air quality, roofing materials, bird population, collection-system type, and other considerations, it can be. So, don't drink rainwater without doing a lot of research first.

FRUGAL FUND-RAISING

Our solicitation for frugal, sensible fund-raising ideas struck a chord. Several readers shared my frustration regarding the waste of kids peddling candy, cookies, and junk door-to-door, with only a tiny percentage of the take going to the worthy cause. They even sent me magazine articles about how parents are fed up with 1) carting their kids around to help them sell, and 2) getting hit up by other kids to buy junk.

Others have told me they dislike pointless "-athons" such as danceathons, playathons, et cetera.

One of the articles suggested that, since parents chose to let their kids get involved in various activities, parents are obliged to pay their own kids' way. In general, I agree, although I know of worthy exceptions. The daughter of a staffer participated in "Odyssey of the Mind." Her group won the state championship and could go on to the world championship in Ohio. In this case, the parents could not have anticipated the huge cost, so it was appropriate for them to resort to fund-raising. In other cases, fund-raising opens activities to children of low-income families. So fund-raising certainly has its place.

Of course, not all fund-raising is for kids' activities. Groups raise funds to, for example, reroof the church, support the local animal shelter, or aid national and international charities such as OxFam. However, the most obnoxious fund-raisers tend to be the ones that support activities for kids.

Good fund-raisers fall into two broad categories. First, there's the type in which you receive something of real value for the money you donate, and most or all of the money goes to the worthy cause. Second, there's the type in which you are persuaded—cleverly, one hopes—simply to donate without personally getting something of value in return.

As a tightwad, I prefer the first type, no matter if I'm the one asking for money or if I'm donating money. But both types have the huge advantages of keeping the money in the community, eliminating the peddling of useless, overpriced junk, and using human energy constructively.

Here are some examples of fund-raisers in which something truly valuable is offered in return for a donation:

Potluck supper/ white elephant auction. Stephanie Takes-Desbiens of Sebago Lake, Maine, wrote that she knew of three such events that raised $200 to $700 in an evening.

There's very little effort involved. Everyone who comes brings a covered dish and a white-elephant item. Volunteers auction and keep records.

I've seen this work well in our community. Each year our school has one of these evenings in which parents also bring baked goods for the auction. I like this because I have the choice to either bring something or buy something—I'd rather donate a giant pumpkin than buy a $20 plate of brownies. Our church took this a step further. In addition to the white-elephant auction, it solicited donations of goods and services from local businesses. The one-time event raised $7,000 to retire the mortgage on a new building.

If your group prefers, it can run a silent auction. Each item is displayed with a bid sheet, which describes the item and lists a minimum bid. Each bidder writes his higher offering on the bid sheet. The time when the bidding is over must be clearly indicated.

Service auctions. Eileen Mierski of Pittsburgh, Pennsylvania, wrote that one of these raised $750 for her church's vacation Bible school. There were no costs involved, but she says organizing the event required about 16 hours. Several weeks before the event, church members made written submissions of services they were willing to donate such as overnight baby-sitting, two hours of math tutoring, a Mexican dinner for up to eight people at the buyer's house, and so on. Twenty-three services were auctioned.

Group yard sales. Patricia Salvanti of Riverdale, New Jersey, wrote that her nursery school received donations from 17 families and raised about $425. Placing an ad was the only cost. Half a dozen parents worked the sale. The unsold stuff was donated to a charity.

Scrip. The organization that needs money—say, a school—buys gift certificates, called scrip, from a national scrip clearinghouse at a discount to their face value. The school then sells them at face value and keeps the difference.

Unlike most gift certificates, these aren't necessarily for overpriced department stores. Karen Marquardt of Caledonia, Wisconsin, sent me a scrip order form that includes listings for grocery stores, gas stations, and long-distance phone companies—in other words, places where you would shop anyway.

This kind of program could be coordinated locally on a store-by-store basis, but most of our readers went through Scrip Plus, a national clearinghouse that negotiates with merchants and sells scrip to nonprofits. Spokesperson Deborah Boyette told us Scrip Plus sells scrip to nonprofits for 1.5 percent to 2 percent over what it pays to the merchants. She said the nonprofits reap from 4 percent to 50 percent profit on scrip sales. Call (800) 800-0700 for more information.

Meals. Spaghetti and baked-bean dinners are common, but breakfast fund-raisers are also popular. Mary Katherine Trevithick of Holualoa, Hawaii, said Easter Sunday and Mother's Day breakfasts worked well for her church youth group. Normally, the food is purchased and the cost subtracted from the take, but for a recent breakfast her church's youth group took the extra step of soliciting donations of hams and eggs from grocers. Charging $5 a plate, the 15 volunteers made $500, all profit. Jamie Bidwell of Kentland, Indiana, added a play to their church supper, transforming it into a dinner-theater event.

I would add from personal experience that it's wise to charge a set price of $3 to $5. If you depend on donations, you will pull in an average of only about $1 per person.

Car wash. Sandi Cunningham of Westminster, California, suggests a refinement on the usual practice of setting up on a street corner and yelling at passing cars (which has always struck me as a bit obnoxious). Her church's youth group makes reservations with church members, which allows the kids to spend 20 to 30 minutes on each car. That gives them enough time to do a great job and consequently get more customers.

Here are some ideas for inspiring people to donate without personally receiving something in return:

You-don't-have-to-come event. Gloria Jackson of Denison, Texas, sent us an invitation to a "Possum Ball." It says, "You are cordially invited to the most forgettable event of the season, a Possum Ball, sponsored by the friends of the Grayson County Humane Society. Date: Whenever you choose. Place: Wherever you are the happiest. Time: Anytime that suits you." The enclosed RSVP says, "I appreciate not having to attend the Possum Ball and herewith enclose ______." It then lists various levels of giving. If you give the highest level, $100, you get to skip not only this year's ball but next year's too. The card points out that since there is no expense for decorations, food, drink, or entertainment, the whole donation will go to caring for homeless and abused animals.

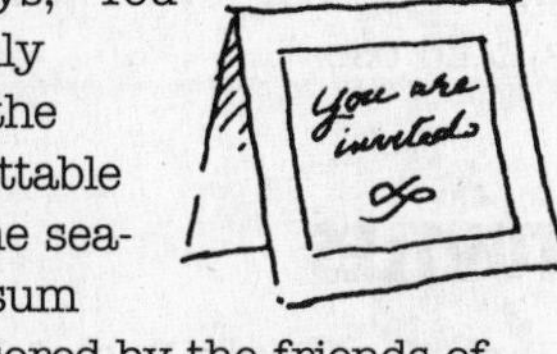

"More money was raised from this effort than from any other form of solicitation in recent years," Gloria writes.

Tea party. In a similar vein, several readers proposed sending a tea bag. Kay Marie Seitz of Orlando, Florida, suggests the accompanying note could read "Have a cup of tea on us instead of coming to an overpriced party."

Coin-collecting strategies. Joan Stansbury of Chambersburg, Pennsylvania, said she had read about a "penny challenge," in which 1,200 students collected almost $3,000 just by bringing pennies to school. Candace Goodman of Albany, New York, writes that her children's school gathered $1,200 for a playground by collecting money in a tire bank. The tire had plexiglass on either side and a slot in the top. The fund-raising committee emptied it weekly and displayed it for a month.

Pie-throw auction. Robin McFetridge says that she and her husband, an army unit commander, were stationed in Germany, looking for a way to raise money for Christmas gifts for soldiers who otherwise would not receive any. They decided to auction off the privilege of throwing a pie at anyone in the unit. The highest bid was $75, which was for the pie to be thrown at her husband. The event raised $750.

The pies were aluminum-foil tins filled with whipped cream or Cool Whip. The total time involved was just three hours to buy the supplies, make the pies, hold the auction, hurl the pies, and clean up.

Bottle collections. Jim has participated in several bottle drives for Scouts. He says 15 parent-Scout pairs can collect $300 worth of bottles in three hours. Lynda Ward of Searsport, Maine, suggests a variation. To raise money for annual class trips, each Friday students in her school brought in returnable juice and soda containers (glass had to be brought in by adults). The containers were collected in the back of the school and were picked up by the local redemption center. One week 126 students brought in 1,179 bottles.

Workathon. Louisa Anderson of Greeley, Colorado, writes that her school organizes workathons. Participants accumulate sponsors on a per-hour or flat-rate basis. They meet on a Saturday morning and perform yard-improvement-type work for five or six hours for elderly or disabled people. Even small children can pick up trash and hold a bag. A variation is cleanup events in which participants gather pledges per bag filled with trash.

Just ask. Finally, Lisa Harris, a "professional fund-raiser turned mom" from Princeton, Massachusetts, says the straightforward approach is often best if an organization needs a *lot* of money for an undeniably worthy cause in a short period of time. She wrote that when her church needed $35,000 for a new roof and paint, it sent out a very straightforward request for funds. She writes, "People praised the honesty of the campaign, and we exceeded a goal we thought we would never reach."

Lisa's letter went on to make many good points about fund-raising. She emphasized that the amount of money needed, as well as the ages and numbers of available volunteers, should be carefully considered before deciding on which type of fund-raiser a group should use.

TURTLES

Charlotte Straub Roe of Gig Harbor, Washington, sent me a copy of her family cookbook. We instantly gravitated toward a unique kid-wowing recipe for "turtles." These are, sort of, chocolate waffles with frosting—when the grid shows through, it resembles a turtle's back.

½ cup melted butter
⅔ cup sugar
2 eggs, well beaten
6 tablespoons cocoa
1 cup flour
½ teaspoon vanilla

Heat waffle iron to medium. Combine the melted butter and sugar in a bowl. Combine the cocoa and flour; add this to the egg mixture. Stir in the vanilla. Drop 1 tablespoon of dough on each of the four sections of the waffle iron. Close and bake for 45 seconds. Remove and cool on racks. Frost while warm with cocoa-and-powdered-sugar frosting (we used leftover green-tinted frosting). Makes 32 cookies.

THE PHENOMENAL FREE PILE

If you've been frugal for many years, you may have discovered that each subsequent yard sale you hold yields a smaller financial return. Our first, 10 years ago, brought in $160—we unloaded the excess from our lives before we were married. The next one netted $100, then $70, and so on. In later years the only time we did better was in the two yard sales when we sold trash-picked stuff.

About the same time I started to notice this diminished return, acquaintances of ours had a yard sale in which they netted about $500. It took me a while to figure out where we "went wrong." I learned the couple was also paying $2,000 per month just to keep up with the interest on credit cards and other debts. Buying a lot of new stuff and selling it at yard-sale prices isn't a financial strategy that I would recommend.

Anyway, after we moved to Maine, holding a yard sale was not a sensible option: Not only did we have less spare stuff, but few people drive down our rural road. But even when I took my loot to a better location for a group yard sale, I still made only $40 and returned home with 90 percent of our stuff. So when I have a free day, I make better use of my time by *going* to yard sales. I save more by buying yard-sale stuff than I earn by selling it.

The loss of the yard-sale option, combined with our town's $1-per-bag disposal fee, has made it more challenging to get rid of stuff inexpensively. We donate our clothes to thrift shops, and we donate saleable stuff to nonprofits holding group yard sales. But even so, there's still a range of unsaleable stuff with which I could not, in good conscience, burden a nonprofit. As waste-disposal fees have risen, there has been an increase in "donations" of trash to charities, thereby burdening them with the disposal fee. When in doubt, *ask* the nonprofit if it wants the donation. Most of my stuff was so ratty that I didn't need to ask. I knew it was my obligation to get rid of it.

So I was interested when, last year, a neighbor up the road put a pile of junk on her lawn next to a

sign that said FREE. Each day I drove by, the pile was noticeably smaller, despite the fact that much of the stuff seemed useless. In the end, she had gotten rid of about 90 percent of the pile.

So we tried it this year. I painted FREE in 8-inch white letters on two scraps of brown Masonite and attached them to two scrap-wood posts. Jim positioned the signs so that they could be seen from a distance from each direction.

Then we put out our junk: baby potty chairs, a box of magazines, broken chairs and tables, an old slide projector, an aquarium, and so on—even four-year-old Brad contributed a pair of his old sneakers. Many of the items we put out were things we had trash-picked, hung on to for years, and ultimately decided we couldn't use. Other stuff, such as the baby equipment, was so battered after being used by six kids that it was not fit for a yard sale.

Then we waited.

At first there seemed to be no takers. The kids worried that no one was coming to our "free sale." But within hours strange cars began stopping. It was as if the message had finally worked its way through the word-of-mouth frugal network.

I was glad that we positioned the pile away from our house but still within eyesight. I found myself committing tightwad voyeurism . . . I would peer and squint though the curtains, overcome with the fascination of watching other tightwads pick through the junk. Once I caught the happy trot of a familiar 12-year-old making off with the old slide projector just before he disappeared into his chicken-coop-turned-science-lab (Alec loves to dismantle anything we allow him to).

Within 24 hours, almost all of the stuff was gone; all that remained were a box of magazines, a couple of baby backpacks, an old, ornate iron headboard, a box of metal junk . . . and Brad's sneakers.

If you live in a more populated area, check with local ordinances to be sure a free pile is okay, and don't leave the stuff out for more than a day or two, out of courtesy to your neighbors. And no matter where you do this, don't put out anything dangerous that kids could get into.

Our experiment was such a success that we have squirreled away our signs—I have a feeling the Dacyczyn free pile will return every summer.

BAKING BASICS

Dear Amy,

I was told by a fellow tightwad that the initial heating of the element in an electric oven is what uses the most energy. Therefore, she had one or two baking days per week. Breads, cookies, and granola were made along with a baked dinner; she used the stove top the rest of the week.

—Yvonne Everly
Newberg, Oregon

DUVET ADDS CACHET

Dear Amy,

My husband and I recently acquired a wood-frame couch with six individual cushions. The frame is beautiful, solid wood, but the coverings on the cushions were well worn. Being newly married, we didn't have money for new cushions or coverings. So we

decided to recover them ourselves with a duvet or comforter cover. A twin size fit all six cushions perfectly, and cleaning is merely machine wash and dry—all for one sixth the price!

—Deeni Hubin
Paxton, Illinois

TOWERING TIGHTWADS

Dear Amy,

A group called the National Institute for Tall People publishes a monthly newsletter called *The NITPicker.* One of its regular features is a clothing exchange, in which tall people from across the country list their used clothing for sale. They also print home-improvement projects, ratings of cars, sources of shoes, and other things that can help tall people save money. The only catch is that you have to be a member to get the newsletter, and the cost is $25 per year, but just one good outfit at a bargain price could pay for the subscription. The address is NITP, P.O. Box 16973, Alexandria, VA 22302, or call (703) 823-3138.

—Lisle Bean
Alexandria, Virginia

FELINE GROOVY

Dear Amy,

I screwed a $1 scrub brush, bristles facing outward, to a wall near a corner, and my cat loves to rub against it. Pet stores sell similar wall-mounted groomers for up to $10. Now whenever my cat wants to be groomed he can do the job himself, plus it keeps cat hair off the furniture. I just vacuum out the brush when I come past it.

—Mary Wallace
Hamilton, Ontario, Canada

A CAN CAN DO

Dear Amy,

You mentioned that you can order a $9 (yikes!) Crock-Pot insert that will bake yeast bread. Try a clean coffee can, as recommended by Mabel Hoffman's classic *Crockery Cookery* available at libraries and yard sales. It works great.

—Julie Narvell
Nashville, Tennessee

MAKE AN EGGS-CEPTION

Dear Amy,

I was out of eggs one day when making a batch of chocolate chip cookies. I decided to make them anyway. I added just enough milk to moisten the batter to make it stick. They came out perfectly!

—Lanise Marrotte
Manchester, New Hampshire

(Eggs can be left out of a lot of baked goods with no significant loss of texture or flavor. Just add a bit more liquid and bake as usual. FZ)

NEW WIFE'S TALE

Dear Amy,

A friend of mine is getting married and found that she could get a significant reduction in the wed-

ding-hall and reception cost if she was willing to be married on Friday the thirteenth! In this case, an "unlucky" Friday the thirteenth saved $500.

—Lisa K. Heller
Richmond, Virginia

YUM-YUM CRUMBS

Dear Amy,

Instead of using Parmesan cheese, which can be expensive, take bread crumbs, toss with a small amount of olive oil, and toast until golden brown. This can keep for a while in the refrigerator. It is delicious and apparently well known in the poorer, southern region of Italy.

—Duncan Masseu
Woodland Hills, California

YOLKLORE

Dear Amy,

Your universal quiche recipe (see page 762) was great. Another way to lower cholesterol in a quiche is to reduce the number of yolks but not whites. One whole egg and two whites in a quiche suffice for me.

—Ruth Ann Weidner
Marblehead, Massachusetts

LEAN AND GREEN

Dear Amy,

We always let two or three of our garden zucchinis get as big as they can at the end of each garden season. We store them in a cool place and wait for Halloween. We carve them like pumpkins but cut their "lids" at their waist. We scoop out seeds from the top and bottom halves and cut a face in the bottom and stars in the top. We reattach the halves with toothpicks. Lined up, leaning against an old crate, they look great, and parents and kids always get a good chuckle.

—Denise Hackney
Ann Arbor, Michigan

OVERNIGHT SUCCESS

Dear Amy,

My husband rushes off to catch a train in the morning and used to like the exorbitant instant flavored oatmeal that comes in packets. Now he is content with my version. I mix a large container full of about five parts oatmeal to one part brown sugar (those packets are really sweet; you can reduce the proportion of sugar to taste). Then I add some cinnamon. Each night, before bed, I mix a serving bowl of oatmeal and milk. Sometimes I add extras: nuts, maple syrup, apples, et cetera. I refrigerate it to "cook" overnight. In the morning, he pops the bowl in the microwave for 90 seconds, and it's as fast as the packet!

—Siri Allison
Beacon, New York

BEETLE JUICE

Dear Amy,

I once read in a little publication called *The Best Garden Tips I Know* of a way to get rid of Japanese beetles. You blend up a pile of them in water, strain, then spray the fil-

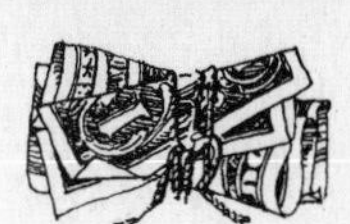

tered water on the affected plants. I didn't use a blender, I just picked 30 beetles off the weeping cherry tree, dunked them in scalding water, and smashed them with a rock. It worked!

—Laurie Lentz-Marino
Belchertown, Massachusetts

SWEEP AND REAP

Dear Amy,

If you're a college student, sign up to clean dorm rooms at the end of the school year. At many schools, dorm-crew members are allowed to keep any items they find. You'd be amazed at what people leave behind. I have friends who have found and have been allowed to keep typewriters, furniture of every description, trunks of clothes (one friend kept the trunk and sold the clothes at a consignment shop for a nice profit), computer printers, books, CD's, you name it!

—Andrea Campbell
Somerville, Massachusetts

COOKING UNDER PRESSURE

I admit it up front: I am not experienced at pressure cooking. While Jim and I are veteran pressure *canners,* the only dish we pressure-cook is the beans-and-rice meal explained on page 229.

But I have met several people who rave about pressure cooking, and a recent letter piqued my interest further. Dr. Laura Geiger of South Pasadena, California, writes, "I am the only person I know besides my mother who uses a pressure cooker, and it is one of my favorite kitchen tools. When I went to college I inherited my mother's cooker, which had been a wedding gift in 1955. The inner ring was old, so I had it and the plug replaced at the local hardware store. My pressure cooker, made by Presto, is now more than 40 years old and going strong."

To get more information, I called National Presto Industries at its Eau Claire, Wisconsin, headquarters and had the company send me some information. I also interviewed JoAnne O'Gara, a Presto home economist. I learned that pressure cooking offers the following advantages:

- It saves energy costs. Laura writes that she cooks potatoes for mashed potatoes in 10 minutes, wild or brown rice in 10 minutes, and pot roast in 35 to 40 minutes. Other times from Presto: steamed vegetables in 1 minute, seafood gumbo in 4 minutes, chicken in 8 minutes. Presto says to convert conventional recipes, a rule of thumb is to reduce cooking time by two thirds. There must always be water or some other liquid in the pressure cooker to produce steam.
- It saves time. "People who don't cook from scratch with healthy ingredients like whole grains frequently cite time as their constraint—not an excuse with the pressure cooker!" writes Laura.
- It saves vitamins, minerals, flavor, and color, according to Presto. The company contends that because the foods cook quickly in an airtight environment, the usual losses of these attributes are largely avoided.

• It saves work. Pressure cooking is very amenable to one-pot cooking. If you want the flavors of, say, chicken and potatoes to remain separate, you can put a rack inside the cooker that holds them above the boiling liquid. If you want the flavors to mix, you can omit the cooking rack.

While pressure cooking is fairly simple and safe, you should follow the directions that come with the cooker. If you have a yard-sale or inherited model, read up on pressure cooking, preferably in a pressure-cooking cookbook; these can be found in libraries.

An important note of caution is that care must be taken when pressure-cooking foods that produce foam, such as dried beans, pearled barley, and macaroni. Beans, for example, must be presoaked, and oil added to the water-and-salt cooking mixture to hold down the froth. Otherwise, Presto says, the vent pipe can clog. While this isn't normally dangerous, as pressure cookers have an "overpressure" plug that pops out in such cases, it is best to avoid overpressure situations. (The pressure-cooker method of cooking beans and rice I wrote about on page 229 specifies preboiling but not presoaking the beans—but preboiling essentially serves the same purpose.)

Should you get one? Some calls to local department stores revealed a range of prices from $29.96 for a 4-quart version made by Mirro to $59.97 for a 6-quart Presto model. At these prices, it would probably take many years to pay back the savings in energy costs. But if you can pick up a cooker on the used market for a few dollars, it would clearly be worthwhile to grab one and start experimenting. And if you already own a pressure canner and don't mind making large quantities, you can use the canner as a cooker.

ARE YOUR KIDS CEREAL KILLERS?

We don't have access to double-coupon grocery stores, so we don't

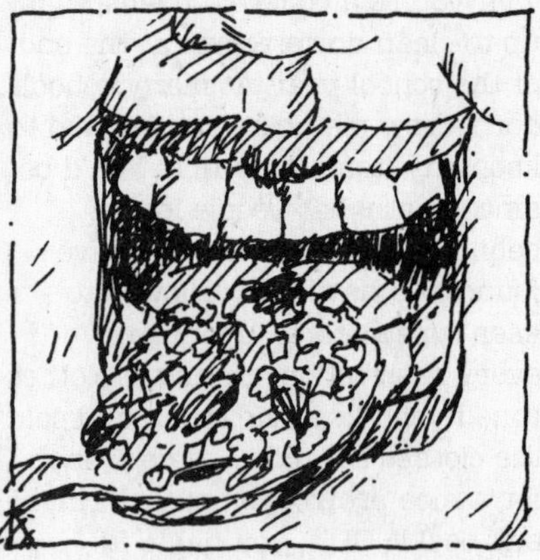

enjoy a range of low-cost cold cereals. Our selection has been limited to homemade granola and $1-per-pound store-brand cornflakes. But lately we've been finding good deals on cold cereal in salvage stores.

I usually don't buy salvage-store cold cereal because it generally still costs about $3 per box. But a few months back we found Grape-nuts with raisins for 99¢ per pound. I theorized that a clerk must have priced the cereal by the box size rather than by the pound. Then Jim and I went to Vermont on family business and spotted a salvage store on our way. We stopped in and found boxes of cereal ranging from 50¢ to $1 per pound. This time it was granola. Again, these

were small, heavy boxes of dense cereal, probably priced low because of the small box size.

So far, so good. But at breakfast we noticed our family would eat about $1.50 worth of this dense cereal in a single sitting—about double the cost of our normal cold-cereal breakfasts. One morning I watched in horror as my big 12-year old started a second heaping bowl of this cereal. I asked him, "Who do you think you are, Jethro?" (That prompted a ten-minute digression to explain about the before-his-time *Beverly Hillbillies* and the character Jethro, who would eat a huge box of cereal in a single sitting.)

So now we have a family rule. Heavy, dense cereals are used as a condiment for cornflakes—as a "mix-in." By doing this, we give variety to the old cornflakes without significantly increasing our breakfasts' costs. And it's really quite good.

THE TIGHTWAD WORKSHOP

Just five months before we closed our business, the post office issued new bulk-mail regulations. One change requires that the mailing trays be bound with plastic banding, which comes on an awkward-to-use, 2-foot-diameter roll. Setting aside his utility-trailer project, Jim turned his attention to building a solution. Using scrap wood, he made a device to hold the roll—it works like a big tape dispenser.

The utility trailer? Jim is building a second utility trailer from a clunker we bought for $40 some time ago. The new body is made from a sawn-in-half oil tank and scrap lumber left over from remodeling our boat. This trailer will be used to haul dirty stuff.

The boat? Yes, we have a 22-foot power boat with a small cabin. Jim and his father bought it 21 years ago. The last time I rode in it I was eight and three quarters months pregnant with Alec . . . it has needed work. This past spring Jim's new workshop was overrun with sundry boat parts and three generations of Dacyczyn males in an extensive remodeling effort.

The new workshop? You knew I was getting to this. Last year Jim built a new, larger workshop in the far corner of the barn; I inherited the old small one in the carriage house.

Jim, the now-world-reknowned handyman, is oft regarded as enormously talented. While there might be a bit of talent in the mix, mostly he's learned from trial and error and from endless childhood hours of watching his yet handier father. But it takes more than skill. Having good tools and a permanent place to work are equally important.

On the following pages is a glimpse into Jim's workshop. It parallels other areas of the tightwad life, consisting of items bought retail, on sale, at yard sales and estate sales. Some things were trash-picked, inherited, or otherwise acquired for free.

Building materials, used to build the workshop or for building things, range in price. To avoid paying retail Jim scavenges whenever possible and watches for cheap sources of new building materials. He acquires tools in a variety of ways. As a general rule, he finds the more necessary the tool, the more he will pay for it as compared with retail.

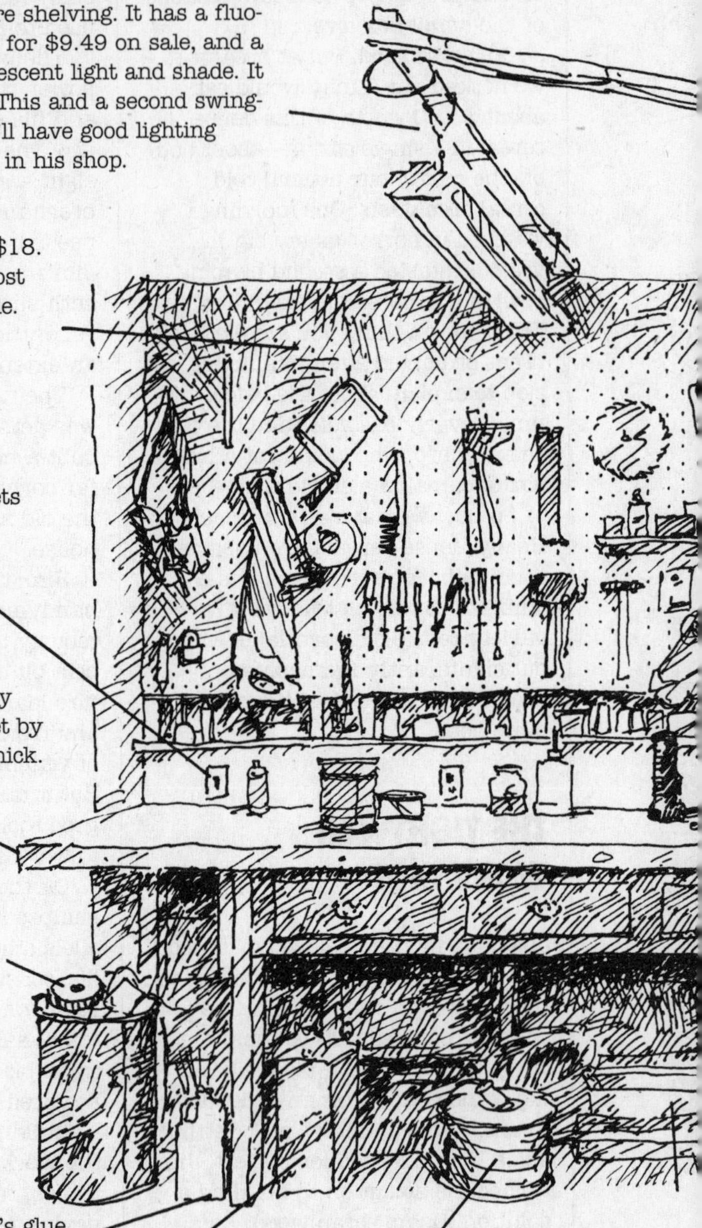

A swing-out light Jim made using uprights from scavenged store shelving. It has a fluorescent light bought for $9.49 on sale, and a trash-picked incandescent light and shade. It swings out 12 feet. This and a second swing-out lamp ensure he'll have good lighting whenever he works in his shop.

Pegboard cost $18. Pegboard hooks cost $.50 at a yard sale.

Recycled outlets and switches.

Counter made of $24 worth of rough-cut, locally sawn hemlock. It's 14 feet by 32 inches and 3 inches thick.

Trash. What ends up here is *really* trash, such as this hopelessly worn training wheel. Jim carefully scavenges useful parts from stuff before he throws it away.

Gallon of carpenter's glue, $2 at yard sale ($18 retail).

Box of miscellaneous scavenged wire, saved for future projects.

Roll of heavy-gauge extension-cord wire, purchased on sale for $.30 a foot (normally $.80 per foot), used to make a 200-foot-long extension cord.

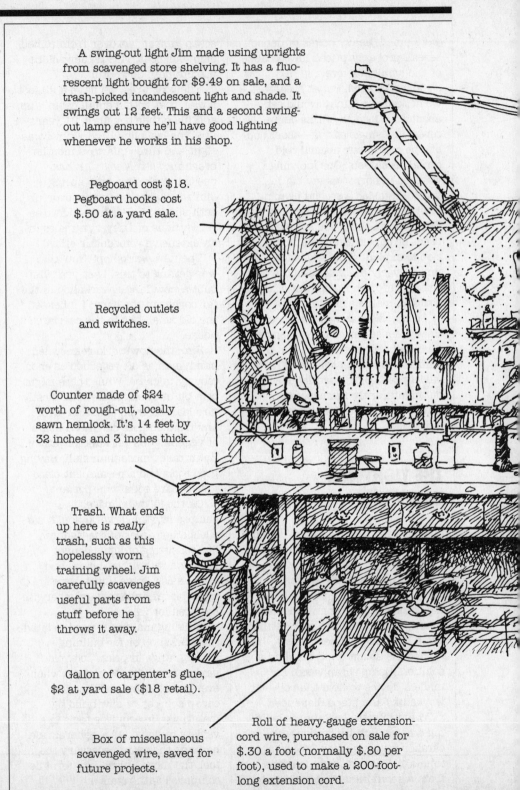

Miscellaneous screws and hardware. When a hardware store had a 70 percent off, going-out-of-business sale, Jim stocked up.

Bar clamps, two for $1 at yard sale ($11.49 each retail).

Cordless drill, purchased on sale for $89 (normally $145). Jim considers this, in combination with drywall screws, a must-have for any serious handyman.

Drawers from a pseudo-colonial-style waterbed purchased at an auction for $1. Lumber from this was used to make a bunk bed, and the waterbed sack was used to make ground covers for camping.

Miter-box saw, free ($28 retail). Jim helped a friend move from her late parents' home into a smaller apartment, and came home with a couple trailer loads of stuff no one else wanted, including a large quantity of tools.

Boxes of miscellaneous new and scavenged electrical junk.

Working antique fan, one of several items in a $1 estate-sale box lot. Doubles as a Salad Shooter. (Just kidding.)

Basic tools such as hammers and handsaws may need to be purchased retail because most people hang on to them until they die. With luck, estate sales (both the auction and yard-sale types) can be a good source of basic tools.

Somewhat necessary tools, such as those owned by serious handymen, can be purchased through the classifieds or by "putting out the word." Items like table saws will be cheaper than retail but not amazingly cheap.

Seldom used tools, such as routers, should be borrowed or rented when needed. However, when such tools show up on the used market they can be so cheap that owning them might be worthwhile.

Below are a few of the finds that are not illustrated:

- Palm sander, $2 at yard sale ($40 retail)—it had an easily fixed loose wire.
- Router and router table bought used for $35 ($140 retail).
- Table saw, purchased for $100 ($280 retail) from a compulsive upgrader. Jim replaced the bad switch for 79¢. Jim upgraded from his ancient freebie saw, mounted on the trash-picked frame of a deep-fat fryer. That saw was inadequate for fine work but did tide him over until he found a better one.
- Miniature lathe, free, inherited from his late uncle.
- Bench grinder, $8 from yard sale ($48 retail).
- Bench-top belt sander, $15 at yard sale ($69 retail), came with $20 worth of belts.
- Pruning saw, $10 at yard sale ($45 retail).
- Tool cabinet, free. When our post office was remodeled, Jim was given the old metal cabinet with pigeonholes. He removed sections of the pigeonhole partitions to make varying-sized places for odd-sized tools.
- Disc sander/grinder, $20 at yard sale. Jim once rented one for $40 a day ($160 retail).
- Drill press, purchased used for $75 ($250 retail).

FREE AS A BIRD

Dear Amy,

When I decided I wanted an Amazon parrot, I let my vet know. Very soon she called me about a lady with a parrot that she would give only to a good home. On the vet's assurance that I am a good pet owner, I got a nice, friendly bird for free that sells for about $1,000 in pet stores.

—Sara Kerwin
South Lyon, Michigan

CHEAP CHIC

Dear Amy,

Looking chic is important to me. I find that I can have my hair cut by Mari the Expensive once a year or so and have my husband take front and back pictures of the cut. The local chain haircutter can duplicate the chic style for $40 less.

—Name withheld by request
Bellevue, Washington

HAND OVER HAND

Dear Amy,

Our four young sons help us create special valentine cards for grandmas each year. We trace each

boy's hand, overlaying the prints so they form a concentric pattern from the smallest to the largest hand. We use four colors of markers to distinguish the prints and always date the card. It's a nice card for our grandmas and gets our boys involved in creating something special.

—Renna Bent
Gardiner, Montana

FROM CHILLER TO CHILI

Dear Amy,

Here's the easiest way to store tomatoes. Right off the vine, put them in a plastic bag and put the bag in your freezer. The frozen tomatoes will resemble big, red marbles. To use, take out as many as you need, scald under hot tap water, and the skin comes right off the still-frozen tomato. Then pop them in the microwave to thaw them, cut out the stem, and they are ready to use.

—Christa Hanson
New Brighton, Minnesota

FREEZER PLEASER

Dear Amy,

A good way to make apple butter for the freezer is to peel, core, and quarter a Crock-Pot full of apples, season with cinnamon and sugar to taste, add a small amount of water, and then let them cook overnight in the Crock-Pot on low. In the morning, let cool, then puree in your blender or food processor, place in containers, and freeze. Fast and easy!

—Nancy A. Myers
Stillwater, Oklahoma

TONER TACTIC

Dear Amy,

Don't replace the toner cartridge on your laser printer or copier as soon as the printer reads "toner low." Gently shake and rock the cartridge a few times to redistribute the toner.

—Karen M. Campbell
Sacramento, California

SAVORY SAVER

Dear Amy,

To save fat, calories, and money, I use liquid smoke in place of bacon or salt pork in recipes such as baked beans. This also lets you skip sterilizing countertops and utensils after using it like you must do with meat products. The liquid smoke saves money and time, and you can't undercook it.

—Denise Hackney
Ann Arbor, Michigan

USE BRAIN, DON'T DRAIN

Dear Amy,

We save the rinse water from one load of laundry and use it in the wash cycle of the next load. We plug the washtub while the rinse cycle drains and then bail it into the washer for the next load. Our water bill has gone from $90 to $41!

—Patty Jacobson
St. Paul, Minnesota

(A less labor-intensive alternative is using a "suds-saver" washer. These suck rinse water from the washtub back into the washer. Lint-buildup

complaints and complex mechanisms have led manufacturers to phase them out in recent years, but many users swear by them. Maytag still makes one, called the "Watersaver." They can also be found on the used market. FZ)

CHEWS WISELY

Dear Amy,

We got a great tip from our dog trainer. Our dog adores Cheerios (actually, the supercheap store-brand version), so we use one or two for treats instead of dog biscuits. They don't fill her up, and they're neat and reasonably healthy. She'll do anything for a Cheerio!

—T.J. Burnside Clapp
Cedar Crest, New Mexico

GREETINGS BY THE GROSS

Dear Amy,

When I was growing up, I remember that my mother always kept a box of inexpensive birthday and all-occasion cards on hand. I looked for these in major discount stores like Wal-Mart but could not find them. Then I tried my luck at some smaller dollar stores and drugstores, like Walgreen's. I found the cards tucked away with the stationery and school supplies. I found that they can be as inexpensive as $1 for a ten-card box. Two brands I have found are Floral Fantasy and English Cards, Ltd. Both companies sell birthday and all-occasion cards.

—Amy Wilder Owen
Nashville, Tennessee

TAMING THE TUBE

Soon after I started the *Gazette,* I began to get letters from readers asking me to address television watching and how it relates to the frugal life. I respectfully read all of these, but ultimately, I set them aside.

Why? Without exception, the writers were antitelevision. I got the sense that they wanted an article only if it focused exclusively on television's negatives, and I did not want to write such a one-sided article.

But, clearly, the issue of TV viewership is on lots of people's minds. TV-blackout weeks are becoming popular in many schools. Books such as *The Plug-In Drug* by Marie Winn contain frightening scenarios of a nation dumbed down by the tube. On the other hand, attempts have been made to put TV's in some classrooms and make viewing some programs mandatory.

So this will be my TV-philosophy article. I hope to bring to the question some balance that may help your family find some balance as well.

Let's start by examining the positives. There are some, really. Television provides:

- Free entertainment. For the mere inconvenience of a few commercials you can see the best performers on earth do their acts—a privilege even kings could not command a century ago.

- Free information. News, magazine shows, documentaries, and talk shows provide an array of valuable information. Print covers similar issues in more depth, but, frankly, we don't always want that

much depth. Television gives us information at the end of our busy days that's more digestible than print.

• Free, quality instruction. Television clearly excels over print in teaching manual skills. When the Frugal Gourmet makes a sauce, he can *show* you the desired consistency. Television instruction in skills such as haircutting, home repair, cooking, sports techniques, and so on is far easier to follow than are the same instructions in print form.

• Greater understanding between people who are "different." The simple fact that intelligent, likable people such as Oprah Winfrey and Bill Cosby have entered millions of homes through TV has contributed to racial understanding in this country. Similarly, some commentators give TV much of the credit for showing Americans and Russians that we are not so different, leading to the end of cold-war hostilities.

• The potential to maximize one's efficiency. Unlike reading, I can do something else at the same time that I am learning something on TV. I often have the TV on while I am making crusts for dozens of little pies, washing dishes, cutting kids' hair, mending, or doing *Tightwad Gazette* illustrations.

Still, there's a lot that's wrong with TV:

• It shows us the worst of human nature. Even during early-evening hours, when children are awake, a surprising amount of modern TV is too graphically violent and/or sexually exploitive.

• It can waste time. Two modern facts are often cited: People are incredibly busy these days, and the average adult watches 4.5 hours of television daily. I believe the second fact *causes* the first fact. To me, TV is like white sugar: The chief harm is not in the stuff itself but that it *replaces* good stuff.

• It's sedentary. It's no coincidence that the average American's weight and TV-watching time have risen in tandem. Even if, like me, you try to keep busy while watching TV, there's a limit on how active you can be and still watch.

• It creates false expectations. In letters that older readers sent in about their Great Depression experiences, the same statement kept popping up: "We never saw ourselves as poor, because everyone we knew was in the same boat." Today the average family depicted on TV shows and commercials is considerably wealthier than the average American family. The affluent images pouring out of TV studios are the major reason why average Americans feel poorer and more victimized, while, in fact, they have more material goods and luxuries than ever before.

One TV Limiting Strategy

• It makes us less social. If the alternative "social life" provided by television were not there, I believe modern American life would be less lonely.

• It can be expensive. Televisions can cost hundreds of dollars. Cable, satellite dishes, pay-per-view, videos (rented or purchased), and/or repair costs boost that total. And many people make foolish purchases inspired by advertising.

Both of these lists could be longer. The point is that TV itself is neither good nor bad; it all depends on how it is used. The best TV is better than a trashy novel.

Further, people's circumstances differ. People are more apt to seek passive entertainment during the cold, dark winter months than during the summer. People who work with their hands are often able to combine television watching with constructive activity. An only child is more likely to become TV-dependent than children with many siblings. Younger people should spend more time developing skills (including reading) and working toward financial security; however, I doubt the number of hours an octogenarian watches will make a great deal of difference in his or her life.

So, no one solution is right for everyone. Here are some possible TV-limiting strategies:

• Restrict viewing to one show/hour per day, or ten hours a week, or to public broadcasting only. This kind of limit forces you to be more selective.

• Give up TV during the summers. Because of the greater variety of activities that come with warm weather and the prevalence of reruns, and because it's for a finite amount of time, this is viable for most families.

• Have kids earn TV time by doing constructive chores. We do have TV limits. But I've allowed a kid to "buy" an extra hour of TV if he, say, does a super job cleaning the two bathrooms.

• Videotape programs you want to watch. Then zap through commercials as well as parts of variety or magazine shows that don't interest you. We used a variation of this during the fluff-laden Olympics. We moved our little TV into the living room and tuned it to the Olympics with the sound off. We watched taped programming on the large TV. When Jim, who was monitoring the small TV, noted that a critical Olympic moment was about to occur, we would switch the big TV over. By doing this, along with zapping though the video, we watched two hours of television in one hour.

• Use TV-privilege withdrawal as a method of discipline for kids over five (the concept is too difficult for younger kids). One of our children, who lost TV for a month, became so good at filling the void that this became an ineffective form of discipline (I was proud of her initiative).

• Have a no-rerun rule. Really, how many shows are worth watching twice?

• Make TV watching less convenient. Have one TV and put it in a closet, so you'll drag it out just for the really good stuff.

• Of course, one can get rid of the TV altogether. This isn't my choice, but I have known families

that have taken this option and are very happy about it.

If this topic strikes a chord with you, you may want to check out an unabashedly anti-TV newsletter called *The White Dot* (P.O. Box 577257, Chicago, IL, 60657-7257), which was the source for a few of the above-mentioned options. Subscriptions to the 12-page quarterly publication are $8 a year.

7-UP, UP AND AWAY

Speaking of good TV, one of my kids' favorite shows is *Bill Nye, The Science Guy* on PBS. It's science in an entertaining format.

Alec picked up a trick from this show that has provided great entertainment—a soda-bottle rocket. To make one you need a large plastic soda bottle (either 1 or 2 liters), a cork or rubber stopper that fits snugly in the bottleneck, the valve stem from an old inner tube (leave a ½-inch circle of rubber at the stem's base), a tire pump, and a patio lounge chair.

Drill a hole through the stopper/cork, and insert the valve stem; it should fit snugly. If you don't have a valve stem, you can drill a smaller hole and substitute an athletic-ball-inflating needle. Fill the bottle one-half to three-fourths full of water, cork it, and attach the tire pump. The lounge chair's back, reclined at a 45-degree angle, serves as the rocket launcher. Stand the upside-down bottle on the seat, resting against the back.

Then pump like mad!

When the bottle builds up enough pressure (it usually takes less than a minute), it will shoot a surprising distance, leaving a trail of exploding water behind. Under the best circumstances, Alec has shot these up to 100 feet.

Alec has found that gluing fins on the sides helps the bottle fly straighter. He has made them from cardboard—it might be wise to avoid making fins from a more rigid material.

Although the results are dramatic, we've found this rounded, soft-plastic rocket to be quite safe as long as no one's nose is in the bottle's trajectory. Our children

have been entertained by these homemade rockets for hours without anything close to a mishap. But it goes without saying that spectators should stand back, and adults should supervise any and all flights if there are young children in the vicinity of the launchpad.

A CHICKEN-AND-EGG QUESTION

Recent visitors to our rural home have asked why, since we have plenty of space in our barn, we don't keep chickens. And some rural readers have asked us to look into the economics of raising chickens to provide eggs.

We don't raise chickens because we spend only $2 a week for two dozen eggs; we don't want to eat more due to cholesterol concerns. So even if there were no costs, the savings are small compared with the hassle (I tended chickens as a kid, so I know).

And, of course, there *are* costs. Consider Frances, one of my staffers, who has 50 hens. It's impractical to keep fewer hens in the northern climates because you'd have to provide heat during the winter. But let's assume you live in a warmer climate and could keep fewer hens. We can use her numbers to roughly determine the cost of producing eggs.

Frances's hens lay an average of 17½ dozen eggs per week, or 910 dozen per year.

During the winter her hens eat 100 pounds, or $13 worth, of laying mash a week. During the summer she grows produce for her hens, so they eat just $7.50 in

mash weekly. So she spends about $533 annually on mash.

Frances replaces her hens every third year at $3 per hen, or $50 annually (she doesn't slaughter for meat, as old hens are tough). Other expenses total $13.

These expenses add up to $596 annually. Dividing $596 by 910 dozen eggs equals 65¢ per dozen, a savings of 35¢ per dozen as compared with $1-per-dozen store-bought eggs. Because our family eats about two dozen eggs a week, we'd need only about six hens. To me, saving 70¢ a week doesn't justify the effort of raising chickens—and that $34.40 annual savings would probably be more than offset by the cost of providing heat for a small flock.

Frances sells her surplus farm-fresh eggs for $1.25 a dozen. So, as a minibusiness/hobby, chicken raising can be viable. But because of the limited number of eggs that small families can eat, chickens are hard to justify solely to lower grocery bills.

There *are* creative ways to cut costs. You can fence off a large "run" so the chickens can scratch for much of their food. You can build a solar-heated coop. You can arrange with grocery stores for old produce for feed. But no matter

how you cut your expenses, you'll save only the amount you currently spend on eggs.

LOAF IS A MANY-SPLENDORED THING

Readers tell me that they have enjoyed my "universal" recipes for muffins, casseroles, quiches, and so on. I like these recipes too—they allow one to use up leftovers, exploit cheap ingredients, and/or accommodate dietary restrictions. So I was pleased when Betsy Bangley of Perrysburg, Ohio, sent me a universal yeast-bread recipe. Most of what follows is from Betsy, but I have made a few additions based on my years of experience as an impromptu bread baker.

These ingredients and proportions will make one loaf or two medium-sized pizza crusts. Remember that making double or triple batches and freezing extra loaves saves time and money.

Liquid. Use 1 to 1½ cups. Water is the most common choice, but other possibilities include potato water, vegetable broth, milk, flat beer, or fruit juice.

Oil and fat. Use up to ¼ cup vegetable or olive oil, melted butter, or melted margarine. Fat-free bread has a chewy crust that many people like, but others prefer the soft texture that comes with the addition of fat. Fat also increases shelf life.

Yeast. Use from 1 teaspoon to 1 tablespoon.

Salt. Use up to 2 teaspoons. Salt regulates the growth of yeast, keeping the dough from rising too rapidly and having uneven internal structure. If you want to eliminate salt, experiment with other yeast inhibitors including cocoa, cinnamon, garlic powder, and onion powder.

Sweetener. Yeast doesn't require any sweetener to grow; it can feed off the flour. But sweeteners make the yeast grow faster, help the crust brown, and, of course, make the dough sweeter. Use 1 to 2 tablespoons sugar or 2 to 4 tablespoons honey for a regular dough; up to ¼ cup sugar or ½ cup honey for a sweet dough. Honey will make your dough sticky even after kneading, so take care not to add too much flour while kneading.

Flour. Use as much flour as required to make a dough that's soft yet holds its own form—usually 3 to 4 cups. This will vary with the flour and the humidity. Choose from white, whole wheat, soy, rye, or other flours. White flour has the most gluten; flours such as whole-wheat, oat (made by grinding rolled oats in a food processor), soy, or rye have less. Gluten makes the bread light and fluffy, so unless you like dense bread, use no more than ½ cup total of low-gluten flour per loaf.

All of the following are optional. For the three kinds of additions immediately below, use just ½ cup of any category. Increase liquid by ¼ cup for every ½ cup of dry additions; reduce liquid by ½ cup for every ½ cup of wet additions:

Dry additions. Dry milk powder, Parmesan or Romano cheese, raw

rolled oats, wheat germ, or sesame seeds.

Moist additions. Grated cheese, mashed potatoes, cooked oatmeal, cooked vegetables, grated carrots, raisins, chopped apples, or dried tomatoes.

Wet additions. Pumpkin, applesauce, or pureed vegetables such as tomatoes or zucchini.

Herbs and flavorings. Use ½ to 2 teaspoons dried herbs (fresh herbs can be used but may color your bread green) or half a medium onion or 1 to 2 cloves of garlic, sauteed before being added to the dough. Sweet dough can be flavored with ½ teaspoon cinnamon and/or ¼ teaspoon nutmeg, cloves, or allspice.

Decorations. Make an egg wash with a beaten egg and a little water. Brush on the dough just before baking. Sprinkle poppy seeds, sesame seeds, or rolled oats on top.

Mixing and baking. Combine and heat liquid, herbs, sweetener, salt, fats/oils, and additions until tepid (95 to 115 degrees). Add yeast and stir. Add flour, one cup at a time at first, mixing well. As the dough thickens, add flour more slowly, stirring until the dough is kneadable. Turn out onto a lightly floured surface, and knead until smooth and elastic, adding flour sparingly to keep the dough from sticking (too much flour will make the dough too firm and the bread bricklike). Cover with plastic wrap or a damp cloth and allow to rise in an oiled bowl until doubled in bulk. Shape into desired form and place in greased pans or baking sheets. Cover and allow to rise again until the dough is not quite as large as you want the final product to be. Mist the loaves with water for a chewier crust. Bake in a preheated 375-degree oven; rolls and breadsticks for 20 to 25 minutes, loaves for 30 to 35 minutes.

The above can be a bit daunting to follow in the midst of bread making, so here's a shorthand version:

1 to 1½ cups liquid
Up to ¼ cup fat
1 teaspoon to 1 tablespoon yeast
Up to 2 teaspoons salt
Up to ¼ cup sugar or up to ½ cup honey
3–4 cups flour
½ cup optional additions
Up to 2 teaspoons flavorings

Finally, Laura Honan of Whitewater, Wisconsin, makes an important point. It's not accurate,

she says, simply to compare the cost of home-baked bread to that of store-bought bread; the actual saving is much greater. Because home-baked bread is so good, it tends to displace not only store-bought bread but also more expensive and often less healthy snack foods such as cookies and crackers. Another family I know that switched to 100 percent home-baked bread a couple of years ago makes the same observation—they noticed a significant drop in their food bill.

HOW CHEAP CAN YOU JET?

Getting cheap airfares can be complicated, but a reader recently informed me about what seems a simple option. Kathryn Tyler Weeks of Northville, Michigan, wrote, "My husband and I have used a consolidator called Cheap Tickets (CT) several times and have been very happy with them. Two years ago, when we called to book a round-trip flight from Detroit to Los Angeles around Christmas, a major airline (Northwest) quoted us $600 per ticket, and other major airlines quoted similar fares. But CT got us a round-trip flight on another major airline, United, for $400 per ticket. This year, we needed to fly to Iowa on short notice. The airline I called wanted $400 for a round-trip flight. Instead, I bought a round-trip ticket through CT for $150. To get the cheapest fare, the CT agent booked me on a different airline each way (American and United). When we fly, we still call all the major airlines to compare, but so far CT has always had the best price."

For more information, I called Greg Gallaher, vice president of reservations for Cheap Tickets Inc. He told me that the company has been in business since 1986 (I confirmed this with the Better Business Bureau) and is the largest consolidator to the public (there are other consolidators who work through travel agents).

Like all consolidators, CT buys seats in bulk, cheaply, from major airlines, marks them up slightly, and sells them for prices that are lower than the airlines' regular prices. Gallaher said CT can book flights all over the world but specializes in flights within the continental United States, and from the continental United States to Hawaii and Europe.

He could not quote a typical savings, saying it depends on many factors. But, like the Weekses, you are likely to find the largest savings on short-notice flights where you can't book two weeks in advance and/or stay over on a Saturday.

To use CT, call (800) 377-1000, let the agent know when and where you want to go, and you will be quoted a price. Cheap Tickets will also quote the airline's normal price, but you don't have to take CT's word for it. Gallaher encourages people to check out regular airline prices themselves before calling his company.

To buy tickets, you give your credit-card number and they are shipped to you overnight, or you can pick them up at one of 12 CT locations nationwide. Tickets are nonrefundable and nontransferable. Gallaher said it is sometimes possible to get frequent-flier-miles credit on tickets purchased through his company.

DON'T WAIT . . . LUBRICATE

One do-it-yourself auto-maintenance task that every tightwad should consider is changing the oil and oil filter. Doing it yourself has several advantages:

- It's usually cheaper. Jim tells me that sometimes, using a coupon, he can get the oil and filter changed in our truck for as little as $11, but if he doesn't find a remarkable deal, he will do it himself. Under normal circumstances, you will pay from $15 to $25 to get this done. But if you get oil and filters on sale (often discount department stores offer lower prices than auto-parts stores), the price can drop to under $7 per change, or $10 for a truck, as these usually need more oil.
- You can choose higher-quality parts. Quick-lube places generally contract with one oil and oil-filter provider, so you don't get a choice. Do it yourself and you can use top-rated products and still save money.
- You'll be more careful. Because it's your car, you will be extra cautious in avoiding under- or overtightening bolts and getting the fill levels exactly right. Generally, garages assign this simple job to the lowest guy on the ladder, and while it *is* simple, it must be done right, or your engine is toast.
- It's faster. With practice, you can change your oil and filter in 20 minutes.
- It's a confidence booster. Changing the oil and filter is a great entry-level activity to teach you more about your car. From there, you may choose to advance to activities such as flushing the radiator.
- Finally, because of all of the advantages listed above, you are more likely to get it done regularly if you do it yourself, and that is crucial. Auto mechanics disagree on lots of things, but on one point they are unanimous: Changing your oil and filter regularly, at least every 4,000 miles, is the #1 way to keep your car running for a long time.

To do this job, you'll need:

1. Oil and filter. You generally cannot go wrong with a good, general-purpose oil such as Castrol. Check your owner's manual to see how much you need, and the proper weight, such as 10W-30. Filters come in different sizes; you must buy the right size for your car. Check the book where oil filters are displayed to find the one that fits your car.

2. An oil-filter wrench. Some oil filters are in easy-to-reach spots, and a strong person can remove and replace them by hand. But usually some kind of wrench is needed. If your filter is in a "hole" formed by wiring and other equipment, you can get a specialized wrench that fits over the filter top like a cap.

3. A ratchet wrench and a socket that fits your oil-pan bolt.

4. A container to catch the old oil. My staffer Brad has one that also serves as an oil reservoir, so he can take his old oil to the dump in it for recycling.

5. Ramps. Available at any auto-parts store and sometimes at yard sales, you drive up on them so you can get under your car.

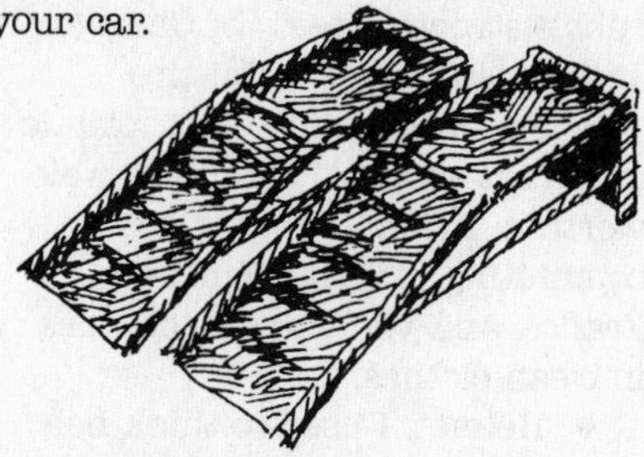

6. Rags and a rubber glove.

7. An old sheet, tarp, or hunk of vinyl flooring (at least 5 feet square) to catch the inevitable spills.

Getting the equipment together is half the battle; actually changing the oil is easy.

First, warm up your car (at least get the temperature needle off of *C*), then drive your front wheels up on the ramps. If your driveway slopes downward, orient the ramps so that the car is as close to level as possible when it is on the ramps. Shut off the engine, put it in gear (or park), and *firmly* set the parking brake.

Open the hood, and remove the oil-fill cap, which is right on top of the engine. This is usually a black plastic cap, and it usually says OIL on it. You are removing it now so that there won't be a drainage-inhibiting vacuum once you start draining the oil.

Slide the tarp under the front of the car, then put the oil-catching container directly under the oil-pan bolt. This bolt is usually easy to find—it's all alone on the underside of the engine.

With the socket wrench, loosen the oil-pan bolt. Since the oil is both messy and *hot,* put on a rubber glove and remove the loosened bolt with the gloved hand. Oil will spill out and fill the container.

While the oil drains, remove the oil filter, turning it counterclockwise, using an oil-filter wrench if needed. You can minimize mess by stuffing a rag under the spot where the filter joins the engine.

Now put the new filter in place. First, dip your finger into some clean oil and rub it around the filter's threads and the rubber ring at its base. Then tighten it onto the engine, according to the instructions on the filter—usually, you should twist it another three fourths to one revolution after the rubber ring first contacts the engine.

Now replace the oil-pan bolt, cinching it firmly, but do not overtighten. Then pour the recommended amount of new oil into the oil-fill hole on top of the engine. Replace the oil-fill cap, back down off the ramps, let the engine run for a few minutes, and look under the car for leaks. Finally, park on a level spot, shut off the engine, and check the oil level with the dipstick, adding more if necessary.

SUCCEED WITH A TEN-SPEED

Todd Barrett of Chicago sent us a detailed letter on the economic benefits of bicycle commuting. For seven and a half years he has traveled 5 miles each way to his job in the city.

"I was curious about how much I was saving," he wrote. "So last year I kept a log of the days I rode to work."

Todd went to his workplace 188 days during 1995 (his job requires

frequent travel, so the other work days were trips to the airport and time spent in other cities). It would have cost $507.60 had he taken public transit daily. But in that year he biked 161 days and took public transportation only 27 days. The fares cost him $72.90, so he saved $434.70. Todd says the twice-daily aerobic workout also saved him the cost of a health club. He points out cycling would save even more money if compared with driving a car.

But serious bike commuting is not expense-free. Costs include:

- Buying a quality bike: A new one will cost between $200 and $300. Clearly, used bikes are available, but after two years of searching the secondhand market for a big-enough bike, my frugal 6-foot 3-inch staffer Brad gave up and bought one new for $240. Not only did it fit, but he was so surprised at how superior bike technology has become since he last had a bike in the mid-1980s, he's never regretted the purchase.
- General maintenance. Because of the severity of Chicago winters, Todd replaces his brake pads and chains each year, which costs $37. Todd also recommends using a pair of tire protectors, such as Mr. Tuffy brand, which cost about $10 each and never wear out. Though he averages 1,600 miles annually on the glass-and-rubble-strewn streets of Chicago, Todd's had only one flat tire.
- Fenders. Lightweight, plastic ones cost about $15 and are well worth it. As Todd says, "This is commuting, not the Tour de France, and you'll arrive at work in clean clothes."
- Helmet. I used to think helmets were for wimps, but a fellow art-school student, last I heard, was still in a coma a decade after his bike-accident head injury. . . . Even so, I didn't start wearing a helmet for my pleasure biking until I learned that a relative's acquaintance incurred a fatal head injury in a bike accident. Todd suggests serious commuters buy a new ANSI- or SNELL-approved bike helmet that fits properly. He says a used helmet might be damaged in a way that isn't visible.
- Specialized biking clothes, such as a waterproof cycling jacket, can be useful but are not a must.
- A top-quality bike lock. A March 1995 article in *Men's Health* magazine challenged a professional bike thief to crack seven bike locks. The three he couldn't break were the Kryptonite Evolution 2000 U-lock (about $50), the Vetta ICS Bad Pack U-lock with two "Bad Bones" antitheft strips (about $50 total), and the Quadrachain (about $100).
- A lightweight backpack to carry your lunch, a fresh shirt, your wallet, and so on.

Aside from saving money, bike commuting can be faster and much more convenient than using public transportation.

Certain factors dictate whether or not bike commuting is a good option for you. Your job has to allow you to wear casual clothing, or you might need access to a shower and business clothes at work. Your job can't require that you must tote a briefcase, portfolio, or other items back and forth. You can't drop kids off at the day-care center. The distance between your home and job might be the most critical factor.

Todd's letter resonated with me. I discovered urban bike commuting after I had lived in Boston about five years, and I thoroughly enjoyed it. In rural areas, biking is purely for recreation, but in the city I rode with an intended destination—I've always preferred constructive exercise.

But more important, after so many years of a sedentary urban life, bike commuting added an outdoorsy, vigorous dimension to my life. It changed my self-image—it made me feel as though I could be forever young.

SURPLUS SOLUTION

Jeanne Buchanan of Hayward, California, writes, "Using some of your strategies and lots of other ideas, we've managed to save about $25,000. We're not quite ready to buy a house yet, but what should we be doing with all that cash now?"

I've stated before that I don't feel qualified to address investment-type questions like this and that this topic is more thoroughly covered in other publications. All I know for sure about Jeanne's specific situation is that the stock market is *not* the place for money like this—it's for long-term investments that can ride out short-term dips.

But so many readers have asked me for investment advice that I feel the least I can do is steer them in the right direction. So I'd like to recommend the works of Jonathan Pond, a nationally known author, lecturer, and columnist on financial planning. I met Pond once in Washington, D.C., when we were both part of a PBS show, and our conversation convinced me that he is not only a whiz at heavy-duty financial topics but also a serious tightwad.

Since then, I've reviewed some of his books and found them quite informative and meticulous. The three that are probably of most interest to tightwads are *Jonathan Pond's Guide to Investment and Financial Planning, The ABC's of Managing Your Money,* and *The New Century Money Book*. Check them out at your library (via interlibrary loan, if necessary) to decide which, if any, is worthwhile for you to purchase.

EXPO YOURSELF

Dear Amy,

Since I have a small business, I go to business expos and trade shows. I take whatever is given out. As a result, I never have to buy pens, pencils, rulers, or notepads. My son has a never-ending supply of hats, tops, flying discs, balls, and yo-yos. My last trip to a show got me the usual take plus three lightbulbs, bottled water, sipper mugs, highlighter markers, a grill-cleaning brush, potholders, a six-pack of soda, lens-cleaning solution, and bandages.

—Michael Gagne
Wallingford, Connecticut

SOCIABLE SEEDS

Dear Amy,

A gift idea: I collect seeds from many nonhybrid plants in my garden that I observe reseeding themselves, such as pole beans, sunflowers, marigolds, hollyhocks, cosmos, et cetera. Last year my four-year-old daughter and I picked the seeds in the autumn after they'd dried on the plants. I made a template for an envelope and cut seed packets out of bright scrap paper. Then we took potatoes, cut them in half, carved a rough design representing each type of plant, dipped them in tempera paint, and made prints on white typing paper, where I had already typed up directions for planting the seeds. We cut out the prints, pasted them on the envelopes, put the envelopes together, and filled them with seeds. We gave them to all the cousins as stocking stuffers, and they were a big hit!

—Meg Bland
Sacramento, California

A DARN GOOD IDEA

Dear Amy,

If you like to sew, you can give everyone a great gift: mending for a year. I have given this gift to about 12 friends for birthdays, and it is very popular. Many people don't have the skills or the right tools, and still they hate to throw clothes away just because of a small rip. This gift is easy to give, because it's usually done in small pieces throughout the year and costs next to nothing.

—Anne Gould
Ukiah, California

RED-MEAT RENDEZVOUS

Dear Amy,

A while back I noticed some 2-pound rolls of sausage were on sale for 99¢ a pound (regularly $5.98 each) on their expiration date. I loaded up and filled my freezer. Next time I shopped, I noted the expiration date of the next batch on my calendar, did my shopping on that day, and received a discount again. Then I used the same method with boneless ham and got it for 99¢ instead of $3.99 a pound. Next, I'm going to try it on bacon!

—Rebecca Novakovich
Dallas, Texas

STREET SMARTS

Dear Amy,

Regarding your yard-sale strategy of marking maps in pencil and then erasing them: Our city's streets are too small and packed together to make that practical, so I made several copies of our surrounding area's section on the copy machine. Now I just highlight the streets with colored pencil and bring along the newspaper section for the house numbers. I could erase the copies for next week, but at 3¢ apiece, I'd rather just start a new page.

—Lisa Rodriguez
San Antonio, Texas

APPEALING SNACKS

Dear Amy,

If you have overripe bananas, try banana pops. Peel a banana and cut it in half to make two short sections. Insert a popsicle stick in the cut end. Spread yogurt on the banana. Roll it in crushed cookies, coating the entire banana with crumbs. Wrap it in plastic wrap and freeze. My five-year-old loves them.

—Inetia Corbin
Tacoma, Washington

THIN TO WIN

Dear Amy,

After I complained about stiff hair spray, a hairdresser suggested I mix the hair spray (from a pump bottle) with water. It can be mixed as much as half and half. I get the same hold with less stiffness, and it's like getting two bottles for the price of one.

—Kathy Davenport
Jackson, Missouri

AVANTE-GARDEN

Dear Amy,

When I pick in the garden, I take two buckets with me. I fill one bucket with veggies, turn on the hose, and wash everything outside, then place the veggies in the second bucket. This keeps the mess out of the kitchen and puts the dirt and water in the garden where they will do the most good.

—Xenia Hallaway
Houston, Texas

GOALS? POST!

Dear Amy,

A note about goals (see "Tending to Goals" [page 837]: Write them down! A study found that people who regularly write down their goals (financial, personal, et cetera) are much more likely to achieve them than people who never write their goals down. I have my major goals on a list on my bedroom door and rewrite them once a month. It's worked for me!

—Polly Laurelchild-Hertig
Somerville, Massachusetts

REVELRY IN REVERSE

Dear Amy,

A "backward" birthday party was a real hit with my eight-year-old son. The invitations were written backward. When people arrived, they were greeted with "Good-bye." We had everyone come dressed backward and started with a backward fashion show. Then we played backward games; a favorite was the three-legged race, where one child faced forward and the other backward. Then we ate lunch, starting with dessert, which was cake with "Happy Birthday" written backward. For prizes, I bought sturdy disposable plastic cups at the salvage store and painted each child's name on them backward. I filled these with small toys (garage-sale and salvage-store finds).

—Elisa Gray
Florence, Oregon

BOBBING AND BONDING

Dear Amy,

I let my artistic 12-year-old trim my short, layered hair one day. Aside from the money saved at my hairdresser, I saw a wonderful, priceless smile on her face as she worked. The trust I showed her was so valuable.

—Eileen Rinehimer
Emmaus, Pennsylvania

CURE FOR BAD-AIR DAYS

Dear Amy,

One of our favorite house-cooling strategies is a whole-house fan. It is simply a 31-inch fan that blows air from a hallway in the center of the house into the attic. You turn it on in the morning and at night, when the air outside is cooler than the air inside. You open all the doors and windows, and the fan draws in cool air from the outside and pushes it up into the attic. This pushes the warm air out of the attic through the ridge or gable vents, reducing the attic temperature by up to 40 degrees. Its cost was $180, and my husband installed it. We recouped that in the first six weeks with savings on our electric bill.

—Suzie Hemphill
Riverside, California

OPULENCE AND SAVING CENTS

In the first issue of *The Tightwad Gazette*, I described a decisive moment when I reacted against cultural mythologies I heard on a TV talk show. Right there, in my living room, I vowed to prove that families *could* make ends meet, and even get ahead, on one average income.

It was a straw-that-broke-the-camel's-back moment. I had heard these same myths repeatedly over the preceding years. And though I had not yet discovered frugality, I had always strongly doubted what I was being told.

Specifically, I recall a debate with one coworker who maintained that two incomes were essential to support a family. Each time he cited an "overwhelming" expense, such as food or shelter, I countered with frugal alternatives such as gardening or fixer-uppers, and he reluctantly agreed with my reasoning. When he told me that kids would need stylish clothing to have good self-esteem, I listed frugal clothing strategies including buying at yard sales. He conceded even this was possible, except that kids should never wear used shoes, which he contended would damage their feet. It was the only point he made that I didn't successfully counter (later I wrote about medical professionals who support the use of secondhand shoes; see pages 371 and 644).

But I must concede that while I was arguing with this guy, I simultaneously imagined that the privilege of being a stay-at-home mom would require a life of bleak sacrifice. I felt this would be a worthwhile trade-off—it would be possible, yet still a struggle, and I resolved to try it.

Now, 15 years later, I've proved that families can live on one average income through the use of many of the strategies I suggested

to my coworker. Yet the quality of this life is not as I imagined it would be.

It is far better.

The thing that I grossly miscalculated was the power of frugality when it is practiced consistently, precisely, and creatively over a period of many years. What I see now is that, very roughly speaking, there are three kinds of people:

First, there are the affluent. This tiny minority of the population can purchase anything they desire at any time.

Second, there is the vast majority of people who have moderate incomes and are frugal only in easy, socially acceptable ways, such as shopping at Wal-Mart, using coupons, and buying new, inexpensive cars.

Third, there are the fanatical, skillful tightwads. They may have moderate or even low incomes but practice power yard-saling, backyard auto repair, extensive gardening, near-100-percent-from-scratch cooking, and so on.

I've been surprised to discover that the third group in some respects more closely resembles the first group than the second group.

Why? Tightwads get things inexpensively through various frugal buying strategies or using do-it-yourself skills. They focus selectively on which quality issues are important to them and direct their energies accordingly. And following those strategies frees up money, so they can buy the quality items that they can't buy or make cheaply.

So while not every area of a black-belt tightwad's life is "opulent," the areas that are most important to him or her can be—and so the resulting feeling of abundance is about the same as that enjoyed by the affluent. Here are a few examples:

- When ten-year-old Jamie had her ears pierced ($8 at a mall included a pair of studs), she eyed expensive earrings in the glass case, but I told her to save her money. We "put out the word" as well as bought at yard sales. The result is that she now has 40 pairs, plus a case to keep them in, all for less than $3.

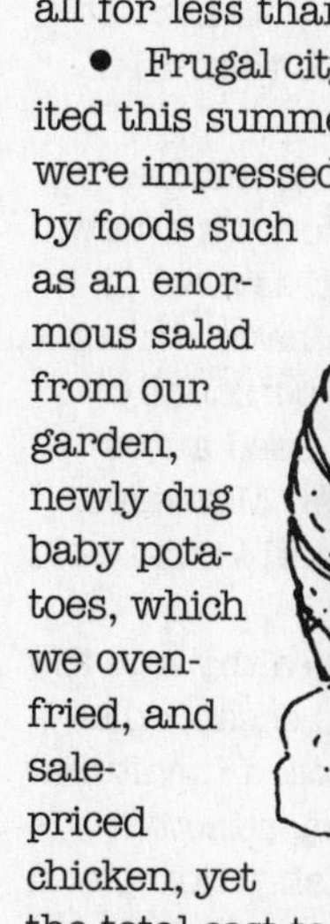
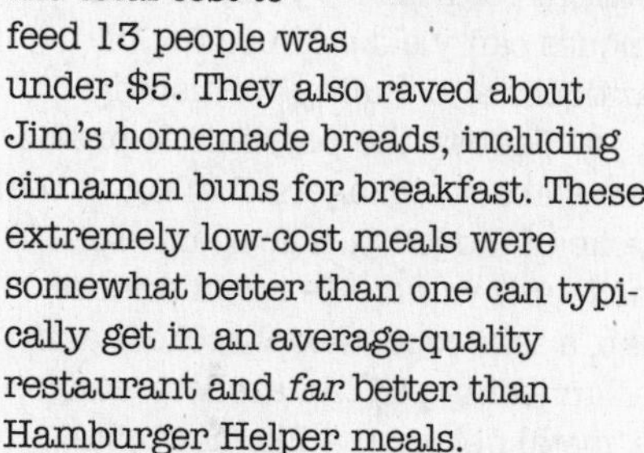

- Frugal city friends visited this summer. They were impressed by foods such as an enormous salad from our garden, newly dug baby potatoes, which we oven-fried, and sale-priced chicken, yet the total cost to feed 13 people was under $5. They also raved about Jim's homemade breads, including cinnamon buns for breakfast. These extremely low-cost meals were somewhat better than one can typically get in an average-quality restaurant and *far* better than Hamburger Helper meals.

- Different frugal friends hit a great yard sale in a wealthy neighborhood a couple of years ago, in which the people were unloading piles of Ralph Lauren Polo for Kids clothing. My friends bought all of it for $10, and it has comprised much of their ten-year-old son's school wear for the last two years. "When he goes to school now, he looks like Prince William," says the

kid's dad. Yard-sale clothing is often superior to new, bargain-priced clothing.

- The same applies to adult clothing. Clothing isn't a priority for me, so I focus most of my yard-saling efforts on finding outfits for my six kids. But a frugal woman I know who enjoys and needs nice clothes has a closet full of blouses, dresses, and slacks that cost up to $300 apiece new. She got them at yard sales for no more than $10 each.
- While the average middle-class family makes do with a new, bottom-of-the-line car, several of my tightwad readers have written that they drive (and personally maintain) expensive used autos such as Volvos or even Mercedes, as these are more durable and hold their value well.
- Both the very wealthy and the intensely frugal avoid cheapo, discount-store, particleboard furniture. Combining yard-saling, selective estate auctioning, trash picking, and patient refurbish-it-yourself techniques can yield a house full of antiques and quality furnishings.
- Despite the pessimistic predictions about teenagers chafing at the yoke of frugality, Alec seems to have few wants. He has a science lab, a telescope, model rockets and a launching pad, an archery range, a metal detector, a like-new bike, cross-country skis, fishing gear, camping equipment, his own kitten, and so on. When we asked him what he wanted for his birthday, all he could come up with was a new watch.
- The final proof, to me, is the fact that, on an average income of under $30,000 a year, we bought the house that once belonged to one of the wealthiest families in this town. Sure, it was a fixer-upper, but with some money and a lot of elbow grease, it is quickly returning to its former glory.

At moments when I note the abundance in our lives, I think back to a media experience I had. On the set of a TV talk show in New York, during a break in the taping, the skeptical TV host asked, in a hostile tone, "How can you live like that?"

I don't recall what I said, but I do know what I thought: Very nicely, thank you.

PASS UP THE PARTY

April Day of Wilder, Kentucky, asks, "How do I tactfully and nicely turn down invitations to home parties like Tupperware, Discovery Toys, Longaberger Baskets, and many more? This should be simple, but I just don't know how to turn down

these invitations without hurting someone's feelings. . . . I go out of obligation and guilt. I just went to a basket party and spent $55 on a basket! Help!"

The key word here is *obligation.* There are many social occasions when we may, in fact, have some obligation to spend money, because we are reciprocating the gifts that others have given to us. Examples include weddings, birthdays, bar mitzvahs, and so on. And if our kids have ever sold Girl Scout cookies to a neighbor, we're obligated, when asked, to buy cookies from the neighbors' kid.

But in April's case, I don't see that there is any social obligation—unless April has hosted a similar type of party, or attends parties and enjoys the refreshments.

The way these parties work is that someone hosts a party for a distributor. The host receives inducements for inviting all her friends to spend money on this expensive stuff.

A case could be made that, when an invitation is offered, April has a right to feel offended, because she has been put in a difficult position by someone who's trying to use her friendship for personal gain. But, at any rate, the host has NO RIGHT to be offended or hurt if her invitation is turned down. If she is, there is little loss to April in jeopardizing this kind of "friendship."

As for a specific response, April could say, "No thank you. I am saving money for (insert worthy goal here) and so, though I'm sure they are very nice, I don't want to buy (insert Tupperware, Discovery toys, or baskets here) at this time."

Personally, I would also seize the opportunity to project my frugality. So I might also nicely say, "I can get lots of nice Tupperware at yard sales. For example, I have six pie-slice containers. Each cost me a quarter or less. I even found a couple in free boxes." There's an art to saying this kind of thing in a smiling, innocent way that gives the other person no clue that I'm trying to educate her. Recently someone observed that the primary message of *The Tightwad Gazette* is "living life on your own terms."

There's no denying that, initially, saying "No" to others can be difficult. I found that by being up-front and open about why I didn't want to spend money, people quickly gave up and left me alone.

JUST THE FAX, MA'AM

I'm a big fan of the lost art of letter writing, but I don't see any particular romance in stuffing the words into an envelope and having them arrive three days later.

Now there are two high-tech, instant-transmission alternatives. One is E-mail, which I wrote about on page 842.

The other is faxing. Generally used for business correspondence, it can be used profitably as a substitute for mailing personal letters.

For example, it takes 30 seconds to fax one page on my Sharp UX-112 fax machine. If I set it to send when my phone rates drop to 10¢ a minute (look in the manual, even inexpensive fax machines usually have a delay feature), the cost for faxing that page is just a dime. That's half the price of a postcard.

Unlike normal mail, *receiving* a fax letter does cost money, but the cost isn't great. I buy six 98-foot rolls of generic fax paper for $16.99—that's 2.8¢ per page.

There are, however, two other expenses to consider. First is the cost of a fax machine; though it's dropped in recent years, a no-frills model still costs about $200. Further, many people purchase a separate phone line for their fax machines, which in this area costs about $16 a month. But there is an alternative. If you get a machine that can respond to a "different ring," it can share the same phone line you normally use. The different-ring option in this area costs $3 a month.

Due to the various expenses required to buy and maintain a fax machine, I can't recommend that you purchase one just to save stamp money. But if you own one for business purposes or can (with permission, of course) use your employer's machine, they can be useful.

And remember; perhaps the greatest advantage of faxing is that, because it's instantaneous, it can be an effective substitute for long-distance calls. If you spend $50 a month to chat with Mom and Dad, faxing instead could save serious money.

SHOULD YOU GIVE IT A WHIRL?

Many readers have pointed out that I once said that a food processor is a valuable tightwad tool and that I would write more on its uses. They've asked for this promised article, so here goes.

We bought our food processor in 1982, back in our tightwad infancy. It's a Robo-Coupe, cost $175 on sale, and came with a 30-year warranty on the motor; it was the company's largest, heaviest-duty model. (Prices have dropped since then. In 1992 *Consumer Reports* gave its top rating to a $114 machine made by Braun.)

While we've *never* regretted this purchase, I don't feel that food processors are essential. Modern American kitchens are stocked with many gizmos such as food processors, blenders, hand-cranked graters, hand-cranked meat grinders, vegetable slicers, mixers, bread machines, bread buckets, and so on. These grate, blend, mix, knead, slice, grind, and so on. Some gizmos do many tasks, others do just one, and there's lots of overlap.

A food processor *does* perform more tasks than any other gizmo, so it can be argued that the cost of one is justified by the gizmos you don't have to buy as well as the space it saves. On the other hand, if you have lots of space, you could buy many of the one-function gizmos for remarkably little at yard sales.

Food processors also pop up at yard sales, but they tend to be priced high (about $30) and are hard to check out on the spot. Yard-sale models also tend to be older and less powerful and to have small feed tubes and bowls that can be inconvenient to use.

So before you buy one, assess your needs, the purchase price, and the gizmos you already own. And remember that because they are a hassle to clean, food processors are best used for handling large quantities of food or for labor-intensive tasks.

Here are some of the tasks for which I use a food processor:

- Grating large quantities of food, such as potatoes, cheese, and

zucchini. I use a hand grater to grate 1 cup or less.

- Blending large quantities of tomatoes (for canned spaghetti sauce) and pumpkin (for puree). I use my blender for smaller quantities. Food processors can also make mashed potatoes and applesauce. I use a potato masher and an applesauce mill instead.
- Kneading bread and pizza dough. If you plan to buy a processor, get one powerful enough for this task. Most breads require ten minutes of hand-kneading, but our food processor kneads dough for two loaves in seconds. Some say you can make good pastry crust with a food processor, but I'm skeptical—pastry is too easy to overmix. They also say you can mix pasta dough in them.
- Grinding. We often make meatloaf in our food processor, particularly when we have tough meat to grind up (a hand-cranked meat grinder can also perform this function). I also use mine to make bread crumbs—I save bread crusts in my freezer, process a large quantity at a time, and keep the crumbs in the freezer. One can make cranberry sauce in a food processor, but I prefer the texture of this when ground in a meat grinder.
- Slicing. One can use a food processor to slice vegetables, but we have a vegetable slicer, which is easier to clean.
- Mixing. Food processors are very handy for mixing frosting. Most other mixing tasks are best done with a bowl and spoon.

The bottom line: We use our machine about twice a week, so its annualized cost of $5.83 a year (assuming it lasts 30 years) works out to about 5¢ per use. The amount of money we save by being able to easily shred and freeze mountains of zucchini or make homemade bread in minutes far outweighs that 5¢ cost.

SMALL VESTS WITH SMALL INVESTMENTS

Whenever I've thought about writing an article on sewing, I've always chuckled when I remember a letter sent to me way back in August 1990. Jean Murray of Whiting, New Jersey, wrote, "I think that the one thing that will save you the most money is being able to sew. You don't like to sew? Well, who said you have to like it? There are a great many things in life that have to be done, whether liked or not." As you might guess from her comment, Jean's no wimpy baby boomer—she identified herself as a 75-year-old Depression survivor.

While sewing remains a valuable money-saving skill, it doesn't save as much as it did in the pre-yard-sale era. Today's high cost of patterns, fabric, and sewing notions makes sewing clothing generally more expensive and time-consuming than buying clothes at yard sales. As a result, I've rarely sewn to make clothing. I do feel sewing is invaluable when it comes to repairing or altering clothing or to making something for my home, such as curtains, cushion covers, quilts, and so on.

But one kind of home-sewn clothing does make economic sense—making kids' clothes from adult-sized garments. This frugal strategy, common during the

Depression, is rare today. But consider: The cheapest new fabric remnants cost at least $1 per yard. A large, yard-sale garment that costs 25¢ (or less) can yield enough fabric to make a child's skirt, vest, or shorts. Further, these adult-sized garments can yield matching zippers, buttons, and other notions to use in your projects. And some home-sewn garments can be made of different fabrics. Amy Salmon of Sacramento, California, suggested that a dress or jumper could be made from a bodice of one fabric and a skirt of another.

I recently used this strategy with success. Despite diligently yard-saling all summer, I had failed to find something special for Jamie to wear on her first day of school. A week before school began, I sorted through my stockpiled children's clothing and found a rejected-by-Jamie vest with (ugh!) floral fabric—her tastes gravitate toward dark, solid colors. But I realized I could use this vest to make a pattern.

Once Jamie gave me her skeptical okay, I proceeded. First, I laid the floral vest on butcher paper and traced the individual pieces (you needn't take the garment apart, just fold so each section can be traced), and then added an extra half inch all around for a seam allowance. The next yard-sale day, I bought a pair of large jeans for 25¢. From this, I was able to cut the two front and two back pieces.

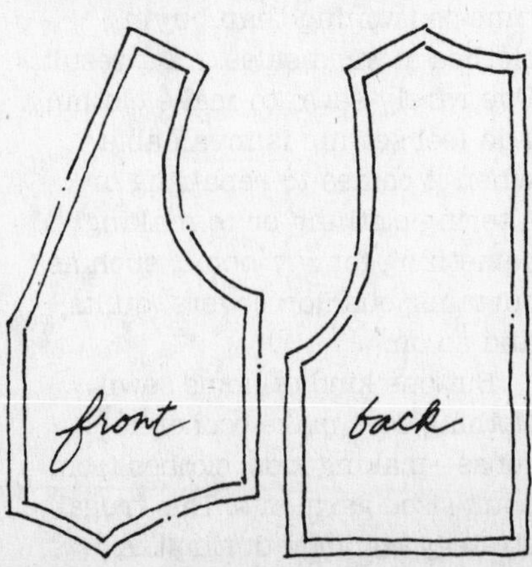

Sewing the vest was actually quite simple. I sewed the rough edge under with a double row of stitching. I also added two pockets with flaps. Store-bought vests usually have an elastic gather in the back; I made a denim tie.

All was going smoothly until I discovered that my button box had long ago been plundered by youthful jewelry makers; white, black, and drab buttons were virtually all that remained.

Well, you know what they say about necessity being the mother of invention. After some pondering, I wondered about my collection of metal blue-jean buttons and snaps. (I cut off and save interesting ones from jeans I'm about to throw away. I have 35, all different.) Jamie liked the idea of varied buttons, so Jim and I brainstormed ways to attach these.

First, Jim had to pull apart the button, removing the old rivet. This was achieved with two pairs of pliers and a fair amount of brute force, yet enough care so as to not damage the buttons.

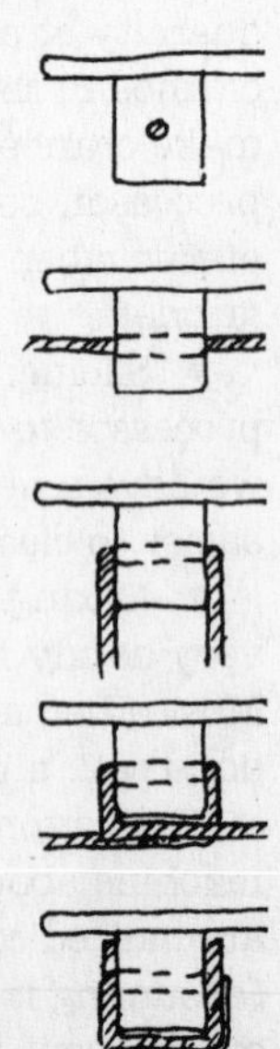

We came up with two methods of attaching the buttons:

1) Riveting. Jim has a pop-rivet tool. He had to drill out the button's rivet hole slightly larger to accommodate his riv-

ets. This is the best method, but not everyone has this tool.

2) Sewing. Jim drilled a tiny hole through the button's shaft. This drilled hole had a sharp metal edge which would cut thread. So, I pushed paper-clip wire through the hole and bent it over the shaft's end so that the button could be sewn on using the paper-clip wire. The wire's sewing section was about $\frac{3}{16}$″ long; to avoid slippage, I sewed the whole width of the wire section. This method was satisfactory, though riveting holds the button tighter to the fabric.

Although I'd made buttonholes only once, at least seven years ago, I was reminded of how easy it is. Because of the thickness of the blue-jean-button's shaft, I used the widest possible setting on my machine and made holes that have a circle on the end.

Jamie picked out seven buttons, including brass, silver, and copper ones of different designs (five down the front and two for the pocket flaps). I marked the position for the buttons, and Jim riveted them on, in the sequence specified by Jamie (this was a nice moment of collaboration between parents and child).

If you use this idea, bear in mind that the shaft lengths can vary, so choose ones that are similar.

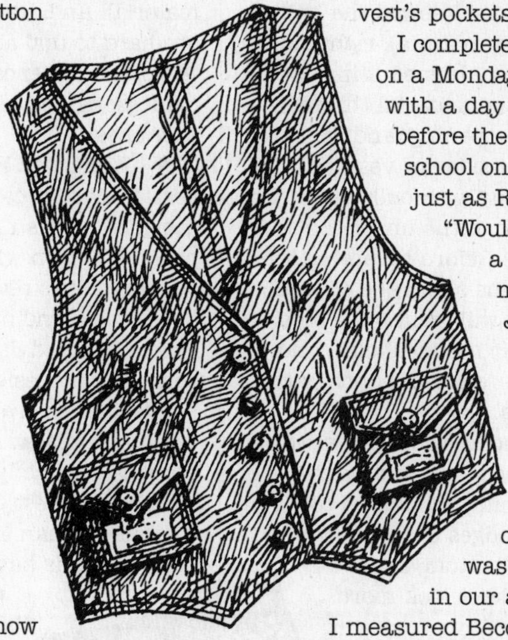

Jamie and I decided her vest needed something else, so we went to the attic and looked for articles of clothing (such as designer jeans) with interesting embroidered patches. We found two small ones she liked. I scavenged the patches and sewed them onto the vest's pockets.

I completed this vest on a Monday night, with a day to spare before the first day of school on Wednesday, just as Rebecca said, "Would you make a vest for me?" Unlike Jamie, Becca prefers flowers, and I told her it depended on what I was able to find in our attic.

I measured Becca from her waist to neck, compared that to the pattern, and then reduced my pattern 10 percent using my copy machine at work the next day. After work, Becca and I rummaged through the attic clothes. I found a pair of flowery cotton pants. These were given to me, and I couldn't imagine any of my children would ever wear them. I also found a black silk item of unknown origin that appeared to be pajama bottoms.

I sewed Rebecca a flowery vest with a black lining. Although a lining seemed daunting, this too was easier than expected. I have a homemade, smaller-than-Becca vest with a lining. I looked carefully to see how it was assembled.

The only visible exterior stitching was a hand-sewn part on the lining's shoulder seam—meaning the remainder was sewn inside out with the machine. I cut four pieces from the flowery material and identical pieces from the lining. I sewed each together except for the shoulder seams. I sewed the lining to the flowery material, right sides together. Then I turned it inside out, pulling the material through one shoulder opening, and ironed the now right-side-out vest. (If you're working with bulkier fabric, reverse through the under-the-arm lining seam.) Before reversing the vest, the seams should be clipped where fabric will want to stretch, such as under the armholes, and trimmed where it will bunch, such as at corners.

Then I machine-sewed the flowery-fabric shoulders and hand-sewed the lining shoulder. I top-stitched the edges of the vest (neck, front, bottom, armholes) to make it look more finished.

I finished sewing buttons on Rebecca's vest at about 9:00 P.M. the night before the first day of school. Including rummaging in the attic for fabric, this vest required four hours of work and cost me just a few cents for the amount of thread I used.

Both of my daughters proudly wore their vests to school. Rebecca said she asked many classmates to guess if the vest was store-bought or homemade; everyone thought it came from a store.

Perhaps more so than any type of garment, vests are ideal for this strategy. The front, back, and (optional) lining do not need to match and so can be made from different garments. Vests require little material. And, I have found, they are hard to find at yard sales.

This experience reinforced some old lessons and taught me some new ones:

- Jamie was happy with her vest, in part, because she "co-designed" it. As I pointed out on page 760, even when looking at clothing in the retail market, Jamie has trouble finding clothes she likes. I realized Jamie and I can solve this by designing clothes to her tastes. Before long, I hope to teach her to sew. And while I was not able to exactly duplicate a storebought vest, I made one more unusual than any that her friends have.
- Sewing is a way to make a quality garment. Rebecca's vest is of a much better quality than the flowery vest I'd bought at a yard sale, which might have cost more than $10 when new. Similarly, adults who need quality business clothing and are unable to find these items through the secondhand market can fill out their wardrobes by sewing—in this case, it can be economical to sew with new fabrics.

• Sewing a simple article of clothing can be accomplished in an evening. I'll think a bit harder about watching an evening of mediocre television.

• A sewing machine need not be expensive. I bought a 1950s black Singer for $50 about 15 years ago. The machine has never needed a professional repair; it's mechanically simple enough for Jim and me to handle any needed maintenance. For instance, in this case, when my buttonhole attachment wouldn't work, Jim examined the unfamiliar mechanism, did minor disassembly, oiled and reassembled it, and it worked fine. In contrast, I've since inherited a fancier machine that does all sorts of tricks I'll never need, and it now needs a too-complex-for-Jim repair that will cost over $100. I recently spotted a mint-condition black Singer for $60 at a yard sale.

• The more you do something, the quicker and better you get at it; the second vest went together much more quickly than the first.

• As with many of my frugal projects, the reward was not just saving the money a new vest would have cost, it was showing my kids that frugality works. So putting in the "extreme" effort at key times is worth it to me.

• Skills of all types are important. One of the aspects I enjoy most about my marriage is that Jim and I frequently combine our ingenuity and technical knowhow to accomplish something great. Our abilities have more to do with having learned skills than having talent. I'm sure Jean would agree that acquiring skills *is* worth your time (and frustration) in the long run.

Since the beginning of the school year, I've completed a second vest for Jamie—this one is made of black velvet—and Becca has requested some new skirts.

FROZEN ASSETS

With seed-catalog season just around the corner, here's a handy seed-storage tip from *Organic Gardening* magazine. This is of special interest to those with small gardens, who may find it difficult to use up whole packets in one year.

Save your seeds in the freezer. According to Kent Whealy of the Seed Savers Exchange in Decorah, Iowa, frozen seeds remain viable up to ten times longer than seeds stored by other methods.

However, for freezing to work, it's crucial that the seeds to be frozen are dry—if they're damp, when the water inside them freezes and expands it will break the cell walls and kill the seed. To test small seeds, flex them; the seed should break rather than bend. Large seeds—beans, for example—should shatter, not smush, when hit with a hammer.

If your seeds are too damp, air-dry them rather than using an

oven, as temperatures over 95 degrees will cause damage. If the humidity is high, here's another way to dry seeds (this isn't from

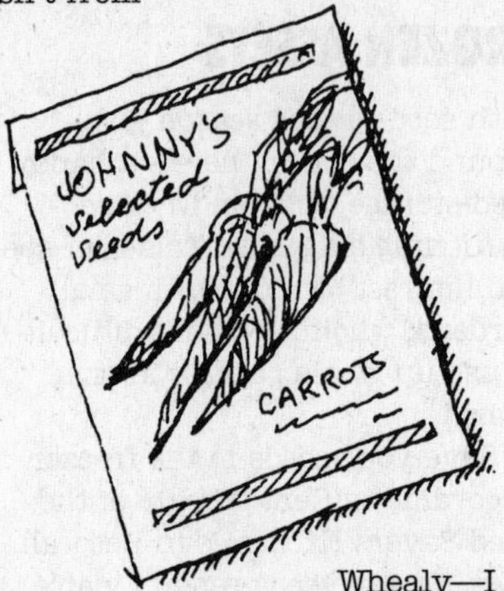

Whealy—I read this somewhere years ago). Put the seeds in an airtight container, such as a Ziploc bag or canning jar, that contains a paper-towel packet of fresh dry milk powder; this will act as a drying agent.

Once seeds are dry, seal them in airtight containers before freezing.

PINNED ON THE MAT

Dear Amy,

You've mentioned (see page 337) using a towel on top of a bureau for a changing table. I use a bath mat instead. The rubber backing keeps it in place when the baby squirms.

—Becky Goodenough
Winsted, Connecticut

CHEAPO IDEA

Dear Amy,

Here is a cheap thrill for young kids while they are in the tub. Rub your hands liberally together with soap. Make an "okay" sign by making an *O* with your thumb and forefinger. Dip the *O* slightly in water until a bubble film forms. Then blow. Voilà! Instant bubbles in the tub. My preschoolers love this, and all are still trying to learn to do it.

—Kelley Reep
Garner, North Carolina

YOU CAN'T CAN?

Dear Amy,

Here's a cheap and easy pizza sauce for nongardeners. Stock up on 8-ounce cans of tomato sauce when they go on sale. To the contents of one can, add 1 teaspoon oregano, 1 teaspoon basil, ¼ teaspoon garlic powder, and ⅛ teaspoon pepper. Makes enough for one 12- to 14-inch pizza.

—Rebecca Novakovich
Dallas, Texas

SALVAGE SOAP

Dear Amy,

I live in an apartment building with community washers and dryers. It's amazing how many people throw away detergent bottles that still have enough detergent left for a

large load. I take bottles from the garbage can and turn them upside down. When the soap has run into the cap, I use it for my own laundry.

—Anne Fasano
Chicago, Illinois

CACHE SAVES CASH

Dear Amy,

Don't pay high prices for sandwiches or fast food if you forget your lunch or have to work late. I bought a case of ramen-noodle packs in assorted flavors at ten for $1 from an Oriental food store and stuffed it into a file cabinet. It isn't so good that I am tempted to eat it, but it suffices in an emergency and cooks up with hot water from the coffeemaker; no microwave needed.

—Karen M. Campbell
Sacramento, California

HAVE A NICE SPRAY

Dear Amy,

Rather than fill the sink with 12 cups of water and 1½ cups of cleaner, which is the minimum required to soak the mop, I now rinse the mop in the sink and use a 1-liter spray bottle of mixture to clean my floors. My cleaner now lasts a little more than three times as long.

—Terri Wedge
Parker, Colorado

DRY AND HUMIDIFY

Dear Amy,

To help beat winter dryness, I put a clothes-drying rack in each bedroom and fill each with wet clothes at night. We no longer have to deal with filling, cleaning, and protecting humidifiers in the kids' rooms, and we have dry clothes by morning. I "screen" the racks with plants, rocking chairs, and dressers and take them down when empty.

—Diana Hyatt
Batavia, New York

COVER STORY

Dear Amy,

I made a seat cover for an old chair by weaving old ties. It looks great.

—Deborah Miller
Wooster, Ohio

FIX FOR A CHEAP MIX

Dear Amy,

With double and triple coupons, I can get cake mixes for pennies, but my family doesn't like boxed cakes. They do love these cookies: Add ½ cup oil plus 2 eggs to one box of cake mix (German chocolate is the best). Add chips, nuts, flavorings if desired. Drop by teaspoonfuls on a cookie sheet. Bake at 350 degrees for 10 to 12 minutes. Makes three dozen soft cookies.

—Tammy Janelle
Caledonia, Mississippi

TIGHTWADS IN TIGHTS

Dear Amy,

Tights are a much better bargain for girls and women than panty hose. I have three pairs of tights I have been wearing for the

past three years; I am lucky to wear a pair of panty hose for a month. Tights are too heavy to be worn in the spring and summer months, but in the fall and winter a pair of navy, black, or cream-colored tights can be worn frequently in place of panty hose. They are a much cheaper fashion choice for any women who must dress up.

—Amy Wilder Owen
Nashville, Tennessee

A LOOK BACK

When I announced that I'd be shutting down *The Tightwad Gazette,* I didn't expect the final 12 months to zip by so quickly. Anyway, in the last months of publishing, I completed an index for the newsletters, a process that forced me to scrutinize past issues. In doing so, I recalled the fun of researching some articles, as well as how tired I was when I did others. The mental connections were amusing. Whenever I look at my article on low-cost funerals I think of the Jimmy Stewart movie *It's a Wonderful Life;* I was watching it as I did the funeral illustrations during a pre-Christmas work marathon.

So it seemed fitting that the final issue should reflect on the *Gazette*'s six-year run: what it's meant to me, the readers, and, just maybe, the country as a whole.

I must concede that all of my memories aren't positive. Obviously, if the whole experience had been ecstatic, I wouldn't have ended it. Yet, many aspects were hugely rewarding. So, let's go way back to the beginning.

In my first issue, I listed the main goals Jim and I had when we married in 1982: a big family, a big house in the country, and no day care. There was a fourth I didn't mention: Jim and I also wanted to start a home-based business to supplement his military pension after he retired in 1991.

For years we had discussed and rejected many options. Then, in February 1990, a couple of months after we moved into our dream home in Leeds, I was trading tightwad ideas with my minister's frugal wife and she said, "There should be a club for tightwads." Something clicked. That evening I said to Jim, "I have an idea for a business, and I don't think it's bad. What about a newsletter for tightwads?"

As we spent a couple of hours discussing it over a pot of tea, we decided it was perfect for us—like a job in a candy factory. For many years I'd had an overwhelming desire to share my frugal ideas, and the purchase of our house on an average income of under $30,000 would serve as tangible proof that frugality does indeed work. Since our frugal lifestyle coupled with Jim's pension meant we'd need only 2,500 subscribers to make a living, it seemed eminently worth a shot.

We launched our business with our meager savings of $3,000 (replenished from a low of a few hundred dollars after we purchased the house). By April I had the June 1990 issue to the printer.

Getting subscribers was our biggest challenge. We took out a few small ads and dropped off freebies in doctors' waiting rooms but had little success. Then an acquaintance in marketing suggested I send out press releases. I thought, "I'll try it,

but the media wouldn't be interested in little old me." Boy, was I wrong.

We sent 14 press releases to Maine newspapers. One immediately resulted in a small story. Then, a full six weeks later, a second journalist called. During that phone call, he said, "I think your newsletter is great. It could be really big. How big do you want it to be?" This writer worked for a local paper but also freelanced for *Parade* magazine. He was sure he could sell our story to *Parade,* which with a circulation of 36 million is one of the biggest publications in the nation. We understood then that our lives could radically change, but there was little we could do to prepare for the unknown amount of business that could result. So we just waited.

Six months later, in March 1991, we were on the cover of *Parade . . .* and if you look closely at the photo (taken a month or so earlier), you can just see the elastic part of my maternity jeans peeking under my sweater. It was (yikes!) twins.

The *Parade* article resulted in 33,000 pieces of mail in two weeks. We hired virtually every available friend we could find to stuff free sample issues into the SASE's we received. We had people crammed into our kitchen, dining room, living room, and front parlor ten hours a day.

Then calls from national television shows started pouring in, including one from *Donahue.* We actually considered passing up that show. Not only were our lives chaotic, but we had received a small amount of extremely negative mail (for example, accusing us of "child abuse") and thought a talk show would be like venturing into the lions' den. We decided to risk it. In retrospect, people remember the negativity of the show, but I felt our appearance succeeded because I had a chance to respond to criticisms—and because my children behaved.

That show, as well as three other national shows that week (*Today, The Home Show,* and *CBS This Morning*), brought us a volume of mail equal to what we had received from the *Parade* article a month earlier.

In June 1991 the twins were born, Jim retired from the Navy, and we had over 40,000 subscribers. We didn't regret the business, but we were not having fun. Our driveway and yard, filled with staffers' vehicles, looked like a used-car lot. We seldom ate supper before 8:00 P.M. The worst moment occurred when a child clogged the upstairs toilet and water filled the kitchen light fixture below and then rained down on a staffer working on the mailing. The year that followed was the most difficult of our entire marriage.

In April 1992 Jim and I moved the business out of our home to a ranch house four miles away, and we hired skilled staff. Among others, that staff included Brad Lemley, the journalist who wrote the *Parade* story. He has worked with me two days a week for the last four years.

Life calmed down somewhat after that. Even so, I estimate I've been interviewed about 750 times. I also did two book tours, each hitting about 20 cities in under a month.

Jim and I had the good sense to keep our success relatively small or it would ruin the quality of life that

we had worked so hard to acquire. So, over the years, I turned down offers to do syndicated columns and speaking engagements, write magazine articles, and have my own radio and television shows.

Our decision to accept a book deal was a turning point in our business. It both allowed and insured that we would not publish forever. We knew our work would be permanently "out there" should we retire, but it also meant we could never repeat material. Early retirement was decided then, way back in 1992.

I've no regrets about this decision, but as our lives have calmed down over the intervening four years, the upsides of our success have become more apparent to me. The biggest, most obvious one is that the newsletter improved, often profoundly, the lives of tens of thousands of people. I also suspect it had a small impact on the culture at large. As compared with the eighties, today I hear less whining on talk shows about how two incomes are essential. In general, my message meets with less resistance than it did when I started in 1990.

I believe that any larger cultural impact we might have made has a great deal to do with the level of access we've given the media to our personal lives. While I have often worried about robbing my kids of their privacy, we've agreed to give journalists the time and access to serve a larger purpose: We want to prove that our quality of life and budget successes are true.

Further, I've found that *being* a journalist is a powerful thing. I've liked having an outlet as well as the resources to research for readers. I am perhaps proudest of some of my research into save-money scams. In one case my contact with law enforcement officials directly contributed to the demise of a major Ponzi scheme sweeping across the country. (These newsletter articles were not included in the books.)

As for other stories, I've hugely enjoyed shredding cultural mythologies, such as "Raising children is so expensive" and "Americans are worse off than ever." I've also enjoyed the highly personal articles about our lives—such as how Jim and I built a bedside table out of scavenged furniture parts. Prior to doing the newsletter, I was often frustrated that we were doing fascinating things and no one knew about it.

I also learned from readers. To name just a few changes, we now make Cuban bread, eat pressure-cooker beans and rice, and recycle coffee grounds.

Although it hasn't always been the candy-factory job I imagined, I'm deeply gratified that the newsletter did so much good. I had initially envisioned it mainly as a support system for people who were *already* frugal. While the newsletter did serve this purpose, I was even more pleased to find that it actually *converted* many people who were major spendthrifts, in some cases drawing them back from the brink of bankruptcy or divorce and putting them on the path to a frugal, fulfilling life.

Altogether, more than 200,000 people subscribed at some time or other. My first three books, to date, have sold half a million copies. Our books are among the most requested at libraries—one woman told me she was thirteenth on her library's waiting list. Most of these newsletters and books were read by more than one person. If a million people changed at least one behavior, collectively, that's a lot of changes for the better.

But the final and perhaps most important point that I want to emphasize about the *Gazette*'s success is that I didn't do it alone. The frugal ingenuity of the readers has always astounded me, and many of the best ideas in the newsletter came from them. It is their insights that made the "Reader's Correspondence" section one of the best parts of the newsletter. In response to my solicitations, they also sent in their own tips on everything from dry cleaning to window treatments.

I also had the opportunity to meet hundreds of readers on book tours and when we opened our home to visitors on the tenth of each month. I discovered there was no typical *TG* reader: They were young and old, wealthy and impoverished, single and married, male and female. But readers were almost universally the kind of people I choose for friends: positive, responsible, hardworking, family-oriented. As much as I am enjoying the peace of retirement, I will miss the connection I had with readers most of all.

SUCCESS STORIES

As I've stated in the past, I've been reluctant to publish the many "success stories" that readers send to me because it would seem self-serving.

But after I did use one—in a cover story, "A Tale of Tightwad Transformation" (see page 628)—several readers wrote to say they wanted more. Why? Because such stories demonstrate that the frugal principles I've been writing about work for a variety of people in a variety of circumstances—and because it's just reassuring to know that others out there are on the same path.

So, here are a few of the success stories we've pulled from a fat, 3-pound file. If you still haven't embraced frugality, I hope you'll recognize yourself in one of these stories and become inspired to make the effort. Also, many of them list specific strategies—so along with encouragement, I hope you'll pick up some useful ideas.

Finally, don't be misled by the fact that many of these writers heap all of their thanks on me. In many cases, *The Tightwad Gazette*

was just a clearinghouse for excellent ideas that the readers sent in. So, to a large extent, these stories are from people who have helped one another to succeed.

Dear Amy,

I have both of your books, and they have been absolutely life-changing for me.

I bought your first book three years ago when my second child (I have two boys) was just two weeks old. I was home on maternity leave and sucked up all the information in that book like a sponge.

Your article "Calculating the Net Value of a Second Income" was eye-popping. My husband and I, on the brink of divorce from stress, figured it out. I was bringing home 50¢ an hour! Within weeks, I quit my job, put the baby in cloth diapers, and started slashing our costs everywhere. We cut our income by 60 percent and lived off my husband's take-home pay of $15,000 a year. It was not easy, but we always had enough. My husband found a better job, our marriage became happier, and the kids became older. This past fall we bought our first house after months of intensive house hunting; a beautiful 70-year-old home with high ceilings, incredible woodwork, wood floors, and no problems.

For our first Christmas, I found a beautiful set of dishes at Goodwill that look antique. They go with our Victorian home, filled with second-hand (and many times antique) furniture.

None of this would have been possible had we not learned the strategies in your books. That's what I love about the way you write; you show people how to apply your methods to their situations.

While we definitely have months when we are more "tightwaddish" than others, we are realizing our dreams. It feels so good to choose tightwaddery, knowing it will get you to your goal. This year we plan to eliminate the last holdover from our spendthrift days: our car loan. Then we will start paying off our mortgage as quickly as we can. Thanks so much for helping us reach our goals!

—Kim Tilley
Peoria, Illinois

Dear Amy,

I am 27 years old. Three years ago I graduated from school with $6,500 in credit-card debt. I barely scraped by for the next 18 months, even though I landed a good job making $21,000 a year.

Then I purchased your first book, and it was amazing! I was totally hooked, elated and excited that things could really change. That it was totally possible to live within your means and *save money!*

I got a new apartment with one of my best friends from church. Together we felt we could overcome the temptation and allow the tightwad inside of ourselves to emerge. We began to cut all costs! We regulate the thermostat (my roommate was used to turning the air conditioning up so far in the summer that she needed a sweater!). We crack the windows and run the fans at night to make it cool enough to sleep. We hang-dry all of our laundry and have turned the

water heater down to the lowest possible setting that still kills germs (FZ note: 120 degrees). When the lightbulb in our refrigerator burned out, we didn't bother to replace it, as that was wasted energy and money!

I've gone from using $16 mascara to the Wal-Mart $2 special. I have found comparable and thrifty substitutes for all my cosmetics to date. I have even let my boyfriend trim my hair! The weird part is that no one can tell the difference!

I could go on and on for pages about the changes in my life in the past two years. But the best part is that I have paid off $3,000 in debt in the past 18 months and will be debt-free in 6 to 8 more months. Now I understand that real deprivation is living from paycheck to paycheck, wondering how I will pay for food or gas until the next payday rolls around. Or lying awake at night, anxious and scared because I need work done on my car and have no idea where to get the money. Or realizing that my twenties are passing me by and I have very little of lasting value to show for it.

I want you to know that you have made a difference! I am on my way not only to solvency but black-belt tightwaddery that will help me fulfill many of my lifelong dreams.

—Rachel J. Pinnow
Tucker, Georgia

Dear Amy,

From the information we gained from you, my husband and I were able to save enough to purchase 3.6 acres and build a new home on one income. We are both 28 and didn't think it would ever be possible.

—Rhonda Hoover
Newburgh, Indiana

Dear Amy,

Our lifestyle has hardly changed. But I have gained self-esteem and power over the ability to save more money, and it feels great. Some of the easy things I have found most helpful include: hanging at least two loads of laundry a week, sharing the trash bill with my neighbor ($91 per year), getting rid of cable TV ($430 per year), getting rid of convenience foods (over $500 per year), cheap birthdays and homemade Christmas ($500 per year), using a price book, and bulk buying ($250 per year), no more Downy, using less detergent, checking the car insurance carefully (I found one item that saved $230 per year), et cetera. Now I ponder every item and put things back on the shelf when I don't need them. My point is, I can't believe how the little things add up. If somebody had told me how much money I could have saved, I would have told them they were crazy.

—Deborah Wallstrom
Anchorage, Alaska

Dear Amy,

We have been tightwadding for two years and have just realized our dream of a 31-acre farm in North Carolina.

Two years ago we both worked full-time, owned no property, and could barely make ends meet. I've been a stay-at-home mom for two

years now, and we are debt-free except for our home, which we got a great deal on.

My decision to stay home cut our income in half, yet my husband, four children, and I all agree that our standard of living has been rising almost daily. No more day-care stress, two-job hustle, fast-food waste. Thanks for the good work. *Tightwad* is a beautiful word in this house.

—Barbara Smith
Westfield, North Carolina

Dear Amy,

My family now eats healthy, homemade food, and my grocery bill has gone from $400 to $100 a month. Thank you.

—J. Maxfield
Millville, New Jersey

Dear Amy,

We have gone from hardly being able to live on my husband's income with credit cards to having money to pay cash for everything and almost have the credit-card balances paid. I enjoy my life now more than I ever have. I get satisfaction from being self-sufficient. I am "making a home" for my family. My children know the value of a dollar and are helpful around the house (most of the time). You have made a big impact on our family.

—Sandra Griego
Mesquite, Texas

Dear Amy,

When I first bought your book a few years ago, I hoped it would save me a few dollars. As I gradually began to incorporate more frugality into my life, I found out what a powerful living tool it can be. We have cut our food bill in half, which is not that remarkable. I am also "retiring" from my work as a nurse to be home with my two (and hopefully three, soon) children—also not very remarkable. What is completely astounding to me is how very easy all of this has been. And the real kicker is that my husband has even joined in. This is the same man who always asked the salesperson the price so that he could make sure he was getting the most expensive product because that must mean it's the best.

Our transformation has included:

- Looking for supermarket sales.
- Making a price book. To be honest, it took me a long time to get myself to do this. I thought it would be too much trouble. What a joke. I have saved more on our grocery bill using this strategy than any other.
- Buying a freezer.
- Bulk buying.
- Yard-saling. We live in the South, and yard sales go from February to November.
- Scratch cooking, including bread. You won't believe this, but in my spendthrift days I bought a bread machine (on a credit card, of course), and we didn't use it because we disliked the taste of the bread it made. Now I use it to knead the dough, then I bake the bread in the oven. Pitiful, huh?
- Buying store brands.
- Eating more meatless and "less-meat" meals. This is the area that helped convert my husband

more than any other. We are really into health and nutrition. We have found that the less we spend on food, the more healthfully we eat.

- Gardening; we will try it this year.
- Using the minimum amount of various detergents, baking ingredients, et cetera.
- Reusing everything.
- Hanging laundry.
- Using cloth diapers.
- Using powdered milk.

There are many, many others.

Despite all of this, and because our lifestyle really hasn't changed much, I never thought of myself as a tightwad. The complete realization came to me the other day as I was talking to my best friend, who is not very frugal. I mentioned needing to weigh a letter to see if I needed to put an extra stamp on it. She said she couldn't believe that I would "go to so much trouble." I told her I would no more waste a stamp than I would throw 32¢ in the trash. Her response: "You are such a tightwad!" I smiled to myself. You know, she's right.

—Michelle Brock
Chattanooga, Tennessee

Dear Amy,

I raised my three children as a single parent for ten years and was financially okay (able to meet my monthly obligations with no room for saving) because of a high-paying career. But due to downsizing, I lost my job in 1993 and could find work at only half the salary. Deep in debt with a mortgage of over $1,000 a month, I was forced to file bankruptcy and lost my home. Then, in 1995, I lost something I had always taken for granted: my health.

Diagnosed with chronic fatigue immune dysfunction syndrome, or CFIDS, I was told by my doctor I could no longer work full-time. But God was on my side, for at that time the man I love asked me to marry him.

The first few months were difficult, as I discovered that the emotional impact of a chronic illness is more devastating than the physical. Having been entirely independent and productive for so long, I had trouble feeling like a useless burden on my family. Then I saw an offer in my book-club flier (from my spendthrift days) for your *Tightwad Gazette II*. I ordered it out of curiosity, and it was the smartest thing I have ever done. I now have both books and subscribe to the newsletter.

Tightwadding has become my career! And a perfect career for someone with this illness. My condition is not as severe for me as for many others who are virtually bedridden. I am unable to work outside the home because the disease comes and goes from day to day; you never know which days will be good and bad. But with tightwadding, I am able to adjust my schedule according to how I feel day-to-day. On my good days I can shop, plan, and even spend the entire day cooking, baking, and freezing meals and snacks for those bad days.

We now feed our five children (three are teenagers) on $60 a week. I know we can do better; I am working on it. We bought an IBM PC at a yard sale for $20, and with my accounting background I've worked out a financial plan for my family.

So, in essence, we are still a two-career family: Mike makes the money, I save it.

We basically do everything you suggest. I even made purple cows (FZ note: mixing powdered milk with grape juice) for the little ones; I'll try anything! My husband went "Dumpster diving" for a five-shelf bookcase that a neighbor had thrown out. I am currently refinishing it.

A neighbor came to me in tears because of overwhelming financial troubles. Using my $20 computer, I restructured her debt and educated her in the fine art of tightwadding. Excited and once again full of hope, she contacts me often to tell of the bargains and strategies she finds. My husband has suggested I become a financial advisor to people like her, and I am seriously considering it. Now there is a purpose in my life, a purpose I thought had been lost to me forever.

None of this would have come about had you not started your newsletter. Through example, my children are receiving a valuable education in money management, which will only make their lives easier; an education that may be handed down to generations to come. Thank you so much, Amy, from all of us.

—Claudette Benoit
Londonderry, New Hampshire

Dear Amy,

Thank you for your continued useful articles for joyful financial salvation without deprivation. Our family now gives much more than previously, yet our savings have more than doubled. Astonishingly, there continues to be even more room for improvement. So many doors open.

Tightwaddery with a flourish truly takes study, alertness, and practice, practice, practice. The possibilities are wonderfully shocking, and the results are satisfying, delightful, and often touching.

—Pearl Nagoshi
Budd Lake, New Jersey

Dear Amy,

You really helped this family. I doubt if my marriage could have survived our economic tough times if I hadn't had *The Tightwad Gazette* as my "black-belt" how-to manual.

—Nancy Strand
Turlock, California

Dear Amy,

Thank you for giving me the inspiration and motivation to:

- Become debt-free in two years (I owed $6,500).
- Save 15 percent of my income through a company-sponsored 401(k) plan.
- Provide significant financial assistance to my parents, who live on Social Security.
- Plan for my retirement in a truly productive way (instead of just daydreaming about growing roses).
- Realize I will need to work at some level when I retire, and plan accordingly.
- Eat more economically and nutritiously (love those rice and beans!). I make the very best pancakes from leftovers; I even freeze

them for quick and easy meals (the best leftover to use in pancakes is spaghetti, without the sauce; cut up in pieces, it extends the batter and adds a wonderful texture).

More specifically:

- I bought my mother a like-new down coat, reversible, at a thrift shop in New York City for $9.99. (I would never have dreamed of shopping in a thrift shop before I got your newsletter.)
- Cut my food bill (single person) by almost half.
- Bought a lovely 4-foot Christmas tree in New York City for $5 on Christmas Eve and started a new family tradition at the same time.
- Instead of gifts, we pool our money and take a trip rather than spending money on stuff we don't need (we *do* need to be together).

But most of all, I am much happier about my future as I now feel I am in control. You are a gifted lady, and I will always be in your debt.

—Marie Mitchell
New York, New York

Dear Amy,

To say you saved our lives would be stretching it. To say you helped to restore order and happiness to our family and marriage would not. Thank you.

—Kathy Wood
Palm Beach Gardens, Florida

Dear Amy,

Thank you! I have chopped my grocery bill, which also includes cleaning products (soap, toothpaste, et cetera) from $800 per month to $350 per month for a family of five. My family does not even notice a difference.

I now use powdered milk mixed with whole to make 1 percent milk, saving $10 a month. I now make homemade spaghetti sauce in very large quantities, in addition to salad dressings, desserts, cookies, and homemade cleaning products. I have also started buying items in bulk. I used to buy small boxes of name-brand cereal. Now I buy large boxes of store-brand for half the price, and my children don't know the difference! And I now purchase all of my meat on sale in the huge family packs and divide it up. My family has also gotten used to eating much healthier food.

We are saving on school lunches; in my town a school lunch costs $1.60 plus and an additional 35¢ for cookies! Since reading your book, I bought, on sale, two reusable fabric lunch bags and two Rubbermaid "Sips" thermoses, which come with their own straws. What a savings!

We have also started home haircuts. Never in a million years did I think that I could give a home haircut. But I got a book out of the library and learned how. My husband bought one of those buzz haircutters and a pair of scissors, which paid for themselves after four haircuts. The haircuts come out great. Last month, one of my friends asked me if I would show her how to do it!

We have paid off all credit cards and have just one more loan to pay off. After that, we should be able to save seriously for a house. You

have really helped us see that our goals can be reached, and I want to thank you for that.

—Mary Malfitano
Nutley, New Jersey

Dear Amy,

Thank you for changing my life. After four marriages, two bankruptcies, seven children, and the squandering of over $250,000 in the past 15 years, I finally bought a copy of your book. It has radically changed my life and my attitude toward money. My current husband (a Spartan tightwad) is much relieved and appreciative. I've read your book many times, loaned it to a friend (reluctantly), she lost it, so I had to buy another one. I'm in the process of converting my sister, brother, and mother. I come from a long line of spendthrifts. I feel like I know you. I can't bear to let the book out of my house.

About a year ago, my husband and I moved to Hawaii for the change in weather. Housing is expensive, but the costs are greatly offset by the lack of bills for heat, winter clothing, shoes, et cetera. We shop carefully and are continuously amazed at how cheaply we can live here. I had started working in September of 1993 but, after reading your book, determined to quit, which I did.

Inspired by my newfound frugality, we parked our van; my husband and I now get around on mopeds. We purchased these for $200 and $250 from friends. They require no insurance, and we're averaging $2 a week in gas. It is amazing what you can stuff into a moped's basket! We trade babysitting with a friend who owns a cab for rides for once-a-month grocery shopping. Honolulu also has an excellent bus system.

Thank you again for what you are doing and the profound change it's making in my life and the life of my family.

—Patrice Dodge
Honolulu, Hawaii

Dear Amy,

I subscribed off and on for the last few years, but I'd never taken tightwaddery seriously. I guess you have to be ready for it, and I couldn't be bothered.

Well, unfortunately, it takes hard times for some of us to "get ready," and that happened to us.

I won't go into too much detail, but I now have both of your books and will be faithful.

I have slashed our food budget by almost half, found great sources of used clothing, and in general learned, and am still learning, new things all the time. I know it's a slow process, but I already feel like we have more money.

At one time I considered a part-time job, but I now feel what I'm doing is worth more than any minimum-wage job that takes me away from my three little boys. My husband is supportive and is thrilled that I've given up that idea.

It will take us a long time to get out of debt, but I feel we now have the tools to do it. Thank you.

—Laura Prolic
Plainfield, Illinois

Dear Amy,

I borrowed your *Tightwad Gazette* book from a friend and

was very encouraged to keep doing many of the money-saving activities I have done for several years. Your article on Baggie washing gave me some ammunition against my skeptical but very sweet mother-in-law, who was convinced that I am the only person on the planet who reuses them. She even bought me a grocery box full of Baggies and said, "Here. Now you can throw them out." That didn't stop me. I stored them in the basement and probably won't have to buy them again in this decade as I continue to wash out and reuse them.

Thank you for what you stand for. There are so few people who will take a stand for frugality and industry in order to have the more important things in life. May the Lord bless you for being such a good steward and teaching others these important life skills as well.

—Ronda Williams
McConnelsville, Ohio

Dear Amy,

I could write you a six-page letter, but let me just say that for the first time, we were able to put $300 in savings (and we've been doing this just one month). I can't begin to tell you what we've saved on food! And we still have money left to buy yard-sale bargains. Our children, ages eight (boy) and five (girl), are even having fun with it! They still point out daily that they brought their Baggies home to be washed!

Thinking back to my childhood, I am amazed at how resourceful my father had been. Needless to say, he is thrilled that I am tightwadding. He's been trying to teach me all his life, and now that I've started, it seems so natural!

—Susan Krause
Wilmington, North Carolina

Dear Amy,

I'm a full-time homemaker, and I haven't been this excited about my career since my last child went to school!

—Patricia Russell
Dawson Springs, Kentucky

Dear Amy,

I must write you and thank you for literally saving my sanity. I had no savings, investments, or assets. Just *debt, debt, debt.* I still have debt, but I've turned my philosophy of money, consumerism, and priorities around in the last few years.

Despite the high cost of living in New York City and two young children, we've learned to get by on less; I'm proud of my accomplishments so far. My daughters are well dressed and have a toy room full of toys, and *none* of it was bought new. My apartment is loaded with furniture I dragged in off the street and refinished. I pursued quality free public education for my children in New York City by networking and researching and working hard to get them into the "best" Upper West Side school program. The city is full of fun, free things to do. We got rid of our car. We eat in, carefully weigh entertainment costs, and fly home to visit my mother only when airfare is dirt cheap.

The *TG* helped me realize the absolute connection between *ecol-*

ogy and frugality. And now I feel that I control the flow of my money, not the reverse.

—Jaclyn von Bleicken
New York, New York

Dear Amy,

We are better off in several ways. Financially, we have more money in savings than when I was working and are paying extra on our house and car loans. Emotionally, our son, 26 months old, is happier at home than at day care. And I'm much happier. And hey, our house is cleaner and more organized!

What's funny is that it's *easy!*

I've read both of your books at least 50 times and say, "Amy says . . ." so much that my family thinks I'm crazy, and that maybe I think you're a close personal friend! It's just that when I need motivation I reread your books.

—Deann Polanco
Austin, Texas

Dear Amy,

I am a testament to the fact that people do change. I am a 37-year-old mother of five who grew up in a large family that gradually rose from the middle to the upper-middle class. My mother did some sewing, but most of our clothing was bought on semiannual trips to Neiman-Marcus. We ate at restaurants fairly regularly. Any broken appliance was tended to by a paid professional. When my parents first bought a VCR, they actually paid an electrician to hook it up for them.

Coming from this environment, I thought frugality meant buying something on sale at a nice retail store.

About six and a half years ago my husband quit his much hated job at IBM to attend law school. During those three years we racked up about $35,000 in debt. When he graduated, he found a job that paid $4,000 a year less than the job he left at IBM and that had no benefits. Two years ago we had our fifth child.

Enter *The Tightwad Gazette.* Now I feel good about doing without things while I wait to find them used or free. We are now trying to find contentment by enjoying the things we have (and *who* we have), by doing things creatively, and by making things we might have bought.

Your humor, creativity, and enthusiasm have somehow worked to shift my entire frame of reference; I think it's called a "paradigm shift." And my husband, who was always more frugal at heart, thanks you.

—Laura Honan
Whitewater, Wisconsin

Dear Amy,

I work at a company that "pays" us in gift certificates for cost-reduction strategies. Since reading your books and newsletters I look at things in a different light not only at home but at work and have come up with more than 100 ideas. For my prizes, I pick gift certificates to stores such as Wal-Mart and Target. I have enough soap, shampoo, and cleaning supplies to last years. People at

work can't believe it, and I have fun doing it.

—Kelly Tardani
Grand Haven, Michigan

Dear Amy,

I want to thank you for your book, which a tactful friend gave me, saying, "It's not a hint or anything. She's funny, and I think you'll find it interesting."

She was right on both counts, and I *needed* the book. My husband and I are spendthrifts for the same reasons most people are: We've been too busy, distracted, or lazy to pay attention to myriad small expenses, and we were too ready to decide we "deserved" the dinner out, too disorganized to plan ahead, and therefore often buying things at the last minute. Same old story.

But you already have us paying a lot more attention. We've switched to store brands on many products, with no loss of enjoyment. We've begun yard-saling with many successes. We are now stocking up when nonperishables go on big sales, tracking prices, bringing lunch more, eating out less, and buying more items used.

We still have a long way to go and many more bad spending habits to change. So much of the battle is just learning to get organized, plan ahead, pay attention to what we spend, and *think* about it. Now that we've made a Dacyczyn to be more frugal (while continuing to be generous) we will be in a much better position to reach our economic and personal goals, like buying a bigger house, starting a college fund, and maybe having a second child. Thank you again. Your creativity, humor, and resourcefulness are an inspiration.

—Elizabeth Michaud
Westford, Massachusetts

Dear Amy,

I am already a tightwad, and proud of it! But your book was an eye-opener. I read it over and over. Every time, I get an adrenaline rush.

—Cheryl Ross
Waldron, Indiana

Dear Amy,

Thank you for a wonderful newsletter! It has changed our life. A year and a half ago my husband and I were in debt, overdrawn and unhappy. Now I am able to stay home with our daughter instead of in a job I hated; my husband is successfully self-employed; we paid off all of our credit cards and just bought our first home: a four-bedroom, pre-1900 farmhouse on two acres, no attached barn. We now have a mortgage to pay off early!

—Ellen LaFleche
Castleton, Vermont

Dear Amy,

I have so much to thank you for that I could go on for pages, but I'll try to keep it short. When I first saw you on *Donahue* in 1991, I had over $7,000 in credit-card debt at 20 percent interest, had no savings account, was 32 years old and living frantically hand-to-

mouth on a gross annual income of $20,000. I had no idea where my money was going, never knew where I would come up with the money for insurance payments, doctor bills, et cetera. I was a financial and emotional wreck, always worried, always feeling out of control.

You gave me hope, practical advice, and a real solution to my problems instead of pie-in-the-sky, get-rich-quick nonsense. I have purchased both books and use them for constant reference and encouragement when I feel impatient.

So, Amy, four years after first hearing of you, I am free of credit-card debt, have a new car that I saved up to pay for, am much more relaxed in general, and have savings totaling over $9,000. I have gained confidence in myself and hope for the fulfillment of my dreams; genuine hopes, not false ones. I fear to think how I would ever have gotten started on the road to financial success if I had not heard of you. And I've had so much fun!

—Laurel Aronson
Richfield, Minnesota

Dear Amy,

I bought the book for myself as a birthday present and enjoy reading it over and over again. We not only use all kinds of strategies to "survive" in today's expensive Switzerland, I also love reading about you and your readers' experiences and ideas. It's like a kind of bond between tightwads all over the world!

—Monika Meyer
Gossau, Switzerland

Dear Amy,

I came to the *Gazette* as a result of surveying the rubble of my economic status after putting my wife through college while raising four children and living in a fairly spendthrift manner.

Your publication has bailed us out of a *very* tight spot. I can say, without exaggerating, that you have found a way to slow or halt the decline of our country, and I'm not saying that lightly. I have considered sending a copy of your book to every elected official who works for me. (Sounds funny, but they do. We all seem to forget that.)

I could write several more pages, but I will close with this. Two years ago I was in the hospital, out of sick leave, and seriously considering bankruptcy. This year I paid my home off a year early, I have six to eight months' worth of groceries in the house (the pantry principle works great), no car payments, and a lot less debt than I would have believed possible in so short a time. The future isn't foreseeable, but I'll be much better prepared for it, thanks to *The Tightwad Gazette.*

—Jerry Anderson
Duluth, Minnesota

Dear Amy,

I'd like to thank you for saving my marriage. When I first ordered the *Gazette*, my husband had just returned to work after two months of unemployment. Although we were thankful he got a job, he was making about 30 percent less than he had at his old job. We had a one-year-old baby at the time, and I stayed home with him full-time.

I was miserable, because we didn't have any money for all the things I wanted. I laid the blame on my husband and, subconsciously, the baby, when I should have been looking at myself. We were all *very unhappy*.

When I started reading the newsletter and putting the ideas to work, my priorities began to change as I realized things could not make me happy. With the spending techniques that I have learned from the newsletter and your book, we find that we can live quite well on my husband's new salary.

Now I have a new appreciation and love for my husband (who has always been somewhat of a tightwad) and my son. We are very happy and planning to add to the family.

—Catherine Sisson
Peachtree City, Georgia

Dear Amy,

I would not have known where to start without your book.

—Laura Ridley
Salt Lake City, Utah

Dear Amy,

I have recently given up my $11-an-hour job to spend more time with my three young sons. Thanks to *The Tightwad Gazette*, we don't miss my income. Our whole family is much happier and healthier since I've been home to take care of things. If I had known it would be this easy, I would have quit sooner.

—Linda Monteith
DeMossville, Kentucky

Dear Amy,

With the help of your newsletter, and following the advice of making and using a price book, packing school lunches, buying secondhand goods, et cetera, we were able to pay off all eight of our credit cards, which were maxed out. We were able to pay cash for a second used car. And now we will be putting 25 percent down on a house.

—Maureen Hill
Hermiston, Oregon

Dear Amy,

I am a stay-at-home mum and thought I would drop you a line to let you know how much our lives have changed since we discovered *The Tightwad Gazette*. Since we have subscribed to your newsletter, we have:

- Made our own Christmas presents.
- Made dog biscuits.
- Dressed ourselves from the thrift shop.
- Preserved tomatoes (bottled).
- Preserved apricots.
- Made apricot jam.
- Used our open fire more.
- Dumpster-dived an artificial Christmas tree.
- Made confetti eggs.
- Made and eaten lentils.
- Put out the word and got a $50 freezer (new $450).
- Slashed our grocery bill.
- Made and used a solar oven.
- Made our own beer.
- Paid thousands off our home loan.

We are a middle-class family but realize that "just because we have it doesn't mean we have to spend it." Thank you for enriching the quality of our family life. It's defi-

nitely true that good times don't have to equal money.

—Judith Koop
Victoria, Australia

Dear Amy,

Not a day goes by when I am not doing something I have learned from your book or one of the newsletters. I have a new attitude and a new outlook, and the great thing is that it makes life a lot more enjoyable and a lot more fun.

—Chelsea A. Leonard-Baum
New Alexandria, Pennsylvania

Dear Amy,

I am convinced that you have changed our lives with your words of tightwaddery almost as much as our new baby will.

—Rachael McLeod Seravalli
Lincoln, Nebraska

Dear Amy,

Thanks to your newsletter, we were able to save for a down payment for some land, then for our house (with affordable payments). We *saved too much* for our house, so we were able to pay off a $3,500 school loan. I now no longer need to work, we're having a second child, and we're still saving! All this within two years!

—Sue DeCoste
Carmel, Maine

Dear Amy,

I'm 36, a single mother with two young children, and thanks to you (and my two and a half years of dedication), I've paid off my mortgage in 5 years instead of 30 and paid off my car loan as well. I work part-time as an occupational therapist earning under $30,000 a year with *no* child support.

—Julie Schulte
Dubuque, Iowa

Dear Amy,

I just wanted to let you know how much I appreciate your newsletter. In the past 18 months my husband and I have been able to:

- Move to the country (realizing an 11-year dream).
- Buy a house (I am still pinching myself).
- I have been able to quit my job and stay home with my four young children.

Being able to accomplish these things has added tremendous quality to our lives. But the thing that graphically demonstrated the value of frugality to me was doing our taxes:

- 1993 income (with me still working): $31,748.
- 1994 income (with me at home): $23,980.

And our savings account is growing!

—Phreddi Goland
Paradise, California

Dear Amy,

I decided it was finally time to let you know how much you have helped me. When I bought your book, I noticed the money-back guarantee if I couldn't save the cost of the book, and I immediately took up your challenge. And happily lost.

I started slowly, first by bypassing my bank and ordering my checks direct from the manufacturer, which saved me $8. Then I spent $32 and six hours of time on a defensive-driving course. That saved me $120 a year in car insurance for three years!

You also taught me how to think differently. At one point I needed more work clothes and dreaded the idea of spending $150 a suit, if I was lucky! But with your book in mind, I was having a chat with a close friend and she mentioned that she had some beautiful suits that she couldn't wear anymore. I tried them on, they fit perfectly, and I bought them from her for $25 apiece (suits in mint condition worth over $200 apiece).

You taught me to be more aware of where the money was going and to keep a list of purchases. In the first two months I was shocked to discover that I had spent around $35 on magazines! And the library carried most of them!

I hardly, if ever, use coupons anymore. The store brands are too good to pass up! I drink dry milk at 40¢ a quart instead of paying 71¢ for whole milk. I eat a lot more vegetarian dishes than I used to, and I like it! And I find that cleaning with baking soda, vinegar, and water for a rinse, and other easy cleaning formulas, keeps the house just as clean. (By the way, my mom and dad, who now live in Florida, are laughing at me because they've been saying this stuff for years. Their 34-year-old daughter finally learned!)

Since I don't go out much, I had basic cable in my apartment, and it cost $25 a month. One day I took the TV schedule and circled all the shows I absolutely must watch. I was totally amazed to find they were all on broadcast TV! So I cut the service down to "reception only," which costs $13 a month, and save $144 a year.

I was absolutely positive that my phone bill was as low as I could get it, but in the interests of being fair, I read it from cover to cover and discovered that I was paying an optional wire-maintenance fee of $1.59 a month. Throwing away $19.08 a year on the phone bill is crazy!

I moved my credit-card balance to a card with a lower rate, and already the savings are making me sleep better at night. The balance is big (for me), and I was a very, very stupid person once upon a time, but I'm dealing with the here and now.

It took time to learn this, and I still have a long way to go. But you are right that the important thing is to have a *goal*. It doesn't work for me to say I'm going to save money in the bank; it's too easy to spend it on instant gratification. But I realized that I want to (1) get out of debt within five years; and (2) buy a large house with land within three years after that. Suddenly, drinking dry milk became a pleasure. Thanks!

—Judy Levinton
Brooklyn, New York

Dear Amy,

Here are the results of six months of tightwaddery:

- Day care: $5,000 last year, $0 so far this year.
- Department store: $10,000 last year, $300 so far this year (for business supplies).
- Groceries: $600 per month last year, $265 per month for the

first four months, $200 per month for the last two months.

Thanks to you our dream house is in sight! The side benefit to tightwaddery is a calmer lifestyle. Because of this, we can now realize another dream of ours; we will be able to home-school our children. What a change from their being raised by a nanny.

—Viki Allin
Albion, Pennsylvania

Dear Amy,

This summer my grocery store had a promotional campaign: Buy $40 worth of groceries at one time, each week, for 10 out of 12 consecutive weeks, and "earn" a $25 gift certificate for that store. Good deal? I couldn't do it! Even though I was shopping for two adults, two teens, and three cats, I could not spend enough to qualify, after using some of your methods and some of mine. Even though I lost the $25 certificate, it's neat to know that in the long run I'll save much more.

—Donna Blakesmith
Lakewood, Ohio

Dear Amy,

I am a divorced, single mother, and I have two children. By using the suggestions you provide, and with the help of a coworker and friend, I am able to rent out a house I own in the inner city, and I bought a lovely three-bedroom raised ranch in the country that was in foreclosure (it was originally offered for $68,000, but I managed to get it for $37,000). My kids love the rural area, because we were living in the inner city where the bullets fly day and night. With my friend's help and yours, I went from being on public assistance to managing nicely on $23,000 a year. Thanks again!

—Lorna Moore
Sodus, New York

Dear Amy,

We have caught a serious case of tightwad fever and have been using the ideas in your books to ruthlessly slash over $560 a month out of our budget! We are using the extra money to pay off our credit cards, and paying them off by Christmas is the best present we will give to each other. After that, we will triple up on my husband's truck payment and pay it off by Christmas 1996. We will then be completely debt-free! After accomplishing this strange new financial status, we plan to save for a house big enough to hold four children (we currently have one child and rent a house).

—Gwen Harrison
Fortson, Alabama

Dear Amy,

Due in great part to the ideas and encouragement found in the two *Tightwad Gazette* books, my husband and I are finally on our way to financial security (peace of mind) and closer to buying the land we've always wanted. We have drastically cut our food bill through bulk buying, comparison shopping of loss-leader prices, cooking from scratch, and eating out less. Before reading your

books, I had never had a yard sale or been to one; can you believe it? Now it is part of my Saturday-morning routine. I can't believe how much money I've wasted. I'll *never* pay full price again.

—Bonita Ward Wimberley
Leland, North Carolina

Dear Amy,

I'd seen you on a talk show and thought, "Sheesh, how extreme can you get?" Then, as our bills piled up and my migraines got worse, I thought, "Sheesh, how extremely are we in debt?"

I went to the library and checked out your book. I trust people who write "help" books about as much as used-car salesmen. But I realized something very different about you: You *live* what you write.

You have never seen such a quick convert from total spendthrift (dropping $200 at a time at a department store) to frugality (spending $13 for two skirts and a pair of leather shoes at Savers' Thrift). I wash Baggies and tinfoil, dropped expanded cable, buy bread at the bakery thrift store, buy in bulk, make pizza—our grocery bills went from over $600 a month to $350, and I'm looking to go even lower.

My dream has always been to have a nice little house on a nice little street in a nice little town. I never had a way or plan to achieve my goal before. Thanks to you and your books, my debts are disappearing at an astounding rate, and we can realistically put away $1,000 a month. That's *reality*. We're doing it, and I can't believe it. I'm the biggest skeptic in the world, and you have won me over with your honesty and personal values.

—Lisa Umstott
Murray, Utah

Dear Amy,

My husband and I used to earn more than twice what we currently bring in and were barely able to make ends meet. Having put into practice most of the material found in your newsletter, we have been able to scale down to one-and-a-bit salaries, make monthly retirement contributions, and make monthly mutual-fund purchases as well as save at least 10 percent of my income. Scaling down allows my husband to stay home with our young baby and thereby accomplish our goal of keeping her out of day care!

—Carolyn Wilding-Eddy
Maple Ridge, British Columbia

Dear Amy,

You have completely changed my attitude. I'm on a debt-reduction plan that most people would call "restrictive." I call it "liberating." Thank you.

—Wendy Howell
Camano Island, Washington

Dear Amy,

I realize that some people have told you that they think you take all of this stuff too far, but I'm here on the other side cheering you on! The fact that you reveal all of your calculations to show how much you save on one item/prac-

tice versus another is actually what helped me the most, and it is what sets you apart from what I feel are inferior "tightwad" topic writers. You've helped me put my lifestyle in a realistic perspective and change my old bad habits. My new joy is the feeling that comes from knowing that I'm smarter than advertisers at grocery stores, et cetera. I choose to buy; I'm not subliminally drawn by fancy packaging.

It is you who have helped me go from being $50,000 in debt to $34,000 today (in a very short time), and it continues to drop as I absorb a little bit more from each of your newsletters.

—Shelly Harris
Pleasanton, California

Dear Amy,

Several years ago, when your story was featured in *Parade* magazine, I was intrigued. Sometime later, having subscribed to the newsletter and purchased your first book, I was hooked. The "snowball" principle especially interested me, as you showed how a couple with a modest income goaled themselves to save a downpayment for a home, and succeeded. Having read and reread that story, I decided to pursue a similar goal and save enough to purchase a home in five years, despite our family's under-$30,000 income.

Within two years we had saved over $10,000 and were able to buy a six-year-old, beautiful home on seven wooded acres.

—Denise Augusto
Northfield, Massachusetts

Dear Amy,

I must tell you what I was like before reading your books. I must warn you, however, because your skin will start to crawl!

I am married and have two teenage daughters. Both girls wore disposable diapers until they were toilet-trained. It's a good thing they didn't make those "Huggies Pull-ups" (plastic potty-training pants) back then because I probably would have bought them too! Both kids always wore brand-new clothes. I was always cursing myself because no sooner did I buy a new item than they would grow out of it!

Cooking has always been my job, and I was the convenience-food queen. I always had a full pantry loaded with Rice-A-Roni, Hamburger Helper, Velveeta Shells and Cheese, Chef Boyardee, et cetera. I have a freezer, but the only things I put in there (which wasn't much) were Pillsbury cookie dough, pie-shell crusts, and those blue freezer-pack things. On the days I didn't cook we would tool over to Burger King, Pizza Hut, or Kentucky Fried Chicken. I should have bought stock in one of those places! Only we could not afford stock, because we were living from week to week; you should have seen the credit and the bills!

But after seeing you on *Donahue,* I bought both books. I read both with intensity! I realized that I was literally throwing money down the sinkhole!

However, I immediately sprang into action to change. It was April, and I packed lunches for the girls for the rest of the year. After-school snacks went from Oreos to homemade apple-spice cake. To top it off, they got involved in baking! Over

the summer we baked cookies, cakes, and homemade dinners together. It was a marvelous experience to be together as a family.

I started a small garden and got to know some older, retired neighbors who gardened. They loved sharing their experience and knowledge with me, and one gave me some pepper and tomato plants he started under his lights. Over the summer we exchanged our produce, and we became terrific friends!

I hung every load of laundry and bought a large quantity of ground beef on sale for 88¢ a pound and froze it in family-sized-meal containers. I also tried many more of your ideas.

My husband has been pretty supportive. He's adapted to his packed lunches. I made a chart on the savings of buying versus packing a lunch. It showed we saved $88.80 a month by taking lunches from home to school and work.

You have truly changed my life! My summer was filled with the enjoyment of my children (whom I had no time for before), my neighbors (whom I didn't know, until now), and my husband (who loves the new, happier me). You are so right, Amy. Tightwaddery is a lifestyle—one that has given me back my sanity, time, and money.

—Karen Jendre
Independence, Ohio

Dear Amy,

It is no small thing to empower people to realize decent and good dreams. Thank you.

—Serena Miller
Portsmouth, Ohio

Index

ABOUT THE AUTHOR

AMY DACYCZYN published a newsletter called *The Tightwad Gazette* from June 1990 until December 1996. Amy is now retired from her writing career. The Dacyczyns and their six children live happily and frugally in Leeds, Maine.